1006. 435
W9-BNZ-137

FOR REFERENCE
NOT TO BE TAKEN FROM THE ROOM

THE
BOWKER
ANNUAL

LIBRARY AND BOOK TRADE ALMANAC

34TH EDITION 1989–90

Publisher • Margaret M. Spier

Consulting Editor • Patricia Harris

Compiled and edited by Filomena Simora

Sponsored by
The Council of National Library and Information Associations, Inc.

R. R. BOWKER
NEW YORK

Published by R. R. Bowker,
a division of Reed Publishing (USA) Inc.

International Standard Book Number 0-8352-2617-4
International Standard Serial Number 0068-0540
Library of Congress Catalog Card Number 55-12434
Printed and bound in the United States of America

ISBN 0-8352-2617-4

Contents

Part 1
Reports from the Field

News of the Year

Special Reports: Ensuring Information's Survival

Federal Agency and Federal Library Reports

Part 3
Library/Information Science Education, Placement, and Salaries

Part 4
Research and Statistics

Library Research and Statistics

Book Trade Research and Statistics

Part 5
Reference Information

Bibliographies

Ready Reference

Distinguished Books

Buyers' Guide, 1988–1989

Part 6
Directory of Organizations

Directory of Library and Related Organizations

Preface

Almanac. *n.* A publication containing statistical, tabular, and general information related to a given calendar year.

For 34 years the *Bowker Annual* has lived up to the definition of an almanac, and now it has taken on a new title that more accurately reflects its contents—*Library and Book Trade Almanac.* In this thirty-fourth edition you will find all the information you have come to rely on: a look at the year's news, reports on funding and legislation, salary statistics, acquisition expenditures, average book and periodical prices, directory information, and much more. And to make this information easier to locate, a "Quick Find Index" and bleed bars have been added. Turn to the last page of the book and you'll find arrows that will lead you directly to the appropriate section.

Another year has passed in which concerns about information's continuing accessibility were raised. Four special reports on the theme "Ensuring Information's Survival" take a look at current issues with long-range effects. Carolyn Clark Morrow, assistant national preservation program officer, Library of Congress, points out some of the successes in preserving library materials, as well as the important work still needed in the areas of environmental control, acid-free paper, and developing national standards. To elucidate the technology picture, Margaret Morrison, coordinator for public services, Torreyson Library, University of Central Arkansas, describes how CD-ROM, online services, optical media, and other new technologies expand access to information while forcing librarians to face the problems created by the transience of electronic material. In his essay on users' rights, C. James Schmidt, vice president, Research Libraries Group, and chairperson, ALA Intellectual Freedom Committee, covers the Library Awareness Program and other government efforts to restrict or monitor access to unclassified information. Fred B. Wood, project director, Office of Technology Assessment (OTA), presents an article based, in part, on the OTA report *Informing the Nation.* Wood discusses the role of the government in disseminating information and the directions that need to be set now to define future roles. The policies being formulated by the government have a strong impact on librarians as information providers.

Advances in computer technology have spawned a unique set of copyright issues. Patrice A. Lyons's article deals specifically with the issues of work-for-hire, infringement, and copy protection devices as they apply to databases and software. William F. Patry's article focuses on other important copyright concerns: the Berne Convention, colorized film, and sovereign immunity.

As in past years, in the News of the Year section of Part 1 you will find JoAn S. Segal's information-packed report on the growth of, and challenges faced by, library networks.

In Part 4 you will find information on how to obtain both ISBNs and ISSNs—important information for both librarians and publishers. You will also find a Buyers' Guide to aid you in locating library suppliers. In the same section, Richard Clare's "High Technology Bibliography" serves as a year in review of technology as well as a bibliography.

Each year the *Bowker Annual* staff apply their editorial, compilation, and production talents to the making of this book. Each year they deserve thanks for a difficult job well done. Filomena Simora, editor and compiler, remains the backbone of the *Annual.* Nancy Bucenec, production editor, continues to keep track of the numerous sections and deadlines with equanimity. And for three years Marjorie Cohen, indexer, has been providing you with access to the wealth of information inside these covers. Patricia Harris, executive director, National Information Standards Organization (NISO), joined us this year as consulting editor and her familiarity with the field, her grasp of current issues, and her clear and incisive input were central to the planning of this year's book.

The greatest thanks are, as always, due to all the contributors to the *Bowker Annual* who work in the interest of professionalism, education, and the importance of information services to society.

Margaret M. Spier
Publisher, Library Reference Books

Part 1
Reports from the Field

News of the Year

LJ News Report, 1988

GraceAnne A. DeCandido
Senior Editor, *Library Journal*

"I had no idea what I had unknowingly unleashed," Paula Kaufman told *LJ.* Kaufman described her encounter with agents of the Federal Bureau of Investigation (FBI) when she was director of academic information services at Columbia University, in letters to the New York Library Association and the American Library Association's Intellectual Freedom Committee. Kaufman and a host of other librarians were visited by FBI agents who questioned library employees about the reading and research habits of persons from countries hostile to the United States. The FBI admitted to a Library Awareness Program of enlisting librarians in research libraries to report the nature of the use of their collections by foreign nationals who could be spies. In the 1987 *"LJ* News Report," the editors wrote glumly that we "have not seen the last" of this kind of intellectual intimidation. How right we were. [See the special report "Rights for Users of Information: Conflicts and Balances among Privacy, Professional Ethics, Law, National Security" by C. James Schmidt, later in Part 1 – *Ed.*]

A Short History of the FBI in Libraries

January 1988

After they were contacted by FBI agents the Brooklyn, Queens Borough, and New York Public Libraries responded with official statements such as that offered by the New York Library Association:

> Once the people of this country begin to fear what they read, view, and make inquiry about may at some future time be used against them or made the object of public knowledge, then this nation will have turned away from the very most basic principle of freedom from tyranny which inspired this union of states.

During the ALA Midwinter conference in San Antonio, a closed meeting was held between agents of the FBI and members of the National Commission on Libraries and Information Science (NCLIS). A transcript of that meeting, with sensitive portions blanked out, was leaked to *LJ.*

Note: Adapted from *Library Journal,* January 1989, where the article was entitled "Library Directions in 1988."

April

The transcript exposed that NCLIS was not hostile to the FBI program. "I am inclined on behalf of what the Bureau is doing," said NCLIS Chair Jerald C. Newman, because "[we are] citizens protecting our democracy and our republic." The FBI's Thomas DuHadway said that he did not wish to interfere with anyone's search for information, but that "we like to know what it is [Soviet agents] are collecting." In the transcript Newman said "the real problem" was the ALA Intellectual Freedom Committee (IFC).

In a well-researched article in the April 9 issue of *The Nation,* Natalie Robins reported that the Library Awareness Program has been around since the mid-1960s. An "Agent X" told Robins that the FBI used appeals to patriotism, threats of hostile foreign agents, and the safety of the free world to enlist library personnel. Agent X said the bureau preferred to approach library clerks rather than librarians, because clerks were easier to intimidate.

May

The Association of Research Libraries condemned the FBI program with a strong statement supporting "unrestricted access to and dissemination of ideas."

June

ALA President Margaret Chisholm asked the Special Libraries Association to help bring the Library Awareness Program "to an end." SLA leaders had claimed the association was "neutral" in the initial SLA statement on the FBI program, but at the SLA conference the membership rebelled. They voted a strong new resolution firmly stating SLA's opposition to the FBI Library Awareness Program. When Robins's article in *The Nation* mentioned the cooperation of the "specialized library association" with the FBI, SLA wrote a strongly worded protest to the bureau and received a reply from FBI Director William Sessions calling the term "generic."

Also in June, a House judiciary subcommittee chaired by Representative (and former FBI agent) Don Edwards (D–Calif.) collected testimony from the library/information community. That testimony indicated a far greater danger to freedom from the FBI than from any Soviet spying.

An unclassified document prepared by the FBI entitled "The KGB and the Library Target, 1962–Present" surfaced. It ended with this statement:

> The FBI must logically pursue any contact between a Soviet national and an American citizen, regardless of where the contact occurs or the profession of the person contacted, and that would include libraries as circumstances require.

July

The American Association of Law Librarians issued a resolution opposing the FBI Library Awareness Program. James H. Geer, assistant director of the FBI's intelligence division, appeared before the Edwards congressional subcommittee and was told by Edwards that the FBI has no appreciation for "the special role of libraries in this society."

Throughout the summer hundreds of articles, columns, cartoons, and editorials from newspapers and magazines across the nation were sent to *LJ.* Most decried the FBI and gave the nation a refreshing and welcome image of librarians as heroes and freedom fighters.

September

The FBI requested a "national security letter" exemption from the proposed Video Privacy and Protection Act. That would have permitted FBI agents access to library patrons' records without a court order. After much lobbying the library portions were struck from the bill, thus denying the FBI. President Reagan signed the results into law in November.

The FBI met with the ALA Intellectual Freedom Committee in September, but 50 typescript pages of transcript revealed little of substance in the discussions. IFC Chair James Schmidt described the meeting as "less sprinkled with fact than I would have liked for it to be."

October

Venerable *LJ* columnist Herb White took on the FBI in his White Papers column.

November

The *New York Times* reported that FBI Director Sessions had agreed to limit the Library Awareness Program to libraries in the New York City area. Neither Edwards nor the library community was satisfied with the new limited focus. During his campaign for the presidency, Michael Dukakis pledged to end the Library Awareness Program. What George Bush will do as president remains to be seen.

To Paula Kaufman and to *LJ*'s writer, the Hydra, the monster of Greek mythology that grew two new heads each time one was cut off, is a fitting symbol for the Library Awareness Program. Make no mistake, the FBI is not done with libraries.

The Soviets: An Alternative View

U.S. librarians often hold a different view of the Soviets from the one promulgated by the FBI. In this time of *glasnost,* cooperation rather than confrontation or infiltration is the key word.

The Library of the U.S.S.R. Academy of Sciences suffered a disastrous fire on February 14, which raged for 19 hours. The library, founded in 1714, lost 400,000 volumes and a quarter of its newspaper collection. Blame was placed on defective electrical wiring.

Along with a more open attitude about the sharing of news, this tragedy also allowed the American library preservation community to share its expertise. Sally Buchanan, preservation officer of the University of Pittsburgh, Don Etherington of Information Conservation, Inc. (Greensboro, N.C.), and Peter Waters of the Library of Congress flew to Leningrad just after the tragedy to offer advice and assistance. Etherington described the Soviet approach as focused on the original item: They would rather restore or repair charred fragments than reformat them, for example, into microform.

A formal session for U.S./U.S.S.R. library cooperation took place in July just before the ALA annual conference. From July 5 to 8, the U.S.-U.S.S.R. Seminar on Access to Library Resources was held at the Library of Congress (LC). E. J. Josey, chair of ALA's International Relations Committee, presided over the 30-person American delegation. The 12-member Soviet delegation was headed by Nikolai S. Kartashov, president of the U.S.S.R. Library Council and director of the Lenin State Library. Cooperative resolutions were issued concerning:

- Adherence to international standards (where they exist) for online public access catalogs;
- The goal of establishing permanent relations between the two countries for the exchange of machine-readable data files; and
- The possibilities of exchange programs for specialists in automation, conservation, library education, and children's services.

[For E. J. Josey's report on the highlights of the seminar, see the International Reports section of Part 1—*Ed.*]

A further agreement, in the form of a protocol signed at ALA in New Orleans, called for the possible exchange of current national bibliographies beginning in 1989. The cataloging and formatting differences between the Library of Congress and a Soviet-supplied magnetic tape were found to be "not insurmountable," according to LC's analysis.

In late spring, SLA's Executive Director David Bender led a group of librarians to the Soviet Union to study the acquisition, documentation, and preservation of art and museum collections. Topics discussed included the standardization of art subject headings and the use of art and culture thesauri.

This kind of intellectual and informational cooperation, fraught with goodwill on all sides, exposes to an even greater degree the plain wrong-headedness of the FBI program.

A New Program at the Library of Congress

The Library of Congress, under new Librarian of Congress (and scholar for Soviet studies) James H. Billington, embarked on a program to review LC's mandate and mission, both internally and externally. A series of forums were held across the country so that librarians might make suggestions regarding LC's future services to the library community as a whole. The Management Planning Committee, composed of LC staff at the middle management level and below, sponsored these forums, one of which was held at the SLA annual conference in Denver in June. The special libraries community offered thoughtful suggestions during a lively and open discussion. Informed sources reported the same sort of enthusiasm at other forums, too.

A special announcement issued from Billington's office in December described the MAP committee and the forums, as well as the review by the Arthur Young management consultants team, as starting a process rather than producing a product. "We have consciously determined that the Library shall have seven institutional values . . . service, quality, effectiveness, innovation, participation, fairness, and staff development. We are, first and foremost, a *service* [italics theirs] institution."

Black Monday Revisited

Just after the October 19, 1987, stock market crash, *LJ* contacted key library finance experts for their assessments of the potential damage to libraries. Most indicated that real difficulties might come later, not immediately. *LJ* went back to some of the same people a year later to see what had happened.

In late 1987, Gregory Long, vice president for public affairs and development at the New York Public Library (NYPL), said his greatest fear was that the personal donor in the $35 to $100 range might be lost to the library. A year later, however, Long and Neil Baldwin, manager of NYPL's annual fund, told us that in reality the crash had its greatest effect on smaller family and private foundations. It was their giving that declined most. Baldwin added that NYPL's fund-raising efforts centered on the importance of the library's mission, and did not refer to external factors. He said that when people had to choose between giving to the library or giving to another institution, the library would win. Corporate giving was described as "flat," neither increasing nor decreasing. Successful as NYPL's efforts are, both Long and Baldwin said they must be seen in the context of the library's enormous size and its huge service, preservation, and education mandate.

Don Sager, city librarian of Milwaukee, reported that while the effect of the crash was much less than he had at first feared, fund-raising is tightening up. He described it as "a holding pattern" and said that alternative sources of revenue must be sought and found. Citing the trend to mergers and acquisitions as one factor, Sager said it was increasingly difficult to get major corporations to commit their support. When local corporations are taken over, often the new controlling managers have no ties in the community and are less willing to donate.

Former ALA Treasurer Pat Schuman, president of Neal-Schuman publishers, told *LJ* that the election had more impact on her business than the stock market crash. The October crash had no visible effect on the library publisher, but Schuman found far more nervousness in the market after the Bush victory than before. Read our lips.

The Bonds of Success

The biggest success of 1988—and it was a huge one—was the bond package passed by 64 percent of the vote in King County, Washington. The $67 million bond issue will pay for nine new libraries, expansion of several others, an online catalog, and an increase in the materials budget. A justifiably gleeful Herb Mutschler, King County Library System director, claimed it was the largest successful library bond issue in U.S. history.

The greatest disappointment of the year was the narrow defeat of the Los Angeles Public Library (LAPL) bond issue. Even in defeat LAPL cornered 62.37 percent of the vote, a massive endorsement, but California's unusual tax laws require two-thirds. A proposed tax increase to reopen the nine Shasta County libraries in California's far north was a more depressing loss. The libraries have been closed for months and could not even capture a majority vote.

Nationally, bond issues did well in 1988. About $130 million in bonds will be sold in Chicago to fund the construction and equipping of the new Harold Washington Library Center. A March referendum gave the Miami-Dade Public Library System (Florida) a half-mill property tax to create a $47 million fund for new library books. A $55 million bond issue for library improvement and expansion passed in Phoenix. The Grosse Point Public Library (Michigan) reversed its 1987 failure to get a tax increase in a June election that will generate $450,000 in additional revenue. Other successful bond issues in the November elections included those in New Mexico, the Chesapeake Public Library System and Chesterfield County in Virginia, Baltimore County in Maryland, and Rochester Hills in Minnesota.

Spiraling Serial Prices

The escalating prices of serials, especially scientific and technical journals from outside the United States, were still a deep and abiding concern. Directors and collection development officers from nine midwestern university libraries met to deal with the question. They plan a shared database of all serials titles priced over $200 to ensure at least one subscription to each in the region. A budget shortfall forced Stanford University Libraries to cancel $100,000 worth of science journals. ARL *Statistics* showed 1986–1987 serials expenditures up to 56 percent of library materials budgets, approaching the 1981 all-time high of 58 percent. A year of debate on the problem and the host of forums planned for 1989 suggest that this issue will not go away for a long time.

An interesting development in contrast to the serials pricing question is the appeal of North American automated systems in Europe. CLSI (Computer Library Services, Inc.) is the vendor of choice in Paris and in Helsinki; Geac will automate the Leningrad Academy of Sciences Library, site of a devastating fire in February 1988.

Preservation Glamour

Preservation has become the glamour issue of the library world, but it might be well for us to consider the older meaning of the word: enchantment or magic. There is no magic that will solve the pressing problems of preserving our cultural heritage, only hard work within a context of sometimes conflicting expert advice.

Many of the most pressing problems in library preservation would be solved if materials were printed on permanent paper. Such paper, which conforms to the American National Standard Z39.48, should last for several hundred years without significant deterioration. All *LJ* book reviews now indicate this information when available. *LJ* has also begun the occasional news column "The Permanent Paper Honor Roll" to bring attention to publishers that have made the commitment to permanent paper.

The need for permanent paper has begun to bring imaginative proposals from many outside of libraries, and a good thing, too. The Center for Paper Permanency has been set up by NYPL to serve as a clearinghouse for information and activity about permanent paper. It is located at 160 Fifth Ave., New York, NY 10010. Author Barbara Goldsmith, who funded the new preservation microfilming lab at NYPL, is spearheading a group of authors who have committed themselves to first printings on permanent paper. Senator Claiborne Pell (D–R.I.) introduced a resolution to establish a national policy on permanent paper, too late in 1988 for action. He is expected to reintroduce that legislation early in 1989.

ALA will issue a pamphlet about library preservation aimed at the general public in the second quarter of 1989. Called "Perishable" and printed on permanent paper, a wide distribution is planned. The preservation teleconference that took place in New York State on April 12 is available in videocassette. The National Endowment for the Humanities Office of Preservation tripled its budget for the microfilming of brittle materials to $12.3 million.

Joseph Grant's preservation comic book, *The Librarian,* has received a big response. Grant reports hundreds of letters and so many phone calls that he had to get an answering machine. He intends to keep publishing *The Librarian,* now in two formats: one on acid-free paper and one in traditional comic book form. Each edition will be published in English and Spanish on facing pages.

Other noteworthy news in library preservation included the development of the Bookkeeper method, a new deacidification process. Deacidification removes acid from paper. It does not restore the paper to its former strength, but it does keep it from deteriorating further. Other processes include DEZ, Wei T'o, and Booksaver; more are surely going to be developed.

The TAPPI conference on paper preservation provided a forum for communication among librarians, paper manufacturers, and conservators. Patricia Battin, president of the Washington, D.C.-based Commission on Preservation and Access, spoke at TAPPI, before a House Subcommittee, and at numerous other public forums about the problem of brittle books and about the commission's plans for addressing that problem. Solutions include a 20-year partnership between the university community and the federal government to preserve 4 million volumes, and a process to institutionalize basic preservation procedures.

[See Carolyn Clark Morrow's special report "Preservation Comes of Age," later in Part 1 – *Ed.*]

Most Favored Gifts

LJ loves to report on gifts to libraries, and there were some truly remarkable ones in 1988. The papers of Ellery Queen (who was actually two people, cousins Frederic Dannay and Manfred Lee) were donated to Columbia University's Rare Books and Manuscripts collection. Queens College (New York) professor Paul Avrich donated his collection of anarchist books, manuscripts, pamphlets, and other memorabilia to the Library of Congress. An archive of materials on homosexuality was donated to Cornell University libraries. Actor Clint Eastwood's papers were given to Wesleyan University in Middletown, Connecticut. *LJ's* very favorite, though, was the gift from the rock group ZZ Top to the Delta Blues Museum, housed in the Carnegie Public Library in Clarksdale, Mississippi. ZZ donated a guitar made from the wood of the cabin where blues musician Muddy Waters lived.

A $1.4 million gift from the estate of William D. Reis assured the conversion of the library card catalogs at Stanford University to its Socrates online system. The Philip Hofer Curatorship of Printing and Graphic Arts at Harvard College Library was funded by a two-year fund drive that raised $1 million. Vaudeville photos will be preserved at the University of Washington (Seattle) libraries through a grant of $144,000 from the Higher Education Act. The Drake Law Library in Des Moines received a $2.3 million gift from the estate of Emily Cartwright, whose husband Harold was an alumnus of the school. The football coach of the University of Georgia, Vince Dooley, contributed $100,000 to create a library endowment fund.

"Great Performances" in Libraries

An A+ goes to all of the libraries that sponsored splendid programs commemorating Black History Month in February 1988. *LJ* gives only a B– for Women's History Month in March; a frantic editorial search revealed that very few libraries even noticed, all of them in the Northeast.

"American Lives: Reflections on Our Values & Ourselves" is an ambitious program sponsored by the Southern Connecticut Library Council. In fall 1988, a panel that included political biographers David McCullough and Herbert Parmet debated the "great man" [sic] theory of history, the question of whether history turns on personality. Led by Robert Stepto, another discussion celebrated Russel Baker's *Growing Up.* Further programs will continue throughout the first half of 1989.

A project called "Adoption and Libraries: A Partnership for Children with Special Needs" produced an information packet focusing on using the library to meet the needs of adopted children and their families. For information on the packet, contact Mady Prowler, The National Adoption Center, 1218 Chestnut St., Philadelphia, PA 19107.

A final bouquet goes to Jefferson County libraries in Lakewood, Colorado, which gave out carnations on Valentine's Day to celebrate the community support that made the Sunday hours possible.

Another View of Video

The Heartland Institute, a Chicago-based public policy research group dedicated to the free-market perspective, published a commissioned study on library video lending. The study, prepared by William B. Irvine, assistant professor of philosophy at Wright State University, Dayton, Ohio, concluded that videocassette lending in public libraries restricts access to other library services. (Nearly 100 requests from libraries in 28 states came into Heartland's offices for the Irvine study, which sells for $4.50 from the Heartland Institute, 59 E. Van Buren, Chicago, IL 60605.) The results of the study are in pointed contrast to the overwhelmingly favorable response, almost across the board, from libraries on the theory and practice of videocassette collections. (The editors might add that the report represents a definite minority view.) The numbers of requests from libraries to Heartland seemed to indicate a willingness to entertain another point of view that was heartening (if the pun can be forgiven).

Self-Supervised Children

Julie Cummins, head of children's services at NYPL, deplores the negative connotation of the term "latchkey children" and prefers to call them "self-supervised" children instead. An awareness of the issue of latchkey children in the library hit the public media in 1988. What seemed a disturbing trend toward defining children at the library without adult caretakers as a problem crept into the library literature. Larry Brandwein, director of the Brooklyn Public Library, refused to reply to a questionnaire sent out by the School of Library and Information Studies at Texas Woman's University because he felt that the wording of the survey clearly defined such children as a problem rather than an opportunity. *LJ*'s November 15 How Do You Manage? entitled "Suffer the Children" provided some interesting answers from an administrative point of view.

AIDS, the Homeless, and Libraries

The dissemination of AIDS information is a task librarians have undertaken with professional rigor. The fact that so many colleagues are threatened, and that so many librarians have already lost friends and coworkers, puts a sharpened focus on these efforts. Numerous state and local library agencies in New York, New Hampshire, California, and other locales have prepared bibliographies and sponsored programs. *LJ*'s How Do You Manage? (September 15, 1988) tackled the question in concrete terms: What do you do when a library employee has AIDS?

Any colleague in almost any public library will tell you that the homeless seek both comfort and information in libraries. In the January 1988 *LJ*, Pat Woodrum described a solution in Tulsa. The Milwaukee Public Library runs the Guest House Drop In Center that provides daytime shelter and regular library services to Milwaukee's homeless.

People in 1988

Ilse Moon became executive secretary for the Association for Library and Information Science Education (ALISE). *P. Tina Lesnick* moved from head of resources, Law Library, Columbia, to chief of acquisitions services for Smithsonian Institution Libraries, Washington, D.C. Municipal librarian *Keith Revelle* of the Anchorage, Alaska, library was fired and replaced by an urban planner. Deputy state librarian in Hawaii, amid some controversy, was *John Penebacker,* who had neither MLS nor library experience. *Richard Dougherty* resigned as director of libraries for the University of Michigan but maintains his appointment at its School of Information and Library Studies.

Elizabeth Stroup left the Library of Congress to go back home to Washington as Seattle city librarian. *Ann E. Prentice* left the deanship of the graduate school of Library and Information Science at the University of Tennessee to become associate vice president for library and information resources at the University of South Florida. *Judith Sessions* left the Meriam Library at California State University, Chico, to become dean and university librarian at Miami University Library in Oxford, Ohio. *Paul Mosher,* formerly deputy director, Stanford University Libraries, is now director of the University of Pennsylvania library system. *Paula Kaufman,* acting vice president for information services at Columbia, moved to Knoxville to become dean of libraries for the University of Tennessee. *Elaine Sloan* moved from the University of Indiana at Bloomington to Columbia, as vice president and university librarian.

Joan Gotwals went from the deputy directorship of the University of Pennsylvania to director of libraries at Emory University, Atlanta. *Susan K. Martin* went from Johns Hopkins library director to executive director of NCLIS.

Rowland Brown, CEO of OCLC, retired and was replaced by *K. Wayne Smith. Milo Nelson* left as editor of *Wilson Library Bulletin* at the end of 1988. *Vartan Gregorian* will leave the presidency of NYPL in spring 1989 to become president of Brown University. *Linda Resnick* resigned from the directorship of the American Society for Information Science effective late winter 1988. *Tom Galvin,* executive director of the American Library Association, tendered his resignation late in 1988. *William Welsh* retired as deputy librarian of Congress.

At *LJ, Nora Rawlinson* left Baltimore County Public Library to become *LJ*'s Book Review Editor. *Susan DiMattia,* library consultant, Stamford, Connecticut, became editor of *Library Hotline. Fred Ciporen* became *LJ*'s new publisher in the spring.

Obituaries 1988

Paul Brawley, editor of *Booklist. John Mackenzie Cory,* retired director of the New York Public Library. *Anne Marie Falsone,* president, Falsone Management Consultants, Denver. *Mildred Lowe,* retired director of the Division of Library and Information Science, St. John's University, Jamaica, New York. *Karl Nyren,* founding editor of *Library Hotline* and former senior editor, *LJ. Everett T. Moore,* librarian emeritus, University of California, Los Angeles. *Thor Wood,* chief of the Performing Arts Research Center, NYPL.

Caution: Future Ahead

The FBI has hampered the free exchange of ideas by creating an unwholesome climate of fear and mistrust. The bureau must bear the burden of having hindered intellectual advancement and slowed the enrichment and diversity of human culture. In sharp contrast, the efforts of Soviet and American librarians to share their knowledge and professional concerns are cause for both hope and cheer. The former director of the Central Intelligence Agency is now our president. What will that mean in terms of resolving this dichotomous dance of U.S./Soviet information?

James Billington has clearly chosen to run the Library of Congress himself. Will there be a new deputy librarian? Will LC's empowered middle management exert real governance? What role will the Library of Congress play in the life of American libraries?

Although fund raising played tag in a skittish market, the support of the voters is obviously behind library bond issues. How can libraries continue to tap that reservoir of deep and abiding support by creative application of bond issues?

LJ expects serials prices to level off, or decrease, perhaps not in 1989, but in the near future. Will publishers heed *LJ*'s cry?

Permanent paper and the growth of processes for deacidification are central concerns in library preservation. Will the conservation community continue its progress toward informing not only the public, but the rest of its library colleagues?

Women's issues remain of deep, pressing, and personal concern. Will Tom Galvin be replaced by a woman? How about Vartan Gregorian? Or Bill Welch?

In 1989, *LJ*'s editors expect to find some answers; or at the least, more questions. Perhaps, with Rilke, we can even learn to love the questions themselves.

SLJ News Report, 1988

Bertha M. Cheatham

News and Features Managing Editor, *School Library Journal*

What began in January as a closed session between the FBI and members of the National Commission on Libraries and Information Science (NCLIS) quickly escalated into a battle between librarians and the FBI. Prominent newspapers were quick to investigate the more unsettling aspects of the innocuously named FBI Library Awareness Program. It was, in fact, the main event of 1988; the resulting media coverage afforded libraries greater visibility among the American public than any issue ever encountered by the library profession, with the possible exception of several highly publicized censorship battles. It was interesting to note the FBI's claim that the program had been in existence over the last 15 years, when in that span no librarian had ever publicly complained.

The problem came to light in fall 1987, when the FBI asked Paula Kaufman, librarian at Columbia University, for circulation records of people reading scientific journals, and, further, to report any "suspicious" activities of foreigners or people with accents or foreign-sounding names. Kaufman refused to cooperate. When this and similar incidents elsewhere were reported in the *New York Times* and circulated by the Associated Press, NCLIS scheduled its closed session without inviting any official of the American Library Association; ALA did obtain a heavily censored transcript, and followed up by demanding that the Bureau drop the program. After some foot dragging, the Special Libraries Association joined with ALA in opposing the Library Awareness Program. But, despite these objections and others raised by the members of ALA's Intellectual Freedom Committee, FBI Director William S. Sessions said that its efforts constituted "an important program" designed "to assure the sanctity and the security of technical, scientific, and military information." FBI officials never quite understood why its recruitment efforts created such a furor; obviously, they had not expected the intensity of the opposition raised by librarians who adhere to confidentiality of patrons' records. At year's end, both sides are at an impasse. ALA has not obtained an uncensored transcript, and the FBI has indicated that it will not scrap the program.

Another FBI matter, one that made the Bureau even less popular with the American public, surfaced during 1988. It was reported in May that FBI investigators had been monitoring the mail and telephone of Todd Paterson, a 17-year-old from North

Note: Adapted from *School Library Journal*, December 1988.

Haledon, New Jersey. When he was 11, Paterson decided to write his own encyclopedia and wrote to 170 countries, including the Soviet Union. Much later, he discovered that the FBI has compiled a file on his activities. Under the Freedom of Information Act, Paterson requested a copy of the contents of the secret file, and received, in return, a heavily censored document. Paterson is suing in federal court asking that his file be expunged. The case is pending. [See the special report "Rights for Users of Information: Conflicts and Balances among Privacy, Professional Ethics, Law, National Security" by C. James Schmidt, later in Part 1—*Ed.*]

Intellectual Freedom

No unusual surge in reports of censorship confrontations occurred in 1988, perhaps because would-be censors are changing tactics and are becoming more sophisticated in the political process. It could be that groups such as the Moral Majority and Eagle Forum have finally reached an awareness that First Amendment rights are difficult to revoke. In the bulk of censorship cases, courts have repeatedly upheld the freedom to read.

Scattered reports from the field reveal that, as in most cases of censorship over the last 15 years, the majority of book banning attempts occurred in the South. In Orange Park, Florida, a principal removed *Cold Sassy Tree* by Olive Ann Burns (Ticknor & Fields, 1984) from the list of recommended titles for a seventh-grade remedial reading class after a student's father complained about a passage on incest. The principal, Stephanie Athens, said this was the first time she had had such a problem: "You have to understand that we are dealing with a very conservative religious community here. Some of the parents are very strict." Athens removed the book to avoid further controversy, saying that it was not appropriate for this age group.

In Charleston, South Carolina, Pat Conroy's *The Prince of Tides* (Houghton Mifflin, 1986) was the target of a Baptist minister who complained that the language in the novel, used in an advanced eleventh-grade English class, would "gag a maggot." The matter was well publicized in the local press. Though the school board refused to ban the novel, it urged teachers to be more cautious in assigning materials for classroom use. Author Conroy responded by saying their action will have a "chilling effect" on teachers' assignments.

In a 5–3 ruling, the Supreme Court upheld the censorship of a Hazelwood, Missouri, high school newspaper. The incident occurred in 1983, when the principal of East High School in the Hazelwood School District deleted two pages from the student-written *Spectrum*. He claimed two articles dealing with divorce and pregnancy were inappropriate for his students and said he took this action to protect a student's identity. Protesting students contended that this violated their First Amendment rights. In the Court's decision, Justice Byron White wrote, "Educators do not offend the First Amendment by exercising editorial control over style and content of student speech. . . ." Many civil libertarians believe this decision opens the door for school administrators to freely censor student-produced materials.

Because it doesn't exempt libraries, ALA's youth divisions and Council have condemned the Omnibus Anti-Pornography Act now before Congress. If enacted, it would allow for the seizure of virtually the entire contents of a bookstore or video chain, based upon one conviction of selling an item considered obscene, and would permit easy federal prosecution of someone who distributes obscene material, even in states that do not consider it a crime.

Education

Education is big business in the United States—costs are rising, much to taxpayers' dismay. Early in 1988, Secretary of Education William J. Bennett predicted that $328 billion will be spent on public and private education in this country, representing a 6.2 percent increase over 1987. The average salary of public elementary and secondary teachers is expected to rise to more than $29,000, and elementary school enrollment is expected to increase 1.4 percent, to 32.8 million.

But Bennett will no longer be in charge of the highest post in education. After a three-year stint, he resigned just after schools opened in early fall. He did not escape without criticism, however. Bennett's main accomplishments were chiefly oratorical. Although he spoke of shortcomings in curricula (a fact that was already evident, following the move toward education reform that was underway when he assumed office), he did not achieve what educators and librarians had wanted most—an increase in federal spending for education. On the plus side, Bennett did leave the Department of Education intact despite Reagan's vow to abolish it; and his *First Lessons* (1987), in which he stated that every child should get and use a library card, was a catalyst in the creation of a national card campaign by ALA. (ALA says that hundreds of thousands of children signed up for library cards in its nationwide campaign; its success was chiefly due to imaginative registration drives held by public and school libraries.)

Reagan appointed, and the Senate unanimously confirmed, Lauro Cavazos as Bennett's replacement. The father of ten children and a native Texan, Cavazos is the first Hispanic official ever named to a cabinet post. He comes from Texas Tech University, where he was president, and before that, Tufts Medical School in Boston, where he was dean. Cavazos's first major project is the distribution of ten drug prevention videos aimed at students in elementary through high school. Approximately 80,000 tapes dealing with drugs such as cocaine, alcohol, and steroids will be distributed to school districts to help teach students to say "no."

Educators and publishers are watching textbook adoptions closely, as many dollars are tied to adoptions by large states such as California and Texas. In 1988, California's State Board of Education is leaning toward texts that contain classic literature. The fact that the state requires books to carry "consumer warning labels" whenever the original selection has been abridged or excerpted will not please intellectual freedom advocates. These labels, possibly the first to be inserted in textbooks, are designed to alert teachers about the dilution of materials and to signal publishers that such "dumbing down" practices are not acceptable. State Superintendent Bill Honig, who coined the phrase, said of California's rejection of "dumbing down" practices: "The sterile prose you see in a lot of the books is out. As a whole, the books that get chosen reflect what we are trying to get—better stories and better characters that grab kids' emotions and get them to think and imagine." His state also adopted improved math and science textbooks.

Elsewhere, school boards are working to strengthen their curricula. Statistics show that, in 1986, only 15 percent of high school students in the United States had taken a physics course, only 30 percent had taken a chemistry course, and only 35 percent had taken algebra. Seeking to improve the scientific literacy of American youth, Congress authorized $250 million for FY 1989 to improve the skills of teachers and the quality of instruction in science and math in elementary and high schools and schools of higher education. Libraries are identified in the legislation as sites that are eligible to receive technical assistance.

Statistics also show that teenagers are still spending a great deal of time watching TV or listening to the radio instead of reading. A 1987 Gallup survey showed that children spent an average of 2 hours and 24 minutes a day watching TV, and another 2 hours listening to the radio. The average time noted for reading books was 1 hour and 6 minutes, newspapers 18 minutes, and magazines 24 minutes. Teenagers with above-average academic standing read an average of 2 hours per day.

To further stimulate reading among children, the Arizona Department of Education announced that it plans to launch a statewide literacy initiative. C. Diane Bishop, state superintendent of public instruction, said programs dealing with reading, writing, library and media services, and early childhood education will capture students "before they lose the desire to learn."

The private sector also joined in the reading efforts. Pizza Hut received an NCLIS recognition award for reaching 14 million children through its Book It! National Reading Incentive Program.

In the wake of the national movement toward school reform, taxpayers have appeared more supportive of schools, and legislatures are more readily passing funding measures. As a result, many school districts are experiencing better times. One such fortunate district is the Irving, Texas, schools, whose director of media services, Mary D. Lankford, had the enviable problem of spending $1 million on books before year's end, in order to comply with a state mandate calling for ten books per pupil.

Public Libraries

The Free Library of Philadelphia received a generous gift of $861,430 from the William Penn Foundation to conduct a project (called "Building Philadelphia's Future: Books for Children and Parents") aimed at children from six months to six years old. The library is replenishing its collection with 75,000 new children's books. Helen Mullen, coordinator of children's services, said "the shiny, new books" plus staff training in outreach will enable the library to reach parents who might not otherwise come into the library.

Funded by an LSCA Library Literacy Grant, the Chicago Public Library has developed a "Parents as Teachers" project, in which participants enroll in continuing education courses held at the library. Instructor Elizabeth Landerholm says the project gets parents involved in reading to their children while improving their own literacy and parenting skills.

The problem of latchkey children who are left unattended in the library isn't new, but it appears to be escalating due to more mothers joining the work force, as well as an influx of children from families that have just emigrated to this country, many of whom are unfamiliar with the normal function of libraries and other options of child care. To help librarians cope, the Public Library Association (PLA) and the Association for Library Services to Children (ALSC) have compiled a booklet explaining how to handle situations where children are left unsupervised in a library. Many public libraries are posting a policy concerning unattended children (in

Atlanta, for example, parents are warned of possible criminal charges of child abandonment, though they do not define the term); and school systems have also begun to grapple with the problem. Recently, the Los Angeles City Council funded a new after-school tutoring program for approximately 2,000 children of working parents in ten elementary schools. A sum of $2 million in urban redevelopment money will go toward initiating the pilot program, which will enable children to participate in 40-minute sessions of homework, athletics, video-watching, and computer study. To expand the program in all 411 elementary schools over the next two years, $220 million will be required. School officials are looking toward the private sector in their efforts to raise the needed funds.

The Prince George's County (Maryland) Memorial Library System has been given a volunteer by the American Home Economics Association's Homesafe Course; her three-day-a-week assignment is to help youngsters age eight to ten learn home-alone skills—kitchen safety, handling appliances, answering the door, and so on. A local supermarket contributes snacks, and library staff contributes booktalks. In Springfield, Illinois, experts on children's self-care skills spoke to parents about its latchkey problem; fire safety and baby-sitting techniques were also covered. In other areas, senior citizens are being enlisted to run after-school activities. The Retired Seniors Volunteer Program is running a reading skills program at the Lakewood Branch of the Dallas Public Library. Other intergenerational programs are being conducted in Utah, Los Angeles, and Chicago.

The public is making good use of libraries. Cuyahoga County (Ohio) Public Library realized a circulation boost of 11.72 percent in the first half of the year as compared to the same period in 1987; program attendance increased by 12 percent over the 1987 total. Patrons of Fairfax County (Virginia) Public Library borrowed 8.2 million books, magazines, tapes, and other materials in 1987. The system serves 725,000 residents. The New York Public Library further updated its circulation system by introducing plastic borrowers' cards in nine automated branches; 72 other branches will be automated by mid-1990. By the year 2000, it is expected that most public libraries will have followed the lead of the larger systems.

[See "Services and Resources for Young Adults in Public Libraries: Report of the NCES Survey" in Part 4—*Ed.*]

School Libraries

After almost three years in the making, and more than 40 years after the first standards were published in 1945, *Information Power: Guidelines for School Library Media Programs* rolled off the press just in time for a national teleconference on April 12. The guidelines, written by a joint committee of members of the Association for Educational Technology (AECT) and the American Association of School Librarians (AASL), were not an unqualified success; some practitioners had wanted more direction as to implementation of specific measures.

Information Power calls for all schools to "adhere to a common district-wide selection policy that has been adopted by the board of education as official district policy." Briefly, among other benefits, this document establishes the legal base for selection and removal of materials; establishes the objective for the selection of materials; identifies the person or personnel who participate in the selection; and includes the process for periodic review and revision of the policy. AASL is holding workshops to train practitioners on how to implement the guidelines; these and other activities received the financial backing of H.W. Wilson Company, which gave a $30,000 grant to assist in training.

Professional Concerns

The shortage of trained librarians is a critical problem. ALA says that a large proportion of librarians will reach retirement age through the year 1990. The number of graduates of ALA-accredited MLS programs is now almost half the level of the mid-1970s. In 1974, there were 6,370 graduates in library science; in 1986, there were only 3,538. New York Public Library, Brooklyn Public Library, and Queens Borough Public Library reported difficulty in finding librarians to fill vacancies—averaging, as of midyear, more than 50 per system.

With the expected growth in the child population between 1990 and 2000, children's and young adult services will soon be faced with a crisis. The greatest increases are expected to be in such states as Arizona, Utah, Washington, California, Louisiana, Oklahoma, and Texas. Already library associations in nine states (Washington, Massachusetts, Michigan, California, New York, New Jersey, Arkansas, Connecticut, and Ohio) are reporting acute shortages in specialists trained to work in children's and young adult services in public libraries. ALA-accredited library schools are just not producing enough graduates in this service area. The most talented appear to be turning to the corporate world, which can provide better salaries, benefits, and opportunities for advancement. The average starting salary in the three metropolitan library systems mentioned above is a paltry $22,800; no one making this amount can cope with the high cost of living in these boroughs.

ALA reports that school library media specialists are in short supply also. Massachusetts will need 200 specialists by 1990, but the state's three accredited library school programs graduated only 30 students in 1987. Shortages are projected in North Carolina, Ohio, and Maryland.

Concerned about the shortage of minority students in the state's libraries, the California Library Association (CLA) has given top priority to the recruitment of blacks and Hispanics into library education programs. Research shows that representation by minorities in California libraries does not conform with the numbers of minorities living in the state. It has been reported that the number of minorities with master's degrees in library science declined 40 percent between 1979 and 1984, and CLA is actively recruiting minority students in MLS degree programs.

But, there is another obstacle—salaries. ALA reports that most starting salaries for librarians are comparable to those of teachers (but this is debatable in many areas). According to a survey conducted last year by *Library Journal,* the top salary for a library director is around $60,000 (in libraries serving a million or more people); an average salary for lower positions ranges from $18,000 (for a branch head of a library with a budget of $250,000) to about $28,000 (for a children's librarian in a high population center).

Following the lead of the University of North Carolina-Chapel Hill and the University of Washington, the Columbia University School of Library Service will expand its master's of library science degree program to two years. Normally 36 credits, the program will require from 48 to 54 credit hours beginning in fall 1989. Reasons given are more emphasis on research methods, greater specialization to enhance students' career prospects, and time for internships.

Literacy

ALA has issued shocking statistics about readers: Seventy-five percent of the unemployed lack basic reading and writing skills; 70 percent of incarcerated adults are also functionally illiterate; 33 percent of aid-to-dependent-children recipients are illiterate; 13 percent of all 17-year-olds can't read; 40 percent of all minority 17-year-olds can't read; 27 percent of all army enlistees can't read material at the seventh-grade level. Among the organizations that continue to promote literacy is Reading Is Fundamental (RIF), which selected Chattanooga, Tennessee, as the site for a model program in 1989. This initiative will spur community involvement in promoting the importance of reading. The year-long campaign, "City of Readers," underwritten by the General Electric Foundation and coordinated by Chattanooga Venture, a nonprofit organization, will feature children's programming, parents' events, and public services. A poster contest illustrating the "Year of the Young Reader" is among the events scheduled; libraries will be involved in a summer reading program.

Publishing

In 1988, trends in children's books reflected social concerns, in both fiction and nonfiction. Because of the need for information on social issues, many more publishers tackled difficult subjects such as AIDS, nuclear threat, ecological issues, and the homeless. Many volumes of masterfully illustrated poetry books and high-quality biographies were produced. Books in series continued to proliferate, causing a dilemma for reviewers and librarians who had to select from among them.

There are big bucks in books. Houghton Mifflin paid packager Ariel Books $801,000 for a retelling of *Swan Lake* by Mark Helprin (to be illustrated by Caldecott Medal winner Chris Van Allsburg), tentatively set for fall 1989 publication. This is believed to be the largest sum ever paid for a children's book.

Another highly publicized first in children's book publishing is the first printing of 250,000 copies, by Farrar Straus & Giroux, of Wilhelm Grimm's *Dear Mili,* illustrated by Maurice Sendak. This demolishes the old record for a first printing—140,000, according to the *New York Times.* The story, previously unpublished, was discovered in an 1816 letter Grimm wrote to a little girl.

Incidentally, Max, the rambunctious preschooler in Sendak's *Where the Wild Things Are,* celebrated his twenty-fifth birthday in 1988.

Technology

The world is rapidly changing; information needs are increasing at a phenomenal rate. Today's graduates must be prepared for a world in which technology predominates. Every year librarians flock to conferences and workshops to learn how to integrate innovations in instruction, only to discover later that the technology or equipment is outmoded and new models are more effective. Experts predict that equipment costs will decrease, but software costs will increase. School systems are opting to buy new equipment rather than fix old machines because repair costs tend to be prohibitive.

Recent reports indicate that the technological revolution has not occurred in education, mainly due to teachers' reluctance to use the equipment and their lack of training; often they receive training long after the children are adept in using new equipment, not before. The revolution in instruction via computers is not yet evident, because many schools are using them for the old "drill and practice," not for active learning. Teachers see mediocre software programs and poor administrative decisions in purchasing and utilizing computers and software as hindrances in school programs. Manufacturers of computers are trying to solve one problem educators face in purchasing software—software that is incompatible with the school's computer equipment. Recently, 12 major U.S. companies agreed to standardization of computers; beginning in 1990, their equipment will be built to comply with an OSI (Open Systems Interconnection) Standard.

Librarians in the nation's public libraries report that the inclusion of so much nonprint material has attracted new library users. A 1987 ALA survey found that 62.5 percent of library systems lend videos. In the Chula Vista, California, Public Library, videos circulate at 15 times the rate of the average book, according to Nora McMartin, head of AV services. However, theft, damage to tapes, and copyright infringement are among the problems inherent in loaning videos; in addition, the acquisition of videos is not cheap. About 30 percent of the public libraries across the country now charge patrons for borrowing videos because the purchase of videocassettes has taken a large chunk out of their budgets.

According to ALA, 49 percent of libraries serving more than 25,000 people have micros available for patron use, 76 percent of public libraries loan books on tape, and almost 25 percent of public libraries are reported to have acquired compact discs.

Computer software budgets are expected to increase for the 1988–1989 school year. Of the 173 school districts surveyed by Quality Education Data (QED) in fall 1987, 54 percent expect to increase their hardware budgets. By 1990, about 51 percent of all large districts plan to use CD-ROM technology. QED also found that 91 percent of schools are now using video, as compared to 86 percent in 1987. Though video collections are much harder to track, QED found that 13,469 schools had collections of more than 500 items, and 29,881 had collections of more than 20 videotapes.

American public schools have acquired nearly 2 million computers in the last decade. Over the last year, new channels of instruction have taken hold. Distance learning, for example, is increasing; 35 states plan to teach either via satellite or another system of electronic communications. One state, North Carolina, has launched a "Distance Learning by Satellite Project." Students in the state's smallest high schools in rural areas will be able to take courses in such subjects as foreign languages, calculus, and art history and appreciation—subjects usually offered only in the largest high schools. The state legislature appropriated $3 million for the cost of equipment, installation, and programming for the 1988–1989 school year, and staff is receiving training.

Computer software budgets, targeted at approximately $3 per student in 1987–1988, are expected to rise in 1988–1989 (mainly in large school districts, according to a QED survey). Approximately $125 million was spent on hardware in the 1987–1988 school year; an increase is expected in 1988–1989. Interestingly, inner-city schools have caught up with more affluent schools: Ninety-six percent of inner-city schools are reportedly now using micros as compared with 79 percent in the 1987–1988 school year.

According to a Knowledge Industry Publications survey, the number of children aged 5 to 13 will increase by 11.5 percent through the turn of the century; publishers and programmers of children's materials (books, videocassettes, and micro software) should therefore expect growth in the elementary school market.

[See the special report "The Promise of New Technology" by Margaret Morrison, later in Part 1—*Ed.*]

ALA Report

Few inroads were made in leadership and recruitment in 1988, the two main themes of Margaret Chisholm's one-year term as ALA president. Efforts are being made by ALA to spotlight librarians, however: 1989 has been named "Year of the Librarian," and the 1989 National Library Week theme is "Ask a Professional. Ask Your Librarian." The simultaneous focus on the library professional is unusual, to say the least. A second National Library Card Campaign, aimed at older readers, will further deepen public awareness of the need for libraries and information services.

Council moved forward with its own agenda in 1988, backing ALA's suit seeking to obtain "vast amounts of information" deleted from the transcript of the clandestine FBI/NCLIS meeting. Council also endorsed the report of a Special Committee on Access to Information, which called for the continuation of the Action Inventory on Access and for a periodic survey report by a permanent Coordinating Committee on Access to Information. In addition, a resolution requesting that the newly elected president, George Bush, affirm a policy of free and open access to information by and about the government, including monitoring of its status, was passed. This matter will continue to demand attention from ALA leadership. Incoming president Bill Summers is planning a program, "Access: The Fifth Freedom," for ALA's 1989 annual conference in Dallas.

Membership in ALA has been climbing: the total now stands at 47,249. A breakdown of members by type of library shows 29.5 percent in public, 13.2 percent in school, and 25.7 percent in academic libraries. A breakdown by job responsibilities shows 20.6 percent in administration, 11.8 percent in reference, and 13.9 percent in youth services. Interestingly, ALA's database shows that an astonishing 41 percent of its members did not indicate any supervisory responsibility; 16.3 percent indicated that they were directors or deans of an institution.

Members' chief concerns, among them demands for better management, centered around ALA's fiscal services. Division members found ALA's new accrual accounting method confusing and are attempting to get a clear idea of just where they stand financially. Other members debated the issue of what kind of accreditation is acceptable, but this was resolved with the acceptance of a policy drawn up by the Standing Committee on Library Education (SCOLE), not, however, without some opposition by the American Association of School Librarians (AASL), representing professionals who work in schools. AASL was fearful that the original policy calling for a master's degree from a program accredited by ALA did not take into account the many who graduate from schools accredited by the National Council for the Accreditation of Teacher Education (NCATE). The result was that Council endorsed both the SCOLE and the AASL statements recognizing school library media specialists who complete NCATE-accredited programs, as well as those who complete an ALA-accredited program.

Membership went on record in opposition to mandatory drug testing of library employees and commended Surgeon General C. Everett Koop for his efforts in informing the public of the causes and effects of AIDS.

ALA's three youth divisions wrestled with fiscal accounting concerns and membership recruitment. AASL was successful in overseeing the acceptance of the curriculum guidelines for school library media specialists developed by the AASL/NCATE Task Force, chaired by Marilyn L. Miller. Implementation of the new guidelines for school library media programs, *Information Power,* was initiated in October, when the first of four planned regional workshops took place. The document is now in its second printing.

ALSC is hopeful that *JOYS,* its jointly published journal (with the Young Adult Services Division), will find new readership among college and university faculty who can now post their articles in the publication, refereed as of fall 1989, for tenure tracks and promotion opportunities. The joint boards approved a three-year trial period; Josette Lyders, the new editor, will oversee the transition of *JOYS* to its refereed status. To provide baseline statistics in children's services (often requested by professionals in the field, but never before obtainable), ALSC and ALA's Office for Research are collaborating with the Department of Education on the development of a fast-response survey.

The YASD/NEH project "Library Programming in the Humanities for Young Adults" is now in its final phase. In 1988, YASD received a $90,000 grant from the National Endowment for the Humanities for training teams of librarians and scholars in how to develop and conduct humanities programs for teenagers. The last training workshops took place in St. Augustine, Florida, and in Philadelphia. Previously, NEH gave $317,294 to YASD to aid in the development of the division's highly successful 1987 preconference workshop "Courtly Love in the Shopping Mall: Young Adult Programming with a Humanities Focus."

Coordinated efforts among the youth divisions are strengthening programs and activities. They are reaching organizations outside the profession in promoting 1989 as The Year of the Young Reader; they also are formulating plans for full participation in the second White House Conference on Library and Information Services, scheduled for 1990.

People in the News

Mae M. Benne, professor of librarianship, Graduate School of Library and Information Science, University of Seattle, retired in June. Russell Freedman won the Newbery Medal for *Lincoln: A Photobiography*; John Schoenherr won the Caldecott Medal for illustrations in *Owl Moon* by Jane Yolen. S. E. Hinton won the first *School Library Journal*/Young Adult Services Division Author Award. Spencer Shaw, storyteller *par excellence* and retired professor in the School of Librarianship, University of Washington, received an honorary membership in ALA. Linda R. Silver, who settled a sex discrimination suit against the board of the Cuyahoga County Public Library, for an undisclosed sum and later resigned her post as CCPL's deputy director, was elected president of Ohio Women's Librarians (OWL). Mildred Taylor won the 1988 Coretta Scott King Award for *The Friendship*, and John Steptoe won for *Mufaro's Daughters.* Lucille Cole Thomas, former assistant director for school library services, New York Board of Education, received ALA's 1988 Grolier Award.

Deaths during 1988 included Margaret A. Edwards, retired adult services coordinator, Enoch Pratt Free Library, Baltimore, where she developed a philosophy for establishing young adult services; Eleanor Estes, author of *The Moffats* and other books; Virginia Haviland, who established the Center for the Study of Literature for Children at the Library of Congress and served as its director until 1981; Clement G. Hurd, illustrator/author; Arnold Lobel, author/illustrator of many award-winning books for young children; Mildred Lowe, library educator; Ursula Nordstrom, noted editor and innovator of children's books and retired vice president of Harper & Row; Karl Nyren, founding editor of *Library Hotline* and retired senior editor of *Library Journal;* and George Allan Woods, former children's book editor of the *New York Times.*

The Outlook for 1989

With the election of Vice President Bush to the U.S. presidency, the mood of the country will likely continue the conservative course begun in the early years of the Reagan administration. Although Bush campaigned as an "education president," he supported his predecessor's proposed $13 billion in education cuts. He did, however, vow to increase appropriations for the newly created Fund for Improvement and Reform of Schools and Teaching, from $12 million to $50 million. One can only wonder where these additional monies will come from; consider, for example, the 1.2 percent drop in appropriations for the Elementary and Secondary Education Act Chapter 2 block grant funds (from the 1988 level of $504,131,000 to $491,728,000 for FY 1989). On the plus side, Barbara Bush is a strong advocate of literacy, so libraries may fare well—if Bush can work with another overwhelmingly Democratic Congress.

PW News Report, 1988

John F. Baker
Editor in Chief, *Publishers Weekly*

One of these years perhaps the restless turbulence in American publishing will subside; but 1988 certainly was not the year. Further major takeovers, purchases and sales of companies, both domestically and internationally, continued apace, top publishing people seemed to be more peripatetic than ever, and the money offered for multiple properties by tried and true best-selling authors reached ever more absurdly astronomical heights. It was a year, in fact, that often seemed to be more about money than books.

The acquisitions began before the first month was out, when Times Mirror bought Richard D. Irwin, the business publisher. The following month Addison-Wesley merged with a U.S. subsidiary of the British Pearson group to form Addison-Wesley Longman. The next acquisition was also a transatlantic affair, as the French

Note: Adapted from *Publishers Weekly,* January 6, 1989, where the article was entitled "Looking Back on '88."

giant Hachette wooed and finally won Grolier, the Danbury, Connecticut-based encyclopedia company.

Robert Maxwell, the British tycoon whose previous U.S. incursions had been the acquisition of a number of printing companies and a failed try for Harcourt Brace Jovanovich, finally established a U.S. publishing beachhead by buying Science Research Associates from IBM in June; in late summer Maxwell began his biggest battle on these shores, as he went after Macmillan. Originally opposed by the Bass group, then by a planned leveraged buyout organized by management through Kohlberg, Kravis Roberts, Maxwell persevered, through courts and upward bids, until he finally prevailed and took over the company in November. Macmillan chairman Edward Evans quit (though most of top management stayed, and were publicly congratulated by Maxwell in a full-page *New York Times* ad for doing so), and as the tycoon named his son Kevin to lead the group he also pledged not to sell off parts of the company piecemeal—though at year's end parts of it had already been sold.

New Domestic Allegiances

Domestically, the biggest news was the conjoining of Random House and Crown, one of the biggest remaining independents. With Crown's vast, and very successful, remaindering and promotional book operations, this gave Random a whole new approach to the market; and within days (although, they insisted, not in reaction) the Bantam Doubleday Dell group established its own remaindering operation. These two moves seemed sure to radically change the shape of the remainder business in the years ahead.

On a smaller scale among takeovers, Harper & Row, which has been rapidly expanding its religious publishing division in San Francisco, bought the Grand Rapids, Michigan, religious house Zondervan; Workman took over the small literary publisher Algonquin Books of Chapel Hill, North Carolina, formerly part of Dallas's Taylor Publishing; Random acquired Vanguard; a New York real estate company (involved also in backing the irreverent *Spy* magazine) purchased Lyle Stuart; and at year's end Zebra Books was looking to buy the assets and contracts of PaperJacks, the Canadian mass market house.

McGraw-Hill announced its plan to sell its trade publishing division, though its assets were diminished when editorial director Gladys Justin Carr departed for Harper, taking McGraw's biggest bestseller, Erma Bombeck, with her. Stein & Day, long embroiled in financial problems and a struggle with a distributor, ceased publishing in late summer, and at year's end Dodd, Mead, which had sold off most of its very considerable backlist assets, also appeared to be out of active operation.

New Agenting Lineups

There was a late-year flurry in the upper levels of agentdom, in which a search for greater clout and a wider international reach seemed to be the prime movers: Morton Janklow and Lynn Nesbit, formerly of ICM, joined forces in a partnership; the London and New York branches of Curtis Brown were amalgamated; and Owen Laster was named to head William Morris's worldwide literary operations.

Discount Changes

In the sometimes acerbic campaign waged by independent booksellers against allegedly preferential discounts offered to the chains by mass market houses, four more publishers announced new discount policies during the year—the Putnam group in November, the Ballantine imprints and Pocket Books and Warner Books all in December, apparently designed to defuse such complaints (which were renewed in a petition campaign against those four mass market firms in September). In the spring Barnes & Noble-B. Dalton said it would no longer deal directly with about 500 smaller publishers for purchase orders, but would instead buy their books through the major distributors and wholesalers.

The Cheever Struggle

One of the year's more unusual legal struggles took place between Academy Chicago, which had contracted for a book of John Cheever's uncollected short stories, and the Cheever family, which complained that the planned book included works the late author would not have approved for republication. The publisher eventually agreed the stories could be chosen by widow Mary Cheever, but at year's end it seemed the sides were still at loggerheads over the length and quality of the collection.

The long-running suit brought by the AAP against 20 dealers in stripped mass market paperback books finally ended after six years when the last of the defendants agreed to cease the practice and to pay fines should it recur.

Improving Book Sales

Book sales seem to be edging upward. The AAP reported that 1987 sales were up 9.2 percent over those in 1986, and the investment bankers Veronis, Suhler & Associates predicted average annual sales increases of slightly more than that—9.4 percent—over the next five years, which would include 1988. Sales figures for most of 1988, up to the last quarter, showed children's paperbacks, adult trade paperbacks, children's hardcovers and adult hardcovers, in that order, with the most impressive gains among major categories; mass market was also performing better than usual, and university press books rose strongly over 1987. Many booksellers reported flat sales in the fall, but early Christmas returns suggested a buoyant season, with some stores reporting sales as high as 25 percent above Christmas 1987.

Our Wealthy Authors

And there was certainly no stopping the upward surge of the sums paid to tried and true authors. Noteworthy contracts signed during 1988 included between $10- and $11 million to Mary Higgins Clark for her next four books (Simon & Schuster), $5.4 million to Thomas Harris for his next two (Dell), $5.2 million to Clive Cussler, also for two (Simon & Schuster), and what is only described as an eight-figure sum to Erma Bombeck for her next three (Harper).

Notable publishing people who died during the year included Fritz Landshoff (Abrams), Joseph Consolino (Random), Grace Bechtold (Bantam), Leon Shimkin

(Simon & Schuster), Sondra Ordover (Pinnacle), and Herbert Alexander (Pocket Books). That, as always, was the saddest side of what was otherwise a lively and reasonably prosperous year.

Library Networking in 1988

JoAn S. Segal
Executive Director
Association of College and Research Libraries
American Library Association

Over the past four years, the work of preparing an annual report on library networking has consisted mainly of finding news pieces, often brief, that, taken together, suggested some trends or important issues. But in 1988, library literature contained many more articles on conceptual aspects of networking than in previous years. The 1988 report begins with a more in-depth analysis of "key articles" than in the past few years, followed by news summaries that reflect a greater emphasis on theory in relation to practice.

One factor underlying the greater output of conceptual work was that in 1988 EDUCOM began to agitate for a "national network" of higher education institutions. Fortunately, a few library networking leaders realized that the network being planned would be built on a different set of protocols than the one planned for librarianship. Several articles explained these events, argued for cooperation, and enlarged the vision of networking for both librarians and administrators.

Believing that librarians need to understand more than a modicum of technical information about networking in order to be alert to such situations and in relation to the efforts of the bibliographic utilities to optimize their telecommunications networks, Larry Learn of OCLC published numerous clear, informative articles about telecommunications. These contain information valuable not only to technological wizards but also to library decision makers.

The prediction that libraries would pull away from networks, using their local systems and suboptimal sources of information for cataloging data, has been fulfilled: Several articles warned of the effects of this practice.

After at least 20 years of automated resource sharing, a restatement of the philosophy of resource sharing was in order. Richard Dougherty made a valuable contribution to the networking literature in reexamining the purpose of networking.

Key Papers

Chris Sugnet asked "eight individuals who are deeply involved in the national networking scene" to "comment on the apparent revolution brewing in their world."[1] Henriette Avram, Rowland Brown, Clifford Lynch, C. James Schmidt, Louella Wetherbee, Bruce Ziegman, Ron Miller, and Susan K. Martin discussed the evolution of a "national network"; historical factors in the formation and development of specific networks; possible impacts on networking of changes in the information marketplace and new technologies; services offered by networks; and relations with the for-profit sector and with other nonprofits. This excellent overview of networking elucidated the present state of library cooperation and made some predictions about its future.

Some common themes emerged from the eight papers. There was agreement about the historical foundation of library networking in the concept of the efficiencies of shared cataloging, about the rapidity of growth, and about the networks' ability to support collective technological developments, lessening the risk to individual institutions. Another area of consensus was that the greatest threat to networks is the defection of members that come to rely on local systems and optically stored databases, rather than to contribute shared cataloging. Schmidt said, ". . . the irony exists that even as the online union catalogs get more recognized and used, their future comprehensiveness, hence attractiveness, is being diminished."[2] The divergence between the networks proposed by administrators and computer center directors in institutions of research and higher education and those developed and actually operating in the libraries in those very institutions also appeared as a potential threat.

The inevitability of change was paramount in these network leaders' vision of a networking future. New services, evolution of qualitatively different databases, new pricing structures, and new technologies all figured in their scenarios. To deal with these, new governance structures are needed, and librarians must provide leadership in shaping the future of networks. The timeliness of this overview article becomes apparent as one reviews the literature of networking in 1988.

The sudden realization that serious efforts at linking campus information systems were developing along different lines from those evolving among the libraries on the same campuses jarred some librarians into action in 1988. From a conceptual point of view, Weiskel warned that there are two contradictory trends in research fostered by increased availability of electronic techniques.[3] The first would encourage interdisciplinary work by allowing scholars to broaden their research interests, since searching techniques for a variety of databases are similar. The second, electronic publishing, makes it easier for scholars to publish their own work and thus may have precisely the opposite effect, that of overspecialization. Weiskel also warned both scholars and librarians that they must learn more about each other's ways of working to create an effective use of an Integrated Scholarly Information System.

Bell reported on the formation of the Federal Coordinating Council for Science, Engineering, and Technology for Computer Research and Applications.[4] He stated, ". . . today most networks are migrating toward DARPA's TCP/IP protocol with a commitment to use the ISO protocols when available."[5] This statement is both disturbing and reassuring to library networkers, who have moved beyond a vague commitment to use the ISO/OSI protocols, having developed several layers of the ISO/OSI as the basis for the Linked Systems Project. The article does not specifically address this gap.

IBM and the University of Michigan announced a $30 million, three-year joint study to develop software to allow end users to send and receive data without special conversion procedures.[6] This software approach might be successful; it might also become part of the development of the upper layers of the OSI/ISO protocols.

The most significant publication in this area during 1988, however, was the Summer/Fall issue of *EDUCOM Bulletin*, with its focus on "Public and Private Initiatives to Create a National Education and Research Network." The issue reported the highlights of the National Net'88 Conference, held in Washington, D.C., in April. The lead article, by Ellen Hancock of IBM, discussed the strategic importance of such a network and argued strongly for cooperation that includes libraries. She specified that the networks "will be able to provide universal access via TCP/IP protocols as an interim step toward OSI and run along high-speed T-1 links, later to become T-3."[7]

In the same issue, Henriette Avram described the evolution of the library networking environment and projected a picture of future network services, stressing the importance of accepting the OSI standards as they are developing and urging collaboration among library networks that exist, those under development, and the evolving national research network.[8]

Avram appeared in the *EDUCOM Bulletin*'s next issue to warn that "because these two distinct networking activities are using different standards to effect computer-to-computer links, and because they are initially being built concentrating on different functions, i.e., technical processing versus reference and research, there is a danger of incompatible national networks developing."[9]

The development of a national research network, and the facilitators and barriers to library participation, generated much serious thought and writing in 1988. Closely related to this was the flow of articles on telecommunications coming one after another from Larry Learn at OCLC in *Library Hi Tech* and *Library Hi Tech News*, clearly dealing with a wide variety of subtopics and developing a coherent set of lessons for librarians and others faced with understanding the medium that carries the information in our networks. The first article set out to describe the telecommunications infrastructure and how it affects future network development.[10] Learn suggested that four spheres – technology, economics, politics, and government – play an important role in telecommunications and will have impact on the future of networks. Learn described aspects of deregulation, their effect on telecommunications, and specific jurisdictional concepts. He discussed three pricing principles: value-based, cost-based, and strategic (market-based), concluding with a note concerning the weak position of libraries and some other businesses to procure telecommunication services.

Learn also pointed out the increased need for data transmission facilities and described the Integrated Services Digital Network (ISDN), which is likely to become available in the 1990s. The ISDN, which is evolving in compliance with the ISO/OSI model, may provide an opportunity for libraries to contain their telecommunications costs to some degree. Concluding, Learn pointed out that "the telecommunications infrastructure is undergoing revolutionary change and development which will have far-reaching effects."[11] Access and delivery costs will increase over the next three to five years, but that period will be followed by new opportunities in a more stable environment.

In a subsequent article, Learn provided an excellent overview of network technologies for the layperson, offering a broad, up-to-date technical review on which to base further study.[12] Learn treated analog and digital signals, synchronous and asynchronous transmission, media and equipment, techniques, multiplexing, network architectures, protocols, and management, and included further references. Learn's assumption is that librarians are going to have to know far more than they now do if they are going to deal with the environment he described in the earlier article, and he has made it much easier for them to do so.

Learn also regularly writes a feature for *Library Hi Tech News* that appears under the title "Telecommunications News and Perspectives." In September, October, and November 1988, he treated serious issues in networking that can only be appreciated by those with some basic knowledge (for example, as might be gained through a familiarity with his two articles discussed above). For instance, one dealt with a possible cap on phone prices and the various pros and cons of a proposed FCC rule to that effect;[13] another treated the Open Network Architecture concept and the development of the provision of information services by common carriers;[14] and the third described the switched network architecture that controls the routing of calls from the local network to the interexchange carrier.[15] These basic lessons have long been needed by networking librarians; Learn has made a major contribution.

In her U.S. Department of Education–funded paper on library networking, Molholt made just this argument: that librarians need to know more about the technical aspects of networking, because the decisions they are making daily will have a decisive impact on the future of resource sharing.[16] She examined the state of networking, including telecommunications and the development and implementation of standards. She identified five major issues in networking of importance to librarians: increased functionality, including adoption of the ISO/OSI protocols and availability of resources on the network; performance reliability based on efficient technology; user assistance based on coordinated end-to-end problem solving; access to all kinds of resources needed by users; and governance participation. She then advocated a leadership role for the Office of Library Programs in interlibrary cooperation, which would be implemented through its influence on state library programs. Here she made a strong argument against purchasing catalog copy from optical-based systems and loading it into a local system only, without entering it into a national database. This, she pointed out, would be a step backward, a form of isolationism that weakens the sharing of resources at the state and national levels. She concluded with a set of recommendations for the Office of Library Programs, including the imposition of certain standards in Library Services and Construction Act (LSCA) regulations (enforcing the building of the national database); the funding of research and development; participation in standards development; cooperation with numerous other federal government groups and agencies and with EDUCOM; development of technical expertise at Library Programs; discretionary funding for state agencies; and creation of an advisory committee. All this would create an information infrastructure parallel with the telecommunications infrastructure being created by the National Science Foundation (NSF) and other federal agencies, to help the country move ahead in the information age.

Another reference to the de-networking trend came from Sheila Intner.[17] Describing a number of alternatives for libraries in dealing with their cataloging needs, Intner concluded that what is most cost-effective in the short run for individual libraries may damage the long-range database-building efforts of all libraries. She foresaw the possible "loss" of an increasing number of items; slower growth of bibliographic utilities' databases and the shift of the burden of collection, cataloging, and interlibrary loan back to the larger libraries; rising costs; the possible rise of smaller, more specialized networks; fragmentation of information and difficulty of access; and the withering away of unique information resources as they are no longer available outside the holding library.

Richard Dougherty reviewed the history of library cooperation, asking the question, "Is resource sharing still a service imperative?"[18] Highlighting the learning of the past 20 years in ten major areas, he concluded that resource sharing must be based on mutual benefit; that ILL transactions account for a very small percentage of total circulation activity; that large databases stimulate greater participation; that libraries will request items they own but that are not currently available; that unique contributions are made by libraries of all sizes; that resource sharing does not produce smaller library materials budgets; that extreme reliance on others is an untenable stance; that quality of output is more important than sheer growth; that both multitype and special-purpose consortia are valid; and that the interdependence of libraries is still problematic among users.

In planning for the future, Dougherty suggested, libraries need to define system capacity and acceptable performance levels. They need to be able to adapt to more growth (including its costs) in ILL as more machine-readable records become available. They need to deal with the question of whether access to materials (as opposed to ownership) is acceptable to their users and to accreditation agencies and whether they can truly revise their collection development behavior in a more cooperative mode.

Finally, Dougherty developed a model of coöperative collection development that stresses coordination to "increase the number of titles available and, through well-designed, shared collection resource programs, minimize the delay and inconvenience of securing publications needed by library users."[19] This expression of the ultimate goal of networking is a modern one; its appearance in an important year of thought about library cooperation is highly significant.

Major Developments in 1988

The major occurrences in networking in 1988 had more to do with gradual changes in interlibrary relationships than with radically new developments. As noted earlier, there was a considerable amount of regrouping, reviewing of position, and looking back over the history and value of networking. Several projects moved forward, however. These included the widespread use of facsimile transmission for interlibrary loan and other purposes, the increased use of CD-ROM both in facilitating and undermining networking efforts, continuation of the National Coordinated Cataloging Program Pilot Project, the Linked Systems Project, and the Network Advisory Committee activities. Some progress was made on standards as well.

Facsimile

If there was much discussion about fax in 1987, in 1988 this long-tested technology finally took off among libraries. Mary Jackson's excellent piece on facsimile transmission concentrated on its use in document delivery but also included a good description of the technique and the history of its development.[20] Especially significant was her coverage of the development of a protocol for facsimile transmission. Jackson addressed key questions, including patron need, processing priorities, copy quality, and cost factors as a prelude to a comparison of delivery methods. Based on a test of five transmission modes, fax compared very favorably in price and was the fastest mode. The article also included information on new developments combining facsimile technology with PCs. Jackson concluded that "only a critical mass of machines will allow facsimile to become just another delivery option," noted that such a mass is fast approaching, and suggested that fax should be given serious consideration as a method for document delivery. A brief article by Elizabeth Fugazzi described the questions raised by the use of facsimile transmission in the library context, especially in the area of fee/free service.[21]

Many examples of the implementation of linked fax systems were described in the library literature in 1988. In Alabama, a Higher Education Act (HEA) Title II-D grant will be used to link 30 OCLC/SOLINET libraries in a document delivery fax network for the state, with heavy participation from the Network of Alabama Academic Libraries (NAAL).[22] In Pennsylvania, the State Library has used LSCA Title III money to back fax projects. The second edition of the state's fax directory, published in 1988, lists 223 libraries of all types and reports 100 percent increases within less than one year in the number of transmissions.[23] The Kansas Library Network's fax-based organization, begun July 1, links eight libraries using Omnifax equipment.[24] The fourth (1988–1989) edition of *Telefacsimile Sites in Libraries in North America* was announced, with a November 1 deadline for inclusion and an expected publication date in December 1988.[25] The Virginia State Library and Archives awarded a contract for a prototype computer facsimile system, including ILL and reference forms in PC memory. Eventually the system is expected to include statistical reporting forms and other features.[26] A consortium of seven Idaho libraries received an LSCA Title III grant to establish and operate a pilot project telefacsimile network.[27]

Eleven Massachusetts public higher education libraries have been linked by a fax network that uses flatbed scanners, thus cutting out the intermediate photocopying step required to create single pages from books or journals, so they can be transmitted. With telecommunications costs subsidized by the State Board of Regents Computer Network, there are plans for connecting the other 18 institutions eventually.[28] The Wyoming State Library purchased 15 fax machines with LSCA monies for use by libraries throughout the state. The use of the state telephone network reduces the cost of transmission on the network, making fax competitive with the U.S. Postal Service. All 23 county library headquarters are expected eventually to have fax machines. Other state agencies are also included on the network.[29]

NCCP

The National Coordinated Cataloging Program (NCCP), a nationwide program for coordinated cataloging sponsored by the Library of Congress, OCLC, and RLG, began a two-year pilot project early in 1988. LC and eight major research libraries are participating in the project, which has as its goal increasing the timeliness of cataloging copy, extending cataloging coverage, reducing duplication of effort, and producing cataloging of a "national-level quality." The libraries will follow agreed-upon practices to create records that will be contributed to the LC database and then distributed to OCLC, RLG, and WLN member libraries on tape and through the Linked Systems Project link. Authority records related to the bibliographic records will also be created, as will LC subject headings and classification numbers.[30, 31] Indiana University Libraries became the first institution to begin contributing authority records to LC under the project.[32]

Linked Systems Project

Three excellent pieces on the Linked Systems Project appeared in 1988, as the project was reaching maturity. In a relatively brief summary article, LC's Ray Denenberg described the history of the project, stressing the Technical Committee, its purposes, structure, and functions.[33] Denenberg pointed out the trail-blazing nature of efforts to define the Standard Network Interconnection (SNI) protocols and expressed the hope that eventually the existence of these protocols will facilitate the development of commercial products that will permit easier networking. He reported on the phased approach to each of the seven layers of the ISO/OSI protocol, describing the status of standards and availability of commercial products at each. Denenberg reviewed the planned "migration" to established standards and the eventual implementation of the "migrated" specifications, emphasizing the importance of these developments, not only to the library world but to telecommunications in general.

Association of Research Libraries

The Association of Research Libraries sponsored a program on linked systems at its May 6, 1988, meeting in Oakland, California, and subsequently published the proceedings.[34] The purpose of the program was to familiarize ARL directors with the opportunities and limitations of some of the new technologies. Three major papers were presented. David Bishop, chair of the LSP Technical Committee, described the history of MARC and the LSP, including the parallels: both were in advance of contemporary technology and both anticipated future developments. Bishop then discussed OSI in terms of four key concepts as an international standard; its potential for enforcing true compatibility among commercially produced systems, rather than relying on emulation programs for each application; the concept of communication among equals; and the notion of minimal prior negotiation, or ease of implementation. He pointed out that OSI is not a *library* standard but is intended to be used for all telecommunications applications. He used analogies to facilitate understanding of the difficult concept of layering, and addressed the issues of interworking, efficiency, and TCI/IP, noting the requirement that there be agreement about which options will be chosen before complete interworking can take place. Bishop went on to explain the conceptual nature of layering, pointing out that there is no reason to believe that efficiency will be a long-term problem in the implementation of OSI. The TCI/IP protocol is widely used and is promoted by many as adequate, making the development of OSI unnecessary. But Bishop stressed that it is *not* a standard and therefore lacks enforceability. He also noted that government agencies, including the National Science Foundation, have been directed to migrate to OSI in the near future and cited the announcement on May 4, 1988, that major computer manufacturers will agree to conform to the OSI standard.

Henriette Avram then recounted the status of the LSP and the library community. Reiterating the theme that librarians need to be knowledgeable about technological developments, Avram identified the project priorities: Complete the Authorities Implementation, develop the means to transfer bibliographic records, synchronize the local system linkages to the systems of the LSP partners, develop the means for intersystem searching to support shared cataloging as we know it today, and develop the means to support interlibrary loan transactions. She mentioned the National Coordinated Cataloging Program (NCCP) pilot project and its demonstration of the advantages of the LSP links and clarified the need for including libraries in the higher education networking picture, but emphasized that library networking is production-oriented, rather than search-oriented, thus creating different needs that must be integrated by working together with the planners of education networks.

The final paper was presented by Dorothy Gregor, who suggested some future directions for the linked systems capability in libraries, particularly by extending the current use of the link, considering Canadian protocol developments, and planning local systems developments.

OCLC

The third major publication on the LSP, a comprehensive treatment of the project, with 12 chapters, each done by experts on an aspect of the topic, came from OCLC.[35] It includes basic information, technical material on the SNI, details about record transfer and information retrieval, authority records and bibliographic records for cataloging, and some brief articles on practical experience with linking, concluding with a discussion of LSP costs with the observation that new developments are incorporated into libraries if they enhance service and if they result in the reduction of other library costs. In the Epilogue, Avram and Wiggins noted that the LSP has reached significant milestones, albeit only a beginning. Possible future applications include use of the LSP to replace large tape-loading operations, such as the exchange of preservation and microfilm set records, CONSER records, or the National Register of Microform Masters Master File. Vendors are beginning to enter the market with OSI products that are "interoperable" with existing systems. The identification of future uses remains open-ended.

Network Advisory Committee

The Library of Congress Network Advisory Committee (NAC) held its regular semiannual meetings in 1988, focusing on key issues in networking and keeping the library networking community in touch with the most advanced developments. One of the lamentable failures during 1988 occurred when, after two years of work on an extremely general "Statement of a Common Vision" to which all the members could assent, the Network Advisory Committee was denied the approval of the American Library Association because some of the language could be interpreted to imply that a fee might be charged.[36] Intellectual property rights, the topic of the May NAC meeting, was covered in an article by Erika Love.[37] The December gathering was a joint meeting with EDUCOM, a historic event in which three common assumptions were agreed upon:

1. Standards and protocols should be compatible so that the network would accommodate library as well as other higher education and research communications;
2. A coalition of higher education, research, information, and library communities would benefit all participants; and
3. Development of such a network will require public/private sector cooperation.[38]

In addition, the groups issued a joint statement and agreed to a continuing working group. EDUCOM announced that its Networking and Telecommunications Task Force would apply for membership in NAC.

Standards

On September 26, at the annual meeting of the National Information Standards Organization (NISO), Peggy Morrison reported on the development of a U.S. standard for a common command language (Z39.58-198X), presenting a comparative analysis of the proposed standard and its international counterpart, ISO/Draft International Standard (DIS) 8777.[39]

Local, State, Regional, National, and International Library Networking in 1988

Local Networking

An increasing number of local networking efforts involved libraries in sharing local automation systems. For instance, members of the Detroit Area Library Network (DALNET), the Wayne State University–based group, share a NOTIS system containing nearly 2 million bibliographic records that tells users if a member library owns a particular title, where a copy of the title is in the system, and whether it is available for loan.[40] Thirty-seven libraries in the Westchester, New York, Library System jointly purchased the UTLAS T/Series 100 System.[41]

Paul Vassallo became executive director of the Washington Research Library Consortium, which is moving ahead on cooperative automation and storage projects.[42] Case Western Reserve University became the hub of a new resource-sharing system under a $75,000 grant from the Pew Charitable Trust. Plans are to link local institutions and then tie them in with other Ohio networks.[43]

The Houston Area Research Library Consortium (HARLiC) received a $100,000 HEA Title II-D grant to develop a CD-ROM catalog of the libraries' combined collections using Marcive for production. The 2.1-million-record union catalog reflects a consortial approach to coordinated collection development and interlibrary cooperation.[44]

In Colorado, several interesting local systems thrive.[45] Least known among them is MARMOT, the multitype network that encompasses the three Regional Library Service Systems on the Western Slope. Using Eyring's system, with software based on CARL, 17 institutions have been linked for circulation and online public access catalog functions. PPRLNET centers on the automated system of the Pikes Peak Library District (Maggie's Place) to link 28 libraries in the Plains & Peaks Regional Library Service System for ILL purposes as well as for database access to the libraries' catalogs and community databases. PLN, the Pueblo Library Network, allows access via dedicated lines or dial-up to its database from public, school, and academic libraries in the area.

Best known of the Colorado networking projects are IRVING and CARL, each exemplifying a totally different approach to cooperation. Each IRVING library maintains a local automated system and database, but these are linked through a Common Network Language. Rick Luce and others described the history of the project, discussed its compatibility with the ISO/OSI protocol standard, and detailed the way the network operates from the perspective of other libraries, that of users, and from a technological viewpoint.[46] They also described the four component parts of the software. Interfaces now exist for CLSI, CARL/Eyring, Dynix, GEAC, NOTIS, and UTLAS. Phase Two of the Dynix interconnection will be funded by LSCA, allowing the provision of actual hardware and telecommunications equipment to complete the project.[47] Electronic verification and transmission of ILL requests are components of IRVING.[48] A contract with Broward County, Florida, announced in March, provides for the linking of public and academic libraries using

IRVING software.[49] An interesting review of IRVING software appeared in September.[50]

CARL made news in 1988 with its Article Access System[51] and its economic development database.[52] The Article Access System allows users to access citations to articles from journals held by the library, employing keywords from titles, article summaries, or author names.[53] Gary Pitkin provided an excellent exposition on the Serials Access and Control project, of which article access is only one part.[54] In addition to the traditional aspects of serials control, the CARL serials system provides access to the content of the articles in each issue, relating each article to the journal title and the status and location of that title. By mid-1989, the project anticipates offering access to articles in more than 10,000 journals and eventually will overcome copyright record-keeping problems and be able to provide the full text of articles to end users. CARL demonstrated the service at the LITA conference in October under the name UnCover.[55] Rebecca Lenzini was named president of CARL Systems, Inc.,[56] which was formed to market this product and the entire CARL system to libraries and information centers.[57] The impact on the circulation services provided by libraries in the CARL system is a testimonial to the efficiencies a good networking effort can yield.[58]

The availability of InfoColorado, a database including published materials on business and economics in Colorado, was announced in October. The database has abstracts of economic development, business, and statistical materials, and will provide an alternative to expensive clipping services for many agencies and businesses.

CLAN. This consortium of 16 libraries in Rhode Island purchased the CLSI CD-CAT to serve its users, which already have access to CLSI's similarly accessed CL-CAT system.[59]

State Networking

Alabama. The Network of Alabama Academic Libraries (mentioned earlier in the section on facsimile) has a number of interesting projects, including retrospective conversion and interlibrary loan. "Major Microform Sets Held in Alabama Libraries" was recently published.[60]

California. Multitype networks were the focus of conferences at four locations in California in September. Although discussions at the conferences were the basis for further work by the California Library Networking Task Force, no reports have yet appeared.[61]

Florida. As mentioned in the earlier description of IRVING, a group of Florida libraries will implement the system. Six public and academic libraries have incorporated as the Southeast Florida Library Information Network (SEFLIN) to provide quick access to information for patrons. Rick Luce, IRVING's former director in Boulder, Colorado, became SEFLIN executive director in October.[62]

Illinois. A plan to link all libraries in the state for voice, data, and video transmission, spearheaded by the Northern Illinois Learning Resources Cooperative, is under development. The network would be implemented as early as 1989–1990.[63]

Michigan. A pilot project funded by the Kellogg Foundation to link seven public libraries in a reference and information delivery operation will focus on community information and outreach as well as typical library information.[64]

Missouri. The Missouri Library Network will distribute BiblioFile Catalog Production Systems and Hitachie CD-ROM readers to libraries throughout the state to support local library service, making a statewide CD-ROM database of holdings available to them.[65]

Nevada. The statewide CD-ROM catalog, prepared by General Research Corporation, includes more than 1.2 million holdings of more than 70 libraries in Nevada. Some 60 LaserGuide work stations have been installed throughout the state for access to the Patron Access Catalog.[66]

South Dakota. In development for over five years, the South Dakota Project for Automated Libraries System (PALS) provides information to ten state-owned libraries. Using UNISYS software, the project is based on the Minnesota-developed (MSUS) system.[67] Four libraries in Sioux Falls, South Dakota, also received a $120,000 challenge grant from the Bush Foundation to assist in planning a statewide automation system.[68]

Vermont. Without counties or other middle-level government, this state has created the Vermont Automated Libraries System, a distributed network of locally owned or institutional computers linked so that the user can access them with a single inquiry. The system now includes an online catalog of five major library collections; electronic mail for communications and ILL; circulation and reserve; automated cataloging links to OCLC; automated booking of films and nonbook materials; and automated services to the visually handicapped. In 1989, rural libraries are receiving additional assistance to enable them to acquire computer equipment and software. The Vermont Department of Libraries reports a rise in user satisfaction, elimination of routine clerical tasks, and a demand for participation from small public libraries. The system is a winner of one of ten 1988 Innovations in State and Local Government Awards, sponsored by the Ford Foundation and Harvard's Kennedy School of Government[69] and carrying a $100,000 prize,[70] which will be used to assist the rural libraries.

Virginia. A new networking review panel, the Virginia Library Networking Task Force, began its work August 29. Its charge is "to plan the growth of the Virginia Library Network by reviewing all relevant material and submitting recommendations for actions that maximize near-term accomplishments and minimize cost."[71] Its *Virginia Networking Notes*, brief newsletters of networking activity in the state, contain information about all aspects of resource sharing and automation.[72] Interesting topics include funding for network planning, search for automation staff, union list details, and retrospective conversion statistics. In December, Brodart published the tenth edition of the microfiche *Catalog of Virginia's Library Resources (CAVALIR)*.[73]

Wisconsin. The state union catalog, formerly on 6,000 microfiche, and weighing 36 pounds per copy, is now available on CD-ROM, on three discs, both formats from Brodart. The state is phasing in the discs and phasing out the fiche.[74]

Regional Networks

AMIGOS

Two 1988 news items had major implications for networking. AMIGOS announced it would contract with a group of its members, the Association for Higher Education of North Texas, to provide a CD-ROM union catalog and cataloging access to it by means of the Library Corporation's Intelligent Catalog.[75] The online public access catalog will include more than 1 million unique holdings and graphics of campus maps and library floor plans.[76] AMIGOS and CLASS also announced an exchange of selected services. AMIGOS members will have search access to the RLIN central bibliographic database, the authorities database, and special databases. In exchange, CLASS members will be eligible for retrospective conversion services through AMIGOS, which means records can be added from the 4.3 million AMIGOS SHARES database or OCLC.[77] Also on the list of exchanged services will be AMIGOS's magnetic tape maintenance and Collection Analysis services.[78]

BCR

LendStats, a shareware program for ILL statistics, was added to the Demonstration Disk Lending Program in 1988.[79] BCR staff now handle almost 2,000 support calls per week and the network offered more than 230 workshops in 1987–1988.[80] The possible pricing structures for networks was discussed with exemplary detail and openness.[81,82] In December, BCR announced that it would generally decrease OCLC prices and offer a volume discount, but also noted that two open staff positions would be frozen and requested that libraries reduce their calls for service.[83] The network reported continuing growth and financial strength.[84] Agreements with Library Technologies, Inc., now provide BCR members with a discount on two LTI products and services: (1) MARC database preparation services, including all aspects of database cleanup for use in online public access catalogs or circulation systems, and (2) Bib-Base software.[85,86] The network also announced a survey of fax users in December.[87]

CAPCON

The CAPCON annual meeting report indicated the network was also battling OCLC Tiered Pricing Structure pressure and was concerned about the ability to provide high-quality OCLC technical services to members.[88]

CLASS

CLASS has a wide variety of CD-ROM programs available at a discount to its members, including Bowker, Dialog, SilverPlatter, and Wilson products.[89] The National Agricultural Library Lending Branch is now accepting ILL requests via CLASS's OnTyme E-mail network.[90] Participants are increasingly using the CLASS OnTyme system for sending orders to vendors.[91]

FEDLINK

Specially discounted prices on Bowker's entire line of CD-ROM products are being made available to FEDLINK libraries, with orders going through the network and being shipped directly to libraries.[92]

Western Library Network

In May, a good overview article appeared on the Western Library Network, generally describing network products and services and emphasizing the LaserCat, a CD-ROM version of the WLN online database, which can be made available for an individual library or for the entire network. The article gives several examples of users, including school libraries, and also describes WLN software for establishing a resource-sharing network, with examples of sites where it is in use.[97] The network added the Archival and Manuscripts Control (AMC) Format to its system in 1988, under a Title II-C grant subcontract from the Washington State University Libraries. WLN now includes all seven USMARC formats.[98]

But the biggest news about WLN was the move from a state agency project to a private, not-for-profit corporation. The action of the Washington State Library Commission in June followed months of discussion among a variety of constituents.[99] Legislative action, which is necessary, will come early in 1989.[100] The new status would provide an added degree of flexibility, broaden governance participation, and open up a variety of funding possibilities.

Other Regionals

Executive Director Laima Mockus left NELINET after ten years of service.[93]

OHIONET announced it would distribute CD-ROM databases of SilverPlatter.[94]

PALINET began a service program to assist its members in integrating CD-ROM into their reference activities. Called CD-ACCESS, the program provides consultation on CD-ROM applications and hardware compatibility; CD-ROM hardware and software/database procurement; hardware and database installation and training; and a series of workshops.[95]

SOLINET also became a designated authorized distributor of SilverPlatter CD-ROM databases.[96]

National Networking

OCLC

The sheer amount of material that appeared in the literature about OCLC in 1988 indicates the extent of activity involving the largest bibliographic utility and the interest it arouses among librarians. Significant activity included new systems developments and investigation of new technologies and their potential for use by libraries, new products and services, publishing, convening of notable meetings, continued work with constituent groups, and international growth. In response to OCLC's ongoing efforts to modify its image, the library community seemed to be softening its attitude in its love-hate relationship with OCLC.

A review of OCLC's situation in *The Chronicle of Higher Education* in July pointed up some of the choices facing the center. Long a source of cataloging and holdings information, OCLC has branched out in recent years to provide reference service products and to become involved in other aspects of librarianship. It faces a serious strategic decision: Should it continue to diversify, moving, for instance, into document delivery and electronic publishing, or should it retrench, concentrating on its cataloging products only and thereby reduce costs? The article suggested that such a decision pits public libraries against academic and research libraries, but the actuality is far more serious. Although the traditional view of economics may be that expansion into new fields is risky, taking the retrenchment step during a period when cataloging revenues are already declining, at least partly because of libraries' failure to upload records from their local systems, is equally risky.[101]

Pricing decisions at the national level prompted a great deal of discussion among libraries and networks on appropriate pricing structures for OCLC products. Tiered pricing concepts caused librarians to give serious consideration to OCLC's revenue sources and costs.[102]

A recent OCLC advertisement indicates how far OCLC has developed in relation to its users. Entitled "Some Simple Truths about OCLC and Libraries," it emphasizes new user options that do not require OCLC membership, stresses that OCLC does more than cataloging, highlights OCLC's commitment to cost-effective library automation, and underscores the fact that libraries don't need special equipment to use OCLC.[103]

Statistically, OCLC logged its eighteen millionth record and noted that 294 million holdings/location listings are recorded for those items.[104] OCLC revenues rose to $85.4 million, an increase of 1.3 percent, and somewhat less than anticipated. However, cost containment resulted in a $2 million contribution to corporate equity. The number of items cataloged online dropped 4.4 percent, to 21.9 million. According to CEO Rowland C. W. Brown, overall system activity and service revenues increased. Although revenues from technical processing activities are flattening out and card production revenue is declining, searching and reference activities are on the upswing. The volume of activity is still phenomenal: 1.9 million cataloging records were added; 3.8 million online interlibrary loan transactions were carried out; online work stations rose to 8,481; and the system now has 9,400 member libraries, including serials union list and group access participants.[105] LS/2000 agreements increased to 105, and 321 libraries are now supported by the local system.[106]

Although OCLC issued its revised "Guidelines for the Use and Transfer of OCLC-Derived Records" late in 1987, the policy began to make news in 1988, as it was realized that member libraries may share records of their own holdings with each other and with nonmember libraries without restrictions.[107] Mason examined the issue of copyright and its application to a compiled electronic database in an article marked by sympathy for the large bibliographic utility that would have been impossible five years ago.[108]

OCLC moved to improve member libraries' ability to link their local systems with OCLC. James Thomas, OCLC Local Systems Division, described three new OCLC products that would have a direct impact on local systems, including a MARC export function that simplifies linking options, a new telecommunications controller, and terminal software for local cataloging functions on the LS/2000 system. Thomas confirmed OCLC's commitment to meeting the needs of its member libraries, with their variety of local systems.[109] This commitment was underscored by progress on the ALIS I and II systems for which OCLC had assumed support responsibility in 1987.[110] A front-page editorial in *Technicalities* also cited these developments, praising OCLC for its cooperative stance.[111]

New Technology Issues

The Users Council Ad Hoc Committee on New Technology examined the impact of the new technologies on libraries, brought the topic before the February Users Council meeting, and prepared a report with recommendations to OCLC. The issues addressed included the current state of the environment, the "haves" and "have nots," the context of change, organizational structure, the economics of information, financing new technology, and the impact of new technology on staff development and on bibliographic control. Recommendations were made in the areas of telecommunications and networking, education and training, research, and new technology support. The intent of the report was to educate and to promote discussion of these issues.[112]

New Online System

Various announcements appeared in 1988 predicting the phasing-in of OCLC's New Online System. In one, Jay Weitz, OCLC quality control librarian, described some of the searching features that will become available.[113]

Products and Services

Several new products and services made news in 1988. The CAT CD450 software provides access to subsets of the OCLC Online Union Catalog (OLUC) on CD-ROM discs.[114] The system also provides access to the Online System, an alternative that is not usually available with CD-ROM-based cataloging systems.[115] Subject and Name Authority Files have been enhanced, Version 4 of the OCLC Cataloging Micro-Enhancer software was released, and Library of Congress minimal level cataloging records became available.[116] The loading of LC subject authority records began in December 1987 and is being updated daily via the Linked Systems Project record transfer component; the file now contains nearly 2 million records.[117]

Reference database developments included enhancements for the Search CD450 System software;[118] the availability of the Education Materials in LIbraries (EMIL) database for use on the Search;[119] the expansion of the EASI Reference database, a multidisciplinary file, available through BRS, of recently published materials in the OCLC;[120] the availability of Macintosh software to search the reference line; the addition of four earth science databases; and the intent to offer a new Online Reference Service in 1989[121] under the name EPIC.[122]

OCLC Link Service, an electronic gateway once needed by libraries for access to online databases, was discontinued in April. The service became less helpful as the use of microcomputers proliferated.[123]

An agreement with Chadwyck-Healey made possible the eventual addition of some 200,000 records to the OCLC Online Union Catalog, representing a collection of nineteenth-century books and pamphlets, now in the British Library and other major research libraries in Britain and the United States. The British publisher will convert the collection to microfiche over a 30-year period. Libraries will have the option of acquiring the records on a machine-readable tape for loading into local systems.[124]

A major cooperative venture between OCLC and the Association of American Publishers began with the naming of OCLC to operate and administer the AAP Electronic Publishing Special Interest Group (EPSIG). EPSIG will promote the adoption of the AAP Electronic Manuscript Standard among publishers, authors, software developers, compositors, libraries, and other groups and will serve as a clearinghouse for information.[125]

Retrospective conversion services have become increasingly sophisticated. OCLC offers several alternatives, including microcomputer-based systems, and a free publication to help libraries prepare for retrocon, which is an expensive process no matter how it's done.[126]

Publications

OCLC has become a formidable publisher of materials for libraries. Not only does it make available materials needed to use its various systems, it issues informative newsletters and special reports about OCLC itself, including an outstanding annual report and an *Annual Review of Research*, reports generated by OCLC activities, and some nonsystem-related materials, usually in technological fields. Some of the publications in 1988 were the *Directory of Software in Higher Education*, compiled from the "Computer Software for Higher Education" column in the *Chronicle of Higher Education*;[127] the second edition of *A Guide to Special Collections in the OCLC Database*;[128] the *Communications and Access Planning Guide*;[129] *Audiovisual Material Glossary*; *The Future of the Public Library: Conference Proceedings*; *Planning in OCLC Member Libraries*;[130] and the *Retrospective Conversion Guidelines for Libraries* (mentioned earlier).[131]

In one of its most important publishing decisions, OCLC acquired the rights to the Dewey Decimal Classification and the assets of its publisher, Forest Press of Albany, New York. The intent is not to move the operation from its present location or to change its management (Peter Paulson will continue as Forest Press executive director). Future possibilities include adding electronic versions of the work.[132] The price of the acquisition was $3.8 million,[133] prompting Art Plotnik to question whether Dewey would have done it, and to answer, "Probably."[134]

Research

Research activities at OCLC were delineated in its *Annual Review of Research*, which identified 17 project reports, 6 external and collaborative research reports, 7 reports of projects sponsored by the Library and Information Science Research Grant Program, and the speeches of the 7 Distinguished Seminar Series speakers. Research at OCLC is focusing on four strategic areas: enhancing OCLC Online Union Catalog use; investigating full-text storage, retrieval, and presentation; strengthening the user-system interface; and statistics.[135]

Meetings

In addition to its usual hosting of the meetings of its constituent groups, OCLC held two major gatherings in 1988. On March 20–22, OCLC sponsored an invitational conference on the Future of the Public Library, which identified a futurist's conception of several possible scenarios for public libraries, featured talks by outstanding public librarians, and gave participants the opportunity to discuss these issues in small groups.[136] The Sixth Annual Conference of Research Library Directors in OCLC was held in Dublin March 27–28, with directors and/or representatives from 67 institutions. The program included presentations on preservation and academic networking and small group discussions on issues confronting research libraries.[137]

Constituent Groups

The proliferation of constituent groups in the library profession over the past several years seems to have been unavoidable, concerned as it is with democratic procedures and open access to information, yet somewhat ironic if one recalls Rowland Brown's statement early in his tenure at OCLC that OCLC was overgoverned and under-managed. Each constituent group meets, discusses developments of particular interest to it, makes (often useful) suggestions that OCLC move in one direction or another, and receives reports from OCLC management on developments. The number of meetings this requires of OCLC staff is phenomenal, and this report will not try to cover all of them.

The Research Libraries Advisory Committee (RLAC) and the Advisory Committee for College and University Libraries (ACCUL) held regular meetings.[138] The Regional OCLC Network Directors Advisory Committee (RONDAC) also met regularly to discuss issues,[139] as did the Users Council.

People

Personnel changes during 1988 included Rowland Brown's departure from OCLC after almost nine years at the helm. In December, it was announced that K. Wayne Smith, former president of World Book, would take over in January 1989. Smith's comments as he assumed the position indicate that OCLC will not retrench; he cited "high hopes for OCLC as an educational and information resource that will move the frontiers of knowledge, further and faster."[140] Smith becomes the third president in OCLC's 22-year history.[141]

Patrick Barkey, founder of PACNET, died May 17. Having served on the OCLC board while at the University of Toledo, he decided to transport OCLC to the West Coast by establishing OCLC's Western Service Center (later PACNET) in 1975. He directed the activity until 1985, served on the Users Council from 1978 to 1986, and was also a founder of ACCUL.[142]

J. Drew Racine, former assistant director for technical services, University of Missouri-Columbia, became program director for research libraries at OCLC in March.[143]

Training Issues

Maxstadt addressed an interesting question of training in OCLC searching in the March issue of *Library Hi Tech News*.[144]

International

A six-month trial project between OCLC and the National Library of Canada will provide a link for interlibrary loan. The U.S. members of the OCLC Northwest Group Access Program will have access to materials in a Canadian collection; Canadian libraries in the group can gain access to the OCLC Online Union Catalog.[145] It is hoped that the collaborative effort will lead to the implementation of an internationally accepted OSI protocol for ILL transactions.[146]

OCLC established an International Office of Marketing and Field Operations, to be headed by David Buckle. The office will coordinate OCLC policies and strategies in relation to "global utility of the OCLC database."[147]

OCLC and the British Library announced the availability of a service for librarians in the United Kingdom and Ireland using the British Library's BLAISE RECORDS services; now they can use the OLUC. Records will be available either online or on magnetic tape. The advantage to the growth of the OCLC database as well as to British and Irish users is exciting.[148]

The Luce Foundation awarded OCLC a three-year grant to create a computerized catalog of materials from the period 1911–1949 held in the National Library of

China, Beijing. The implications for library automation in China, as well as for international cooperation and for access by all OCLC users to a wide range of Chinese resource materials, are impressive.[149]

The National Library of Australia (NLA) and OCLC have agreed to the loading of current-year bibliographic records from the NLA into the OCLC database in U.S. MARC format.[150]

RLIN/RLG

A long-dreamed-of "work-in-progress" database made available by RLIN enables scholars to find out at any time what articles have been accepted in their fields and are awaiting publication.[151] RLIN also made available SAF, the LC subject authorities file. It will be updated through weekly tape distribution of new records from LC.

RLIN was awarded a $1 million NEH grant to support its Great Collections Microfilming Project. The project will involve key scholarly collections at Columbia, Cornell, Michigan, Princeton, Stanford, and Yale universities and the New York Public Library. Subject areas to be covered include American history, German literature, Chinese history, social science, popular culture magazines, Turkish language and literature, and history of science.[152]

Also announced was the addition of the libraries of the Whitney Museum of American Art and the duPont Winterthur Museum to the Research Libraries Group, as special members in its Art and Architecture Program, which now includes more than 40 university and museum libraries.[153]

UTLAS

The University of Toronto completed installation of the UTLAS T/Series 50 Computerized Catalog and Circulation System in February.[154] In doing so, it rounds the circle from the inception of the UTLAS system at the university through the implementation of a major local system using the services of the now-independent and for-profit organization.

CD-CATSS, UTLAS's CD-ROM-based current cataloging system, will provide access to a stand-alone system or can be used in conjunction with the UTLAS online system. Announced at ALA in July, the product is seen as facilitating the use of local systems while maintaining the large utility database.[155]

International Networking

France

The Reseau des Bibliothèques de la Ville de Paris, a network of 49 public and 5 special libraries in Paris with 3.2 million volumes, has contracted with CLSI for its $5 million automation project.[156]

Europe

In late 1987, the Committee of Ministers of the Council of Europe adopted a recommendation for the guidance of libraries of member countries with major implications for cooperation among libraries all over the world. Specific points included are facilitation of the exchange of data, promotion of interconnection, data transfer, and unrestricted access; development and promotion of standards; encouragement of service to users; cooperation in collection development; support for cataloging of all materials; preservation action; exchange of library staff and education of librarians in cooperation; and consideration of a permanent cooperative organization.[157]

Japan

The National Center for Science Information Systems (NACSIS) was established in Tokyo in 1986 to promote cooperation and networking among university libraries. Offering a cataloging service for the construction of a union catalog of books and serials through shared cataloging, NACSIS also has a union catalog containing holdings information and an information retrieval system for university researchers and reference librarians, now containing 13 databases. The center plans to expand coverage on a regular basis. An elaborate computer and telecommunications system serves the network.[158]

Conclusion

Networking and cooperation projects continued to bloom in 1988, as local systems shared by several libraries provided a particularly attractive model for many libraries. Facsimile transmission took off, enhancing interlibrary loan services. But the specter of libraries' failing to upload records into their national bibliographic utility haunted the future of these massive databases, which have become treasures of resources to share. If libraries are to reach Dougherty's lofty goal of ensuring that resources are available for scholars, they may have to take steps even more Draconian than those proposed by Molholt.

Notes

1. Chris Sugnet, "Networking in Transition: Current and Future Issues, a Forum," *Library Hi Tech* 6, no. 4 (1988): 101–119.
2. Ibid., pp. 106–107.
3. Timothy C. Weiskel, "University Libraries, Integrated Scholarly Information Systems (ISIS), and the Changing Character of Academic Research," *Library Hi Tech* 6, no. 4 (1988): 7–27.
4. Gordon Bell, "Steps toward a National Research Telecommunications Network," *Library Hi Tech* 6, no. 4 (1988): 33–36.
5. Ibid., p. 34.
6. "IBM and University of Michigan Begin Project to Enhance Ease of Data Exchange in Computer Networks," *Library Hi Tech News,* no. 54 (November 1988): 13–14.
7. E. M. Hancock, "The Strategic Importance of a National Network," *EDUCOM Bulletin* 23 (2/3) (Summer/Fall 1988): 3–7.
8. Henriette D. Avram, "LSP and Library Network Services in the Future," *EDUCOM Bulletin,* 23 (2/3) (Summer/Fall 1988): 52–58.
9. Henriette D. Avram, "Building a Unified Information Network," *EDUCOM Bulletin* 23, no. 4 (Winter 1988): 11–14.

10. Larry L. Learn, "Networks: The Telecommunications Infrastructure and Impacts of Change," *Library Hi Tech* 6, no. 1 (1988): 13–31.
11. Ibid., p. 26.
12. Larry L. Learn, "NETWORKS: A Review of Their Technology, Architecture and Implementation," *Library Hi Tech* 6, no. 2 (1988): 19–49.
13. Larry L. Learn, "Telecommunications News & Perspectives," *Library Hi Tech News,* no. 52 (September 1988): 1–3.
14. Larry L. Learn, "Open Network Architecture (ONA) or Is It?" *Library Hi Tech News,* no. 53 (October 1988): 7–9.
15. Larry L. Learn, "O's, OO's, and Ohs!: Sorting Out the Operators," *Library Hi Tech News,* no. 54 (November 1988): 3–11.
16. Pat Molholt, *Library Networking: The Interface of Ideas and Actions* (Washington, D.C.: U.S. Department of Education, 1988).
17. Sheila S. Intner, "Bibliographic Triage Revisited," *Technicalities* 8, no. 10 (October 1988): 3–4.
18. Richard M. Dougherty, "A Conceptual Framework for Organizing Resource Sharing and Shared Collection Development Programs," *Journal of Academic Librarianship* 14, no. 5 (November 1988): 287–291.
19. Ibid., p. 291.
20. Mary Jackson, "Facsimile Transmission: The Next Generation of Document Delivery," *Wilson Library Bulletin* 62, no. 9 (May 1988): 37–43.
21. Elizabeth B. Fugazzi, "As a Matter of FAX," *Technicalities* 8, no. 6 (June 1988): 1.
22. "Document Delivery Fax Network," *Library Hotline,* November 7, 1988, p. 4.
23. "Pennsylvania Fax Networks of Libraries Thriving," *Library Hotline,* July 27, 1988, p. 5.
24. "Fax Network Starts Up in Kansas," *Library Hotline,* June 13, 1988, p. 5.
25. "4th Edition of Telefacsimile Directory in Preparation," *Information Retrieval and Library Automation* XXIV, no. 5 (October 1988): 5.
26. "Telefacsimile in Virginia," *Library Hotline,* October 31, 1988, p. 5.
27. "Idaho Experiments with Telefacsimile Network," *Wilson Library Bulletin* 62, no. 9 (May 1988): 22.
28. "Mass. Library Network Adds Facsimile Machines," *Chronicle of Higher Education,* October 26, 1988, p. A22.
29. "Fax Machines Link Libraries around Wyo.," *The Outrider* XX, no. 11 (November 1988): 1–2.
30. "National Coordinated Cataloging Program Pilot Project to Begin This Year," *Advanced Technology/Libraries* 17, no. 1 (January 1988): 5.
31. "Coordinated Cataloging Program Begun," *Information Retrieval and Library Automation* 23, no. 12 (May 1988): 8.
32. "Indiana Inaugurates OCLC's LSP Link with LC," *Information Hotline* 20, no. 8 (September 1988): 11.
33. Ray Denenberg, "The Linked Systems Project and the Maturing of Open Systems Interconnection," *Library Hi Tech News,* no. 48 (April 1988): 1–3.
34. Association of Research Libraries, *Linked Systems* (Washington, D.C.: ARL, 1988).
35. *The Linked Systems Project: A Networking Tool for Libraries,* comp. and ed. Judith G. Fenly and Beacher Wiggins (Dublin, Ohio: OCLC, 1988).
36. "ALA's Network Vision: No Fees," *Library Journal* 113, no. 13 (August 1988): 41.
37. Erika Love, "Intellectual Property Rights in a Network Environment," *MLA News,* no. 208 (September 1988): 1, 12.

38. Joseph Shubert and Carol Henderson, "Report on December 5–7, 1986, NAC/EDUCOM Meeting," Memorandum, December 27, 1988.
39. "NISO Annual Meeting Report," *Voice of Z39* 9, no. 2–3 (November 1988): 12.
40. "DALNET Adds New Members," news release, Wayne State University, Detroit, September 12, 1988.
41. "Westchester and UTLAS Tie the Knot," *Library Hotline,* February 29, 1988, p. 3.
42. "Washington Research Library Consortium Chooses an Executive Director," *Library Hotline,* March 14, 1988, p. 3.
43. "Pew Grant to Make Case Western a New Hub of Resource Sharing," *Library Hotline,* March 14, 1988, p. 5.
44. "HARLIC Wins CD-ROM Union Catalog Grant," *Technicalities* 8, no. 12 (December 1988): 2, 5.
45. Susan Fayad, "Overview of Colorado's Major Automated Library Networks," *Colorado Libraries* 13, no. 4 (December 1987): 9–10.
46. Richard E. Luce, Richard Steele, and Nancy Walters, "The IRVING Library Network: Linking Local Dissimilar Systems," *Library Hi Tech* 6, no. 4 (1988): 47–58.
47. "Dynix/IRVING Phase Two," *MPLA Newsletter* 33, no. 3 (December 1988): 7.
48. Ed Volz, "A Survey of Automated Interlibrary Loan in Colorado," *Colorado Libraries* 13, no. 4 (December 1987): 11–12.
49. "IRVING Interface Expertise Leaps from Colorado to Florida," *Library Hotline,* March 7, 1988, p. 2.
50. "Worth Noting," *Technicalities* 8, no. 9 (September 1988): 8–9.
51. "CARL Announces Article Access System," *Advanced Technology/Libraries* XVII, no. 9 (September 1988): 6.
52. "Colorado Information Database Debuts," *Library Hotline,* October 10, 1988, p. 5.
53. "Automation Roundup," *Library Journal,* October 1, 1988, p. 34.
54. Gary M. Pitkin, "Access to Articles through the Online Catalog," *American Libraries* 19, no. 9 (October 1988): 769–770.
55. "CARL Demonstrated UnCover," *Advanced Technology/Libraries* XVII, no. 11 (November 1988): 3.
56. "Colorado Group Initiates Serials Access and Control Project," *Information Retrieval and Library Automation* 24, no. 2 (July 1988): 6–7.
57. "Automation Roundup," *Library Journal* 113, no. 13 (August 1988): 27.
58. Steve Wrede, "What Hath Automation Wrought? Circulation in the CARL Libraries," *Colorado Libraries* 13, no. 4 (December 1987): 16.
59. "CLAN Network Buys CLSI's CD ROM Catalog," *Advanced Technology/Libraries* 17, no. 8 (August 1988): 7.
60. "Network of Alabama Academic Libraries Points Out Achievements," *Library Hotline,* September 19, 1988, p. 4.
61. "California Calls for Multitype Library Networking," *Library Hotline,* October 31, 1988, pp. 1–2.
62. "New Information Network for Florida," *Library Hotline,* August 22, 1988, pp. 1–2.
63. "Statewide Telecommunications Network Planned for Illinois," *Library Hotline,* March 7, 1988, p. 4.
64. "M-LINK: Linking Michigan's Libraries," flyer (Ann Arbor: University of Michigan Library, 1988?).
65. "Missiouri Library Network Will Distribute BiblioFile Catalog Production Systems and Hitachi CD-ROM Readers to Libraries," *Library Hi Tech News*, no. 47 (March 1988): 9.
66. "Statewide LaserGuide," *MPLA Newsletter* 33, no. 3 (December 1988): 9.

67. "Governor's Involvement Makes South Dakota Network a Reality," *Library Hotline,* August 15, 1988, pp. 1–2.
68. "Sioux Falls, S.D. Gets Automation Funding," *Library Journal,* September 15, 1988:17.
69. Susan W. Johnson, "The Vermont Automated Libraries System," *Information Retrieval & Library Automation* 24, no. 8 (January 1989): 1–3.
70. "Vermont Libraries Win $100,000 Ford Foundation Award," *Library Hotline,* October 24, 1988, p. 2.
71. "Networking Plans," *Virginia Networking Notes*, no. 3 (October 1988): 1.
72. *Virginia Networking Notes* no. 1– (Richmond, Va.: State Network User's Advisory Board, 1988–).
73. "Tenth Edition of CAVALIR to Be Published," *Virginia State Library and Archives News*, no. 64 (November 1988): 3–4.
74. "State of Wisconsin," *Information Retrieval and Library Automation* 24, no. 8 (January 1988): 7.
75. "AMIGOS Moves for Wider Role in Brokering CD-ROM," *Library Hotline,* July 11, 1988, p. 3.
76. "AMIGOS CD-ROM Union Cat. for North Texas Libraries," *Library Journal* 113, no. 13 (August 1988): 26.
77. "AMIGOS, CLASS Exchange Selected Services," *Library Journal* 113, no. 13. (August 1988): 24.
78. "AMIGOS and CLASS to Exchange Services," *Information Hotline* 20, no. 8 (September 1988): 3.
79. "BCR Distributes Lendstats," *Advanced Technology/Libraries* XVII, no. 1 (January 1988): 4.
80. "BCR Task Force on OCLC Pricing and Services Meets," *Action for Libraries* XIV, no. 10 (October 1988): 1.
81. Ibid., pp. 1–3.
82. "OCLC Pricing Task Force Continues to Seek Input," *Action for Libraries* XV, no. 11 (November 1988): 1–2.
83. "BCR Reduces OCLC Prices," *Action for Libraries* XV, no. 1 (January 1989): 1–2.
84. "BCR Audit for FY1987–88 Shows Continuing Growth," *Action for Libraries* XIV, no. 10 (October 1988): 4.
85. "BCR Completes Agreement with LTI for MARC Database Processing Services," *Action for Libraries* XV, no. 11 (November 1988): 2.
86. "Discount Contract Signed for Bib-Base Software," *Action for Libraries* XV, no. 12 (December 1988): 1.
87. "BCR Surveying Fax Users," *Action for Libraries* XV, no. 12 (December 1988): 6.
88. "CAPCON Wary about Its Future with OCLC," *Library Hotline,* July 18, 1988, p. 3.
89. "CLASS Offering Discounts," *Information Today* 5, no. 8 (September 1988): 17.
90. *Library Journal* 113, no. 1 (January 1988): 29.
91. "Library Vendors on Class OnTyme Electronic Mail System," *Electronic Library* 6, no. 2 (April 1988): 75.
92. "Lee County & FEDLINK Utilize Bowker CD-ROM," *Library Journal* 113, no. 1 (January 1988): 31.
93. "Mockus Resigns from NELINET," *Advanced Technology/Libraries* XVII, no. 8 (August 1988): 8.
94. *Library Journal,* February 1, 1988, p. 20.
95. "PALINET Initiates CD-ACCESS Program," *Information Today* 5, no. 8 (September 1988): 17.

96. "SOLINET and SilverPlatter Sign Distribution Agreement," *Electronic Library* 6, no. 2 (April 1988): 71.
97. "The Western Library Network: A Bastion of Information in the Pacific Northwest and Moving Outward," *Information Retrieval and Library Automation* 23, no. 12 (May 1988): 1–5.
98. "Western Library Network Adds AMC Format," *Information Retrieval and Library Automation* 24, no. 3 (August 1988): 6.
99. "Message from the State Librarian," *Washington State Library News* 7, no. 2 (June 1988): 1.
100. "Washington State Library Commission Recommends that WLN Go Private, Non-Profit," *Library Hi Tech News,* no. 52 (September 1988): 7.
101. Judith Axler Turner, "Organization Offering Computerized Services to Libraries Must Choose between Diversifying and Retrenching," *Chronicle of Higher Education,* July 6, 1988, pp. A9, A12.
102. "BCR Task Force on OCLC Pricing and Services Meets," *Action for Libraries* XIV, no. 10 (October 1988): 1–3.
103. "Some Simple Truths about OCLC and Libraries," advertisement, *Wilson Library Bulletin* 63, no. 4 (December 1988): 71.
104. "OCLC Database Logs 18 Millionth Record," *Information Hotline* 20, no. 9 (October 1988): 3–4.
105. "OCLC Service Revenue of $85.4 M," *Advanced Technology/Libraries* 17, no. 12 (December 1988): 6.
106. "OCLC Grows, Changes," *American Libraries* 20, no. 1 (January 1989): 17.
107. "OCLC Issues New Guidelines for Use and Transfer of Cataloging Records," *Library Journal,* February 1, 1988, p. 12.
108. Marilyn Gell Mason, "Copyright in Context: The OCLC Database," *Library Journal* 113, no. 12 (July 1988): 31–34.
109. James Thomas, "Improved Local Systems Links to the OCLC Central System," *Library Hi Tech News,* no. 50 (June 1988): 1–3, 6.
110. "OCLC Reports Progress on Upgrading LS/2 Sites," *Library Hotline,* January 18, 1988, p. 4.
111. "Open Box. Remove Red Tape. Attach Terminals," *Technicalities* 8, no. 10 (October 1988): 1.
112. OCLC Users Council Ad Hoc Committee on New Technology, *New Technology Issues* (Dublin, Ohio: OCLC, 1988).
113. Jay Weitz, "The Future Is (Almost) Now: OCLC Searching Capabilities in Transition," *Library Hi Tech News,* no. 47 (March 1988): 1–3.
114. "OCLC Demonstrates CAT CD450 System," *Advanced Technology/Libraries* 17, no. 2 (February 1988): 5.
115. "OCLC Accepting Orders for CAT CD450 Cataloging System," *Library Hi Tech News,* no. 52 (September 1988): 12.
116. *What's New at OCLC, New Products, Services, and Online System Enhancements from OCLC* (Dublin, Ohio: OCLC, 1988).
117. "OCLC to Provide Online Access to LC Subject Authority Records," *OCLC Newsletter,* no. 171 (January/February 1988): 24.
118. "OCLC Implements Major Enhancements in Search CD450 System CD-ROM Software," *Library Hi Tech News,* no. 44 (January 1988): 5.
119. "OCLC Education Compact Disk Database Available for Use with Search CD450 System," *Library Hi Tech News,* no. 44 (January 1988): 5–6.

120. "OCLC EASI Reference Database Expanded," *Library Hi Tech News,* no. 44 (January 1988): 6.
121. "OCLC Announces Online Reference Service, New Search CD450 Products," *Advanced Technology/Libraries* 17, no. 8 (August 1988): 4.
122. "OCLC Demonstrates EPIC Online Reference Service," *Advanced Technology/Libraries* 17, no. 12 (December 1988): 4.
123. "OCLC LINK Service," *Information Hotline* 20, no. 5 (May 1988): 3.
124. "Microfiches Are Not Dead," *Information Retrieval and Library Automation* 24, no. 4 (September 1988): 7.
125. "OCLC Will Operate AAP's Electronic Publishing Special Interest Group," *Library Hi Tech News,* no. 54 (November 1988): 12.
126. "Retrospective Conversion Aids from OCLC," *Electronic Library* 6, no. 2 (April 1988): 75.
127. "OCLC Publishes Directory of Software in Higher Education," *Technicalities* 7, no. 12 (December 1987): 13.
128. "Special Collections in OCLC," *Library Hotline,* November 7, 1988, p. 5.
129. "OCLC Distributes Communication & Access Planning Guide," *Library Hi Tech News,* no. 48 (April 1988): 13.
130. "OCLC Publishes Three New Monographs," *Library Hi Tech News,* no. 52 (September 1988): 16.
131. *Retrospective Conversion Guidelines for Libraries* (Dublin, Ohio: OCLC, 1988).
132. "OCLC Acquires Dewey Decimal Publisher," *Library Hotline,* August 22, 1988, p. 1.
133. "OCLC Pays $3.8 Million for Dewey Classification," *American Libraries* 19, no. 8 (September 1988): 641.
134. Art Plotnik, "Would Dewey Have Done It?" *American Libraries* 19, no. 8 (September 1988): 736.
135. "OCLC Publishes *Annual Review of Research,*" *Technicalities* 8, no. 10 (October 1988): 2.
136. Nita Dean and Phil Schieber, "Conference on the Future of the Public Library, March 20–22, 1988," *OCLC Newsletter,* no. 173 (May/June 1988): 13–22.
137. "Research Library Directors Urge Expanded Role for OCLC in Providing Access to Scholarly Information at Their 6th Annual Conference," *OCLC Newsletter,* no. 172 (March/April 1988): 5–6.
138. Unpublished minutes (Dublin, Ohio: OCLC, 1988).
139. "Network Directors' Report," *Action for Libraries* XIV, no. 8 (August 1988): 4.
140. "Former Kissinger Aide Takes Helm at OCLC," *American Libraries* 20, no. 1 (January 1989): 14.
141. "OCLC Names K. Wayne Smith President and CEO," *Advanced Technology/Libraries* 18, no. 1 (January 1989): 1–2.
142. "Patrick T. Barkey, Founder of PACNET, Dies," *OCLC Newsletter,* no. 173 (May/June 1988): 10.
143. "J. Drew Racine Named OCLC Program Director for Research Libraries," *OCLC Newsletter,* no. 172 (March/April 1988): 4.
144. John M. Maxstadt, "Staff Training in OCLC Searching: Taking a New Look at an Old Friend," *Library Hi Tech News,* no. 47 (March 1988): 4.
145. "National Library of Canada and OCLC Link for Interlibrary Loan," *Library Hotline,* July 27, 1988, p. 2.
146. "National Library of Canada and OCLC Initiate Trial Interlibrary Loan Referral Project," *Library Hi Tech News,* no. 52 (September 1988): 8.

147. "OCLC Establishes International Office of Marketing and Field Operations," *Library Hotline,* December 12, 1988, p. 3.
148. "OCLC Available via British Library," *Wilson Library Bulletin* 63, no. 2 (October 1988): 10–12.
149. "OCLC Receives Grant from Luce Foundation to Create Chinese Bibliography Program," *Library Hi Tech News,* no. 53 (October 1988): 10–11.
150. "Australian Bibliographic Records to Be Added to OCLC Database," *Library Journal,* October 15, 1988, p. 17.
151. "Scholars at Non-RLG Schools Can Search RLIN's New Service," *Library Hotline,* March 7, 1988, p. 2.
152. "RLIN Offers LC Subject Authorities File," *Advanced Technology/Libraries* 17, no. 11 (November 1988): 5.
153. "Whitney and Winterthur Museums Join Research Libraries Group," *Library Hotline,* October 3, 1988, p. 3.
154. "UTLAS System Installation Complete at University of Toronto," *Library Hi Tech News,* no. 48 (April 1988): 8.
155. "Utlas to Show CD ROM-Based Current Cataloging System at ALA," *Advanced Technology/Libraries* 17, no. 6 (June 1988): 6.
156. "CLSI to Automate Paris Library," *Library Hotline,* December 12, 1988, p. 1.
157. "Cooperation among Research Libraries in Europe," *Information Retrieval and Library Automation* 24, no. 8 (January 1989): 5–6.
158. "Information Systems and Technology in Japan," *Electronic Library* 6, no. 6 (December 1988): 449–51.

Information Standards in 1988

Sally H. McCallum
Network Development and MARC Standards Office
Library of Congress

Communications standards headed the list of activities for the information community in 1988. A decade of work on standards for Open Systems Interconnection was completed by both the National Information Standards Organization (NISO) and the International Organization for Standardization (ISO). Those organizations also held balloting on standards for a common command language for use in online information retrieval systems.

The Organizations: NISO and ISO

NISO, the standards body in the United States responsible for the development of voluntary standards for libraries, information services, publishing, and specialized library equipment, is an affiliate of the American National Standards Institute (ANSI), the U.S. member body in ISO responsible for the development of international standards. All NISO standards are developed according to consensus procedures set by ANSI. The resulting standards are joint ANSI/NISO standards. NISO carries out its standards development activities in Standards Committees (SC) of experts. Draft standards must be reviewed and successfully balloted by the voting members of NISO before being submitted to the ANSI Board of Standards Review for approval. All existing ANSI standards are reviewed every five years by the responsible ANSI affiliates to determine whether the standard should be reaffirmed (as is), revised, or withdrawn.

ISO carries out its work in Technical Committees (TC), such as ISO TC 46, Information and Documentation, the committee responsible for ISO standards for libraries and publishing and information services; and Joint Technical Committee (JTC) 1, Information Processing Systems, which is responsible for standards for computer hardware and systems. ISO standards are balloted at least twice before they become final, first as Draft Proposals (DP) and then by a wider group of member countries as Draft International Standards (DIS). ANSI delegates to NISO the responsibility to advise on ISO TC 46 work and to represent the United States on ISO committees related to NISO's scope.

Open Systems Interconnection Standards

In March 1988, ISO held a press conference in Washington, D.C., to mark the tenth anniversary and completion of the first developmental phase of the Open Systems Interconnection (OSI) protocol, a set of standards that facilitate the interconnection of dissimilar computer systems. The development of OSI began in 1978 with the formation of a standards committee within ISO Joint Technical Committee 1.

Early work on OSI included the formulation of a model for interconnection protocols (which became standard ISO 7498, *Open Systems Interconnection Reference Model*) that divided communication functions into a hierarchy of seven layers and specified the development of a protocol for each. Similar functions are clustered together in the various layers. Functions that are prerequisites for other functions are contained in lower layers. Thus a communication *leaving* a machine to go to another computer passes from the application layer (the highest layer) to the lowest layers of OSI protocol. The communication emerges from the lowest layer in an OSI standardized form and is ready for transmission. At the receiving site it enters the lowest layer, and advances up to the application layer.

In March 1988, the protocols for all seven layers were at last complete, a major first step, and ISO announced that OSI has now been adopted in all major countries. Computer manufacturers also have begun to offer OSI protocol products. A major event in implementation occurred in September 1988, when IBM announced it would offer OSI protocol products in early 1990.

The OSI standards are very important to the information community. Currently, many information systems are isolated from other systems, and thus users of other systems as well, because of differences in computer hardware and software. With OSI, a user on a local library system could access other systems through the local system hardware and software. Depending on the implementation, the user might do this with only slight changes in commands and other elements of user syntax. OSI standards are the basis for communications in the Linked Systems Project (LSP), which currently links the Library of Congress with the Online Computer Library Center (OCLC) and the Research Libraries Information Network (RLIN). For several years, LSP has used the completed OSI protocol standards for the lower layers of its OSI protocol stack and draft OSI standards for the upper layers to support intersystem Record Transfer and Information Retrieval.[1]

Several specialized, application-dependent protocols coexist in the application layer of the OSI model. The protocol that handles connection establishment was developed by JTC 1, and several that are specific to the information community are being developed by NISO and ISO TC 46. In 1988, NISO received final approval on ANSI/NISO Z39.50, *Information Retrieval Service Definition and Protocol Specification for Library Applications.* This standard defines the application protocol for OSI interactions between information retrieval systems running on different computer hardware and software.

In ISO, Draft Proposals for two library specific application protocols were balloted in 1988. The first is the ISO counterpart to Z39.50 in that it supports information retrieval. Care was taken to ensure compatibility between the completed ANSI/NISO Z39.50 and the developing ISO standard. The second ISO Draft Proposal, for an interlibrary loan protocol, was largely drafted in Canada, but agencies in the United States and Europe have been very active in the review process. During 1988, discussion began on two possible pilot projects that would use this emerging protocol if they are carried out. In one pilot group, the National Library of Canada and the British Library would work under the auspices of the International Federation of Library Associations and Institutions (IFLA). The second pilot would be a European Economic Community experiment among DBMIST in France, PICA in the Netherlands, and LASER in England.

Common Command Language

NISO and ISO committees have been working simultaneously on a common command language for information retrieval. These important standards specify the vocabulary, syntax, and operational meaning of commands for use with online interactive retrieval systems. Comments on an early 1988 ballot were resolved and the NISO standard will be sent for reballot in early 1989. The ISO standard was circulated as a Draft International Standard in late 1988. Differences that remain between the two standards reflect both national preferences and the origins of the efforts. In the final round of voting, an attempt will be made to reconcile major points. Fortunately, the commands in the international standard are English-language based, which makes compatibility possible.

New NISO Standards in 1988

Five standards were approved by NISO and ANSI in 1988. One was a revision to an older standard, ANSI/NISO Z39.21, *Book Numbering,* the national standard for the International Standard Book Number (ISBN). The scope of the new ISBN standard was expanded to include all media, not just book format material. The name of the standard and the identification number will retain the word "book," as the acronym is widely known. At an ISO meeting in May 1988, the same changes were introduced into the international counterpart of the standard (ISO 2108).

Approval of ANSI/NISO Z39.59, *Electronic Manuscript: Preparation and Markup,* is a major step forward in standards for publishers. The standard is a specific implementation of the general structure standard for markup languages developed by ISO JTC 1: *Standard Generalized Markup Language* (*SGML*), ISO 8879. It could lead to more efficient publisher/author and publisher/printer interactions. It could also widen publishers' options for printer hardware and software when equipment manufacturers begin to offer generalized products based on the standard.

ANSI/NISO Z39.63, *Interlibrary Loan Data Elements,* was approved for publication in late 1988. This standard specifies data elements that identify both the item requested and the requesting institution in an ILL transaction. The standard is intended to be independent of the transmission medium, supporting both paper and computer interlibrary loan transactions.

ANSI/NISO Z39.64, *East Asian Character Codes* (*EACC*), establishes the computer codes for characters in the Chinese, Japanese, and Korean scripts. The set is currently used in the United States by the systems at RLIN (Research Libraries Information Network) and OCLC and for the bibliographic records for Chinese, Japanese, and Korean material distributed on tape by the Library of Congress.

The fifth new standard for 1988, ANSI/NISO Z39.50, *Information Retrieval Service Definition and Protocol for Library Applications,* is described earlier in the discussion of open systems interconnection standards.

New Publisher for ANSI/NISO Standards

The five standards approved in 1988 and ANSI/NISO Z39.61, *Recording, Use, and Display of Patent Application Data* (completed in 1987), will be the first six to be issued for NISO by Transaction Publishers, Inc. In 1988, NISO signed a three-year contract with Transaction for the publication and marketing of the American National Standards developed by NISO. This major new step for NISO was taken after several years of study by the NISO board. By working with its own publisher, NISO will be able to control the design of the standards documents. NISO also plans to work with Transaction on new ways to advertise the standards, the latter being critical to wider use and adoption of NISO standards. The standards will also continue to be available through ANSI in New York.

New NISO Newsletter

NISO took steps in 1988 to establish the NISO newsletter as an expanded and regularly published source for information on NISO and related standards activities. Late in 1988, the last issue of the *Voice of Z39* was distributed, and in January 1989, volume 1, number 1, of *Information Standards Quarterly* (*ISQ*) was published. *ISQ* will carry status reports on NISO standards work in progress, articles about standards development activities, reports on international standards work, and articles about new areas where standards are needed.

NISO Standards Committee Update

Automation and Interchange

SC CC continued work on a standard serial issue and article identifier to be used in automated systems for serial check-in and ordering and for transmission of serial and article data between systems. A new draft will be ready for circulation in early 1989.

SC W, Holdings Statements for Non-Serial Items, circulated a new draft in late 1988 that is more closely aligned with ANSI Z39.44, *Serial Holdings Statements*. The committee anticipates that this standard will be completed in 1989.

SC DD, Computerized Serials Orders and Claims, sent a draft standard for ballot and subsequently revised it in 1988. In addition to ordering, this serial standard, a companion to ANSI Z39.45, *Computerized Book Ordering,* includes the order response, claim, and claim response messages. It will be circulated to NISO members again in 1989.

SC LL, Circulation Systems Data, held its first meetings in 1988. This standard, which is to be based on work by the Automation Vendor Interface Advisory Committee (AVIAC), will be a dictionary of data elements required in a circulation system to specify the communications format for the data. In order to avoid privacy concerns, NISO has been careful to clarify that standardizing data does not imply that private data will be made available outside a system.

The work of SC G, Common Command Languages, and the newly completed standards ANSI/NISO Z39.50 and ANSI/NISO Z39.64 were discussed in earlier sections.

Publishing Practices

SC FF, Computer Software Description, continued work on a standard that specifies the information that should appear on software packaging and in advertisements for software; SC Z continued with Eye-Legible Information on Microfilm Leaders, Trailers, and Containers. Both standards are especially important to libraries because the information in these items is not eye-legible, making it difficult for staff to catalog and for users to assess the relevance of the material to their needs without equipment.

Five existing standards of special interest to publishers were undergoing revision during 1988. Review of ANSI Z39.10 (*Directories of Libraries and Information Centers*), ANSI Z39.32 (*Information on Microfiche Headings*), and ANSI Z39.22 (*Proof Corrections*) indicated that major revision was not needed. Editors are incorporating suggestions, and the revised standards will be balloted in 1989. Standards committees were formed to make more extensive revisions on two current standards. SC VV will revise ANSI Z39.6, *Trade Catalogs,* which specifies the content and format of trade catalogs. SC NN has been charged with the revision of ANSI Z39.41, *Book Spine Formats.*

Preservation

SC GG, Hard Cover Case Bindings, completed a first draft standard describing methods and materials compatible with reasonable permanence and durability that will be circulated to NISO members in 1989. The draft standard includes specifications for such aspects as grain direction of text paper; inside margin size; endpaper construction; leaf attachment, rounding, backing, and spine lining operations; casemaking and casing-in; and materials used.

New committees are beginning work on two other preservation standards: SC R, Environmental Conditions for Storage of Paper-based Library and Archive Collections, and SC MM, Environmental Conditions for the Exhibition of Library and

Archival Material. SC II continued to work on an addition that would extend ANSI Z39.48, *Permanence of Paper for Printed Library Materials,* to coated papers.

Permanent and Durable Library Catalog Cards (currently numbered ANSI Z85.1) was reviewed in 1988. Ballots recommending the enhancement of the permanence requirement pertaining to acidity and durability were received. The standard will be revised and balloted in 1989.

Description

ANSI Z39.19 (*Guidelines for Thesaurus Structure, Construction, and Use*), ANSI Z39.29 (*Bibliographic References*), and ANSI Z39.1 (*Periodicals: Format and Arrangement*) underwent revision in 1988, with the revision work of SC Q on ANSI Z39.1 progressing to ballot in late 1988. The committee will work to resolve several negative votes in early 1989. Committees were also organized to handle the revisions of the thesaurus and reference standards.

Six NISO standards for romanization were reviewed during 1987–1988. Both ANSI Z39.11, *Romanization of Japanese,* and ANSI Z39.12, *Romanization of Arabic,* were reaffirmed without change. Minor changes were recommended for four standards, largely to bring them closer to the ALA/LC romanization tables. Editors for these four were appointed in 1988 and work should be completed by early 1989. These standards are ANSI Z39.24 (*Romanization of Slavic Cyrillic Characters*), ANSI Z39.25 (*Romanization of Hebrew*), ANSI Z39.35 (*Romanization of Lao, Khmer, and Pali*), and ANSI Z39.37 (*Romanization of Armenian*).

Other NISO Standards Reviewed

Three existing NISO standards for statistics are undergoing revision. ANSI Z39.7, *Library Statistics,* will be revised by SC UU. As comments on ANSI Z39.8, *Compiling Book Publishing Statistics,* were not major, the text was edited and the standard will be recirculated for approval in 1989. ANSI Z39.20, *Library Materials—Criteria for Price Indexes,* was reviewed for reaffirmation in 1988, and NISO voting members called for revision. A committee will be formed to revise that standard.

Two additional NISO standards were reviewed and reaffirmed in 1988: ANSI Z39.33, *Identification Codes for Use by the Bibliographic Community,* and ANSI Z39.30, *Order Form for Single Titles.*

Negative reaffirmation ballots were received on five standards. Editors or committees will be appointed to revise the following standards in 1989: ANSI Z39.23 (*Standard Technical Report Number*), ANSI Z39.46 (*Patent Documents—Identification of Bibliographic Data*), ANSI Z39.45 (*Claims for Missing Issues of Serials*), ANSI Z39.31 (*Format for Scientific and Technical Translations*), and ANSI Z39.34 (*Synoptics*).

New NISO Standards Committees

Charges to four new NISO Standards Committees were developed in 1988, three relating to preservation and one to CDROM.

SC QQ will develop a standard for the physical preparation and binding of theses and dissertations. The purpose of this standard is to ensure long-term retention of the documents by the academic institutions involved. The standard will include specifications for paper, inks, duplication, illustrations, inclusion of oversized material, and bindings.

SC RR will be charged with development of a standard specifying adhesives for affixing identification and security labels to library materials. The standard should specify adhesives that remain permanently bonded without damaging the label, the item, or adjacent items.

SC SS will be formed to develop a standard specifying basic information that vendors should provide when advertising products used to store, rehouse, contain, bind, or repair library materials, including books, pamphlets, sound recordings, videotapes, manuscripts, maps, and photographs. The standard will also specify information that should appear in advertisements for such products.

SC TT was established to develop standards for several groups of data elements included on CDROM and other optical media. These data element sets, called files on the optical media, include the publisher file, data preparer file, copyright file, abstract file, and bibliographic file.

Report on USMARC Standards

The USMARC formats are used for the exchange of bibliographic data in the information community. They have been the keystone for the development of computerized data-sharing networks such as OCLC and RLIN and the proliferation of local library systems such as NOTIS and GEAC. USMARC formats are an application of the NISO standard ANSI Z39.2, *Bibliographic Information Interchange,* which defines a general structure for a flexible data format particularly suited to carry data that are highly variable in length. The family of USMARC formats includes ones for bibliographic data, authority data, and holdings data. They are maintained by the Library of Congress in consultation with a group of representatives from library associations and committees.

Until 1988, the USMARC bibliographic format was a composite of seven material-specific formats that cover all forms of library material—books, serials, maps, visuals (films, two- and three-dimensional visuals), music (scores and sound recordings), and archival material. A major change was approved in 1988 that fully integrates the specifications for all these forms of material.[2] No longer will specialized fields in USMARC be valid only for one form of material, but all fields will be valid across the format. At the same time, a number of data elements were made obsolete.

USMARC bibliographic format integration was carefully planned to ensure that no current records would be invalidated by the changes as there are millions of USMARC-based records in systems and exchanged by systems worldwide. A data element made obsolete in USMARC may continue to appear in records created before the change but should not appear in newly created records. Format integration will enable USMARC to accommodate better the descriptions of nonprint serials such as serially issued computer files, music, or maps; multiformat material such as books that contain records or computer file maps; and nonprint material that is being treated archivally.

During 1988, a project to reedit the USMARC documentation was largely completed by the Library of Congress. New editions of the bibliographic format and code lists for countries, geographic areas, and relators were published. A new document that brings together in one volume briefly annotated USMARC specifications for bibliographic, authority, and holdings data was also completed and published.

To Obtain Standards

USMARC standards are available from the Cataloging Distribution Service, Library of Congress, Washington, DC 20541. Copies of approved ANSI standards developed by NISO may be obtained from Transaction Publishers, Inc., Rutgers University, New Brunswick, NJ 08903; 201-932-2280. Standing orders for ANSI Z39 standards are available. To be placed on a mailing list for information on newly published standards, contact the same address. Copies of *draft* NISO standards described above, information on NISO's program, membership applications, and subscriptions to *ISQ* are available from the NISO office: National Information Standards Organization, Box 1056, Bethesda, MD 20817; 301-975-2814. ISO standards can be obtained from American National Standards Institute, 1430 Broadway, New York, NY 10018.

Notes

1. *The Linked Systems Project: A Networking Tool for Libraries,* comp. and ed. by Judith G. Fenly and Beacher Wiggins (Dublin, Ohio: OCLC, 1988).
2. *Format Integration and Its Effect on the USMARC Bibliographic Format,* prepared by the Network Development and MARC Standards Office (Washington, D.C.: Library of Congress Cataloging Distribution Service, 1988).

Copyright 1988: Databases and Software

Patrice A. Lyons
Haley, Bader & Potts, Washington, DC

Advances in computer technology continued to challenge the U.S. copyright law and administrative practices and required adjustments in well-known copyright doctrine over the course of 1988. While developments having general international repercussions for copyright-dependent industries such as the Berne Convention Implementation Act of 1988 (PL 100-568) captured headlines in intellectual property reports, steady progress was also made in the courts and the Copyright Office of the Library of Congress toward adapting the existing legal framework to the requirements of computer technology.

Deposit of Machine-Readable Copies

When the Copyright Office first adopted regulations to implement Section 407 of the Copyright Act of 1976, pertaining to the deposit of copies and phonorecords of published works for the collections of the Library of Congress, computer software and databases were largely the realm of the specialist. The advent of the personal computer opened the doors of computer technology to the general public and increased the demand for access to information in machine-readable form. To meet the needs of the public, the Library of Congress has established a Machine-Readable Collections Reading Room. The new reading room will provide LC patrons access to computer software in IBM or Macintosh formats "for the purposes of study and evaluation and to obtain information" and to computerized information material, including statistical compendia, serials, or reference works.[1] Generally, automated databases available *only* online in the United States will not be subject to the new deposit requirements.

To alleviate possible burdens on software publishers, the library is proposing to limit the number of deposit copies and will not demand software that requires the use of a password or other special authorization. Further, the Copyright Office and LC will follow developments in technology and confer with industry representatives with a view toward amending the requirement of deposit in IBM or Macintosh formats.

The library has indicated that the terminals in the reading room will be monitored by library staff to ensure that the material is not copied and that the staff, not the patrons, will retain control over the machine-readable copies. Lending of copies to patrons or other institutions is not anticipated.

Computer Screen Displays

Work progressed in 1988 on the application of standard copyright infringement tests to computer programs. Several important suits are now advancing through the courts that may shed some light on the scope of protection to be accorded computer programs under copyright. These so-called look and feel cases have been brought by Lotus Development Corporation, Apple Computer, Inc., and Ashton-Tate Corporation.[2] Decisions in these suits and other similar litigation may clarify whether protection for computer programs extends to what have been termed the externals, that is, the screen displays, or should be limited to copying of the computer code.

The Copyright Office held a hearing in 1988 to consider the proper deposit requirements where a copyright claim in a computer program extends to the screen displays. In its policy decision published June 10, 1988, the Copyright Office announced that it had decided generally to require that "all copyrightable expression embodied in a computer program, including computer screen displays, and owned by the same claimant, be registered on a single application form."[3] The office adopted this regulation in order to discourage "piecemeal" registration of parts of works. However, to establish the most complete public record, the office also decided to permit, but not require, future applicants to deposit visual reproductions of the computer screen displays along with reproductions of any accompanying sounds, together with the identifying material for the program code.

The protection granted a computer screen display was also the subject of a suit challenging the decision of the Register of Copyrights refusing copyright registration to a video game. In *Atari Games Corp.* v. *Oman,* 693 F. Supp. 1204 (D. D.C. 1988), the court considered whether the Register had abused his discretion in denying Atari's application to register a copyright claim in the audiovisual display and accompanying sounds of a game entitled "Breakout." The question presented to the

Register was whether the video game contained the minimal amount of creative expression to be deemed a "work of authorship."

Upholding the Register's decision to refuse registration, the court noted that:

> BREAKOUT can be understood, and apparently was understood by the Register, as little more than a stock description of a paddle-and-ball game, inseparable in any principled manner from the idea which it embodies. This is quite distinct from video games which feature expressive and artistically creative renditions of an idea, and which thereby merit copyright protection. *Id.* at 1207.

Referring to the second circuit decision on copyrightable subject matter in *Financial Information* v. *Moody's Investors Service,* 808 F.2d 204, 207 (2d Cir. 1986), *cert. denied,* ____U.S.____, 108 S.Ct. 79 (1987), the court observed that "[t]he copyrightability of a work is defined not by its financial returns or public favor, but rather by its originality and creativity." *Id.*

Copyrightable Subject Matter

A conflict has been emerging in recent years between the circuit courts of appeals on the issue of "originality" for purposes of copyright protection of databases. Some courts have held that "industrious collection" is sufficient, whereas others have adopted a more restrictive standard, emphasizing the human subjective judgment exercised in the selection and arrangement of the data, rather than the labor and expense incurred in collecting and assembling the material.[4] The Copyright Office follows generally the approach taken by the second circuit for purposes of registration of copyright claims. The office's position on this issue may be found in its policy decision on the copyrightability of digitized typefaces.[5]

In deciding that digitized representations of typeface designs are not registrable under the Copyright Act of 1976 because they do not constitute "original works of authorship," the Copyright Office recalled that the term compilation is defined in Section 101 of Title 17 U.S.C. as "a work formed by the collection and assembling of preexisting materials or of data that are selected, coordinated, or arranged in such a way that the resulting work as a whole constitutes an original work of authorship." Citing the decision in the *Financial Information* case, the office stated: "To be an original work of authorship, a compilation must include subjective elements of human selection and arrangement. . . . Because the typefont data is determined by the ultimate shape of the typeface character, and requires *de minimis,* if any, selection and arrangement, it does not qualify as a compilation or any other original work of authorship."[6]

The "industrious collection" or "sweat of the brow" theory may provide greater protection to databases that are drawn primarily from public domain material than may be available under the standard applied in the *Financial Information* decision. As stated in an early case, *Jeweler's Circular Pub. Co.* v. *Keystone Pub. Co.,* 281 F. 83 (2d Cir. 1922), "[t]he right to copyright a book upon which one has expended labor in its preparation does not depend upon whether the materials which he has collected consist or not of matters which are publici juris, or whether such materials show literary skill or originality, either in thought or in language, or anything more than industrious collection." *Id.* The court reasoned that a work such as a directory would not enjoy full copyright protection where a competitor could freely benefit from the results of a rival's expense and labor.

A recent telephone directory dispute appears to follow the "industrious collection" theory. In *Southwestern Bell Media* v. *Trans World Pub.*, 685 F. Supp. 779 (D. Kan. 1988), the court was asked to determine whether Trans Western Publishing, Inc., and Landmark Publishing Company had infringed Southwestern Bell Media, Inc.'s copyright in its Witchita telephone directory. Recalling an earlier decision involving the same parties, the court noted:

> The information and design of that information contained in a telephone directory may be in the public domain or the property of the advertiser, but the effort involved in preparing artwork and layout, and in the selection, compilation and arrangement of the information contained therein constitutes a work of authorship subject to copyright protection. *Id.* at 784.

In deciding that Trans Western had made a sufficient showing that its yellow pages directory was a product of its own effort, the court considered evidence that, while it had taken Bell Media's data as a starting point, it expended considerable efforts of its own in contacting businesses, drawing up new contracts, creating new business advertisements and deleting unauthorized data. *Id.* The court did not analyze the final product to determine whether it contained sufficient original material to constitute an "original work of authorship."

Whether "originality" should be the standard for computer databases was also deliberated at a recent international meeting convened under the auspices of UNESCO and WIPO. Several participants noted that "there were countries where mere skill and labor were not enough for collections to qualify as works protected by copyright on the basis of the notion of originality prevailing in such countries, but where the significant investments made by data base producers did, on the other hand, need and deserve some kind of protection."[7] It was urged that consideration be given to the adoption of a limited related rights type protection for electronic databases that are not eligible for copyright protection because of their lack of originality. Some participants cautioned, however, that a *sui generis* protection for databases would not be covered by existing international copyright conventions and could result in the dilution of copyright protection. It was also suggested that "states should extend copyright protection to electronically compiled collections of data on the basis of a reasonable standard of originality and should never insist on a higher standard than for traditional compilations."[8] The WIPO/UNESCO meeting did not make a specific recommendation on a reasonable standard of "originality" to be applied in the case of computer databases.

Infringement of Databases

To date, many database infringement cases have involved allegations that the whole or a substantial part of a compilation or arrangement of data has been reproduced for use in a competitive product. The application of the copyright law where only "facts" and other public domain material are taken from a computerized database has also been considered in a few recent cases. Often the courts have been asked to determine whether a taking is a permissible "fair use."

A case decided in August 1988, *United Tel. Co. of Mo.* v. *Johnson Pub. Co.*,

Inc., 855 F.2d 604 (8th Cir. 1988), involved a copying into a computer database of new and updated entries from an existing telephone directory. As a threshold matter, the court found that "United Telephone's compilation or arrangement of annual phone books with new and updated listings is a protected expression of the preexisting names, addresses, and telephone numbers of its subscribers." *Id.* at 608. The court then turned its attention to a "fair use" defense. Analyzing the four elements set forth in Section 107 of the copyright law, Title 17 U.S.C., the court held that the copying was not a fair use of the copyrighted compilation because the new and revised entries were the "heart" of the book's white pages and the copying was for profit. *Id.* at 610.

The copying of allegedly public domain data into a computer database was also considered by the court in *West Pub. Co.* v. *Mead Data Cent., Inc.,* 799 F.2d 1219 (8th Cir. 1986) (settlement reached among parties and case dismissed (1988)). The case involved the impact on West Publishing Company's series of books known as the "National Reporter System" of Mead Data Central, Inc.'s, proposed introduction into LEXIS, its computer-assisted online legal research service, of a "star pagination" feature. Mead Data argued that this new feature did not infringe West's copyright "because its citations to page numbers in West reporters are merely statements of pure fact." *Id.* at 1228.

Finding that Mead Data's proposed addition to its database infringed West's copyright in its arrangement and pagination of cases, the court distinguished between isolated use of factual aspects of a compilation and wholesale appropriation of the arrangement, particularly where the use was for a competitive, commercial purpose. The court observed that " '[i]solated instances of minor infringements, when multiplied many times, become in the aggregate a major inroad on copyright that must be prevented.' . . . The names, addresses, and phone numbers in a telephone directory are 'facts'; though isolated use of these facts is not copyright infringement, copying each and every listing is an infringement." *Id.*

A similar point was considered by the court in *Telerate Systems, Inc.* v. *Caro,* 689 F. Supp. 221 (S.D. N.Y. 1988), albeit couched in a "fair use" analysis. With reference to the third fair use factor (the amount and substantiality of portion used), the court noted that the essence of the database lay in the price quotations of various securities and newsletter-type information. *Id.* at 229. The court found that, while the copying of only a few pages of 20,000 total pages of information in the database may not be deemed quantitatively substantial, "qualitatively, copying those few pages may be substantial in light of the structure and typical use of the database." *Id.*

Generally, the case involved allegations that a competitor marketed a computer program called Excel-A-Rate that permitted a subscriber to the Standard Telerate Network (STN) to use a personal computer to access and analyze the data provided by Telerate Systems, Inc., a provider of computerized financial information. Telerate complained that the use of the Excel-A-Rate program was in violation of the Standard Telerate Agreement between Telerate and STN subscribers. The agreement provided that, without Telerate's authorization, "the subscriber shall not move Telerate equipment and that no foreign equipment shall be interfaced with Telerate equipment." *Id.* at 224.

In addition to fair use, the court also evaluated a defense that, by providing the means for its customers to copy Telerate's database, the defendants were not vicariously liable for any alleged infringement, since its computer program enabled Telerate customers to use a personal computer to analyze the data received from Telerate.

Id. at 228. Citing the decision of the Supreme Court in *Sony Corporation of America* v. *Universal City Studios, Inc.,* 464 U.S. 417 (1984), the court found that the data must be copied in order to be analyzed, and, therefore, "the suggested noninfringing use is in fact the primary infringing activity—copying." The court concluded that, absent a valid defense, copying is an infringement of copyright. *Id.*

Apart from its findings on vicarious liability and fair use, the *Telerate* decision is also noteworthy for its reliance on the Communications Act of 1934 to protect the computer database in question. Telerate alleged that the sale by defendants of the Excel-A-Rate program violated Section 705 of the 1934 act (codified at 47 U.S.C. 605) and, in particular, the first sentence of that provision. In this respect, the court noted that, to establish a violation under the first sentence of Section 705, there must be an unauthorized interception of a communication that is not intended for the general public, and the communication must be divulged or published.

Since it was uncontested that Excel-A-Rate users intercepted Telerate's communications that were not intended for the general public, the court proceeded to address the second requirement under Section 705. Employing the legal fiction that "the act of viewing a transmission that the viewer was not authorized to receive constitutes a publication," *id.* at 231, the court held that the viewing of Telerate data using Excel-A-Rate constitutes a publication for purposes of Section 705. The court also found that the use of Excel-A-Rate in conjunction with a personal computer to receive Telerate data was not an "authorized channel" of transmission and, thus, a violation of Section 705.

Copy Protection Devices

A decision handed down by the Court of Appeals for the Fifth Circuit, *Vault Corp.* v. *Quaid Software, Ltd.,* 847 F.2d 255 (5th Cir. 1988), contains an interesting analysis of the provisions of the Copyright Act of 1976 on the making of adaptations or copies of computer programs. Briefly, Vault developed a program called PROLOK that was designed to prevent unauthorized copying of programs. Quaid's product "CopyWrite" incorporates a feature called RAMKEY that may be used to unlock the PROLOK protection device and facilitate the creation of a fully functional copy of a program placed on a PROLOK diskette.

Among its various claims, Vault alleged that Quaid infringed its copyright in PROLOK by copying the program into the memory of Quaid's computer and contributing to the unauthorized copying of Vault's program and the programs of Vault's customers placed on PROLOK diskettes. Quaid countered that its activities were permitted under the limitations on exclusive rights set forth in Section 117, Title 17 U.S.C.

When Congress enacted a new Section 117 of the copyright law in 1980, it provided generally that the owner of a copy or adaptation of a computer program may make or authorize the making of another copy or adaptation of that program where the new copy or adaptation is created "as an essential step in the utilization of the computer program in conjunction with a machine and that it is used in no other manner," or the copy or adaptation is "for archival purposes only."

The court in the *Vault* case recognized that the copy of Vault's program made by Quaid was not used to prevent the copying of programs placed on a PROLOK diskette, but was actually made for the express purpose of devising a means of defeating this protective function. However, the court declined to limit the scope of the exception in Section 117(1) by requiring that a copy made pursuant to that provision be used only for the purposes intended by the copyright owner.

With respect to the contributory infringement claim that, "because purchasers of programs placed on PROLOK diskettes use the RAMKEY feature of CopyWrite to make unauthorized copies, Quaid's advertisement and sale of CopyWrite diskettes with the RAMKEY feature violate the Copyright Act by contributing to the infringement of Vault's copyright and the copyright owned by Vault's customers," *id.* at 261, the court evaluated whether the RAMKEY feature had substantial noninfringing uses. Noting that the owner of a copy of a computer program is entitled under Section 117(2) to make an archival copy of that program for any reason, provided that the owner uses the copy for archival purposes only and not for an unauthorized transfer, the court found that RAMKEY was capable of substantial noninfringing uses, and, therefore, the advertisement and sale of RAMKEY did not constitute contributory infringement. The court did not restrict the purpose or reason of the owner in making the archival copy.

Vault also relied on what is popularly termed a "shrink wrap" license to prevent Quaid from decompiling or disassembling PROLOK. The court rejected this claim, finding that the license agreement constituted a contract of adhesion under Louisiana law and that, since the particular sections of that law were preempted by the federal copyright statute, the agreement was unenforceable. *See id.* at 268.

Work-Made-for-Hire

Again in 1988, the provisions of the copyright statute on work-for-hire were the subject of litigation. At least one case, *In re Simplified Information Systems* v. *Cannon,* 89 B.R. 538 (W.D. Pa. 1988), involved conflicting claims to copyright in computer software. Analyzing the provisions of the copyright statute on work for hire in that case, the court found that, since the whole purpose of the corporation in question was the creation and marketing of a computer process to assist doctors' staffs in their various clerical duties, the president of the corporation who wrote the program did so as an employee for hire. The fact that he had written the program during off hours, or at another place of business, did not change this result.

The Supreme Court is likely to provide some guidance in 1989 on a proper interpretation of the definition of "work-made-for-hire" in Section 101 of the copyright statute. In November 1988, the Court agreed to review a decision of the Court of Appeals for the District of Columbia Circuit in the case of *Community for Creative Non-Violence* v. *Reid,* 846 F.2d 1485 (D. D.C. 1988), *cert. granted,* ____ U.S. ____ (1988) ("*CCNV*").

The *CCNV* case involves a sculpture of a modern Nativity scene in which the two adult figures and infant appear as contemporary homeless people huddled on a steam grate that is positioned on a pedestal. Discussing the different approaches taken on the meaning of the work-for-hire definition, the appeals court in *CCNV* concluded that the scope of the doctrine was greatly narrowed by the Copyright Act of 1976. Where an individual is not an employee under rules of agency law, and there is no written agreement that the work shall be considered "for hire," the court held that "a copyrightable work of an independent contractor cannot be a work made for hire under the current Act unless the work falls within one of the specific categories enumerated" in Section 101(2) of the law. *Id.* at 1494. Whether the Supreme Court affirms this conclusion remains to be seen.

State Immunity from Copyright Liability

In October 1988, the Court of Appeals for the Eleventh Circuit reached a decision in *BV Engineering* v. *Univ. of Cal., Los Angeles,* 858 F.2d 1394 (9th Cir. 1988). This case involved the unauthorized reproduction by the University of California of copyrighted computer programs created and sold by BV Engineering. In its analysis, the court noted that the issue of Eleventh Amendment immunity of states from liability for copyright infringement was now pending before the Supreme Court, and assumed, without deciding, that Congress could abrogate the states' immunity when acting under an Article I power, but that it did not exercise that power in the Copyright Act of 1976. *Id.* at 1397. Citing the Supreme Court decision in *Atascadero State Hosp.* v. *Scanlon,* 473 U.S. 234 (1985), the court stated that, in order to abrogate states' immunity from suit in federal court, Congress must express its intention "unequivocally." *Id.*

Whether the Eleventh Amendment bars actions against states for damages under the federal copyright law was also the subject of an informative report published by the Register of Copyrights in June 1988.[9] The Register noted that the Supreme Court had recently granted certiorari to review the Third Circuit's decision in *United States* v. *Union Gas Company,* 832 F.2d 1343 (3d Cir. 1987), *cert. granted,* ____ U.S. ____ (1988). The *Union Gas* case raises the issue of congressional authority under its Article I commerce clause powers to abrogate the states' Eleventh Amendment immunity. The Register's recommendations turned on whether *Union Gas* is found to permit Article I abrogation. In the event the Supreme Court does decide favorably on this issue, the Register proposed that Congress amend Section 501 of the copyright statute "to clarify its intent to abrogate states' Eleventh Amendment immunity pursuant to its copyright clause power and thereby make states liable to suit for damages in federal court for copyright infringement."[10] Discussion of this issue will surely continue in 1989.

Notes

1. *Registration of Claims to Copyright Mandatory Deposit of Machine-Readable Copies,* Notice of Proposed Rulemaking, 53 *Fed. Reg.* 29923, 29924 (1988).
2. See *Lotus Development Corp.* v. *Mosaic Software, Inc.,* No. 87-0074-K, and *Lotus Development Corp.* v. *Paperback Software International,* No. 87-0076K, filed Jan. 12, 1987 (D. Mass.); *Apple Computer, Inc.* v. *Microsoft Corp. and Hewlett-Packard Co.,* No. C-88-20149-RPA, filed Mar. 17, 1988 (N.D. Cal.); and *Ashton-Tate Corp.* v. *Fox Software Inc.,* No. 886837-TJH, filed Nov. 1988 (____ Cal.).
3. *Registration Decision; Registration and Deposit of Computer Screen Displays,* Final Registration Decision, Policy, 53 *Fed. Reg.* 21817, 21818 (1988).
4. For scholarly treatment of database protection, see R. C. Denicola, *Copyright in Collections of Facts: A Theory for the Protection of Nonfiction Literary Works,* 81 *Columbia L. Rev.* 516 (1981); and R. A. Gorman, *Fact or Fancy? The Implications for Copyright,* 29 *J. Copr. Socy.* 560, Item 695 (1982).
5. *Policy Decision on Copyrightability of Digitized Typefaces,* Notice of Policy Decision, 53 *Fed. Reg.* 38110 (1988).

6. *Id.* at 38112.
7. *Memorandum Prepared by the Secretariats,* Pt. III, para. 232, Committee of Governmental Experts on the Evaluation and Synthesis of Principles on Various Categories of Works (Geneva, June 27 to July 1, 1988), *reprinted in Copyright (WIPO)* (Nov. 1988); see also *Green Paper on Copyright and the Challenge of Technology,* COM (88) 172 final, Commission of the European Communities, para. 6.6.2, at 215 (June 1988).
8. *Memorandum Prepared by the Secretariats, id.* para. 231.
9. *Copyright Liability of States and the Eleventh Amendment,* Report of the Register of Copyrights (June 1988).
10. *Id.* at 104.

Copyright, 1988

William F. Patry
Policy Planning Adviser, Copyright Office,
Library of Congress

The year 1988 will be remembered as an unusually productive one for copyright issues. Principal among these was passage of the Berne Convention implementation legislation and ratification of the Berne Treaty.

Copyright in Congress

U.S. adherence to the Berne Treaty was effective March 1, 1989. The major changes brought about in U.S. domestic copyright law are (1) abolition of mandatory notice; (2) abolition of recordation as a prerequisite to suit; (3) creation of a "two-tier" system of registration under which Berne Convention works of non-U.S. origin do not have to be registered before bringing suit; and (4) doubling of statutory damages. Although there was considerable pressure to include express moral rights in the legislation, Congress declined to do so, instead leaving existing law unchanged. The sections of the implementing legislation, PL 100-568, may be summarized as follows:

A. **Section 1.* Short Title.**
   Explanation: Title of the Act is given as "Berne Convention Implementation Act of 1988."
B. **Section 2. Declarations.**
   Explanation: Part 1 states that Berne is not self-executing under the Constitution and the laws of the United States.
   Part 2 states that the obligations of the U.S. under Berne may be performed only pursuant to appropriate domestic law.
   Part 3 states that the amendments made by the Act satisfy U.S. obliga-

*The consecutive section numbers here refer to sections of PL 100-568.

tions in adhering to Berne and that no further rights or interests shall be recognized or created for the purpose of adherence.

C. Section 3. Construction of the Berne Convention.
Explanation: By stating that the provisions of Berne are not enforceable under the Convention itself, this section reinforces Section 2, *supra.* This section adds, however, that in addition to Title 17, the provisions of Berne may also be given effect under "any other relevant provision of Federal or State law, including common law"; this is further mentioned in Part (b) of the section, which states that rights to claim authorship, or to object to any distortion, mutilation of, or other derogatory action that would prejudice the author's honor or reputation are neither "expanded or reduced by virtue of, or reliance upon, the provisions of the Berne Convention, adherence of the United States thereto, or the satisfaction of United States obligations thereunder."

D. Section 4. Subject Matter and Scope of Copyrights.
Explanation: This section amends the definition of "pictorial, graphic, and sculptural works" in Section 101 of Title 17 to include architectural plans (but not architectural structures). The section also amends Section 101 by providing the following definition of a "Berne Convention work":

> A work is a "Berne Convention work" if,—
>
> (1) in the case of an unpublished work, one or more of the authors is a national of a nation adhering to the Berne Convention, or in the case of a published work, one or more of the authors is a national of a nation adhering to the Berne Convention on the date of first publication;
>
> (2) the work was first published in a nation adhering to the Berne Convention, or was simultaneously first published in a nation adhering to the Berne Convention and in a foreign nation that does not adhere to the Berne Convention;
>
> (3) in the case of an audiovisual work—
>
> (A) if one or more of the authors is a legal entity, that author has its headquarters in a nation adhering to the Berne Convention; or
>
> (B) if one or more of the authors is an individual, that author is domiciled, or has his or her habitual residence in, a nation adhering to the Berne Convention; or
>
> (4) in the case of a pictorial, graphic, or sculptural work that is incorporated in a building or other structure, the building or structure is located in a nation adhering to the Berne Convention.
>
> For purposes of paragraph (1), an author who is domiciled in, or has his or her habitual residence in, a nation adhering to the Berne Convention is considered to be a national of that nation. For purposes of paragraph (2), a work is considered to have been simultaneously published in two or more nations if its dates of publication are within 30 days of one another.

Tracking Article 5(4) of the Paris text of Berne, the section also amends Section 101 by providing that the United States is the country of origin of a Berne Convention work, for purposes of Section 411, under the following circumstances:

> (1) in the case of a published work, the work is first published—
> (A) in the United States;

(B) simultaneously in the United States and another nation or nations adhering to the Berne Convention, whose law grants a term of copyright protection that is the same as or longer than the term provided in the United States;

(C) simultaneously in the United States and a foreign nation that does not adhere to the Berne Convention; or

(D) in a foreign nation that does not adhere to the Berne Convention, and all of the authors of the work are nationals, domiciliaries, or habitual residents of, or in the case of an audiovisual work legal entities with headquarters in, the United States;

(2) in the case of an unpublished work, all the authors of the work are nationals, domiciliaries, or habitual residents of the United States, or, in the case of an unpublished audiovisual work, all the authors are legal entities with headquarters in the United States; or

(3) in the case of a pictorial, graphic, or sculptural work incorporated in a building or structure, the building or structure is located in the United States.

For the purposes of section 411, the "country of origin" of any other Berne Convention work is not the United States.

As in Sections 2 and 3 of the bill, this section contains a provision declaring that no rights or interests may be claimed under the convention directly, but rather solely under Title 17, other federal or state statutes, or common law. The section concludes by providing a new Section 116A in Title 17 encouraging negotiated jukebox licenses. At the end of the first year following U.S. adherence to Berne, the Copyright Royalty Tribunal is to determine whether voluntarily negotiated or arbitrated licenses are in effect "so as to provide permission to use a quantity of musical works not substantially smaller than the quantity" performed on jukeboxes during the previous year. If the CRT determines that the requisite number of works are not available for licensing, existing Section 116 shall apply with respect to works not the subject of negotiated licenses. The provisions of the negotiated licenses supersede rates set by the CRT.

E. Section 5. Recordation.

Explanation: Section 205(d) of Title 17, which currently requires recordation as a prerequisite to the institution of an infringement action, is abolished, regardless of the nationality of the plaintiff.

F. Section 6. Preemption with Respect to Other Laws Not Affected.

Explanation: Section 301 of Title 17 is amended by adding a new subsection (e):

> The scope of Federal preemption under this section is not affected by the adherence of the United States to the Berne Convention or the satisfaction of the obligations of the United States thereunder.

G. Section 7. Notice of Copyright.

Explanation: The mandatory notice provisions of the Act are eliminated. New subsections (d) are added to Sections 401 and 402, stating that, except as provided in the last sentence of 17 USC Sec. 504(c)(2) (concerning certain nonprofit institutions) an innocent infringer defense asserted in mitigation of damages shall be given no weight where the defendant had access to a copy of a work bearing the specified notice. These new subsections are, however, inapplicable to works consisting predominantly of one or more works of the United States government unless "a statement identifying, either affirmatively or negatively, those portions" embodying protected material is included.

Section 404 (notice for contributions to collective works) is also tied to the revised innocent infringer provisions of new subsections 401(d) and 402(d).

The provisions in Section 405(a) regarding curative steps for omission of notice are amended to apply to distributions before the effective date of the Act, as is the innocent infringer provision of Section 405(b).

H. **Section 8. Library of Congress Deposit.**
Explanation: 17 USC Sec. 407(a) which requires deposit of copies of a work published in the United States with a notice of copyright is revised by deleting the requirement of publication with notice.

I. **Section 9. Copyright Registration.**
Explanation: Section 411, which currently requires registration (or a refusal to register) before institution of an infringement action, has been substantially revised by establishing a two-tier system. Under this system, "works of the Berne Convention" (as defined earlier) whose "country of origin" is the United States (as also defined earlier) will still have to comply with the registration procedures. Works of the Berne Convention whose country of origin is not the United States are, however, exempt from the Section 411 requirements. The incentives for registration found in Section 412 (statutory damages and attorneys fees) remain applicable to all works.

J. **Section 10. Remedies.**
Explanation: 17 USC Sec. 504(c) is amended by doubling the minimum statutory damages from $250 to $500, the maximum nonwillful statutory damages from $10,000 to $20,000, the maximum willful statutory damages from $50,000 to $100,000, and the floor for innocent infringer remission from $100 to $200.

K. **Section 11. Copyright Royalty Tribunal.**
Explanation: This section provides guidance for the new Section 116A negotiated jukebox licenses.

L. **Section 12. Works in the Public Domain.**
Explanation: This section states that "no copyright protection is provided for any work that is currently in the public domain in the United States."

M. **Section 13. Effective Date: Effect on Pending Cases.**
Explanation: Part (a) of this section provides that the legislation takes effect on the day on which the Berne Convention enters into force with respect to the United States. (March 1, 1989). Part (b) provides that any action arising under Title 17 before the effective date of the legislation is governed by the provisions of Title 17 in effect when the cause of action arose.

The issue of moral rights had been raised by film directors in an effort to stop colorization and other material alteration to motion pictures. Although unsuccessful legislatively in this effort, the directors did manage to obtain legislation establishing a

National Film Preservation Board, constituted to select no more than 25 classic films a year for three years for inclusion in a National Film Registry. If a film has been selected for the Registry, it cannot be distributed or performed in a materially altered form without the inclusion of a specified label or notice indicating the alteration.

In other legislation, Congress renewed the Record Rental Act of 1984 for eight years, and established a temporary statutory license for home satellite owners living in unserved areas.

The Copyright Office

The Copyright Office issued final deposit regulations for claims to colorized versions of black-and-white motion pictures, requiring deposit of the best edition of the black-and-white print that formed the basis for the colorized version. The office also issued a policy decision on multiple claims involving computer screen displays, rejecting requests for separate registrations for the underlying computer program and the screen display. It was the office's position that registration for the computer program covered all copyrightable elements. The Copyright Office rejected the request to register certain claims to computer programs and databases relating to digitized typefaces, stating that although it would register claims to computer programs that control the "generic" digitized typeface process, it would not register claims relating to the generation of specific typefaces.

The Copyright Office issued a report on the effect of the Eleventh Amendment on states' liability for infringement of copyrighted works, concluding that if Congress has the authority to abrogate the states' sovereign immunity under Article I of the Constitution, it should amend the Copyright Act to do so in order to conform to recent Supreme Court decisions specifying a strict standard for such statutory abrogation. In another report, the office concluded that only one-third of all jukeboxes are properly licensed. The general pattern of compliance is that large, professional operators with many machines are licensed, and small operators owning a few machines are not. The primary reason for noncompliance was believed to be not ignorance but disregard for the law.

The Courts

Two areas received considerable attention in the courts: sovereign immunity and work made for hire.

Sovereign Immunity

In *BV Engineering* v. *UCLA*, the ninth circuit affirmed a lower court opinion that had held that the Supreme Court's 1985 *Atascadero* decision had effectively overruled its 1979 opinion in *Mills Music* v. *Arizona*. In *Mills Music*, the ninth circuit had concluded that the states were liable for monetary damages in copyright infringement actions. When the decision in *BV Engineering* v. *UCLA* is coupled with the fourth circuit's 1988 decision in *Radford University*, every court of appeals to have addressed the Eleventh Amendment question since 1985 has found that the states are subject to immunity.

Work Made for Hire

Following the fifth circuit's 1987 decision in the Easter Seal case, the District of Columbia Court of Appeals held, in *CCNV* v. *Reid,* that the agency law test is the proper test for determining whether the work of a free-lance artist is that of an independent contractor—governed by subdivision (2) of Section 101's definition of "work made for hire"—or is instead the work of an "employee"—governed by subdivision (1) of that definition. The Supreme Court, however, granted certiorari in the case. A decision is expected by the Court's July recess.

After certiorari was granted in *CCNV* v. *Reid,* the ninth circuit, in *Dumas* v. *Gommerman,* broke new ground, holding that the first subdivision was limited to formal salaried employees and that the works of all free-lancers had to be analyzed under the second subdivision.

Special Reports: Ensuring Information's Survival

Maintaining America's library collections in their original format for as long as needed is at the very heart of ensuring that information resources remain usable. Carolyn Clark Morrow points to three important signs of success in the ongoing battle to preserve library collections: increased use of alkaline paper, increased use of preservation microfilming, and increased use of deacidification. But, as Morrow makes clear, much work still lies ahead to define standards for environmental conditions that contribute to preserving library materials, to persuade publishers to use acid-free paper, to define national strategies and standards for saving nonprint collections, and to share preservation expertise with smaller, local institutions that are important to completing America's historical and cultural record.

Preservation Comes of Age

Carolyn Clark Morrow
Assistant National Preservation Program Officer
Library of Congress

The year 1989 will be a banner year for the preservation of library materials. After decades of contemplating the specter of America's printed heritage at risk, libraries are mounting a concerted attack on all fronts. But as libraries contemplate being able to resolve the acid paper problem forever, what other preservation challenges await them?

Success, Sweet Success: The Attack on Brittle Books

In welcoming participants to a hearing on the problem of brittle books in the nation's libraries on April 21, 1988, Congressman Sidney Yates (D–Ill.) characterized the solution to the acid paper problem as having three major components: first, the production and use of greater quantities of long-lived alkaline paper; second, the use of deacidification technology to neutralize the acids in books en masse and thus provide a cost-effective means to prevent embrittlement; and third, the microfilming of so-called brittle books to ensure the continued availability of the information.

Note: The views expressed in this report are solely those of the author.

The hearing on the problem of brittle books was actually a continuation of the budget hearing for the National Endowment for the Humanities (NEH). In a prepared statement, NEH Chairman Lynne V. Cheney outlined an ambitious proposal for using NEH as the lead agency in mounting an attack on brittle books. Following the formula for a 20-year, 3-million-volume program devised by the independent Commission on Preservation and Access, NEH proposed to use federal funds to increase greatly the amount of preservation microfilming in the nation's largest libraries. Such a program would preserve the core literature published between 1840 and 1920 and at risk from paper deterioration and embrittlement. Both NEH and the Commission on Preservation and Access maintained that the "infrastructure" was in place to tackle the preservation problem on a national scale.

In subsequent months, Representative Yates was instrumental in gaining approval for a threefold increase in funding for the NEH Office of Preservation – from $4.5 million in FY 1988 to $12.4 million in FY 1989. At the same time, Congress gave the Library of Congress funds to double its preservation microfilming effort. Such a dramatic increase in funding for preservation was possible because of pioneer work by such groups as the Commission on Preservation and Access (established in 1985 by the Council on Library Resources expressly to address the brittle book problem), the Association of Research Libraries (ARL), the American Library Association (ALA), and the Research Libraries Group (RLG) – as well as more than two decades of preservation program development in the nation's largest libraries.

A Good Idea Gets Around: Preservation Program Development

The first librarywide approaches to meet the preservation challenge began evolving in the late 1960s in a handful of research libraries. These libraries (New York Public, Yale, Columbia, Library of Congress, and Newberry) began to recognize the enormous task ahead of them – to preserve large aggregate collections of widely divergent physical objects . . . used in different ways . . . at different levels of intensity . . . by a variety of user groups. These libraries were pioneers in preservation. Then, in 1968, 20 years before Congressman Yates held his hearing, the Library of Congress launched its Brittle Books Project with funding from the Council on Library Resources and began to establish the standards and guidelines needed to support a cooperative nationwide program. By 1973, the Conservation Office at the Library of Congress (LC) had invented the "phase box," which along with "storage" quickly became the method of choice for dealing with books with crumbling paper. To the vast majority of libraries, large and small, however, preservation was not an issue.

Preservation as a distinct function of libraries finally caught hold in the late 1970s and early 1980s as the research library community began to define the separate elements of a preservation program and agree on terminology. After years of retrospective buying, even libraries with the younger collections began to notice the insidious "slow fires" of paper deterioration on their shelves. In 1980, the American Library Association (ALA) launched the Preservation of Library Materials Section. In 1981, the Association of Research Libraries (ARL) devised a formal preservation self-study and planning process. In 1982, the Research Libraries Group began the first of its cooperative preservation microfilming projects (the forerunner to the nationwide approach adopted eight years later) and established standards for entering information about a master negative microform in the national bibliographic databases. In 1983, ALA and LC began cosponsorship of a series of four national conferences on the managerial and technical information needed to develop institutional preservation programs. The adoption in 1984 of ARL's "Guidelines for Minimum Preservation Effort" was a strong indication that the research library community agreed, at least in principle, that it had an obligation to develop comprehensive local preservation programs. In 1985 ARL began collecting preservation statistics—a sure indicator of a coming of age.

In 1986, collection development librarians began to join preservation librarians in articulating an intellectual approach to the process of selection for preservation. The 1986 ALA Preconference, "Preservation for Collection Managers," was the forerunner of a 1987 meeting called by RLG to devise a selection strategy for preservation. RLG eventually devised the "Great Collections" approach, whereby libraries would choose their most important, in-depth collections for intensive preservation activity, and do so in coordination with other libraries. In 1987, CLR, NEH, and LC sponsored *Slow Fires: On the Preservation of the Human Record,* an hour-long film documentary aired on public television that captured the attention of literate America and helped galvanize public sentiment for the task of preservation—the task outlined by Congressman Yates in his April 1988 hearing.

Making the Most of Good Fortune—Alkaline Paper

More than a century ago the Industrial Revolution created an information explosion through the introduction of high-speed printing presses and inexpensive wood pulp papers. Unfortunately, the technology of modern papermaking also sowed the seeds of a mammoth preservation problem for libraries. Shorter fibers, residual bleaching compounds, the presence of ground wood fibers, and the use of acidic alum rosin sizing have all contributed to today's brittle book problem. The Industrial Revolution also resulted in the urban pollution that eats away at library collections.

New papermaking technology produced the acid paper problem and new technology was needed to solve it. Although America's recognition of the problem began as early as the 1890s and the cause of acid deterioration was identified in the 1930s at the National Bureau of Standards, it wasn't until 1959, when William J. Barrow published the results of his research, that the precise causes of paper deterioration were clearly understood and generally accepted.

At the same time as Barrow was experimenting with producing permanent paper in his laboratory, the first commercially successful alkaline paper size came on the market, permitting the cost-effective substitution of alkaline size for acidic alum rosin sizing. A combination of other factors has fortunately conspired to increase the number of paper mills "going alkaline." Inexpensive calcium carbonate is available to use as a high-quality alkaline filler to increase opacity and printability. Strict EPA regulations concerning waste treatment and effluent requirements have encouraged mills to switch to an alkaline system.

It is pure good fortune that the papermaking industry continues the trend toward conversion of mills to the alkaline papermaking process. Other challenges remain, however. Traditionally, paper has not been chosen by printers based on its alkaline qualities, but rather for other qualities relating to appearance and printability. Libraries still face an enormous public relations and educational effort to convince publishers to choose alkaline paper over acid paper and to do so consistently for subsequent printings. Second, unless publishers note the use of alkaline paper on the title page, libraries initiating mass deacidification programs for their collections will spend money to treat materials unnecessarily. Finally, the fact that a paper has an alkaline pH does not complete the preservation picture. If the paper contains any ground wood fiber, the impurities will contribute to degradation over time. EPA, along with some states, is developing regulations stipulating the use of recycled paper for government publications. Recycled paper, even produced by an alkaline system, typically has shorter fibers (so the paper is not as durable) and ground wood fibers.

Despite these latest issues, there is considerable progress and promise on the alkaline paper front. In October 1988, the Technical Association of the Pulp and Paper Industry (TAPPI) held a national conference on the topic of permanent paper and deacidification and launched an era of greater understanding and communication among librarians, publishers, and papermakers. Senator Claiborne Pell (D–R.I.) has introduced a Senate joint resolution to establish a "national policy on permanent paper." [See Senator Pell's statement in support of the Senate joint resolution in the Legislation section of Part 2—*Ed.*] On the publishing front, author Barbara Gold Smith has joined forces with the New York Public Library to encourage authors to demand that their work be published on alkaline paper.

Taking a Chance on Mass Deacidification

Research to develop a "whole book" deacidification process has been conducted steadily since the 1940s. Deacidification neutralizes the acid in paper and leaves an alkaline reserve to guard against future acid attack from polluted environments. In combination with increased use of alkaline paper by publishers and microfilming of already brittle books, deacidification completes the preservation picture for America's printed documentary heritage.

Despite the fact that viable mass processes are available, however, libraries have not moved aggressively to incorporate mass deacidification into their long-range preservation plans or to demand access to services. Although few libraries will be able to afford to deacidify their entire collections, every library must determine its own selection guidelines so that materials that should remain in hard copy are chemically stabilized at the time they are acquired. It remains for libraries to develop selection criteria, articulate the rationale for deacidification costs to their parent institutions, and work cooperatively to encourage the development of treatment facilities. Because deacidification is a new concept for libraries, not everything can be known about costs and procedures. But the same was true of library automation in the early days, and the promise of greater access through automation encouraged libraries to take a chance. Today mass deacidification technology promises to ensure access by keeping materials available in their original format for as long as they are needed.

Selling Environmental Control

All organic materials deteriorate. The rate at which they deteriorate depends on the chemical and physical stability of the composite materials and the environment in which they are stored. Because libraries can rarely affect the physical composition of their collections (they collect information, regardless of format), the single most important aspect of preservation is environmental control. Librarians can't *see* the accelerated deterioration of materials due to high temperatures and humidity in their buildings. Furthermore, many of the oldest, largest, and most important library collections are housed in buildings constructed before air conditioning. Adding state-of-the-art environmental control to older buildings can cost hundreds of thousands of dollars. The case for environmental control is difficult to sell to hard-nosed administrators with many competing demands for scarce resources. Yet until libraries improve the storage environment for their collections, it makes little sense to spend large amounts on preservation. The National Information Standards Organization is working to develop a standard for environmental control for library and archives collections. This standard, combined with strategies for graphically demonstrating the loss accrued through inadequate environments, will give library administrators the arguments they need to convince parent institutions.

Beyond Brittle Books – Nonprint Collections

America's documentary heritage is recorded on a vast number of media – from audio transcription discs of early radio broadcasts, to aerial photographs taken from satellites, to the manuscripts of famous American authors, to magnetic computer tape, to name just a few. All of these materials have their own patterns of deterioration and their own preservation strategies. Taken together, they represent the broadest view of America's society and an awesome preservation challenge. Early videotapes of television shows are already showing substantial deterioration due to the separation of the magnetic particles from the base. These visual and audio records, arguably America's most crucial cultural documentation since the 1950s, are the preservation time bomb of the 1990s. Now that libraries are moving beyond brittle books, they must act quickly to form the national strategies and standards for, and acquire the funding to mount a coordinated, concerted attack to ensure, the preservation of nonprint collections.

Taking Preservation to Smaller Collections – Statewide Programs

The largest research libraries have been, appropriately, the site of the most intensive preservation activity during the last two decades. However, the preservation problem extends to every library and historical repository, even the smallest public library and historical society in the nation. Federal funding, such as that available through the Office of Preservation at the National Endowment for the Humanities, cannot reach these smaller institutions. This problem is solved in part through the trickle-down effect, as scores of smaller libraries establish preservation policies and procedures and make use of preservation tools developed in larger libraries. However, authorizing legislation, state appropriations, and the development of coordinated statewide programs, such as was established in New York State in 1984, can result in the distribution of preservation information and services to even the smallest repository. In March 1989, the Library of Congress, the National Archives, the National Endowment for the Humanities, along with a number of other national organizations, cosponsored a conference on the development of statewide preservation programs. This invitational conference was used to alert state archivists, state librarians, heads of state historical agencies, and university librarians to the opportunities inherent in coordinated statewide programs.

Changing Collections – Information, Not Artifacts

In the simplest terms, each library's preservation task is to determine the physical and chemical composition of its collections and assess its preservation needs from a collection development point of view. This process must take place not only for present collections and their users but also for those of the future. Library collections are dynamic, not static, and librarians will apply their professional know-how to meet the preservation challenge in a variety of ways. As the twenty-first century approaches, libraries will face not only the familiar maintenance, reselection, and curatorial responsibilities defined by the preservation programs of the 1980s and 1990s, but also the somewhat intangible (yet very real) problem of preserving not just the physical media that hold information (books, photographs, and so forth) but information itself. Information stored in electronic format is manipulated and frequently even deleted in the course of updating and revision. Will certain kinds of electronic information in its earlier versions ever be needed for review and comparison? Unless guidelines are determined for preserving information as well as objects, we will be forced to stride forward into the next century without the benefit of a complete picture of the past.

Margaret Morrison explores how the use of new technologies – optical media, CD-ROM, online services, microcomputers – poses serious questions about the future of information. On the one hand, Morrison shows, technology provides tremendous advantages by offering wider access and cost savings, but, as she points out, these new technologies also challenge the information profession to safeguard the integrity of information. The use of technology raises concerns about the preservation of the electronic record and will challenge librarians to exercise their best capabilities as experts in information description to ensure access to that information.

The Promise of New Technology

Margaret Morrison
Coordinator for Public Services
Torreyson Library, University of Central Arkansas, Conway, AR

> Walker is my name and I am the same. Riddley Walker. Walking my riddles where ever theyve took me and walking them now on this paper the same.[1]

Russell Hoban's narrator lives three millennia after a nuclear holocaust. Surviving are only remnants of the previous civilization: some machines whose functions are no longer understood, a decayed language based largely on remembered sounds, and stories, told over and over, about the people of that earlier age:

> Counting, counting they wer all the time. They had iron then and big fire. . . . They had machines et numbers up. They fed them numbers and they fractiont out the Power of things. They had the Nos. of the rain bow and the Power of the air all workit out with counting which is how they got boats in the air and picters on the wind. Counting cleverness is what it wer.[2]

Only one written document from those days remains in Riddley Walker's world:

> Onlyes writing I know of is the Eusa Story which that ain't nothing strait but at least it stayed the same. All them other storys tol by mouf they ben put to an took from and changit so much thru the years theyre all bits and blips and all mixt up.[3]

Oral societies, whether from our own preliterate days or from Riddley Walker's far distant future, cannot guarantee that the contents of their stories remain constant, that they do not get "all mixt up." Writing first fixed those stories, and printing allowed those fixed versions to reach an audience much larger than that earlier available. Libraries from ancient times to the present have collected and tried to preserve such written works, thus making our stories, our cumulative store of knowledge, as secure and as permanent as the physical medium upon which they are impressed.

In recent decades, "counting cleverness," in the form of computer technology and more, has come to printing and publishing and to libraries. The conjunction of the new technologies in both publishing and libraries promises great advances in the production and distribution of information. Raymond DeBuse has identified six key technologies that he believes "may well redefine the concept of publishing" and "require libraries to adapt to new conditions as they have never done before."[4] They are powerful and portable computers; "intuitive" user interface software; optical media; hypertext and, more broadly, hypermedia; artificial intelligence; and authoring systems. Ironically, although these technologies will revolutionize the storage and retrieval of information, they raise anew problems of the survival of that information. With sophisticated automated systems, data can now be disseminated widely, with little regard for the location of the information or of the user. Broad access can be granted, perhaps making information more secure and ensuring the growth of knowledge. At the same time, these technologies make it possible for all who have access to information to alter it, to personalize it, thus destroying the integrity of the original source. These new technologies give rise to a strange paradox: More information is available to more people, but the information itself may be more ephemeral than at any time since the days of oral traditions.

Libraries Adopt New Technologies: A Brief Review

Even a brief review of libraries' adoption of the new technologies reveals their staunch commitment to improved access to all sorts of information resources. Access has been the raison d'être for the large bibliographic utilities and commercial database vendors. Current small computers, with their capabilities for downloading and data manipulation, allow a very complex relationship between these online information suppliers and their users. Small, powerful computers, like the new NeXT, that integrate sound and graphics with data and text, will help this relationship flourish. The surprising $353 million paid by Knight-Ridder for DIALOG attests to the worth the information industry puts on such access services, especially as it begins to look beyond the library market.[5]

The desire for better access to basic information drives the continuing growth of the automation of essential library services, such as acquisitions, serials check-in, circulation, and online catalogs. In 1987, 302 online systems, ranging from single-function modules to more comprehensive integrated packages, were installed in libraries, a 56 percent increase over the previous year and the largest single increase ever.[6] These installations brought the total number of working library systems to almost 1,400, with many of those serving more than one library. Added to these are surely many small libraries that are automating their circulation or card preparation with one of the several software packages available for that purpose. Document delivery, too, has improved, with electronic mail systems and a small boom in telefacsimile equipment. A recent count puts the number of FAX services in libraries at nearly 700.[7]

Software

Greater access to computer-based databases and catalogs demands the development of good user interface software. Easy-to-use and easy-to-learn search software has appeared in a number of forms. There are gateway services like Easy Net, end-user databases like BRS After Dark and Knowledge Index, and full services reached through packages like Wilsearch and DialogLink. Macintosh icons have found devotees among many users. Although it is true that user interfaces need not all be the same, the current completion of standards on a common command language by both the International Standards Organization (ISO) and the U.S. National Information Standards Organization (NISO) will bring some consistency to the search process, at least until all search protocols are completely transparent to users.

Expert Systems

Making search protocols transparent has been one of the goals, along with reference and referral, indexing, and cataloging, of a number of expert systems. Although fulfillment of the exciting promises of the field of artificial intelligence still lies in the future, the subfield of expert systems shows considerable usefulness in the present. The National Library of Medicine's CITE, a well-established tool, and the newer Answerman developed at the National Library of Agriculture guide searchers to the most relevant responses to their inquiries. At the 1988 LITA conference, a number of universities, including Case Western Reserve, the University of Houston, and the University of Vermont, discussed their attempts at expert systems. Perhaps the ultimate development of such expert systems will be the "knowbot,"[8] which will know its users' learning styles, preferences, and information needs and will be able to tailor information retrieval to the individual's specifications.

Optical Media

DeBuse adds another wonder to the user-of-the-future's ability to access information: the "Dynabook" or its elegant cousin the "Hyperbook."[9] A hand-held or wall-mounted computer with a high-resolution screen and optical storage, the Dynabook would allow its user to read, manipulate, and save retrieved information. Even more powerful, the Hyperbook would incorporate the nonlinear features of Hypertext to provide user-requested linkages to other information sources in any media. With the development of authoring systems, DeBuse even foresees a new genre of literature utilizing Hypermedia, works for which the structure and order of narrative depend entirely on the choice of the reader. These forms of future publication, in combination with the "knowbot," will indeed make vast quantities of complex information available to users at the push of a button.

Perhaps the biggest recent addition to technologies aimed at increasing access to information has been the optical disk. Optical media, with their tremendous storage capacity, have only recently teased libraries and other information providers with their possibilities. Five years ago the Library of Congress initiated its Optical Disk Pilot Program to enhance access to some of its special collections. The digital print component of the program integrated the full text of selected journal articles with an in-house indexing database. This project had as its primary goal increased efficiency for researchers, with preservation of the journals themselves secondary. The analog nonprint component of the project, however, emphasized the conservation of fragile materials while also affording easier access. The nonprint project reproduced unique photographs, motion picture stills, and films on discs, linking them to an indexing database. The original sources were protected from handling while use of those sources was facilitated.[10] At roughly the same time, the National Agricultural Library developed a version of the *Pork Industry Handbook* that successfully integrated both digital text and analog graphics on a single disc.[11]

CD-ROM

About three years ago, the smaller CD-ROM products began appearing in the popular library press. Although still somewhat inconvenient for large databases, these discs offer the considerable advantage of cost predictability and reasonable user interface software. An estimated 200 CD-ROM products are now on the market. When OCLC surveyed its 9,400 participating members in 1987, 17 percent of the total and 24 percent of academic libraries responded that they had at least one CD-ROM installation.[12] By 1988, that 24 percent had grown to 84 percent, from two to seven of eight academic libraries.[13] The recent High Sierra standard makes compatibility among products more likely, and the information industry is rapidly developing more sophisticated products, such as WORM (Write-Once-Read-Many) and erasable discs, and is planning for a variety of interactive CD products. Even newer products, such as Digital-Audio-Interactive discs and the long-planned Digital-Audio-Tape, are on the horizon.

As with the introduction of earlier information technologies, the advent of compact discs in libraries renews basic questions about the principle of access. At present, utilization of CD-ROM involves considerable expense for libraries. Equipment for one work station may cost $5,000, and although CD-ROM indexes typically cover more than one year of an index and offer features unavailable in print format, annual subscriptions to the discs usually cost far more than their print counterparts. A current subscription to ERIC in disc form, from any of its vendors, costs at least twice as much as the paper subscription; in fact, government document depository libraries may receive the ERIC indexes for free. A subscription to the current PsycLit disc, which corresponds to January 1983 to the present in *Psychological Abstracts,* costs more than $3,500 and is only leased in libraries, making the decision to discontinue the paper format difficult. A disc representing the last six years of the *Readers'*

Guide to Periodical Literature costs ten times the annual print subscription rate, although the cost of unlimited online searches in the *Readers' Guide* database is included in the price of the disc. Many CD-ROM products do not have paper equivalents; their cost can only be evaluated with regard to other similar CD products. Clearly, libraries that wish to offer the advantages of this new technology have to find some way to pay for it.

In addition to cost, there is some concern in libraries about the long-term value of CD-ROM products. One of the earliest evaluations of a CD-ROM index called it "junk food."[14] A more recent study has shown that users fare better with disc searching with some inquiries,[15] and another shows instances where manual searches provide better results.[16] In spite of such mixed responses, libraries seem to appreciate at a minimum the attractiveness of these CD-ROM tools to their users. Since there will undoubtedly be changes in the equipment used to provide access to the discs, in the databases available on discs, and in the interactivity possible with discs, these and other optical media will continue to appeal to libraries.

Keeping Information Alive

In Riddley Walker's world, "tel women" keep alive the legends and lessons of society by relating their stories at every public gathering. In today's world, librarians and publishers keep information alive by making it available to anyone who needs it. Wide distribution and dissemination allow information to be absorbed by many people, "prolonging information's life and its usefulness."[17] Recent technological developments, such as small, powerful computers, good user software, advanced telecommunications, and optical media, make such dissemination possible, and emerging tools, like advanced Hypermedia and expert systems, hold out even greater promise for the future.

The Survival of Computer-Based Information

As the Pentagon discovered in 1988, when a tenacious computer virus invaded its files, sophisticated technology does not guarantee safety of information. The first concerns about the survival of computer-based information appeared in 1984, when Gordon Neavill stated flatly: "The possibility of recording and disseminating written messages electronically, without having to rely on tangible physical objects as the medium of communication is a revolutionary innovation with profound intellectual implications, not all of them salutory."[18] On the following page Neavill stated the problem even more clearly: "The malleability of information that is one of the major advantages of computer-based electronic systems has as its corollary the potential transience of information. Nothing inherent in the technology of computer-based electronic systems ensures that information in the system will survive."[19] Neavill points out that database producers, vendors, and electronic publishers have little incentive to preserve the contents of their databases once their commercial value is exhausted. Questions about the disposition of noncurrent, unused, or discontinued databases and electronic publications will have to be answered.

In addition, unfixed computer-based information may change the nature of research. Although a feared decline in the quality of publications so easily created and disseminated may not come to pass, distinctions between a work in progress and a completed effort blur, and researchers may find it unsettling to have to rely on previous research whose contents may be unverifiable as a result of updates or revisions.

The National Archives and Records Service noted similar concerns when studying the problems of preservation of historical documents in a computerized era. The special Committee on the Records of Government warned, "Because of erasures of electronic records, future historians may know less about the Reagan Administration's 1985 arms control negotiations than about those in 1972 which led to SALT I or, for that matter, those of 1921 which led to the Washington naval treaties."[20]

As information in electronic form may be changed at any point without having the original document reissued, bibliographic description of computer-resident information becomes difficult. The problems of citations of electronic documents became a concern of both ISO and NISO (Z39-00) in 1988. One of the few published suggestions for electronic document citations admits that having proof of citation in electronic form can be tricky, and to address the problem, the authors suggest that one paper copy of every form of an electronic publication be deposited at a national library and a second paper copy at an information clearinghouse.[21] Although this approach does solve the problem of the ephemerality of computer-resident information, the volume of paper and the efforts of classification and maintenance numb the imagination.

Erasures and revisions constitute active destruction of information. The problem of "passive" destruction of data has also been identified.[22] Passive destruction includes cases where data are lost because of incompatibility between hardware and software, between pieces of hardware, and between pieces of software, as well as in the more subtle case where incomplete documentation causes data to be irretrievable. Margaret Cribbs reports that as much as 85 percent of data retained by government-sponsored scientific organizations is useless as a result of hardware or software obsolescence.[23] The solution to this data loss, claim Cribbs and John Mallinson, is the costly and difficult process of regular upgrading and transferring of data files from older to newer systems.[24]

Libraries' response to the threat technology directs toward information survival may be the same as their response to nontechnological challenges to information permanence. "The only guarantee of access is ownership,"[25] bluntly states the solution. "Research libraries will collect databases just as seriously as they collect books—and they will safeguard both,"[26] predict Briscoe et al., who suggest that downloading or archival deposits of databases may be the only security against change, authorized or not. Recalling the role of scribes and libraries of ancient times, Briscoe suggests that the new technological promises for information access need to be supported by policies to ensure information survival. Such policies include the deposit of databases and electronic publications in regional depositories, utilities, consortia, and the Library of Congress to guarantee database security, preservation, and physical access; the reworking of copyright to deal with the issues of computer-based information; and the institution of user fees. In an example of using new technology to preserve data, Cribbs cites the case of NASA, which transfers data collected online to CD-ROM for distribution.[27]

Conclusion

Library technology in all its forms, ranging from photocopiers to telefacsimile machines, from online catalogs, online databases, and CD-ROM products to embryonic electronic publications and expert systems, provides opportunities for access to information that are unequaled in history. American society clearly believes that distribution of and access to all sorts of information sources will aid in the growth of knowledge. Appropriate policy decisions will need to be made to minimize the threats technology poses for information survival. Theodore Roszak, who has cogently analyzed the role of information in American society, especially its often-overlooked limitations, has formulated an eloquent statement of perspective and the library's contribution to the information society. He writes:

> The library is not only there as a socially owned and governed institution, a true people's information service; it is staffed by men and women who maintain a high respect for intellectual values. Because they are also the traditional keepers of the books, the librarians have a healthy sense of the hierarchical relationship between data and ideas, facts and knowledge. They know what one goes to a data base to find and what one goes to a book to find. In their case, the computers might not only generate more information for the public, but information itself is more likely to stay in its properly subordinate place in the culture.[28]

Notes

1. Russell Hoban, *Riddley Walker* (New York: Summit, 1980), p.8.
2. Ibid., p. 19.
3. Ibid., p. 20.
4. Raymond DeBuse, "So That's a Book: Advancing Technology and the Library," *Information Technology and Libraries* 7 (March 1988): 8.
5. Mick O'Leary, "DIALOG's New Era," *Online* 12 (November 1988): 17.
6. Robert A. Walton and Frank R. Bridge, "Automated System Marketplace 1987: Maturity and Competition," *Library Journal,* April 1, 1988, p. 33.
7. Mary Y. Moore et al., "FAX!" *American Libraries* 19 (January 1988): 64.
8. Pat Moholt, "Libraries and the New Technologies: Courting the Cheshire Cat," *Library Journal,* November 15, 1988, pp. 38–40.
9. DeBuse, "So That's a Book," p. 16.
10. Carl Fleischhaur, "A Report on the Optical Disk Pilot Program: The Nonprint Project," *Library of Congress Information Bulletin,* November 11, 1985, p. 336.
11. Pam Q. J. Andre, "Full Text Access and Laser Videodiscs: The National Agricultural Library System," *Library Hi Tech* 4 (Spring 1986): 13.
12. Carol Tenopir, "Decision Making by Reference Librarians," *Library Journal,* October 1, 1988, p. 66.
13. Nancy K. Herther, "Those Lingering Doubts about CD-ROM," *Database* 12 (February 1989): 102.
14. Cynthia Hall, Harriet Talan, and Barbara Pease, "InfoTrac in Academic Libraries: What's Missing in the New Technology?" *Database* 10 (February 1987): 55.
15. Linda Stewart and Jan Olsen, "Compact Disk Databases: Are They Good for Users?" *Online* 12 (May 1988): 48–52.
16. Carol Reese, "Manual Indexes versus Computer-Aided Indexes: Comparing the Reader's Guide to Periodical Literature to InfoTrac," *RQ* 27 (Spring 1988): 386.
17. Margaret Cribbs, "The Invisible Drip . . . How Data Seeps away in Various Ways," *Online* 11 (March 1987): 25.
18. Gordon B. Neavill, "Electronic Publishing, Libraries, and the Survival of Information," *Library Resources and Technical Services* 28 (January/March 1984): 76.

19. Ibid., p. 77.
20. Committee on the Records of Government, *Report* (Washington, D.C.: GPO, 1985), p. 9.
21. Gisle Hannemyr and Even Flood, "Scholarly References to Machine-Readable Documents," *Information Technology and Libraries* 4 (March 1985): 64.
22. Cribbs, "The Invisible Drip," p. 16.
23. Ibid., p. 21.
24. John Mallinson, "On the Preservation of Human- and Machine-Readable Records," *Information Technology and Libraries* 7 (March 1988): 21.
25. Richard D. Hacken, "Tomorrow's Research Library: Vigor or Rigor Mortis?" College and Research Libraries 49 (November 1988): 489.
26. Peter Briscoe et al., "Ashurbanipal's Enduring Archetype: Thoughts on the Library's Role in the Future," *College and Research Libraries* 17 (March 1986): 124.
27. Cribbs, "The Invisible Drip," p. 23.
28. Theodore Roszak, *The Cult of Information* (New York: Pantheon, 1986), p. 176.

What will be the value of the best efforts to preserve information and to widen accessibility through new technologies if users' rights of access are denied? C. James Schmidt chronicles recent events that in his view suggest a pattern of attempts to restrict access to unclassified information. Schmidt describes in detail the FBI Library Awareness Program and the American Library Association's response to it. As chair of the ALA Intellectual Freedom Committee, Schmidt offers an insider's view on these events, which challenge the role of the library in America's democratic society.

Rights for Users of Information: Conflicts and Balances among Privacy, Professional Ethics, Law, National Security

C. James Schmidt
Vice President, Research Libraries Group, Inc.
1200 Villa St., Mountain View, CA 94041-1100

Ensuring the survival of information has many facets, as illustrated by other articles in this volume and elsewhere. Although most perspectives on survival deal with aspects of enduring use and abuse, another aspect—the rights of users—is essential. The issues of survival are not only those of preservation but are also ones of access. Access denied is information unused, therefore unknown, therefore not surviving. This essay will discuss several efforts by the federal government during the 1980s to monitor and/or inhibit access to unclassified information. Such efforts have been justified under three broad categories: national security, economic competitiveness, and necessary reductions in government spending.

Origins of the Recent Concern

Prior to 1979, export restrictions were applied primarily to strategic goods. However, in 1976, a Task Force of the Defense Science Board introduced the concept of "critical technologies," information and techniques as potentially dangerous and therefore suitable for export control—that is, licensing.[1] The concept of "critical technologies" was embodied in the Export Administration Act of 1979 (amended in 1985). The act mandates the use of export controls as necessary "to restrict the export of goods *and technology*" [emphasis added].[2] Technology was defined as

> the *information* [emphasis added] and knowhow (whether in tangible such as models, prototypes, drawings, sketches, diagrams, blueprints, or manuals, or in intangible form such as training or technical services) that can be used to design, produce, manufacture, utilize or reconstruct goods, including computer software and technical data, but not the goods themselves.[3]

Thus, information qua information became subject to export regulation and licensing.[4]

The prevailing philosophy prior to the Export Act had been articulated as early as 1945 by Vannevar Bush:

> . . . sounder foundation for our national security rests in a broad dissemination of scientific knowledge upon which further advances can more readily be made than in a policy of restriction which would impede our further advances in the hope that our potential enemies will not catch up with us.[5]

Two categories of unclassified information have been acknowledged in the regulations issued pursuant to the Export Administration Act (EAR): information arising from "fundamental research" that qualifies for unrestricted export under a "general license"—in effect an exemption—and other information that requires a "validated license" for export. The act represented a major step away from a commitment to security based on openness and toward security based on restriction and secrecy.

Domestic Restrictions

With the Export Administration Act in law and its regulations promulgated, attention turned to other modes of disseminating unclassified information—classification itself, professional conferences, libraries—and means for preventing or monitoring such dissemination.

In 1982, President Reagan issued Executive Order 12356, which laid out the classification guidelines his administration would follow. The Reagan guidelines replaced ones promulgated by President Carter in 1978[6] and differed from them in four significant ways. First, the Reagan guidelines established a presumption *in favor of secrecy* (classification) where there might be doubt about whether secrecy was necessary. Second, the Reagan guidelines eliminated automatic declassification after a prescribed period of time. Third, the Reagan guidelines authorized post facto classification of information already in the public domain. Fourth, the Reagan guidelines encouraged classification, in marginal cases, at a higher rather than lower level, for example, secret rather than confidential.[7] In sum, these guidelines preferred secrecy through classification over openness.

In addition to export controls and the expanded scope of classification, the 1980s also featured attempts, some successful, to control programs and presentations at professional conferences. In 1980, the Commerce Department required application for a "validated license" for the first International Bubble Memory Conference held in Santa Barbara because attendees included computer scientists, mathematicians, and engineers from "communist" countries, including China. Conference organizers were also required to withdraw invitations previously issued to certain of these scientists. In addition to such censoring of unclassified research at conferences, at least seven professional societies have had their proceedings affected by export control regulations.[8]

Restrictions on attendance at conferences and forced withdrawal of selected presentations may have resulted in some delay in access to conference papers, but most such papers are indexed and included in databases. Hence government agencies attempted to monitor usage of databases containing unclassified scientific and technical information and their related document delivery services. In 1986, representatives of the Department of Defense, the Central Intelligence Agency, and the Federal Bureau of Investigation began to visit such database service organizations as Dialog, Mead Data Central, and Chemical Abstracts.[9] The government representatives were seeking the names of users of these services, especially foreigners, and their subject interests.

In October 1986, Admiral John Poindexter, national security adviser, issued a directive (NTISSP No. 2)[10] implementing a then two-year old but little known policy that had been approved by President Reagan in 1984 (NSDD 145).[11] The Reagan policy created a new classification category—"sensitive but unclassified"—and called upon all federal agencies to develop guidelines for its implementation. The Poindexter directive was the first implementation step, disseminating procedures for agencies to follow that had been prepared by an interagency study group. Although the Poindexter directive was withdrawn in March 1987 under congressional pressure, NSDD 145 remains in place.

Another attempt to restrict access to unclassified scientific information occurred in 1988, when NASA officials wrote to the University of California requesting that the university deny access to NASA's unclassified online database to students and faculty who were not citizens. The university declined and transferred its access to the same database via Dialog (at higher cost) where no similar restriction was imposed.

The Library Awareness Program

Concurrent with the attempts to limit access to information at conferences and in databases, libraries became the focus of efforts by FBI agents to monitor activities of foreigners, especially those from East European nations, China, and Cuba.

On Thursday, June 4, 1987, two FBI agents visited the Math/Science Library at Columbia University and questioned the clerk on duty about the use of that library by foreigners. A librarian overheard the conversation, interrupted, and referred the agents to the office of the university librarian. The acting university librarian, Paula Kaufman, reported the visit to the chair of the New York Library Association's Intellectual Freedom Committee, who subsequently reported the incident to ALA's Intellectual Freedom Committee (IFC). This single incident led to a series of disclosures, headlines, congressional hearings, and legislative attempts to secure federal protection for the privacy rights of library users.

During the 1987 annual conference in San Francisco, ALA's Intellectual Freedom Committee discussed the report of the visit at Columbia and decided to write to the acting director of the FBI to secure confirmation that the bureau in fact had an active program of visiting libraries to inquire about foreigners' use of the libraries. On July 31, the bureau confirmed in writing that the Library Awareness Program was indeed active.

On September 18, 1987, the *New York Times* carried a front-page story in all its editions entitled "Libraries Are Asked by FBI to Report on Foreign Agents." Extensive newspaper, magazine, and television and radio coverage of the program followed in all parts of the country and abroad, including a story distributed by TASS, the telegraph agency of the Soviet Union, dated February 25, 1988, entitled "FBI Spying on Library Visitors."

After receiving confirmation from the FBI that such a program was active, the Intellectual Freedom Committee prepared and distributed on October 1, 1987, a statement advising libraries of all types that this program was "an unwarranted government intrusion upon personal privacy . . . that threatened the First Amendment right to receive information." The bureau responded that it "has documented instances, for more than a decade, of hostile intelligence officers who have exploited libraries by stealing proprietary, sensitive, and other information and attemptting (sic) to identify and recruit American and foreign students in American libraries." The IFC's advisory statement reminded libraries of ALA's 1970 policy statement on "Confidentiality of Library Records," and of the provision in ALA's 1981 "Statement on Professional Ethics" for librarians that protects library users' privacy "with respect to information sought or received, and materials consulted, borrowed, or acquired." The advisory statement concluded with a request that libraries visited by FBI representatives report all such visits to ALA's Office for Intellectual Freedom.

On January 14, 1988, at the conclusion of ALA's 1988 Midwinter Conference in San Antonio, the National Commission on Libraries and Information Science held a closed meeting during which its members and staff were briefed by Thomas DuHadway, deputy assistant director of the FBI's Intelligence Division, on the Library Awareness Program. The transcript of this briefing, released under an FOIA request to Toby Macintosh, a reporter for the Bureau of National Affairs, confirmed the existence of the program, provided more extensive justification for it, and indicated that the program was not limited to libraries in the greater New York City area. Both the transcript and the reports received from libraries in response to IFC's advisory statement revealed that FBI representatives had visited libraries across the country during 1987 and had sought to acquire information about specific library patrons, including their subject interests and the materials they had used or borrowed.

In May 1988, Congressman Don Edwards, chair of the House Judiciary Subcommittee on Constitutional and Civil Rights, scheduled hearings on the Library Awareness Program. On June 20, representatives of ALA, the Special Libraries Association, and the Association of Research Libraries testified along with librarians from two universities that had been visited by FBI agents—Columbia and the University of Maryland. On July 13, testimony was taken from James Geer, assistant director of the FBI's Intelligence Division. Geer repeated many of the allegations contained in the transcript of the NCLIS meeting but provided some additional facts. The Library Awareness Program was not the first such effort by the bureau; there had been an earlier one in the 1970s. The program was intended to be limited to libraries with scientific and technical materials in the New York City area; visits to libraries elsewhere in the country were related to investigations of specific individuals.

During ALA's 1988 annual conference in New Orleans, the IFC presented a status report to the executive board and to council. The committee requested and received approval to meet with representatives of the bureau in Washington to express concerns about the program. The committee also requested and was granted authority to take appropriate legal steps to compel disclosure of documents revealing the true extent of the Library Awareness Program. On September 9, 1988, members of the IFC, ALA staff, and counsel met with Geer, DuHadway, and three other representatives of the bureau. ALA's concerns were expressed as was the rationale for the FBI's visits to libraries. Geer agreed to distribute to the bureau's regional and district offices a statement prepared by the IFC setting forth ALA's principles regarding open libraries and privacy rights for library users. The IFC is preparing such a statement. Geer also indicated that future visits to libraries as needed would begin with a library's administrative offices.

In addition to holding hearings on the program, the One-hundredth Congress undertook to develop legislation that would provide federal protection for the privacy rights of library patrons. Such a law would have complemented similar existing laws in 38 states and the District of Columbia by establishing a uniform standard for disclosure—a court order. The legislation (H.R. 4947/S. 2361) also contained protection from disclosure for video rental records. Staff from ALA's Office for Intellectual Freedom worked with the ALA Washington Office, congressional staff, and representatives from other associations to develop the language of the legislation. In the closing days of the One-hundredth Congress, under threat of an amendment that would have made the legislation unacceptable and would have negated existing protection in state laws, ALA's support for the bill was withdrawn and the legislation was adopted containing only the protection from disclosure of video rental records.

Interagency Coordination

Although the FBI's activities received the most publicity, the pattern of attempts to restrict access to unclassified information in the 1980s suggests purposeful, pervasive, and coordinated activity. In his 1982 statement to the Senate Governmental Subcommittee on Investigations studying the issues of technology transfer, Admiral Bobby Inman, then deputy director of the CIA, announced the formation of the interagency Technology Transfer Intelligence Committee (TTIC) to serve as a focal point on all technology transfer issues.[12] The committee was composed of representatives from 22 agencies and had a subcommittee on exchange programs. A corollary group was also established—the NSC Technology Transfer Coordinating Committee—to bring together political, foreign policy, and enforcement perspectives. Together, these two committees provided substantial support to the Department of Commerce's administration of the Export Act.

The TTIC released two reports on technology transfer—one in 1982 and a revised version in 1985.[13] Both reports sought to prove that foreign intelligence officers, especially the Soviets, have large-scale information-gathering programs that have targeted unclassified scientific and technical information such as that available in libraries and databases. An official of the Department of Defense summarized the department's point of view in a 1986 speech at a convention of the Information Industry Association: "The question is not whether there will be restrictions or controls on the use of commercially available on-line databases. The question is how will such restrictions or controls be applied?"[14]

Speaking about libraries, in a letter to the House Judiciary Subcommittee on Constitutional and Civil Rights, William Sessions, director of the FBI, said: "When deemed necessary, the FBI will continue to contact certain scientific and technical libraries (including public and university libraries) in the New York City area concerning hostile intelligence service activities at libraries."[15]

Balancing the Interests

The activities of the 1980s described above attempted to replace established assumptions and expectations with new norms. Unclassified information, previously assumed not to be dangerous, was now regarded as not so benign. Privacy rights assumed to exist for information users, and protected by law in 38 states and the District of Columbia, were presumed to fall in the face of national security needs. Professionals, previously obligated to a code of ethics, were now sought by government agents to serve as informants and operatives.

Conclusion

The debate of the past decade has raised more questions than it has answered. The fundamental premise for the attempts to restrict access to unclassified information is clear: In some cases allowing access could endanger U.S. national security and/or economic competitiveness. The validity of this premise remains to be proven and is argued forcefully on both sides. In 1982, speaking in favor of more restrictions, Assistant Secretary of Commerce Lawrence Brady said:

> Operating out of embassies, consulates, and so-called "business delegations," KGB operatives have blanketed the developed capitalist countries with a network that operates like a gigantic vacuum cleaner, sucking up formulas, patents, blueprints and know-how with frightening precision. We believe these operations rank higher in priority even than the collection of military intelligence. . . . This network seeks to exploit the "soft underbelly"—the individuals who, out of idealism or greed, fall victim to intelligence schemes; our traditions of an open press and unrestricted access to knowledge; and finally, the desire of academia to jealously preserve its prerogatives as a community of scholars unencumbered by government regulation. Certainly, these freedoms provide the underpinning of the American way of life. It is time, however, to ask what price we must pay if we are unable to protect our secrets?[16]

On the side of no restriction:

> Once we accept any restraint . . . we are drawn inexorably, by a series of logical steps, to a total prohibition against public disclosure.[17]

> . . . the openness of the American system is not a weakness, it is our strength.[18]

> . . . the most important question about technology transfer in the long run is whether the receiving side is able to absorb the technology it imports, to diffuse it beyond one or two showcase locations, and to build upon it to generate further technological advances of its own.[19]

A showing of endangerment from unrestricted access to unclassified information has not been made. A showing of pervasive technology transfer at the expense of American economic competitiveness has not been made. An affirmative case for continuing the openness that has historically characterized American policy can be made. The benefits that have accrued from this openness, in terms of scientific, technological, and economic leadership, can be identified, as can the benefits that accrue generally from an informed citizenry.

Notes

1. U.S. Department of Defense, Office of the Director of Defense Research and Engineering, *An Analysis of Export Controls of U.S. Technology—A DoD Perspective: A report of the Defense Science Board Task Force on Export of U.S. Technology* (Washington, D.C.: GPO, 1976).
2. 50 U.S.C. 2402(2) (A) App.
3. 50 U.S.C. 2415 App.
4. The dissemination of certain information had earlier been restricted by law, e.g., the Atomic Energy Act (42 U.S.C. 2014 (y), 2162), the Invention Secrecy Act (35 U.S.C. 181).
5. Vannevar Bush. *Science—The Endless Frontier* (Washington, D.C.: GPO, 1945), p. 182.
6. Executive Order 12065 (1978)
7. For a detailed analysis, see John Shattuck and Muriel Spence, *Government Information Controls: Implications for Scholarship, Science and Technology* (Cambridge, Mass.: Harvard University, 1988), pp. 6–9. Distributed by the Association of American Universities.
8. Ibid., p. 10.
9. "Are Data Bases a Threat to National Security?" *Business Week,* December 1, 1986, p. 39.
10. NTISSP No. 2, "National Policy on Protection of Sensitive, but Unclassified Information in Federal Government Telecommunications and Automated Information Systems," October 29, 1986.
11. National Security Decision Directive 145, "National Policy on Telecommunications and Automated Information Systems Security," September 17, 1984.
12. Reprinted as Appendix H in *Scientific Communication and National Security* (Washington, D.C.: National Academy Press, 1982), pp. 140–142.
13. *Soviet Acquisition of Western Technology* (CIA, 1982); *Soviet Acquisition of Militarily Significant Western Technology* (CIA, 1985); *Washington Post,* June 19, 1983, p. A-12; *New York Times,* September 19, 1985, p. 14.
14. "Pentagon Weighs Curb on Data Bank Access," *New York Times,* November 12, 1986.
15. September 14, 1988, letter to Representative Don Edwards.
16. "Taking Back the Rope: Technology Transfer and National Security," speech presented to Association of Former Intelligence Officers, Washington, D.C., March 29, 1982, pp. 5–6.
17. Robert Park. "Restricting Information: A Dangerous Game," *Issues in Science and Technology* (Fall 1988), 66.

18. Ibid.
19. Thane Gustafson. *Selling the Russians the Rope? Soviet Technology Policy and U.S. Export Controls* (Santa Monica, Calif.: Rand Corporation, 1981), p. 1. See also Roald Sagdeev, "Science and Perestroika: A Long Way to Go," *Issues in Science and Technology* (Summer 1988), reprinted from *Izvestia.*

Fred Wood describes U.S. governmental policy initiatives and possible new programs as America's largest information machine—the federal government—responds to the electronic age. Wood describes the key problems raised by the expanding use of electronic media to store and share information, the specific needs that these problems illustrate, and possible solutions that may contribute to the federal government's future role in information dissemination and potentially enhance the public's access to government information.

Directions in Federal Information Dissemination Policy in 1989

Fred B. Wood

Project Director, Office of Technology Assessment
U.S. Congress, Washington, DC 20510-8025

Federal information is essential to public understanding of many issues facing Congress and the nation, and is used by all sectors of society. Technological advances are opening up many new and potentially cost-effective ways to collect, manage, and disseminate this information. Although traditional ink-on-paper publications will continue to meet important needs for the foreseeable future, many types of federal information—such as statistical, reference, and scientific and technical—are well suited to electronic storage and dissemination. However, the advent of electronic dissemination has generated serious conflicts about how to maintain and strengthen public access to government information and balance the roles of individual federal agencies, governmentwide dissemination mechanisms, and the private sector. Congressional action is urgently needed to resolve federal information dissemination issues and to set the direction of federal activities for years to come. In particular,

Note: This article is based in part on the OTA report *Informing the Nation: Federal Information Dissemination in an Electronic Age,* OTA-CIT-396, October 1988. The views expressed are those of the author and not necessarily those of the OTA, Technology Assessment Board, or U.S. Congress. The focus of the OTA report and this article is on public information, that is, federal information that is or should be in the public domain and is not subject to exemption under the Freedom of Information Act (e.g., due to privacy, security, or confidentiality considerations).

Copies of *Informing the Nation* are available from the Superintendent of Documents, U.S. Government Printing Office, Washington, DC 20402-9325, 202-783-3238. The GPO stock number is 052-003-01130-1; the price is $14.

policy direction is needed to establish the future roles of the U.S. Government Printing Office (GPO) and Superintendent of Documents (SupDocs), the Depository Library Program (DLP, administered by GPO), and the National Technical Information Service (NTIS). Congressional direction is also needed with respect to governmentwide electronic information dissemination policy, use of the Freedom of Information Act in an electronic environment, management of federal information dissemination, and electronic dissemination of congressional information.

Policy Opportunities and Challenges

The U.S. federal government today stands at a major crossroads with respect to the future of federal information dissemination. Technological advances have opened up many new ways to disseminate cost-effectively those types of federal information that are particularly well suited to electronic formats. The technical trends underlying the new opportunities are likely to continue unabated for at least the next three to five years and ten years or more in many cases. These trends include

- Continued, steady improvement in the price/performance of microcomputers, nonimpact printers, scanners, and desktop software
- Rapid proliferations of desktop publishing systems and continued improvement in the ability of desktop systems to produce higher quality, more complex documents
- Rapid growth in networking of desktop and high-end systems, nonimpact printers, and phototypesetters used for more complex, higher volume, and/or larger institutional applications
- Continued increase in the number and use of computerized online information services and online information gateways (that provide the channels for information exchange)
- Rapid advances in optical disk technologies and applications
- Rapid advances in the development of expert systems applicable to many aspects of information dissemination

Many individual federal agencies are already experimenting with and increasingly implementing information dissemination via electronic bulletin boards, floppy disks, compact optical disks, desktop publishing, and electronic printing-on-demand. For example, statistical data are highly suited to electronic formats, and, based on the results of surveys conducted for OTA by the General Accounting Office (GAO), about one-third of the civilian departmental agencies use magnetic tapes or discs, one-fifth floppy disks and electronic data transfer, and one-tenth electronic mail for dissemination of statistical data. Overall, civilian agencies (departmental and independent) reported more than 7,500 information products disseminated electronically, as of FY 1987.

The number of civilian agency publications in paper format appears to be declining slowly, whereas the number of electronic products has more than tripled over the past four years. The GAO survey results suggest that this trend will continue. There already is a significant demand for federal information in electronic formats among various user groups, and particularly within the library community, private industry, the federal agencies themselves, and various groups with specialized needs (such as educators, researchers, and disabled persons). This demand is likely to rise sharply over the next few years, especially among the more technically sophisticated user groups.

The results of the GAO surveys of federal information users document this likely trend in demand. For example, the depository library community (as intermediaries reflecting users and user information needs in university, research, federal, state, local, and public libraries) indicated a strong preference for obtaining increasing percentages of federal information in electronic form and declining percentages in paper and microfiche.

However, technological advances are creating a number of problems and challenges with respect to federal information dissemination:

- At a fundamental level, electronic technology is changing or even eliminating many distinctions between reports, publications, databases, records, and the like, in ways not anticipated by existing statutes and policies. A rapidly growing percentage of federal information exists in an electronic form on a computerized system as part of a "seamless web" of information activities.
- Electronic technology is eroding the institutional roles of governmentwide information dissemination agencies. Although many individual federal agencies disseminate at least some of their information in electronic formats, the central governmentwide dissemination mechanisms (primarily the SupDocs sales program at GPO, DLP, and NTIS) are presently limited largely to paper or paper and microfiche and thus disseminate a declining portion of federal information.
- Technology has outpaced the major governmentwide statutes that apply to federal information dissemination. The Printing Act of 1895, the Depository Library Act of 1962, and Freedom of Information Act of 1966 predate the era of electronic dissemination. The Paperwork Reduction Act of 1980 was amended in 1986 to include information dissemination within its scope, but substantive statutory guidance on electronic information dissemination, per se, is minimal.
- The advent of electronic dissemination raises new equity concerns since, to the extent electronic formats have distinct advantages (e.g., in terms of timeliness and searchability), those without electronic access are disadvantaged. In general, library, research, media, consumer, and related groups argue that the federal government has a responsibility to ensure equity of access to federal information in paper and electronic formats.
- Technological advances complicate the federal government's relationships with the commercial information industry. While those companies that market repackaged or value-added federal information (e.g., with additional indexing or analysis) benefit from access to electronic formats, some of these firms are concerned about possible adverse effects of government competition and oppose government dissemination of value-added information. This conflicts with the long-established government role in producing and disseminating value-added information products in paper format and its logical extension to electronic formats.

Congressional action is urgently needed to resolve these and other federal information dissemination issues and to set the direction of federal activities for the future. Congress needs to provide direction to existing agencies and institutions with respect to electronic information dissemination. Key policy directions are presented below.

Government Printing Office

Historically, GPO has carried out most of the federal government's ink-on-paper printing, either directly or through private contractors, has marketed and sold selected government documents (in paper and microfiche) to the public (through SupDocs), and has distributed government documents to the depository libraries (through DLP). Although GPO already makes extensive use of electronic input and photocomposition, there is very little production or sales of products in electronic formats. GPO does sell (through SupDocs) some agency and congressional products in magnetic computer tape format. It also has ongoing pilot projects involving both online and CD-ROM (compact disc/read-only memory) dissemination and both desktop and high-end electronic publishing.

Defining GPO's future role in the dissemination of electronic formats presents a major opportunity for Congress and GPO. One alternative, mandatory centralization of all electronic dissemination through SupDocs (or any other central government office), would conflict with numerous existing agency activities, would meet strong agency opposition, could precipitate legal and political challenges, and would not appear to be cost-effective. On the other hand, excluding electronic formats from the SupDocs sales program would erode the viability and integrity of the program over time and compromise the ability of SupDocs to facilitate broad public awareness of federal information. A middle ground alternative, with SupDocs including selected electronic formats and products, would appear to strengthen the SupDocs sales program, facilitate public access, and preserve the prerogatives of the agencies to disseminate electronically themselves (and of private vendors to enhance and resell electronic formats).

SupDocs sale of magnetic computer tapes, floppy disks, compact optical disks, and perhaps electronic printing-on-demand products would appear to be straightforward, except for a possible overlap with NTIS. Sales of online services could be more difficult due to staffing, software development, and capital requirements and to more intensive competition with agencies and commercial vendors.

Another challenge is to define GPO's role relative to the growth in agency desktop and high-end electronic publishing systems. GPO could have a key role in standards-setting, training, and innovative activities relevant to electronic publishing, but GPO will be operating in a much more decentralized, competitive environment than has traditionally been the case with conventional ink-on-paper printing. In the medium-term (three to ten years), a significant portion of GPO inplant and procured printing could be suitable for electronic dissemination or vulnerable to competition from electronic formats. GPO will have to be innovative in matching its expertise to agency needs, which are likely to vary widely and change at an increasingly rapid pace.

Other opportunities for improvement in GPO's traditional printing services include more competitive pricing and timely delivery of GPO main plant in-house work for executive agencies, itemized estimating and billing practices, regular surveys of customer needs and problems, and revised and strengthened GPO advisory groups.

National Technical Information Service

NTIS has historically served as the federal government's archive and clearinghouse for scientific and technical reports prepared by federal agencies or contractors, along with related indexes and bibliographies. The bulk of NTIS documents are provided in paper or microfiche format, although, in recent years, NTIS also has served as a clearinghouse for some electronic format products (e.g., software and databases). Also, NTIS performs other related services, such as patent licensing, Japanese literature exchange, and FOIA request and/or information sales processing for a few agencies.

With respect to NTIS, the major opportunity is, quite simply, determining the future of NTIS as a government entity. NTIS faces strategic challenges on several fronts. First, the core NTIS business, as measured by sales of paper and microfiche reports, has been shrinking (by about 40 to 50 percent over the past decade). In part as a result, NTIS prices for these reports have gone up considerably faster than the inflation rate in order to help maintain break-even operations. Over the last few years, NTIS has offset declining revenues from full-text reports and subscription, bibliographic, and announcement products with increasing revenues from services to other agencies (such as order billing and processing), brokerage fees on sales of other agency materials, and sales of computer-related products.

Second, a significant percentage (estimated at one-third to one-half) of federal scientific and technical reports are never provided to NTIS, since agency participation is strictly voluntary. The NTIS collection is thus becoming increasingly incomplete. Third, NTIS is being outdistanced by most of the federal science agencies with respect to use of electronic information technology. And fourth, NTIS has been caught in the middle of the ongoing debate over the privatization of federal information functions.

The Administration has argued that NTIS provides what is essentially a commercial service performed by the government and that it should be contracted out or otherwise privatized. The administration has asserted that the privatization of NTIS would maximize reliance on and minimize competition with the private sector, reduce the cost of government, and/or increase the quality and effectiveness of NTIS services. The academic, research, and scientific communities, however, have argued, in general, that NTIS performs an important and inherently governmental function that is not suitable for privatization, and that no cost savings or service improvement have been demonstrated to occur if NTIS were to be privatized. The federal scientific and technical agencies, the source of NTIS information, have expressed concerns about the viability of NTIS if privatized and whether U.S. and foreign government agencies would continue to cooperate with a privatized NTIS.

The controversy over NTIS precipitated legislative action by the relevant House and Senate authorizing committees to block privatization. Both the House Committee on Science, Space, and Technology and the Senate Committee on Commerce, Science, and Transportation enacted language prohibiting the contracting out of

NTIS, or any major NTIS activities, without explicit statutory approval. This prohibition was included as part of Title V (Technology Competitiveness) of the comprehensive trade legislation (H.R. 4848) signed into law on August 23, 1988. Similar language also was included in the National Bureau of Standards Authorization Act for FY 1989.

NTIS appears to be ideally suited for implementation of an electronic document system (using optical disk storage, electronic printing, and multiformat output—paper, microfiche, and electronic), perhaps using the Defense Technical Information (DTIC) system now under development as a prototype. An electronic document system could help revitalize NTIS if coupled with improved agency participation. Overall, an electronic NTIS should be able to increase greatly the diversity and timeliness of NTIS (and related private vendors) offerings, increase the ability of NTIS (and private vendors) to match information products with potential users, and reduce costs. An electronic NTIS should be better able to serve all users, but especially small and medium-sized businesses and individual researchers.

NTIS and SupDocs could cooperate on implementing electronic technologies that would meet NTIS clearinghouse and archival needs, plus support a broadening of the SupDocs product line to include selected low-demand items. Strengthened NTIS-SupDocs cooperation also could lead to improvements in the indexing, marketing, and international exchange of federal information. And strengthened cooperation seems essential to the extent both agencies pursue sales of electronic format products and that SupDocs enters the low demand market. At present, demand for NTIS documents averages about 10 copies per title, compared to about 2,000 copies per title for items in the SupDocs sales program.

Depository Libraries

The Depository Library Program (DLP) is administered by GPO and serves as a mechanism for dissemination of federal agency documents free of charge to the approximately 1,400 participating libraries. The libraries, in return, provide housing for the documents and access to this information free of charge to the general public. About 55 percent of the depository libraries are university libraries, 23 percent are public libraries, 11 percent are law school libraries, 7 percent are federal libraries, and 4 percent are special libraries and the like.

As with GPO and NTIS, there is a major opportunity to define the future role of the DLP with respect to dissemination of federal information in electronic formats. As agencies make increasing use of electronic formats, limiting the DLP to paper and microfiche products only would, over time, reduce the type and amount of federal information available to the public and erode the legislative intent of the DLP (e.g., as expressed in the legislative history of the Depository Library Act of 1962). The impetus for including electronic information in the DLP is strong. The Joint Committee on Printing has interpreted the DLP statutory provisions as extending to government information in all formats, and other congressional committees concur in the decision to disseminate certain electronic formats to depositories. If it is to succeed, this emerging policy needs to be developed and refined further and have the support of DLP participants (especially libraries, GPO, and the agencies that are the source of most DLP materials). A variety of pilot projects, demonstrations, and tests involving various technologies, financial arrangements, and delivery mechanisms (including possible involvement of the private sector) is warranted. Ultimately, Congress may wish to consider a reorganization or restructuring of the current DLP in light of both electronic information dissemination options now or likely to become available and the evolving nature of libraries and the telecommunication infrastructure.

The results of the GAO survey of federal information users indicate a substantial depository library demand for electronic formats. The vast majority of libraries responding indicated that the *Congressional Record* and *Federal Register,* along with an index to federal information and database of key federal statistical series, would be moderately to greatly useful in both online and CD-ROM formats.

Public Access to Federal Information

A fundamental cross-cutting issue is public access to federal information. Debate over the use of electronic formats, privatization, and the like is obscuring the commitment of Congress to public access. Congress has expressed through numerous public laws the importance of federal information and the dissemination of that information in carrying out agency missions and the principles of democracy and open government. A renewed commitment to public access in an electronic age may be needed.

If Congress wishes to preserve and strengthen the principle of public access to federal information, a number of possible actions warrant consideration. These range from amending specific statutes with respect to electronic formats to articulating an overall statement of congressional intent. For example, if Congress wishes to maintain the integrity of the Freedom of Information Act (FOIA) for electronic as well as traditional paper formats, the option of amending the statute deserves serious consideration and, indeed, may well be essential. (Some illustrative specific electronic FOIA issues that could be addressed by amendments are discussed in a later section.) Similarly, if it is congressional intent that the DLP should include federal information in all formats, then Congress may need to amend appropriate statues to eliminate current ambiguity and controversy.

Another congressional action that warrants serious consideration is the promulgation of congressional views, perhaps in statutory form, on the information dissemination principles addressed in the Office of Management and Budget's (OMB's) Circular A-130, "Management of Federal Information Resources," and the January 1989 draft policy on federal information dissemination. OMB emphasizes the role of the private sector and asserts that, as a general principle, where willing and able, the private sector—not the federal government—should disseminate federal information, especially when such information is in electronic form. And in its draft policy, OMB asserts further that federal agencies should, as a general principle, leave dissemination of "value-added" electronic federal information—that is, the raw data plus searching aids or software enhancements and the like—to the private sector. The statutory authority for the OMB position is unclear at best. The Paperwork Reduction Act, cited by OMB as a general statutory authority, does not specifically speak to the role of the private sector or value-added information.

A major problem with using value-added as a line of demarcation between governmental and private sector roles is that many federal agencies have mandates to develop and disseminate what amounts to value-added information and have been doing so for years or decades. Providing value-added information is a well-established and, indeed, a mandated function of government. Restricting the federal government from providing such information, or from providing such information in electronic form (even if previously available in paper), would appear to diminish substantially the government's role and erode the ability of agencies to carry out numerous statutory responsibilities.

At the same time, however, the concept of multiple levels of value-added may be viable, with the private sector frequently providing additional levels of value or enhancement beyond those provided by the government. Federal agencies would continue to provide information as they do today, using electronic formats where appropriate and desired by users, and employing private sector contractors where cost-effective and/or necessary to provide the desired quality or timeliness. The private information industry would be able to repackage and resell any federal information products and would be able to add further value to create enhanced information products where the market exists, much as the industry does today. The only real difference is that both the governmental and private sector offerings would be moving to a higher and more sophisticated technological level.

The most important policy contribution could be to establish a clearer sense of congressional priority with respect to public access, cost-effectiveness, and privatization. One possible interpretation of congressional intent regarding federal information dissemination is to give highest priority to unimpeded and open dissemination in order to realize the overriding policy goal of public access. This could be achieved as cost-effectively as possible without compromising public access, utilizing the private sector where appropriate as one means to achieve these ends. This interpretation is philosophically somewhat different from that reflected in OMB Circular A-130 or the January 1989 OMB draft dissemination policy, and also from OMB Circular A-76, which requires contracting out of commercially available services when cost-effective to the government. Note that, as in the case of NTIS, the applicability of A-76 to arguably inherent governmental functions such as information dissemination, and the cost-effectiveness of private contracting of such functions, are also in dispute. Clarification or reaffirmation of congressional intent appears warranted, possibly through amendment of relevant statutes such as the Printing Act or Paperwork Reduction Act.

Freedom of Information

The FOIA was enacted in 1966 when paper records were the dominant form of government information. The application of FOIA to electronic formats has created a number of problems. The courts have expressed a need for Congress to clarify gray areas left open by the statute. For example, the case law as applied to paper information establishes that the FOIA does not require agencies to create new records in fulfilling requests. When additional programming is required to extract information from computer systems, agencies and courts have sometimes held that such programming would be analogous to record creation and, therefore, would not be a required part of the FOIA "search" process. In the electronic age, however, some degree of reprogramming or program modification may be essential to obtain access to electronic information.

Another gray area involves defining a "reasonable effort" on the part of the government in searching for records responsive to a FOIA request. In the computer context, the programming/no-programming distinction has begun to separate decisions about "reasonableness" from considerations of effort. This is incongruous with tradition, as significant expenditures of effort continue to be involved in manual FOIA searches. Retrieval of paper documents may involve extensive tracking, communication with various bureaus, consolidation of disparate files, and substantial hand deletions of exempted materials. As computer capabilities for searching, segregating, and consolidating of data become increasingly efficient and cost-effective, computer searches could be broadened and public access enhanced. Agencies may need to focus on new ways to respond more readily to FOIA requests for computer records.

Another issue is whether and under what conditions the advantages of electronic formats are such that access to the format as well as the information itself should be guaranteed. Although the case law and the FOIA fee guidelines have established that computer-stored information is subject to FOIA, requesters are not guaranteed access to the information in formats other than paper. If large quantities of data could be more effectively utilized with the flexibility offered by magnetic tapes, discs, or online retrieval, access to these electronic media may be important.

Congress could amend FOIA to bring electronic formats clearly within the statutory purview, define the scope and limits of FOIA searches in an electronic environment, and clarify fees and procedures for FOIA requests for electronic information. For the 1990s and beyond, Congress may need to decide whether the FOIA should continue to be viewed as an "access to records" statute, or whether it should be perceived more broadly as an "access to information" statute. Due to the explosive growth in electronic information storage, processing, and transmission by the federal government, traditional views about records and searches may need to be modified to ensure even basic access to computerized public information.

Technical/Management Improvements

Several alternatives for improvement of information dissemination management could be implemented in the short term by executive branch action using existing statutory authorities and with the concurrence of Congress, but with no required statutory action. Of course, one or any combination of these alternatives could be incorporated into a legislative package, as amendments to various statutes, should Congress determine that a stronger mandate is needed.

There is a clear consensus that appropriate technical standards for electronic publishing and dissemination are essential if the government wishes to realize potential cost-effectiveness and productivity improvements. Technical standards on text markup, page/document description, and optical disks are especially important. The National Institute of Standards and Technology (NIST), DTIC (or another responsible Department of Defense component), and GPO could be assigned lead responsibility, presumably building on accepted or emerging private sector industry standards to the extent possible and working through the national and international standards organizations.

There is also general consensus in and out of government for the establishment of a governmentwide index to major federal information products—regardless of format—although there are differing views on how to implement an index. GPO and/or NTIS could be assigned lead responsibility to consolidate and upgrade existing indexes, directories, and inventories into one integrated index. The government could contract with private firms or library and information science professionals to carry out some of this work. The index could be made available in multiple formats and disseminated directly from the government as well as via the depository libraries and private vendors (perhaps in enhanced form).

In addition, federal agency officials expressed strong support for much improved mechanisms to exchange learning and experience about technological innovations and user needs relevant to information dissemination. Innovation centers could be designated or established at, for example, DTIC (for the defense sector), NIST and NTIS (for the civilian executive branch), and GPO (for the legislative branch), and under grant or contract to a university or other independent, nonprofit research center. DTIC, NIST, and GPO, along with several mission agencies, already have a variety of laboratory and/or demonstration activities under way. Agencies could be required to conduct "Agency X-2000" studies to explore and develop creatively their own visions of future information dissemination activities.

Information dissemination is still not an effective part of agency information resources management (IRM) programs. A variety of IRM training, career development, budget, and management actions could be implemented to give information dissemination (including printing, publishing, press, public affairs, libraries, and the like) a stronger and better understood role within the IRM concept.

Also, whether within the IRM concept or otherwise, federal agency participation in electronic dissemination of press releases and other time-sensitive information (such as crop reports, weather bulletins, and economic and trade data) could be expanded. Electronic releases could be provided directly to the press, to private electronic news and wire services, and perhaps to depository libraries. A major issue concerns equity of press access and the need to ensure that cost or technical requirements do not discourage smaller, less affluent, and/or out-of-town news organizations from realizing the potential benefits. Although electronic press releases can be more timely and cost-effective than messenger or mail delivery of paper releases, dual format (paper and electronic) would appear to be necessary—at least for a lengthy transition period—for those news outlets without, or lacking interest in, online electronic capability.

Legislative Branch Information

Congress itself is a major source of federal information. Congressional information ranges from the *Record* to congressional calendars and schedules to the status of pending legislation to a wide range of committee reports and numerous documents produced by the analytical support agencies. Most of this information has been and continues to be available in paper formats. However, increasingly, electronic formats offer significant advantages in terms of timeliness and searchability and are being utilized by private vendors and congressional in-house support offices for a growing range of congressional information.

Electronic options offer the potential to make congressional information more quickly and widely available. This can be very important for citizens and organizations—whether consumer, library, research, labor, or business in nature—that desire to follow congressional activity closely and/or participate in the legislative process. As congressional offices automate, increasing amounts of information are created, revised, and stored in electronic form.

Congress has the opportunity to establish a strategic direction for electronic dissemination of legislative branch information. The importance of congressional information to an informed citizenry and the need to ensure equitable channels of access for all interested citizens, including access to electronic formats, are widely accepted in principle. The differences of opinion focus on the means of implementing access to electronic formats.

In setting an overall direction, Congress will need to determine its own level of responsibility for ensuring that electronic congressional information is readily available to the public, and how that information should be made available (by GPO, other congressional offices, and private vendors). For example, because of GPO's growing role in providing electronic formats to Congress as part of the electronic publishing process, GPO is positioned to participate more actively in disseminating electronic congressional information to the depository libraries and the public at large. At the same time, some commercial vendors would like to contract directly with Congress, perhaps on a bulk rate discount basis, for electronic dissemination of congressional information to libraries, the public, and Congress itself.

In many respects, congressional decisions on electronic dissemination of congressional information are just as important as prior decisions on radio and television coverage of congressional hearings and floor sessions.

Conclusion

For most of this nation's history, federal information has been disseminated predominantly in the form of paper documents and, in recent decades, to a lesser extent in microfiche. However, in the last few years, technological advances have resulted in a rapid increase in the use of electronic formats for federal information dissemination. While the electronic technology offers many new opportunities, it also has generated serious conflicts over how to maintain and strengthen public access to government information and balance the roles of individual federal agencies, governmentwide dissemination mechanisms, and the private sector.

Congress has enacted numerous laws that emphasize the importance of broad public access to federal information and assign various information dissemination functions to individual federal agencies and governmentwide clearinghouses. However, the existing statutory and institutional framework was established by Congress largely during the pre-electronic era. It is important, therefore, that Congress review this framework to determine what actions are needed to ensure that legislative intent is carried out in an electronic environment and whether any adjustments in legislative objectives or legislation are needed.

In conducting this policy review, it is appropriate to keep in mind the words of Thomas Jefferson, who, on July 6, 1816, observed: "If a Nation expects to be ignorant and free in a state of civilization, it expects what never was and never will be . . . if we are to guard against ignorance and remain free, it is the responsibility of every American to be informed."

Federal Agency and Federal Library Reports

National Commission on Libraries and Information Science

1111 18 St. NW, Suite 310, Washington, DC 20036

Susan K. Martin
Executive Director

For the U.S. National Commission on Libraries and Information Science (NCLIS), 1988 was a year marked by program accomplishments, internal changes, and controversy. Highlights of the year include enactment of the law calling for a second White House Conference on Library and Information Services (WHCLIS), presentation of the first NCLIS Recognition Award, establishment of a Federal-State Cooperative System for Public Library Data, publication of the NCLIS Hearings on Sensitive but Not Classified Information, and progress in the governance, information age, and information literacy and education programs. A closed session of the year's first NCLIS meeting, at which a representative of the FBI explained the FBI Library Awareness Program, engendered controversy that reflected on the commission and mobilized large segments of the library profession. [See the special report "Rights for Users of Information: Conflicts and Balances among Privacy, Professional Ethics, Law, National Security" by C. James Schmidt, earlier in Part 1—*Ed.*]

Commissioners and Staff

Longtime NCLIS Vice Chairman Bessie Boehm Moore, who has served on the commission since its creation by Congress in 1971, was not reappointed in 1988, and was replaced by Commissioner-designate Charles E. Reid of New Jersey. At a subsequent commission meeting, Moore was voted the title of vice chairman emeritus, a "first" in the history of NCLIS. Commissioner-designate Elinor H. Swaim of North Carolina was appointed to complete the term of Patricia Barbour, who resigned from the commission in April. Both Raymond J. Petersen of Connecticut and sitting Commissioner Julia Li Wu were appointed and confirmed by the Senate, and Commissioners Margaret Phelan and Wanda L. Forbes were reappointed. Commissioners-designate Forbes, Phelan, Reid, and Swaim became full commissioners by recess appointment of President Reagan. Commissioner George H. Nash, scholar-in-residence at the Hoover Institution, saw publication of the critically acclaimed second volume of his biography of Herbert Hoover.

Early in 1988, Executive Director Vivian J. Arterbery resigned to return to the Rand Corporation. Commissioners Margaret Phelan and Daniel H. Carter served consecutive stints as acting executive director until the new executive director, Susan K. Martin, joined the commission in August. Former director of the Milton S. Eisenhower Library of Johns Hopkins University, Martin brings a background in academic librarianship, library networking, and information technologies to NCLIS. Deputy Director David Hoyt and longtime staff members Dorothy Pollet Gray and Marti Quigley also left the commission in 1988.

FBI Library Awareness Program

At its January 14 meeting in the San Antonio Public Library, NCLIS heard a presentation in closed session by FBI agent Thomas DuHadway about the FBI Library Awareness Program. As described by the FBI, this program deploys agents to various academic and scientific and technical libraries to question and elicit the cooperation of library staff members in observing suspicious behavior on the part of potential foreign intelligence operatives. The transcript of this presentation was released, with some portions excised, under a Freedom of Information Act request. Opposition to this program and to NCLIS's perceived tolerance of it mounted in the library and other communities; in response, NCLIS unanimously adopted a resolution reaffirming its commitment to open access to information for all, the right of privacy for all library users, and unequivocal support of First Amendment rights.

WHCLIS II

On August 8, President Reagan signed PL 100-382, authorizing and requesting the president to call and conduct a White House Conference on Library and Information Services (WHCLIS) between September 1, 1989 and September 30, 1991. NCLIS, along with many other individuals and organizations, had supported this bipartisan legislation, which had 72 cosponsors in the Senate and 178 in the House of Representatives. The conference is to be planned and conducted under the direction of NCLIS in cooperation with the entire library/information community. In a 1985 report, the WHCLIS Preliminary Design Group identified library and information services for the three overarching themes of literacy, productivity, and democracy as the focal point of the conference.

The law authorizes a $6 million appropriation to provide states and territories with matching funds for their preconferences and to support the national conference. Maximum flexibility is reserved for state activities, and private fund raising is encouraged. A 30-member Advisory Committee, to be appointed by the president, Speaker of the House, president pro tempore of the Senate, and NCLIS chairman, including the Librarian of Congress and secretary of education, provides policy oversight for the conference. The law also stipulates that conference delegates be drawn equally from four groups: library and information professionals; supporters such as trustees and Friends groups; local, state, and federal government officials; and the general public.

By the end of 1988, 26 members of the advisory committee had been appointed, with two forthcoming each from the Senate and the White House. No action had yet been taken on appropriation of the authorized funds, without which little can be done to move the conference forward.

Recognition Award

The first annual NCLIS Recognition Award, established to honor initiative in improving and promoting the nation's library and information services, was presented to Pizza Hut, Inc., for its "Book It" National Reading Incentive Program. The program, which involves more than 14 million children and their parents and teachers nationwide, provides incentives and rewards for children's reading accomplishments. Pizza Hut was honored at a special ceremony held in the Indian Treaty Room of the White House during the April commission meeting, when Larry Whitt, vice president of public affairs for Pizza Hut, accepted a mounted Steuben crystal bowl engraved with the Great Seal of the United States as a symbol of the award.

Federal-State Cooperative System for Public Library Data

The National Center for Education Statistics and NCLIS have signed a memorandum of understanding (MOU) to continue joint development of the Federal-State Cooperative System for Public Library Data (FSCS). Worked out over the course of the year by a task force chaired by John G. Lorenz, the FSCS action plan builds on and expands the 1987 12-state pilot project conducted by the American Library Association under contract to the Department of Education. This system, when fully developed, will collect and publish public library statistics annually and fill a gap in statistical information that has existed since 1982.

The goal is to initiate a structure in all 50 states for coordinated data-gathering activities related to public library statistics. Subordinate tasks include identifying standard collecting and reporting methodologies; establishing reporting period consistency; adopting uniform definitions and standard reporting formats; and providing effective communication channels among participants at the local, state, regional, and national levels. The current MOU calls for NCLIS and NCES to develop an implementation plan for FSCS, develop communication channels between the states and NCES, develop a process for providing technical assistance to state library agencies, train state data coordinators both at home and in a "hands-on" experience at NCES, and create a user review panel. To this end, NCES will transfer $225,000 to NCLIS in FY 1989.

John Lorenz, who was appointed coordinator of the program within the NCLIS offices, is working closely with NCES staff, the state library data coordinators, and the Chief Officers of State Library Agencies (COSLA). Because NCLIS is not an operating organization, COSLA is seen as a reasonable home for the Federal/State Cooperative System, as fully implemented.

Other Programs

During 1988, NCLIS initiated a number of programs that are still being developed. These include a pilot project with ACTION RSVP (Retired Seniors Volunteer Program), the RSVP Intergenerational Library Assistance Project, which utilizes senior volunteers working with children in after-school public library activities; the Information for Governance program, focusing on three exemplary public library services geared to both citizen and government official information needs; and the Information Age program to convene a series of expert task forces to define the impact of the information age on society and provide recommendations for policy initiatives at the federal level.

The commission received $5,000 from Gaylord and a grant of $20,000 from the Council on Library Resources for an invitational symposium to bring together school librarians, teachers, school administrators, curriculum specialists, and others to suggest major improvements in the education system by incorporating information resources and librarians fully into the teaching process. In the international arena, NCLIS published the previously adopted trilateral Glenerin Declaration and served as the intermediary in securing $216,000 in State Department grants for 12 projects sponsored by various organizations. NCLIS also started a policy of adhering to the permanent paper standard by publishing the *Hearings on Sensitive but Not Classified Information* and its *Annual Report 1986–1987* on alkaline paper.

National Technical Information Service

U.S. Department of Commerce
Springfield, VA 22161

Alan R. Wenberg
Office of Policy and Planning

With a collection of nearly 2 million items, the National Technical Information Service (NTIS) is the central source for public sale of U.S. government–sponsored research, development, and engineering reports, foreign technical reports, and other analyses prepared by U.S. and foreign governments and their contractors worldwide. NTIS's mission is to collect and disseminate this technical information in order to increase U.S. competitiveness in the global economy. NTIS is a relatively small government organization of about 330 employees that is required to price its products and services to fully recover the costs of providing them to users.

All NTIS materials are permanently available. When government agencies, their contractors, and grantees forward their reports and other items to NTIS, they are cataloged, indexed, abstracted into a computer system, and microfilmed for an archival system. The citations are computerized so that the resulting NTIS Bibliographic Database can be accessed by the public through the major commercial online information vendors. Portions of the database are also available on CD-ROM.

Highlights of 1988 Activities

Privatization

In 1988, two laws containing language prohibiting the contracting out of NTIS were enacted by Congress: the Omnibus Trade and Competitiveness Act, PL 100-418, signed August 23, and the National Institute of Standards and Technology (NIST) Authorization Act for FY 1989, PL 100-519, signed October 24. The Authorization Act states: "The functions and activities of the Service [NTIS] . . . are permanent Federal functions to be carried out by the Secretary [of Commerce] through the Service and its employees, and shall not be transferred from the Service . . . without the express approval of the Congress." The new laws also call for modernization and improvements to be madc to NTIS.

Inventory

The National Aeronautics and Space Administration (NASA), the Departments of Defense, Energy, Commerce, Health and Human Services, the Environmental Protection Agency, and more than 200 other federal agencies contribute to the NTIS collection. In 1988, more than 66,000 information items (technical reports, software, numeric databases, patent applications, published searches, and other items) were added, including approximately 22,000 reports from foreign sources. Nearly 2 million different technical publications are now available, none of which is ever out of print. The online NTIS Bibliographic Database contains 1.3 million records, dating back to 1964. But NTIS is more than a secondary source of technical reports. It has a variety of announcement and dissemination products and services to serve the user community.

Technology Applications

NTIS operates the Center for the Utilization of Federal Technology (CUFT) to alert industry and government to technology resulting from U.S. government research and development considered to have potential for commercial or practical use. CUFT's Office of Federal Patent Licensing (OFPL) conducts the most active licensing program in the federal government. Licensable properties come primarily from the Department of Health, Agriculture, Interior, and Commerce. The number of licenses granted increased from 20 in FY 1981 to 66 in FY 1988, a total for those years of 336, and revenues from these licenses have increased each year. Private sector sales of products covered by the granted licenses exceed $200 million of which $70 to $90 million represents exports protected by some of the 1,200 or so foreign patents obtained by OFPL during FYs 1981–1988. Recently, more emphasis has been placed on increasing exclusivity in new licenses to give companies maximum incentive to invest their own funds in rapid commercialization.

CUFT also contains the Office of Applied Technology, which handles specialized information products to aid in transferring technology to the private sector. One of these products is the Federal Applied Technology Database, which provides public access to selected results of U.S. government R&D and engineering activities. Another is the *Federal Technology Catalog* containing carefully evaluated summaries of selected processes, instruments, materials, equipment, software, services, and techniques. In addition, a *Directory of Federal Laboratory and Technology Resources—A Guide to Services, Facilities, and Expertise* has been published.

Foreign Technology

One-third of the information items added to the NTIS collection in 1988 came from foreign sources. NTIS has acquisition agreements with government or private sector organizations in more than 60 countries, including Canada, Western Europe, India, the People's Republic of China, and Japan. The Japanese Technical Literature Act—passed by Congress in 1986 to increase U.S. access to Japanese scientific and technical information—calls for coordination of U.S. government activities in collecting and disseminating that information, for the cataloging and analysis of government and nongovernment activities, and for government agencies to consult with U.S. industry on Japanese information needs. To assist with this activity, NTIS produced the second edition of a directory of Japanese information activities in the United States and a bibliography of Japanese technical information translated into English at U.S. government expense.

The *Foreign Technology Newsletter* now has a new front section with reviews and syntheses of major research programs, activities of specific organizations and laboratories, conference summaries, and descriptions of specific new technologies, processes, and discoveries. In addition to its regular reports on foreign research and development in such fields as advanced microelectronics, structural ceramics, and superconductivity, the newsletter also carries reports from such sources as the Office of Naval Research, the Foreign Broadcast Information Service, and embassies.

NTIS also provides access to the Japanese Online Information System, which consists of many technical databases in English and Japanese. These databases are mounted in Tokyo at the Japan Information Center for Science and Technology (JICST). The JICST/NTIS cooperative agreement allows any interested party in the United States to access the latest Japanese research results.

Library Ordering Program

Virginia Polytechnic Institute and State University Library in Virginia and the University of Texas at Austin Library signed agreements in 1988 to participate in the NTIS Library Ordering Program. These libraries handle orders for NTIS documents as an extension of their services to patrons. Other participants are the University of Colorado/Boulder Government Publications Library, the Detroit Public Library, the Newark Public Library, and the St. Louis Public Library.

Service Improvements

Service improvements made during 1988 included:

- A new, more efficient telephone system.
- Additional workshops and seminars to instruct users in efficient and effective online searching of the NTIS Bibliographic Database. (These were cosponsored by library groups, universities, and vendors of the NTIS Database.)

- Monthly updates to the Federal Research in Progress Database.
- The ability to order NTIS reports on the OCLC system online.

Future Thrust

The NIST Authorization Act for FY 1989 created a Technology Administration within the Department of Commerce. As an integral part of this new organization, NTIS is increasing its efforts to assist the private sector in benefiting from government research and development. The overall goal is to help the United States remain competitive in the global economy by encouraging innovation and stimulating productivity. A primary NTIS strategy to improve information dissemination is to increase the number of joint ventures with private information enterprises. Such alliances offer the information user an added value—government information with improved access, timeliness, quality, and ease of use.

National Archives and Records Administration

Washington, DC 20408
202-523-3000

James Gregory Bradsher
Archivist, Office of Management and Administration

The National Archives and Records Administration is responsible for identifying, preserving, and making available to the federal government and to the people of the United States all forms of government records not restricted by law that have been determined to have sufficient historical, informational, or evidential value to warrant being preserved. All federal agencies of the U.S. government are obliged by law to cooperate with the archives and to transfer all historically valuable federal records more than 30 years old to the archives, if the records are not needed for continuing agency business. In 1978, presidential records, formerly considered the private property of the president who created them, were declared government property and subject to the archives' archival authority. The archives inspects agency records, establishes standards for records retention, and provides guidance and assistance to the agencies with respect to adequate and proper documentation of the policies and transactions of the government.

The National Archives, 1934–Present

When the United States established a National Archives in 1934, it was the last major Western nation to do so. The act of establishment also created the National Historical Publications Commission (renamed the National Historical Publications and Records Commission in 1975), headed by the Archivist of the United States, and directed it to promote the publication of original source material. Since 1975, the commission has aided nonfederal records projects. The Federal Register was created as an office of the archives in 1935. This office provides official notice to the public through various publications of federal laws and administrative regulations, communicates the president's policies by the publication of his official documents and papers, and provides indexes and other finding aids to ensure ready access to all its publications. It also publishes annually *The United States Government Manual,* which provides comprehensive information on the agencies of the legislative, judicial, and executive branches, and includes information on quasi-official agencies, international organizations in which the United States participates, and boards, committees, and commissions. With the creation of the Franklin D. Roosevelt Library in 1939, the presidential libraries system was begun. (See the 1983 edition of *Bowker Annual of Library and Book Trade Information,* pp. 120–123, for a separate report on the presidential libraries.)

The Federal Property and Administrative Services Act of 1949 transferred the National Archives to the newly created General Services Administration and changed the name to the National Archives and Records Service, to reflect the agency's dual responsibilities for records and archives. These responsibilities were clarified and expanded in the Federal Records Act of 1950. In that same year, the National Archives began establishing a series of records centers across the country to hold semiactive federal records at low storage costs. These records are not needed for the daily business of the government but often are required by law to be retained for a fixed period of time, pending final disposition. During the late 1960s, a network of regional archives was created. These depositories, usually located in the same building as regional records centers, hold both microfilm and original records of particular significance to the geographic area in which they are located.

On April 1, 1985, the National Archives and Records Service became an independent agency in the executive branch of the federal government and was renamed the National Archives and Records Administration. This change, which was a return to the status enjoyed by the National Archives from 1935 to 1949, had long been advocated by many users of the archives and by professional organizations associated with the archives.

The National Archives System

The National Archives occupies a massive classic structure on a site bounded by Pennsylvania and Constitution avenues and Seventh and Ninth streets, Northwest, exactly halfway between the White House and the Capitol in Washington, D.C. Designed by John Russell Pope, the building contains 21 levels of stack areas for records, which are controlled for temperature and humidity and equipped with smoke detection devices, sprinkler systems, and, in select areas, a halon gas system to protect against fire. In addition to miles of stacks, the building contains research rooms, office space, laboratory space, a theater, exhibit areas, and the 75-foot-high central rotunda in which the Declaration of Independence, the Constitution, and the Bill of Rights are on permanent display. The 1297 Magna Carta is on indefinite loan and can also be seen in the rotunda.

Several major anniversaries will occasion exhibits in the coming years. "American Voices: Two Hundred Years of Speaking Out," a selection of petitions of American citizens to their government, will be in the circular gallery from March 1989 to March 1990 to celebrate the bicentennial of the federal government. The two-hundredth anniversary of the Bill of Rights will be marked by two exhibits, the first, "This Fierce Spirit of Liberty," opens in the rotunda in May 1989 and continues through 1991. Throughout 1989, an innovative, hands-on exhibit called "Saving Our Sources" will show visitors to the central search room the challenges faced in conserving our heritage.

Five other Washington and suburban locations hold various administrative offices; government cartographic and architectural records and the Richard Nixon presidential materials; and the National Audiovisual Center, which rents and sells to the public motion pictures, slides, and tapes created by many federal agencies.

The National Archives also operates 24 other facilities around the country. Two major national facilities are the Washington National Records Center in Suitland, Maryland, and the National Personnel Records Center in St. Louis. Other National Archives facilities are located in or near Boston, New York City, Philadelphia, Atlanta, Chicago, Dayton, Kansas City, Fort Worth, Denver, San Francisco, Los Angeles, and Seattle. Located within each of these facilities are a regional archives (except for Dayton, which has none, and Philadelphia, where the regional archives is in a separate downtown location) and a federal records center. The nine other National Archives buildings are presidential libraries or museums: the Herbert Hoover Library in West Branch (Iowa), the Franklin D. Roosevelt Library in Hyde Park (New York), the Harry S. Truman Library in Independence (Missouri), the Dwight D. Eisenhower Library in Abilene (Kansas), the John F. Kennedy Library in Columbia Point (Massachusetts), the Lyndon B. Johnson Library in Austin (Texas), the Gerald R. Ford Library in Ann Arbor (Michigan), the Ford Museum in Grand Rapids (Michigan), and the Jimmy Carter Library in Atlanta (Georgia).

The Archivist of the United States, who is appointed by the president with the advice and consent of the Senate, is assisted by a deputy and seven assistant archivists, each having specific program or support function responsibilities. The major organizational elements are Management and Administration, the National Archives, Federal Register, Federal Records Centers, Presidential Libraries, Records Administration, and Public Programs. The executive director of the National Historical Publications and Records Commission is on the level of an assistant archivist. Special staffs reporting to the Archivist are Archival Research and Evaluation, Audits and Compliance, External Affairs, and Legal Services.

The staff of the National Archives numbers approximately 3,500 employees, of whom 2,000 are full-time permanent employees. Most of the 1,500 part-time and intermittent employees work in the federal records centers where they handle reference requests. For 1988, the agency's budget was $116 million, about 35 percent of which was spent on space, utilities, phones, postage, and the like.

An annual description of the activities and finances of the National Archives and Records Administration can be found in the *Annual Report of the National Archives,* which is available from the agency's public information officer.

Holdings of the National Archives and Records Administration

The federal records centers hold more than 15.7 million cubic feet of noncurrent federal records. These records, although in the physical custody of the National Archives, remain under the legal control of the agency of origin. Most of these records are from the Department of Defense, the Department of the Treasury (Internal Revenue Service), the Department of Health and Human Services (Social Security Administration), and the Veterans Administration. Although almost all of the records held by the federal records centers, as well as those that remain in agency custody, will be eventually destroyed, a small portion, those that have been determined to have enduring value, are eventually transferred to the Office of the National Archives, where they become part of the archives of the United States. The National Archives also accepts donated materials from private sources. These materials (except for donated film) are mostly in the presidential libraries; all presidential materials made or received before 1981 are considered private property.

The current estimate of the archival holdings in the National Archives is 1.6 million cubic feet of records, including 3 billion paper documents, 91 million feet of motion pictures, 5.3 million still photographs, 1.8 million maps, 178,000 video and sound recordings, 9.7 million aerial photographs, and 2,600 reels of computer tape containing 6,800 data sets. The records date from the papers of the Continental Congress to the recent past. The presidential libraries estimate their holdings at 210.7 million pages of papers, 13.3 million feet of motion pictures, 3.4 million photographs, 14,559 hours of videotapes, 29,847 hours of sound recordings, 203,193 museum objects, and 184,459 pages of oral history interviews.

The National Archives building and the presidential libraries also have book collections designed to assist researchers working with archival sources. Of particular interest to librarians is the record set of the publications of the federal government, consisting of 1.8 million items, the core of which was formerly the Public Documents Library of the Government Printing Office. This is the most comprehensive set of federal publications in existence—dating from 1790 to 1979—but it is not complete, especially for the years before 1895. The main collection was transferred from the GPO in 1972, and is added to periodically.

Using the Archives

Researchers desiring to consult records in the main archives building are issued a research card, which must be shown when entering the Central Research Room. Those wishing to use only microfilm sign in at the Microfilm Reading Room. Consultants are available to assist researchers, and there are also guides, lists, inventories, indexes, and other finding aids, such as *The Guide to the National Archives of the United States* (1974), which is currently being revised, and *Catalog of National Archives Microfilm Publications,* which is updated annually. Copies of documents or microfilm can be obtained at modest prices, and printed facsimiles of many historical documents are available for purchase. Microfilm of materials of interest primarily to genealogists is available for interlibrary loan through a commercial firm for a modest charge.

The National Archives building is open for research Monday through Friday from 8:45 A.M. to 10:00 P.M. and on Saturdays from 8:45 A.M. to 5:00 P.M.; it is closed Sunday and on every federal holiday. Researchers are also welcome in the regional archives outside Washington and at the presidential libraries, all of which issue their own lists of holdings and maintain their own research rooms. Hours of the regional archives and the presidential libraries vary; researchers should check to determine the exact times. Up-to-date information on accessions and openings of records in all parts of the National Archives and Records Administration can be obtained by consulting the lists published in the quarterly journal *Prologue: Quarterly of the National Archives.*

United States Information Agency Library and Book Programs

Office of Cultural Centers and Resources
301 Fourth St. S.W., Washington, DC 20547

William A. Bate
Special Assistant for American Studies

The United States Information Agency, an independent organization within the executive branch, is responsible for the U.S. government's overseas information, educational exchange, and cultural programs. The work of the agency is carried out by a staff of Foreign Service officers assigned to U.S. missions abroad and by a professional staff of career civil servants in Washington, D.C. Known abroad as USIS (United States Information Service), the agency has 205 posts in 127 countries that are grouped in five geographic areas: Africa; Europe; East Asia and the Pacific; the American Republics; and North Africa, the Near East, and South Asia. Posts in these areas report to area offices in Washington, D.C.

Office of Cultural Centers and Resources

Within the agency's Bureau of Educational and Cultural Affairs, which oversees all academic exchange and international visitor programs, the Office of Cultural Centers and Resources is responsible for USIA's book and library programs. Two of its divisions, the Library Programs Division and the Book Programs Division, are directly concerned with the distribution of American books abroad. Through an extensive network of libraries and reading rooms and through the translation, promotion, and exhibition of American books, the Office of Cultural Centers and Resources provides overseas audiences with authoritative information about U.S. government policies as well as a greater understanding of American society and culture, past and present.

Library Programs

Although individual USIA library services and holdings vary from country to country, depending on post objectives and patron needs, USIS libraries in general perform two separate but mutually supportive functions: to provide the latest and most accurate information about U.S. government policies and to serve as a continuing resource of informed commentary on the origins, growth, and development of

American social, political, economic, and cultural institutions. They seek to explain American actions as well as the cultural and historical background against which such actions are formulated and undertaken.

USIS Library Programs Abroad

USIA currently maintains or supports 156 libraries and reading rooms in 95 countries and a headquarters library in Washington, D.C. In addition, the agency provides substantial support for library programs in 97 binational centers in 24 countries. USIS library collections vary in size from several hundred volumes in a small branch post library to much larger collections, such as the approximately 30,000 volumes in the Benjamin Franklin Library in Mexico City. The system contains an estimated 1 million volumes and 21,000 periodical subscriptions. The libraries are visited by some 4 million persons annually.

Overseas USIS libraries are staffed by more than 480 Foreign Service national (FSN) employees and supported by 21 regional and country librarians, American Foreign Service specialists who assist in designing and administering USIS library programs that are uniquely adapted to local conditions.

USIS libraries continue to move toward the concept of libraries as information centers with access to resources far beyond the scope of a single, finite collection. Such changes reflect not only patron demand but the increased availability of new communications and information-processing technologies. Accordingly, the Library Programs Division continues to experiment with new ways of delivering information to posts. DIALOG, NEXIS, VuText, Legislate, Wilsonline, and other online database systems, including CD-ROM systems, are increasingly essential for coping with the high volume and tight deadlines of reference requests from USIS posts overseas.

Washington Support

USIS posts overseas rely heavily on the 45 librarians and technicians of the USIA Library Programs Division in Washington, D.C.

The division's Bibliographics staff regularly publishes a variety of selection tools to support overseas collection development. The staff is responsible for five regional area documents services, which provide to posts on a subscription basis a steady flow of government reports, think tank documents, and other topical materials that address regional and bilateral concerns; it also issues a weekly alert service to articles from current American periodicals. In fall 1987, the staff began a GPO surplus documents service, which provides copies of government reports to subscribing posts.

Given their distance from the United States and the limited size of their library collections, USIS posts often turn for assistance to the library's Reference Branch for reference assistance. Such support frequently takes the form of assisting with difficult or hard to locate documents, with inquiries that require access to immediately current materials, or with requests for in-depth information not otherwise available to posts. The branch now handles about 150 overseas reference requests per month, transmitted by mail, telegram, telefacsimile, electronic mail, and telephone. In addition, reference staff provide on-site training for USIS librarians abroad in such fields as online searching.

In addition to these services, a central acquisitions staff oversees the complex process of purchasing and delivering books, periodicals, and documents to libraries in every part of the world, while the division's interlibrary loan and document delivery services routinely provide assistance to all USIS libraries, as needed. The division also provides professional cataloging for USIS library materials on request and is developing a worldwide union list of periodical holdings in USIS libraries.

USIA/USIS libraries and offices around the world also access the Public Diplomacy Query System (PDQ), an online interactive database created by the Library Program Division. Developed on a USIA IBM 4381 computer using Information Dimensions, Inc.'s, BASIS information storage and retrieval software, the PDQ system provides timely, comprehensive information about official U.S. foreign policy. More than 40 USIA products, including videotapes, magazine articles, exhibits, films, and pamphlets and acquired material are indexed by the system. PDQ also features online access to the full text of policy statements issued by USIA and other U.S. government agencies.

The number of USIS libraries using personal computers for management, reference, and technical services continues to grow. During 1988, many of these libraries also acquired the capability to use CD-ROM products, expanded library networking through electronic mail systems, and hosted local bulletin boards; other posts, such as Brussels, Tokyo, Jakarta, and Bangkok, are developing microcomputer-based online public access catalogs.

Library Fellows Program

In 1987, the Library Programs Division, in cooperation with the American Library Association, inaugurated an annual program of Library and Book Fellows, which enables U.S. librarians with special expertise to serve in institutions abroad for periods ranging from three months to a year. The general purposes of the program are to improve host country or regional access to important information from and about the United States and to establish wherever possible ongoing linkages between American library professionals and institutions and their overseas counterparts in the interest of improving mutual understanding.

Under the terms of the program, which is administered by the American Library Association through a grant from USIA, prospective host institutions abroad are invited to submit proposals through local USIS posts. The American Library Association then announces the positions available and oversees the recruitment and selection of candidates.

In 1988, fellows served in Argentina, Egypt, France, Liberia, Malawi, Sweden, Thailand, Uganda, Venezuela, and Yemen. Selected projects included providing direction to regional programs designed to teach library skills to children and young adults through public library systems, establishing the organizational framework for a national law library, centralizing cataloging and technical services in an academic library, conducting a countrywide assessment of public library networking requirements, and managing a retrospective bibliographic conversion project.

Book Programs

USIA book programs are also designed to provide foreign audiences with access to a variety of views and information about American life and institutions. The USIA Book Programs Division supports the publication of American books abroad in English and in translation, as well as the export of American books that contribute to a better understanding of the United States. The division works closely with foreign publishers to encourage translations and reprints of important American titles abroad. It works with the American publishing industry in a variety of ways to expand the awareness and availability of American books overseas, including book fairs, circulating book exhibits, and donation of American books to foreign institutions.

Book Translations and Reprints

Translations and reprints of American titles have always been at the heart of USIA overseas book programs. The Book Programs Division works with foreign publishers to produce more than half a million copies annually of full-length U.S. trade books, textbooks, condensations, and serializations in English and in foreign languages. Titles are chosen to reflect a broad range of American thought on subjects of importance to long-term U.S. interests.

To support translations into major world languages, the Book Programs Division operates several regional book offices overseas, in Mexico City, Barcelona, Buenos Aires, and Cairo. French translations are the responsibility of the African Regional Services office in Paris. USIS posts cooperate with USIA book officers in Washington to handle translations and English reprints in other major countries, such as India, China, and Brazil.

Book Promotion

USIA conducts programs to promote the sale and distribution of American books overseas in close cooperation with the book export efforts of the American publishing industry. Circulating book exhibits provide opportunities to acquaint foreign publishers, booksellers, and readers with American books. Up to a half-dozen major exhibits in multiple sets are produced each year for circulation worldwide. Each exhibit is organized around a theme, which for 1988 included "English as a Second Language," "The MBA/MPA Story," and "The American Electoral Process." The exhibits travel to as many as 150 USIS posts overseas, where they are displayed at book fairs, scholarly and professional meetings, and other cultural events. The books are eventually donated to foreign institutions.

Participation in foreign book fairs is also given high priority as a means for increasing the circulation of American books abroad. In 1988, USIA sponsored and organized book exhibits at more than 20 book fairs, including the Frankfurt International Book Fair. During the 1987 Moscow Fair, the agency convened a series of meetings between American publishers and their Soviet counterparts to discuss ways to implement the provisions of the 1985 General Exchanges Agreement, which called for increased activity in the book and library fields. As a result of these discussions, USIA and Goskomizdat (the U.S.S.R. State Committee on Publishing Houses, Printing Plants and the Book Trade) exchanged traveling book exhibits during 1988, opened a permanent U.S. Book Exposition in Moscow, and began an American book translation program in the Soviet Union.

Donated Books

American publishers often donate books with small sales potential to nonprofit organizations. Many of these books have great value overseas, particularly in developing countries where commercial distribution of American books is difficult or impossible. USIA works with private sector organizations to get hundreds of thousands of these books into the hands of both individual and institutional recipients who can benefit from them.

Copyright

USIA has a special interest in encouraging respect for international copyright conventions by all nations. The Book Programs Division works closely on this issue with other government and private entities interested in promoting awareness of the importance of this issue outside the United States.

Information Assistance

American publishers should direct inquiries about export problems, rights, book exhibits, and participation in other USIA book activities to the Book Programs Division, Bureau of Educational and Cultural Affairs, USIA, Washington, DC 20547. Non-U.S. publishers should turn for assistance to the Cultural Affairs Office of the American Embassy in their country, a nearby regional book office, or directly to the Book Programs Division in Washington, D.C.

Federal Library and Information Center Committee

Library of Congress, Washington, DC 20540
202-707-6055

James P. Riley
Executive Director

The year 1988 was one of transition as well as success for the Federal Library and Information Center Committee (FLICC). Contractual services brokered to the federal sector by the committee's operating arm, the Federal Library and Information Network (FEDLINK), grew phenomenally, from $47.9 million in FY 1987 to $97.1 million by the close of FY 1988. In ongoing support of more than 2,500 federal libraries and information centers in the United States and abroad, FLICC sponsored a broad spectrum of educational programs; addressed critical information policy issues; cooperated with other libraries, networks, and information organizations in several joint endeavors; and provided training, technological, and contractual support to members through its network.

History and Organization

The Federal Library and Information Center Committee was established in 1965 (as the Federal Library Committee) by the Library of Congress and the Bureau of the Budget to provide leadership and assistance to the nation's federal libraries and information centers. The FLICC office is part of the National Programs Department of the Library of Congress. The committee chair is Librarian of Congress James H. Billington, and the chair designate is Ruth Ann Stewart, assistant librarian for national programs. The business of the committee is conducted through quarterly meetings of its 40 member libraries and information centers, bimonthly meetings of an Executive Advisory Committee, and concerted action of working groups and ad hoc committees. Twelve FLICC working groups (of which FEDLINK is the first among equals) focus on such areas as educational programs, policy issues, and publishing.

Working Groups

Educational Programs

The highlight of the 1988 education year was the fifth annual FLICC Forum on Federal Information Policies. The theme was "The Impact on Competitiveness." Some 170 library and information leaders from the public and private sectors attended the forum, which was held March 7 at the Library of Congress. The Librarian of Congress opened the forum, and Congressman Sherwood L. Boehlert (R-N.Y.), ranking Republican on the House Science, Research, and Technology Subcommittee, delivered the keynote address. The sessions addressed the acquisition and dissemination of scientific and technical information to improve U.S. productivity and competitiveness and also examined whether the United States is losing its competitive edge in the marketing and export of information products and services. Videotapes of the forum and a published summary of proceedings were released by the FLICC office.

Other events included an Annual Online Meeting, hosted by FLICC at the Library of Congress and sponsored by the Potomac Valley Chapter of the American Society for Information Science (ASIS) on February 4–5; an Executive Management Seminar, held February 18–19 in New Orleans; and a Joint Spring Workshop sponsored by FLICC and five other area library organizations at the Library of Congress on April 26.

Two other programs focused on the latest technology for library applications. Representatives from 15 regional library networks from coast to coast attended the two-day workshop "Microcomputer Applications in Libraries: A Review of the Technology," held August 16–17 at the Library of Congress under FLICC/FEDLINK auspices. Approximately 200 librarians attended the third annual Information Technology Update at the Library of Congress on September 22. FLICC sponsored the meeting in cooperation with the Information Technology Group of the Special Libraries Association, Washington, D.C., chapter. The meeting featured a presentation on electronic imagery for preservation and demonstrations of interactive videodiscs, CD-ROM, hypermedia, and hypertext.

Policy Issues

The Policy Working Group assists the Federal Library and Information Center Committee in adopting a proactive stand on major library and information issues. In 1988, the Policy Working Group studied or took positions on the following issues:

OMB Circular A-76 on Privatization

To monitor the contracting out of library and information services, the Policy Working Group has prepared a two-part survey instrument to be distributed to federal libraries. Defined as "commercial activities" in Circular A-76 of the Office of Management and Budget, libraries are one of the groups targeted for privatization. Position papers protesting the present trend toward full-scale contracting out of federal libraries emphasized the important function served by agency libraries and stated: "FLICC firmly believes that if extensive contracting out of entire libraries continues, the government's primary information resource will be severely weakened, and the public service will lose its ability to cope with the information age."

OTA Study on Federal Information Dissemination

The Policy Working Group reviewed and sent forward suggestions in response to the Office of Technology Assessment's draft report: "Informing the Nation: The Future of Federal Electronic Printing, Publishing, and Dissemination." One primary concern was that OTA did not allow sufficient time for in-depth consideration of proposed important action alternatives, such as the restructuring of the Government Printing Office and the National Technical Information Service (NTIS). OTA was asked to involve FLICC in any task group, forum, or evaluation process in which alternative actions are reviewed, as well as to consider the merger of NTIS with the Library of Congress as a "viable alternative" to other options, one of which is privatization. FLICC is on record as having endorsed the establishment of NTIS as a nonprofit governmental corporation.

Enhanced Service Providers

In April 1988, the Federal Communications Commission (FCC) withdrew its controversial proposal to eliminate the exemption from interstate access charges currently permitted enhanced service providers (ESP). The proposed move would have significantly increased the cost of accessing information through ESP for libraries and information centers in both the public and private sectors. FLICC was one of a number of information entities that had protested the move.

Reference

The Reference Working Group was formed in 1988 to meet the perceived need for cooperative reference action during these times of fiscal constraints and cutbacks. Fifteen reference librarians, from almost as many federal libraries and information centers, met at the Library of Congress on August 4 and voted to come under the aegis of the Federal Library and Information Center Committee as the Reference

Working Group. The group elected Victoria Hill, Library of Congress, as chair, and Wendy Carter, Veterans Administration, as secretary.

Other FLICC Activities

Second White House Conference on Library and Information Services

Federal librarians took action in 1988 to try to influence the agenda for the upcoming second White House Conference on Library and Information Services (WHCLIS), which is to be called by the president no earlier than September 1, 1989, and no later than September 30, 1991. The Federal Library and Information Center Committee task force review group on WHCLIS has proposed that the White House conference focus on one basic issue: "All citizens shall have equal opportunity of access to federal information."

The task force review group has suggested that this one central issue might generate enough support at the second White House conference to emerge as a proposed amendment to the U.S. Constitution. FLICC also has nominated representatives of the federal library community as candidates for appointment to a prestigious 30-member WHCLIS Advisory Committee. The National Commission on Libraries and Information Science (NCLIS) will coordinate the second White House Conference, as it did the 1979 conference.

FLICC delegates took their proposal for a focused conference agenda to the ninth annual meeting of the White House Conference on Library and Information Services Task Force (WHCLIST), held August 24–27 in Minneapolis. There, the FLICC delegates presented their proposal at meetings of five WHCLIST regions, which generally endorsed it. A final FLICC proposal will be prepared by a FLICC task force during the next several months for presentation at the 1989 meeting of WHCLIST in Portland, Oregon.

Library Standards Feasibility Study

The fact-finding phase of a study to determine the feasibility of FLICC drafting new classification and qualification standards for librarians was completed on September 30. Because federal librarians have experienced difficulty in using the Office of Personnel Management's outdated standards (they are 22 years old and make no mention of automation or other changes in the profession), FLICC contracted with consultant Raymond Crosby to study the feasibility of developing standards for the classification and qualification of librarians—librarian series GS-1410 and library technician series GS-1411. Crosby reported on September 30 that he is ready to begin the third and final phase of his study, which will include a comprehensive analysis and recommendations for standards.

Publishing

The FLICC publications office arrived fully in the electronic age in 1988 with desktop publishing in addition to use of other electronic media, including telecommunications, facsimile transmissions, and videotapes. Using desktop publishing applications on a Macintosh, the FLICC publications office began producing illustrated camera-ready copy for all of its publications. The *FLICC Newsletter* is published quarterly, and the *FEDLINK Technical Notes* monthly. Other desktop productions included preparation of the published summary of proceedings of the fifth annual FLICC forum on information, "Federal Information Policies: The Impact on Competitiveness," and in-house bulletins, "Information Alerts."

Videotapes of the FLICC information forum on competitiveness have been circulated by the publications office from Albany, Oregon, to Vienna, Austria, and added to the collections of the Library of Congress. They may be viewed at the Motion Picture, Broadcasting, and Recorded Sound Division (M/B/RS), or federal libraries may borrow them from the FLICC office.

Federal Library and Information Network

FEDLINK is a network organization of cooperating libraries and information centers that offers any federal agency the opportunity to enhance the information resources available to meet the requirements of its personnel. Through FLICC/FEDLINK, federal agencies have cost-effective access to a number of online services—research, cataloging, and interlibrary loan. Through contracts with major vendors, FEDLINK also offers members a wide array of other services and products, including a book ordering service, CD-ROM products, document delivery, gateway services, minicomputer-integrated library systems, microcomputer software for library-related functions, bibliographic data conversion services, serials subscription services, and tape processing services. During FY 1988, FEDLINK participation grew to 1,395 agency libraries, information centers, and offices cooperating in the use of 135 contractual services that resulted in 3,560 interagency agreements for approximately $97.1 million of service. Of the 3,560 agreements, 2,427 were renewals and 1,133 were new. These data represent increases of approximately 32 percent in the number of interagency agreements. (See Figures 1–3.)

Online Services

The growth in the use of online retrieval services, as depicted by interagency agreements, was 11 percent in FY 1988 (see Table 1). Use of the online products and services contract with OCLC continued to expand in 1988. The number of federal libraries using OCLC services increased from 599 in FY 1987 to 654 in FY 1988. From August 1987 to July 1988, FEDLINK libraries cataloged 365,334 items and contributed 72,252 titles to the OCLC Online Union Catalog. Use of the Interlibrary Loan Subsystem (ILL) totaled 220,851 items borrowed and 104,146 items loaned. During this time period, 67 percent of all federal ILL transactions were borrowed items. ILL continues to be an important government-wide library service. To offer members alternative or additional automated/online cataloging and related services, contracts were continued with the Western Library Network (WLN) and with the Research Library Group (RLG) for access to its Research Libraries Information Network (RLIN).

Training

FEDLINK's staff of professional librarians provided 100 training sessions for network librarians. Trainers averaged two out-of-town trips each month. Approximately 75 percent of the classes were on the use of OCLC subsystems. The remaining 25

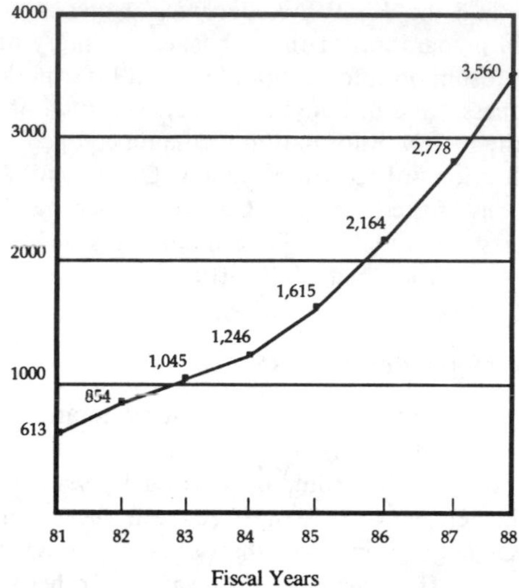

Figure 1 / Interagency Agreements for FEDLINK Services, FYs 1981–1988

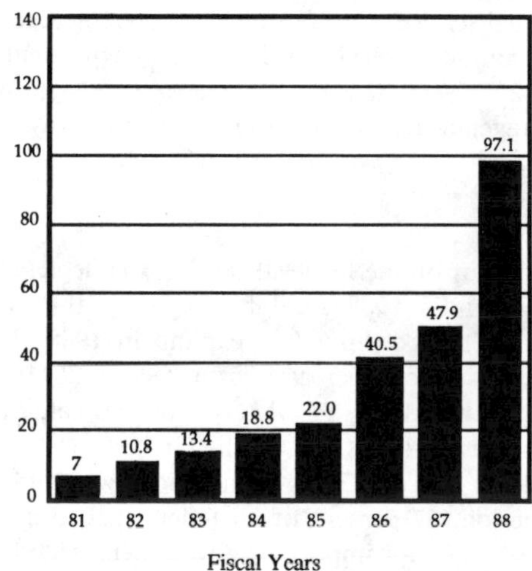

Figure 2 / FEDLINK Service Dollars (in Millions), FYs 1981–1988

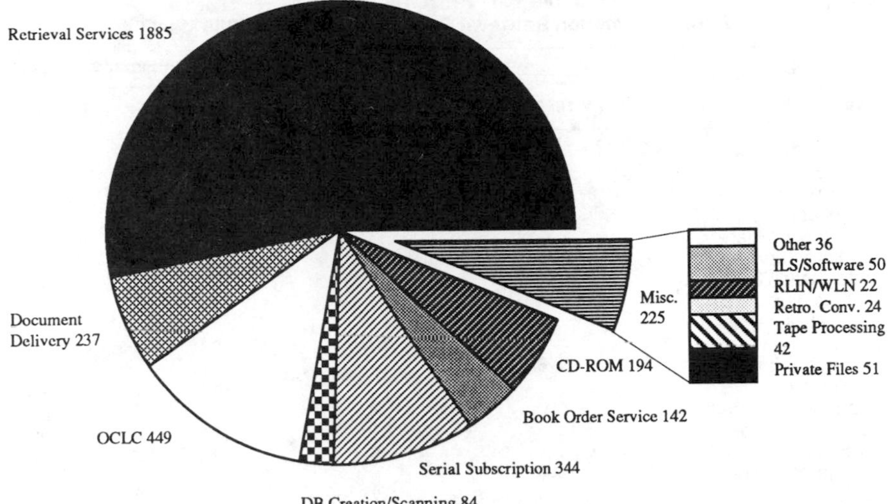

Figure 3 / Interagency Agreements for FEDLINK Services, FY 1988

Table 1 / FEDLINK Growth: Use of Information Retrieval Services, FYs 1985–1988

	No. of Service Requests/Interagency Agreements			
Name of Service	**FY 1985**	**FY 1986**	**FY 1987**	**FY 1988**
AMA/NET	–	–	–	3
Associated Press	–	–	–	2
Aviation/ Aerospace	–	4	8	12
Beth Israel Hospital	–	3	6	5
BRS Information Technologies	212	250	249	240
Chemical Information Systems	–	9	29	28
Commerce Clearing House	–	–	4	4
Compusearch	–	5	20	29
CompuServe	11	10	24	29
Congressional Quarterly	16	23	29	39
Control Data	2	1	2	6
Datatek Corp.	–	1	9	15
Dialcom	4	15	31	27
Dialog Information Services	378	429	477	526
Dow Jones & Co.	8	9	13	15
DMS/Budgetrack	–	0	1	–
Data Resources	11	13	10	5
Dun & Bradstreet	–	–	8	12
EIC/Intelligence	–	–	1	4
Finsbury Data–A Reuters Co.	–	2	8	10
Gannett New Media Services	–	1	2	1
Government Counselling	–	5	4	6
H. W. Wilson Co.	–	21	48	63

Table 1 / FEDLINK Growth: Use of Information Retrieval Services, FYs 1985–1988 *(cont.)*

Name of Service	No. of Service Requests/Interagency Agreements			
	FY 1985	FY 1986	FY 1987	FY 1988
I. P. Sharp	–	–	1	2
Info Globe	–	–	2	2
Information Consultants	–	2	1	–
Information Handling Services	–	3	6	7
Information Services Assoc.	–	2	12	8
Innovative Technology	–	70	104	75
Inventory Locator Service	–	–	11	25
Legi-Slate	29	28	27	25
Mead Data Central	149	151	171	190
NewsNet	1	8	15	22
Pergamon Info-Line	–	7	17	14
NIKKEI TELECOM	–	–	–	2
OCR International	–	–	–	1
Pergamon ORBIT InfoLine	106	89	83	69
Potomac Systems	–	–	4	11
Prentice Hall	–	2	2	3
Questel	–	6	11	9
STN International	–	12	24	43
Telebase Systems	–	2	16	16
The Source Information Network	–	–	–	2
TimePlace	–	5	13	9
United Communications Group	–	–	3	4
United Press International	–	–	–	1
USNI Military Database	–	–	–	32
VeraCorp	–	1	2	2
VideoLog Communications	–	–	–	2
VU/TEXT Information Services	13	19	27	25
West Publishing Co.	98	88	84	96
Western Union Telegraph Co.	–	1	6	13
Ziff-Davis Info Tech. Co.	–	17	68	94
Total	1,038	1,314	1,693	1,885

percent provided instruction on DOS and telecommunications and were conducted in the network's Information Technology Center laboratory. Contracts were continued with other regional networks to train FEDLINK members located outside the mid-Atlantic region.

Information Technology Center Programs and Services

In FY 1988, the FLICC/FEDLINK Information Technology Center produced numerous lists and bibliographies on hypertext, telefax machines, local area networks, multi-user systems, and other new technologies. The network's electronic bulletin board, ALIX, was replaced with a more advanced four-line system that now is receiving between 1,200 and 1,500 calls each month as members use the system to obtain the latest information on FEDLINK services, to share information on new technologies, and to download new public domain computer programs. More than 25 new copyrighted software packages have been added to the center's collection, providing federal librarians with a significant resource for sampling and testing at biweekly workshops conducted in the center's laboratory. Through the efforts of the center, some library-related software packages now are available for procurement through the network program.

National Center for Education Statistics

USOE Office of Educational Research and Improvement
555 New Jersey Ave. N.W., Washington, DC 20208-1404

Lawrence J. La Moure
Coordinator, Library Statistics Program

On April 29, 1988, President Reagan signed PL 100-297, the Hawkins-Safford Elementary and Secondary School Improvement Amendments of 1988. This legislation contained more than two dozen authorizations that will help to make the National Center for Education Statistics (NCES) a more responsive organization to the data needs of the American public. Some of the authorizations will affect the library community.

For the first time, NCES has specific authority to collect data and report on the condition of American libraries, although the kinds of libraries that are to be included in the center's data collection activities is unclear. For the time being, NCES will limit its data collection activities to the three types of libraries—public, academic, and school media centers—mentioned in the legislation. As statistics collection for these libraries improves and as resources develop, NCES plans to gather data for other types of libraries (special, government, cooperatives, and so forth) as well.

Public Libraries

Public Law 100-297 mandates the annual collection of public library data. The statute reads as follows: "The Center, with the assistance of State library agencies, shall develop and support a cooperative system of annual data collection for public libraries. Participation shall be voluntary; however, all States should be encouraged to join the system. Attention should be given to insuring timely, consistent, and accurate reporting."

Prior to the president's signing of the new law, NCES had signed a Memorandum of Understanding with the National Commission on Libraries and Information Science (NCLIS) to develop a federal-state cooperative system for public library data. On September 30, 1988, a task force composed of representatives from NCES, NCLIS, the Library Programs Office of the U.S. Department of Education, library associations, and state library agencies, chaired by John Lorenz, developed an action plan for the new system. Subsequent work by Mary Jo Lynch, director, American Library Association's Office for Research, and 13 pilot states has demonstrated the feasibility of a cooperative system.

The new Federal-State Cooperative System for Public Library Data (FSCS) conducted a test data collection operation in July 1988. The 19 states that participated provided data on 3,648 public libraries. NCES recently made available to the public a data tape containing information from the test. With the release of the data tape, NCES was able to disseminate results of the July test collection four months after the last state library submitted its information. In January 1989, the center plans to release 17 tables through its "ED TAB" publication program. Despite some reporting problems, NCES expects the system to receive data from all 50 states on a consistent and accurate basis in the near future.

In July Emerson Elliott, acting commissioner of education statistics, sent a letter to all state librarians requesting them to name a data coordinator to act as a liaison with NCES on all data issues related to the public libraries of the state. All 50 states plus the District of Columbia responded by naming a coordinator. The coordinators participated in a training workshop held in Annapolis, Maryland, December 5–7, that was based on the action plan described earlier. NCES is planning to hold annual training sessions in order to accommodate change and improvement in the system.

Based on the workshop, NCES expects 40 state libraries to participate in the 1989 data collection effort and the results to be published four to six months after the August 1, 1989, closing date. This cycle will be repeated every year thereafter, with additional states joining as they become more familiar with the reporting procedures. The system, when fully developed, will include three major components: Public Library Universe File (an authority file that will include all public libraries in the state); Local Public Library data survey (the state provides these data for all its local public libraries); State Library Agency Survey (a report about the state library agency). NCES is in the process of developing the coding structure and definitions for the universe file in order to begin data collection in spring 1989 with publication of a directory six months after survey closeout.

Academic Libraries

Since 1980, academic library data have been collected three times (1982, 1985, and 1988). The 1988 data were collected in fall 1988 as part of IPEDS (Integrated Postsecondary Education Data System). NCES expects data collection to be completed in spring 1989, and that data will be available for release in fall 1989.

NCES has requested the Office of Management and Budget (OMB) to approve a two-year data collection cycle for academic libraries instead of the present four-year period. Assuming that OMB agrees with the request, once the two-year cycle begins, academic library data collection will continue to be part of IPEDS and data will be available in the fall for alternate years beginning in 1989.

School Libraries and Media Centers

The last survey of both public and private school libraries and media centers was conducted in 1985–1986, together with the survey of elementary and secondary schools. (School administrators had suggested that NCES combine the school library survey with the school survey to eliminate the need for two separate surveys.) After the 1985–1986 surveys were completed, NCES redesigned its elementary and secondary school surveys. The new Survey of Schools and Staffing (SASS) is a sample survey that will yield state by state data about teacher job experience, work incentives, activities, use of time, compensation, and attitudes. It will also gather data on school incentive programs and college enrollment rates. Principals will be asked about their administration of the school, job preparation and experience, attitudes, and roles. NCES will also be conducting follow-up surveys of a sample of the teachers surveyed to determine turnover rates.

The SASS will be field-tested in fall 1989 with the full-scale survey taking place in 1990. NCES will design two questionnaires for the survey. One will be directed to the school librarian requesting data similar to those requested from the classroom teachers. Another will be completed by the librarian for the school media center and the types of programs it operates. Questions will be added to the school district form regarding staffing concerns. The principal will provide information on his or her objectives and concerns regarding the school media center.

At the present time NCES plans to analyze the results of the study by comparing the responses of the classroom teachers to those of the school media center staff. These comparisons will be done on a state by state basis by type of school (elementary, secondary), racial composition of the school, and social and economic status. A sample of the school librarians who participated in the study will be selected for a follow-up study to determine the turnover rate for the profession, the reasons school librarians leave their jobs, and their present employment status. NCES will also be able to compare the backgrounds of staff who stay in the profession and those who leave, again cross-tabulating with the type of school and other key variables.

NCES will conduct a survey of school media centers every two years, which will include, at a minimum, data on the center and its collections, programs, and services. Every four years NCES plans to expand the survey to the larger study described earlier. As more funding becomes available in future years, additional studies could be conducted for academic, special, and international libraries.

The Library of Congress

Washington, DC 20540
202-707-5000

James DeLorbe
Information Office

Librarian of Congress James H. Billington's appointment of a Management and Planning Committee (MAP) for a major evaluation of all aspects of the library's operations was the highlight of the library's 1988 calendar year. The committee's year-long study promised to be a turning point in the library's history, setting new goals and strategies for moving the library into the twenty-first century. The study was to be the first part of a developing process.

Restructuring

The MAP Committee, consisting of 28 staff members selected from a variety of positions and divisions throughout the library and chaired by Ellen Hahn, chief, General Reading Rooms Division, was charged with defining the "dynamic mission of the institution as a whole" and reaching four specific goals: increasing administrative efficiency and economy, as well as improving job satisfaction; improving the library's service to Congress as well as other branches of the U.S. government; increasing and deepening scholarly use of the institution by the American people; and broadening and rationalizing the library's services to external constituencies, and improving methods for selecting, cataloging, preserving and maintaining collections. During its year-long project, the committee drew on materials provided by two advisory groups. The first, representing the library's broader national and international constituencies, was the National Advisory Committee, a blue-ribbon group consisting of leaders in the academic, legislative, business, judicial, library, and information spheres. The second was Arthur Young, Inc., a private sector management consulting firm, hired to present the library with organizational and procedural options for fulfilling the library's mission most effectively.

During the year the National Advisory Committee identified three overriding areas of concern: the need for improved access to the library's online catalog, the need for greater collaboration with other libraries, and the need to refocus the library's leadership role. Through formal and informal meetings, the MAP Committee drew on suggestions from staff and managers, identifying issues and drafting statements in the process of forming the library's new mission for the year 2000 and beyond. Two management retreats were held for discussion with top library officials. By the end of the year Billington had attended regional forums, visited other libraries, listened to hundreds of recommendations from sources outside the Library of Congress, and reviewed all committee recommendations before they were released to staff members to be used in a continuing process of self-examination, planning, and progress.

Cataloging and Networking

The year 1988 marked the eighty-fifth anniversary of the Library of Congress Cataloging Distribution Service (CDS). The former Card Division began printing and selling cards to other libraries as early as 1898. During 1988, many advances were made in systems designed to ease access to the collections. The library's Subject Authority file is now available on CD-ROM (compact disc/read-only memory). The product, *CD MARC Subjects,* is the first commercial release of a CD-ROM product in the library's history. Two related products were announced for future release: *CD MARC Names* and *CD MARC Bibliographic. CD MARC Names* will be produced on three compact discs. The largest and most ambitious of the three, *CD MARC Bibliographic,* will contain the library's machine-readable bibliographic files, consisting of nearly 4 million cataloging records of books, serials, maps, visual materials, and music scores. With release 2.0 of the National Union Catalog by CDS, bibliographic records can now be submitted in machine-readable format by participating institutions. CDS also released the *National Union Catalog, Books,* a cumulative index of more than 1.4 million titles on diazo microfiche for the years 1983–1987, with access available through subject, title, name, and series.

Two noteworthy publications were released by CDS in 1988. *Library of Congress Rule Interpretations,* a cumulation of all currently valid Library of Congress rule interpretations issued since the implementation of *AACR 2* in 1981, was prepared to assist catalogers in applying *Anglo-American Cataloguing Rules,* second edition (*AACR 2*). The eleventh edition of the *Library of Congress Subject Headings* (*LCSH*), prepared by the Subject Cataloging Division, was released with a new look inside and out. Beginning in 1988 a new edition of the familiar "red book" will be published each year.

To facilitate use of US MARC documentation, CDS published the following new machine-readable cataloging formats: *US MARC Format for Authority Data, US MARC Code List for Languages, US MARC Specifications for Record Structure, Character Sets Tapes,* and *US MARC Format for Bibliographic Data. Intellectual Property Rights in an Electronic Age: Proceedings of the Library of Congress Network Advisory Committee Meeting, April 22–24, 1987,* a five-part, 66-page publication issued in 1988, addresses such topics as challenges posed by new technologies, bibliographic database ownership, and intellectual property rights.

The Linked Systems Project: A Networking Tool for Librarians, a monograph published jointly by the Library of Congress and OCLC (Online Computer Library Center), was released in May. It contains 13 papers describing the LSP (Linked Systems Project)—an ongoing collaborative effort to develop computer-to-computer links among the Library of Congress, the Research Libraries Goup, and OCLC—its underlying concepts, progress, and protocol for use. Other 1988 publications included the thesaurus *Moving Image Materials: Genre Terms,* the first national standard for adding moving-image genre and form terms to MARC records, and the manual *Hebraica Cataloging,* which makes Library of Congress internal descriptive cataloging available for the first time.

In March, the Network Advisory Committee (NAC) conducted a program focusing on the key issues of intellectual property rights for library networks and information providers.

Collections

Several major donations enriched the library's collections during 1988. The greatest composite gift of music materials ever to be received by the Library of Congress (including letters, documents, and a large quantity of autograph music manuscripts dating from the twelfth century to modern times) was bequeathed by the estate of

Hans Moldenhauer, vastly expanding the existing Moldenhauer Archive at the library. The archive was developed for the study of music history from primary sources.

The library's Gershwin Collection received two original strikings of the Congressional Gold Medal, awarded posthumously by President Reagan to George and Ira Gershwin on June 23. The medals were presented to the library by Frances Gershwin Godowsky and Leonore Gershwin.

On March 14 the Fahnestock Expedition Collection of audio recordings, films, and documents obtained by Sheridan Fahnestock's South Pacific Expedition in the early 1940s was presented to the library in a ceremony in the Whittall Pavilion.

Other significant gifts during 1988 included the Berger Collection, consisting of 3,886 recordings, books, and catalogs from Imperial Russia; a collection of anarchist books, periodicals, manuscripts, and memorabilia—the gift of Paul Avrich, Queens College, New York City; and a microform copy of the National Broadcasting Company's Television Program Analysis File, to serve as a guide to its programs in the library's collections.

A three-year trend of decline in appropriated funds for collection development continued in 1988 with a decrease of 1.69 percent in funds for the purchase of general and law materials. This decline is a marked improvement over the 14 percent decline in funds (from $5.2 million in 1985 to $4.51 million) in 1987. However, budgetary constraints and the declining value of the dollar have caused particular concern among those making long-term commitments.

Housing the Collections

The phase I restoration projects of the Thomas Jefferson and John Adams Buildings continued in 1988, to bring the structures into compliance with current health, safety, and access standards while restoring original architectural features and adding modern data communications equipment. Years of overcrowding and numerous temporary modifications to the buildings had obscured many of the original architectural features, which are being restored to their original grandeur. The highlight of the project is the restoration of the Main Reading Room. Phase II is scheduled to begin in October 1989 and be completed in 1992.

Preservation

Work continued throughout 1988 on the diethyl zinc pilot deacidification program for the library's collections. The work is being carried out under contract by a company in Houston, Texas. Treatment procedures have been successfully carried out on quantities of books, including those containing high-gloss paper. The process is designed to preserve and extend the life of printed materials.

The National Preservation Program office worked on a variety of projects to call the brittle book problem to public attention. The library cooperated on the film *Slow Fires: On the Preservation of the Human Record,* aired on the Public Broadcasting System and shown to groups across the nation. Notable treatment projects in the Rare Book Conservation Section included Faden's *North American Atlas; General Sherman's March to the Sea;* and two projects scheduled for completion in 1989—the La Frere and the Rochambeau atlas. The Music Division focused on the

Medieval Manuscript Collection, and the Law Library completed several works, including *Court Roll—Manor of Kellshall, 1661–1678.*

The largest project ever undertaken by the Conservation Office was successfully completed in 1988. It involved the treatment, survey, and refocusing of 28,000 broadsides in the Rare Book and Special Collections Division.

National Outreach Program

Talking Books: Pioneering and Beyond, a new monograph tracing the development of recorded books and playback equipment, was published by the National Library Service for the Blind and Physically Handicapped (NLS/BPH) in 1988. *Birding: An Introduction to Ornithological Delights for Blind and Physically Handicapped Individuals,* the first in a new series of leisure activity booklets, proved an immediate success; other activities to be covered in the series include fishing, skiing, sailing, and horseback riding.

In 1988, NLS/BPH launched an ambitious outreach program to seniors involving market testing, and a public education campaign in the print media, "Take a Talking Book," the most ambitious public-awareness campaign in NLS/BPH history. It also established a World Literature Book Club pilot to circulate cassette recordings of bestsellers and perennial favorites from English-speaking nations other than the United States, rereleased the Alexander Scourby narration of the King James Bible on cassette with tone indexing, and produced year-round schedules of seasonal sporting events in braille in cooperation with various national sports leagues.

The library's Information Office expanded the audience for its weekly *Library of Congress Information Bulletin* by launching an electronic version, accessible online via computers over telephone lines. The service, containing excerpts from the *Bulletin,* was made available on ALIX (Automated Library Information Exchange), the electronic bulletin board of FEDLINK, an arm of the Federal Library and Information Center Committee (FLICC). Some 1,400 FEDLINK members in the United States and more than 100 U.S. armed services libraries abroad now have advance access to articles from the library, with information of national significance and professional importance to the library community. The electronic edition is one of the most popular offerings of the electronic bulletin board.

The Information Office enabled the CBS Television Network to produce more than 100 one-minute "American Treasury" broadcasts, based on facts researched in the library's collections. The office produced 18 radio programs for the "Sounds of the Library of Congress" series on Washington, D.C., radio station WGMS, with sound clips and narration by musicologists, historians, and others on the library's staff. The office also produced the videotape "Conversation with Richard Wilbur, Poet Laureate," for sale to the public, and won an award for the videotape "Tour of the Library of Congress," which is currently being advertised through the Book-of-the-Month Club.

The American Folklife Center (AFC) collaborated with the Lowell Historic Preservation Commission and the Massachusetts Council on the Arts and Humanities to begin documenting the history of Lowell, Massachusetts. Two definitive publications were released by AFC during 1988, *The Grouse Creek Cultural Survey: Integrating Folklife and Historic Preservation Field Research* and *Quilt Collections: A Directory for the United States and Canada.* During the year, the center also sponsored a series of folk concerts and in December held a lecture and workshop on ornaments of the Nordic Christmas season, called "Good Yule, Nordic Christmas Celebrations."

The Children's Literature Center held a program in a joint effort with the Center for the Book to lay the groundwork for "1989—The Year of the Young Reader." Librarian of Congress Billington worked to have a joint resolution passed by the Congress and requested a Presidential Proclamation calling for national participation in programs and activities designed to spark an interest in reading on the part of young people.

The center held a symposium, "Window on Japan: Children, Books, and Television Today," marking the publication of *Japanese Children's Books at the Library of Congress*. On November 17, award-winning author Katherine Peterson spoke on the topic "Celebrating the Young Reader."

Staff Budget and Services

Among the notable arrivals and departures of staff members in 1988 was the retirement of Deputy Librarian of Congress William J. Welsh in October. Welsh, who had completed 41 years of service to the Library of Congress, had held the library's second highest position since February 1976. A related nonstaff appointment was that of Howard Nemerov to the position of Poet Laureate Consultant in Poetry, succeeding Richard Wilbur. Nemerov received the Pulitzer Prize for Poetry in 1978 and has written numerous award-winning collections of poetry.

Publications and Events

In its continuing and expanding effort to share its resources with the public and involve its many and diverse audiences, the Library of Congress sponsored a host of events and exhibits in 1988. *Documenting America: 1935–1943* opened December 15, marking the one-hundred and fiftieth anniversary of the invention of photography, featuring photographs taken in the 1930s and 1940s for the Farm Security Administration. The exhibit, which will be on display through May 15, 1989, includes works by such noted photographers as Dorothea Lang, Ben Shahn, and Marion Post Wolcott. In conjunction with the exhibit, a book of the same title was published in October by the University of California Press.

The library jointly hosted a panel discussion on the Christopher Columbus Quincentennary in cooperation with the Christopher Columbus Quincentennary Jubilee Commission on September 14 in recognition of National Hispanic Heritage Week. The panel, composed of commission members, discussed its purpose and activities as it prepares for the five-hundredth anniversary of Columbus's voyage in 1992.

In recognition of the two-hundredth anniversary of the U.S. Congress in 1989, the library planned a series of events. The first was a presentation to Congress on September 22, 1988, of *The Historical Atlas of Political Parties in the United States Congress, 1789–1989*. Ongoing events include exhibits, seminars, and a major exhibition on the achievements of Congress over the past two centuries.

Other exhibits in 1988 included a commemoration of the millennium of the baptism of Vladimir, ruler of Rus', and the subsequent adoption of Christianity as the state religion of Rus', an area of Eastern Europe encompassed today by the Soviet Union. In conjunction with the exhibit, a major conference of scholars, art historians, theologians, and librarians was held on May 26 and 27 to discuss the impact of Christianity on Russian culture. Librarian of Congress Billington, himself a noted scholar of Russian cultural history, opened the conference.

The seminar "Access to Library Resources through Technology and Preservation" was held July 5–8. The joint effort by the U.S.-U.S.S.R. Commission on Library Cooperation gave librarians from the two countries the opportunity to discuss issues relating to technology, automation, networking, and preservation. The commission was created by an agreement on behalf of the American Council of Learned Societies and the Library Council of the U.S.S.R.

Numerous publications of note were published by the library in 1988. American history is the subject of two major works, one of which is *The American Solution, Origins of the United States Constitution,* the catalog of an important library exhibition. Others, in commemoration of the bicentennial of the U.S. Constitution, are the fourteenth and fifteenth volumes of *Letters of Delegates to Congress: 1774–1789.* In a related work, the Law Library made available reprints of the U.S. Constitution translated into 14 foreign languages.

In response to the Librarian of Congress's call to make the library's resources available to "ever widening circles of our multi-ethnic society," the Publishing Office produced a diversity of works in conjunction with various library divisions, including *Japanese Children's Books at the Library of Congress: A Bibliography of Books from the Post-War Years, 1946–1985; Polish Genealogy & Heraldry: An Introduction to Research; The German Collections of the Library of Congress: Chronological Development;* and *The True Essentials of a Feast: A Collection of Recipes from the Staff of the Library of Congress.*

National Agricultural Library

U.S. Department of Agriculture, NAL Bldg., Beltsville, MD 20705

Robert W. Butler

Assistant Chief, Collection Development Office

The mission and task of the National Agricultural Library (NAL) as set forth in the Organic Act of 1862, which established it, is "to acquire and to diffuse among the people of the United States useful information on subjects connected with agriculture in the most general and comprehensive sense of the word." NAL serves as the nation's chief agricultural information resource and service, as well as the library of the U.S. Department of Agriculture. Under the leadership of Joseph H. Howard since 1983, NAL has enhanced its services to all sectors of the agricultural audience, adapted advanced technologies to expand its services and products, and joined with land-grant universities and other agricultural institutions both in the United States and abroad in coordinating and sharing resources.

NAL Services and Operations

The Library Collection

NAL's collection of materials from all over the world now numbers approximately 2 million volumes. Approximately 27,000 periodical titles are received annually, many through an extensive gift and exchange program with agricultural institutions throughout the world.

The AGRICOLA Database

Indexing agricultural literature worldwide, the AGRICOLA database, containing about 2 million entries, is now available on CD-ROM from two commercial vendors, SilverPlatter Information, Inc., and OCLC Online Computer Library Center, Inc. SilverPlatter offers the complete database from 1970 to the present on four discs: 1970–1976, 1977–1980, 1981–1984, and 1984–present. CRIS (Current Research Information System), an index to current agricultural research produced by U.S.D.A.'s Cooperative State Research Service (CSRS), is planned for inclusion on discs issued in 1989. OCLC has issued the AGRICOLA database on CD-ROM (three discs covering 1979–1982, 1983–1985, and 1986–present) as part of its *Search CD450* Agriculture Series, which also includes CRIS and AgMIL (a selected database of agricultural citations compiled from OCLC's Online Union Catalog). In all, AGRICOLA is available in five formats: (1) machine-readable tape; (2) paper form in the *Bibliography of Agriculture* published by Oryx Press; (3) the U.S. portion that is sent to the Food and Agriculture Organization (FAO) of the United Nations and becomes part of the AGRIS (AGRicultural Information System) database; (4) online via DIALOG and BRS, U.S. database vendors, and DIMDI, a European database vendor. OCLC has the cataloging portion online; and (5) CD-ROM by SilverPlatter and by OCLC.

Although NAL catalogs and indexes items from all countries, it currently is placing highest priority on U.S. publications, following the policy of the international AGRIS system where each country indexes and provides its own publications. Coverage of foreign titles indexed elsewhere is being reduced.

Interlibrary Loan

NAL interlibrary loan consists mainly of providing photocopies of the materials NAL collects and announces both in the United States and overseas. The service is offered on a cost-reimbursable basis. In 1988 more than 116,000 interlibrary loan requests were filled. The turnaround time for most items in the collection is 24 hours.

Cooperative Cataloging Projects

Two cataloging programs exemplify cooperation for more effective access to publications. One concerns state agricultural publications, an underutilized source of valuable information. Following a program initiated by NAL in 1984 to ensure comprehensive coverage of these materials, land-grant university libraries acquire copies of state agricultural documents, catalog those appropriate for full-level cataloging, and serve as the primary source for document requests. Records for all items are incorporated into the AGRICOLA database and are also contributed to AGRIS, providing for worldwide access. Libraries in 43 states are now participating in the project, and ways are being explored to achieve participation by all 50 states and to ensure smoother and easier processing.

In its program for cooperative cataloging of monographs, NAL has established a network of libraries to catalog agricultural monographs using OCLC as the host bibliographic utility. The goal is to include these records in the AGRICOLA database and to follow national cataloging standards so that other institutions can make use of the records and avoid repeating cataloging work.

Advanced Technologies

NAL is adopting and adapting advanced technologies for the development of new information services and products. Twelve-inch laser optical discs are the focus of a project to evaluate their potential to store and disseminate agriculturally related full-text databases. When optical discs are used in conjunction with a microcomputer, each word of the text can be searched. In the first phase, the *Pork Industry Handbook* and 200,000 records from NAL's AGRICOLA database were placed on an optical disc. In the second phase, material was chosen from photocomposition tapes, word processing files, and printed text to test further the conversion and mastering process. Sixteen institutions are participating in phase two and will help evaluate the disc containing the full text (in digital form) and related illustrations (in analog form) of 13 U.S.D.A. and State Extension publications.

The National Agricultural Text Digitizing Project is testing a new method of capturing full text and images in digital format for publication on CD-ROM discs. The purpose is to provide in-depth access to the literature of agriculture and at the same time preserve it from the rapid deterioration affecting most of the world's printed matter. Four thousand pages, both text and images, of noncopyrighted aquaculture publications are being scanned, converted, edited, and indexed. A second disc will contain international agricultural research material from the Consultative Group on International Agricultural Research (CGIAR), a group of research institutions in various countries with a coordinating office in Washington, D.C.; a third will contain the Agent Orange collection at NAL; and a fourth on food irradiation is being planned. Different searching software will be tested for each disc. Forty-two participating land-grant libraries will field-test the CD-ROM products and the search software. After review and refinement of the process, materials on acid rain will be captured on compact disc. Possibilities for electronic document delivery of the digitized collections via telecommunications networks will be examined later.

With the cooperation of the Forest Service and the University of Maryland, NAL has completed a 12-inch videodisc containing 34,000 photographs from the U.S.D.A. Forest Service Historical Photograph Collection. This collection contains photographic documentation on the westward movement in America—farmers, foresters, miners, cowboys, Indians, scientists, and many others. A computer-based, menu-driven, word-searchable database provides quick and efficient image access. This system allows review at local and remote locations without disturbing the originals.

In a similar project, other U.S.D.A. photographs are being put on a WORM (Write Once, Read Many) laser disc. In contrast to the one-time mastering for the videodisc containing the Forest Service photographs, this type of disc allows repeated updating. In both cases, the photographs can be found through index terms stored in a computer.

Laser disc technology has been shown to be very effective for instruction and training. Working with the University of Maryland (University College, Center for Instructional Design and Evaluation), NAL has designed and produced a system using a computer coupled with laser videodisc to provide instruction in searching the AGRICOLA database. This interactive system, called AGRICOLearn, incorporates text, graphics, motion pictures, animation, and sound. The student interacts directly with and controls the system. The stand-alone course provides complete instruction in use of AGRICOLA in DIALOG and BRS at a beginner or advanced level. It is available to land-grant university libraries from NAL or for purchase from the University of Maryland.

NAL staff are creating small-scale microcomputer systems to mimic advisory work done by human experts, in this case subject specialists and reference librarians. These ready-reference systems guide users to appropriate references—books, articles, laws, and the like—or, in some instances, to the answers to specific questions on aquaculture, food and nutrition, and herbs. Several have been developed in cooperation with land-grant university libraries covering Louisiana aquaculture, organic chemistry, and urban forestry. A system addressing anesthesia and analgesia in laboratory animals is being developed with the University of Maryland and one for African aquaculture in cooperation with the Food and Agriculture Organization.

Electronic Bulletin Board

NAL has inaugurated an electronic bulletin board system called ALF (Agricultural Library Forum)—a convenient, low-cost tool for electronically accessing information about NAL products and services and for exchanging agricultural information and resources among libraries, information centers, and other information users. The system supports three basic types of communications: bulletins, messages/conferences, and file transfer. It is available 24 hours per day, 7 days per week, to all those interested in agricultural information issues.

Integrated Library System

A new integrated library information system, ISIS (Integrated System for Information Services), is being implemented at NAL, replacing fragmented, multiple computer operations. A minicomputer-based turnkey system that adheres to national library standards, ISIS will be used to manage the records of the collection. It will include linking modules to perform online reference and cataloging retrieval, online cataloging and catalog maintenance, indexing, serials control, online acquisitions processing, online lending and retrieval control, and preservation control. ISIS will support a linking authority file that meets requirements for national standards. The system used is the Virginia Tech Library System (VTLS), provided by the Virginia Polytechnic Institute and State University.

Specialized Information Centers

Areas of high priority for NAL are served by 12 specialized information centers and a new Youth Development Information Center (YDIC), a joint project with the

U.S.D.A. Extension Service, to provide information services to youth development professionals, supporting the 4-H professional research and knowledge requirements.

The Rural Information Center, established in late 1988, has been expanded to actively involve state and county extension agents in 35 states as coordinators and contact persons working with information center staff in assisting rural officials, community leaders, and economic development organizations. The Animal Welfare Information Center is cooperating in projects for improving the care and management of laboratory animals with Texas Tech University Health Sciences Center, Lubbock, Texas; the Scientists Center for Animal Welfare, Bethesda, Maryland; the Institute of Laboratory Animal Resources of the National Academy of Sciences, Washington, D.C.; and Princeton Scientific Publishing Company, Princeton, New Jersey.

With supplemental funding from several federal agencies, the Aquaculture Information Center is cooperating in the development of expert advisory systems in aquaculture with Louisiana State University and with the Food and Agriculture Organization of the United Nations, and working on publications with the Joint Subcommittee on Aquaculture (representatives from 16 federal agencies) and the National Oceanic and Atmospheric Administration. The National Alternative Farming Systems Information Center is part of a congressionally mandated program on low-input farming systems coordinated by the CSRS. Its information products and services, many developed in cooperation with interested organizations, are aimed at both the investigators for low-input methods and the extension workers and farmers who apply them.

Information Network

An informal system for discussing agricultural information issues has yielded to a new information network, the Agricultural Libraries Information Network, composed of institutions with an interest in agricultural information. (NAL is a coequal participant.) Plans call for participation by agricultural industry libraries, 1,890 land-grant institutions, the National Association of State University and Land Grant Colleges, public, special, and state libraries, and other agriculturally related professional associations. Several individuals from land-grant libraries have been selected by ballot as officers of the network.

National Library of Medicine

8600 Rockville Pike, Bethesda, MD 20894
301-496-6308

Robert B. Mehnert
Public Information Officer

The legislative mandate of the National Library of Medicine (NLM) was significantly enlarged in 1988 when, on November 4, the president signed a law (PL 100-607) directing that a National Center for Biotechnology Information be established at the library. The same legislation authorized a sum of $8 million to carry out the functions of the center in FY 1989. Earlier in 1988, Congress had appropriated $3.8 million for NLM to carry out biotechnology-related programs. Briefly, the center is given the responsibility to create automated systems for knowledge about molecular biology, to conduct research into advanced methods on how to handle biotechnology information, to enable those engaged in biotechnology research and in medical care to use the systems developed, and to coordinate the gathering of biotechnology information worldwide. The organizational structure to fulfill these responsibilities is now authorized in law and will soon be in place.

The same legislation that created the National Center for Biotechnology Information reauthorized the Medical Library Assistance Act – the authority under which NLM makes grants – at a level of $14 million in FY 1989 and "such sums as may be necessary for fiscal year 1990." It also raised the maximum amount that the library can award for a resource grant, from $500,000 to $750,000. In 1988, the library funded 90 grants totaling $14.7 million for research, resources, training, and publications. Included are seven contracts for funding the regional medical libraries.

Online Services

To improve the currency of information offered on its online bibliographic network, NLM moved from monthly to semimonthly updating of the major database, MEDLINE. The number of network users continued its dramatic growth of recent years; for the second straight year the number grew by 50 percent. (There are now more than 20,000 user access codes.) Individual health professionals represent by far the fastest-growing segment of the NLM online network, due to the continuing popularity of the Grateful Med "front-end" software for microcomputers. Version 3.0 of Grateful Med, permitting access not only to MEDLINE (journal article references) and CATLINE (catalog records) but to seven additional databases – including the library's extensive toxicology-related files – was announced in January. By the end of 1988, the number of copies of all versions sold by the National Technical Information Service reached 13,000. An even faster and better looking Grateful Med, Version 4.0, was released at the end of 1988; a Macintosh version will be introduced in 1989.

Usage of the library's MEDLARS/MEDLINE computers grew by 12 to 15 percent in 1988, as measured by hours of use and characters delivered to users' terminals. More than 4 million bibliographic searches were conducted by network users on the library's 25 databases, not including online use of the computers in foreign MEDLARS centers, users of MEDLINE on the systems of domestic information vendors such as DIALOG and BRS, or users of the new commercial MEDLINE CD-ROM (compact discs) services being offered.

The CD-ROM products now on the market (numbering at least half a dozen) are the result of agreements signed by NLM and private companies to produce compact discs containing MEDLINE. In September, the library sponsored a one-day "evaluation forum" to hear from both the producers and the users of the new products.

A new database – AIDSLINE (essentially a subset of MEDLINE) – joined the library's network in July 1988. Plans call for it to be enriched in 1989 with information from other sources. The new file is timely; the same legislation that created the National Center for Biotechnology Information also directed the library to work closely with other federal agencies to establish computerized information services containing the results of AIDS research conducted in the United States and abroad. AIDSLINE will be a part of that effort.

The NLM Collection

The NLM collection grew by some 207,000 items in 1988 – 45,300 volumes and 162,000 other items (audiovisual materials, microforms, pictures, manuscripts, and so forth). The library received and processed more than 153,000 books, serial issues, audiovisual programs, and software packages. Table 1 gives a statistical profile of the library's operations.

Although the number of interlibrary loan requests filled registered a modest 8 percent gain in 1988, the number of circulation requests filled for on-site users dropped significantly (25 percent), due to an imposed limit of ten requests per day from the stacks, coupled with the institution of a fee-based overnight photocopy service for high-volume requestors.

The special emphasis of recent years on preservation continued in 1988. More than 8,000 brittle volumes (1.5 million pages) were committed to microfilm; an additional 777 rare books, manuscripts, and historical films received special conservation treatment. The "National Preservation Plan for the Biomedical Literature" was distributed throughout the Regional Medical Library Network, and several newspaper columns about the peril to library materials printed on acid-based paper were distributed nationwide.

The Permanent Paper Task Force established by NLM on the recommendation of the Board of Regents met twice in 1988. The task force is formulating standards

Table 1 / Selected Statistics*

Library Operation	Volume
Collection (book and nonbook)	3,986,000
Serial titles received	20,800
Articles indexed for MEDLINE	329,000
Titles cataloged	20,200
Circulation requests filled	331,000
For interlibrary loan	147,000
For on-site users	184,000
Computerized searches (all databases)	4,094,000
Online	3,777,000
Offline	317,000

*For the year ending September 30, 1988.

for the making and use of permanent (nonacid) paper and encouraging major medical publishers to use such paper in their books and journals. To date, the efforts of the task force have resulted in a number of news items and articles about the problem of paper deterioration and the publication of the library's acid-free paper program in professional and lay journals, newsletters, and the *Congressional Record.*

Research and Development

Two NLM components engage in research and development into biomedical communications systems, the Lister Hill National Center for Biomedical Communications and the Toxicology Information Program. The projects of the Lister Hill Center fall into three categories: computer and information science as applied to the problems of the library, biomedical research, and health care delivery; biomedical image engineering; and the use of computer and image technologies for education in the health professions. Examples of continuing research and development are the artificial intelligence/expert systems projects (in rheumatology, for example), work on the Unified Medical Language System and related projects concerned with the language aspects of medical communication, the Electronic Document Storage and Retrieval Program, and a variety of prototype interactive videodisc programs intended for use by students of the health professions.

The Toxicology Information Program, which is responsible for developing online databases related to toxicology, pharmacology, and the environment, maintains publicly accessible online data files on two systems—the MEDLARS network and the program's own TOXNET system. Among the databases available are TOXLINE, CHEMLINE, DIRLINE (directory of information resources), and the Hazardous Substances Data Bank. A new databank, the Toxic Release Inventory, being developed in collaboration with the Environmental Protection Agency, will contain names and addresses of industrial sites reporting releases of chemicals into the environment or their transfer to waste treatment sites.

Outreach

Early in 1988, Congress added a new responsibility to NLM's basic mandate—to publicize NLM services—due to concern that the library's online and other information services are not being used to maximum benefit, especially by health professionals in rural and remote areas of the nation. As a first step in this direction, the library decided to update several sections of the Long Range Plan (published in 1986), including those pertaining to education/outreach. An Outreach Planning Panel of experts, chaired by Michael DeBakey, met at the library in November to review NLM's outreach program and make recommendations for improvement. The panel will meet twice more in early 1989.

Publications

Beginning with the January 1989 issue, *Index Medicus,* the library's primary bibliographic publication, will be published in two volumes—a subject volume and a name volume. The selection of journals to be indexed for *Index Medicus* (and the electronic databases) is now the responsibility of a new committee, the Literature Selection Technical Review Committee, which met for the first time in 1988. The committee also provides NLM with policy advice about the literature covered in its bibliographic products.

In addition to the major continuing catalogs and indexes such as *Index Medicus,* NLM issued several special publications in 1988. The collected essays of a one-day sesquicentennial colloquium were published early in the year in *Past, Present, and Future of Biomedical Information.* Special bibliographies on laboratory animal welfare, physical fitness and sports medicine, and compact discs, and a brochure, *Health Hotlines,* listing some 200 health organizations with toll-free telephone numbers, were also published. Finally, two new serial publications made their appearance: the *AIDS Bibliography* (quarterly, to become monthly in 1989) and *Current Bibliographies in Medicine* (about 20 titles per year on a variety of biomedical subjects).

Administration

In FY 1988 the National Library of Medicine had a total budget authority of $72,597,000, including reimbursements from other government agencies. The staff numbered 511 (full-time equivalents). All advisory committees—the Board of Regents, the Biomedical Library Review Committee, and the Board of Scientific Counselors—had their full complement of members and met as scheduled.

Educational Resources Information Center

ERIC Processing and Reference Facility
4350 East-West Hwy., Suite 1100, Bethesda, MD 20814
301-656-9723

Ted Brandhorst
Director

With all 16 ERIC Clearinghouses having been competed in 1987, the remaining competitions for the existing ERIC Processing and Reference Facility (a central editorial and computer processing facility) and for the new "Access ERIC" component (mandated to devote itself to dissemination, marketing, publicity, outreach, etc.) were run in 1988. Competitions in both years were run during the last six months of the year. The ERIC Facility competition (decided on December 15, 1988) was won by ORI, Inc. The "Access ERIC" competition is still in progress at this writing.

Funding for ERIC during both FYs 1988 and 1989 was essentially level at $5.7 million per year (for support of 18 contractors and ERIC's publishing program). In order to support the new "Access ERIC" component within this budget and without additional appropriations, efforts were made to reduce the budgets of virtually all components of the ERIC system, leaving most of ERIC looking ahead to FY 1990 for budgetary salvation.

Organizationally, ERIC's only other initiative toward change was its efforts to establish a set of "ERIC Partners" (each associated with an appropriate Clearinghouse) that would assist ERIC in disseminating its information in return for product discounts and other such conferred advantages. The "ERIC Partners" concept is to be fully worked out and activated by "Access ERIC" in 1989.

During 1988, input into the ERIC database continued its downward trend, falling below 30,000 items per year for the first time since 1969.

	No. of Items Input		
Database	**1966–1987**	**1988**	**Total through 1988**
Resources in Education (RIE)	277,909	12,129 (documents)	290,038
Current Index to Journals in Education (CIJE)	358,804	16,967 (articles)	375,771
	636,713	29,096	665,809

Lexicography

ERIC lexicography witnessed a number of significant developments in late 1987 and in 1988, including the publication of three new thesauri. The National Council for Research on Women and the Business and Professional Women's Foundation jointly published *A Women's Thesaurus* (Harper & Row, 1987). The British Education Index (BEI) published the *British Education Thesaurus* (Leeds University, 1988), which, in its own words, "owes a massive debt to the *Thesaurus of ERIC Descriptors,* which became the other major source document for the new *British Education Thesaurus.*" The Council of Ministers of Education (Canada) and the Canadian Education Index (CEI) published the *Canadian Education Thesaurus* (August 1988). ERIC worked closely with the publishers of the three new thesauri to achieve a measure of compatibility between related indexing vocabularies. ERIC's efforts toward a basic compatibility among the educational thesauri of three English-speaking countries (ERIC, BEI, CEI) may someday facilitate the truly worldwide flow and use of educational information.

Publications and Products

The ERIC database on CD-ROM discs continued to be a popular product and was the subject of numerous journal articles in 1988. SilverPlatter, Inc. (the earliest of three vendors to offer ERIC, the others being DIALOG and OCLC) reported nearly 600 total subscribers to its ERIC product. From the best information available, the online ERIC database appears to be the fifth most used online bibliographic database (in total connect hours), behind such stalwarts as LEXIS, MEDLARS, and Chemical Abstracts.

ERIC Digests (brief, one-page syntheses of practical information) continue to be emphasized as Clearinghouse products. Through 1987, the Clearinghouses had issued a total of 533 Digests (see ERIC Ready Reference no. 10). Future projections are for 150 to 200 new Digests to be issued each year. The full text of selected Digests (about 300) will be made accessible online via DIALOG during 1989.

Two infrequently used Publication Types were provided for in ERIC's database during 1988: "Book/Product Reviews" (code 072) and "Machine-Readable Data Files (MRDF)" (code 102).

During 1988, the new ERIC management initiated the *ERIC Annual Report* to help represent ERIC and its accomplishments both within the Department of Education and to the public. The first report covers 1987; copies can be obtained by writing to the ERIC Facility.

Price Changes

The U.S. Government Printing Office (GPO) continued its practice of making periodic changes in the price of ERIC's monthly abstract journal *Resources in Education (RIE).* The September 1988 change amounted to a 27 percent increase for an annual subscription ($51 to $66) and a 12 percent decrease for an individual issue ($17 to $15), as shown in Table 1.

Table 1 / *Resources in Education* Price Changes, September 1988

	Domestic			Foreign		
Product	Old	New	%	Old	New	%
Monthly subscription (12 issues)	$51.00	$66.00	+27%	$63.75	$82.50	+29%
Single copy (1 issue)	17.00	15.00	−12	21.25	18.75	−12
Semiannual indexes subscription (2 issues)	20.00	20.00	–	25.00	25.00	–
Semiannual index single copy (1 issue)	15.00	15.00	–	18.75	18.75	–

National Associations

American Library Association

50 E. Huron St., Chicago, IL 60611
312-944-6780

F. William Summers
President

Founded in 1876, the American Library Association (ALA) is the world's oldest and largest library association. Its purpose is to provide leadership for the development, promotion, and improvement of library and information services and the profession of librarianship in order to enhance learning and ensure access to information for all. Priority areas of concern include access to information, legislation and funding, intellectual freedom, public awareness, personnel resources, and library services, development, and technology. In 1988, membership reached a record high of 47,249. Of the total, 44,308 are personal members—another record—and 2,941 are organizational members. By type of library, the membership breakdown is 29.5 percent public, 25.7 percent academic, and 13.2 percent school.

Conference Highlights

ALA's One-hundredth and Seventh Annual Conference, held in New Orleans, July 9–14, drew 16,550 members, exhibitors, and guests to the Crescent City. The opening general session featured retired Speaker of the House Tip O'Neill and U.S. Representative Lindy Boggs (D–La.). The conference theme, "Visionary Leaders for 2020: Developing Human Leadership in Resources for Library and Information Science," was reflected in then-President Margaret Chisholm's program, with keynote speaker Harlan Cleveland, former dean of the Humphrey Institute of Public Affairs, and five young librarians selected to reflect emerging leadership. Other conference speakers included pollster Louis Harris and authors Rita Mae Brown, Margaret Truman, and S. E. Hinton.

The 1988 conference was attended by several Soviet participants in a U.S.–U.S.S.R. Seminar on Access to Library Resources through Technology and Preservation, held in Washington, D.C., just before the conference. (U.S. participants in the seminar included Margaret Chisholm, ALA President-elect F. William Summers, and E. J. Josey, chair of ALA's International Relations Committee.) A protocol opening the way for exchange of current national bibliography was signed at the conference by Simmons Library School Dean Robert D. Stueart and Lenin State Library Director Nikolai S. Kartashov, co-chairs of the U.S.–U.S.S.R. Commission on Library Cooperation. [See E. J. Josey's report on the highlights of the jointly sponsored U.S.-USSR seminar in the International Reports section of Part 1—*Ed.*]

Among the more than 80 awards given at the conference was the first-time presentation of the Hugh C. Atkinson Memorial Award for outstanding achievements of an academic librarian who has worked in library automation or management and has made contributions (including risk taking) toward the improvement of library services or to library development or research. The honor went to Richard M. Dougherty of the University of Michigan Library School.

Two ALA divisions held successful conferences during 1988: the Public Library Association met in Pittsburgh April 27–30 and the Library and Information and Technology Association met October 2–6 in Boston.

ALA's 1989 Annual Conference will be held in Dallas June 24–29; the 1990 Midwinter Meeting is set for January 6–11 in Chicago. Upcoming division conferences are the Association of College and Research Libraries, April 5–8, 1989, in Cincinnati; the American Association of School Librarians, October 19–22, in Salt Lake City; and the Public Library Association, March 20–23, 1991, in San Diego.

Council Actions

At the 1988 Annual Conference, ALA Council called for the immediate cessation of the FBI's Library Awareness Program, in which FBI agents have been asking librarians to report library use by persons from countries "hostile to the U.S." (see "Intellectual Freedom," below). Among other actions taken by council in 1988 were resolutions urging Congress to bar further contracting-out of federal libraries; deploring discrimination against or denial of library and information access to persons with AIDS; calling upon the next U.S. president to immediately affirm a policy of free and open access to information by and about the government; opposing mandatory drug testing of library employees; and establishing a new Standing Committee on Freedom and Equality of Access to Information.

Washington Report

In late January, ALA Executive Director Thomas J. Galvin wrote the Office of Management and Budget expressing concern over the Reagan administration's efforts to privatize the National Technical Information Service. Opposition by ALA and others resulted in legislation prohibiting most contracting-out by the agency. [For a discussion of this and other federal information dissemination issues, see the report by Fred B. Wood in the Special Reports secion of Part 1—*Ed.*]

On ALA's fourteenth annual National Library Week Legislative Day, April 19, a record-breaking 603 library supporters from 45 states and the U.S. Virgin Islands visited senators and representatives to lobby for libraries. U.S. Representative Major Owens (D-N.Y.) held his annual National Library Week special order, giving 19 representatives the opportunity to make one-minute speeches about libraries. Despite continued Reagan administration opposition to federal funding for libraries, Congress appropriated a total of $137,200,000 for Library Services and Construction Act and Higher Education Act library programs, up 1.5 percent from FY 1988.

Intellectual Freedom

The FBI's Library Awareness Program dominated ALA's intellectual freedom concerns in 1988. C. James Schmidt, chair of ALA's Intellectual Freedom Committee (IFC), and Judith Krug, director of ALA's Office for Intellectual Freedom, testified against the program at a June 20 hearing of the House Judiciary Subcommittee on Civil and Constitutional Rights. Representatives of the IFC and the FBI met in Washington September 9 to exchange viewpoints on the program; the FBI agents agreed to "sensitize" field agents by distributing a statement describing ALA's ethical concerns. [See the special report "Rights for Users of Information: Conflicts and Balances among Privacy, Professional Ethics, Law, National Security" by C. James Schmidt, earlier in Part 1 – *Ed.*]

ALA representatives also testified before Congress in favor of a bill that would protect the confidentiality of video store and library patron records (the library provision was later dropped) and against a bill restricting the distribution of obscene materials (the bill was later weakened before passage).

Senator Patrick Leahy (D-Vt.) defended freedom of speech and denounced threats to the Freedom of Information Act at an ALA press conference celebrating Freedom of Information Day March 16 in Washington.

The fifth annual Banned Books Week (September 24–October 1) celebrated the freedom to read with the theme "Open Books for Open Minds." Banned Books Week 1989 will be September 23–30. ALA cosponsors the event with the American Booksellers Association, the Association of American Publishers, the American Society of Journalists and Authors, and the National Association of College Stores.

Children's Book Awards

Russell Freedman, author of *Lincoln: A Photobiography* (Houghton Mifflin/Clarion), received the 1988 Newbery Medal for the most distinguished contribution to American literature for children published in 1987. John Schoenherr, illustrator of *Owl Moon* by Jane Yolen (Putnam & Grosset/Philomel), won the 1988 Caldecott Medal for the most distinguished American picture book for children. The awards are presented annually by ALA's Association for Library Service to Children.

The Coretta Scott King Award, given by the Social Responsibilities Round Table to black authors and illustrators for outstandingly inspirational and educational contributions, went to Mildred Taylor, author of *The Friendship* (Dial), and John Steptoe, illustrator of *Mufaro's Beautiful Daughter: An African Tale* (Lothrop, Lee, & Shepard).

The Association for Library Service to Children presented its Mildred L. Batchelder Award, for an outstanding foreign children's book translated into English, to *If You Didn't Have Me,* by Swedish writer Ulf Nilsson.

Public Awareness

The theme of National Library Week 1987 (April 17–23) – "The Card with a Charge . . . Use Your Library" – was designed to boost ALA's national campaign to sign up every child for a library card. During the first year of the campaign, launched in October 1987, hundreds of thousands of children (and adults) received cards – more than 100,000 in the state of West Virginia alone. The Reader's Digest Foundation contributed $135,000 (up from $85,000 in 1987), for phase two of the campaign, aimed at teenagers and older children.

The "Why I Love My Library Card" contest for children in grades K–8 was won by nine-year-old Vivian Safrin. In addition to a $100 cash prize, Vivian received a visit from popular cartoon character Garfield at the Phoenix, Arizona, Hebrew Academy, where she is a fourth-grader.

September marked the first National Library Card Sign-Up Month, an annual campaign to make sure all children have library cards when they return to school.

The 1988 celebrity posters in ALA's popular "Read" series featured basketball star Isiah Thomas, Academy Award–winning actor William Hurt, actor-comedian Steve Martin, and actor Billy Dee Williams. An additional "I got carded at the library" poster, tying in with the library card campaign, featured Keshia Knight Pulliam, who plays Rudy on "The Cosby Show."

During ALA's "Year of the Librarian" in 1989, National Library Week (April 9–15) will focus on the people behind library service with the theme "Ask a Professional. Ask Your Librarian." Campaign materials, including posters, bookmarks, and radio and TV public service announcements, will be available from ALA's Public Information Office.

Another new campaign launched by ALA is aimed at recruiting good candidates into library/information science careers. The campaign delivers its message—"The Future Is Information. Take Charge of the Future"—through posters and brochures profiling six outstanding librarians who chose their careers in recent years.

Special Projects

The ALA Communications Department developed program materials in conjunction with the PBS television series "Voices and Visions," aimed at encouraging an appreciation of American poetry. ALA mailed a kit of information about the series, programming and display ideas, artwork, and an 80-page viewer's guide to some 16,000 public and college libraries. The materials were developed with funding from the Annenberg/CPB Project.

The ALA/PBS partnership was solidified with the introduction of a newsletter, *PBS/Library Pipeline,* and a second mailing of library promotional materials for the fall season.

NEH awarded a $358,000 grant for a demonstration project titled "Voices & Visions: Reading, Viewing and Discussion Programs in America's Libraries," involving 25 public libraries beginning in fall 1988. Each selected library will offer an eight-to-ten-week series of poetry discussion programs with a local humanities scholar and the "Voices and Visions" television programs produced by PBS.

A $374,800 grant from NEH will fund the traveling exhibition "Printing and the French Revolution" to coincide with the bicentennial of the French Revolution. The exhibition, developed with the New York Public Library, will tour 28 libraries between March and December 1989. Reading and discussion materials will be made available to libraries not on the tour.

Six hundred Carnegie libraries received a videocassette player/recorder as part of a $560,000 grant from the Carnegie Corporation of New York to ALA during 1988. The project included publication of *Video for Libraries: Special Interest Video for Small and Medium-Sized Public Libraries,* edited by project director Sally Mason and James Scholtz, two national workshops on libraries and video, two library staff training videos, and the newsletter *Fast Forward.*

In the second year of the Library/Book Fellows Program, supported by the U.S. Information Agency, ten librarians were selected to work abroad in France, Sweden, Uganda, Egypt, North Yemen, Malawi, Liberia, Thailand, Argentina, and Venezuela. The deadline for applications for available 1989–1990 positions is April.

Youth Services

In April the American Association of School Librarians and the Association for Educational Communications and Technology issued new national curriculum guidelines for school library media programs. The document, *Information Power: Guidelines for School Library Media Programs,* comes 13 years after publication of the last joint guidelines. The first of four planned regional workshops on the implementation of the guidelines took place in October. (Copies of *Information Power* are available for $12.95 from ALA's Order Department.)

The problem of latchkey children left unattended in libraries after school was addressed in a position paper prepared by the Service to Children Committee of ALA's Public Library Association. The publication, *Latchkey Children in the Public Library,* resulted in much media attention, with stories appearing in the *New York Times, Chicago Tribune,* and *Detroit Free Press* and on NBC's "Sunday Today" program.

The Young Adult Services Division's first annual YASD *School Library Journal* Author Award went to S. E. Hinton, author of *The Outsiders* and three later books. The $1,000 award, presented at the ALA Annual Conference, recognizes authors whose books have popular appeal with young adults and help to increase their understanding of themselves, their relationships, and the world.

Leadership

F. William Summers, dean of the Florida State University School of Library and Information Studies, took office as ALA 1988–1989 president, choosing as his theme "Commitments—Investing in Our Shared Future." Patricia Berger, chief of the National Bureau of Standards Information Resources and Services Division, was elected ALA vice president/president-elect for 1989–1990. The new ALA treasurer (elected for a four-year term) is Carla J. Stoffle.

Thomas J. Galvin announced in December that he would resign as ALA executive director, effective no later than November 30, 1989. Other resignations included ALA Headquarters Librarian Emily Melton and Manager of Information Technology Publishing Joel Lee, who was replaced by Rob Carlson. New staff appointments include Marla Powers-Gibson, ALA director of personnel, and Sibyl Moses, director of the Office for Library Outreach Services. Evelyn Shaevel, former executive director of ALA's Young Adult Services Division, succeeded Paul Kobasa as assistant director for marketing services for ALA Publishing. Patricia Scarry announced her resignation as director of Membership Services effective February 1989.

Publishing Highlights

ALA Publishing issued 22 new titles and 9 revisions in FY 1987–1988, with sales of more than $2.6 million. A highlight of the year was the 1988 edition of *AACR2.* ALA also produced the CD-ROM version of the *Directory of Library and Information Professionals.*

ALA's membership magazine, *American Libraries,* continued to grow in size and ad revenue, with the number of pages exceeding 1,000 in 1988 for the first time. ALA's review journal, *Booklist,* also had a record-breaking year; and Bill Ott, former managing editor and adult books editor, became editor in chief following the death of longtime editor Paul H. Brawley.

In addition to ALA's ongoing *Library Video Magazine,* 1988 video releases included two ALA-Carnegie Video Project tapes: *The Librarian's Video Primer: Establishing and Maintaining Your Video Collection* and *Fast Forward: Libraries and the Video Revolution.*

Special Libraries Association

1700 18th St. N.W., Washington, D.C. 20009
202-234-4700

David Malinak
Director, Communications

The year 1988 was marked by change, growth, and achievement for the Special Libraries Association (SLA). Among the developments of the year was the implementation of a staff reorganization plan (approved in 1987 by SLA's board of directors), which directed increased emphasis, staff, and funding to SLA's professional development and research programs. In May, just prior to the Reagan-Gorbachev summit, Executive Director David Bender led a team of four art/museum librarians to the Soviet Union on a historic exchange program for special librarians. In June, SLA's board approved the addition of "caucuses" to SLA's structure, "informal groups within SLA intended to serve as a focus for the interaction of members who share a common interest not covered by any Association Division or Committee." By the end of 1988, SLA's first caucus, the Solo Librarians Caucus, had been approved by the board; SLA's expanded Professional Growth Section had premiered its first computer-assisted study program and completed developmental work on the first Executive Development Academy: a networking guide of SLA software users had been published, as had an information kit on small libraries; and research had been initiated on a project to profile top U.S. and Canadian corporate libraries and information centers for publication in early 1989.

The year 1988 also was a turbulent one, with the onslaught of publicity on the FBI's Library Awareness Program. SLA first learned about the Library Awareness

Program in late 1987 when an article appeared in the *Philadelphia Inquirer.* In January 1988, SLA's board of directors reaffirmed its previous stance in support of freedom of access and confidentiality of library records. Unfortunately, as 1988 wore on and the publicity implied a link between SLA and Soviet infiltration of U.S. libraries, the stage was set for a serious discussion of the issue during SLA's Seventy-ninth Annual Conference in Denver. The unexpected tornado that hit Denver during the conference seemed little match for the tempers of SLA chapter and division cabinet members as they received the response of their respective constituents that SLA must go on record in opposition to the FBI's increasingly controversial program. The board received recommendations from SLA's chapter and division cabinets, as well as from individual members. The policy approved by the board at the close of the annual business meeting ended with a simple and strong statement: "The Association opposes the activities of the FBI Library Awareness Program." [See C. James Schmidt's special report "Rights for Users of Information: Conflicts and Balances among Privacy, Professional Ethics, Law, National Security," earlier in Part 1 – *Ed.*]

David Bender best characterized SLA as a key player in the library and information community in his 1988 state-of-the-association address to members at the annual conference. He said, "Our greatest strength as an association is in our diversity. SLA draws its strength from the diversity and individuality of its members." He concluded, ". . . the past year has been a year of continued growth in the services provided by the Association . . . the year has been marked by achievement, and a strengthening of the foundation of the Association."

Highlights of 1988 Activities

Professional Staff Promotions

In January, Richard Battaglia assumed the position of associate executive director, clarifying his position at SLA as second in command. Battaglia assumed a number of new responsibilities, such as guiding the development and direction of the Association Management Team. Kathy Warye was promoted to the position of assistant executive director, Professional Growth, directing the Professional Growth Section, which was expanded to include SLA's research program, the Information Resources Center, and membership development and marketing, as well as the existing professional development program. Tobi Brimsek was promoted to the new position of director, Research and Information Resources.

Professional Development Programs

SLA's continuing education programs continued to provide high-caliber education and related services to SLA members and professionals in the library/information community. In 1988, two regional continuing education programs were offered, New Technology and Its Impact on You (brought back by popular demand) and Managing the One-Person Library. More than 14 continuing education programs were sponsored or coordinated by the association during the year for chapters and related library associations and groups.

The Winter Education Conference, held in Colonial Williamsburg, attracted a record number of attendees to three full-day courses, four half-day workshops, and the "Analytical Tools" unit of the Middle Management Institute. The keynote address by David Penniman of AT&T Bell Laboratories was on strategies for influencing the future and meeting the challenges of our changing technological environment. The Middle Management Institute, SLA's five-unit certificate program, continued to be well attended by professionals desiring the knowledge and skills to advance to midlevel information positions.

Executive Development Academy

After more than a year of development, SLA will offer the Executive Development Academy in collaboration with Carnegie Mellon University in Pittsburgh, Pennsylvania, March 5–11, 1989. The academy is intended for those who seek to develop a top management perspective and to introduce innovative ideas into their organizations. Participants in the academy will broaden their approach to management and learn to plan strategically for the future by evaluating and responding to change. The goal of the academy is to prepare information professionals to advance into executive level positions. At its October 1988 meeting, SLA's board approved the creation of a scholarship for the Executive Development Academy. The first scholarship for the academy will be awarded in 1990.

State-of-the-Art Institute

Now in its third year, SLA's State-of-the-Art Institute is another quality educational opportunity offered by the Professional Growth Section. The 1988 institute, "Global Ties through Information," held October 17–19, 1988, in Washington, D.C., was cosponsored by SLA and six international library associations. The diverse program, highlighted by experts discussing the history of transborder dataflow, current problems and probable solutions, theoretical applications of globalization of data, and a specially designed case study of a fictitious information cartel, attracted an international audience. The 1990 State-of-the-Art Institute, to be held in November in Washington, D.C., will focus on the "economics of information."

New Services

In June, SLA premiered its new computer-assisted study program "Time Management in the Small Library" during the annual conference. SLA embarked on computer-assisted study for those professionals who prefer the convenience of learning in their office or home, or for those individuals who, for whatever reason, are unable to attend a continuing education program. The computer-assisted study program includes a floppy disk and workbook. Other computer-assisted study programs are in the developmental stage.

Another new program initiated in 1988 was the Resume Referral Service. This service utilizes a unique database that will match jobs to potential employees using such variables as specialization, location, and salary. The service, the first of its kind in the library/information community, is available to both members and nonmembers, as well as employers seeking information professionals.

Information Resources Center

Monthly statistics compiled by Information Resources Center (IRC) staff show the astounding growth of the telephone reference service provided to members, the library community at large, the public, and staff. In 1986, the number of monthly calls to the IRC averaged 140; in 1988, the number surpassed the 200 point, an outstanding indicator testifying to the excellence of SLA information services. In October, a new brochure describing IRC services was released with the expectation that calls for reference and referral would increase substantially.

Annual Conference

SLA's Seventy-ninth Annual Conference, held June 11–16, 1988, in Denver, offered the 4,635 participants more than 200 programs, special events, meetings, field trips, breakfasts, luncheons, dinners, speakers, and activities—an educational feast with something for everyone. Keynote speakers Michael Annison, president of Westrends Group, and Roger von Oech, president of CreativeThink, spoke on the conference theme: "Expanding Horizons: Strategies for Information Managers." Annison explained that all institutions are going through restructuring and offered simple advice: ". . . build a strategic vision for the future." Von Oech challenged the audience to think more creatively, to break the rules, take risks and see yourself as a winner.

More than 1,130 individuals were enrolled in the 22 continuing education courses offered at the Denver conference. The Employment Clearinghouse and Career Advisory Service also drew high numbers of participants. Of particular note was the salary range for jobs posted in the clearinghouse—from a low of $18,000 to a high of $72,500. SLA's Exhibit Hall featured 330 booths from 242 companies and organizations, with 32 first-time exhibitors. The Exhibit Hall continued to provide the finest in library and information products and services and current innovations in information technology, ranging from CD-ROM to the latest databases.

Publishing Services

The association's publishing program flourished in 1988 by providing a vast array of publications needed by the information professional. Ten new books or information kits were published during the year:

The Information Profession: Facing Future Challenges (the proceedings from the 1987 State-of-the-Art Institute)
U.S. Government Publications Catalog, Second Edition
Libraries and Information Centers within Women's Studies Research Centers
Managerial Competencies of Twelve Corporate Librarians
Survey of SLA Software Users
Tools of the Profession
SLA Triennial Salary Survey
Directory of Catalogers in the Special Libraries Association
Managing Small Special Libraries, an Information Kit
Who's Who in Special Libraries 1988/89.

SLA's serial publications—*SpeciaList* and *Special Libraries*—continued to provide high-quality information and features for members. The summer issue of *Special Libraries* was a special issue entitled *Governmental Activities and Information Issues.*

In October 1988, SLA member Helen Pile joined the SLA staff as director, Publishing Services. Pile was formerly an editor and research librarian at the American Bankers Association.

Government Relations/Fund Development

SLA's Government Relations and Fund Development Program, directed by Sandy Morton, has firmly established SLA as a valuable source of information on legislation and activities pertinent to the information community. During 1988, SLA presented testimony or prepared statements on a variety of issues, including the proposed privatization of NTIS, changes in the Federal Librarians' Register, the reduction in 1990 census data, the imposition of FCC access charges, and the FBI Library Awareness Program.

In 1988, SLA became an official cosponsor of Legislative Day during National Library Week and celebrated by hoisting a huge banner on the front of the SLA headquarters building saluting National Library Week. To demonstrate support and concern for the association's Canadian members, the SLA board authorized a $10,000 contribution to the Canadian Library Association to assist in efforts to educate members of the Canadian Parliament as they work to make the first revisions in the antiquated copyright laws of Canada. Adding to SLA's government relations network, the board approved the recommendation of the Government Relations Committee to appoint government relations representatives in SLA divisions to complement the work of chapter representatives.

The association's 1988 Fund Development activities included the awarding of two Special Programs Fund Grants totaling $6,350. Tillie Krieger, College of Staten Island, received a grant to study "SLA Members Recruited as Students: What Influenced Their Decision." Marianne Cooper, Queens College, received funding to study "Management of Information in Corporate and Academic Environments in the 1980s." During a "silent auction" held in SLA's Exhibit Hall during the 1988 annual conference, $3,800 was raised to support the Special Programs Fund Grants.

Public Relations Program

In 1988, SLA awarded its first Public Relations Award to David Holmstrom, a freelance author, for his story, "Christine Maxwell: The Business of Knowledge," which appeared in the inflight magazine of American Airlines (*American Way,* March 15, 1987, page 19). The award, sponsored by the Standard & Poor's Corporation and selected by SLA's Public Relations Committee, is given annually to the author of an outstanding article on special librarianship in a general circulation magazine or newspaper. The $1,000 prize is a combination of cash and travel funds to allow the recipient to attend SLA's annual conference. Standard & Poor's Corporation has agreed to sponsor the 1988 award, which will be presented during SLA's 1989 annual conference in New York City.

SLA's media relations program continued to bring recognition to the achievements of SLA members and the profession. A new brochure entitled "Corporate Libraries and Information Centers: The Bottom Line" was prepared for use in promoting the value of special libraries and special librarians. The *Public Relations Handbook,* developed especially for SLA members in 1986, was revised and updated in 1988.

Student Support

Recognizing the growing need for the support of students entering graduate schools of library and information science, the SLA board increased the funding of SLA scholarships for graduate students pursuing careers in special librarianship. Beginning in 1989, SLA will provide four $6,000 scholarships, one of which will be designated an "affirmative action" scholarship. The action raises to $24,000 SLA's annual pledge to graduate education in librarianship.

The number of SLA Student Groups grew to 31 in 1988 with the addition of three new groups: University of California, Berkeley; Catholic University of America; and Rutgers University. SLA's commitment to the development of Student Groups is evidenced by the new services it provides to SLA student members, most notably the publishing of the *Student Group News,* a quarterly newsletter.

Conclusion

Many new programs and services were initiated by SLA for the benefit of its membership and the library and information community in 1988. In light of the accomplishment of many of the goals that had been set by the association's Long-Range Plan in 1985, the board of directors reviewed and revised SLA's future plan, renaming the committee responsible for developing the direction of the association as the Strategic Planning Committee. During its June 1988 meeting, the board approved a new mission statement for the plan that will lead SLA into the year 2000 on a revitalized and reenergized course that reflects the growth and vitality of the association and its members. The statement now reads, "The mission of the Special Libraries Association is to advance the role of its members in putting knowledge to work thus taking a leadership role in shaping the destiny of our Information Society."

Society of American Archivists

600 S. Federal St., Suite 504, Chicago, IL 60605
312-922-0140

Donn C. Neal
Executive Director

During 1988, the Society of American Archivists (SAA) continued to develop several projects of major significance to the archival community. One initiative, expansion of continuing education opportunities for archivists, reached full stride with the creation and offer of a series of short courses and related curricular materials. Funded by the National Historical Publications and Records Commission (NHPRC) and the Andrew W. Mellon Foundation, the project also established an education office within SAA. With the assistance of newly revised graduate education guidelines, the society also moved to strengthen the preappointment training of archivists.

Two projects funded by the National Endowment for the Humanities continued earlier SAA educational initiatives. One, in automation, moved beyond teaching the MARC AMC format to help archivists understand library descriptive standards and to prepare a new edition of *Archives, Personal Papers, and Manuscripts.* The other, in preservation, assisted the society to evaluate its activities in conservation education and to design initiatives to meet future needs in this area.

Work also began in earnest during 1988 on a new series entitled Archival Fundamentals, consisting of seven manuals dealing with the principal archival functions and processes, including archives in society, acquisitions and appraisal, arrangement and description, reference and access, and the administration of archival repositories. The series is partially funded by NHPRC. SAA's existing manual on conservation will be revised to become part of the new series, which will also include a glossary of archival terms.

Two other NHPRC-funded projects nearing completion made significant contributions to archival literature. The Committee on Goals and Priorities published a major report, *An Action Agenda for the Archival Profession,* that identified key initiatives needed in five broad areas of professional work. SAA's Task Force on Institutional Evaluation published a test edition of a workbook for archival managers that, by incorporating data from the 1985 census of archival institutions, will allow managers to assess the strengths and weaknesses of their own institution.

Certification

During 1988, SAA also continued to develop a plan for the voluntary certification of individual archivists. Progress was made on three fronts: the petition process to get certification started; preparation for the certification examination; and increasing awareness of and support for the program among archivists.

SAA's Interim Board for Certification created a petition form to collect information about the education and experience of eligible archivists and established procedures for evaluating information submitted by archivists requesting certification. The forms were distributed at the SAA annual meeting and will be available for a one-year period, ending September 30, 1989, during which certification by petition is possible. The initial group of certified archivists will be announced early in 1989, as the committee reviewing petitions evaluates them and acts. Once 100 archivists are certified, an autonomous Academy of Certified Archivists can be created.

Meanwhile, an experienced testing firm selected by the Interim Board has been assisting in developing an objective, practice-based certification examination, which will be administered for the first time at SAA's 1989 annual meeting and at least once a year thereafter. The process of preparing a reliable and comprehensive examination began with a "role-delineation" meeting at which a group of representative archivists defined the tasks that archivists perform and the knowledge they need to perform them in a competent manner. Once the role-delineation document has been validated by nearly 200 other archivists, it will guide a series of four item-development workshops that will involve still more archivists. Workshop participants will write at least 200 potential examination questions, from which an examination-development committee will select the 100 items for the first examination. In succeeding years, item-development workshops will enlarge and refresh the pool of potential questions to ensure that the examination keeps current with an evolving profession and maintains its integrity.

Both the petition phase of certification and the examination process that will replace it in 1989 will certify an archivist for eight years, after which recertification will be necessary. The fee for either phase, including application fees, is $275.

Along with other proponents of certification, during 1988 the Interim Board worked to increase awareness of the new initiative and its benefits through written communications, presentations at professional meetings, and individual discussions. Not everyone was convinced by their arguments, to be sure; a large minority of archivists remained opposed to certification in principle, skeptical about the announced plan, or dissatisfied with the certification fee. With the SAA Council's final approval of a certification program, however, the issue shifted to whether enough archivists would actually become certified, first through petitions and then by examination. Only time will tell if SAA's venture to provide the archival profession with a visible credential based on an objective standard of archival competence will succeed or fail.

SAA's Annual Meeting

Atlanta was the site of SAA's fifty-second annual meeting, attended by 1,100 persons, which was the occasion for nearly 100 program sessions, numerous preconference workshops, dozens of meetings of all types, and a variety of other professional and cultural activities, as well as the installation of new officers and Council members. SAA also presented its annual awards, as follows:

Distinguished Service Award: Bentley Historical Library/Michigan Historical Collections, University of Michigan

Waldo Gifford Leland Prize: Nancy Gwinn for *Preservation Microfilming*

Philip M. Hamer–Elizabeth Kegan Hamer Award: Nancy Bartlett and Kathleen Koehler, Bentley Historical Library, for *A Book Of Days: 150 Years of Student Life at Michigan*

Sister M. Claude Lane Award: Brother Denis Sennett, S.A., Friars of Atonement

Fellows Posner Prize: Avra Michelson, Smithsonian Institution

Theodore Calvin Pease Award: Gregory Kinney, University of Michigan

C.F. W. Coker Prize: a software system developed by Frederick Honhart at Michigan State University

Colonial Dames Scholarships: Doris Martinson, Knox County Archives, and Margaret Nelson, Smithsonian Institution

Oliver Wendell Holmes Award: Jan Boomgaard (the Netherlands), Alan Ives (Australia), and Ann Pederson (Australia)

Receiving the society's highest individual honor, designation as fellow, were Bruce Dearstyne, Anne Diffendal, Lawrence Dowler, and James Fogerty.

Association of Research Libraries

1527 New Hampshire Ave. N.W., Washington, DC 20036
202-232-2466

Nicola Daval
Program Officer

The Association of Research Libraries (ARL) is an organization of 119 major research libraries in the United States and Canada. ARL is an effective advocate for research libraries in both the library and scholarly communities, as well as in government and the private sector. It serves as a forum for consideration of issues, conducts studies, and develops plans to promote coordinated, collective action among its member institutions as they adapt to change in the world of scholarship and information, to new technological developments, and to increasingly stringent economic conditions.

Highlights of 1988 Activities

The University of Illinois at Chicago became ARL's one-hundred and nineteenth member late in 1988. UIC is the first institution invited to join ARL on the basis of membership criteria adopted by the ARL membership in May 1987.

Duane E. Webster was appointed executive director of the association in February 1988. Webster, who was previously director of the Office of Management Studies and ARL deputy executive director, succeeded Shirley Echelman, who had served as ARL executive director from May 1981 through October 1987. Jeffrey Gardner, formerly associate director of the Office of Management Studies, was appointed director of OMS in May 1988. In June, Jaia Barrett, ARL program officer for federal relations, was appointed ARL assistant executive director, and Susan Jurow, OMS program officer for training, was named OMS associate director.

The ARL Office of Management Studies was renamed in May 1988, and is now the ARL Office of Management Services. The new name reflects more accurately the emphasis of the OMS in helping research libraries meet the challenges of rapidly developing technology, new organizational demands, and changing economic conditions.

ARL held two membership meetings in 1988. The May meeting, held in Oakland, California, had two primary focuses: planning for ARL's future and a program exploring the background, technical aspects, applications, and future implications of linked systems. The papers from the latter session, "Linked Systems," were published during the summer. The one-hundred and thirteenth membership meeting was a joint meeting, held in York, England, with the Standing Conference on National and University Libraries (SCONUL), the British counterpart to ARL. The program, "Collections: Their Development, Management, Preservation, and Sharing," drew a substantial number of ARL and SCONUL directors interested in this unique opportunity to meet and confer with colleagues facing similar challenges and obligations but in very different local environments. The meeting concluded with a call for closer ties between the two organizations. The papers from the York meeting will be published in 1989.

During 1988, ARL initiated the Visiting Program Officer Program, designed to provide personal growth and professional development opportunities for mid- and senior level staff in ARL libraries while at the same time allowing the association to tap the pool of talented staff in its member libraries to work directly on its agenda of issues and projects. The first two participants are Diane H. Smith of the Pennsylvania State Libraries, who will work on access and information policy issues, and Rhonda MacInnes of the National Library of Canada, who will work with the OMS training program. The home institution provides financial support for participants in the program.

The year 1988 was the final year of the ARL five-year plan, adopted by the membership in 1983 and implemented in 1984. The objectives of the plan addressed scholarly communication, access to research materials, preservation, information policy, staffing of research libraries, and management. New planning efforts launched in 1988 will continue into 1989.

Access to Research Resources

Serials Prices

Rapidly rising serials prices continued to be a major ARL focus in 1988. In the spring, ARL contracted with Economic Consulting Services, Inc. (ECS), to conduct analyses of serials prices and the costs of serials publishing as part of a feasibility study on alternative methods of distributing scholarly information, including consideration of alternative publishing organizations and modes and formats for scholarly communication. A major goal of the project is to determine the possibility of introducing new competition into the serials publishing industry in order to moderate pricing behavior. The analyses will look at price trends of a selected group of serials over a 15-year period, and will investigate factors contributing to price increases—for example, currency fluctuations, such increased costs as postage, paper, and staff associated with publication and distribution, and profit motivation. The study will also include a thorough assessment of the impact of serials price trends on research library collections and the libraries' ability to serve their users, the impact on scholarly material in various fields, and the specific responses of libraries.

The serials pricing study grew out of ARL member libraries' concern over the impact of sharply rising serials costs on their ability to serve the research and scholarly communities. The study will clarify the economics of the journal industry and lead to consideration of further strategies for influencing costs and the availability of scholarly communication in both the short and long term. Current ECS efforts are directed toward developing costs indexes for publishing and distributing scientific and technical journals for publishers in the United States and three Western European countries. Price-per-page data from 1973 to the present will also be analyzed for a sample of 165 journal titles, representing four major publishers. The long-term objective of the project is to moderate the rate of serials price increases, particularly those of the commercial sector. A strategic emphasis of the study will be to determine the potential for introducing elements of competition into the technical and scientific journal market in an attempt to moderate the rate of price increases. The report is scheduled for completion in 1989.

An early product of the Serials Project was *ARL Briefing Package 1988-2: Rising Serials Prices and Research Libraries,* distributed to the membership in August.

The briefing package provides member libraries with descriptive, statistical, and analytical information that can be used to inform and educate their various constituencies as to the seriousness of the problems related to rising serials prices.

Collections Inventory

The third phase of the North American Collections Inventory Project (NCIP) ended in June 1988. The project has become an ongoing, self-supporting ARL program. NCIP was designed to develop an online inventory of North American research library collections, building on work of the Research Libraries Group, begun in 1979, and collaborative efforts of RLG and ARL since 1983, to develop a standard approach to describing and assessing research library collections in specific subject areas covering a full range of scholarly interests. This approach has led to a database, the Online Conspectus, that provides information on the location of specific subject collections and relative collection strengths and language coverage. The database, managed by RLG, is also available in printed form. The ARL Office of Management Services operates NCIP and serves as distributor for Conspectus materials to non-RLG libraries.

NRMM Project

During 1987, in partnership with the Library of Congress, ARL negotiated an agreement with the Computer Company of Richmond, Virginia, for retrospective conversion of all monographic reports in the *National Register of Microform Masters.* During the project, the Computer Company will produce about 460,000 machine-readable records, between 30 and 40 percent of them not previously converted. Staff in LC's MARC Editorial and Cataloging Management and Publications Divisions review converted records to ensure that they conform to guidelines established by ARL and LC, based on ARL's *Guidelines for Retrospective Conversion of Bibliographic Records for Monographs.* Beginning in 1989, LC's Cataloging Distribution Services will compile tapes containing the records and sell them with no constraints on further reproductions or distribution to libraries, networks, and any other organization. As of November 30, 1988, 70,000 records had been converted. The project, which is supported by grants from the National Endowment for the Humanities and the Andrew W. Mellon Foundation, is expected to be completed at the end of 1989.

Preservation

The preservation of the intellectual content and, to the extent possible, the physical form of research library materials was one of ARL's six major objectives in 1983. Since then, ARL has supported efforts to increase awareness of preservation problems in the higher education and federal arenas and to work for legislative support for preservation activities. In March 1988, ARL representatives took part in congressional hearings on the brittle books problem and appropriations hearings for the National Endowment for the Humanities, emphasizing the need for accelerated Endowment support for preservation efforts. Growing interest in encouraging publishers to use permanent paper led to ARL's third *Briefing Package* in November 1988, focusing on *Preserving Knowledge: The Case for Alkaline Paper.* The package was produced in conjunction with the Commission on Preservation and Access and the National Humanities Alliance, with funding from the commission. It has been distributed to the ARL membership and to publishers, legislators, scholars, and others interested in the preservation of research materials.

In December, *Meeting the Preservation Challenge,* the papers from the October 1987 ARL membership meeting, was published. The program, "Preservation: A Research Library Priority for the 1990s," covered a number of preservation issues from the perspectives of library directors, preservation administrators, and foundation representatives.

Assisting ARL libraries to improve their preservation activities continued to be a major emphasis for the Office of Management Services. OMS received a three-year grant of $145,167 from the National Endowment for the Humanities to help support the training of six experienced preservation librarians to serve as consultants to libraries in the OMS Preservation Planning Program, the participation of ten member libraries in completing the Preservation Planning Program, and a formal evaluation of the program.

Information Policy

Legislative Affairs

A number of legislative issues captured the attention of ARL during 1988. As in the past, funding for library programs was a primary focus, in particular, appropriations for Title II of the Higher Education Act and the FY 1989 budgets for the Library of Congress, the Government Printing Office, and the National Endowment for the Humanities. Increased funding for library preservation efforts also received substantial attention.

Limitation on access to information continues to be a major ARL concern. ARL issued *Briefing Package 1988-1, The FBI in Libraries* in June, and participated in congressional hearings on the FBI Library Awareness Program. The ARL membership also adopted a "Statement on Library Users' Right to Confidentiality" at the May 1988 membership meeting. ARL continues to monitor other issues such as the Federal Depository Library Program, copyright—including electronic formats—proposed privatization of the National Technical Information Service, and other legislation and federal regulations that affect public access to information.

Government Information in Electronic Format

In May 1988, the ARL membership adopted the following six principles on access to government information in electronic format:

1. The open exchange of public information should be protected.
2. Federal policy should support the integrity and preservation of government electronic databases.
3. Copyright should not be applied to U.S. government information.
4. Diversity of sources of access to U.S. government information is in the public interest and entrepreneurship should be encouraged.

5 Government information should be available at low cost.

6 A system to provide equitable, no-fee access to basic public information is a requirement of a democratic society.

The principles were prepared by the Task Force on Government Information in Electronic Format and issued in the task force's 1987 report, *Technology & U.S. Government Information Policies: Catalysts for New Partnerships.* ARL also has been active in encouraging Congress and the Government Printing Office to proceed with a series of projects to test the use of electronic formats in the Depository Library Program.

Staffing for Research Libraries

Library Education

ARL's commitment to improve staffing for research libraries encompasses both the preparation of new staff and the development of existing staff to meet changing demands. Following the success of its 1984 and 1986 Institutes on Research Libraries for Library and Information Science Faculty, OMS conducted its third such institute in Chicago during summer 1988. Cosponsored by the Association of Library and Information Science Education (ALISE) and the Association of College and Research Libraries (ACRL) and funded by the Council on Library Resources, the 1988 institute concentrated on collection development. Twelve faculty members from the United States and Canada participated.

OMS Training Programs

More than 400 librarians attended OMS training programs in 1988, which included OMS Management Skills Institutes in 11 locations, two Analytical Skills Institutes, and one Managing the Learning Process Institute. Special Focus Workshops, short programs commissioned by individual libraries, focused on a variety of topics, such as team building, motivation, and planning for change. A new program introduced in 1988, the Creativity to Innovation Workshop, focuses on techniques to build personal and organizational capacity for creativity. The workshop is designed to develop creative problem-solving skills among librarians and library managers.

Management of Research Libraries

OMS Programs

The ARL Office of Management Services continued to provide support to research libraries seeking to improve their management and service capabilities through its program of assisted self-studies (e.g., collection analysis, preservation, public services) and its active publications program, as well as the activities already described. Of particular interest is the automation inventory of ARL member libraries, which includes information on automation status, equipment, and expenditures. The data are available in a published report and are being maintained in an online database.

ARL Statistics Program

Maintaining the integrity of its statistical data has been an ARL priority for many years. The Committee on ARL Statistics continues to explore a number of issues, including document statistics, how to collect and display additional data on ARL member library resources, and development of access measures. In 1988, ARL published the 1986–1987 *ARL Statistics,* as well as the *ARL Annual Salary Survey* (for 1986).

Summary

Aware of its important role as a vital force in the library, research, and higher education communities, the Association of Research Libraries will continue its efforts to identify and solve the problems common to large research libraries so that they may serve more effectively the needs of students, faculty, and the research community in general. ARL will also continue its efforts to strengthen and extend the capacity of North American research libraries to provide the recorded information needed both now and in the future by the research community.

American Society for Information Science

1424 16th St. N.W., Washington, DC 20036
202-462-1000

Linda Resnik
Executive Director

Throughout 1988, the American Society for Information Science (ASIS) celebrated its long-awaited fiftieth anniversary with dozens of events, publications, and services for the information community. Incorporating widespread membership participation in a broad range of efforts, including public affairs, membership recruitment, research support, publishing, and state-of-the-art information dissemination, ASIS emphasized its continuing role as the information society for the information age with service to all professionals in the diverse fields of information science. By October, when the anniversary celebration ended in Atlanta at the fifty-first ASIS annual meeting, the membership was infused with a new level of enthusiasm that underpinned the process of setting the profession's agenda for the second 50 years.

"Information and Technology: Planning for the Second 50 Years," the theme of the annual meeting, set the tone for both the technical events at the annual conference as well as members' governance activities. Throughout the week, more than 1,000 members and colleagues discussed the areas of greatest personal and professional interest on which they hoped that ASIS and the information community at large would focus. By the end of the week, the beginnings of the new agenda were firmly in place.

Plenary speakers—including Stewart Brand, author of *The Media Lab: Inventing the Future at MIT*; Robert W. Lucky, executive director of the Communications Sciences Research Division at AT&T Bell Laboratories; Rudy Cypser, director of technical communications at IBM; Toni Carbo Bearman, dean of the School of Library and Information Science at the University of Pittsburgh; Robert Lee Chartrand, senior fellow in Information Policy and Technology, Congressional Research Service; and Edwin Brownrigg, director of computing and information technology at Bond University—spoke of the thresholds in information science and technology and helped their audiences assess the future directions most appropriate to the field.

The Smithsonian Institution, which is building its largest-ever permanent exhibition, entitled "The Information Age: Visions and Realities," offered conference attendees a second exclusive preview of the exhibition in the ASIS Exhibit Hall. Scheduled to open in 1990, "The Information Age" focuses attention on the dimensions of information's role in society.

History of ASIS

When founded in 1937 as the American Documentation Institute (ADI), the society consisted of scientific and professional organizations, foundations, and government agencies with an orientation toward solving information-related problems using a promising new medium—microfilm. At that time, microfilm offered the first practical alternative to paper documentation and represented an exponential increase in the amount of information that could be stored and transmitted.

Over the years, the leaders of ADI recognized that greater opportunities for impact on the burgeoning information profession rested in an emphasis on the *science* of information rather than on the specific *medium* of information. Thus, by the late 1960s, ADI had amended its bylaws to include individual members and had changed the name of the organization to its current American Society for Information Science. In the years since, ASIS has expanded its role within the information profession and, today, is the most active information organization in the development and application of information technologies.

SIGs and Chapters

Since the early 1970s, many ASIS activities have been prepared under the auspices of chapters and Special Interest Groups (SIGs) created by the membership to represent them and their interests in several areas. More than 50 local and student chapters throughout the United States, Canada, Europe, and Asia serve the professional needs of members in specific geographic areas. Each chapter builds its own program of activities geared to the needs of its membership.

In 1988, in honor of ASIS's fiftieth anniversary, chapters played a major role in recognizing the contributions to information science made by many early leaders in information storage, retrieval, and dissemination. The ASIS chapter in Columbus, Ohio, a city in which numerous major information companies operate, celebrated the contributions and achievements of such organizations as Battelle, Chemical Abstracts Service, and ASIS at a day-long symposium. (The speeches presented at the symposium were later published in a booklet.) The Los Angeles Chapter of ASIS held a fiftieth anniversary gala party to honor the dozens of national information leaders who work or live in Southern California.

ASIS Special Interest Groups, which cover virtually every technology and subject area in information storage and retrieval in which developments have been recorded, continued their tradition of providing members with news and updates on the latest research in the various fields of information science and technology emphasizing the potential application of new developments. ASIS SIGs on Medical Information Systems and Biological and Chemical Information Systems, among others, received corporate sponsorship to broaden their reach into new market areas. SIG/Personal Computers introduced an important new service for the information community with its directory of bulletin boards in use in libraries and similiar organizations.

Special Initiatives

At the beginning of her term, Martha E. Williams, professor of information science at the University of Illinois and ASIS president through October 1988, announced plans for an Information Science Indicators project, a scientific effort to quantify information science and establish it as a recognized discipline. As an important step in the process, Williams initiated the ASIS 2000 project, an intensive effort in which the organization's leadership and membership would participate to describe information science as it would be in the year 2000. The results of the effort, which would include elements of a long-range plan for ASIS, would be the basis for the scientific inquiry into information science quantifiers.

In 1988, ASIS also continued its tradition of developing a major information industry topic in depth at the annual midyear meeting. "Artificial Intelligence: Expert Systems and Other Applications" drew some 400 attendees for a detailed view of the new techniques that are redirecting the information profession.

At the end of October 1988, new officers took their seats on the ASIS board of directors. The new ASIS president, W. David Penniman, AT&T Bell Laboratories, announced that he would continue to pursue the Information Science Indicators and ASIS 2000 projects, and would also embark on a major recruitment effort, asking every ASIS member to become a mentor to one new member of the organization.

Awards

Winners of the 1988 ASIS annual awards were honored at the society's fifty-first annual meeting in Atlanta. The 1988 Award of Merit, the society's highest honor, was presented to F. Wilfrid Lancaster, University of Illinois, in recognition of his outstanding contributions as a researcher, teacher, and author. Other 1988 ASIS award winners include Harold Borko, professor at the University of California, Los Angeles, Outstanding Information Science Teacher; *Federal Information Policies in the 1980s: Conflicts and Issues,* by Peter Hernon and Charles R. McClure, published by Ablex, Best Information Science Book; Susanne M. Humphrey and Nancy E. Miller, "Knowledge-Based Indexing of the Medical Literature: The Indexing Aid Project," Best *JASIS* Paper; Stephanie W. Haas, ISI Information Science Doctoral Dissertation Scholarship; Elizabeth DuRoss Liddy and Clifford A. Lynch, Doctoral Forum Award; and Charlotte Weise and Stuart McLean, Student Paper Award. Bonnie C. Carroll, Oak Ridge, Tennessee, received the Watson Davis Award, given annually to an individual or individuals for outstanding continuous service to the society.

Publications

In celebration of its fiftieth anniversary, in June 1988 the society published a special commemorative magazine highlighting many of the accomplishments in information science during the society's first 50 years. Almost an immediate classic, the magazine is being used in library and information science schools throughout the United States as a resource in teaching the history of information science.

New volumes were introduced in two successful ASIS series in 1988: Volume 23 of the prestigious *Annual Review of Information Science and Technology (ARIST),* edited by Martha E. Williams and published for ASIS by Elsevier, and Volume 24 of the *Proceedings of the ASIS Annual Meeting*, edited by Christine Borgman and Edward Pai, published by Learned Information, Inc.

ASIS also continued publication of two leading information science periodicals. The *Journal of the American Society for Information Science*, published for ASIS by John Wiley, is a fully refereed scholarly and technical publication. The *Bulletin of the American Society for Information Science,* published by ASIS, is a newsmagazine focusing on issues affecting information science, pragmatic management reports, opinions, and news of people and events in the information science community.

Association of American Publishers

220 E. 23 St., New York, NY 10010
212-689-8920

2005 Massachusetts Ave. N.W., Washington, DC
202-232-3335

Judith Platt
Director of Communications

Established in 1970 through a merger of the American Book Publishers Council and the American Educational Publishers Institute, the Association of American Publishers (AAP) is the voice of the American book publishing industry. AAP's more than 250 member firms are located in every region of the United States and publish the vast majority of printed materials sold to American schools and colleges, libraries, bookstores, business and industry, and through direct-to-consumer marketing channels. They publish hardcover and paperback books in every field—general trade, educational, reference, religious, scientific, medical, technical, professional, and scholarly. AAP member firms also publish journals, computer software, looseleaf services, and a range of educational materials including classroom periodicals, maps, globes, filmstrips, audio- and videotapes, and testing materials. In 1982 the association's membership was broadened to include publishers of freestanding multimedia products including computer software and online databases.

AAP's basic mandate is to promote and expand the market for American books, journals, and software at home and abroad. In all its programs, the association strives to foster greater understanding and appreciation of the unique place of books in the lives of Americans. AAP sponsors activities to promote intellectual freedom and safeguard First Amendment rights; to provide member publishers with current and useful information on government policies, trade conditions, and legislation affecting their business; and to assist members in the management and administration of their companies by offering practical educational programs. AAP speaks for the industry whenever the publisher's voice needs to be heard—in Washington or elsewhere in the United States and overseas.

AAP's mandate covers both the general and the specific: broad issues with which the entire industry is concerned and those of special import for a particular industry group. The association's core programs deal with matters of general interest to all publishers: domestic and international copyright; postal rates and regulations; First Amendment rights, censorship, and libel; international freedom to publish; tax and trade issues; library and educational funding; and new technology. These programs, which are directed by standing committees, along with a range of membership services including the collection and dissemination of statistical data, group insurance plans, public information, and governmental and press relations, form the core of the association's activities.

Each of AAP's six divisions concerns itself with a specific market area: general trade; mass market paperbacks; elementary and secondary textbooks; higher education—college and graduate school—texts; professional and scholarly publications; and the international marketplace. Each division has its own executive body with an annually elected chairperson to give general direction within the framework of AAP's overall program.

AAP policy is set by an 18-member board of directors elected by the membership for four-year terms under a chairperson who serves for two years. Lawrence Hughes (Hearst Trade Book Group) is currently chairman of the board. Ambassador Nicholas A. Veliotes, president of the association, is AAP's chief operating officer and is responsible for managing the association within the guidelines set by the board. AAP maintains offices in New York and in Washington, D.C., with a total of approximately 30 professional and support staff members.

Highlights of 1988 Activities

AAP's eighteenth annual meeting was held at The Breakers in Palm Beach, Florida, March 20–23, 1988. Featured speakers included journalist and former Assistant Secretary of State Hodding Carter III; Congressman Thomas J. Downey of New York; former Maryland Senator Charles McC. Matthias; New York University law professor Burt Neubourne; Register of Copyrights Ralph Oman; Jack Valenti, president of the Motion Picture Association of America; Alton Crews, superintendent of the Gwinnette County (Georgia) public schools; and management consultant Barbara Toffler.

Nat Wartels, chairman of the Crown Publishing Group, was named to receive the thirteenth annual Curtis Benjamin Award for Creative Publishing.

The AAP board of directors issued a strongly worded resolution stating that efforts to keep American books and educational materials out of South Africa in the cause of fighting apartheid are counterproductive. The resolution, which was unanimously adopted by the board on January 14, restated the association's long-standing commitment to the free flow of ideas and information and the free exchange of books and other publications.

AAP and several individual member houses filed comments with the U.S. Copyright Office on the relationship between copyright infringement and the Eleventh Amendment's "sovereign immunity" provisions. The AAP statement, which was filed jointly with the Association of American University Presses, cites the unfairness of using the Eleventh Amendment to bar copyright suits for damages; it calls upon the Copyright Office to make clear to Congress the law's anticipation of full state liability and subjection to remedies for infringement. The two associations asked the Copyright Office to support the adoption of appropriate remedial legislation if the courts continue to conclude that states are immune.

AAP President Nicholas Veliotes delivered the Brace Memorial Lecture at New York University on April 19, describing the new and complex copyright challenges facing American publishers and the ways in which American publishers are redefining their determination to strengthen the principle of copyright in the face of these challenges.

Pursuant to a decision taken by the board of directors in September 1987, AAP established a new category of affiliate membership and welcomed a number of leading book manufacturers, print and typesetting firms, paper manufacturers, and others closely allied to American book publishers into the association.

AAP testified before both houses of Congress insisting that First Amendment rights be protected in sweeping new federal legislation aimed at curbing the distribution of sexually explicit works.

According to data released by AAP in July, book sales totaled $11,447,220,000 in 1987, an increase of 9.2 percent, or $963 million over the 1986 figure. Trade book sales reflected the highest percentage of increase.

In the wake of Richard Morgan's departure from Scott, Foresman, which left vacant the chairmanship of the AAP board of directors, Lawrence Hughes, chairman of the Hearst Trade Book Group, was unanimously elected on September 28 to serve as AAP chairman for the remainder of Morgan's term, until March 30, 1989, and for an additional year beyond that date.

PUBNET, an applications and data communications network originally developed to serve college publishers and booksellers, was adapted for use by trade publishers and booksellers and was officially introduced in September at a meeting of the Southeast Booksellers Association in Nashville. More than 24 publishers representing over half the trade-mass market business signed on as PUBNET charter members. Some 350 trade book stores are expected to sign up for PUBNET by March 1, 1989.

Divisions

General Publishing Division

The General Publishing Division (GPD), chaired by Howard Kaminsky (Hearst Trade Book Group), represents publishers of fiction, nonfiction, children's literature, and religious and reference books. Its programs, often carried out in conjunction with other AAP divisions, seek to broaden the audience for books, strengthen ties with the bookselling and library communities, and help publishers improve their management and marketing skills. The division maintains close ties with the American Booksellers Association, the National Association of College Stores, and the American Library Association. Joint liaison committees meet on a regular basis to review shared concerns and seek solutions to common problems. Close ties are also maintained with the Children's Book Council, PEN, the Authors Guild, and other groups. The General Publishing Division works closely with the Center for the Book in the Library of Congress seeking ways to promote books and reading, and is an active advocate for literacy promotion projects. The division cosponsored, with AAP's Paperback Publishing Division, an "Evening of Readings" on June 2, 1988, which raised more than $100,000 for the Literacy Volunteers of New York City. The division is a major contributor to the National Book Awards.

In an ongoing effort to strengthen lines of communication between authors and publishers, the division launched a series of workshops in cooperation with PEN. The most recent of these, held in fall 1988, focused on legal aspects of publishing. The division also cosponsored, with the Authors Guild, a series of roundtable forums on such topics as out-of-print, warranty, and indemnification clauses.

Responding to the special concerns of its children's book publisher members, in summer 1988, the division established a special Children's Publishing Committee. Among the areas to be looked at by the new committee are possible development of a national reading initiative and censorship and freedom to read issues as they relate to children's books.

At the 1988 AAP annual meeting, the General Publishing and Paperback Publishing Divisions voted to sponsor the publication *You Can Do Something about AIDS* being put together by Alyson Publications of Boston for distribution by Ingram Books. The 126-page book, which contains chapters written by celebrities and medical experts, is being distributed to the public free of charge.

On September 24 trade publishers and booksellers were offered charter membership in the new Trade PUBNET. The same offer was made at the Mid-Atlantic and New York Regional Booksellers Association meetings and at a meeting of the New England Booksellers Association. More than 24 publishers, representing more than half of the trade–mass market business, signed on as PUBNET charter members. Originally developed to serve college publishers and booksellers, PUBNET is an applications and data communications network that is now expanding into the trade market. The system is available both off- and online. Future enhancements will include an electronic mailbox that will allow publishers to inform customers about author appearances and other news on short notice. Discussions are also being held with two large suppliers of trade software systems, IBID and Wordstock.

The General Publishing Division published its fifteenth annual *Exhibits Directory,* a listing of some 500 meetings of educational, scientific, library, and technical associations of interest to publishers. It continued sponsorship of the "I'd Rather Be Reading" promotional campaign in cooperation with the Center for the Book in the Library of Congress, and it also sponsored a series of informative roundtable publishers' forum luncheon meetings on various subjects of interest to trade publishers.

Higher Education Division

The Higher Education Division (HED) is concerned with all aspects of marketing,

secondary education. Siebert Adams of McGraw-Hill is the current chairman of HED.

PUBNET, the electronic data interchange network designed for the college publishing industry, ended its second and most successful year. During 1988, the PUBNET bookstore base grew from 125 to 380 stores, with total orders processed exceeding 60,000 by year's end. Workshops were held at various college bookstore meetings, with a primary workshop held at the NACS convention in Cincinnati. Workshops were also held for publishers in other segments of the industry to explore the possibilities of expanding the system to serve their needs.

HED sponsors the popular AAP/WEST seminars for publishers west of the Rocky Mountains. The spring seminar held May 4 in San Francisco offered insights to aid in career advancement in publishing. The fall seminar, "Infotech," held October 20, focused on high tech applications specific to the publishing industry and included a vendor fair where selected software and hardware were demonstrated. The division also cosponsored AAP's PubCenter at the National Association of College Stores's 1988 meeting, the largest and most successful to date, with 42 participating publishers occupying 65 booths.

The first annual HED Achievement Awards were presented May 24 at a special dinner in Cambridge, Massachusetts, during the HED annual meeting to honor an outstanding member of the higher education publishing community. James F. Leisy, co-founder and retired CEO of Wadsworth, Inc., and the late William A. Pullin of Harcourt Brace Jovanovich were named to receive awards. The HED annual meeting, which focused on the theme "Beyond Survival: Strategies for the '90's," featured educators, publishers, and representatives of the financial community speaking on organizational change, new technologies, and customer relations.

The division continued its ongoing efforts to increase public awareness of the damage to authors and publishers that results from the sale of complimentary textbook copies. An information kit was mailed by the division in fall 1988 to the presidents of faculty senates at more than 3,000 colleges and universities across the United States. A fact sheet in the kit pointed out that author/professors at American colleges and universities are losing an estimated $10 million in royalties annually as a result of the sale by their colleagues of complimentary and review copies of textbooks. The practice results in greater upward pressure on textbook prices, and does little to benefit students, as the complimentary review copies are usually sold at a minimum of 75 percent of new book prices. The mailing was cited as the latest phase in a productive dialogue which AAP's Higher Education Division initiated last year with the academic community. The information kit also contained an AAP white paper on the problem, along with a proposed "statement on ethical behavior" for possible evaluation by faculty senates. Resolutions against the practice of selling complimentary copies have already been adopted at several universities.

HED's effective public relations program, the AAP Student Service, strengthened ties with college students through a number of popular brochures. The AAP College Textbook Fiche Service began its tenth year of operation, providing college bookstore subscribers with microfiche, updated monthly, of some 88,000 textbook titles available from more than three dozen leading publishers.

International Division

The International Division (ID), chaired by Bernard Finnegan (Macmillan), is concerned with marketing American books and related products overseas through direct sales, copublishing ventures, sales of English-language and translation rights, and the promotion of English as a second language. Among the division's highest priorities are improving trade relations with the Third World; developing members' professional skills through seminars and workshops; developing and strengthening ties with those U.S. government agencies, including USIA and the Departments of State and Commerce, most concerned with promoting American books abroad; fostering international respect for copyright; gathering and disseminating international sales data; and promoting U.S. publisher attendance at and active participation in international book fairs. AAP activities in the international arena in 1988 included several high-level discussions with Mikhail Nenaschev, chairman of the State Committee for Publishing Houses, Printing Plants, and the Book Trade (Goskomizidat), of the U.S.S.R.; the annual meeting with the British Publishers Association during the Frankfurt Book Fair; and meetings with publishers' delegations from Japan and China.

The International Division coordinated AAP activities at the second Beijing International Book Fair in September, including cosponsorship of two seminars that focused on the marketing and distribution of scientific, technical, and medical materials, copyright, and rights and permissions. A bilingual report, "AAP at the Beijing Book Fair, 1988," prepared by the division, was made available to interested publishers.

The International Division once again sponsored its International Visitors' Center at the ABA Convention in Anaheim, California. The center, which is staffed by ID publishers, provides a place for overseas booksellers, publishers, and agents to meet with American publishers. The division held its annual meeting just prior to the opening of ABA. The program featured a full day of reports and discussion on export marketing for U.S. books.

The International Division undertook a joint project with the American Booksellers Association to prepare the directory *Who's Who (Internationally) at ABA '88.* Based on data gathered through questionnaires distributed at Frankfurt, the directory contains a listing of more than 300 foreign publishers, wholesalers, agents, and booksellers who attended the 1988 ABA Convention.

In the wake of the successful international rights meeting in 1987, the division and the Frankfurt Book Fair organization cosponsored a second meeting in October 1988. International experts spoke in four panel sessions. Similar future meetings are planned.

Paperback Publishing Division

The Paperback Publishing Division (PPD) focuses on issues of special pertinence to mass market paperback publishers. The division works to develop and expand the market for paperback books, highlighting their unique value for educational and recreational reading and exploring new approaches to marketing, production, and distribution. The division is chaired by David Shanks (Putnam Berkley Group).

In the belief that Americans' best interests ultimately lie in building a "reading society," PPD actively supports literacy projects such as its recent campaign to place literacy ads in paperback books. With the General Publishing Division it cosponsored an "Evening of Readings" to benefit the Literacy Volunteers of New York City on June 2. It is also a major contributor to the National Book Awards program. The division's ad hoc Publicity Committee sponsors the "I'd Rather Be Reading" promotional campaign in collaboration with the Center for the Book in the Library of Congress. To date, the campaign has disseminated more than 750,000 promotional items to wholesalers, schools, and libraries across the country.

PPD sponsors a highly successful cooperative exhibits program that enables publishers to exhibit books at a number of trade shows for a fraction of the cost of an individual exhibit. The division also sponsors a book previews program at the NACS annual meeting that alerts college bookstore buyers to paperback titles that will be popular on campuses in the coming year. In efforts to open communication between publishers and wholesalers, the division has undertaken sponsorship of a wholesaler/publisher workshop program giving chief executive officers of paperback publishing houses and wholesaler firms a forum in which to discuss industry problems.

In fall 1988, the Paperback Publishing Division sponsored a well-received book training workshop for wholesalers. The four-day session was structured to help sales representatives, marketing managers, and supervisors in the wholesale book business develop more profitable book operations. The workshop will be given again in 1989 on the West Coast and in the Southeast.

A settlement reached in summer 1988 in New York State Supreme Court successfully ended a six-year court battle to halt the illegal sale of "stripped books." The suit, which was coordinated by the Paperback Publishing Division, was originally filed by 13 mass market publishers. In the final settlement all remaining defendants agreed, in a "consent to judgment," to cease all sales of stripped books, to inform publishers if they became aware of such sales by others, and to pay fines should they violate the judgment. The division indicated that it will continue its vigilance on the issue.

In another case coordinated by the division, the U.S. District Court for the northern district of California found book importer J. Ben Stark in contempt for violating an earlier injunction against importing and selling books whose distribution rights were held by American publishers. The decision, handed down in late August, also ordered Stark to pay legal fees incurred by the plaintiffs in seeking to enforce an earlier judgment.

Professional and Scholarly Publishing Division

The Professional and Scholarly Publishing Division (PSP), under the chairmanship of Robert Baensch (American Institute of Physics), is concerned with all aspects of publishing technical, scientific, medical, and scholarly materials. Division members produce books, journals, computer software, loose-leaf services, databases, and CD-ROM products directed primarily, but not exclusively, to the practicing engineer and scientist, the professional business community, and the scholarly and academic communities. Professional societies and university presses play a key role in divisional activities.

The 1988 PSP annual conference was held in Washington, D.C., February 4–6. As part of its commitment to excellence, the division sponsors an annual awards program that acknowledges and promotes outstanding examples of professional and scholarly publishing. Among the presentations at the twelfth annual PSP awards ceremony in Washington was the prestigious R. R. Hawkins Award for an outstanding technical, scientific, or medical book, which went to Macmillan Publishing Company for its *Encyclopedia of Religion.* First place awards were also presented to books in nine subject categories, journal and loose-leaf publications, microcomputer software, and book and journal design and production.

In 1988, the Professional and Scholarly Publishing Division sponsored "An Orientation to Marketing" workshop designed for entry-level personnel in scholarly publishing firms. A 32-page booklet, *The Basics of Book Marketing for Professional and Scholarly Publishing,* was developed as a supplement to the marketing course. During the year, PSP also sponsored seminars on journal copyright, exhibiting and boothmanship, professional and scholarly book exhibits, market planning and management, bar coding for professional and scholarly journals, and a highly successful journals publishing course for middle management, which was cosponsored with the International Group of Scientific, Technical, and Medical Publishers. The *PSP Bulletin,* the division's quarterly newsletter, is now in its second year of publication. In 1988 PSP issued the results of a new survey which it had commissioned to study acquisition practices in American corporate, academic, and public libraries. These results will be reviewed at the 1989 divisional meeting in Boston.

School Division

Under the chairmanship of Alfred McDougal (McDougal Littell), the School Division continued its focus on the production, marketing, and distribution of books, software, and other instructional materials for elementary and secondary schools (kindergarten through twelfth grade). The division works to enhance the role of instructional materials in the educational process, to increase funding for educational materials, and to form a bridge between the publishing and educational communities. One of the division's primary goals is simplification of state adoption procedures for textbooks and instructional materials, and to that end it maintains and directs an effective lobbying network to work with school officials at the state and local levels in key adoption states.

School Division committees work to acquaint parents, educators, and others with the concerns of educational publishers through seminars and publications such as *Parents' Guide to More Effective Schools, How a Textbook Is Made,* and *Standardized Testing.* Public service ads and radio spots are part of the division's grassroots public information campaign. The School Division also sponsors an ongoing series of seminars and workshops on subjects of concern to educational publishers and educators.

The School Division's annual meeting, held in Washington, D.C., in January 1988, was entitled "Publishing for the Next Decade: Doing Your Job More Effectively." The 1988 Mary MacNulty Award to an industry member who has demonstrated both a personal commitment to educational publishing and a special concern for the promotion and development of basic educational skills was presented posthumously to James Carsky, senior vice president of Scholastic, Inc., and was accepted by his widow, Kay Carsky.

With the National Council for Social Studies, the School Division cosponsored a national conference entitled "The Challenge of a Changing World: Implications for Social Studies Curriculum and Instructional Materials." The division's Critical Issues in Educational Publishing Committee sponsored a number of seminars on such subjects as "Tomorrow's Teachers, What Do They Want from Publishers?" and "At-Risk Students: What Can Publishers Do to Meet Their Needs?" The division's Research Committee sponsored two seminars: "Positioning Textbooks in Today's Market" and "Questionnaire Design from Basics to New Technology."

Under a continuing program to encourage research on instructional materials and classroom performance, the School Division awards a maximum of two grants each year to doctoral students at accredited schools of education. In May 1988, two doctoral students received $4,000 research grants.

The division established a Depository Task Force to work with states and state textbook depositories to protect publisher interest in states that require depositories. The Statistics Committee revised the division's statistics program to make statistical information more timely and of greater benefit to School Division members.

Core Activities

Copyright Committee

Under the chairmanship of Myer Kutz (John Wiley), the Copyright Committee continued its work to promote and defend the proprietary rights of authors and publishers. The committee monitors copyright activity in the United States and abroad and acts as an advisory body to the board of directors in formulating AAP policy on legislative issues involving copyright. Working with AAP copyright counsel, the committee prepares congressional testimony. It also sponsors a variety of educational activities, seminars, and workshops to increase awareness of the importance of copyright to the artistic and commercial life of the industry.

Publishers and other segments of the copyright community continue to be concerned over assertions that the Eleventh Amendment to the U.S. Constitution grants to states and state agencies (including universities) protection from damage suits for copyright infringement. AAP has filed amicus briefs in a number of court cases arguing that the copyright clause of the Constitution gives Congress the power to abrogate the states' immunity to suit and that the Copyright Act of 1976 clearly expresses congressional intent to do so. AAP has also filed an amicus brief in the U.S. Supreme Court in a case that, although it does not deal directly with copyright, is seen as critical to the question of whether states can be held liable for copyright infringement. The underlying issue in the case is whether or not Congress does have the power under Article I of the Constitution—the source of the copyright law—to abrogate Eleventh Amendment immunity. The U.S. Copyright Office, in a recently issued report, contends that Congress intended to hold states responsible for infringement under the 1976 Copyright Act. A study by the Copyright Office of the relationship between copyright and the Eleventh Amendment was undertaken in fall 1987 at congressional request.

At the urging of AAP and others, Congress eliminated from the Omnibus Trade Bill language extending the provisions of the countervailing and antidumping duties laws to books that might be regarded as "technical publications." AAP had expressed its objections to this provision, stating that it violated both the letter and the spirit of U.S. obligations under the Florence Agreement.

AAP President Nicholas Veliotes delivered the eighteenth annual Donald C. Brace Memorial Lecture, given under the auspices of the Copyright Society of the U.S.A. and New York University. In the lecture, "A New Round of Challenges," Veliotes discussed copyright in the 1980s from the publishers' point of view, touching on some of the crucial issues facing American publishers, including international piracy, photocopying, and the future of copyright. He stressed the "need to counterbalance whatever forces seek to undermine the principle of copyright," underlining the imperative to seek "solutions that will serve the publishing community, librarians, end users, and society as a whole."

AAP sought the assistance of the U.S. Department of State in ending the British Library's Document Supply Centre's (DSC) unauthorized export to American customers of photocopies of copyrighted journal articles and other materials in apparent violation of U.S. copyright law. In a letter to the State Department on June 1, 1988, AAP President Veliotes described the unlicensed, systematic, and wide-scale photocopying of scientific, medical, and technical journals engaged in by the Document Supply Centre, which then distributes the materials to commercial document delivery services and profit-making corporations. Although such activity is at the present lawful within the United Kingdom, the letter points out that such activity "remains terribly abrasive when viewed in the context of relations and commerce between our two countries," noting that U.S. corporations and profit-making document delivery services are among the DSC's principal customers.

The twenty-third congress of the International Publishers Association (IPA) issued a statement expressing deep concern over the activities of the Document Supply Centre. The IPA statement urged the British government to take steps to end the DSC's illegal export of photocopied material and to heed the advice of its own copyright experts and terminate the legality of such activity within the United Kingdom.

AAP and other information industry representatives participated in a policy discussion concerning the first year's pilot operation of a new Machine-Readable Collection Reading Room at the Library of Congress, which officially opened May 24. Serious researchers will have access to several personal computers and printers to examine and use software programs and data collections on floppy disks and CD-ROM acquired by the library. AAP is submitting comments to the library on publishing industry concerns about the operation of this room.

AAP cooperated in the establishment of the Association for Copyright Enforcement, an independent, nonprofit corporation. The group's objective is to ensure vigorous and consistent enforcement of intellectual property rights under the Copyright Law, with a specific focus on illegal photocopying and copyright infringement deriving from the new technologies. Copyright holders will grant the new agency nonexclusive authorization to act on their behalf in bringing suit to halt illegal copying, recover damages, and bring such copying under license. Funding will be provided by copyright holders from royalties collected on their behalf by the Copyright Clearance Center. AAP President Veliotes will serve on the board of directors.

The copyright implications of "electrocopying" are becoming increasingly significant for publishers, and AAP is taking a close look at the issue. ("Electrocopying" is defined as the storage of preexisting, primarily copyrighted material in electronic or machine-readable form, for example, on videodisc or computer tape, for preservation and possible dissemination, in hard copy and/or electronic format.) A paper identifying issues raised by electrocopying was circulated to the AAP membership.

AAP has been monitoring and responding to a number of legislative proposals, including bills that would amend U.S. copyright law to permit U.S. adherence to the Berne Convention, deal with visual artists' rights, establish a national film commission, and increase statutory damages for copyright infringement. The Copyright

Committee's Rights and Permissions Advisory Committee sponsored two workshops in 1988, one in the spring on the practical implications for American publishers of a number of international issues, and a fall workshop on permissions and the media.

Freedom to Read Committee

AAP's Freedom to Read Committee, under the chairmanship of Erwin Glikes (Free Press), works to promote and strengthen First Amendment rights. The committee plays a major educational role promoting, through its reports and public programs, an understanding and appreciation of these rights. Intervention in court cases, testimony before Congress, and coordinated action with other organizations are some of the ways in which the committee meets the threats of censorship and other encroachments on First Amendment freedoms. At a program sponsored by the Freedom to Read Committee during the 1988 AAP annual meeting, Burt Newbourne of New York University delivered a passionate and provocative defense of the First Amendment.

AAP was gratified by the Supreme Court's 8–0 ruling in February that overturned the damage award to the Reverend Jerry Falwell for "emotional distress" caused by a parody advertisement in *Hustler* magazine. AAP had filed an amicus brief in the case, which was considered an important test of First Amendment protection for the press.

Another issue of major concern is the question of the constitutionality of applying antiracketeering laws to confiscate the assets of bookstores selling sexually explicit materials. Through its Freedom to Read Committee, and other members of the Media Coalition, AAP joined in an amicus brief asking the U.S. Supreme Court to review *Fort Wayne Books* v. *The State of Indiana.* The case involves an Indiana RICO (Racketeering-Influenced Corrupt Organization) statute that allows the state to padlock a bookstore and confiscate its contents, including nonobscene books and periodicals, whenever it can demonstrate that the bookseller, as the amicus brief states, "crossed the grey line between what is obscene and what is not." The Supreme Court has agreed to review the case.

A case in which AAP is a coplaintiff challenges a 1985 amendment to Virginia's "harmful to minors" law (which severely restricts the display of reading materials considered unsuitable for young people). In January, the U.S. Supreme Court, before ruling on constitutional questions, asked the Virginia Supreme Court to clarify its interpretation of key points in this case. The court rendered its decision, stating that the term "harmful to minors" did not apply to any of the 16 books used as exhibits by the bookseller-publisher plaintiffs in the original case (among these books were James Joyce's *Ulysses* and John Updike's *The Witches of Eastwick*). In the latest in a series of convoluted legal maneuvers, the U.S. Supreme Court voided a finding by the Fourth Circuit Court of Appeals that the law is unconstitutional and has sent the case back to the appellate court for review in light of the Virginia Supreme Court interpretation.

In an amicus brief filed in the Supreme Court, AAP argued that censorship of reading materials permitted in federal prisons cannot be left to untrained mailroom employees without violating First Amendment rights of publishers as well as prisoners. The brief, in which AAP was joined by the Authors League and the International Periodical Distributors Association, maintains that the standards for determining whether publications are admissible are "superficial at best" and that these standards reflect judgment and prejudices of mailroom personnel and wardens with no special training. In the case at issue such widely acclaimed books as *The David Kopaye Story* and *Solidad Brother: The Prison Letters of George Jackson* were barred through what the brief maintains is an abuse of official discretionary power.

AAP joined fellow members of the Media Coalition in challenging a feminist, antipornography ordinance recently enacted in Bellingham, Washington. The ordinance restricts books, magazines, and movies that depict "the sexually explicit subordination of women." It is substantially similar to an Indiana law that AAP and other coplaintiffs successfully challenged several years ago and which the U.S. Supreme Court found unconstitutional.

A substantial portion of the committee's time and attention during 1988 was taken up with efforts to modify proposed federal antiobscenity legislation that would have swept within its reach not only targeted publishers and sellers of obscenity, but many legitimate publishers and sellers of protected sexually explicit materials as well. Just prior to adjournment, the One-hundredth Congress approved an amended version of the Child Protection and Obscenity Enforcement Act of 1988 as part of the Omnibus Drug Bill. The final version was a compromise, and although provisions of the legislation are still troubling, some of the more egregious assaults on the First Amendment were modified through the efforts of AAP and other members of the Media Coalition. In making its case to modify obscenity enforcement provisions, AAP reiterated its support for legislation protecting children. For a more detailed analysis of this legislation, see "Legislation and Regulations Affecting Publishing in 1988" in Part 2 of this volume.

Unacceptable major revisions of New York State's "Son of Sam" law (which is intended to deny criminals profits from film or print portrayals of their criminal activities) were staved off in the New York legislature, and a frontal attack on the constitutionality of such legislation, supported by an AAP amicus brief, continues to progress in New York federal courts.

The Freedom to Read Committee collaborated with the American Library Association's Intellectual Freedom Committee in a "freedom to write" presentation by author Margaret Truman during ALA's annual conference in New Orleans. AAP continued to cosponsor with ALA, the American Booksellers Association, the National Association of College Stores, and the American Society of Journalists and Authors, Banned Books Week—Celebrating the Freedom to Read. The theme for the September 1988 observance was "Open Books for Open Minds."

International Copyright Protection Group

Under the chairmanship of Allan Wittman (Macmillan), the International Copyright Protection Group (ICPG) continues to coordinate the campaign against international piracy of AAP members' books, journals, software, and databases. The group gathers and disseminates current information on copyright enforcement and piracy, develops antipiracy strategies, and directs lobbying and educational efforts in Washington. The ICPG also coordinates publisher participation in the International Intellectual Property Alliance (IIPA), a copyright industry coalition that AAP helped organize several years ago.

On recommendation of the International Copyright Protection Group, the AAP board of directors approved proposed copyright enforcement actions in Taiwan and Korea. Two law firms have been retained for this purpose. Although Korea became a member of the Universal Copyright Convention in fall 1987, American publishers are still having problems gaining full protection for their works. At the same time that Korea was becoming a member of the UCC, a massive number of pirated American college textbooks went on sale in Korea, books that were not protected under the new law, but only under "administrative guidance." AAP protested vigorously and the U.S. government intervened to ensure that the Korean government met its bilateral commitment to get pre-1987 pirated books off the market. Continued pressure resulted in raids of major bookstores by the Korean government and stepped-up (but not always effective) efforts by a reluctant Korean government to monitor compliance. Recently, enforcement efforts have lagged again and renewed protests have been made. AAP has also set up an enforcement program to bring legal action against pirates of U.S. books covered by the new law. Due again to Korean government reluctance, such actions have been less than effective.

AAP provided assistance to the U.S. government in its effort to renegotiate the 1946 Treaty of Friendship, Commerce and Navigation (FCN) between the United States and Taiwan under which U.S. works are now protected in Taiwan. The key item for renegotiation is the return to the U.S. copyright owner of an exclusive translation right that had been given up in the 1946 FCN Treaty.

The findings of a study by the U.S. International Trade Commission (ITC) released in February 1988 indicate that American firms are losing billions of dollars in sales worldwide as a result of inadequate protection of U.S. intellectual property abroad. The 193 U.S. companies (including 26 book publishers) that responded to the ITC questionnaire reported losses of $23.8 billion in 1986 as a result of inadequate protection of U.S. intellectual property (including trademarks, copyrights, and patents). Included in that figure are $6.2 billion in lost exports of goods and services, $2 billion in lost royalties, and $9.5 billion in losses resulting from the importation and sale of goods and services into the United States. Administration officials projected that if unsurveyed U.S. companies were factored into the estimates, total U.S. losses could bc bctween $43 and $61 billion. Speaking at a White House press conference at which the study results were released, AAP President Veliotes praised the cooperation between the government and the private sector and noted that "we are only now beginning to realize the full extent of the damage piracy is inflicting on our national economy and the staggering costs of inadequate protection of U.S. intellectual property worldwide."

AAP's International Copyright Protection Group is seeking data on book piracy in the Middle East to be used in preparing a new extensive report by the International Intellectual Property Alliance on copyright piracy in the region.

AAP, acting principally through the Alliance, has been working with the U.S. government to fashion specific standards and enforcement proposals for consideration in the current GATT negotiations. AAP has also been involved in international private sector discussions on intellectual property protection that resulted in the recently issued European-U.S.-Japanese industry trilateral agreement recommending to the three respective governments specific copyright standards of protection modeled closely on the Berne Convention.

AAP was instrumental in having language included in the Omnibus Trade Bill that will aid in the fight against international copyright piracy (a detailed discussion of this legislation can be found in "Legislation and Regulations Affecting Publishing in 1988" in Part 2 of this volume).

International Freedom to Publish

The International Freedom to Publish Committee (IFTP), chaired in 1988 by Roland Algrant (Hearst), is the only group in the world formed by a major publishers' organization for the specific purpose of defending and broadening the freedom of written communication. The committee monitors human rights issues and offers moral support and practical assistance to publishers and authors who are denied basic freedoms. It communicates with members of Congress through correspondence and public testimony on human rights, extends invitations to foreign writers and publishers to visit the United States, and contacts foreign authorities on behalf of publishers and authors. The committee works closely with other human rights groups such as Amnesty International and the Helsinki Watch to promote the freedom of writers to express themselves and have their work published without fear or intimidation.

As part of its continuing effort to support the right of free expression for publishing colleagues in other parts of the world, the International Freedom to Publish Committee participated in a joint fact-finding mission with Helsinki Watch to assess the human rights situation in Turkey in September 1988. Representatives of the IFTP and Helsinki Watch spent ten days in Istanbul and Ankara meeting with more than 80 journalists, writers, editors, publishers, human rights activists, and government officials. IFTP and Helsinki Watch will publish a joint report on the mission.

In 1988 the IFTP committee also became involved in the question of embargoing the sale and shipment of American books to South Africa. The committee is organizing a mission representing a number of groups that will go to South Africa to discuss attitudes there toward the boycott of books and other aspects of press and publishing in South Africa.

Just prior to the 1988 Summer Olympic Games, the International Freedom to Publish Committee, along with American PEN, Asia Watch, and the Fund for Free Expression, sent a protest to South Korean President Roh Tae Woo asking that writers imprisoned in South Korea be released and that the government take "meaningful action" to improve the human rights climate in the Republic of Korea. Such action on the part of the Korean government, the letter noted, would be particularly appropriate in view of the fact that the Fifty-second International PEN Congress was scheduled to be held in Seoul August 28–September 3, to be followed by the Olympic Games. While welcoming "recent measures to relax controls on the media" the four groups expressed concern over the ongoing imprisonment of a number of Korean writers and the confiscation of scores of books because of their political content. The letter pointed to the fact that films and plays are subject to censorship and expressed concern over existing regulations of foreign publications.

The IFTP committee is now involved in planning a special exhibit of American books at the 1989 Moscow Book Fair. Past exhibits have been extraordinarily successful and popular with Soviet citizens. Approximately 300 titles are now being selected for the exhibit, which will also include a Glasnost Library with 35 to 50 titles. The committee also offered some modest support to an independent publishing venture in Poland in 1988.

New Technology

AAP's work in the area of new technology has primarily centered upon development of the industrywide *Standard for the Preparation and Mark-up of Manuscripts in*

Electronic Format, which was published in January 1986. Following publication of the *Standard,* an Electronic Publishing Special Interest Group (EPSIG) was established to facilitate use of and serve as an information clearinghouse on the AAP *Standard* and related products. On August 4, 1988, AAP entered into a contract with the Online Computer Library Center (OCLC) in Columbus, Ohio, under which OCLC took over the administration of the Electronic Publishing Special Interest Group. (EPSIG is an unincorporated voluntary dues-paying group whose members include publishers, software developers, publishing system vendors, database publishers, library service organizations, and others interested in fostering and expanding the use of AAP's electronic manuscript standard.) The AAP *Standard* was formally approved as an ANSI standard (ANSI standard Z39.59) by the American National Standards Organization Institute's Board of Standards Review in August 1988. It will soon be considered for adoption as an international standard as well.

Postal Committee

The Postal Committee under the chairmanship of Stephen Bair (Time-Life Books) coordinates AAP initiatives in the area of postal rates and regulations. The committee monitors the activities of the U.S. Postal Service, the Postal Rate Commission, and the various committees of Congress responsible for postal matters. It serves as an advisory body in formulating AAP policy on postal affairs, prepares testimony for congressional hearings, intervenes in proceedings before the Postal Rate Commission, and ensures that the publishers' voice is heard on postal issues.

The new postmaster general, Anthony Frank, who took office in March 1988, immediately faced a series of service cutbacks and a rate increase intended to keep USPS financially solvent. New postal rate increases for all classes of mail went into effect April 3, 1988. Special rate fourth-class (the book rate) increased 34 percent, the highest percentage increase for any class of mail and higher than the Postal Service had proposed. The increase resulted principally from changes in the Postal Rate Commission's costing analysis. These same costing changes produced substantial increases—averaging 20 percent—in the library rate as well. A bright spot in an otherwise bleak postal year was the $436 million appropriated in "revenue foregone" funds to subsidize nonprofit mailers, including the library rate, for FY 1989.

As part of budget reconciliation legislation passed in late 1987, Congress ordered substantial cutbacks in USPS capital expenditures for FYs 1988–1989 and ordered USPS to cut operating expenses and assume certain pension costs that had been previously paid out of the U.S. Treasury. To meet these requirements, the Postal Service had to institute a number of service cuts. In response to these events, bills were introduced in both houses of Congress to remove the Postal Service from the federal budget and increase its borrowing authority to modernize facilities. Action on the legislation was not completed in the One-hundredth Congress, and the Postal Service has made this a priority item for the One hundred and first Congress, which convenes in January 1989. (The Postal Committee is doing the preliminary groundwork for a new overall rate case expected to be filed in late 1989 or early 1990.)

The Universal Postal Union (UPU) will meet in Washington in November 1989 for the purpose of reviewing the international treaty that governs shipment of international mail. (The UPU meets every five years for this purpose.) Various official organizations also are working to integrate the European postal system as part of the merger of the European Economic Community that will occur in 1992. AAP's Postal

Committee has convened a working group to monitor and plan for related international postal developments.

Administrative Committees

Four administrative committees direct and coordinate AAP member services. Composed of both in-house and outside counsel of AAP member companies, the Lawyers' Committee meets quarterly to consider legal issues affecting publishers in such areas as libel and invasion of privacy, the First Amendment, antitrust, and product liability.

Public Information and Press

The Public Information program serves to keep the trade press, the general press, and the membership informed about AAP activities and initiatives. The program includes regular mailings to press organizations, individual interviews with the media, and organized press coverage of AAP events such as the annual meeting. The AAP *Monthly Report* provides timely and comprehensive information to members on developments in Washington, D.C., in the committees, and in the divisions. The program also develops and issues the AAP *Annual Report,* which each year outlines the association's activities, goals, and accomplishments.

Political Action Committee

The AAP Political Action Committee allows industry members to take an active part in the political process. The committee supports candidates to the House and Senate of both political parties who are responsive to and concerned about issues vital to publishers.

The Compensation Survey Committee oversees preparation of the *AAP Survey of Compensation and Personnel Practices in the Publishing Industry,* which is conducted and published approximately every two years. The survey provides member companies with information on salary and personnel practices in the industry, enabling them to make more informed decisions concerning compensation and benefits.

The Insurance Committee monitors the AAP Group Insurance Plan. With more than 100 participating companies and annual premiums in excess of $6 million, this comprehensive, low-cost group insurance plan offers AAP members a number of coverage options in life, medical, dental, liability, and eye care insurance. The AAP Group Insurance Plan continues to be an important economic benefit of membership in the association.

The Statistics Committee directs activities connected with collection and dissemination of industry statistics. Detailed statistical reports are published monthly and annually, produced by an independent consulting firm under procedures designed to protect confidentiality of financial data reported by individual houses.

American Booksellers Association

137 W. 25th St., New York, NY 10001
212-463-8450

Bernard Rath
Executive Director

For at least the second year in a row, many booksellers reported substantial increases in sales over the same period a year ago. There continued to be soft spots around the country, however, especially in areas where economies had been dependent on oil.

General Economic Conditions

According to *Trends,* the annual publication produced by the Book Industry Study Group, the market share of consumer expenditures on books in bookstores continues to increase, slightly more than 1 percent a year. If this trend continues, by about 1990 or 1991, more than half of the books bought by consumers (which includes libraries, schools, and institutions—that is, all end users) will be bought in bookstores. A number of theories have been suggested to explain why this is happening. First and most obvious is that while the number of bookstores in the United States is ever increasing, the number of book clubs, schools, and libraries remains relatively fixed.

In 1988, 518 prospective members (people who intended to invest money in opening a bookstore in the near future) joined ABA. Booksellers and publishers are promoting books and stores extensively, and advertising in private, regional, and national catalogs, inserts, and newsletters now reaches tens of millions of people annually. (ABA is currently studying how it, too, can heighten public awareness of books and bookstores. Near the end of 1988, it decided to underwrite "A Prairie Home Companion," a weekly show broadcast to 4 million people on more than 213 National Public Radio affiliates nationwide.) Publishers' terms and conditions of sale to bookstores also are more equitable, providing the opportunity for slightly higher gross profit margins than in recent years. Cooperative advertising policies are more generous and easier to use, and some major hardcover publishers—Putnam, Bantam, Doubleday, Viking, Dutton, and New American Library—now include freight to destination in their selling price to bookstores. Simultaneously, booksellers continue to build, expand, and renovate bookstore selling space at a steady pace.

About 20 percent of ABA member bookstores are estimated to have some form of computerized management information system that keeps booksellers better informed on what is selling and how frequently. When combined with databases on CD-ROM, electronic ordering, and ever more efficient wholesalers, this technology is likely to have a positive impact on sales in the immediate future.

Convention and Trade Show

The annual convention and trade show took place in Anaheim, California, from May 28 to May 31. More than 25,000 people attended the event, which required more than 385,000 square feet of space to accommodate nearly 2,000 exhibits from more than 1,000 publishers. Reading rooms were added to the 1988 convention program, where such authors as Raymond Carver, Richard Ford, T. Coraghessan Boyle, Ishmael Reed, and Alice McDermott were able to read from their works in a quiet place, away from the hectic pace of the convention floor. Among the many other authors and celebrities who talked about their work were Maurice Sendak, Judy Blume, William Kennedy, Clyde Edgerton, Carolyn Chute, David Brinkley, Lady Bird Johnson, Nathan Scharansky, and Jonathan Kozol. ABA management is planning for growth of more than 66 percent in the size of the exhibit by 1994, beginning with a 30 percent increase in the space available for exhibits at the 1990 trade show in Las Vegas. The 1989 ABA convention and trade show will take place in Washington, D.C.

Censorship and First Amendment Concerns

The Supreme Court of the United States sent *Virginia* vs. *ABA,* a case dealing with minors' access legislation, back to the Virginia State Court in 1988. The Virginia court was asked to evaluate the breadth of restrictions on minors' ability to view books deemed by the state to be harmful to them and the effect of the legislation on legitimate bookstores seeking to comply with the ordinance. When that court concluded that the effect would be minimal, the U.S. Supreme Court told the state court to reconsider its initial decision in favor of ABA, given the changed circumstances.

ABA, through its membership in both the Media Coalition and Americans for Constitutional Freedom (ACF), fought a drawn-out and emotional battle against one part of the Child Pornography and Obscenity Enforcement Act. The act passed virtually unnoticed as part of a sweeping drug enforcement bill with some minor modifications to protect legitimate booksellers from potential local law enforcement abuse and vigilantism. For the most part, however, it is a serious setback to First Amendment advocates and the constitutionality of many of its parts is expected to be challenged almost immediately. The act's primary goal seems to have been to equate dealing in pornography and/or obscenity with racketeering and to apply forfeiture provisions used in organized crime and drug laws to people and businesses that sell books. Particularly onerous record-keeping provisions, when applied to publishers of books and magazines, will require the maintenance of meticulous records to ascertain the ages of all models and/or subjects who appear frontally nude, whether in art books, photography magazines, or sexual instruction books, produced *after* 1978.

The emotion of the antipornography movement continues to deny reason, as evidenced by the fact that a blatantly unconstitutional ordinance was passed by plebiscite in Bellingham, Washington, after the city council refused to do so on legal advice. This law, identical to the one ruled unconstitutional in Indianapolis in *ABA* vs. *Hudnut,* gives so-called victims of pornography the right to sue authors and publishers for civil and punitive damages if they feel a sexual crime committed against them was inspired by a book plot or magazine article. Additionally, an extraordinarily chilling case came to ABA attention, again from Virginia, in July, when an artist-mother lost custody of her child for having had the local drugstore develop photographs of her naked one-year-old child in what was considered by authorities a sexually provocative pose. Others called them "harmless pictures any parent would take." According to New York lawyer Lawrence Stanley, there is "a mythology of child pornography reminiscent of McCarthyism" gripping this country. The chilling effect the new legislation, scheduled to take effect in August 1989 and retroactive to 1978, will have on First Amendment freedoms is yet to be seen.

ABA Membership

At the end of December 1988, full voting membership of the ABA stood at 4,304 retail bookselling establishments, which registered an additional 716 branches. The total number of members, including nonvoting categories, was 7,072.

Book Industry Study Group, Inc.

160 Fifth Ave., New York, NY 10010
212-929-1393

William Raggio
Assistant Managing Agent

The Book Industry Study Group, Inc. (BISG), is a not-for-profit corporation with a membership of approximately 180 individuals and firms from the various sectors of the book industry: publishers, manufacturers, suppliers, wholesalers, retailers, librarians, industry associations, and others engaged in the development, production, and distribution of books. BISG's goal is to promote and support research in and about the industry so that the various sectors will be better able to realize their professional and business objectives. The group's long-range goal is to increase readership, improve the distribution of books of all kinds, and expand the market for them.

BISG is unique; its membership cuts across all sectors of the industry, because its research is basic to the industry as a whole. Trade and professional associations, such as the American Booksellers Association (ABA), the Association of American University Presses (AAUP), the Association of American Publishers (AAP), the Evangelical Christian Publishers Association (ECPA), and the National Association of College Stores (NACS), are among its members.

The 1988–1989 elected officers are Steven Hill, Houghton Mifflin, chairman; Neil Perlman, Bowker Magazine Group, Cahner's Publishing, vice-chairman; Seymour Turk, Book-of-the-Month-Club, treasurer; Robert W. Bell, Lehigh University Press, secretary. The board of directors is made up of the elected officers and Stephen Adams, Macmillan; Paul Alms, Rand McNally; DeWitt C. Baker, B & H Consulting; James Buick, Zondervan; Jerry Butler, R. R. Donnelley; Carole Cushmore, Silver Burdett Press; Frank Farrell, Grolier; W. Boyd Griffin, Hearst; Richard S. Halsey, SUNY at Albany; J. G. Kaenzig, Jr., Baker & Taylor; Steven J. Mason, Ingram; Henry L. Mollenhauer, S. D. Warren; George Q. Nichols, National Publishing; Serje Seminoff, John Wiley & Sons; Frank Snyder, McGraw-Hill; and Jon Wisotzkey, Little Professor Book Centers, Inc. The four officers and Adams, Butler, and Griffin constitute the executive committee.

Publications and Activities, 1982–1989

Since 1977, BISG has published the annual statistical report *Book Industry Trends* (*Trends*), which has become the industry tool for business planning. *Trends* reviews book sales, in units and dollars, by market segment and product classification for a five-year period and forecasts for an additional five years. The report also includes statistics on library acquisitions, consumer expenditures on books, and publishers' manufacturing expenditures. The 1989 edition will be published in summer 1989 and will include updated and revised data for 1984–1993, based on the 1987 Census of Manufactures. *Trends Update,* published four times a year, provides broad-based statistical analyses on diverse topics including book price trends, paper availability and price trends, Census of Manufactures data (how they are developed and how they will be included in *Book Industry Trends,* 1989), and an update of *Trends* figures. In September 1988, BISG selected a new contractor to compile the 1989 edition of *Trends* and *Trends Update,* the Statistical Service Center (the organization that compiles the annual statistics for the Association of American Publishers).

The Sale of Books through Non-Traditional Retail Outlets, a study sponsored by BISG and conducted by Coopers & Lybrand Strategic Management Services, was published in April 1988. The first of its kind, the study is based on interviews with key players in the nontraditional retailing market and highlights opportunities in these often underutilized channels of distribution.

Since 1982, BISG has sponsored a seminar focused on *Book Industry Trends* statistics and the economy. Now an annual event, the *Trends* seminar brings together leading industry executives and analysts to discuss emerging trends and opportunities in the book industry. The 1989 seminar, cosponsored by *Publishers Weekly,* will be held June 22 in New York City.

The Book Industry Systems Advisory Committee (BISAC) has been instrumental in developing voluntary standardized computer-to-computer communications formats in use throughout the industry and in expanding the acceptance of the International Standard Book Number (ISBN) and the Standard Address Number (SAN) within the publishing, library, and bookselling communities. In 1987, the BISAC Order Acknowledgment format was approved and is now being used within the industry. BISAC is currently working on a hard copy packing slip/invoice format, a front list diskette format, and a sales reporting format.

The Serials Industry Systems Advisory Committee (SISAC) was formed in 1983 to meet the need for computer-to-computer communications formats by journal publishers, subscription agents, librarians, and booksellers. SISAC has developed a serial issue and article identifier, which is to be printed in a machine-readable format on the cover of journals. In conjunction with BISG, the committee has published *Serial Issue Identification: Code and Symbol Guidelines,* a report to help publishers compose and print the Serial Issue Identifier Code on journal covers. It has also developed a computer-to-computer order and claim format, which has been presented for adoption as an American National Standard. Current projects include development of an invoice format and a fixed-length version order and claim format.

Future Projects

BISG is exploring the feasibility of collecting retail sales statistics by subject category on an ongoing quarterly basis. Also under consideration is a study of the effect of state adoption cycles upon elhi manufacturing capacity.

American Society of Indexers, Inc.

1700 18th St. N.W., Washington, DC 20009
718-990-6200

Bella Hass Weinberg
President

The American Society of Indexers (ASI) was founded in 1968 to promote indexing as a profession and to serve as a source of information, guidance, and aid to indexers. ASI acts as an advisory body on the qualifications, training, and remuneration of indexers, and is therefore an organization of interest to authors, editors, and publishers.

Membership

ASI is recognized as *the* society for book indexers, but all kinds of indexers are encouraged to join. Among the more than 750 members listed in the ASI database in 1988 are free-lance indexers, as well as archivists, publishers, information science researchers, and computer programmers. A number of the society's activities in 1988 were designed to increase membership from the database indexing community. As many of its members are self-employed, ASI began to offer group insurance as a membership benefit in 1988. Another change was the establishment of a revolving membership year to obviate the need to supply members who renew late with back issues of serial publications.

Conferences

The ASI by-laws call for a meeting to be held in the spring of each year, but in January 1988, the first midyear meeting was held in San Francisco, cosponsored by the Golden Gate Chapter. President Thomas Jay Kemp spoke on "The Genealogy and Local History Market," and the focus of the meeting was the use of microcomputers in indexing.

Following Kemp's proposal that ASI annual meetings be linked to those of other information organizations, the twentieth ASI annual meeting was listed as a satellite event of the National Online Meeting (NOM), and was held after NOM at the Sheraton Center in New York City on May 13, 1988. More than 200 people from all over the country attended the meeting, which had been organized and was chaired by Bella Hass Weinberg, incoming ASI president. The theme "Indexing: The State of Our Knowledge and the State of Our Ignorance" was designed to cover the full spectrum of indexing theory and practice. Ten invited speakers addressed such topics as "Vocabulary Control" and "Indexing for Print, Online and CD-ROM." The proceedings were recorded by Minute-Tapes International and will be published by Learned Information. Appended to the proceedings will be a history of the society authored by Dorothy Thomas, a former ASI president.

By the end of 1988, plans were well underway for the 1989 annual meeting, scheduled to take place May 19–20 (the two-day format is the first for ASI) in San Francisco under the chairmanship of Nancy Mulvany, ASI vice president/president-elect. The theme of the conference will be "Indexing in the Nineties." Trends in the traditional publishing market and in the growing electronic publishing market will be the focus of the first day's activities, with an emphasis on hypertext indexing techniques. The second day will be devoted to back-of-the-book indexing. Specialists will cover the techniques of indexing various subjects and formats, and entrepreneurial aspects of indexing will also be discussed.

Publications

Among the benefits of ASI membership are receipt of two serial publications and discounts on other ASI publications. Members receive the journal *The Indexer,* which is sponsored by four indexing societies (British, American, Canadian, and Australian), twice a year and the *ASI Newsletter,* which was redesigned in 1988 by editor Nancy Mulvany, five times a year. In addition to news of the society, the *ASI Newsletter* features such columns as "The Electronic Shoebox" by Linda K. Fetters and "What's New in Indexing and Abstracting" by Hans Wellisch. In 1988, the *Newsletter* featured a lively exchange of articles and letters on computer sorting of index entries, as well as a "Survey of Indexer/Abstractor Economics" (March/April), which may be issued as a reprint, in response to frequent requests for the information.

Another important ASI serial publication is the annual *Register of Indexers.* Members offering indexing services pay a nominal fee for a listing in the *Register,* which is indexed geographically, by subject specialty, and by special services such as computer-assisted indexing or database design. *The Register* is distributed free to publishers and others interested in employing professional indexers.

In 1988, the ASI board approved the publication of a directory of ASI members, which will be distributed free to all new members and those who renew their membership at the new rate for personal membership established in fall 1988 ($40; $25 student). The cost of corporate membership remains $150 a year.

ASI periodically revises its directory of indexing courses. The third edition, compiled in 1985 by Bella Hass Weinberg, features course outlines as well as a bibliography of textbooks. Hans Wellisch, chairman of the ASI Education Committee, compiled *Indexing: A Basic Reading List* in 1987.

A new edition of the *Guide to Indexing Software* by Linda K. Fetters, one of ASI's bestselling publications, is being planned. (The 1987 edition is almost sold out.) *Generic Markup of Electronic Index Manuscripts*, a related publication, by Hugh C. Maddocks, was issued in 1988. The author maintains ASI's software library and serves as a director of the society.

A revised edition of A. Cynthia Weber's *Guide to Freelance Indexing* was also issued in 1988. Weber, a former president of the society, chairs its Getting Started in Indexing Committee. A related publication available from the society is *So How Much Will It Cost Me? Estimating Costs and Preparing Bids for Fee-Based Information Services,* by Linda Cooper (1987).

Manuscript editor Dena Sher was appointed in 1988 to assist ASI Publications Chairman Harris Shupak. To lessen the paperwork in processing orders, the board decided that, as of 1989, only prepaid orders would be accepted.

Awards

The American Society of Indexers administers the H. W. Wilson Award for the Best Book Index of the Year. In 1988, the $500 cash award went to Jeanne Moody (of Reston, Virginia), the indexer of *Raptor Management Techniques.* The presentation was made at the twentieth annual ASI meeting in New York City. A citation was also given to the publisher, the National Wildlife Institute. The Best Serial Index of the Year Award is now in the planning stage.

Committees and Chapters

All ASI officers and committee members are volunteers. In 1988, the Membership Committee, with the reloading of its database on an IBM system, and the By-laws Committee were particularly active. As ASI's representative to the National Information Standards Organization, the Standards Committee challenged the Electronic Manuscript Standard, developed by the Association of American Publishers.

With the appointment of new liaisons to a number of information societies, ASI had increased visibility in 1988. The exhibit at the annual meeting of the American Society for Information Science held in Atlanta, Georgia, in October 1988 attracted a great deal of attention. The chapters organized numerous successful meetings, and the board focused its attention on many aspects of chapter policy.

Conclusion

With its clearly defined membership and purpose, the American Society of Indexers looks forward to another active and successful year for the society in 1989, continued growth and increasing visibility in the information and publishing communities as the end of the decade approaches.

International Reports

U.S.–U.S.S.R. Seminar on Access to Library Resources through Technology and Preservation

E. J. Josey
Professor, School of Library and Information Science
University of Pittsburgh, Pittsburgh, Pennsylvania

A jointly sponsored U.S.–U.S.S.R. Seminar on Access to Library Resources through Technology and Preservation, the first meeting of the U.S.–U.S.S.R. Commission on Library Cooperation, was held at the Library of Congress July 5–8, 1988. (The commission had been established by an agreement negotiated between the International Research and Exchanges Board [IREX], on behalf of the American Council of Learned Societies, and the Library Council of the U.S.S.R. in September 1987.) The seminar was organized by the American Library Association's International Relations Committee and was funded by IREX. The 12-member delegation from the U.S.S.R. was headed by Nikolai S. Kartashov, president of the USSR Library Council and director of the Lenin State Library. (Kartashov also co-chairs the U.S.-U.S.S.R. Commission on Library Cooperation, together with Robert D. Stueart, dean of the Graduate School of Library and Information Science, Simmons College, Boston.) Among the U.S. participants were James H. Billington, Librarian of Congress; Margaret E. Chisholm, president of ALA; F. William Summers, then president-elect of ALA; Gerald C. Newman, chair, U.S. National Commission on Libraries and Information Science; E. J. Josey, chair, International Relations Committee of the American Library Association; and many specialists and officials from the library and information community.

A Binational Event

The four-day meeting was a truly binational one, with both an American and a Soviet representative speaking at every session. At the first general session on Automation of Libraries and Information Services, for example, Richard DeGennaro of the New York Public Library described "U.S. Efforts in the Automation of Libraries and Information Services," and Aleksandr S. Sorokin of the State Public Science and Technology Library of the U.S.S.R described related Soviet efforts and successes. Working groups of specialists from both countries dealt with bibliographic standards, online public access catalogs, networking, and preservation, as well as national and international issues in library networking.

The preservation of materials and resources in the libraries of the two countries was of critical interest to all those in attendance. Among the U.S. representatives participating in the working group on preservation were Patricia Battin, president of the Commission on Preservation and Access; Ann Russell, of the Northeast Document Conservation Center; George F. Farr, Jr., National Endowment for the Humanities; and Joseph S. Schubert, of the New York State Library in Albany. The Soviets expressed particular interest in the optical disc project of the Library of Congress.

At the closing session of the meeting, members of the two delegations discussed resolutions drafted by the four working groups, calling for the creation of joint study groups and the exchange of information and expertise between the two countries.

Highlights of the ALA Annual Conference

One of two historic moments at the 1988 ALA annual conference was the gift of 300 books that were on display in the ALA exhibition area by the Soviets to ALA President Margaret Chisholm and the ALA executive board. The second, at the International Relations Committee Program on July 12, was the signing of a protocol for the exchange of current national bibliography by Robert D. Stueart, representing the United States, and Nikolai S. Kartashov, president of the U.S.S.R. Library Council and director of the Lenin State Library.

Future U.S.-Soviet Cooperation

Following the U.S.-U.S.S.R. Seminar on Access to Library Resources through Technology and Preservation, Wesley Fisher, secretary of the IREX Commissions with the U.S.S.R., declared that "work on reconciling the computerized national bibliographies of the two countries proceeded at the seminar and it is clear that the Library of Congress and the All-Union Book Chamber of the U.S.S.R. will be collaborating further to have the national bibliographies of the other country available online for 1989." [*IREX Update,* vol. 2, no. 3 (Fall 1988): 2.] A number of other future U.S.-Soviet cooperative projects had been discussed during the negotiations of the protocol for the July 1988 seminar. These include a seminar on library services to children planned for the Soviet Union in 1989; the exchange of machine-readable bibliographic tapes; microfilming of materials; book exhibits; an exchange of conservators and library educators; collaboration in art and museum librarianship; and the provision of access to library materials and resources.

Conclusion

Glasnost appears to be working in Soviet libraries. American librarians and other specialists reported a new openness in the atmosphere at the seminar and the ALA annual conference. The Soviets appeared frank and honest in their assessment of Soviet programs and critical of their lack of progress in certain areas. By and large, the binational seminar contributed to international librarianship and international understanding.

International Federation of Library Associations and Institutions, 1988

Marjorie E. Bloss
Manager, OCLC Resource Sharing Department

The major conference of any organization is seen as the culmination of that group's activities over a particular period of time. Granted, committee and program work are carried out between conferences. It is at the conference, however, that the various parts of the organization are united into an organic whole. How well those different parts work together varies with the conference—its location, those who are able to attend, the agenda. To the outside world (and sometimes to the members themselves), the conference is viewed as a baseline indicator of the organization's health. Before we assess the health of the International Federation of Library Associations and Institutions (IFLA) as determined from the 1988 conference held in Sydney, some sense of history of the association itself and its various programs is in order.

IFLA—A Historical Perspective

When the International Federation of Library Associations and Institutions was formed in 1927, the organization's participants came predominantly from Europe and North America. Today, IFLA has more than 1,200 members (consisting of associations, institutions, and individual members) in more than 120 countries. It is permanently headquartered in The Hague.

Article 2 of IFLA's *Statutes, Rules of Procedure, Terms of Reference* describes the federation as "an independent international non-governmental association, without profit motive, whose purposes shall be to promote international understanding, cooperation, discussion, research and development in all fields of library activity, including bibliography, information services and the education of personnel, and to provide a body through which librarianship can be represented in matters of international interest." IFLA accomplishes these goals through two primary mechanisms: projects initiated by the federation's 8 divisions, 32 sections, and 10 roundtables and IFLA's five broad core programs that touch all library areas and are of general concern to the library and information service community.

IFLA's Organizational Structure

Coordinating IFLA activities is the general council, or general membership, the federation's highest organ. Member institutions of the organization nominate candidates for the executive board, the governing body, with elections held at council meetings every two years. The executive board is responsible for the federation's general policy, management and finance, and external communications.

When associations and institutions join IFLA, they indicate membership in specific sections of the organization. The member associations and institutions may then nominate individuals whom they wish to serve as section or standing committee members. The officers of each section (consisting of a chairperson and a secretary) make up the coordinating board. The professional board, consisting of one representative from each division, is responsible for the professional program, including all divisional programs.

In order to identify the various section programs and projects, the professional board has published a document listing those activities over a six-year period. The *Medium-Term Programme (1986–1991)* is recommended reading for anyone interested in ILFA's divisional and sectional goals and objectives. This booklet also identifies IFLA's five core programs, programs that are seen as basic to all library activities. All IFLA activities are planned with particular core programs in mind.

IFLA's Core Programs

In 1983, a special IFLA task force defined six core programs that, it felt, reflected the major library and information science professional concerns: Universal Availability of Publications (UAP), Universal Bibliographic Control (UBC), International MARC (IM), Transborder Data Flow (UDT), Preservation and Conservation (PAC), and Advancement of Librarianship in the Third World (ALP). Two of the programs (UAP, UBC) were already in existence in less defined form before the task force was created; consequently they have a much longer record of accomplishments than some of the newer programs that are just now beginning to gather momentum (UDT, ALP). The activities of two of the original programs, UBC and IM, became so intertwined that, in 1986, they were merged into one. A short description of each program and its objectives follows.

Universal Availability of Publications (UAP)

Universal Availability of Publications (UAP) is based on two primary principles: that access to information is essential for the economic, social, cultural, and scientific and technological development of nations and for the personal development of individuals and that present systems for providing information are inadequate. Consequently, the major objectives of the UAP program focus on ensuring access and availability of library materials to users at the national and international levels through improved acquisition, repository, and interlending policies and practices.

Universal Bibliographic Control International MARC (UBCIM)

The aim of the Universal Bibliographic Control International MARC (UBCIM) program is to promote the exchange and use of compatible bibliographic records. The UBC portion of the program concerns itself with the standardization of bibliographic descriptions (ISBDs) and the choice and form of access points within those bibliographic descriptions. Although national bibliographic databases have, up to this point, been the primary thrust of the UBCIM program, it is only a matter of time before the library committee takes advantage of the Open System Interconnection protocols and standards for the transfer of bibliographic data. Therefore, UBCIM's emphasis on the standardization of bibliographic information will become even more critical.

The International MARC portion of the UBCIM program focuses on the MARC tagging of fields for the purposes of machine communication. Its main objectives are the creation and maintenance of standards for bibliographic data exchange and the studies into the international transfer of bibliographic data. The UNIMARC format is the vehicle used for the storage and maintenance of these data. The program not only promotes the use of this format, it also encourages its further development and enhancement.

Universal Dataflow and Telecommunications (UDT)

The Universal Dataflow and Telecommunications (UDT) program aims to promote the international electronic transfer of data for storage and/or processing by computers. It deals with two types of databases—reference databases (containing citations and/or abstracts) and source databases (numeric, textual-numeric, and full-text databases). The focus of the program is to aid in the development of national and international guidelines for transferring information, to improve the technology for such purposes, and to study the economic implications for users. UDT has become a sensitive topic politically, as it raises questions of privacy rights, national security, tariff barriers, and the transfer of technological information.

Preservation and Conservation (PAC)

The Preservation and Conservation (PAC) program has two primary concerns: to ensure the permanent preservation of domestic publications at the national level for consultation or loan and to develop methods of preserving information in formats other than the original. PAC is concerned not only with preserving information from the past, but also with conserving information of the present and future. As a result, its activities require close cooperation among librarians, publishers, printers, and binders alike.

Advancement of Librarianship in the Third World (ALP)

The general objective of the Advancement of Librarianship in the Third World (ALP) program is to improve librarianship in Third World countries (Africa, Asia, Latin America, and the Caribbean). To accomplish this, ALP hopes to identify a cohesive program to address the specific needs of libraries in developing countries. The following tasks are emphasized: support and advice to librarians, library schools, and library associations in those countries; the strengthening of regional cooperation through the creation of standing committees and information centers; and the furthering of professional education and training. Of the core programs, ALP is perhaps the most abstract and therefore the most difficult to define.

IFLA's Relationship with Other Organizations

The very fact that IFLA is composed of library organizations and associations from all over the world points to great interdependency between IFLA and a variety of organizations with related subject interests. Working closely with a number of organizations provides IFLA with the opportunity for regular exchanges of information and perspectives on issues of mutual concern. IFLA has been granted consultative status with UNESCO, and the working relationship between the two organizations has been particularly close. IFLA also has consultative status with such organizations as the International Organization for Standardization (ISO), the International Council of Scientific Unions, FID (International Federation of Documentation), and ICA (International Council on Archives). Given its cooperative relationships and the composition of its membership, IFLA truly is an organization international in scope.

The 1988 IFLA Conference

With the backdrop of IFLA's history and structure in place, and some of the organizations with which it deals closely identified, the 1988 IFLA conference can now be described in some perspective. The conference had several unusual features. For one, it was the first conference ever held back-to-back with a national conference: The Library Association of Australia (LAA) held its annual conference from August 27 to August 30; the IFLA Conference followed immediately afterward, from August 30 to September 3. The two conferences shared the general theme "Living Together" with only the subtitle differentiating them. LAA focused on living together through "people, persuasion, power." IFLA emphasized "people, libraries, information." Second, because the conference was held in Sydney, Australia, the conference had a much larger than usual number of attendees from Asian/Pacific countries (and fewer attendees from Europe or North America). Still, more than 1,600 people from 60 countries participated in the two conferences—a solid showing. Third, IFLA attendees were able to participate not only in association gatherings but in Australia's celebration of its bicentennial as well.

IFLA elections for the executive and professional boards and for sections are held every two years at IFLA conferences. This year, 1988, was not an election year. Consequently, there was little of the political jockeying for position evident at the 1987 conference in Brighton, England. This, coupled with the Australian "laid back" attitude, resulted in a more relaxed atmosphere for conference attendees.

The Conference Opening

The IFLA conference was opened at the Sydney Opera House on the afternoon of August 30 by IFLA President Hans-Peter Geh. In his remarks, Geh emphasized the root of libraries, information services, and education—the book. He spoke of the close working relationship among IFLA, UNESCO, FID, and ICA and identified two activities that pointed to major IFLA involvement. The first was the help offered to and accepted by the Leningrad Academy of Sciences when a fire destroyed nearly 400,000 volumes and necessitated the restoring of 7 million more. The second was a happier event—participation by IFLA at a ceremony where the cornerstone was laid for the new Alexandrian library in Egypt.

Core Program Reports

Reports updating the activities of three of the five core programs were presented during the conference. The Universal Availability of Publications (UAP) program has primarily been focusing on research and publication of three documents: *Measuring the Performance of Document Supply Systems* by Maurice Line; a revision of a 1984 document by Priscilla Oakeshott and Brenda White, *The Impact of New Technology on the Availability of Publications,* to be undertaken by Line and UAP Programme Officer Marie-France Plassard; and a joint statement of European librarians and publishers, *The Use of Optical Media for Publication of Full Text: Cooperation between Publishers and Librarians.* The UAP report concluded by acknowledging that as new technologies and methods of storing information are developed, methods of making information universally available will also change. UAP must be fully aware of the impact and the implications of these changes.

The Universal Dataflow and Telecommunications (UDT) report emphasized two major projects: the creation of an Open Systems Interconnection (OSI) Technical Working Group and the Interlibrary Loan (ILL) Demonstration Project. The latter is a two-phase project intended to demonstrate the use of the OSI-based interlibrary loan protocol for the international exchange of electronic ILL messages.

The National Library of Canada and the British Library/Document Supply Centre are the two project participants in the ILL Demonstration Project. The objectives of this project are to show that such a system can connect libraries beyond their own borders and is an efficient means of exchanging information. One additional objective is to gather information for the coordination and planning of other OSI projects in general and ILL projects in particular.

The Universal Bibliographic Control International MARC (UBCIM) program reported the first tangible results from the ISBD five-year reviews in the publication of revised ISBDs for monographs, cartographic materials, nonbook materials, and serials. Drafts of the ISBDs for printed music and antiquarian materials are currently under review, and work continues on a new ISBD for computer files. Last but not least, 1988 saw the long-awaited publication of *Guidelines for the Application of the ISBD's to the Description of Component Parts.*

The program's primary UNIMARC-related activity has been the sale of the 1987 revision of the *UNIMARC Manual.* The UNIMARC Format for Authorities is currently under worldwide review.

Sectional Programs

In addition to the reports on IFLA's core programs, each IFLA section (or standing committee) and division reported on its own subject-specific programs. Attendees heard presentations on technical subjects (the OSI protocol, cataloging, serials, acquisitions), on public service concerns (interlibrary loan and reference), on information concerning types of libraries (public, medical, legal, etc.), and on country-specific "how things work/don't work in my country" topics.

Although the conference presentations contained no surprises, serving more as a review of activities than as an unleashing of new concepts, the receptions they received from attendees who view or handle activities differently from those described were the highlights of the conference. The opportunity to hear, learn about, and share diverse perspectives with people whose goals are similar but whose methods of attaining those goals are very different is an essential quality of the IFLA conference.

Conclusion

Conferences always have several different level of attendance. First, there is the general conference goer—the person who attends for the papers and presentations. (IFLA attendees have the advantage of taking home the printed version of those presentations, permitting them the luxury of analyzing the texts at a later date and freeing them to listen carefully and observe during the conference.) Second is the committee member—the person who is an active member of one of IFLA's committees responsible for program or project implementation. Third is the social level of the conference. IFLA conference organizers, knowing that attendees who are comfortable with one another socially will be more productive professionally, encourage attendees to meet their counterparts from different countries. As a result, social events are an integral part of every IFLA conference.

The IFLA 1988 conference was not as dynamic or volatile as some of the recent conferences because of its location, the shorter than usual duration of the conference (a result of time sharing with the LAA), and the fact that it was not an IFLA election year. Plans are already well underway for the 1989 conference in Paris where IFLA will help celebrate another bicentennial. From all indications, this is a conference not to miss.

Frankfurt Book Fair, 1988: Back on an Even Keel

Herbert R. Lottman

International Correspondent, *Publishers Weekly*

Countless thousands of book people from the world over assembled in Frankfurt for its fortieth postwar book fair October 5–10. Was it worth it? A *PW* reporter queried frequent fairgoers from the United States to learn that the presence of a single publishing executive—not counting salary—can cost between $5,000 and $10,000. "It doesn't pay," one of the most experienced added, "unless you can calculate the value of getting a feel for the business." "It's too expensive," the financial officer of a major group agreed. "But we have to be here!"

Space was once more at a premium, for fair attendees had again smashed their own record, with a growth of nearly 10 percent in exhibitors. The fair was a true labyrinth for the newcomer, agreed author Umberto Eco, star of the fair (because Italy was its theme, and because he had another bestseller in the shops). An expert on literary and semantic labyrinths, Eco told *PW* how he had forgotten the site of an appointment and just kept walking until his date spotted him and shouted "Umberto!"

It didn't help the real business of the fair that the general public was allowed entry on three full fair days, Friday through Sunday. Some exhibitors (including Germans) regretted that the doors had been opened too widely, slowing down what even German exhibitors see as the fair's true business: meetings with booksellers, the working press—and, of course, colleagues from abroad. One thing was clear: Frankfurt would stay in Frankfurt; the organizers of the fair had worked out a satisfactory arrangement with the official fairground authority. The effect on stand rentals will

Note: Adapted from *Publishers Weekly,* October 28, 1988.

be minimal, and fair director Peter Weidhaas believes that exhibitors' costs won't rise at all in the next couple of years—though the question of how to manage expansion has yet to be dealt with. Certainly there has never been a better layout than in 1988. Some first-time British exhibitors were placed on the "American" floor, because a few U.S. houses had actually requested smaller stands, and mergers had reduced the number of U.S. imprints. But everywhere else expansion was the name of the game, and the fair's technical director Franz-Josef Fenke told *PW:* "We could rent 20 percent more space if we had it."

Is This Meeting Necessary?

Space and cost weren't the only considerations. For a couple of years publishing people have been asking themselves (and each other) whether an annual face-to-face meeting was still necessary in the electronic age of instant transmission of synopses, options, and offers. But a new situation has developed with the merger wave: a need to meet the new men and women in charge. And to counter the impression of faceless groups, heads of houses were often to be seen out front of their collectives greeting people—Octopus's Paul Hamlyn here, Ian Chapman of Collins there, Penguin's newly smokeless Peter Mayer everywhere. "It's inevitable; you can't stop it," Hamlyn remarked of the mergers. But is there a choice? Hamlyn thinks there is; though big companies get bigger, small ones keep cropping up all the time.

Attorney-agent Morton Janklow, who attends Frankfurt fairs not to close on blockbusters but to pursue contacts ("I see more Americans here than I do in New York"), found a new use for the fair: to get a feel of the situation in the groups. He agreed that it was inevitable that the biggest books are going to large entities with hardcover/softcover potential; why sell to a trade house which will then sell off mass market rights less profitably than the agent can, with a loss to the author? Still, Peter Mayer regretted the decline of a mix between large and small houses. At lunches and dinners, "big groups meet big groups; we don't even have the time to see the others."

PW encountered a number of former officers of merged or raided groups who were now on their own, and smiling, like Fred Kobrak, Macmillan's international man, who has joined with Adrian Higham (ex-Wiley International) in a newly formed international consultancy agency. And some of the busiest people in town were the marriage brokers who put together buyers and sellers of companies.

The 1988 Frankfurt fair seemed less frenetic to many. "There was a time," remembered Alfredo Machado of Brazil's Editora Record, "when you couldn't buy a book in New York in the three months before Frankfurt. American rights managers would say, 'Wait for the fair.' With telex and FAX machines they can't do that anymore." There were the planned big books, and some came off according to plan: Nancy Reagan's memoirs, Yves Saint Laurent's autobiography. Agent-scout Lynn Franklin confirmed the rush to nonfiction, the active blind bidding; she mentioned the 25 pages of the Andy Warhol diaries on the Warner stand.

Fair Business

The Inevitable Sleeper

There was even a fair sleeper, the kind of book that set the juices running in times past. Rave reviews in the German press had drawn scouts and editors to small Greno Verlag in Nördlingen, near Munich, which had a 34-year-old Austrian author, Christoph Ransmayr, whose historical novel about the Roman poet Ovid had drawn the raves. "Obviously everyone is looking for another Patrick Süskind [author of *Perfume*]," commented Gerhard Beckmann of Vienna's Paul Zsolnay. Greno was accepting bids—but planned not to close with any foreign partner until the end of October.

The Other Big Books

The other big books had been sold before the fair, or would certainly go to present publishers—the Umberto Eco (*Foucault's Pendulum*), a revised *Perestroika* by Mikhail Gorbachev (apparently to be followed by a "Son of *Perestroika*").

Gerhard Beckmann of Zsolnay made a point of staying out of the chase for big books. He tried to identify projects that would "really work" in the German-language market, and for these he'd pay considerable advances.

"There are always 20 or 30 good books I want to buy immediately," confessed Michael Krüger of Carl Hanser Verlag. "Books are getting better and better, even in Germany. Booksellers are asking for nonfiction 500 pages long." One result is that the big groups have moved in, fighting each other with good literature, even promoting it in a way an independent such as Hanser cannot.

Bookselling

Frankfurt is also, and importantly, a bookselling event, and the importers and exporters were talking about good or even very good business. Paul E. Feffer, who sells for America via Feffer & Simons (a Baker & Taylor company), gives some of the credit to the lower cost of dollars to most of the biggest buying nations. Meanwhile *PW* learned that some importers remained unhappy with U.S. terms, and a few were going to do something about it. Import booksellers from Germany had banded together in an Association for the Import of Scientific Publications, and just before the fair they decided to bypass U.S. publishers that mark up their books for European continental sales by working through an American wholesaler—the name was kept a precious secret—who would buy for them Stateside and then ship abroad.

The fair provides many such opportunities for underdogs to explain themselves. Publishing countries in crisis were present at the fair, even as active contenders for books and rights, but they came with information too. For a nation like Argentina, which is experiencing economic problems unimaginable in the United States or in today's Europe, the solution is copublishing (with other Latin American countries) and exportation. Javier Vergara, of his own Buenos Aires imprint, told *PW* that he exports 70 percent of his production, and the biggest customer is Spain.

Soviet Salesmanship

Perhaps 1988 was the year that Frankfurt acquired a new and potentially significant trading partner: the U.S.S.R. The message of Gorbachev has been heard by Moscow's publishers: Move fast into the world of hard currency. One of the Soviet Union's top book officers, Dimitri Mamleev, who ran the U.S.S.R. collective exhibit at Frankfurt, reported that the increased rights business had made it necessary to build more private rooms into the stand area, and even that wasn't enough. More publishing folk than ever were present from Moscow; a number of them (like Leningrad's prestigious art house Aurora) were involved in one-on-one talks with Western counterparts. And a rights manager who notices such things told *PW*'s reporter that the VAAP representative had been invited to five cocktail parties one evening. . . .

The adventurous soul who wandered into the U.S.S.R. collective was quickly surrounded by Soviet book officials pushing projects that, in the past, they themselves would have denounced as dissident literature. Progress Publishers of Moscow, once a leading producer of political propaganda in book form, was handing out expensively produced synopses with titles such as *The Life and Tragedy of Nikolai Bukharin* and *Lives Cut Short,* "biographies of revolutionaries of the Leninist type . . . whose fate was affected by Stalin's personality cult." The Novosty Press Agency, whose reason for being was glorification of the regime, had a still glossier presentation for projects such as a two-volume biography of Stalin based on heretofore closed archives (by military historian Dmitri Volkogonov); a startled *PW* visitor watched as George Weidenfeld and associate Ann Getty sat with Soviet officials smack in the middle of the U.S.S.R. booth to negotiate purchase (it will be done by Aaron Asher at Grove in New York).

The new dispensation was apparent all over International Hall 4. Harper's Simon Michael Bessie threw a stand party for publishers of *Perestroika,* and a simultaneous party on the Addison-Wesley stand saw the exchange of editions of *The Home Planet* (a collection of photographs taken from satellites by the United States and U.S.S.R., printed handsomely by Pizzi in Italy). Just before the Frankfurt fair Americans had met with their Moscow counterparts in bilateral media talks in a number of areas, including books. The day before the bilateral talks began, William Begell of Hemisphere Publishing negotiated for a 30-volume encyclopedic reference series to be done in coproduction with Mechanical Engineering Press in Moscow, each partner to furnish an editor in chief and material. Begell revealed that he also has the green light for a *Who's Who in the Soviet Union.*

1992 and All That

Frankfurt had its buzzword, at least on the American and British floors of Hall 4: The word was "Europe." The European Economic Community had been around for a long time, but suddenly Americans had discovered its existence, perhaps because they had learned that their British friends were nervous about it. Just prior to the fair London's *Bookseller* reported the decision of Penguin to go out for exclusive all-European rights in the future, anticipating the elimination of trade barriers within Europe—including the United Kingdom—by the end of 1992. The point was that a book introduced into any member state—which on the Continent meant France, Italy, Spain, West Germany, the Netherlands, Belgium, Denmark, Portugal, Greece, or Luxembourg—would be able to enter Britain unhampered by territorial considerations. One top British agent confessed that she had hoped another couple of years would go by before Americans realized what they could do now—or soon. As Lynette Owen, rights director for the Longman group, explained it, in theory even today an American book sold to France could move into the United Kingdom in defiance of territorial agreements, and a British publisher for its part cannot honor a contract barring sale into a Community country. British publishers will henceforth have to refuse open market agreements if they are to keep American books out of Britain.

John Clement, group managing director of Collins, confirmed the seriousness with which the British are taking the single market. Unless there is exceptional legislation, and this seemed unlikely, the British publisher will have to be protected by a United Kingdom-and-Continent contract, or it won't be protected at all. "I'll surely be instructing our people to buy U.K. and European rights, and then we'll pay full royalties rather than an export royalty on Continental sales." In the end, Clement predicted a lot more trading in world English rights.

Britain's trade has a watchdog in the Publishers Association, whose chief executive Clive Bradley points out that 1992 is the deadline for getting rid of nonfiscal barriers (such as standards and formalities), now that the *fiscal* tariffs have already disappeared among member states of the Community. But what is important about 1992 is the change in psychology: Member states will no longer consider themselves as separate markets but as a single one. Bradley admitted that ever since the Treaty of Rome went into effect, anything that could be sold in France, say, could go into Britain. But interpretations are changing, and as a result, the typical U.S.-U.K. publishing contract leaving the Continent as an open market cannot lawfully be enforced; American books can make their way into the United Kingdom. Parallel importations are clearly increasing, to the prejudice of publishers on both sides of the Atlantic, as effective marketing requires that one be able to exploit one's own copyrights. The PA's Ian Taylor told *PW* that British publishers are seeking a "block exemption" for books under the Community's law. Mark Barty-King of Britain's Bantam Press suggested that agents will henceforth prefer to sell world rights so as not to get "ensnared." Mort Janklow: "The world English deal is clearly on the way, and the world deal isn't much further away."

On the European continent there was also considerable movement. Fabbri's recent acquisition of a major Spanish partwork house, Orbis, was motivated in part by a wish to enter another lucrative Community market; Fabbri has also set up companies in Paris, Hamburg—and London. With Lumen of Barcelona, and using Fabbri's affiliate Bompiani as the copublisher, Fabbri will do the Spanish translation of the certain 1989 bestseller, Umberto Eco's *Foucault's Pendulum.*

Party Time

The ubiquitous Umberto was doing wonders for himself and his publisher at the fair. He was one of several authors utilized by a prime publisher to bring together fellow publishers—in a sense to ensure brand loyalty. And so there was a lunch at the quaint Palmengarten, where, as it happened, Eco celebrated his marriage 26 years ago. Among guests was HBJ's Rubin Pfeffer, who announced publication of William Weaver's English translation of *Foucault's Pendulum* for September 1989. In Italy the novel had been released October 3 and all 25,000 copies in the stores were sold that day.

Curtis Brown (London) hosted a sit-down affair to honor Hammond Innes, whom it has been representing for 50 years. Other authors present and working for their publishers included Tom Wolfe (*Bonfire of the Vanities*) and Yugoslavia's Milorad Pavić (whose strange *Dictionary of the Khazars* was just published by Knopf). Rizzoli gave a party for Giulio Einaudi, whose brief memoir of a publisher's life it is going to publish.

Then there were the regular parties. The elite of trade publishers knows that

Tuesday night means a reception in the offices of Frankfurt's own S. Fischer Verlag, and Wednesday is the Stecher-Konsalik late-night affair in the Frankfurter Hof's big ballroom. The hottest tickets are for the Bertelsmann Friday and the Reader's Digest Saturday (limited, for space reasons, to non-Americans). Munich's Heyne also hosts a Saturday party, Gustav Lübbe a middle-European Sunday night banquet.

One amused fairgoer noted that Robert Maxwell threw a posh party at the Union Club on Friday (Bertelsmann's night, and therefore a possible instance of hostile party takeover). And for the first time Collins and its sister company Harper & Row joined forces for an end-of-the-day reception in the Plaza's largest space—surely a way to stress to the world that it was all one large family now. Another notable event for the elite was the dinner party hosted by Italy's Inge Feltrinelli for the eightieth birthday of Heinrich M. Ledig-Rowohlt.

Some publishers used the fair to launch projects. Denmark's Lindhardt & Ringhof and a Danish Bonnier group affiliate were joint hosts at the launching (in the Hessischer Hof's swank Jimmy's Bar) of a major Danish book club, a one-book-of-the-month to compete with the large Gyldendal clubs whose catalogs were offering many books a month. Most big German publishers held parties for their domestic customers as well as foreign friends (e.g., the traditional Friday morning Springer-Verlag reception, also at the Hessischer).

Focus on Italy

Although there had been cultural themes at earlier Frankfurt fairs, 1988 saw the launching of a new cycle of country themes requiring a major effort on the part of the country concerned. Italy arrived with a bang; indeed, the enormous cost of mounting the Italian pavilion and ancillary exhibits, concerts, lectures, and other cultural events around the city had been widely criticized in the Italian press. The pavilion itself consisted of a cluster of outsized sets built by Cinecittà designers and architects; the overall effect was of Disneyland.

But Italy was the theme in more ways than its cultural authorities had bargained for. The weeks before Frankfurt had seen major changes in the publishing world, changes that became apparent only as publishing partners encountered Milan colleagues in the aisles, or looked for them on the wrong stands. For one thing, the top editorial people at Rizzoli had left (or were leaving), including publisher Marco Polillo, who had returned to his old firm Mondadori. Polillo had taken Rizzoli editorial director Gianni Ferrari with him. Polillo will run the book division of Mondadori and Ferrari will be editor in chief. Meanwhile former Mondadori book division chief Leonardo Mondadori was buying actively for a new imprint he was calling Leonardo (he had engaged one of New York's top scouts, Lynn Franklin, and had a first list coming in February that included Philip Roth's *The Facts*). Giovanni Ungarelli had left Mondadori to become CEO of Rizzoli's book division.

The acquisition of the Linder agency (Milan's Agenzia Letteraria Internazionale) by Donatella Barbieri of Sperling & Kupfer had been announced just before the fair. Now it became known that Rosaria Carpinelli was moving into Barbieri's editorial functions at Sperling (and Frassinelli), while Roberto Santachiara was leaving Bompiani to assist Donatella Barbieri at ALI; veteran agent Piero Cecchini had died suddenly after a brief illness. Everybody was watching the situation at Einaudi, acquired by Mondadori and Electra in 1988 in a deal challenged in the courts by minority shareholders. And during the fair Mondadori was the target of a raid by part-owner Carlo De Benedetti.

Talking Rights

In what was called a follow-up to the 1987 first international rights seminar, the book fair management, with assistance from AAP's international division, staged a half-day conference on the afternoon preceding the fair opening. There were four panels, each of which ran four hours, devoted, respectively, to fiction/nonfiction, art/illustrated books, children's books, and sci-tech and professional. Spot checks, notably at the session on fiction/nonfiction chaired by Katerina Czarnecki of Macmillan (New York), suggested that the conference was largely a dialogue between haves and have-nots, perhaps even between Americans and the rest of the trading world. The main problem seemed to be that American acquisition contracts—born of that litigious society—were harder and harder to follow, while Americans would sell via the simplest of arrangements. Czarnecki admitted that Americans sell their books all over the world but are reluctant to try new things, particularly from difficult languages.

International Association Meetings

The general assembly of STM, the International Group of Scientific, Technical and Medical Publishers, took place as always on the Tuesday morning preceding the opening of the fair. STM secretary Paul Nijhoff Asser presented the report of the group executive, which stressed the effects of the "merger wave" on membership.

In a report on copyright, M.F.J. Pijnenborg of Elsevier stressed the need for an STM policy on the concept of publishers' rights, in order to influence legislation. He also warned of the new threat of electrocopying, more of a challenge to traditional print publishing than photocopying ever was, and he urged fellow publishers to demand contractual arrangements with libraries and other users. With the International Publishers Association (IPA), STM is planning a second international symposium on copyright, stressing economics, to be held in France in 1990.

In another report to members, Jolana von Hagen of Springer-Verlag called attention to the increasing hostility of librarians; publishers could fight back by correcting misinformation, but they also have to take positive steps, such as helping librarians to understand publishers' problems (and trying to understand theirs). "The future of scientific publishing is going to be electronic in one way or another," *Nature*'s John Maddox summed up.

During the fair the IPA international committee agreed to set up a new category of members for countries unable to comply entirely with the IPA charter, and the Hungarian Book Publishers Association was voted in as the first member in the new category; apart from Western-oriented Yugoslavia, Hungary is IPA's first member from Eastern Europe. One requirement is that the country concerned accept private publishing, and Hungary now does—at least in principle. In another area, IPA is working with and on UNESCO to put teeth into the Florence Agreement on free flow; in recent years impediments in the form of duties or taxes have actually turned back the clock. Finally, IPA resolved to try to move UNESCO to campaign on behalf of "copyright awareness."

That unique institution, the Motovun group of copublishers, held its annual breakfast on Frankfurt Sunday. Participating publishers (including new member Hugh Levin of his own New York firm) heard of plans for a Motovun group visit to China in April, a follow-up to the 1980 visit that brought back some significant projects. The regular annual gathering will take place in the medieval Istrian hilltop village that gave the group its name, late in June.

Remembering the Pioneers

One of Germany's most respected novelists, Siegfried Lenz, got the German book trade's annual peace prize. And in a touching ceremony fair director Peter Weidhaas, in the presence of his predecessor Sigfred Taubert, honored book people who had been present at the very first fair in 1949. Thirty-two of them were present, including publisher Klaus Piper and veteran Hanser editor Fritz Arnold (apparently no non-German-speaking publisher had attended fair one).

Some said the 1988 fair was quiet; no one said it was bad. "I've never seen so much activity!" declared Ann Martyn of the Tuttle-Mori agency. "Of course it was quiet," Milan agent Antonella Antonelli said, "but I like that." "The point," said Jonathan Lloyd of Grafton, "is not to get caught up by the bidding hysteria."

The test of a good fair is the last day. Would *PW* find important fair users on their stands that day? In the American area on Sunday afternoon, the reporter spotted Roger Straus selling briskly from his stand and watched André Schiffrin at the back of a booth with Penguin's Peter Carson. "The fair isn't really that long," explained Gerhard Beckmann of Zsolnay, "so it's not surprising that people are still around." Of course the best of the agents, rights managers, and acquiring editors were still talking away as afternoon turned into evening. Were they going to stay around until next year's fair, which takes place October 11–16, 1989?

Part 2
Legislation, Funding, and Grants

Legislation

Legislation and Regulations Affecting Libraries in 1988

Eileen D. Cooke
Director, Washington Office, American Library Association

Carol C. Henderson
Deputy Director, Washington Office, American Library Association

Libraries claimed the attention of Congress and federal agencies to an unusual extent in 1988. At times, the attention was inappropriate, as in the case of the FBI Library Awareness Program, which came under attack not only from library associations, but from several congressional committees. Some of the attention was welcome but problematic, as in the Reagan administration's finally acknowledging a positive federal role in support of libraries. As the administration's proposed Library Improvement Act came so late and followed six years of zero budgets, it was a foregone conclusion that Congress would not pay serious attention in the administration's final year, choosing instead to continue the current programs.

A new School Improvement Act made libraries a strong component of two major federal elementary/secondary education programs—Chapter 1 aid to disadvantaged schoolchildren and the Chapter 2 school block grant. The same act made library surveys a required part of the newly reorganized National Center for Education Statistics. Congress prohibited the privatization of the National Technical Information Service. With little fanfare, the first electronic government information products went out to depository libraries. Congress recognized the seriousness of the brittle books problem with a major increase in preservation funding through the National Endowment for the Humanities. The Year of the Young Reader will be officially celebrated in 1989. Finally, in a long-range planning step, legislation was approved authorizing a second White House Conference on Library and Information Services.

Funding, FY 1989

In a major shift in policy, the Reagan administration proposed a modest federal role in support of libraries. The FY 1989 budget for libraries was based on a legislative proposal later submitted to Congress as the Library Improvement Act. Designed to replace the Library Services and Construction Act and the Higher Education Act Title II (for which a total of $135 million was appropriated in FY 1988), the $76 million proposal would authorize $45 million for Title I Services to Disadvantaged People through state formula grants, $30 million for Title II Resource Sharing ($20 million in state formula grants, $10 million in direct discretionary grants), and $1 million for Title III Research and Assessment direct discretionary grants.

Coming after six years of attempts to eliminate library programs, the Library Improvement Act was viewed with skepticism by both the library community and Congress. Senator Dan Quayle (R–Ind.) introduced it (S. 2579) at the request of the administration. The bill did not receive hearings or congressional action, nor did it influence FY 1989 funding decisions.

For the first time since FY 1977, Congress completed work on all 13 appropriations bills before the October 1 start of the 1989 fiscal year. The task was made easier by having military and domestic totals for FY 1989 set in the budget summit agreement between the administration and congressional leaders in fall 1987, following the October stock market collapse.

The total FY 1989 funding for LSCA and HEA library programs was $137.2 million, up 1.5 percent from the previous year. However, program-by-program results were uneven, as Table 1 indicates. The HEA II-B training and research and II-C research library funding show the effects of across-the-board cuts imposed on programs under their jurisdiction by the House and Senate Labor-HHS-Education Appropriations subcommittees. To keep funding within the subcommittees' allocated totals, House-Senate conferees generally split the difference between the House- and Senate-passed amounts and then applied a cut of 1.2 percent on all programs. A year before, the conferees used a similar technique, except the across-the-board cut to the initial conference totals was 4.2 percent. The process shaves any intended increases and erodes programs intended to be level funded. For instance, two years ago, HEA II-B was at $1 million and II-C was $6 million.

The vulnerability of consolidated programs and block grants to budget cuts in a deficit reduction climate was vividly demonstrated in the education funding bill (HR 4783). Four amendments in the Senate raided the Chapter 2 school block grant to fund various small programs in the new School Improvement Act (HR 5, PL 100-

Table 1 / Funding for Selected Federal Library Programs, FY 1989
(Amounts in thousands)

		FY 1989				
Program	FY 1989 Approp.	FY 1989 Budget	1989 House Passed	1989 Senate Passed	1989 Initial Conference	FY1988 Final
LSCA I	$ 78,986	$ -0-	$ 85,000	$ 78,986	$ 81,993	$ 81,009
LSCA II	22,595	-0-	22,595	22,595	22,595	22,324
LSCA III	18,669	-0-	20,000	18,669	19,334	19,102
LSCA VI	4,787	-0-	4,787	4,787	4,787	4,730
HEA II-B	718	-0-	718	718	718	709
HEA II-C	5,744	-0-	5,744	5,744	5,744	5,675
HEA II-D	3,590	-0-	3,800	3,590	3,695	3,651
ESEA I Ch. 2	504,131	567,500	517,430	476,000	497,700	491,728
NCLIS	718	755	750	750	750	741
NLM	58,496	60,836	64,836	60,836	64,836	64,058
MLAA	9,414	9,790	defer	9,790	9,790	9,673

297). As a result, Chapter 2 wound up at $476 million in the Senate, $31 million less than the subcommittee recommended and $41.4 million less than the House figure.

Funding details for these and other programs are shown in Table 2; some details are highlighted under other headings in this article.

Contracting Out

Additional federal libraries contracted out to commercial firms during 1988 included those of the Department of Labor and the National Oceanic and Atmospheric Administration Central Library. The NOAA library outcome followed years of controversy on the study process, the award to a subsidiary of a foreign company, and the assumption in the winning low-cost bid that there would be increasing use of "volunteers" to operate one of the federal government's major technical research libraries. The contract was later awarded to the low bidder based on compensated personnel.

The libraries of the Department of Education, Department of Interior, the General Services Administration, and the Immigration and Naturalization Service were all under review for contracting out at year's end. Such reviews usually involve a hiring freeze, which can hasten the process, since activities with staffs of fewer than ten persons are exempt from the formal review process and can be contracted out immediately. The Office of Management and Budget Circular A-76, through which contracting-out procedures are implemented, was revised in September 1988 (see October 14 *Federal Register,* pp. 40370–40375) to comply with a congressional requirement for a more accurate comparison of private and federal benefit costs and pay raise assumptions in cost comparison studies. In a first, as far as is known, the National Institute of Standards and Technology Research Information Center was designated as a governmental activity in the NIST Authorization Act for FY 1989 (PL 100-519).

Copyright

After lengthy consideration in the One-hundredth Congress, the U.S. joined the Berne Convention for the Protection of Literary and Artistic Works, a 102-year-old international agreement to promote improved copyright standards. Long-standing differences between Berne Convention standards and U.S. law were reduced by the passage of the 1976 Copyright Act and the expiration of the manufacturing clause. Other factors adding some urgency were U.S. trade deficits and growing foreign copyright piracy.

The Senate version could have had a major impact on Library of Congress collections, heavily dependent on copyright deposit copies, because the Senate eliminated the registration requirement as a formality prohibited by Berne. A compromise created a two-tier solution: Registration of copyright was continued as a prerequisite to suit by U.S. authors, but foreign origin works were excepted from this requirement. The mandatory notice of copyright requirement was eliminated and replaced with an incentive for voluntary notice.

In end-of-session action, Congress approved an extension for eight years of the provisions of the Record Rental Amendment of 1984. PL 100-617 continued the prohibition against the commercial rental, lease, or lending of audio recordings without

Table 2 / Appropriations for Library and Related Programs, FY 1989

(Figures in thousands)

Library Programs	FY 1988 Appropriation	FY 1989 Budget	FY 1989 House	FY 1989 Senate	FY 1989 Appropriation
Elementary and Secondary Education Act I					
Chapter 2 (including school libraries)	$ 504,131	$ 567,500[1]	$ 517,430	$ 476,000	$ 491,728
GPO Superintendent of Documents	24,662	26,800	25,155	25,155	25,155
Higher Education Act	10,052	0[2]	10,262	10,052	10,079
Title II-A, College Libraries	0	0	0	0	0
Title II-B, Training & Research	718	0	718	718	709
Title II-C, Research Libraries	5,744	0	5,744	5,744	5,675
Title II-D, Technology	3,590	0	3,800	3,590	3,651
Library of Congress	247,971	274,198	256,883	257,278	257,278
Library Services and Construction Act	125,037	0[2]	132,382	125,037	127,165
Title I, Public Library Services	78,986	0	85,000	78,986	81,009
Title II, Public Library Construction	22,595	0	22,595	22,595	22,324
Title III, Interlibrary Cooperation	18,669	0	20,000	18,669	19,102
Title IV, Indian Library Services	(funded at 2% of appropriations for LSCA I, II, & III)				
Title V, Foreign Language Materials	0	0	0	0	0
Title VI, Library Literacy Programs	4,787	0	4,787	4,787	4,730
Medical Library Assistance Act	9,414	9,790	defe[illegible]	9,790	9,673
National Agricultural Library	12,194	13,599	13,446	14,682	13,268[3]
National Commission on Libraries & Information Science	718	755	750	750	741
National Library of Medicine	58,496	60,836	64,836	60,836	64,058

Library-Related Programs

Adult Education Act	134,036	150,000	166,754	167,180	162,210
Bilingual, Immigrant, Refugee Education	191,751	200,504	201,782	197,009	199,791
ESEA Chapter 1 (Disadvantaged Children)	4,327,927	4,566,084	4,663,719	4,589,800	4,570,246
Education of Handicapped Children (state grants)	1,431,737	1,474,239	1,478,539	1,508,200	1,475,449
Educational Research	46,573	51,531	50,343	44,960	47,079
HEA Title III, Developing Institutions	152,370	136,978	180,000	169,978	174,577
Title IV-C, College Work Study	588,249	600,014	635,000	600,014	610,097
Title VI, International Education	25,419	25,419	25,419	25,419	25,114
National Archives and Records Administration	112,000	117,862	121,962	113,862	117,900
National Center for Education Statistics	20,953	32,869[1]	33,169	29,500	31,122
National Endowment for the Arts	167,731	167,731	169,000	168,631	169,090
National Endowment for the Humanities	140,435	140,435	153,700	144,235	153,000
National Historical Publications and Records Commission	4,000	0	4,000	4,000	4,000
Postal Revenue Forgone Subsidy	517,001	19,023[4]	436,417	436,417	436,417
Postsecondary Education Improvement Fund	11,645	13,645	13,645	11,645	11,856
Science & Math Education	119,675	119,675	119,675	139,000	137,332
Star Schools	19,148	0	19,148	10,000	14,399
VISTA Literacy Corps	2,872	0	2,872	2,872	2,838
Women's Educational Equity	3,351	0	3,351	2,620	2,985

[1]Request revised following enactment of School Improvement Act.
[2]Administration proposed $76 million Library Improvement Act to replace LSCA and HEA II.
[3]Congress approved $14,268,000, but by error, the amount signed into law was $13,268,000.
[4]Free mail for blind and overseas voters only.

the copyright owner's permission. Also extended was an exemption for noncommercial rental, lease, or lending by nonprofit libraries or educational institutions.

FBI Visits to Libraries

In 1987, reports from librarians and articles in the national press brought attention to the Federal Bureau of Investigation Library Awareness Program, under which the bureau was approaching U.S. academic and public libraries, requesting the assistance of library personnel in conducting surveillance of "suspicious-looking" persons who may be from countries "hostile to the United States." The American Library Association Intellectual Freedom Committee issued an October 1987 advisory statement vigorously protesting the FBI program, pointing out that 36 states (now 38 plus the District of Columbia) have enacted "Confidentiality of Library Records" statutes.

At its January 14, 1988, meeting in San Antonio, Texas, the National Commission on Libraries and Information Science held a closed session on the Library Awareness Program with Thomas DuHadway, deputy director of operations for foreign intelligence for the FBI. Through a Freedom of Information Act request, a reporter obtained a transcript of the NCLIS meeting with the FBI and wrote an article about the meeting. The transcript soon generated numerous articles in the general and library press and considerable controversy in the library community when it revealed that some commissioners had made remarks critical of ALA and the Intellectual Freedom Committee (IFC).

The general media, the library press, several library associations, information industry representatives, higher education institutions and associations, and several members of Congress all expressed outright opposition or serious reservations about the FBI program in 1988. The IFC documented numerous instances of FBI "fishing expeditions" in libraries across the country, indicating the library program is much less focused and more widespread than the narrow descriptions of it provided by DuHadway or by FBI Director William Sessions at congressional hearings.

The program was strongly criticized at congressional hearings in March, April, and May. At a June 20 hearing of the House Judiciary Subcommittee on Civil and Constitutional Rights, FBI library-related activities were uniformly criticized by the several librarians testifying. Witnesses said the program posed a threat to the free flow of information that was greater than the threat of Soviet espionage. The scheduled FBI witness did not appear, although a statement was released at the hearing; the FBI testified on July 13.

In a September 14 letter to Representative Don Edwards (D–Calif.), chairman of the House Judiciary Subcommittee on Civil and Constitutional Rights, Sessions indicated some procedural changes in the FBI library activities (not circumventing library management, not asking generally about people with foreign-sounding names or accents or with suspicious or anomalous behavior, not asking for circulation records). However, he said that when deemed necessary, the FBI will continue to contact certain scientific and technical libraries (including university and public libraries) in the New York City area concerning hostile intelligence service activities at libraries. Edwards shared this letter with interested organizations and noted in a cover memo that libraries do not have to cooperate with these FBI requests for information without a warrant.

The FBI's willingness to set some limits on its library activities in September contrasted with its efforts in October to obtain a "national security letter" exemption to the then pending Video and Library Privacy Protection Act (see the section later in this article on the bill). Serving notice that Congress will consider curbs on FBI activity, Representatives Edwards and John Conyers (D–Mich.) introduced HR 5369 on September 23 to make it clear that the FBI must not monitor First Amendment activities of American citizens and organizations without some reason to believe criminal activity is involved.

Freedom of Information Day

Senator Patrick Leahy (D–Vt.) gave a stirring defense of freedom of speech and the Freedom of Information Act as the keynote speaker at a press conference sponsored by ALA to mark March 16, James Madison's birth date, as Freedom of Information Day. Leahy said the FOIA was part of the First Amendment freedom to get knowledge, speak it, and use it. "No other country has such absolute guarantees," he said. ALA released a media "starter kit" on government information titled "Information: The Currency of Democracy," containing a cumulation of ALA chronologies, "Less Access to Less Information by and about the U.S. Government: A 1981–1987 Chronology," and statements from some of the 43 organizational members of the ALA-developed Coalition on Government Information. The president issued a proclamation designating March 16 FOI Day, following congressional passage of S.J.Res. 126.

Government Information

Early in 1988, the Government Printing Office (GPO), at the request of the congressional Joint Committee on Printing (JCP), suspended a plan to give information vendors at no cost the tapes GPO was selling, in return for making them available to depository libraries on a limited basis. JCP indicated support for distribution of government publications in electronic formats, but requested GPO to develop a broader plan. The broader plan, published in July for comment, involved distribution of three federal CD-ROM products and access for a limited number of depository libraries to two existing government databases. The Depository Library Program entered the age of electronic information dissemination in September, when a Census Bureau CD-ROM product was distributed to selected depository libraries.

In October, the congressional Office of Technology Assessment concluded a two-year study with a report, *Informing the Nation: Federal Information Dissemination in an Electronic Age*. The advent of electronic dissemination, according to OTA, has generated serious conflicts over how to maintain and strengthen public access to government information and balance the roles of the federal government and the private sector. OTA concluded that congressional action is urgently needed to resolve federal information dissemination issues, and to set the direction of federal activities for years to come. Key policy alternatives were listed for GPO, the National Technical Information Service, and the Depository Library Program. (Copies are available for $14 from GPO, Washington, DC 20402-9325, stock number 052-003-01130-1.)

A revised fee policy for patent information was set in a Patent and Trademark

Office extension bill (PL 100-703). The measure authorized the establishment of "reasonable fees for access by the public to automated search systems of the Patent and Trademark Office. . . . If such fees are established, a limited amount of free access shall be made available to all users of the systems for purposes of education and training." Fees may be waived for an individual upon a showing of need or hardship, and if such waiver is in the public interest. The prohibition was maintained against charging the public fees for the use of paper and microform collections of U.S. patents and foreign documents and U.S. trademark registrations arranged to permit search for and retrieval of information. Fees may not be imposed for use of such collections or for use of public patent or trademark search rooms and libraries.

Library Services and Construction Act

In October, Congress gave final approval to HR 4416, the reauthorization for FY 1989 without change of the two expiring Library Services and Construction Act titles (Title V for foreign-language materials and Title VI for library literacy projects). Enactment of HR 4416, now PL 100-569, means that all titles of LSCA are now on the same reauthorization schedule—authorized through September 30, 1989, with an automatic one-year extension for FY 1990 under the General Education Provisions Act.

An interesting, but problematic, approach to the growing numbers of latchkey children being left in public libraries for lack of adequate day care was introduced in October by Representative Olympia Snowe (R–Me.). HR 5486 would provide for demonstration programs to match older volunteers with libraries interested in developing after-school literacy and reading skills programs for latchkey children. The program would be funded by reallocating $5 million in unobligated carryover funds from Title II (public library construction) of the Library Services and Construction Act. No action was taken, but Snowe plans a revised version in 1989 in connection with LSCA reauthorization.

Medical Libraries

Legislation to reauthorize the Medical Library Assistance Act (MLAA) was included in an omnibus health programs extension bill (S. 2889) passed by Congress in October. PL 100-607 extended the current authorization level of $14 million for MLAA for two years through FY 1989 and 1990. It also raised the cap on grants for basic medical library resources from $500,000 to $750,000.

PL 100-607 also authorized $8 million for FY 1989 and such sums as necessary for FY 1990 for a new National Center for Biotechnology Information in the National Library of Medicine. The center is to support the development of improved and enhanced database services related to biotechnology. The legislative history of this provision can be found in S. 1966 (S. Rept. 100-359 and H. Rept. 100-992) and HR 4502 (H. Rept. 100-993). In appropriations action, Congress provided the full $8 million for the center within the NLM budget.

Overall, NLM received $73,731,000 for FY 1989, including $9,673,000 for MLAA. The total is an increase over FY 1988 of 8.6 percent, and more than the administration request of $70,626,000.

National Agricultural Library

Legislation (HR 5056) to clarify the statutory authority for the National Agricultural Library was passed by the House by voice vote on September 26. However, no action was taken by the Senate, which had a similar bill (S. 2138) pending. The House NAL provisions, originally included in HR 1435, introduced in 1987 by Agriculture Committee Chairman E. de la Garza (D–Tex.), were combined with other provisions in the Agricultural Research Act of 1988. The committee's report on HR 5056 (H. Rept. 100-978, Part 1) indicated that the NAL provisions respond to the recommendations of a 1982 blue-ribbon panel which recommended that legislation relating to NAL be reviewed, consolidated, and revised to better support the library's mission.

House-Senate conferees on the FY 1989 agriculture appropriations bill (HR 4784, PL 100-460) agreed to $14,268,000 for NAL, which would have been an increase of 8.8 percent over FY 1988 and more than the administration request of $13,599,000. However, a last-minute error in the version that reached the president for signature left NAL with $13,268,000, $1 million short of the intended amount. At year's end, the library and the Department of Agriculture were exploring ways to get the $1 million reinstated. The permanent loss of the funds would be a disaster for NAL, according to library officials.

NARA and NHPRC

FY 1989 funding for the National Archives and Records Administration was $121,900,000, up from $116 million in FY 1988, although the increased total includes some one-time funding for transfer of Reagan administration papers to California and construction work at the Kennedy Presidential Library. NARA also was authorized to construct a new facility on a donated site at the University of Maryland to relieve severe overcrowding in its current location. The facility would be lease-purchased over a period of time.

Of the NARA total, $4 million was earmarked for the grant programs of the National Historical Publications and Records Commission. In separate legislation (S. 1856, PL 100-365), the NHPRC grant programs were extended for five years at authorization levels of $6 million in FY 1989, $8 million in FY 1990, and $10 million each year for FY 1991, 1992, and 1993. The fields of expertise from which two of the fifteen NHPRC members may be chosen were expanded to include the arts and archival or library science in addition to the existing social or physical sciences.

National Technical Information Service

As part of legislation to reauthorize the National Bureau of Standards (HR 4417, PL 100-519), Congress prohibited privatization of the National Technical Information Service. The provision originated in an amendment by Representative Doug Walgren (D–Pa.), who said, "Information cannot be valued only by its for-profit nature; in fact, it must be evaluated and stored and made available for those circumstances unpredictable in the future when that piece will be the key ingredient to advancing knowledge further."

NTIS received an updated charter and was maintained as a self-supporting clearinghouse in the Commerce Department for the collection and dissemination of unclassified federal technical reports. The provision required that NTIS bibliographic information products be made available in a timely manner to GPO depository libraries. Some exceptions to the ban on contracting out were permitted: NTIS can enter into joint ventures and into contracts for the marketing and promotion of NTIS materials and for equipment to modernize.

The legislative history of the provision is complex but represents the outcome of a long controversy over administration attempts to privatize NTIS. Congress criticized the contracting out of NTIS at hearings in February and May 1988. Earlier bills proposed restructuring NTIS as a government corporation. The Walgren amendment in PL 100-519 repealed such an earlier NTIS-related development. The omnibus trade bill signed into law in August (PL 100-418) prohibited NTIS from entering into contracts for more than $250,000.

Postal Rates

A general postal rate increase took effect April 3, raising a first-class stamp from 22¢ to 25¢. For the fourth-class library rate, a two-pound book package went from 73¢ to 87¢. In congressional funding of the postal revenue forgone appropriation, $436,417,000 was provided for FY 1989, enough to continue free mail for the blind and preferred mail at April 3 rates through September 30, 1989. Revenue forgone funding makes up the difference between full cost and reduced rates for certain preferred classes of mail, such as the library rate.

Preservation

The president signed HR 4867, the Interior Appropriations Bill, into law (PL 100-446) on September 27, with an $8 million increase for the Office of Preservation at the National Endowment for the Humanities—from $4.5 million to $12.5 million. Of this total, $170,000 will be used for administration, leaving $12,330,000 to fund a variety of preservation activities. This significant increase will allow NEH to initiate a multiyear plan to support coordinated preservation efforts, with the emphasis on microfilming brittle books. Congress also restored the administration-requested cut in the NEH Humanities Projects in Libraries and Archives. Details on NEH funding are shown in Table 3.

The NEH preservation increase resulted in large part from a hearing on April 21 held by House Interior Appropriations Subcommittee Chairman Sidney Yates

Table 3 / National Endowment for the Humanities Funding, FY 1989
(Amounts in thousands)

Program	FY 1988 Approp.	FY 1989 Budget	89 House Passed	89 Senate Passed	FY 1989 Final
NEH total	$140,435	$140,435	$153,700	$144,235	$153,000
Humanities projects in libraries and archives	2,900	2,100	2,900	2,800	2,800
Office of Preservation	4,500	4,495	12,500	4,495	12,500
Research grants	16,400	16,400	16,400	16,400	16,400
Challenge grants	16,500	16,700	16,700	16,700	16,700

(D–Ill.). In a wide-ranging, open-forum setting, the hearing explored the microfilming of brittle books, deacidification, and use of alkaline paper. Yates had invited representatives from NEH, LC, the Commission on Preservation and Access, several large research libraries, conservation centers, foundations, associations, GPO, and paper manufacturers. Although NEH had officially requested $4.5 million for its Office of Preservation, Yates requested and received a "Capability Budget" for the Office for FY 1989–1993 showing what could be done with an increase in funding.

FY 1989 appropriations for the Library of Congress allowed it to double its annual rate of preservation microfilming from 11,000 to 22,000 volumes. Congress also approved the library's request to contract with the private sector for a mass deacidification facility, but not for a "sole source" technology solution. LC was commended for advancing the state of the art, but any procurement is to specify, in addition to the safety, mass production and quality standards required by LC and the library community, only the results or product required, not the technology to be used. Total funding for LC in the Legislative Branch Appropriations bill (PL 100-458) was $257,278,000, including $13,034,000 from receipts and $680,000 for the Speaker's Civic Achievement Awards Program administered by LC. The total represents a 3.8 percent increase over FY 1988.

On October 11, Senator Claiborne Pell (D–R.I.) introduced a senate joint resolution establishing as national policy that books and other publications of enduring value be published on acid-free paper. Pell plans to reintroduce the resolution in January 1989, and hopes public hearings will be held soon thereafter.

School Improvement Act

An omnibus five-year reauthorization and amendment of several elementary and secondary education programs was signed into law in April (HR 5, PL 100-297). Popularly known as the School Improvement Act, the official title is the Augustus F. Hawkins-Robert T. Stafford Elementary and Secondary School Improvement Amendments of 1988. The act dropped the Education Consolidation and Improvement Act in favor of the previous name for the programs, the Elementary and Secondary Education Act.

Within ESEA title I, school library resources were retained as one of six targeted areas of assistance under the Chapter 2 school block grant to the states (with 80 percent of state funding earmarked for redistribution to local educational agencies on a formula basis). Training of librarians was added as an eligible Chapter 2 activity, and librarians were added to Chapter 2 state advisory committees. The inexpensive book distribution program for reading motivation (Reading Is Fundamental) was retained as part of the secretary of education's discretionary fund. Library resources and librarian training also were added to Chapter 1 aid to disadvantaged children, and library components were added to several other programs in the School Improvement Act.

"National" was restored to the title of the Center for Education Statistics, and NCES was reorganized and strengthened as a semi-independent entity within the Department of Education. The center was charged with developing and supporting a cooperative system of annual data collection for public libraries with the assistance of state library agencies, and libraries and librarians were added to NCES data collection activities. Within NCES, a National Cooperative Education Statistics System was established to produce and maintain, with the cooperation of the states, comparable and uniform education information and data useful for policymaking at the federal, state, and local levels. Data on the availability and use of school libraries and their resources are among those to be collected. The chairman of the National Commission on Libraries and Information Science was added as a member of the Advisory Council on Education Statistics.

Trade Bill

After an earlier trade bill was vetoed, Congress approved in August a revised Omnibus Trade and Competitiveness Act of 1988 (HR 4848, PL 100-418). Several of its provisions are of interest to librarians. The trade bill reauthorized the president to implement the Nairobi Protocol to the Florence Agreement. The Florence Agreement provides for duty-free trade in certain educational, cultural, and scientific materials and articles for the blind and physically handicapped. The Nairobi Protocol provides for the removal of import duties among adhering countries on audiovisual and microform materials and materials for the blind and physically handicapped not included in the original agreement.

The act authorized an additional $2.5 million for FY 1988 (and such sums for the next three years) for the Higher Education Act II-D College Library Technology and Cooperation grants for "activities that will enable libraries to participate more fully in the initiative funded under the Education and Training for American Competitiveness Act of 1987" (Title VI, the education title of the trade bill). Other programs in Title VI for which authorization was newly provided or increased included various literacy programs such as workplace literacy and a student literacy corps, foreign-language assistance, and technology transfer centers.

Video and Library Privacy Protection

The Video Privacy Protection Act of 1988 provides that personally identifiable information relating to videotape rental or sale records may not be disclosed except under certain narrowly defined circumstances, including with the customer's permission, or under a properly executed warrant, grand jury subpoena, or court order. Approved by Congress in October and signed into law on November 5 (PL 100-618), S. 2361 was known as the "Bork Bill" because of wide publicity over a reporter's story about the videotapes the Supreme Court nominee Judge Bork and his family had rented at a local video store.

As originally introduced, S. 2361 and a related House bill, HR 4947, would have included library patron records, but several developments led to the removal of the library provisions from the bill. The House Judiciary Subcommittee on Courts, Civil Liberties, and the Administration of Justice began to mark up HR 4947 on September 22. According to Subcommittee Chairman Robert Kastenmeier (D–Wis.), the FBI had informally indicated that it wanted an amendment to give the bureau a "national security letter" exemption. Such a letter from the FBI director or a designee would provide sufficient authority to obtain access to library patron records and would exempt the FBI from having to obtain a court order. On October 4, the subcommittee approved HR 4947 without the requested "national security letter" exemption. Kastenmeier said he would not seek full committee or floor action on the bill.

The Senate Judiciary Committee, anticipating that a similar exemption amendment would be offered at markup on October 5, stripped the library portion of S. 2361, leaving video privacy protection intact and avoiding the national security amendment. The revised S. 2361 was then reported out of committee. It passed the Senate without any further attempt to add a "national security letter" exemption. ALA supported the Video and Library Privacy Protection Act as originally introduced, but agreed that if the "national security letter" amendment were added, it would be better to have the library portion of the bill removed entirely and rely on state statutes to secure the privacy rights of library users.

White House Conference

On August 8 the president signed legislation (H.J.Res. 90, now PL 100-382) authorizing the calling of a White House Conference on Library and Information Services (WHCLIS) to be held between September 30, 1989, and September 30, 1991. The next step is separate legislation for federal funding of the conference; $6 million is authorized.

According to the new law, participants in the WHCLIS are to be one-fourth library and information professionals; one-fourth active library and information supporters, including trustees and Friends groups; one-fourth government officials; and one-fourth delegates from the general public. State or territorial conferences may be held but are not required. The conference, to be planned and conducted under the direction of the National Commission on Libraries and Information Science, is for the purpose of developing recommendations for the further improvement of the library and information services of the nation and their use by the public.

To assist and advice NCLIS in planning and conducting the conference, the act also calls for a 30-member advisory committee that is to be broadly representative of all areas of the United States and is to include the secretary of education and the Librarian of Congress, eight members appointed by the NCLIS chair, five by the speaker of the House (whose appointments may include up to three representatives), five by the president pro tempore of the Senate (with up to three senators), and ten by the president. A number of appointments had been made by the end of 1988.

Year of the Young Reader

At a December 5 White House ceremony, President Reagan issued Proclamation 5920 calling upon parents, educators, librarians, publishers, and others to observe 1989 as The Year of the Young Reader. "Families and schools," he said, "can make reading materials a familiar part of youngsters' surroundings and can suggest regular visits to libraries." The proclamation followed passage by Congress of S.J.Res. 315 (now PL 100-662). Representative Mary Rose Oakar (D–Ohio) sponsored the House companion measure. A joint effort of the Center for the Book and the Children's Literature Center in the Library of Congress, The Year of the Young Reader will be used as a theme by state centers for the book, the American Library Association, and other groups.

The week of November 28 through December 5, 1988, was designated National Book Week, by S.J.Res. 342, passed by Congress, signed into law (PL 100-635), and given a strongly worded Proclamation 5914 by the president on November 23: ". . .

Table 4 / Status of Legislation of Interest to Librarians
(100th Congress, 2nd Session, Convened January 25, 1988, Adjourned October 22, 1988)

Legislation	House					Senate					Final Action		
	Introduced	Hearings	Reported by Subcommittee	Committee Report No. (H. Rept. 100–)	Floor Action	Introduced	Hearings	Reported by Subcommittee	Committee Report No. (S. Rept. 100–)	Floor Action	Conference Report (H. Rept. 100–)	Final Passage	Public Law (PL 100–)
Anti-Drug Abuse Act (incl. Child Protection . . .)	HR 5210				X	HR 5210				X	none	X	690
Child Protection and Obscenity Enforcement Act	HR 3889	X				S 2033			none	X			
Competitiveness (new trade bill)	HR 4848				X	S 2558, 2613				X	none	X	418
Copyright – Berne Convention	HR 4262	X		609	X	S 1301	X	X	352	X	none	X	568
Copyright – Computer Programs Rental	HR 1743					S 2727							
Copyright – Record Rental	HR 4310	X	X	776	X	S 2201		X	361	X	none	X	617
E1/Sec Education Programs reauthorization	HR 5	X	X	95	X	S 373	X	X	222	X	567	X	297
FBI First Amendment Protection Act	HR 5369												
Intergenerational Library Literacy Act	HR 5486												
Library Improvement Act						S 2579							
LSCA V and VI Extension	HR 4416			666	X	HR 4416			none	X	none	X	569
Medical Library Assistance Act reauthorization	S 2889					S 2889	X		363	X		X	607

National Agricultural Library	HR 5056			978	X	S 2138							
National Book Week, Nov. 28–Dec. 5, 1988	HJRes 595			none	X	SJRes 342			none	X	none	X	635
NHPRC reauthorization	HR 3933	X	X	533	X	S 1856	X		330	X	none	X	365
National Library Card Sign-up Month	HJRes 549					SJRes 298			none	X			
National Library of Medicine – Biotech. Info. Ctr.	HR 4502			993		S 1966	X		359	X		X	607
NTIS/NBS Authorization	HR 4417, 5183	X		673	X	S 2701	X		466	X	none	X	519
Patent and Trademark Office authorization	HR 4972			none	X	HR 4972			none	X	none	X	703
Pay Equity	HR 387	X	X	914	X	S 552			301				
Permanent Paper resolution						SJRes 394							
Tax Reform Act – Technical Corrections	HR 4333			795	X	S 2238			445	X	1104	X	647
Video (and Library) Privacy Protection Act	HR 4947	X	X		X	S 2361	X	X	599	X	none	X	618
WHCLIS II	HJRes 90	X		121	X	SJRes 26	X		156	X	765	X	382
Year of the Young Reader, 1989	HJRes 565			none	X	SJRes 315			none	X	none	X	662
Appropriations, FY 1989													
Agriculture	HR 4784	X	X	690	X	HR 4784	X	X	389	X	990	X	460
Commerce, State Department	HR 4782	X	X	688	X	HR 4782	X	X	388	X	979	X	459
HUD, Independent Agencies	HR 4800	X	X	701	X	HR 4800	X	X	401	X	817	X	404
Interior	HR 4867	X	X	713	X	HR 4867	X	X	410	X	862	X	446
Labor-HHS-Education	HR 4783	X	X	689	X	HR 4783	X	X	399	X	880	X	436
Legislative	HR 4587	X	X	621	X	HR 4587	X	X	382	X	1000	X	458
Treasury, Postal	HR 4775	X	X	679	X	HR 4775	X	X	387	X	881	X	440

For a free copy of bills, reports, and laws, write: House Documentation Room, H-226 Capitol, Washington, DC 20515; Senate Documentation Room, B-04 Senate Office Building, Washington, DC 20510.

the printed word is an implacable enemy of tyranny, whether that tyranny comes in the form of official censorship by government or fashionable neglect by academia. . . . Our free society, then, must prize its libraries just as it values its liberties."

The Senate passed S.J.Res. 298 to designate September 1988 as National Library Card Sign-Up Month, but by October when the House acted on the related measures above, September had passed and no final action was taken. The measure was designed to promote the campaign by NCLIS and ALA to register every child for a public library card, picking up on published advice by then Secretary of Education William Bennett.

Other Legislative and Regulatory Activity

Child Protection and Obscenity Enforcement Act provisions were tacked onto an end-of-session omnibus Anti-Drug Abuse Act (HR 5210, PL 100-890). The original S. 2033, on which the amendments were based, had the potential for imposing criminal penalties and forfeiture provisions on innocent booksellers and librarians who were found to be in possession of materials later determined obscene. As included in the drug bill, the provisions were considerably modified to reduce such impact, but the effect is still uncertain and of concern.

A House tax subcommittee discussed various options for revision of the unrelated business income tax on nonprofit organizations, but took no legislative action. The House passed a measure (HR 387) providing for a pay equity study of the federal wage and classification system, but the Senate did not take action. Legislation on which no action was taken included HR 1743 and S. 2727, prohibiting the commercial rental, lease, or lending of a particular copy of computer software, and HR 2050, S. 1940, and S. 2160, to restore a tax deduction for artwork or manuscripts donated by their creators to libraries and museums.

Regulations were published for Higher Education Act library programs to implement changes made by the Higher Education Amendments of 1986. In April, the Federal Communications Commission announced the closure of CC Docket 87-215, in which the FCC had proposed to impose access charges on enhanced service providers or value-added networks such as Telenet, CompuServe, and similar services. Libraries would have paid an estimated $4.47 per hour in added costs to access remote databases under the proposal, which was said to have generated the most letters ever to the FCC on a telephone issue.

Table 4 shows the status of legislation of interest to librarians at the end of the One-hundredth Congress.

Legislation and Regulations Affecting Publishing in 1988

Judith Platt
Director of Communications

and Members of the AAP Washington Staff*

Tax Issues

Treatment of Certain Prepublication Costs

An unanticipated consequence of passage of the 1986 Tax Reform Act was a ruling by the Treasury Department requiring the capitalization of a number of prepublication costs that had heretofore been expensed. Efforts were begun almost two years ago to allow educational and professional publishers to treat certain prepublication costs as research and development expenses. Despite widespread bipartisan congressional support, spearheaded by Representative Thomas Downey (D–N.Y.), and ongoing discussions with high-level Treasury officials, legislative relief was not forthcoming in the One-hundredth Congress, because such relief would result in estimated "revenue losses" to the U.S. Treasury of between $350 and $400 million over a five-year period. This issue will be raised again in the One-hundredth and First Congress when it convenes in January.

Postal Issues

Mail-Order Sales/Use Tax

AAP called on Congress to reject bills that would authorize state and local jurisdictions to impose sales and use taxes on mail-order sales. The legislative proposals are seen as particularly injurious for book clubs and other direct book marketers, and counterproductive in light of long-standing congressional policy to promote the dissemination of books and other educational and cultural materials. A strong lobbying effort in support of the legislation has been mounted by state and local governments with the support of some members of Congress, who view the proposal as an attractive way to raise revenues without using federal funds. AAP will actively oppose the legislation if, as expected, it is reintroduced in the new Congress.

Postal Funding

AAP and its allies were able to hold the line on "revenue foregone" funding, permitting a continuation of the subsidy for certain nonprofit mailers.

Removing USPS from the Federal Budget

Bills were introduced in both houses of Congress to remove the U.S. Postal Service from the federal budget and increase its borrowing authority to modernize facilities.

*Contributors to this article include the following members of the Washington professional staff of the Association of American Publishers: Richard P. Kleeman, Diane Rennert, and Carol A. Risher.

USPS had been put back into the federal budget when the Gramm-Rudman-Hollings deficit reduction legislation took effect several years ago. The bill passed the House overwhelmingly but never made it to the Senate floor for consideration prior to adjournment. The U.S. Postal Service has made removal of its funding from the federal budget a top priority for the new Congress.

Copyright

Berne Convention

In the closing hours of the One-hundredth Congress, the Senate ratified the Berne Convention for the Protection of Literary and Artistic Works. The oldest and most comprehensive of the international copyright conventions, Berne went into effect in 1886. Legislation implementing U.S. adherence to the convention was signed into law by President Reagan on October 31.

Long advocated by various segments of the copyright community, U.S. adherence to Berne had been precluded by legal technicalities under earlier U.S. copyright laws. It was not until wide-ranging changes in domestic law were accomplished through passage of the 1976 Copyright Act that U.S. accession to Berne began to appear an attainable goal. The U.S. Register of Copyrights has said that U.S. ratification of the Berne treaty sends a "clear and unmistakable signal to foreign pirates that we will insist upon fair trade in copyrights based upon the minimum guarantees of the Berne Convention." After completion of diplomatic formalities, the United States is expected to become a member of the Berne Union in March 1989.

Visual Artists' Rights

Although the Visual Artists' Rights Act of 1987, sponsored by Senator Edward Kennedy (D–Mass.), ostensibly would apply only to original works of fine art, AAP is still not comfortable with legislation that would introduce a new, inalienable right that would supersede traditional copyright and contractual arrangements. The new Congress is expected to take a new look at this legislation in the context of a comprehensive "moral rights" framework that will also include work-for-hire. [See *Bowker Annual, 1988*, p. 216, for a description of the provisions of the proposed bill.]

Work-for-Hire

Senator Thad Cochran (R–Mass.) introduced a bill that would not only amend the work-for-hire provisions of the copyright law but would regulate certain aspects of author-publisher contractual relationships. Although no hearings were held on the bill during the One-hundredth Congress, Senator Cochran obtained a commitment during the debate on Berne that hearings on a new work-for-hire bill would be held early in the new Congress. AAP will continue to work with a broad-based coalition to fight the legislation.

Omnibus Trade Bill

AAP was instrumental in having language included in the new Omnibus Trade Bill, signed into law by President Reagan in August 1988, which will aid in the fight against international copyright piracy and open overseas markets for U.S. copyrighted works. Four years in the making, the legislation is the most sweeping revision of U.S. trade law since the end of World War II, and mandates a tougher stance by the U.S. government against the unfair trade practices of other nations. Of specific concern to publishers are provisions strengthening Section 301 of the 1974 Trade Act to combat piracy and open foreign markets unfairly closed to U.S. intellectual property industries. The new provisions will broaden and strengthen existing trade law with regard to the protection of intellectual property by requiring the U.S. Trade Representative to identify "priority" countries in which the level of piracy and/or the lack of fair market access create a significant export barrier for U.S. firms. The process of negotiating improvements with these "priority" countries and of recommending remedial action to the president will be accelerated. The legislation also provides the Reagan administration and future administrations with negotiating authority in the ongoing Uruguay round of trade talks under the General Agreement on Tariffs and Trade.

Education

Elementary and Secondary School Improvements Amendment

Signed into law in April 1988, the Elementary and Secondary School Improvements Amendment renews for the next five years virtually all major federal elementary and secondary educational programs. The new law recognizes the importance of instructional materials as a key component of effective educational programs and contains many provisions AAP fought for during the lengthy legislative process. Among them are several programs designed specifically to combat illiteracy; a clearly stated commitment of Chapter Two funds for instructional materials; provisions to improve the gathering and analysis of educational statistics; and an extension of the inexpensive book distribution program.

"Even Start" Literacy Program

AAP strongly supported legislation to authorize the "Even Start" Literacy Program, based on the concept of integrating early childhood education with adult literacy efforts, developing the reading skills of parents at the same time their children are learning to read. A pared-down program, funded at $14 million, was incorporated into the FY 1989 Education Appropriations Bill.

First Amendment

Child Protection and Obscenity Enforcement Act of 1988

In the hours just prior to adjournment, Congress approved an amended version of the Child Protection and Obscenity Enforcement Act of 1988 as part of the Omnibus Drug Bill. The final version was a compromise, and while provisions of the legislation are still troubling, some of the more egregious assaults on the First Amendment were modified. AAP, along with the Media Coalition and other publishing industry entities, closely followed efforts to enact this sweeping new federal legislation, which was aimed at curbing both child pornography and distribution of sexually explicit works to the general population. In testimony before committees of both houses of

Congress, AAP (through its Freedom to Read Committee) made known its support for tougher child pornography sanctions but expressed strong reservations about an expanded federal enforcement role outside of that area. Of special concern to AAP were proposals to create a new federal offense for mainstream publishers, distributors, or booksellers in "possession with intent to distribute" of material which could later be found to be obscene; the imposition of severe criminal and civil penalties and fines arising out of such possession; and the potential forfeiture of major business assets—including First Amendment-protected works—as one of those penalties.

Members of the Media Coalition (including AAP) and other media groups succeeded in persuading lawmakers to change the language regarding criminal forfeiture of materials in obscenity cases. The original Senate version of the bill called for mandatory forfeiture of not only the obscene material but any property purchased with the gross profits of a violation of the obscenity laws and any property used to "commit or to promote" such an offense. The provision generated real concern that a bookseller could lose his or her entire store from mistakenly selling one work later judged to be obscene. The final version approved by Congress leaves the decision to forfeit property used to "commit or to promote" a violation to a judge, who is required to make the determination in light of the "nature, scope, and proportionality of the use of the property in the offense." This change is seen as a safeguard for mainstream booksellers and wholesalers.

The final version also eliminated the Senate provision for civil fines of up to $250,000 for individuals and $500,000 for corporations for *each* defense (each obscene book or magazine would have constituted a separate offense). The compromise also deleted the use of civil forfeiture proceedings to confiscate obscene materials. Finally, the compromise bill seems to draw a distinction between mainstream booksellers and wholesalers and those who deal in obscene materials "as a regular course of business." The bill, as passed, provides that only those "engaged in the business of selling or transferring obscene matter" can be prosecuted for receipt or possession.

Responding to AAP's urging to clarify potentially troubling loophole language with respect to the definition of "engaging in the business" of distributing obscenity, Congressman William J. Hughes (D-N.J.), chairman of the House Judiciary Committee's Subcommittee on Crime, made extended remarks that were published in the *Congressional Record* "to guide the public, the Department of Justice, and the courts in the enforcement of the new law." These remarks significantly narrowed the scope of the legislation so that "the severe penalties upon those in the obscenity business are not to be imposed upon those who are legitimate retailers or publishers who might possess on a single occasion items in inventory that are subsequently judged obscene." Senator Joseph R. Biden (D-Del.), chairman of the Senate Judiciary Committee, made a similar, helpful statement that was also carried in the *Congressional Record.*

Legislation and Regulations Affecting the Information Industry in 1988

David Y. Peyton
Director, Government Relations
Information Industry Association

By the end of 1988, four areas of ongoing concern to the information industry had been confirmed as having primary importance to the U.S. information industry's future: copyright, telecommunications, availability of government records, and avoidance of government duplication of private services. International and state issues also emerged clearly for the first time as having a major bearing on the industry's prospects.

Copyright

Clearly, the major development of the year, from the standpoint of all parties, was U.S. ratification of the Berne Copyright Convention of 1886, effective March 1, 1989, and the associated implementing legislation. The United States will be gaining strong copyright relations with 24 countries where relations are now unclear or nonexistent, plus an enhanced voice in international copyright consultations. To comply with treaty requirements, Congress had to amend the U.S. Copyright Act in several ways. Notably, the copyright notice will no longer be required; and registration and recording of transfers with the Copyright Office will no longer be required for foreign works, although retained for domestic works. The information industry strongly supported adherence.

Congress also passed the Intellectual Property Licensing Bankruptcy Protection Act, which overruled a much-criticized bankruptcy decision, *Lubrizol* vs. *Richmond Metal Finishers.* That case had held that a trustee in bankruptcy could withdraw an exclusive license based on intellectual property protection, even against the will of the licensee. For example, a compact disc publisher relying on a small outside firm for its search software could have had that software revoked in a bankruptcy proceeding, with the result that it would have had to withdraw its CDs from licensees such as libraries. Under the new law, such revocation can no longer happen, provided the licensee continues to make royalty payments.

Government Automation and Information Dissemination

Perhaps the most significant legislative development in the area of government information dissemination was the creation, by the massive Omnibus Trade and Competitiveness Act, of a National Trade Data Bank in the Commerce Department. The authorizing language reflects the basic principles of *Office and Management Circular A-130,* "The Management of Information Resources," in that duplication of services already offered by the private sector is to be avoided. The Information Industry Association (IIA) and its members are in continuing discussions with Commerce about the shape of this major new export-related database.

Other agencies pursuing major automation efforts include the Patent and Trademark Office (PTO) and the Customs Bureau. In authorizing the PTO for three years, Congress reversed an earlier prohibition against the imposition of any fees for use of automated facilities in the PTO's public search rooms. Legislative history also made clear that the PTO would have to get permission from copyright owners before entering copyrighted works into its own databases. Customs's efforts to automate vessel manifests raised different questions. To promote computerization by port authorities, Customs proposed to provide only them, and not companies in the information industry, with direct access to data, either online or by daily tape. Despite industry objections, Customs held to this plan until successfully sued by a company seeking access.

The future of the National Technical Information Service (NTIS) has been in question for several years, and Congress finally settled the matter in the authorizing legislation for the National Institute of Standards and Technology (formerly National Bureau of Standards). Opting essentially for keeping NTIS largely as is, Congress rejected both administration plans for large-scale contracting out or "privatization" and the idea to turn NTIS into a government corporation. The law imposes a dollar ceiling on NTIS contracts and reinforces the short NTIS organic statute, to provide for distribution of NTIS's bibliography to federal depository libraries.

Another agency whose information dissemination activities came under review was the Department of Energy, which is responsible for the output of its system of national laboratories. A number of times over the years, the Reagan administration has sought limitations or exemptions to the release of unclassified government technical data, claiming that release of such data would compromise national technological or economic security. The most recent reflection of that concern came in bills to promote superconductor activities at the laboratories. Congress finally passed a National Superconductivity and Competitiveness Act without any new authority for national laboratory directors to withhold unclassified technical data or software. A wide range of private groups, including the information industry, had objected to such provisions as unsupported and dangerous. However, an unpassed broad DOE authorization bill introduced in the closing days of Congress contained similar language, suggesting that the issue would return next Congress.

Telecommunications

In 1988, voice information services rose to occupy significant congressional attention. To the dismay of companies offering uncontroversial services, from dial-a-diet to stock market quotations, Congress passed sweeping and strict legislation to deal with sexually oriented services, or dial-a-porn. Language in the Department of Education authorization banned not only obscene but also "indecent" communications interstate. The standard dealing with indecency was immediately and successfully challenged in federal court on First Amendment grounds. The emotional election year atmosphere proved fatally inhospitable to efforts to reach a middle-ground compromise, under which telephone companies would make "good faith" efforts to prevent sexually oriented programming from reaching minors. The evident unconstitutionality of the provision that was passed left the future of the matter in some doubt.

The future of the Regional Bell Operating Companies (RBOCs) continued to occupy the foreground of telecommunications policy. The primary arena continued to be federal district court in Washington, with Judge Harold Greene issuing a major ruling on the Justice Department's petition to remove most line-of-business restrictions on the RBOCs. While rejecting the better part of Justice's request—which was strongly supported by the companies themselves—the judge did allow the companies to start offering gateway services, including menus and billing. Not satisfied with this step, however, the RBOCs pressed for appellate reversal of Judge Greene's decision and also sought relief in Congress. A House resolution to the effect that the restrictions should be removed attracted widespread opposition from numerous groups, including the information industry, and did not pass. However, there were indications that similar legislation might be reintroduced in the One Hundred and First Congress.

In regulatory matters, the Federal Communications Commission formally dropped a plan to impose special access charges on lines used to provide enhanced or information services, such as database and data processing services. The FCC's theory had been that all users should contribute to the access charges paid by interexchange carriers to local carriers, but industry successfully countered that there was no reason to create a new and distinct rate class for enhanced service providers, apart from other business users. Furthermore, the dramatically increased rates would certainly stunt industry and service growth.

However, many apprehended that the substance of the special access charge proposal was reappearing in the FCC's proposed order on Open Network Architecture (ONA) plans, voted on but not yet released by the year's end. The ONA plans from the seven RBOCs overhaul numerous tariffs so as to unbundle various service elements for the benefit of users. The troublesome provision would allow telephone companies to charge customers, for the first time, on a usage-sensitive basis.

Other Domestic Issues

Computer security grabbed attention at year's end as a computer virus penetrated Internet, the university and research network, largely bringing it to a halt for a whole day. It remained to be seen whether the suspect could be successfully prosecuted under the existing federal Computer Fraud and Abuse Act, which did not specifically contemplate viruses. If not, then chances would seem high for reintroduction of legislation to amend the act to deal with viruses, introduced but not taken up in the last Congress.

Libel arose as an issue for the information industry in the case of *Blue Ridge National Bank* vs. *Veribanc*. There, a bank sued a small database publisher for libel on the grounds that it had erroneously predicted that the bank was headed toward insolvency. The publisher, for its part, has relied on standard federal reports from the Federal Reserve. The IIA filed a friend of the court brief on behalf of the defendant, arguing that it stood to be put under an impossible burden of going beyond the level of information required in federal reports.

International Issues

International issues of import to the information industry mirror those important domestically. As the information business becomes a more global one, the same conditions necessary for industry success in the United States also apply worldwide: adequate copyright protection, competitive provision of telecommunications, availability of government records, and forbearance by government from duplication of privately offered services.

With regard to copyright, U.S. accession to the Berne Convention immediately boosted the credibility of U.S. positions in critical proceedings. The first is the attempt by the United States and other developed nations to gain addition of an intellectual property code to the General Agreement on Tariffs and Trade (GATT). At the Montreal meeting of GATT trade ministers in December 1987, India continued to lead Third World opposition to such a code. However, the United States planned to keep the issue alive by negotiating with countries, both developed and developing, that saw the need for more orderly trade in intellectual property. Also, the World Intellectual Property Organization (WIPO), the United Nations agency that administers the Berne Convention, is well along toward writing a model copyright law, with conclusive meetings set for late February 1989. Prospects looked good for the model law to specify copyright protection for software and databases.

In telecommunications, the United States successfully concluded negotiations with both Britain and Japan for essentially unrestricted use of leased lines to provide value-added services such as delivered by the information industry. This was a major step forward for liberalization. In late November and early December, the International Telecommunications Union (another UN agency) assembled a diplomatic World Administrative Telephone and Telegraph Conference (WATTC) in Melbourne. Many U.S. business groups had been apprehensive that the conference would produce more restrictive rules for international value-added services.

The result was somewhat ambiguous, with a final text seeming to permit national governments to impose such rules if they saw fit, but not requiring such a result. The United States was able to sign the text with a reservation that it understood the rules to apply only to government telecommunications administrations and so-called Recognized Private Operating Agencies. Also of significance was the parallel attempt by the United States and other developed countries to add a GATT code on trade in services, including telecommunications-based services. The Montreal outcome was more favorable, with negotiators reaching a tentative framework for a GATT agreement on services.

The conclusion of a Free Trade Area between the United States and Canada, however, marked the first binding international document on trade in services, including those based on telecommunications. Earlier documents on free or relatively free international information flows had only been hortatory. This new treaty, however, provides real prospective rights and guarantees about being able to conduct information business internationally without nontariff trade barriers.

State Issues

Finally, state information policy emerged as a true subject in 1988, with a first conference on the subject organized by the Council on State Governments. The most controversial issue arose in New York, where the state government proposed, over strenuous industry objections, to stop making Uniform Commercial Code information available in machine-readable form, in favor of an in-house government dial-up service. The proposal, unresolved at year's end, would have spelled the end of most commercial information services offering business credit information about New York State. In addition, Florida, still the only state to have amended its public records law explicitly to provide for online and tape availability of public records, announced hearings early in 1989 to assess the progress of its policies.

A National Policy on Permanent Paper: An Idea Whose Time Has Come

Claiborne Pell
Chairman, Joint Committee on the Library, U.S. Senate

Many of us in the legislative branch are becoming increasingly concerned about the fact that we are facing the loss of an enormous part of our historical, cultural, and scientific record because of the self-destruction of the acidic papers on which books and other publications have been printed since the mid-nineteenth century. I have been particularly concerned about this problem in my role as chairman of the Joint Committee on the Library in the One-hundredth Congress over the past two years.

The Library of Congress is a pioneer in developing the technology for mass deacidification of its collections through the use of diethylzinc (DEZ). A pilot plant utilizing this process is now being tested in Houston, with the expectation that a large-scale facility will soon be in operation under license from the library. The present goal is to begin treatment of all LC's new acquisitions by 1991 and to start retrospective treatment at the same time of existing publications in American history.

The National Archives and Records Administration and the National Library of Medicine are also making vigorous efforts to deal with the problem, either through deacidification or through microfilming books and publications that are already too brittle to save. Congress has already appropriated more than $100 million in support of these efforts, and we should be prepared to provide more. At stake is nothing less than the preservation of the whole record and literary output of the most remarkable century of human experience to date.

It makes little sense, though, to continue the remedy without attempting to curb the basic problem. And that is why I have introduced a resolution to establish a national policy to promote and encourage the printing of books and other publications of enduring value on nonacidic paper. In a figurative sense, it locks the library door against prospective invasion by publications printed on acidic paper.

The resolution declares it to be a policy of the United States that all federal records, books, and publications of enduring value be produced on acid-free papers. In furtherance of that objective, the resolution urgently recommends that federal agencies require the use of archival quality papers for permanently valuable federal records, and the use of permanent papers for other publications of enduring value. The resolution would also urgently recommend that American publishers voluntarily adhere to the American National Standard for permanent paper in printing publications of enduring value, and that the use of such paper be noted in the publication, in advertisements, and in standard bibliographic listings. Finally, the resolution would urge the compilation of reliable statistics on the production of permanent paper and on the volume of production required to meet the objectives of the national policy established by the bill. And it would direct the Librarian of Congress and the Archivist of the United States, together with the directors of the National Libraries of Medicine and Agriculture, to monitor progress in implementing the national policy and report annually to Congress.

It is worth noting that some progress is already being made toward implementing the national policy. The recent excellent study of Book Preservation Technologies prepared by the Office of Technology Assessment estimated that 15 to 25 percent of the books currently being published in the United States are printed on acid-free paper. The Library of Congress and many university presses are among those already publishing on acid-free papers, as is the National Historical Publications and Records Commission. As a former member of the commission, I am proud to have had a role in establishing its policy of publishing on permanent paper.

Clearly, the technology exists to implement the national policy. I am advised that permanent papers with a life of several hundred years can be produced at prices generally competitive with acid papers. The implementation of a national policy with respect to federal records and publications surely would stimulate an expansion of production of nonacidic papers and, it is hoped, would lead to increasingly competitive prices.

Finally, it should be noted that the implementation of the national policy, by attacking the problem prospectively, will have the effect of reducing the long-range costs of deacidification. Every book produced on acid-free paper today frees up preservation resources that can be used to attack the crumbling backlog of publications dating back to 1850.

For all of these reasons, it seems to me that the establishment of a national policy on permanent papers is an idea whose time has come. I hope that my resolution will be favorably considered in the Senate in 1989, and I welcome any support that the library and book trade community may see fit to extend.

Funding Programs and Grant-Making Agencies

Council on Library Resources

Ellen B. Timmer
Editor

The Council on Library Resources (CLR), a private operating foundation, was founded in 1956 with support from the Ford Foundation to put "emerging technologies to use in order to improve operating performance and expand library services." While continuing its initial concentration on technological applications in academic and research libraries, the council has gradually expanded its focus to reflect changing needs and opportunities in areas such as linking computer systems, making library management more effective, improving access to library materials, addressing international concerns, exploring cooperative approaches, and enhancing the skills of librarians. One of CLR's most important undertakings in 1987–1988 was to review the CLR program and to establish council direction for the next few years. Following the review, thc CLR program was restructured into two categories: (1) library management and operations and (2) librarianship and professional education.

During FY 1987–1988, CLR received financial support from the Ford Foundation, the J. Paul Getty Trust, the William and Flora Hewlett Foundation, the Andrew W. Mellon Foundation, the Pew Charitable Trusts, the Alfred P. Sloan Foundation, and the H. W. Wilson Foundation. Support for the Commission on Preservation and Access (mentioned later in this report) was received from the Getty Grant Program, the William and Flora Hewlett Foundation, the Andrew W. Mellon Foundation, the H. W. Wilson Foundation, participants in the New York State Preservation Program, and nine universities.

The council's board of directors is composed of 20 individuals from academic institutions, research libraries, business, and the professions. CLR officers are Maximilian W. Kempner, chairman; Charles D. Churchwell, vice chairman; Warren J. Haas, president; Deanna B. Marcum, vice president; and Mary Agnes Thompson, secretary and treasurer.

Highlights of FY 1988

Research

The council's research program has three components: *Institutional grants* stimulate and encourage collaborative projects among various units of the university—departments, schools, institutes—and the university library. *Individual grants* are made in response to proposals by researchers. A newly formed Research Library Committee is charting a plan that will result in *commissioned studies* of the future of academic information services.

The council's grant to the University of California, Los Angeles, continues to stimulate strategic planning for future information services required by the several schools and departments of the university. Most recently, these planning efforts have contributed to the university-wide effort at UCLA to develop an Academic Strategic Plan.

A 1987 grant to the University of Minnesota supports collaborative efforts among the university libraries, the Hubert H. Humphrey Institute of Public Affairs, and the Curtis L. Carlson School of Management. The objective is to develop an integrated information center to serve the needs of faculty and graduate students of the Humphrey Institute.

A grant to Carnegie Mellon University in 1987 supported a study group, involving the university libraries, the Department of Computer Science, and the Laboratory for Computational Linguistics, which investigated problems in the structuring of electronic text. The purpose of this grant was to identify and explore the issues involved in making large amounts of text available for distribution through electronic media.

A fourth institutional grant, to the University of Illinois at Chicago, enabled two members of the university library staff to spend a year as participants at the university's Institute for the Humanities. The objective was to begin a process of engaging faculty in exploring, with the library, questions pertaining to the methods and informational tools they use to do their research, how they communicate their work, and how that work is disseminated.

Recipients of the first individual grant in the research program, Elizabeth Liddy and Robert Oddy of Syracuse University, continued their research on two related topics: how to represent better the information content of documents and how to assist users to present better their needs to an information system. At the University of Missouri-Columbia, MaryEllen Sievert, assistant professor of information science, and Donald Sievert, professor of philosophy, began a study of the information requirements of philosophy faculty and graduate students at a number of universities in the Midwest.

Early in 1988, the council organized a Research Library Committee composed of more than two dozen individuals—university presidents, provosts, deans, librarians, scholars from several fields, foundation officers, and information scientists—with the active collaboration of the American Council of Learned Societies, the Association of American Universities, and the Social Science Research Council. The committee is developing a plan for a schedule of investigations, studies, and probing position papers whose end is the specifications for the research library of the future.

Access to Information

The Access to Information program has been funded for the past five years by a grant from the Ford Foundation. The council has initiated activities and awarded grants to libraries and individuals to promote equitable access to information and to study all aspects of information delivery systems that provide the resources needed by library users. In 1987–1988, CLR grantees produced guides to previously unavailable resources, conducted experiments to improve and facilitate online catalog access, and studied the information-seeking behavior of several disciplinary groups. Lawrence Dowler, archivist at the Harvard University Library, began a study of how scholars use archives and what their research needs are likely to be in the future.

The British Library received a grant for an international conference on increasing access to Japanese scientific and technical information. As a result of the grant, the proceedings of the conference will be available to U.S. libraries at reduced cost.

CLR staff met with directors of 60 liberal arts colleges at Grinnell College (Iowa) in October 1987. Participants were especially interested in access to research resources and machine-readable data for collegiate institutions.

Bibliographic Services

Substantial CLR resources have been invested over the years in a bibliographic system configuration that will allow library patrons at any location to have complete access to bibliographic information, no matter what its source. Since the Bibliographic Service Development Program has ended, two coordinating committees—the LSP Policy Committee and the LSP Technical Committee—are overseeing the work required to install the Linked Systems Protocols that ultimately will allow the exchange of bibliographic records from one network to another.

The National Coordinated Cataloging Project, aided by a CLR grant to the Library of Congress, moved into training and operational phases in 1988. Eight research libraries agreed to contribute original cataloging records for certain categories of materials directly to the Library of Congress for immediate distribution via MARC (Machine-Readable Cataloging) tapes. To monitor the work of the Coordinated Cataloging Project and to ensure that managerial concerns are addressed, CLR appointed a Bibliographic Services Study Committee (Carol Mandel, Columbia University, chair; Dorothy Gregor, University of California, San Diego; Martin Runkle, University of Chicago; and Paul Kantor, Tantalus, Inc.). The group met three times during the year to plan a survey of ARL libraries to determine the variations in practices between original and copy cataloging and to predict the subsequent financial savings in copy cataloging. Methods and practices that seem to be cost-effective will be reported for the benefit of other libraries. In the longer term, the committee will study several aspects of equitable access to bibliographic information, including the need to enhance the bibliographic structure for humanistic scholarship.

Karen Markey (University of Michigan) and Diana Vizine-Goetz (OCLC, Inc.) produced an interim report on their study of automated techniques for linking subject terms entered by users of online catalogs with the controlled vocabulary of the online catalog.

Librarianship and Librarians

Basic professional education and continuing education for those already at work in libraries were the subjects of much discussion within CLR during 1988. In 1989, the council will continue to develop the long-term program that is required to enhance professional skills among those who must guide the transformation of research libraries.

During 1987–1988, several grants made under the Internships for Recent Graduates program were completed. The multi-institutional program in Chicago was conducted for a third and final year, and the University of Missouri-Columbia's two-year program was also completed. Thus far in the program, 51 relatively new librarians have been given the opportunity to learn more about the library in the context of the research university. Program activities at the University of Georgia will continue for another year, and an internship program at Columbia University is being planned.

Yale University, with a CLR grant, offered summer internships for three of its undergraduates in 1987 to introduce them to librarianship as a possible career. The results were encouraging, and a second grant was made to continue the program in summer 1988.

In March 1988, three librarians were selected to participate in CLR's Academic Library Management Intern Program for the 1988–1989 academic year: Patricia Iannuzzi of Yale University, to work with Joseph A. Rosenthal, director, University Library, University of California, Berkeley; Sarah Pritchard, Library of Congress, to work with Donald W. Koepp, university librarian, Princeton University; and Sarah Watstein of Hunter College, to work with Norman D. Stevens, director of the University of Connecticut Library.

Two cycles of Faculty/Librarian Cooperative Research grants in 1987–1988 resulted in funding for 15 teams of researchers. These grants continue to stimulate productive collaboration between practicing librarians and teaching faculty who have jointly identified library problems that can be addressed by a research project. The reports, generally of high quality, have been distributed widely through the professional literature and the ERIC Clearinghouse.

The University of Chicago's Graduate Library School implemented its curriculum concentration in library automation and information systems with ongoing funding from the council. Other grants were made to the Association of Research Libraries' Office of Management Studies to conduct a third Institute for Library Educators and to the Senior Fellows program at the University of California, Los Angeles, to host a fifth class in 1989.

Preservation

At the end of FY 1988, the Commission on Preservation and Access, created in 1986 by CLR following a two-year study of the scope of national preservation needs, was incorporated as a separate nonprofit organization. The commission will retain appropriate functional ties to CLR, and the CLR president will serve as a member of the commission's board of directors.

With the arrival in August 1987 of the commission's first president, Patricia Battin, the work of the organization expanded, and two immediate tasks emerged: responding to increased congressional interest in funding a nationwide preservation microfilming program through the National Endowment for the Humanities' Office of Preservation and seeking nongovernmental funding for the commission's programs. At the same time, development of a structure for a nationwide preservation microfilming program continued. During 1988, the commission also worked to establish links with commercial and university publishers, writers, and paper manufacturers to encourage the increased production and use of alkaline paper.

The problem of deteriorating scientific literature was addressed in a daylong meeting sponsored by the commission in October 1987. Medical and scientific literature often requires coated paper for proper display of graphic information, and most coated paper used in such publications is acidic.

A variety of projects were funded during 1988, including broadcasting the preservation film "Slow Fires" on the national Public Broadcasting System. Also funded was a project to determine the feasibility of developing an international database of bibliographic records of materials on microfilm. The Mid-Atlantic Preservation Service received funds to develop archival standards for the use of 105mm microfiche film.

Major New Grants and Contracts, FY 1987–1988

Educational Broadcasting Corporation	
Public broadcast of the film "Slow Fires"	$14,950
International Federation of Library Associations and Institutions	
Joint Colloquium on Newspaper Resource Sharing	$11,700
Mid-Atlantic Preservation Service	
Start-up and capital equipment support	$47,956
Study of microfiche production standards	$24,131
Hans Rütiman	
Development of an international bibliographic records database on preservation activity	$50,000
Simmons College	
Symposium on solutions to the problems of recruiting, educating, and training cataloging librarians	$15,000
University of California, Los Angeles	
Study of microcomputer-based digital imaging as a technique for preservation of library materials	$20,500
Senior Fellows conference, 1988	$25,000
Senior Fellows program, 1989	$30,000
University of Missouri-Columbia	
Study of information needs of philosophers	$34,625
Yale University	
Undergraduate Internship Program	$16,000

U.S. Department of Education Library Programs, 1988

Anne J. Mathews

Director, Library Programs
Office of Educational Research and Improvement
U.S. Department of Education

555 New Jersey Ave., N.W., Washington, DC 20208-5571
202-357-6293

The Library Programs Office in the U.S. Department of Education makes a major contribution to the improvement of the nation's libraries and library education by administering the ten programs under the Library Services and Construction Act (LSCA) and the Higher Education Act (HEA). These ten programs

- Promote resource sharing and cooperation among all types of libraries by facilitating development and access to databases that permit individuals to find and use books and other materials from libraries around the country
- Help state library agencies to improve local library services for all citizens, yet focus on underserved populations such as the elderly and handicapped
- Provide financial assistance for construction of new public library facilities and modification of existing ones
- Improve library services to native populations, including Indian tribes, Alaskan native villages, and Hawaiian natives
- Support adult literacy projects conducted by state library agencies and local public libraries
- Strengthen major research libraries, including those of postsecondary institutions, by helping them improve access to important collections, preserve deteriorating materials, and acquire unique, distinctive, and specialized materials
- Advance the education of librarians through fellowships and training institutes
- Encourage colleges and universities to promote and develop exemplary uses of technology for resource sharing and networking
- Fund research and demonstration projects on library and information science issues

Higher Education Act (HEA, PL 99-498)

Title II of the Higher Education Act has been the backbone of federal financial assistance to college and university libraries for two decades. With the enormous expansion of resources and demand on higher education libraries, Title II has been a vital element in helping these libraries preserve, acquire, and share resources and

Note: The following staff members of Library Programs assisted in writing and/or compiling data for this article: Pat Alexander, Carol Cameron, Yvonne Carter, Adrienne Chute, Beth Fine, Clarence Foglestrom, Donald Fork, Barbara Humes, Robert Klassen, Dorothy Kittel, Linda Loeb, Sandy Pemberton, Jan Owens, Trish Skaptason, Frank Stevens, Louise Sutherland, and Diane Villines.

train and retrain personnel to improve services or use new technology. In 1986, HEA Title II was reauthorized and some parts rewritten to accommodate further change, including the establishment of a new program, the College Library Technology and Cooperation Grants program (HEA, Title II-D). In 1987, these amendments were implemented fully through revisions in the regulations and the development of new regulations for the II-D program.

College Library Resources Program (HEA, Title II-A)

During its reauthorization in Congress in 1986, the Title II-A portion of the Higher Education Act was amended to award grants to institutions of higher education strictly on the basis of need. To date, no funds have been appropriated.

Library Career Training Program (HEA, Title II-B)

The Library Career Training Program (Title II-B of the Higher Education Act) authorizes a program of federal financial assistance to institutions of higher education and other library organizations and agencies to assist in training persons in librarianship and to establish, develop, and expand programs of library and information science. Grants are made for fellowships and traineeships at the associate, bachelor, master, postmaster, and doctoral levels of training in librarianship. Grants may also be used to assist in covering the costs of institutes or courses, to upgrade the competencies of persons serving in all types of libraries, information centers, or instructional materials centers offering library and information services, and those serving as educators. In FY 1988, Congress appropriated $718,000 for the two programs in HEA Title II-B. Of this amount, $410,000 was allocated for the Library Career Training Program. Table 1 shows the Library Career Training Grants awarded in FY 1988.

Fellowship Program

In FY 1988, $282,800 was awarded for fellowships under HEA Title II-B. Twenty awards were made to support 23 fellowships (14 master's, and 9 doctoral). Stipend levels were $5,400 for master's, $7,400 for postmaster's, and $7,400 for doctoral training. Institutions receive an amount equal to the stipend to cover the cost of training. Between 1966 and 1988, institutions of higher education were awarded 1,081 doctoral, 243 postmaster's, 2,751 master's, 16 bachelor's, and 53 associate's fellowships and 77 traineeships, totaling 4,221 awards. Table 2 reviews the fellowship program since it began in FY 1966.

Institute Program

The institute program provides long- and short-term training and retraining opportunities for librarians, media specialists, information scientists, and persons desiring to enter these professions. Many institutes have given experienced practitioners the opportunity to update and advance their skills in a given area of librarianship. Institute programs have been supported since FY 1968 under the Higher Education Act of 1965 and since FY 1973 under further amendments included in the Education Amendments of 1972 and the Higher Education Amendments of 1986. Due to lim-

Table 1 / HEA Title II-B, Library Career Training Program, FY 1988

Institution	Fellowships	
	No. and Level	Amount
University of California, Los Angeles	1 master's	9,200
Florida State University	1 doctoral	14,800
Atlanta University	1 master's	10,800
University of Illinois	1 doctoral	14,800
Indiana University	1 master's	10,800
Indiana University	2 doctoral	29,600
Louisiana State University	1 master's	10,800
University of Maryland	1 master's	10,800
University of Michigan	1 master's	10,800
Rutgers University	1 master's	10,800
Rutgers University	1 doctoral	14,800
Columbia University	1 master's	10,800
CUNY, Queens College	1 master's	10,800
Syracuse University	1 master's	10,800
University of Pittsburgh	2 doctoral	29,600
North Texas State University	1 doctoral	14,800
Texas Woman's University	1 master's	10,800
University of Texas	1 master's	10,800
University of Wisconsin, Madison	1 doctoral	14,800
University of Wisconsin, Milwaukee	2 master's	21,600
Subtotals	14 master's 9 doctoral	
Total	23 fellowships	$282,800
Institutes		
West Virginia University		$27,509
University of Wisconsin, Madison		72,658
University of Wisconsin, Milwaukee		26,909
Total		$127,076

ited funds, no invitations were made for applications for institutes between 1979 and 1986. In FY 1987, however, applications for institutes were invited to determine the degree of interest and need. Eight proposals were received and two were funded to serve 40 participants. No priorities were established for the competition.

In FY 1988, applications were invited again, and 23 proposals were received. Three were funded, totaling $127,076. The institutes were carried out during the 1988–1989 school year at the University of West Virginia for school librarians, at the University of Wisconsin, Madison, for children's services librarians, and at the University of Wisconsin, Milwaukee, for urban academic and public librarians.

Library Research and Demonstration Program (HEA Title II-B)

The Library Research and Demonstration Program (Title II-B of the Higher Education Act) authorizes the award of grants and contracts for research and demonstration projects related to the improvement of libraries, training in librarianship, and the dissemination of information derived from these projects. Title II, Part B, of the Higher Education Act was amended by the Higher Education Amendments of 1986 and, in 1987, the Research and Demonstration regulations were amended to implement the statutorily mandated change deleting "information technology" from the

Table 2 / HEA Title II-B, Library Education Fellowship/Traineeship Program, Academic Years 1966–1988

Academic Year	No. of Insti-tutions	Fellowship/Traineeship						
		Doctoral	Master	Post-Master	Bachelor	Asso-ciate	Total	FY
1966/67	24	52	25	62	–	–	139	1966
1967/68	38	116	58	327	–	–	501	1967
1968/69	51	168	47	494	–	–	709	1968
1969/70	56	193	30	379	–	–	602	1969
1970/71	48	171	15	200	20*	–	406	1970
1971/72	20	116	6	–	20*	–	142	1971
1972/73	15	39	3	20*	–	–	62	1972
1973/74	34	21	4	145 + 14*	–	20	204	1973
1974/75	50	21	3	168 + 3*	–	5	200	1974
1975/76	22	27	6	94	–	–	127	1975
1976/77	12	5	3	43	–	–	51	1976
1977/78	37	18	3	134	–	5	160	1977
1978/79	33	25	9	139	10	5	188	1978
1979/80	36	19	4	134	2	3	162	1979
1980/81	32	17	5	72	–	7	101	1980
1981/82	34	13	2	59	–	5	79	1981
1982/83	33	13	2	56	–	3	74	1982
1983/84	33	8	7	56	4	–	75	1983
1984/85	41	5	4	67	–	–	76	1984
1985/86	38	11	4	57	–	–	72	1985
1986/87	39	14	3	51	–	–	68	1986
1987/88	29	10	5	45	–	–	60	1987
1988/89	20	9	0	14	–	–	23	1988
Total		1,091	248	2,796 + 37*	16 + 40*	53	4,281	

*traineeships.

list of authorized research and demonstration project subjects. This amendment precludes research on or about information technology, but allows the use of technology to accomplish the goals of a research or demonstration project.

Fiscal year 1987 was the first year since 1980 that field-initiated applications were sought. In FY 1988, 49 proposals were submitted and 5 were selected for funding, totaling $307,323. Four of the projects are research based and one is a demonstration. These projects are:

University of Alaska, Project director: Patricia Book. *Summer Institutes of Circumpolar Studies—A Demonstration:* The University of Alaska proposes to involve anthropologists, geographers, historians, and librarians in an institute on "People of the Circumpolar North." The Circumpolar North studies involve special circumstances not usually found in U.S. regional studies. The institute will demonstrate the use of multidisciplinary activities involving explorations, government, scientific and academic research, administrative studies, and their continuing interaction with native traditions and lifestyles. The resulting research papers and bibliographies will analyze specific aspects of life in the Circumpolar North and, at the same time, will provide details on search strategy and the primary and secondary sources used. *Grant award:* $63,646.

University of Chicago, Project director: Don Swanson. *Medical Literature as a Source of New Knowledge:* The goal of this project is to extend work already in progress to develop and describe systematic techniques of literature exploration that can lead to the discovery of new knowledge. The specific objectives are (1) to demonstrate more examples, within the biomedical literature, of unnoticed logical connections that are potential sources of new knowledge; (2) to develop further and describe online search strategies that can aid, stimulate, and systematize the discovery of such connections; and (3) to develop requirements for representing logical relationships in the process of indexing biomedical articles for entry into online databases. *Grant award:* $41,248.

Rutgers University, School of Communication, Information, and Library Studies, Project director: Tefko Saracevic. *Nature and Improvement of Libraries—User Interaction and Online Searching for Information Delivery in Libraries:* The aim of the study is to provide guidelines and insight leading to improvement of information delivery to users in libraries, specifically in the area of library online information services, by exploring cognitive decisions and human-system and human-human interactions by librarians and users in information seeking and searching. The objectives are (1) to analyze the nature and pattern of online searches that are optimized for a given set of questions and user-evaluated answers; (2) to analyze the nature and patterns of discourse in librarian user interactions connected with information seeking and searching; (3) to provide guidelines and explanations of improved searches and interactions and conduct pilot tests of those; and (4) to actively disseminate results through papers, presentations and construction of model courses. *Grant award:* $84,823.

Clarion State University, Project director: Bernard Vavrek. *Assessing Information Needs of Rural Americans:* In a majority of rural communities no other information/educational resource exists outside the public library. To enable rural public libraries to become more efficient in serving their constituencies, the following data are needed: What do rural people think about their public libraries? What are the information needs of rural Americans? To what extent do rural public libraries meet the information needs of their users? Training materials for the rural public "librarian" will be developed and disseminated based on these data. *Grant award:* $57,443.

Indiana University Foundation, Project director: Verna Pungitore. *Dissemination of Public Library Planning Process:* This project proposes to document the effort that went into the development, evaluation, refinement, and dissemination of *The Planning Process* (a manual developed by the Public Library Association and funded under HEA, II-B, in 1980) and its second phase, *The Public Library Development Project* (begun in July 1987). It will also explore the factors that tend to inhibit and those that facilitate the dissemination and utilization of administrative innovations among smaller public libraries. The proposal includes a content analysis of the professional literature to determine whether a small group of core journals exists through which *The Planning Process* was promoted and debated, and whether trends can be observed in the number and nature of references to *The Planning Process* in the literature during the specified eight-year period. The various parts of the study should, in combination, provide insight into the ways in which information flows among members of the public library profession and suggestions concerning which techniques and channels appear to be the most productive for future diffusion projects. *Grant award:* $57,143.

Three projects awarded in FY 1986— "Issues in Library Research: Proposals for the Nineties," "Readers Are Leaders," and "Libraries and Literacy Education"—and three projects funded in FY 1987—"Facilitating Information through Cognitive

Models of the Search Process," "The Effectiveness of Libraries: The Public Library," and "The Evaluation of Adult Literacy Programs"—continued through FY 1988.

Table 3 summarizes the Research and Demonstration Program.

Strengthening Research Library Resources Program (HEA Title II-C)

The Strengthening Research Library Resources Program, funded by Title II-C of the Higher Education Act, promotes high-quality research and education throughout the United States by providing grants to help major research libraries maintain and strengthen their collections and make their holdings available to other libraries and to individual researchers and scholars outside their primary clientele.

In authorizing the Strengthening Research Library Resources Program, Congress recognizes that the expansion of educational and research programs, together with the rapid increase in the production of recorded knowledge, places unprecedented demands on major research libraries by requiring programs and services beyond the financial capabilities of the individual and collective library budgets. Further, the nation's major research libraries are acknowledged as essential elements to advanced and professional education and research. Major research libraries are defined as public or private nonprofit institutions having collections available to qualified users that make a significant contribution to higher education and research, are unique in nature and contain material not widely available, are in sub-

Table 3 / HEA II-B, Library Research and Demonstration Program, FY 1967–1988

FY	Appropriation	Grants and Contracts Obligations	Numbers of Grants (and Contracts)†
1967	$3,550,000	$ 3,381,052	38
1968	3,550,000	2,020,942	21
1969	3,000,000	2,986,264	39
1970	2,171,000	2,160,622	30
1971	2,171,000	2,170,274	18
1972	2,750,000	2,748,953	31
1973	1,785,000	1,785,000	24
1974	1,425,000	1,418,433	20
1975	1,000,000	999,338	19
1976	1,000,000	999,918	19
1977	1,000,000	995,193	18
1978	1,000,000	1,000,000	17
1979	1,000,000	980,563	12
1980	*	319,877	4
1981	*	239,954	12(2)
1982	*	243,438	(1)
1983	*	237,643	(4)
1984	*	240,000	(2)
1985	*	363,900	(3)
1986	*	345,126	(3)
1987	*	282,485†	3
1988	*	307,303	5
Total		$26,226,218	335

Note: The Library Research and Demonstration Program has, in the past, operated primarily as a grant program. Both contracts and grants are issued, depending on the administrative decision.

* Included in the II-B training appropriation.

† Numbers of contracts are in parentheses.

stantial demand by researchers and scholars not connected with the institution, and are of national or international significance for research.

In FY 1987, the amendment regarding eligibility, added in FY 1986 with the reauthorization of the Higher Education Act, was implemented. Institutions that do not qualify under the criteria listed in the program regulations can provide additional information or documentation to demonstrate the national or international significance for scholarly research of the particular collection described in the grant application.

During the 11 years of program operation, $64,238,264 has been awarded to acquire rare and unique materials; to augment special collections in demand by researchers and scholars; to preserve fragile and deteriorating materials not generally available elsewhere; and to provide access to research collections by converting bibliographic information into machine-readable form and entering the records into national databases. Overall, 980 applications have been received, and of these, 360 were funded, benefiting 369 institutions.

In FY 1988, 93 applications requesting more than $17 million were received. With an allotment of $5,744,000, 34 new and 5 continuation grants were awarded, supporting project activities at 53 institutions. Bibliographic control emerged as the major activity again in FY 1988, accounting for 84 percent of the funds. Preservation was the secondary activity, accounting for 15 percent of total funds; collection development accounted for only 1 percent of total funds. Tables 4, 5, and 6 summarize the Strengthening Research Library Resources Program.

College Library Technology and Cooperation Grants Program (HEA, Title II-D)

During the reauthorization of the Higher Education Act in 1986, Title II-D was added to award grants to institutions of higher education for technological equipment to enhance resource-sharing activities among colleges and universities. In FY 1987, $3,590,000 was appropriated for Title II-D, the first year of program funding.

The College Library Technology and Cooperation Grants Program is designed to encourage the development of exemplary uses of technological equipment in libraries of institutions of higher education. The secretary awards grants to institutions of higher education that demonstrate a need for special assistance for the planning, development, acquisition, installation, maintenance, or replacement of technological equipment (including computer hardware and software) necessary to participate in networks for sharing of library resources; to combinations of institutions of higher education that demonstrate a need for special assistance in establishing and strengthening joint-use library facilities, resources, or equipment; to other public and private nonprofit organizations that provide library information services to institutions of higher education on a formal cooperative basis for the purpose of establishing, developing, or expanding programs that improve the services they supply to institutions of higher education; to institutions of higher education conducting research or demonstration projects to meet special programs that improve the services they supply to institutions of higher education; and to institutions of higher education conducting research or demonstration projects to meet special national or regional needs in utilizing technology to enhance library or information sciences.

In FY 1988, 331 applications requesting more than $26 million were received. In the Networking Equipment Grant category, 160 applications were evaluated, totaling approximately $8.5 million; in the Joint-Use Grant category, 74 applications were evaluated, totaling $10 million; in the Services to Institutions Grant category, 15 applications were evaluated, totaling $500,000; and in the Research and Demonstration Grant category, 53 applications were evaluated, totaling approximately $7 million. Based on the appropriation of $3,590,000 and the dollars requested the following grants were awarded in the first competition: 20 Networking Equipment Grants, averaging $52,339, for a total of $1,046,776; 14 Joint-Use Grants, averaging $104,367, for a total of $1,461,420; 3 Services to Institutions Grants, averaging $23,915, for a total of $71,744; and 9 Research and Demonstration Grants, averaging $112,229, for a total of $1,010,057 (see Table 7).

Table 4 / HEA Title II-C, Strengthening Research Library Resources: Analysis of FY 1988 Grants, by Major Activity

		Program Activity		
Institution	**Total**	**Bibliographic Control**	**Preservation**	**Collection Development**
Total	$5,744,000	$4,804,408	$850,570	$89,022
Auburn University	$ 112,577	$ 112,577	$ —	$ —
Brandeis University	100,051	100,051	—	—
Brown University	197,653	197,653	—	—
Carnegie Institute	108,142	68,393	39,749	—
Duke University	44,106	44,106	—	—
Georgetown University	69,552	69,552	—	—
Harvard University	120,861	45,671	75,190	—
Indiana University	506,839	506,839	—	—
Indiana University	103,956	103,956	—	—
Johns Hopkins University	64,798	64,798	—	—
Missouri Botanical Garden	253,320	252,120	1,200	—
New-York Historical Society	61,125	52,125	9,000	—
New York Public Library	207,574	149,076	58,498	—
Ohio University	104,705	104,705	—	—
Princeton University	105,749	67,320	38,429	—
Southern Illinois University	130,000	130,000	—	—
Stanford University	400,121	400,121	—	—
Stanford University, Hoover Institution	86,000	45,672	40,328	—
Stanford University, Hoover Institution	166,693	—	166,693	—
State Historical Society of Wisconsin	111,246	107,244	4,002	—
State University of New York at Buffalo	104,246	104,246	—	—
State University of New York at Buffalo	163,000	163,000	—	—
Tulane University	102,708	102,708	—	—
University of California, Berkeley	155,243	86,399	33,793	35,051
University of California, Berkeley	269,159	269,159	—	—

Table 4 / HEA Title II-C, Strengthening Research Library Resources: Analysis of FY 1988 Grants, by Major Activity *(cont.)*

		Program Activity		
Institution	Total	Bibliographic Control	Preservation	Collection Development
University of California, Berkeley	$192,283	$162,023	$30,260	$ –
University of Hawaii	64,345	51,907	6,282	6,156
University of Illinois, Urbana	191,556	168,421	23,135	–
University of Maryland	500,226	500,226	–	–
University of Michigan	60,706	363	60,343	–
University of New Mexico	64,000	58,023	5,977	–
University of Oklahoma	115,689	86,767	28,922	–
University of South Carolina	45,683	45,683	–	–
University of Southern California	146,288	146,288	–	–
University of Vermont	100,000	18,663	65,509	15,828
University of Washington	179,378	179,378	–	–
University of Wisconsin, Madison	114,929	16,829	66,113	31,987
University of Wisconsin, Madison	77,083	22,346	54,737	–
Virginia Historical Society	42,410	–	42,410	–

Table 5 / Projects Funded Under HEA II-C, Strengthening Research Library Resources Program, FY 1988

Institution and Project Director(s)	Grant Award	Project Description
Auburn University, Ralph Brown Draughon Library, Auburn University, AL Boyd Childress, Social Services Librarian, and Harmon Straiton, Head, Microforms & Documents Dept.	$112,577	In cooperation with the University of Alabama, to catalog records for individual titles included in Confederate imprints and French Revolutionary pamphlets.
Brandeis University, Waltham, MA Bessie Hahn, Director, Library Services	$100,051	To increase national awareness and access to more than 17,000 scientific offprints collected by the distinguished mathematician Vito Volterra; monographs and serials will be cataloged into a database that will be available to researchers in print and electronic form.
Brown University, University Libraries, Providence, RI Merrily Taylor, University Librarian	$197,653	To continue the retrospective conversion of the monographic holdings of the John Hay Library; most records will be from the Harris Collection of American Poetry and Plays.

Table 5 / Projects Funded Under HEA II-C, Strengthening Research Library Resources Program, FY 1988 *(cont.)*

Institution and Project Director(s)	Grant Award	Project Description
Carnegie Institute, Carnegie Museum of Natural History, Pittsburgh, PA Elizabeth Kwater, Music Librarian	$108,142	To catalog retrospectively two major monograph collections, Botany and Entomology, and to conserve and rebind. Published catalogs will disseminate result of the project.
Duke University, Perkins Library, Durham, NC Steven Hensen, Assistant Curator for Technical Services	$ 44,106	To contribute records for manuscript collections dealing with southern history to OCLC and RLIN.
Georgetown University, University Library, Washington, DC Jon Reynolds, University Archivist	$ 69,552	To catalog and prepare a computer-based index to Jesuit and Jesuit-related manuscripts and archival record groups that offer important research resources in many areas of American history, culture, sciences, and other fields.
Harvard University, Holyoke Center, Cambridge, MA Sidney Verba, Director, Library	$120,861	To film and provide bibliographic access to 250,000 pages of valuable research material too rare or fragile for lending. Specific collections to be filmed include Chinese studies, landscape architecture, church history, and women's studies.
Indiana University, Bloomington, IN David Fenske, Head, Music Library	$506,839	In cooperation with Eastman School of Music, Harvard, Stanford University, University of California at Berkeley, and Yale, Indiana will retrospectively convert manual bibliographic records for printed music for entry into OCLC and RLIN.
Indiana University, Bloomington, IN David Fenske, Head, Music Library	$103,956	To continue cataloging significant additional materials of its collection of operatic recordings.
Johns Hopkins University, Milton S. Eisenhower Library, Baltimore, MD Johanna Hershey, Acting Director	$ 64,798	To complete online cataloging of the Yale University Library collection of German Baroque literature.
Missouri Botanical Garden, Library, St. Louis, MO Constance Wolf, Librarian	$253,320	To continue the FY 1986 and FY 1987 projects to enable the libraries of the Missouri Botanical Garden and the New York Botanical Garden to enter into the OCLC database full bibliographic records and/or locations for more than 80,000 titles, especially primary botanical research literature, including rare books, monographs, and serials.
New-York Historical Society, New York, NY James Mooney, Librarian	$ 61,125	To continue cataloging and conserving its Rufus King Library collection of eighteenth- and nineteenth-century revolutionary and constitutional history materials and to enter the records into RLIN.
New York Public Library, Rodgers & Hammerstein Archives of Recorded Sound, New York, NY Christine Hoffman, Assistant Chief	$207,574	To catalog and conserve a portion of its collection of noncommercial recordings in the Rodgers and Hammerstein Archives of Recorded Sound.

Table 5 / Projects Funded Under HEA II-C, Strengthening Research Library Resources Program, FY 1988 *(cont.)*

Institution and Project Director(s)	Grant Award	Project Description
Ohio University, Alden Library, Athens, OH Hwa-Wei Lee, Director, Libraries	$104,705	To continue to catalog and input into OCLC international online union catalog Southeast Asian monographic and serial titles from the Library of Congress Jakarta Field Office.
Princeton University, Princeton, NJ Dorothy Pearson, Associate University Librarian	$105,749	To produce master preservation microfilm and catalog and create machine-readable records for pamphlets, monographs and serials, posters, broadsides, and fliers that collectively document the socioeconomic and political life of primarily twentieth-century Latin America.
Southern Illinois University, Morris Library, Carbondale, IL David Koch, University Archivist, and Kenneth Peterson, Dean, Library Affairs	$130,000	To continue to catalog rare and fugitive pamphlets and printed ephemera, briefs, correspondence, and manuscripts relating to the First Amendment freedoms dating from the seventeenth century to the present. Records will be entered into OCLC and the Illinois Library Computer System.
Stanford University, Green Library, Stanford, CA David Weber, Director, University Library	$400,121	In cooperation with the University of California, Berkeley, University of Florida, University of Texas, and Yale University, Stanford will create machine-readable bibliographic records for Latin American library materials now represented only in each institution's local card catalog.
Stanford University, Hoover Institution, Stanford, CA Judith Fortson, Head, Conservation Services	$166,693	To continue the FY 1986 and FY 1987 projects to preserve its rare international political poster collection as well as its newspaper collection dealing with specific events during times of political unrest or development.
Stanford University, Hoover Institution, Stanford, CA Charles Palm, Associate Director, Library and Archival Operations	$ 86,000	To continue to preserve and catalog its collection of materials related to the Russian revolutions of 1905 and 1917, the provisional government, and the Russian civil war.
State Historical Society of Wisconsin, Madison, WI John Peters, Acting Head Librarian	$111,246	To continue a two-year project to catalog and conserve material in the Cutter Pamphlet Collection and to enter full MARC records into OCLC for all items not now in the database.
State University of New York, Buffalo, NY Barbara von Wahlde, Associate Vice President, University Libraries	$163,000	To continue to create machine-readable records for monographs in the microform sets that comprise the Latin American Documents Collection. All records created will be tapeloaded into the OCLC database.
State University of New York, Buffalo, NY Robert Bertholf, Curator, Poetry/Rare Books Collection	$104,246	To process and produce MARC records of the poetry collection and input them into the RLIN database. These records include working manuscripts, drafts of poems, and the letters of twentieth-century poets.

Table 5 / Projects Funded Under HEA II-C, Strengthening Research Library Resources Program, FY 1988 *(cont.)*

Institution and Project Director(s)	Grant Award	Project Description
Tulane University, Howard-Tilton Memorial Library, New Orleans, LA Clifton Johnson, Executive Director	$102,708	To make collections of the Amistad Research Center accessible through machine-readable records and original processing. Materials are on ethnic history, civil rights, and race relations.
University of California, Berkeley, CA Donald Shively, Head, East Asiatic Library	$192,283	To continue a two-year project to catalog Japanese titles from the Mitsui Library and the Endo Collection and to conserve the Mitsui books and manuscript collection.
University of California, Berkeley, CA Joseph Rosenthal, University Librarian, Bancroft Library	$269,159	To conduct the second of a four-year project to convert card catalog records of the two collections of internationally recognized distinction in the Bancroft Library into machine-readable form. Records created will be entered into OCLC and RLIN.
University of California, Berkeley, CA James Sphorer, Librarian	$155,243	To enrich, preserve, and improve bibliographic access for the Germanic collections.
University of Hawaii, Honolulu, HI John Haak, University Librarian	$ 64,345	To enhance scholarly access to the Tsuzaki Reinecke Creole Collection by providing subject and keyword access to these unique published and unpublished creolist materials and by loading records tapes to OCLC.
University of Illinois, Urbana, IL Carol Boast, Agriculture Librarian	$191,556	To complete a project to improve national and international access to hard copy sets of U.S. Department of Agriculture and State Experiment Station agricultural materials dating from 1862 to date through series analytics on OCLC and RLIN databases and indexing on AGRICOLA and AGRIS databases.
University of Maryland, College Park, MD Marietta Plank, Associate Director, Technical Services	$500,226	To continue the FY 1986 and FY 1987 projects to provide machine-readable full cataloging records for Segment 2 of the Goldsmiths'-Kress Library of Economic Literature microfilm collection in cooperation with University of Delaware and the New York State Library.
University of Michigan, Ann Arbor, MI Robert Warner, Interim Director	$ 60,706	To microfilm or otherwise preserve 2,500 monographs in its homeopathy collection, none of which is available elsewhere in either reprint or microform.
University of New Mexico, General Library, Albuquerque, NM Christopher Sugnet, Head, Monographic Cataloging Department	$ 64,000	To catalog, preserve, strengthen, and made available materials pertaining to the history and culture of the Mexican state of Oaxaca.
University of Oklahoma, Norman, OK Lynda Kaid, Director, Department of Communication	$115,689	To preserve and catalog its unique collection of videocassettes, films, and audio recordings of political commercials.

Table 5 / Projects Funded Under HEA II-C, Strengthening Research Library Resources Program, FY 1988 *(cont.)*

Institution and Project Director(s)	Grant Award	Project Description
University of South Carolina, Thomas Cooper Library, Columbia, SC Elizabeth Lange, Assistant Director, Technical Services	$ 45,683	To catalog analytically titles from a collection of rare and significant serials and enter them into OCLC.
University of Southern California, University Library, Boeckmann Center, Los Angeles, CA Barbara Robinson, Curator, Latin American Collection	$146,288	To catalog its collection of Central American materials and to make it available through OCLC and RLIN.
University of Vermont, Bailey/Howe Library, Burlington, VT Nancy Eaton, Director, Libraries	$100,000	To continue to acquire original copies or photocopies of all the Canadian documents on acid rain and to catalog them into OCLC database. The documents will then be scanned and digitized, and CD-ROM discs will be distributed to 42 land-grant libraries.
University of Washington, Libraries, Seattle, WA Steve Hiller, Head, Science Department	$179,378	To catalog the collections of cartographic materials relating to the Pacific Northwest held in the libraries of the University of Washington and the University of Oregon, and to develop and apply an innovative method of microcomputer-based graphic access to aerial photography holdings.
University of Wisconsin, Madison, WI D. Kaye Gapen, Director, General Library System	$114,929	To expand its research collections through creation of a video archive that will acquire a core collection of approximately 600 videotapes produced in South and Southeast Asia and to produce circulating copies for loan.
University of Wisconsin, Madison, WI D. Kaye Gapen, Director, General Library System	$ 77,083	To preserve by microfilming highly brittle social science serials and monographs published in Germany in the four zones of military occupation from 1945 to 1949 and in the German Democratic Republic since 1949. Films will become a part of the exchange program with libraries in East Germany.
Virginia Historical Society, Richmond, VA Paulette Thomas, Librarian, Books and Serials	$ 42,410	To implement a phased comprehensive conservation program to increase access to and prolong use of its rare book and serials collection.

Library Services and Construction Act

Title IV, Library Services for Indian Tribes and Hawaiian Natives

More than 180 Indian tribes and more than 170,000 Hawaiian natives benefited from the $2.4 million awarded in FY 1988 under LSCA Title IV. In 29 states, funds are improving access to public library services by supporting activities that include surveys to determine the library needs of tribal and Hawaiian native communities, pay-

(text continues on page 254)

Table 6 / HEA Title II-C, Strengthening Research Library Resources: Summary of Funding, by Major Activity, FY 1978–1988

Fiscal Year	Total Funding	Bibliographic Control	Percent of Funding	Preservation	Percent of Funding	Collection Development	Percent of Funding
Total	$64,238,264	$46,949,226	73	$13,219,195	21	$4,069,843	6
1978	$ 4,999,996	$ 2,864,339	57	$ 1,340,554	27	$ 795,103	16
1979	6,000,000	3,978,366	66	1,393,201	23	628,433	11
1980	5,992,268	4,345,765	73	805,383	13	841,120	14
1981	6,000,000	4,249,840	71	1,298,542	22	3,451,618	7
1982	5,760,000	4,042,549	70	1,521,258	27	196,193	3
1983	6,000,000	4,738,575	79	909,612	15	351,813	6
1984	6,000,000	4,526,772	76	1,044,973	17	428,255	7
1985	6,000,000	4,236,695	70	1,729,997	29	33,308	(*)
1986	5,742,000	4,429,374	77	1,122,409	20	190,217	3
1987	6,000,000	4,732,543	79	1,202,696	20	64,761	1
1988	5,744,000	4,804,408	84	850,570	15	89,022	1

* Less than 1 percent.

Table 7 / Projects Funded Under HEA II-D, College Library Technology and Cooperation Grants Program, FY 1988

Institution and Project Director(s)	Grant Award	Project Description
	Networking	
Southern Methodist University, Dallas, TX Carolyn Kacena, Director, Academic Support Automation	$220,073	To install the NOTIS integrated library system at SMU for better internal and external access to its bibliographic data, the third largest academic library holdings in Texas.
Pensacola Junior College, Pensacola, FL Mike Whaley, Systems Librarian	$ 17,334	To purchase the equipment necessary to access the Florida State University System database of library holdings, the largest bibliographic database in the Southeast.
Montana State University Libraries, Bozeman, MT Laurie A. Stack, Systems Coordinator	$ 89,958	To purchase equipment to extend the accessibility of MSU's CatTrac, the only automated catalog in the state, to decentralized, off-campus users via direct dial-up capabilities.
Eastman School of Music, University of Rochester, Rochester, NY Mary Wallace Davidson, Principal Investigator, and Joan Swanekamp, Project Director	$ 24,121	To replace, upgrade, and add to equipment currently used to participate in OCLC networking activities, including cataloging, retrospective conversion, and resource sharing via interlibrary loan, as well as the related activities of collection development, and remote searching in bibliographic databases.
Mayville State University Library, Mayville, ND Betty J. Karaim, Director, Library Services	$ 35,757	To develop the first stage of a statewide online library catalog by a cooperative effort with the University of North Dakota libraries to create an online, shared library catalog between the two universities. This project will provide the base for future library automation and will permit the universities to link with databases in Minnesota, South Dakota, and Manitoba.
Lewis-Clark State College, Lewiston, ID Paul Krause, Director, the Library	$ 48,275	To extend resource sharing and networking activities by increasing access to the holdings of the college and local consortium via implementation of OPACs (online public access catalogs) in seven strategic locations throughout the state that will support the off-campus programs of the college.
North Carolina State University Libraries, Raleigh, NC John E. Ulmschneider, Head, Library Systems	$ 36,357	To support enhanced functionality within, and expanded access to, the distributed online catalog Bibliographic Information Systems (BIS) by upgrading computer hardware and software, and thereby increasing access to information users throughout the state.
Guilford Technical Community College, Jamestown, NC Beverly Glass, Coordinator, Library Services	$ 15,697	To enable GTCC libraries to participate fully in statewide library resource sharing. The purchase of five telefacsimile machines will enable GTCC to bring document delivery in line with resources available through the North Carolina Information Network (NCIN).

Table 7 / Projects Funded Under HEA II-D, College Library Technology and Cooperation Grants Program, FY 1988 *(cont.)*

Institution and Project Director(s)	Grant Award	Project Description
	Networking (cont.)	
Daytona Beach Community College, Daytona Beach, FL Mercedes Clement	$ 53,340	To improve services to library users by making their bibliographic records available via the University of Central Florida system and other state and local systems, and to connect the five community colleges in the FCLA system.
University of Virginia, Charlottesville, VA Douglas Hurd, Interlibrary Loan Coordinator	$ 77,000	To develop a telefacsimile resource-sharing network among 15 state-supported institutions of higher education, creating the first stage of a multitype library network in Virginia.
Waldorf College, Forest City, IA Christina Cosgriff, Librarian, Voss Memorial Library, and Oscar T. Lenning, Executive Vice President & Dean, Academic Affairs	$ 30,000	To purchase the equipment necessary to implement a network connecting Voss Memorial Library with local, regional, state, and national libraries by using the Iowa Locator and Data Trek systems.
Roanoke-Chowan Community College, Ahoskie, NC Peggy Lefler, Assistant Dean	$ 37,118	To plan, purchase, and install the equipment necessary to participate in the North Carolina Information Network (NCIN), which will allow resource sharing and networking activities via the NC On-line Union catalog, OCLC Selective Users, Western Union Easylink, and Telefacsimile networks.
Morton College, Learning Resources Center, Cicero, IL Wanda K. Johnston, Director, Learning Resources	$ 47,134	To purchase and install the computer equipment necessary to contribute its bibliographic records to the Suburban Library System's SLS/CLSI Automated Circulation Control System, a combined resource sharing and circulation system, resulting in increased and expedited access to the holdings of the 58 member libraries.
East Tennessee State University, Sherrod Library and Medical Library, Johnson City, TN Fred. P. Borchuck, Director, Libraries	$ 30,010	To replace and upgrade the OCLC work stations, terminals, peripherals, and telecommunications capabilities to allow continued and increased participation in the new, redesigned OCLC Online System via its regional network, SOLINET.
University of Montana, Mike and Maureen Mansfield Library, Missoula, MT Ruth J. Patrick, Dean, Library Services	$ 30,000	To develop the Montana Business Education Consortium by creating a shared business information collection with Eastern Montana College via leasing InfoTrac CD-ROM work stations and subscribing to the General Periodicals Database. Telefacsimile capabilities will also be included to improve business education programs and promote resource sharing throughout the state.
University of Maine System Libraries, Fogler Library, Orono, ME	$ 40,454	To create a document delivery network connecting eight campus libraries and eleven remote off-

Table 7 / Projects Funded Under HEA II-D, College Library Technology and Cooperation Grants Program, FY 1988 *(cont.)*

Institution and Project Director(s)	Grant Award	Project Description
	Networking (cont.)	
Marilyn Lutz, Systems Librarian		campus centers using telefacsimile transmission to speed the exchange of intercampus loans.
University of Detroit, Main Campus Library, Detroit, MI Jean Houghton, Assistant Director, Technical Services	$125,529	To participate in DALNET, a cooperative automated library network of eight major Detroit area libraries, that will include the creation of an OPAC, circulation, acquisitions, and serials control systems.
Southwestern College, Winfield, KS Gregory Zuck, Library Director	$ 30,173	To create a microcomputer work station that will enable the database of library holdings to be shared with the systemwide CD-ROM union catalog. This will also allow participation in the Kansas Information Circuit (KIC) network.
Westminster College, Fulton, MO William E. Marquardt, Head Librarian, Reeves Library	$ 22,446	In cooperation with William Woods College, to purchase equipment necessary for continued participation in OCLC and in Missouri's new statewide interlibrary lending system.
Catonsville Community College, Catonsville, MD Timothy McDonald	$ 36,000	To acquire the resources necessary to participate in a statewide telefacsimile network and to provide a model document delivery service. This will enable CCC to provide students and staff access to thousands of additional information sources from 14 other Maryland institutions.
	Combination Grants	
University of Tennessee, Knoxville, TN Linda L. Phillips, Head, Science and Technology Services, Knoxville Libraries	$108,417	To expand resource-sharing efforts between the University of Tennessee and Vanderbilt University through improved bibliographic access to collections, more efficient delivery of materials, and a program of cooperative collection development in the areas of science, technology, agriculture, and medicine.
Swarthmore College, Swarthmore, PA Linda G. Bills, Tri-College Library Automation Coordinator, Bryn Mawr College Library	$174,000	In cooperation with Bryn Mawr and Haverford Colleges, to defray the telecommunications costs of installing an integrated automated library system for the three campuses, using a single, merged database of 1 million bibliographic records.
Illinois Library Computer Systems Organization (ILCSO), c/o Edward Meachen, North Central College, Osterle Library, Naperville, IL	$ 87,265	To support the expansion of remote access to ILLINET Online, a statewide union catalog and library resource-sharing network, 40 dial access ports will be installed

Table 7 / Projects Funded Under HEA II-D, College Library Technology and Cooperation Grants Program, FY 1988 *(cont.)*

Institution and Project Director(s)	Grant Award	Project Description
	Combination Grants (cont.)	
David F. Bishop, University Librarian, University of Illinois, Urbana-Champaign		throughout the state to enable academic library users to access the network from personal work stations.
Network of Alabama Academic Libraries, Alabama Commission on Higher Education, Montgomery, AL Sue O. Medina, Director	$ 89,239	To install a statewide telefacsimile network to improve document delivery for interlibrary loan among NAAL members. NAAL is a consortium of the Alabama Commission on Higher Education and 17 of the state's academic institutions that offer graduate education.
Bridgewater State College, Bridgewater, MA Ratna Chandrasekhar	$122,576	A collaborative resource-sharing project with Southeastern Massachusetts University designed to increase access to the holdings and to automate the card catalogs and circulation systems for both institutions' libraries.
Bismarck State College, Library Excellence in North Dakota (LEND), Bismarck, ND Valarie Morehouse	$110,000	To automate the 1.6-million-record database of North Dakota college and university library holdings through the development of a statewide online library catalog that will also link the North Dakota State University catalog, the Minnesota State University library system, and the South Dakota State System.
PICKLE Consortium, Doane College, Crete, NE Peggy Brooks Smith, Director, Library	$ 47,887	To coordinate the collection development of periodicals and serials for a consortium of nine private college libraries. State-of-the-art telefacsimile machines will be used by each participating library to increase access and make interlibrary loan of expensive serials and periodicals possible.
University of Wisconsin, Madison, WI D. Kaye Gapen, Dean, Libraries, and Erwin Welsch, Assistant Director, Research	$127,815	To improve the University of Wisconsin-Madison Libraries' resource-sharing program through the creation of a user-transparent network utilizing telefacsimile and electronic mail in document delivery, online reference, and collection development for the University of Wisconsin System.
Associated College Libraries of Central Pennsylvania (ACLCP), Elizabethtown, PA Charles Townley, Pennsylvania State University	$ 76,794	To expand the consortium's interlibrary loan network through the creation of a union catalog, using CD-ROM technology.
New Hampshire College and University Council, Manchester, NH Douglas W. Lyon, Vice President	$108,525	To increase access for New Hampshire academic libraries to the minicomputer-based NH Automated Information System via a cost-effective microwave communications system.

Table 7 / Projects Funded Under HEA II-D, College Library Technology and Cooperation Grants Program, FY 1988 *(cont.)*

Institution and Project Director(s)	Grant Award	Project Description
	Combination Grants (cont.)	
New England Law Library Consortium, Cambridge, MA Elizabeth A. Snyder, Coordinator	$133,159	To produce a CD-ROM database containing holdings information for the 16 consortium member libraries. The database will be used for public access, interlibrary loan, and as an aid in making collection development decisions.
Houston Area Research Library Consortium (HARLIC), University of Houston Libraries, Houston, TX Robin N. Downes, Director	$100,000	To create a state-of-the-art CD-ROM union catalog for over 9 million volumes that will develop and improve resource sharing among the eight participating member libraries.
Sweet Briar College, Tri-College Consortium of Central Virginia, Sweet Briar, VA John G. Jaffee, Director, Libraries	$ 99,046	To improve resource-sharing activities of three college libraries by combining the records of their holdings on a single database in CD-ROM format, to be updated monthly, and to acquire the necessary equipment for 24 work stations at the participating libraries.
Mid-America Law School Library Consortium Inc., c/o Washburn University of Topeka, School of Law Library, Topeka, KS John E. Christensen, Project Chief	$ 76,600	To strengthen regional resource sharing through the development of a CD-ROM cooperative catalog among 18 university law schools in 7 midwestern states.
	Services to Institution Grants	
Oak Ridge Schools, Oak Ridge, TN Eleanor S. Chandler, Director, Staff Development, Grants/Research and Communication Services	$ 24,997	To expand the services of the Oak Ridge Schools Professional Library to instructors and students enrolled in five area colleges and universities by implementing optical scan technology and by acquiring CD-ROM databases and hardware.
Pittsburgh Regional Library Center, Pittsburgh, PA H. E. Broadbent III	$ 21,747	To extend PRLC's microcomputer and OCLC training programs to member libraries of institutions of higher education in West Virginia, thereby enhancing local, regional, and national resource sharing and improving the quality of library services at participating institutions.
West Virginia Library Commission, Charleston, WV Judith M. Prosser	$ 25,000	To extend the commission's online Union Catalog and network to the ten board of regents institutions of higher education without online access to the catalog via WVNET, allowing improved access to bibliographic data statewide.
	Research and Demonstration	
Ohio State University Foundation, Ohio State University Libraries System, Columbus, OH Virginia Tiefel	$117,558	To expand upon a FIPSE project to develop a prototype microcomputer program to teach and guide students in the application of informa-

Table 7 / Projects Funded Under HEA II-D, College Library Technology and Cooperation Grants Program, FY 1988 *(cont.)*

Institution and Project Director(s)	Grant Award	Project Description
Research and Demonstration (cont.)		
		tion search strategies using an online public catalog (OPAC) and computerized and print reference sources.
University of Alabama, Tuscaloosa, AL Frances Benham	$ 84,545	To develop comparative research data on two methods of library instruction to determine if course-integrated library instruction utilizing CD-ROM and end-user online searching is positively associated with improvement in student capabilities in retrieving, evaluating, and communicating information on engineering topics.
University of Alaska, Anchorage, AK Jack O'Bar	$101,622	In conjunction with the University of Alaska Computer Network, to demonstrate the usefulness of telefacsimile-computer technology and the effectiveness of this technology as a means of enhancing library resource-sharing activities already in place.
Drexel University, College of Information Studies, Philadelphia, PA Thomas A. Childers and Belver C. Griffith	$102,643	To measure the effectiveness of the Tri-College Library Automation Project on library users and staff and on the quality of collection development and services. The Tri-College project is a collaborative effort to integrate the library resources of the colleges and expand services into the community.
Rutgers University, School of Communication, Information and Library Studies, New Brunswick, NJ Nicholas Belkin and Tefko Saracevic	$106,987	To develop guidelines and features for the design of third-generation Online Public Access Catalogs (OPACS) and for improvement of existing ones, based on library users and their information-seeking behavior.
SUNY Buffalo, University Libraries, Buffalo, NY Robert J. Bertholf	$175,746	To evaluate the efficacy of incorporating telefacsimile and optical scanning technologies into ongoing interlibrary loan and resource-sharing activities.
University of Michigan Libraries, Ann Arbor, MI Yvonne Wulff, Assistant Director, Collection Management	$ 77,652	To investigate the ability of a major research library to deliver rapidly by telefacsimile materials requested by faculty from both remote divisional libraries and off-campus locations.
Cornell University, A. R. Mann Library, Ithaca, NY Jan Olsen	$153,866	To design and implement a computer system to provide interactive, online access through the Cornell campus telecommunications network to data files in the biological and agricultural sciences via the creation of front-end software.
George Washington University, Washington, DC	$ 89,438	In conjunction with George Mason University, to design, test, and

Table 7 / Projects Funded Under HEA II-D, College Library Technology and Cooperation Grants Program, FY 1988 *(cont.)*

Institution and Project Director(s)	Grant Award	Project Description
	Research and Demonstration (cont.)	
Patricia M. Kelley, Assistant University Librarian, Programs and Services		implement an electronic means of capturing bibliographic data from an online union catalog and to transmit the request and patron information to system-selected institutions to facilitate interlibrary loan transactions for a large and diverse clientele and to distribute more equitably ILL requests among participating libraries.

ment of salaries of library personnel, training of library personnel, purchase of library materials, as well as the renovation or construction of library facilities.

Funding is authorized by PL 98-480. Two percent of the appropriations for LSCA Titles I, II, and III is set aside as the available funding for LSCA IV (1.5 percent for Indian tribes and 0.5 percent for Hawaiian natives). Federally recognized Indian tribes and Alaskan villages and organizations that serve Hawaiian natives that are recognized by the governor of Hawaii are eligible to apply for assistance. Two types of discretionary awards are available—Basic Grants and Special Projects Grants. The Basic Grant is noncompetitive, and the amount is determined by dividing the number of eligible applicants into available funds.

For the past four years, the only organization recognized by the governor of Hawaii, Alu Like, Inc., has applied for the entire appropriation under the Basic Grant program, which in FY 1988, was $601,250. The funds support several outreach programs to Hawaiian natives, as well as improvement of Hawaiian and Pacific collections and the training of library professionals.

For Indian tribes, the established amount is determined by dividing the number of eligible tribes into available funds. In FY 1988, the amount was $3,550; 175 grants were awarded to benefit 183 Indian tribes and Alaskan villages.

As only 36 percent of the federally recognized tribes applied, about $1.1 million remained after Basic Grants were awarded. This residual funding is always used for Special Projects awards to tribes that have received Basic Grants. Seventeen tribes successfully competed for Special Projects funds. The Special Projects awards range from more than $20,000 to the Crow Tribe in Montana to purchase specialized resources relating to the Northern Plains Indians, to more than $160,000 to the Lummi Tribe in Washington for the renovation of a building to use as a library facility.

Awards for FY 1988 Basic Grants were made in February 1988, and for Special Projects, in August 1988 (grant period of 12 months began October 1, 1988).

Title VI, Library Literacy

Title VI of the Library Services and Construction Act authorizes a discretionary grant program to provide support to state and local public libraries for literacy programs. The program is in its third year and received an appropriation of $4,787,000 for FY 1988.

The Library Literacy Program is the only federal library program under which state and local public libraries apply directly to the U.S. Department of Education and compete for grant awards. State and local public libraries may apply for grants of up to $25,000 for literacy programs. State public libraries may use grant funds to coordinate and plan library literacy programs and to arrange for the training of librarians and volunteers to carry out such programs. Local public libraries may use grant funds to promote the use of the voluntary services of individuals, agencies, and organizations in providing literacy programs and to acquire library materials, use library facilities, and train volunteers for local literacy programs.

By August 1988, 224 grants totaling $4.78 million were awarded to 203 local public libraries and 21 state libraries. The grants were reviewed by a panel of 74 literacy experts representing local and state libraries, literacy councils, state departments of education, institutions of higher education, and private or other literacy efforts. Grants ranged in size from $1,000 to the maximum amount of $25,000. The average amount awarded was $21,370. All projects planned and coordinated their efforts with literacy councils, schools, private agencies, and other literacy providers in the state or community. Grantees were also encouraged to coordinate their activities with those supported by Title I of the Library Services and Construction Act.

Specific Projects funded in FY 1988 include the following:

- $4,412 to the Sterling Municipal Library in Baytown, Texas, to increase the number of tutor training sessions in response to student demand and to produce a quarterly literacy magazine that uses students' contributions for its content. This periodical is used to teach creative writing, grammar, and reading.
- $19,850 to the Fremont County Library in Fremont County, Wyoming, to provide support to existing literacy programs through development of a resource and referral center for literacy volunteers and learners. The library will also build a resource collection of adult new reader materials to be housed at two branch libraries.
- $25,000 to the State Library of Ohio to assist public libraries in developing countywide literacy coalitions.
- $25,000 to the Allen Public Library in Allen, Texas, for a regional conference to provide information and training in management skills for the increasing number of literacy providers in the region.
- $24,991 to Rutland Free Library in Rutland, Vermont, to organize writing seminars for adult new readers and to produce a selected number of students' stories for publication. The manuscripts will be illustrated, printed, bound, and distributed to the 210 libraries in Vermont.

LSCA State-Administered Programs

Over a 30-year period, the LSCA program has supported improvements in public library services. The Title I formula grant funds are used by states to provide improved public library access for all persons who, by reason of distance, residence, handicap, or other disadvantaged perspective, are unable to benefit from basic public library services. Title II funds are used for construction of new public library facilities and modification of existing buildings, and Title III funds promote resource sharing and cooperation among all types of libraries.

Plans and programs from the state library administrative agencies support the extension of library services in these legislated categories:

Title I

- Areas without public library services
- Areas with inadequate public library services
- Physically handicapped
- Other types of handicapped conditions
- State institutionalized
- Disadvantaged
- Limited English-speaking proficiency
- Elderly
- Literacy
- Strengthening state library administrative agencies
- Strengthening metropolitan public libraries serving as regional resource centers
- Strengthening major urban resource libraries
- Community information referral centers
- Administrative costs related to all titles

Title II

- Construction
- Remodeling
- Acquisition costs, land purchases, and architectural fees

Title III

- Development and establishment of cooperative library networks
- Promotion of resource sharing through coordination among public, academic, school, and special libraries

The Library Programs Staff has the federal management responsibility for these programs. The staff administrative librarians provide technical assistance to the states during the grant period and then analyze their annual reports, providing information on some of the trends and notable projects.

Almost $118 million was available to the states from the FY 1988 appropriation (Table 8) and nearly 3,000 projects were supported by these funds. More than 25 percent of the Title I funds were spent directly to improve public library services for special population groups, such as the functionally illiterate, the handicapped and the elderly. In addition, Title II funds were used to stimulate more than 200 local public library construction projects, and Title III provided some support to 500 regional, state, or local library cooperative projects.

To provide some perspective on these activities, the staff have reviewed the state

Table 8 / LSCA Titles I, II, and III, FY 1988

State	Title I	Title II	Title III
Alabama	$ 1,308,448	$ 379,461	$ 308,221
Alaska	343,861	136,270	74,182
Arizona	1,079,979	321,859	252,936
Arkansas	850,407	263,980	197,384
California	7,464,167	1,931,431	1,797,765
Colorado	1,091,278	324,708	255,669
Connecticut	1,073,916	320,330	251,468
Delaware	371,421	143,218	81,480
District of Columbia	371,697	143,288	81,547
Florida	3,311,876	889,604	797,844
Georgia	1,846,688	515,161	438,462
Hawaii	489,651	173,027	110,089
Idaho	476,698	169,761	106,955
Illinois	3,379,554	901,625	809,381
Indiana	1,715,780	482,156	406,785
Iowa	993,993	300,180	232,128
Kansas	874,935	270,164	203,319
Kentucky	1,227,699	359,102	288,680
Louisiana	1,436,325	411,700	339,163
Maine	521,070	180,948	117,692
Maryland	1,410,695	405,239	332,961
Massachusetts	1,803,695	504,321	428,058
Michigan	2,704,619	731,461	646,062
Minnesota	1,355,300	391,272	319,557
Mississippi	920,409	281,628	214,323
Missouri	1,587,627	449,847	375,775
Montana	427,367	157,323	95,017
Nebraska	642,332	211,520	147,034
Nevada	458,234	165,106	102,487
New Hampshire	475,321	169,413	106,621
New Jersey	2,283,784	625,360	544,229
New Mexico	599,890	200,820	136,764
New York	5,090,732	1,333,044	1,223,447
North Carolina	1,925,784	535,102	457,601
North Dakota	388,783	147,596	85,681
Ohio	3,161,833	846,733	756,697
Oklahoma	1,111,121	329,711	260,471
Oregon	940,252	286,631	219,124
Pennsylvania	3,469,399	924,276	831,121
Rhode Island	466,502	167,190	104,487
South Carolina	1,119,114	331,726	262,405
South Dakota	395,122	149,194	87,215
Tennessee	1,513,768	431,225	357,902
Texas	4,716,748	1,238,756	1,132,952
Utah	653,356	214,299	149,702
Vermont	347,444	137,173	75,678
Virginia	1,771,450	496,192	420,256
Washington	1,414,829	406,281	333,961
West Virginia	733,830	234,588	169,175
Wisconsin	1,516,248	431,850	358,502
Wyoming	340,554	135,436	74,011
American Samoa	49,729	22,453	12,354
Guam	73,016	28,324	17,989
Puerto Rico	1,101,200	327,209	258,070
Marshall Islands	19,162	7,470	4,722
Virgin Islands	69,627	27,469	17,169
Micronesia	45,331	17,672	11,171
North Marianas	45,126	21,292	11,240
Palau	7,504	2,925	1,849
Total	$77,406,280	$22,143,100	$18,295,620

reports in a number of LSCA program areas. These descriptions are designed to give the reader, for example, a more thorough understanding of the Major Urban Libraries (MURLs) and Metropolitan Public Libraries LSCA I provisions; to identify some trends in some of the LSCA "priority areas"; and to reflect the tremendous breadth and scope of LSCA project activity as found in the state reports.

Public Library Services (LSCA Title I)

Major Urban Libraries (MURLs) and Metropolitan Public Libraries

In FY 1987, 157 cities out of a possible 180 with populations over 100,000 that were eligible under the LSCA program were designated as Major Urban Resource Libraries (MURLs) in 41 states. As a program requirement, such a city library must agree to serve users throughout the regional area in which the city is located. For example, Florida had nine cities with populations over 100,000. Five of the city libraries—Jacksonville, Miami, Tampa, Fort Lauderdale, and Orlando—had already been funded by the state under the 1970 LSCA Title I provision for "strengthening metropolitan public libraries which serve as national or regional resource centers" to support the state's collection development policy. With the 1984 availability of MURL funds, this statewide effort was considerably enhanced, with the state again designating that these local libraries provide

- Interlibrary loan and information service free of charge to all libraries that are members of the Florida Information Network (FLIN). Such interlibrary loans are handled in accordance with protocols, procedures, and standards established by the State library administrative agency.
- General open access for nonresidents of the taxing jurisdiction to collections of all their library materials.
- Reference and information service to nonresidents on the same basis as residents.

From FY 1984 through FY 1987, the five Florida MURLS expended $469,481 and obligated $164,235 for FY 1988, for a total of $633,716. Under the regional resource center provisions, $1,210,000 was expended and $302,500 obligated for FY 1988, for a total of $1,512,500 or combined total of MURL and Regional Resource funds of $2,146,216. The funds have been spent to purchase bibliographic materials, personnel costs for interlibrary loan services to other Florida libraries, purchase of business and science technology materials, genealogy, local history, online computer database searching, literature and literacy criticism, microform readers, microcomputer terminals, and specialized reference and information sources that other libraries could not afford or would not often use. This is an outstanding example of using LSCA funds from two legislated LSCA categories to serve the statewide library information needs.

Following are the amounts expended for MURL purposes from FY 1984 through FY 1987 and the amount obligated in FY 1988.

FY	Amount
1984	$2,142,102
1985	$4,256,151
1986	$4,189,392
1987	$4,992,614
1988	$4,992,614

In the 1970 congressional reauthorization deliberations adopting the "metropolitan public library provision," Congress had hoped that the new provision would be important to the success of statewide interlibrary cooperation. In fact, states do continue to reflect this focus in designating local metropolitan libraries to serve regional needs. Following are the amounts expended by these States for "metropolitan public libraries" from FY 1984 through FY 1987 and the estimated amount programmed by states from FY 1988 funds.

FY	Amount
1984	$2,226,236
1985	$3,371,749
1986	$3,637,353
1987	$3,083,483
1988	$3,150,893

Services to Special Populations: The State Institutionalized

The following are the noted trends in library services to the state institutionalized from the state reports:

- More institutions are relying on service from a nearby public library or library system. Although this tends to bring significant professional service to the institutionalized, it also is limited by the hours the public library provides services.
- The majority of the funds for general library services are used to purchase materials, especially paperbacks.
- Audiovisuals and computer software still head the list as the most needed materials.
- Libraries serving mental hospitals must constantly reevaluate the appropriateness of their collections for their users. Mainstreaming and other changes in this field have caused shifts in the population makeup of the institutions, requiring many changes in collection development policies. Devices, realia, games, and the like, are the mainstay of most library collections in this category rather than printed materials.
- Fewer state library administrative agencies have consultant services available for the institutionalized programs. Whether this is because it is now so common that it is taken for granted, or because of basic cutbacks in state staff is not known.

The expenditures for library services to the institutionalized are listed in Table 9.

Table 9 / LSCA Title I, Funds for the State Institutionalized, FY 1987

State	Federal	State	Local	Total
Alabama	$ 14,852	$ 41,989	$ 0	$ 56,841
Alaska	0	56,000	0	56,000
Arizona	0	203,640	0	203,640
Arkansas	50,649	21,979	19,505	92,133
California	186,315	1,932,428	0	2,118,743
Colorado	82,675	212,529	0	295,204
Connecticut	50,965	153,285	0	204,250
Delaware	3,689	111,368	0	115,057
District of Columbia*	0	15,189	0	15,189
Florida	337,475	315,792	0	653,267
Georgia	56,166	16,793	5,041	78,000
Hawaii	0	287,966	7,321	295,287
Idaho*	0	99,250	0	99,250
Illinois	152,353	1,863,860	0	2,016,213
Indiana	110,676	322,776	0	433,452
Iowa	12,596	18,902	411,748	443,246
Kansas	39,509	1,429	0	40,938
Kentucky	39,500	50,000	0	89,500
Louisiana	65,332	76,354	0	141,686
Maine	59,979	157,186	0	217,165
Maryland*	132,348	230,500	0	362,848
Massachusetts	17,470	281,431	0	298,901
Michigan	54,366	39,528	0	93,894
Minnesota*	43,259	770,578	0	813,837
Mississippi	36,687	78,915	0	115,602
Missouri	58,526	290,776	26,000	375,302
Montana	33,795	55,990	0	89,785
Nebraska	25,029	329,501	0	354,530
Nevada	30,154	64,139	0	94,293
New Hampshire	27,000	96,830	0	123,830
New Jersey	118,216	325,326	1,000,000	1,443,542
New Mexico	38,000	43,148	0	81,148
New York	80,444	2,552,461	0	2,632,905
North Carolina	34,228	146,969	0	181,197
North Dakota	36,316	78,000	0	114,316
Ohio	118,189	38,636	384,058	540,883
Oklahoma	88,154	219,542	0	307,696
Oregon	0	316,175	0	316,175
Pennsylvania	27,816	1,297,328	0	1,325,144
Rhode Island*	33,040	175,889	0	208,929
South Carolina	50,345	499,655	0	550,000
South Dakota	38,254	73,056	0	111,310
Tennessee	35,000	17,500	0	52,500
Texas	45,395	324,364	0	369,759
Utah	29,997	87,250	0	117,247
Vermont	18,101	84,618	0	102,719
Virginia	520	170,000	0	170,520
Washington	30,000	677,160	0	707,160
West Virginia	2,299	189,187	0	191,486
Wisconsin	89,259	815,257	0	904,516
Wyoming	31,257	58,314	0	89,571
Guam	9,000	18,935	0	27,935
Puerto Rico	52,922	71,005	0	123,927
Virgin Islands	8,498	49,008	0	57,506
Total	$2,736,615	$16,525,686	$1,853,673	$21,115,974

* Report not available: figures based on program plans.

Literacy

Significant Title I commitments to literacy programs were made in California, Illinois, New York, Michigan, Massachusetts, Oklahoma, Florida, South Carolina, and Wisconsin. The noted trends from the state reports reflect

- The increased use of computers, videos, cable television, and audio devices in providing literacy services
- The use of a traditional one-to-one tutoring approach
- The emphasis on services for those reading below the fourth-grade level
- English for new Americans preparing for citizenship
- Literacy programs in state institutionalized settings such as prisons
- The establishment of many statewide literacy coalitions
- The increasing recognition of interdisciplinary literacy programming between libraries and other types of literacy providers, such as adult basic educators and other private sector interests
- Innovative programming focusing on incorporating basic writing skills, tutoring the deaf and learning disabled, literacy theater, the development of support groups for illiterate students, and intergenerational and workplace literacy efforts

Other LSCA Title I Project Activities

The diversity of LSCA Title I project activities is reflected in the following projects:

Audiovisual Programming

Life Skills Video Series to Reduce Functional Illiteracy. Bartow County Library System, Cartersville, Georgia.

Funds were used to produce four 30-minute videos for a Life Skills Video Series on the subjects of "Getting a Job/Job Interview," "Managing Your Family Finances," and "Being a Good Parent: Meeting Your Child's Physical and Emotional Needs." In addition to teaching skills, the videos included information on stress management, time management, family and marital communication, home safety, family planning, self-esteem, and human relations. Library personnel received training in the use of equipment and production techniques. The target group was the young adult and adult population of functionally illiterate residents of Bartow County. $6,375.

Programming through Cable Access TV. Eugene Public Library, Eugene, Oregon.

The purpose was to make available to the community libraries videotapes showing the local culture and to keep these tapes for future archival use. Eleven videos were shown to an estimated audience of 4,000. Approximately 50 half-hour shows were converted from ¾-inch to ½-inch, which made it possible for them to be seen at home on patrons' VCRs. The reduced size made it easy for parents of young children to take home tapes on child rearing that were produced earlier. $9,065.

Bookmobile/Books-by-Mail Projects

Project Plus. Niles Public Library District, Niles, Illinois.

Bookmobile library service was established at no cost to residents of the unincorporated areas adjoining the Niles Public Library District with a view to annexing the area to the library district. The service involved making 200 stops at 11 locations with 14 stops at one shut-in location. A concerted effort was also made to improve the bookmobile collection of library materials. $50,000.

Mediamobile. New Hampshire State Library, Concord, New Hampshire.

Funds were used to purchase a fuel-efficient van for the delivery of library materials to homes, post offices, country stores, nursing homes, and several other rural service points. Books, films, and talking books were delivered at the community stops to individuals with no library services. Included were handicapped children and adults, senior citizens, and housebound persons. $86,830.

The Business Community

Business Information Center to the World Trade Center. Lexington Public Library, Lexington, Kentucky.

Focusing on the recent World Trade Center activities in Lexington, the library used its MURL grant to purchase business and trade-related reference materials. By improving its national and international business collection, the library was able to play a significant role as a business information provider to both the World Trade Center and businesses in the Bluegrass region. $12,360.

Taking Care of Business. Illinois Coalition of Library Advocates, Springfield, Illinois.

This project represented a public awareness effort that called attention to library services to businesses in the community. Project activities included assembling a "think tank" of experienced librarians and others skilled in public relations to identify key business leaders who would support the effort; acquiring advertising space in Illinois business periodicals; preparing a public relations manual for the use of participating libraries; and distributing a press release package to newspapers covering the Illinois Press Association, the Chicago-Metro and Central Illinois regions, and 34 southern and 22 northern counties. $38,000.

Children's Services

The Quiz Bowl. Division of State Library, North Carolina Department of Cultural Resources, Raleigh, North Carolina.

The Quiz Bowl program reached hundreds of North Carolina students in more than 150 high schools participating in intramural, local, district, and state competitions and involved teachers, librarians, and many other citizens. Forty-seven public library systems representing 77 percent of the state's 100 counties participated in the program. The Quiz Bowl Committee worked with the state library's youth services consultant to plan and coordinate all aspects of the Quiz Bowl Program. The program encouraged library use by young adults and promoted public libraries working directly with high school students. $46,200.

The Child's Place. Brooklyn Public Library, Brooklyn, New York.

The funds were used to help preschool children develop basic communication and social skills so that they could engage in positive relationships with peers and adults outside the family. In an effort to expand their vocabulary, the children were exposed to books, stories, rhymes, and songs. All the Child's Place activities were designed to ease the children's entry into formal schooling and to sharpen their awareness of everything around them. $6,100.

Community Health Efforts

Consumer Health Information Network. Lyman Maynard Stowe Library, University of Connecticut Health Center, Farmington, Connecticut.

The funds supported a network of public libraries, statewide health associations and agencies, and other appropriate health organizations to make health information available to all Connecticut's residents. Programs and services included workshops for librarians to help them develop consumer health information services; evaluations of consumer health materials; a publication of a health newsletter to inform librarians of new material; community health forums at local libraries; and subject bibliographies on consumer health topics. $32,100.

Alzheimer's Disease Information Project. Champaign Public Library, Champaign, Illinois.

The library established a print and nonprint collection on Alzheimer's disease. A quick referral file was developed providing access to over 8,000 periodical articles on the topic. An information booklet on Alzheimer's disease was compiled, published, and distributed to all Illinois libraries, and workshops were held featuring gerontological specialists. $8,500.

Community Information and Referral

Twenty-four Hour Library. Bloomington Public Library, Bloomington, Illinois.

The project provided 24-hour information service to anyone who had access to a touchtone telephone. A microcomputer-based system allowed users to dial into the library and receive a variety of messages about library service, including notification of reserves, programs, and overdues. The service was also made available to other local agencies for the purpose of presenting their community messages. $20,000.

ACCESS: A Computer-based Information Service. Spokane Public Library, Spokane, Washington.

Funds were used to develop a computerized community information service for Spokane residents in the areas of job searching and skills developments; formal and informal educational opportunities; and cultural and recreational resources and opportunities. The project functioned as a publicly owned source of local data ranging from job-hunting information to the location of tickets for live performances; from a directory of crisis help services to a listing of available small business accounting courses. $40,000.

Community Outreach

Creation of a Homework Center. Augusta Regional Library, Augusta, Georgia.

The funds supported the facilities and volunteers for the homework center. Project activities included coordinating with schools and day-care centers, recruiting volunteers for the tutorial program, and establishing a homework center council of community, school, and library workers to provide policy direction for the homework center. A workshop for training volunteers was conducted by school personnel. New books were added to the reference and general collection, and a significant portion of the budget was used to purchase teaching aids such as games, flash cards, and workbooks. $18,000.

Field Services Project. South Carolina State Library, Columbia, South Carolina.

The program supported staff development for the state staff consultants, including the director, the children's consultant, and the audiovisual consultant. They participated in a number of workshops, institutes, and conferences on lifelong learning issues and programming for preschoolers. The consultants were committed to working on the design to improve library services all library systems in the state. $24,000.

Computer-Related Projects

Network Technical Training and Development. Indiana Cooperative Library Services Authority, Indianapolis, Indiana.

This program supported microcomputer training and development; local planning and development; and information retrieval aimed at improving and extending library networking. Training emphasized the role of microcomputers in network links for small libraries. $110,000.

Oregon Index. Oregon State Library, Salem, Oregon.

This project allowed participating libraries to convert their card files of indexes to newspapers, magazines, and other materials to online files accessible through the state library's computer system. All libraries were then able to use microcomputers to dial into the state library's computer to access the Oregon Index. $21,000.

Continuing Education

Advanced Professional Training Program. Case Western Reserve University, Cleveland, Ohio.

A series of workshops were designed to provide training for state library staff in management, organizational development, and local area network assessment. The program focused particularly on managing in a union environment and developing special managerial skills and working on professional attitudes awareness. $69,960.

Certification Program for Library Personnel. Delaware Division of Libraries, Dover, Delaware.

Two workshops were held on reference skills in business resources and collection development. These workshops were offered for certification/recertification credit for library staff, as well as providing them with needed knowledge and skills and techniques to improve library services. Thirty-six librarians attended the reference skills workshop and 25 attended the collection development seminar. $14,800.

Drug Abuse Prevention

Programs on Drug Abuse and Related Problems. Arrowhead Library System, Janesville, Wisconsin.

The project focused on programs concerning family violence, child abuse, drug abuse, alcoholism, and teenage pregnancy. Funds supported an audiovisual directory on these issues, story hour presentations, and the distribution of newsletters. Project staff also worked closely with area agencies to help residents with drug problems. $25,000.

Educational Materials on Drug Abuse. Kinchafoonee Regional Library, Dawson, Georgia.

The funds were used to purchase materials and equipment for drug abuse education. A community planning committee suggested a wide range of materials to help educate the community and to make them aware of effective deterrents to the use of drugs. Materials on the problem of illiteracy were purchased because it was felt that it was a related problem. $21,000.

Early Child/Parent Relationship

Model Parenting Center. Chicago Public Library, Chicago, Illinois.

The project sought to accomplish four objectives: to develop a love for books and reading; to develop cognitive and manipulative skills in young children; to enlighten parents to the value of play as a learning experience; and to promote the library as a learning center for parents and children. Some of the project activities included a bedtime story hour when children were invited to the center dressed for bed to listen to bedtime stories and a workshop on child development and training conducted by a pediatrician. $40,500.

Parent/Child Workshops. Queens Borough Public Library, Jamaica, New York.

Six workshops were held to assist parents in their roles as primary educators of their children. Project activities included using qualified professionals in the field of health care and child development to work with parents as they play with their children, using games and toys to develop cognitive and motor skills; providing supplies and instructions for simple crafts to be done by parents and children working together; and promoting the use of the library as a resource center for information on child development, nutrition, physical fitness, home safety, latchkey children, and reading readiness. $50,000.

The Elderly

Homecare and Nutrition Programs. Brigham Memorial Library, Sharon, Wisconsin.

The project identified a group of 38 persons over 65 years of age for special library services. Funds were used to purchase over 200 large print titles, magnifiers, and a cassette carousel. Most of these items focused on local homecare and nutrition programs. A weekly home delivery service was also instituted. $75,000.

Volunteer Program for the Elderly. Kokomo-Howard County Public Library, Kokomo, Indiana.

The project trained volunteers to serve the elderly in their homes. The volunteers assisted in providing books, cassettes, recordings, and health slide programs to institutions, apartment complexes, and older adult clinics. An additional dozen informational slide program kits were developed and made available to the elderly. $49,500.

Employment Assistance

Computerized Guidance Information System. New Haven Public Library, New Haven, Connecticut.

A computerized guidance information system was used to provide information on job openings, career and educational paths, training, and vocational programs. Target groups included the unemployed, the underemployed, unskilled adults, and people making career decisions and changes. New books on careers, colleges and vocational schools, job-hunting strategies, and interviewing techniques were added to the library collection. A bulletin board displayed job listings, and a manual was produced outlining job-hunting resources. The project was designed to help lower the local unemployment rate and help reduce the number of people living below the poverty level. $18,000.

Minority Recruitment. California State Library, Sacramento, California.

Californians of ethnic minority background were placed in a master's program at one of the state's three graduate schools of library science. Awards of $5,000 were made to nine Asian, black, Hispanic, or Native American candidates sponsored by a public library or the library school. Graduates from the program in the past had held positions in public, academic, and other libraries and, in some cases, had risen to middle management or directorship positions. $44,800.

The Farming Community

Farm Information Center. Jefferson County Public Library, Monticello, Florida.

Funds were used to purchase over 150 basic agricultural books and periodicals of interest to farmers. In addition, local farmers donated many books on gardening and small farming to strengthen the collection. The funds also helped farmers and their families to become computer literate through the purchase of a microcomputer with color monitor, internal modem, and printer to make an online agricultural database readily available to the farming community. $35,000.

Computer Aid for Farmers. Onawa Public Library, Onawa, Iowa.

This was a training program to improve farm management and accounting practices. Through the library use of computers and agricultural software, farmers, aided by a team of community advisers, were able to develop skills on the computers and improve their management decisions. Ultimately, they learned to develop their own financial accounting system on computers at home. $27,000.

Handicapped Persons

High Tech Facilities for Developmentally Disabled Persons. Hamburg Center-Client Library, Hamburg, Pennsylvania.

The project was designed to use mobile video and computer equipment with the developmentally handicapped persons in the library. The computer was used as a teaching tool and as a means of communication with the clients, and the video was used for tracking, as well as for leisure-time activity. $10,000.

UPDATE Radio Reading Service. Chautauqua-Cattaraugus Library System, Jamestown, New York.

Programming for this 45 hours per week broadcast served 300 listeners with consumer news, information for the disabled, grocery shopping news, current books, and local newspaper articles. The most popular programs were the daily newspaper (a two-hour reading that was repeated in the evening), the weekly grocery advertisements, and local history programs. $28,500.

Library Administration

Support for Improved Evaluation of Library Programs. Massachusetts Board of Library Commissioners, Boston, Massachusetts.

Funds were used to support the statewide Advisory Council on Libraries, which advised the board on the evaluation of library programs, services, and activities under the state plan. Funds supported were a needs assessment of LSCA target population and areas; the development of criteria for applicant eligibility for LSCA funds; and the development of reliable and valid techniques for evaluating LSCA-funded programs. $101,000.

Grants Management Manual. Mississippi Library Commission (MLC), Jackson, Mississippi.

Funds were used to hire a consulting firm that worked with key state library personnel in producing a grants manual. The manual pulled together in one place information that a subgrantee would need on ED financial management requirements, including funding methods, property management, reporting requirements, and internal controls. Examples of all applications and reporting forms were included with instructions for their use. The MLC also outlined a program evaluation plan that in part focused on the extent to which LSCA funds were properly allocated, obligated and expended. $33,000.

Library Public Relations Efforts

Public Relations Information Team. Kentucky Department for Libraries and Archives, Frankfort, Kentucky.

The team included representatives from each of the state library's divisions and major program areas. Project activities included expanding the state library newsletter mailing list; issuing timely press releases pertaining to services and funds available through the state library; and purchasing for each public library and branch library a National Library Week kit, including a handbook of publicity ideas, and developing a publicity handbook to encourage residents to take time to read and use their library. $13,500.

Comprehensive Marketing Program. Lancaster County Library, Lancaster, Pennsylvania.

Funds were used to provide the resources and leadership for the in-service training of key library staff, to partially support a public relations officer and graphic artist, and to purchase new printing equipment and supplies. The marketing program called for a number of library surveys, including a citizens' telephone survey. The public relations officer's responsibilities were to design and produce more than 80,000 brochures for use by the Library Friends Groups and to coordinate and distribute press releases for library programs and activities. $19,000.

Literacy

Library Literacy Project. Kansas State Library, Topeka, Kansas.

The state library worked cooperatively with other state, regional, and local agencies to expand existing or newly created literacy programs throughout the state. A literacy coordinator helped to develop specialized library programs for functionally illiterate persons, purchase literacy materials, and train volunteers, who in turn trained other volunteers. A toll-free hotline was set up to provide patrons with information on literacy programs available to them. $33,000.

Literacy Center. Graham County Public Library, Stafford, Arizona.

A literacy center for Graham County was developed to train tutors in basic reading, ESL and GED preparation; develop a community coalition for literacy; hire a part-time coordinator; reach 20 to 30 students per year; and provide coping skills materials, including obtaining a driver's license and getting a job. A center for adult basic educational materials was developed with over 500 books and nonprint items. The tutor training workshops were held and 17 tutors were trained. Sixty percent of the tutors were matched with students within one month of the training. $8,000.

Minority Language Groups

Services to Non-English Speaking. Rhode Island Department of State Library Services, Providence, Rhode Island.

This project provided improved library assistance and information to ethnic groups from Asia, Central and South America, and Africa. Project activities included developing, maintaining, and distributing to public libraries a list of non-English-speaking people by language groups; and publishing a directory of bilingual librarians in Rhode Island. $16,290.

Expansion of Library Services for Vietnamese, Cambodians, and Mexicans. Carol Stream Public Library, Carol Stream, Illinois.

Books and audiovisual materials were purchased in the spoken languages of Vietnamese, Cambodian, and Spanish. In addition, the funds were used to provide appropriate staff for patrons with special language needs and to expand and update the library's community resources file to provide local reference and referral services. $7,300.

Preschoolers

Toddler Time Program. Mobile Public Library, Mobile, Alabama.

Funds were used to acquire materials for a six-week "Toddler Time" program for parents and toddlers. Printed booklists and handouts explaining the program were distributed. Parents with preschool children were encouraged to register in the library for the summer preschool program resulting in a 31 percent increase in preschool registration. $7,300.

Special Preschoolers Project. Carthage Free Public Library, Carthage, Illinois.

Funds were used to acquire a collection of books, kits, records, games, and other materials especially useful in serving both normal and handicapped preschool children. Project activities included two six-week series of story hours for preschool children at the library; story hours for each class of special education preschoolers at the Union Douglas School; and story hour programs for groups at a special education day camp. $9,000.

Public Library Construction (LSCA Title II)

During FY 1987, $10.4 million was obligated by the states for local public library construction projects, which left $11.6 million available for projects in FY 1988. At the end of FY 1988, more than $9.3 million of these funds will have been obligated. During FY 1987, 27 states completed 111 public library construction projects, significantly fewer than the 157 projects completed in FY 1986. This may be because fewer projects are now emanating from the large $50 million Emergency Jobs Act for public library construction enacted more than five years ago.

The combined (state, local, federal) funding for completed public library construction projects receiving LSCA Title II assistance during FY 1987 totaled $45.3 million. Of this amount, almost 20 percent of the total construction costs for projects completed in FY 1987 was funded with LSCA Title II funds. When compared with FY 1986 combined expenditures, the figures reveal a reduction of approximately 5 percent in the amount of LSCA funds that were used to support Title II projects and a proportionate increase in state and local support for construction activity.

Combined matching funds from state and local sources amounted to more than $36.2 million from state and local sources and provided more than 80 percent of the total costs for completed public library construction project in FY 1987. Of this amount, local contributions made up by far the largest percentage (77 percent of $35.1 million).

Table 10 is a partial listing of completed LSCA II projects reported during FY 1987.

Table 10 / LSCA Title II, Public Library Construction Projects, FY 1987: A Partial Listing

State	Project	Federal	Local	State	State/Local	Total (FSL)
AL	Anniston	$ 15,202	$ 15,203	$ 0	$ 15,203	$ 30,405
AL	Carrollton	75,000	81,906	0	81,906	156,906
AL	Kenan	15,000	15,251	0	15,251	30,251
AL	Monroe	81,000	152,248	0	152,248	233,248
AL	Oneonta	25,000	25,095	0	25,095	50,095
AK	Kenai	168,586	405,893	0	405,893	574,479
AZ	Miami	15,600	15,600	0	15,600	31,200
AZ	Pinal	35,000	35,000	0	35,000	70,000
AZ	Pomeroy	4,800	4,800	0	4,800	9,600
CO	Idaho Springs	28,200	32,192	0	32,192	60,392
DE	Dover	287,446	427,364	0	427,364	714,810
FL	Eustis	200,000	319,540	0	319,540	519,540
FL	Indian River	24,050	24,413	0	24,413	48,463
FL	Jefferson Co.	100,000	77,000	100,000	177,000	277,000
FL	North Miami	200,000	218,445	0	218,445	418,445
GA	Avondale Marta	52,500	52,500	0	52,500	105,000
GA	Cochran	95,854	153,333	316,667	470,000	565,854
ID	Boise	25,218	33,878	0	33,878	59,096
ID	Prairie	1,000	2,188	0	2,188	3,188
ID	Priest River	5,500	8,175	0	8,175	13,675
ID	Weiser	912	913	0	913	1,825
IL	Daugherty	161,856	242,784	0	242,784	404,640
IL	Mackinaw	79,200	119,770	0	119,770	198,970
IL	Nichols	184,200	474,063	0	474,063	658,263
IL	Oak Lawn	200,000	538,286	0	538,286	738,286
IL	Peru	250,000	654,361	0	654,361	904,361
IN	Anderson	250,000	7,130,441	0	7,130,441	7,380,441
IN	Anderson-Stony	158,000	163,723	0	163,723	321,723
IN	Geneva P.L.	42,000	42,000	0	42,000	84,000
IN	Geneva	40,000	40,000	0	40,000	80,000
IN	Huntington	235,000	1,453,000	0	1,453,000	1,688,000
IN	Plainfield	217,915	1,510,189	0	1,510,189	1,728,104
IN	Scott Co.	265,000	413,957	0	413,957	678,957
IA	Drake	75,000	104,911	0	104,911	179,911
IA	Hampton	85,500	92,263	0	92,263	177,763
IA	Nashua	112,500	114,908	0	114,908	227,408
IA	Ottumwa	20,910	20,910	0	20,910	41,820

Table 10 / LSCA Title II, Public Library Construction Projects, FY 1987: A Partial Listing *(cont.)*

State	Project	Federal	Local	State	State/Local	Total (FSL)
KS	Eudora	2,234	3,275	0	3,275	5,509
KS	Goddard	61,100	164,888	0	164,888	225,988
KS	Kingman	78,222	271,921	0	271,921	350,143
KS	Leavenworth	10,430	11,460	0	11,460	21,890
KS	Minneola	28,555	33,285	0	33,285	61,840
KS	Mound Valley	40,000	9,500	0	9,500	49,500
KS	Sheridan Co.	57,000	167,645	0	167,645	224,645
ME	Turner	14,740	14,740	0	14,740	29,480
MA	Mashpee	99,770	505,000	0	505,000	604,770
MS	Hernando	119,333	119,333	0	119,333	238,666
MS	Okolona	75,000	75,000	25,000	100,000	175,000
MS	Pascagoula	115,196	2,500,000	0	2,500,000	2,615,196
NE	Ashland	4,575	7,759	0	7,759	12,334
NE	Ceresco	3,000	5,001	0	5,001	8,001
NE	Gordon	66,634	77,866	0	77,866	144,500
NE	La Vista	3,675	3,795	0	3,795	7,470
NE	Morton-James	22,500	22,500	0	22,500	45,000
NE	Oakland	15,000	62,699	0	62,699	77,699
NE	Scribner	6,500	6,500	0	6,500	13,000
NE	Sutton	26,413	26,413	0	26,413	52,826
NE	Woods	6,994	6,944	0	6,944	13,938
NH	Amherst	36,500	1,030,000	0	1,030,000	1,066,500
NH	Campton Grange	50,000	165,000	0	165,000	215,000
NH	Concord	12,500	12,500	0	12,500	25,000
NH	Holderness	17,000	20,300	0	20,300	37,300
NH	Manchester	15,000	15,000	0	15,000	30,000
NJ	Asbury Park	16,500	30,350	7,000	37,350	53,850
NJ	Dover	14,320	10,762	3,558	14,320	28,640
NJ	Franklin	34,800	34,800	0	34,800	69,600
NJ	Haddonfield	75,000	75,452	0	75,452	150,452
NJ	Jersey City	46,000	161,910	0	161,910	207,910
NJ	New Brunswick	15,000	15,000	0	15,000	30,000
NJ	Woodbridge	30,500	121,300	0	121,300	151,800
NM	Hatch	60,000	22,000	100,000	122,000	182,000
NM	Silver City	138,596	213,170	0	213,170	351,766
NV	Elko	4,971	6,589	0	6,589	11,560
NV	Elko Co.	121,768	62,000	200,512	262,512	384,280

NV	Sparks	73,100	19,067	77,605	96,672	169,772
NV	Washoe	19,388	25,928	0	25,928	45,316
NV	Wendover	46,368	60,000	159,120	219,120	265,488
NC	Columbus	221,413	226,106	0	226,106	447,519
NC	Cumberland	497,000	3,973,542	10,000	3,983,542	4,480,542
NC	Rockingham	90,500	897,035	60,300	957,335	1,047,835
NC	Rowan Co.	150,000	276,000	34,771	310,771	460,771
OH	Bluffton	262,377	305,600	0	305,600	567,977
OH	Schiappa	199,792	1,067,847	0	1,067,847	1,267,639
OK	Chandler-Watts	100,000	118,247	0	118,247	218,247
OK	Noble	125,000	305,000	0	305,000	430,000
OR	Brandon	75,000	88,645	0	88,645	163,645
OR	Clatskanie	51,000	69,650	0	69,650	120,650
OR	Manzanita	98,265	105,000	0	105,000	203,265
OR	Yachats	17,500	20,720	0	20,720	38,220
SD	Wessington	648	648	0	648	1,296
TN	Cleveland	150,000	495,056	0	495,056	645,056
TN	Collierville	122,313	195,170	0	195,170	317,483
TN	Jonesborough	150,000	180,592	0	180,592	330,592
TN	Scott Co.	121,365	90,000	0	90,000	211,365
TX	Cedar Hill	100,000	793,151	0	793,151	893,151
TX	Corrigan	100,000	280,388	0	280,388	380,388
TX	Gilbreath	100,000	302,875	0	302,875	402,875
TX	McKinney	200,000	1,427,362	0	1,427,362	1,627,362
TX	Montgomery Co.	100,000	225,000	0	225,000	325,000
TX	Montrose	80,591	1,649,000	0	1,649,000	1,729,591
TX	Rains Co.	100,000	104,464	0	104,464	204,464
TX	Werner	100,000	320,555	0	320,555	420,555
UT	Cedar City	950	953	0	953	1,903
UT	Ephraim	695	695	0	695	1,390
UT	Fillmore	950	1,045	0	1,045	1,995
UT	Milford	950	950	0	950	1,900
UT	Monroe	950	951	0	951	1,901
UT	Mt. Pleasant	970	1,027	0	1,027	1,997
UT	Price City	950	1,012	0	1,012	1,962
UT	Richfield	950	1,000	0	1,000	1,950
WV	White Sulphur Springs	144,940	260,911	0	260,911	405,851
Total		$8,982,200	$35,199,352	$1,094,533	$36,293,885	$45,276,085

Interlibrary Cooperation and Resource Sharing (LSCA Title III)

The states reported actual expenditures of $14.4 million Title III activities in FY 1987. Although the federal funds expended on networking and resource-sharing activities are a relatively small amount, states have used these funds to investigate, experiment, plan, and initiate a great variety of resource-sharing activities. The kinds of activities reported by the states include

- Planning and evaluating statewide automation programs
- Establishing, expanding, and operating networks
- Implementing interlibrary loan and document delivery services
- Converting bibliographic holdings to machine-readable records
- Automating circulation and other resource-sharing systems
- Fostering cooperative library acquisition plans
- Increasing involvement of school library/media centers in networking activities

Grants most often supported activities initiated in one year, then developed and expanded or altered in succeeding years, with the ultimate goal being statewide coverage with significant nonfederal financial support. An immediate example taken from the Illinois State report is SILO, the union list of serials for the state of Illinois. It was begun in 1982 with an LSCA grant of $144,491 to Northern Illinois University from the Illinois State Library with a primary goal of increasing resource sharing among the state's libraries, using the OCLC's Serials Control System. The SILO list now has 340 libraries as contributors and 204,393 serials holdings in its database. Staff at the university entered local data records, trained the staff of the new member OCLC libraries, and administered the project. Major goals for SILO met during its first five years included establishing the OCLC holdings list as a viable statewide tool; increasing the number of participants to include a substantial number of Illinois libraries; producing customized printed lists of serials holdings; and moving the work activity with SILO to a public service area to enhance its public use. During 1987, the staff undertook the transition of the administration of the SILO project from the university library to the Illinois State Library. It will now continue within the ILLINET/OCLC Services unit as the primary focus for statewide resource sharing.

A listing of other exemplary state-supported LSCA III projects follows.

Establishing, Expanding, and Operating Networks

Washington. The LSCA grant, made to the Lower Columbia College Library, established and implemented an automated and integrated shared cooperative network between Longview Public Library and the college library forming the Longview Integrated Library System (LILS). Formed through the installation of Longview Public Library's integrated library computer system at the college library, both libraries now have improved access to each other's collections, and each library can now make more effective use of its materials budget through coordinated acquisitions. In addition, the public library users have access to the titles in the more specialized holdings at Lower Columbia College. The project produced the "LILS User Manual," which incorporates data entry protocols and cataloging standards, and "Guide to Services" brochures for users in each of the libraries. $112,042.

Maine. An intensive study of Maine's library-related computer activity and its future was completed in FY 1987. This study was based on the 1986 Epstein Report, which inventoried computer-related activity among Maine's libraries and reviewed the Maine library scene as a whole. An Ad-Hoc Statewide Automation Committee is implementing the Epstein Report, working with the projected network based on:

1 Five nodes or databases, with interconnections, as follows: one each at the three Area Reference and Resource Centers—Bangor, Portland, and the state library—serving their respective geographic areas; one at the University of Maine at Orono serving the seven state campus libraries; and one serving the large private college libraries at Colby, Bates, and Bowdoin; and

2 A coordinated holding listed using MINIMARC and concentrating on the collections of 30 middle-sized libraries (the larger libraries are mostly on OCLC) using optical disk technology.

A library microcomputer consultant continued workshops and marketplace monitoring. Directories of computers and computer magazines in Maine libraries were maintained. $112,154.

Connecticut. A continuation project initiated in 1966, the Interlibrary Loan Center served 349 Connecticut libraries during the year and received 27,680 requests for identification, location, and loan of materials. The center participated in the OCLC/ILL System and, as a third party borrower, in the ALANET electronic mail system. During the year, the teletype machines at nine libraries were removed as they were superseded by the OCLC/ILL dial access system to three additional Connecticut shared bibliographic databases, increasing the number of libraries in the state that cooperate as statewide lenders from 75 to 150. $90,292.

Automated Circulation/Resource-Sharing System

Nevada. LSCA funds were granted to the Clark County Library District to purchase equipment, including CD-ROM readers, players, and terminals; a scanner with light pens; a computer with printers; and software to improve the library's circulation control system for the benefit of all cooperating libraries. $22,438.

West Virginia. The West Virginia network was expanded with the addition of two more libraries: Marshall University's James E. Morrow Library was provided access to the state network via Cabell County Public Library by expanding the microwave link between Charleston and Huntington. This link provided university access to all public libraries, as well as public library access to Marshall University. The West Virginia Institute of Technology library joined in the sharing of a common bibliographic database for circulation. Access was provided to Tech students both in the library and in the dorms via 12 channels into network concentrators at the Library Commission. The sharing of resources between the commission and WV Tech marks the first sharing of resources within the state university system and the commission. $165,000.

Converting Bibliographic Holdings to Machine-Readable Records

Nevada. The Washoe County School District purchased a computer and software to study ways in which the holdings of school libraries, which constitute the largest collection of books in the state, can be made more accessible to other types of libraries in the state. $4,300.

New Mexico. Cooperative cataloging and interlibrary loan services for 14 libraries and the state library were purchased from AMIGOS/OCLC. $107,000.

Massachusetts. The purpose of this project was to transfer a paper copy of a regional holdings list of serials into a machine-readable format for NELINET's New England Union List of Serials (NEULS) project, a serial subset of OCLC. Holdings of 38 libraries were placed into the NEULS database and a hard copy and microfiche copy of the completed union list were produced and distributed to special, public, and academic libraries in western Massachusetts. $26,599.

Tennessee. This is the first year of a project that will provide statewide up-to-date access to holdings in specified periodical collections of both OCLC and non-OCLC members. Creating, maintaining, and updating the system will be accomplished at the Memphis State University Library and will provide access to an estimated 64,000 periodical titles in the state. The first year of the project was devoted to the installation of equipment, contact with libraries represented in the project, training of personnel for decision making, and preparing data for entry into the database. However, the holdings of four libraries (one large university, two state community colleges, and one large public) were almost completed, with completion estimated at the end of November 1987. $121,000.

Arkansas. Funds were used to contract with AMIGOS Bibliographic Council, Inc., to coordinate all aspects for the production of a cumulative issue of member records from OCLC/AMIGOS multiinstitutional data tapes and the conversion of these records. Funds also were used to maintain the online Arkansas Union List of Serials through payment of AMIGOS/OCLC related costs and funding of the third production of OCLC off line products, that is, 150 microfiche copies distributed to participants and subscribers. $184,413.

Connecticut. The grant to Western Connecticut State University allowed the conversion of 8,000 items in the collections not widely held in Connecticut to be entered into the Bilbiomation database. These items are in the fields of health, aging, foreign languages, business, music, and computer science. At present, more than 70 percent of the university's 300,000 circulating collection is available to statewide borrowers through this database. The remaining items will be converted using state funding. $10,000.

Interlibrary Loan and Document Delivery Services

New Mexico. The grant helped support the state's electronic bulletin board network now connecting 31 multitype libraries throughout New Mexico. The network was used to process over 5,700 interlibrary loan requests during the last year and has become a standard communication mechanism for resource sharing in the state. $11,894.

Mississippi. The LSCA grant continued the electronic interlibrary loan network. The database was moved offline and changed from microfiche to laser disc. This allowed interaction between the Mississippi Union Catalog and the Mississippi Automated Interlibrary Loan System (MAILS). In addition, five universities received funds to enable them to acquire telefacsimile copiers. This made possible the immediate delivery of documents and allowed for better communication among the university libraries, the state library, and other libraries in the state having similar equipment. $270,764.

Louisiana. The funds supported the development and maintenance of the laser disc statewide interlibrary loan network, consultation with participating libraries, and production of a written manual. The project continued to coordinate the operation of the system and to facilitate the adding of libraries to the network. It also contributed to the automation of the state library. $10,277.

Iowa. The Southeast Iowa Resource Sharing Project is a demonstration designed to address the needs of users among seven libraries through faster interlibrary loan services. In addition, the project sought means to expand networking service in Iowa. The objectives were to carry on interlibrary loan activities among member libraries of different types using the CD-ROM Iowa Locator and electronic mail and to study the impact of this activity. Records generated from participating libraries will be available for the next edition of the Iowa Locator. $10,028.

Continuing Education and Staff Development

North Dakota. A Kodak overhead projector was purchased to attach to a computer for statewide workshops on automation. Demonstrations were given to 53 public, academic, school, and special librarians on nine different online library computer systems for the purpose of developing a statewide online computer network. $989.

New Hampshire. A professional librarian was made available to provide consultation and assistance to libraries participating in the multitype New Hampshire Automated Information System. With the assistance of the librarian consultant, an increasing number of libraries are accessing the statewide automated database. $11,280.

New York. The South Central Research Library Council received a grant to develop a training program for coordinated collection development in the allied health sciences subject area and to produce a regional plan for all types of libraries. The librarians were trained in collection assessment procedures and techniques, analysis of user needs, identification of interlibrary loan patterns, and interpretation of the data from the OCLC holdings tapes for participating libraries. Participants learned to collect and develop more meaningful statistical data on the usage of their collections. A major benefit was that the data were comparable among libraries and provided a basis for a coordinated collection development plan. $16,438.

National Endowment for the Humanities Support for Libraries, 1988

1100 Pennsylvania Ave. N.W., Washington, DC 20506
202-786-0438

The National Endowment for the Humanities (NEH), an independent federal grant-making agency created by Congress in 1965, supports research, education, and public understanding in the humanities through grants to organizations, institutions, and individuals. According to the legislation that established the Endowment, the term "humanities" includes, but is not limited to, the study of archaeology, ethics, history, the history and criticism of the arts, the theory of the arts, jurisprudence, language (both modern and classical), linguistics, literature, philosophy, comparative religion, and those aspects of the social sciences that have humanities content and employ humanistic methods.

The Endowment's grant-making operations are conducted through five major divisions: (1) The Division of Research Programs provides support for the preparation for publication of important texts in the humanities, for the organization of collections and the preparation of reference materials, for the conduct of collaborative or coordinated research, and for the development of potential research through specific regrant programs. (2) The Division of Fellowships and Seminars, through several programs, provides stipends that enable individual scholars, teachers, and members of nonacademic professions to undertake study and research in the humanities that will enhance their capacity as teachers, scholars, or interpreters of the humanities and that will enable them to make significant contributions to thought and knowledge in the humanities. (3) The Division of Education Programs supports projects that promise to improve humanities teaching at all levels of instruction. (4) The Division of General Programs endeavors to fulfill the Endowment's mandate to foster public appreciation and understanding of the humanities. The division includes programs that assist institutions and organizations in developing humanities projects for presentation to general audiences, including adults and young adults. The division is composed of Museums and Historical Organizations, Media, Humanities Projects in Libraries, and the Public Humanities Program. Applications must meet published deadlines. (5) Finally, the Division of State Programs makes grants to citizens' committees in each state to provide support for local humanities projects, primarily directed toward general audiences.

In addition to support through each of the five divisions, support is also available to libraries through two offices, the Office of Preservation and the Office of Challenge Grants. The Office of Challenge Grants helps institutions to develop new and increased nonfederal, long-range sources of support in order to improve the quality of their humanities resources and activities to strengthen their financial stability. The Office of Preservation makes grants for a variety of preservation activities in libraries and other repositories.

Table 1 shows examples of grants made by the Challenge Grants office, the Division of Research Programs, the Division of General Programs, and the Division of Education Programs that were in effect as of December 1988 and are wholly or partially for library support.

Categories of Support

The NEH seeks to cooperate with libraries in strengthening the general public's knowledge and use of the humanities through its various programs. A description of these programs follows.

Division of General Programs

The single program within the division that supports libraries directly is Humanities Projects in Libraries, though other programs offer indirect support. The program encourages public, academic, or special libraries to plan and present humanities pro-

Table 1 / Examples of Current NEH Library Grants, December 1988

Recipient	Project Description	Amount
Office of Challenge Grants		
American Antiquarian Society Worcester, MA	To establish an endowment whose income will support library acquisitions, the salaries of a professional conservator and intern, the enhancement of staff salaries and the hiring of two new catalogers, and the basic administrative costs of the society's associate director for research and publication.	$500,000
John Carter Brown Library Providence, RI	To support the completion of a four-story annex to the library's present building and renovation of its present facilities, which will improve scholarly access to its humanities collections and their continuing maintenance.	$400,000
Clemson University Clemson, SC	To establish an endowment for library acquisitions in the humanities, faculty development and research, and special programs and events that would deepen understanding of the humanities at the university.	$300,000
Iowa City Public Library Foundation Iowa City, IA	To establish an endowment to increase the library's budget for humanities materials.	$125,000
Division of Education Programs		
Newberry Library Chicago, IL	To support faculty study of the historical and intellectual origins of European reconnaissance of the New World, the existence and influences of American cultures, the history of America before 1492, the forces that produced and the consequences that proceeded from European discovery, and the dialogue that ensued between European and American peoples.	$292,661
French Library in Boston Boston, MA	To support a unique collaborative project for improving the teaching of French at the seventh- and eighth-grade levels. The project concentrates on the history and culture of Paris as it is delineated in Marivaux's *Le Paysan parvenu,* Prevost's *Manon Lescaut,* Balzac's *Le Pere Goriot,* and Zola's *L'Assommoir.*	$182,529
Division of General Programs		
Clinton-Essex-Franklin Library System Plattsburgh, NY	To support reading and discussion programs in 56 libraries in New York State about social mobility, change, and dreams in America and about the decades of the 1920s, 1930s, and 1940s.	$125,000
Delaware Library Association Newark, DE	To support scholar-led reading discussion programs on six themes in 40 libraries on the Delmarva Peninsula of Delaware, Maryland, and Virginia.	$147,860
University of Minnesota Libraries Minneapolis, MN	To support planning of a traveling exhibition, an interpretive catalog, and concomitant print and media material about the emergence of a new Afro-American identity during the Harlem Renaissance of the 1920s.	$15,000
Division of Research Programs		
University of Illinois Champaign-Urbana, IL	To support microfilming of a private Arabic manuscript collection in Boutilimiṭ. Mauritania, and prepare a finding aid for the collection.	$83,449
Brown University Providence, RI	To complete the last two volumes of *European Americana,* a chronological guide to European writings on the Americas printed before 1750.	$122,327

grams. Cooperative projects between public, academic, or special libraries and between libraries, museums, historical societies, and other cultural institutions are also encouraged. Programs may take place at locations other than the library, but the primary objective of using library resources to enhance the understanding and appreciation of the humanities must be evident in the design of any project.

Among the many possible ways applicants to Humanities Projects in Libraries might fulfill the Endowment's mandate to foster public understanding and appreciation of the humanities are the following: Investigate the history of systems of thought; explore language as a reflection of culture; pose a philosophical debate concerning fundamental human rights; trace the development of the origins of social, political, or religious systems or institutions; and examine central themes such as love, war, family, or work through literature that illustrates such themes. A variety of methods and formats may be employed for the exploration of topics within the disciplines of the humanities. Some formats that have proven useful include reading and discussion groups; lecture series; conferences; film series accompanied by discussion groups and supplementary readings; exhibitions of library material or small exhibitions subordinate to other program formats; and such written materials as anthologies devoted to specific themes, essays illuminating specific topics, annotated bibliographies, or reading lists.

Applicants are urged to consider carefully the most appropriate means of implementing their projects and to discuss them with Endowment staff. Projects should involve the active collaboration of scholars from the appropriate disciplines of the humanities during both the planning and presentation of programs. They should create an opportunity for thoughtful examination of scholarly work or dialogue between the scholarly community and the general public based on the existing collections of humanities resources of the library.

The division also encourages libraries to design out-of-school projects for groups of young people of high school or junior high school age. By involving youth in projects, libraries can help them to acquire and apply new knowledge and skills in the disciplines of the humanities. Projects for this age group are intended to encourage a lifelong interest in the humanities on the part of young people by introducing them to the range of resources and activities in the humanities that are available to them outside of school.

Division of Education Programs

Libraries may receive Division of Education Programs grants directly or may be part of a college or university effort to strengthen teaching in the humanities. Direct grants to libraries usually support humanities institutes at which elementary and secondary school teachers or college and university faculty use the library's resources as part of a program of study directed by recognized scholars. The Folger Shakespeare Library and the Library of the University of Missouri are recent grantees. The division also encourages applications for projects to foster greater cooperation between libraries and humanities departments on individual college and university campuses.

Division of Fellowships and Seminars

The Division of Fellowships and Seminars' fellowship programs provide support for persons who wish to work individually; the division's seminar programs enable individuals to pursue their work and to exchange ideas in the collegial atmosphere of a community of scholars.

NEH fellowships provide opportunities for individuals to pursue independent study and research that will enhance their capacity as teachers, scholars, or interpreters of the humanities and that will enable them to make significant contributions to thought and knowledge in the humanities. These 6- to 12-month fellowships free people from the day-to-day responsibilities of teaching and other work for extended periods of uninterrupted investigation, reflection, and often writing. The programs are designed to support a range of people from those who have made significant contributions to the humanities to those at the beginning of their careers. Projects too may cover a range of activities from general study to specialized research.

Fellowships for University Teachers are for faculty members of departments and programs that grant the Ph.D. and faculty members of postgraduate professional schools. The annual application deadline is June 1.

Fellowships for College Teachers and Independent Scholars are for faculty members of two-year, four-year, and five-year colleges, faculty members of departments and programs in universities that do not grant the Ph.D., individuals affiliated with institutions other than colleges and universities, and scholars and writers working independently. The annual application deadline is June 1.

Summer Stipends provide support for faculty members in universities and two-year, four-year, and five-year colleges and for others working in the humanities to pursue two consecutive months of full-time study or research. Applicants may propose projects that can be completed during the stipend period or that are part of a long-range endeavor. Each college and university in the United States may nominate three members of its faculty for the summer stipend competition. Nonfaculty college and university staff members are eligible for this program and may apply without nomination, provided that they have no teaching duties during the year of their application. The annual application deadline is October 1.

Summer Seminars for College Teachers provide opportunities to teachers in two-year, four-year, and five-year colleges and universities and to others who are qualified to do the work of the seminar and make a contribution to it. Participants, working under the direction of distinguished scholars and teachers at institutions with libraries suitable for advanced study, pursue research in their own fields or in fields related to their interests. The seminars last six or eight weeks and are broadly distributed throughout the country. Seminars have been held at independent research libraries such as the Newberry and Huntington. The annual application deadline for participants and directors is March 1.

Summer Seminars for School Teachers provide opportunities for teachers of grades K through 12 and other full- or regular part-time school personnel to work in their areas of interest with accomplished teachers and active scholars studying seminal works in the humanities systematically and thoroughly. The seminars last four, five, or six weeks, depending on the individual seminar, and are held at institutions broadly distributed throughout the country. The annual application deadline for participants is March 1, and for directors is April 1.

Graduate Study Fellowships for Faculty at Historically Black Colleges and Universities are offered by the Endowment in response to President Reagan's initiative (Executive Order 12320) regarding historically black colleges and universities. These fellowships are intended to strengthen the teaching of the humanities at these colleges and universities by providing one year of support for teachers to work toward the completion of a doctoral degree in one of the disciplines of the humanities. The annual application deadline is March 15.

The *Travel to Collections Program* offers small grants to scholars who must travel to use research collections of libraries, archives, museums, and other repositories. Awards are made to help defray the costs of transportation, subsistence and lodging, reproduction and photoduplication, and associated research. Annual application deadlines are January 15 and July 15.

Younger Scholars Awards provide for secondary school and undergraduate students to carry out projects of research and writing in the humanities during the summer. Recipients work under the close supervision of a humanities scholar, and no academic credit may be taken for this work. The annual application deadline is November 1.

Division of Research Programs

The Texts Program provides support for the preparation for publication of works that promise to make major contributions to the study of the humanities. The Editions category supports various stages of the preparation of authoritative and annotated editions of works and documents of significant value to humanities scholars and general readers. The Translations category supports individual or collaborative projects to translate into English works that provide insight into the history, literature, philosophy, and artistic achievements of other cultures and that make available to scholars, students, and the public the thought and learning of those civilizations. Grants in the Publication Subvention (of scholarly books) category support the publication and dissemination of distinguished scholarly works in all fields of the humanities. Applications are particularly encouraged for projects that will be of significance to general readers as well as scholars, and for projects of lasting value. Applications must demonstrate that the work is important and likely to be influential.

The Reference Materials Program provides support for projects that promise to facilitate research in the humanities by organizing essential resources for scholarship and by preparing finding aids and other reference materials that improve scholarly access to information and collections. Grants in the Tools category support the creation of dictionaries, historical or linguistic atlases, encyclopedias, concordances, *catalogues raisonnés*, linguistic grammars, descriptive catalogs, databases, and other materials that codify information essential to research in the humanities. In the Access category, the Endowment supports projects that promise to increase the availability of important research collections and other significant source material in all fields of the humanities. Priority is given to projects that provide access to materials that are national in scope or import. Support is provided for such activities as archival arrangement and description; bibliographies (including bibliographic databases); records surveys; cataloging projects involving print, graphic, film, sound, and artifact collections; indices; foreign microfilming; other guides to humanities documentation; and projects to improve the ways in which libraries, archives, and other repositories make research documentation available. The Endowment encourages proposals for the compilation of comprehensive guides to the bibliographic and archival resources in broadly conceived subjects or fields. Historically black colleges and universities that possess collections of their own records or other significant primary source materials are invited to contact Access Program staff for information on types of projects eligible for support.

The Interpretive Research Program provides support for important, original research in all fields of the humanities. The Projects category supports research that will advance knowledge and deepen or enlarge critical understanding of an important topic in the humanities. In the Humanities, Science and Technology category, the Endowment supports research that employs the theories and methods of humanities disciplines to study science, technology, and medicine. The Endowment encourages proposals for the preparation of manuscripts leading to the publication of guided studies of historically significant scientific writings.

The Regrants Program awards funds to organizations that regrant those funds according to an effective and coherent plan for improving the state of research in a particular area or topic in the humanities. The Conferences category supports conferences designed to advance the state of research in a field or topic of major importance in the humanities. Through grants in the Centers for Advanced Study category, the Endowment supports interrelated research efforts in well-defined subject areas at independent research libraries and museums, American research centers overseas, and centers for advanced study. Through the Regrants for International Research category, the Endowment provides funds to national organizations and learned societies to enable American scholars to pursue research abroad, to attend or participate in international conferences, and to engage in collaborative work with foreign colleagues. Through Regrants in Selected Areas, the Endowment supports three kinds of regrants offered by the American Council of Learned Societies: ACLS fellowships, grants-in-aid, and research fellowships for recent recipients of the Ph.D.

Office of Challenge Grants

Libraries are eligible for support within the Endowment's Challenge Grants program, now (1988) in the twelfth year of funding. By inviting libraries to appeal to a broader funding public, challenge grants assist them to increase long-term financial stability and capital support and thereby improve the quality of humanities activities and collections. To receive each federal dollar, a challenge grant recipient must raise \$3 or \$4 from new or increased nonfederal funding sources. Both federal and nonfederal funds may be used to support the costs of renovation and construction, and the purchase of equipment. All funds may be invested in interest-bearing accounts to ensure annual revenues to support programs in the humanities in perpetuity. Awards in this category are limited to two per institution; second awards require four to one matching.

Office of Preservation

Grants are made to institutions to address the problems posed by the disintegration of significant humanities resources: books, newspapers, journals, manuscripts, documents, maps, and similar paper materials, as well as photographs, film, sound recordings, and tape.

Awards have been made to support cooperative preservation microfilming at a number of institutions as well as the preservation of important single collections; the conservation of original materials in certain special instances; efforts to provide professional training in preservation administration; the work of regional preservation services; research undertaken to improve preservation technology and procedures; and projects designed to increase public understanding of the preservation problem. The Office of Preservation also provides funds for the U.S. Newspaper program in states and territories for the preservation and bibliographic control of U.S. newspapers.

Division of State Programs

The Endowment annually makes grants to state humanities councils in the 50 states, the District of Columbia, Puerto Rico, and the U.S. Virgin Islands. The state councils, in turn, award regrants to institutions and organizations within each state according to guidelines and application deadlines determined by each council. Most grants are for projects that promote public understanding and appreciation of the humanities. Guidelines and application deadlines may be obtained by contacting the appropriate state council directly.

State Humanities Councils

Alabama Humanities Foundation
Robert Stewart, Exec. Dir.
Leslie Wright Fine Arts Center, 2 fl., Box 2280, Samford University, 800 Lakeshore Dr., Birmingham, AL 35229. 205-870-2300

Alaska Humanities Forum
Gary Holthaus, Exec. Dir.
430 W. Seventh Ave., Anchorage, AK 99501. 907-272-5341

Arizona Humanities Council
Lorraine W. Frank, Exec. Dir.
2828 N. Central, Suite 1111, Phoenix, AZ 85004. 602-279-3593

Arkansas Endowment for the Humanities
Jane Browning, Exec. Dir.
Baker House, 109 W. Fifth N., Little Rock, AR 72114. 501-372-2672

California Council for the Humanities
James Quay, Exec. Dir.
312 Sutter St., Suite 601, San Francisco, CA 94108. 415-391-1474

Colorado Endowment for the Humanities
James Pierce, Exec. Dir.
1836 Blake St., #200, Denver, CO 80202. 303-292-4458

Connecticut Humanities Council
Bruce Fraser, Exec. Dir.
41 Lawn Ave., Wesleyan Sta., Middletown, CT 06457. 203-347-6888

Delaware Humanities Forum
Henry Hirschbiel, Exec. Dir.
2600 Pennsylvania Ave., Wilmington, DE 19806. 302-573-4410

D.C. Community Humanities Council
Francine Cary, Exec. Dir.
1331 H St. N.W., Suite 310, Washington, DC 20005. 202-347-1732

Florida Endowment for the Humanities
Ann Henderson, Exec. Dir.
3102 N. Habana Ave., Suite 300, Tampa, FL 33607. 813-272-3473

Georgia Endowment for the Humanities
Ronald E. Benson, Exec. Dir.
1556 Clifton Rd. N.E., Emory University, Atlanta, GA 30322. 404-727-7500

Hawaii Committee for the Humanities
Annette M. Lew, Exec. Dir.
First Hawaiian Bank Bldg., Rm. 23, 3599 Waialae Ave., Honolulu, HI 96816. 808-732-5402

Idaho Humanities Council
Thomas H. McClanahan, Exec. Dir.
Len B. Jordan Bldg., Rm. 300, 650 W. State St., Boise, ID 83720. 208-345-5346

Illinois Humanities Council
Frank Pettis, Exec. Dir.
618 S. Michigan Ave., Chicago, IL 60605. 312-939-5212

Indiana Committee for the Humanities
Kenneth L. Gladish, Exec. Dir.
1500 N. Delaware St., Indianapolis, IN 46202. 317-638-1500

Iowa Humanities Board
Donald Drake, Exec. Dir.
Oakdale Campus, University of Iowa, N210 OH, Iowa City, IA 52242. 319-335-4153

Kansas Committee for the Humanities
Marion Cott, Exec. Dir.
112 W. Sixth St., Suite 210, Topeka, KS 66603. 913-357-0359

Kentucky Humanities Council, Inc.
Ramona Lumpkin, Exec. Dir.
417 Clifton Ave., University of Kentucky, Lexington, KY 40506-0414. 606-257-5932

Louisiana Committee for the Humanities
Michael Sartisky, Exec. Dir.
1001 Howard Ave., Suite 3110, New Orleans, LA 70113. 504-523-4352

Maine Humanities Council
Dorothy Schwartz, Exec. Dir.
Box 7202, Portland, ME 04112. 207-773-5051

Maryland Humanities Council
Naomi F. Collins, Exec. Dir.
516 N. Charles St., #201, Baltimore, MD 21201. 301-625-4830

Massachusetts Foundation for the Humanities and Public Policy
David Tebaldi, Exec. Dir.
One Woodbridge St., South Hadley, MA 01075. 413-536-1385

Michigan Council for the Humanities
Ronald Means, Exec. Dir.
Nisbet Bldg., Suite 30, 1407 S. Harrison Rd., East Lansing, MI 48824. 517-355-0160

Minnesota Humanities Commission
Cheryl Dickson, Exec. Dir.
580 Park Square Ct., Sixth and Sibley Sts., St. Paul, MN 55101. 612-224-5739

Mississippi Committee for the Humanities
Cora Norman, Exec. Dir.
3825 Ridgewood Rd., Rm. 111, Jackson, MS 39211. 601-982-6752

Missouri Humanities Council
Christine Reilly, Exec. Dir.
Lindell Professional Bldg., Suite 210, 4144 Lindell Blvd., Saint Louis, MO 63108. 314-531-1254

Montana Committee for the Humanities
Margaret Kingsland, Exec. Dir.
Box 8036, Hellgate Sta., Missoula, MT 59807. 406-243-6022

Nebraska Committee for the Humanities
Jane Renner Hood, Exec. Dir.
Lincoln Center Bldg., Suite 422, 215 Centennial Mall S., Lincoln, NE 68508. 402-474-2131

Nevada Humanities Committee
Judith K. Winzeler, Exec. Dir.
Box 8029, Reno, NV 89507. 702-784-6587

New Hampshire Council for the Humanities
Charles G. Bickford, Exec. Dir.
Walker Bldg., 15 S. Fruit St., Concord, NH 03301. 603-224-4071

New Jersey Committee for the Humanities
Miriam L. Murphy, Exec. Dir.
73 Easton Ave., New Brunswick, NJ 08901. 201-932-7726

New Mexico Endowment for the Humanities
John Lucas, Exec. Dir.
Onate Hall, Rm. 209, University of New Mexico, Albuquerque, NM 87131. 505-277-3705

New York Council for the Humanities
Jay Kaplan, Exec. Dir.
198 Broadway, 10 fl., New York, NY 10038. 212-233-1131

North Carolina Humanities Council
Alice Barkley, Exec. Dir.
112 Foust Bldg., UNC-Greensboro, Greensboro, NC 27412. 919-334-5325

North Dakota Humanities Council
Everett Albers, Exec. Dir.
Box 2191, Bismarck, ND 58502. 701-663-1948

Ohio Humanities Council
Charles C. Cole, Jr., Exec. Dir.
Box 06354, Columbus, OH 43206. 614-461-7802

Oklahoma Foundation for the Humanities
Anita May, Exec. Dir.
Executive Terrace Bldg., Suite 500, 2809 Northwest Expressway, Oklahoma City, OK 73112. 405-840-1721

Oregon Committee for the Humanities
Richard Lewis, Exec. Dir.
418 S.W. Washington, Rm. 410, Portland, OR 97204. 503-241-0543

Pennsylvania Humanities Council
Craig Eisendrath, Exec. Dir.
320 Walnut St., Suite 305, Philadelphia, PA 19106. 215-925-1005

Fundacion Puertorriquena de las Humanidades
Arturo Morales Carrion, Exec. Dir.
Box S-4307, Old San Juan, PR 00904. 809-721-2087

Rhode Island Committee for the Humanities
Thomas H. Roberts, Exec. Dir.
60 Ship St., Providence, RI 02903. 401-273-2250

South Carolina Committee for the Humanities
Randy L. Akers, Exec. Dir.
Box 6925, Columbia, SC 29260. 803-738-1850

South Dakota Committee on the Humanities
John Whalen, Exec. Dir.
Box 7050, University Sta., Brookings, SD 57007. 605-688-6113

Tennessee Humanities Council
Robert Cheatham, Exec. Dir.
1003 18th Ave. S., Nashville, TN 37212. 615-320-7001

Texas Committee for the Humanities
James Veninga, Exec. Dir.
100 Nueces, Austin, TX 78701. 512-473-8585

Utah Endowment for the Humanities
Delmont Oswald, Exec. Dir.
Broadway Bldg., Suite 900, 10 W. Broadway, Salt Lake City, UT 84101. 801-531-7868

Vermont Council on the Humanities
Victor R. Swenson, Exec. Dir.
Grant House, Box 58, Hyde Park, VT 05655. 802-888-3183

Virgin Islands Humanities Council
David Barzelay, Exec. Dir.
Market Sq., Conrad Bldg., Suite 6, 4 fl., #6 Torvet Straede, Box 1829, St. Thomas, VI 00801. 809-776-4044

Virginia Foundation for the Humanities and Public Policy
Robert C. Vaughan, Exec. Dir.
1939 Ivy Rd., Charlottesville, VA 22903. 804-924-3296

Washington Commission for the Humanities
Hidde Van Duym, Exec. Dir.
Lowman Bldg., Suite 312, 107 Cherry St., Seattle, WA 98104. 206-682-1770

Humanities Foundation of West Virginia
Charles Daugherty, Exec. Dir.
Box 204, Institute, WV 25112. 304-768-8869

Wisconsin Humanities Committee
Patricia Anderson, Exec. Dir.
716 Langdon St., Madison, WI 53706. 608-262-0706

Wyoming Council for the Humanities
Robert Young, Exec. Dir.
Box 3972, University Sta., Laramie, WY 82071-3972. 307-766-6496

National Science Foundation Support for Research in Information and Technology, 1988

Bruce H. Barnes
Deputy Division Director
Division of Information, Robotics and Intelligent Systems
National Science Foundation
1800 G. St. N.W., Washington, DC 20550

The National Science Foundation (NSF) is an independent agency of the federal government, established by Congress in 1950 to maintain the health and promote the progress of science in the United States. For many years, NSF supported research in the vital areas of information science and technology, primarily through the Information Science and Technology Division in the Directorate for Biological Sciences. In October 1986, recognizing the increasing need to advance research in information- and computer-related fields, NSF created a new Directorate for Computer and Information Science and Engineering (CISE), responsible for the coordination of all computer-related research programs in the foundation. The Division of Information, Robotics and Intelligent Systems (IRIS), one of the five divisions in CISE, has the broad responsibility of supporting research central to the progress of information science and technology, with an increasing emphasis toward the emerging areas of automation and machine intelligence.

The Division of Information, Robotics and Intelligent Systems

Information, in the context of modern technologies, takes many forms: language, speech, images, and various types of signals or sensory data, including text, numbers, and symbols. The impact of information and the technologies developed to process information is most dramatically seen when vast amounts of data from different sources must be efficiently organized, accessed, and possibly combined to enhance the ability to work and live in a knowledge-intensive society. Research supported by the IRIS Division primarily focuses on various information processes.

"Information processes" are understood to include the origination, capture, storage, and transmission of information and the transformation, aggregation, propagation, and interpretation of information-bearing structures. Special attention is given to the computing and communications technologies, including software, employed to manage these processes in the representation and processing of knowledge. Research in this field is highly interdisciplinary, drawing on mathematics, the computer sciences and engineering, and the biological, behavioral, and cognitive sciences. It reflects the state of the art in microelectronics, large-scale and distributed computation, user input/output, and networking. Rapid prototyping and real-time experimentation ensure the relevance and applicability of its abstract theories and concepts to significant problems in the national economy, in organizations, in the physical world, and in the interaction of individuals with computing systems.

Knowledge and Database Systems Program

The Knowledge and Database Systems program includes two distinct programmatic areas: Knowledge Models and Cognitive Systems support research fundamental to the design of computational systems that can learn, reason, and solve problems.

Representative topics supported by this area include formal models of information, knowledge, and reasoning; representation of knowledge and uncertainty; natural language processing; and learning and problem solving. Database and Expert Systems support research fundamental to the design, development, management, and use of databases and knowledge-based systems. Typical topics funded by this area are conventional database and knowledge base extensions; database support in distributed systems; expert systems; and information retrieval.

Robotics and Machine Intelligent Program

The Robotics and Machine Intelligent Program supports research in the design of computational systems that can adapt to a perceived situation by planning and executing complex tasks. Building such systems requires a fundamental knowledge of machine vision, pattern recognition, and speech understanding; planning of paths and trajectories; and manipulation, locomotion, and sensor-based control.

Interactive Systems Program

User-system dialogue and the cognitive and machine processes on which it rests is the main focus of the Interactive Systems Program. Communication across the user-system interface and interaction modalities through which it can be accomplished as well as the methodological problem of arriving at valid empirical generalizations about user-system interaction are important topics of research in this program.

Information Technology and Organization Program

The Information Technology and Organization Program supports research fundamental to the design and use of computational and communications systems to coordinate work and decision making. Representative topics are theory and models of information processing in organizations; information systems in environments of networked, decentralized computing; and social impacts and policy implications of information technology in the United States and in regard to international trade and development.

Coordination Theory and Technology is a special emphasis of the Information Technology and Organization Program. This initiative is motivated by three scientific issues that have been the focus of separate research efforts but may benefit by collaborative research. The first is the effort to discover the principles underlying how people collaborate and coordinate work efficiently and productively in environments characterized by a high degree of decentralized computation and decision making. The second is to gain a better fundamental understanding of the structure and outputs of organizations, industries, and markets that incorporate sophisticated, decentralized information and communications technology as an important component of their operations. The third is to understand problems of coordination in decentralized, or open, computer systems.

A Multidisciplinary Program

The research supported by the IRIS division is multidisiciplinary and crosses departmental boundaries. Many projects deal with research that requires expertise in psychology, economics, mathematics, computer and information sciences, as well as several fields of engineering. The division also participates in a number of initiatives designed to improve the knowledge base and human resources for teaching and learning science and engineering. Computers, multiprocessors, and information networks are critical instruments for experimental information science and technology research. The division seeks resources to meet such needs for those researchers whose work explores these new technologies.

Library-Related Research

Although the IRIS Division has expanded its scope of research to include a broad range of information science and technology projects, many of the research projects sponsored by the division have and will continue to have a significant impact on modern library science and related activities. A list of the FY 1986 research projects with relevance to library science follows.

Don S. Batory, University of Texas, Austin, Genesis: A Project to Develop Reconfigurable Database Management Systems, $119,097.

William J. Baumol, New York University, The Role of Computers & Scientific & Technical Information in Comparative Economic Development, $171,476.

Peter Buneman, University of Pennsylvania, Combining Object-Oriented and Relational Database Programming, $117,882.

Tomasz Imielinski, Rutgers University, New Brunswick, Complexity Tailored Information Systems, $149,996.

Paris Kanellakis, Brown University, Logic, Databases and Parallel Computation, $105,961.

George P. Lakoff, University of California, Berkeley, Lexical Network Theory, $100,278.

David Maier, Oregon Graduate Center, Presidential Young Investigator Award, $62,500.

Gary Marchionini, University of Maryland, College Park, Mental Models for Adaptive Search Systems: A Theory for Information Seeking, $70,732.

Richard S. Marcus, Massachusetts Institute of Technology, Advanced Models and Techniques for Expert Interactive Retrieval Assistance, $55,044.

Douglas P. Metzler, University of Pittsburgh, An Expert System Approach to Syntactic Parsing and Information Retrieval, $76,122.

Sergei Nirenburg, Carnegie Mellon University, Acquisition and Maintenance for Knowledge Bases for Natural Language Processing Systems, $97,621.

Vijay Raghavan and Jitender S. Deogun, University of SWLA, Cluster-Based Adaptive Information Retrieval System, $69,013.

Victor Raskin, Purdue University, Acquisition and Maintenance for Knowledge Bases for Natural Language Processing Systems, $96,506.

Fred S. Roberts, Rutgers University, New Brunswick, Scales of Measurement and the Limitations They Place on Information Processing, $49,712.

James B. Rule, Bank Street College of Education, The New Uses of Information: Impact in Organizations, $14,088.

Gerard Salton, Cornell University, Interface Tools and User-System Interaction in Automatic Information Retrieval, $139,553.

William M. Shaw and Judith B. Wood, University of North Carolina, Chapel Hill, An Evaluation and Comparison of Term and Citation Indexing, $75,487.

Fredrick N. Springsteel, University of Missouri, Columbia, Entity-Relationship Design of Information Systems, $58,435.

T. Toffoli, Massachusetts Institute of Technology, Information Mechanics, $77,000.

Jeffrey D. Ulman, Stanford University, Research into the Design and Implementation of Knowledge-Based Systems, $205,443.

Yorick Wilks, New Mexico State University, Machine Tractable Dictionaries as Tools and Resources for Natural Language Processing, $127,990.

Robert T. Winkler, Duke University, Combining Dependent Information: Models and Issues, $96,554.

Part 3
Library/Information Science Education, Placement, and Salaries

Guide to Library Placement Sources

Margaret Myers
Director, Office for Library Personnel Resources
American Library Association

The 1989 guide to library placement sources updates the listing in the 1988 *Bowker Annual* with information on new services and changes in contact information for previously listed groups. The sources listed primarily assist librarians in obtaining professional positions. A few also assist paraprofessionals, but they tend to be recruited through local sources.

General Sources of Library Jobs

Library Literature

Classified ads of library job vacancies and positions wanted are carried in many national, regional, and state library journals and newsletters. Members of associations can sometimes list position wanted ads free of charge in association publications. Listings of available positions are regularly found in *American Libraries, Chronicle of Higher Education, College & Research Libraries News, Library Journal,* and *Library Hotline.* State and regional library association newsletters, state library journals, foreign library periodicals, and other types of periodicals carrying such ads are listed in later sections of this guide.

Newspapers

In addition to the regular classifieds, the Sunday *New York Times* carries ads for librarians in the "Week in Review" section. Local newspapers, particularly the Sunday editions in large cities, such as the *Washington Post, Los Angeles Times,* and *Chicago Tribune,* often carry listings of job vacancies in libraries, both professional and paraprofessional.

Library Joblines

Library joblines or job hotlines give recorded telephone messages of job openings in a specific geographic area. Most tapes are changed once a week on Friday afternoon, although individual listings may sometimes be carried for several weeks. Although the information is fairly brief and the cost of calling is borne by the individual job seeker, a jobline provides a quicker and more up-to-date listing of vacancies than is usually possible through printed listings or journal ads.

Note: The author wishes to thank Maxine Moore, OLPR administrative assistant, for her help in updating the guide.

Most joblines carry listings for their state or region only, although some occasionally accept out-of-state positions if there is room on the tape. A few list technician and other paraprofessional positions, but the majority are for professional jobs only. When calling the joblines, one might occasionally find a time when the telephone keeps ringing without any answer; this usually means that the tape is being changed or there are no new jobs for that period. The classified section of *American Libraries* carries jobline numbers in each issue.

The following joblines are in operation: *American Association of Law Libraries* 312-939-7877; *Arizona State Library Association* 602-278-1327; *Association of College and Research Libraries* 312-944-6795; *British Columbia Library Association* 604-430-6411 (British Columbia listings only); *California Library Association* 916-443-1222 for northern California and 818-797-4602 for southern California (identical lists); *California Media and Library Educators Association* 415-697-8832; *Colorado State Library* 303-866-6741 (Colorado listings only, includes paraprofessional); *Connecticut* 203-645-8090 (Connecticut jobs only); *Delaware Library Association* 800-282-8696 (in-state), 302-736-4748 ask for jobline (out-of-state); *Drexel University College of Information Studies* 215-895-1672; *State Library of Florida* 904-488-5232 (in-state listings only); *Library Jobline of Illinois* 312-828-0930 professional positions, 312-828-9198 support staff positions (cosponsored by the Special Libraries Association Illinois Chapter and Illinois Library Association); *Indiana Statewide Library Jobline* 317-926-6561; *Kansas State Library Jobline* 913-296-3296 (also includes paraprofessional and out-of-state); *Maryland Library Association* 301-685-5760; *Metropolitan Washington Council of Governments Library Council* (D.C.) 202-223-2272; *Michigan Library Association* 517-694-7440; *Midwest Federation of Library Associations* 317-926-8770 (also includes paraprofessional and out-of-state if room on tape; cosponsored by four state library associations – Illinois, Indiana, Minnesota, Ohio); *Missouri Library Association* 314-442-6590; *Mountain Plains Library Association* 605-677-5757; 800-356-7820 available from all MPLA states except South Dakota (includes listings for Arizona, Colorado, Kansas, Montana, Nebraska, Nevada, North and South Dakota, Utah, and Wyoming; also paid listings from out-of-region institutions); *Nebraska* 402-471-2045 (during regular business hours); *New England Library Jobline* 617-738-3148 (New England jobs only); *New Jersey Library Association* 609-695-2121; *New York Library Association* 212-227-8483; *North Carolina State Library* 919-733-6410 (professional jobs in North Carolina only); *Oklahoma Jobline* (Oklahoma Department of Libraries) 405-521-4202 (5 P.M.–8 A.M. Monday–Friday and all weekend); *Oregon Library Association* 503-585-2232; *Pacific Northwest Library Association* 206-543-2890 (Alaska, Alberta, British Columbia, Idaho, Montana, Oregon, and Washington; includes both professional and paraprofessional and other library-related jobs); *Pennsylvania Cooperative Jobline* 717-234-4646 (cosponsored by the Pennsylvania Library Association, Medical Library Association Pittsburgh group, and West Virginia Library Association; also accepts paraprofessional out-of-state listings); *Public Library Association (PLA) Jobline* 312-664-5627; *Special Libraries Association* 202-234-3632; *Special Libraries Association, New York Chapter* 212-214-4226; *Special Libraries Association, San Andreas-San Francisco Bay Chapter* 408-378-8854 or 415-391-7441; *Special Libraries Association, Southern California Chapter* 818-795-2145; *Texas Library Association Job Hotline* 512-328-1518 (5:30 P.M. Friday–8:00 A.M. Monday, weekends only); *Texas State Library Jobline* 512-463-5470 (Texas listings only); *University of South Carolina College of Library and Information Science* 803-777-8443; *Virginia Library Association Jobline* 703-370-7267 (Virginia libraries only); *University of Western Ontario School of Library and Information Science* 519-661-3543.

For those employers who wish to place vacancy listings on the jobline recordings, the following numbers can be called: *ACRL* 312-944-6780, ext. 286; *Arizona* 602-269-2535; *California* 916-447-8541; *Colorado* 303-866-6740; *District of Columbia* 202-223-6800, ext. 230; *Florida* 904-487-2651; *Illinois* 312-644-1896; *Maryland* 301-727-7422 (Monday–Thursday, 9:30 A.M.–2:30 P.M.); *Michigan* 517-694-6615; *Missouri* 314-449-4627; *New York/SLA* 212-880-9716; *North Carolina* 919-733-2570; *Oklahoma* 405-521-2502; *Pennsylvania* 717-233-3113 ($15 per week for nonmembers); *PLA Jobline* 312-944-6780; *San Andreas-San Francisco/SLA* 415-620-4919; *Southern California/SLA* 818-356-6704; *Special Libraries Association* 202-234-4700; *Texas* 512-463-5465 or write: Library Development, Box 12927, Austin, TX 78711.

Write: *American Association of Law Libraries,* 53 W. Jackson Blvd., Suite 940, Chicago, IL 60604 or telex 312-431-1097 or use ABA/net 7603; *British Columbia Library Association Jobline,* 300-3665 Kingsway, Vancouver, B.C. V5R 5W2, Canada, 604-430-6010; *California Media and Library Educators Association,* 1575 Old Bayshore Hwy., Suite 204, Burlingame, CA 94010; *Colorado State Library Jobline,* 201 E. Colfax, 3rd fl., Denver, CO 80203; *Connecticut Library Association,* 638 Prospect Ave., Hartford, CT 06105; *Delaware Library Association,* Box 1843, Wilmington, DE 19899; *State Library of Florida,* R. A. Gray Bldg., Tallahassee, FL 32399-0251; *Library Jobline of Illinois,* Illinois Lib. Assn., 33 W. Grand Ave., Suite 301, Chicago, IL 60610 ($20 fee/2 weeks); *Kansas State Library Jobline,* c/o Roy Bird, 3rd fl., State Capitol, Topeka, KS 66612; *Maryland Library Association,* 115 W. Franklin St., Baltimore, MD 21201; *Michigan Library Association,* 1000 Long Blvd., Suite 1, Lansing, MI 48911 ($10 fee/week); *Missouri Library Association,* Parkade Plaza, Suite 9, Columbia, MO 65201 ($10 fee for nonmember libraries); *Mountain Plains Library Association,* c/o I. D. Weeks Lib., Univ. of South Dakota, Vermillion, SD 57069; *Nebraska Job Hotline,* Lib. Commission, 1420 P St., Lincoln, NE 68508; *New England Library Jobline,* c/o James Matarazzo, GSLIS, Simmons College, 300 The Fenway, Boston, MA 02115; *New Jersey Library Association,* Box 1534, Trenton, NJ 08607; *New York Library Association,* 15 Park Row, Rm. 434, New York, NY 10038 ($10 fee/listing/week for nonmembers); *Oregon Library Association JOBLINE,* Oregon State Lib., State Library Bldg., Salem, OR 97310; *PNLA Jobline,* c/o Grad. School of Lib. & Info. Science, Univ. of Washington, FM-30, Seattle, WA 98195, 206-543-1794; *Texas Library Association Job Hotline,* 3355 Bee Cave Rd., Suite 603, Austin, TX 78746; *University of South Carolina, College of Library and Information Science,* Admissions & Placement Coord., Columbia, SC 29208 (no geographic restrictions); *Virginia Library Association Jobline,* 80 S. Early St., Alexandria, VA 22304; *University of Western Ontario* 519-661-3542. For the *Midwest Federation Jobline,* employers should send listings to their own state library association executive secretary or call 317-926-6561. There is a $10 fee for the first week and $5 per listing each week thereafter. Paraprofessional positions are also accepted.

Specialized Library Associations and Groups

The National Registry for Librarians, formerly housed in the Illinois State Job Service at 40 W. Adams St., Chicago, IL 60603, is no longer in operation. Referral service will still be carried out through state and local Job Service offices, but no independent registry will be maintained for librarians.

Advanced Information Management, 444 Castro St., Suite 320, Mountain View, CA 94041, 415-965-7799. This personnel agency, specializing in library personnel, offers work on a temporary, permanent, and contract basis for both professional librarians and paraprofessionals in the special, public, and academic library marketplace. It supplies consultants who can work with special projects in traditional libraries or manage library development projects and also offers a résumé-writing service geared toward people in the library field.

American Association of Law Libraries, 53 W. Jackson Blvd., Suite 940, Chicago, IL 60604, 312-939-4764. The AALL monthly *Newsletter* publishes lists of openings and persons available. A placement listing up to eight lines of typeset copy is free; for more than eight lines, the charge is $2.50 per line. An advance subscription service for job listings is available for $1.25 a month. A Career Hotline gives a recorded message featuring descriptions of positions available; call 312-939-7877 to hear the listings, which run for a two-week period. Employers are invoiced $25 for the first 60 words; $5 for each additional 10 words.

American Libraries, "Career LEADS EXPRESS," c/o Beverly Goldberg, 50 E. Huron St., Chicago, IL 60611. Advance galleys (3–4 weeks) of classified job listings to be published in next issue of *American Libraries.* Early notice of approximately 100 "Positions Open" sent about the seventeenth of each month does not include editorial corrections and late changes as they appear in the regular *AL* LEADS section, but does include some "Late Job Notices." For each month, send $1 check made out to AL EXPRESS, self-addressed, standard business-size envelope (4 × 9), and 45¢ postage on envelope.

American Libraries, ConsultantBase (CBase). An *AL* service that helps match professionals offering library/information expertise with institutions seeking it. Published quarterly, CBase appears in the Career LEADS section of the January, April, June, and October issues of *AL.* Rates: $4.50/line—classified; $45/inch—display. Inquiries should be made to Beverly Goldberg, LEADS Ed., *American Libraries,* 50 E. Huron St., Chicago, IL 60611, 312-944-6780, ext. 326.

American Library Association, Association of College and Research Libraries, 50 E. Huron St., Chicago, IL 60611-2795, 312-944-6780, ext. 286. In addition to classified advertising each month in *College & Research Libraries News,* ACRL lists job openings in academic and research libraries in the *Fast Job Listing Service,* a monthly bulletin that announces positions one month before they appear in *C&RL News,* as well as positions that do not appear elsewhere because of early application deadlines. $10 to ACRL members (indicate ALA/ACRL membership number); $15 to nonmembers. Renewable after six months.

Also available is the ACRL Jobline, a recorded telephone message updated each Friday. Call 312-944-6795 to hear the recording; 312-944-6780, ext. 286, to place a listing for a two-week period.

American Library Association, Office for Library Personnel Resources, 50 E. Huron St., Chicago, IL 60611, 312-944-6780. A placement service is provided at each annual conference (June or July) and midwinter meeting (January). Request job seeker or employer registration forms prior to each conference. Persons not able to attend the conference can register with the service and can also purchase job and applicant listings sent directly from the conference site. Information included when requesting registration forms. Handouts on interviewing, preparing a résumé, and other job-seeking information are available from the ALA Office for Library Personnel Resources.

In addition to the ALA conference placement center, ALA division national conferences usually include a placement service. See *American Libraries* "Datebook" for dates of upcoming divisional conferences, since these are not held every year.

American Library Association, ASCLA/SLAS State Library Consultants to Institutional Libraries Discussion Group, Institutional Library Mailed Jobline. Monthly compilation of job openings in institutional libraries throughout the United States and territories. Send self-addressed, stamped envelope(s) to Institutional Library Jobline, c/o S. Carlson, Rhode Island Dept. of State Lib. Services, 300 Richmond St., Providence, RI 02903. Send job postings to same or call 401-277-2726. Listings appear for one month unless resubmitted.

American Society for Information Science, 1424 16 St. N.W., Rm. 404, Washington, DC 20036, 202-462-1000. An active placement service is operated at ASIS annual (usually October) and mid-year (usually May) meetings (locales change). All conference attendees (both ASIS members and nonmembers), as well as ASIS members who cannot attend the conference, are eligible to use the service to list or find jobs. Job listings are also accepted from employers who cannot attend the conference. Interviews are arranged and special seminars are given. Throughout the year, current job openings are listed in *ASIS JOBLINE,* a monthly publication sent to all members and available to nonmembers on request.

Art Libraries Society/North America (ARLIS/NA), c/o Exec. Dir., 3900 E. Timrod St., Tucson, AZ 85711, 602-881-8479. Art librarian and slide curator jobs are listed in the *ARLIS/NA UPDATE* (4/yr.) and a job registry is maintained at society headquarters. (Any employer may list a job with the registry, but only members may request job information.)

Associated Information Managers, c/o Paul Oyer, Exec. Dir., 2026C Opitz Blvd., Woodbridge, VA 22191, 703-490-4246. *AIM Career Exchange Clearinghouse* lists positions open and wanted on a monthly basis in conjunction with the *AIM Network.* Applicants send résumé and cover letter to AIM for forwarding to employers. Employers listing available positions may list their organization name, contact person, and telephone number, or they may request that AIM serve as the clearinghouse. Reference numbers for all listings are assigned by AIM. The *Career Exchange Clearinghouse* distribution is open to AIM members only, but nonmembers may list position vacancies.

Association for Educational Communications & Technology, Placement and Referral Service, 1126 16 St. N.W., Washington, DC 20036, 202-466-4780. A referral service is available at no charge to AECT members. A placement center operates at the annual conference, free to all conference registrants. In addition, there are placement bulletin boards on TechCentral, AECT's electronic mail and information system, listing job vacancies and positions desired. Members receive a free monthly newsletter of job vacancies.

Black Caucus Newsletter, c/o George C. Grant, Rollins College, Campus Box 2654, Winter Park, FL 32789. Lists some job vacancy notices. Free to members; $5 to others. Published bimonthly. Paid vacancy announcements are also accepted.

C. Berger and Company, 327 E. Gundersen Dr., Carol Stream, IL 60188, 312-653-1115. CBC represents clients nationwide in filling permanent positions in library or information management, supervision, or subject specialty areas. Professional and support personnel can also be supplied to special, academic, and public libraries on a temporary basis or in a maintenance capacity. Teams of qualified specialists and project management services are also available under contract.

Canadian Association of Special Libraries and Information Services/Ottawa Chapter Job Bank, c/o Coord., CASLIS, 66C Brockington Crescent, Nepean, Ont. K2G 5L1, Canada. Those looking for a job should send résumé; employers with a job to list should call 613-237-3688.

Catholic Library Association, 461 W. Lancaster Ave., Haverford, PA 19041, 215-649-5250. Personal and institutional members of CLA are given free space (35 words) to advertise for jobs or to list job openings in *Catholic Library World* (6/yr.). Others may advertise at $15 per printed line (36 characters).

Center for the Study of Rural Librarianship, College of Library Science, Clarion Univ. of Pennsylvania, Clarion, PA 16214, 814-226-2383. *Rural Libraries Jobline,* monthly listing. Send $1 for each monthly listing as desired.

Council on Library/Media Technicians, c/o Shirley Daniels, Newsletter Ed., 5049 Eighth St. N.E., Washington, DC 20017. *COLT Newsletter* appears quarterly and accepts listings for library/media technician positions. However, correspondence relating to jobs cannot be handled.

Gossage Regan Associates, Inc., 15 W. 44 St., New York, NY 10036, 212-869-3348. Gossage Regan Associates works with library trustees and faculty search committees or with library directors, systems heads, library search committees, chief executive officers of corporations, higher education institutions, and other organizations to locate, screen, assess, and recommend candidates for library management positions such as directors, division heads, or information specialists. In the New York/New Jersey/Connecticut metropolitan area, Gossage Regan provides temporary librarians and information specialists, paraprofessionals, and clericals to special, academic, and public libraries for long- and short-term assignments. GRA People, a Gossage Regan Associates subsidiary, is a registered employment agency for permanent placement of library and information personnel operating nationwide.

GRAPEVINE, c/o Beverly Goldberg, *American Libraries,* 50 E. Huron St., Chicago, IL 60611. Online database of job openings on ALANET updated every Monday. Short-entry job alert, which includes job title, institution, date available, application deadline, salary, and contact person. Limited Boolean search flexibility. GRAPEVINE ads do not automatically appear in *American Libraries* LEADS; employers can choose one or both services. $25 for GRAPEVINE ad; $10 if also advertised with LEADS. Can be read on ALANET by typing ⟩VINE at system level or from within the Units menu (ALANET4).

HBW Library Recruiters, 214-559-4291. A firm of professional librarians that works exclusively for libraries and information centers seeking to fill executive positions. HBW assists library boards, county administrators, city managers, faculty search committees, library directors, and personnel officers with the selection of key administrative and managerial staff. HBW assists with the development of position guidelines and requirements, candidate lists, screening, credential checks and verification, and preliminary interviewing through final selections. There is no obligation for an exploratory discussion.

Indiana Jobline, Area Library Services Authority, 1100 W. 42 St., Indianapolis, IN 46208, 317-926-6561. Computer-based listing of library jobs in all types of libraries in Indiana. Indiana libraries may access through ALANET. A printed copy of job listings is available for a nominal charge. Sort can be requested by type of library or geographic region within state.

Information Exchange System for Minority Personnel (IESMP, Inc.), Box 90216, Washington, DC 20090. Nonprofit organization designed to recruit minority librarians for EEO/AA employers. *Informer,* quarterly newsletter. Write for membership categories, services, and fees.

Library Associates, 2600 Colorado Blvd., Suite 160, Santa Monica, CA 90404, 213-453-5583 or 5270. A consulting firm owned and operated by librarians, the agency will provide personnel on a temporary or contract basis to fill vacancies, substitute for regular staff, and so on, in addition to providing expertise for such projects as automation, systems analysis, records retention and organization, cataloging, indexing/abstracting, thesauri construction, marketing strategy, and implementing marketing plans for vendors who sell information products.

Medical Library Association, 6 N. Michigan Ave., Suite 300, Chicago, IL 60602, 312-419-9094. *MLA News* (10 issues/yr., June/July and November/December combined issues) lists positions wanted and positions available in its "Employment Opportunities" column. The position available rate is $12.50 per line for nonmembers and for any advertisements received through an employment agency, advertising agency, or any other third party. Up to 10 free lines for MLA members plus $11 per line over 10 lines. Positions wanted rates are $8.50 per line for nonmembers; $7.50 per line for members, with 20 free lines. Advance mailings of "Employment Opportunities" may be requested for a period of six months. This service is available for a prepaid fee: MLA members, $15; nonmembers, $25. MLA also offers placement service at annual conference each spring.

Midwest Federation of Library Association (MFLA) Jobline, 317-926-8770. Telephone jobline listing job openings in all types of libraries throughout the Midwest. Libraries wishing to list job openings should contact their state library association for listing forms and guidelines, or contact MFLA Jobline, c/o Central Indiana ALSA, 1100 W. 42 St., Suite 305, Indianapolis, IN 46208, 317-926-6561.

North American Serials Interest Group, Job Connections Service, c/o Marla Edelman, 3800 Walker Ave., Greensboro, NC 27403. Free to NASIG members (dues $15; applicants with interest in serials are welcome). Job seeker placement forms are kept on file for up to six months and sent to employers who send a job description and handling fee.

Online, Inc., c/o June Thompson, 11 Tannery Lane, Weston, CT 06883, 203-227-8466; Electronic Mail—TCU 202 (The Source), CLASS.ONLINE (ONTYME); TFHN (BRS); ALANET mailbox is ALA0795. Jobline is available for positions sought and positions available in the online/library field through the Online Chronicle (file 170) on DIALOG. All postings are free.

Pro Libra Associates, Inc., 6 Inwood Place, Maplewood, NJ 07040, 201-762-0070. A multiservice agency, Pro Libra specializes in placement of temporary and permanent personnel.

REFORMA, National Association to Promote Library Service to the Spanish-Speaking. The REFORMA jobline publication is no longer issued. Employers wishing to do direct mailings to the REFORMA membership (500+) may obtain mailing labels arranged by zip code for $125 per set from REFORMA, Box 832, Anaheim, CA 92815-0832. An alternative is selective mailings of job fliers to the members of the REFORMA Executive Board (20–25). A set of mailing labels for the executive board is available for $5.

Rhode Island Library Association Bulletin, Jobline, c/o Charlotte Schoonover, Kingston Free Lib., 2605 Kingstown Rd., Kingston, RI 02881, 401-783-8254. Jobline appears monthly in *RILA Bulletin,* listing positions in southeast New England, including paraprofessional and part-time jobs. Job seekers desiring copy of most recent monthly jobline, send self-addressed, stamped envelope. Groups of envelopes may also be sent. To post a notice, contact C. Schoonover at above address.

School Library Career Awareness Network (SCAN), School of Info. Studies, Syracuse, NY 13244, 315-443-2740. In coordination with the New York Library Association School Library Media Section, Syracuse operates a clearinghouse for recruitment and placement of school library media specialists in New York State. *SCANsheet* is mailed biweekly from April through September and on a monthly basis from October to March. The fee for members of the New York Library Association School Library Media Section is $8, for nonmembers $12. *SCANfolio* gives school administrators information from database directory of participating library media specialists seeking positions. *SCANline* is a 24-hour hotline. Employers are not charged for listing jobs; $20 charge for a SCANfolio search. A fee of $8/yr. (nonmembers $12) entitles registrants to all SCAN services.

Society of American Archivists, 600 S. Federal, Suite 504, Chicago, IL 60605, 312-922-0140. The *SAA Newsletter,* sent to members only six times annually, lists jobs, as well as details of professional meetings and courses in archival administration. The "Employment Bulletin," sent to members who pay a $12 subscription fee, alternates with the *Newsletter.*

Special Libraries Association, 1700 18 St. N.W., Washington, DC 20009, 202-234-4700. SLA operates the Resume Referral Service for information professionals and employers and also maintains a telephone jobline, SpeciaLine, 24 hours a day, 7 days a week, 202-234-3632. Most SLA chapters have employment chairpersons who act as referrals for employers and job seekers. Several SLA chapters have joblines. The association's monthly newsletter, *The SpeciaList,* carries classified advertising. SLA also offers a conference employment clearinghouse at the June annual conference.

Theresa M. Burke Employment Agency, 23 W. 39 St., Suite 710, New York, NY 10018, 212-398-9250. The first employment service for information personnel (founded in 1949), the agency is New York City–based and has an international reputation. The majority of library openings are in the New York City metropolitan area in special libraries and require related experience. Records management positions are available in law firms, corporations, and government agencies. Ask for Frances McMeen or Catherine Kenny. All fees are paid by the employer.

State Library Agencies

In addition to the joblines mentioned previously, some of the state library agencies issue lists of job openings within their area. These include Colorado (biweekly, sent on receipt of SASE); Indiana (monthly on request); Iowa (*Joblist,* monthly on request); Massachusetts (*Massachusetts Position Vacancies,* monthly, sent to all public libraries in-state and to interested individuals on a one-time basis); Minnesota (*Position Openings in Minnesota and Adjoining States,* semimonthly, sent to public and academic libraries); Mississippi (job vacancy list, monthly); and Ohio (*Library Opportunities in Ohio,* monthly, sent to accredited library education programs and interested individuals upon request).

The North Carolina and South Carolina state libraries have an electronic bulletin board service that lists job openings in the state. North Carolina can be accessed in-state and nationally by Western Union Easylink system users (use NCJOBS).

South Carolina can be accessed in-state by users of the South Carolina Library Network.

Some state library newsletters and journals occasionally list vacancies. These include: Alabama (*Cotttonboll,* bimonthly); Alaska (*Newspoke,* bimonthly); Arizona (*Libraries News Week*); Indiana (*Focus on Indiana Libraries,* 11 times/yr.); Iowa (*Footnotes*); Kansas (*Kansas Libraries,* monthly); Louisiana (*Library Communique,* monthly); Missouri (*Show-Me Libraries,* quarterly); Nebraska (*Overtones*, 10 times/yr.); New Hampshire (*Granite State Libraries,* bimonthly); New Mexico (*Hitchhiker,* weekly); North Carolina (*NEWS FLASH,* monthly, public libraries only); Utah (*Directions for Utah Libraries,* monthly); and Wyoming (*Outrider,* monthly).

Many state library agencies refer applicants informally when vacancies are known to exist, but do not have formal placement services. The following states primarily make referrals to public libraries only: Alabama, Arizona, California, Georgia, Idaho, Louisiana, North Carolina, Pennsylvania, South Carolina (institutional also), Tennessee, Utah, Vermont, and Virginia. Those who refer applicants to all types of libraries are Alaska, Delaware, Florida, Illinois, Kansas, Maine, Maryland, Massachusetts, Mississippi, Montana, Nebraska, Nevada (largely public and academic), New Hampshire (public, school, academic), New Mexico, North Dakota, Ohio, Pennsylvania, Rhode Island, South Dakota, West Virginia (public, academic, special), and Wyoming.

The following state libraries post job vacancy notices for all types of libraries on a bulletin board: California, Connecticut, Florida, Indiana, Iowa, Michigan, Montana, Nevada, New York, Ohio, Utah, and Washington. Addresses of the state agencies are found in the *Bowker Annual* or *American Library Directory.*

State and Regional Library Associations

State and regional library associations often make referrals, run ads in association newsletters, or operate a placement service at annual conferences, in addition to the joblines sponsored by some groups. When jobs are known, the following associations refer applicants: Arkansas, Delaware, Hawaii, Louisiana, Michigan, Nevada, Pennsylvania, South Dakota, Tennessee, Texas, and Wisconsin. Although listings are infrequent, job vacancies are placed in the following association newsletters or journals when available: Alabama (*Alabama Librarian,* 9 times/yr.); Arkansas (*Arkansas LA Newsletter,* 6 times/yr.); Connecticut (*Connecticut Libraries,* 11 times/yr.), Delaware (*Delaware Library Association Bulletin,* 3 times/yr.), District of Columbia (*Intercom,* 11 times/yr.); Florida (*FLASH*); Indiana (*Focus on Indiana Libraries,* 11 times/yr.); Iowa (*Catalyst,* 6 times/yr.); Kansas (*KLA Newsletter,* 6 times/yr.); Minnesota (*MLA Newsletter,* 10 issues/yr.); Missouri (bimonthly); Mountain Plains (*MPLA Newsletter,* bimonthly, lists vacancies and position wanted ads for individual and institutional members or area library school students); Nevada (*Highroller,* 4 times/yr.); New Hampshire (*NHLA Newsletter,* 6 times/yr.); New Jersey (*NJLA Newsletter,* 10 times/yr.); New Mexico (shares notices via state library's *Hitchhiker,* weekly); New York (*NYLA Bulletin,* 10 times/yr.); Rhode Island (*RILA Bulletin,* 10 times/yr.); South Dakota (*Bookmarks,* bimonthly); Vermont (*VLA News,* Box 803, Burlington, VT 05402, 10 issues/yr.); Virginia (*Virginia Librarian,* quarterly); and Wyoming (*Roundup,* 3 times/yr.).

At their annual conference the following associations have indicated some type of placement service, although it may consist only of bulletin board postings: Alabama, California, Connecticut, Idaho, Illinois, Indiana, Kansas, Louisiana, Maryland, Massachusetts, Midwest Federation, Mountain Plains, New England, New Jersey, New York, North Carolina, Oregon, Pacific Northwest, Pennsylvania, South Dakota, Tennessee, Texas, Vermont, and Wyoming.

The following associations have indicated they have no placement service at this time: Georgia, Kentucky, Middle Atlantic Regional Library Federation, Minnesota, Mississippi, Montana, Nebraska, Nevada, New Mexico, and North Dakota. State and regional association addresses are found in the *Bowker Annual.*

Library Education Programs

Library education programs offer some type of service for their current students as well as alumni. Most schools provide job-hunting and résumé-writing seminars. Many have outside speakers representing different types of libraries or recent graduates relating career experiences. Faculty or a designated placement officer offer individual advising services or critiquing of résumés.

Of the ALA-accredited programs, the following handle placement activities through the library school: Atlanta, British Columbia, Clarion, Columbia, Dalhousie, Drexel, Emporia, Hawaii, Illinois, Louisiana, McGill, Michigan, Missouri, Pittsburgh (Department of Library Science only), Queens, Rhode Island, Rosary, Rutgers, St. John's, South Carolina, Syracuse, Tennessee, Texas-Austin, Toronto, Western Ontario, Wisconsin-Madison, and Wisconsin-Milwaukee.

The central university placement center handles activities for the following schools: California-Berkeley and Pittsburgh (Department of Information Science only). However, in most cases, faculty in the library school still do informal job counseling.

In some schools, the placement services are handled in a cooperative manner; in most cases the university placement center sends out credentials while the library school posts or compiles the job listings. Schools utilizing both sources include Alabama, Albany, Alberta, Arizona, Brigham Young, Buffalo, Catholic University of America, Chicago, Clarion, Emporia, Florida State, Indiana, Iowa, Kent State, Kentucky, Long Island, Maryland, Montreal, North Carolina Central, North Carolina-Chapel Hill, North Carolina-Greensboro, University of North Texas, Northern Illinois, Oklahoma, Pittsburgh, Pratt, Queens, St. John's, San Jose, Simmons, South Florida, Southern Connecticut, Southern Mississippi, Syracuse, Tennessee, Texas Woman's, UCLA, Washington, Wayne State, and Wisconsin-Milwaukee.

In sending out placement credentials, schools vary as to whether they distribute these free, charge a general registration fee, or request a fee for each file or credentials sent out.

Those schools that have indicated they post job vacancy notices for review but do not issue printed lists are Alabama, Albany, Alberta, Arizona, Atlanta, British Columbia, Buffalo, Catholic University of America, Chicago, Columbia, Dalhousie, Florida State, Hawaii, Kent State, Kentucky, Long Island, Louisiana, Maryland, McGill, Montreal, North Carolina Central, North Carolina-Chapel Hill, North Carolina-Greensboro, Northern Illinois, University of North Texas, Oklahoma, Pratt, Queens, Rosary, Rutgers, St. John's, San Jose, Simmons, South Carolina, South Florida, Southern Mississippi, Syracuse (general postings), Tennessee, Texas Woman's, Toronto, Washington, Wayne State, Western Ontario, and Wisconsin-Milwaukee.

In addition to job vacancy postings, some schools issue a printed listing of positions open that is distributed primarily to students and alumni and only occasionally available to others. The following schools issue listings free to students and alumni *only* unless indicated otherwise: Albany (weekly to SLIS grads registered with Placement Office); Brigham Young; British Columbia (uses BLCA Jobline, 604-430-6411); California-Berkeley (alumni receive weekly out-of-state listings if registered; $55 fee for service, also a weekly California jobline, call 415-642-1716 to list positions); Clarion (free to students and with SASE to alumni); Drexel (job hotline listing local jobs only, 215-895-1672—changed each Monday); Florida State (free to students and alumni); Illinois (free in office; 8 issues by mail for $4 and 8 self-addressed, stamped no. 10 envelopes to alumni, $8 and 8 SASEs to nonalumni); Indiana (free for one year following graduation; alumni and others may send self-addressed stamped envelopes); Iowa (weekly, $15/yr. for registered students and alumni); Long Island (listing from Career Services, $35/yr. includes handling résumé, seminars, etc.); Michigan (free for one year following graduation, all other grads, $15/yr., 24 issues, $20 to others); Missouri (Library Vacancy Roster, monthly printout, 50¢ an issue, with minimum of 5 issues, to anyone); University of North Texas ($5/6 mo., students and alumni); Pittsburgh (free online placement to alumni, frequency by request); Rhode Island (monthly, $3/yr.); Rosary (*Placement News* every 2 weeks, free for 6 months following graduation, $15/yr. for students and alumni, $25 to others; *Placement News* is also on Lincolnet and can be accessed via telephone lines); Simmons operates the New England Jobline, which announces professional vacancies in New England, call 617-738-3148; southern Connecticut (printed listing twice a month, free in office, mailed to students/alumni free); Syracuse (School Media-New York State Listings—$8 NYLA members; $12 nonmembers); Texas-Austin (bimonthly placement bulletin free to alumni and students one year following graduation, $10/6 mo. or $17/yr. thereafter; Austin area Job-Hunters List—$6/6 mo., $11/1 yr., free to students and alumni up to one year following graduation, full job descriptions sent out as often as jobs are received; particular job announcements are sent to graduates interested in a specific type and location of job if qualifications match and are registered for this service); UCLA (alumni—every 2 weeks by request, renew every 3 months); Wisconsin-Madison (subscription $12/yr. for 12 issues, to anyone). Western Ontario operates the SLIS Jobline, which announces openings for professionals, call 519-661-3543; to list positions, call 519-661-3542. Wisconsin-Milwaukee sends copies of particular job announcements to graduates who are interested in the type and location of the job, who seem to meet the qualifications, and have registered with the school for this service. It has also developed a job database for remote access on the university's mainframe using terminals in the school, or dial access.

Employers often list jobs with schools only in their particular geographic area; some library schools give information to nonalumni regarding their specific locales, but as they are not staffed to handle mail requests information is usually given in person. Schools that allow librarians in their area to view listings are Alabama, Albany, Alberta, Arizona, Brigham Young, British Columbia, Buffalo, California-Berkeley, Catholic University of America, Chicago, Clarion, Columbia, Dalhousie, Drexel, Emporia, Florida State, Hawaii, Illinois, Indiana, Iowa, Kent State, Kentucky, Long Island, Lousiana, Maryland, McGill, Michigan, Missouri, Montreal, North Carolina Central, North Carolina-Chapel Hill, North Carolina-Greensboro, University of North Texas, Northern Illinois, Oklahoma, Pittsburgh, Pratt, Queens, Rhode Island, Rutgers, Simmons, St. John's, San Jose, South Carolina, Southern California, Southern Connecticut, Southern Mississippi, Syracuse, Tennessee, Texas-Austin, Texas Woman's, Toronto, UCLA, Washington, Wayne State, Western Ontario, Wisconsin-Madison, and Wisconsin-Milwaukee.

A list of accredited programs is included in Part 3 of the *Bowker Annual*. Individuals interested in placement services of other library education programs should contact the schools directly.

Federal Library Jobs

Consideration for employment in many federal libraries requires establishing civil service eligibility and being placed on the Office of Personnel Management (OPM) register in the geographic area in which you wish to be considered. As of November 1987, OPM terminated its nationwide register and the OPM network of area offices became responsible for meeting librarian hiring needs within each office's area of responsibility.

Eligibility can be obtained by meeting specific education and/or experience requirements and submitting appropriate forms to OPM during designated "open" periods. Interested applicants should contact their local Federal Job Information/Testing Center (FJI/TC) periodically to find out when the next open period will be and to obtain the proper forms for filing. The FJI/TC is listed under "U.S. Government" in major metropolitan telephone directories. A listing of FJI/TCs is also available from ALA Office for Library Personnel Resources. For the Washington, D.C., area register, ask for the librarian packet from the OPM Washington Area Service Center, Rm. 1416, 1900 E St. N.W., Washington, DC 20415, 202-653-8468. The packet includes an SF171 form, a supplemental qualifications form, and a computer-generated form.

Applications are evaluated for the grade(s) for which applicants are qualified. Information on beginning salary levels can be obtained from the FJI/TC. To qualify for librarian positions, applicants must possess: (1) a master's degree in library science; (2) a fifth-year bachelor's degree in library science; or (3) 30 semester hours of graduate study in library science. *Note:* If you have a combination of qualifying education and/or experience, you may qualify to take the written subject-matter test. This test is administered in the Washington, D.C., metropolitan area. To receive consideration for librarian positions and testing outside the D.C. metropolitan area, contact your local Federal Job Information Testing Center.

The OPM office that maintains the register refers names but does not hire and, consequently, is unaware of actual vacancies until an agency requests candidates to fill them. Applications are evaluated according to the agency's specific requirements. OPM refers only the most highly qualified candidates to an agency for consideration.

In addition to filing the appropriate forms, applicants can attempt to make personal contact directly with federal agencies in which they are interested. Over half the vacancies occur in the Washington area. Most librarian positions are in three agencies—Army, Navy, and Veterans Administration.

The Veterans Administration employs more than 350 professional librarians at 176 health care facilities located throughout the United States and Puerto Rico. Although most VA positions require training in medical librarianship, many entry-level GS-9 positions require no previous experience; GS-11/13 positions require experience specific to the duties of each vacancy. The VA has now been delegated examinating authority for librarian positions throughout the agency. This register is open continuously. To receive information and application forms, contact the VA Special Examining Unit, Box 24269, Richmond, VA 23224, or call 1-800-368-6008; in Virginia, call 1-800-552-3045. For a copy of the current vacancy list, call 202-233-2820 Monday through Friday, 8:00 A.M.-4:30 P.M. EST.

Some "excepted" agencies are not required to hire through the usual OPM channels. Although these agencies may require the standard forms, they maintain their own employee selection policies and procedures. Government establishments with positions outside the competitive civil service include Board of Governors of the Federal Reserve System; Central Intelligence Agency; Defense Intelligence Agency; Department of Medicine and Surgery; Federal Bureau of Investigation; Foreign Service of the United States; General Accounting Office; Library of Congress; National Science Foundation; National Security Agency; Tennessee Valley Authority; U.S. Nuclear Regulatory Commission; U.S. Postal Service; Judicial Branch of the Government; Legislative Branch of the Government; U.S. Mission to the United Nations; World Bank and IFC; International Monetary Fund; Organization of American States; Pan American Health Organization; and United Nations Secretariat.

The Library of Congress, the world's largest and most comprehensive library, is an excepted service agency in the Legislative Branch and administers its own independent merit selection system. Job classifications, pay, and benefits are the same as in other federal agencies, and qualifications requirements generally correspond to those used by the U.S. Office of Personnel Management. The library does not use registers, but announces vacancies as they become available. A separate application must be submitted for each vacancy announcement. For most professional positions, announcements are widely distributed and open for a minimum period of 30 days. Qualifications requirements and ranking criteria are stated on the vacancy announcement. The Library of Congress, Recruitment and Placement Office, is located at Rm. LM-107, James Madison Memorial Bldg., 101 Independence Ave. S.E., Washington, DC 20540, 202-287-5627.

Guide to Federal Jobs, 2nd ed., by Rod W. Durgin (Toledo, Ohio: Resource Directories, 1988), lists general procedures for finding a job with the government. The *Federal Times, Federal Career Opportunities, Federal Jobs Digest,* and the Sunday *Washington Post* sometimes list federal library openings.

Additional General and Specialized Job Sources

Affirmative Action Register, 8356 Olive Blvd., St. Louis, MO 63132. The goal is to "provide female, minority, handicapped and veteran candidates with an opportunity to learn of professional and managerial positions throughout the nation and to assist employers in implementing their Equal Opportunity Employment programs." Free distribution of monthly bulletin is made to leading businesses, industrial and academic institutions, and over 4,000 agencies that recruit qualified minorities and women, as well as to all known female, minority, and handicapped professional organizations, placement offices, newspapers, magazines, rehabilitation facilities, and over 8,000 federal, state, and local governmental employment units with a total readership in excess of 3.5 million (audited). Individual mail subscriptions are available for $15 per year. Librarian listings are in most every issue. Sent free to libraries on request.

The Chronicle of Higher Education (48 times/yr., 2-week breaks in August and December), 1255 23 St. N.W., Washington, DC 20037, 202-466-1000. Publishes a variety of library positions each week, including administrative and faculty jobs.

Education Information Service, Box 662, Newton Lower Falls, MA 02162. Instant Alert service for $35 will send individual 12 notices of domestic or overseas openings on same day EIS learns of opening. Also publishes periodic list of educational openings including librarian openings worldwide. Library jobs are small portion of this publication. $8.

National Faculty Exchange, 4656 W. Jefferson, Suite 140, Fort Wayne, IN 46804. The program brokers exchange of faculty and staff at U.S. institutions. Librarians interested in participation should ascertain if their academic institution is a member.

School Libraries. School librarians often find that the channels for locating positions in education are of more value than the usual library ones, for example, contacting county or city school superintendent offices. The *School Library Media Quarterly* (11, 63–65, Fall 1982) contains a discussion in the "Readers' Queries" column on recommended strategies for seeking a position in a school library media center. Primary sources include university placement offices that carry listings for a variety of school system jobs and *local* information networks among teachers and library media specialists. A list of commercial teacher agencies may be obtained from the *National Association of Teachers' Agencies,* Eugene Alexander, CPC, CTC, Secy./Treas., c/o 11 Firethorne Lane, Valley Stream, NY 11581-1799, 516-791-1390.

Overseas

Opportunities for employment in foreign countries are limited, and immigration policies of individual countries should be investigated. Employment for Americans is virtually limited to U.S. government libraries, libraries of U.S. firms doing worldwide business, and American schools abroad. Library journals from other countries sometimes list vacancy notices. Some persons have obtained jobs by contacting foreign publishers or vendors directly. Non-U.S. government jobs usually call for foreign-language fluency. "Job-Hunting in the UK" by Diane Brooks, *Canadian Library Journal* (45, 374–378, December 1988), offers advice for those interested in the United Kingdom.

Council for International Exchange of Scholars (CIES), 3400 International Dr., Washington, DC 20008-3097, 202-686-4000. Administers U.S. government Fulbright awards for university lecturing and advanced research abroad; usually 10 to 15 awards per year are made to specialists in library science. Many countries also offer awards in any specialization of research or lecturing for which specialists in library and information science may apply. Open to U.S. citizens with university or college teaching experience. Applications and information may be obtained, beginning in April each year, directly from CIES.

Department of Defense, Dependents Schools, 2461 Eisenhower Ave., Alexandria, VA 22331-1100. Overall management and operational responsibilities for the education of dependent children of active duty U.S. military personnel and DOD civilians who are stationed in foreign areas. Also responsible for teacher recruitment. For complete application brochure, write to above address.

Education Information Service, Box 662, Newton Lower Falls, MA 02162. Provides a monthly update on overseas education openings, including positions for librarians, media center directors, and audiovisual personnel. Also includes openings in school/college libraries in the United States.

Instant Alert, 15 Orchard St., Wellesley Hills, MA 02181. Notifies clients of library openings in U.S. overseas schools, international schools, and college and universities. Applicants indicate their specific requirements and as fast as the service learns of a position that meets these requirements, a personal notice is mailed.

International Association of School Librarianship, Box 1486, Kalamazoo, MI 49005. Informal contacts can be established through this group.

International Schools Services, Box 5910, Princeton, NJ 08543, 609-452-0990. Private, not-for-profit organization founded in 1955 to serve American schools overseas, other than Department of Defense schools. These are American elementary and secondary schools enrolling children of business and diplomat families living away from their homeland. ISS seeks to register men and women interested in working abroad in education who meet basic professional standards of training and experience. Specialists, guidance counselors, department heads, librarians, supervisors, and administrators normally need one or more advanced degrees in the appropriate field as well as professional experience commensurate with position sought. ISS also publishes a comprehensive directory of overseas schools and a monthly newsletter, *NewsLinks,* for those interested in the intercultural educational community. Information regarding these publications and other services may be obtained by writing to the above address.

Library/Book Fellows Program, c/o Robert Doyle, American Library Assn., 50 E. Huron St., Chicago, IL 60611, 312-944-6780. ALA administers a grant from the U.S. Information Agency for a program that places American library and book service professionals in institutions overseas for periods of several months to one year. Assignments vary, depending on projects requested by host countries. Persons with foreign-language skills, technical expertise, and international interests or expertise are sought. Positions announced in January, interviews held in May, and Fellows start assignments in mid-September.

Peace Corps, 1990 K St. N.W., 9th fl., Washington, DC 20526. Need several professionals with work experience in medicine, agriculture, automated systems, cataloging, and technical service in rural areas. For brochure and application form, call toll-free 800-424-8580, ext. 93, or write the above address.

U.S. Information Agency (USIA), U.S. Information Service (USIS) overseas. Seeks librarians with MLS and at least four years' experience for regional library consultant positions. Candidates must have a master's degree in librarianship from an ALA-accredited graduate library program, proven administrative ability, and skills to coordinate the overseas USIS library program with other information functions of USIS in various cities worldwide. Some practical work experience in at least one of the major functional areas of adult library services is required. Additional relevant experience might include cooperative library program development, community outreach, public affairs, project management, and personnel training. USIA maintains more than 130 libraries in more than 80 countries, 1 million books, and 400 local library personnel worldwide. Libraries provide reference service and publications about the United States for foreign audiences. U.S. citizenship required. Benefits include overseas allowances and differentials where applicable, vacation leave, term life insurance, and medical and retirement programs. Send standard U.S. government application (SF-171) to Special Services Branch, USIA, 301 Fourth St. S.W., Washington, DC 20547.

Overseas – Exchange Programs

Most exchanges are handled by direct negotiation between interested parties. A few libraries have established exchange programs for their own staff. In order to facilitate exchange arrangements, the *IFLA Journal* (February, May, August, and November) provides a listing of persons wishing to exchange positions *outside* their own country. All listings must include the following information: full name, address, present position, qualifications (with year of obtaining), language, abilities, preferred country/city/library, and type of position. Send to International Federation of Library Associations and Institutions (IFLA) Secretariat, Box 95312, 2509 CH, The Hague, Netherlands.

A two-page "Checklist for Preparing for an International Exchange," prepared by the ALA IRC/IRRT, is available from the ALA Office for Library Personnel Resources or the ALA International Relations Committee. Under the auspices of the International Relations Committee/International Relations Round Table Joint Committee on International Exchange of Librarians and Information Professionals, Linda E. Williamson has written *Going International: Librarians' Preparation Guide for a Work Experience/Job Exchange Abroad* (1988, 74 pp., ISBN 0-8389-7268-3, $15 from ALA Order Services, 50 E. Huron St., Chicago, IL 60611).

Additional clearinghouses for information on exchanges are

American Libraries, Professional Exchange, 50 E. Huron St., Chicago, IL 60611, 312-944-6780, ext. 326. Classified section for persons who wish to place ad if interested in trading jobs and/or housing on a temporary basis. Rate: $6/line. Inquiries should be made to Beverly Goldberg, LEADS Ed.

American Library Association, Association of College and Research Libraries, ACRL Exchange Librarian Program, 50 E. Huron St., Chicago, IL 60611, 312-944-6780. Maintains file of American and foreign academic libraries that might be interested in providing opportunity for librarians to work on their staff in an exchange arrangement, as a temporary replacement, or nonsalaried visitor.

Bureau for International Staff Exchange, c/o A. Hillier, College of Librarianship Wales, Llanbadarn Fawr, Aberystwyth, Dyfed SY23 3AS, Wales, Great Britain. Assists in two-way exchanges for British librarians wishing to work abroad and for librarians from the United States, Canada, European Economic Community countries, the British Commonwealth, and as many other countries as possible who wish to work in Britain.

Using Information Skills in Nonlibrary Settings

A great deal of interest has been shown in alternative careers or in using information skills in a variety of ways in nonlibrary settings. These jobs are not usually found through the regular library placement sources, although many library schools are trying to generate such listings for their students and alumni. Job listings that do exist may not call specifically for "librarians" by that title so that ingenuity may be needed to search out jobs where information management skills are needed. Some librarians are working on a free-lance basis by offering services to businesses, alternative schools, community agencies, legislators, and the like; these opportunities are usually not found in advertisements but are created by developing contacts and publicity over a period of time. A number of information brokering business firms have developed from individual free-lance experiences. Small companies or other organizations often need one-time service for organizing files or collections, bibliographic research for special projects, indexing or abstracting, compilation of directories, and consulting services. Bibliographic networks and online database companies are using librarians as information managers, trainers, researchers, systems and database analysts, online services managers, and so on. Jobs in this area are sometimes found in library network newsletters or data processing journals. Librarians can be found working in law firms as litigation case supervisors (organizing and analyzing records needed for specific legal cases); with publishers as sales representatives, marketing directors, editors, and computer services experts; with community agencies as adult education coordinators, volunteer administrators, grants writers. A listing of job titles is included in the three-page handout "Alternative Career Directions for Librarians," available from OLPR/ALA, 50 E. Huron St., Chicago, IL 60611.

Classifieds in *Publishers Weekly* and *The National Business Employment Weekly* may lead to information-related positions. One might also consider the Sunday classified ad sections in metropolitan newspapers in their entirety to locate descriptions calling for information skills but under a variety of job titles.

The Directory of Fee-Based Information Services is an annual publication that lists information brokers, free-lance librarians, independent information specialists, and institutions that provide services for a fee. Individuals do not need to pay to have listings; the 1989 directory is available for $34.95 prepaid plus $2 postage and handling (foreign postage, $5) from Burwell Enterprises, 3724 FM 1960 West, Suite 214, Houston, TX 77068 (713-537-9051). It is supplemented by *The Information Broker* ($35, foreign postage, $5). *The Information Broker* includes articles by, for, and about individuals and companies in the fee-based information field, book reviews, calendar of upcoming events, issue-oriented articles, and new listings for companies that will appear in subsequent annual editions of the *Directory*.

The Independent Librarians Exchange Round Table is a unit within the American Library Association that serves as a networking source for persons who own their own information businesses, are consultants, or work for companies providing support services to libraries or providing other information services outside traditional library settings. Dues are $5 in addition to ALA dues and include a newsletter, *ILERT Alert*. The Association of Independent Information Professionals was formed in 1987 for individuals who manage for-profit information services. Contact Marilyn Levine, 324 E. Wisconsin Ave., Suite 1438, Milwaukee, WI 53202, 800-545-4141, ext. 387.

A growing number of publications are addressing opportunities for librarians in the broader information arena. "The Information Broker: A Modern Profile" by Mick O'Leary, *Online*, November 1987, pp. 24–30, provides an overview on the practice of information brokerage. *Mind Your Own Business: A Guide for the Information Entrepreneur* by Alice Sizer Warner (New York: Neal-Schuman, 1987, 165 pp., ISBN 1-55570-014-4, $24.95) describes planning for and managing an information business, including marketing, sales, and record keeping. *Careers in Other Fields for*

Librarians . . . Successful Strategies for Finding the Job by Rhoda Garoogian and Andrew Garoogian is a 1985 publication from ALA (ISBN 0-8389-0431-9; 171 pp., $15). Chapters discuss bridging traditional and nontraditional employment; opportunities in business, government, education, and entrepreneurship; and employment techniques (where to look for jobs, résumés and letters, interviewing). Of particular interest is the chapter describing the translation process of traditional library tasks and skills with new types of job responsibilities. Scattered throughout are sample job descriptions in other fields where information functions are found. *New Options for Librarians: Finding a Job in a Related Field,* edited by Betty-Carol Sellen and Dimity S. Berkner (New York: Neal-Schuman, 1984, ISBN 0-918212-73-1, 300 pp., $27.95) covers how to prepare for and initiate a job search and examines career possibilities in publishing, public relations, abstracting and indexing, association work, contract service companies, information management, and more. Included also are a survey of librarians working in related fields and an annotated bibliography. "Librarians in Alternative Work Places" (*Library Journal,* February 15, 1985, pp. 108–110) summarizes the survey.

Careers in Information, edited by Jane F. Spivack (White Plains, N.Y.: Knowledge Industries, 1982, ISBN 0-914236-70-9, $34.50), includes chapters on the work of information specialists, entrepreneurship in the information industry, and information professionals in the federal government, as well as guidance on finding a job, placements, and salaries in both librarianship and the broader information field. "Atypical Careers and Innovative Services in Library and Information Science," edited by Walter C. Allen and Lawrence W. S. Auld, is an entire issue of *Library Trends* [32 (Winter 1984): 251–358] focusing on new directions for librarians and some of the implications for the changing role of the information professional.

Information Broking: A New Career in Information Work by Marshall Jean Crawford (London: Library Association, 1988) is available through ALA Order Services for $14 (ISBN 0-85365-718-1, 36 pp.).

Infomediary, an international, professional quarterly journal edited by Susan Klement and published by Elsevier/North Holland, began in 1985. Its focus is on information brokerage, consulting, and the entrepreneurial aspects of the library and information field. Subscription price is Dfl. 299. Contact Elsevier Science Publishers BV, Journals Dept., Box 211, 1000 AE Amsterdam, the Netherlands.

Other publications include *What Else You Can Do with a Library Degree,* edited by Betty-Carol Sellen (New York: Neal-Schuman and Gaylord Brothers, 1979); *The Information Brokers: How to Start and Operate Your Own Fee-Based Service* by Kelly Warnken (New York: R. R. Bowker, 1981); and *Abstracting & Indexing Career Guide* (1986, 63 pp.), available for $15 from National Federation of Abstracting & Information Services, 1429 Walnut St., Philadelphia, PA 19102.

Temporary/Part-Time Positions

Working as a substitute librarian or in temporary positions may be an alternative career path or an interim step while looking for a regular job that can provide valuable contacts and experience. Organizations that hire library workers for part time or temporary jobs include Pro Libra Associates, Inc., 6 Inwood Place, Maplewood, NJ 07040 (201-762-0070); C. Berger and Company, 327 E. Gundersen Dr., Carol Stream, IL 60188 (312-653-1115) in the Chicago area; Gossage Regan Associates, Inc., 15 W. 44 St., New York, NY 10036 (212-869-3348); Library Associates, 2600

Colorado Blvd., Suite 160, Santa Monica, CA 90404 (213-453-5583 or 5270); and Advanced Information Management, 444 Castro St., Suite 503, Mountain View, CA 94041 (415-965-7799).

Part-time jobs are not always advertised, and are often found by canvassing local libraries and leaving applications.

Job Hunting in General

Wherever information needs to be organized and presented to patrons in an effective, efficient, and service-oriented fashion, the skills of professional librarians can be applied, whether or not they are in traditional library settings. However, an individual must invest considerable time, energy, imagination, and money before finding a satisfying position in a conventional library or other type of information service. Usually, no one job-hunting method or source can be used alone.

"How to Find a Job Online" by Ann J. Van Camp (*Online* 12: 26–34, July 1988) offers guidance on databases that might lead to library- and information-related position listings.

Public and school library certification requirements often vary from state to state; contact the state library agency for such information in a particular state. Certification requirements are summarized in *Certification of Public Librarians in the United States* (4th ed., 1989), available from the ALA Office for Library Personnel Resources. A summary of school library/media certification requirements by state is included in *Requirements for Certification,* edited by Mary P. Burks and published annually by the University of Chicago Press. "School Library Media Certification Requirements: 1988 Update" by Patsy H. Perritt (*School Library Journal,* 34, June/July 1988, 31–39, and August 1988, 32–40) also provides a two-part compilation. State supervisors of school library media services may also be contacted for information on specific states; see Part 6 of the *Bowker Annual* for a list of these contact persons.

Civil service requirements either on a local, county, or state level often add another layer of procedures to the job search. Some civil service jurisdictions require written and/or oral examinations; others assign a ranking based on a review of credentials. Jobs are usually filled from the top candidates on a qualified list of applicants. Since the exams are held only at certain time periods and a variety of jobs can be filled from a single list of applicants (e.g., all Librarian I positions regardless of type of function), it is important to check whether a library in which one is interested falls under civil service procedures.

If one wishes a position in a specific subject area or in a particular geographic location, remember those reference skills to ferret information from directories and other tools regarding local industries, schools, subject collections, and so on. Directories such as the *American Library Directory, Subject Collections, Directory of Special Libraries and Information Centers, The North American Online Directory,* and *Directory of Federal Libraries,* as well as state directories and directories of other special subject areas, can provide a wealth of information for job seekers. Some students have pooled resources to hire a clipping service for a specific time period in order to get classified librarian ads for a particular geographic area.

For information on other job-hunting and personnel matters, request a checklist of personnel materials available from the ALA Office for Library Personnel Resources, 50 E. Huron St., Chicago, IL 60611.

Placements and Salaries, 1987: The Upswing Continues

Carol L. Learmont
Associate Dean, School of Library Service, Columbia University

Stephen Van Houten
Head, Cataloging Department, Library of Health Sciences, University of Illinois at Chicago

Fifty-five of the 60 eligible schools responded to all or part of the questionnaire for this thirty-seventh annual report on placements and salaries of graduates of American Library Association–accredited library school programs. One southeastern, one southwestern, one western, and two Canadian schools did not participate.

In 1987, the average beginning level salary was $22,247, based on 1,610 known full-time permanent professional salaries. Salaries for 1987 improved over 1986. For the fifth year the increase in the average beginning salary was higher than the increase in the cost of living. In 1987 it was 7% higher. The 1987 salaries increased at the rate of 7% compared to 6% in 1986, and 5% in 1985.

In 1987, the average (mean) beginning salary for women was $22,045, a 6% increase over 1986; for men, $23,013, a 7% increase. The median salary was $21,116 for all graduates; for women $21,000; and for men $22,000. For new graduates with relevant prior experience the average beginning salary was $24,018, up from $21,971 in 1986; without experience, $20,402, up from $19,457 in 1986. The number of graduates continues to rise, the average salary increase is the highest since 1981, and there are many more jobs than qualified people to fill them. There were 279 temporary professional placements reported in 1987 compared with 240 in 1986 and 272 in 1985. In tables 1–12, when included, Canadian salaries are given in U.S. dollar equivalents. The category "other information specialties" includes a wide variety of nontraditional positions.

Placement Statistics

First professional degrees were awarded to 3,702 graduates of the 55 schools reporting in 1987 (Table 1). In 1986, the 53 reporting schools awarded 3,538 first professional degrees; in 1985, the 58 reporting schools awarded 3,484 first professional degrees. In 1987, the average number of graduates of schools reporting was 67; in 1986 it was 67; in 1985 it was 60. (A total of 126 foreign students from 31 countries were reported among the graduates in 1987.)

Table 1 shows permanent and temporary professional placements, as well as nonprofessional library placements, and the totals for the three. These are library or information-related positions. Table 1 also shows the number of graduates reported who were not in library positions or whose employment status was unknown at the beginning of April 1988. Of these, 10% were known not to be in library positions compared with 10% in 1986 and 13% in 1985. In April 1988, the whereabouts of 23% were unknown compared with 23% in April 1987 and 21% in April 1986.

Note: Adapted from *Library Journal*, October 15, 1988.

Table 1 / Status of 1987 Graduates, Spring 1988*

	No. of Graduates			Not in Library Positions			Empl. Not Known			Permanent Prof. Placements			Temp. Prof. Placements			Nonprof. Library Placements			Total in Library Positions		
	Women	Men	Total	Women	Men	Total	Women	Men	Total	Women	Men	Total	Women	Men	Total	Women	Men	Total	Women	Men	Total
United States	2462	742	3314	237	81	321	517	169	788	1499	434	1938	154	45	199	55	13	68	1708	492	2205
Northeast	948	286	1323	66	24	90	242	76	406	580	167	748	48	16	64	12	3	15	640	186	827
Southeast	467	108	593	35	16	53	90	24	128	309	63	374	29	5	34	4	0	4	342	68	412
Midwest	616	197	815	80	29	109	133	46	179	364	110	476	22	6	28	17	6	23	403	122	527
Southwest	188	56	245	30	4	35	24	9	33	114	36	150	7	4	11	13	3	16	134	43	177
West	243	95	338	26	8	34	28	14	42	132	58	190	48	14	62	9	1	10	189	73	262
Canada	296	89	388	33	15	49	53	12	67	147	37	184	57	23	80	6	2	8	210	62	272
All Schools	**2758**	**831**	**3702**	**270**	**96**	**370**	**570**	**181**	**855**	**1646**	**471**	**2122**	**211**	**68**	**279**	**61**	**15**	**76**	**1918**	**554**	**2477**

*Includes placements undifferentiated by sex.

Table 2A / Placements and Salaries of 1987 Graduates—Summary by Region*

	Placements	Salaries			Low Salary			High Salary			Average Salary			Median Salary		
		Women	Men	Total	Women	Men	Total	Women	Men	Total	Women	Men	Total	Women	Men	Total
United States	1865	1162	314	1477	9500	13000	9500	44000	72000	72000	22217	23268	22440	21252	22000	21588
Northeast	709	455	106	561	10000	16000	10000	44000	45000	45000	23214	24248	23410	22750	23000	22800
Southeast	363	223	44	267	12600	13513	12600	36000	31000	36000	21556	20984	21462	20800	20500	20800
Midwest	459	285	86	372	9500	13000	9500	40000	38000	40000	20933	21856	21147	20000	21000	20000
Southwest	150	96	32	128	13500	17400	13500	34200	54500	54500	21155	24451	21979	20500	22500	21008
West	184	103	46	149	14000	16047	14000	40000	72000	72000	23783	25012	24162	22907	23200	23000
Canada	174	110	23	133	13575	15837	13575	35709	27149	35709	20224	19526	20103	20362	20362	20362
All Schools	**2039**	**1272**	**337**	**1610**	**9500**	**13000**	**9500**	**44000**	**72000**	**72000**	**22045**	**23013**	**22247**	**21000**	**22000**	**21116**

*Includes placements undifferentiated by sex.

Table 2B / Placements and Salaries of 1987 Graduates*

Schools	Placements	Salaries			Low Salary			High Salary			Average Salary			Median Salary		
		Women	Men	Total	Women	Men	Total	Women	Men	Total	Women	Men	Total	Women	Men	Total
Alabama	29	21	5	26	16000	13513	13513	31880	25000	31880	21294	19363	20922	20225	19800	20000
Albany	44	34	10	44	17000	19000	17000	33800	33000	33800	22349	23385	22584	21000	22500	22000
Atlanta	26	20	6	26	16500	21000	16500	26588	26000	26588	22173	22817	22321	22000	22000	22000
Brigham Young	37	23	12	35	15898	18000	15898	40000	29000	40000	23650	23267	23519	21600	23200	22000
British Columbia	15	0	0	0	0	0	0	0	0	0	0	0	0			
Buffalo	26	15	5	20	16000	16000	16000	31200	21900	31200	21670	19180	21048	21600	18500	21358
California (Berk.)	41	19	14	33	14000	20400	14000	34200	72000	72000	24098	30739	26915	23664	25000	24960
California (L.A.)	38	20	4	24	18500	18000	18000	40000	34452	40000	24900	23863	24728	24000	18000	24000
Catholic	27	22	3	25	16000	21500	16000	42000	32000	42000	25059	28375	25457	23760	31625	23899
Chicago	26	12	9	21	16731	18300	16731	28500	25000	28500	21725	21830	21770	21828	22000	22000
Clarion	21	20	1	21	16000	24600	16000	27570	24600	27570	21029	24600	21199	20000	24600	20000
Columbia	58	29	17	46	17650	21000	17650	38000	26000	38000	25022	23427	24433	25000	23000	24000
Dalhousie	12	10	0	10	16591	0	16591	27816	0	27816	21241	0	21241	19608		19608
Drexel	68	45	15	60	17000	16500	16500	44000	35000	44000	24457	23202	24143	22000	20600	22000
Emory	22	20	1	21	18179	23500	18179	31512	23500	31512	22957	23500	22983	22008	23500	22500
Emporia	16	9	4	13	17500	18500	17500	30000	36000	36000	22002	24250	22694	19800	19500	19800
Florida State	29	25	1	26	14000	21240	14000	35000	21240	35000	22872	21240	22809	21600	21240	21240
Hawaii	28	16	5	21	15000	17297	15000	31500	31500	31500	21822	23316	22177	20000	19000	20000
Illinois	64	43	16	59	16000	17000	16000	25000	37500	37500	19991	23031	20815	20000	22000	20000
Indiana	58	30	9	39	15600	14700	14700	31000	29000	31000	20355	21842	20699	19982	20800	20000

Iowa	32	15	8	23	16000	19000	16000	25200	24000	25200	19397	21188	20020	18900	20500	20000
Kent State	63	50	9	59	15000	16000	15000	39000	24000	39000	20787	21163	20844	18500	22000	19400
Long Island	34	24	3	27	18000	20528	18000	42000	28000	42000	26090	24466	25909	25000	24870	25000
Louisiana State	38	27	9	36	16700	15600	15600	26004	28000	28000	19752	21287	20135	19000	20000	19200
McGill	37	25	7	32	13575	15837	13575	30166	21116	30166	18914	18638	18854	18854	18854	18854
Maryland	41	30	6	36	17500	18798	17500	35000	32400	35000	23960	23292	23849	23000	21252	23000
Michigan	70	48	15	63	14000	14700	14000	38800	27000	38800	21300	21007	21230	20000	20500	20000
Missouri	16	10	4	14	9500	18000	9500	40000	27000	40000	20310	22000	20793	19000	21000	20000
North Carolina	28	22	6	28	16000	18600	16000	32000	27000	32000	19896	20542	20035	19100	19000	19000
N.C. Greensboro	33	0	0	0	0	0	0	0	0	0	0	0	0			
N.C. Central	9	7	2	9	18281	18300	18281	25260	30000	30000	20734	24150	21493	20000	18300	20000
North Texas State	46	28	7	35	16340	19500	16340	29000	37200	37200	20772	25753	21768	19416	21500	20400
Northern Illinois	17	12	2	14	16000	18000	16000	34250	38000	38000	21261	28000	22224	20000	18000	20000
Oklahoma	27	16	4	20	13500	17500	13500	25000	25000	25000	18938	22500	19650	17500	22500	17500
Peabody	29	0	0	0	0	0	0	0	0	0	0	0	0			
Pittsburgh	79	16	10	26	14000	16000	14000	28900	45000	45000	22214	27850	24382	21718	25000	24000
Pratt	17	3	4	7	22800	22000	22000	31500	40750	40750	25767	28888	27550	23000	22802	23000
Queens	15	9	0	9	19500	0	19500	28000	0	28000	24944	0	24944	25300		25300
Rosary	49	23	3	27	17000	13000	13000	39000	21828	39000	22975	17609	22314	22000	18000	21800
Rutgers	89	77	11	88	17496	17500	17496	43000	32000	43000	23524	23108	23472	22836	22080	22800
St. John's	9	6	2	8	10000	28000	10000	26070	39000	39000	20479	33500	23734	20000	28000	22803
Simmons	119	81	12	93	13000	16000	13000	33761	32000	33761	21731	21777	21737	21430	21000	21430
South Carolina	60	49	8	57	12600	16000	12600	35400	31000	35400	21474	19964	21262	21000	18000	20857
South Florida	26	20	3	23	16000	18500	16000	36000	23000	36000	22944	21300	22730	21000	22400	21420
S. Connecticut	37	29	6	35	12000	21000	12000	35500	42000	42000	22683	28633	23703	23485	25400	23500
S. Mississippi	16	12	3	15	15686	18100	15686	33595	21500	33595	21517	19367	21087	20500	18500	20500
Syracuse	25	15	1	16	18000	23000	18000	30000	23000	30000	21677	23000	21760	20500	23000	20500
Tennessee	18	0	0	0	0	0	0	0	0	0	0	0	0			

Table 2B / Placements and Salaries of 1987 Graduates* (cont.)

Schools	Placements	Salaries			Low Salary			High Salary			Average Salary			Median Salary		
		Women	Men	Total	Women	Men	Total	Women	Men	Total	Women	Men	Total	Women	Men	Total
Texas	53	32	18	50	15000	17400	15000	34200	54500	54500	22236	24304	22980	21008	22500	22500
Texas Woman's	24	20	3	23	17500	22000	17500	30000	30670	30670	21737	24890	22148	21000	22000	21100
Toronto	39	33	5	38	17345	17345	17345	26395	27149	27149	21284	20211	21143	20739	18854	20739
Washington	40	25	11	36	16524	16047	16047	40000	26000	40000	24026	20817	23046	21500	20000	21000
Western Ontario	71	42	11	53	13575	16968	13575	35709	20362	35709	19928	19779	19897	19985	20362	20362
Wisconsin (Mad.)	34	19	7	26	15600	18000	15600	30520	25250	30520	20590	21313	20785	19200	20500	19569
Wisconsin (Milw.)	14	14	0	14	16800	0	16800	32541	0	32541	21889	0	21889	19800		19800

*Includes placements undifferentiated by sex.

Of the 1987 graduates, 67% were known to be employed either in professional or nonprofessional positions in libraries or information-related work, as were 66% of the 1986 graduates and 69% of the 1985 graduates. Of the 1987 graduates, 57% were known to be employed in permanent professional positions, compared with 57% of the 1986 graduates and 57% of the 1985 graduates.

Employment distribution of 2,001 of the 3,702 graduates (54%) is shown in Tables 3, 4, and 11. In all, 2,122 permanent full-time professional placements were reported and 279 temporary placements. Of the 2,122 people finding permanent professional positions, 594 (28%) found jobs before graduation; 607 (29%) reported actively searching for less than 90 days for professional employment after getting their degrees; 123 people (6%) looked for three or four months; 88 (4%) looked from four to six months; and 52 (2%) looked for more than six months. A total of 421 people (20%) went back to their previous positions. The length of time it took the 237 others (11%) to find employment is not known.

In 1987, 2.1% of the graduates were in nonprofessional library and related positions (Table 1). In 1986, 2.7% were in this category, down from 4% in the seven previous years. Within the category, 80% are women and 20% are men.

Placements by type of library showed a notable decrease for college and university libraries in 1987, and a modest increase for the other types. In actual numbers the increase and decrease are more marked than in recent years as shown in Table 4. Table 4 does not include 43 foreign professional placements and 78 placements undifferentiated by type of library that do appear in Table 1 in the Permanent Professional Placements category (a total of 2,122 placements).

Comparisons of U.S. and Canadian placements appear in Table 5. Table 6, showing special placements, gives a rough picture of hiring activity in various specialties in 1987.

Openings and Applicants

A total of 61,063 listings of open library positions was reported received by 40 schools, ranging in number of listings from 100 to 5,000. The listings were for positions at all levels, and many were duplicated in several places. In 1986, 40 schools reported 60,807 listings.

Twenty-one schools reported increases in position listings in 1987 over 1986. Increases reported in 1987 ranged from 1% to 345%. The median was 15%. Fourteen schools reported no significant change from 1986; four reported a decrease ranging from 5.2% to 10%. Forty-three placement officers reported no major difficulty in placing 1987 graduates, but two reported major difficulty. Two others indicated having more difficulty placing graduates in 1987 than in 1986. Thirteen reported having less difficulty, and 30 reported about the same level of difficulty in both years.

The strong demand for children's and young adult specialists in public and school libraries continues, as does the demand for technical services specialists, particularly catalogers, and people with an information science background. Other specialties mentioned as still in demand are science, law, medical, archival, and systems analysis. Undergraduate majors that make graduates especially attractive to employers continue to be science (all types), math, languages, engineering, business, computer science, art, and music.

Table 3 / Placements by Type of Library*

Schools	Public			Elementary & Secondary			College & Univ.			Special			Other			Total		
	Women	Men	Total	Women	Men	Total	Women	Men	Total	Women	Men	Total	Women	Men	Total	Women	Men	Total
Alabama	10	3	13	5	0	5	5	2	7	3	1	4	0	0	0	23	6	29
Albany	7	4	11	18	0	18	3	3	6	4	2	6	2	1	3	34	10	44
Atlanta	3	2	5	5	0	5	6	1	7	6	3	9	0	0	0	20	6	26
Brigham Young	9	1	10	6	4	10	7	4	11	3	1	4	0	2	2	25	12	37
British Columbia	5	0	5	0	0	0	3	2	5	4	1	5	0	0	0	12	3	15
Buffalo	7	2	9	4	0	4	3	2	5	5	2	7	1	0	1	20	6	26
California (Berk.)	6	3	9	0	0	0	3	6	9	8	2	10	4	4	8	21	15	36
California (L.A.)	8	1	9	0	0	0	9	2	11	12	1	13	4	1	5	33	5	38
Catholic	3	1	4	4	0	4	3	0	3	13	2	15	1	0	1	24	3	27
Chicago	2	2	4	1	0	1	7	5	12	5	3	8	1	0	1	16	10	26
Clarion	4	0	4	13	1	14	0	0	0	3	0	3	0	0	0	20	1	21
Columbia	7	8	15	0	0	0	7	5	12	20	9	29	2	0	2	36	22	58
Dalhousie	5	0	5	2	0	2	2	0	2	2	0	2	1	0	1	12	0	12
Drexel	6	4	10	6	1	7	8	4	12	13	3	16	17	4	21	50	16	66
Emory	10	0	10	4	0	4	4	1	5	2	0	2	0	1	1	20	2	22
Emporia	5	0	5	1	0	1	4	4	8	1	1	2	0	0	0	11	5	16
Florida State	8	0	8	9	1	10	6	1	7	3	0	3	1	0	1	27	2	29
Hawaii	3	3	6	9	1	10	3	0	3	4	2	6	1	2	3	20	8	28
Illinois	25	2	27	1	0	1	14	11	25	3	1	4	5	2	7	48	16	64
Indiana	23	2	25	1	2	3	12	5	17	7	5	12	1	0	1	44	14	58
Iowa	9	1	10	2	1	3	7	8	15	2	2	4	0	0	0	20	12	32
Kent State	26	5	31	13	0	13	4	1	5	8	3	11	2	1	3	53	10	63
Long Island	4	3	7	15	2	17	4	0	4	5	1	6	0	0	0	28	6	34
Louisiana State	7	5	12	4	0	5	13	2	15	4	1	5	0	1	1	28	9	38
McGill	8	1	9	4	1	5	9	2	11	7	3	10	2	0	2	30	7	37
Maryland	7	1	8	3	1	4	5	1	6	18	3	21	1	1	2	34	7	41

Michigan	21	8	29	7	0	7	13	8	22	10	1	11	1	0	1	52	17	70
Missouri	5	1	6	2	0	2	3	3	6	1	0	1	1	0	1	12	4	16
North Carolina	7	2	9	3	0	3	6	4	10	5	0	5	1	0	1	22	6	28
N.C.Greensboro	7	1	8	17	0	17	1	1	2	3	2	5	1	0	1	29	4	33
North Carolina Central	2	0	2	1	0	1	2	1	3	2	0	2	0	1	1	7	2	9
North Texas State	8	5	13	11	1	12	6	2	8	8	2	10	0	0	0	33	10	43
Northern Illinois	6	1	7	2	0	2	3	1	4	3	0	3	0	0	0	14	2	16
Oklahoma	4	1	5	11	2	13	5	2	7	2	0	2	0	0	0	22	5	27
Peabody	6	1	7	5	0	5	7	4	11	5	0	5	1	0	1	24	5	29
Pittsburgh	11	4	15	3	0	3	3	1	4	8	1	9	19	26	45	44	32	76
Pratt	3	3	6	0	1	1	0	0	0	6	4	10	0	0	0	9	8	17
Queens	3	0	3	2	1	3	2	0	2	2	0	2	1	0	1	10	1	11
Rosary	12	3	15	7	1	8	7	1	8	5	0	6	2	1	3	33	6	40
Rutgers	32	7	39	14	0	14	13	1	14	15	2	17	4	1	5	78	11	89
St. John's	0	1	1	3	0	3	1	0	1	1	1	2	0	1	1	5	3	8
Simmons	28	2	30	11	2	13	28	5	33	33	8	41	2	0	2	102	17	119
South Carolina	15	5	20	23	2	26	5	1	6	7	0	7	1	0	1	51	8	60
South Florida	7	1	8	10	1	11	3	1	4	2	0	2	0	0	0	22	3	25
Southern Connecticut	12	0	12	9	3	12	2	1	3	7	2	9	1	0	1	31	6	37
Southern Mississippi	5	1	6	5	1	6	1	1	2	1	1	2	0	0	0	12	4	16
Syracuse	5	0	5	5	1	6	1	1	2	1	1	2	0	0	0	12	4	16
Tennessee	4	1	5	1	0	1	3	1	4	3	2	5	2	1	3	13	5	18
Texas	7	4	11	11	1	12	4	8	12	7	2	9	3	3	6	32	18	50
Texas Woman's	7	1	8	5	1	6	2	1	3	7	0	7	0	0	0	21	3	24
Toronto	20	0	20	1	0	1	1	0	1	11	2	13	1	3	4	34	5	39
Washington	9	4	13	5	0	5	6	7	13	8	0	8	0	0	0	28	11	39
Western Ontario	17	2	19	3	0	3	9	2	11	20	10	30	3	4	7	52	18	70
Wisconsin (Madison)	9	3	12	5	0	5	6	4	10	4	2	6	0	0	0	24	9	33
Wisconsin (Milwaukee)	5	0	5	4	0	4	4	0	4	1	0	1	0	0	0	14	0	14
Total	**494**	**116**	**610**	**321**	**32**	**355**	**300**	**133**	**434**	**354**	**94**	**449**	**91**	**62**	**153**	**1560**	**437**	**2001**

* Includes placements undifferentiated by sex or type of library

Table 4 / Placements by Type of Library, 1951–1987

Year	Public	School	College & Universities	Other Library Agencies*	Total
1951-1955**	2076 (33.0%)	1424 (23.0%)	1774 (28.0%)	1000 (16.0%)	6264
1956-1960**	2057 (33.0)	1287 (20.0)	1878 (30.0)	1105 (17.0)	6327
1961-1965	2876 (30.0)	1979 (20.0)	3167 (33.0)	1600 (17.0)	9622
1966-1970	4773 (28.0)	3969 (23.0)	5834 (34.0)	2456 (15.0)	17032
1971	999 (29.0)	924 (26.0)	1067 (30.0)	513 (15.0)	3503
1972	1117 (30.0)	987 (26.0)	1073 (29.0)	574 (15.0)	3751
1973	1180 (31.0)	969 (25.0)	1017 (26.0)	712 (18.0)	3878
1974	1132 (31.0)	893 (24.0)	952 (26.0)	691 (19.0)	3668
1975	994 (30.0)	813 (24.0)	847 (25.0)	714 (21.0)	3368
1976	764 (27.1)	655 (23.2)	741 (26.3)	657 (23.2)	2817
1977	846 (28.4)	673 (22.6)	771 (25.9)	687 (23.1)	2977
1978	779 (26.1)	590 (19.8)	819 (27.4)	798 (26.7)	2986
1979	778 (27.4)	508 (17.9)	716 (25.3)	835 (29.4)	2837
1980	659 (27.1)	473 (19.5)	610 (25.1)	687 (28.3)	2429
1981	642 (27.3)	451 (19.2)	556 (23.6)	704 (29.9)	2353
1982	588 (28.5)	358 (17.4)	505 (24.5)	612 (29.7)	2063
1983	501 (28.0)	308 (17.3)	424 (23.8)	552 (30.9)	1785
1984	548 (27.9)	284 (14.4)	551 (28.0)	583 (29.7)	1966
1985	565 (29.4)	300 (15.6)	522 (27.2)	533 (27.8)	1920
1986	576 (30.3)	288 (15.2)	488 (25.7)	548 (28.8)	1900
1987	610 (30.5)	355 (17.7)	434 (21.7)	602 (30.1)	2001

*From 1951 through 1966 these tabulations were for "special and other placements" in all kinds of libraries. From 1967 to 1979 these figures include only placements in library agencies that do not clearly belong to one of the other three groups; in the 1980 through 1987 report these figures include the sum of responses to placements in special libraries and in other information specialties.
**Figures for individual years are reported in preceding articles in this series.

Table 5 / U.S. and Canadian Placements Compared
(Percents may not total 100 because of rounding)

	Placements	Public Libraries	School Libraries	College & University Libraries	Special Libraries	Other Info. Specialties
All Schools*	2001	610 (30.5)	355 (17.7)	434 (21.7)	449 (22.4)	153 (7.6)
Women	1560	494 (31.7)	321 (20.6)	300 (19.2)	354 (22.7)	91 (5.8)
Men	437	116 (26.5)	32 (7.3)	133 (30.4)	94 (21.5)	62 (14.2)
U.S. Schools*	1828	522 (30.2)	344 (18.8)	404 (22.1)	389 (21.3)	139 (7.6)
Women	1420	439 (30.9)	311 (21.9)	276 (19.4)	310 (21.8)	84 (5.9)
Men	404	113 (28.0)	33 (7.7)	127 (31.4)	78 (19.3)	55 (13.6)
Canadian Schools*	173	58 (33.5)	11 (6.4)	30 (17.3)	60 (34.7)	14 (8.1)
Women	140	55 (39.3)	10 (7.1)	24 (17.1)	44 (31.4)	7 (5.0)
Men	33	3 (9.1)	1 (3.0)	6 (18.2)	16 (48.5)	7 (21.2)

*Includes placements undifferentiated by sex.

Table 6 / Special Placements*

	Women	Men	Total
Government Jurisdictions (U.S. and Canada)			
Other government agencies (except USVA hospitals)	30	15	45
National libraries	19	15	34
State and provincial libraries	17	4	21
Overseas agencies (incl. Armed Services)	3	1	4
Armed Services libraries (domestic)	2	0	2
Library Science			
Advanced study	11	9	20
Teaching	7	3	10
Other			
Children's services (school libraries)	132	6	138
Business, (finance, industrial, corporate, banking, insurance, oil, etc.)	78	22	100
Law	80	18	98
Children's services (public libraries)	78	9	87
Systems analysis; automation	44	30	74
Youth services (school)	64	3	67
Youth services (public libraries)	53	11	64
Audiovisual and media centers	39	12	51
Science and technology	32	18	50
Bibliographic instruction	43	6	49
Medicine (incl. nursing schools)	42	3	45
Communications industry (advertising, newspaper, etc.)	31	6	37
Information services (nonlibrary)	21	9	30
Art and museum	24	4	28
Bookstore	3	24	27
Rare books, manuscripts, archives	12	13	25
Social sciences	16	9	25
Historical agencies and archives	15	9	24
Records management	19	5	24
Government documents	15	8	23
Religion (seminaries, theological schools)	12	11	23
Outreach activities and services	18	3	21
Hospitals (incl. USVA hospitals)	16	4	20
Research and development	14	4	19
Databases (publishing, servicing)	15	3	18
Indexing & abstracting	12	4	16
Correctional institutions	11	2	13
Theater, motion pictures, dance, music	4	9	13
Architecture	11	1	12
Conservation/Preservation	9	2	11
Children's services (other)	8	1	9
International relations (incl. area studies)	5	3	8
Professional associations	8	0	8
Pharmaceutical	4	3	7
Public affairs information specialist	7	0	7
Free-lance	4	2	6
Library services to the handicapped	5	0	5
Networks and consortia	5	0	5
Spanish-speaking centers	4	1	5
Technical writing	2	2	4
Genealogical	2	1	3
International agencies	2	1	3
Sales	3	0	3
Consulting	2	0	2
Maps	1	0	1
Total Special Placements	**1114**	**330**	**1444**

*Includes special placements in all types of libraries.

Several respondents emphasized the diverse enrollment in their schools, indicating that as many as one-third to one-half of the students have postbachelor's degrees and thus enter the MS programs with specialized subject strengths and often with excellent employment experience.

The Bottom Line

Only salaries reported as full-time annual salaries are included in this report. Variables such as vacations and other fringe benefits, which may be part of the total compensation, were excluded. Salaries do not reflect differences in hours worked per week. Such information might provide more precise comparability, but is probably beyond the needs of most library schools. In any case, the validity of this analysis rests on comparable statistics collected since 1951.

All of the 55 reporting schools provided some salary data. Not all schools could provide all the information requested, nor could they supply it for all employed graduates. Data for graduates in irregular placements, such as those for graduates from abroad returning to posts in their homelands, appointments in religious orders or elsewhere where remuneration is in the form of some combination of salary plus living, and all salaries for part-time employment, were excluded as best the authors can tell. (The exclusions are included in the number of salaries not known or not reported.) Salary information was provided for 1,610 of the 1987 graduates (1,272 women, 337 men, and one undifferentiated by sex). This represents 79% of the known placements and 43% of all graduates reported. The response ratios have remained fairly constant for the past few years. In 1986 salary information was reported for 75% of the known placements, representing 43% of the number of graduates reported.

Salary data (in U.S. dollars) as reported by the 55 schools are contained in Table 2 and summarized in Table 7.

Average (Mean) Salaries

The average salary for all 1987 graduates was $22,247, an increase of $1,373 (7%) over the 1986 average of $20,874. This is the largest increase since 1981. The average salary for women was $22,045 and the average for men was $23,013, a difference of $968 (Table 7). Table 8 shows the annual changes in average salaries since 1967, and includes a beginning salary index figure that may be compared with the annual Cost of Living (COL) Index report issued by the U.S. government. The COL Index for 1987 was 340.4, an increase of 12 points over the 1986 figure of 328.4, a gain of

Table 7 / Salary Data Summarized

	Women	Men	Total
Average (Mean) Salary	$22045	$23013	$22247
Median Salary	21000	22000	21116
Individual Salary Range	9500–44000	13000–72000	9500–72000

3.7%. The comparable increase in the beginning salary index was 19 points, 7.0 above the increase in the cost of living, the second largest gain in several years.

Average salaries for women in 1987 ranged from a low of $9,500 to a high of $44,000, a difference of $34,500; for men, the range was $13,000 to $72,000, a $59,000 difference. In the 48 schools that reported average salaries for both men and women, the women's average salary was higher in 19 schools; the men's average salary was higher in 29 schools. In 1986, the women's average salary was higher in 20 schools, and the men's in 30 schools. In Table 11, the average salary is higher for men (the difference ranging from $722 to $4,056) in all but the "Special Libraries" category where the average salary for women was higher by only $110.

Median Salaries

The median salary for all graduates in 1987 was $21,116, an increase of $1,116 over the 1986 median of $20,000. The median for women was $21,000; for men, $22,000. Of the 48 schools reporting on both men and women, the median salary for women was higher in 21 schools; for men in 25; and the same in two.

Salary Ranges

A wide range between high and low individual salaries continued in 1987. (For the purposes of the survey, prior experience, if known, consisted of work of a professional and/or subject nature of a year or more.) In 1987, the range (Table 7) was from a low of $9,500 (a public library) to a high of $72,000, (in the category "Other Library agencies"), a difference of $62,500. The range of high salaries reported was from $25,000 to $72,000, a difference of $47,000. The high range in 1986 was from $18,126 to $61,859, a difference of $43,733.

In 1987, 42 schools showed high salaries of $30,000 or more. Of these, 37 went to women and 21 to men. The median high salary for all graduates was $35,000 (up from $30,000 in 1986); for women, $32,000 (up from $29,689 in 1986); for men, $28,000 (up from $26,850 in 1986). The category "Special Libraries" accounted for 25% of the 51 highest salaries (18% in 1986) and the category "Other Information Specialties" accounted for 24% (10% in 1986). School libraries accounted for 41% (39% in 1986); academic libraries accounted for 6% (20% in 1986); public libraries had a 4% share (12% in 1986). The positions were scattered geographically and included 25 states, the District of Columbia, and two Canadian provinces; New York accounted for seven positions, California for five, and the rest for one, two, or three each.

The lowest reported beginning-level salaries from each school ranged from $9,500 to $22,000. (The 1986 range was from $11,200 to $21,000.) The median low salary was $16,000 ($15,000 in 1986) for all graduates. Forty-eight schools reported low salaries for both men and women; of these, 38 reported that the lowest low was received by a woman; eight reported that the lowest low was received by a man; two schools reported that both received the same. Public libraries accounted for 40% of the lowest salaries reported (44% in 1986); academic libraries accounted for 24% (21% in 1986); special libraries accounted for 18% (23% in 1986); school libraries for 16% (6% in 1986); and other information specialties for 2% (6% in 1986). Twenty-five states and four provinces were represented. New York led with five placements; Illinois and Georgia had three; the rest had one or two.

Table 8 / Average Salary Index: Starting Library Positions, 1967–1987

Year	Library Schools	Fifth-Year Graduates	Average Beginning Salary	Increase in Average	Beginning Index
1967	40	4030	$7305	—	—
1968	42	4625	7650	$355	105
1969	45	4970	8161	501	112
1970	48	5569	8611	450	118
1971	47	5670	8846	235	121
1972	48	6079	9248	402	127
1973	53	6336	9423	175	129
1974	52	6370	10000	617	137
1975	51	6010	10594	554	145
1976	53	5415	11149	555	153
1977	53	5467	11894	745	163
1978	62	5442	12527	633	171
1979	61	5139	13127	600	180
1980	63	4396	14223	1096	195
1981	65	4512	15633	1410	214
1982	64	4050	16583	950	227
1983	60	3494	17705	1122	242
1984	57	3529	18791	1086	257
1985	58	3484	19753	962	270
1986	54	3538	20874	1121	286
1987	55	3702	22247	1373	305

Table 9 / High Salaries by Type of Library

	Public			School			College & Univ.			Special			Other		
	Women	Men	Total	Women	Men	Total	Women	Men	Total	Women	Men	Total	Women	Men	Total
14,000								1	1		1	1			
15,000					1	1									
16,000		2	2	1	1	2	1	1	1	2		2	2	2	2
17,000	1	1	2				2		2						
18,000		1	1	1		1		5	5	2	3	5	2		2
19,000	5	3	8	1		1	3		3	1	1	2			
20,000		2	2	1			7	3	10	5	2	7	3	1	4
21,000	5	6	11	1	2	3	2	3	5	2	2	4	1		1
22,000	9	7	16	1	2	3	2	1	3	3	1	4	2	1	3
23,000	12	6	18				7	3	9	1	3	4		3	3
24,000	4	3	7		2	2	7	2	9	2	4	6	1		1
25,000	3	2	5	4	1	5	4	8	12	2	3	5	1		1
26,000	4		4	5		5	2	3	5	3	2	5	3		3
27,000	2	1	3	4		4	3	4	7	2		2		1	1
28,000	2	1	3				4		4	4	3	7	6	2	8
29,000				2	3	5	3		3	1	1	2	1		1
30,000	1	2	3	7	1	8	1	1	2	5		5	1	1	2
31,000	1		1	3	2	5				2		2	1		1
32,000				3		3				1	4	5		1	1
33,000				1		1	2	1	3	2		2			
34,000				1		1		2	2	2		2	1		1
35,000				3		3		1	1	4		4	1	1	2
36,000				1		1					1	1			
37,000				1		1					1	1		1	1
38,000				1		1		1	1	2		2			
39,000	1		1	1		1								1	1
40,000				1		1				1	1	2	1		1

Table 9 / High Salaries by Type of Library *(cont.)*

	Public			School			College & Univ.			Special			Other		
	Women	Men	Total	Women	Men	Total	Women	Men	Total	Women	Men	Total	Women	Men	Total
41,000															
42,000					1	1				2		2			
43,000				1		1									
44,000													1		1
45,000														1	1
54,000														1	1
72,000														1	1

Table 10 / Low Salaries by Type of Library

	Public			School			College & Univ.			Special			Other		
	Women	Men	Total	Women	Men	Total	Women	Men	Total	Women	Men	Total	Women	Men	Total
9,000	1		1												
10,000															
11,000				1		1									
12,000	1		1	1		1				1		1			
13,000	3		3	1		1	1	1	2	2	1	3			
14,000	2	1	3				2		2	1	1	2		1	1
15,000	6	1	7	4	1	5	2	1	3	1	1	2		1	1
16,000	13	4	17	2	1	3	9	2	11	9	2	11	3		3
17,000	7	5	12	7	1	8	11	2	13	3	1	4	1		1
18,000	8	5	13	5		5	10	13	23	11	3	14	3	2	5
19,000	2	5	7	4	1	5	4	3	7	8	1	9			
20,000	2	2	4	5		5	4	3	7	4	5	9	5	3	8
21,000	2	5	7	1	2	3	2	3	5	2	2	4	2		2
22,000	3	5	8	4	3	7	1	3	4	1	3	4	2	1	3
23,000		2	2	4		4	1	2	3	3	4	7		3	3
24,000					2	2	1		1	2	2	4	2	1	3
25,000		1	1	2	2	4		5	5		1	1			
26,000				2		2				1	1	2	2		2
27,000										1		1			
28,000											1	1	4	2	6
29,000					1	1					1	1			
30,000		1	1	1	1	2							1	1	2
31,000					1	1				1	1	2	1	1	2
32,000														1	1
33,000															
34,000							1		1						
35,000															
36,000								1	1				1		1
37,000											1	1			
38,000															
39,000								1	1					1	1
40,000											1	1	1		1

Table 11 / Comparison of Salaries by Type of Library*

	Placements	Salaries Known			Low Salary			High Salary			Average Salary			Median Salary		
		Women	Men	Total	Women	Men	Total	Women	Men	Total	Women	Men	Total	Women	Men	Total
Public Libraries																
United States	552	372	92	464	9500	147000	9500	39000	30784	39000	20052	20801	20200	19900	21000	20000
Northeast	179	121	30	151	12680	16000	12680	28600	28000	28600	20563	21341	20718	21000	21500	21000
Southeast	113	70	18	88	13900	15600	13900	30056	23600	30056	19784	19458	19717	19500	19200	19500
Midwest	176	124	23	147	9500	14700	9500	39000	27000	39000	19577	20529	19726	19000	21000	19569
Southwest	37	25	10	35	13500	17400	13500	23000	30670	30670	19325	21225	19868	19489	20072	19500
West	47	32	11	43	15898	17297	15898	31000	30784	31000	21111	21714	21265	20328	21719	20500
Canada	58	45	2	47	13575	19231	13575	26395	21116	26395	20178	20174	20178	20362	19231	20362
All Schools	610	417	94	511	9500	14700	9500	39000	30784	39000	20066	20788	20198	21000	20000	20000
School Libraries																
United States	344	251	24	275	10000	16500	10000	43000	42000	43000	23908	25525	24049	23485	25000	23700
Northeast	127	100	9	109	10000	16500	10000	43000	42000	43000	23663	25586	23830	23000	24870	23000
Southeast	99	68	4	72	12600	21000	12600	36000	31000	36000	23844	23375	23852	23500	21500	23300
Midwest	50	35	2	37	15000	19200	15000	39000	29000	39000	25672	24100	25587	25000	19200	25000
Southwest	43	33	4	37	13500	22000	13500	29657	29326	29657	22181	24707	22454	22500	22500	22500
West	25	15	5	20	15000	25000	15000	40000	31500	40000	25507	27700	26055	23000	27000	25000
Canada	11	9	1	10	17345	15837	15837	35709	15837	35709	24823	15837	23924	26018	15837	21116
All Schools	355	260	25	285	10000	15837	10000	43000	42000	43000	23939	25138	24045	23485	25000	23700
College/Univ. Libraries																
United States	404	224	106	330	13000	13000	13000	33595	38000	38000	20794	22219	21252	20000	21240	20300
Northeast	108	70	20	90	13000	18000	13000	29000	33000	33000	21444	22995	21789	21000	22650	21500

Southeast	83	48	14	62	16300	16000	16000	33595	27000	33595	20781	20896	20807	20000	19000	20000
Midwest	136	73	42	115	14000	13000	13000	27000	38000	38000	19797	21289	20342	19700	20500	20000
Southwest	30	13	11	24	16500	18100	16500	22000	35000	35000	18762	23645	21000	18700	22500	20000
West	47	20	19	39	17500	16047	16047	33000	34452	34452	23513	23607	23559	23000	23880	23000
Canada	30	18	4	22	14706	17345	14706	27903	20362	27903	18804	19608	18950	18854	20362	19231
All Schools	434	242	110	352	13000	13000	13000	33595	38000	38000	20646	22124	21108	20000	21000	20100
Special Libraries																
United States	389	253	61	315	12000	13513	12000	42000	40750	42000	23976	24155	24002	23000	23500	23000
Northeast	195	126	31	157	12000	16000	12000	42000	40750	42000	25207	24728	25113	24000	23000	24000
Southeast	56	34	6	40	16000	13513	13513	35400	26000	35400	22014	21102	21877	21000	22000	21000
Midwest	69	41	15	57	15000	14700	14700	38900	36000	38900	22214	24408	22774	21000	24000	22000
Southwest	28	22	4	26	16340	24000	16340	34200	37200	37200	22704	27812	23490	22500	24048	23000
West	41	30	5	35	14000	18000	14000	40000	25000	40000	24367	20580	23826	24000	20400	24000
Canada	60	32	10	42	13575	15837	13575	29412	21116	29412	19814	18778	19568	20254	18476	20211
All Schools	449	285	71	357	12000	13513	12000	42000	40750	42000	23508	23398	23480	23000	23000	23000
Other Libraries																
United States	139	59	30	89	16000	18000	16000	44000	72000	72000	25921	31106	27669	26000	28000	26500
Northeast	87	36	16	52	18000	22000	18000	44000	45000	45000	26890	29525	27701	26500	28000	26500
Southeast	11	3	2	5	16000	28000	16000	22800	30000	30000	18267	29000	22560	16000	28000	22800
Midwest	17	12	3	15	16400	20000	16400	40000	37500	40000	23658	27000	24327	22000	23500	23500
Southwest	6	3	3	6	20700	18000	18000	26500	54500	54500	24133	33333	28733	25200	27500	25200
West	18	5	6	11	28000	20000	20000	34200	72000	72000	30040	36964	33817	30000	31992	30000
Canada	14	6	6	12	17722	18854	17722	21116	27149	27149	20111	21116	20613	20362	20362	20362
All Schools	153	65	36	101	16000	18000	16000	44000	72000	72000	25385	29441	26831	24500	27149	25000

* Includes placements undifferentiated by sex

Table 12 / Effects of Experience on Salaries*

	Salaries Without Previous Experience (40 Schools)			Salaries with Previous Experience (48 Schools)		
	Women	Men	Total	Women	Men	Total
Number of Positions	333	83	416	470	134	605
Range of Low Salaries	$10000–24000	$14700–38000	$10000–24000	$9500–37200	$13000–41400	$9500–37200
Mean (Average)	17002	20453	17060	19456	22320	19092
Median	18000	21252	18000	17500	20000	17500
Range of High Salaries	$18000–39000	$18000–38000	$18120–39000	$22519–43000	$18100–72000	$25200–72000
Mean (Average)	24857	24174	26065	31812	29902	34669
Median	20945	25303	24870	35000	28000	35000
Range of Average Salaries	$16780–25242	$16760–38000	$17262–28000	$18122–38600	$17414–56700	$19315–48800
Mean (Average)	20094	21635	20402	23785	24858	24018
Median	19486	23278	20557	24757	24420	24541

*Includes placements undifferentiated by sex.

1988 Predictions

Placement officers at 20 schools predict little or no change in the number of job vacancy listings for the class of 1988. Nineteen officers think that there will be increases ranging from 1% to 170%; two predict decreases ranging from 9% to 51%. Placement officers at 27 schools expect the same difficulty placing 1988 graduates as they had placing 1987 graduates; two expect more difficulty; 19 expect less.

Salaries for 1988 will be higher according to 28 placement officers. Estimates range from $500 to $5,000. Most estimates are in the $1,000 to $2,000 range. Seventeen officers do not think salaries will be higher in 1988.

The following table indicates the increase or decrease in hiring rates of various types of libraries as perceived by the placement officers.

Type of Placement	No. of Schools Responding	
	Increase	Decrease
Public libraries	18	1
School libraries	18	2
Academic libraries	10	2
Special libraries	12	1
Other information specialties	5	0

Accredited Library Schools

This list of graduate schools accredited by the American Library Association was issued in October 1988. A list of more than 300 institutions offering both accredited and nonaccredited programs in librarianship appears in the forty-first edition of the *American Library Directory* (R. R. Bowker, 1988).

Northeast: Conn., D.C., Mass., Md., N.J., N.Y., Pa., R.I.

Catholic University of America, School of Lib. and Info. Science, Washington, DC 20064. Pauline A. Cochrane, Acting Dean. 202-635-5085.

Clarion University, College of Lib. Science, Clarion, PA 16214. Bernard Vavrek, Interim Dean. 814-226-2271.

Columbia University, School of Lib. Service, New York, NY 10027. Robert Wedgeworth, Dean. 212-280-2292.

Drexel University, College of Info. Studies, Philadelphia, PA 19104. Richard H. Lytle, Dean. 215-895-2474.

Long Island University, Palmer School of Lib. and Info. Science, Brookville, NY 11548. Lucienne G. Maillet, Dean. 516-299-2855, 2856.

Pratt Institute, Grad. School of Computer, Info. and Lib. Sciences, Brooklyn, NY 11205. S. Michael Malinconico, Dean. 718-636-3702.

Queens College, City University of New York, Grad. School of Lib. and Info. Studies, Rosenthall Rm. 254, Flushing, NY 11367. Thomas T. Surprenant, Dir. 718-520-7194.

Rutgers University, School of Communication, Info., and Lib. Studies, 41 Huntington St., New Brunswick, NJ 08903. Patricia G. Reeling, Chpn. 201-932-7917.

St. John's University, Div. of Lib. and Info. Science, Jamaica, NY 11439. Emmett Cory, Dir. 718-990-6200.

Simmons College, Grad. School of Lib. and Info. Science, Boston, MA 02115. Robert D. Stueart, Dean. 617-738-2225.

Southern Connecticut State University, School of Lib. Science and Instructional Technology, New Haven, CT 06515. Emanuel T. Prostano, Dean. 203-397-4532.

State University of New York at Albany, School of Info. Science and Policy, Albany, NY 12222. Richard S. Halsey, Dean. 518-442-5115.

State University of New York at Buffalo, School of Info. and Lib. Studies, Buffalo, NY 14260. George S. Bobinski, Dean. 716-636-2412.

Syracuse University, School of Info. Studies, Syracuse, NY 13244-2340. Donald A. Marchand, Dean. 315-423-2911.

University of Maryland, College of Lib. and Info. Services, College Park, MD 20742. Claude E. Walston, Dean. 301-454-5441.

University of Pittsburgh, School of Lib. and Info. Science, Pittsburgh, PA 15260. Toni Carbo Bearman, Dean. 412-624-5230.

University of Rhode Island, Grad. School of Lib. and Info. Studies, Kingston, RI 02881. Elizabeth Futas, Dir. 401-792-2947.

Southeast: Ala., Fla., Ga., Ky., La., Miss., N.C., S.C., Tenn.

Atlanta University, School of Lib. and Info. Studies, Atlanta, GA 30314. Lorene B. Brown, Dean. 404-653-8698.

Florida State University, School of Lib. and Info. Studies, Tallahassee, FL 32306. F. William Summers, Dean. 904-644-5775.

Louisiana State University, School of Lib. and Info. Science, Baton Rouge, LA 70803. Kathleen M. Heim, Dean. 504-388-3158.

North Carolina Central University, School of Lib. and Info. Science, Durham, NC 27707. Benjamin F. Speller, Jr., Dean. 919-683-6485.

University of Alabama, Grad. School of Lib. Service, Tuscaloosa, AL 35487. Philip M. Turner, Dean. 205-348-4610.

University of Kentucky, College of Lib. and Info. Science, Lexington, KY 40506-0039. Thomas J. Waldhart, Acting Dean. 606-257-8876.

University of North Carolina, School of Info. and Lib. Science, Chapel Hill, NC 27599-3660. Evelyn H. Daniel, Dean. 919-962-8062.

University of North Carolina at Greensboro, Dept. of Lib. and Info. Studies, Greensboro, NC 27412. Marilyn L. Miller, Chair. 919-334-5100.

University of South Carolina, College of Lib. and Info. Science, Columbia, SC 29208. Fred W. Roper, Dean. 803-777-3858.

University of South Florida, School of Lib. and Info. Science, Tampa, FL 33620. Robert Grover, Dir. 813-974-3520.

University of Southern Mississippi, School of Lib. Science, Hattiesburg, MS 39406. Jeannine Laughlin, Dir. 601-266-4228.

University of Tennessee, Knoxville, Grad. School of Lib. and Info. Science, Knoxville, TN 37996-4330. Gary R. Purcell, Dir. 615-974-2148.

Midwest: Ill., Ind., Iowa, Kans., Mich., Minn., Mo., Ohio, Wis.

Emporia State University, School of Lib. and Info. Management, Emporia, KS 66801. Martha L. Hale, Dean. 316-343-1200.

Indiana University, School of Lib. and Info. Science, Bloomington, IN 47405. Herbert S. White, Dean. 812-335-2848.

Kent State University, School of Lib. Science, Kent, OH 44242. Rosemary R. Dumont, Dean. 216-672-2782.

Northern Illinois University, Dept. of Lib. and Info. Studies, DeKalb, IL 60115. Cosette N. Kies, Chpn. 815-753-1733.

Rosary College, Grad. School of Lib. and Info. Science, River Forest, IL 60305. Michael E. D. Koenig, Dean. 312-366-2490.

University of Chicago, Grad. Lib. School, Chicago, IL 60637. Don R. Swanson, Acting Dean. 312-962-8272.

University of Illinois, Grad. School of Lib. and Info. Science, 1407 W. Gregory, 410 DKH, Urbana, IL 61801. Leigh Estabrook, Dean. 217-333-3280.

University of Iowa, School of Lib. and Info. Science, Iowa City, IA 52242. Carl F. Orgren, Dir. 319-335-5707.

University of Michigan, School of Info. and Lib. Studies, Ann Arbor, MI 48109-1092. Robert M. Warner, Dean. 313-764-9376.

University of Missouri, Columbia, School of Lib. and Info. Science, Columbia, MO 65211. Mary F. Lenox, Dean. 314-882-4546.

University of Wisconsin-Madison, School of Lib. and Info. Studies, Madison, WI 53706. Jane B. Robbins, Dir. 608-263-2900.

University of Wisconsin-Milwaukee, School of Lib. and Info. Science, Milwaukee, WI 53201. Mohammed M. Aman, Dean. 414-229-4707.

Wayne State University, Lib. Science Program, Detroit, MI 48202. Joseph J. Mika, Dir. 313-577-1825.

Southwest: Ariz., Okla., Tex.

Texas Woman's University, School of Lib. and Info. Studies, Denton, TX 76204. Brooke E. Sheldon, Dean. 817-898-2602.

University of Arizona, Grad. Lib. School, Tucson, AZ 85719. Charles D. Hurt, Dir. 602-621-3565.

University of North Texas, School of Lib. and Info. Sciences, Denton, TX 76203. Raymond F. Vondran, Dean. 817-565-2445.

University of Oklahoma, School of Lib. and Info. Studies, Norman, OK 73019. Robert D. Swisher, Dir. 405-325-3921.

University of Texas at Austin, Grad. School of Lib. and Info. Science, Austin, TX 78712-1276. Ronald E. Wyllys, Dean. 512-471-3821.

West: Calif., Colo., Hawaii, Utah, Wash.

Brigham Young University, School of Lib. and Info. Sciences, Provo, UT 84602. Nathan M. Smith, Dir. 801-378-2977.

San Jose State University, Div. of Lib. and Info. Science, San Jose, CA 95192-0029. James S. Healey, Dir. 408-277-2490.

University of California, Berkeley, School of Lib. and Info. Studies, Berkeley, CA 94720. Robert C. Berring, Dean. 415-642-1464.

University of California, Los Angeles, Grad. School of Lib. and Info. Science, Los Angeles, CA 90024. Robert M. Hayes, Dean. 213-825-4351.

University of Hawaii, School of Lib. and Info. Studies, Honolulu, HI 96822. Miles M. Jackson, Dean. 808-948-7321.

University of Washington, Grad. School of Lib. and Info. Science, Seattle, WA 98195. Margaret Chisholm, Dir. 206-543-1794.

Canada

Dalhousie University, School of Lib. and Info. Studies, Halifax, N.S. B3H 4H8. Mary Dykstra, Dir. 902-424-3656.

McGill University, Grad. School of Lib. and Info. Studies, Montreal, P.Q. H3A 1Y1. Helen Howard, Dir. 514-398-4204.

Université de Montréal, Ecole de bibliothéconomie et des sciences de l'information, Montréal, P.Q. H3C 3J7. Marcel Lajeunesse, Dir. 514-343-6044.

University of Alberta, Faculty of Lib. and Info. Studies, Edmonton, Alta. T6G 2J4. Sheila Bertram, Acting Dean. 403-432-4578.

University of British Columbia, School of Lib., Archival, and Info. Studies, Vancouver, B.C. V6T 1Y3. Basil Stuart-Stubbs, Dir. 604-228-2404.

University of Toronto, Faculty of Lib. and Info. Science, Toronto, Ont. M5S 1A1. Ann H. Schabas, Dean. 416-978-3202.

University of Western Ontario, School of Lib. and Info. Science, London, Ont. N6G 1H1. Jean M. Tague, Dean. 519-661-3542.

Library Scholarship Sources

For a more complete list of scholarships, fellowships, and assistantships offered for library study, see *Financial Assistance for Library Education* published annually by the American Library Association.

American Association of Law Libraries. (1) A varying number of scholarships of a minimum of $1,000 for graduates of an accredited law school who are degree candidates in an accredited library school; (2) a varying number of scholarships of varying amounts for library school graduates working on a law degree, nonlaw graduates enrolled in an accredited library school, and law librarians taking a course related to law librarianship; (3) a stipend of $3,500 for an experienced minority librarian working toward an advanced degree to further a law library career. For information, write to: School and Grants Committee, AALL, 53 W. Jackson, Suite 940, Chicago, IL 60604.

American Library Association. (1) The David H. Clift Scholarship of $3,000 is given to a varying number of U.S. or Canadian citizens who have been admitted to accredited library schools. For information, write to: Staff Liaison, David H. Clift Scholarship Jury, ALA, 50 E. Huron St., Chicago, IL 60611; (2) the Louise Giles Minority Scholarship of $3,000 is given to a varying number of minority students who are U.S. or Canadian citizens and have been admitted to accredited library schools. For information, write to: Staff Liaison, Louise Giles Minority Scholarship Jury, ALA, 50 E. Huron St., Chicago, IL 60611; (3) the ACRL Doctoral Dissertation Fellowship of $1,000 for a student who has completed all coursework in the area of academic librarianship. For information, write to: Program Officer, ACRL/ALA, 50 E. Huron St., Chicago, IL 60611; (4) the Samuel Lazerow Fellowship of $1,000 for a librarian currently working in acquisitions or technical services in an academic or research library. For information, write to: Program Officer, ACRL/ALA, 50 E. Huron St., Chicago, IL 60611; (5) the Nijhoff International West European Specialist Study Grant pays travel expenses, room, and board for a 10-day trip to the Netherlands and two other European countries for an ALA member. Selection based on proposal outlining purpose of trip. For information, write to Program Officer, ACRL/ALA, 50 E. Huron St., Chicago, IL 60611; (6) Bound-to-Stay Bound Books Scholarship of $2,000 for two students admitted to an ALA-accredited program who will work with children in a library for one year after graduation. For information, write to: Exec. Dir., ALSC/ALA, 50 E. Huron St., Chicago, IL 60611; (7) EBSCO/JMRT Scholarship of $1,000 for a U.S. or Canadian citizen and member of the ALA Junior Members Round Table. Based on financial need and professional goals. For information, write to: Pat Brill, 171 N. Pleasant Ave., Bloomingdale, IL 60108; (8) LITA/CLSI Scholarship in Library and Information Technology of $1,500 for a student who may not have completed more than 12 hours toward a degree in library science before June 1, 1989. Foreign students may apply. For information, write to: LITA/ALA, 50 E. Huron St., Chicago, IL 60611; (9) Bogle International Library Travel Fund grant of $300 for a varying number of ALA members to attend a first international conference. For information, write to: Robert P. Doyle, ALA, 50 E. Huron St., Chicago, IL 60611; (10) PLA/CLSI International Study Award of up to $5,000 for a PLA member with five years' experience in public libraries. For information, write to: PLA/ALA, 50 E. Huron St., Chicago, IL 60611.

American-Scandinavian Foundation. Fellowships and grants for 25 to 30 students, in amounts from $2,000 to $8,000, for advanced study in Denmark, Finland, Iceland, Norway, or Sweden. For information, write to: Exchange Div., American-Scandinavian Foundation, 127 E. 73 St., New York, NY 10021.

Association for Library and Information Science Education. A varying number of research grants of $2,500 (maximum) for members of ALISE. For information, write to: Ilse Moon, Exec. Secy., ALISE, 5623 Palm Aire Dr., Sarasota, FL 34243.

Beta Phi Mu. (1) The Sarah Rebecca Reed Scholarship of $1,500 for a person accepted in an ALA-accredited library program; (2) the Frank B. Sessa Scholarship of $750 for a Beta Phi Mu member for continuing education; (3) the Harold Lancour Scholarship of $1,000 for graduate study in a foreign country related to the applicant's work or schooling. For information, write to: Exec. Secy., Beta Phi Mu, Grad. School of Lib. and Info. Science, Univ. of Pittsburgh, Pittsburgh, PA 15260.

Canadian Library Association. (1) The Howard V. Phalin-World Book Graduate Scholarship in Library Science of $2,500; (2) the H. W. Wilson Foundation Scholarship of $2,000; and (3) the Elizabeth Dafoe Scholarship of $1,750 are given to a Canadian citizen or landed immigrant to attend an accredited Canadian library school. For information, write to: Scholarships and Awards Committee, Canadian Lib. Assn., 200 Elgin St., Ottawa, Ont. K2P IL5, Canada.

Catholic Library Association. (1) Rev. Andrew L. Bouwhuis Scholarship of $1,500 for a person with a B.A. degree who has been accepted in an accredited library school; (2) World Book-Childcraft Award: one scholarship of a total of $1,500 to be distributed among no more than four recipients for a program of continuing education. Open to CLA members only. For information, write to: Scholarship Committee, Catholic Lib. Assn., 461 W. Lancaster Ave., Haverford, PA 19401.

Church and Synagogue Library Association. Two Muriel Fuller Memorial Scholarships of $66 each for a correspondence course offered by the Univ. of Utah Continuing Education Div. Write to: CSLA, Box 19357, Portland, OR 97219.

Information Exchange System for Minority Personnel. Scholarship of $500, intended for minority students, for graduate study. For information, write to: Dorothy M. Haith, Chpn., Clara Stanton Jones School, Box 90216, Washington, DC 20090.

Medical Library Association. (1) A scholarship of $2,000 for graduate study in medical librarianship, with at least one-half of the program yet to be completed; (2) a scholarship of $2,000 for a minority student for graduate study; (3) a varying number of Research, Demonstration and Development Project grants of $100–$500 for U.S. or Canadian citizens who are ALA members; (4) continuing education awards of $100–$500 for U.S. or Canadian citizens who are ALA members. For information, write to: Scholarship Committee, Medical Lib. Assn., Suite 300, 6 N. Michigan Ave., Chicago, IL 60602.

The Frederic G. Melcher Scholarship (administered by Association of Library Service to Children, ALA). Two scholarships of $4,000 each for a U.S. or Canadian citizen admitted to an accredited library school who plans to work with children in school or public libraries. For information, write to: Exec. Secy., Assn. of Lib. Service to Children, ALA, 50 E. Huron St., Chicago, IL 60611.

Mountain Plains Library Association. Varying number of grants of $500 (maximum) each for residents of the association area. Open only to MPLA members with at least two years of membership. For information, write to: Joseph R. Edelen, Jr., MPLA Exec. Secy., Univ. of South Dakota Lib., Vermillion, SD 57069.

Natural Sciences and Engineering Research Council. (1) A varying number of scholarships of $12,500 each; and (2) a varying number of scholarships of varying amounts for postgraduate study in science librarianship and documentation for a Canadian citizen or landed immigrant with a bachelor's degree in science or engineering. For information, write to: Scholarships and International Programs, Natural Sciences and Engineering Research Council, 200 Kent St., Ottawa, Ont. K1A 1H5, Canada.

REFORMA, the National Association to Promote Library Services to the Spanish-Speaking. Two scholarships of $1,000 each to attend an ALA-accredited program. For information, write to: Marta-Luísa Sclar, Outreach, Valencia Park Lib., 101 50th St., San Diego, CA 92114.

Southern Regional Education Board. (1) A varying number of grants of varying amounts to cover in-state tuition for West Virginia residents for undergraduate, graduate, or postgraduate study in an accredited library school; (2) a varying number of grants of varying amounts to cover in-state tuition for residents of West Virginia, Alabama, Mississippi, Oklahoma, or South Carolina for postgraduate study in an accredited library school; (3) a varying number of grants of varying amounts to cover in-state tuition for residents of Georgia and South Carolina for undergraduate study in an ALA-accredited library school. For information, write to SREB, 592 Tenth St., Atlanta, GA 30318-5790.

Special Libraries Association. (1) Two $6,000 scholarships for U.S. or Canadian citizens, accepted by an ALA-accredited library education program, who show an aptitude for and interest in special libraries; (2) two $1,000 scholarships for U.S. or Canadian citizens with an MLS and an interest in special libraries who have been accepted in an ALA-accredited Ph.D. program. For information, write to: Scholarship Committee, SLA, 1700 18 St. N.W., Washington, DC 20009; (3) a scholarship of $6,000 for a minority student with an interest in special libraries. Open to U.S. or Canadian citizens only. For information, write to: Positive Action Program for Minority Groups, 1700 18 St. N.W., Washington, DC 20009.

Library Scholarship and Award Recipients, 1988

AASL/Baker & Taylor President's Award—$2,000. For demonstrating excellence and providing an outstanding national or international contribution to school librarianship and school library development. *Offered by*: ALA American Association of School Librarians. *Donor*: Baker & Taylor. *Winner*: Margaret I. Rufsvold.

AASL/Encyclopaedia Britannica National School Library Media Program of the Year Award. *Offered by*: ALA American Association of School Librarians. *Winners*: West Bloomfield Schools, West Bloomfield, Mich. (medium school); Round Rock Independent School District, Round Rock, Tex. (large school).

AASL/Follett Microcomputer in the Media Center Award. *Offered by*: American Association of School Librarians. *Winners*: Nancy Everhart and Linda Hartman.

AASL/SIRS Distinguished Library Service Award for School Administrators. For exemplary leadership in the development and support of library media programs at the building and district levels. *Offered by*: ALA American Association of School Librarians and Social Issues Resources Series, Inc. *Winner*: Ralph E. Ricardo, Supt., Ascension Parish School Board, Donaldsville, La.

AASL/SIRS Intellectual Freedom Award—$1,000. For a school library media specialist who has upheld principles of intellectual freedom. *Offered by*: ALA American Association of School Librarians and Social Issues Resources Series, Inc. *Winner*: Nancy Quesada Moreno.

ACRL Academic/Research Librarian of the Year Award—$2,000. For an outstanding national or international contribution to academic and research librarianship and library development. *Offered by*: ALA Association of College and Research Libraries. *Donor*: Baker & Taylor. *Winner*: Edward G. Holley, Chapel Hill, N.C.

ACRL Doctoral Dissertation Fellowship. For research in academic librarianship. *Offered by*: ALA Association of College and Research Libraries. *Winner*: Sarla Murgai, University of Tennessee, Knoxville.

AIA/ALA-LAMA Library Buildings Award. *Offered by*: ALA Library Administration and Management Association. *Winners*: Not awarded in 1988.

ALA Equality Award—$500. For an outstanding contribution toward promoting equality between women and men in the library profession. *Donor*: Scarecrow Press. *Offered by*: American Library Association. *Winner*: Kathleen Weibel.

ALA Honorary Life Membership Award. *Offered by*: American Library Association. *Winners*: Ralph E. Ellsworth and Spencer G. Shaw.

ALA Map and Geography Honor Award. *Offered by*: ALA Map and Geography Round Table. *Winner*: Ralph E. Ehrenberg.

ALISE Award for Outstanding Professional Contributions to Library and Information Science Education. *Offered by*: Association for Library and Information Science Education. *Winner*: Samuel Rothsten (British Columbia).

ALISE Doctoral Dissertation Competition. For excellence and for providing the opportunity for exchange of research ideas. *Offered by*: Association for Library and Information Science Education. *Winner*: Eugenia Brumm.

ALISE Doctoral Students Dissertation Awards – $400. To promote the exchange of research ideas between doctoral students and established researchers. *Offered by*: Association for Library and Information Science Education. *Winners:* Prudence Dalrymple, University of Wisconsin-Madison, and Anthony Olden, University of Illinois.

ALISE Research Grant Award – $2,500. For a project that reflects ALISE goals and objectives. *Offered by*: Association for Library and Information Science Education. *Winners*: John V. Richardson, Jr., and Donald Case, University of California, Los Angeles.

ALISE Research Paper Competition – $500. For a research paper concerning any aspect of librarianship or information studies by a member of ALISE. *Offered by*: Association for Library and Information Science Education. *Winners*: Verna L. Pungitore, University of Indiana, and Pamela Spence Richards, Rutgers University.

ALISE Service Award. For evidence of regular and sustained service to the association. *Offered by*: Association for Library and Information Science Education. *Winner*: Mohammed M. Aman (Wisconsin–Milwaukee).

ALTA Literacy Award. For an outstanding contribution to the extirpation of illiteracy. *Offered by*: ALA American Library Trustee Association. *Winners*: Richard C. Torbert, Swarthmore, Pa., and Tyrone Bryant, Fort Lauderdale, Fla.

ALTA Major Benefactors Honor Awards. *Offered by*: ALA American Library Trustee Association. *Winners*: Rhoda Krasner, Wheatride, Colo., Denver Public Library, and Fred K. Darrah, Little Rock, Ark., public libraries throughout Arkansas.

ASCLA Exceptional Achievement Award. For recognition of leadership and achievement in the areas of library cooperation and state library development. *Offered by*: ALA Association of Specialized & Cooperative Library Agencies. *Winner*: Not awarded in 1988.

ASCLA Exceptional Service Award. For exceptional service to ASCLA or any of its component areas of service, namely, services to patients, the homebound, medical, nursing, and other professional staff in hospitals, and inmates; demonstrating professional leadership, effective interpretation of program, pioneering activity, or significant research or experimental projects. *Offered by*: ALA Association of Specialized & Cooperative Library Agencies. *Winner*: Not awarded in 1988.

ASIS Award of Merit. For an outstanding contribution to the field of information science. *Offered by*: American Society for Information Science. *Winner*: F. Wilfrid Lancaster.

ASIS Best Information Science Book. *Offered by*: American Society for Information Science. *Winners*: Peter Hernon and Charles R. McClure, for "Federal Informaiton Policies in the 1980s: Conflicts and Issues."

ASIS Best Information Science Teacher Award – $500. *Offered by*: American Society for Information Science. *Winner*: Harold Borko, University of California, Los Angeles.

ASIS Doctoral Forum Award. *Offered by*: American Society for Information Science. *Winners*: Elizabeth Liddy, Syracuse University, for "The Discourse-Level Structure of Natural Language Text: An Exploratory Study of Empirical Abstracts," and Clifford Lynch, University of California, Berkeley, for "Extending Relational Database Management Systems for Information Retrieval Applications."

Advancement of Literacy Award. *Offered by*: Public Library Association. *Winner*: Gannett Foundation.

Aggiornamento Award. For an outstanding

contribution to the growth of parish librarianship. *Offered by*: Catholic Library Association Parish and Community Libraries Section. *Winner*: Orbis Books of Maryknoll Publishers.

Hugh C. Atkinson Memorial Award. *Offered by*: ALA divisions. *Winner*: Richard M. Dougherty.

Carrol Preston Baber Award—$10,000. For an innovative research project that will improve library services to a specific group of people. *Offered by*: American Library Association. *Donor:* Eric Baber. *Winners:* Melvin Bowie, University of Georgia; David Loertscher, Libraries Unlimited; May Leir Ho, University of Arkansas.

Bill Backer Memorial Scholarships. *Offered by*: American Association of School Librarians and SIRS, Inc. *Winners*: Barbara J. Burgess, Deborah Levitov, Grace E. Stamper, Joie Taylor.

Baker & Taylor Conference Grants. *Offered by*: ALA Young Adult Services Division. *Winners*: Barbara A. Carmody and Gloria L. Rhodes.

The Best of LRTS Award. *Offered by*: ALA Resources and Technical Services Division. *Winner*: Not awarded in 1988.

Beta Phi Mu Award—$500. For distinguished service to education for librarianship. *Offered by*: ALA Awards Committee. *Donor*: Beta Phi Mu Library Science Honorary Association. *Winner*: Samuel Rothstein.

Blackwell North America Resources Section Scholarship Award (formerly National Library Service Resources Section Publication Award). Presented to the author/authors of an outstanding monograph, published article, or original paper on acquisitions pertaining to college or university libraries. *Offered by*: ALA Resources and Technical Services Division, Resources Section. *Donor*: Blackwell North America. *Winners*: Joe A. Hewitt and John S. Shipman.

Bogle International Library Travel Fund. *Offered by*: ALA International Relations Committee. *Winners*: Maria Otero-Boisvert, Robert K. Bruce, Ann Kelsey, Carolyn A. W. Snyder, Betty L. Tsai.

Bound to Stay Bound Books Scholarship. *Offered by*: Association for Library Service to Children. *Winners*: Birgit Nicolaisen and Susan Valtfort.

Rev. Andrew L. Bouwhuis Scholarship—$1,500. For a person with a B.A. degree who has been accepted in an accredited library school. (Award is based on financial need and proficiency.) *Offered by*: Catholic Library Association. *Winner*: Kathleen Hintz, Catskill, N.Y.

R. R. Bowker/Ulrich's Serials Librarianship Award. *Offered by*: ALA Resources and Technical Services Division. *Winner*: Marjorie E. Bloss.

Estelle Bradman Award. *Offered by*: Medical Library Association. *Winner*: Audrey Powderly Newcomer.

John Brubaker Memorial Award. *Offered by*: Catholic Library Association. *Winner*: Rev. Roy M. Gasnick, OFM, dir. of Public Relations, Franciscan Communications, Los Angeles, Calif.

CACUL Distinguished Librarian Award. *Offered by:* Canadian Association of College and University Libraries. *Winner:* Alan MacDonald, University of Calgary Library.

CALA Distinguished Service Award. *Offered by*: Chinese-American Librarians Association. *Winner*: Tze-chung, dean and professor, Graduate School of Lib. and Information Science, Rosary College, River Forest, Ill.

CASLIS Award for Special Librarianship in Canada. *Offered by*: Canadian Association of Special Libraries and Information Services. *Winner*: Shirley B. Elliott, Halifax, N.S.

CIS/GODORT/ALA Documents to the People Award—$1,000. For effectively encouraging the use of federal documents in support of library services. *Offered by*: ALA Government Documents Round Table. *Donor*: Congressional Information Service, Inc. *Winner*: Agnes Ferruso.

CLA Dafoe Scholarship—$1,750. For a Canadian citizen or landed immigrant to attend an accredited Canadian library school. *Offered by*: Canadian Library Association. *Winner*: Kathryn Abbott, Vancouver, B.C.

CLA High School Library Section Certificate of Merit. For an outstanding contribution to high school librarianship. *Offered by*: Catholic Library Association. *Winner*: Rev. John T. Catoir, pres., Christophers, New York, N.Y.

CLA Outstanding Service to Librarianship Award. *Offered by:* Canadian Library Association. *Winner:* Ronald F. Yeo, chief librarian, Regena Public Library.

CLA Outstanding Service to Public Libraries Award. *Offered by*: Canadian Library Association. *Winner*: Diane MacQuarrie, Halifax City Regional Library.

CLR Grants. For a list of the recipients of CLR grants for the 1987–1988 academic year, see the report from the Council on Library Resources, in Part 2.

CSLA Award for Outstanding Congregational Librarian. For distinguished service to the congregation and/or community through devotion to the congregational library. *Offered by*: Church and Synagogue Library Association. *Winner*: Charles Snyder, Perkasie, Pa.

CSLA Award for Outstanding Congregational Library. For responding in creative and innovative ways to the library's mission of reaching and serving the congregation and/or the wider community. *Offered by*: Church and Synagogue Library Association. *Winners*: Pathfinders Memorial Library, Chapelwood UMC, Houston, Tex.

CSLA Award for Outstanding Contribution to Congregational Libraries. For providing inspiration, guidance, leadership, or resources to enrich the field of church or synagogue librarianship. *Offered by*: Church and Synagogue Library Association. *Winner*: Ruth Turney, Bethel, Conn.

CSLA Distinguished Service Award for School Administrators. *Offered by:* Canadian School Libraries Association. *Winner:* Geraldine Roe, St. John's Roman Catholic School Board.

Francis Joseph Campbell Citation. For an outstanding contribution to the advancement of library service to the blind. *Offered by*: Section on Library Service to the Blind and Physically Handicapped of the Association of Specialized and Cooperative Library Agencies. *Winner*: James Chandler.

Canadian Library Trustee Merit Award. For exceptional service as a trustee in the library field. *Offered by:* Canadian Library Association. *Winner:* Nancy Bennett, British Columbia Library Association.

Carnegie Reading List Grants. *Offered by*: ALA Publishing Committee. *Winners*: Association for Library Service to Children, for "Summertime Family Reading," $1,600; Association for Library Service to Children, for "Professional Literature for Children's Librarians," $1,200; American Association of School Librarians, for "Selection Tools: A Guide for Choosing Materials for K–12 Students," $2,265; Office of Library Outreach Services, for *Coretta Scott King Award Books*, $2,065; Young Adult Services Division, in conjunction with the ALA Public Information Office, for "A Series of Genre Booklists for Young Adults," $5,675.

James Bennett Childs Award. For a distinguished contribution to documents librarianship. *Offered by*: ALA Government Documents Round Table. *Winner*: Patricia Reeling.

David H. Clift Scholarship—$3,000. For a worthy student to begin a program of library education at the graduate level. *Offered by*: ALA Awards Committee, Standing Committee on Library Education. *Winners*: Linda Hilton, Pottstown, Pa.; Donna Chen, Storm Lake, Iowa; Sheryl Davis, Redlands, Calif.

Cunningham Fellowship—$3,500. A six-month grant and travel expenses in the United States and Canada for a foreign librarian. *Offered by*: Medical Library Association. *Winner*: Not awarded in 1988.

John Cotton Dana Award. For exceptional support and encouragement of special librarianship. *Offered by*: Special Libraries Association. *Winners*: Beryl L. Anderson, Ron Coplen (posthumously), Paul Klinefelter, Enid Thompson.

John Cotton Dana Library Public Relations Award. *Offered by*: American Library Association. *Winners: Academic Library Category*—McGoogan Library of Medicine, Omaha, Nebr.; University of Texas Library, Arlington. *Consortia Category*—Montana's libraries, Bozeman. *Public Library Category*—Alameda County Library, Hayward, Calif.; Dauphin County Library System, Harrisburg, Pa.; East Brunswick Public Library, N.J.; Farmers Branch Manske Library, Tex.; Greenville County Library, Greenville, S.C.; John C. Hart Memorial Library, Shrub Oak, N.Y.; Louisville Free Public Library, Ky.; Middle County Public Library, Centereach, N.Y.; Orange County Library, Orange, Calif.;

San Francisco Public Library, Calif.; Sierra Madre Public Library, Calif. *School Library Category*—Kenmore West High School Library, Buffalo, N.Y. *Service Library Category*—Cargill Information Center, Minneapolis, Minn. *Special Library Category*—RAF Upper Heyford Base Library, APO, N.Y.

Louise Darling Medal. *Offered by*: Medical Library Association. *Winner*: Dorothy R. Hill.

Dartmouth Medal. For achievement in creating reference works of outstanding quality and significance. *Offered by*: ALA Reference and Adult Services Division. *Winner*: *Encyclopedia of Religion* (Macmillan), Mircea Eliade, ed. in chief.

Watson Davis Award. For a significant long-term contribution to the American Society for Information Science. *Offered by*: American Society for Information Science. *Winner*: Bonnie C. Carroll.

Melvil Dewey Medal. For recent creative professional achievement, particularly in library management, library training, cataloging and classification, and the tools and techniques of librarianship. *Offered by:* ALA Awards Committee. *Donor:* Forest Press. *Winner:* Herbert Goldhor.

Janet Doe Lectureship—$250. *Offered by*: Medical Library Association. *Winner*: Gerald J. Oppenheimer.

Vincent H. Duckles Award—$350. For the best book-length bibliography or music reference work. *Offered by*: Music Library Association. *Winner*: *The New Grove Dictionary of American Music*, ed. by H. Wiley Hitchcock and Stanley Sadie (Macmillan, 1986).

Miriam Dudley Bibliographic Instruction Award. For leadership in academic library instruction. *Offered by*: American Library Association. *Winner*: Sharon A. Hogan, Louisiana State University.

Ida and George Eliot Prize—$100. For an essay published in any journal in the preceding calendar year that has been judged most effective in furthering medical librarianship. *Offered by*: Medical Library Association. *Donor:* Login Brothers Books. *Winners:* Ellen Gay Detlessen and Thomas J. Galvin.

FLRT Achievement Award. For leadership or achievement in the promotion of library and information service and the information profession in the federal community. *Offered by*: Federal Librarians Round Table. *Winner*: Anne A. Heanue.

Facts on File Award—$1,000. For a librarian who has made current affairs more meaningful to adults. *Offered by*: ALA Reference and Adult Services Division. *Winner*: Chicago Public Library, Ralph W. Schneider, dir.

Frederick Winthrop Faxon Scholarship—$3,000. *Offered by*: American Library Association. *Winner*: Michael Whetzel, Miami, Fla.

Fellows' Posner Prize. For the best article in the *American Archivist Journal*. *Offered by*: Society of American Archivists. *Winner*: Avra Michelson, Smithsonian Institution.

Muriel Fuller Scholarship. *Offered by*: Church and Synagogue Library Association. *Winner*: Linda Altman, Clearlake, Calif.

Gale Research Company Financial Development Award—$2,500. *Offered by*: American Library Association. *Donor*: Gale Research Co. *Winners*: Sterling C. Evans Library of Texas, A & M University, Irene B. Hoadley, dir., and Charlene K. Clark, Dept. of Development, for "Library Excellence Dinners."

Walter Gerboth Award—$500. To support research in the first five years as a music librarian. *Offered by*: Music Library Association. *Winner*: David A. Day, Harold B. Lee Library, Brigham Young University, for an annotated catalog of the printed and manuscript opera and ballet collection of the Théâtre de la Monnaie at the Archives de la ville, Brussels.

Louise Giles Minority Scholarship—$3,000. For a worthy student who is a U.S. or Canadian citizen and is also a member of a principal minority group. *Offered by*: ALA Awards Committee, Office for Library Personnel Resources Advisory Committee. *Winners*: Victor Lui, Haslett, Minn.; Stephanie Sterling, Culver City, Calif.; Rita Jiminez, Tucson, Ariz.

Murray Gottlieb Prize—$100. For the best unpublished essay submitted by a medical librarian on the history of some aspect of health sciences or a detailed description of a library exhibit. *Offered by*: Medical Library Association. *Donor*: Ralph and Jo Grimes. *Winner*: Not awarded in 1988.

Grolier Award for Research in School Librarianship in Canada—$1,000. For theoretical or applied research that advances the field of school librarianship. *Offered by*: Canadian Library Trustees Association. *Winner*: Melvyn Rainey, University of British Columbia.

Grolier Foundation Award—$1,000. For an unusual contribution to the stimulation and guidance of reading by children and young people through high school age, for continuing service, or one particular contribution of lasting value. *Offered by*: ALA Awards Committee. *Donor*: Grolier Foundation. *Winner*: Lucille C. Thomas.

Grolier National Library Week Grant. *Offered by*: ALA National Library Week Committee. *Winner*: Kentucky Library Association.

G. K. Hall Award for Library Literature. *Offered by*: American Library Association. *Winner*: Wayne A. Wiegand, for *Politics of an Emerging Profession 1876–1917* (Greenwood Press, 1986).

Philip M. Hamer-Elizabeth Hamer Kegan Award. For outstanding work by an editor of a documentary publication. *Offered by*: Society of American Archivists. *Winners*: Nancy Bartlett and Kathleen Koehler, Bentley Historical Library, for *A Book of Days: 150 Years of Student Life at Michigan*.

Hammond Incorporated/Magert Award. *Offered by*: ALA Map and Geography Round Table. *Winner*: Not awarded in 1988.

Frances Henne Award. *Offered by*: American Association of School Librarians. *Winner*: Jane Louise Thomas.

(John Ames) Humphry/Forest Press Award. *Offered by*: ALA International Relations Committee. *Winner*: Joel C. Downing.

ISI Information Science Doctoral Dissertation Scholarship—$1,000. *Offered by*: American Society for Information Science. *Winner*: Stephanie W. Haas, University of Pittsburgh.

ISI Scholarship—$1,000. For beginning doctoral candidates in library/information science. *Offered by*: Special Libraries Association. *Donor*: Institute for Scientific Information. *Winner*: Not awarded in 1988.

John Phillip Imroth Memorial Award for Intellectual Freedom—$500. For a notable contribution to intellectual freedom and remarkable personal courage. *Offered by*: ALA Intellectual Freedom Round Table. *Donor*: Intellectual Freedom Round Table. *Winner*: Elliot Goldstein and Eleanor Goldstein of SIRS, Inc.

Intellectual Freedom Round Table State Program Award. *Offered by*: ALA Intellectual Freedom Round Table. *Winner*: New York Library Association, Intellectual Freedom Committee and Intellectual Freedom Round Table.

JMRT Professional Development Grant. *See* 3M/JMRT Professional Development Grant.

J. Morris Jones–World Book Encyclopedia–ALA Goal Award. *See* World Book Encyclopedia–ALA Goal Award.

LITA/Gaylord Award for Achievement in Library and Information Technology. For distinguished leadership, notable development or application of technology, superior accomplishments in research or education, or original contributions to the literature of the field. *Offered by*: Library and Information Technology Association. *Winner*: Barbara E. Markuson.

Harold Lancour Scholarship—$1,000. For graduate study in a foreign country related to the applicant's work or schooling. *Offered by*: Beta Phi Mu. *Winner*: Pamela Spence Richards.

Sister M. Claude Lane Award. For outstanding work by a religious archivist. *Offered by*: Society of American Archivists. *Winner*: Brother Denis Sennett, S.A., Friars of Atonement.

Samuel Lazerow Fellowship—$1,000. For outstanding contributions to acquisitions or technical services in an academic or research library. *Offered by*: ALA Association of College and Research Libraries and the Institute for Scientific Information. *Winner*: Carol M. Kelly, Texas Tech University.

Joseph Leiter Lectureship. *Offered by*: Medical Library Association. *Winner*: Alvin M. Weinberg.

Waldo Gifford Leland Prize. For an outstanding published work in the archival field. *Offered by*: Society of American Archivists. *Winner*: Nancy Gwinn, for *Preservation Microfilming*.

Joseph W. Lippincott Award—$1,000. For distinguished service to the profession of librarianship, such service to include outstanding participation in the activities of professional library associations, notable published professional writing, or other significant activity on behalf of the profession and its aims. *Offered by*: ALA Awards Committee. *Donor*: Joseph W. Lippincott. *Winner*: Henriette D. Avram.

MLA Award. For the best article-length bibliography or article on music librarianship. *Offered by*: Music Library Association. *Winner*: Carol June Bradley, "Notes of Some Pioneers: America's First Music Librarians" in *Notes* 43/2 (December 1986): 272–291.

MLA Citation. For significant contributions to music librarianship. *Offered by*: Music Library Association. *Winner*: Donald W. Krummel, University of Illinois, Champaign-Urbana, School of Library and Information Science.

MLA Continuing Education Award. *Offered by*: Medical Library Association. *Winner*: Rick B. Forsman.

MLA Distinguished Public Service Award. *Offered by*: Medical Library Association. *Winner*: The Honorable Claude D. Pepper, U.S. House of Representatives.

MLA Doctoral Fellowship. *Offered by*: Medical Library Association. *Winner*: Beth Paskoff.

MLA President's Award. For an outstanding contribution to medical librarianship. *Offered by*: Medical Library Association. *Winner*: Alison Bunting.

MLA Scholarship—$2,000. For graduate study in medical librarianship at an ALA-accredited library school. *Offered by*: Medical Library Association. *Winner*: Colleen Anne Marty.

John P. McGovern Award Lectureship—$500. *Offered by*: Medical Library Association. *Winner*: Robert Wedgeworth.

Margaret Mann Citation. For outstanding professional achievement in the area of cataloging and classification. *Offered by*: ALA Resources and Technical Services Division/Cataloging and Classification Section. *Winner*: Ben R. Tucker.

Allie Beth Martin Award—$2,000. For an outstanding librarian. *Offered by*: ALA Public Library Association. *Donor*: Baker & Taylor. *Winner*: Daniel O. Robles.

Frederic G. Melcher Scholarship—$4,000. For young people who wish to enter the field of library service to children. *Offered by*: ALA Association for Library Service to Children. *Winners*: Lisa Griest and Jeffrey Dufty.

Margaret E. Monroe Library Adult Services Award. *Offered by*: ALA Reference and Adult Services Division. *Winner*: Jane K. Hirsch.

Isadore Gilbert Mudge Citation. For a distinguished contribution to reference librarianship. *Offered by*: ALA Reference and Adult Services Division. *Winner*: James R. Rettig.

Gerd Muehsam Memorial Award. For the best paper on a subject related to art or visual resources librarianship. *Offered by*: Art Libraries Society of North America. *Winner*: Not awarded in 1988.

Martinus Nijhoff International West European Specialist Study Grant. *Offered by*: Association of College and Research Libraries. *Winner*: Not awarded in 1988.

Marcia C. Noyes Award—$250 and travel expenses to MLA annual meeting. For an outstanding contribution to medical librarianship. *Offered by*: Medical Library Association. *Winner*: Gertrude Lamb.

Eunice Rockwell Oberly Award. For the best bibliography in agriculture or related sciences. *Offered by*: ALA Association of College and Research Libraries. *Winner*: Not awarded in 1988.

Eli M. Oboler Memorial Award. *Offered by*: ALA Intellectual Freedom Round Table. *Winner*: "Choosing Equality: The Case for Democratic Schooling," edited by Ann Bastian et al. (Temple University Press, 1986).

Shirley Olofson Memorial Award. For individuals to attend their second annual conference of ALA. *Offered by*: ALA Junior Members Round Table. *Winners*: James L. Huessmann and Judy Jeng.

Doris Orenstein Memorial Fund. *Offered by*: Association of Jewish Libraries. *Winners*: David Lecourt, Helen Rutenberg, Cindy Silver.

Howard V. Phalin-World Book Graduate Scholarship in Library Science—$2,500 (maximum). For a Canadian citizen or landed immigrant to attend an accredited library school in Canada or the United States. *Offered by*: Canadian Library Association. *Winner*: Gail Bunt, Saskatoon, Sask.

Esther J. Piercy Award. For contribution to librarianship in the field of technical services by younger members of the profession. *Offered by*: ALA Resources and Technical Services Division. *Winner*: Karen Markey.

Plenum Scholarship—$1,000. For graduate study leading to a doctorate in library and information science. *Offered by:* Special Libraries Association. *Winner:* Beth M. Paskoff.

Herbert W. Putnam Award—$500. A grant-in-aid for an American librarian of outstanding ability for travel, writing, or any other use that might improve his or her service to the profession. *Offered by*: ALA. *Winner:* Charles A. Seavey.

Putnam Publishing Group Award. To attend the ALA annual conference. *Offered by*: ALA Association for Library Service to Children. *Winners:* Katherine Louise Kan, Cynthia M. Olsen, Lesly A. Kaplan, Timothy R. Wadham.

Sarah Rebecca Reed Scholarship—$1,500. For study at an ALA-accredited library school. *Offered by*: Beta Phi Mu. *Winner*: Victor Liu.

Reference Service Press Award. *Offered by*: ALA Reference and Adult Services Division. *Winner*: Elfreda A. Chatman, for "Opinions Leadership, Poverty, and Information Sharing," *RQ* 26 (3) (Spring 1987): 341–353.

Catherine J. Reynolds Award. *Offered by*: ALA Government Documents Round Table. *Winners*: Barbara L. Bell, Karen W. Fachan, Diane L. Garner.

Rittenhouse Award—$200. For the best unpublished paper on medical librarianship submitted by a student enrolled in, or having been enrolled in, a course for credit in an ALA-accredited library school, or a trainee in an internship program in medical librarianship. *Offered by*: Medical Library Association. *Donor*: Rittenhouse Medical Bookstore. *Winner*: Catherine Burroughs.

Frank Bradway Rogers Information Advancement Award—$500. For an outstanding contribution to knowledge of health science information delivery. *Offered by*: Medical Library Association. *Donor*: Institute for Scientific Information. *Winner*: Charles M. Goldstein.

SAA Distinguished Service Award. *Offered by*: Society of American Archivists. *Winner*: Bentley Historical Library/Michigan Historical Collections, University of Michigan.

SLA Minority Stipend—$3,000. For graduate study leading to a master's degree in the field of special librarianship. *Offered by*: Special Libraries Association. *Winners*: Carrie Robinson and Jacquelyn Cenacveira.

SLA Public Relations Award—$1,000. For an outstanding article on special librarianship. *Offered by*: Special Libraries Association. *Winner*: David Holmstrom, for "Christine Maxwell: The Business of Knowledge," *American Way*, March 15, 1987, p. 19.

SLA Scholarships—$6,000. For students with financial need who show potential for special librarianship. *Offered by*: Special Libraries Association. *Winners*: Debra Kay Barnes and Christopher D. Forney.

K. G. Saur Award for Best College and Research Libraries Article. *Offered by:* ALA Association of College and Research Libraries. *Winners:* Robert Boice, Jordan M. Scepanski, and Wayne Wilson, for "Librarians and Faculty Members: Coping with Pressures to Publish," for *College & Research Libraries,* 28, no. 6.

Margaret B. Scott Memorial Award—$400. For the development of school libraries in Canada. *Offered by*: Canadian School Library Association and Ontario Library Association. *Winner*: Donald Hamilton, University of Victoria Library.

John Sessions Memorial Award. For significant efforts to work with the labor community. *Offered by*: ALA Reference and Adult Services Division. *Winner*: Southern Labor Archives.

Jesse H. Shera Award for Research. *Offered by*: ALA Library Research Round Table. *Winners*: Danny P. Wallace and Bert R. Boyce, for "Holdings as a Measure of Journal Value."

Pat Tabler Memorial Award. *Offered by*: Church and Synagogue Library Association. *Winner*: Clydia D. DeFreese, Decatur, Ala.

3M/JMRT Professional Development Grant. To encourage professional development and participation of new librarians in ALA and JMRT activities. To cover expenses for recipients to attend ALA conferences. *Offered by*: ALA Junior Members Round

Table. *Winners*: Joan L. Dobson, Nancy Clemente Palma, Linda Scott.

Trustee Citations. For distinguished service to library development whether on the local, state, or national level. *Offered by*: ALA American Library Trustee Association. *Donor*: ALA. *Winners*: Jane Norcross, Atlanta, Ga., and Frances H. Naftalin, Minneapolis, Minn.

Voice of Youth Advocates Research Grant—$1,000. *Offered by*: ALA Young Adult Services Division. *Winner*: Not awarded in 1988.

Whitney-Carnegie Fund Grants. *Offered by*: ALA Publishing Committee. *Winners*: Bettina J. Manzo, for *Guide to the Animal Rights Movement in the United States, 1972–1987* ($1,650); Blanche E. Woolls, for *Reference Sources to Aid Public Librarians in Small Libraries to Meet the Needs of Small Business in Their Communities* ($2,498); Robert L. Wick, for *Bibliography on Electronic and Computer Music* ($1,540); Rod Henshaw and Mary E. Jackson, for *Creating Access: A Bibliographic Guide to the Purposes and Practices of Library Resource Sharing* ($2,000); Susan Steadman, for *Feminist Dramatic Criticism, 1972–1988: An Annotated Bibliography* ($1,000); Joni Bodart-Talbot, for *Researching Adolescence: Resources across the Disciplines* ($2,000).

H. W. Wilson Co. Scholarship—$2,000. Available to Canadian citizen or landed immigrant for pursuit of studies at an accredited Canadian library school. *Offered by*: Canadian Library Association. *Winner*: Roberta Todd, Mt. Brydges, Ont.

H. W. Wilson Library Periodical Award—$500. To a periodical published by a local, state, or regional library, library group, or library association in the United States or Canada that has made an outstanding contribution to librarianship. *Offered by*: ALA Awards Committee. *Donor:* H. W. Wilson Co. *Winner: California State Library Foundation Bulletin*, Gary E. Strong, ed.

H. W. Wilson Library Staff Development Grant—$2,500. *Offered by*: ALA Awards Committee. *Winners*: Fairfax County Public Library, Springfield, Va., Edwin S. Clay III, dir., and Nancy C. Woodall, trng. coord., for "Recognizing Cultural Differences: A Training Program for Staff."

Justin Winsor Prize. *Offered by*: ALA Library History Round Table. *Winner:* Brother Thomas O'Connor, St. Mary's College of California, for "Library Service to the American Commission to Negotiate Peace and to the Preparatory Inquiry, 1917–1919."

World Book Encyclopedia-ALA Goal Award—$5,000. To support programs that recognize, advance, and implement the goals and objectives of the American Library Association. *Offered by:* American Library Association. *Donor:* World Book-Childcraft International, Inc. *Winners*: Chapter Relations Committee, CLENE RT, and the Chapter Relations Office, for "Improving Chapter Conferences"; Committee on the Status of Women in Librarianship, for "Minority Women Librarians' Personal Perspectives on Librarianship."

World Book Inc. Grant—$1,500. For continuing education in school or children's librarianship; distributed among no more than four recipients (candidates must be members of Catholic Library Association). *Offered by*: Catholic Library Association. *Winners*: Margaret Golub, OSU, Bellerose, N.Y., and Nancy K. Schmidtmann, Hicksville, N.Y.

Part 4
Research and Statistics

Library Research and Statistics

Research on Libraries and Librarianship in 1988

Mary Jo Lynch
Director, ALA Office for Research (OFR)

In the 1987 *Bowker Annual,* the ALA Office for Research announced a new project, "Topics in Library Research—Proposals for the Nineties," in which the Library Programs office of the Department of Education would consult experts to identify issues that must be resolved if libraries are to maintain a position of leadership in the information society. Four meetings of experts held during 1987 generated a list of 200 researchable questions, which were organized into ten major subject areas:

- Education and Training of Librarians
- Information Needs/Users
- Archives and Preservation
- Organizing, Indexing and Retrieving Materials
- Library Funding and Economics
- Libraries and Education
- Library Models
- Role of the Public Services Librarian
- Policy Issues
- Access to Information

Experts were then commissioned to write a paper on their area of expertise. The papers and the reviews by other experts at the first draft stage and again upon completion offer alternative approaches to each subject area and cite areas in need of research. The results of this work are now available from the Government Printing Office in the two-volume publication *Rethinking the Library in an Information Age: Issues in Library Research—Proposals for the 1990s.* Volume I includes abstracts of nine papers and lists of questions related to the ten topics generated from the four meetings of experts. Volume II contains the full text of the papers, comments by reviewers, and a report on the teleconference held with three U.S. embassy posts in Germany to discuss the issues. A third volume will be published in 1989 to report results of a "Workshop on Creating a Library Research Infrastructure," held in Washington, D.C., on October 31 and November 1, 1988. The volume will include a summary of the workshop proceedings and recommendations prepared by Robert Hayes, along with the text of the four papers, on the possible components of a library research infrastructure prepared by four task forces for discussion at the workshop. The topics of the papers (and the task force chairs) are:

- The Role of Professional Associations (Julie Virgo)
- The Creation of a Library-Oriented Think-Tank (Duane Webster)
- Research Institute in Library Consortia or Large Research Libraries (Jerome Yavarkowsky)
- Library School Based Centers (Kathleen Heim and Abe Bookstein)

Reviewing and discussing the papers at the workshop was an invited group of task force participants and federal officials.

A remarkable similar view of an infrastructure or framework for research was presented in early November by Pat Molholt in the Samuel Lazerow Memorial Lecture at the University of Pittsburgh. Molholt, associate director of the Rensselaer Polytechnic Institute's Folsom Library, spoke about "Structuring Models of Research for Information Science: Attitudes Perceptions and Values," criticizing the field for lacking both "research-mindedness" and an infrastructure capable of executing any coordinated research agenda. The research framework Molholt proposes has four principal components: research centers, library schools, teaching libraries and extension services. According to Molholt, any or all of these four can help to improve library and information science research, which she believes to be "a major weak spot in our efforts to seek a leadership role in the Information Age."

Title II-B Funded Research

Library Programs awarded HEA Title II-B funding to four projects in FY 1988. Verna Pungitore of the Indiana University School of Library and Information Science is studying the diffusion of PLA's public library planning process. Pungitore's work will document the methods and channels used on the national, state, and regional level to disseminate information, train planners, and promote the adoption of the process.

Research on another aspect of public library service has been conducted by Bernard Vavrek of the School of Library Science at Clarion State University. Vavrek's project, "Assessing Information Needs of Rural Americans," investigates such questions as What do rural people think about their public libraries? What are the information needs of rural Americans? To what extent do rural libraries meet those needs? Based on the answers to these questions, training materials will be developed to enable rural librarians to become more efficient in serving their constituencies. [See Bernard Vavrek's report on the results of his study later in this section—*Ed.*]

Tefko Saracavic, of the Rutgers School of Communication, Information, and Library Studies, is studying "User Interaction and On-line Searching for Information Seeking in Libraries." Using data and results from an earlier grant to Betty Turock and Carol Kuhlthau at the same institution plus original data, Saracavic is analyzing the nature and pattern of online searches and the nature and patterns of discourse in librarian user interactions to provide guidelines for improved searches and interactions, conduct pilot tests of the guidelines, and disseminate the results through papers, presentations, and construction of model courses.

More theoretical research involving online searching is being conducted by Don Swanson of the University of Chicago's Graduate Library School in a project entitled "Medical Literature as a Source of New Knowledge." The announcement of the award notes that Swanson's work is based on the belief that "the fragmentation of science into specialties and the resulting isolation of specialized literatures from one another, suggest that there may exist many implicit, unintended and unnoticed logical relationships between such literatures. Moreover, as the scientific literature grows, and specialties proliferate, the number of potential relationships between pairs of specialties increases at a much higher rate, proportional to the square of the number of specialties." Swanson will extend work already in progress to meet three objectives:

- To demonstrate more examples, within the biomedical literature, of unnoticed logical connections that are potential sources of new knowledge
- To further develop and describe online search strategies that can aid, stimulate, and systematize the discovery of such connections
- To develop requirements for representing logical relationships in the process of indexing biomedical articles for entry into online databases

Anne Mathews, director of library programs at the U.S. Department of Education (DOE), spoke about funding for research on two occasions in 1988: at the January meeting of the Association for Library and Information Science Research, where she presented "An Analysis of Issues and Proposals in Library and Information Science Research," and at the ALA annual conference in New Orleans, where she spoke on "The Role of the U.S. Department of Education in Developing a Core of Library Science Research" at a program sponsored by the Library Research Round Table.

Public Libraries

Two survey reports published in 1988 provide information about aspects of public library service that had not been previously documented. The National Center for Education Statistics (NCES) published results of its Fast Response Survey of public library service to young adults (12–18 years). The survey questionnaire, which was brief (as it is in all Fast Response Surveys), was mailed in September 1987 to a stratified random sample that included both main libraries and branches. [The text of the survey report, "Services and Resources for Young Adults in Public Libraries," is reprinted later in this section of Part 4—*Ed.*] A copy of the full report, which includes 15 tables, is available from the Government Printing Office. Some of the key findings of the survey are

- One out of every four public library patrons in 1986–1987 was a young adult (between the ages of 12 and 18).
- Only 11 percent of the nation's public libraries have the services of a young adult librarian.
- Eighty-four percent of libraries offer a section or collection of materials specially designated for young adults. In 74 percent of these libraries, the young adult section or collection was moderately or heavily used.

In late 1988, work began on a similar Fast Response Survey on Public Library Service to Children.

In September ALA published the report of another public library survey, *Nontax Sources of Revenue for Public Libraries.* The study was funded by the H. W. Wilson Foundation and conducted by the ALA Office for Research (OFR) with an advisory committee of members and staff from two ALA divisions, the Library Administration and Management Association and the Public Library Association (PLA). The questionnaire, sent to a stratified random sample of public libraries from all regions and serving populations of all sizes, asked about nontax revenue in three catagories: user charges; fines, contracts, and sales; and fundraising and financial development. An executive summary of the report includes the following key findings:

- More than 49 percent of respondents reported no revenue from user charges and more than 94 percent reported that less than 5 percent of their operating expenditures came from that source.
- More than 85 percent of respondents reported income from one or more of ten sources of fund raising and financial development listed on the questionnaire. "Individuals" and "Friends groups" were the most likely sources.
- Only 2.7 percent of respondents reported no revenue from any nontax source.

The 42-page report contains text, 22 tables, and 6 figures presenting results as well as an annotated bibliography.

The results of the survey were first revealed by OFR Director Mary Jo Lynch in a presentation at PLA's April 1988 national conference. Several other programs at that conference also featured research reports. Douglas Zweizig and Debora Wilcox Johnson presented the results of the Department of Education–funded survey of adult literacy programs in public libraries, community college/technical school libraries, state institutional libraries, and state library agencies. Sharon Baker of the University of Iowa School of Library & Information Science reported on research showing that fiction classification increases circulation and alleviates information overload among browsers. Another program, "Answers from Managers: New Data for Decision Making," repeated a format popular at previous PLA conferences. Three presentations showed how research provides key management information for planning and decision making. Both research and management perspectives were presented for each study.

Academic Libraries

The major news on academic libraries comes from the Council on Library Resources. As part of its program on Library Management and Operations, CLR announced two research grants to individuals in 1988. Elizabeth Liddy and Robert Oddy of Syracuse University received support for research on two related topics: how to represent better the information content of documents and how to assist users to present better their needs to an information system. Mary Ellen Sievert and Donald Sievert of the University of Missouri at Columbia received CLR support for a study of the information requirements of philosophy faculty and graduate students at a number of universities in the Midwest.

The research component of the CLR program entered a new phase in 1988 with the formation of the Research Library Committee, in partnership with the American Council of Learned Societies, the Social Science Research Council, and the Association of American Universities. Members of the new committee include university presidents and provosts, faculty members from the humanities and social sciences, librarians, and archivists. CLR's 1988 annual report gives examples of topics under consideration by the committee, as an indication of the committee's interests:

- The process of establishing policy for library and information services in research universities
- The relationship between library functions and practices, on the one hand, and the needs and styles of use of individuals and disciplines on the other
- Legal rights and constraints affecting the application of information technologies, consortial activities, preservation, and public policy
- The costs and funding of "public good" undertakings
- The effect of publishing practices on scholarship and library operations
- The kinds and quality of services to scholarship provided by the Library of Congress and other national agencies
- Alternative future forms for research libraries and implications of each for costs, funding, performance, and institutional organization

The efforts of the Research Library Committee, its subcommittees, consultants, staff, and grantees should help the academic community understand the issues, and through their recommendations promote broadly based support for specific courses of action.

CLR also supports research as part of its program on librarianship and professional education. The following grants were listed under the Faculty/Librarian Cooperative Research program in CLR's 1988 annual report:

Arlene G. Taylor and Angela Giral, Columbia University

To determine the overlap between the Avery Index to Architectural Periodicals and the Architectural Periodicals Index.

Mary Biggs, Columbia University, and Victor Biggs, Brookdale Foundation

To explore the attitudes and experiences of library school faculty regarding research and publishing.

Joseph McDonald and Lynda B. Micikas, Holy Family College

To test a previously developed prototype method of analyzing syllabi as a way to identify collection strengths and weaknesses and encourage faculty participation in collection development.

Rita Millican and Michael Carpenter, Louisiana State University

To explore methods of recognizing depreciation of library collections.

Beth Paskoff and Anna Perrault, Louisiana State University

To use shelflist sampling in four university libraries to construct multidimensional profiles as a possible basis for cooperative collection development.

Shirley Fondiller, Mid-Atlantic Regional Nursing Association, and Jeanne D. Fonseca, Interagency Council on Library Resources for Nursing

To compile an inventory of libraries and archives that hold historical papers and documents on nursing and nurses.

Barbara Stein, North Texas State University, and Julia Rholes, Texas A&M University

To compare the cognitive styles of reference librarians and students in database searching classes to aid in the selection and training of online searchers.

Mary Grosch, Northern Illinois University, and Terry L. Weech, University of Illinois at Urbana-Champaign

To determine the perceived value of advanced subject degrees by librarians who hold such degrees.

Marjorie Murfin, Ohio State University, and Charles A. Bunge, University of Wisconsin-Madison

To build a cost-effectiveness model into a previously developed reference survey instrument.

Caryn Carr and Gaynelle Winograd, Pennsylvania State University

To assess the needs and perceptions of library users affiliated with the department of speech communication, as part of a collection development effort in that field.

Carol Tenopir and Christine Tomoyasu, University of Hawaii at Manoa

To study library users of full-text databases and to determine how such databases will be used in libraries.

Barbara Finkelstein and Danuta A. Nitecki, University of Maryland

To compare two microcomputer-based systems for use by teachers in evaluating potential curricular materials.

Ridley R. Kessler, Jr., and Evelyn H. Daniel, University of North Carolina at Chapel Hill

To study the U.S. regional depository libraries to establish baseline data and to determine the relationship of these libraries to one another and to the library community.

Jerry D. Saye and Eric C. Palo, University of North Carolina at Chapel Hill

To examine the relationship of subject-related online catalog searches to circulation patterns and profiles of the collection.

Susan E. Searing and Margo Anderson, University of Wisconsin

To examine the information-seeking behaviors of scholars in women's studies.

Technical Services and Technology

The Council on Library Resources provided $2,000 to the School of Information Science and Policy, State University of New York at Albany, to assist in publishing the proceedings of an international conference on classification in the computer age. Other sponsors of the conference were OCLC-Forest Press, the H. W. Wilson Foundation, and the SUNY Research Foundation. At the conference, held November 18–19, experts presented papers offering a variety of disciplinary perspectives on classification, including biology, artificial intelligence, philosophy, computer science, mathematics, linguistics, as well as librarianship, covering current research; ways in which classification is being affected by information technology; and implications for library and information science education, information processing, and access. The conference proceedings will be published in April 1989. An outgrowth of the conference, the Albany Classification Research Organization (ACRO), will promote colloquia to examine such issues as the economic impact of mis- and nonclassification, the feasibility of creating a single unified system for electronically stored and distributed materials, and the development of improved interfaces between users and databases.

The changing technology of library technical services has provided an unprecedented opportunity to record unobtrusively the interactions of system and user. One of the technical sessions at the October conference of the Library and Information Technology Association (LITA) focused on "How Systems Are Used: Research Results." Speakers described the creation and use of transaction logs in the following institutions: OCLC, University of California, Columbia University, Princeton University, and the University of Illinois at Chicago.

Research at OCLC

The third *Annual Review of OCLC Research* describes a wide variety of work underway at OCLC or being conducted elsewhere with OCLC support. The following sample of project titles indicates the multifaceted nature of the work in progress at OCLC: Automated Document Structure Analysis; Clustering Equivalent Bibliographic Records; Duplicates Detection and the "Species" Problem; Nonfiction Book Use; and Scholars Cross-Reference System. The 1987–1988 *Annual Review* contains both brief abstracts and fuller summaries of these and 12 other projects.

OCLC also supports work done elsewhere. A number of projects were described in the 1988 *Bowker Annual.* Among those not yet reported are: Niall Teskey of the Information Technology Research Institute at Brighton Polytechnic is supplementing work being done at OCLC in "Extensions to the Advanced Interface Management Project." Both OCLC and the British Library Research and Development Department funded work on a methodology to assess subject resources for a narrow subject specialty in the OCLC Online Union Catalog in a project entitled "Latvian Bibliographic Records in the Online Union Catalog" conducted by Inese Auzina Smith at the Loughborough University of Technology. Carnegie Mellon University and OCLC are collaborating on a project entitled "Mercury: An Electronic Library" that will deliver information needed for research to a scholar's work station. As described in the *Annual Review:*

> The goal of this ambitious project is to demonstrate that the electronic library of the future is feasible today using current technology. Implementing the system will test accepted and emerging protocols for intersystem communications, remote call procedures, and sophisticated database searching on multiple databases using various storage media. The system will also function as an electronic library to support research in computer science by delivering information to the scholar's desktop workstation.

In a third aspect of its research program OCLC assists schools of library and information science through the Library and Information Science Research Grant

Program (LISRG), initiated in 1988 to replace the earlier Library School Research Equipment Support program. The LISRG program funds grants of up to $10,000 to cover release time from teaching for the principal investigator, research assistants, travel, equipment, and other project-related expenditures. The latest *Annual Review* lists three projects funded in 1988 and provides preliminary reports on seven projects funded under the earlier program.

The final component in OCLC's research program is a Distinguished Seminar Series of lectures, open to OCLC staff and interested members of the library and information science community, that serves as a stimulus for discussion of current research topics. The following speakers conducted seminars at OCLC in 1987–1988: Sandra A. Mamrack, Toni Carbo Bearman, W. David Penniman, Nicholas J. Belkin, Michael Lesk, William S. Cooper, and W. Bruce Croft. Summaries of these events are included in the *Annual Review.*

Awards

The first library and information science awards of the year were presented in January at the annual meeting of the Association for Library and Information Science Education (ALISE), which preceded the ALA midwinter meeting in San Antonio. Two research paper awards were presented. Pamela Spence Richards (Rutgers) won an award for "ASLIB at War: The Brief but Intrepid Career of a Library Organization as a Hub of Allied Scientific Intelligence, 1942–1945." Verna L. Pungitore (Indiana) also won an award for "The Flow of Information among Public Library Directors and Library Change Agents: An Exploratory Study." John V. Richardson (UCLA) described the work he and Donald O. Case (UCLA) would do with the support of the 1988 Research Grant Award. Their project is "Gender and Ethnic Determinates of Success in Graduate School: A Mathematical Modeling of the Admissions Process in Library and Information Science."

Two doctoral dissertations won ALISE Doctoral Students Dissertation Awards. Prudence W. Dalrymple (Wisconsin-Madison) won an award for "Retrieval by Reformulation in Two Library Catalogs: Toward a Cognitive Model of Searching Behavior." Edward Anthony Older (Illinois) also won an award for "The Beneficiaries of Library and Information Policy in British and Ex-British Africa: Steps from the White Women's League to the Electronic Library."

At the midwinter meeting, the ALA Library Research Round Table (LRRT) held a reception to honor Jesse Shera and raise funds to support the annual Jesse H. Shera Award for Research, the new name for the 12-year-old LRRT Research Award. At the annual conference in New Orleans, the first Shera Award was given to Danny P. Wallace and Bert Boyce of the Louisiana State University School of Library and Information Science for the paper "Holdings as a Measure of Journal Value." The award was presented at the LRRT-LHRT (Library History Round Table) joint awards program where LHRT also presented its Justin Winsor Award to Thomas F. O'Connor of St. Mary's College (California) for the paper "Library Service to the American Commission to Negotiate Peace and to the Preparatory Inquiry, 1917–1919."

Two award winners were announced at the ACRL President's Program in New Orleans. The ACRL Doctoral Dissertation Fellowship was won by Sarla Murgai, doctoral candidate at the University of Tennessee, Knoxville. Murgai's proposed dissertation is entitled "Management Motivation and Career Aspirations of Library/

Information Science Students." The Samuel Lazerow Fellowship for Research in Acquisitions or Technical Services was won by Carol M. Kelly, head of acquisitions at Texas Tech University. Kelly will examine CD-ROM versions of *Books in Print Plus* and *Ulrichs Plus* to identify information not previously available. She will also investigate the application of CD-ROM sources to acquisitions and try to identify other ways to use these sources.

ALA's largest award for research, the Carroll Preston Baber Grant, was given at the inaugural banquet to a team of researchers from three different institutions. Melvin Bowie (University of Georgia, Instructional Technology Department), David Loertscher (Libraries Unlimited), and May Leir Ho (University of Arkansas, College of Education) will use the $10,000 Baber Grant to complete the training phase of a project entitled "Computerized Collection Development Research in School Libraries." The project uses a microcomputer to first produce a visual "map" of the school library media center collection, revealing strengths and weaknesses, and then create a structured acquisition system that will generate data needed to assess library purchases in terms of curricular demands. The system has already been designed and pilot-tested. The Baber Grant will enable the researchers to conduct training seminars on-site or communicate by teleconference with up to 200 school librarians on the techniques of the computerized collection development system and work with them to implement it. After this work is completed (i.e., after the Baber Grant), the research team will spend several years tracking the impact of the system on the ability of participating libraries to meet curricular demands.

Three awards for research were presented at the October meeting of the American Society for Information Science at Atlanta. Stephanie W. Hass of the University of Pittsburgh Interdisciplinary Department of Information Science won the Information Science Doctoral Dissertation Scholarship for a proposal on "A Procedure for Porting Natural Language Interfaces, Using a Case Hierarchy for Domain Analysis." Two other doctoral students won Doctoral Forum Awards. Elizabeth Du Ross Liddy, Syracuse University, for "The Discourse-Level Structure of Natural Language Texts: An Exploratory Study of Empirical Abstracts," and Clifford A. Lynch, University of California, Berkeley, for "Extending Relational Database Management Systems for Information Retrieval Applications."

Statistics

The most important event in 1988 related to the future of library statistics was the passage, in April, of the Hawkins-Stafford Elementary and Secondary School Improvement Amendments of 1988, which became PL 100-297. The new law gives greater power and responsibility to the National Center for Education Statistics (NCES) and also restores "National" to its name. Libraries are mentioned six times in the law. Although it had always been assumed that libraries were part of education, and statistics about libraries had been collected by NCES, the new law specifically mandates library statistics for the first time.

Public Libraries

Even before PL 100-297 was passed, NCES began to increase its activity in the area of public library statistics. In February 1988, NCES and the National Commission on Libraries and Information Science (NCLIS) signed a Memorandum of Understanding, whereby NCLIS would organize a task force to plan the development of what was later named the Federal-State Cooperative System (FSCS). Serving on the task force would be Daniel Carter, commissioner, NCLIS; Eileen Cooke, ALA Washington Office; Ray Fry, Library Programs, U.S. Department of Education; Carol Henderson, ALA Washington Office; Mary Jo Lynch, ALA Office for Research; Ann Mathews, director of library programs, U.S. Department of Education; Amy Owen, director, Utah State Library; Richard Palmer, Ohio State Library; Margaret Phelan, commissioner, NCLIS; Charlie Robinson, director, Baltimore County Library; Joseph Shubert, State Librarian Development and Services; Peter Young, chair, LAMA Statistics Section and director of academic information services at Faxon; and Barratt Wilkins, Florida State Librarian.

Between March and November 1988, the task force met seven times to draft an action plan based on groundwork done by the ALA Office for Research in a 1985–1987 pilot project. The pilot project had examined the feasibility of a system that would combine the annual collection of statistics from public libraries in the 50 states with the periodic reporting of national statistics on public libraries by NCES. By the end of 1987, data for FY 1986 had been received at CES in machine-readable form from 12 states and transferred to the CES mainframe. Early in 1988 NCES analyzed the data, sent reports back to participating states, and met with state data coordinators to discuss ways to improve future data collection and reporting.

In November, the task force approved a final draft of the technical report of its work prepared by Richard Palmer of the Ohio State Library and critiqued the first draft of a popular version. The technical report, in draft form, had been presented to the Chief Officers of State Library Agencies (COSLA) at their October meeting, and COSLA had agreed to begin acting as the coordinating agency for the system in late 1989. Also in November, NCES and NCLIS signed a second Memorandum of Understanding, whereby NCLIS will begin implementation of the plan while COSLA is setting up procedures to do so. The first step was a training workshop for state data coordinators held in Annapolis, Maryland, in early December. Forty-eight states and the District of Columbia sent representatives to the highly successful event.

A second project involving public library statistics was implemented by the Public Library Association (PLA). The design for a Public Library Data Service (PLDS), the statistical component of PLA's Public Library Development Program, was tested during 1987. Early in 1988, PLA sent a questionnaire to all public libraries serving populations of 100,000 or more, all libraries that contributed to the Public Library Development Program, and any others requesting participation early. The first annual report, published by PLA in July 1988, contains statistics for 422 individual public libraries on their resources, services, and expenditures, plus summary statistics on these variables and graphs of the summary statistics.

School Libraries

No new national data were published on school libraries in 1988, but steps were taken to ensure the availability of such data in 1989 and beyond. NCES began negotiations with the ALA Office for Research regarding a contract to design several new components of the biennial School and Staffing Survey (SAS) conducted by the NCES Elementary and Secondary Education Division. Existing questionnaires will be modified and new instruments developed to collect data about various aspects of school library media centers and their staffs. The NCES data will eventually provide a regular and comprehensive view of school library media centers.

A more limited but very valuable view has been provided in the biennial report on "Budgeting and Expenditures for Materials in School Library Media Centers," based on data gathered by Marilyn Miller in a survey of subscribers to *School Library Journal (SLJ).* Questionnaires were sent out in late 1988 for the fourth report to be published in the June–July 1989 issue of *SLJ.*

Academic Libraries

For many years NCES has conducted a periodic survey of academic libraries as part of the Higher Education General Information Survey (HEGIS). HEGIS has now been replaced by IPEDS (Integrated Postsecondary Education Data System), which will collect data on many topics from all postsecondary institutions, those offering accredited degrees (the HEGIS universe) as well as any others offering education beyond the baccalaureate degree. A library survey will continue to be part of IPEDS. Questionnaires for the first survey were mailed in summer 1988, and a report is expected in late 1989.

Special Libraries

Statistics on special libraries have been sadly lacking. In 1988, however, the Special Libraries Association (SLA) took the first steps toward filling the gap. The SLA staff position of director, research and information resources, approved in October 1987, was filled in January 1988 by Tobi Brimsek. The report of SLA's Special Committee on Research, accepted by the SLA board in June, recommended a research agenda that included "developing baseline demographic data" on special libraries and librarians.

NISO Standard on Library Statistics

All national, periodic statistical reports on libraries will be influenced by work begun in 1988 to revise the 1983 standard library statistics established by Committee Z39 of the American National Standards Institute, the forerunner of the National Information Standards Organization (NISO). All NISO standards must be either reaffirmed, revised, or withdrawn every five years. When the library statistics standard came up for review in 1988, a revision committee was established, cochaired by Mary Jo Lynch, director of ALA's Office for Research, and Peter Young, director of academic information services at Faxon and current chair of the ALA Library Administration and Management Association's Statistics Section. Also serving on the committee are Tobi Brimsek, Special Libraries Association; Jan Feye-Stukas, Minnesota Department of Education, Library Development and Services; Dean Hollister, R. R. Bowker Company; Richard Lyders, executive director, Houston Academy of Medicine-Texas Medical Center Library; Marilyn Miller, chair, Department of Library and Information Studies, University of North Carolina at Greensboro; and Kendon Stubbs, associate librarian, University of Virginia. The committee met for the first time in November 1988. It hopes to complete its work within a year.

New Ventures

Two research developments were announced in late 1988. The Special Libraries Association has established a standing Committee on Research, following the recommendation of the report of the SLA Special Committee on Research. Miriam Drake, director of libraries at the Georgia Institute of Technology, will chair the new committee. Also, plans for a new periodical were revealed when Steven Roberts of the School of Library and Information Studies at Ealing College of Higher Education (London) invited people to serve on the editorial board of the *International Journal of Information and Library Research.* The new journal will appear three times a year and will endeavor to be truly international in scope, scientific in the widest sense, and a source of significant contributions to research in the field. All the papers will be refereed. Topics of potential interest include information and library systems and their users, information technology, man-machine interfaces, the architecture and environment of systems, information design, media and communication studies, freedom of information, copyright, sociolegal and political aspects of information, transnational information flow, the economics of information and information services, funding, artificial intelligence, knowledge-based systems, information management, classification and indexing, information retrieval, traditional and innovative service delivery, general theory, research methodology, statistical analysis and bibliometrics, the information work force, human resources in information systems, organizational and behavioral aspects of information systems, management information systems, the psychology of information, policymaking, strategy and forecasting, the management of change, technological innovation studies, subject-based studies of information and communication, education and training, public relations, the marketing of systems and services, and information and user education.

Selected Characteristics of the U.S. Population

W. Vance Grant

Specialist in Education Statistics, Education Information Branch
Office of Educational Research and Improvement
U.S. Department of Education

Item	Number	Percent
Total U.S. population (July 1, 1988)[1]	246,113,000	100.0
Resident population, 50 states and D.C.	245,602,000	99.8
Armed forces overseas	511,000	0.2
Resident population, outlying areas of the U.S. (July 1, 1987)[2]	3,587,000	–
U.S. population, 5 years old and over, including armed forces overseas (July 1, 1987)[3]	225,663,000	100.0
5–9 years	17,661,000	7.8
10–14 years	16,485,000	7.3
15–19 years	18,497,000	8.2
20–24 years	19,984,000	8.9
25–64 years	123,201,000	54.6
65 years and over	29,834,000	13.2
Public and private school enrollment (fall 1987)[4]	58,168,000	100.0
Elementary and secondary schools	45,624,000	78.4
Public	40,024,000	68.8
Private	5,600,000	9.6
Institutions of higher education	12,544,000	21.6
Public	9,706,000	16.7
Private	2,838,000	4.9
Estimated enrollment and teaching staff (fall 1988)[5]	62,020,000	100.0
Elementary and secondary schools	48,450,000	78.1
Enrollment	45,800,000	73.8
Teachers	2,650,000	4.3
Institutions of higher education	13,570,000	21.9
Enrollment	12,850,000	20.7
Senior instructional staff[6]	720,000	1.2
Educational attainment of the population 25 years old and over (March 1987)[7]		
Total	149,144,000	100.0
With 4 or more years of college	29,637,000	19.9
With 1 to 3 years of college	25,478,000	17.1
With 4 years of high school or more	112,784,000	75.6
With less than 4 years of high school	36,358,000	24.4

Item	Number	Percent
Population residing in and outside metropolitan areas		
(July 1, 1984)[8]	236,158,000	100.0
Nonmetropolitan areas	56,435,000	23.9
Metropolitan areas	179,723,000	76.1
In central cities	74,476,000	31.5
Outside central cities	105,247,000	44.6
Employment status[9]		
Total noninstitutional population 16 years old and over (November 1988)	186,949,000	–
Civilian labor force[10]	122,572,000	100.0
Employed[10]	115,976,000	94.6
Unemployed[10]	6,595,000	5.4

[1]Estimates of the Bureau of the Census, *Current Population Reports*, Series P-25, No. 1034.
[2]Estimates of the Bureau of the Census, *Current Population Reports*, Series P-25, No. 1030.
[3]Estimates of the Bureau of the Census, *Current Population Reports*, Series P-25, No. 1022.
[4]Data are from the National Center for Education Statistics, *Digest of Education Statistics*, 1988 edition. Also includes estimates for private elementary and secondary schools and preliminary figures for institutions of higher education.
[5]Derived from early estimates of the National Center for Education Statistics and the *Digest of Education Statistics*, 1988 edition.
[6]Includes instructional faculty with the rank of instructor or above. Excludes graduate and teaching assistants.
[7]Data from the Bureau of the Census, *Current Population Reports*, Series P-20, No. 428.
[8]Estimates of the Bureau of the Census, *Current Population Reports*, Series P-25, No. 976.
[9]Data from the Bureau of Labor Statistics, published in *Economic Indicators*, December 1988.
[10]Data are seasonally adjusted.
Note: Because of rounding, details may not add to totals.

Number of Libraries in the United States and Canada

Statistics are from the forty-first edition of the *American Library Directory* (*ALD*) edited by Jaques Cattell Press (R. R. Bowker, 1988). In addition to listing and describing more than 34,479 individual libraries, the forty-first edition of *ALD* lists more than 350 library networks, consortia, and other cooperative library organizations, including processing and purchasing centers and other specialized organizations. Data are exclusive of elementary and secondary school libraries. The directory does not list public libraries with holdings of fewer than 500 volumes. Law libraries with fewer than 10,000 volumes are included only if they specialize in a specific field.

Libraries in the United States

A. Public Libraries	15,013*
Public libraries, excluding branches	9,094
Main public libraries that have branches	1,301
Public library branches	5,919
B. Academic Libraries	4,647*
Junior college libraries	1,249
Departmental	87
Medical	7
Religious	3
University and college	3,398
Departmental	1,486
Law	178
Medical	224
Religious	110
C. Armed Forces Libraries	488*
Air force	134
Medical	16
Army	198
Law	1
Medical	35
Navy	156
Medical	22
D. Government Libraries	1,683*
Law	426
Medical	227
E. Special Libraries (excluding public, academic, armed forces, and government)	8,886*
Law	587
Medical	1,870
Religious	944
F. Total Special Libraries (including public, academic, armed forces, and government)	9,860
Total law	1,196
Total medical	2,405
Total religious	1,058
G. Total Libraries Counted (*)	30,717

Libraries in Regions Administered by the United States

A. Public Libraries	32*
Public libraries, excluding branches	12
Main public libraries that have branches	2
Public library branches	20
B. Academic Libraries	54*
Junior college libraries	7
University and college	47
Departmental	23
Law	2
C. Armed Forces Libraries	4*
Air force	1
Army	1
Navy	2

**Note:* Numbers followed by an asterisk are added to find "Total libraries counted" for each of the three geographic areas (United States, U.S.-administered regions, and Canada). The sum of the three totals is the "Grand total of libraries listed" in the *ALD* (shown in the Summary). For details on the count of libraries, see the preface to the fortieth edition of the *ALD*–*Ed.*

D. Government Libraries..... 8*
Law 1
Medical................. 2

E. Special Libraries (excluding public, academic, armed forces, and government)....... 15*
Law 1
Medical................. 4
Religious................ 1

F. Total Special Libraries (including public, academic, armed forces, and government........ 19
Total law................ 4
Total medical 6
Total religious 1

G. Total Libraries Counted (*) 113

Libraries in Canada

A. Public Libraries.......... 1,684*
Public libraries, excluding branches 760
Main public libraries that have branches...... 168
Public library branches.... 924

B. Academic Libraries....... 508*
Junior college libraries 141
Departmental.......... 41
Medical............... 2
Religious.............. 3
University and college 367
Departmental.......... 184
Law 20
Medical............... 25
Religious.............. 23

C. Government Libraries..... 346*
Law 19
Medical................. 3

D. Special Libraries (excluding public, academic, and government). 1,111*
Law 72
Medical................. 224
Religious................ 68

E. Total Special Libraries (including public, academic, and government). 1,250
Total law 111
Total medical 254
Total religious 94

F. Total Libraries Counted (*) 3,649

Summary

Total of U.S. Libraries........ 30,717
Total of Libraries Administered by the United States........ 113
Total of Canadian Libraries ... 3,649
Grand Total of Libraries Listed 34,479

Library Acquisition Expenditures, 1987–1988: Public, Academic, Special, and Government Libraries

For almost two decades, the R. R. Bowker Company has been compiling statistics on public and academic library acquisition expenditures (Tables 1 and 2) from information reported in the *American Library Directory* (*ALD*). Since 1987, statistics also have been compiled for special and government libraries (Tables 3 and 4). The information in Tables 1-4 is taken from the forty-first edition of the directory (1988) and in most cases reflects expenditures for the 1987–1988 period. The total number of libraries listed in the forty-first edition of *ALD* is as follows: 9,094 public libraries; 4,647 academic libraries; 8,886 special libraries; and 1,683 government libraries.

Understanding the Tables

Number of libraries includes only those libraries in *ALD* that reported annual acquisition expenditures (7,217 public libraries; 3,326 academic libraries; 3,341 special libraries; 866 government libraries). Libraries that reported annual income but not expenditures are not included in the count. Academic libraries include university, college, and junior college libraries. Special academic libraries, such as law and medical libraries, that reported acquisition expenditures separately from the institution's main library are counted as independent libraries.

Total acquisition expenditures for a given state is always greater than the sum of the categories of expenditures. This is because the total acquisition expenditures amount also includes the expenditures of libraries that did not itemize by category.

Figures in *categories of expenditure* columns represent only those libraries that itemized expenditures. Libraries that reported a total acquisition expenditure amount but did not itemize are only represented in the total acquisition expenditures column.

Unspecified includes monies reported as not specifically for books, periodicals, audiovisual, microform, or binding (e.g., library materials). This column also includes monies reported for categories in combination, for example, audiovisual *and* microform. When libraries report only total acquisition expenditures without itemizing by category, the total amount is not reflected as unspecified.

Special Note for 1987–1988: Users of the tables will note that the total number of libraries as well as the state-by-state totals in Tables 1–4 are somewhat lower for 1987–1988 than for previous years. Because of an earlier deadline for return of 1987–1988 questionnaires, data for many libraries received after the deadline could not be included in the tables. Despite the decrease in the number of libraries, however, the percentages of acquisition expenditures for 1987–1988 remain consistent with those of previous years.

Table 1 / Public Library Acquisition Expenditures

			Categories of Expenditure			
State	**Number of Libraries**	**Total Acquisition Expenditures**	**Books**	**Other Print Materials**	**Periodicals**	**Manuscripts & Archives**
Alabama	95	$ 5,375,411	$ 2,962,118	$ 35,280	$ 428,705	$ 519
Alaska	25	1,967,120	891,124	116,812	187,666	–
Arizona	65	9,812,217	5,344,572	77,574	747,507	16,000
Arkansas	30	2,146,679	995,794	9,354	125,368	3,000
California	184	62,088,375	37,601,608	355,618	7,107,987	26,000
Colorado	97	9,754,186	7,075,500	19,505	839,809	21,996
Connecticut	136	10,298,529	5,962,907	24,849	843,608	550
Delaware	22	1,388,986	578,782	44	87,632	–
District of Columbia	2	28,389,000	1,322,651	–	167,349	–
Florida	111	20,936,854	12,547,423	56,701	2,394,694	2,000
Georgia	50	12,245,024	6,420,592	16,028	435,473	–
Hawaii	2	2,255,159	1,559,468	–	396,983	–
Idaho	75	1,882,302	1,126,996	2,664	130,388	–
Illinois	504	38,837,828	18,751,201	246,206	3,436,940	582
Indiana	196	14,869,269	8,432,219	57,439	1,337,140	4,100
Iowa	325	6,415,109	3,793,192	36,942	539,224	–
Kansas	208	6,786,681	3,445,925	471,790	571,051	1,456
Kentucky	103	4,553,074	3,050,310	4,156	343,568	79
Louisiana	58	7,707,475	4,885,857	6,500	754,806	–
Maine	132	2,271,729	1,299,681	2,095	192,142	–
Maryland	29	14,726,783	12,007,035	272,108	685,690	50,100
Massachusetts	289	22,154,653	14,369,233	19,927	2,143,762	3,230
Michigan	300	29,685,610	14,330,007	139,899	2,425,896	–
Minnesota	120	11,711,285	7,227,490	148,005	873,328	–
Mississippi	42	3,392,217	1,462,480	17,496	230,834	–
Missouri	104	11,167,461	6,170,935	15,189	1,301,323	22
Montana	62	1,928,069	1,069,146	10,237	112,846	200
Nebraska	151	3,149,609	1,542,177	7,066	301,134	–
Nevada	21	2,360,826	1,608,903	81,377	264,702	–
New Hampshire	163	2,732,602	1,497,958	10,133	163,764	150
New Jersey	267	40,001,148	13,149,654	309,523	2,220,619	8,600
New Mexico	44	2,750,678	933,188	430	201,269	3,280
New York	579	77,490,553	57,867,593	330,800	5,079,959	20,047
North Carolina	102	13,338,135	8,288,392	32,419	1,122,802	582
North Dakota	23	846,538	511,195	340	81,566	–
Ohio	214	40,406,862	25,331,523	147,541	4,214,392	658
Oklahoma	62	5,929,751	3,702,513	6,556	624,702	–
Oregon	86	6,639,467	3,537,037	9,300	605,208	–
Pennsylvania	340	20,538,870	11,541,562	277,952	2,155,006	200
Rhode Island	44	2,359,178	1,675,916	6,180	263,291	6,000
South Carolina	37	5,340,871	3,663,842	5,996	463,733	100
South Dakota	49	1,594,736	806,100	850	132,727	–
Tennessee	90	6,924,850	4,444,206	56,211	614,754	250
Texas	342	33,746,967	18,785,683	194,966	3,289,361	652
Utah	35	3,593,895	2,382,603	41,104	213,454	500
Vermont	131	1,669,200	862,061	2,756	105,661	9,103
Virginia	81	26,319,438	20,024,389	62,395	1,466,747	249
Washington	65	14,653,884	7,501,321	39,918	1,526,567	–
West Virginia	71	2,647,046	1,635,025	9,800	234,249	10,000
Wisconsin	312	12,515,879	6,785,463	102,654	1,081,317	2,160
Wyoming	24	2,128,460	943,449	25,291	102,962	500
Pacific Islands	1	102,000	80,000	5,000	14,000	–
Puerto Rico	2	219,049	192,537	–	16,263	–
Virgin Islands	1	78,188	43,338	–	30,000	–
Total U.S.	7,217	$768,040,966	$431,443,593	$4,401,728	$61,939,413	$285,753
Estimated Percent of Acquisition			71.55	.73	10.27	.05

Table 1 / Public Library Acquisition Expenditures *(cont.)*

Categories of Expenditure						
AV Materials	AV Equipment	Microform	Machine-Readable Materials	Preservation	Database Fees	Unspecified
$ 377,256	$ 28,047	$ 319,353	$ 9,912	$ 92,413	$ 21,627	$ 270,405
172,787	17,425	190,153	6,975	21,425	36,731	6,000
372,774	42,628	61,088	75,483	152,082	249,341	1,836,039
27,295	500	27,230	850	10,267	58,492	52,882
3,520,444	115,923	885,397	168,413	630,299	928,721	868,079
334,094	78,071	64,660	103,546	56,367	151,488	10,355
663,929	73,364	113,670	22,390	57,963	300,951	161,853
25,726	7,412	5,138	18,000	1,030	6,286	5,522
40,000	–	–	–	–	–	–
1,044,072	44,408	458,202	41,789	128,491	114,683	76,695
233,348	65,932	87,275	–	47,337	14,376	30,887
258,604	9,798	9,878	–	–	–	–
78,606	6,998	38,849	12,007	22,548	86,894	3,565
2,339,530	303,744	548,827	67,424	317,253	486,170	276,758
1,148,835	127,842	256,772	76,760	137,075	143,665	188,388
393,790	64,568	58,141	77,242	32,395	93,093	72,727
251,589	75,514	748,245	22,416	40,901	99,550	228,486
324,639	24,648	72,956	4,894	27,936	86,053	111,488
349,902	41,188	51,970	4,930	84,959	30,585	11,827
44,140	3,774	18,221	1,704	31,533	35,740	6,335
1,158,203	15,173	105,946	32,490	85,372	33,521	45,384
854,402	85,808	160,394	37,624	73,702	169,643	241,289
1,406,859	87,753	170,254	62,606	181,467	356,617	521,423
696,700	49,790	177,344	220,250	57,999	234,560	26,195
184,245	16,046	22,028	8,146	20,477	9,920	15,243
663,455	69,312	271,517	38,518	81,635	88,910	172,137
12,622	5,780	5,295	3,560	3,797	33,442	174,469
104,924	14,908	22,280	2,010	12,797	83,201	47,619
2,439	–	20,500	4,150	3,514	13,500	22,851
80,204	19,562	37,615	6,568	24,487	1,440	38,690
954,058	141,757	348,434	145,150	174,952	387,609	17,598,233
67,975	5,709	12,255	1,868	12,337	164,215	150
3,062,732	227,875	795,197	140,843	463,326	519,163	724,339
787,834	150,679	162,077	76,322	116,894	108,634	129,981
41,219	5,100	11,600	2,000	6,576	22,000	–
4,290,497	167,244	877,131	149,227	622,637	359,455	136,592
355,334	21,249	104,063	11,833	50,463	192,619	150,931
249,260	3,861	66,083	4,352	38,056	1,015,939	13,685
947,740	105,148	727,138	41,060	270,048	389,953	1,122,224
108,446	15,814	38,830	14,680	27,303	20,271	2,300
316,830	39,889	41,986	1,010	52,735	24,247	61,273
173,853	17,285	21,716	3,921	9,358	199,585	24,774
494,806	21,800	114,998	3,798	63,578	82,987	117,926
1,713,332	222,257	419,682	123,248	323,233	216,063	819,417
281,736	83,943	51,822	1,600	31,948	103,166	137,394
30,123	1,221	21,080	1,300	9,200	500	8,095
804,232	152,270	396,919	72,740	126,527	130,212	396,276
446,632	32,090	101,520	23,589	32,950	164,269	41,016
229,029	40,985	15,063	2,153	20,541	5,290	116,692
834,992	57,585	113,366	57,992	80,308	383,282	840,709
72,366	5,960	17,956	12,238	20,597	11,970	27,489
–	–	–	–	–	–	–
–	–	–	–	–	–	–
–	4,850	–	–	–	–	–
$39,523,530	$4,515,311	$10,009,415	$2,173,411	$7,368,210	$9,177,284	$32,178,973
6.55	.75	1.66	.36	1.22	1.52	5.34

Table 2 / Academic Library Acquisition Expenditures

State	Number of Libraries	Total Acquisition Expenditures	Categories of Expenditure: Books	Other Print Materials	Periodicals	Manuscripts & Archives
Alabama	51	$ 13,802,426	$ 4,755,447	$ 54,805	$ 6,363,212	$ 2,579
Alaska	7	2,197,060	769,856	–	826,691	500
Arizona	26	11,844,352	4,509,004	326,515	4,936,900	683
Arkansas	32	6,966,937	1,989,412	43,525	3,285,409	45,312
California	241	108,922,696	41,428,538	1,044,089	41,857,476	38,564
Colorado	50	13,356,572	4,497,551	91,821	6,216,837	500
Connecticut	62	23,366,780	7,276,976	1,356,581	8,871,096	1,215,678
Delaware	11	4,310,275	2,090,609	21,718	1,745,394	50
District of Columbia	32	16,010,256	6,005,101	307,266	6,373,445	16,976
Florida	87	29,645,030	10,629,618	216,063	10,217,182	22,179
Georgia	68	18,104,376	4,961,161	39,243	7,940,363	157,982
Hawaii	14	4,934,561	1,355,416	6,771	2,119,340	–
Idaho	10	3,547,382	1,307,199	10,332	1,659,195	–
Illinois	124	46,800,806	15,257,774	300,036	19,425,666	3,600
Indiana	66	21,013,814	7,100,617	530,408	9,885,285	20,590
Iowa	53	13,628,863	4,426,608	31,906	6,472,280	52,750
Kansas	51	11,026,832	4,046,961	74,129	5,012,592	23,629
Kentucky	52	13,128,019	4,239,763	723,445	5,669,834	1,500
Louisiana	39	14,412,057	4,540,343	2,163	7,522,099	3,344
Maine	25	4,329,954	1,784,177	183,019	1,877,931	6,000
Maryland	54	19,858,645	6,205,705	421,308	7,586,553	500
Massachusetts	117	52,410,623	20,985,746	2,188,855	20,528,509	16,785
Michigan	94	29,777,936	8,441,634	114,978	11,172,095	24,384
Minnesota	64	18,892,322	7,066,690	607,011	8,034,945	9,104
Mississippi	36	7,681,815	1,810,740	107,982	3,440,526	21,564
Missouri	84	21,087,274	5,556,848	289,908	8,284,367	9,508
Montana	16	2,405,343	633,491	11,840	1,491,985	1,000
Nebraska	32	7,351,416	2,027,841	26,730	3,636,717	468
Nevada	10	2,865,718	973,212	1,871	1,155,897	–
New Hampshire	26	6,324,058	2,203,857	1,100	3,526,522	–
New Jersey	74	22,912,717	5,876,733	263,856	6,321,991	–
New Mexico	24	5,803,678	1,884,157	6,750	2,969,157	–
New York	207	87,179,303	24,997,530	1,463,428	30,600,637	42,196
North Carolina	106	33,859,331	11,462,495	127,966	13,527,996	7,843
North Dakota	16	2,778,706	824,365	16,000	1,549,702	–
Ohio	143	40,950,136	14,266,089	123,592	18,726,399	10,899
Oklahoma	45	10,940,304	3,396,993	45,983	4,923,043	1,000
Oregon	41	11,524,146	3,059,214	4,948	5,511,315	1,400
Pennsylvania	176	47,776,809	14,539,971	146,469	20,162,673	28,858
Rhode Island	15	6,268,571	2,611,467	5,000	2,868,362	5,000
South Carolina	54	11,463,779	3,245,131	441,136	4,005,333	5,012
South Dakota	18	2,515,501	757,206	160,459	1,133,935	1,500
Tennessee	74	18,491,010	5,538,507	220,792	7,703,178	6,300
Texas	161	59,893,787	17,078,616	656,649	19,556,289	48,014
Utah	12	10,734,260	1,926,065	230,980	3,066,646	15,000
Vermont	23	3,918,805	1,522,712	800	1,828,143	750
Virginia	79	29,472,407	10,746,867	108,281	14,028,295	16,400
Washington	51	16,646,622	4,822,261	171,038	7,867,827	20,470
West Virginia	28	5,061,511	1,714,206	51,810	2,357,535	988
Wisconsin	74	22,439,153	9,787,538	83,313	7,864,888	4,500
Wyoming	8	3,594,386	1,622,381	–	1,684,477	–
Pacific Islands	2	202,188	40,000	–	78,000	–
Puerto Rico	34	4,834,023	1,938,948	3,000	2,163,536	–
Virgin Islands	2	406,729	93,000	1,600	58,500	–
Total U.S.	3,326	$1,131,213,080	$367,497,568	$13,969,915	$458,293,554	$1,913,532
Estimated Percent of Acquisition			37.83	1.44	47.18	.20

Table 2 / Academic Library Acquisition Expenditures (*cont.*)

Categories of Expenditure						
AV Materials	AV Equipment	Microform	Machine-Readable Materials	Preservation	Database Fees	Unspecified
$ 207,050	$ 161,020	$ 329,676	$ 4,255	$ 482,726	$ 219,174	$ 447,224
20,545	3,500	13,752	1,500	90,489	155,792	81,858
227,186	116,969	229,044	21,329	543,726	77,056	46,924
60,783	43,791	186,418	12,712	167,803	147,421	51,893
1,155,175	1,105,504	1,966,842	302,660	4,927,077	1,119,043	5,445,621
138,871	65,226	345,944	91,523	295,109	121,955	54,019
117,625	58,217	1,287,571	14,893	1,120,438	400,698	161,974
21,248	59,537	59,200	28,920	156,840	47,850	33,916
187,624	58,112	299,789	28,496	226,878	159,667	108,563
638,910	397,962	516,357	60,074	713,008	299,802	239,277
200,144	155,809	572,397	179,639	304,698	331,190	357,786
68,717	243,792	122,853	8,410	209,886	31,200	190,061
29,138	21,994	50,148	1,200	84,603	47,239	168,644
1,040,326	732,233	515,002	228,270	1,195,285	742,922	342,853
181,506	210,880	218,006	14,308	869,404	310,938	216,168
269,860	114,094	181,470	32,836	309,669	101,898	135,899
150,702	66,975	77,978	20,962	389,290	306,322	36,401
216,501	191,690	192,219	39,296	415,173	468,864	376,517
73,964	79,158	163,955	26,761	709,938	188,119	302,973
83,833	59,387	94,462	3,100	97,438	48,612	27,308
359,322	120,939	346,750	109,811	552,580	216,606	1,772,074
820,082	326,165	675,264	162,142	1,213,732	912,331	291,322
358,133	416,875	382,387	56,503	763,837	397,241	254,949
411,375	317,862	164,541	27,724	988,187	209,827	380,284
151,942	145,699	249,626	44,849	84,740	200,777	31,179
293,460	123,766	432,917	162,377	324,328	273,486	2,224,461
25,909	2,500	17,743	12,000	61,970	61,817	–
96,609	108,898	42,772	1,964	254,566	171,440	100
63,978	41,642	84,293	825	61,268	12,763	–
53,257	34,041	109,972	29,362	141,234	40,053	90,833
298,937	145,747	333,604	46,600	572,004	290,513	915,392
119,812	34,981	33,340	4,050	154,834	116,535	124,318
853,767	933,446	1,301,345	324,668	2,805,858	1,295,552	4,392,850
955,181	639,149	665,402	55,522	745,366	489,434	244,814
34,270	16,475	53,646	–	39,842	74,755	86,267
621,837	559,552	456,462	91,635	1,514,090	437,265	425,906
97,521	78,935	157,346	29,077	183,387	166,758	729,219
220,013	80,800	238,935	99,296	332,441	248,029	83,156
710,196	1,239,405	890,564	96,522	1,826,981	561,798	706,956
37,070	24,707	74,794	5,000	269,797	160,397	29,305
118,467	70,611	196,576	38,163	358,283	128,172	56,725
19,884	26,991	5,132	8,742	66,733	51,819	53,721
308,319	149,133	368,083	66,185	489,822	231,616	157,411
1,572,905	451,141	744,781	225,423	792,549	1,087,171	787,812
63,792	40,524	25,183	63,750	102,955	96,826	28,794
56,354	26,544	114,479	4,600	124,791	119,394	15,377
592,524	101,872	959,445	79,758	734,917	305,706	475,831
345,268	481,668	310,135	75,068	192,849	328,766	434,704
100,055	68,984	153,224	16,585	43,845	79,132	190,410
678,228	254,437	431,257	39,729	459,326	318,847	873,168
82,911	8,646	9,246	17,000	102,096	34,485	1,739
20,000	–	15,000	–	1,000	5,000	26,188
193,603	87,630	47,968	45	136,472	32,650	40,736
500	–	5,000	–	8,000	675	–
$17,004,351	$11,709,162	$17,903,026	$3,238,869	$32,927,293	$15,645,417	$31,278,212
1.75	1.21	1.84	.33	3.39	1.61	3.22

Table 3 / Special Library Acquisition Expenditures

State	Number of Libraries	Total Acquisition Expenditures	Books	Other Print Materials	Periodicals	Manuscripts & Archives
			Categories of Expenditure			
Alabama	17	$ 946,019	$ 187,168	$ –	$ 478,601	$ –
Alaska	3	5,220	1,600	–	400	–
Arizona	45	1,522,338	258,070	146,645	238,591	3,050
Arkansas	7	119,445	14,400	–	8,500	368
California	266	17,559,397	3,901,413	316,692	5,200,877	42,924
Colorado	59	2,230,180	471,140	3,933	628,057	–
Connecticut	70	2,757,835	689,287	22,315	845,682	45,706
Delaware	10	372,075	83,700	–	92,075	–
District of Columbia	80	6,984,234	2,106,633	12,460	1,923,100	5,300
Florida	80	2,345,035	739,088	10,603	664,564	17,300
Georgia	40	2,722,730	257,165	217,971	202,448	238
Hawaii	17	550,560	93,796	1,668	264,483	1,500
Idaho	10	131,090	25,700	–	37,700	–
Illinois	163	9,644,295	2,007,206	550,339	2,938,146	66,450
Indiana	62	1,342,247	264,662	7,800	278,017	200
Iowa	36	1,104,844	270,909	17,970	270,449	750
Kansas	26	345,451	118,896	3,470	89,273	–
Kentucky	23	657,654	235,314	5,500	109,404	20,000
Louisiana	19	464,587	60,492	1,925	155,379	–
Maine	26	674,347	141,910	900	287,677	2,065
Maryland	77	1,960,217	713,522	15,250	452,944	3,200
Massachusetts	157	8,385,556	2,543,181	172,608	2,020,976	15,450
Michigan	92	5,924,396	1,040,601	179,840	1,381,371	1,250
Minnesota	63	2,746,529	775,890	230,669	674,623	13,250
Mississippi	7	133,068	29,000	1,350	79,250	1,000
Missouri	55	4,302,643	698,816	53,150	1,667,361	4,365
Montana	12	156,982	22,154	1,000	34,764	–
Nebraska	20	349,442	93,794	5,133	17,021	–
Nevada	9	141,735	43,300	5,028	46,352	400
New Hampshire	12	475,710	173,367	249	210,060	2,800
New Jersey	94	5,305,023	1,561,577	82,850	1,939,689	32,000
New Mexico	34	1,248,267	819,925	25,550	114,699	120
New York	342	20,807,985	3,180,887	695,994	5,163,041	14,920
North Carolina	42	1,154,007	169,424	3,725	322,641	–
North Dakota	6	142,668	43,108	2,400	56,123	–
Ohio	140	6,629,916	1,666,982	349,277	1,599,051	11,800
Oklahoma	19	603,123	68,574	1,661	350,930	300
Oregon	27	515,597	82,785	10,450	61,190	–
Pennsylvania	191	7,049,354	1,794,675	452,953	2,232,260	21,003
Rhode Island	15	183,412	58,354	75	69,930	1,100
South Carolina	22	572,680	138,653	1,400	223,482	2,000
South Dakota	14	207,554	64,968	2,000	63,937	–
Tennessee	42	2,946,517	785,851	36,000	1,445,598	1,100
Texas	120	6,368,370	1,492,430	138,376	1,662,045	12,800
Utah	10	362,350	18,670	–	50,630	–
Vermont	19	223,671	31,949	3,649	33,680	900
Virginia	86	2,943,966	703,781	70,349	759,415	42,738
Washington	47	1,953,276	304,803	16,483	863,733	3,538
West Virginia	17	673,001	180,056	3,168	318,874	–
Wisconsin	83	2,271,192	323,866	14,572	511,285	1,050
Wyoming	9	66,237	22,600	85	25,650	300
Pacific Islands	1	80,686	77,195	–	729	–
Puerto Rico	1	5,500	1,500	–	–	–
Virgin Islands	1	7,650	3,500	150	1,500	–
Total U.S.	3,341	$168,700,209	$38,539,750	$4,228,452	$53,706,138	$431,735
Estimated Percent of Acquisition			31.63	3.47	44.07	.35

Table 3 / Special Library Acquisition Expenditures *(cont.)*

Categories of Expenditure						
AV Materials	AV Equipment	Microform	Machine-Readable Materials	Preservation	Database Fees	Unspecified
$ 680	$ –	$ 12,000	$ 3,000	$ 23,200	$ 50,500	$ 500
–	–	–	–	1,500	–	–
12,374	5,000	19,050	2,456	18,680	237,080	2,200
6,100	–	–	–	1,077	–	–
135,346	85,465	124,145	188,527	203,315	1,315,798	777,519
79,111	18,280	8,500	15,225	33,738	221,943	105,694
94,431	46,570	94,275	11,914	69,011	183,724	28,300
2,070	900	3,900	–	11,430	7,000	14,000
24,247	12,011	76,052	22,840	41,499	549,691	22,250
41,518	24,574	19,974	12,594	22,966	191,195	47,423
14,179	14,784	24,246	11,100	153,549	49,173	25,243
4,791	–	1,905	–	22,677	29,446	550
–	500	470	600	3,600	51,520	500
71,211	40,143	509,899	41,000	484,255	409,527	192,205
35,992	6,129	8,500	60	15,450	99,579	4,000
43,346	10,000	5,450	4,000	18,390	151,651	8,830
3,906	6,000	2,400	3,778	9,169	15,802	643
21,230	4,500	5,600	4,988	9,300	28,815	272
6,151	300	650	–	6,600	10,710	1,000
26,344	11,915	20,395	7,190	11,410	37,600	1,637
97,884	47,655	45,721	1,070	27,353	169,564	30,650
81,031	74,522	72,740	30,400	179,790	753,298	112,173
85,936	64,240	83,350	36,292	77,077	277,252	50,053
52,306	31,102	73,200	25,265	23,215	225,053	26,350
1,800	1,500	2,500	10,000	1,500	82	–
66,465	12,872	67,663	2,500	180,236	76,570	92,819
6,000	–	540	–	5,524	5,458	1,700
3,615	1,000	1,350	525	3,443	12,974	1,146
1,038	9,205	8,334	545	6,800	3,780	15,953
1,300	–	7,811	17,878	18,470	16,694	2,000
61,097	44,958	125,762	43,818	65,005	356,600	24,200
29,891	17,607	500	200	46,760	85,036	8,750
186,439	42,984	171,093	46,204	468,869	1,689,078	926,029
44,224	6,300	3,200	–	23,708	151,571	31,295
7,800	1,345	7,500	4,195	4,247	14,990	–
98,060	57,573	95,780	67,825	167,277	373,608	182,757
5,250	20,000	11,078	–	2,350	2,405	300
25,318	8,000	8,325	–	5,300	20,800	729
117,929	86,133	125,035	48,350	150,145	692,737	181,940
2,316	1,700	1,000	–	10,077	15,360	–
22,970	6,020	22,000	20	6,814	18,251	2,000
1,237	1,000	3,100	–	838	16,184	2,549
16,956	8,407	13,938	2,573	29,743	59,422	953
72,542	24,722	58,881	18,319	129,399	737,879	95,535
2,000	6,000	500	–	200	2,000	40,000
4,400	25,800	1,000	190	3,400	6,801	1,401
42,845	8,271	96,839	40,850	51,076	244,931	200,392
17,900	16,500	19,455	14,000	54,168	69,605	21,440
9,375	6,000	9,000	–	4,305	109,116	842
189,233	32,650	31,379	2,900	34,369	152,096	97,479
23	–	3,000	–	587	8,457	–
1,487	–	1,275	–	–	–	–
–	–	–	–	500	–	3,500
500	500	1,000	–	500	–	–
$2,293,372	$1,081,137	$2,421,795	$856,104	$3,213,366	$11,348,932	$3,735,098
1.88	.89	1.99	.70	2.64	9.31	3.07

Table 4 / Government Library Acquisition Expenditures

			Categories of Expenditure			
State	Number of Libraries	Total Acquisition Expenditures	Books	Other Print Materials	Periodicals	Manuscripts & Archives
Alabama	8	$ 323,117	$ 147,318	$ 55	$ 113,095	$ –
Alaska	11	863,550	91,996	700	744,535	–
Arizona	18	1,140,275	257,550	351,500	111,560	–
Arkansas	3	157,004	47,655	–	60,931	–
California	62	6,274,878	1,688,899	396,162	1,383,141	103,500
Colorado	17	1,016,525	181,465	4,720	412,756	–
Connecticut	7	126,997	19,305	–	33,840	–
Delaware	3	196,900	37,933	–	106,000	–
District of Columbia	36	10,881,735	2,895,211	48,100	2,746,748	–
Florida	36	1,981,598	611,182	35,600	610,287	10,000
Georgia	12	958,711	141,940	20,818	427,571	181
Hawaii	5	453,335	421,407	–	9,600	1,000
Idaho	1	28,000	4,900	–	18,000	–
Illinois	16	1,211,682	160,972	1,200	302,300	–
Indiana	10	396,869	77,357	–	38,571	–
Iowa	9	232,859	84,180	4,154	84,036	20
Kansas	8	482,552	114,601	82,091	97,926	500
Kentucky	4	500,932	12,730	3,000	55,500	–
Louisiana	8	529,807	100,405	–	248,443	–
Maine	3	279,807	39,201	–	179,184	–
Maryland	26	11,275,623	1,766,962	80,000	4,760,635	8,600
Massachusetts	21	3,370,518	2,736,054	32,000	190,723	–
Michigan	11	528,089	130,825	600	101,914	–
Minnesota	11	1,269,879	118,275	463,400	435,254	16,000
Mississippi	9	482,694	221,834	–	73,500	–
Missouri	8	396,382	148,732	–	132,800	–
Montana	10	449,652	203,434	1,036	120,111	–
Nebraska	4	83,950	10,050	–	14,900	–
Nevada	6	595,809	332,812	–	53,345	–
New Hampshire	2	78,830	10,750	–	13,542	–
New Jersey	12	754,756	235,680	15,000	102,520	–
New Mexico	8	353,448	276,348	450	40,750	200
New York	57	3,867,808	1,323,364	2,750	439,352	–
North Carolina	10	971,602	302,249	–	398,632	–
North Dakota	1	1,800	600	–	1,200	–
Ohio	22	2,110,131	600,196	8,450	605,674	–
Oklahoma	7	229,378	91,905	–	47,642	–
Oregon	11	793,806	155,985	560	317,547	–
Pennsylvania	34	2,164,233	1,192,326	2,650	213,645	–
Rhode Island	4	292,204	32,589	–	5,515	–
South Carolina	5	197,387	90,572	257	15,808	–
South Dakota	8	122,984	35,063	–	45,469	–
Tennessee	7	248,973	74,116	4,000	97,157	–
Texas	19	1,117,224	500,567	189,628	244,363	3,000
Utah	6	126,100	30,400	–	69,200	–
Vermont	5	71,956	22,319	1,759	25,806	–
Virginia	18	1,229,614	307,459	7,840	483,893	–
Washington	19	1,381,308	517,846	800	153,730	10,000
West Virginia	4	474,000	194,300	200	48,200	–
Wisconsin	20	718,187	373,604	3,850	139,235	–
Wyoming	7	182,569	133,653	1,000	22,503	–
Puerto Rico	4	770,123	294,340	152,968	267,415	–
Total U.S.	866	$86,887,761	$23,884,786	$2,072,655	$25,471,738	$158,501
Estimated Percent of Acquisition			35.32	3.06	37.67	.23

Table 4 / Government Library Acquisition Expenditures *(cont.)*

Categories of Expenditure						
AV Materials	**AV Equipment**	**Microform**	**Machine-Readable Materials**	**Preservation**	**Database Fees**	**Unspecified**
$ 22,336	$ –	$ 3,000	$ –	$ 2,826	$ 16,686	$ –
295	6,393	1,632	300	8,745	3,925	1,609
13,350	2,400	25,586	500	3,500	45,400	26,166
16,362	–	5,000	–	–	23,082	974
84,441	9,842	90,373	9,466	71,370	80,796	135,466
21,914	4,738	4,115	1,000	9,600	100,536	–
20,549	–	1,792	–	2,478	5,081	3,000
–	–	6,000	–	900	–	–
41,000	1,500	227,000	33,500	117,072	1,191,904	953,100
22,798	13,500	20,360	25,180	19,707	61,410	37,464
1,259	19,034	9,855	1,500	93,918	23,028	5,107
400	–	171	–	–	2,000	–
75	–	–	–	2,700	–	2,325
6,880	55,550	–	2,600	9,200	26,200	8,600
11,780	–	4,994	–	500	2,179	3,000
4,884	6,252	–	–	6,205	2,000	2,607
4,000	1,000	–	–	13,745	7,189	–
2,150	–	12,100	–	2,500	6,400	9,700
2,852	1,393	3,545	50	9,815	12,663	6,401
8,145	5,300	6,225	–	5,850	21,500	13,702
1,249,392	30,800	113,195	15,825	1,270,550	818,357	935,657
21,389	13,700	24,416	6,120	144,258	34,832	35,261
27,601	2,975	6,100	100	3,821	8,358	–
1,600	6,148	50,800	2,000	10,550	68,050	1,600
5,000	2,200	15,000	–	5,600	6,710	400
28,800	–	400	–	6,300	13,300	11,150
11,830	–	16,570	4,045	11,500	9,120	9,815
50,000	8,000	–	–	1,000	–	–
5,833	–	2,519	–	2,370	37,930	1,000
1,750	–	19,500	–	30,850	2,073	–
5,000	–	5,000	–	8,900	53,000	–
7,200	–	25,000	700	2,700	–	–
31,850	8,400	77,167	–	18,427	36,700	29,100
35,000	11,000	34,678	–	5,193	141,000	–
–	–	–	–	–	–	–
19,066	58,217	37,456	3,500	2,250	45,293	13,042
1,309	3,084	25,875	–	1,200	3,200	2,962
20,727	7,090	14,533	–	2,700	141,031	2,175
27,718	–	29,500	9,000	19,775	54,288	90,000
–	–	–	–	5,400	1,000	–
6,000	–	–	–	700	44,000	–
10,680	5,923	4,750	–	750	600	2,439
19,000	6,300	–	1,500	8,230	–	–
37,263	7,679	20,171	–	14,993	63,582	5,400
1,500	–	2,000	–	6,000	16,900	–
300	–	6,300	–	6,000	200	–
21,565	10,000	136,115	20,000	9,080	64,825	2,029
14,709	1,500	5,492	–	29,200	53,311	–
–	–	30,500	–	7,000	31,000	1,800
34,310	4,960	17,435	–	4,400	34,546	1,883
3,633	–	–	–	–	3,057	–
11,000	2,000	20,000	2,000	17,000	2,000	–
$2,364,910	$419,178	$2,087,155	$277,101	$2,251,285	$5,358,820	$3,279,995
3.50	.62	3.09	.41	3.33	7.92	4.85

Price Indexes for School and Academic Library Acquisitions

Kent Halstead
Research Associates of Washington, 2605 Klingle Rd. N.W., Washington, DC 20008

The School Price Index (SPI) and the Higher Education Price Index (HEPI) report changes in the prices of goods and services purchased by elementary and secondary schools (SPI) and colleges and universities (HEPI) for their current operations.* Of relevance to the library community are the components of the indexes that report price changes in new acquisitions. These data can be used to project estimated future funding required to offset anticipated price increases. Also, past expenditures can be compared with price movements to ascertain whether spending has kept pace with price level changes. A decline in constant dollars means that the library's acquisitions budget has lost real purchasing power.

The Indexes and Database

Tables 1 and 2 show prices and indexes of new acquisitions for school and academic libraries. In both tables, the Library Acquisitions Price Index (LAPI) is a weighted aggregative index number with "fixed," or "constant," weights, often referred to as a "market basket" index. The LAPI measures price change by repricing each year and comparing the aggregate costs of the library materials bought by institutions in the base year. For college and university libraries the base year for establishing the market basket weights is 1971–1972; for elementary and secondary schools the 1973–1974 buying pattern has been used. Because the academic index was first published nearly a decade earlier, its composition is not as sophisticated as the index for schools.

Both the amount and the quality of the various items that compose the acquisitions market basket must remain constant so that only the effects of price changes are reflected. Weights are changed infrequently—only when there is clear evidence of a shift in the relative *amounts* of various items purchased, or when new items are introduced. Institutions with substantially different buying patterns may wish to construct a tailored composite index using weights based on their own budget proportions. However, once established for a selected base year, the weights must be held constant.

The indexes for each acquisitions category (books, periodicals, and so on) are calculated with FY 1983 as the base. This means that current prices are expressed as a percentage of prices for 1983. An index of 110 means that prices have increased 10 percent since the base year. The index may be converted to any desired base period by dividing each index number to be converted by the index for the desired base period.

Sources of the price series are listed in the tables. Prices for library materials are generally quoted for the calendar year. The corresponding fiscal years are also listed for budget year identifications.

*See Kent Halstead, *Inflation Measures for Schools and Colleges*, National Institute of Education, U.S. Department of Education, 1983, 183 pp. Available from the Superintendent of Documents, U.S. Government Printing Office, Washington, DC 20402, Document #065-000-00186-01, $6 includes shipping. Available in microfiche from the ERIC Document Reproduction Service, Box 190, Arlington, VA 22210, ED #230083, $.98 plus $.22 postage. The HEPI and SPI are updated annually by Research Associates of Washington.

Table 1 / Average Prices and Indexes for Elementary and Secondary School Library Acquisitions, FYs 1976–1988

Year (1983 = 100)		Hardcover Books					Mass Market Paperback Books				
		Elementary[1]		Secondary[2]			Elementary[1]		Secondary[2]		
Calendar	Fiscal	Av. Price	Index	Av. Price	Index	Total Index[3]	Av. Price	Index	Av. Price	Index	Total Index[4]
1975	1976	$ 5.82	65.6	$16.19	52.9	59.0	$1.07	53.0	$1.46	49.5	51.2
1976	1977	5.87	66.2	17.20	56.2	61.0	1.22	60.4	1.60	54.2	57.3
1977	1978	6.64	74.9	18.03	58.9	66.6	1.41	69.8	1.71	58.0	63.9
1978	1979	6.59	74.3	20.10	65.7	69.8	1.47	72.8	1.91	64.7	68.8
1979	1980	7.13	80.4	22.80	74.5	77.3	1.48	73.3	2.06	69.8	71.6
1980	1981	8.21	92.6	23.57	77.1	84.5	1.65*	81.7	2.50	84.7	83.2
1981	1982	8.29	93.5	26.63	83.3	88.2	1.79	88.6	2.65	89.8	89.2
1982	1983	8.87	100.0	30.34	100.0	100.0	2.02	100.0	2.95	100.0	100.0
1983	1984	9.70	109.4	31.19	102.0	105.5	2.24	110.9	3.13	106.1	108.5
1984	1985	10.11	114.0	29.82	97.5	105.4	2.28	112.9	3.38	114.6	113.7
1985	1986	9.89	111.5	31.44	102.8	107.0	2.67	132.2	3.59	121.7	127.0
1986	1987	10.51	118.5	32.43	106.0	112.0	2.71	134.2	3.87	131.2	132.7
1987	1988	11.59	130.7	35.35	115.6	122.8	2.80	138.6	3.98	134.9	136.8

Year		U.S. Periodicals					Audiovisual Materials							
		Elementary[5]		Secondary[6]			Microfilm[8]		16mm Film[9]		Videocassettes		Filmstrip[10]	
Calendar	Fiscal	Av. Price	Index	Av. Price	Index	Total Index[7]	Av. Price	Index	Av. Price	Index	Av. Price	Index	Av. Price	Index
1975	1976	4.69	47.4	$14.36	60.0	54.0	$.1190	54.5	$12.85	85.6	—	—	$73.91	90.6
1976	1977	5.32	53.7	15.24	63.7	58.9	.1335*	61.1	12.93	86.1	—	—	58.41	71.6
1977	1978	5.82	58.8	16.19	67.7	63.4	.1475*	67.5	13.95	92.9	—	—	76.26	93.4
1978	1979	6.34	64.0	17.26	72.1	68.3	.1612	73.8	12.56	83.7	—	—	62.31	76.3
1979	1980	6.70	67.7	18.28	76.4	72.2	.1750*	80.1	13.62	90.7	—	—	65.97	80.8
1980	1981	7.85	79.3	19.87	83.0	81.2	.1890*	86.5	12.03	80.1	$ 7.58	72.4	67.39	82.6
1981	1982	8.56	86.5	21.83	91.2	88.9	.2021	92.5	16.09	107.2	14.87	142.0	71.12	87.1
1982	1983	9.90	100.0	23.93	100.0	100.0	.2184	100.0	15.01	100.0	10.47	100.0	81.62	100.0
1983	1984	11.49	116.1	26.43	110.4	113.1	.2274	104.1	15.47	103.1	11.04	105.4	79.57	97.5
1984	1985	12.21	123.3	27.90	116.6	119.8	.2450	112.2	16.93	112.8	8.44	80.6	85.76	105.1
1985	1986	13.31	134.4	26.41	110.4	121.9	.2612	119.6	16.50	109.9	10.24	97.8	83.50	102.3
1986	1987	13.76	139.0	26.95	112.6	125.3	.2750	125.9	16.85	112.3	7.44	71.1	85.33	104.5
1987	1988	15.19	153.4	27.79	116.1	134.0	.2888	132.2	17.00	113.3	6.79	64.9	112.15	137.4

Table 1 / Average Prices and Indexes for Elementary and Secondary School Library Acquisitions, FYs 1976–1988 *(cont.)*

Year (1983 = 100)		Audiovisual Materials (cont.)						Free Textbooks to Students†				
		Prerecorded Cassette Tape		Multimedia Kits				Hardbound		Paperbound		
Calendar	Fiscal	Av. Price	Index	Av. Price	Index	Total Index[11]	Library Acquisitions Price Index[12]	Av. Price	Index	Av. Price	Index	Total Index[13]
1975	1976	$10.32	98.1	$140.25	NA	89.5	64.5	$4.10	57.7	$2.08	58.4	57.8
1976	1977	12.08	112.5	93.63	NA	76.1	63.8	4.67	65.7	2.27	63.8	65.3
1977	1978	10.63	99.0	93.65	NA	93.0	71.7	5.23	73.6	2.40	67.4	72.4
1978	1979	12.57	117.0	117.38	NA	79.9	71.8	5.78	81.3	2.70	75.8	80.2
1979	1980	12.58	117.1	85.70	NA	84.3	78.1	6.12	86.1	2.87	80.6	85.0
1980	1981	9.34	87.0	92.71	NA	81.9	83.5	6.42	90.3	3.05	85.3	89.4
1981	1982	12.48	116.2	46.99	NA	95.4	89.9	6.64	93.4	3.23	90.7	92.9
1982	1983	10.47	100.0	57.52	NA	100.0	100.0	7.11	100.0	3.56	100.0	100.0
1983	1984	11.23	104.6	Discontinued		99.2	105.1	7.80	109.7	3.75	105.3	108.9
1984	1985	9.99	93.0			103.5	107.1	8.40	118.1	4.05	113.8	117.3
1985	1986	8.99	83.7			101.6	108.6	9.12	128.1	—[a]	120.3	126.6
1986	1987	10.61	98.8			102.5	112.6	9.88	138.8	5.57	134.5	138.0
1987	1988	8.50	79.1			125.0	125.3	10.85	152.4	6.24	150.7	152.1

*Estimates

†Price series for free hardbound and paperbound textbooks, 1974–1984, was substantially altered in 1985.

[1]Juvenile book category (age 8 or younger, fiction).

[2]All book categories. The price for all book categories is considerably higher than the price of books selected for school libraries. However, the price trend for all books is considered parallel and is used as a proxy for a school library book price series, which is not available.

[3]Weighted average: elementary (K–6) books, 47.9 percent; secondary (7–12) books, 52.1 percent. Weights based on data reported in the National Center for Education Statistics, *Statistics of Public School Library Media Centers, 1973–1974.*

[4]Weighted average: elementary (K–6) paperback, 50.2 percent; secondary (7–12) paperback, 49.8 percent. Weights based on data reported in the National Center for Education Statistics, *Statistics of Public School Library Media Centers, 1973–1974.*

[5]Children's periodicals (approx. 75 titles).

[6]General interest periodicals (approx. 175 titles).

[7]Weighted average: elementary (K–6) periodicals, 47.9 percent; secondary (7–12) periodicals, 52.1 percent. Weights based on data reported in the National Center for Education Statistics, *Statistics of Public School Library Media Centers, 1973–1974.*

[8]Average price per foot, 35mm positive microfilm.

[9]Average cost per minute, color purchase.

[10]Average cost of filmstrip set (cassette).

[11]Weighted average: 16mm film, 12.3 percent; videocassettes, 7.9 percent; filmstrips, 73.5 percent; prerecorded tapes, 6.3 percent; multimedia kits, 25.9 percent. Based on industry sales data from *Survey of 1975 Educational Media Sales,* Association of Media Producers, Washington, D.C.

[12]Weighted average: hardcover books, 61.2 percent; paperback books, 3.6 percent; periodicals, 11.7 percent; microfilm, 3.3 percent; audiovisual materials, 21.2 percent. Weights based on data reported in the National Center for Education Statistics, *Statistics of Public School Library Media Centers, 1973–1974.*

[13]Weighted average: hardbound textbooks, 80.5 percent; softbound textbooks, 19.5 percent. Weights based on data for 1974 reported in *Trends in Textbook Markets—Status Reports*, Paine Webber Mitchell & Hutchins, Inc., New York.

[a]Change in database invalidates comparisons of current year price to previous series.

Sources: Prices of hardcover books, and of mass market paperback books before 1980, are based on books listed in *Publishers Weekly* Weekly Record for the calendar year with an imprint for the *same* year (usually cited as *preliminary* data). After 1980 data on mass market paperbacks are taken from *Paperbound Books in Print.* Not included in the hardcover category are government documents and certain multivolume encyclopedias. The average prices are compiled by the R. R. Bowker Company. Prices of U.S. periodicals are compiled by Norman B. Brown and Jane Phillips. Prices of microfilm are compiled by Imre T. Jarmy from the *Directory of Library Reprographic Services: A World Guide* and supplemental data. Prices of audiovisual materials are compiled by David B. Walch based on information derived from selected issues of *Choice, School Library Journal*, and *Booklist.* Prices of hardbound and softbound textbooks are from J. Kendrick Noble, Jr., *Trends in Textbook Markets—Status Report,* prepared for the Book Industry Study Group, Inc., published by Paine Webber Mitchell & Hutchins, Inc., New York. All prices, except for textbook prices, are published in Part 4 of *The Bowker Annual of Library and Book Trade Information.*

Table 2 / Average Prices and Indexes for College and University Library Acquisitions, FYs 1976–1988

Year (1983 = 100)		U.S. Hardcover Books		U.S. Periodicals		Foreign Monographs[1]		Library Acquisitions Price Index[3]
Calendar	Fiscal	Av. Price	Index[2]	Av. Price	Index[2]	Av. Price	Index[2]	
1975	1976	$16.19	53.5	$38.94	49.9	$ 7.59	63.7	53.6
1976	1977	17.20[a]	56.8	41.85	53.6	7.91	66.4	57.0
1977	1978	18.03	59.5	45.14	57.8	8.89	74.7	61.0
1978	1979	20.10	66.4	50.11	64.2	9.41	79.0	67.3
1979	1980	22.80	75.3	57.23	73.3	11.52	96.7	77.5
1980	1981	23.57	77.8	67.81	86.9	13.05	109.6	85.2
1981	1982	26.88	88.6	73.89	94.7	13.84	116.2	94.4
1982	1983	30.34	100.0	78.04	100.0	11.91	100.0	100.0
1983	1984	29.00[b]	102.8	82.47	105.7	12.09	101.5	103.6
1984	1985	29.96	106.2	86.10	110.3	11.78	98.9	107.5
1985	1986	31.77	112.6	92.32	118.3	11.66	97.9	112.6
1986	1987	33.66	119.3	104.69	134.2	13.52	113.5	123.6
1987	1988	36.93	130.9	117.75	150.9	15.94	133.8	138.1

[1]All hardcover books, paperbacks, and pamphlets purchased during the fiscal year by the Library of Congress from approximately 100 foreign countries.

[2]Indexes are not fixed-weight indexes; they reflect changes in the type and mix of books and periodicals from year to year. The fiscal year index refers to average price in the previous calendar year due to the normal time delay between published date and purchase.

[3]Weighted average based on the estimated proportion of the total acquisitions budget expended for each category. Weights used—U.S. hardcover books, 52 percent; U.S. periodicals, 34 percent; and foreign monographs, 14 percent.

[a]In 1976, *Publishers Weekly* reported a book price of $17.39 for an 18-month period (1976–1977). An adjusted value of $17.20 for calendar year 1976 was determined from the trend line.

[b]New price series introduced. FY 1984 index based on 1984 series price of $31.19.

Sources: Prices of hardcover books, 1974–1982, are published in *The Bowker Annual of Library and Book Trade Information,* R. R. Bowker, New York, based on books listed in the Weekly Record section of *Publishers Weekly* for the calendar year with an imprint for the same year. Not included are mass market paperbacks, government documents, and certain multivolume encyclopedias. Prices of hardcover books purchased by colleges and universities, 1983–present, are reported by Kathryn A. Soupiset, Trinity College, from book reviews appearing in *Choice.* U.S. periodicals are priced by the F. W. Faxon Co. and reported by F. F. Clasquin in an October issue of *Library Journal.* Foreign monographs are priced according to an unpublished price series prepared by the Library of Congress.

Library Buildings, 1988

Bette-Lee Fox
Managing Editor, *Library Journal*

Ann Burns and Michael Rogers
Staff Editors, *Library Journal*

Reginald E. Pruitt
Production Editor, *Library Journal*

Each year *LJ* editors approach the architectural issue with expectations of more and bigger projects and more funding than ever before. They are never disappointed. The 1988 report features 47 new academic projects (a 42 percent increase over 1987) and 238 public projects (98 new buildings and 140 additions and renovations) completed between July 1, 1987 and June 30, 1988. What continues to amaze is the number of buildings in progress (see Tables 8 and 9); 796 buildings will be completed within the next four to five years. The asterisked (*) projects in Tables 1–7 are those that were in progress in 1987. The largest academic project in 1988 was the Benjamin S. Rosenthal Library of Queens College of the City University of New York. Designed by the architectural firm of Gruzen Samton Steinglass, at a cost of $54.6 million, it occupies 252,000 square feet. The largest new public projects are the Kern County Library, Bakersfield, California ($19.5 million) and the Virginia Beach Central Library, Virginia ($12.3 million). The largest public additions and renovations are also in California: the City of Cerritos Public Library and the Redwood City Public Library, each about $8.2 million.

Perhaps it is in keeping with the pace of the 1980s that more libraries are being built in shopping malls. Several new and renovated projects are sharing space with merchants and boutiques. Most of the libraries find the locale ideal for patrons, and that use of the libraries has increased. Another, perhaps more unsettling fact is that several libraries have been built out of renovated churches.

Money for buildings is still predominantly from local government, amounting to more than $186 million. Total funding reached $243 million in 1988, up from $217 million in 1987. Money is definitely available, and the future of libraries appears bright as far as construction is concerned.

Note: Adapted from *Library Journal*, December 1988.

Table 1 / New Public Library Buildings, 1988

Symbol code: B–Branch library; BS–Branch and system headquarters; M–Main library; MS–Main and system headquarters; S–System headquarters; n/a–Not available

Community	Pop. in M	Code	Project Cost	Const. Cost	Gross Sq. Ft.	Sq.Ft. Cost	Equip. Cost	Site Cost	Other Costs	Volumes	Reader Seats	Federal Funds	State Funds	Local Funds	Gift Funds	Architect
ALABAMA																
* Auburn	28	M	$1,147,071	$947,290	12,835	$73.80	$131,781	Owned	$68,000	40,000	66	0	$154,400	$960,890	$31,781	Moss & Assocs.
* Birmingham	16	B	934,783	715,278	8,100	88.31	125,762	Owned	93,743	48,230	56	154,400	0	780,383	0	David Jones Jr.
* Hamilton	5	B	251,215	171,215	4,730	36.20	31,000	35,000	14,000	10,000	16	0	77,200	108,015	66,000	Barr, Tune, Wynne
CALIFORNIA																
* Bakersfield	511	M	19,480,000	13,015,000	127,000	102.48	3,130,000	2,345,000	990,000	500,000	445	0	0	17,980,000	1,500,000	Parsons Brinckerhoff . . .
Hawaiian Grdns	12	B	15,213	9,875	1,800	5.00	1,056	Leased	4,282	10,000	16	0	0	15,213	0	not reported
* Los Angeles	18	B	91,000	85,166	2,200	38.71	923	Leased	4,911	7,000	12	0	0	91,000	0	Starkman & Assocs.
* San Diego[1]	37	B	1,886,466	1,381,592	10,244	134.87	183,097	Owned	321,777	35,000	90	1,886,466	0	0	0	Rob W. Quigley
CONNECTICUT																
Marlborough	5	M	944,232	836,442	5,200	160.85	42,262	Owned	65,528	24,000	56	0	200,000	300,000	444,232	Galliher & Baier
FLORIDA																
* Casselberry	100	MS	3,365,303	2,158,307	50,000	43.17	441,536	346,633	418,827	150,000	193	0	0	3,365,303	0	Rogers, Lovelock & Fritz
Clearwater	50	B	1,210,000	970,000	15,000	64.67	175,000	Owned	65,000	70,000	65	0	0	1,210,000	0	Williams Architects
Crystal River	43	B	1,025,000	754,000	15,000	50.27	125,000	100,000	46,000	50,000	113	0	0	925,000	100,000	Alan R. Wolfe
* Edgewater	15	B	626,000	461,849	10,000	46.18	84,000	45,811	35,000	48,000	48	200,000	50,000	376,660	0	Dana A. Smith
Ft. Lauderdale[2]	85	B	3,079,357	1,347,759	14,500	92.95	254,357	1,411,241	66,000	70,000	105	0	0	3,079,357	0	Rodney North Green
Inverness	46	B	1,015,000	754,000	15,000	50.27	125,000	90,000	46,000	50,000	113	0	0	1,015,000	0	Alan R. Wolfe
* Lake Helen	5	B	210,321	143,518	3,458	41.50	25,000	11,000	30,803	15,000	24	100,000	20,000	36,000	54,321	James L. Mitchell
* Lake Mary	25	B	1,178,479	938,032	12,000	78.17	79,114	Owned	161,333	68,000	65	0	0	1,178,479	0	Rogers, Lovelock & Fritz
* Longwood	51	B	1,416,084	867,242	12,000	72.24	108,559	300,000	140,283	127,000	73	0	0	1,416,084	0	Rogers, Lovelock & Fritz
* Oviedo	50	B	1,229,884	882,115	12,000	73.51	77,624	130,129	140,016	93,000	59	0	0	1,229,884	0	Rogers, Lovelock & Fritz
* Palm Harbor	55	M	1,100,000	650,000	16,000	40.63	130,000	250,000	70,000	100,000	110	0	200,000	770,000	130,000	Prindle Assocs.
* Sanford	31	B	1,168,522	876,068	12,000	73.01	57,712	130,005	104,737	50,000	70	0	0	1,168,522	0	Rogers, Lovelock & Fritz
GEORGIA																
Barnesville	13	B	680,450	532,000	8,926	59.60	68,000	30,000	50,450	30,000	56	0	550,215	0	130,235	Spangler & Manley
* Jonesboro[3]	184	MS	3,283,870	2,484,050	32,500	76.43	586,115	Owned	213,705	140,000	241	0	2,221,429	1,062,441	0	Scogin Elam & Bray
Metter	8	B	467,733	324,408	5,884	55.13	76,611	25,000	41,714	17,196	46	0	383,059	59,674	25,000	James W. Buckley
* Monroe	16	B	998,000	662,400	12,000	55.20	278,000	Owned	57,600	35,000	82	0	778,000	220,000	0	Taylor & Williams
* Monticello	6	B	477,330	341,560	6,800	50.23	71,878	Leased	63,892	20,000	40	0	429,597	10,000	37,733	John Tuten & Assocs.
Newnan	49	B	2,347,077	1,766,894	23,000	76.82	338,877	Owned	241,306	117,000	180	0	1,661,595	685,482	0	Kirkman & Assocs.
Social Circle	12	B	462,541	356,454	7,800	45.70	70,424	Owned	35,663	20,000	40	0	413,679	1,077	47,785	Brittain, Thompson . . .
* Tifton	85	S	486,570	332,745	8,511	39.10	112,962	Owned	40,863	65,000	28	0	437,913	48,657	0	Thomson & Assocs.
* Winder	70	MS	1,360,487	1,009,440	16,200	62.31	253,159	20,000	77,888	75,000	94	0	1,104,095	377,048	20,000	Winford Lindsay

ILLINOIS																
Chicago	31	B	1,825,000	1,350,000	11,500	117.39	150,000	125,000	200,000	45,000	98	0	1,250,000	575,000	0	Chicago Bureau of Arch.
Glenwood	18	M	669,579	651,263	3,880	167.85	n/a	Leased	18,316	28,000	43	250,000	0	419,579	0	Alan R. Clapp
Round Lake[4]	23	M	2,442,960	1,797,010	27,680	64.92	258,644	11,395	375,911	60,000	96	56,816	250,000	2,136,144	n/a	Thomas Bleck
INDIANA																
* Franklin[5a]	35	M	2,579,408	1,575,000	21,500	73.26	261,000	66,500	676,308	78,000	125	131,909	0	2,447,499	0	InterDesign Group
Greenwood[5b]	45	B	2,744,909	1,720,000	23,500	73.19	290,000	58,000	676,309	120,000	160	131,908	0	2,613,001	0	InterDesign Group
Middlebury	10	M	590,309	469,903	7,776	60.43	67,642	Owned	52,764	25,000	40	0	0	589,301	49,719	Borger Jones Leedy
Mooresville	7	M	991,945	716,331	12,000	59.69	126,576	50,000	99,038	32,000	80	0	0	980,620	11,325	Robert Porter
IOWA																
Des Moines[6]	3000	M	3,986,205	2,739,100	28,600	95.77	700,000	343,180	203,925	65,400	100	0	0	0	3,986,205	Brown Healey Bock
KANSAS																
Towanda	1	M	89,187	83,752	3,000	29.72	0	0	5,435	10,100	20	0	0	84,187	5,000	Gerald Starr
LOUISIANA																
Folsom	5	B	283,737	166,737	2,000	83.37	52,000	50,000	15,000	12,500	16	0	0	283,737	0	W. Freddie Boothe
* Metairie	30	B	1,467,424	763,624	10,000	76.36	200,000	408,003	95,797	45,000	73	0	0	1,417,424	50,000	Grimball/Savoye
MARYLAND																
* Elkton	67	MS	1,887,629	1,519,235	25,000	60.77	291,084	Owned	77,310	160,000	97	448,263	0	1,439,366	0	Smeallie, Orrick . . .
* Upper Marlboro	25	B	70,000	17,000	4,725	3.60	53,000	Leased	0	20,000	30	0	0	70,000	0	none
* Walkersville	7	B	353,508	305,806	2,500	122.32	23,700	Owned	24,002	12,000	20	0	0	353,508	0	Landon M. Proffitt
MINNESOTA																
* Cloquet	11	M	1,214,087	1,004,640	12,000	83.72	92,444	1	117,002	50,000	60	200,000	0	800,000	250,000	Steve McNeill
* Coon Rapids[7]	21	B	724,570	522,570	7,010	74.55	80,736	107,329	13,935	45,000	40	0	0	724,570	0	Sirny Architects
* Maple Grove	36	B	1,620,337	935,210	10,000	93.52	135,731	294,975	254,421	40,000	39	0	0	1,620,337	0	Freerks, Sperl, Flynn
New York Mills	3	M	209,686	146,689	3,310	44.32	14,765	29,400	18,832	10,000	24	69,197	0	30,727	107,262	Brian Phellps
Rush City	4	B	200,530	96,446	3,450	27.96	12,179	87,800	4,105	10,000	24	63,525	0	41,725	95,280	Jack Ovick
MISSOURI																
Blue Springs	40	B	1,308,003	932,153	17,500	53.27	117,499	228,607	29,744	80,000	136	0	0	1,308,003	0	Tognascioli/Gross/Jarvis
Gladstone	40	B	1,670,826	1,206,591	22,500	53.63	127,038	300,011	37,186	100,000	100	0	0	1,670,826	0	Tognascioli/Gross/Jarvis
Grandview	26	B	1,021,837	733,050	13,050	56.17	118,452	148,637	21,698	50,000	96	0	0	1,021,837	0	Tognascioli/Gross/Jarvis
Kansas City	41	B	1,655,287	1,057,602	14,100	75.01	156,779	316,356	124,550	50,000	112	6,739	0	1,648,548	0	Devine Architects
* Mt. Vernon	10	B	304,488	257,049	5,996	42.87	26,327	6,003	15,109	39,681	39	89,400	0	0	215,088	Warren & Goodin
Smithville	10	B	343,297	269,562	4,000	67.39	25,585	37,503	10,647	30,000	24	0	0	343,297	0	Tognascioli/Gross/Jarvis
NEBRASKA																
Omaha	41	B	2,461,736	1,824,056	20,000	91.20	257,680	215,000	165,000	80,000	194	0	0	2,461,736	0	Bahr, Vermeer . . .
NEVADA																
* Henderson	35	B	2,459,089	1,942,163	21,700	89.50	132,026	140,000	244,900	70,000	96	0	1,159,544	1,159,544	140,000	Architronics
* Las Vegas	75	B	2,556,142	2,146,835	22,900	93.75	167,235	85,000	157,072	75,000	85	0	1,278,071	1,278,071	0	Architronics
West Wendover	3	B	243,400	217,600	3,800	57.26	25,800	Owned	0	10,000	34	46,368	137,032	60,000	0	J.D. Long

Table 1 / New Public Library Buildings, 1988 *(cont.)*

Symbol code: B–Branch library; BS–Branch and system headquarters; M–Main library; MS–Main and system headquarters; S–System headquarters; n/a–Not available

Community	Pop. in M	Code	Project Cost	Const. Cost	Gross Sq. Ft.	Sq.Ft. Cost	Equip. Cost	Site Cost	Other Costs	Volumes	Reader Seats	Federal Funds	State Funds	Local Funds	Gift Funds	Architect
NEW HAMPSHIRE																
Exeter	12	M	$2,490,000	$2,141,263	21,000	$101.97	$155,000	Owned	$193,737	80,000	125	$60,000	0	$2,380,000	$50,000	Stahl Assocs.
NEW JERSEY																
* Thorofare	18	M	2,013,000	1,705,000	18,300	93.17	144,077	Owned	163,923	90,000	100	0	227,500	1,725,500	60,000	Faridy, Thorne, Maddish
NEW YORK																
* Center Moriches[8]	7	M	1,859,106	1,594,990	14,418	110.63	39,814	$75,000	149,302	60,000	52	0	21,500	1,655,292	182,314	Banwell, White . . .
E. Bloomfield	3	M	331,538	238,001	4,455	53.42	29,841	24,900	28,796	19,000	32	0	0	19,539	311,999	David Beinetti
* Hopewell Junction	18	M	1,026,000	860,000	9,000	95.56	80,000	35,000	51,000	50,000	35	0	9,401	616,599	400,000	Remick Architects
* Oriskany	2	M	407,673	274,749	3,356	81.87	38,000	50,000	44,924	12,000	28	43,724	17,199	328,750	18,000	Alesia & Crewell
* Syracuse[9]	464	MS	6,579,400	3,369,400	122,788	27.44	2,800,000	Leased	410,000	400,000	460	700,000	0	5,849,400	30,000	Quinlivan, Pierik . . .
Tully	5	M	165,398	149,541	3,568	41.91	0	Owned	15,857	10,000	22	50,000	41,707	8,000	65,691	Bennetts & Turner
* West Amherst	109	M	1,842,339	1,438,339	13,365	107.62	200,000	125,000	79,000	100,000	119	334,499	0	1,382,840	125,000	David Varecka
Wyandanch	13	M	1,437,238	1,271,074	16,580	76.66	40,000	Owned	126,164	60,000	80	0	37,238	1,400,000	0	Arktek Assocs.
NORTH CAROLINA																
Fuquay-Varina	10	B	432,000	370,000	4,065	91.02	62,000	Owned	n/a	40,000	30	0	0	432,000	0	Haskins, Rice . . .
* Lillington	63	MS	876,764	567,653	13,800	41.13	85,905	135,000	88,206	86,000	70	243,878	227,020	405,867	0	George M. Smart
* Newport	8	B	224,000	181,210	3,500	51.77	25,000	Owned	17,790	10,000	35	99,500	3,000	97,000	24,500	William J. Hedrick
OHIO																
* Amanda	5	B	181,631	134,390	2,400	56.00	29,241	15,000	3,000	10,000	16	0	0	0	181,631	Jon Lynch
* Bellville	4	B	203,901	146,901	2,500	58.76	18,000	25,000	14,000	17,000	20	0	0	203,901	0	Alexander Seckel
* Dayton	11	B	502,486	391,718	4,600	85.16	41,768	35,000	34,000	23,000	40	0	0	502,486	0	Gary Dunker
* Garrettsville	10	MS	794,186	606,479	11,000	55.13	100,707	Owned	87,000	50,000	31	323,247	0	470,939	0	Holzheimer & Assocs.
* New Matamoras	2	B	374,119	298,473	3,512	84.99	21,638	23,333	30,675	10,788	21	0	0	373,334	785	John Southwick
Norton	30	B	1,163,703	823,489	10,830	76.04	93,149	102,085	144,980	60,000	61	0	0	1,141,953	21,750	T.C. Architects
* Waynesville	11	M	735,209	536,053	8,300	64.58	135,417	Owned	63,739	45,000	48	0	0	730,063	5,146	Kleski & Assocs.
OKLAHOMA																
* Kingfisher	14	M	502,000	323,000	10,165	31.78	90,000	25,000	64,000	65,000	60	0	4,000	239,000	265,000	James L. Butcher
* Stroud[10]	30	M	213,445	135,000	2,200	61.36	30,020	Owned	48,425	5,000	23	167,185	0	46,260	0	MNT Robert Thomas
PENNSYLVANIA																
Monongahela	15	M	650,000	476,000	6,500	73.23	35,000	54,000	85,000	35,000	46	225,000	0	0	425,000	Lorenzi, Dodds . . .
Paoli	16	B	226,870	145,522	3,400	42.80	64,748	Leased	16,600	20,000	28	0	0	184,334	42,536	Robert V. Hamilton

SOUTH CAROLINA																
* Darlington	19	MS	1,099,461	894 199	15,000	59.61	94,193	25,469	85,600	60,000	77	150,000	0	949,461	0	F. Earle Gauldin
TEXAS																
* Bedford	45	M	1,820,752	1,149 352	17,000	67.61	93,049	482,110	96,241	86,000	83	200,000	0	1,670,927	0	Albert S. Komatsu
Crosby	17	B	668,660	536 906	10,500	51.13	73,244	Owned	58,510	n/a	n/a	0	0	668,660	0	PBR Architects
* Crosbyton	9	M	402,006	319,472	6,111	52.28	30,379	25,000	27,155	20,000	28	100,000	0	0	302,006	Mike Briggs
Emory	6	M	204,464	153,669	5,000	30.73	30,449	Owned	20,346	20,000	39	100,000	0	0	104,464	Charles J. Muller III
Georgetown	16	M	1,700,000	1,240,890	17,000	72.99	383,347	Owned	75,763	100,000	126	200,000	0	1,500,000	0	Gregory S. Ibanez
Santa Fe[11]	9	M	473,094	401,915	6,400	62.80	16,500	20,302	34,377	25,000	17	0	0	16,500	456,594	Reed & Clements
Seabrook	14	B	559,668	442,729	7,217	61.34	80,363	Owned	36,576	35,000	60	0	0	559,668	0	Richard Ainslie
VIRGINIA																
Lovingston	12	B	$353,377	$288,545	4,000	$72.14	$17,399	$19,275	$28,158	16,000	24	$70,551	0	$116,476	$166,350	S. Cabell Burks
* Virginia Beach	380	M	12,362,636	7,469,000	95,000	78.62	3,000,000	457,800	1,435,836	375,000	n/a	0	0	12,362,636	0	Design Collaborative
WASHINGTON																
* Coupeville	10	M	269,625	185,625	2,660	69.78	38,500	20,000	25,500	13,000	22	62,840	0	148,285	58,500	Lewis-Nelson Assocs.
* Mountlake Terrace	16	B	1,517,831	1,141,824	12,842	88.91	104,479	141,510	130,018	50,000	88	0	0	1,497,831	20,000	Lewis-Nelson Assocs.
WEST VIRGINIA																
Franklin	8	M	408,063	327,508	6,300	52.00	27,415	35,000	18,040	31,000	30	140,127	183,873	35,000	49,063	J.D. King
New Haven	2	B	387,557	338,394	4,100	82.68	22,881	Leased	25,682	20,000	24	121,568	179,552	60,000	26,437	Wilson & Goff
WISCONSIN																
Dodgeville	5	M	699,045	551,596	13,000	42.43	44,000	64,402	39,047	18,000	42	125,000	0	574,045	0	The Durant Group
St. Francis	10	M	1,097,788	922,768	19,200	48.06	116,100	Owned	58,920	35,000	124	0	0	912,688	185,100	Potter Design Group

*Projects that were in progress in 1987 and are now completed.

Table 2 / Public Libraries: Additions and Renovations, 1988

Symbol code: B–Branch library; BS–Branch and system headquarters; M–Main library; MS–Main and system headquarters; S–System headquarters; n/a–Not available

Community	Pop. in M	Code	Project Cost	Const. Cost	Gross Sq. Ft.	Sq.Ft. Cost	Equip. Cost	Site Cost	Other Costs	Volumes	Reader Seats	Federal Funds	State Funds	Local Funds	Gift Funds	Architect
ALABAMA																
* Alexander City	15	M	$87,884	$61,495	10,810	$5.69	$21,389	Owned	$5,000	47,000	44	0	$43,425	$17,985	$26,474	Seay, Seay & Litchfield
* Andalusia	46	M	215,000	213,379	3,790	56.30	0	Owned	1,720	80,000	110	0	115,800	62,402	36,898	Seymour & Lisenby
Arab	10	M	129,496	92,841	2,160	42.98	28,050	1,178	7,427	26,750	34	0	88,992	37,648	2,856	Pearson, Humphries . . .
Dadeville	170	BS	139,324	106,686	5,467	19.51	20,000	Owned	12,638	93,060	24	0	82,015	0	57,309	Earl Lancaster
* Gadsden	103	M	253,834	224,000	3,600	62.22	11,334	Owned	18,500	10,000	50	0	154,400	99,434	0	Ronald G. Cannon
Gurley[12]	2	B	5,750	2,500	1,500	1.67	750	Leased	2,500	7,500	10	0	0	2,500	3,250	not reported
Sheffield	12	M	150,000	120,000	9,380	12.79	10,000	15,000	5,000	35,000	42	0	75,000	25,000	50,000	Thomas Donaldson
ALASKA																
Valdez	3	M	452,939	347,000	4,000	86.75	23,943	Owned	81,996	3,000	30	0	0	452,939	0	Arch Fry
ARIZONA																
* Scottsdale	129	M	3,426,583	2,125,630	44,000	48.31	475,160	Owned	825,793	300,000	232	0	0	3,265,583	161,000	Dean, Hunt, Krueger . . .
ARKANSAS																
Eureka Springs[13]	17	B	98,670	89,502	n/a	n/a	0	Owned	9,168	n/a	n/a	24,000	0	15,000	59,670	John Mott
CALIFORNIA																
Cerritos	57	M	8,200,000	5,800,000	41,500	139.76	1,500,000	Owned	900,000	180,000	270	0	0	8,200,000	0	Charles Walton
* Redwood City[14]	60	M	8,116,000	5,614,000	45,000	124.76	775,000	947,000	780,000	175,000	239	0	0	8,105,350	10,650	Ripley Assocs.
* Rosemead	46	B	114,885	70,139	1,000	70.14	44,746	Owned	0	1,300	4	0	0	114,885	0	none
COLORADO																
* Steamboat Springs	10	M	$650,000	$504,000	9,500	$53.05	$104,000	Owned	$42,000	40,000	75	$41,200	0	$603,800	$5,000	William Rangitch
CONNECTICUT																
Middlefield	3	M	46,808	39,979	225	177.68	0	Owned	6,829	n/a	n/a	12,847	8,564	21,411	3,986	Peter Able, Inc.
* Newington[15]	30	M	3,300,023	2,344,650	24,730	94.81	390,000	131,000	435,373	102,000	153	100,000	350,000	2,776,469	73,554	Kaestle Boos Assocs.
DELAWARE																
* Milton	7	B	51,344	47,344	728	65.03	0	Owned	4,000	n/a	n/a	0	22,500	28,844	0	Calvin Clendaniel
Seaford	21	M	265,315	230,861	3,000	76.95	23,742	Owned	10,712	45,000	32	0	60,000	23,300	182,015	Moeckel Carbonell
FLORIDA																
Brooksville	80	MS	490,000	380,000	10,000	38.00	60,000	Owned	50,000	80,000	32	200,000	0	289,500	500	Friedman McKenna
Cross City[16]	9	B	56,000	46,451	2,869	16.19	0	5,500	4,049	14,000	24	0	45,000	0	11,000	Jackson Reeger Inc.
* Daytona Beach	259	MS	740,000	679,000	13,500	50.29	8,000	Owned	53,000	28,000	35	200,000	0	220,000	320,000	Gee & Jenson

* Deltona	12	B	257,032	136,703	2,200	62.14	22,000	Owned	98,329	50,000	63	0	90,000	47,032	120,000	Gee & Jenson
Oakland Park	26	M	684,847	554,182	12,000	46.19	77,217	Owned	53,448	70,000	94	0	0	623,064	61,783	Oscar Vagi & Assocs.
Quincy	47	MS	369,442	267,176	8,105	32.96	67,725	Leased	34,541	24,000	77	0	301,717	67,725	0	Barrett Daffin . . .
* Sanford	250	M	60,305	53,911	5,000	10.79	4,000	Owned	2,394	n/a	n/a	0	0	60,305	0	Rogers, Lovelock & Fritz
Tampa[17]	30	B	177,000	147,000	5,600	26.25	15,000	Leased	15,000	30,000	20	0	0	177,000	0	Fletcher, Valenti . . .
GEORGIA																
* Albany	30	B	266,902	218,972	10,000	21.90	0	Owned	47,930	40,000	72	114,274	0	152,628	0	Floyd Smith
* Cordele	21	B	942,165	714,898	15,000	47.66	151,477	Owned	75,790	60,000	120	0	560,976	287,488	93,701	Michael V. Parker
* Eatonton	12	B	499,770	349,835	8,000	43.72	91,944	Owned	57,991	20,000	40	0	449,793	49,977	0	W. Lane Greene
Statesboro	39	MS	121,532	91,854	1,070	85.84	19,524	Owned	10,154	3,750	10	50,000	0	0	71,532	James W. Buckley . . .
* Toccoa	21	B	532,943	409,616	10,975	37.32	87,579	Owned	35,748	57,000	93	0	476,667	47,276	9,000	Bailey & Assocs.
* Tucker	38	B	761,974	544,616	12,140	44.86	137,000	Owned	80,358	58,000	106	125,000	449,974	167,000	20,000	Christian/Foley
IDAHO																
Blackfoot	20	M	828,955	624,234	19,500	32.01	73,107	98,614	33,000	45,000	50	0	0	0	828,955	Sundberg & Assocs.
Filer	2	M	85,337	61,545	2,400	25.64	0	19,849	3,943	n/a	n/a	37,027	20,282	28,028	0	Russ Lively
Garden Valley	1	M	11,787	11,787	674	17.48	0	Owned	0	12,000	20	5,537	0	1,000	5,250	Ellery Brown
ILLINOIS																
* Calumet Park	9	M	44,500	34,500	1,000	34.50	0	Owned	10,000	30,000	32	0	22,250	22,250	0	Edwin H. Lugowski
Chicago	97	B	2,150,000	1,750,000	16,000	109.37	150,000	Owned	250,000	105,000	122	1,054,000	0	1,096,000	0	Lempp Kerbis
Chicago	78	B	1,525,000	1,150,000	12,000	95.83	150,000	Owned	225,000	70,000	59	1,100,000	0	425,000	0	Wendell Campbell Assocs.
Kewanee	17	M	128,041	106,690	14,500	7.35	0	Owned	21,351	n/a	n/a	0	48,805	79,236	0	Landes, Benson, Parkins
* Oreana	1	M	64,004	23,099	1,272	18.16	1,721	33,962	5,221	5,500	12	25,000	0	18,904	20,100	Bradley, Likins . . . .
Streamwood	47	M	863,597	564,030	15,500	36.39	173,417	0	126,150	220,000	204	0	250,000	613,597	0	Robert Hunter
Wilmette	28	M	3,637,972	3,159,945	32,426	97.45	225,390	Owned	252,637	259,000	255	0	250,000	3,372,972	15,000	Frye Gillan Molinaro
Woodstock	20	M	1,871,786	1,530,691	22,114	69.22	37,793	Owned	303,302	80,600	115	0	250,000	1,621,786	0	O'Donnell Wicklund . . .
INDIANA																
* Batesville	4	M	1,573,900	1,252,900	8,850	141.57	130,000	Owned	191,000	108,000	96	0	0	0	1,573,900	Stephen Ford . . . .
Muncie	80	M	194,724	190,024	12,000	15.83	0	Owned	4,700	n/a	n/a	0	0	85,560	109,164	James H. Gooden
Princeton	12	M	544,846	498,412	5,600	89.00	0	Owned	46,434	50,000	18	182,000	0	362,846	0	Bill Gaisser Designs
KANSAS																
Ellis	2	M	45,459	43,172	1,056	40.88	2,287	Owned	0	n/a	n/a	0	0	0	45,459	not reported
Russell	8	M	129,111	100,590	9,572	10.51	15,456	Owned	13,065	44,485	72	46,352	0	81,559	1,200	Don Marrs
KENTUCKY																
* Bedford	6	M	114,531	95,860	1,500	63.91	9,649	Owned	9,022	n/a	60	0	49,508	64,523	500	Quinton Biagi
LOUISIANA																
Arcadia	17	M	466,176	414,427	13,430	30.86	21,813	Owned	29,936	75,000	53	0	0	466,176	0	Allen J. Kelly
MAINE																
Cumberland	5	M	700,000	552,866	8,100	68.25	29,971	Owned	117,163	44,500	84	0	0	700,000	0	Terrien Architects

Table 2 / Public Libraries: Additions and Renovations, 1988 *(cont.)*
Symbol code: B—Branch library; BS—Branch and system headquarters; M—Main library; MS—Main and system headquarters; S—System headquarters; n/a—Not available

Community	Pop. in M	Code	Project Cost	Const. Cost	Gross Sq. Ft.	Sq.Ft. Cost	Equip. Cost	Site Cost	Other Costs	Volumes	Reader Seats	Federal Funds	State Funds	Local Funds	Gift Funds	Architect
MARYLAND																
Oxon Hill	165	B	149,000	130,000	7,000	18.57	16,000	Owned	3,000	200,000	118	0	0	149,000	0	none
St. Michaels	8	B	192,709	147,242	3,000	49.08	20,049	1.00	25,417	11,000	22	0	0	0	199,497	Rurik Ekstrom & Assocs.
MASSACHUSETTS																
Ashburnham	4	M	833,974	763,814	10,000	76.38	0	Owned	70,160	50,000	45	84,055	13,138	640,766	96,015	Preservation Partnership
* Eastham	4	M	697,365	584,915	8,632	67.76	50,000	Owned	62,450	30,000	51	0	0	693,665	3,700	Gaffney Assocs.
* Wayland	12	M	1,696,000	1,515,000	13,000	116.53	56,000	Owned	125,000	75,000	64	150,000	16,000	1,450,000	80,000	A. Anthony Tappe & Assocs.
MICHIGAN																
Constantine	4	M	$179,795	$119,285	3,400	$35.08	$18,734	$30,000	$11,776	16,000	30	$62,500	0	$87,295	$30,000	Brooks Architectural
Temperance	25	B	600,000	500,000	14,800	33.78	0	Owned	100,000	n/a	125	0	0	600,000	0	David O. Peters
MINNESOTA																
* Forest Lake	11	M	339,044	289,898	3,190	90.88	27,943	Owned	21,203	40,000	50	105,000	0	234,044	0	Adkins Assn.
McIntosh	1	B	16,148	12,093	1,064	11.37	4,055	Owned	0	n/a	13	0	0	11,188	4,960	not reported
MISSISSIPPI																
Ridgeland	47	B	63,890	30,000	1,190	25.21	32,000	Owned	1,890	15,000	34	0	0	64,000	0	Charles P. McMullan
MISSOURI																
Galena	14	M	33,403	33,403	1,960	17.04	0	Owned	0	n/a	10	0	0	15,403	18,000	not reported
MONTANA																
* Hamilton	37	M	375,797	292,248	7,600	38.45	12,620	35,000	35,929	40,000	40	79,958	0	57,427	238,412	Mark L. Young
NEVADA																
* Beatty	1	M	34,386	29,416	596	49.35	0	Owned	4,970	13,500	21	14,620	7,965	11,801	0	Charles Sullivan
Elko	30	MS	388,368	359,600	5,800	62.00	0	Owned	28,768	19,000	30	121,768	204,600	69,000	3,000	J.D. Long
* Las Vegas	25	B	2,547,110	2,073,941	24,260	85.48	74,266	317,643	81,260	80,000	65	0	1,273,555	1,273,555	0	Congdon & Assocs.
* Reno	10	B	77,000	18,000	6,000	3.00	59,000	Owned	0	30,000	38	0	0	77,000	0	not reported
* Reno	40	B	345,087	241,087	12,000	20.09	104,000	Owned	0	22,000	50	45,087	0	300,000	0	not reported
* Sparks	55	B	184,500	144,500	2,180	66.28	40,000	Owned	0	79,000	273	77,605	76,021	30,874	0	Paul Huss
NEW HAMPSHIRE																
Newport	6	M	582,229	502,535	4,000	125.63	22,716	Owned	56,978	35,000	61	40,000	0	43,013	499,216	Sheerr & McCrystal
NEW MEXICO																
Bosque Farms	18	M	46,663	43,009	1,875	22.93	3,654	Owned	0	20,000	13	20,000	0	13,209	18,000	John Friedman
* Silver City	15	M	322,000	297,000	4,000	74.25	4,000	Owned	21,000	45,000	68	138,596	0	179,404	4,000	Jay Hill & Assocs.

NEW YORK																	
Allegany	4	B	63,985	57,353	2,304	24.89	6,632	Owned	0	30,000	n/a	3,300	60,685	0	0	R. John
* Baldwin	32	M	1,159,627	622,334	20,400	30.50	50,000	432,163	55,130	200,000	61	267,955	31,672	860,000	0	Plushnick & Tsue Architects
Bayville	8	M	56,079	52,860	900	58.73	2,535	Owned	684	40,000	54	4,841	0	0	51,238	Leonard T. Kurkowski
Blauvelt	5	M	233,500	198,000	1,000	198.00	15,500	Owned	20,000	9,000	25	0	10,000	180,000	43,500	Remick Architects . . .
Brentwood	68	M	6,000,750	4,665,750	51,800	90.07	847,500	Owned	487,500	225,000	70	0	21,000	5,979,750	0	Arktek Associates
* Brooklyn	2231	MS	4,353,000	3,873,000	21,000	184.42	200,000	Owned	280,000	n/a	n/a	700,000	0	3,653,000	0	Renato Severino
* Brooklyn	26	B	767,461	668,461	7,225	92.53	55,000	Leased	44,000	34,720	68	0	0	767,461	0	Designers Quad
* Cambridge	2	M	172,500	152,750	1,200	81.92	2,000	Owned	17,750	10,000	30	0	23,441	51,788	97,271	Richard E. Jones Assocs.
* Croton	8	M	594,000	540,000	3,500	154.29	n/a	Owned	54,000	75,000	65	82,298	20,591	277,111	214,000	LML Architects
Cutchogue	5	M	537,613	410,257	3,560	115.24	92,613	Owned	34,743	20,000	34	0	5,000	462,000	70,613	Ward Assocs.
* Gowanda	10	M	44,453	81,481	2,176	37.45	1,208	Owned	5,764	14,006	28	30,000	33,000	1,453	24,000	Trevor W. Rogers
Irondequoit	57	M	429,864	373,375	6,000	62.22	21,489	Owned	35,000	100,000	40	97,756	49,743	282,365	0	Passero Assocs.
* Jericho	15	M	2,909,500	2,353,955	27,938	84.26	207,117	10,500	337,928	103,076	133	0	57,000	2,852,500	0	Lee Harris Pomeroy Assocs.
LeRoy	12	M	279,386	240,850	8,895	27.07	0	Owned	38,536	50,000	80	57,884	65,000	156,542	0	Clark, Clark, Millis & Gilson,
* Marlboro	10	M	555,429	514,092	5,740	89.56	0	Owned	41,337	32,295	36	89,753	29,750	279,000	156,926	Peter R. Hoffman
New York	57	B	916,956	584,313	7,163	81.57	233,941	Owned	98,702	21,470	72	0	0	666,956	250,000	Gwathmey, Siegel & Assocs.
* Old Forge	2	M	138,715	119,682	3,329	35.95	9,149	Owned	9,884	14,867	30	0	50,000	13,902	74,813	Robert Noble
* Patchogue	46	M	136,045	32,933	1,451	22.70	85,367	Owned	17,745	50,000	0	43,750	0	92,295	0	Gibbons Heidtmann . . .
* Peru	6	M	130,909	117,909	3,746	31.48	3,000	Owned	10,000	18,700	30	0	75,000	21,720	34,189	Ronald DeLair
* Ransomville	14	M	130,000	80,000	1,400	57.14	20,000	23,000	7,000	20,000	25	26,000	38,000	50,000	16,000	Mesch Assocs.
* Rome	44	M	256,916	160,105	1,500	106.73	80,904	Owned	16,717	120,000	60	57,956	0	167,727	31,233	Robert W. Trowell
* Sandy Creek	3	M	78,025	69,715	1,120	62.25	0	1,000	7,310	9,800	20	0	13,701	28,000	36,324	Stephen Yaussi . . .
* Schenectady	288	MS	137,500	123,500	8,812	14.06	0	Owned	14,000	67,775	n/a	46,662	90,838	0	0	Thun Associates
Wantagh	19	M	504,877	454,710	18,304	24.84	0	Owned	50,167	110,685	108	129,789	0	375,088	0	Arthur Petterino
* Westhampton	M	8	352,000	302,000	7,240	41.71	15,000	Owned	35,000	50,000	60	0	17,500	154,500	180,000	Garrett Strang
* Woodstock	7	M	97,578	96,178	1,050	91.60	0	Owned	1,400	4,000	24	0	15,750	43,153	38,675	John Rovere
NORTH CAROLINA																
* Cary	50	B	257,806	176,000	11,780	14.94	81,206	Owned	n/a	100,000	110	0	0	257,806	0	Hager, Smith & Huffman
Valdese	8	BS	323,742	259,468	6,181	41.98	40,402	Owned	23,872	30,732	35	80,000	80,000	62,540	101,202	Robert B. Salsbury Assocs.
OHIO																
Ashland	46	M	2,177,000	1,763,975	20,880	84.48	249,916	Owned	163,109	100,000	127	0	0	2,177,000	0	Alexander Seckel
* Butler	3	B	143,308	112,808	2,880	39.17	15,000	Owned	15,500	15,000	15	0	0	143,308	0	Alexander Seckel
Carey	6	M	163,000	140,200	3,100	45.23	5,000	Owned	17,880	24,600	40	0	0	103,000	60,000	Bruce Wobser
Centerburg	4	M	122,028	105,117	5,000	21.02	7,450	Owned	9,461	24,000	20	0	0	114,578	0	Marr Knapp & Crawtis
Franklin	34	M	567,692	424,692	5,700	74.51	143,000	Owned	0	50,000	64	120,000	0	447,692	0	Comaco
* Lexington	13	B	603,658	393,158	6,322	62.19	58,500	105,000	47,000	38,000	71	0	0	603,658	0	Alexander Seckel
* Minerva	8	M	189,122	160,731	10,000	16.07	28,391	Owned	0	65,000	60	0	0	137,886	51,236	Robert Wilson
* Newton Falls	10	M	606,335	502,889	7,856	64.01	67,000	Owned	36,446	20,000	38	206,094	0	400,241	0	Frank Pliska
Ontario	10	B	139,138	106,838	2,935	36.40	22,500	Owned	9,800	21,000	15	0	0	139,138	0	Alexander Seckel
Wadsworth	19	M	1,671,017	1,367,744	19,650	69.61	22,668	Owned	280,605	85,000	120	0	0	1,671,017	0	William D. Koster
OKLAHOMA																
* Durant	12	M	451,000	396,000	8,900	44.49	30,000	Owned	25,000	39,000	60	148,000	0	283,000	20,000	Jack Nusbaum
Hobart	12	M	403.708	351.123	6.900	50.89	30,518	Owned	22,067	42,000	54	0	57,560	0	346,148	Jack Nusbaum

Table 2 / Public Libraries: Additions and Renovations, 1988 *(cont.)*

Symbol code: B–Branch library; BS–Branch and system headquarters; M–Main library; MS–Main and system headquarters; S–System headquarters; n/a–Not available

Community	Pop. in M	Code	Project Cost	Const. Cost	Gross Sq. Ft.	Sq.Ft. Cost	Equip. Cost	Site Cost	Other Costs	Volumes	Reader Seats	Federal Funds	State Funds	Local Funds	Gift Funds	Architect
* Miami	14	M	333,712	280,685	3,750	74.85	35,399	Owned	17,628	60,000	76	125,000	33,000	95,712	80,000	Jack Mann
* Tonkawa	4	M	253,225	210,133	4,758	44.16	11,879	15,000	9,163	20,000	25	0	500	28,600	231,175	Howard & Porch
PENNSYLVANIA																
Phoenixville	25	B	890,000	719,300	9,634	74.66	14,000	Owned	156,700	70,000	150	80,000	0	226,000	584,000	Dagit Saylor
Telford	31	M	897,638	645,275	20,000	32.26	83,820	Owned	168,543	44,000	60	0	0	0	897,638	Diseroad & Wolff
Upper St. Clair	19	M	1,320,000	1,000,000	23,724	42.15	120,000	Owned	200,000	90,000	164	0	0	1,120,000	200,000	Ruprecht, Schroeder . . .
TENNESSEE																
Alamo	15	M	86,536	72,329	1,610	44.93	6,849	Owned	7,356	18,180	20	0	38,487	21,410	26,638	Troy Williams
Bristol	6	B	37,946	28,585	489	58.46	7,361	Owned	2,000	12,021	13	0	15,000	18,028	4,918	Norris Guthrie
Jasper	24	M	120,828	105,438	1,915	55.06	6,225	Owned	9,165	3,720	14	52,858	0	67,970	0	Klaus Peter Nentwig
Lynchburg	5	M	95,846	85,975	1,400	61.41	1,800	Owned	0	35,000	24	45,156	0	0	52,491	Jerry Stroud
TEXAS																
Columbus	6	M	228,838	207,469	4,141	50.10	5,208	Owned	16,161	32,030	54	0	0	0	228,838	R. Bruce Simmons
Crockett	24	MS	96,521	82,295	1,104	74.54	6,082	Owned	8,152	5,000	24	0	0	3,879	92,642	Gremer & Sumner
* Devine	7	M	384,000	296,700	5,013	59.19	3,900	37,000	46,400	26,480	28	100,000	0	100,000	184,000	Jesse Fernandez & Assocs.
* Dickinson	11	M	337,500	150,000	8,600	17.44	0	162,500	25	30,000	33	100,000	0	40,000	197,500	Rodney Mackey
Farmersville	3	M	35,950	33,000	2,100	15.71	1,500	Owned	1,450	18,500	50	0	0	19,950	16,000	Baseshore, Bashton . . .
Houston	45	B	1,963,500	1,332,000	15,100	88.21	350,000	151,500	130,000	60,000	126	80,000	0	1,732,000	151,500	Ray Bailey
* League City	35	M	2,530,000	1,965,651	29,285	67.12	564,349	Owned	0	135,000	123	0	0	2,500,000	30,000	Mackey & Co.
Matador	19	M	37,365	27,729	2,400	11.55	1,636	8,000	0	10,900	14	0	0	0	37,365	none
* N. Richl'nd Hills	45	M	5,500,000	742,000	87,000	8.53	212,000	4,300,000	246,000	200,000	110	0	0	5,500,000	0	Komatsu & Assocs.
UTAH																
Milford	1	M	$1,900	$1,900	180	$10.56	0	Owned	0	1,200	28	$950	0	$950	0	none
VIRGINIA																
* Glouster	30	M	384,000	318,000	6,000	53.00	31,000	Owned	35,000	38,000	44	94,000	33,000	20,000	237,000	Caro, Monroe, & Liang
Roanoke	29	MS	562,000	465,000	13,239	35.12	45,000	Owned	52,000	92,000	142	0	0	562,000	0	Rogers & Reynolds
WASHINGTON																
Burbank	3	B	77,762	6,894	900	7.66	50,590	Leased	20,278	20,000	20	63,836	0	11,926	2,000	none
Cathlamet	2	M	30,000	18,000	1,408	12.78	12,000	Owned	0	9,000	28	0	0	0	30,000	none
* Seattle	48	B	766,002	605,660	9,300	65.13	19,200	Owned	141,142	22,000	52	0	0	680,002	86,000	Bassetti, Norton, Metler . . .
* Seattle	40	B	804,606	662,453	11,300	58.62	20,700	Owned	121,453	16,800	65	0	0	714,606	90,000	Bassetti, Norton, Metler . . .

Table 2 / Public Libraries: Additions and Renovations, 1988 *(cont.)*

Symbol code: B–Branch library; BS–Branch and system headquarters; M–Main library; MS–Main and system headquarters; S–System headquarters; n/a–Not available

Community	Pop. in M	Code	Project Cost	Const. Cost	Gross Sq. Ft.	Sq.Ft. Cost	Equip. Cost	Site Cost	Other Costs	Volumes	Reader Seats	Federal Funds	State Funds	Local Funds	Gift Funds	Architect
WISCONSIN																
Cross Plains	6	M	225,709	182,318	3,640	50.09	22,955	Owned	20,436	25,000	28	23,103	0	189,411	13,195	K. Brink
Galesville	3	M	202,720	173,500	4,540	38.22	8,860	Owned	20,860	18,000	50	48,600	0	113,400	40,720	Schute-Larson Inc.
Three Lakes	2	M	163,000	160,000	2,028	78.90	3,000	Owned	n/a	12,000	4	0	0	3,000	160,000	Wergin Co., Inc.

*Projects that were in progress in 1987 and are now completed.

References (Tables 1 and 2)

1. Winner of S.D. Chapter AIA Design Award.
2. Library on second-floor level with parking beneath.
3. Winner of Award for Excellence, South Atlantic Region, AIA.
4. Value unknown for two acres of land donated by Park District.
5. Both libraries planned, designed, and constructed as one project.
6. Total funding from donations and Iowa State Lottery.
7. Located in a shopping complex.
8. All furniture and equipment plus site were donated.
9. Five-level building in The Galleries of Syracuse, a shopping mall in the downtown area.
10. Located on Indian tribal land, the emphasis is on Native American cultures.
11. Building and site financed and donated by Sante Fe resident Mae S. Bruce.
12. Renovated cafe.
13. Handicapped access to historic Carnegie building.
14. Forty thousand square feet of new construction added to renovated fire station, a brick and terra cotta 65-year-old landmark.
15. New construction added to existing 1939 building attached by skylight, creating a building inside a building.
16. Renovated bank; correctional institution labor used to "gut" bank building and refurbish it.
17. First branch library in Hillsborough County to be located in major shopping mall.

Table 3 / Public Libraries: Six-Year Cost Summary

Symbol code: B–Branch library; BS–Branch and system headquarters; M–Main library; MS–Main and system headquarters; S–System headquarters; n/a–Not available

	Fiscal 1983	Fiscal 1984	Fiscal 1985	Fiscal 1986	Fiscal 1987	Fiscal 1988
Number of new bldgs.	54	48	99	71	101	98
Number of ARRs[1]	42	63	125	120	149	140
Sq. ft. new bldgs.	835,211	800,252	852,831	1,141,957	1,370,479	1,400,597
Sq. ft. ARRs	369,351	523,963	1,227,063	1,189,319	1,567,121	1,271,285
NEW BLDGS.						
Construction cost	$48,761,130	$64,370,118	$52,799,143	$73,092,317	$101,016,870	$97,485,013
Equipment cost	6,426,618	6,451,298	6,585,913	9,799,996	17,958,318	19,680,354
Site cost	2,741,248	1,622,534	4,085,764	4,211,461	5,047,659	10,393,705
Other costs	6,018,787	6,397,740	5,728,714	10,869,097	12,096,087	11,600,724
Total—Project cost	63,947,783	78,841,690	70,583,649	97,972,871	136,952,501	139,169,136
ARRs—Project cost	18,769,475	30,762,934	69,256,835	59,634,921	79,208,109	103,570,287
NEW & ARR PROJECT COST	$82,717,258	$109,604,624	$139,840,484	$157,607,792	$215,457,355	$242,739,423
FUND SOURCES						
Federal, new bldgs.	$4,401,647	$2,274,957	$9,803,398	$6,367,559	$5,757,098	$7,352,110
Federal, ARRs	1,046,490	2,227,355	8,086,819	4,753,052	4,677,400	7,261,967
Federal, total	$5,448,137	$4,502,312	$17,890,217	$11,120,611	$10,434,498	$14,614,077
State, new bldgs.	$8,175,330	$4,340,803	$4,139,433	$1,863,277	$7,710,681	$13,707,819
State, ARRs	3,160,159	2,784,153	1,607,519	7,054,676	5,060,877	6,822,165
State, total	$11,335,489	$7,124,956	$5,746,952	$8,917,953	$12,771,558	$20,529,984
Local, new bldgs.	$47,544,033	$71,043,181	$47,914,637	$73,997,971	$117,135,870	$107,313,990
Local, ARRs	10,640,891	22,921,592	49,096,264	42,971,936	62,974,065	78,807,645
Local, total	$58,184,924	$93,964,773	$97,010,901	$116,969,907	$180,109,935	$186,121,635
Gift, new bldgs.	$3,957,736	$1,169,101	$8,766,333	$15,771,620	$7,182,656	$11,074,832
Gift, ARRs	3,171,935	2,838,892	10,490,099	4,982,621	6,734,422	10,745,494
Gift, total	$7,129,671	$4,007,993	$19,256,432	$20,754,241	$13,917,078	$21,820,326
TOTAL FUNDS USED	$82,098,221	$109,600,034	$139,904,502	$157,762,712	$217,233,069	$243,086,022

[1] Additions, remodelings, and renovations.

Table 4 / New Academic Libraries, 1988

Name of Institution	Project Cost	Gross Area	Sq.Ft. Cost	Construction Cost	Equipment Cost	Book Capacity	Seating Capacity	Architect
Queens College, City University of New York, Flushing	$54,600,000	252,000	$136.71	$34,450,000	n/a	850,000	n/a	Gruzen Samton Steinglass
Lasalle University, Philadelphia	11,500,000	107,000	86.30	9,233,971	100,000	500,000	996	Shepley Bulfinch . . .
* Arizona State University West Campus, Glendale	10,817,000	95,113	83.81	7,971,374	822,000	300,000	900	Anderson DeBartolo Pan
* Macalester College, St. Paul	10,374,000	92,000	85.58	7,873,190	830,000	450,000	600	Shepley Bulfinch . . .
Fayetteville State University, N.C.	7,567,000	77,191	62.40	4,816,618	780,296	489,650	700	Clinton Gravely & Assocs.
* Florida State University, Tallahassee[1]	7,472,132	107,050	57.19	6,122,132	1,350,000	450,000	350	Schweizer & Assocs.
* Florida International University, North Miami[2]	7,369,954	82,330	83.74	6,894,024	257,258	232,000	657	Miller, Meier, Kenyon, Cooper
* Wright State University, Dayton, Ohio	7,300,000	47,000	146.81	6,900,000	400,000	200,000	300	John Ruetschle Assocs.
Annenberg Research Institute for Judaic & Near Eastern Studies, Philadelphia	7,000,000	36,000	162.78	5,860,000	1,140,000	200,000	25	Geddes, Brecher . . .
* Texas Wesleyan College, Fort Worth	6,962,000	84,395	75.15	6,342,000	620,000	350,000	474	Cannady, Jackson & Ryan
Centennial Science & Engineering Library,[3] University of New Mexico, Albuquerque	n/a	63,000	67.37	4,244,310	1,260,000	300,000	800	Dean Hunt Assocs.
Academy of the New Church, Bryn Athyn, Pa.	3,900,000	35,000	101.60	3,556,000	250,027	150,000	185	H2L2 Architects

Table 4 / New Academic Libraries, 1988 *(cont.)*

Name of Institution	Project Cost	Gross Area	Sq.Ft. Cost	Construction Cost	Equipment Cost	Book Capacity	Seating Capacity	Architect
* Allentown College, Center Valley, Pa.	3,816,900	36,000	97.33	3,504,000	190,000	270,000	343	Breslin Ridyard & Federo
* Assumption College, Worcester, Mass.	3,368,000	43,743	70.87	3,100,000	268,000	260,000	350	O.E. Nault & Sons
Southern Maine Vocational-Technical Inst., Portland	2,800,000	7,500	n/a	n/a	75,000	14,000	90	Portland Design Team
Brenan College & Academy, Gainesville, Ga.	2,500,000	42,000	35.71	1,500,000	1,000,000	250,000	400	not reported
* Southern Illinois University, Carbondale	1,622,500	32,035	45.88	1,469,775	5,620	500,000	6	Fischer Stein Assocs.
* Science-Technology Library, University of Texas at Arlington	n/a	14,800	80.66	1,193,768	236,926	140,000	107	Albert S. Komatsu & Assocs.
Art & Architecture Library, University of Texas at Arlington	n/a	6,000	n/a	n/a	91,200	38,000	72	Pratt, Box & Henderson
South Atlantic Regional Resource Center, Florida Atlantic University, Plantation	3,000	100	n/a	n/a	1,500	2,000	6	not reported

*Projects that were in progress in 1987 and are now completed.

[1]Total area includes fourth floor and dean's suite; library portion, 85,000 sq. ft.

[2]Library part of 82,330 sq. ft. project: 70,270 sq. ft.

[3]Part of $11,553,744 Electrical & Computer Engineering/Science Library project.

Table 5 / Academic Libraries: Additions and Renovations, 1988

Name of Institution		Project Cost	Gross Area	Sq.Ft. Cost	Construction Cost	Equipment Cost	Book Capacity	Seating Capacity	Architect
Princeton University	Total	$13,800,000	69,700	$155.52	$10,840,000	$990,000	465,000	155	Fred Koetter
	New	n/a	47,700	205.24	9,790,000	n/a	n/a	n/a	
	Renovated	n/a	22,000	47.73	1,050,000	n/a	n/a	n/a	
D'Angelo Law Library, Univ. of Chicago	Total	10,500,000	121,305	78.00	9,461,789	n/a	650,000	431	not reported
	New	6,000,000	74,555	n/a	n/a	n/a	200,000	n/a	
	Renovated	4,500,000	46,750	n/a	n/a	n/a	450,000	n/a	
* University of Missouri-Columbia	Total	n/a	128,435	60.63	7,787,574	331,778	100,000	n/a	Peckham Guyton
	New	n/a	70,568	n/a	n/a	n/a	40,000	n/a	Albers & Viets, Inc.
	Renovated	n/a	57,867	n/a	n/a	n/a	60,000	n/a	
Claremont University Center, Calif.	Total	7,791,000	65,474	113.91	7,458,000	333,000	500,000	397	Skidmore, Owings &
	New	7,400,000	54,968	128.57	7,067,000	333,000	500,000	340	Merrill
	Renovated	391,000	10,506	37.22	391,000	0	0	57	
University of Alabama at Birmingham	Total	7,750,013	165,000	38.47	6,347,991	700,000	1,200,000	1,200	Hellmuth, Obata . . . &
	New	6,750,013	105,000	50.93	5,347,991	700,000	970,000	765	Davis, Speake
	Renovated	1,000,000	60,000	16.67	1,000,000	0	230,000	435	
* Hope College, Holland, Mich.	Total	n/a	92,000	81.97	7,540,820	700,000	430,000	691	Shepley Bulfinch . . .
	New	n/a	80,000	n/a	n/a	n/a	n/a	661	
	Renovated	n/a	12,000	n/a	n/a	n/a	n/a	30	
Southwestern University, Georgetown, Tex.	Total	6,850,000	73,955	63.97	4,730,803	708,715	265,245	472	Skidmore, Owings &
	New	5,385,898	41,706	96.42	4,021,182	396,880	136,245	320	Merrill
	Renovated	1,464,102	32,249	22.00	709,621	311,835	129,000	152	
Dallas Theological Seminary	Total	5,801,680	58,392	56.72	3,312,190	1,073,215	250,000	584	Tom F. Dance
	New	5,427,534	37,496	85.51	3,206,348	804,911	212,000	312	
	Renovated	374,146	20,896	5.07	105,842	268,304	38,000	272	
Gordon College, Wenham, Mass.	Total	n/a	72,000	77.51	5,581,000	416,000	162,000	468	Roman Assocs.
	New	5,500,000	52,000	99.63	5,181,000	416,000	75,000	252	
	Renovated	n/a	20,000	20.00	400,000	0	87,000	216	

Table 5 / Academic Libraries: Additions and Renovations, 1988 *(cont.)*

Name of Institution		Project Cost	Gross Area	Sq.Ft. Cost	Construction Cost	Equipment Cost	Book Capacity	Seating Capacity	Architect
University of Evansville, Ind.	Total	n/a	84,000	82.21	4,717,000	716,000	400,000	551	Jack H. Kinkel
	New	n/a	56,000	65.70	3,679,260	558,480	n/a	n/a	
	Renovated	n/a	28,000	37.01	1,037,740	157,520	n/a	n/a	
Moorhead State University, Minn.	Total	3,394,000	131,000	24.19	3,168,500	369,000	400,000	900	Yeater Hennings Ruff
	New	n/a	28,000	63.50	1,778,000	79,000	250,000	200	
	Renovated	n/a	103,000	13.50	1,390,500	290,000	150,000	700	
* Southern College of Technology, Marietta, Ga.	Total	n/a	59,000	52.54	3,100,000	350,000	200,000	600	Sizemore & Floyd
	New	n/a	34,000	67.65	2,300,000	n/a	100,000	400	
	Renovated	n/a	25,000	32.00	800,000	n/a	100,000	200	
* Ouachita Baptist University, Arkadelphia, Ark.	Total	1,512,694	40,699	34.40	1,399,992	112,702	292,560	410	Steve Kinzler of Blass Chilcote . . .
	New	n/a	28,263	n/a	n/a	n/a	129,570	246	
	Renovated	n/a	12,436	n/a	n/a	n/a	162,990	164	
Seton Hill College, Greensburg, Pa.	Total	n/a	30,250	51.80	1,567,000	75,000	n/a	n/a	Roach, Wolfish & Tetrich
	New	n/a	10,600	70.00	742,000	n/a	n/a	n/a	
	Renovated	n/a	19,650	41.99	825,000	n/a	n/a	n/a	
Virginia Baldwin Orwig Music Library, Brown University, Providence, R.I.	Total	1,296,500	10,686	76.04	812,600	154,300	61,000	116	Shepley Bulfinch . . .
	New	n/a	1,972	n/a	n/a	n/a	n/a	60	
	Renovated	n/a	8,714	n/a	n/a	n/a	n/a	56	
Lincoln Memorial University, Harrogate, Tenn.	Total	n/a	25,886	38.63	1,000,000	100,000	158,000	200	Allan Assocs.
	New	n/a	12,058	n/a	n/a	n/a	85,000	150	
	Renovated	n/a	13,828	n/a	n/a	n/a	73,000	50	
San Diego State University	Total	n/a	8,450	n/a	n/a	n/a	52,440	97	SDSU Facilities
	New	57,250	3,050	n/a	n/a	n/a	23,640	37	
	Renovated	n/a	5,400	n/a	n/a	n/a	28,800	60	

*Projects that were in progress in 1987 and are now completed.

Table 6 / Academic Libraries: Additions Only, 1988

Name of Institution	Project Cost	Gross Area	Sq.Ft. Cost	Construction Cost	Equipment Cost	Book Capacity	Seating Capacity	Architect
Georgia State University, Atlanta	$12,000,000	122,515	$80.14	$9,818,000	$514,071	400,000	400	Jova, Daniels & Busby
College of William & Mary, Williamsburg, Va.	3,040,841	32,130	89.20	2,866,161	443,000	150,000	334	Perry, Dean, Rogers
* Babson College, Wellesley, Mass.	2,600,000	13,860	165.94	2,300,000	188,000	n/a	270	Arrowstreet, Inc.
Earth & Atmospheric Science Library, Purdue University, West Lafayette, Ind.	n/a	5,375	88.26	474,397	96,000	19,900 +	38	Walter Scholer & Assocs.
Commerce Library, University of Virginia, Charlottesville	n/a	n/a	n/a	n/a	n/a	8,904	68	Hartman & Cox
Biology/Psychology Library, University of Virginia, Charlottesville	n/a	4,407	n/a	n/a	n/a	20,832	79	Kliment & Halsbend

*Projects that were in progress in 1987 and are now completed.

Table 7 / Academic Libraries: Renovations Only, 1988

Name of Institution	Project Cost	Gross Area	Sq.Ft. Cost	Construction Cost	Equipment Cost	Book Capacity	Seating Capacity	Architect
George Washington Univ., Washington, D.C	$1,900,000	58,714	$23.84	$1,400,000	$480,000	107,820 +	392	Mills, Clagett & Wening
* California State University, Chico	836,543	46,820	n/a	n/a	18,000	110,000	450	Statford, King & Assocs.
St. John's University, Collegeville, Minn.	128,810	22,400	n/a	n/a	28,964	n/a	n/a	Hamilton Smith
University of Texas at Austin	20,860	13,835	1.38	19,080	1,780	25,000	n/a	not reported

*Projects that were in progress in 1987 and are now completed.

Table 8 / Public Library Projects in Progress, 1988

NAME OF LIBRARY	STAGES 1	2	3	4	5	6	7	8
ALABAMA								
Hoover PL, Birmingham [1990]	✓	✓		✓		✓		
Boaz PL [1988]	✓	✓	✓	✓	✓	✓	✓	✓
Demopolis PL [1990]	✓	✓		✓	✓			
Eufaula Carnegie Library [?]	✓	✓		✓	✓			✓
Gardendale PL [1989]	✓	✓	✓	✓	✓			
Irondale PL [1989]	✓	✓	✓	✓	✓	✓	✓	✓
Lineville City Library [1989]			✓					
Madison PL [1989]			✓		✓			
Rainsville PL [1990]	✓			✓				
Saraland PL [1989]	✓	✓	✓	✓	✓	✓	✓	✓
ALASKA								
Homer PL [?]			✓	✓	✓			
Hope Community Library [1988]	✓	✓	✓	✓	✓	✓	✓	✓
Haines Borough PL [1988]	✓	✓	✓	✓	✓	✓	✓	✓
Juneau PL [1989]	✓	✓	✓	✓	✓	✓	✓	✓
ARKANSAS								
Arkansas River Valley Regional Lib., Dardanelle [1988]	✓	✓	✓	✓	✓	✓	✓	✓
Columbia County Lib., Magnolia [1988]	✓	✓	✓	✓	✓	✓	✓	✓

NAME OF LIBRARY	STAGES 1	2	3	4	5	6	7	8
Jackson County Lib., Newport [1989]	✓	✓	✓	✓	✓			
North Logon Country Lib., Paris [1989]	✓	✓	✓	✓	✓	✓	✓	✓
Randolph County Lib., Pocahontas [1988]	✓	✓	✓	✓	✓	✓	✓	✓
Pope County Lib., Russellville [1989]	✓	✓	✓	✓	✓			
Sherwood Municipal Library [1988]	✓	✓	✓	✓	✓	✓	✓	✓
ARIZONA								
Tucson PL [1989]	✓	✓	✓	✓	✓	✓	✓	✓
CALIFORNIA								
Beverly Hills PL [1989]	✓	✓	✓	✓	✓	✓	✓	✓
Carlsbad City Library [1991]	✓		✓					
Lancaster Library [?]	✓	✓						
Lawndale Library [?]	✓	✓		✓	✓	✓	✓	
Oceanside PL [1989]	✓	✓	✓	✓	✓	✓	✓	✓
Sacramento PL [1990]	✓	✓	✓	✓	✓			
San Fernando Library [1988]	✓	✓		✓	✓	✓	✓	✓
West Hollywood Library [?]	✓	✓		✓				
South Whittier Lib., Whittier [1988]	✓	✓	✓	✓	✓	✓	✓	✓
Willits Regional Library [1989]	✓	✓	✓	✓	✓	✓	✓	✓
CONNECTICUT								
Fairfield Woods PL, Fairfield [1990]	✓	✓	✓	✓	✓			

Predesign stage: (1) preliminary investigation, (2) program filed, (3) project funded, (4) architect selected. *Design stage*: (5) design stage in progress, (6) construction documents completed, (7) bidding complete, (8) contracts awarded.

The date following the library name represents the estimated year of completion.

Table 8 / Public Library Projects in Progress, 1988 *(cont.)*

NAME OF LIBRARY	STAGES								NAME OF LIBRARY	STAGES							
	1	2	3	4	5	6	7	8		1	2	3	4	5	6	7	8
David Milbunt Lib., Falls Village [1991]	✓	✓		✓	✓				Roddenbery Memorial Library, Cairo [1989]	✓	✓	✓	✓	✓	✓	✓	✓
Greenwich Library [1989]					✓	✓			Calhoun/Gordon County Lib., Calhoun [1989]	✓	✓	✓	✓	✓	✓	✓	✓
Harwinton PL [1989]	✓	✓	✓	✓	✓	✓	✓	✓	R.T. Jones Memorial Library, Canton [1990]	✓	✓						
E.C. Scranton Memorial Lib., Madison [1989]								✓	Embry Hills Library, Chamblee [1990]	✓	✓	✓	✓	✓			
Mystic & Noank Lib., Mystic [1989]	✓	✓		✓					Clarkston Library [1990]	✓	✓	✓	✓				
New Haven Free PL [1989]								✓	South Fulton Lib., College Park [1989]	✓	✓	✓	✓	✓	✓		
East Lyme PL, Niantic [1989]	✓	✓	✓	✓	✓	✓	✓	✓	Nancy Guinn Library, Conyers [1990]	✓	✓	✓	✓	✓			
Prospect PL [?]	✓	✓	✓	✓	✓				Madison County Library, Danielsville [1989]	✓	✓	✓	✓	✓	✓	✓	✓
Plumb Memorial Lib., Shelton [1990]	✓	✓							Avondale Mall Library, Decatur [1989]	✓	✓	✓	✓	✓			
Sherman Library [1990]	✓	✓		✓	✓				Covington Library, Decatur [1990]	✓	✓	✓	✓	✓			
Fairchild-Nichols Branch, Trumbull [1990]					✓				Maud M. Burrus Lib., Decatur [1991]	✓	✓	✓	✓				
Trumbull Library [?]	✓								Scott Candler Library, Decatur [1990]	✓		✓	✓	✓			
Windsor Locks PL [1990]	✓	✓	✓	✓	✓				Northlake PL, Decatur [1990]	✓	✓	✓	✓	✓			
DELAWARE									South DeKalb Area Library, Decatur [1990]	✓	✓	✓	✓	✓			
Greenwood PL [1988]			✓			✓	✓	✓	Southwest DeKalb Library, Decatur [1990]	✓	✓	✓	✓	✓			
Selbyville PL [1988]	✓	✓	✓	✓				✓	Dunwoody PL [1988]	✓	✓	✓	✓	✓	✓	✓	✓
DISTRICT OF COLUMBIA									Jones County PL, Gray [1988]	✓	✓	✓	✓	✓	✓	✓	✓
Library of Congress [1992]	✓	✓	✓	✓	✓	✓	✓	✓	Salter Memorial Library, Hahira [1988]	✓	✓	✓	✓	✓	✓	✓	✓
Shepherd Park Branch [1989]	✓	✓	✓	✓	✓	✓	✓	✓	Hart County Library, Hartwell [1989]	✓	✓	✓	✓	✓	✓		
FLORIDA									Towns County PL, Hiawassee [?]	✓	✓	✓	✓	✓	✓	✓	✓
Boynton Beach City Library [1989]	✓	✓	✓	✓	✓	✓	✓	✓	Lakes Library, Lake Park [1989]	✓	✓	✓	✓	✓			
Brandon Regional Library [1990]	✓	✓	✓	✓	✓				Lithonia Library [1990]	✓		✓	✓	✓			
Hugh Embry Library, Dade City [1990]	✓	✓	✓	✓	✓				Salem/Panola Library, Lithonia [1990]	✓	✓	✓	✓	✓			
Deerfield Beach Branch [1990]	✓	✓	✓	✓	✓				O'Kelly Memorial Library, Loganville [1989]							✓	
DeLand Area PL [1989]	✓	✓	✓	✓	✓	✓	✓	✓	Morgan Cty. Lib., Madison [1988]								✓
Hudson Area Library [1989]			✓	✓		✓	✓	✓	Moultrie-Colquit Cty. Lib., Moultrie [1989]	✓	✓	✓	✓	✓			
Land O'Lakes Branch Library [1990]	✓	✓	✓	✓	✓				Nicholson PL [1989]	✓	✓	✓	✓	✓			
Madison County PL, Madison [1989]			✓	✓	✓	✓	✓	✓	East DeKalb Area Library, Redan [1990]	✓	✓	✓	✓	✓			
Melbourne PL [1989]	✓	✓	✓	✓	✓	✓	✓	✓	Redan/Hairston Library [1990]	✓	✓	✓	✓	✓			
Ormond Beach PL [1989]	✓	✓	✓	✓	✓				Sara Hightower Regional Lib., Rome [1988]	✓	✓	✓	✓	✓	✓	✓	✓

Putnam County Lib. System, Palatka [?]	✓	✓						
Regency Park Branch, Port Richey [1989]	✓	✓	✓	✓				✓
Sunrise Branch Library [?]	✓	✓	✓	✓	✓			
Leon County PL, Tallahassee [1990]	✓	✓	✓	✓	✓	✓		
College Hill Branch, Tampa [1988]	✓	✓	✓	✓	✓			
Thonotosassa Branch [1989]	✓	✓	✓	✓	✓	✓	✓	✓
GEORGIA								
Cook County Library, Adel [1989]	✓	✓	✓	✓	✓			
Southside Branch, Albany [1989]	✓	✓	✓	✓	✓	✓	✓	✓
Tallulah Massey Branch, Albany [1989]	✓	✓	✓	✓	✓			
Alpharetta Branch [1989]	✓	✓	✓	✓	✓	✓	✓	✓
Victoria Evans Memorial Lib., Ashburn [1988]	✓	✓	✓	✓	✓	✓	✓	✓
Athens Regional Library [1991]	✓	✓	✓	✓				
Auburn Avenue Library, Atlanta [1990]	✓	✓	✓					
Briarcliff Library, Atlanta [1990]	✓	✓	✓	✓	✓			
Brookhaven Library, Atlanta [1990]	✓		✓	✓	✓			
Buckhead Library, Atlanta [1989]	✓	✓	✓	✓	✓	✓	✓	
Central Library, Atlanta [1990]	✓	✓	✓	✓				
Central Library, Atlanta [1989]	✓	✓	✓	✓	✓	✓	✓	✓
Chamblee PL, Atlanta [1989]	✓	✓	✓	✓	✓	✓	✓	✓
Cleveland Avenue Lib., Atlanta [1989]	✓	✓	✓	✓	✓			
Collier Heights Lib., Atlanta [1989]	✓	✓	✓	✓	✓	✓	✓	✓
Dogwood Library, Atlanta [1989]	✓	✓	✓					
Gresham Homework Center Lib., Atlanta [1990]	✓	✓	✓	✓	✓			
Northside Library, Atlanta [1989]	✓	✓	✓	✓	✓	✓	✓	✓
Ponce de Leon Lib., Atlanta [1989]	✓	✓	✓	✓	✓	✓	✓	
Public Housing Libraries, Atlanta [1989]	✓	✓	✓					
Sandy Springs Regional Lib., Atlanta [1989]	✓	✓	✓	✓	✓	✓	✓	✓
Southwest Regional Lib., Atlanta [1989]	✓	✓	✓	✓	✓	✓	✓	✓
West End Library, Atlanta [1989]	✓	✓	✓					
West Hunter Library, Atlanta [1989]	✓	✓	✓					
Union County PL, Blairsville [?]	✓	✓	✓	✓	✓	✓	✓	✓
Warren P. Sewell Memorial Lib., Bowdon [1988]	✓	✓	✓	✓				✓
Warren P. Sewell Memorial Lib., Bremen [1988]	✓	✓	✓	✓				✓

Roswell Library [1989]	✓	✓	✓	✓	✓	✓	✓	✓
Hancock Cty. Lib., Sparta [1989]								✓
Sue Kellogg PL, Stone Mountain [1988]	✓	✓	✓	✓	✓	✓	✓	✓
Screven County Library, Sylvania [1988]	✓	✓	✓	✓	✓	✓	✓	✓
Haralson County Civic Lib., Tallapoosa [1990]	✓	✓						
Warren County Library, Warrenton [1989]	✓	✓	✓	✓	✓	✓		
Woodstock PL [1989]	✓	✓	✓	✓	✓	✓	✓	✓
Pike County Library, Zebulon [1989]	✓	✓	✓	✓	✓			
IDAHO								
Boise PL [1989]	✓	✓	✓	✓	✓			
Kootenai County Libs., Hayden [?]	✓							
East Bonner County Lib., Sandpoint [1990]	✓	✓		✓	✓			
ILLINOIS								
Belleville PL [1989]					✓			✓
Bement Township Library [1989]	✓	✓	✓	✓	✓	✓	✓	✓
Bridgeview PL [1988]	✓	✓	✓	✓	✓	✓	✓	✓
Hope Weltry Twp. Lib., Cerro Gordo [1988]	✓	✓	✓	✓	✓	✓	✓	✓
Chester PL [1989]	✓	✓	✓	✓	✓	✓	✓	✓
Chicago PL [1991]	✓	✓	✓	✓	✓			
Hegewisch Branch, Chicago [?]	✓	✓	✓	✓	✓			
Kelly Branch Library, Chicago [1988]	✓	✓	✓	✓				✓
Logan Square Branch, Chicago [1989]	✓	✓	✓	✓				✓
Mount Greenwood Branch Lib., Chicago [?]	✓	✓	✓	✓	✓			
Pilsen Branch Library, Chicago [1988]	✓	✓	✓	✓				✓
Portage-Cragin Branch Lib., Chicago [1989]	✓	✓	✓	✓		✓		
Uptown Branch Library, Chicago [1990]	✓	✓	✓	✓	✓			
Elmwood Park PL [1989]	✓	✓	✓	✓		✓		
Fairview Heights PL [1989]	✓	✓	✓	✓	✓	✓		
Franklin Park PL [1988]	✓	✓	✓	✓	✓	✓	✓	✓
Schmaling Memorial PL Dist., Fulton [1989]	✓	✓	✓	✓	✓	✓	✓	✓
DuPage Library System, Geneva [1988]	✓	✓	✓	✓	✓	✓	✓	✓
Heyworth PL District [1988]	✓	✓	✓	✓	✓	✓	✓	✓
Highland Park PL [1989]	✓	✓	✓	✓	✓	✓	✓	✓
Hinsdale PL [1989]	✓	✓	✓	✓	✓	✓	✓	✓

Table 8 / Public Library Projects in Progress, 1988 *(ccnt.)*

NAME OF LIBRARY	STAGES							
	1	2	3	4	5	6	7	8
Homewood PL [1989]	✔	✔	✔	✔	✔	✔	✔	✔
La Grange Park PL [1989]						✔		
Palos Heights PL [1988]	✔	✔	✔	✔	✔	✔	✔	✔
Lakeview Branch, Peoria [1988]	✔	✔	✔	✔	✔	✔	✔	✔
Riverdale PL District [1989]	✔	✔	✔	✔	✔	✔	✔	✔
St. Charles PL District [1989]	✔	✔	✔	✔	✔	✔	✔	✔
St. Joseph Township-Swearingen Memorial Lib. [1988]	✔	✔	✔	✔	✔	✔	✔	✔
South Beloit PL [1988]	✔	✔	✔	✔	✔	✔	✔	✔
Towanda District Library [1988]	✔	✔	✔	✔	✔	✔	✔	✔
INDIANA								
Alexandria-Monroe PL [1989]	✔	✔	✔	✔	✔	✔	✔	
Bloomfield-Eastern Greene County PL [1990]	✔	✔	✔	✔	✔			
Clinton PL [1993]	✔							
Evansville-Vanderburgh County PL [1990]	✔		✔	✔				
Goshen PL [1989]	✔	✔	✔	✔	✔			
Hagerstown-Jefferson Twp. Library [1989]	✔	✔	✔	✔	✔	✔		
Hammond PL [1988]	✔	✔	✔	✔	✔	✔	✔	✔
Hartford City PL [1989]	✔	✔	✔	✔	✔	✔	✔	✔
Jasper PL [1990]	✔			✔				
Jeffersonville Twp. PL [1988]	✔	✔	✔	✔	✔	✔	✔	✔
Tippecanoe Cty. PL, Lafayette [1989]	✔	✔	✔	✔	✔	✔	✔	✔
La Porte County PL [1990]	✔	✔		✔	✔	✔	✔	
Magan County PL., Marlinsville [1990]	✔			✔	✔			
Peru PL [1988]						✔		
Rushville PL [1989]	✔	✔	✔	✔	✔	✔	✔	✔
South Bend PL [1990]	✔	✔		✔	✔			
Syracuse-Turkey Creek Twp. PL [?]	✔							
Switzerland Co. PL., Vevay [?]	✔							
Winchester Community Library [1990]	✔	✔		✔	✔			
KANSAS								
Americus Twp. Library [?]			✔	✔		✔		

NAME OF LIBRARY	STAGES							
	1	2	3	4	5	6	7	8
Napoleon Library, New Orleans [1939]			✔	✔	✔			
Navra Library, New Orleans [1989]			✔	✔		✔		
Nix Library, New Orleans [?]			✔	✔	✔			
St. John the Baptist Parish Lib., Reserve [1988]			✔	✔			✔	✔
Shreve Memorial Lib., Shreveport [1988]	✔	✔	✔	✔	✔	✔	✔	✔
Slidell Branch Library [1988]	✔	✔	✔	✔	✔	✔	✔	✔
Live Oak Branch, Waggaman [1989]	✔	✔	✔	✔	✔	✔	✔	✔
MAINE								
Lewiston PL [1990]	✔	✔						
MARYLAND								
Anne Arundel Cty. Library, Annapolis [1991]	✔	✔	✔	✔				
Crofton Area Library, Annapolis [1995]	✔							
Edgewater Branch, Annapolis [1990]	✔	✔	✔	✔	✔			
Severna Park Branch, Annapolis [1990]	✔	✔	✔	✔	✔			
Bel Air Branch [1990]	✔	✔	✔					
Little Falls Community Library, Bethesda [1990]	✔	✔	✔	✔	✔			
Brunswick PL [1989]			✔	✔		✔	✔	✔
Chevy Chase Community Library [1990]	✔	✔	✔	✔	✔			
Damascus Community Library [1990]	✔	✔	✔	✔	✔			
Germantown Community Library [1990]	✔	✔	✔	✔	✔			
Greenbelt Branch [1988]								✔
Hyattsville Branch [1989]								✔
Kensington Park Comm. Lib., Kensington [1990]	✔	✔	✔					
Laurel Branch [1990]	✔			✔				
Aspen Hill Community Library, Rockville [1989]	✔	✔	✔	✔	✔			
Rockville Regional Library [1992]	✔	✔						
Twinbrook Community Lib., Rockville [19991]	✔	✔						
Fairland Community Lib., Silver Spring [1992]	✔	✔	✔					
White Oak Community Lib., Silver Spring [1989]	✔	✔	✔	✔	✔	✔	✔	✔
Largo-Kettering Branch, Upper Marlboro [?]	✔							
Whiteford Branch [1990]	✔		✔					
MASSACHUSETTS								

Mc Cracken PL [1989]						✓		
KENTUCKY								
Boyd County PL, Ashland [1988]	✓	✓	✓	✓	✓	✓	✓	✓
Bowling Green PL [1988]	✓	✓	✓	✓	✓	✓	✓	✓
Harrison County PL, Cynthiana [1989]	✓	✓	✓	✓	✓			
Danville-Boyle Cty. PL [1989]	✓	✓	✓	✓	✓	✓	✓	✓
Pike County PL, Elkhorn City [1989]	✓	✓	✓	✓	✓	✓		
Todd Cty. PL, Elkton [1989]	✓	✓	✓	✓	✓			
Henry Cty. PL, Eminence [1989]	✓	✓	✓	✓	✓	✓	✓	✓
Boone Cty. PL, Florence [1989]	✓	✓	✓	✓	✓	✓		
Paul Sawyier PL, Frankfort [1988]	✓	✓	✓	✓	✓	✓	✓	✓
Perry Cty. PL, Hazard [1989]	✓	✓	✓	✓	✓			
Breathitt Cty. PL, Jackson [1989]	✓	✓	✓	✓	✓			
Russell Cty. PL, Jamestown [1989]	✓	✓	✓	✓	✓	✓	✓	✓
Lexington PL [1988]	✓	✓	✓	✓	✓	✓		
Casey County PL, Liberty [?]	✓	✓		✓	✓			
Louisville Free PL [1989]	✓	✓	✓	✓	✓	✓		
Campbell County PL, Newport [1988]	✓	✓	✓	✓	✓	✓	✓	✓
Paris-Bourbon County PL, Paris [1989]	✓	✓	✓	✓	✓	✓	✓	✓
Madison Cty. PL, Richmond [1989]	✓	✓	✓	✓	✓			
Magoffin Cty. PL, Salyersville [1989]	✓	✓	✓	✓	✓			
LOUISIANA								
Ascension Parish Lib., Donaldsonville [?]	✓			✓				
West Bank Regional Lib., Harvey [1989]	✓	✓	✓	✓	✓	✓	✓	✓
Claiborne Parish Library, Homer [1988]	✓	✓	✓	✓	✓	✓	✓	✓
Vernon Parish Library, Leesville [?]	✓			✓	✓			
East Bank Regional Lib., Metairie [1990]	✓	✓	✓	✓	✓	✓	✓	✓
Webster Parish Library, Minden [?]	✓							
Algiers Point Library, New Orleans [1989]			✓	✓		✓		
Algiers Regional Lib., New Orleans [1989]			✓	✓		✓		
Broadmoor Library, New Orleans [1990]			✓					
East New Orleans Lib., New Orleans [1988]			✓	✓				
Latter Library, New Orleans [1989]			✓	✓	✓			

Jones Library, Amherst [1990]	✓	✓	✓	✓	✓			
Memorial Hall Library, Andover [1988]								✓
Robbins Library, Arlington [1992]	✓	✓		✓	✓			
Attleboro PL [1991]					✓			
Bellingham PL [1989]	✓	✓	✓	✓	✓	✓	✓	✓
Boston PL [1993]	✓	✓	✓	✓	✓			
Chelmsford PL [?]	✓	✓		✓	✓			
Chelsea PL [1989]	✓	✓	✓	✓	✓	✓	✓	✓
Chilmark PL [1990]	✓	✓		✓	✓			
Gale Free Library, Holden [1989]	✓	✓	✓	✓	✓	✓	✓	✓
Lancaster Town Library [1988]					✓			
Lincoln PL [1989]	✓	✓	✓	✓	✓	✓	✓	✓
Reuben Hoar Lib., Littleton [1989]	✓	✓	✓	✓	✓	✓	✓	✓
Hubbard Memorial Library, Ludlow [?]	✓	✓	✓	✓	✓			
Malden PL [1988]								✓
Mansfield PL [1989]								✓
Middleborough PL [1990]	✓	✓		✓	✓			
Monson Free Library [1989]	✓	✓	✓	✓				✓
Newton Free Library [1990]	✓	✓	✓	✓	✓	✓		
Stevens Memorial Lib., North Andover [?]	✓	✓		✓	✓			
Pembroke PL [1990]	✓	✓	✓	✓	✓			
Provincetown PL [1988]			✓	✓		✓	✓	✓
Richard Sugden Library, Spencer [?]	✓		✓	✓	✓			
Conant PL, Sterling [1989]						✓		✓
Joshua Hyde Library, Sturbridge [1989]			✓	✓		✓	✓	
Wareham Free Library [1990]	✓	✓	✓	✓	✓	✓		
G.A.R. Memorial Lib., West Newbury [1988]	✓	✓	✓	✓	✓	✓	✓	✓
J.V. Fletcher Lib., Westford [1989]	✓	✓	✓	✓	✓	✓	✓	✓
Whitman PL [1988]	✓	✓	✓	✓	✓	✓	✓	✓
Fiske PL, Wrentham [?]				✓				
MICHIGAN								
Auburn Hills PL [1989]					✓			
Howe Memorial Library, Breckenridge [?]	✓				✓			

Table 8 / Public Library Projects in Progress, 1988 *(cont.)*

NAME OF LIBRARY	STAGES 1	2	3	4	5	6	7	8
Burr Oak Twp. Library [1989]	✓			✓	✓			
Canton PL [1988]	✓	✓	✓	✓	✓	✓	✓	✓
Charlotte PL [1989]				✓	✓			
Mason/Union Branch, Edwardsburg [1988]	✓	✓	✓	✓	✓	✓	✓	✓
Fennville District Lib. & Enrichment Ctr. [1989]						✓		
Georgetown Twp. PL, Jenison [1989]	✓	✓	✓	✓	✓			
Orion Township PL, Lake Orion [1988]	✓	✓	✓	✓	✓	✓	✓	✓
Library of Michigan, Lansing [1988]								✓
Livonia PL [1988]								✓
Milford Twp. Library [1989]		✓	✓	✓		✓	✓	✓
Oakland Cty. Library, Pontiac [1991]	✓	✓		✓				
MINNESOTA								
Detroit Lakes PL [1989]	✓	✓	✓	✓		✓	✓	✓
Minnetonka Community Library [1989]		✓	✓	✓		✓	✓	✓
Moorhead PL [1988]	✓	✓	✓	✓	✓	✓	✓	✓
Pelican Rapids PL [1989]	✓	✓	✓	✓	✓	✓	✓	✓
MISSISSIPPI								
Hancock County Library System, Bay St. Louis [1988]	✓	✓	✓	✓	✓	✓	✓	✓
Bude PL [1988]								✓
VanCleave Mem. Lib., Centreville [1988]	✓	✓	✓	✓	✓	✓	✓	✓
Robinson-Carpenter Memorial Library, Cleveland [1989]	✓	✓	✓	✓	✓	✓		
Elizabeth Jones PL, Grenada [1989]	✓		✓	✓	✓	✓	✓	✓
Newhebron PL [1989]								✓
Ridgeland PL [1988]	✓	✓	✓	✓	✓	✓	✓	✓
Ricks Memorial Library, Yazoo City [1989]	✓		✓	✓	✓	✓		
MISSOURI								
Bonne Terre Memorial Library [1989]	✓	✓	✓	✓	✓			
Kansas City PL, Independence [1988]								✓

NAME OF LIBRARY	STAGES 1	2	3	4	5	6	7	8
Afton Free Library [?]	✓							
Allegany PL [1989]	✓	✓						
Amityville PL [1990]	✓	✓		✓	✓			
Stevens Memorial Library, Attica [1990]	✓	✓						
Babylon PL [?]	✓	✓		✓	✓			
Barker Free Library [1990]	✓	✓			✓			
Bellmore Memorial Library [1989]	✓	✓	✓	✓	✓			
Byron-Bergen PL, Bergen [1989]	✓	✓	✓	✓	✓	✓		
Bethpage PL [1990]	✓							
Broome Cty. PL, Binghamton [?]	✓							
Bay Shore PL, Brightwaters [1988]	✓	✓	✓	✓	✓			
Bristol Library [?]	✓							
Seymour Library, Brockport [?]	✓	✓						
Brookhaven Free Library [1988]	✓	✓	✓	✓	✓	✓	✓	
Mott Haven Branch, Bronx [?]	✓							
Brighton Beach Branch, Brooklyn [1989]	✓	✓	✓	✓	✓			
Brower Park Branch, Brooklyn [1989]	✓	✓	✓	✓	✓			
Canarsie Branch, Brooklyn [1990]	✓	✓						
Clarendon Branch, Brooklyn [1989]	✓	✓	✓	✓	✓	✓	✓	✓
Cypress Hills Branch, Brooklyn [1990]	✓	✓						
East Flatbush Branch, Brooklyn [?]	✓	✓	✓	✓	✓	✓	✓	✓
Gerritsen Beach Branch, Brooklyn [1992]	✓	✓						
Homecrest Branch, Brooklyn [1990]	✓	✓	✓					
McKinley Park Branch, Brooklyn [1991]	✓	✓	✓					
Ulmer Park Drive Branch, Brooklyn [1990]	✓	✓	✓					
Canajoharie Library [1989]	✓	✓	✓	✓	✓			
Wood Library, Canandaiqua [?]	✓							
Cazenovia PL [?]	✓	✓		✓	✓			
Cheektowaga PL [1991]	✓	✓						
Riga Free Library, Churchville [1989]	✓	✓	✓	✓	✓	✓		
Clayville Library [?]	✓							

Mid-Continent PL, Independence [1988]								✓
Kansas City PL [1988]								✓
South Branch, Kansas City [1988]								✓
St. Louis Cty. Library, Ladue [1989]	✓	✓	✓	✓	✓	✓	✓	✓
Ray County Lib., Richmond [?]			✓				✓	✓
Boonslick Regional Lib., Sedalia [1988]	✓	✓	✓	✓	✓	✓	✓	✓
Scenic Regional Library, Union [?]	✓							
MONTANA								
Chouteau Cty. Free Lib., Fort Benton [1988]			✓	✓		✓	✓	✓
Lewis and Clark PL, Helena [1988]	✓	✓	✓	✓	✓	✓	✓	✓
Laurel PL [1988]								✓
Polson City Library [1988]	✓	✓	✓	✓	✓	✓	✓	✓
NEVADA								
Las Vegas Library/ Discovery: Children's Museum [1990]		✓	✓	✓		✓	✓	✓
West Las Vegas Library [1988]	✓	✓	✓	✓		✓	✓	✓
NEW HAMPSHIRE								
Dover PL [1988]	✓	✓	✓	✓		✓	✓	✓
Hancock Town Library [1988]	✓	✓	✓	✓	✓	✓	✓	✓
Laconia PL [1989]	✓	✓	✓	✓	✓	✓	✓	✓
Orford Social Library [1988]								✓
Sanbornton PL [1988]	✓	✓	✓	✓	✓	✓	✓	✓
Whitefield PL [1988]	✓	✓	✓	✓	✓	✓	✓	✓
Wilton PL-Gregg Free Library [1988]	✓	✓	✓	✓	✓	✓	✓	✓
NEW JERSEY								
Eastern Branch Lib., Shrewsbury [1990]	✓	✓	✓	✓	✓	✓	✓	✓
NEW MEXICO								
Thomas Branigan Lib., Las Cruces [1988]	✓	✓	✓	✓	✓	✓	✓	✓
Rio Rancho PL [1989]	✓		✓	✓				
Roswell PL [1989]	✓	✓	✓	✓	✓	✓	✓	✓
Villa Linda Mall, Santa Fe [1988]	✓	✓	✓	✓	✓			
Truth or Consequences PL [1988]	✓	✓	✓	✓	✓	✓	✓	✓
NEW YORK								
Addison PL [1992]	✓	✓						

Shenendehowa PL, Clifton Park [1990]	✓	✓						
Kirkland Town Lib., Clinton [?]	✓	✓						
Copiague Memorial PL [1989]	✓	✓	✓	✓	✓	✓	✓	✓
Cornwall PL, Cornwall-on-Hudson [1990]	✓	✓		✓	✓			
Cortland Free Library [?]	✓	✓	✓					
Hammond Library, Crown Point [1989]	✓	✓	✓	✓	✓	✓	✓	✓
Cutchogue Free Library [1989]	✓	✓	✓	✓	✓	✓	✓	✓
Bethlehem PL, Delmar [1990]	✓	✓						
Half Hollow Hills Comm. Lib., Dix Hills [1989]	✓	✓	✓	✓	✓	✓	✓	✓
East Syracuse Free Library [1988]	✓	✓	✓	✓	✓	✓	✓	✓
West Harrison Library, East White Plains [1991]	✓	✓						
Eden Library [1989]	✓	✓		✓	✓			
Floral Park PL [1989]	✓	✓	✓					
Freeport Memorial Library [1989]	✓	✓						
Geneva Free Library [?]	✓	✓						
Glen Cove PL [1990]	✓	✓	✓	✓	✓			
Grand Island Memorial Library [1989]	✓	✓	✓	✓	✓	✓	✓	✓
Floyd Memorial Lib., Greenport [1989]	✓	✓						
Guilderland Free Library [?]	✓							
Hamburg PL [1991]	✓	✓						
Hampton Bays PL [1990]	✓	✓		✓	✓			
Louise Read Memorial Lib., Hancock [1989]	✓	✓	✓	✓	✓			
Harrison PL [1989]	✓	✓		✓	✓			
Haverstraw King's Daughters PL [1990]	✓							
Hewlett-Woodmere PL [1991]	✓	✓		✓	✓			
Hicksville PL [1989]	✓	✓		✓	✓			
Highland PL [?]	✓							
Highland Falls Library [1991]	✓							
Sachem PL, Holbrook [1991]	✓	✓						
Hornell PL [?]	✓							
Huntington PL [1989]	✓	✓						
Island Park PL [?]	✓	✓						
Finger Lakes Lib. System, Ithaca [?]	✓		✓					
Queens Borough PL, Jamaica [1989]	✓	✓		✓	✓			

Table 8 / Public Library Projects in Progress, 1988 *(cont.)*

NAME OF LIBRARY	STAGES 1	2	3	4	5	6	7	8
Queens Borough PL, Jamaica [1990]	✓	✓		✓	✓			
Jeffersonville PL [1991]	✓	✓	✓	✓	✓	✓	✓	
Katonah Village Library [1990]	✓	✓						
Lackawanna PL [?]	✓	✓						
Orleans PL, La Fargeville [?]	✓							
Island Trees PL, Levittown [1989]	✓	✓		✓	✓			
Lewiston PL [1990]	✓	✓		✓	✓			
Liverpool PL [1993]	✓							
Livonia PL [1991]	✓	✓						
Nioga Library System, Lockport [1989]	✓	✓	✓		✓			
William Sanford Town Lib., Loudonville [1989]	✓	✓	✓	✓	✓	✓	✓	✓
Lynbrook PL [1989]	✓	✓		✓	✓			
Massapequa PL [1989]	✓	✓						
Mechanicville District PL [?]	✓	✓						
Melville Branch Library [1989]	✓	✓	✓	✓	✓	✓	✓	✓
Merrick Library [?]	✓	✓		✓	✓			
Longwood PL, Middle Island [1988]	✓	✓	✓	✓	✓	✓	✓	✓
Weller Library, Mohawk [?]	✓	✓						
Montauk Library [1989]	✓	✓	✓	✓	✓			
Nanuet PL [1989]	✓	✓	✓	✓	✓			
New Berlin Library [1988]	✓	✓	✓	✓	✓	✓	✓	✓
New City Library [1988]				✓		✓	✓	✓
New Hartford PL [?]	✓	✓						
Hillside PL, New Hyde Park [?]	✓	✓						
New York PL/Research Libraries [1989]	✓	✓	✓	✓	✓	✓	✓	✓
Countee Cullen Regional Lib., New York [1989]	✓	✓	✓	✓	✓	✓	✓	✓
Jefferson Market Branch, New York [?]	✓	✓	✓					
Ninety-Sixth Street Regional Branch, New York [1989]	✓	✓	✓	✓	✓			
Tompkins Square Branch, New York [?]	✓	✓	✓					
Newark PL [?]	✓							

NAME OF LIBRARY	STAGES 1	2	3	4	5	6	7	8
Schenectady County PL [1991]	✓	✓		✓	✓			
Rotterdam Branch Lib., Schenectacy [?]	✓	✓	✓	✓	✓	✓	✓	✓
Glenville Branch, Scotia [1989]	✓	✓	✓	✓	✓	✓		
Seaford PL [1991]	✓	✓						
Sherburne PL [?]	✓							
Mastics-Moriches-Shirley PL, Shirley [1990]	✓	✓		✓	✓			
John C. Hart Memorial Library, Shrub Oak [1989]	✓	✓	✓	✓	✓			
Smithtown Library [?]	✓	✓		✓	✓			
Rogers Memorial Lib., Southampton [1992]	✓	✓		✓	✓			
Southold Free Library [1990]	✓	✓		✓	✓			
Ogden Farmers' Library, Spencerport [1989]	✓	✓		✓	✓			
Staatsburg Library [?]	✓							
Tottenville Branch Lib., Staten Island [?]	✓	✓	✓					
Mary E. Seymour Memorial Free Lib., Stockton [1989]	✓	✓						
Stony Creek Free Library [1989]	✓	✓	✓					
Mundy Branch Library, Syracuse [1989]	✓	✓	✓	✓	✓	✓	✓	✓
Tappan Library [?]	✓							
Troy PL [1991]	✓	✓		✓	✓			
Tuxedo Park Library [1989]	✓	✓						
Utica PL [1989]	✓	✓	✓	✓	✓	✓		
Valley Cottage Free Library [1992]	✓	✓		✓	✓			
Waldinger Memorial Lib., Valley Stream [?]	✓			✓				
Vestal PL [?]	✓	✓		✓	✓			
Victor Free Library [?]	✓	✓						
Voorheesville Central Sch. Dist. Lib. [1989]	✓	✓	✓	✓	✓	✓	✓	✓
William B. Ogden Free Lib., Walton [1990]	✓	✓	✓	✓	✓	✓		
Warsaw PL [1988]	✓	✓	✓	✓	✓	✓	✓	✓
Westport Library Association [?]	✓	✓		✓	✓			
Wolcott Civic Free Library [1989]	✓	✓		✓	✓			

North Bellmore PL [1989]	✓	✓	✓	✓	✓	✓	✓	✓
North Collins Memorial Library [1990]	✓	✓		✓	✓	✓		
Northport-East Northport PL [1991]	✓	✓		✓	✓			
Northport PL [1989]	✓	✓		✓	✓			
Oceanside Free Library [1990]	✓							
Oneida Library [?]	✓	✓						
Orchard Park PL [?]	✓	✓						
Ossining PL [?]	✓	✓		✓	✓			
Oyster Bay-East Norwich PL [1990]	✓	✓						
Pearl River PL [?]	✓	✓	✓	✓	✓			
Pelham PL [?]	✓							
Perry PL [?]	✓	✓						
Phoenix PL [?]	✓							
Pittsford Community Library [1989]	✓							
Plainview-Old Bethpage PL [?]	✓	✓		✓	✓			
Port Jefferson Free Library [1989]	✓	✓	✓					
Port Washington PL [?]	✓	✓						
Adriance Memorial Lib., Poughkeepsie [1991]	✓							
Rego Park Branch [1989]	✓	✓	✓	✓	✓	✓	✓	✓
Brighton Memorial Library, Rochester [?]	✓	✓						
Chili PL, Rochester [1990]	✓	✓						
Gates PL, Rochester [1992]	✓	✓						
Greece PL, Rochester [1990]	✓	✓						
Lincoln Branch, Rochester [1989]	✓	✓						
Maplewood Branch, Rochester [1991]	✓	✓						
Marketview Branch, Rochester [1991]	✓	✓						
North Hampton Branch, Rochester [?]	✓	✓						
Rochester PL [1992]	✓	✓						
Sully Branch, Rochester [1992]	✓	✓						
Rockville Centre PL [1990]	✓	✓	✓	✓	✓	✓	✓	✓
Roosevelt PL [1989]	✓	✓	✓	✓	✓	✓	✓	✓
Bryant Library, Roslyn [?]	✓	✓						
Saratoga Springs PL [1991]	✓	✓						
Arvilla E. Diver Memorial Lib., Schaghticoke [?]	✓	✓	✓	✓	✓			

NORTH CAROLINA								
Wake County PL, Apex [1989]	✓	✓	✓	✓	✓			
Pender County PL, Burgaw [1989]	✓	✓	✓	✓		✓		
Canton Branch Library [1990]	✓	✓	✓	✓		✓		
Chapel Hill PL [1992]	✓	✓	✓	✓				
Charlotte & Mecklenburg Cty. Lib. [1989]	✓	✓						
Charlotte & Mecklenburg Cty. Lib. [1989]	✓	✓	✓	✓	✓	✓	✓	✓
Charlotte & Mecklenburg Cty. Lib. [1990]	✓	✓	✓	✓				
Rosenboro Library, Clinton [1989]	✓	✓	✓	✓	✓			
Granville Cty. Library System, Creedmoor [1988]	✓	✓	✓	✓	✓	✓	✓	✓
Danbury PL [1989]						✓		
Northwest Branch, Fayetteville [1990]	✓	✓	✓	✓				
Macon County PL [1990]	✓	✓		✓	✓			
Wake County PL [1988]	✓	✓	✓	✓	✓	✓	✓	✓
Sheppard Memorial Lib., Greenville [1989]	✓	✓	✓	✓	✓	✓		
Caldwell County PL, Lenoir [1989]	✓	✓	✓	✓	✓			
Kill Devil Hills Branch, Manteo [1990]	✓	✓	✓	✓	✓	✓		
Cameron Village Regional Lib., Raleigh [1989]	✓	✓	✓	✓	✓	✓		
Richard B. Harrison Library, Raleigh [1989]	✓	✓	✓	✓	✓	✓	✓	✓
Roanoke Rapids PL [1988]	✓	✓	✓	✓	✓	✓	✓	✓
Rowan PL, Salisbury [1989]	✓	✓	✓	✓	✓	✓	✓	✓
Cleveland Cty. Memorial Lib., Shelby [1990]	✓	✓	✓	✓	✓			
Thomasville PL [1990]	✓	✓	✓	✓	✓			
Wake County PL, Wendell [?]	✓	✓	✓	✓	✓	✓	✓	✓
Martin Memorial Library, Washington [1991]	✓	✓		✓	✓			
NORTH DAKOTA								
Bismarck Veterans Memorial PL [1989]							✓	✓
Minot PL [1988]	✓	✓	✓	✓	✓	✓	✓	✓
OHIO								
Bellevue PL [1988]	✓	✓	✓	✓	✓	✓	✓	✓
Berea Branch [1989]	✓	✓	✓	✓	✓	✓	✓	✓
Blanchester PL [1989]	✓	✓	✓	✓	✓	✓	✓	✓
Brecksville Branch [1990]	✓	✓	✓	✓	✓			

Table 8 / Public Library Projects in Progress, 1988 *(cont.)*

NAME OF LIBRARY	STAGES							
	1	2	3	4	5	6	7	8
Bristol PL, Bristolville [1990]				✓	✓			
Bucyrus PL [1989]			✓	✓		✓	✓	✓
Caldwell PL [1989]	✓	✓	✓	✓		✓	✓	✓
Mercer Cty. District PL, Celina [1989]	✓	✓		✓	✓			
Chagrin Falls Branch [1989]	✓	✓	✓	✓	✓	✓	✓	✓
Cleveland PL [1989]	✓	✓	✓	✓	✓	✓	✓	✓
Cuyahoga Cty. PL, Cleveland [1991]	✓	✓	✓	✓	✓			
Grandview Heights PL, Columbus [1989]	✓	✓	✓	✓	✓	✓	✓	✓
Karl Road Branch, Columbus [1988]	✓	✓	✓	✓	✓	✓	✓	✓
Main Library, Columbus [?]	✓	✓	✓	✓	✓			
Parsons Branch, Columbus [?]	✓	✓	✓	✓	✓			
Taylor Memorial PL, Cuyahoga Falls [1989]	✓	✓	✓	✓	✓	✓	✓	✓
Dublin Branch [?]		✓	✓	✓	✓			
Findlay-Hancock County PL, Findlay [1990]	✓	✓		✓	✓	✓		
Birchard PL, Fremont [1989]	✓	✓	✓	✓	✓	✓	✓	✓
Dr. Samuel L. Bossard Memorial Lib., Gallipolis [?]	✓							
Mary P. Shelton PL, Georgetown [1989]	✓	✓	✓	✓		✓	✓	✓
Lima PL [1990]	✓	✓	✓	✓	✓			
London PL [1989]			✓	✓		✓		
Madison Branch, Mansfield [1989]	✓	✓	✓	✓	✓	✓	✓	✓
Mansfield-Richland County PL [1988]	✓	✓	✓	✓	✓	✓	✓	✓
Massillon PL [1989]	✓	✓	✓	✓		✓	✓	✓
Massillon PL [?]	✓	✓						
Mount Vernon PL [1989]	✓	✓	✓	✓		✓	✓	✓
Nelsonville PL [1988]								✓
New Breman Branch Lib. [1989]					✓			
Tuscarawas County PL, New Philadelphia [1990]	✓	✓		✓	✓			
Oberlin PL [1990]		✓		✓	✓			

NAME OF LIBRARY	STAGES							
	1	2	3	4	5	6	7	8
Hermiston PL [1989]	✓	✓	✓	✓	✓	✓	✓	✓
North Bend PL [1989]	✓	✓	✓	✓	✓	✓	✓	✓
Sisters Branch Library [1989]	✓		✓					
Stayton PL [1989]	✓			✓	✓			
West Linn PL [1989]	✓	✓	✓	✓	✓			
PENNSYLVANIA								
Bucks County Free Lib., Doylestown [1988]	✓							
Wolfsohn Memorial Library, King of Prussia [1989]	✓	✓	✓	✓	✓	✓	✓	✓
Samuel Pierce Branch, Perkasie [1988]	✓							
RHODE ISLAND								
East Greenwich Free Library [?]	✓							
Greenville PL [1989]	✓	✓		✓	✓			
Hope Library [1989]	✓	✓		✓	✓			
Kingston Free Library [1991]	✓							
Newport PL [?]	✓							
South Kingstown PL, Peace Dale [1989]	✓	✓	✓	✓				✓
Providence PL [1988]	✓	✓	✓	✓	✓	✓	✓	✓
N. Smithfield PL, Slatersville [1989]	✓	✓	✓	✓	✓	✓	✓	✓
Robert Beverly Hale Branch, Wakefield [1990]	✓							
West Warwick PL System [1990]	✓	✓						
SOUTH CAROLINA								
Aiken County PL [1989]	✓	✓	✓	✓	✓	✓	✓	✓
Kershaw County Library, Camden [1988]		✓			✓			
Charleston County Library [1990]	✓	✓	✓	✓	✓			
James A. Rogers Library, Florence [1988]	✓	✓	✓	✓	✓	✓	✓	✓
Georgetown County PL [1989]	✓	✓	✓	✓	✓	✓		
Great Falls Branch [1988]	✓	✓	✓	✓	✓	✓	✓	✓
Greenville County Library [1990]	✓							

Orwell PL, Grand Valley [?]			✓	✓		✓	✓	
Parma Heights Branch [1989]	✓	✓	✓	✓	✓	✓	✓	✓
Paulding County Carnegie Library [1989]		✓						
Meigs County PL, Pomeroy [1989]	✓		✓	✓	✓	✓	✓	✓
Reynoldsburg Branch [?]	✓	✓	✓	✓	✓	✓		
Rocky River PL [1989]	✓	✓	✓	✓	✓	✓	✓	✓
Domonkas Branch, Sheffield Lake [1990]					✓			
Marvin Memorial Library, Shelby [1990]	✓	✓	✓	✓	✓			
Clark County. PL, Springfield [1988]	✓	✓	✓	✓	✓	✓	✓	✓
PL of Steubenville & Jefferson Cty. [1988]	✓	✓	✓					✓
Streetsboro Branch Library [1988]	✓	✓	✓	✓	✓	✓	✓	✓
Tiffin-Seneca PL [1988]	✓	✓	✓	✓	✓	✓	✓	✓
Toronto Branch Library [?]	✓	✓		✓	✓			
Carnegie PL, Washington Court House [1989]	✓	✓		✓				
Wayne County. PL, Wooster [1989]						✓		
John McIntire PL, Zanesville [1990]	✓			✓				
OKLAHOMA								
Anadarko PL [1989]	✓	✓		✓	✓			
Grace M. Pickens Library, Holdenville [?]	✓	✓	✓	✓	✓	✓	✓	✓
Hominy PL [1989]		✓	✓		✓			
Grove PL, Muskogee [1988]	✓	✓	✓	✓	✓	✓	✓	✓
Warner PL, Muskogee [1989]	✓	✓	✓	✓		✓		
Belle Isle Branch, Oklahoma City [1989]	✓	✓	✓	✓	✓	✓		
Village Branch, Oklahoma City [1990]	✓	✓	✓	✓	✓			
Ponca City Library [1989]	✓	✓	✓	✓	✓	✓	✓	✓
Sallisaw PL [?]	✓							
Shawnee PL [1989]	✓	✓	✓	✓	✓			
Stilwell PL [1988]								✓
Waurika PL [1989]	✓		✓	✓	✓			
Woodward PL [1988]	✓	✓	✓	✓	✓	✓	✓	✓
Yale PL [1989]	✓		✓	✓	✓			
OREGON								
Siuslaw PL, Florence [1990]	✓	✓		✓	✓			

Laurens County Library [1989]	✓	✓	✓	✓	✓		✓	✓
Nancy Carson Library, North Augusta [1989]	✓	✓	✓	✓	✓	✓		
Orangeburg County Library [1989]					✓			
York County Library, Rock Hill [1989]	✓	✓	✓	✓	✓	✓	✓	✓
York County Library, Rock Hill [1988]	✓	✓	✓	✓	✓	✓	✓	✓
Spartanburg County PL [?]	✓	✓		✓	✓			
TENNESSEE								
Irving Meek Jr. Lib., Adamsville [1989]	✓	✓	✓	✓	✓			
Southeast Branch Library, Antioch [?]	✓		✓	✓				
Bluffton-Wells County PL [1990]	✓			✓				
Bicentennial Library, Chattanooga [1989]	✓	✓	✓	✓	✓			
Houston County PL, Erin [1989]	✓	✓	✓	✓	✓			
Fairview PL [1989]	✓	✓	✓	✓	✓			
S. Cheatham Branch, Kingston Springs [1989]	✓							
Lebanon-Wilson County PL [1989]	✓							
Loretto Branch Library [1988]	✓	✓	✓	✓	✓	✓	✓	✓
Manchester PL [1989]	✓							
C.E. Weldon PL, Martin [1989]	✓	✓	✓		✓			
Mt. Juliet-Wilson Cty.-Harvey Freeman Memorial Lib. [1989]								✓
Linebaugh PL, Murfreesboro [?]	✓	✓	✓	✓				
PL of Nashville & Davidson Cty. [?]	✓	✓	✓	✓	✓	✓	✓	✓
Giles County PL, Pulaski [1989]	✓	✓	✓	✓	✓	✓	✓	
Argie Cooper PL, Shelbyville [1988]								✓
Gorham-Mac Bane PL, Springfield [1988]								✓
Lannom Memorial PL, Tullahoma [1989]								✓
TEXAS								
Allen PL [1989]	✓	✓	✓	✓	✓	✓	✓	✓
Atlanta PL [1988]			✓	✓		✓	✓	✓
Central Library, Garland[1988]	✓	✓	✓	✓	✓	✓	✓	✓
W.O. Haggard Jr. Library, Plano [1988]	✓	✓	✓	✓	✓	✓	✓	✓
Shepherd PL [1988]			✓	✓			✓	✓
Vidor PL [?]			✓					✓

Table 8 / Public Library Projects in Progress, 1988 *(cont.)*

NAME OF LIBRARY	STAGES 1	2	3	4	5	6	7	8
Nicholas P. Sims Library, Waxahachie [1989]	✓	✓	✓	✓	✓	✓	✓	✓
Whitehouse Community Library [1988]		✓	✓	✓	✓	✓	✓	✓
VERMONT								
Ilsley PL, Middlebury [1988]	✓	✓	✓	✓	✓	✓	✓	✓
VIRGINIA								
Arlington County PL [1991]			✓	✓	✓			
Central Rappahannock Regional Lib., Fredericksburg [?]	✓	✓		✓				
Central Rappahannock Regional Lib., Fredericksburg [1989]		✓						
Lancaster County PL, Kilmarnock [?]	✓	✓		✓	✓			
Russell County PL, Lebanon [1988]	✓							
Leesburg PL [1991]	✓	✓	✓	✓	✓			
Eastern Loudoun PL, Loundoun County [1991]	✓	✓	✓	✓	✓			
Lovettsville PL [1990]	✓	✓	✓	✓	✓	✓		
Middleburg PL [1990]	✓	✓	✓	✓	✓			
Purcellville PL [1991]	✓	✓	✓	✓	✓			
Gayton Library, Richmond [1988]	✓	✓	✓	✓	✓	✓	✓	✓
Kempsville Area Lib., Virginia Beach [1989]	✓	✓	✓	✓	✓	✓	✓	✓
Rappahannock County Lib., Washington [?]	✓							
WASHINGTON								
Bellevue Library [?]	✓		✓					
Lake Hills Library, Bellevue [1991]			✓	✓	✓			
Cheney Community Library [1988]	✓	✓	✓	✓	✓	✓	✓	✓
Darrington Library [1989]		✓						
Des Moines Library [1988]			✓	✓				✓
Everett PL [1990]	✓	✓	✓	✓	✓			
South Everett Branch, Everett [1989]	✓	✓	✓	✓	✓			
Peninsula Branch Lib., Gig Harbor [1989]	✓	✓	✓	✓		✓		
Kent Library [1991]				✓	✓	✓		
Parkland Branch Library [1989]	✓	✓	✓	✓	✓			

NAME OF LIBRARY	STAGES 1	2	3	4	5	6	7	8
Processing & Administrative Center, Parkland [1990]	✓	✓	✓	✓	✓			
Douglass-Truth Library, Seattle [1988]	✓							
Fremont Library, Seattle [1988]	✓							
Green Lake Library, Seattle [1989]								✓
Queen Anne Library, Seattle [1989]								✓
South Hill Branch Library [1990]	✓	✓	✓	✓	✓			
North Spokane Library, Spokane [1989]	✓	✓	✓	✓	✓			
Buckley Branch Library, Tacoma [1990]	✓	✓	✓	✓	✓			
Eatonville Branch Library, Tacoma [1990]	✓	✓	✓	✓	✓			
Fern Hill Branch, Tacoma [1989]								✓
McCormick Branch, Tacoma [?]	✓							
Main/Carnegie, Tacoma [1990]								✓
Dr. Martin Luther King Jr. Branch, Tacoma [?]						✓		
Moore Branch, Tacoma [1988]								✓
Mottet Branch, Tacoma [1989]								✓
South Hill Branch, Tacoma [1988]	✓	✓	✓	✓	✓			
South Tacoma Branch, Tacoma [1988]	✓							
Swan Creek Branch, Tacoma [1988]								✓
Swasey Branch, Tacoma [1989]								✓
Tacoma PL [1989]						✓		
Woodinville Library [1991]	✓		✓					
WISCONSIN								
Matheson Memorial Lib., Elkhorn [1989]						✓		
Lakes County PL, Lakewood [1989]	✓	✓	✓	✓				
Lodi Woman's Club Free Library [1989]	✓	✓	✓	✓	✓			
Middleton PL [1990]	✓	✓	✓	✓	✓			
New Berlin PL [1989]	✓	✓	✓	✓	✓			
Oostburg PL [1989]	✓	✓	✓	✓	✓	✓	✓	✓
Racine PL [1990]	✓	✓	✓	✓	✓			
WYOMING								
Johnson County Library, Buffalo [1989]	✓	✓	✓	✓	✓	✓	✓	✓

Table 9 / Academic Library Projects in Progress, 1988

NAME OF LIBRARY	STAGES 1	2	3	4	5	6	7	8
ALABAMA								
Jacksonville State University [1988]	✓	✓	✓	✓	✓	✓	✓	✓
Huntingdon College, Montgomery [1989]	✓	✓	✓	✓	✓	✓	✓	✓
Science/Engineering Lib., Univ. of Alabama, Tuscaloosa [1989]	✓	✓	✓	✓			✓	
ALASKA								
Univ. of Alaska-Southeast, Juneau [1989]	✓	✓	✓	✓	✓	✓	✓	✓
ARIZONA								
Northern Arizona University, Flagstaff [1990]	✓	✓	✓	✓	✓			
Arizona State University, Tempe [1989]	✓	✓	✓	✓	✓	✓	✓	✓
Arizona State University, Tempe [1989]	✓	✓	✓	✓	✓	✓		
Architecture/Environmental Design Lib., Arizona State University, Tempe [1989]	✓	✓	✓	✓	✓	✓	✓	✓
Music Lib., Arizona State University, Tempe [1990]	✓	✓	✓					
CALIFORNIA								
Science Lib., University of California, Irvine [1992]	✓	✓	✓	✓	✓			
Univ. of California–San Diego, La Jolla [1991]	✓	✓		✓	✓			
Naval Postgraduate School, Monterey [1991]	✓	✓	✓	✓	✓			
California State Univ., Northridge [1990]		✓	✓	✓	✓	✓		

NAME OF LIBRARY	STAGES 1	2	3	4	5	6	7	8
Mills College, Oakland [1989]	✓	✓	✓	✓		✓	✓	✓
California State Univ., Sacramento [1990]	✓	✓	✓	✓	✓	✓	✓	✓
Univ. of California, San Francisco [1990]								✓
Univ. of California, Santa Cruz [1990]	✓	✓	✓	✓	✓	✓		
Cal. State–Stanislaus, Turlock [1989]	✓	✓	✓	✓	✓	✓	✓	✓
CONNECTICUT								
W. Connecticut State Univ., Danbury [?]	✓			✓				
DISTRICT OF COLUMBIA								
The American University/ Washington College Law Lib. [1992]	✓				✓			
Georgetown University [1988]	✓	✓	✓	✓	✓	✓	✓	✓
FLORIDA								
Embry-Riddle Aeronautical Univ., Daytona Beach [1988]	✓	✓	✓	✓	✓	✓	✓	✓
GEORGIA								
Health Sciences Center Lib., Emory University, Atlanta [1990]	✓	✓	✓	✓	✓	✓	✓	✓
IDAHO								
Lewis Clark State Coll., Lewiston [1991]	✓	✓		✓	✓			
University of Idaho, Moscow [1988]	✓	✓	✓	✓	✓	✓	✓	✓

Table 9 / Academic Library Projects in Progress, 1988 *(cont.)*

NAME OF LIBRARY	STAGES 1	2	3	4	5	6	7	8
ILLINOIS								
Saint Xavier College, Chicago [1988]	✓	✓	✓	✓	✓	✓	✓	✓
Greenville College [1990]	✓	✓		✓	✓			
Augustana Coll., Rock Island [1990]	✓	✓	✓	✓	✓	✓	✓	✓
INDIANA								
Indiana Univ.–Purdue Univ. at Indianapolis [1991]		✓		✓	✓			
Indiana University at South Bend [1988]	✓	✓	✓	✓	✓	✓	✓	✓
IOWA								
Coe College, Cedar Rapids [1988]	✓	✓	✓	✓	✓	✓	✓	✓
KANSAS								
University of Kansas, Lawrence [1989]	✓	✓	✓	✓	✓	✓	✓	✓
Wichita State University [1989]	✓	✓	✓	✓	✓	✓	✓	✓
KENTUCKY								
Lib. of Engineering/Physical Science/Technology, University of Louisville [1989]						✓		
MAINE								
Coll. of the Atlantic, Bar Harbor [1988]								✓
University of Maine, Machias [1989]	✓	✓	✓	✓		✓	✓	✓
Univ. of Southern Maine, Portland [?]	✓							
MARYLAND								
Univ. of Maryland, College Park [1989]	✓	✓	✓	✓		✓	✓	✓
Western Maryland Coll., Westminster [1991]					✓			
MASSACHUSETTS								
Northeastern University, Boston [1990]	✓	✓	✓	✓	✓	✓	✓	✓
Mass. Inst. of Technology, Cambridge [1990]	✓	✓	✓	✓	✓			
Lib. on the History of Women in America, Radcliffe College, Cambridge [1988]	✓	✓	✓	✓	✓	✓	✓	✓
MICHIGAN								
Wayne State University, Detroit [1992]				✓	✓			
NORTH CAROLINA								
Univ. of North Carolina, Asheville [1990]							✓	
North Carolina State Univ., Raleigh [1989]	✓		✓	✓	✓	✓	✓	✓
OHIO								
Univ. of Akron School of Law [1989]	✓	✓	✓	✓	✓	✓	✓	✓
College of Applied Science, University of Cincinnati [1989]	✓	✓	✓	✓	✓	✓		
Geology/Physics Library, University of Cincinnati [1989]	✓	✓	✓		✓	✓	✓	
Ohio State College of Law Lib. [1992]	✓	✓	✓	✓	✓			
Shawnee State Univ., Portsmouth [1990]	✓	✓	✓	✓	✓			
OKLAHOMA								
Langston University [?]			✓	✓	✓			
University of Oklahoma, Norman [1989]	✓	✓	✓	✓	✓	✓	✓	✓
OREGON								
Architecture & Allied Arts Lib., University of Oregon, Eugene [1990]	✓	✓	✓	✓	✓			
Science Lib., Univ. of Oregon, Eugene [1990]	✓	✓	✓	✓	✓	✓	✓	✓
University of Oregon, Eugene [1991]	✓	✓		✓	✓			
Eastern Oregon State Coll., LaGrande [1989]	✓	✓	✓	✓	✓	✓	✓	✓
George Fox College, Newberg [1988]	✓	✓	✓	✓	✓	✓	✓	
Reed College, Portland [1989]	✓	✓	✓	✓	✓	✓	✓	✓
PENNSYLVANIA								
Muhlenberg College, Allentown [1988]	✓	✓	✓	✓	✓	✓	✓	✓
Ursinus College, Collegeville [1989]	✓	✓	✓	✓	✓	✓	✓	✓
Elizabethtown College [1990]	✓	✓		✓	✓			
Behrend College Lib., Pennsylvania State Univ. at Erie [1991]				✓	✓			
Franklin & Marshall Coll., Lancaster [1990]	✓	✓	✓	✓	✓			
Pennsylvania State Univ. at Great Valley,								

Michigan State Univ., East Lansing [1992]	✓	✓	✓	✓	✓			
Western Michigan Univ., Kalamazoo [1990]	✓	✓	✓	✓	✓	✓	✓	✓
Oakland University, Rochester [1989]	✓	✓	✓	✓	✓	✓	✓	✓
MINNESOTA								
Univ. of Minnesota, Minneapolis [1995]	✓							
Univ. of Minnesota, Minneapolis [1990]		✓						
College of St. Thomas, St. Paul [1991]	✓	✓	✓	✓	✓			
MISSISSIPPI								
Millsaps College, Jackson [1990]		✓		✓	✓			
MISSOURI								
Park College, Kansas City [1988]	✓		✓					✓
Univ. of Missouri–Kansas City [1990]	✓		✓	✓	✓			
Kirksville Coll. of Osteopathic Medicine [1988]	✓	✓	✓	✓		✓	✓	✓
Northeast Missouri State Univ., Kirksville [1989]	✓	✓	✓	✓	✓	✓	✓	✓
University of Missouri, St. Louis [1989]			✓	✓	✓	✓	✓	✓
Missouri Western State Coll., St. Joseph [1989]	✓	✓	✓	✓	✓			
NEW MEXICO								
New Mexico Institute of Mining and Technology, Socorro [?]		✓						
NEW YORK								
University of Albany [1989]								✓
New York State Coll. of Ceramics at Alfred University [1992]		✓	✓	✓	✓			
State University of New York College at Fredonia [?]	✓	✓	✓	✓	✓			
Sch. of Hotel Administration Lib., Cornell University, Ithaca [1988]	✓	✓	✓	✓	✓	✓	✓	✓
Cornell Univ. Law Lib., Ithaca [1988]	✓	✓	✓	✓	✓	✓	✓	✓
Baruch College, New York [?]	✓	✓	✓	✓	✓			
Niagara University [1989]	✓	✓	✓	✓	✓	✓	✓	✓
Hartwick College, Oneonta [1990]								✓
Rochester Institute of Technology [1991]				✓	✓			
U.S. Military Academy, West Point [1988]								✓

Malvern [1988]	✓	✓	✓	✓	✓	✓	✓	✓
Mansfield University [1991]				✓	✓			
Susquehanna University, Selinsgrove [1989]	✓		✓	✓	✓	✓	✓	✓
RHODE ISLAND								
University of Rhode Island, Kingston [1992]	✓	✓						
Salve Regina College, Newport [1989]	✓	✓	✓	✓	✓			
TENNESSEE								
Tennessee Tech. Univ., Cookeville [1989]	✓	✓	✓	✓	✓	✓	✓	✓
TEXAS								
Houston Baptist University [1989]	✓	✓	✓	✓	✓	✓	✓	✓
LeTourneau College, Longview [?]	✓							
VIRGINIA								
Randolph-Macon College, Ashland [1988]	✓	✓	✓	✓	✓	✓	✓	✓
University of Virginia, Charlottesville [?]	✓			✓	✓			
Mary Washington Coll., Fredericksburg [1988]	✓	✓	✓	✓	✓	✓	✓	✓
Christopher Newport College, Newport News [1991]	✓	✓		✓	✓			
Norfolk State University [1992]	✓	✓	✓	✓	✓			
Virginia Wesleyan College, Norfolk [1988]	✓	✓	✓	✓	✓	✓	✓	✓
Roanoke College, Salem [1990]	✓	✓		✓	✓	✓		
WASHINGTON								
Evergreen State College, Olympia [1988]	✓	✓	✓	✓	✓	✓	✓	✓
Washington State Univ., Pullman [1993–95]	✓			✓				
University of Washington, Seattle [1990]								✓
Gonzaga University, Spokane [1992]	✓	✓	✓					
Whitworth College, Spokane [1991]	✓	✓		✓	✓			
WEST VIRGINIA								
Bethany College [?]	✓							
WISCONSIN								
Gateway Technical College, Elkhorn [?]		✓		✓	✓			
Univ. of Wisconsin-Madison [1990]	✓	✓	✓	✓	✓	✓	✓	✓
Wisconsin Lutheran College, Milwaukee [1988]	✓	✓	✓	✓	✓	✓	✓	✓

Role Setting for Rural Public Libraries

Bernard Vavrek
Coordinator, The Center for the Study of Rural Librarianship,
Clarion University of Pennsylvania

In fall 1987, the Center for the Study of Rural Librarianship (CSRL) undertook a survey to determine the relevance of the American Library Association/Public Library Association publication *Planning and Role Setting for Public Libraries, 1987* to rural libraries and the degree to which the roles cited in that publication are put into practice. The investigation focused on three areas: (1) the impressions of public librarians involved in establishing roles for their respective institutions; (2) the degree to which planning is accomplished; and (3) the compilation of current socioeconomic data relevant to rural libraries. For surveying purposes, the eight library roles cited in the publication were reorganized.

Five hundred and eighty-eight questionnaires were mailed to public librarians across the United States in rural and near rural communities of 25,000 or fewer individuals. Selections based on resident population, not population served, were drawn randomly from the *American Library Directory.* The study's data base consisted of ($n = 373$) completed questionnaires.

"My library is a focal point for community activities," the first statement to which individuals were to respond, perhaps set the tone for the entire study. (Respondents were usually asked to answer on a scale of options from "strongly agree" to "strongly disagree.") Although 51 percent (179) of those answering indicated some form of agreement, approximately 49 percent (171) were either neutral or expressed disagreement. The response is not startling: Most small libraries simply do not have the facilities to function as community centers. Other surveys have had similar results, for example, as an explanation of why the frequency of adult-oriented programs is sometimes dismal. However, a collateral effect to this physical inadequacy may be that other efforts to transform the public library into the community's information center become particularly troublesome. This is reflected in the response to the survey's second statement: "My library works closely with other community organizations to provide a program of recreational services." Although 47 percent (156) indicated some form of agreement, at least 53 percent (174) were either neutral or disagreed. Limitations of space, staff, and money are clearly among the reasons.

In a more positive regard, almost three-fourths of those surveyed indicated that their library ". . . responds to community needs with specialized services provided inside the library building." The most frequently cited activities were story hours for children and literacy programs. The response was a little different, however, when individuals were asked about ". . . specialized services provided outside of the library." Approximately 51 percent (164) were in agreement as to the appropriateness of this role, but an almost equal number of respondents—49 percent (158)—were either neutral or disagreed. The favorite external service was book delivery to nursing homes, shut-ins, and so on.

About 94 percent (346) of the respondents agreed with the statement "My library assists elementary and secondary students in meeting educational objectives established during formal courses of study." Seventy-seven percent (270) of those surveyed in public libraries that serve college and university students agreed with a similar statement. "My library assists literacy and/or adult basic education students in meeting educational objectives established during formal courses of study" elicited an agreement rate of 71 percent (245), and "assists with continuing education students" achieved an 80 percent (284) approval rate. Finally, "My library supports out of school adults who pursue a program of learning independent of any formal educational provider" also elicited agreement from 80 percent (280) of the respondents.

Continuing with the strong emphasis on education, 99 percent (367) agreed that their library ". . . encourages young children to develop an interest in reading." Likewise, 96 percent (355) of the respondents said yes to "My library provides parents and other adult caregivers with materials on reading for children." Although slightly more than three-fourths of those responding to the survey indicated that the library cooperates "with child care agencies in the community on an ongoing basis," the sense of collective agreement would probably be even higher if it were not for the paucity of social agencies dealing with children in some communities.

In evaluating the informational role of the typical rural public library, 92 percent (339) of the respondents agreed that "My library provides timely information to community residents in their respective areas of interest." One must bear in mind, however, that "timely information" includes both an item obtained through interlibrary loan over the period of one week and the real-time response to a reference question. Also, the two audiences (librarians and clients) see the same situation differently, and librarians seldom have the necessary feedback to judge their own effectiveness. The true litmus test would be to ask library users about their community information center. In a current study of rural library usage in Pennsylvania, preliminary data suggest a high level of approval of overall services by library clients but only a modest reliance on the library's resource collection for current information. Bestsellers seem to be in greater demand than, for example, information dealing with community ordinances or the decisions of local governing authorities. The Pennsylvania study will be used as the basis for a national investigation being supported by the U.S. Department of Education in 1988–1989.

Ninety-three percent (344) of the respondents agreed that "My library promotes its reference services (within the library) to aid users in locating needed information," and more than three-fourths (275) of those surveyed agreed or strongly agreed with the statement "My library promotes telephone reference services to aid users in locating needed information." Two factors affected the response to the latter role statement: First, some libraries continue to be without telephone service (the latest data suggest approximately six percent) and, second (quoting one of the respondents), "A limited staff does not allow us to encourage telephone service." (One rural library staff member indicated that the library's telephone number was unlisted—the telephone was really intended for administrative purposes rather than for promoting information access.)

Although 67 percent (233) of those surveyed indicated that they ". . . assist researchers to conduct in-depth studies in a specific subject," the typical rural library has a modest resource collection (approximately 25,000 volumes) and no more than three (in most cases only one) full-time personnel. As one respondent indicated, "We don't get many in-depth requests." Data collected by CSRL suggest that no more than three questions are asked by clients in the typical rural library on an hourly basis. Also, only 25 percent of the full-time staff working in rural libraries are academically certified at the master's level, and reference training remains a priority goal among state, district, and regional library providers. Less than half of the respondents (170) indicated the availability of an in-depth collection within the library, but public libraries continue to maintain a responsibility for providing information on state and local history. Sixteen percent (61) of those surveyed identified local history and genealogy as subjects provided by their libraries, and six percent (22) listed a state history collection.

Library Planning

Unfortunately, results from the library planning section of the survey suggest that rural librarians are only modestly involved in planning for library services, showing little improvement over the last six years. Only 22 percent (81) of those surveyed indicated that a community analysis had been conducted over the last five years. The leading reasons were insufficient time, not enough staff, and not enough money. On the question of whether the library had a multiyear plan, only 23 percent (86) answered affirmatively. The leading explanations were "it is in process," "lack of time," and "lack of money"; 5 percent (19) of the respondents commented that the "trustees are not interested."

Only 25 percent (88) of those participating in the survey indicated using output measures in their libraries. A range of answers was given to explain the nonuse, but the major explanation, 13 percent (48), was lack of familiarity/lack of awareness. Although 48 respondents is a small sample, uncertainty may well be the most frequent reason for the lack of implementation of output measures in rural libraries. Despite the American Library Association's plans to jointly publish (with the Public Library Association) a revised edition of *Output Measures,* the original concept of measuring the output of libraries continues to be in the seminal stages of application (and not just in small libraries).

Socioeconomic Data

In a continuing effort to gather data about the communities in which rural librarians live, the survey included a variety of general questions. For example, because of the interest in rural revitalization, the survey instrument included a question regarding the community's industry(ies) of primary importance: 26 percent (96) indicated farming; tourism was next, at 7 percent (25); and metal industries was third, at 4 percent (15). Although students of rural America are cognizant of the shift from agriculture to a variety of other economic bases, small-town America has not entirely escaped its roots. When the respondents were asked to name community problems, not surprisingly, 80 percent (167) indicated unemployment as the major difficulty. Twenty percent (43) identified rapid population growth as the greatest challenge. Only 25 percent (83) thought that their problems would be solved in the near future.

The final questions were directed at the librarians. One question concerned involvement in library associations. Forty-one percent (151) of those answering indicated membership in the American Library Association, but 80 percent (294) belong to their state organizations. The typical rural librarian has lived in her or his community for an average of 17 years, although the range in the survey was from one month to 64 years. Further, she or he has been employed in the library for an average of more than ten years. The range in this latter response was also one month to 64 years. And what about current salary? Although 13 percent (42) earn $30,000 or more,

more than 56 percent (181) earn between $5,000 and $19,000, and 39 percent (125) earn between $5,000 and $14,000. (The library profession should reflect on the fact that for a family of four, $14,000 is at the poverty level.) The final survey question asked for the librarian's age. Fifty-five percent (207) are between the ages of 20 and 49. Only 3 percent (12) are under 30 years of age.

Conclusion

There appears to be a consistent lack of planning—of both short and long duration—among librarians in communities of 25,000 or fewer people, which represents most of the public libraries in the United States. Librarians in small and medium-sized institutions are simply not planning for future library services. A partial explanation is that staff members are too busy delivering services. (How much is to be expected of the one-person library manager?) Without planning, local surveying, and so forth, the public library becomes an extension of the librarian's views rather than those of the community. Another practical concern is that public librarians may be taking on too many roles. Because of the high level of commitment, there is an inherent tendency to want to accept more and more responsibility. It may not be clear in some libraries, for example, that literacy programs are not possible without compromising other library services.

The final question becomes one, then, of how planning is facilitated. It is, of course, a responsibility at all sectors of library administration. But library associations at the national, and particularly at the state, level could have a profound effect by making planning, and its collateral aspects, a sustaining goal. One of the weaknesses of American librarianship is that library administrators fail to plan over a calculated period of time. It should not be surprising that symptoms of the same deficiencies are seen throughout thc countryside.

Library Statistics, 1870 to 1990: Retrospective and Outlook

Frank L. Schick
Consultant, Bethesda, MD
Former Chief, Learning Resources Branch,
National Center for Education Statistics

The Office (more recently, the Department) of Education has been collecting, analyzing, and publishing national data dealing with libraries since 1870. In the early 1980s, however, support for the library statistics program in the National Center for Education Statistics (NCES) was substantially reduced: The unit responsible for library statistics was given new assignments, and staff and funding were decreased. Then in 1983 the unit was completely abolished; the few ongoing studies were parceled out to other parts of NCES where they were slowly completed. When the disappearance of an administrative library statistics unit and the dissatisfaction in the general educational community with NCES's performance in the collection and dissemination of statistics were brought to the attention of Congress, the Hawkins-Stafford Elementary and Secondary School Improvement Amendments (PL 100-297) were passed in 1988. These amendments changed the status of NCES within the Department of Education and spelled out a mandate for the collection of library statistics. A new unit and two staff members were appointed in 1988 to carry out this mandate.

Library Statistics, 1870–1964

The federal government created the Office of Education (OE) in 1870 to conduct statistical surveys of all phases of education in order to provide educational opportunities for Civil War veterans. OE conducted regular periodic studies and surveys of public, society, and school libraries, as well as occasional surveys of college and university libraries. Until 1938, OE had no separate library unit, and library surveys were undertaken by the staff responsible for educational statistics; advice regarding subjects related to libraries was obtained from the American Library Association and other national library organizations.

In 1938, OE established a separate unit for all library-related activities, including research and statistics. Surveys of different types of libraries were published in four- to six-year cycles. In 1956, the Library Services and Construction Act was passed and the administration of this grant program for public libraries was added to the functions of the Library Services Branch; programs for academic and school libraries were also initiated. Between 1958 and the mid-1960s, financial support and professional staff for library development increased substantially. Library statistics were used to support developing federal legislation concerning public, academic, and school libraries and library education. Academic libraries were surveyed annually, public and school libraries approximately every two to four years, to keep Congress and the library community informed about the progress and scope of these programs.

Library Statistics, 1965–1988

In 1965, the responsibility for all statistical surveys, including those relating to libraries, was transferred from OE to the newly created National Center for Education Statistics (NCES). The library grants program continued as a separate unit in the Office of Libraries and Learning Technologies, without formal connection to the statistics program; informal contacts, however, resulted in many joint projects. Between 1965 and 1968, ongoing library surveys were continued. In order to eliminate data overlaps in the many separate educational surveys that had previously been undertaken, NCES was starting to implement two large survey systems: HEGIS (Higher Education General Information Survey) and ELSEGIS (Elementary and Secondary Education General Information Survey).

In the late 1960s and early 1970s, preparations for LIBGIS (the Library General Information Survey), a library data system similar to HEGIS and ELSEGIS, were initiated. An essential step for the implementation of LIBGIS was the standardization of terminology done by the ALA Statistics Coordinating Project, with funds from the Council of Library Resources, in which OE, ALA, and the Special Libraries Association (SLA) cooperated. This project resulted in the publication of *Library Statistics: A Handbook of Concepts, Definitions and Terminology.*[1]

In June 1966, the American Library Association and NCES held a National Conference on Library Statistics that covered a broad range of topics, including national and international library statistics standards.[2] In the late 1960s, NCES contracted with ALA to develop the design of LIBGIS; the resulting report was published in 1971[3]. Herner and Company conducted an extensive study of library and information center statistics practices on national, state, and local levels for NCES; the report of this study appeared in two volumes in 1972.[4]

A LIBGIS demonstration project to test the proposed NCES survey instruments for all types of libraries, and a state participation project to test the cooperative potential between NCES and state library agencies, were conducted by the Illinois State Library in 1972 and 1973. With these studies, LIBGIS preparations were completed and the system was ready for implementation in 1974.

The LIBGIS system provided three major features: (1) simultaneous collection of comparable basic data items for the three key types of libraries (public, college and university, and public elementary and secondary schools) on a biennial basis and for other types of libraries at longer intervals; (2) cooperation with state agencies in the areas of survey development, data collection, and manual editing; and (3) sharing of collected and edited data with state agencies to provide uniform statistics to users at the local, state, and national levels.

LBGIS I (FY 1975) included surveys of public libraries, public school libraries/ media centers, and academic libraries. LIBGIS II (FY 1976) covered surveys of library cooperatives, consortia and networks (first-time survey), academic libraries, libraries serving state governments (first-time survey), state library agencies, and special libraries in commerce and industry (a first-time universe study). LIBGIS III (FY 1977) surveyed academic, public, and school libraries and initiated a survey of all federal libraries. LIBGIS IV (FY 1978) funded the *Library Data Base Handbook* to provide uniform library statistics terminology conforming with the international UNESCO and the US ANSI/Z39 standards, updating the *Library Statistics Handbook* of 1966. LIBGIS V (FY 1979) saw the completion of the cooperative and library network survey and the handbook study, the initiation of the first private school library survey, and a library human resources survey. Plans were made to survey special libraries in commerce and industry and religious school libraries. Twenty-three library surveys were completed between 1960 and 1969; 24 were completed between 1970 and 1979.[5]

In May 1977, in an effort to reduce funds expended by NCES, the Office of Management and Budget questioned the need for government involvement in the collection of library statistics, stating in an article in the *Statistical Reporter:*

> The Library General Information Survey (LIBGIS) collects systematic data on virtually all types of libraries in the United States. . . . Arrangements are currently being completed for the collection of . . . data which will round out the statistics on library resources. . . . While the relative level of effort expended by NCES on library statistics is not substantial, the need for the expansive current and proposed program of library statistics has not been adequately justified in the face of unaddressed competing priorities. It is recommended that a study of the uses and users of the information gathered on libraries be conducted as a basis for determining appropriate levels of effort to be ex-

pended and types of data to be collected on the role and contribution of libraries to the educational system.[6]

In an apparent response to this article, the name of the Library Surveys Branch was changed to Learning Resources Branch; educational technology and museums were added to the branch responsibilities without additional funding or staff. A study on "Uses and Users of Library Statistics" was authorized by NCES; it was conducted by Robert D. Little, professor of library science at Indiana State University, and was completed in 1979. The study recommended that "the Learning Resources Branch should conduct at least four to six surveys annually; surveys dealing with topics in support of the Office of Libraries and Learning Resources programs should be conducted for public, school and academic libraries every two to three years and for other programs (i.e. state libraries) when needed."[7]

In spite of these recommendations and complaints from members of Congress, the library community, government agencies, and the publishing and other library-related industries, the library statistics program continued on a downward trend in the 1980s. Staff members with a library background were replaced by lower-grade personnel with unrelated experience, and experienced staff members were transferred to other positions. The Learning Resources Branch was phased out; the Division of Elementary and Secondary Education became responsible for school library surveys and the Division of Postsecondary Education Statistics for college, university, and public library surveys. At most, ten library surveys will have been produced by NCES between 1980 and the end of 1989.

The disappearance of federal agencies or subagencies and their programs without the knowledge or approval of Congress is not rare. It happens when administrations change, when Congress has not provided for specific activities with sufficient legislative detail, or when there is no immediate public protest. One of the best known examples occurred in the mid-1950s when the Bureau of Vital Statistics in the Department of Health, Education, and Welfare was phased out in an economy move. At first, nobody seemed to notice, but as people continued to be born, to die, and to immigrate, and insurance companies and other agencies using population data found it difficult to issue actuarially sound reports and projections, in response to increasing protest, the government tried to reassemble the bureau's dispersed staff, hired new people, and reactivated the phased-out programs, at a substantially increased cost to the taxpayers.

NCES generally failed to live up to the expectations of its data user community, which had hoped that the implementation of large automated systems would make coordinated, reliable data on all aspects of education more quickly available, while reducing the burden on responding institutions to reply to a multitude of uncoordinated questionnaires. The realities of budget constraints, system coordination, the tedious processes of contract procurement and monitoring, ever more stringent clearance procedures, and restrictions on publications resulted in many delays and complaints by Congress and organizations interested in obtaining educational data on a regular basis. This prompted the Office of the Assistant Secretary for Educational Research and Improvement to ask the National Academy of Sciences to undertake an evaluation of NCES in 1985. The report, *Creating a Center for Education Statistics: A Time for Action,* published in 1986, was highly critical of nearly all aspects of the center.[8]

The Future of Library Statistics

When NCES was created in 1965, its legislative mandate was to collect and disseminate statistics and other data related to education in the United States and other countries. Library statistics were not specifically mentioned. PL 100-297, which was passed in 1988, established NCES as a semi-independent unit in the Department of Education, comparable to the Bureau of Labor Statistics in the Department of Labor. Section 406(a) of PL 100-297 specifically mentions libraries among the subjects on which NCES is mandated to "acquire and diffuse useful statistical information." This will make it more difficult for library statistics programs in NCES to quietly disappear again. Lawrence J. La Moure, coordinator of the new library statistics program, and statistician Arthur Podolsky are hoping to get enough support to produce comprehensive data on public libraries in a timely fashion. ALA's 1984 report, *Analysis of Library Data Collection and Development of Plans for the Future,* recommended that NCES "maintain close communication with the library community at all stages of the survey process," and "publish results as soon as possible after data are collected."[9] Although the new unit undoubtedly will try to follow these recommendations, it is questionable whether federal budgets of the 1990s will allow it to "collect data annually from each type of library"[10] as recommended by ALA. Do changes from year to year warrant such survey expenses?

Notes

1. *Library Statistics: A Handbook of Concepts, Definitions and Terminology* (Chicago: American Library Association, 1966).
2. *National Conference on Libary Statistics* (Chicago: American Library Association, 1967).
3. *Planning for a Nationwide System of Library Statistics,* David Palmer, ed., report of a project of the Library Administration Division, American Library Association, prepared under contract with the National Center for Education Statistics, 1970 (OE-15070).
4. *National Inventory of Library Statistics Practices: Volume 1—Data Collection on the National, State and Local Levels: Volume II—Agency Profiles and Individual Site Descriptions,* 1972 (OE 74–188).
5. Frank L. Schick, "Developments in Library Statistical Activities," *Bowker Annual, 1982* (New York: R. R. Bowker, 1982), p. 310.
6. "Education Statistics," *Statistical Reporter,* no. 77–78 (May 1977), 332.
7. Rober David Little, "The Collection of Nationwide Library Statistics in the United States," *Libri.* 30, no. 2, 138.
8. Mary Jo Lynch, "Research on Libraries and Librarianship in 1986," *Bowker Annual, 1987* (New York: R. R. Bowker, 1987), p. 350.
9. Mary Jo Lynch, "Analysis of Library Data Collection and Development of Plans for the Future: A Project Summary," *Bowker Annual, 1985* (New York, R. R. Bowker, 1985), p. 410.
10. Ibid.

Services and Resources for Young Adults in Public Libraries: Report of the NCES Survey

Ray M. Fry
Senior Advisor for Library Programs
Office of Educational Research and Improvement
U.S. Department of Education
555 New Jersey Ave. N.W., Washington, DC 20208
202-357-6300

In summer 1987, an urgent call came to the Department of Education Library Programs (LP) Division from a researcher at the Chapin Hall Center for Children at the University of Chicago for information on how public libraries were serving teenagers. The researcher, who had already contacted the American Library Association with no results, was assisting in a major national study for the William T. Grant Foundation Commission on Work, Family, and Citizenship. One section of the survey was to address young adults' access to community facilities. The Department of Education had already received other similar requests but it could not supply any national data because the Library Programs Division had never collected data on young adult (YA) services through its public library surveys. As of fall 1987, however, Library Programs was able to report that a Fast Response Survey on library services and resources for young adults was being conducted by the National Center for Education Statistics.

Introduction

A high (84) percentage of public libraries have special sections or collections for young adults, which may reflect considerable interest in giving special attention to the age group. These collections are primarily books, and 85 percent of the books are classified "juvenile/young adult" with only 15 percent classified "adult." Is this a good ratio if one of the major goals of young adults programs is to introduce teenagers to adult reading?

Only 11 percent of libraries have a trained YA librarian, however. Most YAs are served by generalists and adult librarians. Fewer of these librarians (16 percent vs. 42 percent) are required to participate in continuing education to improve their capacity to serve young adults. Compounding the issue of the lack of training for librarians serving young adults is the fact that 49 percent of libraries without a young adult librarian also do not have the assistance of a young adult coordinator or consultant.

Across all library characteristics young people are a most significant proportion of library patrons and they are not only moderate or heavy users of the young adult collections but also of adult reference and adult circulation collections. This is especially true in libraries employing a young adult librarian. As was expected, teenagers are heavy users of readers' advisory services for assistance with school assignments but also, when a young adult librarian is on staff, they show considerable use of readers' advisory services for assistance with independent needs and interests.

With a young adult librarian on staff, cooperative activities with schools and other community organizations and agencies are more likely to occur and with greater frequency. The major barriers to library use by young adults, according to the survey, are lack of service/programs for their age group, disinterest, and competition from other activities. Perhaps there is a correlation between the first two.

This first national survey of services and resources for young adults can be used by library administrators, educators, researchers, and young adult librarians. It can also be utilized by community leaders, school administrators, state librarians, and organizations and agencies at all levels of government interested in educational and recreational opportunities for young people. Because of the limitations of the Fast Response Survey System, the study may raise more questions than it answers, but it does have some stark and stimulating facts on young adult services. It moves us in the right direction toward a more in-depth study of the services and resources public libraries are, or should be, offering young people.

Survey Report

This report presents the findings from a fall 1987 survey of public libraries. Among the key findings are

- One out of every four public library patrons in 1986–1987 was a young adult (between the ages of 12 and 18).
- Only 11 percent of the nation's public libraries have the services of a young adult librarian.
- Eighty-four percent of libraries offer a section or collection of materials specially designated for young adults. In 74 percent of these libraries, the young adult section or collection was moderately or heavily used.
- Libraries that employ a young adult librarian were more likely to report moderate or heavy use of library services by young adults, including
  - Use of the library after school, evenings, and on weekends
  - Use of the reference, adult circulation, and children's sections of the library
  - Use of most library services including readers' advisory services for both school and independent needs, study space, and college and career information
- In libraries without a young adult librarian on staff, young adults are primarily served by generalists. Only 16 percent of libraries that do not employ a young adult librarian require continuing inservice training in young adult services and materials.

The survey was performed under contract by Westat, Inc., for the National Center for Education Statistics (NCES), U.S. Department of Education, through its Fast Response Survey System (FRSS).[1] It was requested by the Office of Library Programs in the Office of Educational Research and Improvement. Questionnaires were sent to 846 libraries (540 main libraries and 306 branch libraries), and data were collected for individual library buildings rather than for library systems. Survey items included the availability of young adult sections in libraries and the kinds of materials they contain; staff resources for young adults; the availability and use of library services for young adults; amount of library cooperation with schools and other youth-serving organizations; and perceived barriers to increased use of the library by 12- to 18-year-olds.

Survey findings are presented for all library buildings, and by the following characteristics of library buildings: patrons per week (a measure of library size),[2] type of library (main without branches, main with branches, and branch), whether or not the library had a young adult section or collection, and whether or not a library had a young adult librarian.

Based on the findings, statements about associations between survey items and libraries with different characteristics can be made (e.g., libraries with young adult librarians are more likely to report moderate or heavy use by young adults after school than libraries that do not have young adult librarians). Statements about causal relationships, however, *cannot* be made (e.g., the presence of the young adult librarian produces an increase in library use by young adults). FRSS surveys are not designed to show cause-and-effect relationships, only associations.

Characteristics of libraries are often interrelated. For example, whether the library has a young adult librarian is related to the number of patrons per week and type of library. Estimates for libraries with a young adult librarian often are similar to those of libraries with 1,000 or more patrons per week and those of main libraries with branches. Because of the relatively small size of the sample, it is difficult to separate the independent effects of each of these characteristics.[3] In addition, the presence or absence of a young adult librarian may be related to other factors not covered in the survey; those other factors may be the true causes of apparent differences regarding young adult services and resources.

Some of the data obtained in this survey are based on librarians' opinions. For example, "heavy," "moderate," and "light use" were not defined; the definitions of these terms were left to the judgment of librarians who may have interpreted these categories somewhat differently. However, because of the wide variation in the size of libraries and the exploratory nature of this survey, subjective evaluations were considered more appropriate than more objective measures.

Young Adult Sections or Collections

Most public libraries (84 percent) have a section or collection of materials for young adults.[4] On average, 91 percent of these collections are books, 6 percent are other printed materials, and 3 percent are audiovisual materials. Among the books, an average of 60 percent in young adult collections are hardback and 40 percent paperback; 73 percent are fiction and 27 percent nonfiction; and 85 percent are juvenile/young adult and 15 percent adult.[5]

The proportion of paperbacks is greater in libraries with heavy patronage (1,000 or more patrons per week) and in those with a young adult librarian. In libraries with heavy patronage, 50 percent of the young adult collection is paperback, compared with 36 percent in libraries with moderate patronage (200 to 999 patrons per week) and 37 percent in those with light patronage (less than 200 patrons per week). Similarly, the young adult collection in libraries with a young adult librarian is 48 percent paperback on average; the average young adult collection in libraries without a young adult librarian is 38 percent paperback.

Availability of Young Adult Librarians in Public Libraries

Only 11 percent of public libraries have a young adult librarian on staff. Young adult librarians are most commonly found in libraries with heavy patronage and in main libraries with branches. One-fourth (26 percent) of libraries with heavy patronage have a young adult librarian on staff, compared with only 2 percent of libraries with light patronage and 9 percent of those with moderate patronage.[6] Young adult librarians are also found more often in main libraries with branches (19 percent) than in main libraries without branches (8 percent).

In libraries without a young adult librarian, young adults are served by generalists (45 percent of libraries), adult librarians (22 percent), children's librarians (12 percent), reference librarians (5 percent), and adult/young adult librarians (3 percent).[7] Thus, librarians are twice as likely to report that young adults are served by a generalist than by any other type of librarian.

The use of generalists decreases as the volume of patronage increases. Generalists are the primary providers of services to young adults in 59 percent of libraries with light patronage, but only 28 percent of libraries with heavy patronage. In libraries with heavy patronage, young adults are as likely to be served by children's librarians or adult librarians as they are to be served by generalists.

Main libraries with branches are less likely to have generalists serving young adults (26 percent) than branch libraries (50 percent) or main libraries without branches (44 percent). They are more likely, however, to serve young adults with children's librarians (26 percent) than other types of libraries (8 percent in branch libraries and 13 percent in main libraries without branches).

Young Adult Coordinators or Consultants

Assistance from a young adult coordinator or consultant is available to 51 percent of all libraries. These coordinators are provided by local system headquarters (51 percent), regional system headquarters (40 percent), and state library agencies (41 percent).[8]

The assistance of a coordinator is available from local system headquarters more often for branch libraries than main libraries. Almost three-fourths of branch libraries (73 percent) have coordinators available from this source, compared with 30 percent of main libraries without branches and 44 percent of main libraries with branches.

Regional system headquarters provide assistance primarily for main libraries without branches. About half (52 percent) of these libraries have coordinator assistance available from regional headquarters, while only 24 percent of main libraries with branches and 30 percent of branches have coordinators available from this source.

Young adult coordinators may be a valuable resource for libraries—particularly for those without a young adult specialist on staff. However, coordinators are more often available for libraries with a young adult librarian than for those without one. While coordinators are available for 65 percent of libraries with a young adult librarian, they are available for only 49 percent of libraries without a young adult librarian.

Almost half (45 percent) of all libraries have neither a young adult librarian nor the assistance of a young adult coordinator.

Continuing Training for Librarians Serving Young Adults

One in five libraries (19 percent) requires continuing in-service training in young adult materials and services for young adult librarians or other librarians primarily serving young adults. Required continuing training is more common in libraries with a young adult librarian than in libraries without a young adult librarian (42 percent vs. 16 percent). Also, libraries with a young adult section require continuing training more often than those without this section: 21 percent compared with 6 percent.

Patterns of Library Use by Young Adults

Librarians reported that 25 percent of library patrons in 1986–1987 were young adults.[9] This proportion did not vary greatly across library characteristics. For example, libraries with light patronage indicated that 23 percent of their patrons were 12- to 18-year-olds, libraries with moderate patronage reported 26 percent, and libraries with heavy patronage reported 25 percent. Similarly, there were no significant differences in the proportion of young adult patrons by type of library, presence of a young adult section, or presence of a young adult librarian.

Figure 1 shows the relative frequency with which various sections of the library were used by young adults during 1986–1987. Young adult and adult reference sections were used most heavily: About three-fourths (74 and 75 percent, respectively) of libraries reported moderate or heavy use of these sections by young adults.[10] About two-thirds (68 percent) of libraries reported moderate or heavy use of adult circulation by young adults and 38 percent for children's sections.

Proportionately more libraries with a young adult librarian reported moderate or heavy use of the following sections of the library compared with libraries without a young adult librarian:

- Adult reference (89 percent vs. 73 percent)
- Adult circulation (78 percent vs. 66 percent)
- Children's (54 percent vs. 36 percent)

Libraries with heavy patronage reported moderate or heavy use of all library sections more often than those with light patronage. For example, young adult use of

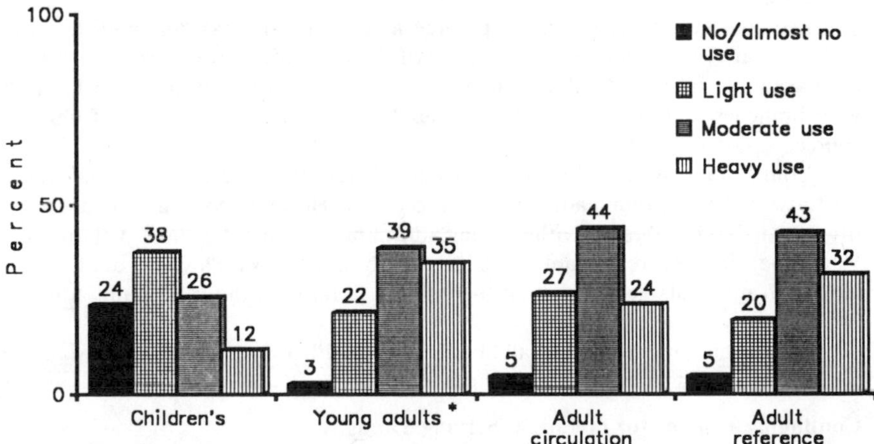

Figure 1. Percentage of Public Libraries Reporting Level of Use for Various Sections of the Library by 12- to 18-Year-Olds: United States, Fall 1987

adult reference was moderate or heavy in 88 percent of libraries with heavy patronage, compared with 58 percent of libraries with light patronage.

Library Use during School Year and Vacations

Figure 2 presents data for young adult use of the library at various times during 1986–1987. During the school year, young adult use of the library was generally heaviest after school (from 3 to 6 P.M.). Three-fourths (76 percent) of libraries reported moderate or heavy use of the library after school, compared with 53 percent during evening hours, 48 percent on weekends, and only 12 percent during school hours. During vacations, libraries were about evenly divided between those with moderate or heavy young adult use (54 percent) and those with almost no or light use.

Young adult use of libraries during the school year is correlated with amount of patronage and the presence of a young adult librarian. Ninety-two percent of libraries with a young adult librarian reported moderate or heavy library use by young adults after school, compared with 74 percent of those without a young adult librarian. Evening use and weekend use were moderate or heavy in about three-fourths (79 and 78 percent) of libraries with a young adult librarian, compared with 50 percent for evening and 45 percent for weekend use in libraries without a young adult librarian.

Libraries with heavy patronage were more likely to report moderate or heavy use by young adults during evenings and weekends than libraries with moderate or light patronage. Libraries with heavy or moderate patronage were used more heavily after school (from 3 to 6 P.M.) than those with light patronage. However, proportionately more libraries with light patronage reported moderate or heavy use by young adults during vacations than libraries with heavy patronage.

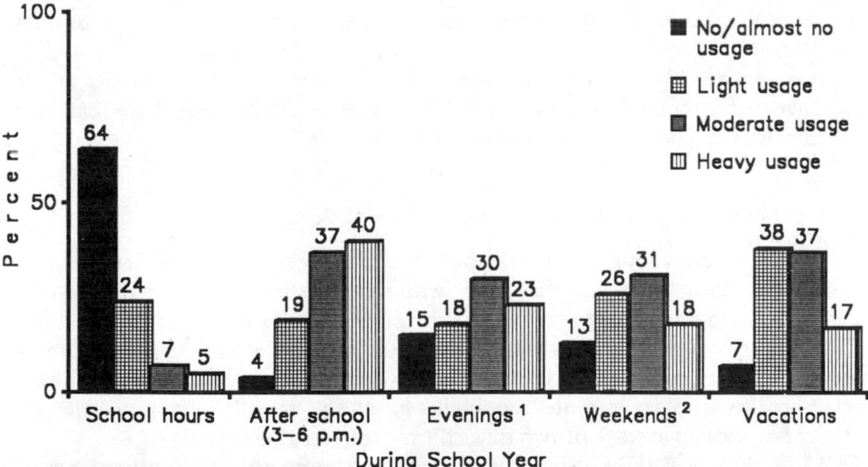

[1] Percentages do not sum to 100 because 13 percent of libraries are closed during evening hours.

[2] Percentages do not sum to 100 because 13 percent of libraries are closed on weekends.

NOTE: Percentages may not add to 100 because of rounding.

Figure 2. Percentage of Public Libraries Reporting Level of Use at Various Times during the Last 12 Months by 12- to 18-Year-Olds: United States, Fall 1987

Availability and Use of Services

Besides lending books, most libraries offer the following services for young adults:

- Study space (94 percent)
- College and career information (92 percent)
- Readers' advisory service for independent needs (88 percent)
- Readers' advisory service for school needs (87 percent)

The following services are also widely available: reading lists or booklists (78 percent), displays (71 percent), and audio recordings or cassettes (68 percent). Other library services, however, are less often available. Less than half of libraries provide meeting rooms (48 percent), videocassettes (34 percent), special collections (29 percent), and personal computers (26 percent).

The services for which libraries most often reported moderate or heavy use by young adults during 1986–1987 were book loans (76 percent), readers' advisory service for school needs (65 percent), and study space (61 percent.)[11]

Where there was a young adult librarian on staff, libraries reported moderate or heavy use of 9 out of 12 listed services more often than libraries without a young adult librarian. Only book loans, use of videocassettes, and meeting rooms showed no differences between libraries with or without a young adult librarian.

Reported use of library services during 1986–1987 also varied by amount of patronage. Libraries with heavy patronage were more likely than those with light patronage to report moderate or heavy use of more than half the services, including readers' advisory services for school needs and independent needs, personal computers, college and career information, loans of audio recordings or cassettes, book loans, and study space.

Main libraries with branches also reported greater use of the following services than main libraries without branches: college and career information, readers' advisory service for school needs and independent needs, and loans of audio recordings or cassettes.

According to librarians in 55 percent of all libraries, services to young adults have increased compared with three years ago. In 40 percent, services have remained the same, and in 5 percent they have decreased.[12]

Cooperation with Schools and Other Youth-Serving Agencies

On average, libraries cooperated with about half of the schools in their service areas during 1986–1987. Cooperative activities with schools enrolling 12- to 18-year-olds included hosting class visits to the library, visits by a librarian to classes for booktalks or other activities to promote reading, and meetings with school staff to promote reading or library usage. Libraries hosted an average of six class visits to the library for 12- to 18-year-olds, presented booktalks in schools about three times, and met with school staff an average of two times during the last 12 months.

Main libraries with branches hosted class visits more often than other types of libraries. These libraries reported an average of 23 class visits (or about three per school in their service area). In contrast, branch libraries average six class visits (about one per school), and main libraries without branches averaged three (again, one per school).

Libraries also indicated whether they had cooperated with the following youth-serving organizations during 1986–1987 by organizing activities, providing space, referrals, or providing information: scouting or other clubs or associations (51 percent); volunteer or service organizations (41 percent); literacy programs (41 percent); community or other recreational centers (33 percent); tutoring programs (31 percent); school-sponsored after-school programs (20 percent); health education groups (20 percent); and YMCAs or YWCAs (7 percent).

Barriers to Increased Use of the Library by 12- to 18-Year-Olds

Librarians were also asked for their opinions on the degree to which various factors were barriers to increased library use by young adults. Competition from extracurricular activities, disinterest on the part of young people, and lack of services or programs for young adults were viewed as the most serious: between 67 and 87 percent considered these factors moderate or major barriers (Figure 3).

Lack of transportation was believed a major or moderate barrier in 48 percent of public libraries, and hours of operation was perceived as a barrier in 36 percent. Least frequently cited was lack of encouragement by library staff (22 percent).

Across library characteristics, there is a strong consensus regarding perceived barriers. Thus, only three significant differences occur.

- Main libraries (71 to 77 percent) are more likely to consider lack of services or programs a barrier than branch libraries (59 percent).
- Main libraries with branches consider lack of transportation a barrier (60 percent) more often than main libraries without branches (45 percent).
- Libraries with light patronage find hours of operation a barrier (51 percent)

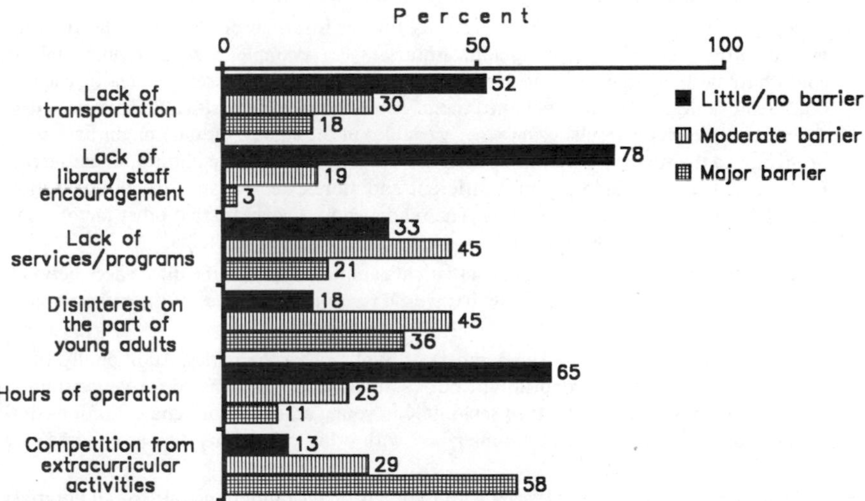

NOTE: Percentages may not add to 100 because of rounding.

Figure 3. Percentage of Public Libraries Indicating the Extent to Which Various Factors Are Perceived as Barriers to Increased Use of the Library by 12- to 18-Year-Olds: United States, Fall 1987

more often than libraries with moderate or heavy patronage (32 percent and 21 percent).

Conclusion

Although the results of the survey, published in July 1988, were too late for use in the Chapin Hall study, national data are now available on how public libraries are serving young people. The data are limited but they do represent nationally representative samples. According to consistent estimates across all types of libraries, 25 percent of public library patrons during the year surveyed are young adults. They are there to be served!

For the complete survey report, which includes 15 tables and a copy of the questionnaire, contact Helen Ashwick, Office of Educational Research and Improvement, National Center for Education Statistics, 555 New Jersey Ave. N.W., Washington, DC 20208, 202-357-6325.

Notes

1. The NCES Fast Response Survey System is a special service that, upon request, quickly obtains, from nationally representative samples, policy-relevant data from short surveys to meet the needs of U.S. Department of Education policy officials.
2. Number of patrons per week was obtained from the survey and used as a measure of size. The term patron was not defined on the questionnaire. Number of patrons per week and percentage of patrons 12 to 18 years old are based on door counts or similar counts of the number of persons entering the library rather than on circulation or other measures of library use. These figures are duplicated counts, and include persons entering library buildings to attend activities or meetings and those using no library services.
3. Other types of analyses might have given us further information regarding the findings related to the presence of a young adult librarian. For example, a demographic analysis could have been conducted of the number of young adults in the service area of each library relative to the responses obtained there. A multivariate analysis could have been carried out on the survey results using other variables in the survey. Or data might have been brought into the survey from other sources on library budgets, expenditures, or resources. Each of these topics would require a different and more extensive analysis, and collection of data beyond the scope of this study. The reader should be aware that other factors may temper our results, but the basic finding, with no further analysis, holds.
4. Because the estimates are based on a statistical sample, there may be differences between the responses of the sample and those that would result from a survey of the entire population.
5. Percentages for books are based on numbers of books rather than titles. Additionally, these percentages represent the proportion of books in collections designated for young adults. These collections include those filed separately in young adult sections and collections designated for young adults which are interfiled with other collections such as children's or adults'.
6. It should be noted that many libraries with light patronage (about one-third of all libraries) may be small libraries with only one librarian on staff.
7. Fourteen percent of libraries selected the "other" category, and specified other librarian specialties, administrators, and nonprofessionals.

8. Percentages add to more than 100 because the assistance of a young adult coordinator may be available from multiple sources.
9. Proportion of young adult patrons represents the mean percentage reported by libraries. Percentages of patrons 12 to 18 years old are based on door counts or similar counts of the number of patrons entering the library, rather than on circulation or other measures of library usage.
10. The percentage of libraries reporting moderate or heavy usage of the young adult section is based on libraries that have a young adult section or collection – 84 percent of all libraries.
11. Percentages are based on all libraries including those that reported that services were not available.
12. This question obtains perceptions of change rather than measuring actual change in amount of service or quality of services. Moreover, it does not distinguish between addition of new services and increased usage of existing services.

Book Trade Research and Statistics

Book Title Output and Average Prices: 1988 Preliminary Figures

Chandler B. Grannis
Contributing Editor, *Publishers Weekly*

Preliminary figures from R. R. Bowker Company sources on U.S. book title output in 1988 (Tables 1–5) suggest that final totals will be somewhere near those of 1987. In 1987, a record overall total of 56,027 titles in all areas and formats was recorded, which marked an increase of more than 3,000 over the 1986 total and was a record up to that time. So far in 1988, a possible decrease in mass market paperback titles is indicated and may turn out to affect the final overall total. (The final compilation of 1988 data should be ready for publication by late summer 1989.) There are few surprises among the categories (Table 1), but the extreme volatility in the travel book market is indicated by the fact that the preliminary total of new editions for 1988 already eclipses the final total for 1987—a sure indicator of a record year. A similar result can be seen in new editions of business books. Among translations (Table 5), books translated from the French, which surpassed translations from German in 1984, seem to be drawing ahead solidly, with Russian continuing to gain in third place.

Average 1988 prices that Bowker has now recorded (Tables A–C) appear to have changed little except among mass market paperbacks, where the preliminary 1988 average is 14% over the final 1987 figure. Worthy of note is that, at least in these preliminary figures, the average trade paperback price seems to have leveled out after actually declining between 1986 and 1987. Science and technology titles, closely followed by medicine, remain the highest priced among the various categories. Table D, based on manual counting of books advertised in *PW* Fall Announcement issues, shows only one noteworthy 1988 change from 1987, a 12.9% rise in the median price of hardcover novels.

Each of the 23 standard subject groups used here represents one or more specific Dewey Decimal Classification numbers as follows:

Agriculture, 630–639, 712–719; Art, 700–711, 720–779; Biography, 920; 929; B; Business, 650–659; Education, 370–379; Fiction; General Works, 000–099; History,

Note: Adapted from *Publishers Weekly,* March 10, 1989, where the article was entitled "Title Output and Prices."

Table 1 / American Book Title Production, 1986–1988

CATEGORY	1986 ALL HARD & PAPER	1987 FINAL HARD & TRADE PAPER			1987 FINAL ALL HARD & PAPER	1988 PRELIMINARY HARD & TRADE PAPER			1988 PRELIMINARY ALL HARD & PAPER
		Books	Editions	Totals		Books	Editions	Totals	
Agriculture	564	548	97	645	652	488	85	573	575
Art	1,697	1,460	226	1,686	1,693	1,157	166	1,323	1,338
Biography	2,152	1,903	292	2,195	2,259	1,674	253	1,927	1,994
Business	1,604	1,088	346	1,434	1,462	993	370	1,363	1,375
Education	1,029	906	161	1,067	1,081	830	134	964	979
Fiction	5,578	3,264	402	3,666	6,298	2,953	253	3,206	5,144
General Works	2,484	2,232	307	2,539	2,620	1,741	290	2,031	2,083
History	2,471	2,310	544	2,854	2,882	2,117	410	2,527	2,550
Home Economics	1,103	930	136	1,066	1,168	733	123	856	929
Juveniles	4,516	4,000	278	4,278	4,642	3,699	206	3,905	4,212
Language	668	544	103	647	699	434	88	522	534
Law	1,385	1,149	392	1,541	1,544	820	305	1,125	1,129
Literature	2,145	2,024	293	2,317	2,358	1,717	231	1,948	1,982
Medicine	3,445	3,281	668	3,949	3,995	2,761	577	3,338	3,376
Music	356	283	66	349	352	222	50	272	273
Philosophy, Psychology	1,669	1,424	282	1,706	1,845	1,352	209	1,561	1,656
Poetry, Drama	1,278	1,141	80	1,221	1,236	979	81	1,060	1,106
Religion	2,788	2,474	360	2,834	2,850	2,004	287	2,291	2,306
Science	3,360	3,046	607	3,653	3,658	2,575	535	3,110	3,118
Sociology, Economics	7,912	6,987	1,049	8,036	8,115	6,180	878	7,058	7,119
Sports, Recreation	1,192	901	184	1,085	1,263	702	107	809	941
Technology	2,698	2,259	468	2,727	2,756	1,813	375	2,188	2,216
Travel	543	484	132	616	629	400	137	537	554
Total	52,637	44,638	7,473	52,111	56,027	38,344	6,150	44,494	47,489

Note: Figures for mass market paperbound book production are based on entries in *Paperbound Books in Print*. Other figures are from the *Weekly Record (American Book Publishing Record)* database.

Table 2 / Mass Market Paperbacks, 1986–1988

CATEGORY	1986 FIN.	1987 FIN.	1988 PREL.
Agriculture	6	7	2
Art	3	7	15
Biography	76	64	67
Business	31	28	12
Education	20	14	15
Fiction	2,424	2,632	1,938
General Works	61	81	52
History	33	28	23
Home Econ.	97	102	73
Juveniles	461	364	307
Language	17	22	12
Law	4	3	4
Literature	35	41	34
Medicine	43	46	38
Music	10	3	1
Philosophy, Psychology	82	139	95
Poetry, Drama	27	15	46
Religion	25	16	15
Science	14	5	8
Sociology, Economics	55	79	61
Sports, Recreation	160	178	132
Technology	36	29	28
Travel	10	13	17
Total	3,730	3,916	2,995

900–909, 930–999; Home Economics, 640–649; Juveniles; Language, 400–499; Law, 340–349; Literature 800–810, 813–820, 823–899; Medicine, 610–619; Music, 780–789; Philosophy, Psychology, 100–199; Poetry, Drama, 811, 812, 821, 822; Religion, 200–299; Science, 500–599; Sociology, Economics, 300–339, 350–369, 380–399; Sports, Recreation, 790–799; Technology, 600–609, 620–629, 660–699; Travel, 910–919.

Table 3 / Paperbacks (Excluding Mass Market), 1986–1988

CATEGORY	1986	1987 FINAL			1988 PRELIMINARY		
	TOTALS	NEW BOOKS	NEW ED'NS	TOTALS	NEW BOOKS	NEW ED'NS	TOTALS
Fiction	431	295	87	382	269	112	381
Nonfiction	15,502	13,463	2,855	16,318	11,470	2,526	13,996
Total	15,933	13,758	2,942	16,700	11,739	2,638	14,377

Table 4 / Imported Titles, 1986–1988: Hard and Trade Paper Only

CATEGORY	1986	1987 FINAL			1988 PRELIMINARY		
	TOTALS	BOOKS	ED'NS	TOTALS	BOOKS	ED'NS	TOTALS
Agriculture	124	116	19	135	95	19	114
Art	168	117	11	128	102	7	109
Biography	188	152	21	173	154	9	163
Business	159	128	26	154	140	33	173
Education	220	263	13	276	193	15	208
Fiction	247	219	72	291	197	59	256
General Works	346	348	34	382	267	27	294
History	384	411	71	482	378	56	434
Home Econ.	42	32	7	39	26	2	28
Juveniles	112	104	5	109	75	2	77
Language	334	180	21	201	165	20	185
Law	190	179	46	225	140	29	169
Literature	261	277	18	295	259	27	286
Medicine	665	693	64	757	542	57	599
Music	60	59	7	66	56	5	61
Philosophy, Psychology	263	306	25	331	305	15	320
Poetry, Drama	216	168	12	180	150	33	183
Religion	141	139	24	163	126	13	139
Science	1,214	1,154	148	1,302	980	119	1,099
Sociology, Economics	1,635	1,617	119	1,736	1,397	122	1,519
Sports, Recreation	110	86	11	97	61	9	70
Technology	618	586	65	651	489	60	549
Travel	46	45	11	56	37	5	42
Total	7,749	7,379	850	8,229	6,334	743	7,077

Table 5 / Translations into English, 1986–1988: Hard and Trade Paper Only

	ARABIC	CHINESE	DANISH	DUTCH	FINNISH	FRENCH	GERMAN	HEBREW	ITALIAN	JAPANESE	LATIN	NORWEGIAN	RUSSIAN	SPANISH	SWEDISH	YIDDISH	OTHER	TOTALS
1984 Final	16	27	27	38	10	355	425	28	97	64	42	4	181	97	21	10	N/A	1,466
1985 Final	8	27	17	40	5	416	369	29	92	59	30	13	182	86	28	15	N/A	1,412
1986 Final	29	29	26	48	3	485	470	45	110	116	36	9	185	93	26	11	N/A	1,791
1987 Final	33	39	24	45	3	580	486	45	115	65	38	16	245	130	36	9	N/A	1,908
1988 Prel.	27	29	21	42	4	495	428	38	112	85	36	11	204	112	42	8	N/A	1,634

Note: "Total" covers only the languages listed here.

Table A / Hardcover: Average Per-Volume Prices, 1986–1988*

CATEGORY	1977	1986		1987		1988 PRELIMINARY		
	PRICES	VOLS.	PRICES	VOLS.	PRICES	VOLS.	$ TOTAL	PRICES
Agriculture	$16.24	391	$39.26	423	$46.24	377	$18,418.91	$48.85
Art	21.24	996	35.41	1,004	37.71	816	32,506.23	39.83
Biography	15.34	1,446	22.96	1,542	25.04	1,369	35,327.60	25.80
Business	18.00	1,115	30.72	1,032	33.31	966	36,321.44	37.59
Education	12.95	559	26.11	669	31.58	549	18,400.23	33.51
Fiction	10.09	2,212	16.84	2,499	18.19	1,992	35,544.73	17.84
General Works	30.99	1,511	38.97	1,623	43.81	1,250	61,609.44	49.28
History	17.12	1,598	28.44	1,954	31.74	1,722	57,226.88	33.24
Home Economics	11.16	532	18.97	558	20.13	411	8,864.43	21.56
Juveniles	6.65	3,066	10.64	3,162	11.48	3,003	35,802.31	11.92
Language	14.96	351	32.80	361	37.80	298	11,657.93	39.12
Law	25.04	958	49.20	1,097	49.65	812	40,549.15	49.93
Literature	15.78	1,359	25.73	1,537	28.70	1,310	40,364.20	30.81
Medicine	24.00	2,643	49.99	3,065	57.68	2,565	165,933.49	64.69
Music	20.13	222	32.59	224	35.82	177	6,507.03	36.76
Philosophy, Psychology	14.43	991	29.65	1,090	33.32	950	33,347.24	35.10
Poetry, Drama	13.63	617	25.11	699	28.46	586	15,935.55	27.19
Religion	12.26	1,171	21.60	1,226	24.51	1,003	26,978.99	26.89
Science	24.88	2,559	55.65	2,815	62.16	2,455	163,165.31	66.46
Sociology, Economics	29.88	5,043	30.34	5,393	34.38	4,791	174,568.61	36.43
Sports, Recreation	12.28	573	23.25	586	23.96	438	11,192.75	25.55
Technology	23.61	1,904	55.00	1,988	60.24	1,635	103,471.03	63.28
Travel	18.44	218	24.32	227	28.07	179	4,786.46	26.74
Total	$19.22	32,035	$32.43	34,774	$36.28	29,654	$1,138,499.94	$38.39

*From *Weekly Record Listings of Domestic and Imported Books*

Table A-1 / Hardcover: Average Per-Volume Prices—Less Than $81, 1986–1988

CATEGORY	1985	1986		1987		1988 PRELIMINARY		
	PRICES	VOLS.	PRICES	VOLS.	PRICES	VOLS.	$ TOTAL	PRICES
Agriculture	$29.99	356	$31.89	363	$32.44	300	$ 9,614.61	$32.04
Art	30.05	961	31.63	959	33.07	773	26,092.23	33.75
Biography	20.81	1,431	21.66	1,514	22.75	1,347	32,092.15	23.82
Business	27.27	1,088	28.44	1,007	30.48	925	30,736.69	33.22
Education	24.02	556	25.75	654	29.37	539	17,193.23	31.89
Fiction	15.24	2,197	15.89	2,470	17.02	1,989	35,194.73	17.69
General Works	29.05	1,441	31.86	1,518	34.22	1,139	41,435.54	36.37
History	25.41	1,578	27.04	1,906	29.58	1,684	51,640.48	30.66
Home Economics	17.11	528	18.41	554	19.23	410	8,749.43	21.34
Juveniles	9.95	3,062	10.47	3,157	11.29	3,001	35,628.66	11.87
Language	27.61	340	30.24	345	33.26	284	10,062.03	35.42
Law	35.87	863	37.28	953	37.40	704	26,609.90	37.79
Literature	23.46	1,346	24.63	1,515	28.97	1,292	37,824.70	29.27
Medicine	36.29	2,235	37.34	2,405	38.33	1,832	74,037.56	40.41
Music	27.72	217	26.30	216	31.92	173	5,988.08	34.61
Philosophy, Psychology	27.34	980	28.48	1,062	31.48	916	29,862.64	32.60
Poetry, Drama	20.90	610	22.82	679	24.99	577	14,975.55	25.95
Religion	18.88	1,162	20.08	1,210	23.09	994	25,986.64	26.14
Science	40.06	2,122	40.96	2,186	43.02	1,765	76,014.66	43.06
Sociology, Economics	27.91	4,978	28.89	5,266	31.65	4,650	155,960.40	33.53
Sports, Recreation	21.36	571	21.77	582	23.32	438	11,192.75	25.55
Technology	38.60	1,630	39.88	1,622	41.68	1,259	53,646.86	42.61
Travel	22.07	216	23.74	221	24.45	177	4,446.46	25.12
Total	$26.57	30,468	$27.15	32,364	$28.96	27,168	$814,985.98	$29.99

Table B / Mass Market Paperbacks: Average Per-Volume Prices, 1986–1988

CATEGORY	1986	1987		1988 PRELIMINARY		
	PRICES	VOLS.	PRICES	VOLS.	$ TOTAL	PRICES
Agriculture	$ 6.04	6	$ 3.56	2	$ 8.45	$ 4.23
Art	9.80	7	12.38	15	150.24	10.02
Biography	5.15	62	5.10	67	416.35	6.21
Business	7.73	28	6.39	12	92.00	7.67
Education	7.28	14	5.99	15	107.80	7.19
Fiction	3.46	2,571	3.59	1,938	7,747.56	4.00
General Works	5.07	80	5.40	52	355.80	6.85
History	5.17	28	4.90	23	163.05	7.09
Home Economics	6.23	99	6.69	73	480.70	6.59
Juveniles	2.71	363	2.80	307	963.90	3.14
Language	5.28	22	4.94	12	79.50	6.63
Law	3.98	3	3.98	4	18.35	4.59
Literature	4.92	40	4.50	34	183.95	5.41
Medicine	7.18	46	6.28	38	264.75	6.97
Music	4.21	3	7.45	1	7.95	7.95
Philosophy, Psychology	5.07	137	4.96	95	576.05	6.06
Poetry, Drama	5.76	13	5.05	46	184.90	4.02
Religion	3.84	16	3.71	15	72.00	4.80
Science	5.91	5	4.55	8	44.15	5.52
Sociology, Economics	5.32	78	5.63	61	343.60	5.63
Sports, Recreation	4.09	175	4.97	132	780.25	5.91
Technology	12.08	29	11.52	28	493.15	17.61
Travel	5.02	13	7.15	17	185.15	10.89
Total	$3.86	3,838	$4.00	2,995	$13,719.60	$4.58

Table C / Trade Paperbacks: Average Per-Volume Prices, 1986–1988

CATEGORY	1977	1986		1987		1988 PRELIMINARY		
	PRICES	VOLS.	PRICES	VOLS.	PRICES	VOLS.	$ TOTAL	PRICES
Agriculture	$ 5.01	149	$13.22	190	$14.21	169	$ 2,879.21	$17.03
Art	6.27	641	15.46	640	15.21	487	7,471.88	15.34
Biography	4.91	591	11.32	608	10.18	529	5,882.44	11.11
Business	7.09	421	18.56	376	17.53	376	6,808.59	18.10
Education	5.72	412	14.01	376	18.29	402	6,032.72	15.00
Fiction	4.20	897	8.64	1,124	9.26	1,171	11,999.71	10.24
General Works	6.18	828	28.44	871	21.57	737	17,385.51	23.58
History	5.81	766	14.55	843	13.51	769	10,514.41	13.67
Home Economics	4.77	450	9.96	491	10.26	431	5,022.27	11.65
Juveniles	2.68	906	5.71	1,024	11.66	829	5,018.07	6.05
Language	7.79	287	14.31	270	14.15	212	3,231.02	15.24
Law	10.66	364	17.46	384	22.02	286	7,029.71	24.57
Literature	5.18	712	13.19	730	12.53	610	7,950.76	13.03
Medicine	7.63	692	19.34	838	17.74	738	14,066.70	19.06
Music	6.36	117	13.67	117	13.29	90	1,251.40	13.90
Philosophy, Psychology	5.57	564	13.36	588	12.96	580	7,682.18	13.24
Poetry, Drama	4.71	596	10.02	500	9.33	458	4,688.60	10.23
Religion	3.68	1,525	9.26	1,576	9.24	1,257	12,714.41	10.11
Science	8.81	707	23.27	762	22.04	602	13,570.27	22.54
Sociology, Economics	6.03	2,597	16.76	2,490	15.79	2,140	35,330.72	16.50
Sports, Recreation	4.87	430	11.49	476	11.51	364	4,443.82	12.20
Technology	7.97	682	25.55	688	25.69	523	11,958.54	22.86
Travel	5.21	299	10.91	377	10.99	351	4,042.45	11.51
Total	$5.93	15,633	$14.86	16,339	$14.55	14,111	$206,975.39	$14.66

Table D / Average and Median Prices for Three Cloth Categories: *PW* Fall Announcements, 1982–1988

NOVELS*	AVG.	MED.	BIOGRAPHY**	AVG.	MED.	HISTORY***	AVG.	MED.
1988—209 vols./39 pubs.	$18.48	$18.95	1988—132 vols./55 pubs.	$25.29	$22.50	1988—154 vols./68 pubs.	$27.17	$24.95
1987—198 vols./42 pubs.	$17.90	$16.95	1987—115 vols./64 pubs.	$25.30	$19.95	1987—182 vols./66 pubs.	$27.05	$24.95
1986—305 vols./53 pubs.	$17.13	$16.95	1986—125 vols./53 pubs.	$22.28	$19.95	1986— 73 vols./24 pubs.	$28.99	$24.95
1985—219 vols./49 pubs.	$16.53	$16.95	1985—137 vols./60 pubs.	$22.09	$19.50	1985—179 vols./70 pubs.	$24.25	$25.00
1984—172 vols./42 pubs.	$16.46	$15.95	1984—134 vols./60 pubs.	$21.75	$18.95	1984—149 vols./79 pubs.	$24.77	$22.50
1983—214 vols./42 pubs.	$15.27	$14.95	1983—150 vols./62 pubs.	$20.74	$18.50	1983—172 vols./51 pubs.	$21.90	$20.00
1982—177 vols./41 pubs.	$14.75	$14.95	1982—140 vols./62 pubs.	$20.43	$18.95	1982—152 vols./64 pubs.	$22.88	$19.50

*Not Mystery, Western, SF, Light Romances.

**Includes letters, diaries, memoirs.

***Not art books.

Book Sales Statistics: Highlights from AAP Surveys, 1987 and 1988

Chandler B. Grannis
Contributing Editor, *Publishers Weekly*

U.S. book publishers' sales in 1987 amounted to more than $11.4 billion, according to compilations by the Association of American Publishers. This represented a 9.2% increase over the 1986 total, which had been a modest 5.8% above the 1985 figure, which, in turn, had been 8.3% over the 1984 total. (See accompanying table.)

The trade book categories (adult and children's books in hardcover and paperback), totaling more than $2.4 billion, made up 21.2% of 1987 sales and were 15.9% over the 1986 sales. Professional books reached $1.84 billion in sales, were 16% of the total, and gained 7.1% over their 1986 sales figure. Elhi texts, at $1.7 billion, made up near 15% of the total, rising by 6.3%. College text sales, over $1.52 billion, showed a 7.9% increase and accounted for more than 13.2% of the 1987 total.

AAP's full report for 1988 was not complete as this edition of *The Bowker Annual* went to press. Unweighted data from those publishers reporting to AAP on a monthly basis suggest, however, that adult hardcover sales experienced only a slight gain in 1988 over a strong 1987 total. It should be kept in mind in any case that the monthly report and the full annual report are not truly comparable, although the monthly reports are helpful indicators of trends.

Category	% change, December	% change, Year to Date
Adult hardcover	−8.6	1.8
Adult paperback	−2.5	18.2
Juvenile hardcover	8.3	18.6
Juvenile paperback	−1.0	20.5
University Press hardcover	10.5	15.9
University Press paperback	12.8	20.9
Bibles, etc.	39.5	3.4
Mass market paperback	17.5	10.0
Book club	−3.2	0.0
Mail order	9.4	10.5
Sci-tech	−2.5	9.0
College texts	12.8	11.1
School texts	−2.1	5.0

Note: Adapted from *Publishers Weekly,* July 22, 1988, "Book Sales Rise 9.2% to $11.45 Billion in 1987," and *Publishers Weekly,* February 17, 1989, chart p. 14.

Table 1 / Estimated Book Publishing Industry Sales, 1972, 1977, 1982, 1986–1987
(Millions of Dollars)

	1972	1977	1982		1986		1987			
Category	$	$	$	% Change from 1977	$	% Change from 1982	$	% Change from 1986	% Change from 1982	% Change from 1977
Trade (total)	444.8	887.2	1,355.5	52.8	2,095.5	54.6	2,428.5	15.9	79.2	173.7
Adult hardbound	251.5	501.3	671.6	34.3	1,025.8	52.7	1,211.5	18.1	80.4	141.7
Adult paperbound*	82.4	223.7	452.0	102.1	683.5	51.2	767.6	12.3	69.8	243.1
Juvenile hardbound	106.5	136.1	180.3	32.5	290.1	60.9	334.5	15.3	85.5	145.8
Juvenile paperbound	4.4	26.1	51.5	97.3	96.1	86.6	114.9	19.6	123.1	340.2
Religious (total)	117.5	250.6	390.0	55.6	475.5	21.9	539.3	13.4	38.3	115.2
Bibles, testaments, hymnals, and prayer books	61.6	116.3	163.7	40.8	182.9	11.7	210.7	15.2	28.7	81.2
Other religious	55.9	134.3	226.2	68.4	292.6	29.4	328.6	12.3	45.3	144.7
Professional (total)	381.0	698.2	1,230.5	76.2	1,722.5	40.0	1,845.2	7.1	50.0	164.3
Technical and scientific	131.8	249.3	431.4	73.0	579.1	34.2	635.9	9.8	47.4	155.1
Business and other professional	192.2	286.3	530.6	85.3	747.5	40.9	796.8	6.6	50.2	178.3
Medical	57.0	162.6	268.5	65.1	395.9	47.4	412.5	4.2	53.6	153.7
Book clubs	240.5	406.7	590.0	45.1	698.4	18.4	779.4	11.6	32.1	91.6
Mail-order publications	198.9	396.4	604.6	52.5	620.6	2.6	627.4	1.1	3.8	58.3

Mass market paperback rack-sized	250.0	487.7	685.5	40.6	792.3	15.6	893.7	12.8	30.4	83.2
University presses	41.4	56.1	122.9	119.1	160.5	30.6	172.1	7.2	40.0	206.8
Elementary and secondary text	497.6	755.9	1,051.5	39.1	1,604.0	52.5	1,705.1	6.3	62.2	125.6
College text†	375.3	649.7	1,142.4	75.8	1,409.8	23.4	1,521.2	7.9	33.2	134.2
Standardized tests	26.5	44.6	69.7	56.3	96.6	38.6	101.9	5.5	46.2	128.5
Subscription reference	278.9	294.4	396.6	34.7	501.2	26.4	516.2	3.0	30.2	75.3
AV and other media (total)	116.2	151.3	148.0	−2.2	211.1	42.6	213.0	0.9	43.9	40.8
Elhi	101.2	131.4	130.1	−1.0	177.4	36.4	174.7	−1.5	34.3	33.0
College	9.2	11.6	7.9	−31.9	13.5	70.9	15.1	11.5	91.1	30.2
Other	5.8	8.3	10.0	20.5	20.2	102.0	23.2	14.9	132.0	179.5
Other sales	49.2	63.4	77.1	21.6	96.5	25.2	104.2	8.0	35.1	64.4
Total	3,017.8	5,142.2	7,864.3	52.9	10,484.5	33.3	11,447.2	9.2	45.6	122.6

Source: Association of American Publishers, 1987 *Annual Statistics.*

*Includes non-rack-sized sales by mass market publishers of $113.5 million in 1982, $172.9 million in 1986, and $200.0 million in 1987. The added reporting of certain mass market publishers in 1985 and 1986 has given this survey data from *all* major MMPB publishers. Based on this information, it would seem that AAP's estimates of the industry sales were virtually on the mark. However, to allow for the few small nonreporting MMPB publishers, AAP has increased its 1982 estimate by $20 million, and its 1986 estimate by $30 million.

†The Higher Education Division of AAP has requested the Statistical Service Center to conduct an independent survey of college publishers. For 1987, this survey of 50 college publishers, which in the opinion of the Higher Education Division Statistics Committee represent the majority of known college publishers, reported sales of $1,249.1 million.

U.S. Book Exports and Imports, 1987

Chandler B. Grannis
Contributing Editor, *Publishers Weekly*

In 1987, following a year in which U.S. book imports exceeded exports for the first time in memory, exports recovered enough to bring the two totals almost into balance. The value of shipments of American books aboard was at least $739.3 million, and book imports were valued at about $743.8 million. The export-to-import ratio for 1987 was about 49.8 to 50.2, compared with 46 to 54 in 1986. In contrast, the 1982 exports had shown a 67 to 33 ratio to imports.

According to William F. Lofquist of the International Trade Administration, U.S. Department of Commerce, the export trend is increasingly favorable. In the first five months of 1988, he reports, book exports rose 20%-25% in both dollars and units, while imports were up about 10% in dollars and down about 5% in units. (Lofquist supplied *Publishers Weekly* with the Department of Commerce printouts from which Tables 1-4 were produced.)

The 1987 export totals were 22.4% higher in dollar value than those of 1986; the import figure also rose, but by only 6%. U.S. international trade in books is actually larger than the figures shown in Tables 1-4 can indicate, but how much larger is impossible to say; the U.S. Department of Commerce, which compiles the figures, does not take into account the undoubtedly sizable number of export shipments valued under $500 or import shipments valued under $250.

Table 1 shows export increases in most Department of Commerce categories, with declines in the Bibles and Encyclopedias groups. Table 2 shows increases in all reported categories except books in languages other than English.

Shifts in business with individual countries show interesting differences. Table 3 shows major increases in 1987 export sales to Taiwan, Canada, Japan, the United Kingdom, India, Brazil, Saudi Arabia, and other nations and sharp declines in shipments to the People's Republic of China and Mexico.

Table 4 shows spectacular increases in 1987 imports from the Republic of Korea, Taiwan, and Singapore, and large increases for Hong Kong, Israel, and Colombia. Several of these countries have recently increased the amount of printing they are doing for U.S. publishers, which is reflected in the figures. This, as Lofquist points out, is partly because the demise of the manufacturing clause in the copyright law makes it possible to buy more printing abroad, and partly because governments in these countries are giving support to their printers. Some of the same countries that print for U.S. publishers are also among those that are buying more U.S. books—because of both the decline in the dollar and U.S. government efforts to combat massive book piracy.

Note: Adapted from *Publishers Weekly*, September 9, 1988, where the article was entitled "Balancing the Books: U.S. Exports, Imports, Almost Equal in 1987."

Table 1 / U.S. Book Exports, 1986–1987
Shipments Valued over $500

	$ 1986	$ 1987	% Change	1986 Units	1987 Units	% Change
Bibles, Testaments, and other religious books (2703020)	$33,874,307	$31,768,687	−6.2	46,275,876	37,722,886	−18.5
Dictionaries and thesauruses (2703040)	4,725,970	5,528,987	+17.0	724,196	798,145	+7.5
Encyclopedias (2703060)	32,356,436	29,567,216	−8.6	5,536,458	4,587,352	−17.1
Textbooks, workbooks, and standardized tests (2703070)	112,377,028	140,853,541	+25.3	16,347,662	19,158,094	+17.2
Technical, scientific, and professional books (2703080)	156,555,078	194,187,973	+24	29,857,731	38,625,832	+29.4
Paperbound mass market books (2704020)	40,898,773	51,845,636	+28.8	33,299,603	43,574,972	+30.9
Books not specially provided for (2704040)	210,787,351	269,796,403	+28.0	87,205,160	114,410,535	+31.2
Children's picture and coloring books (7375200)	7,555,664	9,274,858	+22.8	—	—	—
Total Exports	$604,033,069	$739,314,267	+22.4	—	—	—

Note: Source for Tables 1, 2, and 3: Department of Commerce; compiled by Chandler B. Grannis from printouts supplied by William S. Lofquist, Industry Specialist (Printing and Publishing), International Trade Administration.

Table 2 / U.S. Book Imports, 1986–1987
Shipments Valued over $250

	$ 1986	$ 1987	% Change	1986 Units	1987 Units	% Change
Bibles, prayer books (2702520)	$ 15,038,156	$16,086,429	+7.0	12,859,531	14,049,275	+9.3
Books, foreign language (2702540)	37,738,941	35,278,985	−6.5	22,114,817	22,442,193	+1.5
Books, not specially provided for, wholly or in part the work of an author who is a U.S. domiciliary (2702560)	26,128,615	29,850,263	+14.2	57,982,639	58,633,432	+1.1
Other books (2702580)	607,969,899	644,708,677	+6.0	510,550,155	505,322,125	−1.0
Children's picture and coloring books (7375200)	14,567,999	17,891,266	+22.8	–	–	–
Total Imports	$701,438,610	$743,815,620	+6.0	–	–	–

Table 3 / U.S. Book Exports, 1986–1987
Shipments Valued over $500

	$ 1986	$ 1987	% Change
Canada	$206,203,780	$289,741,297	+40.5
United Kingdom	79,067,346	109,132,002	+38.0
Australia	56,945,259	58,194,896	+2.2
Japan	34,827,058	50,514,449	+45.0
Netherlands	22,177,779	23,592,807	+6.4
West Germany	14,467,329	17,930,210	+23.9
India	10,477,379	13,890,950	+37.5
Brazil	9,702,609	13,322,612	+37.3
France	9,913,069	11,730,366	+18.3
Philippines	9,624,891	11,671,740	+21.3
Mexico	15,799,004	11,654,640	−26.2
Singapore	10,477,379	10,810,067	+3.2
South Africa	6,860,296	8,036,522	+17.1
Ireland	7,345,706	7,764,495	+5.7
China (PRC)	17,505,469	5,913,697	−66.2
Hong Kong	5,550,831	5,869,945	+5.7
New Zealand	4,523,415	5,743,458	+27.0
Italy	4,122,343	4,950,574	+20.1
Saudi Arabia	3,516,641	4,740,794	+34.8
China (Taiwan)	2,842,508	4,470,620	+57.3
Total*	$604,033,669	$739,314,267	+22.4

*Includes figures for the countries not specifically listed here.

Table 4 / U.S. Book Imports, 1986–1987
Shipments Valued over $250

	$ 1986	$ 1987	% Change
United Kingdom	$175,113,256	$188,301,480	+7.5
Japan	125,925,445	129,344,395	+2.7
Canada	104,293,065	97,354,793	−6.7
Hong Kong	54,284,854	74,542,998	+37.3
Italy	47,908,722	42,796,144	−10.7
West Germany	35,037,710	36,400,360	+3.9
Singapore	15,953,384	26,363,319	+65.3
Republic of Korea	7,880,650	14,399,067	+82.7
Netherlands	12,760,656	13,953,242	+9.3
Belgium	18,160,365	11,783,656	−35.1
France	12,362,195	11,431,722	−7.5
China (Taiwan)	6,289,152	10,713,170	+70.3
Switzerland	10,344,613	7,682,728	−25.7
Mexico	8,942,945	6,742,875	−24.6
Israel	4,433,522	5,897,993	+33.0
Colombia	4,164,476	5,383,768	+29.3
Total*	$701,438,619	$743,815,620	+6.0

*Includes figures for the countries not specifically listed here.

British Book Production, 1988

The number of book titles published in the United Kingdom in 1988 was a record on both bases on which the figures are calculated. As Tables 1 and 2 show, 56,514 titles were issued: 43,188 of them were new books and 13,326 new editions including paperbacks. This was a 3.2 percent increase on the 1987 total of 54,746, which was itself a 4.1 percent rise on the 1986 figure.

So the remorseless rise continued, particularly with new books, which were up by 1,738. New editions were almost static, increasing by only 30. The proportion of U.S.-originated titles handled by stockholding U.K. distributors remained constant at about 27–28 percent. These figures relate to titles published and notified to Whitaker in the year 1988. As noted in 1987, Whitaker no longer includes—as it previously did—laggard notifications from the earlier year in the figures for the current year. If this is done, as for the sake of continuity it is in Table 3, which shows growth in title output over the past 42 years, the total figures are yet more alarming: 62,063 titles, of which 14,594 are new editions.

Given the overall situation of continued daunting growth that is evidenced in almost every category in Table 2, it is perhaps surprising that travel fell by nearly 2 percent. But this is probably a reaction to the 1987 figure: travel grew then by 22 percent.

Table 1 / British Book Production by Subject, 1987 and 1988

	1987	1988	+ or –
Art	1,573	1,703	+130
Biography	1,880	2,131	+251
Chemistry and physics	811	839	+28
Children's books	5,014	5,063	+49
Commerce	1,898	2,033	+135
Education	1,226	1,429	+203
Engineering	1,604	1,604	—
Fiction	6,389	6,496	+107
History	2,015	2,153	+138
Industry	460	456	–4
Law and public administration	1,904	1,932	+28
Literature	1,412	1,574	+162
Medical science	3,345	3,423	+78
Natural sciences	1,254	1,199	–55
Political science	4,451	4,307	–144
Religion	2,028	2,047	+19
School textbooks	1,881	2,007	+126
Sociology	1,118	1,284	+166
Travel and guidebooks	1,355	1,333	–22
Total new books	41,450	43,188	+1,738
Total new editions	13,296	13,326	+30
Overall total	54,746	56,514	+1,768

Note: Adapted from *The Bookseller* (12 Dyott St., London WC1A 1DF, England), February 3, 1989, where the article is entitled "Publishers' Output Goes Up Again."

Table 2 / British Book Title Output, 1988

Classification	December 1988				January–December 1988			
	Total	Reprints & New Editions	Trans.	Limited Editions	Total	Reprints & New Editions	Trans.	Limited Editions
Aeronautics	26	4	—	—	258	54	1	—
Agriculture and forestry	39	6	—	—	457	91	6	—
Architecture	66	20	1	—	378	86	6	—
Art	139	24	3	—	1,703	292	58	4
Astronomy	32	3	—	—	136	27	—	—
Bibliography and library economy	102	20	—	1	811	124	2	2
Biography	196	48	10	2	2,131	594	79	8
Chemistry and physics	137	19	2	—	839	163	10	—
Children's books	296	65	10	—	5,063	1,203	151	7
Commerce	232	52	10	—	2,033	514	15	2
Customs, costumes, folklore	24	9	1	—	189	40	9	2
Domestic science	68	32	1	—	830	220	9	—
Education	211	28	—	—	1,429	204	5	—
Engineering	195	37	3	—	1,604	354	13	—
Entertainment	79	18	6	—	668	150	37	—
Fiction	494	252	20	—	6,496	3,076	270	3
General	130	19	2	—	961	131	7	—
Geography and archaeology	31	9	—	—	520	152	3	1
Geology and meteorology	52	15	—	—	259	52	1	—
History	205	30	7	—	2,153	412	76	4
Humor	30	3	1	—	286	33	1	—
Industry	74	17	1	—	456	99	7	1
Language	72	11	3	—	747	198	8	—
Law and public administration	244	65	2	—	1,932	441	13	—
Literature	143	13	3	—	1,574	216	44	3
Mathematics	117	22	4	—	927	185	21	—
Medical science	446	98	4	—	3,423	729	29	—
Military science	40	22	1	—	316	100	6	—
Music	39	12	2	—	421	100	14	—
Natural sciences	140	9	—	—	1,199	194	8	2
Occultism	40	6	1	—	413	108	12	—
Philosophy	133	15	3	—	752	141	45	—
Photography	15	—	—	—	204	24	5	2
Plays	24	8	3	—	280	67	36	3
Poetry	113	9	12	14	834	97	68	23
Political science and economics	581	96	17	—	4,307	778	68	1
Psychology	136	26	1	—	887	156	19	—
Religion and theology	217	44	17	—	2,047	331	117	2
School textbooks	217	51	1	—	2,007	332	16	—
Science, general	18	6	1	—	91	20	2	—
Sociology	164	17	3	—	1,284	168	27	—
Sports and outdoor games	74	15	1	1	888	200	7	1
Stockbreeding	38	8	2	—	317	74	5	—
Trade	51	12	—	—	472	123	—	1
Travel and guidebooks	113	23	—	—	1,333	426	17	—
Radio and television	15	4	—	—	199	47	2	—
Totals	6,048	1,322	159	18	56,514	13,326	1,355	72

Table 3 / British Title Output, 1947–1988

Year	Total	Reprints & New Editions
1947	13,046	2,441
1948	14,686	3,924
1949	17,034	5,110
1950	17,072	5,334
1951	18,066	4,938
1952	18,741	5,428
1953	18,257	5,523
1954	18,188	4,846
1955	19,962	5,770
1956	19,107	5,302
1957	20,719	5,921
1958	22,143	5,971
1959	20,690	5,552
1960	23,783	4,989
1961	24,893	6,406
1962	25,079	6,104
1963	26,023	5,656
1964	26,154	5,260
1965	26,358	5,313
1966	28,883	5,919
1967	29,619	7,060
1968	31,470	8,778
1969	32,393	9,106
1970	33,489	9,977
1971	32,538	8,975
1972	33,140	8,486
1973	35,254	9,556
1974	32,194	7,852
1975	35,608	8,361
1976	34,434	8,227
1977	36,322	8,638
1978	38,766	9,236
1979	41,940	9,086
1980	48,158	10,776
1981	43,083	9,387
1982	48,307	10,360
1983	51,071	12,091
1984	51,555	11,309
1985	52,994	11,740
1986	57,845	13,671
1987	59,837	14,185
1988	62,063	14,594

Number of Book Outlets in the United States and Canada

The *American Book Trade Directory* has been published by the R. R. Bowker Company since 1915. Revised annually, it features lists of booksellers, wholesalers, periodicals, reference tools, and other information about the U.S. book market as well as markets in Great Britain and Canada. The data provided in Tables 1 and 2 for the

United States and Canada, the most current available, are from the 1988 edition of the directory.

The 23,983 stores of various types shown in Table 1 are located in approximately 6,300 cities in the United States, Canada, and regions administered by the United States. All "general" bookstores are assumed to carry hardbound (trade) books, paperbacks, and children's books; special effort has been made to apply this category only to bookstores for which this term can properly be applied. All "college" stores are assumed to carry college-level textbooks. The term "educational" is used for outlets handling school textbooks up to and including the high school level. The category "mail order" has been confined to those outlets that sell general trade books by mail and are not book clubs; all others operating by mail have been classified according to the kinds of books carried. The term "antiquarian" covers dealers in old and rare books. Stores handling only secondhand books are classified by the category "used." The category "paperback" represents stores with more than 80 percent of their stock in paperbound books. Other stores with paperback departments are listed under the major classification ("general," "department store," "stationer," etc.), with the fact that paperbacks are carried given in the entry. A bookstore that specializes in a subject to the extent of 50 percent of its stock has that subject designated as its major category.

Table 1 / Bookstores in the United States (and Canada)

Category	United States	Canada	Category	United States	Canada
Antiquarian	1,295	(89)	Medical	36	(2)
Mail-order antiquarian	649	(24)	Museum store and art gallery	412	(25)
College	3,117	(169)	Newsdealer	152	(5)
Department store	346	(72)	Office supply	77	(15)
Drugstore	21	(7)	Paperback[1]	667	(33)
Educational	125	(39)	Religious	3,846	(234)
Exporter-importer	16	(1)	Remainders	14	(3)
Foreign language	121	(29)	Rental	1	(0)
General	6,561	(990)	Science-technology	37	(4)
Gift shop	181	(26)	Special[2]	2,295	(204)
Juvenile	275	(52)	Stationer	119	(34)
Law	42	(2)	Used	1,140	(91)
Mail order (general)	404	(25)	*Totals*		
			Bookstores	21,808	(2,175)
			Bookstore chain headquarters[3]	1,092	(95)
			Bookstore chain branches[3]	6,795	(728)
			Independent bookstores	14,066	(1,352)

[1]This figure does not include used paperback bookstores, paperback departments of general bookstores, department stores, stationers, drugstores, or wholesalers handling paperbacks.

[2]This indicates stores specializing in subjects other than those specifically given in the list.

[3]These chain headquarters and branches include wholesalers.

Table 2 / Wholesalers in the United States (and Canada)

Category	United States	Canada
Total listed	1,235	(177)
General wholesalers	955	(139)
Paperback wholesalers[1]	280	(38)

[1]This figure is the total of all wholesalers who indicated in the survey that at least 51 percent of total title volume was accounted for by paperbound sales.

Book Review Media Statistics

Number of Books Reviewed by Major Book-Reviewing Publications, 1987–1988

	Adult		Juvenile		Young Adult		Total	
	1987	1988	1987	1988	1987	1988	1987	1988
Booklist[1]	4,507	4,639	1,662	2,016	1,545	1,764	7,714	8,419
Bulletin of the Center for Children's Books	–	–	485	896	300	–	785	896
Chicago Sun Times	800	992	250	48	–	–	1,050	1,040
Chicago Tribune	800	1,000	200	150	–	–	1,000	1,150
Choice[2]	6,803	6,769	–	–	–	–	6,803	6,769
Horn Book	7	13	292	324	78	109	375	446
Kirkus Services[3]	4,000	3,000	–	1,000	–	–	4,000	4,000
Library Journal	4,500	4,000	–	–	–	–	4,500	4,000
Los Angeles Times	2,600	1,200	125	100	–	–	2,725	1,300
New York Review of Books	400	350	–	–	–	–	400	350
New York Times Sunday Book Review[4]	2,250	2,250	250	250	–	–	2,500	2,500
Publishers Weekly[5]	5,479	5,239	936	698	–	–	6,415	5,937
School Library Journal	237	223	2,540	2,575	–	–	2,777	2,798
Washington Post Book World	1,607	1,731	173	160	–	–	1,780	1,891

[1]All figures are for a 12-month period from September 1 to August 31; 1987 figures are for September 1, 1986–August 31, 1987. Totals include reference and subscription books. In addition, *Booklist* publishes reviews of nonprint materials–911 in 1987 and 1,033 in 1988–and of special bibliographies–4,300 in 1987 and 4,750 in 1988.

[2]All figures are for a 12-month period beginning September and ending July/August; 1988 figures are for September 1987–August 1988. Total for 1987 includes 322 nonprint materials; total for 1988 includes 316 nonprint materials.

[3]Adult figures include both adult and juvenile books.

[4]Adult figures include paperbacks reviewed in "New & Noteworthy" column. Figures for 1987 and 1988 are estimates based on counts done in previous years.

[5]Includes reviews of paperback originals and reprints.

Prices of U.S. and Foreign Published Materials

Kathryn Hammell Carpenter
Chair, ALA RTSD Library Materials Price Index Committee

Prices for library materials continued to rise in 1988, although in several instances the rate of increase was a moderate one. The price of U.S. hardcover books increased 5.8%, of North American academic books 6%, and of U.S. college books (including reference titles) 8.8%. Trade (higher priced) paperbacks, which had decreased 2.1% in 1987, rose .8% in 1988. After a 3.1% increase in 1987, prices for mass market paperbacks shot up 15% in 1988. The rate of increase for U.S. Periodicals (excluding Soviet translations) remained stable but high at 9.1%, 2.2 times the rate of inflation in 1988 marked by the 4.1% increase in the Consumer Price Index (CPI). The changes in indexes for the principal categories of U.S. materials are as follows:

U.S. Materials	Index Change	Percent Change
Consumer Price Index*	13.6	4.1
Periodicals	26.5	9.1
Hardcover books	10.9	5.8
Academic books	10.1	6.0
College books	17.1	8.8
Mass market paperbacks	22.6	15.1
(Higher priced) paperbacks	2.0	.8

*Adjusted to base year 1977

A three year comparison of these data shows a rate of increase higher in most cases than the increase in the CPI.

	Percent Change		
U.S. Materials	1986	1987	1988
Consumer Price Index*	1.9	3.7	4.1
Periodicals	8.9	9.9	9.1
Hardcover books	-.76	9.0	5.8
Academic books	5.9	9.9	6.0
College books	7.1	5.0	8.8
Mass market paperbacks	6.6	3.1	15.1
(Higher priced) paperbacks	6.3	-2.1	.8

*Adjusted to base year 1977

U.S. Published Materials

Tables 1 and 2 show 1988 average prices and price indexes for U.S. periodicals and serials services, respectively. (Comparative figures for 1989 will be published in the April 15, 1989, issue of *Library Journal*.) Table 3 reports on U.S. hardcover books, Table 4 on North American academic books, Table 5 on U.S. college books, Table 6 on U.S. mass market paperbacks, Table 7 on U.S. trade (higher priced) paperbacks, and Table 8 on U.S. nonprint media. Price indexes for library microfilm and newspapers were resumed in 1988. Tables 9 and 10 contain retrospective data on library microfilm and newspapers from 1985 to 1987. Unless otherwise indicated, the base year for the price indexes is 1977.

Periodicals and Serials Prices

The U.S. Periodicals Price Index for 1988 was produced by the Faxon Company in collaboration with members of the ALA RTSD Library Materials Price Index Committee. Subscription prices for 1988 are list prices obtained directly from publishers that do not include customer discounts or service charges. The complete report, which includes breakdowns by subject, multiyear comparisons, and rankings by rate of increase and average price, is published annually in the April 15 issue of *Library Journal*. Average prices for periodicals (excluding Soviet translations) increased from $71.41 in 1987 to $77.93 in 1988, an increase of 9.1%. When Soviet translations are

Table 1 / U.S. Periodicals: Average Prices and Price Indexes, 1985–1988*
(Index Base: 1977 = 100)

Subject Area	1977 Average Price	1985 Average Price	1985 Index	1986 Average Price	1986 Index	1987 Average Price	1987 Index	1988 Average Price	1988 Index
U.S. periodicals									
Excluding Soviet translations†	$24.59	$59.70	242.8	$65.00	264.3	$71.41	290.4	$77.93	316.9
Including Soviet translations†	33.42	80.78	241.7	87.38	261.5	96.36	288.3	105.45	315.5
Agriculture	11.58	26.05	225.0	28.71	247.9	31.14	268.9	33.56	289.8
Business and economics	18.62	44.41	238.5	47.15	253.2	50.39	270.6	53.89	289.4
Chemistry and physics	93.76	238.43	254.3	264.05	281.6	294.05	313.6	329.99	352.0
Children's periodicals	5.82	13.31	228.7	13.76	236.4	15.19	261.0	16.39	281.6
Education	17.54	37.81	215.6	40.47	230.7	43.30	246.9	47.95	273.4
Engineering	35.77	84.38	235.9	92.66	259.0	103.49	289.3	114.83	321.0
Fine and applied arts	13.72	27.03	197.0	28.28	206.1	30.58	222.9	32.43	236.4
General interest periodicals	16.19	26.41	163.1	26.95	166.5	27.79	171.6	28.29	174.7
History	12.64	25.55	202.1	26.04	206.0	27.64	218.7	30.16	238.6
Home economics	18.73	41.04	219.1	45.59	243.4	48.67	259.9	54.73	292.2
Industrial arts	14.37	35.09	244.2	39.75	276.6	41.45	288.4	44.20	307.6
Journalism and communications	16.97	46.08	271.5	47.54	281.1	50.66	298.5	53.39	314.6
Labor and industrial relations	11.24	34.75	309.2	37.14	330.4	38.65	343.9	44.06	392.0
Law	17.36	35.13	202.4	36.44	209.9	39.82	229.4	43.33	249.6
Library and information sciences	16.97	40.66	239.6	42.82	252.3	48.42	285.3	51.61	304.1
Literature and language	11.82	24.18	204.6	25.21	213.3	26.21	221.7	28.04	237.2
Mathematics, botany, geology, and general science	47.13	116.93	248.1	129.95	275.7	146.08	310.0	159.33	338.1
Medicine	51.31	137.92	268.8	151.77	295.8	169.36	330.1	180.67	352.1
Philosophy and religion	10.89	24.30	223.1	24.85	228.2	25.60	235.1	27.09	248.8
Physical education and recreation	10.00	23.72	237.2	24.78	247.8	26.67	266.7	28.60	286.0
Political science	14.83	32.72	220.6	35.19	237.3	39.95	269.4	41.55	280.2
Psychology	31.74	76.34	240.5	83.71	263.7	92.05	290.0	100.57	316.9
Sociology and anthropology	19.68	50.87	258.5	56.31	286.1	60.29	306.4	64.27	326.6
Soviet translations†	175.41	453.47	258.5	483.09	275.4	537.54	306.4	592.22	337.6
Zoology	33.69	90.75	269.4	102.83	305.2	112.91	335.1	127.33	377.9
Total number of periodicals									
Excluding Soviet translations†	3,218	3,731		3,731		3,731		3,731	
Including Soviet translations†	3,418	3,942		3,942		3,942		3,942	

*Compiled by Leslie C. Knapp and Rebecca T. Lenzini. For further comments see *Library Journal,* April 15, 1988, "Price Indexes for 1988: U.S. Periodicals," by Leslie C. Knapp and Rebecca T. Lenzini. Note that Table 1 uses a one-year (1977), rather than a three-year (1977–1979), base, conforming to the practice of the Bureau of Labor Statistics and making these price indexes comparable to the consumer price indexes. For average prices for years prior to 1985, see previous editions of the *Bowker Annual.*

†The category Soviet translations was added in 1986. Data for U.S. periodicals including Soviet translations are based on the total group of titles included in the indexes of this table; data for U.S. periodicals excluding Soviet translations are based on the total group of titles minus the Soviet translation titles.

Table 2 / U.S. Serial Services: Average Prices and Price Indexes, 1977–1988*
(Index Base: 1977 = 100)

Year	Number of Titles	Average Price	Percent Increase	Index	Year	Number of Titles	Average Price	Percent Increase	Index
U.S. Serial services[a]					Science and technology				
1977	1,432	$142.27	–	100.0	1977	297	$141.16	–	100.0
1978	1,426	153.95	8.2	108.2	1978	289	160.61	13.8	113.8
1979	1,450	171.06	11.1	120.2	1979	290	173.96	8.3	123.2
1980	1,470	194.21	13.5	136.5	1980	288	191.35	10.0	135.6
1981	1,477	219.75	13.2	154.5	1981	287	214.01	11.8	151.6
1982	1,494	244.52	11.3	171.9	1982	286	229.98	7.5	162.9
1983	1,525	274.72	12.4	193.1	1983	282	270.94	17.8	191.9
1984	1,537	295.13	7.4	207.4	1984	281	295.36	9.0	209.2
1985–1987	na	na	na	na	1985–1987	na	na	na	na
1988	1,310	341.32	na	239.9	1988	302	378.37	na	268.0
Business					Social sciences[b]				
1977	255	$216.28	–	100.0	1977	134	$145.50	–	100.0
1978	262	222.45	2.9	102.9	1978	136	153.94	5.8	105.8
1979	270	249.05	12.0	115.2	1979	139	169.55	10.1	116.5
1980	279	294.00	18.0	135.9	1980	143	190.07	12.1	130.6
1981	271	343.29	16.8	158.7	1981	144	215.12	13.2	147.8
1982	276	371.03	8.1	171.6	1982	149	249.03	15.8	171.2
1983	286	417.83	12.6	193.2	1983	159	266.43	7.0	183.1
1984	289	437.07	4.6	202.1	1984	159	283.82	6.5	195.1
1985–1987	na	na	na	na	1985–1987	na	na	na	na
1988	281	458.33	na	211.9	1988	156	441.67	na	303.6
General and humanities					U.S. documents				
1977	113	$90.44	–	100.0	1977	204	$62.88	–	100.0
1978	113	94.88	4.9	104.9	1978	196	72.52	15.3	115.3
1979	114	118.83	25.2	131.4	1979	198	75.87	4.6	120.7
1980	118	124.28	4.6	137.4	1980	197	78.87	4.0	125.4
1981	120	142.04	14.3	157.1	1981	200	84.48	7.1	134.4
1982	119	160.03	12.7	176.9	1982	202	99.05	17.2	157.5
1983	120	186.67	16.6	206.4	1983	203	101.24	2.2	161.0
1984	122	196.55	5.3	217.3	1984	203	97.37	–3.8	154.9
1985–1987	na	na	na	na	1985–1987	na	na	na	na
1988	116	225.95	na	249.8	1988	190	101.88	na	162.0

Table 2 / U.S. Serial Services: Average Prices and Price Indexes, 1977–1988* *(cont.)*
(Index Base: 1977 = 100)

Year	Number of Titles	Average Price	Percent Increase	Index	Year	Number of Titles	Average Price	Percent Increase	Index
Law					Wilson Index[c]				
1977	229	$126.74	–	100.0	1977	18	$87.51	–	100.0
1978	235	137.91	8.8	108.8	1978	18	95.99	9.7	109.7
1979	241	158.65	15.0	125.2	1979	19	104.68	9.1	119.6
1980	248	184.38	16.2	145.5	1980	19	114.05	9.0	130.3
1981	251	212.85	15.4	167.9	1981	19	122.30	7.2	139.8
1982	256	232.61	9.3	183.5	1982	19	132.55	8.4	151.5
1983	268	249.64	7.3	197.0	1983	19	139.93	5.6	159.9
1984	272	275.23	10.3	217.2	1984	19	155.77	11.3	178.0
1985–1987	na	na	na	na	1985	19	176.98	13.6	202.2
1988	265	338.13	na	266.8	1986	19	193.54	9.4	221.2
					1987	19	203.59	5.2	232.6
					1988	19	211.31	3.8	241.5

*Compiled by Mary Elizabeth Clack, Harvard College Library, from data supplied by the Faxon Company, publishers' price lists, and library acquisition records.

The definition of a serial service has been taken from the *American National Standard Criteria for Library and Information Services and Related Publishing Practices–Library Materials–Criteria for Price Indexes* (ANSI Z39.20–1983).

[a] Excludes "Wilson Index." Soviet translations (a category of journal titles) were removed from this index and have been part of the U.S. Periodicals Index since 1985.

[b] The average price includes two expensive titles, "Leading National Advertiser Multi-media Report Service" at $8,750 and "LNA-PIB Magazine Service," priced at $7,300. If these titles are omitted, the average price drops to $343.18.

[c] The 1988 average price and index are estimated figures.

included, the average price in 1988 was $105.45, compared with $96.36 in 1987, a 9.4% increase (Table 1). In 1988, for the first time, the average price for periodical titles in all subjects was 300% higher than in 1977. Since 1979, titles in science and technology have risen an average of 11.6% per year, a rate that continues to be higher than that observed for prices in other broad subject divisions. The rate of increase by subject category varies from year to year, revealing no clear pattern. In 1988, prices of titles concerned with labor and industrial relations increased the highest percentage (14.0%), followed by zoology (12.8%) and home economics (12.5%). The ranking by subject categories remains remarkably consistent from year to year, with Soviet translations having the highest average price, followed by chemistry and physics and medicine.[1]

The U.S. Serial Services Price Index was resumed in 1988 after being suspended from 1985 to 1987 while the ALA RTSD Library Materials Price Index Committee investigated its scope and usefulness. As 1988 was the first year of production, it is not possible to calculate and annual rate of change in prices. In 1988, the average annual price for a serial service was $341.32, an increase of $46.19 over the 1984 average price; this represents a cumulative increase of 15.6% over the 1984 price (Table 2), which is quite low for a five-year period, especially if rates for periodicals for the same time period are examined.[2]

Book Prices

U.S. hardcover books increased in price at a rate of 5.8% in 1988 (Table 3), based on data supplied by the R. R. Bowker Company. Business titles showed the highest rate of increase—12.9%—reaching an average price of $37.60. The average price of general works was $49.29, a 12.5% increase. The average price of three subject areas decreased, with travel books showing the greatest decrease—4.7%—falling to $26.74 in 1988.

The 1988 rate of increase for North American academic books was 6.0%. Data for this index is provided by Baker & Taylor, Coutts Library Services, and Blackwell/North America from approval plan statistics collected by each firm. At an average price of $58.66, general works showed the highest rate of increase—42.6% (Table 4). Prices for titles in 8 of the 29 subject categories reflect double-digit inflation. Titles in two categories, anthropology and physical education and recreation, decreased in price, although the decreases were quite modest—.8% and .7%, respectively. For readers interested in price comparisons with local data, an explanation of the methodology used to compile this index is available in the Summer 1986 issue of *Book Research Quarterly*.[3]

Book reviews appearing in *Choice* constitute the database for the U.S. college books price index. The rate of increase for college books is 5.2%, a rate consistent with that of other categories of books reviewed. Data for two categories do not cover the entire year; political science was divided into four new categories in March 1988 and law was a separate category from January to March 1988 only. Titles concerned with the performing arts rose from $24.58 in 1987 to $84.24 in 1988, an unusual increase of 342.7%, which was due in part to a single title priced over $200. In language and literature, prices dropped 25.2%, from an average of $40.88 in 1987 to $30.57 in 1988 (Table 5). Reference materials had a lower rate of increase in 1988 than in 1987, that of 10.7% compared to 15.6%. When reference titles are excluded, the average price increased 8.8% in 1988 compared to 3.6% in 1987. Compiler Kathryn

Table 3 / U.S. Hardcover Books: Average Prices and Price Indexes, 1985–1988*
(Index Base: 1977 = 100)

Category	1977 Average Price	1985 (Final) Volumes	1985 (Final) Average Price	1985 (Final) Index	1986 (Final) Volumes	1986 (Final) Average Price	1986 (Final) Index	1987 (Final) Volumes	1987 (Final) Average Price	1987 (Final) Index	1988 (Preliminary) Volumes	1988 (Preliminary) Average Price	1988 (Preliminary) Index
Agriculture	$16.24	368	$36.77	226.4	391	$39.26	241.7	423	$46.24	284.7	377	$48.86	300.9
Art	21.24	908	35.15	165.5	996	35.41	166.7	1,004	37.71	177.5	816	39.84	187.6
Biography	15.34	1,298	22.20	144.7	1,446	22.96	149.7	1,542	25.04	163.2	1,369	25.81	168.3
Business	18.00	1,040	28.84	160.2	1,115	30.72	170.7	1,032	33.31	185.1	966	37.60	208.9
Education	12.95	602	27.28	210.7	559	26.11	201.6	669	31.58	243.9	549	33.52	258.8
Fiction	10.09	1,800	15.29	151.5	2,212	16.84	166.9	2,499	18.19	180.3	1,992	17.84	176.8
General works	30.99	1,632	37.91	122.3	1,511	38.97	125.8	1,623	43.81	141.4	1,250	49.29	159.1
History	17.12	1,506	27.02	157.8	1,598	28.44	166.1	1,954	31.74	185.4	1,722	33.24	194.2
Home economics	11.16	594	17.50	156.8	532	18.97	170.0	558	20.13	180.4	411	21.57	193.3
Juveniles	6.65	2,529	9.95	149.6	3,066	10.64	160.0	3,162	11.48	172.6	3,003	11.92	179.2
Language	14.96	347	28.68	191.7	351	32.80	219.3	361	37.80	252.7	298	39.12	261.5
Law	25.04	955	41.70	166.5	958	49.20	196.5	1,097	49.65	198.3	812	49.94	199.4
Literature	15.78	1,181	24.53	155.4	1,359	25.73	163.1	1,537	28.70	181.9	1,310	30.81	195.2
Medicine	24.00	2,798	44.36	184.8	2,643	49.99	208.3	3,065	57.68	240.3	2,565	64.69	269.5
Music	20.13	238	28.79	143.0	222	32.59	161.9	224	35.82	177.9	177	36.76	182.6
Philosophy and psychology	14.43	895	28.11	194.8	991	29.65	205.5	1,090	33.32	230.9	950	35.10	243.2
Poetry and drama	13.63	563	22.14	162.4	617	25.11	184.2	699	28.46	208.8	586	27.19	199.5
Religion	12.26	1,100	19.13	156.0	1,171	21.60	176.2	1,226	24.51	199.9	1,003	26.90	219.4
Science	24.88	2,556	51.19	205.7	2,559	55.65	223.7	2,815	62.16	249.8	2,455	66.46	267.1
Sociology and economics	29.88	4,761	33.33	111.5	5,043	30.34	101.5	5,393	34.38	115.1	4,791	36.44	122.0
Sports and recreation	12.28	530	23.43	190.8	573	23.25	189.3	586	23.96	195.1	438	25.55	208.1
Technology	23.61	1,693	50.37	213.3	1,904	55.00	233.0	1,988	60.24	255.1	1,635	63.29	268.1
Travel	18.44	210	24.66	133.7	218	24.32	131.9	227	28.07	152.2	179	26.74	145.0
Total	$19.22	30,104	$31.46	163.7	32,035	$32.43	168.7	34,774	$36.28	188.8	29,654	$38.39	199.7

*Compiled by Dennis E. Smith and Sue Plezia, University of California, from data supplied by the R.R. Bowker Company. Price indexes on Tables 3 and 7 are based on books recorded in the R.R. Bowker Company's *Weekly Record* (cumulated in the *American Book Publishing Record*). The 1988 preliminary figures include items listed during 1988 with an imprint date of 1988. Final data for previous years include items listed between January of that year and June of the following year with an imprint date of the specified year.

Table 4 / North American Academic Books:* Average Prices and Price Indexes, 1986-1988
(Index Base: 1979-80 = 100)

Subject	LC Class	1979-1980 Number of Titles	1979-1980 Average Price	1985-1986† Number of Titles	1985-1986† Average Price	Index
Agriculture	S	1,275	$22.80	1,419	$37.45	164.3
Anthropology	GN	688	18.23	698	27.94	153.3
Botany	QK	428	30.06	393	52.26	173.9
Business and economics	H	6,980	18.92	9,277	28.75	152.0
Chemistry	QD	950	43.44	936	70.82	163.0
Education	L	2,682	14.37	2,500	22.47	156.4
Engineering and technology	T	5,277	28.83	5,907	47.45	164.6
Fiction and children's literature	PZ	572	11.47	1,151	16.18	141.1
Fine and applied arts	M, N	4,846	21.82	4,269	31.69	145.2
General works	A	322	22.71	249	35.14	154.7
Geography	G	554	23.22	541	35.08	151.1
Geology	QE	475	31.59	630	47.25	149.6
History	C,D,E,F	5,713	18.95	6,173	27.87	147.1
Home economics	TX	492	16.71	560	22.12	132.4
Industrial arts	TT	111	16.14	105	18.00	111.5
Law	K	1,122	19.82	1,174	34.75	175.3
Library and information science	Z	774	21.82	850	32.73	150.0
Literature and language	P	8,823	15.43	11,316	23.32	151.1
Mathematics and computer science	QA	2,281	24.62	4,207	32.82	133.3
Medicine	R	6,636	26.02	8,896	41.07	157.8
Military and naval science	U,V	599	18.14	1,052	25.46	140.4
Philosophy and religion	B	3,319	15.63	4,266	24.01	153.6
Physical education and recreation	GV	1,391	12.43	944	18.38	147.9
Physics and astronomy	QB	1,114	35.63	1,556	51.30	144.0
Political science	J	2,861	17.25	3,004	26.69	154.7
Psychology	BF	1,752	18.84	1,513	31.26	165.9
Science (general)	Q	313	22.85	391	34.05	149.0
Sociology	HM	4,851	16.87	4,184	25.34	150.2
Zoology	QH,QL, QP,QR	2,982	32.70	3,551	52.64	161.0
Average for all subjects		70,183	$21.98	81,712	$33.60	152.9
Canadian history		348	$9.17	465	$15.97	174.2
Canadian literature		540	5.37	668	8.14	151.6

*Compiled by Dora Biblarz, Arizona State University, from data collected from approval plan statistics supplied by Baker & Taylor, Coutts Library Services, and Blackwell/North America. Baker & Taylor and Blackwell/North America used a fiscal year from July 1 to June 30. Coutts Library Services used a fiscal year from June 1 to May 31 from 1979-1980 to 1982-1983; in 1983-1984 Coutts changed its fiscal year to February 1 to January 31. Table 4 covers titles published or distributed in the United States and Canada. Baker & Taylor data include continuations (series, serials, and sets) and paperbacks of 48 pages or less. "General Supplementary" and "Extra-curricular" (nonacademic) categories are included by Baker & Taylor in 1979-1980 but excluded beginning with 1980-1981.

Table 4 / North American Academic Books: Average Prices and Price Indexes, 1986–1988* (cont.)
(Index Base: 1979–80 = 100)

1986–1987				1987–1988			
Number of Titles	Average Price	Percent Increase	Index	Number of Titles	Average Price	Percent Increase	Index
1,540	$40.09	7.0	175.8	1,686	$42.40	5.8	186.0
742	30.75	10.1	168.7	798	30.49	−0.8	167.3
391	54.00	3.3	179.6	487	59.54	10.3	198.1
9,681	30.98	7.8	163.7	10,410	33.62	8.5	177.7
947	69.71	−1.6	160.5	1,100	75.03	7.6	172.7
2,399	24.62	9.6	171.3	2,861	26.85	9.1	186.8
6,896	50.38	6.2	174.7	7,279	54.12	7.4	187.7
1,228	17.34	7.2	151.2	1,407	17.91	3.3	156.1
4,409	33.37	5.3	152.9	5,001	35.68	6.9	163.5
276	41.29	17.5	181.8	321	58.86	42.6	259.2
522	37.64	7.3	162.1	598	43.21	14.8	186.1
565	48.94	3.6	154.9	597	58.55	19.6	185.3
6,760	27.94	0.3	147.4	7,995	28.14	0.7	148.5
625	23.88	8.0	142.9	636	24.00	0.5	143.6
174	21.39	18.8	132.5	184	22.38	4.6	138.7
1,322	34.23	−1.5	172.7	1,663	39.46	15.3	199.1
911	33.65	2.8	154.2	1,022	34.72	3.2	159.1
12,723	24.59	5.4	159.4	14,612	25.47	3.6	165.1
4,576	36.11	10.0	146.7	5,277	39.30	8.8	159.6
8,898	45.10	9.8	173.3	9,355	50.96	13.0	195.8
1,155	27.82	9.3	153.4	1,252	28.93	4.0	159.5
4,906	25.83	7.6	165.3	5,568	27.90	8.0	178.5
960	19.41	5.6	156.2	1,049	19.28	−0.7	155.1
1,675	54.67	6.6	153.4	1,837	60.50	10.7	169.8
3,048	28.66	7.4	166.1	3,460	31.09	8.5	180.2
1,528	31.67	1.3	168.1	1,517	34.25	8.1	181.8
465	36.79	8.0	161.0	533	39.67	7.8	173.6
4,206	27.83	9.8	165.0	4,691	28.98	4.1	171.8
3,439	55.47	5.4	169.6	3,745	63.86	15.1	195.3
86,967	$36.93	9.9	168.0	96,941	$39.14	6.0	178.1
491	$19.63	22.9	214.1	327	$16.40	−16.5	178.8
1,086	11.80	45.0	219.7	678	9.41	−20.3	175.2

Table 5 / U.S. College Books: Average Prices and Price Indexes, 1986–1988*

(Index Base for all years: 1978 = 100. 1987 also indexed to 1986; 1988 also indexed to 1987)

	1978		1986			1987				1988			
***Choice* Subject Categories**	**Number of Titles**	**Average Price per Title**	**Number of Titles**	**Average Price per Title**	**Prices Indexed to 1978**	**Number of Titles**	**Average Price per Title**	**Prices Indexed to 1978**	**Prices Indexed to 1986**	**Number of Titles**	**Average Price per Title**	**Prices Indexed to 1978**	**Prices Indexed to 1987**
General	47	$15.25	9	$32.22	211.3	8	$24.93	163.5	77.4	11	$26.23	172.0	105.2
Humanities	92	16.14	33	31.64	196.0	21	28.71	177.9	90.7	18	36.06	223.4	125.6
Art	315	26.60	278	45.43	170.8	259	46.58	175.1	102.5	266	47.55	178.8	102.1
Photography[a]	–	–	28	37.46	–	17	35.07	–	93.6	29	39.88	–	113.7
Communication arts	71	14.03	35	25.46	181.5	37	28.00	199.6	110.0	33	34.89	248.7	124.6
Classical studies[b]	–	–	84	35.58	–	106	22.41	–	63.0	103	39.14	–	174.7
Language and literature	97	13.38	93	26.87	200.8	87	40.88	305.5	152.1	98	30.57	228.5	74.8
Linguistics[c]	22	15.07	–	–	–	–	–	–	–	–	–	–	–
Classical[d]	18	13.41	–	–	–	–	–	–	–	–	–	–	–
English and American	834	12.42	609	23.40	188.4	709	25.64	206.4	109.6	626	27.97	225.2	109.1
Germanic	51	12.35	39	20.54	166.3	32	27.39	221.8	133.3	42	26.47	214.3	96.6
Romance	101	12.27	102	23.28	189.7	136	24.61	200.6	105.7	120	24.46	199.3	99.4
Slavic	46	13.22	32	25.63	193.9	36	26.89	203.4	104.9	39	25.95	196.3	96.5
Other	67	13.03	53	22.81	175.1	49	24.80	190.3	108.7	67	25.65	196.9	103.4
Performing arts	16	15.07	7	27.14	180.1	5	24.58	163.1	90.6	4	84.24	559.0	342.7
Dance	21	12.95	9	28.22	217.9	18	36.97	285.5	131.0	13	40.67	314.1	110.0
Film	80	15.70	60	28.42	181.0	73	30.94	197.1	108.9	60	32.31	205.8	104.4
Music	138	15.10	141	31.43	208.1	118	35.58	235.6	113.2	128	34.31	227.2	96.4
Theater	34	13.84	35	28.09	203.0	48	35.13	253.8	125.1	51	36.27	262.1	103.2
Philosophy	197	14.21	141	30.04	211.4	197	32.53	228.9	108.3	218	35.22	247.9	108.3
Religion	300	11.98	191	26.14	218.2	201	25.70	214.5	98.3	198	30.74	256.6	119.6
Total humanities	2,500	14.86	1,970	29.11	195.9	2,149	30.40	204.6	104.4	2,113	33.00	222.1	108.6
Science and technology	102	21.31	136	36.15	169.6	130	40.93	192.1	113.2	121	42.96	201.6	105.0
History of science and technology	85	17.37	76	34.18	196.8	85	33.80	194.6	98.9	89	36.34	209.2	107.5
Astronautics and astronomy	22	23.78	20	26.40	111.0	22	47.27	198.8	179.1	13	36.06	151.6	76.3
Biology	231	23.67	94	39.27	165.9	91	47.25	199.6	120.3	100	46.10	194.8	97.6
Botany[a]	–	–	36	47.28	–	32	54.54	–	115.4	38	49.36	–	90.5
Zoology[a]	–	–	33	38.52	–	35	60.04	–	155.9	34	57.94	–	96.5
Chemistry	95	28.59	16	53.69	187.8	27	57.69	201.8	107.5	17	87 51	306.1	151.7

Table 5 / U.S. College Books: Average Prices and Price Indexes, 1986–1988* *(cont.)*

	1978		1986			1987				1988			
***Choice* Subject Categories**	**Number of Titles**	**Average Price per Title**	**Number of Titles**	**Average Price per Title**	**Prices Indexed to 1978**	**Number of Titles**	**Average Price per Title**	**Prices Indexed to 1978**	**Prices Indexed to 1986**	**Number of Titles**	**Average Price per Title**	**Prices Indexed to 1978**	**Prices Indexed to 1987**
Earth science	84	29.99	47	50.36	167.9	32	51.27	171.0	101.8	39	59.94	199.9	116.9
Engineering	241	25.75	157	55.52	215.6	101	55.49	215.5	99.9	98	59.81	232.3	107.8
Health sciences	92	14.88	127	29.76	200.0	116	30.90	207.7	103.8	109	33.72	226.6	109.1
Information and computer science	53	20.37	81	34.77	170.7	93	32.47	159.4	93.4	79	36.44	178.9	112.2
Mathematics	70	22.54	43	42.86	190.2	60	48.56	215.4	113.3	62	43.80	194.3	90.2
Physics	47	28.77	21	50.10	174.1	24	42.81	148.8	85.4	27	42.05	146.2	98.2
Sports and physical education	73	10.32	28	25.25	244.7	21	25.65	248.5	101.6	20	26.21	254.0	102.2
Total sciences	1,195	22.77	915	40.27	176.9	869	42.88	188.3	106.5	846	44.89	197.1	104.7
Social and behavioral sciences	156	16.37	137	28.00	171.0	140	31.15	190.3	111.3	142	32.75	200.1	105.1
Anthropology	102	16.97	104	32.97	194.3	143	33.28	196.1	100.9	120	33.82	199.3	101.6
Business, management, and labor	136	14.36	175	30.62	213.2	166	30.30	211.0	99.0	127	32.41	225.7	107.0
Economics	242	17.65	303	32.83	186.0	315	34.45	195.2	104.9	301	37.85	214.4	109.9
Education	129	12.48	71	24.75	198.3	82	26.73	214.2	108.0	52	36.02	288.6	134.8
History, geography, and travel	116	16.26	91	38.01	233.8	66	33.43	205.6	88.0	66	39.01	239.9	116.7
Ancient (including archaeology)[d]	67	21.79	–	–	–	–	–	–	–	–	–	–	–
Africa	38	16.34	40	32.43	198.5	41	32.33	197.9	99.7	43	33.11	202.6	102.4
Asia and Oceania	78	19.03	68	33.81	177.7	74	36.52	191.9	108.0	65	35.59	187.0	97.5
Europe	308	16.52	299	32.81	198.6	316	35.25	213.4	107.4	314	39.97	241.9	113.4
Latin America and the Caribbean	47	15.82	44	35.32	223.3	39	31.02	196.1	87.8	46	33.67	212.8	108.5
Middle East and North Africa	40	16.80	44	31.95	190.2	35	33.88	201.7	106.0	33	43.91	261.4	129.6
North America	275	16.08	327	28.43	176.8	329	27.55	171.3	96.9	344	30.02	186.7	109.0
Political Science	281	14.74	551	28.60	194.0	620	29.41	199.5	102.8	127	32.61	221.2	110.9
Law[e]	–	–	–	–	–	33	34.08	–	–	16	32.47	–	95.3
Comparative politics[f]	–	–	–	–	–	–	–	–	–	183	37.01	–	–
International relations[f]	–	–	–	–	–	–	–	–	–	172	34.71	–	–
Political theory[f]	–	–	–	–	–	–	–	–	–	56	33.14	–	–
United States politics[f]	–	–	–	–	–					151	28.18	–	–
Psychology	142	15.39	137	31.92	207.4	211	32.76	212.9	102.6	149	37.18	241.6	113.5
Sociology	280	14.69	192	27.20	185.2	183	31.19	212.3	114.7	181	35.93	244.6	115.2
Total social and behavioral sciences	2,437	15.98	2,583	30.51	190.9	2,793	31.51	197.2	103.3	2,688	34.91	218.5	110.8
Total (excluding reference)	6,179	16.83	5,477	31.64	188.0	5,819	32.79	194.8	103.6	5,658	35.67	211.9	108.8
Reference	453	34.15	528	51.63	151.2	540	59.70	174.8	115.6	501	66.07	193.5	110.7
Grand total	6,632	$18.02	6,005	$33.40	185.3	6,359	$35.07	194.6	105.0	6,159	$38.14	211.7	108.8

*Compiled by Kathryn A. Soupiset, Trinity University, from book reviews appearing in *Choice* during the calendar year indicated. The cooperation of the *Choice* editorial staff is gratefully acknowledged. Additional information about these data appears in the March 1988 issue of *Choice*.

Table 6 / U.S. Mass Market Paperbacks: Average Prices and Price Indexes, 1985–1988*
(Index Base: 1981 = 100)

	1981	1985 (Final)			1986 (Final)			1987 (Final)			1988 (Preliminary)		
	Average Price	Total Volumes	Average Price	Index	Total Volumes	Average Price	Index	Total Volumes	Average Price	Index	Total Volumes	Average Price	Index
Agriculture	$2.54	7	$5.76	226.8	6	$6.04	237.8	6	$3.56	140.2	2	$4.23	166.5
Art	5.49	3	9.80	178.5	3	9.80	178.5	7	12.38	225.5	15	10.02	182.5
Biography	3.82	79	4.81	125.9	76	5.15	134.8	62	5.10	133.5	67	6.21	162.6
Business	4.63	26	7.57	163.5	31	7.73	167.0	28	6.39	138.0	12	7.67	165.7
Education	3.96	12	6.07	153.3	20	7.28	183.8	14	5.99	151.3	15	7.19	181.6
Fiction	2.47	2,524	3.24	131.2	2,424	3.46	140.1	2,571	3.59	145.3	1,938	4.00	161.9
General works	3.63	86	4.63	127.5	61	5.07	139.7	80	5.40	148.8	52	6.84	188.4
History	3.53	31	5.34	151.3	33	5.19	147.0	28	4.90	138.8	23	7.09	200.8
Home economics	4.35	101	5.65	129.9	97	6.23	143.2	99	6.69	153.8	73	6.58	151.3
Juvenile	1.79	427	2.71	151.4	461	2.71	151.4	363	2.80	156.4	307	3.14	175.4
Language	3.42	14	4.28	125.1	17	5.28	154.4	22	4.94	144.4	12	6.63	193.9
Law	3.09	6	6.62	214.2	4	3.98	128.8	3	3.98	128.8	4	4.59	148.5
Literature	3.42	35	4.76	139.2	35	4.92	143.9	40	4.50	131.6	34	5.41	158.2
Medicine	3.66	36	6.65	181.7	43	7.18	196.2	46	6.28	171.6	38	6.97	190.4
Music†	5.68†	9	5.68	100.0	10	4.21	74.1	3	7.45	131.2	1	7.95	140.0
Philosophy and psychology	2.84	112	4.22	148.6	82	5.07	178.5	137	4.96	174.6	95	6.06	213.4
Poetry and drama	3.22	16	4.88	151.6	27	5.76	178.9	13	5.05	156.8	46	4.02	124.8
Religion	2.70	24	3.22	119.3	25	3.84	142.2	16	3.71	137.4	15	4.80	177.8
Science	4.45	15	4.83	108.5	14	5.91	132.8	5	4.55	102.2	8	5.52	124.0
Sociology and economics	3.43	44	4.77	139.1	55	5.32	155.1	78	5.63	164.1	61	5.63	164.1
Sports and recreation	3.05	149	3.80	124.6	160	4.09	134.1	175	4.97	163.0	132	5.91	193.8
Technology	4.20	42	12.29	292.6	36	12.08	287.6	29	10.69	254.5	28	17.61	419.3
Travel	3.23	9	4.93	152.6	10	5.01	155.4	13	6.88	213.0	17	10.89	337.2
Total	$2.65	3,807	$3.62	136.6	3,730	$3.86	145.7	3,833	$3.98	150.2	2,995	$4.58	172.8

*Compiled by Dennis E. Smith and Sue Plezia, University of California, from data supplied by the R. R. Bowker Company. Average prices of mass market paperbacks are based on listings of mass market titles in *Paperbound Books in Print*.

†1982 is used as the index base for Music.

Table 7 / U.S. Trade (Higher Priced) Paperback Books: Average Prices and Price Indexes, 1985–1988*
(Index Base: 1977 = 100)

	1977	1985 (Final)			1986 (Final)			1987 (Final)			1988 (Preliminary)		
	Average Price	No. of Books	Average Price	Index	No. of Books	Average Price	Index	No. of Books	Average Price	Index	No. of Books	Average Price	Index
Agriculture	$5.01	198	$ 9.50	189.6	149	$13.22	263.9	190	$14.21	283.6	169	$17.04	340.1
Art	6.27	593	14.04	223.9	641	15.46	246.6	640	15.21	242.6	487	15.34	244.7
Biography	4.91	536	10.78	219.6	591	11.32	230.5	608	10.18	207.3	529	11.12	226.5
Business	7.09	425	16.83	237.4	421	18.56	261.8	376	17.53	247.2	376	18.11	255.4
Education	5.72	440	12.98	226.9	412	14.01	244.9	376	18.29	319.8	402	15.01	262.4
Fiction	4.20	726	13.66	325.2	897	8.64	205.7	1,124	9.26	220.5	1,171	10.25	244.0
General works	6.18	1,123	19.13	309.5	828	28.44	460.2	871	21.57	349.0	737	23.59	381.7
History	5.81	729	14.08	242.3	766	14.55	250.4	843	13.51	232.5	769	13.67	235.3
Home economics	4.77	513	9.22	193.3	450	9.96	208.8	491	10.26	215.1	431	11.65	244.2
Juveniles	2.68	767	5.20	194.0	906	5.71	213.1	1,024	11.66	435.1	829	6.05	225.7
Language	7.79	252	13.25	170.1	287	14.31	183.7	270	14.15	181.6	212	15.24	195.6
Law	10.66	339	18.46	173.2	364	17.46	163.8	384	22.02	206.6	286	24.58	230.6
Literature	5.18	694	14.04	271.0	712	13.19	254.6	730	12.53	241.9	610	13.03	251.5
Medicine	7.63	698	16.01	209.8	692	19.34	253.5	838	17.74	232.5	738	19.06	249.8
Music	6.36	113	12.20	191.8	117	13.67	293.6	117	13.29	209.0	90	13.90	218.6
Philosophy and psychology	5.57	523	13.25	237.9	564	13.36	239.9	588	12.96	232.7	580	13.25	237.9
Poetry and drama	4.71	550	8.86	188.1	596	10.02	212.7	500	9.33	198.1	458	10.24	217.4
Religion	3.68	1,373	9.30	252.7	1,525	9.26	251.6	1,576	9.24	251.1	1,257	10.11	274.7
Science	8.81	677	19.78	224.5	707	23.27	264.1	762	22.04	250.2	602	22.54	255.8
Sociology and economics	6.03	2,402	16.30	270.3	2,597	16.76	277.9	2,490	15.79	261.9	2,140	16.51	273.8
Sports and recreation	4.87	447	10.66	218.9	430	11.49	235.9	476	11.51	236.3	364	12.21	250.7
Technology	7.97	722	21.08	264.5	682	25.55	320.6	688	25.69	322.3	523	22.87	287.0
Travel	5.21	235	10.48	201.2	299	10.91	209.4	377	10.99	210.9	351	11.52	221.1
Total	$5.93	15,075	$13.98	235.8	15,633	$14.86	250.6	16,339	$14.55	245.4	14,111	$14.67	247.4

*Compiled by Dennis E. Smith and Sue Plezia, University of California, from data supplied by the R. R. Bowker Company. Price indexes on Tables 2 and 6 are based on books recorded in the R. R. Bowker Company's *Weekly Record* (cumulated in the *American Book Publishing Record*). The 1988 preliminary figures include items listed during 1988 with an imprint date of 1988. Final data for previous years include items listed between January of that year and June of the following year with an imprint date of the specified year.

Soupiset notes that science and technology titles increased the least in price in 1988, 4.7%, whereas humanities titles increased the most, 8.6%, reversing the trend of previous years. Additional data are published in the March issue of *Choice*.

Data on paperback prices provided by R. R. Bowker Company are compiled by Dennis Smith and Sue Plezia, who report that the average price of mass market paperbacks leaped 15.1% from $3.98 in 1987 to $4.58 in 1988. The highest increases were a 60.0% increase (to $7.95) in the average price of music titles and a 44.7% increase (to $7.09) for history titles (Table 6). Of the categories showing a decline in price, poetry and drama showed the greatest decrease (20.4%), dropping from $5.05 in 1987 to $4.02 in 1988. Conversely, prices of trade (higher priced) paperbacks increased only .8%, from $14.55 in 1987 to $14.67 in 1988. When subject is considered, the price of agriculture titles increased 20.1%, from $14.21 in 1987 to $17.04, and for home economics the increase was 13.5%, from $10.26 in 1987 to $11.65 in 1988. The most dramatic decrease for trade paperbacks was a 48.1% decrease in the price of juvenile titles, from $11.66 in 1987 ($n = 1,024$) to $6.05 in 1988 ($n = 829$).

In summary, with the exception of trade paperbacks, prices for the categories of books examined showed moderate increases in 1988, with a wide range of increases and decreases for titles by finer subject breakdowns. Readers are encouraged to examine data for individual categories as well as the summary data for each index.

Prices of Other Media

The Nonprint Media Price Index is compiled from data published in selected issues of *Choice, School Library Journal,* and *Booklist.* All costs associated with video format increased in 1988. The average cost of a video in 1988 ($262.08) was 9.1% higher than the average cost ($240.16) in 1987 (Table 8). According to compiler David Walch, this increase follows a decline in cost over the previous four years. Although there has been an increase in the "purchase cost per minute" for 16mm film, the average price has decreased due to a reduction in overall length from 30.3 minutes in 1986 and 1987 to 26.3 minutes in 1988. Walch further notes that the number of 16mm films produced has declined rapidly and only in a few instances are 16mm films available without a video counterpart. Walch also points out that the cost of renting 16mm film has escalated substantially. The average price of sound recordings increased from $8.50 in 1987 to $10.12 in 1988, an increase of 19.1%.

Previously unpublished data on microfilms for 1985–1987 are included in Table 9. Production problems have been resolved and the price index for microfilm was resumed in 1988. The Microfilm Price Index is compiled from data obtained from the acquisitions records of 57 research libraries. The cost to libraries of negative microfilm rose from $0.1601 per exposure in 1987 to $0.1614 in 1988, an increase of .8%. Since the index was calculated in 1984, the increase in cost has been 29.1% (Table 9). The cost of positive microfilm decreased from $0.2450 per exposure in 1984 to $0.2352 in 1988 (a decrease of 4%), but actually increased 6.5% in 1988 from the 1987 low of $0.2198.

Table 10 shows previously unpublished data on newspapers for 1985–1987. The Newspaper Price Index was also resumed in 1988. The average subscription rate reported for daily newspapers of $198.20 per year in 1988 reflects a substantial increase of 15.8% over the 1987 cost of $171.21. Since these data last appeared in 1984, the average price has increased 81.0%, from $109.52.

Table 8 / U.S. Nonprint Media: Average Prices and Price Indexes, 1983–1988*
(Index Base: 1977 = 100)

Category	1977	1983		1984		1985		1986		1987		1988	
	Average Price	Average Price	Index	Average Price	Index	Average Price	Index	Average Price	Index	Average Price	Index	Average Price	Index
16mm films													
Rental cost per minute	$1.23	$1.82	148.0	$1.81	147.2	$2.15	174.8	$ 2.00	162.6	$1.86	151.2	$2.54	206.5
Purchase cost per minute	13.95	15.47	110.9	16.93	121.4	16.50	118.3	16.85	120.8	17.00	121.9	18.96	135.9
Cost of film	308.85	423.87	137.2	470.65	152.4	475.07	153.8	507.19	164.2	515.78	167.0	499.22	161.6
Length per film (min.)	22.1	27.4	—	27.8	—	28.8	—	30.1	—	30.3	—	26.33	—
Videocassettes													
Purchase cost per minute	7.58†	11.04	145.6	8.44	111.3	10.24	135.1	7.44	98.2	6.79	89.6	7.21	95.1
Cost of video	271.93†	320.16	117.7	333.38	122.6	333.94	122.8	274.54	101.0	240.16	88.3	262.08	96.4
Length per video (min.)	—	29.0	—	39.5	—	32.6	—	36.9	—	35.4		36.35	
Filmstrips													
Cost of filmstrip	18.60	28.60	153.8	33.04	177.6	32.41	174.2	34.13	183.5	39.49	212.3	37.54	201.8
Cost of filmstrip set	72.26	79.57	110.1	85.76	118.7	83.50	115.6	85.33	118.1	112.15	155.2	74.45	103.0
Number of film-strips per set	4.1	2.8	—	2.6	—	2.6	—	2.5	—	2.8	—	2.0	—
Number of frames per filmstrip	64.2	70.7	—	67.0	—	66.7	—	65.9	—	65.1	—	66.1	—
Sound recordings													
Average cost per cassette	10.63	11.23	105.6	9.99	94.0	8.99	84.6	10.61	99.8	8.50	80.0	10.12	95.2

*Compiled by David B. Walch, California Polytechnic State University, from selected issues of *Choice*, *School Library Journal*, and *Booklist*.
†1980 is used as the base year for videocassettes.

Table 9 / U.S. Library Microfilm: Average Prices and Price Indexes, 1981–1988*
(Index Base: 1978 = 100)

Year	Negative Microfilm (35mm)			Positive Microfilm (35mm)		
	Average Rate per Exposure	Index Value	Change in Index	Average Rate per Foot	Index Value	Change in Index
1978	$0.0836	100.0	+0.0	$0.1612	100.0	+0.0
1981	0.0998	119.4	19.4	0.2021	125.4	25.4
1982	0.1067	127.6	8.2	0.2184	135.5	10.1
1983	0.1100	131.6	4.0	0.2274	141.1	5.6
1984	0.1250	149.5	17.9	0.2450	152.0	10.9
1985	0.1290	154.3	4.8	0.2612	162.0	10.0
1986	0.1550	185.4	31.1	0.2350	145.8	−16.2
1987	0.1601	191.5	6.1	0.2198	136.4	−9.4
1988	0.1614	193.1	1.6	0.2352	145.9	+9.5

*Compiled by Imre T. Jármy, Library of Congress, from data secured from the staff of the 57 indexed libraries.

Table 10 / Selected U.S. Daily Newspapers: Average Prices and Price Indexes, 1981–1988*
(Index Base: 1978 = 100)

Year	Average Rate	Index Value	Change in Index
1978	$76.4391	100.0	+0.0
1981	98.5521	128.9	28.9
1982	103.6382	135.6	6.7
1983	107.4728	140.6	5.0
1984	109.5210	143.3	2.7
1985	111.3121	145.6	2.3
1986	141.6235	185.3	39.7
1987	171.2084	224.0	38.7
1988	198.1954	259.3	35.3

*Compiled by Imre T. Jármy, Library of Congress, from data secured from 131 newspapers published in the continental United States, and Alaska and Hawaii.

Foreign Prices

Average prices and price indexes for British academic books are presented in Table 11 and for German academic books in Table 12. Both indexes have been compiled using subject categories that have changed since 1987. A summary of Latin American prices is presented in Table 13.

British Prices

Prices for British academic books are compiled from information supplied by B. H. Blackwell. In 1988, a more detailed subject breakdown is being published than in prior years, and retrospective figures are also supplied. The average price was £25.44 in 1988, which reflects an increase of 6.8% over the 1987 price of £23.81. As with U.S. books in all categories, the rate of increase varies widely over subject areas, ranging from an increase of 60.4% (to £33.81) in 1988 for titles in military science to a decrease of 39.2% (to £20.82) for miscellaneous applied social sciences. This category covers a wide range of social issues, including urbanism, population, poverty, housing, race relations, women, youth, age, leisure, and drugs and alcohol. Compiler Curt Holleman notes that if the inflationary increase in price of 6.8% is added to the average loss in value of the dollar compared to the pound during 1988 (8.7%), U.S. libraries had to expand 16.1% more to keep up with British academic book production in 1988 than in 1987.

German Prices

Prices for German academic books are compiled from data supplied by Otto Harrassowitz, Wiesbaden, West Germany. Harrassowitz's data are based on titles supplied to approval plan customers in North America, representing a selection of what has been published in West and East Germany, Austria, and Switzerland rather than the complete publishing record. All prices are given in German marks.

The average price for a German title increased 6.3% from DM70.76 in 1987 to DM75.22 in 1988 (Table 12). The deletion of the miscellaneous, or xxx, subject category has made a significant difference in the German Price Index in 1988, making it

Table 11 / British Academic Books: Average Prices and Price Indexes, 1985–1988*

(Index Base: 1985 = 100)

Subject Category	1985		1986			1987			1988		
	Number of Titles	Average Price	Number of Titles	Average Price	Index	Number of Titles	Average Price	Index	Number of Titles	Average Price	Index
General works	29	£30.54	41	£48.36	158.3	40	£35.29	115.6	34	£45.40	148.7
Fine arts	329	21.70	324	21.44	98.8	420	22.22	102.4	448	21.28	98.1
Architecture	97	20.68	119	21.70	104.9	100	22.93	110.9	99	24.67	119.3
Music	136	17.01	111	19.97	117.4	142	19.82	116.5	136	20.95	123.2
Performing arts (except music)	110	13.30	99	15.60	117.3	88	16.33	122.8	98	17.63	132.6
Archaeology	146	18.80	146	21.04	111.9	207	23.35	124.2	213	23.24	123.6
Geography	60	22.74	46	24.66	108.4	55	22.66	99.6	46	25.13	110.5
History	1,123	16.92	1,124	19.94	117.8	1,276	21.31	125.9	1,302	22.54	133.2
Philosophy	127	18.41	127	23.76	129.1	119	21.83	118.6	144	25.91	140.7
Religion	328	10.40	310	12.06	116.0	335	12.68	121.9	334	14.21	136.6
Language	135	19.37	104	19.51	100.7	134	22.16	114.4	122	23.99	123.9
Miscellaneous humanities	59	21.71	52	20.53	94.6	62	28.16	129.7	65	31.17	143.6
Literary texts (excluding fiction)	570	9.31	408	10.12	108.7	418	11.86	127.4	411	12.10	130.0
Literary criticism	438	14.82	395	17.85	120.4	440	19.49	131.5	541	21.25	143.4
Law	188	24.64	273	26.06	105.8	283	29.05	117.9	235	31.07	126.1
Library science and book trade	78	18.69	99	20.91	111.9	114	26.65	142.6	123	21.86	117.0
Mass communications	38	14.20	67	15.34	108.0	66	15.85	111.6	74	18.86	132.8
Anthropology and ethnology	42	20.71	46	21.95	106.0	54	24.35	117.6	51	26.92	130.0
Sociology	136	15.24	147	20.65	135.5	174	20.33	133.4	157	20.90	137.1
Psychology	107	19.25	117	19.74	102.5	135	20.48	106.4	129	24.63	127.9
Economics	334	20.48	401	25.89	126.4	409	28.25	137.9	429	30.75	150.1
Political science and international relations	314	15.54	350	18.29	117.7	404	19.57	125.9	410	22.11	142.3
Miscellaneous social sciences	20	26.84	16	26.60	99.1	24	22.26	82.9	22	25.30	94.3
Military science	83	17.69	96	19.43	109.8	121	21.08	119.2	134	33.81	191.1
Sports and recreation	44	11.23	67	11.77	104.8	68	11.75	104.6	57	13.48	120.0

Table 11 / British Academic Books: Average Prices and Price Indexes, 1985–1988* *(cont.)*
(Index Base: 1985 = 100)

	1985		1986			1987			1988		
Subject Category	**Number of Titles**	**Average Price**	**Number of Titles**	**Average Price**	**Index**	**Number of Titles**	**Average Price**	**Index**	**Number of Titles**	**Average Price**	**Index**
Social service	56	12.17	76	12.42	102.1	80	14.15	116.3	74	15.70	129.0
Education	295	12.22	323	13.88	113.6	364	16.84	137.8	351	16.87	138.1
Management and business administration	427	19.55	422	23.30	119.2	484	29.27	149.7	450	26.12	133.6
Miscellaneous applied social sciences	13	9.58	12	17.38	181.4	10	34.25	357.5	23	20.82	217.3
Criminology	45	11.45	49	14.63	127.8	60	17.54	153.2	53	15.54	135.7
Applied inter-disciplinary social studies	254	14.17	300	16.11	113.7	331	18.92	133.5	327	20.11	141.9
General science	43	13.73	51	29.00	211.2	42	31.52	229.6	49	30.94	225.3
Botany	55	30.54	42	29.93	98.0	58	27.70	90.7	65	34.16	111.9
Zoology	85	25.67	100	25.73	100.2	84	28.21	109.9	71	29.67	115.6
Human biology	35	28.91	32	27.88	96.4	32	27.63	95.6	44	32.75	113.3
Biochemistry	26	33.57	31	41.67	124.1	43	43.23	125.8	35	36.34	108.3
Miscellaneous biological sciences	152	26.64	154	31.81	119.4	163	27.35	102.7	162	34.92	131.1
Chemistry	109	48.84	88	46.82	95.9	110	54.53	111.7	105	64.66	132.4
Earth sciences	87	28.94	87	33.80	116.8	102	38.96	134.6	82	40.12	138.6
Astronomy	43	20.36	27	26.19	128.6	27	25.65	126.0	49	29.87	146.7
Physics	76	26.58	106	29.70	111.7	84	35.11	132.1	73	36.82	138.5
Mathematics	123	20.20	142	24.36	120.6	134	24.30	120.3	136	26.36	130.5
Computer sciences	150	20.14	179	22.60	112.2	193	27.80	138.0	208	33.26	165.1
Inter-disciplinary technical fields	38	26.14	56	23.87	91.3	64	36.39	139.2	82	27.85	106.5
Civil engineering	134	28.68	155	35.26	122.9	141	36.15	126.0	173	38.74	135.1
Mechanical engineering	27	31.73	22	40.95	129.1	39	41.59	131.1	33	51.98	163.8
Electrical and electronic engineering	100	33.12	92	35.66	107.7	129	35.80	108.1	118	41.29	124.7
Materials science	54	37.93	75	52.94	139.6	89	46.34	122.2	101	50.75	133.8
Chemical engineering	24	40.48	17	33.17	81.9	36	45.92	113.4	29	44.50	109.9
Miscellaneous technology	217	36.33	256	38.85	106.9	289	41.90	115.3	256	44.61	122.8

Food and home economics	38	23.75	58	25.46	107.2	70	28.16	118.6	57	32.27	135.9
Non-clinical medicine	97	18.19	94	21.29	117.0	124	19.96	109.7	108	24.43	134.3
General medicine	73	21.03	79	27.38	130.2	81	27.91	132.7	77	31.20	148.4
Internal medicine	163	27.30	170	28.15	103.1	174	31.91	116.9	184	34.17	125.2
Psychiatry and mental disorders	71	17.97	70	18.21	101.3	69	21.88	121.8	95	22.82	127.0
Surgery	50	29.37	82	35.08	119.4	46	40.22	136.9	49	40.26	137.1
Miscellaneous medicine	292	22.08	288	24.36	110.3	282	27.33	123.8	258	26.77	121.2
Dentistry	20	19.39	22	18.10	93.3	19	20.61	106.3	20	22.95	118.4
Nursing	71	8.00	66	10.50	131.3	71	9.44	118.0	64	11.38	142.3
Agriculture and forestry	78	23.69	74	28.98	122.3	73	28.63	120.9	87	31.74	134.0
Animal husbandry and veterinary medicine	34	20.92	40	22.46	107.4	45	22.14	105.8	46	20.48	97.9
Natural resources and conservation	58	22.88	81	25.61	111.9	82	23.25	101.6	54	31.28	136.7
Total	9,049	19.07	9,428	22.09	115.8	10,408	23.81	124.9	10,413	25.44	133.4

*Compiled by Curt Holleman, Southern Methodist University, from data supplied by Chris Tyzack of B. H. Blackwell and Peter H. Mann of Loughborough University of Technology. The Committee uses 1985 as the base year because that is the first year that the BHB database was used as the source of prices.

†Includes other small categories not listed in this table.

Table 12 / German Academic Books: Average Prices and Price Indexes, 1986–1988*
(Index Base: 1984 = 100)

Subject	LC Class	1984 Average Price	1986 No. of Titles	1986 Average Price	1986 Index
Agriculture	S	DM50.00	261	DM60.44	120.9
Anthropology	GN	70.11	128	69.14	98.6
Botany	QK	120.10	53	103.96	86.6
Business and economics	H-HJ	55.96	1,469	60.10	107.4
Chemistry	QD	102.87	116	118.15	114.9
Education	L	50.50	530	44.33	87.8
Engineering and technology	T	74.87	946	80.51	107.5
Fine and applied arts	M-N	57.24	2,217	57.97	101.3
General works	A	47.07	28	77.73	165.1
Geography	G	75.57	282	52.65	69.7
Geology	QE	60.01	74	84.38	140.6
History	C,D,E,F	82.02	959	77.02	93.9
Home economics	TX	70.94	21	64.88	91.5
Industrial arts	TT	1,456.29	7	57.51	3.9
Law	K	100.60	1,188	88.98	88.4
Library and information science	Z	272.14	166	221.70	81.5
Literature and language	P	56.26	2,520	62.21	110.6
Mathematics and computer science	QA	63.30	430	71.04	112.2
Medicine	R	86.25	1,249	92.51	107.3
Military and naval science	U-V	63.79	117	58.90	92.3
Natural history	QH	96.00	99	102.31	106.6
Philosophy and religion	B	84.76	946	72.59	85.6
Physical education and recreation	GV	172.34	90	41.52	24.1
Physics and astronomy	QB-QC	98.42	208	75.64	76.9
Physiology	QM-QR	119.30	162	127.14	106.6
Political science	J	51.56	409	56.18	109.0
Psychology	BF	47.25	173	52.67	111.5
Science (general)	Q	57.33	75	64.52	112.5
Sociology	HM-HX	48.19	769	41.28	85.7
Zoology	QL	114.04	55	101.56	89.1
Total		DM71.77	15,747	DM70.16	97.8

*Compiled by Steven E. Thompson, Brown University, from approval plan data supplied by Otto Harrassowitz. Data represent a selection of materials relevant to research and documentation published in East and West Germany, Austria, and Switzerland (see text for more information regarding the nature of the data). Unclassified material (xxx code) that appeared as a subject category in 1987 has been removed from the index. Average prices and indexes have been recalculated. The revised 1985 figures are: average price DM69.90, index 96.9. See text for details of this change. The index is not adjusted for high priced titles. High priced titles may in some years skew some subject areas.

Using the Price Indexes

Librarians are encouraged to monitor trends in the publishing industry as well as changes in economic conditions when preparing budget projections. To make these data on publishing trends readily available, the ALA RTSD Library Materials Price Index Committee sponsors the annual compilation and publication of price data contained in Tables 1–13. The price indexes for different categories of library materials document the rate of price change at the national level of newly published materi-

Table 12 / German Academic Books: Average Prices and Price Indexes, 1986–1988*
(Index Base: 1984 = 100)

1987				1988			
No. of Titles	Average Price	Percent Increase	Index	No. of Titles	Average Price	Percent Increase	Index
227	DM53.84	−10.9	107.7	203	DM53.49	−0.7	107.0
119	67.75	−2.0	96.6	79	72.06	6.4	102.8
53	101.25	−2.6	84.3	70	116.63	15.2	97.1
1,426	75.27	25.2	134.5	1,423	66.48	−11.7	118.8
93	99.51	−15.8	96.7	92	122.57	23.2	119.2
513	38.91	−12.2	77.0	521	41.08	5.6	81.3
802	78.50	−2.5	104.8	941	77.27	−1.6	103.2
1,850	62.43	7.7	109.1	1,919	68.19	9.2	119.1
40	82.48	6.1	175.2	48	347.85	321.7	739.0
236	51.70	−1.8	68.4	247	102.09	97.5	135.1
58	80.42	−4.7	134.0	66	74.53	−7.3	124.2
877	76.36	−0.9	93.1	916	73.34	−4.0	89.4
23	89.20	37.5	125.7	25	78.88	−11.6	111.2
11	66.09	14.9	4.5	5	151.40	129.1	10.4
1,186	81.96	−7.9	81.5	1,397	80.16	−2.2	79.7
131	293.92	32.6	108.0	154	312.97	6.5	115.0
2,670	58.89	−5.3	104.7	2,345	59.84	1.6	106.4
360	68.87	−3.1	108.8	383	63.81	−7.3	100.8
1,547	86.12	−6.9	99.8	1,422	83.50	−3.0	96.8
135	55.61	−5.6	87.2	77	71.07	27.8	111.4
90	80.32	−21.5	83.7	80	101.27	26.1	105.5
964	68.08	−6.2	80.3	832	87.80	29.0	103.6
104	37.46	−9.8	21.7	112	37.38	−0.2	21.7
193	98.42	30.1	100.0	191	72.32	−26.5	73.5
159	149.99	18.0	125.7	187	145.70	−2.9	122.1
524	57.53	2.4	111.6	460	57.58	0.1	111.7
198	51.71	−1.8	109.4	155	58.75	13.6	124.3
87	64.84	0.5	113.1	85	56.66	−12.6	98.8
735	41.62	0.8	86.4	593	62.77	50.8	130.3
64	116.09	14.3	101.8	50	172.52	48.6	151.3
15,475	DM70.76	0.9	98.6	15,078	DM75.22	6.3	104.8

als against those of earlier years. They are useful benchmarks against which local costs may be compared, but because they reflect retail prices in the aggregate, they are not a substitute for price data that reflect the collecting patterns of individual libraries.

In part, differences arise due to the inclusion of discounts, service charges, or shipping and handling fees in library price indexes that are not included in the national indexes. Discrepancies may also emerge that relate to subject focus, mix of current and retrospective materials, and the proportion of foreign imprints that are acquired. These variables have an impact on the average price paid by a particular library; however, it is not possible to predict that the rate of increase that they influence will be significantly different from the rate of increase shown by the national price indexes. The ALA RTSD Library Materials Price Index Committee is interested in pursuing correlation of studies of a particular library's prices with national prices and would appreciate being informed about any studies undertaken. The committee has begun an investigation of price indexes for foreign periodicals and would especially like to review any library studies of prices for these materials. The committee also welcomes interested parties to its meetings at the ALA annual and midwinter conferences.

necessary to recalculate the index from 1986 to the present. The xxx material represents such titles as textbooks, political pamphlets, ephemeral contributions, agitprop, and so forth that had not been subject coded, based on the assumption that they were of little interest to general academic libraries. In the past year, due to budget limitations, Harrassowitz has supplied fewer of these titles to libraries that formerly collected comprehensively. The elimination of these titles in 1988 reduced the number of lower priced titles included in the study and so contributed to an artificially high rate of increase in a single year. The recalculation of the index for 1986 and 1987 makes more realistic cost comparisons possible.

Latin American Prices

The data reported for Latin American books are compiled from acquisitions records of nine large research libraries and so are not a true price index based on the publishing output of these nations. Many of these libraries pursue comprehensive coverage in all countries, although some collect selectively in certain countries. For 1988, the libraries reported acquiring a range of 54 books for Surinam to 7,835 books for Brazil; the average price ranged from $7.29 for titles from Guyana to $23.33 for titles from Surinam (Table 13). In addition to collecting profiles, other factors may influence the prices recorded, including how developed the book trade is in each country, the lack of meaningful list prices for many countries, varying rates of inflation, currency revaluations, inconsistent reporting of shipping, handling, and binding charges in the cost of materials, changes in the scope of dealer coverage, and other inconsistencies in reporting practices.

U.S. Purchasing Power Abroad

The strength of the dollar against foreign currencies improved somewhat in 1988, but the gains did not offset the dramatic loss of purchasing power in 1987. The value of the dollar increased 6.5% in exchange for Canadian currency, showed modest improvements in relation to the British pound, Japanese yen, and Spanish preseta, but continued to weaken in the exchange for French, West German, and Dutch currencies. Libraries are most aware of this loss of purchasing power when renewing periodical subscriptions, but it has also affected their ability to obtain foreign monographic imprints as well. In the chart that follows, exchange rates are expressed in U.S. dollars and are based on quotations from the Banker's Trust Company reported daily in the *Wall Street Journal.* Readers interested in quotations for earlier years may examine earlier volumes of *The Bowker Annual.*

Country	1/31/87	12/31/87	% Change	1/31/88	12/13/88	% Change
Canada	$.7474	$.7965	+ 6.6	$ .8382	$.7348	−6.4
France	.1639	.1881	+14.8	.16504	.1765	+6.9
United Kingdom	1.5135	1.8870	+24.6	1.8085	1.7660	−2.4
Germany	.5466	.6371	+16.6	.5638	.5951	+5.5
Japan	.006515	.008264	+26.8	.008001	.007871	−2.3
Netherlands	.4860	.5677	+16.8	.4981	.5298	+6.4
Spain	.007722	.009346	+21.0	.008826	.008790	−0.4

Table 13 / Number of Copies and Average Cost of Latin American Books Purchased by Nine Selected U.S. Libraries in FYs 1987 and 1988*

	Number of Books		Average Cost†		Percent Increase/ Decrease in Cost over 1987
	FY 1987	FY 1988	FY 1987	FY 1988	
Argentina	5,416	3,266	$10.21	$10.63	4.08
Bolivia	1,469	1,532	9.72	10.46	7.65
Brazil	7,900	7,835	7.91	10.55	33.49
Chile	2,743	2,609	10.89	12.23	12.33
Colombia	4,128	3,069	11.42	11.79	3.26
Costa Rica	1,088	1,086	11.94	12.29	2.95
Cuba	418	619	13.10	8.36	−36.15
Dominican Republic	676	653	10.46	12.57	20.14
Ecuador	1,617	1,200	9.59	8.12	−15.31
El Salvador	284	381	9.51	10.38	9.18
Guatemala	357	229	13.38	12.88	−3.71
Guyana	159	178	7.94	7.29	−8.21
Haiti	176	227	12.63	20.14	59.45
Honduras	332	523	9.61	7.89	−17.86
Jamaica	370	390	7.77	8.35	7.47
Mexico	6,614	6,548	10.21	11.08	8.46
Nicaragua	449	300	7.79	9.62	23.47
Panama	211	221	13.54	14.02	3.53
Paraguay	631	582	10.24	11.04	7.87
Peru	2,736	2,511	10.44	11.36	8.84
Puerto Rico	513	359	13.45	14.44	7.40
Surinam	11	54	26.91	23.33	−13.31
Trinidad	90	135	11.06	9.76	−11.73
Uruguay	1,928	1,581	11.78	15.59	32.34
Venezuela	2,564	1,697	9.97	9.42	−5.53
Other Caribbean	1,892	3,114	12.44	11.58	−6.89

*Compiled by David Block, Seminar on the Acquisition of Latin American Library Materials (SALALM) Acquisition Committee, from reports on the number and cost of current monographs purchased by the libraries of New York Public Library, Library of Congress, University of Arizona, University of Texas, University of Florida, University of Minnesota, Cornell University, University of Wisconsin, and University of Illinois.

†Some figures include binding costs.

As in the past, the data in Tables 1–13 were compiled on a personal computer that computes to 15 decimal places. As a result, users may encounter minor discrepancies with the data reported in earlier years.

The current members of the Library Materials Price Index Committee are Kathryn Hammell Carpenter (chairperson), Stephen Bosch, Dana D'Andraia, Curt Holleman, Pamela Mason, Marilyn Mitchell, and Jana Stevens. Consultants to the committee are Dora Biblarz, Mary Elizabeth Clack, Rebecca Lenzini, and Kathryn Soupiset. Exofficio consultants who contribute their time to index production include David Block, Imre Jarmy, Dennis Smith, Steven E. Thompson, David Walch, and Peter Young.

Notes

1. Leslie C. Knapp and Rebecca T. Lenzini, "Price Index for 1988: U.S. Periodicals," *Library Journal,* April 15, 1988, pp. 35–41.
2. Mary Elizabeth Clack, "Price Index for 1988: U.S. Serial Services," *Library Journal,* April 15, 1988, pp. 41–42.
3. Dora Biblarz, "Reporting Book Prices," *Book Research Quarterly* 2 (Summer 1986).

Part 5
Reference Information

Bibliographies

The Librarian's Bookshelf

Olha della Cava
Librarian, School of Library Service Library
Columbia University, New York

This bibliography is intended as a buying and reading guide for individual librarians and as a selection tool for staff library collections. A few of the titles listed are core titles that any staff development collection might contain, but most are titles published since 1986 with an emphasis on continuing education. Bibliographic tools that most libraries are likely to have for day-to-day operations and special issues of journals devoted to one theme have been excluded from this list. Four key areas of professional concern—online catalogs, library automation, expert systems and microcomputers in libraries—also are omitted, because they are treated in the "High Technology Bibliography," which immediately follows "The Librarian's Bookshelf."

Books

General Works

ALA World Encyclopedia of Library and Information Services. 2nd ed. Ed. by Robert Wedgeworth. Chicago: American Library Association, 1986. $165.

ALA Yearbook of Library and Information Services, 1988. Vol. 13. Ed. by Roger Parent. Chicago: American Library Association, 1988. $80.

ARBA Guide to Library Science Literature, 1970–1983. Ed. by Donald G. Davis, Jr., and Charles D. Patterson. Littleton, CO: Libraries Unlimited, 1987. $65.

Advances in Librarianship. Vol. 14. Ed. by Wesley Simonton, Orlando, FL: Academic Press, 1986. $67.50.

Alternative Library Literature, 1986/1987: A Biennial Anthology. Ed. by Sanford Berman and James P. Danky. Jefferson, NC: McFarland, 1988. $35.

American Libraries: 1986: U.S. and Canadian Libraries. Ed. by Barbara Fischer et al. New York: K. G. Saur, 1986. $36.

American Library Directory, 1988–89. 41st ed. 2 vols. New York: R. R. Bowker, 1988. $156.70.

Books in Our Future: Perspectives and Proposals. Ed. by John Cole. Washington, DC: Library of Congress, 1987. $16.

Bowker Annual of Library and Book Trade Information, 1988. 33rd ed. New York: R. R. Bowker, 1989. $109.50.

Corry, Emmett. *Grants for Libraries: A Guide to Public and Private Funding Programs and Proposal Writing Techniques*. 2nd ed. Littleton, CO: Libraries Unlimited, 1986. $35.

Crawford, Walt. *Technical Standards: An Introduction for Librarians*. White Plains, NY: Knowledge Industry, 1986. $36.50.

DeGennaro, Richard. *Libraries, Technology and the Information Marketplace: Selected Papers*. Boston: G. K. Hall, 1987. $36.50

Directory of Library and Information Professionals. 2 vols. Woodbridge, CT: Research Publications, published in collaboration with American Library Association, 1988. $345.

Encyclopedia of Information Systems and Services. 8th ed. 3 vols. Ed. by Amy Lucas and Annette Novallo. Detroit, MI: Gale, 1988. $399.

Encyclopedia of Library and Information Science. New York: Marcel Dekker, 1968–1988. Vols. 1–43. $75 per vol.

Harrod's Librarians' Glossary of Terms Used in Librarianship, Documentation and the Book Crafts and Reference Books. 6th ed. Comp. by Ray Prytherch. Aldershot, Hampshire, England; Brookfield, VT: Gower, 1987. $79.50.

Libraries and Information Science in the Electronic Age. Ed. by Hendrik Edelman. Philadelphia: ISI Press, 1986. $39.95.

Libraries in the Age of Automation: A Reader for the Professional Librarian. White Plains, NY: Knowledge Industry, 1986. $36.50.

Library and Information Science Annual 1988, Vol. 4. Ed. by Bohdan S. Wynar. Englewood, CO: Libraries Unlimited, 1988. $37.50.

Library Lit. 17—The Best of 1986. Ed. by Bill Katz. Metuchen, NJ: Scarecrow, 1988. $22.50.

Lynch, Mary Jo. *Libraries in an Information Society: A Statistical Summary.* Chicago: American Library Association, 1987. Price unknown.

Prytherch, Raymond. *Sources of Information in Librarianship and Information Science.* 2nd ed. Brookfield, VT: Gower, 1987. $37.

Riggs, Donald E. *Libraries in the '90s: What the Leaders Expect.* Phoenix, AZ: Oryx, 1988. $24.95.

Stevens, Norman D. *A Guide to Collecting Librariana.* Metuchen, NJ: Scarecrow, 1986. $19.50.

Wertsman, Vladimir F. *The Librarian's Companion: A Handbook of Thousands of Facts and Figures on Libraries, Librarians, Books, Newspapers, Publishers, Booksellers.* Westport, CT: Greenwood, 1987. $35.

Academic and Research Libraries

ACRL University Library Statistics, 1985–86 & 1986 "100 Libraries" Statistical Survey. Comp. by Robert E. Molyneux. Chicago: American Library Association/Association of College and Research Libraries, 1987. $30.

ARL Statistics 1985–86. Comp. by Nicola Daval and Alexander Lichtenstein. Washington, DC: Association of Research Libraries, 1987. $6.

Adams, Roy J. *Information Technology & Libraries: A Future for Academic Libraries.* London; Dover, NH: Croom Helm, 1986. $29.

Association of College and Research Libraries. National Conference (Fourth, 1986, Baltimore). *Energies for Transition.* Ed. by Danuta A. Nitecki. Chicago: Association of College and Research Libraries/American Library Association, 1986. $30.

Campus of the Future. Conference on Information Resources. Dublin, OH: OCLC, 1987. $9.

Cummings, Martin Marc. *The Economics of Research Libraries.* Washington, DC: Council on Library Resources, 1986. $5.

Directory of Agencies Collecting Statistical Data from College & University Libraries. Ed. by Lynn B. Labrake. Chicago: American Library Association/Library Administration and Management Association, Statistics Section, Statistics for College and University Libraries Committee, 1986. $15.

Hyatt, James A. *University Libraries in Transition.* Washington, DC: National Association of College and University Business Officers, 1987. $15.

Leadership for Research Libraries: A Festschrift for Robert M. Hayes. Ed. by Anne Woodsworth and Barbara von Wahlde. Metuchen, NJ: Scarecrow, 1988. $25.

Library Statistics of Colleges and Universities, 1985: National Summaries, State Summaries, Institutional Tables. Chicago: American Library Association/Association of College and Research Libraries, 1987. $30.

Person, Roland C. *A New Path: Undergraduate Libraries at United States and Canadian Universities, 1949–1987.* New York: Greenwood, 1988. $29.95.

Public Access Microcomputers in Academic Libraries: The Mann Library Model at Cornell University. Ed. by Howard Curtis. Chicago: American Library Association, 1987. $30.

Research Libraries: The Past 25 Years, the Next 25 Years: Papers for a Festschrift Honoring L. W. Anderson, Director of Libraries, Colorado State University. Ed. by Taylor E. Hubbard. Boulder, CO: Colorado Associated University Press, 1986. $25.

SPEC Kits. Washington, DC: Association of Research Libraries. 1973- . Nos. 1- . $10 for members, $20 for nonmembers. (Recent kits have been on such topics as building use policies, remote access to online catalogs, approval plans, and performance evaulation in reference services.)

The Smaller Academic Library: A Management Handbook. Ed. by Gerard B. McCabe. New York: Greenwood, 1988. $49.95.

Administration and Personnel

Advances in Library Administration and Organization. Vol. 7. Ed. by Gerard B. McCabe and Bernard Kreissman. Greenwich, CT: JAI Press, 1988. $58.50.

Alvarez, Robert S. *Library Boss: Thoughts on Library Personnel.* San Francisco: Administrator's Digest Press, 1987. $20.95.

Auld, Lawrence W. S. *Electronic Spreadsheets for Libraries.* Phoenix, AZ: Oryx, 1986. $37.50.

Cargill, Jennifer S. *Managing Libraries in Transition.* Phoenix, AZ: Oryx, 1988. $29.50.

Clayton, Marlene, *Managing Library Automation.* Brookfield, VT: Gower, 1987. $53.95.

Conroy, Barbara. *Improving Communication in the Library.* Phoenix, AZ: Oryx, 1986. $25.

Creth, Sheila D. *Effective On-the-Job Training: Developing Library Human Resources.* Chicago: American Library Association, 1986. $15.95.

Dewey, Barbara I. *Library Jobs: How to Fill Them, How to Find Them.* Phoenix, AZ: Oryx, 1987. $26.50.

Dollars and Sense: Implications of the New Online Technology for Managing the Library. Ed. by Bernard F. Pasqualini. Chicago: American Library Association, 1987. $10.

Euster, Joanne R. *The Academic Library Director: Management Activities and Effectiveness.* New York: Greenwood, 1987. $35.

Foster, Donald L. *Managing the Catalog Department.* 3rd ed. Metuchen, NJ: Scarecrow, 1987. $20.

Handbook of Library Training Practice. Ed. by Ray Prytherch. Aldershot, Hampshire, England; Brookfield, VT: Gower, 1986 (U.S. dist. by Lexington Books, Lexington, MA). $68.95.

The How-to-Do-It Manual for Small Libraries. Ed. by Bill Katz. New York: Neal-Schuman, 1988. $39.95.

Jones, Noragh. *Staff Management in Library and Information Work.* 2nd ed. Brookfield, VT: Gower, 1987. $35.

Kohl, David F. *Cataloging and Catalogs: A Handbook for Library Management.* Santa Barbara, CA: ABC-Clio, 1986, $35.

______ *Library Education and Professional Issues: A Handbook for Library Management.* Santa Barbara, CA: ABC-Clio, 1986. $35.

Kusack, James M. *Unions for Academic Library Support Staff: Impact on Workers and the Workplace.* New York: Greenwood, 1986. $25.85.

Library Management in Review. 2 vols. Ed. by Alice Bruemmer. New York: Special Libraries Association, 1981–1987. $13.75 per vol.

The Library Microcomputer Environment: Management Issues. Ed. by Sheila S. Intner and Jane Anne Hannigan. Phoenix, AZ: Oryx, 1988. $27.50.

Performance Evaluation: A Management Basic for Librarians. Ed. by Jonathan A. Lindsey. Phoenix, AZ: Oryx, 1986. $35.

Ramsey, Inez L. *Library Planning and Budgeting.* New York: Watts, 1986. $19.95.

Rooks, Dana C. *Motivating Today's Library Staff: A Management Guide.* Phoenix, AZ: Oryx, 1988. $27.50.

St. Clair, Guy. *Managing the One-Person Library.* London, Boston: Butterworths, 1986. $19.95.

Schauer, Bruce P. *The Economics of Managing Library Services.* Chicago: American Library Association, 1986. $24.

Simpson, I. S. *Basic Statistics for Librarians.* 3rd ed. Chicago: Library Association/American Library Association, 1988. £19.50.

Stueart, Robert D. *Library Management*. 3rd ed. Littleton, CO: Libraries Unlimited, 1987. $35.

T.I.P. Kit: Topics in Personnel. Chicago: Office for Library Personnel Resources, ALA, 1982- . $10. (Recent kits have been on such topics as hiring library staff and pay equity.)

Thompson, James. *An Introduction to University Library Administration*. 4th ed. London: Clive Bingley, 1987. £24.

Archives, Preservation, and Special Collections

Buchanan, Sally A. *Disaster Planning: Preparedness and Recovery for Libraries and Archives*. Paris: UNESCO General Information Programme and UNISIST, 1988. Price unknown.

Conservation of Library and Archive Materials and the Graphic Arts. Ed. by Guy Petherbridge. Boston: Butterworths, 1987. $129.95.

Cook, Michael. *Archives and the Computer*. 2nd ed. Stoneham, MA; Kent, UK: Butterworths, 1986. $49.95.

______ *The Management of Information from Archives*. Brookfield, VT: Gower, 1986. $41.50.

Couture, Carol. *The Life of a Document: A Global Approach to Archives and Records Management*. Montreal: Vehicule Press, 1987. Price unknown.

Kantor, Paul B. *Costs of Preservation Microfilming at Research Libraries: A Study of Four Institutions*. Washington, DC: Council on Library Resources, 1986. $3.

McCleary, John M. *Vacuum Freeze-Drying, A Method Used to Salvage Water-Damaged Archival and Library Materials: A RAMP Study with Guidelines*. Paris: UNESCO General Information Programme and UNISIST, 1987. Free.

Morris, John. *The Library Disaster Preparedness Handbook*. Chicago: American Library Association, 1986. $20.

Morrow, Carolyn C. *Conservation Treatment Procedures: A Manual of Step-by-Step Procedures for the Maintenance and Repair of Library Materials*. 2nd ed. Littleton, CO: Libraries Unlimited, 1986. $20.

Preservation Microfilming: A Guide for Librarians and Archivists. Ed. by Nancy E. Gwinn for the Association of Research Libraries. Chicago: American Library Association, 1987. $40.

Preservation of Library Materials: Conference Held at the National Library of Austria, Vienna, April 7–10, 1986. Ed. by Merrily A. Smith. Munich, New York: K. G. Saur, 1987. $70.

Preservation Planning Program: An Assisted Self-Study Manual for Libraries. Expanded ed. Prepared by Pamela W. Darling and Duane E. Webster. Washington, DC: Association of Research Libraries, Office of Management Studies, 1982, c. 1987. $15.

Preservation Planning Program Resource Notebook. Comp. by Pamela W. Darling. Rev. ed. by Wesley Boomgaarden. Washington, DC: Association of Research Libraries, Office of Management Studies, 1987. Price unknown.

Scham. A. M. *Managing Special Collections*. New York: Neal-Schuman, 1986. $35.

Stielow, Frederick J. *The Management of Oral History Sound Archives*. Westport, CT: Greenwood, 1986. $35.

Wallace, Patricia E., et. al. *Records Management: Integrated Information Systems*. 2nd ed. New York: Wiley, 1987. Price unknown.

Bibliographic Instruction

Beasley, David R. *How to Use a Research Library*. New York: Oxford University Press, 1988. $24.95.

Berge, Patricia. *Basic College Research*. New York: Neal-Schuman, 1987. $19.95

Bibliographic Instruction: The Second Generation. Ed. by Constance A. Mellon. Littleton, CO: Libraries Unlimited, 1987. $27.50.

Conceptual Framework for Bibliographic Education: Theory into Practice. Ed. by Mary Reichel and Mary Ann Ramey. Littleton, CO: Libraries Unlimited, 1987. $25.

Cook, Sybilla A. *Instructional Design for Libraries: An Annotated Bibliography*. New York: Garland, 1986. $27.

Felknor, Bruce L. *How to Look Things Up and Find Things Out*. New York: Morrow, 1988. $19.95.

Gates, Jean Key. *Guide to the Use of Li-*

braries and Information Sources. 6th ed. New York: McGraw-Hill, 1988. $17.95.

Hauer, Mary G., et al. *Books, Libraries, and Research.* 3rd ed. Dubuque, IA: Kendall/Hunt, 1987. $15.95.

Jay, M. Ellen. *Building Reference Skills in the Elementary School.* Hamden, CT: Library Professional Publications, 1986. $24.50.

Mann, Thomas. *A Guide to Library Research Methods.* New York: Oxford University Press, 1987. $14.95.

Marketing Instruction Services: Applying Private Sector Techniques to Plan and Promote Bibliographic Instruction: Papers Presented at the Thirteenth Library Instruction Conference Held at Eastern Michigan University, May 3 & 4, 1984. Ed. by Carolyn A. Kirkendall. Ann Arbor, MI: Pierian, 1986. $19.50.

A Place to Stand: User Education in Canadian Libraries. Ed. by Elizabeth Frick. Ottawa: Canadian Library Association, 1988. $30.

Shih, Tian-Chu. *Library Instruction: A Bibliography, 1975 through 1985.* Jefferson, NC: McFarland, 1986. $14.95.

Svinicki, Marilla D. *Designing Instruction for Library Users: A Practical Guide.* New York: Marcel Dekker, 1988. $55.

Teaching Librarians to Teach: On-the-job Training for Bibliographic Instruction Librarians. Ed. by Alice S. Clark and Kay F. Jones. Metuchen, NJ: Scarecrow, 1986. $18.50.

User Instruction in Academic Libraries: A Century of Selected Readings. Comp. by Larry L. Hardesty et al. Metuchen, NJ: Scarecrow, 1986. $29.50.

Wolf, Carolyn E. *Basic Library Skills.* 2nd ed. Jefferson, NC: McFarland, 1986. $12.95.

Children's and Young Adult Services and Materials

Elementary School Library Collection: A Guide to Books and Other Media, Phases 1-2-3. Ed. by Lois Winkel. 16th ed. Williamsport, PA: Brodart, 1988. $79.95.

England, Claire. *Childview: Evaluating and Reviewing Materials for Children.* Littleton, CO: Libraries Unlimited, 1987. $19.50.

Ettlinger, John R.T. *Choosing Books for Young People: Vol. 2: A Guide to Criticism and Bibliography, 1976–1984.* Phoenix, AZ: Oryx, 1987, $43.50.

Fiction, Folklore, Fantasy & Poetry for Children 1876–1985: Author Index, Illustrator Index, Title Index, Awards Index. 2 vols. New York: R. R. Bowker, 1986. $499.95.

Field, Carolyn W. *Values in Selected Children's Books of Fiction and Fantasy.* Hamden, CT: Library Professional Publications, 1987. $27.50.

Helbig, Alethea. *Dictionary of American Children's Fiction, 1960–1984: Recent Books of Recognized Merit.* New York: Greenwood, 1986. $65.

Kohn, Rita T. *Once Upon—A Time for Young People and Their Books: An Annotated Resource Guide.* Metuchen, NJ: Scarecrow, 1986. Price unknown.

Library Service to Children. Ann Gagnon, series ed. Ottawa: Canadian Library Association, 1987. $5 per series issue. (Topics covered include budgeting for children's services, library service to toddlers, preschool story time, and audiovisual media for children.)

Lukenbill, W. Bernard. *Youth Literature: An Interdisciplinary, Annotated Guide to North American Dissertation Research, 1930–1985.* New York: Garland, 1988. Price unknown.

Marshall, Margaret R. *An Introduction to the World of Children's Books.* 2nd ed. Aldershot, Hampshire, England; Brookfield, VT: Gower, 1988. $39.60.

Reference Books for Young Readers: Authoritative Evaluations of Encyclopedias, Atlases, and Dictionaries. Ed. by Marion Sader. New York: R. R. Bowker, 1988. $47.45.

Sutherland, Zena. *The Best in Children's Books: The University of Chicago Guide to Children's Literature, 1979–1984.* Chicago: University of Chicago Press, 1986. $35.

Wilms, Denise M. *A Guide to Non-sexist Children's Books, Volume II, 1976–1985.* Chicago: Academy Chicago, 1987. $16.95.

Collection Development

Blazek, Ron. *The Humanities: A Selective Guide to Information Sources.* 3rd ed. Englewood, CO: Libraries Unlimited, 1988. $23.

Collection Development: Cooperation at the Local and National Levels. Papers of the Twenty-ninth Annual Meeting of the Seminar on the Acquisition of Latin American Library Materials, University of North Carolina, Chapel Hill, North Carolina, June 3–7, 1984. Ed. by Barbara G. Valk. Madison, WI: SALALM Secretariat, 1987. Price unknown.

Collection Development Organization and Staffing in ARL Libraries. SPEC Kit No. 131. Washington, DC: System and Procedures Exchange Center, Association of Research Libraries, Office of University Management Studies, 1987. $20.

Collection Management and Development Committee, Resources and Technical Services Division. *Guide for Writing a Bibliographer's Manual.* Chicago: American Library Association, 1987. $4.75.

English and American Literature: Sources and Strategies for Collection Development. Ed. by William McPheron. Chicago: American Library Association/Association of College and Research Libraries, 1987. $29.95.

Evans, G. Edward. *Developing Library and Information Center Collections.* 2nd ed. Littleton, CO: Libraries Unlimited, 1987. $29.50.

Selection of Library Materials in Applied and Interdisciplinary Fields. Ed. by Beth J. Shapiro and John Whaley. Chicago: American Library Association, 1987. $42.

Slavens, Thomas P. *A Great Library through Gifts.* New York: K. G. Saur, 1986. $40.

Spiller, David. *Book Selection: An Introduction to Principles and Practice.* 4th ed. London: Clive Bingley, 1986 (U.S. dist. by Shoe String Press, Hamden, CT). £14.75.

Comparative and International Librarianship

Comparative and International Librarianship. Ed. by P. S. Kawatra. New York: Envoy, 1987. $30.

Coombs, Douglas. *Spreading the Word: The Library Work of the British Council.* London, New York: Mansell, 1988. $60.

Developments in International and Comparative Librarianships, 1976–1985. Ed. by Inese A. Smith. Birmingham: International and Comparative Librarianship Group, Library Association, 1986. £13.

Essen Symposium (9th: 1986). *Impact of New Information Technology on International Library Cooperation: Essen Symposium, 8 September–11 September 1986.* Ed. by Ahmed H. Helal. Essen, West Germany: Essen University Library, 1987. Price unknown.

Essen Symposium (10th: 1987). *International Library Cooperation: Essen Symposium, 19 October–22 October 1987.* Ed. by Ahmed H. Helal. Essen, West Germany: Essen University Library, 1987. Price unknown.

Gassol de Horowitz, Rosario. *Librarianship: A Third World Perspective.* New York: Greenwood, 1988. $37.95.

Gorman, G. E. *Guide to Current National Bibliographies in the Third World.* 2nd rev. ed. London, New York: K. G. Saur, 1987. £45.

Information Consultants in Action. Ed. by J. Stephan Parker. London, New York: Mansell, 1986. $56.

International and Comparative Librarianship: An Annotated Selective Bibliography on the Theme of the LACUNY 1986 Institute. Shrinking World/Exploding Information: Developments in International Librarianship. Comp. and ed. by Mimi B. Penchansky and Adam Halicki-Conrad. New York: Library Association of the City University of New York, 1986. Price unknown.

Kabir, Abulfazal M. Fazle. *The Libraries of Bengal, 1700–1947.* London, New York: Mansell, 1987. $40.

Kumar, Girja. *Library Development in India.* New Delhi: Vikas, 1986. $45.

McCarthy, Cavan M. *The Introduction of Automated Library and Information Services in a Newly Industrialized Country: A Case Study of the Brazilian Experience.* Halifax, N.S.: Dalhousie University, University Libraries, School of Library Service, 1986. $16.50.

New Information Professionals: Proceedings of the Singapore-Malaysia Congress of Librarians and Information Scientists, Singapore, 4–6 September 1986. Ed. by Ajita Thuraisingham. Aldershot, Hampshire; Brookfield, VT: Gower, 1987. $77.95.

Pain, Helen. *School Librarianship in the United Kingdom.* Boston Spa, Wetherby, West Yorkshire: British Library Research and Development Department, 1987. £12.

Parker, J. Stephen. *Asking the Right Questions: Case Studies in Library Development Consultancy.* London, New York: Mansell, 1988. $59.

Plumbe, Wilfrid J. *Tropical Librarianship.* Metuchen, NJ: Scarecrow, 1987. Price unknown.

Readings in Canadian Library History. Ed. by Peter F. McNally. Ottawa, Ont.: Canadian Library Association, 1986. $25.

Rochester, Maxine K. *Foreign Students in American Library Education: Impact on Home Countries.* Westport, CT: Greenwood, 1986. $35.

Sardar, Ziauddin. *Information and the Muslim World: A Strategy for the Twenty-first Century.* London, New York: Mansell, 1988. $60.

Sharma, Ravindra N. *Indian Academic Libraries and Dr. S. R. Ranganathan: A Critical Study.* New Delhi: Sterling, 1986. Price unknown.

Sibai, Mohamed Makki. *Mosque Libraries: An Historical Study.* London, New York: Mansell, 1987. $56.

Copyright

Library Reproduction of Copyrighted Works (17 U.S.C. 108). Second Report: Report of the Register of Copyrights. Washington, DC: Library of Congress, Copyright Office, 1988. Price unknown.

Reed, Mary H. *The Copyright Primer for Librarians and Educators.* Chicago: American Library Association, Washington, DC: National Education Association, 1987. $7.95.

Reproduction of Copyrighted Works by Educators and Librarians (Circular 21). Washington, DC: Copyright Office, Library of Congress, 1988. Price unknown.

Talab, R. S. *Commonsense Copyright: A Guide to the New Technologies.* Jefferson, NC: McFarland, 1986. $14.95.

Document Delivery and Fee-Based Services

Charging for Services in Academic Libraries: Proceedings of a Seminar Held at Teeside Polytechnic Library on 22nd October 1986. Ed. by Eimer Tomlinson. Newcastle upon Tyne: Library Association, University and Research Section, Northern Group, 1987. £7.

Fee-based Services: Issues and Answers: Second Conference on Fee-based Research in College and University Libraries. Proceedings of the Meetings Held at the University of Michigan, Ann Arbor, Michigan, May 10–12, 1987. Comp. by Anne K. Beaubien. Ann Arbor: Michigan Information Transfer Source, University of Michigan, 1987. $28.

Education for Librarianship and Information Management

Boaz, Martha T. *Librarian/Library Educator: An Autobiography and Planning for the Future.* Metuchen, NJ: Scarecrow, 1987. $27.50.

Education for Professional Librarians. Ed. by Herbert S. White. White Plains, NY: Knowledge Industry, 1986. $36.50.

Education of Library and Information Professionals: Present and Future Prospects. Ed. by Richard K. Gardner. Littleton, CO: Libraries Unlimited, 1987. $27.50.

Financial Assistance for Library Education: Academic Year 1987–1988. Chicago: American Library Association/SCOLE, 1986. $1.

Griffiths, José-Marie. *New Directions in Library and Information Science Education.* White Plains, NY: Knowledge Industry, 1986. $45.

Internationalizing Library and Information Science Education: A Handbook of Policies and Procedures in Administration and Curriculum. Ed. by John F. Harvey and Frances Laverne Carroll. New York: Greenwood, 1987. $49.94.

Library and Information Science Education: An International Symposium. Papers Presented at the International Conference on Library and Information Science Education Sponsored by the Department and Graduate Institute of Library Science, National Taiwan University, November 29–30, 1985. Ed. by James S. C. Hu. Metuchen, NJ: Scarecrow, 1987. $27.50.

Library and Information Services Council. *Professional Education and Training for Library and Information Work: A Review.*

London: Library Association, 1986. £17.50.

Paris, Marion. *Library School Closings: Four Case Studies*. Metuchen, NJ: Scarecrow, 1988. $20.

Rehman, Sajjad ur. *Management Theory and Library Education*. New York: Greenwood, 1987. $29.95.

Reid, William H. *Four Indications of Current North American Library and Information Doctoral Degree Programs*. Champaign: University of Illinois, Graduate School of Library and Information Science, 1987. $3.50.

Government Documents

Collins, Mae S. *A Practical Guide to the Superintendent of Documents Classification System*. Washington, DC: Classification and Cataloging Branch, Library Programs Service, Superintendent of Documents, US GPO, 1986, Su.Doc. No. GP 3.29:Pr88. Price unknown.

Directory of Government Document Collections & Librarians. 5th ed. Ed. by Barbara Kile. Bethesda, MD: Congressional Information Service, 1987. Price unknown.

Evinger, William R. *Federal Statistical Data Bases: A Comprehensive Catalog of Current Machine-Readable and Online Files*. Phoenix, AZ: Oryx, 1988, $115.

Government Information, an Endangered Resource of the Electronic Age: Papers Presented at the First Annual State-of-the-Art Institute, October 19–22, 1986, Washington, D.C. Washington, DC: Special Libraries Association, 1986. $21.75.

Government Infostructures: A Guide to the Networks of Information Resources and Technologies at Federal, State, and Local Levels. Ed. by Karen B. Levitan. New York: Greenwood, 1987. $45.

Guide to U.S. Government Publications. 1988 ed. Ed. by John L. Androit. McLean, VA: Documents Index, 1988. Price unknown.

International Information: Documents, Publications, and Information Systems of International Governmental Organizations. Ed. by Peter I. Hajnal. Englewood, CO: Libraries Unlimited, 1988. $27.50.

Lane, Margaret T. *Selecting and Organizing State Government Publications*. Chicago: American Library Association, 1987. $35.

Less Access to Less Information by and about the U.S. Government: A 1981–1987 Chronology. Prepared by the American Library Association Washington Office. Washington, DC, 1988. Price unknown.

McClure, Charles R., et al. *Linking the U.S. National Technical Information Service with Academic and Public Libraries*. Norwood, NJ: Ablex, 1986. $29.50.

Richardson, John. *Government Information: Education and Research, 1928–1986*. New York: Greenwood, 1987. $35.

Schorr, Alan E. *Federal Documents Librarianship, 1879–1987*. Juneau, AK: Denali, 1988. $27.

Schwartz, Julia. *Easy Access to Information in United States Government Documents*. Chicago: American Library Association, 1986. $12.95.

Sears, Jean L. *Using Government Publications*. 2 vols. Phoenix, AZ: Oryx, 1985–86. $67.50 each.

Stratford, Juri. *Guide to Statistical Materials Produced by Governments and Associations in the United States*. Alexandria, VA: Chadwyck-Healey, 1987. $75.

Turner, Carol A. *Current Approaches to Improving Access to Government Documents*. Washington, DC: Association of Research Libraries, Office of Management Studies, 1987. $15.

Williams, Wiley J. *Subject Guide to Major United States Government Publications*. 2nd ed. rev. and exp. Chicago: American Library Association, 1987. $21.95.

Zwirn, Jerrold. *Congressional Publications and Proceedings: Research on Legislation, Budgets, and Treaties*. 2nd ed. Englewood, CO: Libraries Unlimited, 1988. $27.50.

Indexing and Abstracting

Aitchison, Jean. *Thesaurus Construction: A Practical Manual*. 2nd ed. London: ASLIB, 1987. £19.50.

Craven, Timothy C. *String Indexing*. Orlando, FL: Academic Press, 1986. $29.95.

Lancaster, F. Wilfrid. *Vocabulary Control for Information Retrieval*. 2nd ed. Arlington, VA: Information Resources Press, 1986. $27.50.

PRECIS: A Recent Application. Ed. by Mary Dykstra. Halifax, N.S.: School of Library Service, Dalhousie University, 1986. $14.50

Rowley, J. E. *Abstracting and Indexing.* 2nd ed. London: Clive Bingley, 1988. £16.

Wellisch, Hans H. *Indexing: A Basic Reading List.* Washington, DC: American Society of Indexers, 1987. Price unknown.

Information and Society

Beniger, James R. *The Control Revolution: Technological and Economic Origins of the Information Society.* Cambridge, MA: Harvard University Press, 1986. $25.

Hernon, Peter. *Federal Information Policies in the 1980's: Conflicts and Issues.* Norwood, NJ: Ablex, 1987. $35.

The Ideology of the Information Age. Ed. by Jennifer Daryl Slack and Fred Fejes. Norwood, NJ: Ablex, 1987. Price unknown.

Klapp, Orrin E. *Overload and Boredom: Essays on the Quality of Life in the Information Society.* New York: Greenwood, 1986. $29.95.

Wolpert, Samuel A. *Economics of Information.* New York: Van Nostrand Reinhold, 1986. $35.

Information Management and Technology

Annual Review of Information Science and Technology. Vol. 22. 1987. Ed. by Martha E. Williams. Amsterdam, New York: Elsevier for American Society for Information Science, 1987. $69.50.

CD-ROM: The New Papyrus, the Current and Future State of the Art. Ed. by Steve Lambert and Suzanne Ropiequet. Redmond, WA: Microsoft, 1986. $34.95.

Cortez, Edwin M. *Managing Information Systems & Technologies: A Basic Guide for Design, Selection, Evaluation, and Use.* New York: Neal-Schuman, 1986. $35.

Directory of Information Management Software for Libraries, Information Centers, Record Centers. 1987/88 ed. Comp. and ed. by Edward John Kazlauskas. Studio City, CA: Pacific Information, 1987. $49.

Information Technology and Information Use: Towards a Unified View of Information and Information Technology. Ed. by Peter Ingwersen et al. London: Taylor Graham, 1986. £37.

McQueen, Judy. *Videodisc and Optical Digital Disk Technologies and Their Applications in Libraries: 1986 Update.* Chicago: American Library Association, 1986. $25.

Marsterson, William A. J. *Information Technology and the Role of the Librarian.* London, Dover, NH: Croom Helm, 1986. $32.50.

New Methods and Techniques for Information Management. Ed. by Mary Feeney. London: Taylor Graham, 1986. $43.50.

Rowley, J. F. *The Basics of Information Technology.* London: Clive Bingley, 1988. £9.95.

Taylor, Robert S. *Value-added Processes in Information Systems.* Norwood, NJ: Ablex, 1986. $39.50.

Intellectual Freedom

American Library Association. Commission on Freedom and Equality of Access to Information. *Freedom and Equality of Access to Information: A Report to the American Library Association.* Chicago: American Library Association, 1986. $10.95.

Banned Books Week 1988: Celebrating the Freedom to Read. A Resource Book. Chicago: American Library Association, 1988. $15.

Freedom to Read. Ed. by Haig A. Bosmajian. New York: Neal-Schuman, 1987. $37.50.

Government Information, an Endangered Resource of the Electronic Age: Papers Presented at the First Annual State-of-the-Art Institute, October 19–22, 1986, Washington, D.C. Washington, DC: Special Libraries Association, 1986. $21.75.

Hernon, Peter. *Federal Information Policies in the 1980's: Conflicts and Issues.* Norwood, NJ: Ablex, 1987. $54.50.

Information for All: Access and Availability: Proceedings of the Annual Conference of the Institute of Information Scientists, Peebles, 1986. Ed. by Brenda White. London: Taylor Graham, 1987. £15.

Information: The Currency of Democracy. Chicago: American Library Association, 1988. Free.

Reichman, Henry. *Censorship and Selection:*

Issues and Answers for Schools. Chicago: American Library Association; Arlington, VA: American Association of School Administrators, 1988. $12.95.

Unequal Access to Information Resources: Problems and Needs of the World's Information Poor. Proceedings of the Congress for Librarians, February 17, 1986. Division of Library and Information Science, St. John's University, Jamaica, New York. Ed. by Jovian P. Lang. Ann Arbor, MI: Pierian, 1988. $35.

West, Mark I. *Trust Your Children: Voices against Censorship in Children's Literature.* New York: Neal-Schuman, 1988. $19.95.

Library and Information Science Research

Alley, Brian. *Librarian in Search of a Publisher: How to Get Published in the Library and Information Field.* Phoenix, AZ: Oryx, 1986. $18.50.

Current Research for the Information Profession 1986/87. Ed. by Pirkko Elliot. London: Library Association, 1987. $80.

Mann, Thomas. *A Guide to Library Research Methods.* New York: Oxford University Press, 1987. Price unknown.

Moore, Nick. *Research and Practice: 21 Years of Library Research in the UK.* Library and Information Research Report No. 55. London: British Library, 1987. £16.50.

Research and the Practice of Librarianship: An International Symposium. Ed. by G. G. Allen and F. C. A. Exon. Perth: Western Australian Institute of Technology, 1986. $35.

Stewart, Linda. *The Dissemination of Library and Information Research and Development to the Practitioner: An Investigation into Public Libraries.* Loughborough: Centre for Library and Information Management, 1987. Price unknown.

Library Automation

See the "High Technology Bibliography," following in Part 5.

Library Buildings and Space Planning

Boss, Richard W. *Information Technologies and Space Planning for Libraries and Information Centers.* Boston: G. K. Hall, 1987. $28.50.

Library Buildings Consultant List. Ed. by Jane G. Johnson. Chicago: Library Administration and Management Association/American Library Association, 1987. $15.

Metcalf, Keyes DeWitt. *Planning Academic and Research Library Buildings.* 2nd ed. Ed. by Philip D. Leighton and David C. Weber. Chicago: American Library Association, 1986. $55.

Public Library Buildings, 1975–1983. Ed. by K. C. Harrison. London: Library Services, 1987. £29.50.

Tucker, Dennis C. *From Here to There: Moving a Library.* Bristol, IN: Wyndham Hall, 1987. $34.95.

Working Papers on Building Planning. Ed. by Don Revill. Oxford, England: Council of Polytechnic Librarians, 1987. £10.50.

Library History

Balbi, Adriano. *A Statistical Essay on the Libraries of Vienna and the World.* Trans. by Larry Barr and Janet L. Barr. Jefferson, NC: McFarland, 1986. $25.95.

British Library History: Bibliography 1981–1984. Ed. by Denis F. Keeling. London: Library Association, 1987. £16.

Buzas, Ladislaus. *German Library History, 800–1945.* Trans. by William D. Boyd. Jefferson, NC: McFarland, 1986. $55.

Dickson, Paul. *The Library in America: A Celebration in Words and Pictures.* New York: Facts on File, 1986. $35.

Frisbie, Margery. *This Bookish Inclination: The Story of the Arlington Heights Memorial Library, 1887–1987.* Arlington Heights, IL: Friends of the Arlington Heights Memorial Library, 1987. Price unknown.

Greene, Jack P. *The Intellectual Heritage of the Constitutional Era: The Delegates' Library.* Philadelphia: Library Company of Philadelphia, 1986. Price unknown.

Humanities' Mirror: Reading at the New-

berry, 1887–1987. Ed. by Rolf Achilles. Chicago: Newberry Library, 1987. $16.95.

Libraries, Books, and Culture: Proceedings of Library History Seminar VII, 6–8 March 1985, Chapel Hill, North Carolina. Ed. by Donald G. Davis, Jr. Austin, TX: Graduate School of Library and Information Science, University of Texas, 1986. $15.

Young, Arthur P. *American Library History: A Bibliography of Dissertations and Theses*. 3rd rev. ed. Metuchen, NJ: Scarecrow, 1988. $39.50.

Library Profession and Professionals

Academic and Public Librarians—Data by Race, Ethnicity and Sex. Chicago: American Library Association, Office for Library Personnel Resources, 1986. $4.

Academic Status: Statements and Resources. Chicago: Association of College and Research Libraries/American Library Association, 1988. $8.

Activism in American Librarianship, 1962–1973. Ed. by Mary Lee Bundy and Frederick J. Stielow. New York: Greenwood, 1987. $38.

Burrington, Gillian. *Equal Opportunities in Librarianship? Gender and Career Aspirations*. London: Library Association, 1987. (U.S. dist. by American Library Association, Chicago). $28.

Dale, Doris C. *A Directory of Oral History Tapes of Librarians in the United States and Canada*. Chicago: American Library Association, 1986. $15.

Dewey, Barbara I. *Library Jobs: How to Fill Them, How to Find Them*. Phoenix, AZ: Oryx, 1987. $26.50.

Harring, Mark Y. *Controversial Issues in Librarianship: An Annotated Bibliography, 1960–1984*. New York: Garland, 1987. $45.

Hauptman, Robert. *Ethical Challenges in Librarianship*. Phoenix, AZ: Oryx, 1988. $22.50.

Heim, Kathleen M. *Opportunities in Library and Information Science*. Lincolnwood, IL: VGM Career Horizons, 1986. $9.95.

Lynch, Mary Jo, and M. Meyers. *ALA Survey of Librarian Salaries, 1988*. Chicago: American Library Association, 1988. $40.

Warner, Alice S. *Mind Your Own Business: A Guide for the Information Entrepreneur*. New York: Neal-Shuman, 1987. $24.95.

Webb, Sylvia P. *Personal Development in Information Work*. London: ASLIB, 1986. £12.

Wiegand, Wayne A. *Members of the Club: A Look at One Hundred ALA Presidents*. Urbana: University of Illinois GSLIS, 1988. $3.50.

Wiegand, Wayne A. *The Politics of an Emerging Profession: The American Library Association, 1876–1917*. Westport, CT: Greenwood, 1986. $39.95.

Winter, Michael F. *The Culture and Control of Expertise: Toward a Sociological Understanding of Librarianship*. New York: Greenwood, 1988. $37.95.

Marketing Library and Information Services

Great Library Promotion Ideas III: JCD Library Public Relations Award Winners and Notables 1986. Ed. by John W. Berry and Beverly J. Bagan. Chicago: Library Administration and Management Association/ American Library Association, 1987. $9.95.

Heath, Alan. *Off the Wall: The Art of Book Display*. Littleton, CO: Libraries Unlimited, 1987. $19.50.

Kies, Cosette N. *Marketing and Public Relations for Libraries*. Metuchen, NJ: Scarecrow, 1987. $14.50.

Liebold, Louise C. *Fireworks, Brass Bands, and Elephants: Promotional Events with Flair for Libraries and Other Nonprofit Organizations*. Phoenix, AZ: Oryx, 1986. $29.50.

Schmidt, Janet. *Marketing the Modern Information Center: A Guide to Entrepreneurship for the Information Manager*. New York: Find/SVP, 1987. Price unknown.

Tuggle, Ann M. *Grand Schemes and Nitty-Gritty Details: Library PR That Works*. Littleton, CO: Libraries Unlimited, 1987. $19.50.

Virgo, Julie A. C. *A Marketing Study for Five Public Libraries*. Chicago: Carroll Group, 1987. $29.95.

Weingand, Darlene E. *Marketing/Planning Library and Information Services*. Littleton, CO: Libraries Unlimited, 1987. $23.50.

Wood, Elizabeth J. *Strategic Marketing for Libraries: A Handbook.* New York: Greenwood, 1988. $37.50.

Microcomputers in Libraries

See the "High Technology Bibliography," following in Part 5.

Networks, Interlibrary Cooperation, and Resource Sharing

Advances in Library Automation and Networking: A Research Annual. Ed. by Joe A. Hewitt. Vol. 1. Greenwich, CT: JAI Press, 1987. $56.50. Vol. 2. Greenwich, CT: JAI Press, 1988. $58.50.

Ballard, Thomas H. *The Failure of Resource Sharing in Public Libraries and Alternative Strategies for Service.* Chicago: American Library Association, 1986. $20.

Binkowski, Edward S. *Satellite Information Systems.* Boston: G. K. Hall, 1988. $38.50.

Hafter, Ruth. *Academic Librarians and Cataloging Networks: Visibility, Quality Control and Professional Status.* Westport, CT: Greenwood, 1986. $29.95.

Holligan, Patrick J. *Access to Academic Networks.* London: Taylor Graham, 1986. $26.50.

Impact of New Information Technology on International Library Cooperation. Essen Symposium 8–11 September 1986. Essen, West Germany: Universitatsbibliothek Essen, 1987. Price unknown.

Kemper, Marlyn. *Networking: Choosing a LAN Path to Interconnection.* Metuchen, NJ: Scarecrow, 1987. $37.50.

The Linked Systems Project: A Networking Tool for Libraries. Comp. and ed. by Judith G. Fenly and Beacher Wiggins. Dublin, OH: OCLC Online Computer Library Center, 1988. $13.50.

Martin, Susan K. *Library Networks, 1986–1987: Libraries in Partnership.* White Plains, NY: Knowledge Industry, 1986. $36.50.

Morris, Leslie R. *Interlibrary Loan Policies Directory.* 3rd ed. New York: Neal-Schuman, 1988. $75.

Not Alone . . . But Together: A Conference on Multitype Library Cooperation. Ed. by Alphonse F. Trezza. Talahassee: Florida State University, School of Library and Information Studies, 1987. $15.

Open Systems Interconnection: The Communications Technology of the 1990's: Papers from the Pre-Conference Seminar held at London, August 12–14, 1987. Ed. by Christine H. Smith. Munich, New York: K. G. Saur, 1988. Price unknown.

Telecommunications for Information Management and Transfer: Proceedings of the First International Conference Held at Leicester Polytechnic, April 1987. Ed. by Mel Collier. Aldershot, Hampshire, England; Brookfield, VT: Gower, 1988. £16.50.

Telecommunications Networks: Issues and Trends. Ed. by M. E. L. Jacob. White Plains, NY: Knowledge Industry for the American Society for Information Science, 1986. $36.50.

Toward a Common Vision in Library Networking: Proceedings of the Library of Congress Network Advisory Committee Meeting, December 9–11, 1985. Washington, DC: Network Development and MARC Standards Office, Library of Congress, 1986. Free.

Townley, Charles Thomas. *Human Relations in Library Network Development.* Hamden, CT: Library Professional Publications, 1988. Price unknown.

Nonprint Materials

AVMP Audio Video Market Place, 1988. New York: R. R. Bowker, 1988. $65.

Casciero, Albert J. *Audiovisual Technology Primer.* Littleton, CO: Libraries Unlimited, 1988. $22.50.

Daily, Jay E. *Organizing Non Print Materials.* 2nd ed. New York: Marcel Dekker, 1986. $49.75.

Educational Media and Technology Yearbook, 1986. Vol. 12. Ed. by Elmwood E. Miller. Littleton, CO: Libraries Unlimited, 1986. $47.50.

The Equipment Directory of Audio-Visual, Computer and Video Products, 1987–88. 33rd ed. Fairfax, VA: International Communications Industries Association, 1986. $35.

Markey, Karen. *Subject Access to Visual Resources Collections: A Model for Com-*

puter Construction of Thematic Catalogs. New York: Greenwood, 1986. $35.

Nonbook Media: Collection Management and User Services. Ed. by John W. Ellison and Patricia Ann Coty. Chicago: American Library Association, 1987. $35.

Online Catalogs

See the "High Technology Bibliography," following in Part 5.

Periodicals and Serials

Advances in Serials Management: A Research Annual. Vol. 2. Ed. by M. Tuttle. Greenwich, CT: JAI Press, 1988. $56.50.

Automating the Newspaper Clipping Files: A Practical Guide. Comp. by members of the Newspaper Division, Special Libraries Association. Washington, DC, 1987. $30.

Heynen, Jeffrey. *The CONSER Project: Recommendations for the Future: Report of a Study Conducted for the Library of Congress.* Washington, DC: Library of Congress, 1986. $7.50.

Newspapers in the Library: New Approaches to Management and Reference Work. Ed. by Lois N. Upham. New York: Haworth, 1988. $29.95.

Page, Gillian. *Journal Publishing: Principles and Practice.* London; Boston: Butterworths, 1987. $79.95.

Serials Control and Deselection Project. SPEC Kit No. 147. Washington, DC: Office of Management Studies, Association of Research Libraries, 1988. $15.

Thomas, Nancy G. *Notes for Serials Cataloging.* Littleton, CO: Libraries Unlimited, 1986. $17.50.

Public Libraries

Bakewell, K. G. B. *Business Information and the Public Library.* Brookfield, VT: Gower, 1987. $37.

Collection Management in Public Libraries: Proceedings of a Preconference to the 1984 ALA Annual Conference, June 21–22, 1984, Dallas, Texas. Ed. by Judith Serebrick. Chicago: American Library Association, 1986. $9.95.

Gervasi, Anne. *Handbook for Small, Rural, and Emerging Public Libraries.* Phoenix, AZ: Oryx, 1988. $27.50.

Guidelines for Public Libraries. 3rd ed. Munich; New York: K. G. Saur, 1986. $14.

Kim, Choong Han. *Public Library Users and Uses: A Market Research Handbook.* Metuchen, NJ: Scarecrow, 1987. $29.50.

Libraries, Coalitions & the Public Good. Ed. by E. J. Josey. New York: Neal-Schuman, 1987. $29.95.

The Library Trustee: A Practical Guidebook. 4th ed. Ed. by Virginia G. Young. Chicago: American Library Association, 1988. Price unknown.

McClure, Charles R., et al. *Planning and Role Setting for Public Libraries: A Manual of Options and Procedures.* Chicago: American Library Association, 1987. $14.

O'Donnell, Peggy. *Public Library Development Program: Manual for Trainers.* Chicago: American Library Association, 1988. $20.

Riechel, Rosemarie. *Improving Telephone Information and Reference Service in Public Libraries.* Hamden, CT: Library Professional Publications, 1987. $21.50.

Rubin, Richard. *In-house Use of Materials in Public Libraries.* Champaign: University of Illinois, Graduate School of Library and Information Science, 1986. Price unknown.

Shavit, David. *The Politics of Public Librarianship.* New York: Greenwood, 1986. $29.95.

Shuman, Bruce A. *River Bend in Transition: Managing Change in Public Libraries.* Phoenix, AZ: Oryx, 1987. $27.50.

Van House, Nancy A., et al. *Output Measures for Public Libraries: A Manual of Standardized Procedures.* 2nd ed. Chicago: American Library Association, 1987. $12.50.

Reference Services and Online Searching

Alberico, Ralph. *Microcomputers for the Online Searcher.* Westport, CT: Meckler, 1987. $24.95.

Benham, Frances. *Success in Answering Reference Questions: Two Studies.* Metuchen, NJ: Scarecrow, 1987. $29.50.

End-User Searching: Services and Providers. Ed. by Martin Kesselman and Sarah B. Watstein. Chicago: American Library Association, 1988. $26.

Harter, Stephen P. *Online Information Retrieval: Concepts, Principles, and Techniques.* Orlando, FL: Academic Press, 1986. $46.

Hawley, George S. *The Referral Process in Libraries: A Characterization and an Exploration of Related Factors.* Metuchen, NJ: Scarecrow, 1987. Price unknown.

Hernon, Peter. *Unobtrusive Testing and Library Reference Services.* Norwood, NJ: Ablex, 1987. $35.

Humphrey, Susanne M. *Databases: A Primer for Retrieving Information by Computer.* Englewood Cliffs, NJ: Prentice-Hall, 1986. $29.95.

Improving Reference Management: Papers Based upon a Conference Sponsored by the Southeastern Library Association and the Reference and Adult Services Division. Ed. by Trish Ridgeway et al. Chicago: Reference and Adult Services Division/American Library Association, 1986. $15.

Information Seeking: Basing Services on Users' Behaviors. Ed. by Jana Varlejs. Jefferson, NC: McFarland, 1987. $9.95.

Jennerich, Elaine Z. *The Reference Interview as a Creative Art.* Littleton, CO: Libraries Unlimited, 1987. $24.50.

Katz, William A. *Introduction to Reference Work.* 5th ed. New York: McGraw-Hill, 1987. $28.95.

Managing Online Reference Services. Ed. by Ethel Auster. New York: Neal-Schuman, 1986. $35.

Manual of Online Search Strategies. Ed. by C. J. Armstrong and J. A. Large. Boston: G. K. Hall, 1988, $57.

Palmer, Roger C. *Online Reference and Information Retrieval.* 2nd ed. Littleton, CO: Libraries Unlimited, 1987. $25.

Prytherch, Ray J. *The Basics of Readers' Advisory Work.* London: Clive Bingley, 1988. £9.95.

Reference and Information Services: A Reader for Today. Comp. by Bill Katz. Metuchen, NJ: Scarecrow, 1986. $19.

Rowley, Jennifer E. *Organising Knowledge: An Introduction to Information Retrieval.* Brookfield, VT: Gower, 1987. $53.95.

Sieburth, Janice F. *Online Search Services in the Academic Library: Planning, Management, and Operation.* Chicago: American Library Association, 1988. $30.

Stevens, Rolland E. *Reference Work in the University Library.* Littleton, CO: Libraries Unlimited, 1986. $37.50.

Watson, Paula D. *Reference Services in Academic Research Libraries.* Chicago: Reference and Adult Services Division/American Library Association, 1986. $15.

Yates, Rochelle. *A Librarian's Guide to Telephone Reference Service.* Hamden, CT: Library Professional Publications, 1986. $19.50.

School Libraries/Media Centers

Adams, Helen R. *School Media Policy Development: A Practical Process for Small Districts.* Littleton, CO: Libraries Unlimited, 1986. $23.50.

Benedict, Emma L. *The Reading Consultant/Library Media Specialist Team: Building the Reading Habit.* Hamden, CT: Library Professional Publications, 1987. $27.50.

Costa, Betty. *A Micro Handbook for Small Libraries and Media Centers.* 2nd ed. Littleton, CO: Libraries Unlimited, 1986. $28.

Craver, Kathleen W. *The Changing Instructional Role of the High School Librarian.* Champaign: University of Illinois, Graduate School of Library and Information Science, 1986. $3.

Eble, Mary M. *New Dimensions in School Library Media Service.* Metuchen, NJ: Scarecrow, 1988. Price unknown.

The Elementary School Library Collection: A Guide to Books and Other Media, Phases 1-2-3. 16th ed. Ed. by Lois Winkel. Williamsport, PA: Brodart, 1988. $79.95.

Gillespie, John T. *The Senior High School Paperback Collection.* Chicago: American Library Association, 1986. $22.50.

Herring, James E. *School Librarianship.* 2nd ed. London: Clive Bingley, 1988. $20.43.

Information Power: Guidelines for School Library Media Programs. Prepared by the American Association of School Librarians and Association for Educational Communications and Technology. Chicago: ALA, Washington, DC: AECT, 1988. $12.95.

Jay, M. Ellen. *Motivation & the School Library Media Teacher.* Hamden, CT: Library Professional Publications, 1988. $26.50.

Loertscher, David V. *Computerized Collection Development for School Library Media Centers.* Fayetteville, AR: Hi Willow

Research and Publishing, 1986. $40.

______ *Taxonomies of the School Library Media Program.* Englewood, CO: Libraries Unlimited, 1988. $28.

The Microcomputer Facility and the School Library Media Specialist. Ed. by E. Blanche Woolls and David V. Loertscher. Chicago: American Library Association, 1986. $15.

The Microcomputer, the School Librarian and the Teacher: An Introduction with Case Studies. Ed. by James E. Herring. London: Clive Bingley, 1987. £13.75.

Prostano, Emanuel T. *The School Library Media Center.* 4th ed. Littleton, CO: Libraries Unlimited, 1987. $28.50.

School Library and Media Center Acquisitions Policies and Procedures. 2nd ed. Ed. by Betty Kemp. Phoenix, AZ: Oryx, 1986. $44.50.

School Library Media Annual, 1987. Vol. 5. Ed. by Shirley L. Aaron and Pat R. Scales. Littleton, CO: Libraries Unlimited, 1987. $40.

Silverman, Eleanor. *Trash into Treasure: Recycling Ideas for Library/Media Centers, Containing 100 Easy-to-Do Ideas.* Rev. and enl. ed. Metuchen, NJ: Scarecrow, 1988. Price unknown.

Van Orden, Phyllis. *The Collection Program in Schools: Concepts, Practices, and Information Sources.* Englewood, CO: Libraries Unlimited, 1988. $24.50.

Wilson, Patricia J. *Happenings: Developing Successful Programs for School Libraries.* Littleton, CO: Libraries Unlimited, 1987. $19.

Woolls, Blanche. *Grant Proposal Writing: A Handbook for School Library Media Specialists.* New York: Greenwood, 1986. $29.95.

Wynar, Christine G. *Guide to Reference Books for School Media Centers.* 3rd ed. Littleton, CO: Libraries Unlimited, 1986. $35.

Yesner, Bernice L. *The School Administrator's Guide to Evaluating Library Media Programs.* Hamden, CT: Library Professional Publications, 1987. $26.

Services for Special Groups

Dee, Marianne. *Library Services to Older People.* London: British Library, 1986 (U.S. dist. by Longwood, Dover, NH). £12.50.

Library Services for Hispanic Children: A Guide for Public and School Librarians. Ed. by Adela Artola Allen. Phoenix, AZ: Oryx, 1987. $30.

Library Services to Housebound People. Ed. by Julied Ryder. London: Library Association, 1987. £18.50.

Special Libraries

Ahrensfeld, Janet L. *Special Libraries: A Guide for Management.* 2nd ed., rev. Washington DC: Special Libraries Association, 1986. $15.50.

Bailey, Martha J. *The Special Librarian as a Supervisor or Middle Manager.* 2nd ed. Washington, DC: Special Libraries Association, 1986. $18.95.

Baxter, Paula A. *International Bibliography of Art Librarianship: An Annotated Compilation.* Munich, New York: K. G. Saur, 1987. £14.

Coyle, William. *Libraries in Prisons: A Blending of Institutions.* New York: Greenwood, 1987. $29.95.

Directory of Special Libraries and Information Centers. 11th ed. 3 vols. Ed. by Brigitte Darnay. Detroit, MI: Gale, 1988. $895 for 3 vols.

Jones, Lois S. *Art Libraries and Information Services: Development, Organization, and Management.* Orlando, FL: Academic Press, 1986. $39.50.

Keaveney, Sydney Starr. *Contemporary Art Documentation and Fine Arts Libraries.* Metuchen, NJ: Scarecrow, 1986. $17.50.

Larsgaard, Mary L. *Map Librarianship: An Introduction.* 2nd ed. Littleton, CO: Libraries Unlimited, 1987. $43.50.

Lavin, Michael R. *Business Information: How to Find It, How to Use It.* Phoenix, AZ: Oryx, 1987. $49.50.

Manual of Law Librarianship: The Use and Organization of Legal Literature. 2nd ed. Ed. by Elizabeth M. Moys, Boston: G. K. Hall, 1987. £47.50.

A Manual of Local Studies Librarianship. Ed. by Michael Dewe. Aldershot, Hampshire; Brookfield, VT: Gower, 1987. $89.95.

Medical Librarianship in the Eighties and Beyond: A World Perspective. Ed. by Fiona

Mackay Picken and M. C. Kahn. London, New York: Mansell, 1986. $58.

Prison Librarianship: A Selective, Annotated, Classified Bibliography, 1945–1985. Comp. by Fred R. Hartz et al. Jefferson, NC: McFarland, 1987. $19.95.

Pruett, Nancy J. *Scientific and Technical Libraries.* 2 vols. Orlando, FL: Academic Press, 1986. $90.

SLA Triennial Salary Survey. Washington, DC: Special Libraries Association, 1986. $25.

Viet, Fritz. *Presidential Libraries and Collections.* New York: Greenwood, 1987. $29.95.

Technical Services

Bush, B. J. *Integration of Public and Technical Services Functions: Observations on Organizational Change in Six Member Libraries of the Association of Research Libraries.* Washington, DC: Office of Management Studies, Association of Research Libraries, 1986. $20.

Hahn, Harvey. *Technical Services in the Small Library.* Chicago: American Library Association, 1987. $3.95.

Statistical Applications in Library Technical Services: An Annotated Bibliography. Ed. by Sue A. Burkholder. Chicago: Library Administration and Management Association/American Library Association, 1987. $25.

Technical Services: Acquisitions

Block, David. *A Directory of Vendors of Latin American Library Materials.* 2nd ed, rev. and enl. Madison: Secretariat, Seminar on the Acquisition of Latin American Library Materials, Memorial Library, University of Wisconsin, 1986. $12.

Peet, Terry C. *A Guide to Spanish Correspondence for Acquisition Librarians.* Madison: Secretariat, Seminar on the Acquisition of Latin American Library Materials, Memorial Library, University of Wisconsin, 1987. $22.

Pricing and Costs of Monographs and Serials: National and International Issues. Ed. by Sul H. Lee. New York: Haworth, 1987. $29.95.

Technical Services: Cataloging and Classification

Authority Control Symposium: Papers Presented during the 14th Annual ARLIS/NA Conference, New York, NY, February 10, 1986. Ed. by Karen Muller. Tucson, AZ: ARLIS/NA, 1987. $20.

Bauer, Mary Celia. *Dewey Classification: 200 Schedules Expanded for Use.* Rev. and exp. Haverford, PA: Catholic Library Association, 1988. $25.

Cataloging Special Materials: Critiques and Innovations. Ed. by Sanford Berman. Phoenix, AZ: Oryx, 1986. $32.50.

Chan, Lois Mai. *Library of Congress Subject Headings: Principles and Application.* 2nd ed. Littleton, CO: Libraries Unlimited, 1986. $45.

Cochrane, Pauline A. *Improving LCSH for Use in Online Catalogs: Exercises for Self-Help with a Selection of Background Readings.* Littleton, CO: Libraries Unlimited, 1986. $35.

The Complete Cataloguing Reference Set. Collected Manuals of the Minnesota AACR 2 Trainers. 2 vols. Ed. by Nancy B. Olson and Edward Swanson. DeKalb, IL: Minnesota Scholarly Press, 1988. $285.

Guidelines on Subject Access to Microcomputer Software. Comp. by the Ad Hoc Subcommittee on Subject Access to Microcomputer Software, Cataloging and Classification Section, RTSD/ALA. Chicago: American Library Association, 1986. $5.

Hoffman, Herbert H. *Small Library Cataloging.* 2nd ed. Metuchen, NJ: Scarecrow, 1986. $18.50.

Hunter, Eric J. *Classification Made Simple.* Aldershot, Hampshire, England; Brookfield, VT: Gower, 1988. $12.95.

LC Rule Interpretations of AACR2, 1978–1986. Comp. by Sally C. Tseng. 2nd cumulated ed. 1st update. Metuchen, NJ: Scarecrow, 1987. $32.50.

Manheimer, Martha L. *OCLC: An Introduction to Searching and Input.* 2nd ed. New York: Neal-Schuman, 1986. $17.95.

Parker, Elisabeth B. *LC Thesaurus for Graphic Materials: Topical Terms for Subject Access.* Washington, DC: Cataloging Distribution Service, Library of Congress, 1987. $30.

Piggott, Mary. *Topography of Cataloguing: Showing the Most Important Landmarks, Communications and Perilous Places.* London: Library Association, 1988. $27.50 (U.S. dist. by American Library Association, Chicago).

Policy and Practice in Bibliographic Control of Nonbook Media. Ed. by Sheila S. Intner and Richard P. Smiraglia. Chicago: American Library Association, 1987. $24.95.

Research Libraries and Their Implementation of AACR2. Ed. by Judith Hopkins and John A. Edens. Greenwich, CT: JAI Press, 1986. $49.50.

Rogers, JoAnn V. *Nonprint Cataloging for Multimedia Collections: A Guide Based on AACR2.* 2nd ed. Littleton, CO: Libraries Unlimited, 1987. $23.50.

Rowley, J. E. *Organising Knowledge: An Introduction to Information Retrieval.* Aldershot, Hampshire, England; Brookfield, VT: Gower, 1987. $53.95.

Satija, Mohinder P., and John P. Comaromi. *Introduction to the Practice of Dewey Decimal Classification.* New York: Envoy, 1987. $22.50.

Smiraglia, Richard P. *Cataloging Music: A Manual for Use with AACR2.* 2nd ed. Lake Crystal, MN: Soldier Creek Press, 1986. $35.

Subject Cataloging Manual: Shelflisting. Prep. by the Subject Cataloging Division, Library of Congress. Washington, D.C., 1987. $30.

Taylor, Arlene G. *Cataloging with Copy: A Decision-Maker's Handbook.* 2nd ed. Englewood, CO: Libraries Unlimited, 1988. $35.

Turner, Christopher. *Organizing Information: Principles and Practice.* London: Clive Bingley, 1987. $27.50.

Periodicals

The list of journals that follows may be viewed as a core collection in a professional library or may be used by librarians as a selection tool for personal subscriptions. Titles used primarily as acquisition tools have been omitted.

ALA Washington Newsletter
American Archivist
American Libraries
Archival Informatics Newsletter
Archival Informatics Technical Reports
Audiovisual Librarian
Behavioral and Social Sciences Librarian
The Bottom Line
Business Information Review
Business Library Management
CD-ROM Librarian
CD-ROM Review
Cataloging and Classification Quarterly
Collection Building
Collection Management
College and Research Libraries
Community and Junior College Libraries
Conservation Administration News
Current Research in Library and Information Science
Database
Database Alert
Database Searcher
Government Information Quarterly
Health Libraries Review
IATUL Quarterly: A Journal of Library Management and Technology
IFLA Journal
The Indexer
Infomediary
Information and Referral
Information Development
Information Processing and Management
Information Technology and Libraries
Information Today
International Library Review
International Review of Children's Literature and Librarianship
Journal of Academic Librarianship
Journal of Education for Library and Information Science
Journal of Library Administration
Journal of Youth Services in Libraries
Laserdisk Professional
Libraries and Culture
Library Acquisitions: Practice and Theory
Library Administration and Management
Library and Archival Security
Library and Information Science Research
Library Automation
Library Currents
Library Hi Tech
Library Hi Tech News
Library Hotline
Library Journal
Library Management
Library of Congress Information Bulletin

Library Personnel News
Library Quarterly
Library Resources and Technical Services
Library Technology Reports
Library Trends
Library Video Magazine (video recording)
Microfilm Review
Newsletter on Intellectual Freedom
Online
Online Libraries and Microcomputers
Online Review
Public Library Quarterly
RQ
RSR (Reference Services Review)
Rare Book and Manuscript Librarianship
The Reference Librarian
Resource Sharing and Information Networks
SLJ (School Library Journal)
School Library Media Quarterly
Science and Technology Libraries
Serials Librarian
Serials Review
Special Libraries
Technical Services Quarterly
Wilson Library Bulletin

High Technology Bibliography

Richard W. Clare, III
Associate Librarian for Automation and Collection Maintenance
SUNY College of Technology at Utica/Rome, Utica, NY 13504-3051

No article-length bibliography can hope to encapsulate all noteworthy trends and relevant citations. This review has been assembled with the aim of highlighting the major areas of activity in high technology likely to be of interest to library personnel exploring the available technologies and applying them within library settings. The materials cited fall into two general categories: the most recent reviews as of the time of composition and current writing on specific aspects of the topic that represent "hot spots" or critical issues.

Introduction

The year in high technology as it applies to libraries was characterized by a greater interest in improvements in interdevice and intersystem connectivity. The development of the multitasking concept, for individuals and groups of users, has had the effect of a nearly geometric increase in the performance demands upon both the hardware and software for personal computers. To facilitate the performance and the monitoring of these demanding applications, the computer display screen has been liberated from its fixed task of representing the current, individual processing to provide an overview of concurrent, multiple processing. The use of on-screen menus and icons to manage and command the activities of the system has been largely accepted as a convenient and graceful method for enabling general users to maintain their bearings within the more complex processing environment and to maximize their potential productivity. These advances in the complexity of the processing environment and the demands for equivalent development in the areas of displays and output technologies, all the while maintaining brisk response times, have strained the performance capacity of the majority of personal computers. The additional software overhead necessary to coordinate these functions has proven more difficult to create and debug than had been originally anticipated.

Gosney, Michael, and Linnea Dayton. *Making Art with the Macintosh II: Maximizing the MAC II for Graphic Art and Desktop Publishing.* Glenview, IL: Scott, Foresman, 1989. pap. $22.95. ISBN 0-673-38159-5.

Sanders, William B. *Compute's Guide to Sound & Graphics on the Apple IIGS.* Radnor, PA: Compute! Publications, 1987. 233 pp. illus. $18.95. ISBN 0-87455-096-3.

Thorell, Lisa G., and Wanda J. Smith. *Using Computer Color Effectively: An Illustrated Reference to Computer Color Interface.* Englewood Cliffs, N.J.: Prentice-Hall, 1988. 224 pp. illus. $42.67, pap. $39.95. ISBN 0-13-939878-3. pap. ISBN 0-13-939852-X.

Hardware

Various theoretical and practical strategies have been employed, in almost every aspect of computer design and construction, in order to meet today's lofty performance requirements. One computing economy that has proven successful in a number of environments has been the use of "reduced instruction set computers," or RISC, to decrease the amount and variety of superfluous system activity, in order to hasten the performance of a more restricted subset of computing problems. Increased amounts of random access memory (RAM) have been provided to maintain swift fetches of ever-larger volumes of data and application programs. Disk caching likewise seeks to accelerate access to data and/or program information otherwise stored more remotely on fixed or floppy disks.

The debate among personal computer manufacturers regarding the characteristics of the main data channel or system bus, which connects the major components of the system, has direct bearing upon the overall performance characteristics of the machine. The 80286 and 80386 chip designs offer increased speeds and greater throughput than existing 8086 or 8088 class devices. The 286 is robust enough for individual multitasking but is presently wanting in capacity when multiuser, multitasking is the issue. IBM's Micro Channel Architecture, MCA, is a radical response to the issue of bus design, as it is incompatible with the existing, de facto, standard. A rival design championed by Compaq and eight other manufacturers seeks to maintain the existing 32-bit bus while permitting multiusers and multitasking and preserving compatibility.

Gimarc, Charles E., and Veliko M. Milutinovic. "A Survey of RISC Processors and Computers in the Mid-1980s," *Computer,* 20, no. 9 (September 1987), 59–69.

Interfaces

Machine-independent user and application interfaces are being developed and installed to maximize the compatability of existing hardware and software, to cushion users as they move from system to system or application to application, and to advance the goals of multitasking and interconnectivity. Windows, X Windows, and the Presentation Manager are products that bring some measure of uniformity to the user interface. Application program interfaces are presented as menus that transparently permit users to issue commandlike instructions to programs, allowing the programs to interact, without necessitating the use of formal command codes or syntax. The actual interfaces lie beneath the menus at the nexus of the operating system accessing the software and the programs identified at the menu.

Operating Systems and Networking

The drive to maximize the ease of data and device sharing in order to harness any underutilized computing capacity is most pronounced in institutions with extensive automation expertise and the budgetary leeway to consider expenditures for increasingly sophisticated, and expensive, local area networks. The evolution of local area network management continues, with increasing attention being paid to automated network management.

The choice of an operating system, which has been largely moot due to the overall dominance of DOS, has resurfaced again due to the waning interest in networking. DOS appears to possess the potential of quite complete and powerful networking architecture; however, the software to exploit these features has not exactly exploded from the developers' ateliers. This attention to networked multitasking has provoked something of a renaissance of interest in Unix, which has much the same potential and a substantial body of established software. A fancifully christened "multiple standards environment" is threatening to emerge as AT&T and a camp of followers and the Open System Foundation contend for hegemony in the promulgation of the "standard" Unix operating system. This multiplicity of standards, and the "Extended Industry Standard Architecture" springing up around the Ur-286 chip and the "new and improved 286," are simply music to the black box industry.

Computerworld. "Local Area Networks," *Spotlight,* January 25, 1988, pp. S1–S16.

King, Stephen. "Network Complexity," *PC Tech Journal,* 6, no. 6 (June 1988), 44–52.

______. "Novell Advances," *PC Tech Journal,* 6, no. 6 (June 1988), p. 58–72.

Hardware and Communications Technologies

Hardware for library applications, a belated after-market of commercial and scientific "iron," has followed in their wake. Personal computers built upon 286 chips are being designed to run at ever-higher frequencies, achieving greater throughput. PCs employing 386 chips offer a wider data path and higher speeds, while presenting individual users with the option of multitasking, running programs in virtual and protected modes. The NeXT computer, a relative of the well-established and powerful tribe of work stations, appears to feature a host of artfully combined, innovative components. Laptop computers are thought to be nearing the point in terms of power/price/weight of becoming viable "first" machines for a larger market of users; if this is the case, increasing numbers of "carry-in" users can be expected to occupy more space in libraries with the expectation of connecting their machines to decent electrical power and local and national information sources. The cleavage in the personal computer industry precipitated by the advent of the PS/2 machines has prompted several manufacturers to propose enhancing the longevity and vitality of 286-based machines through the so-called "Extended Industry Standard Architecture" (EISA) standard. Whether the goal of these manufacturers is at odds with the trend toward networked computing remains to be seen. Peripherals have continued to show incremental improvements. Innovative storage devices such as the "floptical" disk drives have made their commercial appearance. Whether this type of storage medium succeeds in the marketplace or becomes another high-potential but low-impact innovation, à la the compact disc, in terms of widespread user and vendor support will have to be seen. In this as in other innovations, such as the PS/2 machines, the mass of the installed base has increased the difficulty of marketing compelling products that sweep up the gamut of users with a clear market mandate.

The entire gauge of telecommunications technologies is moving to ever-higher baud rates and wider bandwidths in order to move and manipulate the increasing volume and types of data being generated, processed, and stored. Commercially available modems, operating at speeds of 9,600 baud and above, are being manufactured for personal computers. This upward ratcheting will continue for the foreseeable future, as additional fiber optic capacity and subsequent generations of chips or other technologies make greater processing speeds possible. The utility of processing and sorting many different types of data—alphanumeric characters, audio, and video within a unified database or easily accessible from other, standardized sources—is being gradually appreciated by the entire computing community. How long it will take before sufficient data are codified and made available, whether transformed into the electronic equivalent of library materials or over economical telecommunications facilities, is anybody's guess. A full-blown encyclopedia that presented the user with the spectrum of data streams as a well-integrated whole would be a revolutionary product. The evoluting communications networks are proceeding to offer the foundations of a unitary data stream, at 9.6K bits per second, by means of the Integrated Services Digital Network. This telecommunications network proposes to transmit an increasingly broader data spectrum, ripe for access and manipulation by the developing technologies described in this review and elsewhere.

Bocker, Peter, *ISDN—The Integrated Services Digital Network.* New York: Springer-Verlag, 1988, xi. 258 pp. illus. $64.50. ISBN 0-387-17446-X.

Finneran, Michael. "ISDN: What's Here Now." *Computerworld,* June 6, 1988, pp. 71, 74–75, 78.

Sharrock, Suzanne Marie. *Integration of Voice, Data, and Video in LAN-Based Systems.* Minneapolis, MN: University Microfilms International, 1987. 163 leaves. illus. pap. $28. No. GAX87-18663.

Compact Disc Technology

The library market continues to be faced with the inconvenience and unnecessary expense of competing physical standards for CD-ROMs. This stalemate, where no manufacturer of CD players or CD vendor has been able to establish an industrywide standard by means of marketing success, has hobbled the acceptance and utility of this truly valuable storage medium. Whether this forthcoming "year of the CD-

ROM" heralds any breakthrough in the reduction of differences without distinction remains to be seen. An interesting new product, CD-Net, from Meridian Data of Capitola, California, promises to allow multiple-user access to individual CDs. Such a product appears to broaden significantly the distribution and access channels to this attractive but technology-intensive resource. The costs of CD-ROM library catalogs is still rather higher than most libraries can justify. The publication of the Library of Congress's Subject Headings on CD-ROM discs, searchable through a variety of keys, represents a measure of progress. The question of timeliness of the headings themselves and the frequency and cost of updates to the discs remain to be resolved. This product would seem to be an ideal candidate for large cataloging departments, distributed via a dedicated machine to cataloging work stations or smart terminals.

Alpert, Mark. "500,000 Pages on One Erasable Disk," *Fortune,* January 2, 1989, pp. 99–101.

Cinnamon, Barry. *Handbook of Optical Disk Storage and Retrieval Systems.* Silver Spring, MD: Association for Information and Image Management, 1988. iii. 98 pp. illus. $28 members, $35 nonmembers. ISBN 0-89258-116-6.

Lambert, Steve, and Suzanne Ropiequet, eds. *CD ROM: The New Papyrus.* Redmond, WA: Microsoft, 1986. xiii. 619 pp. illus. pap. $21.95. ISBN 0-914845-74-8.

Saffady, William. *Optical Storage Technology 1988: State of the Art Review.* Westport, CT: Meckler, 1988. x. 155 pp. illus. $39.50. ISBN 0-88736-344-X.

Computer Security and Disaster Preparedness

The entire computing community was chastened in 1988 by the episodic appearance of computer viruses and security breaches. Computer hackers have always attempted to gain unauthorized access to databases as a test of their expertise or for more sinister and malicious ends. The international dimensions of this phenomenon, where a West German citizen penetrated systems associated with the Department of Defense at the Lawrence Livermore labs, among others, have justifiably alarmed the community. The compromise of national defense cannot be condoned; unfortunately, there seems to be no clear-cut safeguards to be adopted without imposing a burdensome amount of system overhead in the form of encryption and associated costs for secure, or "hardened," equipment. The pace and relative collegiality of networked computing for sensitive projects will undoubtedly be set back until the next moat of security has been put into place. Mischievous programmers and destructive computer programs, known as computer viruses, have been an unhappy aspect of computing from the onset. What distinguished these misguided bursts of creativity in 1988 was the widespread impact of one virus on an academic computing network. A graduate student from Cornell University is alleged to have brought a national system to its knees by means of a not so very elegant program inserted into a known weakness of the operating system. This combination of moderate expertise, a flawed but effective program, and the consequences of a less than vigilant approach toward system security has jostled the networks' sense of well-being. What price we will all have to pay for this is unclear. The oscillation between rigid and flexible system access and the reciprocating nature of the struggle between hackers and systems designers will doubtless continue. The consequences of carefree importation of programs and data files within individual machines and systems can clearly be disastrous. Systems administrators must take their responsibilities to heart, by educating systems users to the risks associated with "unknown" programs and by scrutinizing the security of their own sites in the light of the increasing level of sophistication of the computing population at large. The expenses associated with heightened security must be evaluated against the costs, tangible and otherwise, of disruptive or debilitating attacks upon the system.

Gasser, Morrie. *Building a Secure Computer System.* New York: Van Nostrand Reinhold, 1988. xvi. 288 pp. illus. $34.95. ISBN 0-442-23022-2.

Highland, H. "How to Evaluate Microcomputer Encryption Software and Hardware." *Computer Security,* 6, no. 3 (June 1987), 229–244.

"Out of Harm's Way: Security Planning Can Save Your Business," *Computerworld,* April 6, 1988, pp. 1–40.

The general computing community is beginning to take the issue of disaster preparedness seriously. The impact of the fire in an Illinois switching center that interrupted telecommunication service was felt nationwide. Disaster recovery services are projected to become a multi-million-dollar industry, with computer manufacturers and independent agents offering backup "hot sites" and additional emergency services to subscribers. Such recovery service is coming to be marketed as a logical extension of the existing hardware maintenance agreement.

Computerworld. "Disaster Prevention and Recovery," *Spotlight,* July 11, 1988, pp. S1–S16.

Usdin, S. "Like It or Not, Plan for Disaster Recovery." *Office,* 105, no. 3 (March 1987), 90, 92.

Word Processing and Graphics Software

Word processing software continues to develop a more comprehensive array of features and functions. Successive releases of these programs show a definite trend toward providing increased compatibility with the more popular database management systems. These products are being enhanced to utilize the increasingly powerful hard- and software options available to users. For instance, the results of a comprehensive report created from various in-house databases may be displayed in several different fashions, graphed and printed in numerous colors, seamlessly incorporated within a different report, reformatted for use as a presentation graphic, faxed to another location, and there treated to an additional cycle of processing.

Barrett, Edward, ed. *Text, ConText, & Hypertext: Writing with & for the Computer.* Cambridge, MA: MIT Press, 1988, xxv. 368 pp. illus. $35. ISBN 0-262-02275-3.

Foley, Mary Jo. "PC Word Processing: The Era of New & Improved," *Datamation,* May 1, 1988. pp. 75–77.

Hewson, David. *Introduction to Desktop Publishing: A Guide to Buying & Using a Desktop Publishing System.* San Francisco: Chronicle Books, 1988. 112 pp. illus. pap. $18.95. ISBN 0-87701-565-1.

Jones, Robert. *DTP: The Complete Guide to Corporate Desktop Publishing.* New York: Cambridge University Press, 1988. 132 pp. illus. $39.50. pap. $19.95. ISBN 0-521-35179-0. pap. ISBN 0-521-35973-2.

Database Management Systems

The waxing sophistication of database management systems (DBMSs) has brought with it some disincentives for some individual, established consumers. The major programs are now so feature-rich that many users are wondering if the additional learning necessary to exploit them is truly justifiable. The complexity of these DBMSs has also lengthened the design, debugging, and distribution time frames, resulting in some consumer antipathy and cynicism. Considering the increasing pervasiveness of institutional computing, the benefits that might accrue from an economical in-house network, and the probability that existing databases are likely to contain redundant or poorly coordinated information, we seem to be getting to the point where a well-synthesized version of the enterprise's computing activities is merited. Although this would seem to be a cyclical process, no more radical than previous revisions to institutional record-keeping/statistical practices, it is daunting due to the practical and theoretical ramifications associated with computerized activities. Given the fact that not every director has either the desire or the expertise to devote to such a critical undertaking, outside consultants, with a firm grip on the standards pertinent to libraries and attuned to contemporary as well as future institutional initiatives, ought to be available to suggest incremental, evolutionary paths to achieve these ends. More research and publication are needed to address these issues.

Gorman, Michael. *Managing Databases: DBMS Evaluation and Selection,* vol. 2. Wellesley, MA: QED Information Science, 1988. 350 pp. $34.50. ISBN 0-89435-236-9.

Relational Database Management Systems

Relational database managers (RDBMSs) have been developed to employ the powers inherent in set theory to integrate relevant data, without requiring the "programmer" to explicitly call every individual item from the data file or files. Structured query language packages (SQLs) have been created to permit microcomputers to interrogate mainframes and large databases in a logical and reliable manner to achieve this end. The two levels of ANSI standard SQL have not been fully implemented as a commercially available product for computers of any size at the time of this writing. The largest barrier to the acceptance of SQLs at the present time is compatibility; very few databases are in this format and no products or programs appear to be capable of transforming or atomizing a DBMS into an RBMS. Some practical concerns, reflecting theoretical limitations of SQL, are yet to be resolved.

Ageloff, Roy. *Primer on SQL.* St. Louis, MO: Mosby, 1988. xv. 173 pp. illus. pap. $17.95. ISBN 0-8016-0085-5.

American National Standards Institute. *American National Standard for Information Systems: Database Language SQL, Approved October 16, 1986.* New York, 1986. 104 pp. $25. $5 shipping & handling. ANSI X3.135-1986.

Codd, E. F. "Fatal Flaws in SQL," Part 1, *Datamation,* August 15, 1988, pp. 45–48.

______. "Fatal Flaws in SQL," Part 2, *Datamation,* September 1, 1988, pp. 71–74.

Finkelstein, Richard, and Fabian Pascal. "SQL Database Management Systems," *Byte,* 13, no. 1 (January 1988) 111–144ff. Reviews six RBMSs.

Gardarin, Georges, and Patrick Valduriez. *Relational Databases and Knowledge Bases.* Reading, MA: Addison-Wesley, 1988. 416 pp. illus. $24.75. ISBN 0-201-09955-1.

Harrington, Jan L. "Concurrency Control in Multi-User Microcomputer Environments Database Management Systems," *Information & Management,* 13, no. 5 (December 1987), 223–232.

Jackson, Glenn A. *Relational Database Design with Microcomputer Applications.* Englewood Cliffs, NJ: Prentice-Hall, 1988. xii. 207 pp. illus. $27. ISBN 0-13-771841-1.

Kitsuregawa, Masaru, and Hidehiko Tanaka, eds. *Database Machines and Knowledge Base Machines.* Boston: Kluwer Academic, 1988. ix. 689 pp. illus. $85. ISBN 0-89838-257-2.

Sweet, Frank. *Consultant's Handbook of Database Design.* Jacksonville, FL: Boxes & Arrows, 1988. 80 pp. illus. pap. $6.50. ISBN 0-939479-03-6.

Hypertext

Hypertext is a form of associative database construction that relies upon a combination of hard- and software to manually and automatically knit information together in order to retrieve or discover related ideas and facts. This technology appears to be the realization of Vannevar Bush's Memex, the idealized scholarly work station. The sophistication of the various hardware and software packages varies considerably. The goal of these efforts is to facilitate the marshalling of relevant data, whether the data have been explicitly linked or through synthetic means. Personal information managers and Hypertext-like products are constructed to support extratextual annotations, buttons, that can be called upon through several different search keys, to retrieve data related to the inquiry. More solid theory and methodology will have to be developed and demonstrated before this software becomes widespread. The ability and willingness of the user to abstract and note the salient aspects of the data files in a way that will prove to be both apt and cogent have hardly been reduced to clear practice. More experience and experimentation are needed in order to generalize such a demanding application for the average user. Whether the average user, or successive user, is prepared to manage and effectively cope with such a potentially dynamic form of a database, and how this product category is ultimately related to the construction of expert systems and the tools of artificial intelligence, await considerable research.

Barker, D. "Digitalize Sound, Put It in Hypercard (MacRecorder)," *Byte,* (special edition), 13 (August 1988) 7–8ff.

Communications of the ACM, 31, no 7. The entire issue is devoted to Hypertext.

Conklin, Jeff. "Hypertext: An Introduction and Survey," *Computer,* 20 (September 1987) 17–41.

Harmon, Paul, and Ric Mayer. *Evaluating Knowledge Engineering Tools.* Menlo Park, CA: American Association for Artificial Intelligence, 1988. 75 pp. illus. $5. ISBN 0-929280-14-8.

Skuce, Doug, and John Sowa. *Knowledge Representation: Design Issues.* Menlo Park, CA: American Association for Artificial Intelligence, 1988. 85 pp. illus. $5. ISBN 0-929280-24-5.

Swaine, Michael. *Dr. Dobb's Essential Hypertalk Handbook.* Redwood, CA: M&T Publishing, 464 pp. illus. $24.95. ISBN 0-934375-98-4. $39.95 including disk. ISBN 0-934375-99-2.

Video Technology

High-definition television screens and ever-higher resolution CRTs are expected to become more widely available and affordable as research and market pressure bring these devices into greater circulation. The graphic outputs from descriptive and analytical programs are straining the existing resolution of personal computer displays. The beauty and power of the image is being increasingly appreciated and exploited through integrated "presentation" video programs that can generate and export quality graphics as slides and overhead projections. The challenge of aesthetically employing these increasingly sophisticated imaging programs during computation and for effective presentation—be it a slide, an illustration within the text of document, or a desktop publication—is in achieving the impression of a balanced, unified document, in combination with the appropriate amount of detail, clear layout, and the suppression of superfluous or distracting typefaces or ornamentation. The burden of synthesizing the overall postproduction of documents would seem to be coming to the point that individuals will only master the array of niceties after a protracted apprenticeship in a number of programs. Whether so-called "group ware" or networked document formulation is an answer to this quandary will be seen in the fullness of time.

Sweet, Frank. *Handbook of Data Driven Screen Design.* Jacksonville, FL: Boxes & Arrows, 1988. 80 pp. pap. $6.50. ISBN 0-939479-03-6.

Tufte, Edward R. *The Visual Display of Quantitative Information.* Cheshire, CT: Graphics Press, c1983. 197 pp. illus. $32. ISBN 0-9613921-0-X. A classic.

Printer Technology

The price/performance ratio of laser printers has continued to fall, with the increased interest in graphics and desktop publishing systems spurring software developers to provide sophisticated programs for nontechnical users. Color printers remain too costly for the majority of libraries, but the trend of decreasing prices is encouraging.

Tanaka, Y., and T. Abe. "Quantitative Analysis of Print Quality Features," *Journal of Imaging Technology,* 13, no. 6 (December 1987), 202–207.

Optical Character Recognition

Optical recognition systems or scanners are likewise witnessing a reduction in price. These devices offer users the opportunity to import extensive back files of data without incurring enormous inputting costs. Unlike manual input where the per unit cost of data acquisition remains approximately constant, the per unit costs of scanned data decline as more and more use is made of the device. As libraries extend their in-house databases to include scanned data it would be a signal service to alert peer institutions to the availability of these resources in order to minimize the duplication of these efforts. More and more of these devices are capable of transforming their inputs into ASCII characters, suitable for word processing and retrieval.

Kavan, S., T. Pavlidis, and H. Baird. "On the Recognition of Printed Characters of Any Font and Size," *IEEE Transactions on Pattern Analysis and Machine Intelligence,* 9, no. 2 (March 1987), 274–288.

Stover, Richard N. "Improved Scanners Challenge Manual Digitalizers," *Machine Design,* April 21, 1988, pp. 151–155.

Wright, Maury. "Affordable Image Scanners and Software Simplify the Design of Imaging Systems," *EDN,* March 31, 1987, pp. 75ff.

Audio Technology

Digital tape recording is currently the subject of intense scrutiny by the recording industry and the audio community. These devices offer the potential of vivid recordings, similar to that achieved in CD audio discs, and digitalized output suitable for manipulation and analysis by all manner of computers. Although their precise applications are difficult to predict, it seems safe to say that these devices will contribute to the overall digitalization of the environment. Libraries specializing in sound recordings will want to pay particular attention to this emerging product category. Voice recognition systems are continuing to make slow progress toward the goal of "conversational" computing. A great deal of fundamental research remains to be done.

Bristow, Geoff, ed. *Electronic Speech Recognition: Techniques, Technology and Applications.* New York: McGraw-Hill, 1986. xix. 395 pp. illus. $48.50. ISBN 0-07-007913-7.

Clements, M. A. "Voice Recognition Systems Can Be Designed to Serve a Variety of Purposes," *Industrial Engineering,* 19, no. 9 (September 1987), 44–57.

Herther, N. "Much Ado about DAT . . . Including an Interview about DAT (Digital Audio Tape)," *Database,* 10, no. 3 (June 1987), 116–121.

Klatt, D. H. "Review of Text-to-Speech Conversion for English [with a Recording of Selected Examples of the Historical Development of Synthetic Speech]," *Journal of the Acoustical Society of America,* 82 (September 1987), 737–793.

Lalonde, Daniel, and A. Duane Donnelly. "Voice Technology Speaks for Itself," *Computerworld,* May 16, 1988, pp. 71, 74–75, 78.

Facsimile Technology

Facsimile machines, faxes, have been enjoying a welcome renaissance. This technology, originally developed in the 1840s, has become a progressively more economical and widespread vehicle for document delivery. The protocols for this method of information exchange are still being worked out among participating institutions; no standard has emerged. The various packagings available for fax equipment—standalone models, add-in boards for personal computers, and portable models—have rapidly transformed this machine into a ubiquitous and virtually essential business tool.

Meeks, Brock N. "Fax Board Faire (10 Facsimile Transmission Add-on Boards)," *Byte,* 13, no. 9 (September 1988), 203–208ff.

Voros, G. L. "The Future Fax: A System-Solution Approach Needed." *Office,* 105, no. 5 (May 1987), 65–66.

Integrated Library Systems

No earthshaking innovation in the area of automated integrated library systems appeared in 1988. Each provider or developer has continued to strive to improve its product, without precipitating a stampede. One of the most deficient aspects of the automated library systems currently on the market is the want of support for or access to collateral word processing, spreadsheets, and nonbibliographic databases. A reasonably priced product such as this might do rather well at the low end of the market, garnering support from institutions that have yet to automate and those libraries that cannot justify two sets of machinery to pursue their automation goals.

Hildreth, C. R. "Library Networking in North America in the 1980s. Part I. The Dreams, the Realities," *The Electronic Library,* 5, no. 4 (August 1987), 222–228.

______. "Library Networking in North America in the 1980s. Part II. The Response of Bibliographic Utilities to Local, Integrated Systems," *The Electronic Library,* 5, no. 5 (October 1987), 270–275.

Martin, Susan K. "Library Networks: Trends and Issues," *Journal of Library Administration,* 8, no. 2 (Summer 1987), 27–34.

Summary and Outlook

The NeXT machine appeared to be the synthesis of high technology for personal computers in 1988, offering an array of advanced components in a sleek package. Whether the Mach kernel melded with version 4.3 BSD (the Berkeley extension of Unix) proves a popular choice, with users and developers alike, remains to be seen. Even if this aspect of the system is less than a howling success, the machine itself is likely to be quite influential within the personal computer design community. Users can expect to see emulations, clones, and "act-likes" offered in the future. That segment of the academic community with relatively deep pockets and the ambition to utilize the spectrum of technologies and types of information that can be addressed by the various components found in the machine can be expected to review it quite favorably. The marketing psychology—continue to tantalize after the initial roll-out—ought to give way after the evaluations are in and production capacity has been firmly established. This machine, and the trends its designers have sought to epitomize, should continue to be a significant locus of comment and activity in personal computing. More powerful personal computers partaking of the characteristics of work stations are going to be increasingly common. Considerable care will be required to size each machine for present and anticipated use within the institutional setting. The challenge to administrators to divine the correct mix of strategic, tactical, and operational computing capacity and personnel has never been greater.

Elsewhere, the electrons look to be in for another year of feverish transit.

Lancaster, Ian, and Villard McCarty, eds. *The Humanities Computing Yearbook.* New York: Oxford University Press, 1988. 404 pp. $59. ISBN 0-19-824442-8.

Tucker, Michael Jay. "Ready for What's Next?" *Unixworld,* 5, no. 11 (November 1988), 38–49.

Webster, Bruce F. "What's Next? Redefining Our Expectations of Personal Computing," *Macworld,* 6, no. 1 (January 1989), 108–117.

Williams, Michael R. *A History of Computing Technology.* Englewood Cliffs, NJ: Prentice-Hall, 1985. xi. 432 pp. $29. illus. ISBN 0-13-389917-9. Covers computing, broadly conceived, from the origins of numerical systems to 1968. Ample illustrations document the evolving machinery.

Zuboff, Shoshana. *In the Age of the Smart Machine: The Future of Work and Power.* New York: Basic Books, 1988. xix. 468 pp. illus. $19.95. ISBN 0-465-03212-5.

General Sources for Information about High Technology

Byte. Peterborough, NH: McGraw-Hill Information Systems. $29.95. ISSN 0360-5280. Twelve issues per year with supplement(s).

Communicationsweek. Box 2070, Manhasset, NY: CMP Publications. $75. ISSN 0746-8121. Fifty-two issues per year.

Computerworld. Framingham, MA: D. G. Communications. $48. ISSN 0010-4841. Fifty-two issues per year with additional supplements and special numbers.

Electronics. New York: McGraw-Hill Information Systems. $32. ISSN 0888-4909. Twenty-six issues per year.

Infoworld. Menlo Park, CA: C. W. Communications. $100. ISSN 0199-6649. Fifty-two issues per year.

Science. Washington, DC: American Association for the Advancement of Science. $75. ISSN 0036-8075. Fifty-two issues per year.

Scientific American. New York: Scientific American. $24. ISSN 0036-8733. Twelve issues per year. The October issues are devoted to the general topics of computing and computer technologies.

Technology Review. Cambridge, MA: Massachusetts Institute of Technology, Alumni Association. $27. ISSN 0040-1698. Eight issues per year.

Wall Street Journal. New York: Dow Jones. $250. ISSN 0270-9910. Five days a week.

Useful General Indexes

ACM Guide to Computing Literature. New York: Association for Computing Machinery. $150. ISSN 0149-1199. Annual.

CompuMath Citation Index. Philadelphia: Institute for Scientific Information. $950. ISSN 0730-6199. Three issues per year.

Computer & Control Abstracts. Piscataway, NJ: INSPEC/Institute of Electrical and Electronic Engineers. $880. ISSN 0036-8113. Twelve issues per year.

Computer and Information Systems Abstracts Journal. Bethesda, MD: Cambridge Scientific Abstracts. $800. ISSN 0191-9776. Twelve issues per year.

Computer Literature Index. Phoenix, AZ: Applied Computer Research. $148. ISSN 0270-4046. Four issues per year.

Micro Computer Index. Mountain View, CA: Database Services. $85. ISSN 8756-7040. Six issues per year.

A raft of more specific journals exist for virtually every heading employed in the bibliography.

Basic Publications for the Publisher and the Book Trade

Jean Peters
Librarian, R. R. Bowker Company

Bibliographies of the Book Trade

Gottlieb, Robin. *Publishing Children's Books in America, 1919–1976: An Annotated Bibliography.* New York: Children's Book Council, 1978. pap. $10.

Lee, Marshall. *Bookmaking: The Illustrated Guide to Design/Production/Editing.* New York: R. R. Bowker, 1980. $49.95. Bibliography is divided into four parts: Part 1 covers books and includes a general bibliography as well as extensive coverage of books on all technical aspects of bookmaking; Part 2 lists periodicals; Part 3 lists films, filmstrips, etc.; Part 4 lists other sources.

The Reader's Adviser: A Layman's Guide to Literature. 13th ed. New York: R. R. Bowker, 1986–88. $375. (Vols. 1–6); $75 each vol. Vol. 1. *The Best in American and British Fiction, Poetry, Essays, Literary Biography, Bibliography, and Reference,* edited by Fred Kaplan. Vol. 2. *The Best in American and British Drama and World Literature in English Translation*, edited by Maurice Charney. Vol. 3. *The Best in the Reference Literature of the World*, edited by Paula Kaufman. Vol. 4. *The Best in the Literature of Philosophy and World Religions*, edited by William Reese. Vol. 5. *The Best in the Literature of Science, Technol-*

ogy, and Medicine*, edited by Paul T. Durbin. Vol. 6. Index.

Tanselle, G. Thomas. *Guide to the Study of United States Imprints.* 2 vols. Cambridge, MA: Belknap Press of Harvard University Press, 1971. $90. Includes sections on general studies of American printing and publishing as well as studies of individual printers and publishers.

Trade Bibliographies

American Book Publishing Record Cumulative, 1876–1949: An American National Bibliography. 15 vols. New York: R. R. Bowker, 1980. o.p.

American Book Publishing Record Cumulative, 1950–1977: An American National Bibliography. 15 vols. New York: R. R. Bowker, 1979. o.p.

American Book Publishing Record Cumulative, 1876–1982. New York: R. R. Bowker. Microfiche $999.

American Book Publishing Record Five-Year Cumulatives. New York: R. R. Bowker, 1970–1974 Cumulative. 4 vols. $150. 1975–1979 Cumulative. 5 vols. $175. 1980–1984 Cumulative. 5 vols. $199. Annual vols.: 1979–1984, $100 ea.; 1985, $119.95; 1987, $123.45.

Books in Print. 7 vols. New York: R. R. Bowker, ann. $279.95. fiche $699.

Books in Print Supplement. New York: R. R. Bowker, ann. $159.95.

Books in Series in the United States. 4th ed. New York: R. R. Bowker, 1984. 6 vols. $349.

British Books in Print. New York: R. R. Bowker, 1985. $261.25 (plus duty where applicable).

Canadian Books in Print, edited by Marian Butler. Toronto: University of Toronto Press, ann. $70.

Canadian Books in Print: Subject Index, edited by Marian Butler. Toronto: University of Toronto Press, ann. $55.

Complete Directory of Large Print Books and Serials. New York: R. R. Bowker, ann. $66.95.

Cumulative Book Index. New York: Wilson. Monthly with bound semiannual and larger cumulations. Service basis.

El-Hi Textbooks and Serials in Print. New York: R. R. Bowker, ann. $85.

Forthcoming Books. New York: R. R. Bowker. $162. Bimonthly supplement to *Books in Print* and *Subject Guides to Books in Print.*

On Cassette: A Comprehensive Bibliography of Spoken Word Audiocassettes. New York: R. R. Bowker, 1988/89. $90.25.

Paperbound Books in Print. New York: R. R. Bowker. Spring, 1988, 3-vol. set $123.45. Fall, 1988, 3-vol. set $132.95.

Publishers' Trade List Annual. New York: R. R. Bowker, ann. 4 vols. $179.95.

Reginald, Robert, and Burgess, M. R. *Cumulative Paperback Index, 1939–59.* Detroit: Gale, 1973. $64.

Small Press Record of Books in Print, edited by Len Fulton. Paradise, CA: Dustbooks, 1988. $35.95.

Subject Guide to Books in Print. 4 vols. New York: R. R. Bowker, ann. $189.95.

Book Publishing

Education and Practice

Bailey, Herbert S., Jr. *The Art and Science of Book Publishing.* Austin: University of Texas Press, 1980. pap. o.p.

Biggs, Mary. *Publishers and Librarians: A Foundation for Dialogue.* Chicago: University of Chicago Press, 1984. pap. $5.95.

Bodian, Nat G. *Bodian's Publishing Desk Reference: A Comprehensive Dictionary of Practices and Techniques for Book and Journal Marketing and Bookselling.* Phoenix, AZ: Oryx, 1988. $49.

______. *Book Marketing Handbook: Tips and Techniques for the Sale and Promotion of Scientific, Technical, Professional, and Scholarly Books and Journals.* New York: R. R. Bowker, 1980. $64.95.

______. *Book Marketing Handbook, Volume Two: 1,000 More Tips and Techniques for the Sale and Promotion of Scientific, Technical, Professional, and Scholarly Books and Journals.* New York: R. R. Bowker, 1983. $64.95.

______. *Copywriter's Handbook: A Practical Guide for Advertising and Promotion of Specialized and Scholarly Books and Journals.* Philadelphia: ISI Press, 1984. pap. $29.95.

Carter, Robert A. *Trade Book Marketing: A Practical Guide.* New York: R. R. Bowker, 1983. pap. $24.95.

Dessauer, John P. *Book Publishing: What It Is, What It Does.* New York: R. R. Bowker, 1981. $29.95. pap. $19.95.

Glaister, Geoffrey. *Glaister's Glossary of the Book: Terms Used in Paper-Making, Printing, Bookbinding, and Publishing.* 2nd ed., completely rev. Berkeley: University of California Press, 1979. $75.

Grannis, Chandler B., ed. *What Happens in Book Publishing.* 2nd ed. New York: Columbia University Press, 1967. $40.

Greenfeld, Howard. *Books: From Writer to Reader.* Rev. ed. 1988. New York: Crown, pap. $12.95.

Gross, Gerald. *Editors on Editing.* Rev. ed. New York: Harper & Row, 1985. $22.45. pap. $13.95.

Huenefeld, John. *The Huenefeld Guide to Book Publishing.* Bedford, MA: Huenefeld, 1986. $185.

McCormack, Thomas. *The Fiction Editor, the Novel, and the Novelist.* New York: St. Martin's Press, 1988. $12.95.

Mora, Imre. *Publisher's Practical Dictionary in 20 Languages.* Munich: K. G. Saur, 1984. $65.

Peters, Jean, ed. *Bookman's Glossary.* 6th ed. New York: R. R. Bowker, 1983. $34.95.

Powell, Walter W. *Getting into Print: The Decision-making Process in Scholarly Publishing.* Chicago: University of Chicago Press, 1985. $19.95.

Poynter, Dan. *The Self-Publishing Manual: How to Write, Print and Sell Your Own Book.* Santa Barbara, CA: Para, 1986. $14.95.

______, and Kent, Charles. *Publishing Contracts: Sample Agreements on Disk.* Santa Barbara, CA: Para, 1987. $29.95.

Richards, Pamela Spence. *Marketing Books and Journals to Western Europe.* Phoenix, AZ: Oryx, 1985. pap.

Smith, Datus. *A Guide to Book Publishing.* Rev. ed. Seattle: University of Washington Press, 1989. $25. pap. $12.50.

Analysis, Statistics, Surveys

Altbach, Philip G., Arboleda, Amadio A., and Gopinathan, S., eds. *Publishing in the Third World: Knowledge and Development.* Portsmouth, NH: Heinemann Educational Books, 1985. $35.

Altbach, Philip G., and Rathgeber, Eva-Marie. *Publishing in the Third World: Trend Report and Bibliography.* New York: Praeger, 1980. $40.95.

Arthur Andersen & Co. *Book Distribution in the U.S.: Issues and Perceptions.* New York: Book Industry Study Group, 1982. $60.

Association of American Publishers 1987 Industry Statistics. New York: Association of American Publishers, 1988. Nonmemb. $350.

Association of American Publishers. *1989 Survey of Compensation and Personnel Practices in the Publishing Industry.* Prepared and conducted by Sibson & Co., Inc. New York: Association of American Publishers, 1989. Available only to AAP members. $225 (participating members); $435 (others).

Bowker Annual of Library and Book Trade Information. New York: R. R. Bowker, ann. $110.

Center for Book Research. University of Scranton. *Book Industry Trends 1988.* New York: Book Industry Study Group, 1988. $200; $40 to members.

Coser, Lewis A., Kadushin, Charles, and Powell, Walter W. *Books: The Culture and Commerce of Publishing.* Chicago: University of Chicago Press, 1985. pap. $13.95.

Fox, Mary F., ed. *Scholarly Writing and Publishing: Issues, Problems, and Solutions.* Boulder, CO: Westview, 1985. $39. pap. $17.95.

Geiser, Elizabeth, and Dolin, Arnold, eds. *The Business of Book Publishing.* Boulder, CO: Westview, 1985. $46.

Kozol, Jonathan. *Illiterate America.* Garden City, NY: NAL; 1986. pap. $6.95.

Long, Elizabeth. *The American Dream and the Popular Novel.* Boston: Routledge & Kegan Paul, 1985. $22.50.

Machlup, Fritz, and Leeson, Kenneth W. *Information through the Printed Word: The Dissemination of Scholarly, Scientific, and Intellectual Knowledge,* 4 vols. Vol. 1. *Book Publishing.* Vol. 2. *Journals.* Vol. 3. *Libraries.* Vol. 4. *Books, Journals, and Bibliographic Services.* New York: Praeger, 1978. Vol. 1, $44.95; Vol. 2, $44.95; Vol. 3, $42.95; Vol. 4, $44.95.

Nell, Victor. *Lost in a Book: The Psychology of Reading for Pleasure.* New Haven, CT: Yale University Press, 1988. $32.50.

1983 Consumer Research Study on Reading and Book Purchasing. New York: American Booksellers Association, 1984. 3 vols. $35. $19.95 to members.

Publishing—The Future, edited by Peter Owen. A collection of essays by leading publishers, issued to coincide with the International Publishers Congress, June 1988. London: Peter Owen, 1988. pap. £6.95.

Shatzkin, Leonard. *In Cold Type: Overcoming the Book Crisis.* Boston: Houghton Mifflin, 1983. pap. $8.95.

Trends Update, prepared by Robert F. Winter Statistical Services Center for the Book Industry Study Group. New York: BISG, irreg. Expands upon statistics in the annual *Book Industry Trends* and explains forecasting techniques. $240/year; $25 to members.

Walters, Ray. *Paperback Talk.* Derived from the author's column "Paperback Talk" and articles contributed by him to *The New York Times Book Review.* With an introduction by Ian and Betty Ballantine. Chicago: Academy Chicago, 1985. $19.95. pap. $9.95.

Whiteside, Thomas. *The Blockbuster Complex.* Middletown, CT: Wesleyan University Press. Dist. by Columbia University Press, 1981. o.p.

History

Bruccoli, Matthew J. *The Fortunes of Mitchell Kennerley, Bookman.* San Diego, CA: Harcourt Brace Jovanovich, 1986. $24.95.

Cave, Roderick. *The Private Press.* New York: R. R. Bowker, 1983. $64.95.

Cerf, Bennett. *At Random: The Reminiscences of Bennett Cerf.* New York: Random House, 1977. $16.45.

Crider, Allen Billy. *Mass Market Publishing in America.* Boston: G. K. Hall, 1982. $40.50.

Davis, Kenneth C. *Two-Bit Culture: The Paperbacking of America.* Boston: Houghton Mifflin, 1984. $18.95. pap. $9.95.

Dennison, Sally. [*Alternative*] *Literary Publishing: Five Modern Histories.* Iowa City: University of Iowa Press, 1984. $18.50. pap. $10.95.

Dzwonkoski, Peter, ed. *American Literary Publishing Houses, 1900–1980: Trade and Paperback.* (*Dictionary of Literary Biography,* vol. 46). Detroit: Gale, 1986. $95.

______. *American Literary Publishing Houses, 1638–1899.* 2 vols. (*Dictionary of Literary Biography,* vol. 49). Detroit: Gale, 1986. $190.

Hall, Max. *Harvard University Press: A History.* Cambridge, MA: Harvard University Press, 1986. $22.50; pap. $8.95.

Haydn, Hiram. *Words & Faces.* New York: Harcourt Brace Jovanovich, 1974. $8.95.

Joyce, Donald F. *Gatekeepers of Black Culture: Black-owned Book Publishing in the United States.* Westport, CT: Greenwood, 1983. $35.

Madison, Charles. *Jewish Publishing in America.* New York: Hebrew Publishing Co., 1976. $15.

Morpurgo, J. E. *Allen Lane: King Penguin.* New York: Methuen, 1980. $25.

Regnery, Henry. *Memoirs of a Dissident Publisher.* New York: Regnery Gateway, 1979. $12.95.

Silverman, Al, ed. *The Book of the Month: Sixty Years of Books in American Life.* Boston: Little, Brown, 1986. $17.95.

Tebbel, John. *Between Covers: The Rise and Transformation of Book Publishing in America.* New York: Oxford University Press, 1987. $24.95.

______. *A History of Book Publishing in the United States.* 4 vols. Vol. 1. *The Creation of an Industry, 1630–1865.* Vol. 2. *The Expansion of an Industry, 1865–1919.* Vol. 3. *The Golden Age between Two Wars, 1920–1940.* Vol. 4. *The Great Change, 1940–1980.* New York: R. R. Bowker, 1972, 1975, 1978, 1981. o.p.

Book Design and Production

Grannis, Chandler B. *The Heritage of the Graphic Arts.* New York: R. R. Bowker, 1972. o.p.

Lee, Marshall. *Bookmaking: The Illustrated Guide to Design and Production.* 2nd ed. New York: R. R. Bowker, 1980. $49.95.

Mintz, Patricia Barnes. *Dictionary of Graphic Arts Terms: A Communication Tool for People Who Buy Type & Printing.* New York: Van Nostrand Reinhold, 1981. $26.95.

Rice, Stanley. *Book Design: Systematic Aspects.* New York: R. R. Bowker, 1978. $29.95.

______. *Book Design: Text Format Models.* New York: R. R. Bowker, 1978. $29.95.

White, Jan. *Editing by Design.* 2nd ed. New

York: R. R. Bowker, 1982, pap. $34.95.

Williamson, Hugh. *Methods of Book Design: The Practice of an Industrial Craft.* 3rd ed. New Haven, CT: Yale University Press, 1983. $45. pap. $14.95.

Wilson, Adrian. *The Design of Books.* Layton, UT: Gibbs M. Smith, 1974. pap. o.p.

Bookselling

Coopers & Lybrand. *Non-traditional Retail Outlet Sales Study.* New York: Book Industry Study Group, 1988. $450; $50 to members.

Gilbert Dale L. *Complete Guide to Starting a Used Bookstore.* Chicago: Chicago Review Press, 1986. $11.95.

Hale, Robert D. *Manual on Bookselling: How to Open and Run a Bookstore.* 4th ed. New York: American Booksellers Association, 1987. Dist. by Harmony Books. $16.95.

Censorship

de Grazia, Edward, comp. *Censorship Landmarks.* New York: R. R. Bowker, 1969. o.p.

The First Freedom Today: Critical Issues Relating to Censorship and Intellectual Freedom, edited by Robert B. Downs and Ralph F. McCoy. Chicago: American Library Association, 1984. $40.

Gregorian, Vartan. *Censorship: Five Hundred Years of Conflict.* New York: Oxford University Press, 1984. $32.50.

Haight, Anne Lyon. *Banned Books.* 4th ed., updated and enlarged by Chandler B. Grannis. New York: R. R. Bowker, 1978. o.p.

Hentoff, Nat. *The First Freedom: The Tumultuous History of Free Speech in America.* New York: Delacorte, 1980. $16.95.

Hurwitz, Leon. *Historical Dictionary of Censorship in the United States.* Westport, CT: Greenwood, 1985. $56.95.

Jenkinson, Edward B. *Censors in the Classroom: The Mind Benders.* New York: Avon, 1982. pap. $3.50.

Copyright

Johnston, Donald F. *Copyright Handbook.* 2nd ed. New York: R. R. Bowker, 1982. $34.95.

Strong, William S. *The Copyright Book: A Practical Guide.* Cambridge, MA: MIT Press, 1984. $14.95.

Editing

Barzun, Jacques. *Simple and Direct: A Rhetoric for Writers.* New York: Harper & Row, 1985. $15. pap. $7.95.

Bernstein, Theodore. *The Careful Writer.* New York: Atheneum, 1965. pap. $12.95.

The Chicago Manual of Style, 13th rev. ed. Chicago: University of Chicago Press, 1982. $37.50.

Fowler, H. W. *Dictionary of Modern English Usage.* 2nd rev. ed. New York: Oxford University Press, 1987. $22.95.

Jordan, Lewis. *The New York Times Manual of Style and Usage.* New York: Times Books, 1982. pap. $6.95.

Plotnik, Arthur. *The Elements of Editing: A Modern Guide for Editors and Journalists.* New York: Macmillan, 1986. pap. $4.95.

Skillin, Marjorie E., and Gay, Robert M. *Words into Type.* Rev. ed. Englewood Cliffs, NJ: Prentice-Hall, 1974. $35.95.

Strunk, William, Jr., and White, E. B. *The Elements of Style.* 3rd ed. New York: Macmillan, 1979. pap. $3.95.

Zinsser, William. *On Writing Well: An Informal Guide to Writing Nonfiction.* 3rd ed. New York: Harper & Row, 1985. $12.95.

Editors, Agents, Authors

Appelbaum, Judith. *How to Get Happily Published.* New York: Harper, 3d ed., 1988. $8.95.

Berg, A. Scott. *Max Perkins: Editor of Genius.* New York: Washington Square Press, 1983. pap. $5.95.

Commins, Dorothy Berliner. *What Is an Editor? Saxe Commins at Work.* Chicago: University of Chicago Press, 1978. pap. $5.95.

Curtis, Richard. *How to Be Your Own Literary Agent.* Boston: Houghton Mifflin, 1983. $12.95. pap. $8.95.

Dill, Barbara. *The Journalist's Handbook on Libel and Privacy.* New York: Free Press, 1986. $19.95.

Henderson, Bill, ed. *The Art of Literary Publishing: Editors on Their Craft.* Yonkers, NY: Pushcart, 1980. $15.

Meyer, Carol. *Writer's Survival Manual: The Complete Guide to Getting Your Book Published.* New York: Crown, 1982. $13.95. Bantam, 1984, pap. $4.50.

Unseld, Siegfried. *The Author and His Publisher.* Chicago: University of Chicago Press, 1980. $15.

Electronic Publishing

Bove, Tony. *The Art of Desktop Publishing: Using Personal Computers to Publish It Yourself.* New York: Bantam, 1986. $18.95.

CD-ROMs in Print. Westport, CT: Meckler, 1989. $37.50.

Desktop Publishing Bible, edited by James Stockford. Indianapolis, IN: Howard W. Sams, 1987. $24.95.

Kleper, Michael L. *The Illustrated Handbook of Desktop Publishing and Typesetting.* Blue Ridge Summit, PA: TAB Professional and Reference Books, 1987. $49.95; pap. $29.95.

Lichty, Tom. *Design Principles for Desktop Publishers.* Glenview, IL: Scott, Foresman, 1989. $19.95.

Standera, Oldrich. *The Electronic Era of Publishing: An Overview of Concepts, Technologies, and Methods.* New York: Elsevier, 1987. $39.95.

White, Jan V. *Graphic Design for the Electronic Age.* New York: Watson-Guptill, 1988. $24.95.

Book Trade Directories and Yearbooks

American and Canadian

American Book Trade Directory, 1988–89. New York: R. R. Bowker, ann. $159.95.

Chernofsky, Jacob L., ed. *AB Bookman's Yearbook.* Clifton, NJ: AB Bookman's Weekly, ann. $20; free to subscribers to *AB Bookman's Weekly.*

The Community of the Book: A Directory of Selected Organizations and Programs, compiled by Maurvine Williams; edited and with an introduction by John Y. Cole. Rev. ed. Washington, DC: Library of Congress, 1989. Price not set.

Fulton, Len, and Ferber, Ellen. *Directory of Poetry Publishers, 1985–86.* Paradise, CA: Dustbooks, 1985. pap. $9.95.

Kim, Ung Chon. *Policies of Publishers.* Metuchen, NJ: Scarecrow, 1982. pap. $16.50.

Kremer, John. *Directory of Book, Catalog, and Magazine Printers.* Fairfield, IA: Ad-Lib, 1987. $15.

Literary Agents of North America. New York: Author Aid-Research Associates, 1988. $19.95.

Literary Market Place, 1988, with Names & Numbers. New York: R. R. Bowker, ann. $85.

Publishers Directory, edited by Linda S. Hubbard. Detroit: Gale, 1989. $195; Supp. $155.

Publishers, Distributors, & Wholesalers of the United States: A Directory. New York: R. R. Bowker, 1988–1989. $95.

Foreign and International

International Directory of Little Magazines and Small Presses 1988–89. Paradise, CA: Dustbooks. ann. $22.95.

International ISBN Publishers' Directory. Berlin: International ISBN Agency, 1988. Dist. by R. R. Bowker. $175.

International Literary Market Place 1988–89. New York: R. R. Bowker. $119.95.

Publishers' International Directory. 2 vols. New York: K. G. Saur, 1988. $275.

Taubert, Sigfred, ed. *The Book Trade of the World.* Vol. I. *Europe and International Sections.* Vol. II. *U.S.A., Canada, Central and South America, Australia and New Zealand.* Vol. III. *Asia.* Vol. IV. *Africa.* New York: K. G. Saur. Vol. I, 1972, $70; Vol. II, 1976, $70; Vol. III, 1980, $70; Vol. IV, 1984, $70.

UNESCO Statistical Yearbook, 1988. Lanham, MD: Unipub, 1989. pap. Price not set.

Newspapers and Periodicals

Directory of Small Magazine-Press Editors and Publishers, edited by Len Fulton and Ellen Ferber. Paradise, CA: Dustbooks, 1987. $16.95.

Editor and Publisher International Year Book. New York: Editor and Publisher. ann. 1988. $70.

Gale Directory of Publications, 1988. Detroit: Gale. $145.

The Serials Directory: An International Reference Book. 3 vols. Birmingham, AL: Ebsco, 1988–1989. $289.

Sources of Serials: An International Publisher and Corporate Author Directory to Ulrich's and Irregular Serials. New York: R. R. Bowker, 1981. o.p.

Standard Periodical Directory, edited by Patricia Hagood. New York: Oxbridge Communications, 1988. $325.

Ulrich's International Periodicals Directory including Irregular Serials & Annuals. 3 vols. New York: R. R. Bowker, 1988–1989. $279.95.

Working Press of the Nation: Newspapers, Magazines, Radio and TV, and Internal Publications. Chicago: National Research Bureau, 1988. 5 vols. $260.

Periodicals

AB Bookman's Weekly (weekly including yearbook). Clifton, NJ: AB Bookman's Weekly. $70.

American Book Publishing Record (monthly). New York: R. R. Bowker. $90.

The American Bookseller (monthly). New York: American Booksellers Association. $24.

Book Research Quarterly. New Brunswick, NJ: Transaction Periodicals Consortium. Individuals $30; institutions $50.

BP Report: On the Business of Book Publishing (weekly). White Plains, NY: Knowledge Industry Publications. $315.

EP&P: Electronic Printing & Publishing (bimonthly) Chicago: Maclean Hunter. $35.

Electronic and Optical Publishing Review (quarterly). Medford, NJ: Learned Information, Inc. $75.

Publishers Weekly. New York: R. R. Bowker. $94.

Scholarly Publishing: A Journal for Authors & Publishers (quarterly). Toronto: University of Toronto Press. $37.50.

Small Press: The Magazine and Book Review of Independent Publishing (bimonthly). Westport, CT: Meckler. $29.95.

Weekly Record. New York: R. R. Bowker. $110. A weekly listing of current American book publications, providing complete cataloging information.

American National Standards for Libraries, Publishers, and Information Services

National Information Standards Organization (NISO)
Box 1056, Bethesda, MD 20817
301-975-2814

The American National Standards that follow were developed by the National Information Standards Organization. For 50 years, NISO has developed voluntary consensus standards that are used by libraries, information services, and publishers. These American National Standards cover many aspects of library science, publishing, and information services, such as information transfer, forms and records, identification systems, publication formats, transliteration, and preservation of materials. These standards address the application of both traditional and new technologies to information services. All of them may be obtained at the prices noted from Transaction Publishers, Rutgers University, New Brunswick, New Jersey 08903 (201-932-2280). For more information on the work of the National Information Standards Organization, contact NISO, Box 1056, Bethesda, MD 20817. A list of new standards now in development is free on request.

American National Standards

Book Production and Publication

Z39.4-1984 Basic Criteria for Indexes, $14
Z39.6-1983 Trade Catalogs, $10
Z39.8-1977 Compiling Book Publishing Statistics, $10 (reaffirmed 1982)
Z39.13-1979 Describing Books in Advertisements, Catalogs, Promotional Materials, and Book Jackets, $10 (reaffirmed 1984)
Z39.14-1979 Writing Abstracts, $12 (reaffirmed 1987)
Z39.15-1980 Title Leaves of a Book, $10
Z39.20-1983 Price Indexes for Library Materials, $10
Z39.21-1980 Book Numbering (ISBN), $10
Z39.22-1981 Proof Corrections, $14
Z39.29-1977 Bibliographic References, $30
Z39.30-1982 Order Form for Single Titles of Library Materials in a 3-Inch by 5-Inch Format, $12
Z39.40-1979 Compiling U.S. Microform Publishing Statistics, $10 (reaffirmed 1987)
Z39.41-1979 Book Spine Formats, $10
Z39.43-1980 Identification Code for the Book Industry, $10
Z39.49-1985 Computerized Book Ordering, $30
Z39.52-1987 Standard Order Form for Multiple Titles of Library Materials, $14

Codes and Numbering Systems

Z39.9-1979 International Standard Serial Numbering, $10 (reaffirmed 1984)
Z39.21-1980 Book Numbering (ISBN), $10
Z39.23-1983 Standard Technical Report Number (STRN), Format and Creation, $10
Z39.27-1984 Structure for the Representation of Names of Countries, Dependencies, and Areas of Special Sovereignty for Information Interchange, $10
Z39.33-1977 Development of Identification Codes for Use by the Bibliographic Community, $10 (reaffirmed 1988)
Z39.43-1980 Identification Code for the Book Industry (SAN), $10
Z39.47-1985 Extended Latin Alphabet Coded Character Set for Bibliographic Use (ALA Character Set), $16
Z39.53-1987 Codes for the Representation of Languages for Information Interchange, $30

Indexes and Thesauri

Z39.4-1984 Basic Criteria for Indexes, $14
Z39.19-1980 Guidelines for Thesaurus Structure, Construction and Use, $12
Z39.20-1983 Price Indexes for Library Materials, $10

Microforms

Z39.26-1981 Advertising of Micropublications, $10
Z39.32-1981 Information on Microfiche Headings, $12

Z39.40-1979	Compiling U.S. Microform Publishing Statistics, $10 (reaffirmed 1987)

Acquisitions and Ordering

Z39.30-1982	Order Form for Single Titles of Library Materials, $12
Z39.49-1985	Computerized Book Ordering, $30
Z39.52-1987	Standard Order Form for Multiple Titles of Library Materials, $14

Romanization

Z39.11-1972	Romanization of Japanese, $10 (reaffirmed 1983)
Z39.12-1972	Romanization of Arabic, $10 (reaffirmed 1984)
Z39.24-1976	Romanization of Slavic Cyrillic Characters, $10
Z39.25-1975	Romanization of Hebrew, $12
Z39.35-1979	Romanization of Lao, Khmer, and Pali, $12
Z39.37-1979	Romanization of Armenian, $10

Technical Reports and Papers

Z39.16-1979	Preparation of Scientific Papers for Written or Oral Presentation, $12 (reaffirmed 1985)
Z39.18-1987	Scientific and Technical Reports—Organization, Preparation, and Production, $20
Z39.23-1983	Standard Technical Report Number (STRN), Format and Creation, $10
Z39.29-1977	Bibliographic References, $30
Z39.31-1976	Format for Scientific and Technical Translations, $10 (reaffirmed 1983)
Z39.46-1983	Identification of Bibliographic Data on and Relating to Patent Documents, $10
Z39.61-1987	Recording, Use, and Display of Patent Application Data in Printed and Computer-Readable Publications and Services, $30

Serial Publications

Z39.1-1977	Periodicals: Format and Arrangement, $12
Z39.5-1985	Abbreviation of Titles of Publications, $12
Z39.9-1979	International Standard Serial Numbering, $10 (reaffirmed 1984)
Z39.16-1979	Preparation of Scientific Papers for Written or Oral Presentation, $12 (reaffirmed 1985)
Z39.20-1983	Criteria for Price Indexes for Library Materials, $10
Z39.29-1977	Bibliographic References, $30
Z39.30-1982	Order Form for Single Titles of Library Materials in a 3-Inch by 5-Inch Format, $12
Z39.34-1977	Synoptics, $12 (reaffirmed 1983)
Z39.39-1979	Compiling Newspaper and Periodical Publishing Statistics, $10 (reaffirmed 1988)

Z39.44-1986 Serials Holdings Statements, $30
Z39.45-1983 Claims for Missing Issues of Serials, $12
Z39.46-1983 Identification of Bibliographic Data on and Relating to Patent Documents, $10
Z39.61-1987 Recording, Use, and Display of Patent Application Data in Printed and Computer-Readable Publications and Services, $30

Statistics

Z39.7-1983 Library Statistics, $20
Z39.8-1977 Compiling Book Publishing Statistics, $10 (reaffirmed 1982)
Z39.39-1979 Compiling Newspaper and Periodical Publishing Statistics, $10 (reaffirmed 1988)
Z39.40-1979 Compiling U.S. Microform Publishing Statistics, $10 (reaffirmed 1987)

Automation

Z39.2-1985 Bibliographic Information Interchange, $12
Z39.44-1986 Serials Holdings Statements, $30
Z39.45-1983 Claims for Missing Issues of Serials, $12
Z39.49-1985 Computerized Book Ordering, $30
Z39.50-1988 Information Retrieval Service Definition and Protocol Specification for Library Applications, $35
Z39.52-1987 Standard Order Form for Multiple Titles of Library Materials, $14
Z39.53-1987 Codes for the Representation of Languages for Information Interchange, $30

Development and Approval of NISO Standards

The American National Standards in the preceding list were developed by the National Information Standards Organization. They were prepared by volunteer Standards Committees, which draw on expert opinion from a variety of disciplines. NISO standards are reviewed regularly and revised when necessary. NISO's voting membership, which participates in the formal review and approval of these standards, includes the following organizations:

American Association of Law Libraries
American Chemical Society
American Library Association
American Psychological Association
American Society for Information Science
American Society of Indexers
American Theological Library Association
Apple Computer, Inc.
Aspen Systems Corporation
Association for Information and Image Management (AIIM)

Association for Recorded Sound (ARSC)
Association of American Publishers (AAP)
Association of American University Presses (AAUP)
Association of Information and Dissemination Centers
Association of Jewish Libraries
Association of Research Libraries
AT&T Bell Laboratories
Blue Bear Group, Inc.
Book Manufacturers' Institute
CAPCON Library Network
Catholic Library Association
Colorado Alliance of Research Libraries (CARL)
Cooperative College Library Center (CCLC)
Council of Biology Editors
Council of National Library and Information Associations
Data Research Associates, Inc.
DYNIX, Inc.
EBSCONET
Faxon, Inc.
Geovision, Inc.
Indiana Cooperative Library Services Authority (INCOLSA)
Information Industry Association
Information Workstation Group, Inc.
Library Binding Institute
Library of Congress
Medical Library Association
MINITEX
Music Library Association
National Agricultural Library
National Archives and Records Administration
National Commission on Libraries and Information Science (NCLIS)
National Federation of Abstracting and Information Services (NFAIS)
National Institute of Standards and Technology Research Information Center, Information Resources and Services Division
National Library of Medicine
OCLC, Inc.
OHIONET
Optical Publishing Association
PALINET
Philips New Media Systems
Pittsburgh Regional Library Center (PRLC)
Reference Technology, Inc.
Research Libraries Group, Inc.
Society for Technical Communication
Special Libraries Association
SUNY/OCLC Network
U.S. Department of Commerce, National Technical Information Service (NTIS)
U.S. Department of Commerce, Printing and Publishing Division
U.S. Department of Defense, Army Library Management Office

U.S. Department of Defense, Defense Standardization Program Office
U.S. Department of Energy, Office of Scientific & Technical Information (OSTI)
U.S. ISBN Maintenance Agency
University Microflims, Inc.
University of Pittsburgh
Waldenbooks
H. W. Wilson Company

New Standards in Development

The draft standards listed below were developed by (and can be ordered from) the National Information Standards Organization.

Z39.1 (revision) *Periodicals: Format and Arrangement,* $25. Recommends publication practices to facilitate identification and use of periodicals and their component parts and access to and retention of publications over time.

Z39.41 (revision) *Book Spine Format,* $25. Specifies the information that should be shown on the spine of a book and the manner in which it should be displayed, so that book designers and publishers can produce spine formats that will facilitate the locating of books by librarians, scholars, and others.

Z39.55 (new) *Computerized Serials Orders, Claims, Cancellations, and Acknowledgements,* $25. Presents a variable-length format for placing computerized serials orders, claims, cancellations, and acknowledgments, and also provides a fixed-record structure. Covers monographic series, annuals, periodicals, journals, reports, proceedings, and so on.

Z39.56 (new) *Serial Issue and Article Identifier,* $15. Defines the requirements for providing in coded form an identifier for each issue of a serial and each item published in a serial.

Z39.57 (new) *Holdings Statements for Non-Serial Items,* $25. Sets forth display requirements for holdings statements for nonserial items to promote consistency in the communication and exchange of such information by institutions. All formats of material are covered by the standard, and provisions are set out for both compressed and itemized holdings statements. The standard defines a basic structure for nonserial holdings statements consisting of five data areas (Item Identification Area, Location Data Area, Extent of Holdings Area, Note Area, and Date Area), of which only the first two are mandatory. The document includes an appendix with examples of holdings statements created according to the standard.

Z39.58 (new) *Common Command Language for Online Interactive Information Retrieval,* $25. Specifies the vocabulary, syntax, and operational meaning of commands in a command language for use with online interactive information retrieval systems. The text of the standard is intended to give guidance to designers of information retrieval systems, including online library catalogs and "gateway" or "front-end" database access and search facilities.

Z39.62 (new) *Eye Legible Information on Microfilm Leaders and Trailers and on Containers of Processed Microfilm on Open Reels,* $25. Specifies the eye-readable information on leaders and trailers of microfilm and on the containers of processed microfilm. The standard specifies the location of elements, the order of elements in each location, and the minimum type size.

Ready Reference

Publishers' Toll-Free Telephone Numbers

Publishers' toll-free numbers continue to play an important role in ordering, verification, and customer service. This year's list comes from *Publishers, Distributors, and Wholesalers of the United States* (R. R. Bowker) and includes distributors and regional toll-free numbers, where applicable.

Publisher/Distributor	Toll-Free No.
ABC-Clio, Santa Barbara, CA	800-422-2546; CA 800-824-2103
ACS Publications, San Diego, CA	800-637-2312; CA 800-826-1085
AFCEA International Press, Fairfax, VA	800-336-4583
APL Press, Rockville, MD	800-592-0050
A.R.E. Press, Virginia Beach, VA	800-368-2727
ASQC Quality Press, Milwaukee, WI	800-952-6587
Abbeville Press, New York, NY	800-227-7210
Abilene Christian University Press, Abilene, TX	800-444-4228
Abingdon Press, Nashville, TN	800-251-3320
Wm. Abrahams Books, New York, NY	800-526-0275
Harry N. Abrams, New York, NY	800-345-1359
Academic Press, San Diego, CA	800-321-5068
Accent Books, Denver, CO	800-525-5550
Accent Publications, Scituate, MA	800-525-5550
Access Press, New York, NY	800-222-3774
Acropolis Books, Washington, DC	800-451-7771; DC 800-621-5199
Ad-Lib Publications, Fairfield, IA	800-624-5893
Adama Publishers, New York, NY	800-672-6672
Addison-Wesley Publishing Co., Reading, MA	800-447-2226
Adler's Foreign Books, Evanston, IL	800-235-3771
Agape, Carol Stream, IL	800-323-1049
Agency for Instructional Technology, Bloomington, IN	800-457-4509
AgriData Resources, Milwaukee, WI	800-558-9044
Agrinde Publications, New York, NY	800-251-4000
Alemany Press, Hayward, CA	800-227-2375
Alfred Publishing Co., Van Nuys, CA	800-292-6122; CA 800-821-6083
Allyn & Bacon, Needham Heights, MA	800-223-1360
Alternate Source, Lansing, MI	800-253-3200, ext. 700
American Assn. for Medical Transcription, Modesto, CA	800-982-2182
American Assn. on Mental Retardation, Washington, DC	800-424-3688

Publisher/Distributor	Toll-Free No.
American Bible Society, New York, NY	800-543-8000
American Chemical Society, Washington, DC	800-227-5558
American College of Laboratory Animal Medicine, Hershey, PA	
Dist: Academic Press	800-321-5068
American Correctional Assn., College Park, MD	800-222-5646
American Educational Trust, The, Washington, DC	800-368-5788
American Geophysical Union, Washington, DC	800-424-2488
American Guidance Service, Circle Pines, MN	800-328-2560
American Institute of Physics, New York, NY	800-247-7497
American Institute of Small Business, Minneapolis, MN	800-328-2906
American Law Institute, Philadelphia, PA	800-253-6397
American Library Assn., Chicago, IL	800-545-2433; IL 800-545-2444
	Canada 800-545-2455
American Mathematical Society, Providence, RI	800-556-7774
American Medical Assn., Chicago, IL	800-621-8335
American Numismatic Assn., Colorado Springs, CO	800-367-9723
American Nurses Assn., Kansas City, MO	800-233-2428
American Phytopathological Society, St. Paul, MN	800-328-7560
American Polygraph Assn., Severna Park, MD	800-272-8037
American Psychiatric Press, Washington, DC	800-368-5777
American Society of Civil Engineers, New York, NY	800-548-2723
American Technical Publications, Homewood, IL	800-323-3471
American Travel Publications, Carlsbad, CA	
Dist: Sunset Books	800-227-7346
Amphoto, New York, NY	800-526-3641
Anaheim Publishing Co., Belmont, CA	800-831-6996
Ancestry, Salt Lake City, UT	800-531-1790
John Mackenzie Anderson, Cincinnati, OH	800-732-2663
Robert D. Anderson Publishing Co., Sacramento, CA	800-532-2332
Anderson Publishing Co., Cincinnati, OH	800-543-0883
Andrews & McMeel, Kansas City, MO	800-826-4216
Annual Reviews, Palo Alto, CA	800-523-8635
Antioch Publishing Co., Yellow Springs, OH	800-543-2397
Apollo Books, Poughkeepsie, NY	800-431-5003; NY 800-942-8222
Apollo Editions, New York, NY	
Dist: Harper & Row Publishers	800-242-7737; PA 800-982-4377
Applause Theatre Book Publications, New York, NY	800-873-6775
Appleton & Lange, East Norwalk, CT	800-423-1359
Arbit Books, Milwaukee, WI	800-558-6908
Archway Paperbacks, New York, NY	800-223-2336
Ariel Press, Canal Winchester, OH	800-336-7769
Arista Corp., Elmsford, NY	800-227-1606
Arno Press, New York, NY	800-242-7737
Art Institute of Chicago, Chicago, IL	800-621-2736
Artech House, Norwood, MA	800-225-9977
Ash-Kar Press, San Francisco, CA	
Dist: Bookpeople	800-227-1516; CA 800-624-4466

Publisher/Distributor	Toll-Free No.
Ashton-Tate Publishing Group, Torrance, CA	800-437-4329
Dist: Triton Products	800-227-6900
Aspen Publishers, Rockville, MD	800-638-8437
Associated Booksellers, Bridgeport, CT	800-232-2224
Association for Library Service to Children, Chicago, IL	800-545-2433
Association of College and Research Libraries, Chicago, IL	800-545-2433; IL 800-545-2445
Atheneum Publishers, New York, NY	800-257-5755
Atlantic Monthly Press Books, Boston, MA	800-343-9204
Auerbach Publishers, New York, NY	800-922-0066
Augsburg Publishing House, Minneapolis, MN	800-328-4648; MN 800-752-8153
Aura Enterprises, Los Angeles, CA	
Dist: Bookpeople	800-227-1516; CA 800-624-4466
New Leaf Distributing	800-241-3829
Automobile Quarterly, Wyomissing, PA	800-523-0236
Aviation Book Co., Glendale, CA	800-423-2708; CA 800-542-6657
Avon Books, New York, NY	(customer service) 800-238-0658; (orders) 800-223-0690
BMH Books, Winona Lake, IN	800-348-2756
BUC International Corp., Fort Lauderdale, FL	800-327-6929
Backcountry Publications, Woodstock, VT	800-635-5009
Baha'i Publishing Trust, Wilmette, IL	800-999-9019
Baker Book House, Grand Rapids, MI	800-253-7283
Ballantine Books, New York, NY	800-638-6460
Ballinger Publishing Co., Cambridge, MA	800-242-7737
Balsam Press, New York, NY	
Dist: Kampmann & Co.	800-526-7626
Bantam Books, New York, NY	800-223-6834
Barbacoa Press, Kansas City, MO	800-255-0513
Dist: Publishers Group West	800-982-8319
Barbour & Co., Westwood, NJ	800-221-2648
Dist: Ingram Book Co.	800-251-5900
Barnes & Noble Books, New York, NY	800-242-7737
Barre Publishing Co., New York, NY	
Dist: Crown Publishers	800-526-4264
Barron's Educational Series, Hauppauge, NY	800-645-3476; NY 800-257-5729
Basic Books, New York, NY	800-242-7737
Battelle Press, Columbus, OH	800-451-3543
Beacon Press, Boston, MA	
Dist: Harper & Row Publishers	800-242-7737
Bear & Co., Santa Fe, NM	800-932-3277
Dist: New Leaf Distributing	800-241-3829
Inland Book Co.	800-243-0138
Spring Arbor	800-521-3690
Beau Bayou Publishing Co., Lafayette, LA	800-624-0466
Beaufort Books, New York, NY	
Dist: Kampmann & Co.	800-526-7626
Peter Bedrick Books, New York, NY	800-982-8319

Publisher/Distributor	Toll-Free No.
Beginner Books, New York, NY	800-638-6460
Behrman House, West Orange, NJ	800-221-2755
Matthew Bender & Co., New York, NY	800-223-1940
Robert Bentley, Cambridge, MA	800-423-4595
Bergh Publishing Group, Indianapolis, IN	800-526-0275
Berkley Publishing Group, New York, NY	800-223-0510
Berlitz Publications, New York, NY	800-428-7267
Bernan Associates, Lanham, MD	800-274-4888
Bethany House Publications, Minneapolis, MN	800-328-6109
Bethel Publishing Co., Elkhart, IN	800-348-7657
Bibli O'Phile Publishing Co., New York, NY	800-255-1660
Bicycle Books, Mill Valley, CA	
Dist: Kampmann & Co.	800-526-7626
Bookpeople	800-227-1516; CA 800-624-4466
Bilingual Books, Seattle, WA	
Dist: Cliffs Notes	800-228-4078
Bishop Graphics, Westlake Village, CA	800-222-5808
Blacksmith Corp., Chino Valley, AZ	800-531-2665
Basil Blackwell, New York, NY	
Dist: Harper & Row Publishers	(trade orders) 800-242-7737
Blackwell Scientific Publications, Boston, MA	800-325-4177
John F. Blair, Winston-Salem, NC	800-222-9796
Blood-Horse, Lexington, KY	800-354-9207
Blue Mountain Press, Boulder, CO	800-525-0642
Clark Boardman Co., New York, NY	800-221-9428
Edward Marshall Boehm, Trenton, NJ	800-257-9410
Books on Demand, Ann Arbor, MI	800-521-0600
Books on Tape, Newport Beach, CA	800-626-3333
R. R. Bowker Co., New York, NY	800-521-8110; Canada 800-537-8416
Marion Boyars Publishers, New York, NY	
Dist: Kampmann & Co.	800-526-7626
Bradbury Press, New York, NY	
Dist: Macmillan Publishing Co.	800-257-5755
Branchemco, Jacksonville, FL	800-874-5990; FL 800-342-1259
Breakthrough Publications, Briarcliff, NY	800-824-5000
Brentwood Communications Group, Columbus, GA	800-334-8861
Brethren Press, Elgin, IL	800-323-8039
Brigham Young University Press, Provo, UT	800-453-3235
Broadman Press, Nashville, TN	800-251-3225
Broadway Play Publishing, New York, NY	800-752-9782 (exc. NY, HI, AK)
Brodart Co., Williamsport, PA	800-233-8467
Paul H. Brookes Publishing Co., Baltimore, MD	800-638-3775
Brooks/Cole Publishing Co., Monterey, CA	800-354-9706
Broude Brothers, New York, NY	800-225-3197
Brownlow Publishing Co., Fort Worth, TX	800-433-7610
Bull Publishing Co., Palo Alto, CA	
Dist: Publishers Group West	800-365-3453
Bureau of National Affairs, Washington, DC	800-372-1033

Publisher/Distributor	Toll-Free No.
Business Publications, Homewood, IL	
Dist: Richard D. Irwin	800-323-4560
Business Research Services, Lombard, IL	800-325-8720
Butterworth Legal Publications, St. Paul, MN	800-333-3839
Butterworth Legal Publications, Stoneham, MA	800-548-4001
Butterworth Pubs. (Med, Sci, Tech), Stoneham, MA	800-544-1013
CBP Press, St. Louis, MO	800-351-2665
C.C. Publications, Chicago, IL	800-547-4800
CIBA Medical Education Div., West Caldwell, NJ	800-631-1162
CRC Press, Boca Raton, FL	800-272-7737
CRC Publications, Grand Rapids, MI	800-333-8300
C. S. S. of Ohio, Lima, OH	800-537-1030
Caedmon, New York, NY	800-223-0420
Cajun Publishers, New Iberia, LA	800-551-3076
Calibre Press, Northbrook, IL	800-323-0037
California College Press, National City, CA	800-221-7374
Callaghan & Co., Wilmette, IL	800-323-1336; (edit.) 800-323-8067
Cambridge Book Co., New York, NY	800-221-4764
Cambridge University Press,	
New York, NY	800-227-0247; orders 800-872-7423
Canter & Associates, Santa Monica, CA	800-262-4347
Capitol Publishing, Alexandria, VA	800-327-7203
Carcanet Press, New York, NY	
Dist: Harper & Row Publishers	800-242-7737; PA 800-982-4377
Career Publishing, Orange, CA	800-854-4014; CA 800-821-0543
CareerTrack Publications, Boulder, CO	800-334-1018
Carolina Biological Supply Co., Burlington, NC	800-334-5551
Caroline House, Naperville, IL	800-245-2665
Carolrhoda Books, Minneapolis, MN	800-328-4929
Carroll and Graf Publishers, New York, NY	800-982-8319
Cassell Communications, Fort Lauderdale, FL	800-351-9278; FL 800-851-3392
Castle Books, Secaucus, NJ	800-526-7257
Marshall Cavendish Corp., Freeport, NY	800-821-9881
Celestial Arts Publishing Co., Berkeley, CA	800-841-2665
Centennial Press, Lincoln, NE	800-228-4078
Charismatic Renewal Services, South Bend, IN	800-348-2227
Chartwell Books, Secaucus, NJ	800-526-7257
Chase Publications, San Francisco, CA	
Dist: Bookpeople	800-227-1516; CA 800-624-4466
Chatsworth Press, Chatsworth, CA	800-262-7367
Dist: Publishers Group West	800-982-8319
Bookpeople	800-227-1516; CA 800-624-4466
Children's Press, Chicago, IL	800-621-1115
Chilton Book Co., Radnor, PA	800-345-1214
Christian Books Publishing House, Auburn, ME	800-228-2665
Christian Publishing Services, Tulsa, OK	800-331-3647
Citadel Press, Secaucus, NJ	800-LS-Books

Publisher/Distributor		Toll-Free No.
Clarion Books, New York, NY		
Dist: Houghton Mifflin Co.		800-225-3362
Cliffs Notes, Lincoln, NE		800-228-4078
Close Up Foundation, Arlington, VA		800-336-5479
Cold Spring Harbor Laboratory, Cold Spring Harbor, NY		800-843-4388
Collector Books, Paducah, KY		800-626-5420
College Press Publishing Co., Joplin, MO		800-641-7148
College Skills Center, Baltimore, MD	(orders only)	800-638-1010
College Survival, Rapid City, SD		800-528-8323
Collier Books, New York, NY		800-257-5755
Colorado School of Mines, Golden, CO		800-446-9488
Columbia Pictures Publications, Hialeah, FL		800-327-7643
Colwell Systems, Champaign, IL		800-248-7000
Comedy Center, The, Wilmington, DE		800-441-7098
Communication Channels, Atlanta, GA		800-241-9834
Communication Networks, Richmond, VA		800-882-4800
CompCare Publications, Irvine, CA		800-328-3330
Computer Information, Kailua, HI		800-528-3665
Concordia Publishing House, St. Louis, MO		800-325-3040
Conference Board, The, New York, NY		800-872-6273
Congdon & Weed, New York, NY		800-221-7945
Congressional Information Service, Bethesda, MD		800-638-8380
Consumer Guide Books/Publications Intl., Lincolnwood, IL		
Dist: Crown Publishers		800-526-4264
Continuum Publishing Co., New York, NY		
Dist: Harper & Row Publishers	800-242-7737; PA	800-982-4377
David C. Cook Publishing Co., Elgin, IL		800-533-2201
Cornell Maritime Press, Centreville, MD		800-638-7641
Council Oak Books, Tulsa, OK		800-247-8850
Countryman Press, Woodstock, VT		800-635-5009
Crain Books, Chicago, IL		800-323-4900
Crawford Press/Econo-Clad Books, Topeka, KS		800-255-3502
Creative Homeowner Press, Upper Saddle River, NJ		800-631-7795
Creative Teaching Press, Cypress, CA		800-732-1548
Crestwood House, Mankato, MN		800-535-4393
Crittenden Publishing, Novato, CA		800-421-3483
Crossroad Publishing, New York, NY		800-982-4377
Dist: Harper & Row Publishers	800-242-7737; PA	800-982-4377
Thomas Y. Crowell, New York, NY		800-242-7737
Dist: Harper & Row Publishers	800-242-7737; PA	800-982-4377
Crown Publishers, New York, NY		800-526-4264
Cy De Cosse, Minnetonka, MN		800-328-3895
DAW Books, New York, NY		800-526-0275
D&S Publishers, Clearwater, FL	800-237-9707; FL	800-282-8118
DOK Publishers, East Aurora, NY		800-458-7900
D.A.T.A., San Diego, CA		800-854-7030
Da Capo Press, Jersey City, NJ		800-221-9369

Publisher/Distributor	Toll-Free No.
Dance Magazine, New York, NY	800-331-1750
Dartnell Corp., Chicago, IL	800-621-5463
Datar Publishing Co., Sulphur Springs, MO	800-633-8378
F. A. Davis Co., Philadelphia, PA	800-523-4049
Dealer's Choice Books, Land O'Lakes, FL	800-238-8288
Marcel Dekker, New York, NY	800-228-1160
Delacorte Press, New York, NY	800-221-4676
Delgren Books, Tucson, AZ	800-528-4923
Dell Publishing Co., New York, NY	800-255-4133
Delmar Co., Charlotte, NC	800-438-1504
Delmar Publishers, Albany, NY	800-347-7707; NY 800-252-2550
DeLorme Mapping Co., Freeport, ME	800-227-1656
Dembner Books, New York, NY	800-223-2584
T. S. Denison & Co., Minneapolis, MN	800-328-3831
Deseret Book Co., Salt Lake City, UT	800-453-3876
Devin-Adair, Greenwich, CT	800-251-4000
Dial Books for Young Readers, New York, NY	800-526-0275
Dial Press, New York, NY	800-645-6156
Dialogue House Library, New York, NY	800-221-5844
Digital Press, Bedford, MA	800-343-8322/8321
Dillon Press, Minneapolis, MN	800-328-8322, ext. 687
Directories Publishing Co., Clemson, SC	800-222-4531
The Distributors, South Bend, IN	800-348-5200 (exc. IN)
Dodd, Mead & Co., New York, NY	800-237-3255
Dog-Master Systems, Agoura Hills, CA	800-824-7888
Donning Co. Publishers, Norfolk, VA	800-446-8572
Dormac, Beaverton, OR	800-547-8032
Dorset House Publishing Co., New York, NY	800-342-6657
Dorsey Press, Chicago, IL	800-245-7524
Doubleday & Co., New York, NY	800-223-5780; (sales service) 800-255-4133
Dover Publications, New York, NY	800-223-3130
Dow Jones-Irwin, Homewood, IL	800-323-4560
Drivers License Guide Co., Redwood City, CA	800-227-8827
Dryden Press, Hinsdale, IL	800-323-7437
Dun's Marketing Services, Parsippany, NJ	800-526-0651
Duquesne University Press, Pittsburgh, PA	800-345-8112
Dushkin Publishing Group, Guilford, CT	800-243-6532
E. P. Dutton, New York, NY	
Dist: New American Library	800-526-0275
EBSCO Industries, Birmingham, AL	800-633-6088
EDC Publishing, Tulsa, OK	800-331-4418
EIC/Intelligence, New York, NY	800-521-8110
EMC Publishing, St. Paul, MN	800-328-1452
ERA/CCR Corp., Nyack, NY	800-845-8402
ESP, Jonesboro, AR	800-643-0280
Ecco Press, New York, NY	800-223-2584
Economics Press, Fairfield, NJ	800-526-2554

Publisher/Distributor	Toll-Free No.
Educational Activities, Baldwin, NY	800-645-3739
Educational Design, New York, NY	800-221-9372
Educational Ministries, Brea, CA	800-221-0910
Educational Service, Stevensville, MI	800-253-0763
Educators Publishing Service, Cambridge, MA	800-225-5750
Wm. B. Eerdman's Publishing Co., Grand Rapids, MI	800-253-7521
Elek-Tek, Chicago, IL	800-621-1269
Encyclopaedia Britannica, Chicago, IL	800-554-9862
Encyclopaedia Britannica Educational Corp., Chicago, IL	800-554-9862
Europa Publications, Detroit, MI	800-521-0707
M. Evans & Co., New York, NY	
Dist: Henry Holt & Co.	800-343-9204
Faber & Faber, Winchester, MA	
Dist: Harper & Row Publishers	800-242-7737; PA 800-982-4377
Facts on File, New York, NY	800-322-8755
Family Circle Books, New York, NY	800-678-2680
Farrar, Straus & Giroux, New York, NY	800-242-7737
Fawcett Book Group, New York, NY	800-638-6460
Faxon Co., Westwood, MA	800-225-6055
Federal Document Retrieval, Washington, DC	800-368-1009
Fielding Travel Books, New York, NY	800-843-9389
Dist: William Morrow & Co.	(orders) 800-631-1199
Film Communicators, North Hollywood, CA	800-621-2131
Forest Publishing, Lake Forest, IL	800-323-9442
Reginald Bishop Forster & Associates, Sacramento, CA	800-328-5091; CA 800-321-9789
Fortress Press, Philadelphia, PA	800-367-8737
Forward Movement Publications, Cincinnati, OH	800-543-1813
The Foundation Center, New York, NY	800-424-9836
Charles Franklin Press, Edmonds, WA	800-992-6657
Free Press, New York, NY	800-257-5755
Fromm International Publishing Corp., New York, NY	
Dist: Kampmann & Co.	800-526-7626
Fulcrum, Golden, CO	800-992-2908
Funk & Wagnalls Co., New York, NY	800-888-8818
GP Publishing, Columbia, MD	800-638-3838
Gale Research Co., Detroit, MI	800-223-4253
Gallaudet University Press, Washington, DC	800-451-1073
Garden Way Publishing Co., Pownal, VT	800-242-7737
Geneva Press, Philadelphia, PA	800-523-1631
Geological Society of America, Boulder, CO	800-472-1988
C. R. Gibson Co., Norwalk, CT	800-243-6004
Ginn Press, Lexington, MA	800-848-9500
Glencoe Publishing Co., Mission Hills, CA	800-423-9534
Peter Glenn Publications, New York, NY	800-223-1254
Global Engineering Documents, Irvine, CA	800-854-7179
Globe Book Co., New York, NY	800-848-9500

Publisher/Distributor	Toll-Free No.
Globe Pequot Press, Chester, CT	800-243-0495; CT 800-962-0973
Golden-Lee Books, Brooklyn, NY	800-221-0960
Good Apple, Carthage, IL	800-435-7234
Good Books, Intercourse, PA	800-762-7171
Good Money Publications, Worcester, VT	800-535-3551
Goodheart-Willcox Co., South Holland, IL	800-323-0440
Gospel Publishing House, Springfield, MO	800-641-4310
Graphic Arts Center Publishing Co., Portland, OR	800-452-3032
Great Plains National Instructional Television Library, Lincoln, NE	800-228-4630
Great Plains Software, Fargo, ND	800-345-3276
Stephen Greene Press, Lexington, MA Dist: Viking Penguin, Inc.	800-526-0275
Green Tiger Press, San Diego, CA	800-424-2443
Greenhaven Press, San Diego, CA	800-231-5163
Greenwich Press, Trumbull, CT	800-243-4246
Greenwillow Books, New York, NY	800-631-1199
Grove Press, New York, NY	800-638-6460
Groves Dictionaries of Music, New York, NY	800-221-2123
M. Grumbacher, Cranbury, NJ	800-346-3278
Grune & Stratton, Orlando, FL	800-782-4479
Gryphon House, Mount Rainier, MD	800-638-0928
Guilford Press, New York, NY	800-221-3966
Hadley School for the Blind, Winnetka, IL	800-323-4238
Hafner Press, New York, NY	800-257-5755
G. K. Hall & Co., Boston, MA	800-343-2806
Hammond, Maplewood, NJ	800-526-4953
Happiness Unlimited Publications, Virginia Beach, VA	800-777-3529
Harcourt Brace Jovanovich, San Diego, CA	800-543-1918
Harmony Books, New York, NY	800-526-4264
Harper & Row Publishers, New York, NY	800-242-7737; PA 800-982-4377
Harris Publishing Co., Twinsburg, OH	800-888-5900
Harrison Co., Norcross, GA	800-241-3561; GA 800-282-9867
Harrison House, Tulsa, OK	800-331-3647
Harvard Business School Press, Boston, MA Dist: Harper & Row Publishers	800-242-7737; PA 800-982-4377
Harvest House Publishers, Eugene, OR	800-547-8979
Hastings House Publishers, New York, NY Dist: Kampmann & Co.	800-526-7626
Haworth Press, New York, NY	800-342-9678
Hazelden Foundation, Center City, MN	800-328-9000
D. C. Heath Co., Lexington, MA	800-235-3565
William S. Hein & Co., Buffalo, NY	800-828-7571
Heinle & Heinle Publishers, Boston, MA	800-237-0053
Hemisphere Publishing Corp., New York, NY	800-821-8312
Herald House, Independence, MO	800-821-7550
Herald Press, Scottdale, PA	800-245-7894

Publisher/Distributor	Toll-Free No.
Hewlett-Packard Co., Sunnyvale, CA	800-367-4772
Hideaways International, Littleton, MA	800-843-4433
Hill & Wang, New York, NY	800-638-3030
History of Science Society, Philadelphia, PA	800-341-1522
Holman Bible Publishers, Nashville, TN	800-251-3225
Holt, Rinehart & Winston, Orlando, FL	800-782-4479
Home Planners, Farmington Hills, MI	800-521-6797
Hope Publishing Co., Carol Stream, IL	800-323-1049
Horizon Publishers & Distributors, Bountiful, UT	800-453-0812
Horn Book, Boston, MA	800-325-1170
Houghton Mifflin Co., Boston, MA	800-225-3362
Hubbard Scientific, Northbrook, IL	800-323-8368
Hudson Hills Press, New York, NY	
Dist: Rizzoli International Publications	800-433-1238
Human Resource Development Press, Amherst, MA	800-822-2801
Humanics, Atlanta, GA	800-874-8844
Humanities Press International, Atlantic Highlands, NJ	(orders) 800-221-3845
Hunter Books, Kingwood, TX	800-231-3024
Huntington House, Lafayette, LA	800-572-8213
ICS Press, San Francisco, CA	
Dist: Kampmann & Co.	800-526-7626
IEEE Computer Society Press, Washington, DC	(orders only) 800-272-6657
IHRDC, Boston, MA	800-327-6756
ISI Press, Philadelphia, PA	800-523-1850
Ibis Publishing, Charlottesville, VA	800-582-0026
Imported Publications, Chicago, IL	800-345-2665
Incentive Publications, Nashville, TN	800-421-2830
Independence Press, Independence, MO	800-821-7550
Institute for Palestine Studies, Washington, DC	800-874-3614
Institute for the Study of Human Knowledge, Cambridge, MA	800-222-4745
Institute of Early American History and Culture, Williamsburg, VA	800-223-2584
Institute of Modern Languages, Lincolnwood, IL	800-323-4900
Intel Corp., Santa Clara, CA	800-548-4725
Inter/Face Associates, Durham, CT	800-433-1116
International Aviation Publications, Casper, WY	800-443-9250
International Publications Service, Philadelphia, PA	800-821-8312
International Specialized Book Services, Portland, OR	800-547-7734
Interport USA, Portland, OR	800-233-5729
Interstate Printers & Publishers, Danville, IL	800-843-4774
Interweave Press, Loveland, CO	800-272-2193
Investor Publications, Cedar Falls, IA	800-553-1789
Investrek Publishing, Huntington Beach, CA	800-334-0854, ext. 864
Iron Crown Enterprises, Charlottesville, VA	800-325-0479
Richard D. Irwin, Homewood, IL	800-323-4560; (orders) 800-634-3961
Ivory Tower Publishing Co., Watertown, MA	800-322-5016
JA Micropublishing, Eastchester, NY	800-227-2477
Jalmar Press, Rolling Hills Estates, CA	800-662-9662

Publisher/Distributor	Toll-Free No.
Jamestown Publishers, Providence, RI	800-872-7323
Janus Book Publishers, Hayward, CA	800-227-2375
Jefferson Law Book Co., Washington, DC	800-543-0883
Jesuit Historical Institute, Chicago, IL	800-621-1008
Johnson Institute, Minneapolis, MN	800-231-5165; (Canada) 800-447-6660
Johnson Reference Books, Alexandria, VA	(orders only) 800-851-2665
Johnson Reprint Corp., New York, NY	800-543-1918
Joint Center for Political Studies, Washington, DC	800-323-5277
Jones & Bartlett Publishers, Boston, MA	800-832-0034
Jove Publications, New York, NY	800-223-0510
Judson Press, Valley Forge, PA	800-331-1053
Jury Verdict Research, Solon, OH	800-321-6910
KC Publications, Las Vegas, NV	800-626-9673
K-Dimension Publishers, Decatur, GA	800-241-4702
KET, Lexington, KY	800-354-9067
Kalmbach Publishing Co., Milwaukee, WI	800-558-1544
Kampmann and Co., New York, NY	800-526-7626
Kar-Ben Copies, Rockville, MD	800-452-7236
Kaypro Corp., Del Mar, CA	800-452-9776
J. J. Keller Associates, Neenah, WI	800-558-5011
Kent State University Press, Kent, OH	800-666-2211
Key Book Service, Bridgeport, CT	800-243-2790
Key Curriculum Press, Berkeley, CA	800-338-7638
Keystone Publications, New York, NY	800-223-0935
Neil A. Kjos Music Co., San Diego, CA	800-854-1592
Kluwer Law Book Publishers, New York, NY	800-821-4526
Knapp Press, New York, NY	800-526-4264
Alfred A. Knopf, New York, NY	800-638-6460
Knowledge Industry Publications, White Plains, NY	800-248-5474
John Knox Press, Atlanta, GA	800-334-6580
Kodansha International USA, New York, NY	800-638-3030; (exc. MD)
Kraus Reprint & Periodicals, Millwood, NY	800-223-8323
Kregel Publications, Grand Rapids, MI	800-253-5465
Lane Publishing Co., Menlo Park, CA	800-227-7346
Lawyers Cooperative Publishing Co., Rochester, NY	800-527-0430
Lea & Febiger, Philadelphia, PA	800-433-3850
Learning Publications, Holmes Beach, FL	800-222-1525
Learning Well, Roslyn Heights, NY	800-645-6564
Learning Works, The, Santa Barbara, CA	800-235-5767
Lederer Enterprises, Asheville, NC	800-258-7160
Hal Leonard Publishing Corp., Milwaukee, WI	800-642-6692
Lerner Publications Co., Minneapolis, MN	800-328-4929
Lewis Publishers, Chelsea, MI	800-525-7894
Lexington Books, Lexington, MA	800-235-3565
Libraries Unlimited, Englewood, CO	800-237-6124
Library of America, New York, NY	800-631-3577
Light & Life Press, Winona Lake, IN	800-348-2513

Publisher/Distributor	Toll-Free No.
Light Impressions Corp., Rochester, NY	800-828-6216; NY 800-828-9629
Liguori Publications, Liguori, MO	(orders) 800-325-9521
Limelight Editions, New York, NY	800-426-0489
Linch Publishing, Orlando, FL	800-327-7055; FL 800-434-0399
Dist: Ingram Book Co.	(orders only) 800-251-5900
Linden Publishing Co., Fresno, CA	800-345-4447
Lineal Publishing Co., Fort Lauderdale, FL	800-222-4253
J. B. Lippincott Co., Philadelphia, PA	800-242-7737
Lippincott Junior Books, New York, NY	800-242-7737
Little, Brown & Co., Boston, MA	800-343-9204
Liveright Publishing Corp., New York, NY	800-233-4830
Llewellyn Publications, St. Paul, MN	800-843-6666
Lodestar Books, New York, NY	
Dist: New American Library	800-526-0275
Lomond Publications, Mount Airy, MD	800-443-6299
Lothrop, Lee & Shepard Books, New York, NY	800-843-9389
Loyola University Press, Chicago, IL	800-621-1008
McCutchan Publishing Corp., Berkeley, CA	800-227-1540
McDonnell Douglas Information Systems Group, St. Louis, MO	800-325-1087
David McKay Co., New York, NY	800-327-4801
Macmillan Publishing Co., New York, NY	800-257-5755
MacRae's Blue Book, New York, NY	800-622-7237
Madrona Publishers, Seattle, WA	
Dist: Slawson Communications	800-367-8420
Magickal Childe, New York, NY	800-243-0138
Ralph Maltby Enterprises, Newark, OH	800-848-8358; OH 800-762-1831
Management Information Source, Portland, OR	(orders only) 800-626-8257
Mansell, Bronx, NY	800-367-6770
Market Data Retrieval, Shelton, CT	800-243-5538
Marquis Who's Who/Macmillan Directory Div., Wilmette, IL	800-621-9669
Master Books, El Cajon, CA	800-999-3777
Masterco Press, Ann Arbor, MI	800-443-0100, ext. 230
Mastery Education Corp., Watertown, MA	800-225-3214
Math House, Glen Ellyn, IL	800-222-3547
Media Materials, Baltimore, MD	800-638-1010
Media Press, Chatsworth, CA	800-262-7367; CA 800-272-7367
Medical Economics Books, Oradell, NJ	800-223-0581
Medical Manor Books, Philadelphia, PA	800-343-8464
Dist: Ingram Book Co.	800-251-5900
Bookpeople	800-227-1516; CA 800-624-4466
Quality Books	(libraries only) 800-323-4241
Merriam-Webster, Springfield, MA	800-828-1880
Merrill Publishing Co., Columbus, OH	800-848-1567; 800-848-6205
Merrimack Publishing Corp., Bridgeport, CT	800-232-2224
Julian Messner, New York, NY	800-223-2336
Minerva Books, New York, NY	800-345-5946
Minnesota Historical Society Press, St. Paul, MN	800-647-7827

Publisher/Distributor	Toll-Free No.
Mitchell Publishing, Santa Cruz, CA	800-435-2665
Modern Curriculum Press, Cleveland, OH	800-321-3106
Money Market Directories, Charlottesville, VA	800-446-2810
Montezuma Micro, Dallas, TX	800-527-0347; TX 800-442-1310
Moody Press, Chicago, IL	800-621-5111; IL 800-621-4323
Thomas More Press, Chicago, IL	800-835-8965
Morgan-Rand Publications, Philadelphia, PA	800-354-8673
Morrison-Peterson Publishing, Kailua, HI	800-528-3665
Wm. Morrow & Co., New York, NY	800-843-9389
C. V. Mosby Co., St. Louis, MO	800-325-4177; (orders) 800-633-6699
Mother Earth News, Hendersonville, NC	800-438-0238
Motorbooks International, Osceola, WI	800-826-6600 (exc. WI and AK)
Multnomah Press, Portland, OR	800-547-5890
Dist: Riverside Bk. & Bible Hse.	800-247-5111
Mike Murach & Associates, Fresno, CA	800-221-5528; CA 800-221-5527
Museum of Western Art, Denver, CO	800-525-7047
S. D. Myers, Akron, OH	800-321-9580
Mysterious Press, New York, NY	
Dist: Ballantine Books	800-638-6460
NAL Penguin, New York, NY	800-526-0275
National Assessment of Educational Progress, Princeton, NJ	800-223-0267
National Assn. of Home Builders, Washington, DC	800-368-5242
National Assn. of Social Workers, Silver Spring, MD	800-638-8799
National Bureau of Economic Research, Cambridge, MA	
Dist: University of Chicago Press	800-621-2736
National Center for Constitutional Studies, Salt Lake City, UT	800-522-6227
National Center for State Courts, Williamsburg, VA	800-446-8952
National Clearinghouse for Bilingual Education, Wheaton, MD	800-647-0123
National Fire Protection Assn., Quincy, MA	800-344-3555
National Geographic Society, Washington, DC	800-638-4077
National Health Publishing, Owings Mills, MD	800-446-2221
National League for Nursing, New York, NY	800-847-8480
National Learning Corp., Syosset, NY	800-645-6337
National Nursing Review, Los Altos, CA	800-221-4093
National Register Publishing Co., Wilmette, IL	800-323-6772
National Society to Prevent Blindness, Schaumburg, IL	800-221-3004
National Textbook Co., Lincolnwood, IL	800-323-4900
National Underwriter Co., Cincinnati, OH	800-543-0874
Naval Institute Press, Annapolis, MD	(customer service) 800-233-USNI
Thos. Nelson Publishers, Nashville, TN	800-251-4000
New Classics Library, Gainesville, GA	800-336-1618
New Directions Publishing Corp., New York, NY	
Dist: W. W. Norton Co.	800-533-7978
New Leaf Press, Green Forest, AR	800-643-9535
New Readers Press, Syracuse, NY	800-448-8878
New York Academy of Sciences, New York, NY	800-843-6927
New York Graphic Society Books, Boston, MA	800-922-NYGS

Publisher/Distributor	Toll-Free No.
New York Zoetrope, New York, NY	800-242-7546
Newberry Library, Chicago, IL	800-621-2736
Newbury House Publishers, New York, NY	
Dist: Harper & Row, Publishers	(wholesale only) 800-242-7737; 800-638-3030
Newmarket Press, New York, NY	
Dist: Harper & Row Publishers	800-242-7737; PA 800-982-4377
Nightingale Paperbacks, Boston, MA	800-343-2806
Norse Press, Sioux Falls, SD	800-843-1300, ext. 890
North Light Books, Cincinnati, OH	800-543-4644
North Point Press, Berkeley, CA	
Dist: Farrar, Straus & Giroux	800-242-7737
Northland Press, Flagstaff, AZ	800-346-3257; AZ 800-462-6657
Jeffrey Norton Publishers, Guilford, CT	800-243-1234
W. W. Norton & Co., New York, NY	800-223-2588
Ohara Publications, Burbank, CA	800-423-2874
Oil Daily, Washington, DC	800-368-5803
Oliver-Nelson, Nashville, TN	800-251-4000
Open Court Publishing Co., Peru, IL	800-435-6850; 800-892-6831
Orbis Books, Maryknoll, NY	800-258-5838
Ken Orr & Associates, Topeka, KS	800-255-2459
Oryx Press, Phoenix, AZ	800-457-6799
Osborne/McGraw-Hill, Berkeley, CA	800-227-0900
Outlet Book Co., New York, NY	800-526-4264
Overlook Press, New York, NY	
Dist: Viking Penguin	800-526-0275
Oxford University Press, New York, NY	800-451-7556
Oxmoor House, Birmingham, AL	800-633-4712
PSG Publishing Co., Littleton, MA	800-225-5020
PSI Research, Milpitas, CA	800-228-2275
PWS Kent Publishing Co., Boston, MA	800-343-2204
Pacific Search Press, Seattle, WA	800-858-0628
Paladin Press, Boulder, CO	(retail only) 800-351-1700
Pantheon Books, New York, NY	
Dist: Random House	800-638-6460
Paraclete Press, Orleans, MA	800-451-5006
Parenting Press, Seattle, WA	800-992-6657
Pasha Publications, Arlington, VA	800-424-2908
Patchwork Publications, Las Vegas, NV	800-634-6268
Pathway Press, Cleveland, TN	800-251-7216
Peachtree Publishers, Atlanta, GA	800-241-0113; GA 800-282-0255
Pegasus, Indianapolis, IN	800-428-3750
Pelican Books, New York, NY	800-526-0275
Penguin Books, New York, NY	800-631-3577
Peregrine Smith Books, Layton, UT	800-421-8714
Perennial Library, New York, NY	800-242-7737
Perma Bound Books, Jacksonville, IL	800-637-6581
Thomas W. Perrin, Rutherford, NJ	800-321-7912

Publisher/Distributor	Toll-Free No.
Peterson's Guides, Princeton, NJ	800-338-3282
Picture Book Studio, Saxonville, MA	800-462-1252
Pierian Press, Ann Arbor, MI	800-443-5915
Pilot Publications, Ocala, FL	800-521-2120
Plenum Publishing, New York, NY	800-221-9369
Pocket Books, New York, NY	800-223-2336
Clarkson N. Potter Books, New York, NY	800-526-4264
Predicasts, Cleveland, OH	800-321-6388
Prentice Hall Press, Englewood Cliffs, NJ	800-634-2863
Price Stern Sloan, Los Angeles, CA	800-421-0892; CA 800-227-8801
Princeton Architectural Press, New York, NY	800-458-1131
Print Media Services, Elk Grove, IL	800-323-8899
Professional Education Systems, Eau Claire, WI	800-647-8079
Professional Resource Exchange, Sarasota, FL	800-443-3364
Prometheus Books, Buffalo, NY	800-421-0351
Psychological Assessment Resources, Lutz, FL	800-331-8378
Public Media, Chicago, IL	800-323-4222
Publishers Group West, Emeryville, CA	800-982-8319
Puffin Books, New York, NY	800-526-0275
Pushcart Press, Wainscott, NY	
Dist: W. W. Norton Co.	800-233-4830
Putnam Publishing Group, New York, NY	800-631-8571
QED Information Sciences, Wellesley, MA	800-343-4848
Quality Books, Lake Bluff, IL	(libraries only) 800-323-4241
Que Corp., Carmel, IN	800-428-5331
Queue, Bridgeport, CT	800-232-2224
Quill, New York, NY	
Dist: Wm. Morrow & Co.	800-843-9389
Quinlan Press, Boston, MA	800-551-2500
Quintessence Publishing Co., Lombard, IL	800-621-0387
Raintree Publishers, Milwaukee, WI	800-558-7264
Rand McNally & Co., Chicago, IL	800-678-7263
Randall Book Co., Orem, UT	800-453-1356
Randall House Publications, Nashville, TN	800-251-5762; TN 800-624-6538
Random House, New York, NY	800-638-6460
Rawson Associates, New York, NY	800-257-5755
Reader's Digest Assn., Pleasantville, NY	800-431-1246
Reader's Digest Press, Pleasantville, NY	
Dist: Random House	800-638-6460
Realtors National Marketing Institute, Chicago, IL	800-621-7035
Redwood Records, Emeryville, CA	800-888-7664
Regal Books, Ventura, CA	800-235-3415
Regnery Gateway, Washington, DC	800-448-8311
Research Publications, Phoenix, AZ	800-528-0559
Research Publications, Woodbridge, CT	800-732-2477
Resource Applications, Baltimore, MD	800-826-1877
Resource Publications, San Jose, CA	800-228-2028

Publisher/Distributor	Toll-Free No.
Retail Reporting Bureau, New York, NY	800-251-4545
Fleming H. Revell Co., Old Tappan, NJ	800-631-1970
Richardson, Steirman, & Blackwell, New York, NY	800-526-7626
Rittenhouse Book Distributors, King of Prussia, PA	800-345-6425
Riverside Publishing Co., Chicago, IL	800-323-9450
Rizzoli International Publications, New York, NY	800-433-1238
Rodale Press, Emmaus, PA	800-441-7761
Roscoe Pound Foundation, Washington, DC	800-424-2725
Roth Publishing, Great Neck, NY	800-327-0295
Fred B. Rothman & Co., Littleton, CO	800-457-1986
Running Press, Philadelphia, PA	800-428-1111
Russell Sage Foundation, New York, NY	800-242-7737
Wm. H. Sadlier, New York, NY	800-221-5175
St. Luke's Press, Memphis, TN	(orders) 800-524-5554, ext. 4617
St. Martin's Press, New York, NY	800-221-7945
St. Mary's Press, Winona, MN	800-533-8095
Salem House Publishers, Topsfield, MA	(orders) 800-624-8947
Salem Press, Englewood Cliffs, NJ	800-221-1592
Howard W. Sams & Co., Indianapolis, IN	800-428-7267
Santillana Publishing Co., Northvale, NJ	800-526-0107
Saybrook Publishing Co., Dallas, TX	
Dist: W. W. Norton Co.	800-223-2588
Scala Books, New York, NY	800-242-7737
Schirmer Books, New York, NY	
Dist: Macmillan Publishing Co.	800-257-5755
Scholarly Resources, Wilmington, DE	800-772-8937
Scholastic, New York, NY	800-392-2179
Scott Publications, Livonia, MI	800-458-8237
Scott Publishing Co., Sidney, OH	800-448-3611; OH 800-327-1259
Chas. Scribner's Sons, New York, NY	800-257-5755
Scripture Press, Wheaton, IL	800-323-9409
Sentinel Publishing Co., Lubbock, TX	800-858-4602
Shambhala Publications, Boston, MA	
Dist: Random House	800-638-6460
M. Shanken, New York, NY	800-227-1617
Harold Shaw Publishers, Wheaton, IL	800-742-9782
Sheed & Ward, Kansas City, MO	800-444-8910; (orders) 800-333-7373
Shepard's/McGraw-Hill, Colorado Springs, CO	800-525-2474
Shipley Associates, Bountiful, UT	800-343-0009
Showcase Publishing Co., Benicia, CA	800-526-0275
Sierra Club Books, San Francisco, CA	
Dist: Random House	800-638-6460
Signs of the Times Publishing Co., Cincinnati, OH	800-543-1925
Silver Burdett Press, Englewood Cliffs, NJ	800-631-8081; 800-624-4843
Simmons-Boardman Books, Omaha, NE	800-228-9670
Simon & Schuster, New York, NY	800-223-2348; (orders only) 800-223-2336
Gibbs M. Smith, Layton, UT	800-421-8714

Publisher/Distributor	Toll-Free No.
W. H. Smith Publishers, New York, NY	800-932-0070; NY 800-645-9990
Smithsonian Books, Washington, DC	800-223-2584
Social Issues Resources Series, Boca Raton, FL	800-327-0513
Society for Visual Education, Chicago, IL	800-621-1900
Somerset Press, Carol Stream, IL	800-323-1049
South-Western Publishing Co., Cincinnati, OH	800-543-0487
Spizzirri Publishing Co., Rapid City, SD	800-325-9819
Springer-Verlag New York, New York, NY	800-526-7254
Springhouse Publishing Co., Springhouse, PA	800-346-7844
Squadron Signal Publications, Carrollton, TX	800-527-7427
Stackpole Books, Harrisburg, PA	800-732-3669
Standard Publishing Co., Cincinnati, OH	800-543-1301; OH 800-582-1385
Robert A. Stanger Co., Shrewsbury, NJ	800-631-2291
Stanton & Lee Publishers, Madison, WI	800-356-4600; WI 800-362-5464
Star-Gate Enterprises, Orinda, CA	800-824-2222, ext. 35
Steinway & Sons, Long Island City, NY	800-223-6017
Stewart, Tabori & Chang, New York, NY	
Dist: Workman Publishing Co.	800-722-7202
Stillpoint Publishing, Walpole, NH	800-847-4014
Stockton Press, New York, NY	800-221-2123
Stoeger Publishing Co., South Hackensack, NJ	800-631-0722
Storey Communications, Pownal, VT	800-441-5700
Story House Corp., Charlottesville, NY	800-847-2105; NY 800-428-1008
Lyle Stuart, Secaucus, NJ	800-572-6657
Stubs Publications, New York, NY	800-223-7565
Sunburst Communications, Pleasantville, NY	800-431-1934
Sunset Books/Lane Publishing Co., Menlo Park, CA	800-227-7346
Swansea Press, Philadelphia, PA	800-792-6732
Sweet Publishing, Ft. Worth, TX	800-531-5220; TX 800-252-9213
Sybex, Alameda, CA	800-227-2346
TAB Books, Blue Ridge Summit, PA	800-233-1128
TSR, Lake Geneva, WI	800-372-4667; MD 800-492-0782
Taft Group, The, Washington, DC	800-424-3761
Jeremy P. Tarcher, Los Angeles, CA	800-225-3362
Taunton Press, Newtown, CT	800-243-7252
Taylor & Francis, New York, NY	800-821-8312
Taylor & Ng, Fairfield, CA	800-227-4090
Technical Data Corp., Boston, MA	800-237-8931
Technology Marketing Corp., Norwalk, CT	800-243-6002
Technomic Publishing Co., Lancaster, PA	800-233-9936
Ten Speed Press, Berkeley, CA	800-841-2665
Thames & Hudson, New York, NY	
Dist: W. W. Norton & Co.	800-223-4830
Thorndike Press, Thorndike, ME	800-223-6121
Ticknor & Fields, New York, NY	800-225-3362
Tidewater Publishers, Centreville, MD	800-638-7641
Time-Life Books, Alexandria, VA	800-621-7026

Publisher/Distributor	Toll-Free No.
Times Books, New York, NY	800-242-7737
Todd & Honeywell, Great Neck, NY	800-233-3361
Tor Books, New York, NY	
Dist: St. Martin's Press	800-221-7945
Torah Aura Productions, Los Angeles, CA	800-238-6724
Treasure Chest Publications, Tucson, AZ	800-223-5369, ext. 239
Tree Communications, South Salem, NY	800-242-7737
Triad Publishing Co., Gainesville, FL	800-874-7777, ext. 10
Trimark Publishing Co., New Castle, DE	800-874-6275
Trinet, Parsippany, NJ	800-874-6381
Troll Associates, Mahwah, NJ	800-526-5289
Twayne Publishers, Boston, MA	800-343-2806
Twenty-Third Publications, Mystic, CT	800-321-0411
Tyndale House Publishers, Wheaton, IL	800-323-9400
UMI Research Press, Ann Arbor, MI	800-521-0600
Ungar Publishing Co., New York, NY	
Dist: Harper & Row Publishers	800-242-7737
UNIPUB, Lanham, MD	800-274-4888; (Canada) 800-233-0504
Unique Publications, Burbank, CA	800-332-3330
U.S. Catholic Conference, Washington, DC	800-235-8722
U.S.-China Peoples Friendship Assn., Washington, DC	800-368-5883
University Books, Secaucus, NJ	800-LS-BOOKS
University Microfilms, Ann Arbor, MI	800-521-0600; Canada 800-343-5299
University of California Press, Berkeley, CA	800-822-6657
University of Chicago Press, Chicago, IL	800-621-2736
University of Missouri Press, Columbia, MO	800-666-2211
University of Notre Dame Press, Notre Dame, IN	800-426-0489
University of Oklahoma Press, Norman, OK	800-627-7377
University of Pittsburgh Press, Pittsburgh, PA	
Dist: Harper & Row Publishers	800-242-7737; PA 800-982-4377
University of Utah Press, Salt Lake City, UT	800-662-0062, ext. 6771 (exc. WA, HI, AK)
University of Washington Press, Seattle, WA	800-441-4115
University Press of Kentucky, Lexington, KY	800-666-2211
University Publications of America, Frederick, MD	800-692-6300
Unwin Hyman, Winchester, MA	800-223-1360
VC Publishing, Hudson, FL	800-472-9336
Vadare Publishing Co., Dix Hills, NY	800-645-1112
Valley of the Sun Publishing Co., Malibu, CA	800-421-6603; CA 800-225-4717
Veterinary Medicine Publishing Co., Lenexa, KS	800-255-6864
Victor Books, Wheaton, IL	800-323-9409
Viking Penguin, New York, NY	800-631-3577
Wadsworth Publishing Co., Belmont, CA	800-354-9706
Frank R. Walker Co., Lisle, IL	800-458-3737
Frederick Warne & Co., New York, NY	
Dist: Viking Penguin	800-631-3577
Warner Books, New York, NY	800-638-6460

Publisher/Distributor	Toll-Free No.
Warner Press, Anderson, IN	800-428-6427; (orders) 800-428-6409
Washington Square Press, New York, NY	800-223-2336
Watson-Guptill Publications, New York, NY	800-451-1741
Franklin Watts, New York, NY	800-672-6672
Weidenfeld & Nicolson, New York, NY	800-521-0178
Samuel Weiser, York Beach, ME	(orders only) 800-423-7087
Wesleyan University Press, Middletown, CT	800-638-3030
West Publishing Co., College & School Div., St. Paul, MN	(customer service) 800-328-2209; 800-328-9424
Westcliffe Publications, Englewood, CO	800-523-3692
Westin Communications, Woodland Hills, CA	800-421-1893
Westminster Press, Philadelphia, PA	800-523-1631; PA 800-462-0405
Whatever Publishing, San Rafael, CA	(retail orders only) 800-227-3900 CA 800-632-2122
Dist: Bookpeople	800-227-1516; CA 800-624-4466
Whitaker House, Springdale, PA	800-444-4484
White Dove Publishing Co., San Diego, CA	800-621-0852
Albert Whitman & Co., Niles, IL	800-255-7675
Whitney Library of Design, New York, NY	800-526-3641
Whole World Publishing, Deerfield, IL	800-323-4305
Wildwood Publications, Traverse City, MI	800-447-7367
Williams & Wilkins, Baltimore, MD	800-638-0672
Dist: J. A. Majors Co.	800-345-4366; GA 800-241-6551; TX 800-527-3492
Matthews Medical Book Co.	800-633-2665
Willow Creek Press, Wautoma, WI	800-341-7770
H. W. Wilson, Bronx, NY	800-367-6770
Windsor Publications, Northridge, CA	800-423-5761
Harry Winston, New York, NY	800-223-2305
Winston-Derek Publishers, Nashville, TN	800-826-1888
Wonder-Treasure Books, Los Angeles, CA	800-421-0892; CA 800-227-8801
Wordware Publishing, Plano, TX	800-231-7467
Workman Publishing Co., New York, NY	800-722-7202
World Book, Chicago, IL	800-621-8202
Writer's Digest Books, Cincinnati, OH	800-543-4644; OH 800-543-8677
Year Book Medical Publishers, Chicago, IL	800-621-9262
Zebra Books, New York, NY	800-221-2647

International Standard Book Number (ISBN)

Emery Koltay
Director, United States ISBN Agency

The International Standard Book Numbering (ISBN) system was introduced into the United Kingdom by J. Whitaker & Sons, Ltd., in 1967, and into the United States in 1968 by R. R. Bowker Company. The Technical Committee on Documentation of the International Organization for Standardization (ISO TC 46) defines the scope of the standard as follows:

> . . . the purpose of this standard is to coordinate and standardize the use of identifying numbers so that each ISBN is unique to a title, edition of a book, or monographic publication published, or produced, by a specific publisher, or producer. Also, the standard specifies the construction of the ISBN and the location of the printing on the publication.
>
> Books and other monographic publications may include printed books and pamphlets (in various bindings), mixed media publications, other similar media including educational films/videos and transparencies, books on cassettes, microcomputer software, electronic publications, microform publications, braille publications and maps. Serial publications and music sound recordings are specifically excluded, as they are covered by other identification systems. [ISO Standard 2108]

The ISBN is used by publishers, distributors, wholesalers, book stores, and libraries, among others, in 64 countries to expedite such operations as order fulfillment, electronic point-of-sale checkout, inventory control, returns processing, circulation/location control, file maintenance and update, library union lists, and royalty payments.

Construction of an ISBN

An ISBN consists of ten digits separated into the following parts:

1. Group identifier—national, geographic, language, or other convenient group
2. Publisher or producer identifier
3. Title identifier
4. Check digit

When an ISBN is written or printed, it should be preceded by the letters ISBN, and each part should be separated by a space or hyphen. In the United States, the hyphen is used for separation, as in the following example: ISBN 0-394-57327-7. In this example, 0 is the group identifier, 394 is the publisher identifier, 57327 is the title identifier, and 7 is the check digit. The group of English-speaking countries, which includes the United States, Australia, Canada, New Zealand, and the United Kingdom, uses the group identifiers 0 and 1.

The ISBN Organization

The administration of the ISBN system is carried out at three levels—through the International ISBN Agency in Berlin, West Germany; the national agencies; and the publishing houses themselves. Responsible for assigning country prefixes and for coordinating the worldwide implementation of the system, the International ISBN Agency in Berlin has an advisory panel that represents the International Organization for Standardization (ISO), publishers, and libraries. The International ISBN Agency publishes the *ISBN System User's Manual*—the basic guide for all national agencies—and the *Publishers International ISBN Directory,* which is distributed in the United States by the R. R. Bowker Company. As the publisher of *Books in Print,* with its extensive and varied database of publishers' addresses, the R. R. Bowker Company was the obvious place to initiate the ISBN system and from which to provide the service to the U.S. publishing industry. To date, the U.S. ISBN Agency has entered more than 45,000 publishers into the system.

ISBN Assignment Procedure

Assignment of ISBNs is a shared endeavor between the U.S. ISBN Agency and the publisher. The publisher is provided with an application form, an Advanced Book Information (ABI) form, and an instruction sheet. After an application is received and verified by the agency, an ISBN publisher prefix is assigned, along with a computer-generated block of ISBNs. The publisher then has the responsibility to assign an ISBN to each title, to keep an accurate record of the numbers assigned by entering each title in the ISBN Log Book, and to report each title to the *Books in Print* database. One of the responsibilities of the ISBN Agency is to validate assigned ISBNs and to retain a record of all ISBNs in circulation.

ISBN implementation is very much market driven. Wholesalers and distributors, such as Baker and Taylor, Brodart, and Ingram, as well as such large retail chains as Waldenbooks and B. Dalton, recognize and enforce the ISBN system, by requiring all new publishers to register with the ISBN Agency before accepting their books for sale. Also, the ISBN is a mandatory bibliographic element in the International Standard Bibliographical Description (ISBD). The Library of Congress Cataloging in Publication (CIP) Division directs publishers to the agency to obtain their ISBN prefixes.

Location and Display of the ISBN

On books, pamphlets, and other printed material, the ISBN shall be on the verso of the title leaf or, if this is not possible, at the foot of the title leaf itself. It shall also appear at the foot of the outside back cover if practicable and at the foot of the back of the jacket if the book has one (the lower right-hand corner is recommended). If neither of these alternatives is possible, then the number shall be printed in some other prominent position on the outside. The ISBN shall also appear on any accompanying promotional materials following the provisions for location according to the format of the material.

On other monographic publications, the ISBN shall appear on the title or credit frames and any labels permanently affixed to the publication. If the publication is issued in a container that is an integral part of the publication, such as a cassette or microcomputer software, the ISBN shall be displayed on the label. If it is not possible to place the ISBN on the item or its label, then the number should be displayed on the bottom or the back of the container, box, sleeve, or frame. It should also appear on any accompanying material, including each component of a multitype publication.

Printing of ISBN in Machine-Readable Coding

In the last few years, much work has been done on machine-readable representations of the ISBN, and many books now carry ISBNs in optical character recognition (OCR) form and in bar code. The rapid worldwide extension of bar code scanning has brought into prominence the 1980 agreement between the International Article Numbering, formerly the European Article Numbering (EAN), Association and the International ISBN Agency, which allows the ISBN to be translated into an EAN bar code.

All EAN bar codes start with a national identifier (00–09 representing the United States), *except* those on books and periodicals. The agreement replaces the usual national identifier with a special "Bookland" identifier represented by the digits 978 for books (see example) and 977 for periodicals. The 978 Bookland/EAN prefix is followed by the first nine digits of the ISBN. The check digit of the ISBN is dropped and replaced by a check digit calculated according to the EAN rules (see Figure 1).

ISBN 0-8352-2477-5

Figure 1. Printing the ISBN in Bookland/EAN Symbology.

The following is an example of the conversion of the ISBN to ISBN Bookland/EAN:

ISBN	0-8352-2477-5
ISBN without check digit	0-8352-2477
Adding EAN flag	978083522477
EAN with EAN check digit	9780835224772

Five-Digit Add-on Code

In the United States, a five-digit add-on code is utilized for additional information. In the publishing industry, this code can be used for price information or some other specific coding. The lead digit of the five-digit add-on has been designated a currency identifier, when the add-on is used for price. Number 5 is the code for the U.S. dollar; number 6 is for the Canadian dollar. Currency identifiers for other English-speaking countries will be determined in the future. Publishers that do not want to indicate price in the add-on should print the code 90000 (see Figure 2).

978 ISBN Bookland/EAN Prefix
039475835 ISBN Minus check digit
0 = New EAN check digit
5 = Code for U.S.$
1195 = $11.95

90000 means no information in the add-on code

Figure 2. Printing the ISBN Bookland/EAN Number in Bar Code with the Five-Digit Add-on Code.

Reporting the Title and the ISBN

After the publisher reports a title with the ISBN Agency, the number is validated and the title is listed in the many R. R. Bowker Company hard copy and electronic publications, including: *Books in Print, Forthcoming Books, Paperbound Books in Print, Books in Print Supplement, Books Out of Print, Books in Print Online, Books in Print Plus-CD ROM, Children's Books in Print, Subject Guide to Children's Books in Print, On Cassette: A Comprehensive Bibliography of Spoken Word Audiocassettes, Variety's Complete Home Video Directory, Software Encyclopedia, Software for Schools,* and other specialized publications.

For an ISBN application form and additional information, write to United States ISBN Agency, R. R. Bowker Company, 245 W. 17 St., New York, NY 10011; or call 212-337-6971.

International Standard Serial Number (ISSN)

Julia C. Blixrud
Head, National Serials Data Program,
Library of Congress

Nearly two decades ago, the rapid increase in the production and dissemination of information and an intensified desire to exchange information about serials in computerized form among different systems and organizations made it increasingly clear that a means to identify serial publications at an international level was needed. The International Standard Serial Number (ISSN) was developed and has become the internationally accepted code for the identification of serial publications. The number itself has no significance other than brief, unique, and unambiguous identification. It is an international standard, ISO 3297, as well as a U.S. standard, ANSI Z39.9, and has been in use since 1971. The ISSN consists of eight digits in arabic numerals 0 to 9, except for the last or check digit, which can be an X. The numbers appear as two groups of four digits separated by a hyphen and preceded by the letters ISSN – for example, ISSN 1234-5679.

The ISSN is not self-assigned by publishers. Administration of the ISSN is coordinated through the International Serials Data System (ISDS), an intergovernmental organization established within the framework of the UNESCO/UNISIST program. ISDS is a network of national and regional centers, coordinated by an international center. Centers have the responsibility to register serials published in their respective countries.

Since serials are generally known and cited by their titles, the assignment of the ISSN is inseparably linked to a key title. This title is a standardized form of the title derived from information appearing in the serial issue. Only one ISSN can be assigned to a title; if the title changes, a new ISSN must be assigned. Centers responsible for the assignment of ISSN also construct the key title and create an associated bibliographic record for each assignment.

The ISDS International Center handles ISSN assignments for international organizations and for those countries that do not yet have a national center. It also maintains and distributes the collective ISDS database that contains bibliographic records corresponding to each ISSN assignment as reported by the rest of the ISDS network. The ISDS database contains more than 400,000 records.

In the United States, the National Serials Data Program (NSDP) at the Library of Congress is responsible for the assignment and maintenance of ISSN to all U.S. serial titles. Publishers wishing to have an ISSN assigned can either request an application form from or send a current issue of their publication to the program and ask for an assignment to be made. The assignment of the ISSN is free and there is no charge for its use.

The ISSN is currently used all over the world by serial publishers to distinguish similar serial titles from each other. It is used by subscription services and libraries to manage their files for orders, claims, and back issues. It is used in automated check-in systems by libraries that wish to process receipts more quickly. Copyright centers use the ISSN as a means to collect and disseminate royalties. It is also used as an identification code by postal services and legal deposit services. The ISSN is included as a verification element in interlibrary lending activities and for union catalogs as a collocating device. In recent years, the ISSN is being incorporated into bar codes for optical recognition of serial publications and into the standards for the identification of issues and articles in serial publications.

For further information about the ISSN or the ISDS network, U.S. libraries and publishers should contact the National Serials Data Program, Library of Congress, Washington, DC 20540 (202-707-6452). Non-U.S. parties should contact the ISDS International Center, 20 rue Bachaumont, 75002 Paris, France (1) 42.36.73.81.

Distinguished Books

Notable Books of 1988

This is the forty-second year in which this list of distinguished books has been issued by the Notable Books Council of the Reference and Adult Services Division of the American Library Association.

Fiction

Allende, Isabel. *Eva Luna.* Trans. from the Spanish by Margaret Sayers Reden. Knopf. $18.45.

Carver, Raymond. *Where I'm Calling From: New and Selected Stories.* Atlantic Monthly Press. $19.95.

DeLillo, Don. *Libra.* Knopf. $19.95.

Dexter, Pete. *Paris Trout.* Random. $17.95.

Dubus, Andre. *Selected Stories.* David Godine. $19.95.

Erdrich, Louise. *Tracks.* Holt. $18.95.

Garcia Marquez, Gabriel. *Love in the Time of Cholera.* Translated from the Spanish by Edith Grossman. Knopf. $18.95.

Greenberg, Joanne. *Of Such Small Differences.* Holt. $18.95.

Lessing, Doris. *The Fifth Child.* Knopf. $16.95.

Mukherjee, Bharati. *The Middleman and Other Stories.* Grove. $15.95.

Naylor, Gloria. *Mama Day.* Ticknor & Fields. $18.95.

Powers, J. F. *Wheat That Springeth Green.* Knopf. $18.95.

Sexton, Linda Gray. *Points of Light.* Little, Brown. $16.95.

Smith, Lee. *Fair and Tender Ladies.* Putnam. $17.95.

Spark, Muriel. *A Far Cry from Kensington.* Houghton. $17.95.

Tyler, Anne. *Breathing Lessons.* Knopf. $18.45.

Nonfiction

Berton, Pierre. *The Arctic Grail: The Quest for the North West Passage and the North Pole, 1818–1909.* Viking. $24.95.

Cagin, Seth, and Philip Dray. *We Are Not Afraid: The Story of Goodman, Schwerner, and Chaney and the Civil Rights Campaign for Mississippi.* Macmillan. $22.50.

Ellmann, Richard. *Oscar Wilde.* Knopf. $24.95.

Gay, Peter. *Freud: A Life for Our Time.* Norton. $25.00.

Goodwin, Richard N. *Remembering America: A Voice from the Sixties.* Little, Brown. $19.95.

Hansen, Eric. *Stranger in the Forest: On Foot across Borneo.* Houghton. $8.95.

Lester, Julius. *Lovesong: Becoming a Jew.* Holt. $17.95.

Maddox, Brenda. *Nora: The Real Life of Molly Bloom.* Houghton. $24.95.

McPherson, James M. *Battle Cry of Freedom: The Civil War Era.* Oxford. $35.00.

Pagels, Elaine. *Adam, Eve, and the Serpent.* Random. $17.45.

Sharansky, Natan. *Fear No Evil.* Trans. by Stefani Hoffmann. Random. $18.95.

Best Young Adult Books of 1988

Each year a committee of the Young Adult Services Division of the American Library Association compiles a list of best books for young adults selected on the basis of young adult appeal. These titles must meet acceptable standards of literary merit and provide a variety of subjects for different tastes and a broad range of reading levels. *School Library Journal (SLJ)* also provides a list of best books for young adults. The 1988 list was compiled by the Adult Books for Young Adults Committee, made up of public and school librarians, and was published in the December 1988 issue of the journal. The following list combines the titles selected for both lists. The notation ALA or *SLJ* following the price indicates the source of each selection.

American Sports Poems. Selected by R. R. Knudson and May Swenson. Orchard. $14.95. ALA.

Ashabranner, Brent. *Always to Remember: The Story of the Vietnam Veterans Memorial.* Dodd. Price not available. ALA.

At the Heart of the White Rose: Letters and Diaries of Hans and Sophie Scholl. Ed. by Inge Jens. Harper. $21.45. ALA.

Bova, Ben. *Welcome to Moonbase.* Ballantine. $9.95. ALA.

Brown, Rita Mae. *Starting from Scratch: A Different Kind of Writer's Manual.* Bantam. $16.95. ALA.

Cable, Mary. *The Blizzard of '88.* Atheneum. $19.95. ALA.

Cagin, Seth, and Philip Dray. *We Are Not Afraid: The Murder of Goodman, Schwerner and Chaney and the Civil Rights Campaign for Mississippi.* Macmillan. $22.50. ALA.

Cheneviere, Alain. *Vanishing Tribes: Primitive Man on Earth.* Dolphin/Doubleday. $35. *SLJ.*

Cleary, Beverly. *A Girl from Yamhill.* Morrow. $14.95. ALA.

Coman, Carolyn, and Judy Dater. *Body and Soul: Ten American Women.* Hill. $27.50. ALA.

Cormier, Robert. *Fade.* Delacorte. $15.95. ALA.

Davis, Jenny. *Sex Education.* Orchard/Watts. $13.95. *SLJ.*

Dillard, Annie. *An American Childhood.* Harper. $17.95. *SLJ.*

Dorris, Michael. *Yellow Raft in Blue Water.* Holt. $16.95. *SLJ.*

Edgerton, Clyde. *The Floatplane Notebooks.* Algonquin. $16.95. ALA.

Fagan, Brian M. *The Great Journey: The Peopling of Ancient America.* Thames and Hudson. $19.95, pap. $10.95. *SLJ.*

Feldbaum, Carl B., and Ronald J. Bee. *Looking the Tiger in the Eye.* Harper. $14.95. ALA.

Flanigan, Sara. *Alice.* St. Martin's. $16.95. ALA.

Fleischman, Paul. *Joyful Noise: Poems for Two Voices.* A Charlotte Zolotow Book, Harper. $11.95. ALA.

Freedman, Russell. *Buffalo Hunt.* Holiday. $16.95. *SLJ.*

______. *Lincoln: A Photobiography.* Clarion. $15.95. ALA.

Garfield, Leon. *The Empty Sleeve.* Delacorte. $14.95. *SLJ.*

Gelman, Rita Golden. *Inside Nicaragua: Young People's Dreams and Fears.* Watts. $13.90. ALA.

Giddings, Robert. *The War Poets.* Crown/Orion Books. $24.95. ALA.

Gies, Miep. *Anne Frank Remembered.* Simon & Schuster. $17.95. *SLJ.*

Gordon, Jacquie. *Give Me One Wish: A True Story of Courage and Love.* Norton. $18.95. ALA.

Greenberg, Joanne. *Of Such Small Differences.* Holt. $18.95. ALA.

Greene, Marilyn, and Gary Provost. *Finder: The True Story of a Private Investigator.* Crown. $18.95. ALA.

Hailey, Kendall. *The Day I Became an Autodidact.* Delacorte. $15.95. ALA.

Hambly, Barbara. *Those Who Hunt the Night.* Ballantine/Del Rey. $16.95. ALA.

Hamilton, Virginia. *Anthony Burns: The Defeat and Triumph of a Fugitive Slave.* Knopf. $11.95. ALA, *SLJ.*

______. *In the Beginning: Creation Stories from around the World.* Harcourt. $18.95. ALA.

Hartmann, William, and Ron Miller. *Cycles of Fire.* Workman. $27.50. *SLJ.*

Haskins, James, and Kathleen Benson. *The 60s Reader.* Viking/Kestrel. $13.95. ALA.

Heller, Nancy G. *Women Artists: An Illustrated History.* Abbeville. $19.95. *SLJ.*

Hillerman, Tony. *A Thief of Time.* Harper & Row. $15.95. ALA.

Hinton, S. E. *Taming the Star Runner.* Delacorte. $14.95. ALA.

Hoffman, Alice. *At Risk.* Putnam. $17.95. ALA.

Hoover, H. M. *The Dawn Palace: The Story of Medea.* Dutton. $15.95. ALA.

Hotze, Sollace. *A Circle Unbroken.* Clarion. $13.95. ALA.

Huggan, Isabel. *The Elizabeth Stories.* Viking. $15.95, pap. $6.95. *SLJ.*

Humphreys, Josephine. *Rich in Love.* Viking. $16.95, pap. $7.95. *SLJ.*

Jacobs, Paul Samuel. *Born into Light.* Scholastic. $12.95. *SLJ.*

Janeczko, Paul B., sel. *The Music of What Happens: Poems That Tell Stories.* Orchard/Watts. $14.95. *SLJ.*

Kahn, Albert E. *The Matusow Affair: Memoir of a National Scandal.* Moyer Bell. $18.95, pap. $9.95. *SLJ.*

Katz, Welwyn Wilton. *False Face.* McElderry/Macmillan. $12.95. *SLJ.*

Kennedy, William P. *Toy Soldiers.* St. Martin's. $19.95. ALA.

Kingsolver, Barbara. *The Bean Trees.* Harper. $16.95. ALA.

Koertge, Ron. *The Arizona Kid.* Little, Brown. $14.95. ALA.

Komunyakaa, Yusef. *Dien Cai Dau.* Wesleyan University/Harper. $9.95. ALA.

Kozol, Jonathan. *Rachel and Her Children: Homeless Families in America.* Crown. $17.95. ALA.

Langone, John. *AIDS: The Facts.* Little, Brown. pap. $8.95. ALA.

Lasky, Kathryn. *The Bone Wars.* Morrow. $12.95. *SLJ.*

Lyon, George Ella. *Borrowed Children.* Orchard/Watts. $12.95. *SLJ.*

MacKay, Donald A. *The Building of Manhattan: How Manhattan Was Built over Ground and Underground from the Dutch Settlers to the Skyscraper.* Harper. $16.95. ALA.

McKinley, Robin. *The Outlaws of Sherwood.* Greenwillow. $11.95. ALA.

Madaras, Lynda. *Lynda Madaras Talks to Teens about AIDS: An Essential Guide for Parents, Teachers and Young People.* Newmarket/Harper. $12.95, pap. $5.95. ALA, *SLJ.*

Mahy, Margaret. *Memory.* Margaret K. McElderry Books. $13.95. ALA, *SLJ.*

Mazer, Norma Fox. *Silver.* Morrow. $11.95. ALA.

Meltzer, Milton. *Rescue: The Story of How Gentiles Saved Jews in the Holocaust.* Harper. $12.95. ALA, *SLJ.*

Mills, Judie. *John F. Kennedy.* Watts. $14.95. ALA, *SLJ.*

Mitgang, Herbert. *Dangerous Dossiers.* Donald I. Fine. $16.95. *SLJ.*

Mowat, Farley. *Woman in the Mists.* Warner. $19.50, pap. $10.95. *SLJ.*

The Music of What Happens: Poems That Tell Stories. Sel. by Paul Janeczko. Orchard. $14.95. ALA.

Myers, Walter Dean. *Fallen Angels.* Scholastic. $12.95. ALA, *SLJ.*

______. *Scorpions.* Harper. $12.95. ALA.

Ngor, Haing, and Roger Warner. *Haing Ngor: A Cambodian Odyssey.* Macmillan. $19.95. ALA.

Nilsson, Lennart, and Jan Lindberg. *The Body Victorious.* Delacorte. pap. $25. *SLJ.*

Noonan, Michael. *McKenzie's Boots.* Orchard. $13.95. ALA.

Palmer, Laura. *Schrapnel in the Heart.* Random. $17.95, pap. $7.95.

Paulsen, Gary. *The Island.* Orchard. $17.95, pap. $7.95. ALA.

Penman, Sharon Kay. *Falls the Shadow.* Holt. $18.45. *SLJ.*

Pringle, Terry. *The Preacher's Boy.* Algonquin. $15.95. ALA.

Pullman, Philip. *Shadow in the North.* Knopf. $12.95. ALA.

Rendell, Ruth. *Heartstones.* Harper. $10.95. *SLJ.*

Rhythm Road: Poems to Move To. Sel. by Lillian Morrison. Lothrop, Lee & Shepard. $11.95. ALA.

Riddles, Libby, and Tim Jones. *Race across Alaska: First Woman to Win the Iditarod Tells Her Story.* Stackpole. pap. $14.95. ALA.

Rinaldi, Ann. *The Last Silk Dress.* Holiday House. $15.95. ALA.

Ritter, Lawrence S. *The Babe: A Life in Pictures*. Ticknor & Fields. $39.95. ALA.

Rogasky, Barbara. *Smoke and Ashes: The Story of the Holocaust*. Holiday House. $16.95. ALA, *SLJ*.

Ruskin, Cindy. *The Quilt: Stories from the NAMES Project*. Pocket Books. $22.95. ALA.

Rylant, Cynthia. *A Kindness*. Orchard. $13.95. ALA, *SLJ*.

Salzman, Mark. *Iron and Silk*. Random. $16.95, pap. $5.95. *SLJ*.

Sattler, Helen Roney. *Hominids: A Look Back at Our Ancestors*. Illus. by Christopher Santoro. Lothrop. $15.95. *SLJ*.

Severin, TIm. *The Ulysses Voyage: Sea Search for the Odyssey*. Dutton. $21.95. ALA.

Shilts, Randy. *And the Band Played On*. St. Martin's. $24.95. *SLJ*.

Sleator, William. *The Duplicate*. Dutton. $12.95. ALA, *SLJ*.

Somehow Tenderness Survives: Stories of Southern Africa. Collected by Hazel Rochman. Harper. $12.95. ALA.

Spielberg, Nathan, and Byron D. Anderson. *Seven Ideas That Shook the World*. Wiley. $22.95, pap. $14.95. *SLJ*.

Tolan, Stephanie S. *A Good Courage*. Morrow. $11.95. *SLJ*.

Vare, Ethlie Ann, and Greg Ptacek. *Mothers of Invention: From the Bra to the Bomb: Forgotten Women & Their Unforgettable Ideas*. Morrow. $17.95. ALA.

The Wall: Images and Offerings from the Vietnam Veterans Memorial. Ed. by Sal Lopes. Collins. $24.95. ALA.

Willeford, Charles. *I Was Looking for a Street*. Countryman. $14.95. ALA.

Wolff, Virginia E. *Probably Still Nick Swansen*. Holt. $13.95. ALA, *SLJ*.

Wyss, Thelma Hatch. *Here at the Scenic-Vu Motel*. Harper. $11.70. ALA.

Xiyang, Tang. *Living Treasures: An Odyssey through China's Extraordinary Nature Reserves*. Bantam. $29.95. ALA.

Best Children's Books of 1988

A list of notable children's books is selected each year by the Notable Children's Books Committee of the Association for Library Service to Children of the American Library Association (ALA). The committee is aided by suggestions from school and public children's librarians throughout the United States. The book review editors of *School Library Journal (SLJ)* also compile a list each year, with full notations, of best books for children. The following list is a combination of ALA's Notable Children's Books of 1988 and *SLJ*'s selection of "Best Books 1988," published in the December 1988 issue of *SLJ*. The source of each selection is indicated by the notation ALA or *SLJ* following each entry. [See "Literary Prizes" later in Part 5 for Newbery, Caldecott, and other award winners—*Ed.*]

Ackerman, Karen. *Song and Dance Man*. Illus. by Stephen Gammell. Knopf. $11.99. ALA.

Agee, Jon. *The Incredible Painting of Felix Clousseau*. Farrar. $13.95. ALA.

Alcock, Vivien. *The Monster Garden*. Delacorte. $13.95. ALA.

Apfel, Necia H. *Nebulae: The Birth and Death of Stars*. Lothrop. $13.95. *SLJ*.

Arnosky, Jim. *Sketching Outdoors in Winter*. Lothrop. $12.95. ALA.

Ashabranner, Brent. *Always to Remember: The Story of the Vietnam Veterans Memorial*. Dodd. o.p. ALA.

Ballard, Robert D. *Exploring the Titanic*. Scholastic. $14.95. *SLJ.*

Banish, Roslyn. *Let Me Tell You about My Baby*. Harper. $12.70. *SLJ.*

Barton, Byron. *I Want to Be an Astronaut*. Crowell. $7.95. ALA.

Bawden, Nina. *Henry*. Illus. by Joyce Powzyk. Lothrop. $13. ALA.

Berry, James. *A Thief in the Village and Other Stories*. Orchard. $12.95. ALA.

Bjork, Christina. *Linnea's Windowsill Garden*. Trans. by Joan Sandin. Illus. by Lena Anderson. R & S Books. $10.95. ALA.

Booth, Jerry. *The Big Beast Book*. Illus. by Martha Weston. Little, Brown. $14.95. ALA.

Byars, Betsy. *The Burning Questions of Bingo Brown*. Viking. $11.95. *SLJ.*

Carroll, Lewis. *Alice's Adventures in Wonderland*. Illus. by Anthony Browne. Knopf. $19.95. *SLJ.*

Chaucer, Geoffrey. *Canterbury Tales*. Adapt., sel., and trans. by Barbara Cohen. Illus. by Trina Schart Hyman. Lothrop. $17.95. *SLJ.*

Cleary, Beverly. *A Girl from Yamhill: A Memoir*. Morrow. $14.95. ALA.

Colman, Warren. *Understanding and Preventing AIDS*. Children's Press. $14.60, pap. $6.95. ALA.

Cooney, Barbara. *Island Boy*. Viking. $14.95. *SLJ.*

deRegniers, Beatrice Schenk, and others, eds. *Sing a Song of Popcorn: Every Child's Book of Poems*. Illus. by Marcia Brown and others. Scholastic. $16.95. *SLJ.*

Dickinson, Peter. *Merlin Dreams*. Illus. by Alan Lee. Delacorte. $19.95. ALA.

Ellis, Sarah. *A Family Project*. McElderry. $12.95. ALA.

Fleischman, Paul. *Joyful Noise: Poems for Two Voices*. Illus. by Eric Bellows. Harper. $11.95. ALA.

Fox, Paula. *The Village by the Sea*. Orchard/Watts. $13.95. ALA, *SLJ.*

Freedman, Russell. *Buffalo Hunt*. Holiday. $16.95. ALA, *SLJ.*

Fritz, Jean. *China's Long March*. Putnam. $14.95. ALA.

Giblin, James Cross. *Let There Be Light: A Book about Windows*. Crowell. $14.95. ALA.

Goble, Paul. *Her Seven Brothers*. Bradbury. $13.95. *SLJ.*

______. *Iktomi and the Boulder: A Plains Indian Story*. Orchard. $13.95. ALA.

Greenfield, Eloise. *Grandpa's Face*. Illus. by Floyd Cooper. Philomel. $13.95. ALA, *SLJ.*

______. *Under the Sunday Tree*. Paintings by Amos Ferguson. Harper. $13.95. ALA.

Haldane, Suzanne. *Painting Faces*. Dutton. $13.95. ALA.

Hamilton, Virginia. *In the Beginning: Creation Stories from around the World*. Illus. by Barry Moser. Harcourt. $18.95. ALA.

Hansen, Joyce. *Out from This Place*. Walker. $13.95. ALA.

Hartling, Peter. *Crutches*. Trans. by Elizabeth D. Crawford. Lothrop. $11.95. ALA.

Henkes, Kevin. *Chester's Way*. Greenwillow. $11.95. ALA.

Hughes, Shirley. *Out and About*. Lothrop. $13. ALA.

Hutchins, Pat. *Where's the Baby?* Greenwillow. $11.95. *SLJ.*

Jacobs, Paul Samuel. *Born into Light*. Scholastic. $12.95. *SLJ.*

Jones, Diana Wynne. *The Lives of Christopher Chant*. Greenwillow. $11.95. ALA.

Kasza, Keiko. *The Pigs' Picnic*. Putnam. $13.95. *SLJ.*

Katz, Welwyn Wilton. *False Face*. McElderry/Macmillan. $12.95. *SLJ.*

Larrick, Nancy, comp. *Cats Are Cats*. Illus. by Ed Young. Philomel. $17.95. ALA.

______. *Sea Swan*. Illus. by Catherine Stock. Macmillan. $13.95. *SLJ.*

Lester, Julius, retel. *More Tales of Uncle Remus: Further Adventures of Brer Rabbit, His Friends, Enemies, and Others*. Illus. by Jerry Pinkney. Dial. $15. ALA, *SLJ.*

Little, Jean. *Little by Little: A Writer's Education*. Viking Kestrel. $11.95. ALA.

Loh, Morag. *Tucking Mommy In*. Illus. by Donna Rawlins. Orchard. $12.95. ALA.

Lowry, Lois. *All about Sam*. Illus. by Diane deGroat. Houghton. $12.95. *SLJ.*

Lyon, George Ella. *Borrowed Children*. Orchard/Watts. $12.95. *SLJ.*

Macaulay, David. *The Way Things Work*. Houghton. $24.95. ALA, *SLJ.*

McKinley, Robin. *The Outlaws of Sherwood*. Greenwillow. $11.95. ALA.

McKissack, Patricia. *Mirandy and Brother Wind*. Illus. by Jerry Pinkney. Knopf. $12.95. ALA.

MacLachlan, Patricia. *The Facts and Fictions of Minna Pratt*. Harper. $11.95. ALA.

Marshall, James, retel. *Goldilocks and the Three Bears*. Dial. $10.50. ALA, *SLJ*.

Meltzer, Milton. *Benjamin Franklin: The New American*. Watts. $14.90. ALA.

Moore, Lilian. *I'll Meet You at the Cucumbers*. Illus. by Sharon Wooding. Atheneum. $12.95. *SLJ*.

Morrison, Lillian, sel. *Rhythm Road: Poems to Move to*. Lothrop. $11.95. ALA.

______. *Me, Mop, and Moondance Kid*. Delacorte. Price not set. ALA.

______. *Scorpions*. Harper. $12.95. ALA.

The Nativity. Illus. by Julie Vivas. Harcourt. $13.95. ALA.

Opie, Iona, and Peter Opie, eds. *Tail Feathers from Mother Goose: The Opie Rhyme Book*. Little, Brown. $19.45. ALA, *SLJ*.

Owens, Mary Beth. *A Caribou Alphabet*. Dog Ear Press. $13.95. ALA.

Parker, Steve. *Skeleton*. Knopf (Eyewitness). $12.95. ALA.

Paxton, Tom. *Aesop's Fables*. Illus. by Richard Rayevsky. Morrow. $12.95. *SLJ*.

Pople, Maureen. *The Other Side of the Family*. Holt. $13.45. *SLJ*.

Rogasky, Barbara. *Smoke and Ashes: The Story of the Holocaust*. Holiday. $16.95. ALA, *SLJ*.

Roth-Hano, Renee. *Touch Wood: A Girlhood in Occupied France*. Four Winds. Price not set. ALA.

Sattler, Helen Roney. *Hominids: A Look Back at Our Ancestors*. Illus. by Christopher Santoro. Lothrop. $15.95. ALA, *SLJ*.

Schwartz, Amy. *Annabelle Swift, Kindergartner*. Orchard/Watts. $12.95. ALA, *SLJ*.

Scott, Elaine. *Ramona: Behind the Scenes of a Television Show*. Morrow. $13.95. ALA.

Sleator, William. *The Duplicate*. Dutton. $12.95. ALA, *SLJ*.

Smith, Janice Lee. *The Show-and-Tell War: And Other Stories about Adam Joshua*. Illus. by Dick Gackenbach. Harper. $10.70. *SLJ*.

Snyder, Dianne. *The Boy of the Three-Year Nap*. Illus. by Allen Say. Houghton. $14.95. ALA, *SLJ*.

Steig, William. *Spinky Sulks*. Farrar. $13.95. ALA.

Thiele, Colin. *Farmer Schulz's Ducks*. Harper. $12.95. ALA.

______. *Shadow Shark*. Harper. $12.95. ALA.

Thomas, Jane Resh. *Saying Goodbye to Grandma*. Illus. by Marcia Sewell. Clarion. $13.95. ALA.

Tolan, Stephenie S. *A Good Courage*. Morrow. $11.95. *SLJ*.

Trezise, Percy, and Dick Roughsey. *Turramulli the Giant Quinkin*. Gareth Stevens. $15. ALA.

Vincent, Gabrielle. *Feel Better, Ernest!* Greenwillow. $11.95. *SLJ*.

Wells, Rosemary. *Shy Charles*. Dial. $11.60. *SLJ*.

White, Ruth. *Sweet Creek Holler*. Farrar. $11.95. ALA.

Wiesner, David. *Free Fall*. Lothrop. $13.95. ALA.

Williams, Vera B. *Stringbean's Trip to the Shining Sea*. Illus. by the author and Jennifer Williams. *Greenwillow*. $11.95. ALA, *SLJ*.

Yorinks, Arthur. *Bravo, Minski*. Illus. by Richard Egielski. Farrar. $13.95. *SLJ*.

______. *Company's Coming*. Illus. by David Small. Crown. $11.95. ALA.

Bestsellers of 1988: Hardcover Fiction and Nonfiction

Daisy Maryles
Executive Editor, *Publishers Weekly*

No new significant sales records were set by the 1988 crop of hardcover bestsellers, although just maintaining some of those established in previous years is a cause for celebration. The news for 1987 was in the sheer breadth of titles with sales of more than 100,000 copies, and the same can be said for 1988. In fiction, 51 books had sales claims of more than 100,000, just one notch down from the 1987 record of 52. In nonfiction, 76 made it to the six-figure count, easing out the record 72 set in 1987.

In 1988, three books went over the million-copy mark compared with four in 1987 and five in each of the two years prior. Sales were also down for books selling over the 500,000 figure—in 1988, 12 topsellers made this claim, compared with 17 in 1987. Also, sales for the top 30 nonfiction titles have fallen off. In 1987, the top dozen were over the 400,000 mark and the top 30 enjoyed sales of more than 200,000 copies. In 1988, only seven books sold more than 400,000 copies and 25 went over 200,000.

Fiction, however, enjoyed a surge of sorts, though not at the higher counts. In the top 15 rankings, 1987 figures for novels matched or surpassed the numbers set in 1988—three over the 1-million mark in both years; ten over 500,000 in 1987, compared with six in 1988. But novels with reported sales over 200,000 copies stood at 25 in 1988, compared with 18 in 1987, and 39 novels sold more than 150,000 copies in 1988, compared with 23 in 1987.

The books and subjects that comprise these topsellers haven't changed. In fiction, nearly all the authors among the top 15 have held top rankings in previous years. "Newcomers" included Wilhelm Grimm and Maurice Sendak, author and illustrator, respectively, of *Dear Mili.* The only new novelist among the fiction books selling more than 100,000 was actress Joan Collins, hardly an unknown writer.

In fact, several thespians enjoyed long runs on *PW's* weekly nonfiction list, resulting in high rankings among the coveted end-of-the-year slots. They included George Burns, Elizabeth Taylor, Michael Jackson, Kirk Douglas, and Shirley Temple Black. The nonfiction topsellers were also dominated by celebrities from the business and political fields as well as by familiar nonfiction bestselling authors. The surprise title in the nonfiction group was *A Brief History of Time: From the Big Bang to Black Holes* by Stephen W. Hawking, a prominent and highly regarded theoretical physicist whose academic and professional achievements are even more spectacular considering his 20-year affliction with Lou Gehrig's disease.

"Shipped and Billed" Figures

The books on *PW's* annual bestseller lists, including all the runners-up, are based on sales figures supplied by publishers for new books published in 1987 and 1988. These figures, according to the publishers, reflect only 1988 U.S. *trade* sales—that is, sales

Note: Adapted from *Publishers Weekly,* March 10, 1989.

to bookstores, wholesalers, and libraries. Publishers were carefully instructed not to include book club, overseas, and direct-mail sales transactions in their sales figures. Some books appear in the listings without sales figures; these were submitted to *PW* in confidence, for use only in placing the titles in their correct positions on a specific list.

"Sales" as used on these lists refers to books shipped and billed in calendar year 1988. Publishers were asked to take into account returns made through February 1, 1989. In many cases, the 1988 sales figures include books still on bookstore and wholesalers' shelves, books on the way back to the publishers' warehouses, and/or books already stacking up on returns piles but not yet calculated.

All the top 15 fiction bestsellers of the year were highly visible on weekly charts. The same is true for 14 of the 15 runners-up, the exception being Alex Haley's *A Different Kind of Christmas.* Three titles among the top 15 nonfiction bestsellers in 1988 and two runners-up have yet to make it onto a weekly *PW* bestseller chart. They include two Weight Watchers titles, *The Sackett Companion, Life in Camelot,* and *Nightmares in the Sky.*

The Fiction Bestsellers

1 *The Cardinal of the Kremlin* by Tom Clancy (Putnam, 7/26/88; *1,277,000*)
***2** *The Sands of Time* by Sidney Sheldon (Morrow, 11/10/88)
3 *Zoya* by Danielle Steel (Delacorte, 6/3/88; *1,025,000*)
4 *The Icarus Agenda* by Robert Ludlum (Random House, 3/15/88; *827,849*)
5 *Alaska* by James A. Michener (Random House, 6/27/88; *795,429*)
6 *Till We Meet Again* by Judith Krantz (Crown, 9/15/88; *506,697*)
7 *The Queen of the Damned* by Anne Rice (Knopf, 10/31/88; *398,773*)
8 *To Be the Best* by Barbara Taylor Bradford (Doubleday, 7/4/88; *358,913*)
***9** *One: A Novel* by Richard Bach (Morrow/Silver Arrow Books, 10/14/88)
10 *Mitla Pass* by Leon Uris (Doubleday, 11/11/88; *343,921*)
11 *The Bonfire of the Vanities* by Tom Wolfe (Farrar, Straus & Giroux, 11/9/87; *335,493*)
12 *Final Flight* by Stephen Coonts (Doubleday, 1/7/88; *328,068*)
13 *Rock Star* by Jackie Collins (Simon & Schuster, 4/18/88; *308,000*)
14 *Dear Mili* by Wilhelm Grimm with illustrations by Maurice Sendak (Farrar, Straus & Giroux/Michael di Capua Books, 10/24/88; *275,990*)
15 *Hot Money* by Dick Francis (Putnam, 3/4/88; *256,300*)

Thanks to Stephen King's decision not to publish any new hardcover fiction titles in 1988, Tom Clancy was finally able to capture the lead spot with *The Cardinal of the Kremlin.* In 1987 and 1986, Clancy came in second after King despite sales over the 1-million mark. His impressive sales of 1,277,000 for *The Cardinal* were his best sales performance yet.

*Sales figures were submitted to *PW* in confidence, for use only in placing the title in its correct position on a list.

The other 2-million-copy performances were by seasoned veterans whose books regularly make it to the top slots of these end-of-year lists. For Sidney Sheldon, his ninth bestseller, *The Sands of Time,* is also his most successful hardcover; Sheldon had never before experienced first-year sales of 1 million. In 1987, *Windmills of the Gods* made it to number 6 with reported sales of more than 700,000. Danielle Steel heads up the list of bestselling female authors both in output and sales. *Zoya,* her twenty-third novel, is her second to go over the 1-million mark. According to the *1989 Guinness Book of World Records,* Steel holds the record for consecutive weeks on a national bestseller list, hardcover or paperback—381, beginning December 1981 through July 1988.

Seasoned novelists with well-worn tracks on bestseller charts also abound in the other top slots. Robert Ludlum's books continue to gain in sales and his fourteenth, *The Icarus Agenda,* is also his most successful, with sales of 827,849, enough for the number 4 spot. Back in 1979, Ludlum's *The Matarese Circle* enjoyed the top fiction slot with sales of only 250,000 copies. For James A. Michener, his sales of 795,429 for *Alaska* and his number 5 ranking could be considered low numbers. Excluding his 175-page celebration of the two-hundredth anniversary of the U.S. Constitution in 1987, his major historical opuses usually place in the first and second spots and have gone over the seven-figure mark (*Texas* was number 2 in 1985 with sales of 1,373,933).

Although Judith Krantz's fifth novel, *Till We Meet Again,* missed a chance atop a weekly bestseller chart because of an ill-timed shipment of books, the book proved to be a crowd pleaser nonetheless. With sales of 506,697, enough for the number 6 spot of the year, it compares favorably with her previous successes and is her bestselling hardcover to date.

Leon Uris returned to the turbulent Middle East with his latest opus, *Mitla Pass,* number 10 with sales of 343,921. This time it's the Suez crisis in 1956. This is Uris's tenth novel in more than 30 years, beginning with *Battle Cry* in 1953 (number 4 that year) and more recently *The Haj* in 1984 (number 12 that year with sales of 250,000).

A veteran of both the fiction and nonfiction end-of-year lists, Richard Bach returned with another allegoric fantasy novel, *One,* in the number 9 position. His last appearance was in 1984—number 14 on the nonfiction list with *The Bridge Across Forever.* Bach led the end-of-year list two years running, in 1972 and 1973, with *Jonathan Livingston Seagull.*

Jackie Collins made it to the number 13 slot for *Rock Star* with sales of 308,000; *Hollywood Husbands* sold 517,000 copies in 1986, enough for the number 5 position. Collins's first appearance on an annual list was in 1983 with *Hollywood Wives* (number 9 with sales of 226,505). Barbara Taylor Bradford's *To Be the Best,* number 8 with sales of 358,913, is the third book in her Hart Family Trilogy, which began with her first novel, *A Woman of Substance,* in 1975, followed by *Hold the Dream* in 1985. A novel outside the trilogy, *Act of Will,* was number 14 in 1986 with sales of 205,000. Making a first appearance on the end-of-the-year list is Anne Rice with her third and most successful tale in The Vampire Chronicles, *The Queen of the Damned,* number 7 with sales of 398,773. Blood drinkers proved stronger than missile mongers, at least on these bestseller charts, as Rice's book knocked Clancy off the top of *PW*'s weekly bestseller list.

In 1987, Farrar, Straus & Giroux had two first novels among the top 15 in fiction, a remarkable feat on these annual lists. In 1988, one of the novels, *The Bonfire of the Vanities,* made a reappearance at the number 11 position with sales of 335, 493; total sales for the hardcover are more than 700,000 copies. The Tom Wolfe novel also enjoyed the longest run on the weekly fiction hardcover lists in 1988—48 consecutive weeks. FSG's second entry in the top 15 is one of those books for children of all ages—recently discovered Grimm tale, illustrated by Maurice Sendak. Sales of 275,990 earned it the number 14 spot.

The other two slots on the list are taken up by authors new to the top 15 but who have been runners-up in previous years. Stephen Coonts, another popular author in the techno-thriller genre, scored a hit with his second novel, *Final Flight;* sales of 328,068 gave it the number 12 position. In 1986, his first book, *The Flight of the Intruder,* was number 22 with sales of more than 158,800. Dick Francis made it in 1988 with his twenty-sixth thriller, *Hot Money,* number 15 with sales of 256,300. In 1987 *Bolt* landed at number 20 with sales of 179,000.

The Fiction Runners-Up

The second tier of the year's bestsellers is also dominated by well-known authors with considerable time spent on bestseller charts both in 1988 and preceding years. Gabriel García Márquez, the acclaimed Latin American writer, had a 34-week run on *PW*'s weekly charts. Rosamunde Pilcher had a 33-week run on *PW*'s weekly charts with her twelfth and most successful novel. *Timothy's Game* is Lawrence Sanders's eleventh book; each of his previous titles have been either among the top 15 or one of the runners-up.

16 *Lightning* by Dean R. Koontz (Putnam, 1/88; *251,100*)

17 *Love in the Time of Cholera* by Gabriel García Márquez (Knopf, 4/88; *248,041*)

18 *Anything for Billy* by Larry McMurtry (Simon & Schuster, 10/88; *248,000*)

19 *Doctors* by Erich Segal (Bantam, 8/88; *246,000*)

20 *Breathing Lessons* by Anne Tyler (Knopf, 9/88; *234,284*)

21 *Treasure* by Clive Cussler (Simon & Schuster, 4/88; *229,000*)

22 *Prime Time* by Joan Collins (Simon & Schuster, 10/88; *225,000*)

23 *Koko* by Peter Straub (Dutton, 9/88; *222,246*)

24 *Timothy's Game* by Lawrence Sanders (Putnam, 7/88; *202,100*)

25 *A Different Kind of Christmas* by Alex Haley (Doubleday, 12/88; *201,115*)

26 *Tapestry* by Belva Plain (Delacorte, 5/88; *190,000*)

27 *The Shell Seekers* by Rosamunde Pilcher (St. Martin's/A Thomas Dunne Book, 1/88; *182,445*)

28 *Shining Through* by Susan Isaacs (Harper & Row, 8/88; *181,148*)

29 *Dragonsdawn* by Anne McCaffrey (Del Rey Hardcover, 11/88; *181,000*)

30 *People Like Us* by Dominick Dunne (Crown 6/88; *180,824*)

Four titles with reported sales of more than 100,000 failed to make even a single appearance on *PW*'s weekly charts, including *Faerie Tale, Blossom Comes Home, Killing Time in St. Cloud,* and *Fast Copy.*

Nine titles had sales of more than 150,000 for 1988: *Inheritance* by Judith Michael (Poseidon Press); *The Last Princess* by Cynthia Freeman (Putnam); *The Si-*

lence of the Lambs by Thomas Harris (St. Martin's); *Crimson Joy* by Robert B. Parker (Delacorte); *Spock's World* by Diane Duane (Pocket Books); *Prelude to Foundation* by Isaac Asimov (Doubleday); *Demon Lord of Karanda* by David Eddings (Del Rey); *The Tommyknockers* by Stephen King (Putnam); and *Mortal Fear* by Robin Cook (Putnam). Three novels reported sales of more than 120,000: *King of the Murgos* by David Eddings (Del Rey); *Sword Point* by Harold Coyle (Simon & Schuster); and *Spy Hook* by Len Deighton (Knopf). Nine more 1988 novels reported sales of 100,000 plus: *Faerie Tale* by Raymond Feist (Doubleday); *The Tenants of Time* by Thomas Flanagan (Dutton/A William Abrahams Book); *Blossom Comes Home* by James Herriot (St. Martin's); *The Aviators* by W.E.B. Griffin (Putnam); *Scorpius* by John Gardner (Putnam); *Killing Time in St. Cloud* by Judith Guest and Rebecca Hill (Delacorte); *A Thief of Time* by Tony Hillerman (Harper & Row); *Fast Copy* by Dan Jenkins (Simon & Schuster); and *Tracks* by Louise Erdrich (Henry Holt).

Nonfiction Leaders

1 *The 8-Week Cholesterol Cure* by Robert E. Kowalski (Harper & Row, 8/31/87; *961,221*)

2 *Talking Straight* by Lee Iacocca with Sonny Kleinfield (Bantam, 7/29/88; *747,000*)

3 *A Brief History of Time: From the Big Bang to Black Holes* by Stephen W. Hawking (Bantam, 4/2/88; *729,000*)

4 *Trump: The Art of the Deal* by Donald J. Trump with Tony Schwartz (Random House, 12/14/87; *610,812*)

5 *Gracie: A Love Story* by George Burns (Putnam, 11/14/88; *582,800*)

6 *Elizabeth Takes Off* by Elizabeth Taylor (Putnam, 2/15/88; *512,750*)

*7 *Swim with the Sharks without Being Eaten Alive* by Harvey MacKay (Morrow, 3/23/88)

8 *Christmas in America* edited by David Cohen (Collins, 11/1/88; *381,000*)

9 *Weight Watchers Quick Success Program Cookbook* by Jean Nidetch (NAL,1/89; *349,640*)

10 *Moonwalk* by Michael Jackson (Doubleday, 4/20/88; *341,748*)

11 *All I Really Need to Know I Learned in Kindergarten: Uncommon Thoughts on Common Things* by Robert Fulghum (Villard, 10/13/88; *334,960*)

*12 *For the Record: From Wall Street to Washington* by Donald T. Regan (Harcourt Brace Jovanovich, 5/23/88)

13 *The Sackett Companion: A Personal Guide to the Sackett Novels* by Louis L'Amour (Bantam, 11/1/88; *285,000*)

14 *Weight Watchers Quick and Easy Menu Cookbook* by Weight Watchers International (NAL, 1/88; *260,000*)

*15 *Seven Stories of Christmas Love* by Leo Buscaglia (Morrow/Slack, 10/15/87)

*Sales figures were submitted to *PW* in confidence, for use only in placing the title in its correct position on a list.

The extraordinary sales of the number 1 nonfiction bestseller of the year, *The 8-Week Cholesterol Cure,* was such that Harper & Row cancelled plans to publish a trade paperback edition and instead will publish a revised and expanded hardcover edition in August. The book's jacket includes the right blend of endorsements—from readers and the medical establishment—and promise—lower your blood cholesterol by up to 40 percent. The book has been on *PW*'s weekly charts 79 times and continues strong.

The sleeper of the year is *A Brief History of Time,* number 3 with sales of 729,000 copies. An impressive feat for a book that was published April 2 with a first printing of 50,000. Although the publisher claims to have expected the book to become an important bestseller, it never anticipated its becoming a phenomenon. Reviews and stories about the book and its remarkable author—a Cambridge physicist confined to a wheelchair and able to communicate only with the assistance of a computerized voice synthesizer—have filled an entire file cabinet drawer at Bantam, according to the publisher.

The battle for the bestselling 1988 business book seems to have been won by Lee Iacocca, who took the number 2 spot for his *Talking Straight* with sales of 747,000—excellent numbers, except when compared to his first book, *Iacocca: An Autobiography,* which claimed the number 1 spot in 1984 and 1985 with sales well over 1 million copies each year. Coming in second was Donald Trump, at the number 4 spot with sales of 610,812. But if you add the 1987 sales of Trump's book—about 240,000 copies— the real estate mogul's first book did better than the supreme car salesman's second.

Business also figured in two other topsellers, *Swim with the Sharks without Being Eaten Alive,* number 7, and Donald T. Regan's *For the Record,* number 12. Morrow successfully sold the first book despite a money back guarantee to anyone who didn't agree that the book delivers what it promises—"how to outsell, outmanage, outmotivate and outnegotiate your competition." Although Regan, the former White House chief of staff, included details about the Iran-contra scandal and the inner workings of the Reagan White House in *For the Record,* the single fact that propelled the book onto the bestseller lists was the revelation of Nancy Reagan's consultations with an astrologer regarding her husband's presidential activities.

George Burns's loving reminiscences of his wife, Gracie, were his most successful book, with sales of 582,800, enough for the number 5 slot. Actress Elizabeth Taylor's successful—at least for a while—battle with the bulge was frank and credible, making it one of the bestselling books of the year, number 6 with sales of 512,750, and one of the most successful celebrity diet books in the last decade. Michael Jackson shared some of his personal thoughts and family photographs and 341,748 fans bought the book, enough to garner it the number 10 spot—nice, but not where he lands on the music charts.

Although traditional bookstores certainly accounted for some of the 381,000 copies sold of *Christmas in America,* sales at K-Mart outlets around the country were particularly brisk. The world's second largest retailer mounted a special promotional program for its 2,000 stores centered on the book. In 1987, Collins had two books among the top 15—*A Day in the Life of America* with sales of 570,000 copies and *A Day in the Life of the Soviet Union* with 420,000 copies sold.

An ordained minister, Robert Fulghum, was as surprised as his publishers by the success of his first book, *All I Really Need to Know I Learned in Kindergarten.* In 1988, the book sold 334,960, enough for the number 11 spot. A familiar figure on these end-of-year lists is Leo Buscaglia. He rounds out the top 15 with a 1987 book,

Seven Stories of Christmas Love, that sold more than 240,000 in 1988. In 1987, approximately the same rate of sales gave it a number 20 ranking.

Two recent Weight Watchers cookbooks placed at number 9 and number 14. Although neither book has made it to *PW*'s weekly list, individual bookstores often report it among their lead sellers.

Another no show on the weekly lists was Louis L'Amour's *The Sackett Companion,* number 13 with sales of 285,000 copies. Interestingly, it outsold another L'Amour-based hardcover, *A Trail of Memories: The Quotations of Louis L'Amour,* number 21 on the list with sales of 221,000. The latter was on *PW*'s weekly charts for more than two months.

Guinness's Record Sale

PW's annual lists reflect 1988 sales of new hardcover titles published in 1988 or 1987 and do not include annuals, but it is still fitting to note that the 1989 edition of *Guinness Book of World Records* edited by David Boehm sold 363,429 copies for Sterling in 1988, the book's highest sales figure in recent years. A book that does not qualify because of publication date but had an astounding sales rate is *Webster's Ninth New Collegiate Dictionary*—1988 sales were 988,745 copies.

The Nonfiction Runners-Up

The books in the group of runners-up represent the usual blend of subjects that make up a nonfiction bestseller list—books by or about well-known personalities, business and how-to categories, books by writers who have previously written bestsellers. A welcome new subject is a book of photographs and impressions of earth, *The Home Planet,* by the astronauts and cosmonauts who have viewed and studied the planet from the vantage point of Space.

16 *Child Star: An Autobiography* by Shirley Temple Black (McGraw-Hill, 11/88; *237,759*)

17 *The Home Planet* edited by Kevin W. Kelley for the Association of Space Explorers (Addison-Wesley, 10/88; *235,419*)

18 *The Lives of John Lennon* by Albert Goldman (Morrow, 9/88)

19 *All You Can Do Is All You Can Do but All You Can Do Is Enough* by A. L. Williams (Oliver-Nelson, 9/88; *229,022*)

20 *Press On! Further Adventures in the Good Life* by General Chuck Yeager and Charles Leerhsen (Bantam, 10/88; *229,000*)

21 *A Trail of Memories: The Quotations of Louis L'Amour* compiled by Angelique L'Amour (Bantam, 6/88; *221,000*)

22 *The Rise & Fall of The Great Powers* by Paul Kennedy (Random House, 12/87; *220,506*)

23 *The Last Lion, 1932–1940* by William Manchester (Little, Brown, 10/88; *217,305*)

24 *The Ragman's Son* by Kirk Douglas (Simon & Schuster, 8/88; *204,000*)

25 *The Dictionary of Cultural Literacy* by E. D. Hirsch Jr., Joseph F. Kett, and James Trefil (Houghton Mifflin, 10/88; *200,541*)

26 *Life in Camelot* by Philip Kunhardt Jr. (Little, Brown, 9/88; *197,815*)

27 *Nightmares in the Sky* by Stephen King and photographs by f-stop Fitzgerald (Viking Studio Books, 10/88; *196,352*)

28 *Transformation: The Breakthrough* by Whitley Strieber (Morrow/Beech Tree Book, 9/88)

29 *Surviving the Great Depression of 1990* by Ravi Batra (Simon & Schuster, 9/88; *196,000*)

30 *First Salute* by Barbara W. Tuchman (Random House, 9/88; *194,029*)

The 46 Nonfiction Almost-Rans

Thirteen of the 46 almost-rans never achieved a position on any weekly *PW* bestseller list. Whether that reflects the stiff competitive nature of the weekly charts, the veracity of the publishers supplying the numbers, or "shipped and billed" figures that include only the tip of the returns iceberg, only the publishers know for sure. At any rate, books by Madden, Nelson, Terkel, Solt, Carter, Stewart, King, Edwards, Mandino, Ohrbach, Morris, Kunhardt, and the book on Robert Kennedy's talks have yet to achieve a spot on *PW*'s weekly charts.

Eleven books with reported sales over 150,000 include *The Boz* by Brian Bosworth with Rich Reilly (Doubleday); *Goldwater* by Barry M. Goldwater and Jack Casserly (Doubleday); *A Bright Shining Lie* by Neil Sheehan (Random); *Don't Bend Over in the Garden, Granny, You Know Them Taters Got Eyes* by Lewis Grizzard (Villard); *One Size Doesn't Fit All* by John Madden (Villard); *Washington Goes to War* by David Brinkley (Knopf); *The Duchess of Windsor* by Charles Higham (McGraw-Hill); *Controlling Cholesterol* by Dr. Kenneth Cooper (Bantam); *Imagine: John Lennon* by Andrew Solt and Sam Egan (Macmillan); *Willie: An Autobiography* by Willie Nelson with Bud Shrake (Simon & Schuster); and *Riding the Iron Rooster* by Paul Theroux (Putnam).

Nine books reported sales over the 125,000-copy mark: *The Great Divide* by Studs Terkel (Pantheon); *What's Next?* by Paul Erdman (Doubleday); *Citizen Cohn: The Life and Times of Roy Cohn* by Nicholas von Hoffman (Doubleday); *Landslide: The Unmaking of the President, 1984–1988* by Jane Mayer and Doyle McManus (Houghton Mifflin); *An Outdoor Journal* by Jimmy Carter (Bantam); *Senatorial Privilege: The Chappaquiddick Cover-Up* by Leo Damore (Regnery Gateway); *Martha Stewart's Quick Cook Menus* by Martha Stewart (Potter); *Generation of Swine* by Hunter S. Thompsn (Summit); and *A Day in the Life of California* by Rick Smolan and David Cohen (Collins).

Twenty-six more books claimed 1988 sales figures of 100,000 plus: *A Season Inside* by John Feinstein (Villard); *Wilderness* by Jim Morrison (Villard); *Getting Together* by Roger Fisher and Scott Brown (Houghton Mifflin); *Whales* by Jacques-Yves Cousteau and Yves Paccalet (Abrams); *The Portable Curmudgeon* compiled by Jon Winokur (NAL Books); *"What Do You Care What Other People Think?"* by Richard P. Feynman with Ralph Leighton (Norton); *Being a Woman* by Dr. Toni Grant (Random); *The National Geographic Society* by C.D.B. Bryan (Abrams); *Donnie Brasco: My Undercover Life in the Mafia* by Joseph D. Pistone with Richard Woodley (NAL); *Capote: A Biography* by Gerald Clarke (Simon & Schuster); *Speaking Out* by Larry Speakes with Robert Pack (Scribners); *1999: Victory without War* by Richard M. Nixon (Simon & Schuster); *Picasso: Creator and Destroyer* by A. S.

Huffington (Simon & Schuester); *Tell it to the King* by Larry King with Peter Occhiogrosso (Putnam); *Priscilla, Elvis and Me* by Michael Edwards (St. Martin's); *The Greatest Salesman in the World* by Og Madino (Bantam); *Chaos* by James Gleick (Viking); *Battle Cry of Freedom: The Civil War Years* by James M. McPherson (Oxford University Press); *They Went That Away* by Malcolm Forbes with Jeff Bloch (Simon & Schuster); *The Frugal Gourmet Cooks American* by Jeff Smith (Morrow); *A Token of Friendship* by Barbara Milo Ohrbach (Potter); *Catlore* by Desmond Morris (Crown); *The Way Things Work* by David Macaulay (Houghton Mifflin); *Life Laughs Last* by Philip B. Kunhardt, Jr. (Simon & Shuster); *Winfield: A Player's Life* by Dave Winfield with Tom Parker (Norton); and *Robert Kennedy in His Own Words* edited by Edwin O. Guthman and Jeffrey Shulman (Bantam).

Literary Prizes, 1988

ASCAP-Deems Taylor Awards. *Offered by:* American Society of Composers, Authors, and Publishers. *Winners:* Bruce Bastin for *Red River Blues* (Univ. of Illinois); Paul E. Bierley for *John Philip Sousa, American Phenomenon* (Integrity); Jane Bowers and Judith Tick for *Women Making Music* (Univ. of Illinois); Elise K. Kirk for *Music at the White House* (Univ. of Illinois); H. Wiley Hitchcock and Stanley Sadie for *The New Grove Dictionary of American Music* (Grove's Dictionaries of Music); Kim Kowalke for *A New Orpheus—Essays on Kurt Weill* (Yale Univ.); Sigmund Levarie for *Early Music* (Da Capo); Kay Kaufman Shelemay for *Music, Ritual, and Falasha History* (Michigan State Univ.); Martin Torgoff for American Fool—John Cougar Mellencamp (St. Martin's).

Academy of American Poets Fellowship Award. For distinguished poetic achievement. *Winner:* Donald Justice.

Nelson Algren Award. For a work of fiction in progress. *Offered by:* PEN American Center. *Winner:* Steve Schwartz for "Madagascar."

American Academy and Institute of Arts and Letters Awards in Literature. *Winners:* William Barrett, David Bottoms, Rosellen Brown, David Cope, John Clellon Holmes (posthumous), John McCormick, James Seay, William Weaver, Norman Williams.

American Academy in Rome Fellowship in Literature. *Offered by:* American Academy and Institute of Arts and Letters. *Winner:* Edward Hirsch.

American Literary Translators Association. For a translation of a work by an American author into a foreign language. *Winners:* Red Hill Press of San Francisco for the translation of *Portfolio* by Paul Vangelisti into Italian (translator: Peter Carravetts); Folder Editions of New York City for the translation of *A Golden Story* by Daisy Alden into German (translator: Dr. Ernst Rippmann); Black Sparrow Press of Santa Rosa, California for the translation of *West of Rome* by John Fante into German (translator: Doris Engelke); McPherson & Company Publishers of New Paltz, New York for the translation of *Transparent Tree: Fictions* by Robert Kelly into

French (translator: Pierre Joris); Cross Cultural Communications of Merrick, New York for the translation of *On the Edge of the Hudson* by Laura Boss into Italian (translator: Nat Scammacca); Cross Cultural Communications for the translation of *Monologues: Women of Fact and Fantasy Speak their Minds* by Enid Dame into Italian (translator: Nat Scammacca with Nina Scammacca); and Chantry Press of Midland Park, New Jersey for the transation of *Winter Light* by Maria Gillan into Italian (translators: Nat and Nina Scammacca).

American Society of Journalists and Authors Author of the Year Award. *Winner:* Randy Shilts for *And the Band Played On: People, Politics, and the AIDS Epidemic* (St. Martin's).

Anisfield-Wolf Book Award. *Winners:* (fiction) Toni Morrison for *Beloved* (Knopf) and Nadine Gordimer for *A Sport of Nature* (Knopf); (Scholarly or technical work) Abigail M. Thernstrom for *Whose Votes Count? Affirmative Action and Minority Voting Rights* (Harvard Univ.) and Walter F. Morris, Jr., and Jay Foxx for *Living Maya* (Abrams).

Associated Writing Programs Award. For book-length manuscript to be published by a university press. *Winner:* (fiction) Duff Brena for *Mamie Beaver* (Univ. of Iowa); (poetry) Christopher Davis for *The Tyrant of the Past* (Texas Tech); (short fiction) Roland Sodowsky for "Things We Lose" (Univ. of Missouri).

Robert S. Ball Award. *Offered by:* Aviation/Space Writers Association. *Winner:* Neil McAleer for *Omni Space Almanac.*

Bancroft Prizes. For books of exceptional merit and distinction in American history, American diplomacy, and the international relations of the United States. Offered by: Columbia University. *Winners:* Peter R. Kolchin for *Unfree Labor: American Slavery and Russian Serfdom* (Harvard Univ.) and Michael S. Sherry for *The Rise of American Air Power: The Creation of Armegaddon* (Yale Univ.).

Mildred L. Batchelder Award. For an American publisher of a children's book originally published in a foreign language in a foreign country and subsequently published in English in the United States. *Winner:* Margaret McElderry Books for *If You Didn't Have Me* by Ulf Nilsson, translated from the Swedish by Lone Thygesen Blecher and George Blecher.

Bay Area Book Reviewers Association. *Winners:* (fiction) Lynn Freed for *Home Ground* (Summit); (poetry) William Dickey for *The King of the Golden River* (Pterodactyl); (arts and letters) Alex Zwerdling for *Virginia Woolf and the Real World* (Univ. of California); (contemporary issues) William Finnegan for *Crossing the Line* (Harper); (children's book) Gayle Pearson for *Fish Friday* (Atheneum); (community service citation) Raymond Lifchez for *Rethinking Architecture* (Univ. of California); (translation citations) Chana Bloch and Stephen Mitchel for *Selected Poetry of Yehuda Amichai* (Harper); Czeslaw Milosz and Robert Hass for *Unattainable Earth* by Czelsaw Milosz (Ecco Press); Reginald Zelnik for *A Radical Worker in Tsarist Russia: The Autobiography of Semen Ivanovich Kanatchikov* (Stanford Univ.).

Before Columbus Foundation American Book Awards. For literary achievement by people of various ethnic backgrounds. *Winners:* Jimmy Santiago Baca for *Martin and Meditations on the South Valley* (New Directions); Daisy Bates for *The Long Shadow of Little Rock* (Univ. of Arkansas); Allison Blakely for *Russia and the Negro: Blacks in Russian History and*

Thought. (Howard Univ.); David Halberstam for *The Reckoning* (Avon/Morrow); Marlon Hom for *Songs of Gold Mountain* (Univ. of California); Salvatore La Puma for *The Boys of Bensonhurst* (Univ. of Georgia); Wing Tek Lum for *Expounding the Doubtful Points* (Bamboo Ridge); Toni Morrison for *Beloved* (Knopf); Charles Olson (George Butterick, ed.) for *The Collected Poems of Charles Olson* (Univ. of California); Ed Sanders for *Thirsting for Peace in a Raging Century: Poems 1961–1985* (Coffee House); Kesho Scott, Cherry Muhanji, and Egyirba High for *Tight Spaces* (Spinsters/Aunt Lute); Ronald Sukenick for *Down and In* (Beech Tree/Morrow); Gerald Vizenor for *Griever: An American Monkey King in China* (Fiction Collective); Opal Whiteley for *The Singing Creek Where the Willows Grow* (Warner).

Boston Globe–Horn Book Awards. For excellence in text and illustration. *Winners:* (fiction) Mildred Taylor for *The Friendship,* illus. by Max Ginsburg (Dial); (illustration) Dianne Snyder for *The Boy of the Three-Year Nap,* illus. by Allen Say (Houghton Mifflin); (nonfiction) Virginia Hamilton for *Anthony Burns: The Defeat and Triumph of a Fugitive Slave* (Knopf).

Witter Bynner Foundation Prize for Poetry. *Offered by:* American Academy and Insitute of Arts and Letters. *Winner:* Andrew Hudgins.

CLA Book of the Year (Canada). *Offered by:* Canadian Library Association. *Winner:* Kit Pearson for *A Handful of Time* (Penguin).

Caldecott Medal. For the artist of the most distinguished picture book. *Offered by:* R. R. Bowker Company. *Winner:* John Schoenherr, illus. of *Owl Moon* by Jane Yolen (Philomel).

John W. Campbell Award. For an author whose first professional story was published in the preceding two years. *Offered by:* World Science Fiction Convention. *Winner:* Judith Moffett.

Italo Calvino Award. *Offered by:* Columbia Univ. *Winner:* Rina Ferrarelli for *Light without Motion* by Giorgio Chiesura (Owl Creek).

Campion Award. *Offered by:* Catholic Book Club. *Winner:* Robert Giroux, editor and publisher.

Catholic Book Awards. For an outstanding religious book. *Winners:* Lawrence S. Cunningham for *The Catholic Faith: An Introduction* (Paulist Press); Leonardo Boff for *Passion of Christ, Passion of the World* (Orbis); Bernard L. Marthaler for *The Creed* (Twenty-Third Publicatons); George Pixley for *On Exodus* (Orbis); *Alternative Futures for Worship Series* (seven vols.) (Liturgical Press); Dean Hoge for *Future of Catholic Leadership: Responses to the Priest Shortage* (Sheed & Ward); Mary Kathleen Glavich for *Leading Students into Scripture* (Twenty-Third Publications); Harry W. Paige and Don Doll for *Land of the Spotted Eagle: A Portrait of the Reservation Sioux* (Loyola Univ.).

Christopher Book Awards. For books that affirm the highest values of the human spirit. *Winners:* Alicia Appleman-Jurman for *Alicia: My Story* (Bantam); Sara Lawrence Lightfoot for *Balm in Gilead: Journey of a Healer* (Addison Wesley); James M. McPherson for *Battle Cry of Freedom* (Oxford Univ.); Edwin Mickleburgh for *Beyond the Frozen Sea: Visions of Antarctica* (St. Martin's); Natan Sharansky for *Fear No Evil* (Random); Nan Robertson for *Getting Better: Inside Alcoholics Anonymous* (Morrow); Irina Ratushinskaya for *Grey Is the Color of Hope* (Knopf); Tolbert McCarroll for *Morning Glory Babies: Children with AIDS and the*

Celebration of Life (St. Martin's); Donna Whitson Brett & Edward T. Brett for *Murdered in Central America: The Stories of Eleven U.S. Missionaries* (Orbis); Garret Keizer for *No Place but Here: A Teacher's Vocation in a Rural Community* (Viking); Taylor Branch for *Parting the Waters: America in the King Years 1954–63* (Simon & Schuster); Jonathan Kozol for *Rachel and Her Children: Homeless Families in America* (Crown); Sidney Callahan for *With All Our Heart & Mind: The Spiritual Works of Mercy in a Psychological Age* (Crossroad).

Christopher Children's Book Awards. *Winners:* Judith Viorst for *The Good-Bye Book* (Atheneum); Thomas Locker for *Family Farm* (Dial); Ann E. Weiss for *Lies, Deception and Truth* (Houghton Mifflin); Carl B. Feldbaum and Ronald J. Bee for *Looking the Tiger in the Eye: Confronting the Nuclear Threat* (Harper).

Cleveland Arts Prize. *Winner:* Eleanor Munro for *On Glory Roads* (Thames and Hudson).

Common Wealth Award. For distinguished service in literature. *Winner:* Andrei Andreevich Voznesensky.

Commonwealth Writers' Prize. *Winner:* Festus Iyayi for *Heroes* (Longman).

Thomas Cook Travel & Guide Book Awards. *Winners:* (travel) John Underwood and Pat Underwood for *Landscapes of Madeira* (Sunflower Books); (illustrated travel book) Richard B. Fisher for *The Marco Polo Expedition* photographed by Tom Ang (Hodder and Stoughton).

T. S. Eliot Award. For creative writing. *Offered by:* Ingersoll Foundation. *Winner:* Walker Percy.

Maurice English Poetry Award. *Winner:* David Ray for *Sam's Book* (Wesleyan Univ. Press).

English-Speaking Union Ambassador Book Awards. *Winners:* Tom Wolfe for *Bonfire of the Vanities* (Farrar, Straus); Robert Lowell for *Collected Prose* (Farrar, Straus); Joan Didion for *Miami* (Simon & Schuster); Brendan Gill for *Many Masks: A Life of Frank Lloyd Wright* (Putnam).

Armand G. Erpf Awards. *Offered by:* Columbia University. *Winners:* Barbara Goldberg for *On Top of the Cliff* by Moshe Dor (Mosaic Press) and Siv Hennum for *Semmelweis* by Jens Bjornboe (Angel).

European Prize. For an exceptional translation of poetry. *Winner:* Edmund Keeley for *Exile and Return: Selected Poems, 1967–1974* (Ecco Press).

Faulkner Award for Fiction. *Offered by:* PEN American Center. *Winner:* T. Coraghessan Boyle for *World's End* (Viking).

Dorothy Canfield Fisher Children's Book Award. For a children's book by a distinguished Vermont author selected by Vermont schoolchildren. *Offered by:* Vermont Department of Libraries and Vermont Congress of Parents and Teachers. *Winner:* Mary Downing Hahn for *Wait till Helen Comes* (Clarion).

E. M. Forster Award. *Winner:* Blake Morrison.

George Freedley Memorial Award. *Offered by:* Theatre Library Association. *Winner:* Charles Shattuck for *Shakespeare on the American Stage, Vol. II: From Booth and Barrett to Sothern and Marlowe* (Folger/Associated Univ. Presses).

Freedom-to-Write Awards. *Winners:* Maina wa Kinyatti, Kenya, and Pramoedya Ananta Toer, Indonesia.

Friends of Literature Award. *Winner:* John Conroy for *Belfast Diary* (Beacon).

Gay Book Award. *Offered by:* American Library Association Social Responsibilities Round Table Gay Task Force. *Winners:* Joan Nestle for *A Restricted Country* (Firebrand) and Randy Shilts for *And the Band Played on: Politics, People, and the AIDS Epidemic* (St. Martin's).

Golden Kite Awards. *Offered by:* Society of Children's Book Writers. *Winners:* (fiction) Lois Lowry for *Rabble Starkey* (Houghton Mifflin); (nonfiction) Rhoda Blumberg for *The Incredible Journey of Lewis and Clark* (Lothrop, Lee); (picture/illustration) Arnold Lobel for *The Devil and Mother Crump,* by Valerie S. Carey (Harper).

Golden Spur Awards. *See* Spur Awards.

Great Lakes Colleges Association New Writers Awards. *Winners:* (poetry) Charlie Smith for *Red Roads* (Dutton); (fiction) Brett Laidlaw for *Three Nights in the Heart of the Earth* (Norton).

Grolier Poetry Peace Prize. *Offered by:* Ellen LaForge Memorial Poetry Foundation. *Winner:* Charles Atkinson.

Heartland Prize. *Offered by: Chicago Tribune. Winners:* (fiction) Eric Larsen for *An American Memory* (Algonquin); (nonfiction) Donald R. Katz for *The Big Store* (Viking).

Ernest Hemingway Foundation Award. *Offered by:* PEN American Center. For a work of first fiction by an American. *Winner:* Lawrence Thornton for *Imagining Argentina* (Doubleday).

David Higham Prize (U.K.). For a first work of fiction. *Winner:* Carol Birch for *Life in the Palace* (Macmillan).

James S. Holmes Award. *Winner:* Shirley Kaufman for *But What: Selected Poems of Judith Herzberg* (Oberlin College).

Amelia Frances Howard-Gibbon Award (Canada). For the illustrator of an outstanding book. *Offered by:* Canadian Library Association, Canadian Association of Children's Librarians. *Winner:* Marie-Louise Gay for *Rainy Day Magic* (Stoddard).

Hugo Awards. *Offered by:* World Science Fiction Convention. *Winners:* (novel) David Brin for *The Uplift War* (Phantasia/Bantam); (novella) Orson Scott Card for "Eye for Eye"; (novelette) Ursula K. Le Guin for "Buffalo Gals, Won't You Come Out Tonight"; (short story) Lawrence Watt-Evans for "Why I Left Harry's All-Night Hamburgers"; (nonfiction) Michael Whelan for *Michael Whelan's Works of Wonder* (Ballantine); (semiprozine) Charles N. Brown, ed., for *Locus;* (other forms) Alan Moore and Dave Gibbons for *Watchmen* (Warner).

International Reading Association Children's Book Awards. For a first or second book of fiction or nonfiction by an author of promise. *Winners:* (children) Leslie Baker for *The Third-Story Cat* (Little, Brown); (young adults) Philip Pullman for *The Ruby in the Smoke* (Knopf).

Iowa Poetry Prizes. *Offered by:* University of Iowa. *Winners:* Mary Ruefle for *The Adamant* (Univ. of Iowa) and Bill Knot for *Outremer* (Univ. of Iowa).

Iowa Short Fiction Award. *Offered by:* University of Iowa Press. *Winner:* Sharon Dilworth for *The Long White* (Univ. of Iowa).

Jerard Fund Award. *Winner:* Hollis Giammatteo for *On the Line* (Knopf).

Chester H. Jones Award for Poetry. *Winners:* Lynne McMahon for "An Elvis for the Eighties" and Kathleen Peirce for "Need Increasing Self."

Margaret Jones Fiction Award. *Winner:* Jack Driscoll for "Flea to Jesus" (*Black Ice,* issue no. 4).

Sue Kaufman Prize. For a first work of fiction. *Offered by:* American Academy and Institute of Arts and Letters. *Winner:* Kaye Gibbons for *Ellen Foster* (Algonquin).

Ezra Jack Keats Award. *Winner:* Barbara Reid.

Robert F. Kennedy Book Award. For works that reflect Robert Kennedy's purposes. *Winner:* Toni Morrison for *Beloved* (Knopf) and Pauli Murray for *Song in a Weary Throat* (Harper).

Coretta Scott King Award. For a work that promotes the cause of peace and brotherhood. *Offered by:* American Library Association Social Responsibilities Round Table. *Winners:* Mildred D. Taylor for *The Friendship* (Dial) and John Steptoe, illus. of *Mufaro's Beautiful Daughters: An African Tale* (Lothrop, Lee).

Ruth Lilly Poetry Prize. *Winner:* Anthony Hecht for *The Venetian Vespers* (Atheneum).

Locus Awards. *Offered by:* Locus Publications. *Winners:* (science fiction novel) David Brin for *The Uplift War* (Phantasia/Bantam); (fantasy novel) Orson Scott for *Seventh Son* (Tor); (first novel) Emma Bull for *War for the Oaks*; (nonfiction) Alan Moore and Dave Gibbons for *Watchmen* (Warner); (novella) Robert Silverberg for "The Secret Sharer" (Isaac Asimov's *SF* Magazine); (novelette) Pat Murphy for "Rachel in Love" (Isaac Asimov's *SF* Magazine); (short story) Pat Cadigan for "Angel"; (collection) Lucius Shepard for *The Jaguar Hunter* (Arkham); (anthology) Gardner Dozois, ed., for *The Year's Best Science Fiction,* Fourth Annual Collection; (artist) Michael Whelan; (magazine) Isaac Asimov's *SF* Magazine; (all-time author) Robert A. Heinlein; (eighties' author) David Brin.

Los Angeles Times Book Awards. To honor literary excellence. *Winners:* (fiction) Gabriel Garcia Marquez for *Love in the Time of Cholera,* translated by Edith Grossman (Knopf); (poetry) Richard Wilbur for *New and Collected Poems* (Harcourt); (history) Eric Foner for *Reconstruction: America's Unfinished Revolution, 1863–1877* (Harper); (biography) Brenda Maddox for *Nora: The Real Life of Molly Bloom* (Houghton Mifflin); (current interest) William Greider for *Secrets of the Temple: How the Federal Reserve Runs the Country* (Simon & Schuster).

Edward MacDowell Medal. For excellence in the arts. *Winner:* William Styron.

Mary McNulty Award. *Offered by:* Association of American Publishers. *Winner:* James B. Garsky (Scholastic).

Lenore Marshall/Nation Award. For an outstanding book of poems published in the United States. *Offered by: The Nation* and the New Hope Foundation. *Winner:* Josephine Jacobsen for *The Sisters: New and Selected Poems* (Bench Press).

Emil/Kurt Maschler Award. *Winner:* Anthony Browne for *Alice's Adventures in Wonderland* by Lewis Carroll.

Medicine Pipe Bearer Award. For the best western, historical, or juvenile first novel. *Offered by:* Western Writers of America, Inc. *Winner:* Elaine Long for *Jenny's Mountain* (St. Martin's).

Milkweed Editions National Fiction Prize. *Winner:* Susan Lowell for *Ganado Red* (Milkweed Editions).

Frank Luther Mott-Kappa Tau Alpha Award. For the best researched book dealing with the media. *Offered by:* National Journalism Scholarship Society. *Winner:* James L. Baughman for *Henry R. Luce and the Rise of the American News Media* (Twayne).

National Arts Club Gold Medal of Honor for Literature. *Winner:* Carlos Fuentes.

National Book Awards. *Winners:* (fiction) Peter Dexter for *Paris Trout* (Random); (nonfiction) Neil Sheehan for *A Bright Shining Lie: John Paul Vann and America in Vietnam* (Random).

National Book Critics Circle Awards. *Winners:* (fiction) Philip Roth for *The*

Counterlife (Farrar); (nonfiction) Richard Rhodes for *The Making of the Atomic Bomb* (Simon & Schuster); (biography/autobiography) Donald R. Howard for *Chaucer: His Life, His Works, His World* (Dutton); (criticism) Edwin Denby for *Dance Writings* (Farrar); (poetry) C. K. Williams for *Flesh and Blood* (Farrar); (reviewing) Josh Rubins.

National Jewish Book Awards. *Winners:* (contemporary Jewish life) Paul Cowan with Rachel Cowan for *Mixed Blessings: Marriage Between Jews and Christians* (Doubleday); (fiction) Philip Roth for *The Counterlife* (Farrar, Straus); (holocaust) Susan Zucotti for *The Italians and the Holocaust: Persecution, Rescue, Survival* (Basic Books); (Israel) Shabtai Teveth for *Ben-Gurion: The Burning Ground 1886–1948* (Houghton Mifflin); (Jewish history) Robert Chazan for *European Jewry and the First Crusade* (Univ. of California); (Jewish thought) Rabbi Marc D. Angel for *The Orphaned Adult: Confronting the Death of a Parent* (Insight Books/Human Sciences Press); (scholarship) Daniel M. Friedenberg for *Medieval Jewish Seals from Europe* (Wayne State Univ.); (visual arts) Lester D. Friedman for *The Jewish Image in American Film* (Citadel Press/Lyle Stuart); (children's book) Sonia Levitin for *The Return* (Atheneum); (illustrated children's book) Charles Mikolaycak for *Exodus,* adapt. by Miriam Chaikin (Holiday).

National Medal of Arts. *Winner:* Saul Bellow.

Nebula Awards. For outstanding works of science fiction. *Offered by:* Science Fiction Writers of America. *Winners:* (novel) Pat Murphy for *The Falling Woman* (Tor Books); (novella) Kim Stanley Robinson for "The Blind Geometer"; (novelette) Pat Murphy for "Rachel in Love"; (short story) Kate Wilhelm for "Forever Yours, Anna"; (Grand Master Award) Alfred Bester.

Nene Award. For an outstanding children's book selected by Hawaii's schoolchildren. *Offered by:* Hawaii Association of School Librarians and the Hawaii Library Association Children's and Youth Section. *Winner:* Patricia Hermes for *You Shouldn't Have to Say Goodbye* (Harcourt).

Neustadt International Prize for Literature. *Winner:* Rajo Rao.

John Newbery Medal. For the most distinguished contribution to literature for children. *Donor:* ALA Association for Library Service to Children. *Medal contributed by:* Daniel Melcher. *Winner:* Russell Freedman for *Lincoln: A Photobiography* (Clarion).

Nobel Prize for Literature. For the total literary output of a distinguished writer. *Offered by:* Swedish Academy. *Winner:* Nagiub Mahfouz.

Flannery O'Connor Award. For an outstanding book-length collection of short stories. *Offered by:* University of Georgia. *Winners:* Gail Galloway Adams for *The Purchase of Order* (Univ. of Georgia) and Carole L. Glickfield for *Useful Gifts* (Univ. of Georgia).

Scott O'Dell Award. *Winner:* Patricia Beatty for *Charley Skadaddle* (Morrow).

Helen Keating Ott Award. For outstanding contribution to children's literature. *Offered by:* Church and Synagogue Library Association. *Winners:* Carolyn W. Field and Jaqueline S. Weiss.

Guy Owen Poetry Prize. *Offered by: Southern Poetry Review. Winner:* Sue Ellen Thompson for "Easier."

PSP Awards. For the most outstanding books in the fields of science, medicine, technology, and business. *Offered by:* Professional and Scholarly Publishing Division, Association of

American Publishers. *Winners: Encyclopedia of Artificial Intelligence* (Wiley); Cervin Robinson & Joel Herschman for *Architecture Transformed: A History of the Photography of Buildings from 1839 to the Present* (MIT Press/Architectural League of N.Y.); John Stachel, ed., for *The Collected Papers of Albert Einstein, Vol. 1: The Early Years, 1879–1902* (Princeton Univ.); Wayne A. Sinclair, Warren T. Johnson, Howard H. Lyon for *Diseases of Trees and Shrubs* (Cornell Univ.); James H. Jandl for *Blood: A Textbook of Hematology* (Little, Brown); *The Probabilistic Revolution* (MIT Press); Robert Gilpin for *The Political Economy of International Relations* (Princeton Univ.); *The History of Cartography, Vol. 1: Cartography in Prehistoric, Ancient, and Medieval Europe and the Mediterranean* (Univ. of Chicago); *The Founders' Constitution* (five volumes) (Univ. of Chicago).

Parents Magazine Best Book for Babies Award. *Winner:* Sarah Pooley for *A Day of Rhymes* (Bodley Head).

Robert Payne Award. *Offered by:* Columbia University. *Winner:* Seymour Levitan for *Paper Roses: Selected Poems of Rachel Korn* (Aya Press).

PEN Book of the Month Translation Award. *Winners:* Madeline Levine and Francine Prose for *A Scrap of Time* by Ida Fink (Pantheon).

PEN Medal for Translation. *Winner:* Ralph Manheim.

Vincent Perischetti Award. For an outstanding publisher of music and/or educational books. *Winner:* Clair Brook, W. W. Norton Company.

Poggioli Award. *Offered by:* PEN American Center. For an outstanding translation. *Winner:* James Marcus for *La Valigia Vuota* by Sergio Ferrero (in progress).

Present Tense/Joel H. Cavior Literary Awards. *Awarded by:* American Jewish Committee. To honor authors and translators of works that reflect humane Jewish values. *Winners:* (fiction) Phillip Roth for *The Counterlife* (Penguin); (autobiography/biography) Dan Vittorio Segre for *Memoirs of a Fortunate Jew* (Adler); (history) David Sorkin for *The Transformation of German Jewry* (Oxford); (religious thought) Nehama Aschkenasy for *Eve's Journey* (Univ. of Pennsylvania); (special citation for lifetime achievement) Cynthia Ozick.

Pulitzer Prizes in Letters. To honor distinguished works by American writers, dealing preferably with American themes. *Winners:* (fiction) Toni Morrison for *Beloved* (Knopf); (general nonfiction) Richard Rhodes for *The Making of the Atomic Bomb* (Simon & Schuster); (biography) David H. Donald for *Look Homeward: A Life of Thomas Wolfe* (Little, Brown); (history) Robert V. Bruce for *The Launching of Modern American Science, 1846–1876* (Knopf); (poetry) William Meredith for *Partial Accounts* (Knopf).

John Llewellyn Rhys Memorial Prize. *Winner:* Matthew Yorke for *The March Fence* (Viking).

Roethke Memorial Prize. *Offered by:* Theodore Roethke Memorial Foundation. *Winner:* Carolyn Kizer.

Richard and Hilda Rosenthal Foundation Award. For a work of fiction that is a considerable literary achievement though not necessarily a commercial success. *Offered by:* American Academy and Institute of Arts and Letters. *Winner:* Thomas McMahon.

Delmore Schwartz Memorial Poetry Award. *Offered by:* New York University College of Arts and Science. *Winner:* Deborah Digges.

Science Book Prizes. For books in the English language published for the first time in the United Kingdom. *Of-*

fered by: Science Museum and the Committee on the Public Understanding of Science. *Winners:* (book for young people) *Living Things* by Robin Kerrod; (book with general readership) *Living with Risk* by British Medical Association Board of Science.

Sheaffer-PEN New England Award. *Winner:* Allen Grossman.

John Simmons Short Fiction Award. *Offered by:* Univ. of Iowa Press. *Winner:* Michael Pritchett for *The Venus Tree* (Univ. of Iowa).

Society of Midland Authors Award. For outstanding books about the Midwest or by midwestern authors. *Winners:* (fiction) Jon Hassler for *Grand Opening* (Morrow); (nonfiction) John Conroy for *Belfast Diary* (Beacon); (biography) Frederick J. Blue for *Salmon P. Chase: A Life in Politics* (Kent State Univ.); (children's fiction) Violet Olson for *View from the Pighouse Roof* (Atheneum/Macmillan); (children's nonfiction) Beverly Butler for *Maggie by My Side* (Dodd, Mead); (poetry) David Wojahn for *Glassworks* (Univ. of Pittsburgh); (drama) Jon Klein for *T Bone N Weasel* (produced by Actors' Theatre, Louisville, Kentucky).

Soros Translation Award. *Offered by:* Columbia University. *Winner:* Ivan Sanders for *The Story of My Wife* by Milan Fust (PAJ Publications/Farrar Straus).

Spur Awards. *Offered by:* Western Writers of America. *Winners:* (novel) Tony Hillerman for *Skinwalkers* (Harper); (historical novel) Robert Flynn for *Wanderer Springs* (TCU): (nonfiction) Pamela Herr for *Jessie Benton Fremont* (Franklin Watts); (juvenile) Joan Lowery Nixon for *The Orphan Train* (Bantam); (short fiction) Max Evans for "Orange County Cowboys" (*South Dakota Review*); (short nonfiction) Joyce Gibson Roach for "A High-toned Woman" (Texas Folklore Society); (cover art) Sam Abell for *C. M. Russell's West* (Thomasson-Grant); (screenplay) Gordon Dawson for "Independence"; (first novel) Elaine Long for *Jenny's Mountain* (St. Martin's).

Jean Stein Award. *Offered by:* American Academy and Institute of Arts and Letters. *Winner:* Andre Dubus.

Teachers as Writers Award. *Offered by:* Teachers USA. *Winner:* Ted Anton for *Barrio Numbers* (Teachers USA).

Theatre Library Association Award. For the outstanding book in the field of motion pictures and broadcasting. *Winner:* John Canemaker for *Winsor McCay: His Life and Art* (Abbeville).

Translation Center Awards. *Winners:* Al Poulin, Jr., for *Anne Hebert: Selected Poems* (Boa Editions) and Ritva Poom for *Fog Horses* by Eeva-Liisa Marner (Cross-Cultural Communications).

University of Iowa. *See* Iowa Short Fiction Award.

Harold D. Vursell Memorial Award. *Offered by:* American Academy and Institute of Arts and Letters. *Winner:* Jonathan Maslow.

Washington Post/Children's Book Guild Nonfiction Award. *Winner:* Jim Arnosky.

Wheatland Prize. For a notable contribution to international literary exchange. *Winner:* Gregory Rabassa.

Whitbread Literary Awards (Great Britain). For literature of merit that is readable on a wide scale. *Offered by:* Booksellers Association of Great Britain. *Winner:* Paul Sayer for *The Comforts of Madness* (Constable).

William Allen White Children's Book Award. *Winner:* Betsy Byars for *Cracker Jackson* (Viking Penguin).

Walt Whitman Award. For an American poet who has not yet published a book of poems. *Winner:* April Bernard for *Blackbird Bye Bye* (Random).

Thornton Niven Wilder Prize. *Offered*

by: Columbia University. *Winners:* Olov Jonason and Hassan Shahbaz.

H. H. Wingate Award. *Winners:* (nonfiction) Anton Gill for *The Journey Back from Hell* (Grafton) and (fiction) Amos Oz for *Black Boy* (Chatto and Windus).

George Wittenborn Memorial Award. For excellence of content and physical design of an art book, exhibition catalog, and/or periodical published in North America. *Offered by:* Art Libraries Society of North America. *Winners: The Eloquent Object* (Philbrook Museum of Art) and *The Art That Is Life* (Museum of Fine Arts, Boston).

Women's Studies Award. *Offered by:* Crossroad/Continuum Publishing Group. *Winner:* Rita Nakashima Brock for *Journeys by Heart: A Christology of Erotic Power* (Crossroad/Continuum).

World Science Fiction Convention Hugo Awards. *See* Hugo Awards.

YASD/*SLJ* Author Achievement Award. *Offered by:* American Library Association Young Adult Services Division and *School Library Journal. Winner:* S. E. Hinton.

Morton Dauwen Zabel Award for Criticism. *Offered by:* American Academy and Institute of Arts and Letters. *Winner:* Clement Greenberg.

Buyers' Guide, 1988–1989

The *Library Journal* 1988–1989 Buyers' Guide presents the most up-to-date purchasing information on products and services for libraries. *LJ* asked each company listed to supply its own 20-word annotation of either specific products, general product or service line, special discounts, or information librarians should know. Each company listing includes a contact person to whom all inquiries should be addressed. When contacting any of these companies, please mention or note *LJ* as the source of the inquiry. It helps *LJ* know how its readers are using this guide.

The Directory of Products is arranged by product or service categories, subdivided by more specific product names, with cross-references to the common terminology. The Directory of Suppliers includes contact person, complete address, telephone number(s), FAX and telex numbers, and a brief description. Companies that advertised in the August 1988 issue of *LJ* are indicated by a ★ with the page number of the ad in parentheses after the company name.

Directory of Products

ABSTRACTING
Magazine Article

ACCESSION BOOKS & SHEETS
Data Trek • Gaylord • Highsmith

ACID-FREE MATERIALS (see Restoration & Preservation)

ACQUISITIONS SYSTEMS
Advanced Library • Brodart • Comstow • CLSI • Data Research • Data Trek • Dynix • E B S • Faxon • Fordham • Info Dimensions • INLEX • Innovative Interfaces • NSC • Right On • Ringgold • UNISYS • Universal Library • Utlas • VTLS

ADDING MACHINES
Highsmith

ADDRESSING MACHINES
Heyer

ADHESIVE
ACID-FREE (see also Restoration & Preservation): Demco • Gaylord • Highsmith • Kapco • Seal
APPLICATORS: Gaylord • Highsmith • Larlin • 3M Office Supply
ARCHIVAL: Demco • Fordham • Highsmith • Seal
BOOK LABEL: Demco • Follett Software • Fordham • Gaylord • G M Assocs • Highsmith • Larlin
CALL NUMBER LABEL: Data Recall • Data Trek • Demco • Fordham • Gaylord • Highsmith • Kapco • Larlin
CLOTH: Gaylord • Highsmith • Larlin
DISPLAY: Fordham • Highsmith
GLUE: Brodart • Demco • Fordham • Gaylord • Highsmith • Larlin
PASTE: Brodart • Demco • Fordham • Gaylord • Highsmith • Seal
PLASTIC: Brodart • Fordham • Gaylord • Highsmith • Larlin • Library Store • Seal
POLYESTER FILM JACKET: Brodart • Gaylord • Highsmith • Larlin • Library Store
PRESSURE SENSITIVE: Data Recall • Gaylord • Highsmith • Kapco • Larlin • Scott • Seal • 3M Office Supply
RUBBER CEMENT: Brodart • Demco • Fordham • Gaylord • Highsmith • Larlin • Library Store
SPRAY: Brodart • Demco • Fordham • Gaylord • Highsmith • Larlin • Library Store • Seal • 3M Office Supply

Note: Reprinted from *Library Journal*, August 1988.

VINYL: Gaylord • Highsmith
WAX: Lectro-Stik • Stikki-Wax

ADHESIVE DISPENSERS (see Dispensers)

ADHESIVE TAPE
Brodart • Demco • Fordham • Gaylord • Highsmith • Kapco • Kole • Larlin • Scott • Seton Name Plate • 3M Office Supply

APPLICATION CARDS (see Cards, Circulation)

ARCHIVAL MATERIALS
Dahle • Demco • Fordham • Franklin • Gaylord • Highsmith • Larlin

ART REPRODUCTIONS (see Prints & Reproductions)

ASH STANDS & TRAYS
Block • Fordham • Lawrence Metal

ATLAS CASES
Buckstaff • Fordham • Gaylord • Heller • Highsmith • Library Bureau • Porta-Structures • Texwood • Tuohy

ATLASES
Graphic Learning • Hammond • Nystrom • Rand McNally

AUDIOTAPE (see also "On Cassette," published by Bowker)
BLANK (cassettes & reel to reel): Brodart • Central AV • Demco • Fordham • Highsmith • Larlin • Radmar • Select AV • 3M Office Supply
CLEANERS: Brodart • Central AV • Demco • Highsmith • Select AV
DISPLAY RACKS: Alps • Brodart • Demco • Educational Servs • Fordham • Gaylord • Gressco • Hannecke • Highsmith • Liberty • Library Bureau • Nieman Design • Video Space • Worden
DUPLICATION SERVICE: Highsmith • Radmar
DUPLICATORS: Brodart • Central AV • Highsmith • Select AV
INVENTORY CONTROL: Alps • Phelps • Seton Name Plate
PRERECORDED: Applause • Avedex • Books on Tape • Caedmon • Educational Servs • Ingram • KECCō • Listening Library • Live Oak • Metacom • Norton • Nystrom • Perma-Bound • Potentials Unltd • Fay Inst • Professional Media • Soper Sound • Telesensory • Troll • Westport Media
PROCESSING KITS: Jon-Tone • Professional Media
RECORDERS & PLAYERS: Avedex • Brodart • Central AV • Highsmith • Select AV
REELS: Brodart • Central AV • Demco • Fordham • Gaylord • Highsmith • Select AV
SLIDE/SYNC RECORDERS: Highsmith • Select AV
SPLICERS: Brodart
STORAGE CABINETS (FILES): Alps • Brodart • Demco • Fordham • Gressco • Highsmith • Larlin • Library Bureau • Neumade • Select AV • Video Space • Worden
TAPE MAINTENANCE KITS: Brodart • Central AV • Gaylord • Highsmith

AUDIOVISUAL (AV)
AIDE PINS: Highsmith • Larlin
CARDS & FORMS (see Cards, Audiovisual & Forms)
CARRYING BAGS: Demco • Fordham • Gaylord • Highsmith • Keystone • Larlin • Monaco
CASES: Brodart • Demco • Dukane • Fordham • Gaylord • Highsmith • Larlin • Professional Media • Select AV
CATALOGING SERVICES (see Cataloging Services)
CONTROL BOARDS: Data Trek • Fordham • Highsmith • Select AV
DISSOLVES: Highsmith • Select AV • Sharp
EQUIPMENT (see listing for specific article, e.g., projector, record player, etc. See also "Audiovisual Market Place: A Multimedia Guide," Bowker)
EQUIPMENT CARTS: Brodart • Demco • Esselte • Fordham • Garrett • Gaylord • Highsmith • Larlin • Library Store • Neumade • Select AV • Wheelit • Worden
FURNITURE: Bretford • Brodart • Demco • Elden • Fordham • Gaylord • Heller • Highsmith • Larlin • Mohawk Midland • Neumade • Redpath • Select AV • Texwood • Tufnut • Wheelit • Worden
INFORMATION SYSTEMS: Advanced Library • Data Trek • Highsmith
LAMPS: Sitler's
MOBILE RESOURCE CENTERS (see also Learning Systems): Garrett • Gaylord • Highsmith • Select AV
PROCESSING KITS: Highsmith • Professional Media • Specialized Service & Supply
PROGRAM CONTROL DEVICES: Data Trek • Highsmith • Select AV
SOFTWARE (see "Feature Films on 8mm & 16mm," Bowker)
STORAGE: Elden • Franklin • Gaylord • Heller • Highsmith • Larlin • Monaco • Select AV • Worden

AUTOMATION & SYSTEMS DESIGN
Auto-Graphics • Brodart • Carlyle • CLSI • Computer Co • Comstow • Data Recall • Data Research • Data Trek • Dynix • Eyring • Gaylord • INLEX • Innovative Interfaces • Library Corp • NSC • Sirsi • SOLINET • Universal Library • VTLS

AWARD PINS & RIBBONS
Arch Bronze • Demco • Fordham • Highsmith • Larlin • Riverside • Seton Name Plate

BADGES, CONFERENCE
Block • Data Recall • Demco • Fordham • Library Sign • Seton Name Plate

BEST SELLER LIST, LUCITE
Fordham

BIBLIOGRAPHIC SERVICE SYSTEMS (Data Processing)
Advanced Library • Auto-Graphics • Blackwell NA • Brodart • Computer Co • Data Trek • Dynix • Hendershot • Library Corp • OCLC • Shelfmark • Sirsi • Utlas • VTLS

BICYCLE RACKS
Am Playground • Fordham

BINDER STRIPS
Larlin

BINDERS
BOOKJACKET: Brodart • Demco • Fordham • Gaylord • Highsmith • Larlin
CASSETTE: Brodart • Demco • Fordham • Gaylord • Highsmith • Larlin • Professional Media • Vulcan
CLEANER: Fordham • Gaylord
DECORATIVE INSERTS: Fordham
DISKETTE: Devoke • Esselte • Fordham • Gaylord • Highsmith • Vulcan
EASEL BACK: Esselte • Fordham • Franklin • Highsmith • Molex • Vulcan
LOCKABLE: Brodart • Franklin • Gaylord • Highsmith • Larlin
LOOSE-LEAF: Brodart • Esselte • Fordham • Franklin • Highsmith • Larlin • Vulcan
MAGAZINE: Brodart • Demco • EBSCO Subscription Services • Fordham • Franklin • Gaylord • Highsmith • Larlin • Library Store • Vulcan
NEW BOOK LISTER: Fordham
NEWSPAPER: Fordham • Franklin • Highsmith • Portage • Vulcan
PAMPHLET: Brodart • Demco • Fordham • Gaylord • Highsmith
PHONODISCS: Demco • Highsmith • Professional Media
SHEET MUSIC: Brodart • Demco • Gaylord • Highsmith • Vulcan
SINGLE- & DOUBLE-STITCHED: Brodart • Demco • Gaylord • Highsmith
TRANSPARENT: Brodart • Demco • Esselte • Fordham • Gaylord • Highsmith • Larlin

BINDING MATERIALS & EQUIPMENT
BINDER'S BOARD: Highsmith
CLOTH: Brodart • Gaylord • Highsmith • Johnson Bookbinding • Vulcan
GENERAL SUPPLIERS: Brodart • Fordham • Gaylord • Highsmith • Johnson Bookbinding
LEATHER: Vulcan
MACHINES: Brodart • Gaylord • Permaseal
PAPER: Highsmith • Johnson Bookbinding • Vulcan
PAPERBACK REINFORCING: Baker & Taylor • Brodart • Highsmith • Kapco • Permaseal • Plastic Window
PREBINDING SUPPLIES: Hertzberg • Highsmith
PRESERVATIVE, LEATHER: Gaylord
SLIDE-ON SPINES: Vulcan
SPIRAL SPINES: Gaylord • Multigraphics • Vulcan

BINDING SERVICES
CERTIFIED BINDERS (for addresses of nearest certified binders write to Library Binding Inst, 8013 Centre Park Dr, Austin, TX 78754)
CLASS A BINDING: Atlantic • Bridgeport • Campbell-Logan • Crawford • E B S • Library Bindery of PA • San Val • Wallaceburg
LEATHER BINDING: Atlantic • Bridgeport • Campbell-Logan • Crawford • E B S • Library Bindery of PA • Publishers Book Bindery • Wallaceburg
PICTURE BINDINGS: Atlantic • Bridgeport • San Val
PREBINDERS, HARDBACKS: Atlantic • Baker & Taylor • Bound To Stay Bound • Bridgeport • E B S • Mook & Blanchard
PREBINDERS, MAGAZINES: Atlantic • Baker & Taylor • Bridgeport
PREBINDERS, PAPERBACKS: Atlantic • Baker & Taylor • Bound To Stay Bound • Bridgeport • E B S • Emery-Pratt • Hertzberg • San Val • Story House
RESTORATION BINDING: Atlantic • Bridgeport • Campbell-Logan • Crawford • E B S • Library Bindery of PA

BLACKBOARDS & ACCESSORIES
Arch Bronze • Brodart • Demco • Fordham • Ghent • Highsmith • Pryor

BLIND, MATERIALS FOR (see Physically Challenged)

BOOK BLOCKS
Brodart • Gaylord • Highsmith • Larlin

BOOK CARDS (see Cards, Circulation)

BOOK CARRYING BAGS
CANVAS: Brodart • Demco • Gaylord • Highsmith • Keystone • Larlin
PLASTIC: Brodart • Continental Extrusion • Demco • Fordham • Gaylord • Highsmith • Larlin

BOOK CARRYING CASES
Highsmith • Larlin

BOOK CATALOG SERVICES
Auto-Graphics • Catalog Card • E B S • Marcive • Pathway • VTLS

BOOK CHARGING SYSTEMS (see Circulation Control Systems)

BOOK CLEANERS
Brodart • Demco • Highsmith

BOOK COATING, PLASTIC
Brodart • Fordham • Gaylord • Highsmith • Larlin

BOOK COPYING SERVICE (see Book Reproduction)

BOOK CRADLES (for Microfilming)
Buk Mark • Micobra

BOOK DROPS (see Book Returns)

BOOK EXHIBITS
Buk Mark • Gaylord • Learned Information • Nieman Design • Porta-Structures

BOOK HANDLING EQUIPMENT (see item desired, e.g., Book Carts, Shipping Cases, etc)

BOOK HOLDERS & DISPLAYERS
Brodart • Demco • Elm • Fordham • Gaylord • Hannecke • Heller • Nieman Design • Porta-Structures • Roberts • Worden

BOOK IMPORTERS (see Booksellers, Importers)

BOOK LACQUER (see Lacquer)

BOOK MAILING BAGS
Brodart • Gaylord • Kole • Larlin • Library Store

BOOK MARKING EQUIPMENT & SUPPLIES (see Marking Equipment & Supplies)

BOOK ORDER CARDS (see Cards, Book Order & Forms)

BOOK PROCESSING KITS (see also Cataloging Services)
Baker & Taylor • Bound To Stay Bound • Demco • E B S • Emery-Pratt • Marcive • Modern Book • Pathway • Shelfmark • Specialized Service & Supply

BOOK RENTAL (see Rental, Books)

BOOK REPAIRING
EQUIPMENT: Demco • Fordham • Gaylord • Hertzberg • Highsmith • Larlin
KITS: Brodart • Demco • Gaylord • Hertzberg • Highsmith • Kapco
MATERIALS (see item desired , e.g., Book Cleaners, Binding Materials & Equipment, Tape, Lacquer, Book, etc)

BOOK REPRODUCTION (including periodicals) (see On-Demand Publishing)

BOOK RETURNS
BUILT-IN: Fordham • Gaylord • Heller • Highsmith • Library Bureau • Worden
FINE ENVELOPES: Gaylord
OUTDOOR: Brodart • Demco • Fordham • Gaylord • Highsmith

BOOK REVIEW CARDS
Larlin

BOOK SHELLAC (see Shellac, Book)

BOOK SUPPORTS
MAGNETIC: Acme • Adjustable Steel
METAL: Acme • Adjustable Steel • Brodart • Demco • Fordham • Gaylord • Highsmith • Larlin • Library Bureau • Library Prods • Library Store
PLASTIC: Brodart • Buk Mark • Demco • Fordham • Gaylord • Highsmith • Larlin • Library Prods • Library Store • Roberts
SPRING-TENSION: Brodart • Gaylord • Highsmith • Library Bureau

BOOK TRUCKS
DEPRESSIBLE (see Furniture, Library)
LOCKING: Brodart • Buckstaff • Highsmith • Library Bureau • Worden
METAL: Brodart • Buckstaff • Demco • Equipto • Fordham • Garrett • Gaylord • Highsmith • Larlin • Library Store
PORTABLE: Bretford • Buckstaff • Equipto • Gaylord • Heller • Highsmith • Larlin
SELF-LEVELING: Buckstaff • Gaylord • Highsmith • Worden
STEP STOOL: Brodart • Buckstaff • Fordham • Gaylord • Highsmith • Library Store
WIRE: Equipto • Fordham • Gaylord • Highsmith
WOOD: Brodart • Buckstaff • Fordham • Gaylord • Heller • Highsmith • Library Bureau • Porta-Structures • Texwood • Tuohy • Worden

BOOK-WEEK MATERIALS (see Publicity Services & Materials)

BOOKCARTS, FOLDING
Brodart • Highsmith • Putnam

BOOKCASES (see also Shelving)
Adjustable Steel • Brodart • Buckstaff • Equipto • Fordham • Gaylord • Heller • Highsmith • Larlin • Library Bureau • Library Prods • Library Store • Porta-Structures • Putnam • Texwood • Tuohy • Vecta • Worden

BOOKCOVER MEASURING BOARDS
Bridgeport • Brodart • Gaylord

BOOKCOVERS
ACETATE: Demco • Highsmith
DECORATIVE: Fordham • Highsmith
PAPER: Fordham • Highsmith
PLASTIC: Fordham • Franklin • Gaylord • Highsmith • Kapco • Library Store
POLYESTER FILM: Brodart • Demco • Fordham • Gaylord • Highsmith • Kapco • Larlin • Library Store
SELF-ADHESIVE: Brodart • Fordham • Gaylord • Highsmith • Kapco • Larlin • Library Store • Plastic Window
VINYL: Brodart • Fordham • Gaylord • Highsmith • Larlin • Library Store

BOOKJACKET BINDERS (see Binders)

BOOKJACKET PASTING MACHINES
Highsmith

BOOKLIST DISPLAYERS (see Pamphlet Display Case, Lucite)

BOOKLISTS (see also Publicity Services & Materials)
Blackwell NA

BOOKMARKS
Brodart • Buk Mark • Demco • Gaylord

BOOKMOBILES
NEW: Moroney • Ohio Bus • Terra Transit • Thomas Built
REBUILDING: Moroney • Ohio Bus
REPAIR: Moroney • Ohio Bus
TRAILER LIBRARIES: Moroney
USED: Moroney • Ohio Bus

BOOKPLATES
Brodart • Demco • Fordham • Gaylord • Highsmith • Kidstamps

BOOKPOCKET PASTING MACHINES
Brodart • Demco

BOOKPOCKETS
GUMMED BACKS: Brodart • Demco • Fordham • Gaylord • Highsmith • Larlin • Library Store
PRESSURE-SENSITIVE: Brodart • Demco • Fordham • Gaylord • Highsmith • Library Store • Molex
REGULAR: Brodart • Demco • Fordham •

Gaylord • Highsmith • Larlin • Library Store

BOOKRACKS (see Furniture, Library)

BOOKRESTS (see Book Holders & Displayers)

BOOKS-BY-MAIL

Afro-Am • Fay Inst • Internat Bookfinders • McNaughton • Modern Book • Pendragon

"BOOKS I HAVE READ"—NOTEBOOK

Demco • Gaylord

BOOKS PROCESSED (see Cataloging Services, Books)

BOOKSELLERS (for additional booksellers, "American Book Trade Directory," published by Bowker)

BOOK IMPORTERS: Accents • Applause • Blackwell NA • E B S • Emery-Pratt • Fay Inst • Fiesta • French & European • Kraus • Pendragon

FOREIGN: Applause • Blackwell NA • Emery-Pratt • Fay Inst • Fiesta • French & European • Kraus • Pendragon • Perma-Bound

OUT OF PRINT BOOKS: Blackwell NA • Colonial • French & European • Internat Bookfinders • Kraus • Larlin • UMI

REMAINDERS: French & European • Ingram

REPRINTS: Baker & Taylor • Blackwell NA • Emery-Pratt • Kraus • Larlin

REPRODUCED BOOKS (see On-Demand Publishing)

WHOLESALE, HARDBACK & PAPERBACK: Accents • Baker & Taylor • Blackwell NA • Bound To Stay Bound • Bowker • Digital Pr • E B S • EBSCO Publishing • Emery-Pratt • Ingram • Larlin • Marshall Cavendish • Meckler • Modern Book (juv) • Mook & Blanchard • Pathway • Perma-Bound • Story House

WHOLESALE, PAPERBACK: Baker & Taylor • Blackwell NA • E B S • Emery-Pratt • Ingram

BOOKSHELVING, STACKS & ACCESSORIES (see Shelving)

BOXES

BOOK, SHIPPING: Demco • Highsmith • Kole

GENERAL (see specific type, i.e., Files, Microfilm, Shipping Cases, etc)

PHASE: Bridgeport

BRAQUETTE (see Picture, Frames, Adjustable)

BROWSER BINS

Brodart • Demco • Gaylord • Highsmith • Library Bureau • Redpath

BULLETIN BOARDS

CHANGEABLE (see Signs, Movable Letters)

CORK: Arch Bronze • Block • Brodart • Demco • Designers Sign • Fordham • Gaylord • Ghent • Highsmith • Larlin • Pryor • Scott

ELECTRONIC: Arch Bronze • Demco • Designers Sign • Highsmith • Multiverse • Pryor • Scott • Video Space

HOOK 'N' LOOP: Arch Bronze • Designers Sign • Fordham • Highsmith

MAGNETIC: Arch Bronze • Brodart • Designers Sign • Fordham • Ghent • Highsmith • Pryor • Video Space

PLASTIC: Arch Bronze • Brodart • Demco • Designers Sign • Fordham • Gaylord • Highsmith • Pryor

UPHOLSTERED: Worden

BUSINESS MACHINES (see machine desired, Addressing, etc)

CABINETS, CARD CATALOG (see Furniture, Library)

CABINETS, STORAGE STATIONERY (see also Files & Furniture, Office)

Adjustable Steel • Brodart • Buckstaff • Central AV • Demco • Equipto • Esselte • Fordham • Foster • Gressco • Hannecke • Heller • Kole • Larlin • Liberty • Library Bureau • Micobra • Putnam • Tuohy • Vecta • Worden

CALCULATORS, ELECTRONIC

Demco • Gaylord • Highsmith • Sharp

CALENDARS

Block • Demco • Highsmith • Ingram • Kole

CALL NUMBER LABEL PROTECTORS

Brodart • Demco • Fordham • Gaylord • Highsmith • Kapco • Larlin • Library Store

CALL NUMBER LABELS (see Labels, Call Number)

CALL NUMBER STAMPING MACHINES (see Marking Equipment & Supplies)

CAMERAS, CATALOGING

Demco • Extek • Minolta

CARD SORTER (see Sorting Equipment)

CARDS

AUDIOVISUAL, ACQUISITION: Advanced Library • Data Trek • Fordham • Highsmith

AUDIOVISUAL, FILM BOOKING: Data Trek • Fordham • Highsmith

AUDIOVISUAL, INSTRUCTIONAL MATERIALS: Data Trek • Fordham • Highsmith

AUDIOVISUAL, LOCATOR: Data Trek • Fordham • Highsmith

AUDIOVISUAL, RECORDING BOOKING: Data Trek • Fordham • Highsmith

BOOK CARD PROTECTORS: Brodart • Demco • Fordham • Gaylord • Highsmith • Larlin

BOOK ORDER: Brodart • Demco • Fordham • Gaylord • Highsmith • Larlin

BOOKCOVER/SIGNALS: Brodart • Fordham • Gaylord • Highsmith

CATALOG: Advanced Library • Bound To Stay Bound • Brodart • Catalog Card • CLSI • Data Trek • Demco • Fordham • Gaylord • Highsmith • K-12 Micromedia • Larlin • Library Store • Right On

CATALOG, ACID-FREE: Brodart • Fordham • Gaylord • Gen Microfilm • Highsmith • Larlin • Library Store

CATALOG, COLOR-BANDED: Brodart • Demco • Follett Software • Fordham • Gaylord • Highsmith • Library Store

CATALOG, COMPUTER-PRINTED: Data Trek • Fordham • Highsmith • K-12 Micromedia • Library Store • Marcive
CATALOG, CROSS REFERENCE: CLSI • Data Trek • Highsmith • Woods
CATALOG, DISPLAY: Data Trek • Demco • Fordham • Highsmith
CATALOG, DUPLICATED: Data Trek • Gen Microfilm • Highsmith • Library Reproduction
CATALOG FLAG: Brodart • Data Trek • Fordham • Larlin
CATALOG, LIBRARY OF CONGRESS, MACHINE-READABLE ORDER FORMS: Catalog Card • Data Trek • Demco • Gaylord
CATALOG, PRINTED: Data Trek • EBSCO Subscription Services • Marcive • Modern Book • Specialized Service & Supply
CATALOG, PROTECTORS: Brodart • Demco • Gaylord • Larlin • Library Store
CATALOG, SHEET OR STRIP FORM: Brodart • Fordham • Gaylord
CATALOG, TEMPLATES (XEROX): Library Corp
CATALOG, XEROX COPYING: Brodart • Gaylord
CIRCULATION, APPLICATION OR REGISTRATION: Brodart • CLSI • Data Trek • Gaylord • Larlin • NSC
CIRCULATION, BOOK: Brodart • Data Trek • Demco • Gaylord • Larlin • Library Store • Modern Book • Specialized Service & Supply
CIRCULATION, BORROWERS': Brodart • Data Trek • Demco • Follett Software • Gaylord • Larlin • Library Store
CIRCULATION, DATE DUE: Brodart • Data Trek • Demco • Gaylord • G M Assocs • Larlin • Library Store
CIRCULATION, IDENTIFICATION: Brodart • Data Trek • Demco • Gaylord • Larlin
CIRCULATION, MAGAZINE CHARGING: Brodart • Data Trek • Fordham • Gaylord • Larlin • Library Store
CIRCULATION, OVERDUE FINE: Brodart • Data Trek • Gaylord • Larlin
CIRCULATION, OVERDUE POST CARDS: Brodart • Data Trek • Demco • Gaylord
COIN MAILING: Brodart • Gaylord
DOCUMENT RECORD: Data Trek • Gaylord • Larlin
MAGAZINE RECORD: Brodart • Data Trek • Fordham • Gaylord
MICROFILM APERTURE: Extek
PRACTICE (INDEX): Brodart • Fordham • Gaylord • Larlin
RESERVE BOOK: Brodart • Fordham • Gaylord • Larlin
SHELFLIST: Auto-Graphics • Brodart • Gaylord • Marcive • Modern Book • Specialized Service & Supply
SUBJECT HEADING CATALOG GUIDE: Brodart • Gaylord • Larlin • Science Pr
TIME: Phelps

CARPETING
Demco • Seton Name Plate

CARRELS
ACOUSTICAL: Buckstaff • Demco • Fordham • Gaylord • Highsmith • Library Bureau • Library Prods • Mohawk Midland • Worden
AUDIOVISUAL ("Wet") (see also Learning Systems): Buckstaff • Demco • Fordham • Heller • Highsmith • Library Bureau • Library Prods • Mohawk Midland • Texwood • Tuohy • Worden
BOOKTRUCK (see Book Trucks, Locking)
DOUBLE-LEVEL: Heller • Highsmith • Mohawk Midland • Worden
PORTABLE, TABLE: Buckstaff • Fordham • Highsmith • Library Prods • Worden
STANDARD ("Dry"): Brodart • Buckstaff • Demco • Fordham • Heller • Highsmith • Library Bureau • Library Prods • Mohawk Midland • Porta-Structures • Texwood • Tuohy • Worden
WHEELCHAIR-SEATED: Brodart • Buckstaff • Demco • Fordham • Gaylord • Highsmith • Library Bureau • Mohawk Midland • Porta-Structures • Texwood • Worden

CARROUSELS
HARDBACKS: Brodart • Fordham • Gaylord • Highsmith • Larlin • Porta-Structures
MICROFILM: Highsmith
PAPERBACKS: Brodart • Fordham • Gaylord • Highsmith • Larlin • Library Store • Porta-Structures
ROTATING: Brodart • Demco • Fordham • Gaylord • Highsmith • Library Store • Porta-Struc-tures

CARTON
SIZERS & CUTTING KNIVES: Demco • Kole

CASES
EXHIBIT (see Exhibit Cases)
SHIPPING (see Shipping Cases)

CASH BOXES
Block • Demco • Fordham • Highsmith

CASH REGISTERS
Block

CASH SORTER
Block • Demco • Fordham • Highsmith

CASSETTES (see Recordings or Audio)

CATALOG CARD COPY HOLDER (for typewriters)
Gaylord

CATALOG CARD FILES (see Furniture, Library)

CATALOG CARDS (see Cards, Catalog)

CATALOG CARD SETS (see Book Processing Kits)

CATALOG GUIDES (see Guides, Catalog)

CATALOGING SERVICES
AUDIOVISUAL MATERIALS: Brodart •

Jon-Tone • Marcive • Professional Media • Specialized Service & Supply
BOOKS (see also Book Processing Kits): Auto-Graphics • Blackwell NA • Bound To Stay Bound • Brodart • Catalog Card • Emery-Pratt • Gen Research • Library Corp • Marcive • Mook & Blanchard • Pathway • Shelfmark • Specialized Service & Supply • Utlas • VTLS

CD-ROM
Auto-Graphics • Bowker • CLSI • Disclosure • E B S • EBSCO Electronic Info • EBSCO Subscription Services • Faxon • Gaylord • Gen Research • Inst for Scientific Info • Learned Information • Library Corp • Magazine Article • Marcive • Meridian Data • NewsBank • Sirsi • Turner • UMI • Utlas • VTLS

CHAIRS (see Furniture, Library)

CHANGEMAKERS (see Coin Operated Equipment)

CHARGING DESKS (see Furniture, Library)

CHARGING SYSTEMS (see Circulation Control Systems)

CHARGING TRAY GUIDES (see Guides, Charging Trays)

CHARGING TRAYS (see Trays, Charging)

CHILDREN'S READING PROGRAMS
Larlin • Live Oak • Modern Book • Perma-Bound • Troll

CIRCULATION CONTROL SYSTEMS
AUTOMATIC: Brodart • CLSI • Comstow • Data Recall • Gaylord • Innovative Interfaces
COMPUTER-BASED: Auto-Graphics • Bar Code • Brodart • Catalog Card • CLSI • Data Recall • Data Research • Data Trek • Dynix • Eyring • Follett Software • Gen Research • Info Dimensions • INLEX • Innovative Interfaces • Library Corp • Nichols • NSC • Ringgold • Sirsi • UNISYS1• Universal Library • Utlas • VTLS
THERMOGRAPHIC: Brodart
VISIBLE: Gaylord

CLASSIFICATION GUIDES
Auto-Graphics • Brodart • Demco • Gaylord • Larlin • Professional Media • Woods

CLEANING PRODUCTS
Demco • Evans • Garnet • Larlin

CLIPPING & PICTURE ENVELOPES (see Envelopes, Clipping & Picture)

CLOCKS, TIME RECORDING
Demco • Dukane • Highsmith

COAT RACKS
Highsmith • Lawrence Metal • Library Bureau • Vogel

COIN-OPERATED EQUIPMENT
BILL CHANGERS: Standard Change
CHANGE DISPENSERS: Hamilton • Standard Change
CHANGEMAKERS: Hamilton • Standard Change
COIN COUNTERS: Nadex
COPYING MACHINES: Campus Copies • XCP
LAMINATING MACHINES: Brodart
MICROFILM READER-PRINTERS: Brodart • Minolta • UMI

COIN SORTERS
Block • Demco • Fordham • Highsmith

COLLATING MACHINES
Demco • Highsmith

COMMEMORATIVE TABLETS (see Signs, Metal)

COMPACT DISCS (see also CD-ROM)
DISC CLEANER: A A A Record • Brodart • Gaylord • Highsmith • Jon-Tone
DISC PLAYERS: Brodart • CLSI • Highsmith • Sharp • TEAC
DISCS: A A A Record • French & European • Gaylord • Ingram • Jon-Tone • Professional Media • Soper Sound
STORAGE CABINETS: A A A Record • Brodart • Equipto • Fordham • Gaylord • Gressco • Hannecke • Highsmith • Liberty • Library Store • Nieman Design

COMPUTERS (see Data Processing, Computers)

CONSULTING SERVICES
Brodart • Computer Co • Fay Inst • Garnet • Gossage Regan • Heller • Jaeger • Natl Inst for Rehabilitation • OPL • Porta-Structures • Ringgold • Sexton • Shelfmark • Sirsi

COPIER CONTROL
Copicard • Harris/3M • XCP

COPYING MACHINES
BOND COPIER: Campus Copies • Highsmith • Kole • Sharp
COIN-OPERATED (see Coin-Operated Equipment)
COLOR PHOTOCOPIER: Campus Copies • Multigraphics • Sharp
DUAL SPECTRUM: Campus Copies • Harris/3M
ELECTROSTATIC: Harris/3M
PLAIN PAPER: Campus Copies • Canon • Harris/3M • Kole • Sharp
THERMAL: Highsmith

COPYING SERVICE
Campus Copies

CORK BOARDS (see Display, Panels)

CORNER GUARDS
Heller • Kole • Larlin • Tepromark

CORRECTION FLUID, CATALOG CARD MATCHING
Brodart • Demco • Gaylord • Highsmith • Larlin • Library Store

COUPON CUTTER
Highsmith • Larlin

COVERS, PROTECTIVE
BOOK (see Bookcovers)
BOOK CARD (see Cards, Book Card Protectors)
CATALOG CARD (see Cards, Catalog Protectors)
COMPUTER TERMINAL: Gaylord • High-

smith • Natl Inst for Rehabilitation • Tech-Cessories
DISKETTE: Gaylord • Highsmith • Natl Inst for Rehabilitation
DOCUMENT: Gaylord • Highsmith
ENCYCLOPEDIA: Highsmith
MICROFILM: Highsmith • Library Store
PAGE: Brodart • Demco • Gaylord • Highsmith
PAPERBACKS (see Binding Materials, Paperback Reinforcing)
PERIODICAL: Brodart • Gaylord • Highsmith • Larlin
PHONOGRAPH RECORD: Brodart • Gaylord • Highsmith • Library Store
PICTURE: Brodart • Highsmith
PLASTIC: Gaylord • Highsmith • Larlin • Library Bindery of PA • Library Store

CUMULATIVE BOOK INDEX (CBI) CABINET (see Furniture, Library)

DATABASES (see Automation & Systems Design; Bibliographic Service Systems; Circulation Control Systems [Computer-Based]; MARC Tape Storage & Retrieval Systems; Online Systems; & Retrieval Systems Design)

DATA PROCESSING—EQUIPMENT, SERVICES, & SUPPLIES
ANTIGLARE & ANTISTATIC SCREENS: Devoke • Gaylord • Natl Inst for Rehabilitation
ANTISTATIC MATS & PADS: Brodart • Devoke • Follett Software • Gaylord • Mat Makers • Tech-Cessories • 3M Office Supply
ANTISTATIC SPRAY: Evans
CD READER: Disclosure • Library Corp • NewsBank • Sirsi
CLEANING PRODUCTS: Brodart • Demco • Devoke • Evans • Extek • Garnet • Gaylord • Larlin • 3M Office Supply
COMPUTERS: Auto-Graphics • Data Trek • Eyring • Follett Software • INLEX • Innovative Interfaces • Learned Information • NewsBank • Sharp • Natl Inst for Rehabilitation • Sirsi • Telesensory • UNISYS • Universal Library • VTLS
CONTROL: Copicard
DATA BINDING SUPPLIES: Demco • Devoke • Esselte • Gaylord
DATA COLLECTING MACHINES: NewsBank
FURNITURE: Brodart • Demco • Devoke • Fordham • Foster • Gaylord • Heller • Highsmith • Larlin • Mohawk Midland • Texwood • Vecta • Wheelit • Worden
GENERAL: Block • Document Control • Gaylord • Larlin
MINI & PERSONAL COMPUTERS: Data Trek • Document Control • INLEX • Natl Inst for Rehabilitation • NewsBank • NSC • Sharp • Sirsi • UNISYS
PROCESSORS: CLSI • Extek • Sirsi • Telesensory • UNISYS • Universal Library
PRINTERS: CLSI • Data Trek • INLEX • Natl Inst for Rehabilitation • NewsBank • Sirsi • Telesensory • UNISYS • Universal Library
SCREENS: Demco • Larlin • Natl Inst for Rehabilitation • NewsBank • Sirsi • Telesensory • UNISYS • Universal Library
SECURITY CABINETS: Devoke • Fordham • Gaylord • Heller • Highsmith • Kole • Larlin • Nieman Design • Southsafe
SECURITY SYSTEMS: Gaylord • Sentronic • Telmark • Tufnut
SHIPPING SUPPLIES: Kole • Larlin
SOFTWARE: Data Trek • Document Control • Eyring • Fay Inst • Follett Software • Info Dimensions • INLEX • Innovative Interfaces • Inst for Scientific Info • Larlin • Library Corp • Micro Data Base • Natl Inst for Rehabilitation • Nichols • Right On • Sirsi • Telesensory • UNISYS • Universal Library • Wallaceburg
STORAGE & RETRIEVAL SYSTEMS: Acme • ATLIS • Brodart • Document Control • Eyring • Gillotte • Kole • Library Corp • NewsBank • Sirsi • TEAC • Telesensory • UNISYS • VTLS • Wallaceburg
SURGE SUPPRESSORS: Brodart • Devoke • Follett Software • Fordham • Gaylord • Highsmith • Natl Inst for Rehabilitation • Teledyne • UNISYS • Universal Library • Worden
TERMINALS: CLSI • Document Control • INLEX • NewsBank • Sirsi • UNISYS • Universal Library
TERMINAL PROTECTORS: Highsmith • UNISYS • Universal Library

DATE CARD HOLDERS
Demco • Gaylord • Larlin • Stanger

DATE DUE CARDS & SLIPS (see Cards, Circulation)

DATERS
AUTOMATIC: Block • Demco • G M Assocs • Highsmith • Pryor
BAND: Brodart • Demco • Fordham • Gaylord • Highsmith • Larlin • Library Store • Pryor
NUMBERING STAMPS: Brodart • Demco • Gaylord • Highsmith • Pryor
SELF-INKING: Brodart • Demco • Fordham • Gaylord • Highsmith • Larlin • Pryor

DATEPOCKET (combination bookpocket & date slip)
Demco • Larlin • Library Store

DECORATIVE BOOKCOVERS (see Bookcovers, Decorative)

DEHUMIDIFIERS (see Humidifiers)

DESKS (see Furniture, Library, Office)

DICTIONARY STANDS (see Furniture, Library)

DIRECTORY BOARDS (see Signs, Movable Letters)

DISPENSERS
ADHESIVE: Fordham • Highsmith • Larlin • 3M Office Supply
LABEL: Data Recall • Demco • Fordham • G M Assocs • Highsmith • Larlin • Seton Name Plate

PRESSURE-SENSITIVE TAPE: Brodart • Demco • Gaylord • Highsmith • Kole • Larlin • Library Store • Seton Name Plate • 3M Office Supply

DISPLAY

ADHESIVES (see Adhesive, Display)
BOOKRACKS (see Furniture, Library)
CARD HOLDERS: G M Assocs • Lawrence Metal
CASES (see Exhibit Cases)
FASTENERS: Demco • G M Assocs
LETTERS (see Letters, Display)
LIGHTING FIXTURES (see Lighting Fixtures)
MATERIALS, GENERAL SUPPLIERS: Demco • Designers Sign • Larlin • Library Sign
MODULAR DISPLAY SYSTEMS: Brodart • Fordham • Gressco • Hannecke • Nieman Design • Video Space • Walker
PANELS: Demco • Fordham • Hannecke • Highsmith • Walker
RACKS, AUDIO (see Audiotape)
RACKS, CASSETTE (see Audiotape)
RACKS, LITERATURE: Brodart • Demco • Fixturecraft • Fordham • Gaylord • Hannecke • Highsmith • Kole • Larlin • Lawrence Metal • Library Bureau • Library Sign • Library Store • R & D • Texwood
RACKS, METAL (book, magazine, newspaper): Brodart • Demco • Equipto • Fixturecraft • Fordham • Gaylord • Highsmith • Larlin • Library Store • Nieman Design
RACKS, MOBILE: Brodart • Fordham • Gaylord • Highsmith • Larlin
RACKS, PAPERBACKS: Brodart • Fixturecraft • Fordham • Gaylord • Gressco • Hannecke • Highsmith • Larlin • Library Bureau • Library Store • Nieman Design • Texwood
RACKS, RECORDING (see Recordings)
RACKS, VIDEOCASSETTE (see Video)
RACKS, WIRE (book, magazine, newspaper): Brodart • Equipto • Fixturecraft • Fordham • Gaylord • Highsmith • Larlin • Library Store • Perma-Bound
RACKS, WOOD (book, magazine, newspaper): Brodart • Fordham • Gaylord • Gressco • Heller • Highsmith • Larlin • Liberty • Library Store • Texwood • Worden
SUPPORTS, VERTICAL POLES: Walker
WHEELCHAIR-SEATED: Gaylord

DOCUMENT

BOXES, ACID-FREE (see Restoration & Preservation)
FUMIGATORS (see Restoration & Preservation)
PROTECTORS (see Covers, Protective)
RECORD CARDS (see Cards, Document Record)

DOOR CLOSER CONTROLS

Motorola

DOOR COUNTERS, ELECTRIC

Laser

DRAFTING EQUIPMENT

FURNITURE: Fordham
GENERAL: Dahle • Fordham

DRY-MOUNTING EQUIPMENT & SUPPLIES (see Laminating)

DUPLICATING EQUIPMENT & SUPPLIES

CORRECTION FLUID: Gaylord • Heyer
GENERAL: Demco • Heyer • Multigraphics • Sharp
INK: Heyer • Multigraphics
MICROFILM: Extek • Micobra • Xidex
MIMEOGRAPH: Heyer
MULTIGRAPH: Multigraphics
OFFSET PLATEMAKING EQUIPMENT: Gaylord • Multigraphics
SILVER FILM DUPLICATOR: Extek • Multigraphics
SPIRIT: Heyer
STENCIL DUPLICATOR: Heyer • Larlin

DUPLICATING SERVICE (see Audiotape & Slides)

EASELS (see Blackboards & Accessories)

EDGE PASTERS (see Margin Gluers)

EDUCATIONAL MATERIALS (including Special Education Materials)

Afro-Am • Applause • Asia Society • Audio Language • Demco • E M E • Fairchild • Fay Inst • Fordham • Garnet • Guidance Assocs • Highsmith • Internat Film • K-12 Micromedia • Kidstamps • Larlin • Live Oak • Merit AV • Norton • Nystrom • Pathway • Perma-Bound • Pied Piper • Radmar • Right On • Society for Visual Ed • Teacher Support • Troll • Vocational Media • Westport Media

EMBOSSING

MACHINES & TAPE (see Labelmakers)
STAMP (see Stamps, Library Embossing)

EMPLOYMENT AGENCIES

Gossage Regan

ENVELOPES

ACID-FREE (see Restoration & Preservation)
CLIPPING & PICTURE: Brodart • Fordham • Gaylord • Highsmith • Larlin
MICROFICHE (see Microfiche, Envelopes)
STORAGE: Demco • Foster • Gaylord • Highsmith • Molex
TRANSPARENT: Demco • Highsmith
WINDOW, INTERLIBRARY LOAN: Brodart • Demco • Follett Software • Gaylord • Highsmith

ERASERS

ELECTRIC: Brodart • Demco • Fordham • Gaylord • Larlin
STEEL: Brodart • Fordham • Gaylord

EXHIBIT CASES

INDOOR: Arch Bronze • Brodart • Buckstaff • Fordham • Gaylord • Heller • Highsmith • Worden
OUTDOOR: Fordham • Highsmith

FACSIMILE (FAX) TRANSMITTERS

Demco • Harris/3M • Omnifax • Sharp

FILES

AUTOMATED ELECTRONIC: Document

Control • Eyring
CARD CATALOG (see Furniture, Library)
COMPUTER DISK: Esselte • Gaylord • Highsmith
ENVELOPE: Esselte • Foster • Gaylord • Highsmith
FILM (see Films)
FILMSTRIPS (see Filmstrips)
MAP: Fordham • Gaylord • Highsmith • Library Bureau
MICROFICHE (see Microfiche)
MICROFILM (see Microfilm)
MICRO-OPAQUE (see Micro-Opaque)
NEWSPAPER: Fordham • Gaylord • Gillotte • Heller • Highsmith • Library Bureau • Portage • Worden
OPEN-SHELF: Acme • Adjustable Steel • Brodart • Gaylord • Heller • Highsmith • Library Bureau • Worden
PAMPHLET: Brodart • Demco • Fordham • Gaylord • Gillotte • Highsmith • Larlin • Library Bureau • Magafile • Worden
PERIODICAL: Adjustable Steel • Brodart • Demco • Fordham • Gaylord • Gillotte • Heller • Highsmith • Larlin • Library Bureau • Magafile • Worden
PERIODICAL (LIBRARY TECH PROG): Gaylord
PRINCETON: Brodart • Demco • Fordham • Gaylord • Highsmith • Larlin
PUNCHED CARDS (see Tabulating Cards, Equipment & Supplies)
RECORDINGS (see Recordings)
ROTARY: Acme • Brodart • Fordham • Highsmith
ROTARY INDEX: Acme • Brodart • Highsmith
SLIDES (see Slides)
STEEL: Acme • Brodart • Foster • Gaylord • Highsmith • Kole
STORAGE: Acme • Adjustable Steel • Brodart • Demco • Equipto • Fordham • Foster • Gaylord • Gillotte • Highsmith
TRAYS: Acme • Demco • Gaylord • Highsmith • Molex • Russ Bassett • Worden
VERTICAL: Acme • Demco • Fordham • Foster • Gaylord • Gillotte • Highsmith • Worden
VISIBLE: Acme • Brodart • Demco • Fordham • Gaylord • Highsmith • Worden
WOOD: Adjustable Steel • Demco • Fordham • Gaylord • Heller • Highsmith • Putnam • Worden

FILING

DRAWER DIVIDERS, STEEL: Acme • Brodart • Cel-U-Dex • Esselte
EQUIPMENT: Acme • Adjustable Steel • Cel-U-Dex • Demco • Esselte • Fordham • Gaylord
FLAGS, CARD CATALOG: Brodart • Gaylord • Highsmith • Larlin
MAINTENANCE: Garnet
SIGNALS (see Signal Tabs)
SUPPLIES: Brodart • Cel-U-Dex • Esselte • Garnet • Gaylord • Kole

FILM

CAMERAS: Extek • Gaylord
CANS: Brodart • Demco • Highsmith • Larlin • Neumade
CARRYING BAGS: Demco • Gaylord • Highsmith • Jones West • Keystone
CLEANERS, PRESERVATIVES & PRESERVATION SERVICES: Extek • Highsmith • Neumade
DUPLICATING SERVICE: Radmar
EDUCATIONAL: Coronet/MTI • Highsmith • Internat Film • Larlin • Merit AV • Nystrom • Radmar
8mm FILM LOOP PROJECTORS: Gaylord • General AV • Highsmith
8mm PROJECTORS: Demco • Fordham • Highsmith
GENERAL SUPPLIERS: Gaylord • Highsmith • Neumade
INSPECTION & CLEANING EQUIPMENT: Extek • Highsmith • Neumade
PERFORATION REPAIR SYSTEM: Gaylord • Neumade
POLYESTER: Larlin
POST-PRODUCTION SUPPLIES: Neumade
PREVIEWERS: Highsmith
PROJECTOR LENSES: Gaylord • Highsmith
PROTECTORS: Brodart • Franklin • Highsmith
RECORD CARDS (Acquisition, Booking, etc) (see Cards, Audiovisual)
REELS: Brodart • Demco • Gaylord • Highsmith • Larlin • Neumade • Select AV
RENTAL: Cable • Internat Film • Select AV
REWINDERS: Brodart • Demco • Gaylord • Highsmith • Kalart • Neumade
SEPARATOR RACKS: Brodart • Demco • Highsmith • Neumade
SHIPPING CASES: Brodart • Demco • Gaylord • Highsmith • Larlin • Neumade
16mm FILM LIBRARY: Applause • Brodart • Cable • Eastin Phelan
16mm PROJECTORS: Brodart • Demco • Fordham • Gaylord • Highsmith • Kalart
SPLICERS: Brodart • Demco • Fordham • Gaylord • Highsmith • Kalart • Neumade
VIEWERS: Brodart • Fordham • Highsmith • Neumade

FILMS, PRODUCERS & DISTRIBUTORS (see "Audiovisual Market Place: A Multimedia Guide," & "Feature Films on 8mm & 16mm," both by Bowker)

FILMSTRIP

BLANK FILMSTRIPS: Fordham • Highsmith • Larlin
PROTECTION & REPAIR: Gaylord • Highsmith
SILENT PROJECTORS: Brodart • Central AV • Demco • Dukane • Fordham • Gaylord • Highsmith • Radmar • Select AV
SOUND PROJECTORS: Brodart • Central AV • Demco • Dukane • Fordham • Gaylord • Highsmith • Radmar • Select AV
STORAGE CASES, RACKS & FILES: Brodart • Central AV • Demco • Fordham • Gaylord • Highsmith • Larlin •

Neumade • Worden
VIEWERS: Brodart • Central AV • Demco • Dukane • Fordham • Gaylord • General AV • Highsmith
WRITE-ON: Demco • Highsmith • Larlin

FILMSTRIPS, SILENT & SOUND, PRODUCERS & DISTRIBUTORS (see "Audiovisual Market Place: A Multimedia Guide," Bowker)

FINES CALCULATOR
Gaylord

FINGERTIP MOISTENERS
Evans • Highsmith • Larlin

FIRE PROTECTION
ALARMS: Kidde • Motorola
EQUIPMENT: Detex • Kidde
EXTINGUISHERS: Devoke • Kidde
INFORMATION: Kidde
SMOKE DETECTION: Detection Systems • Kidde

FLAGS (pennants, banners, etc)
Fordham • Highsmith

FLANNEL BOARDS & ACCESSORIES (see Blackboards & Accessories)

FLOOR COVERINGS
Demco

FLOOR MAINTENANCE SUPPLIES
Demco

FLOOR MATS
Block • Demco • Fordham • Highsmith • Kole • Ludlow • Preston • Seton Name Plate • Tepromark

FLOOR STANDS
Brodart • Demco • Fordham • Heller • R & D

FOLDING MACHINES
Heyer

FOREIGN BOOKSELLERS (see Booksellers, Foreign)

FORMS
AUDIOVISUAL: Brodart • Gaylord • Highsmith • Larlin
BOOK ORDER, NO CARBON REQUIQUIRED: Brodart • Demco • Fordham • Gaylord • Highsmith • Larlin • Library Store • Right On
BOOK ORDER, OPTICAL CHARACTER RECOGNITION: Fordham • Gaylord • Highsmith • Larlin
BOOK ORDER, REGULAR: Gaylord • Highsmith • Larlin
CIRCULATION: Brodart • Follett Software • Gaylord • Highsmith • Larlin
COMPUTER: Brodart • Highsmith • Right On
GENERAL OFFICE: Block • Highsmith
INTERLIBRARY LOAN: Brodart • Demco • Fordham • Gaylord • Highsmith • Larlin • Library Store • Right On
OVERNIGHT BOOK SLIPS: Brodart • Fordham • Gaylord • Highsmith • Larlin
PHOTODUPLICATION ORDER: Demco • Gaylord • Larlin
PRINTED TO ORDER: Gaylord
RECORDINGS (DISCS & TAPES): Phelps
REPRODUCIBLE:
SCHOOL LIBRARY: Fordham • Gaylord • Larlin
STATISTICAL REPORTS: Gaylord

FREE EDUCATION MATERIALS, GUIDES
Larlin

FURNITURE
AUDIOVISUAL: Brodart • Buckstaff • Central AV • Demco • Fordham • Gaylord • General AV • Heller • Highsmith • Mohawk Midland • Neumade • Redpath • Select AV • Wheelit • Worden
AUDITORIUM: Buckstaff • Highsmith • Vecta • Worden
COMPUTER & DATA PROCESSING: Block • Brodart • Buckstaff • Fordham • Foster • Garrett • Gaylord • Heller • Highsmith • Kewaunee • Mohawk Midland • Texwood • Wheelit • Worden
IMPORTED: Buckstaff • Demco • Gaylord • Highsmith • Worden
JUVENILE: Artisans' Guild • Brodart • Buckstaff • Demco • Fordham • Gaylord • Heller • Highsmith • Porta-Structures • Tuohy • Worden
LIBRARY: Artisans' Guild • Brodart • Buckstaff • Demco • Fordham • Gaylord • Heller • Highsmith • Library Prods • Mohawk Midland • Porta-Structures • Putnam • Texwood • Tuohy • Worden
LOUNGE: Brodart • Buckstaff • Demco • Fordham • Gaylord • Heller • Highsmith • Mohawk Midland • Porta-Structures • Tuohy • Vecta • Worden
METAL: Brodart • Buckstaff • Equipto • Esselte • Fordham • Foster • Garrett • Gaylord • Highsmith • Kewaunee • Neumade • Nieman Design • Porta-Structures • Vecta • Worden
MODULAR PANELS: Buckstaff • Demco • Fordham • Gaylord • Highsmith • Porta-Structures • Vecta • Vogel • Worden
OFFICE: Adjustable Steel • Buckstaff • Demco • Fordham • Gaylord • Heller • Highsmith • Porta-Structures • Putnam • Tuohy • Vecta • Worden
OUTDOOR: Am Playground • Buckstaff • Demco • Fordham • Highsmith • Worden
SCHOOL: Brodart • Buckstaff • Demco • Fordham • Gaylord • Heller • Highsmith • Worden
WHEELCHAIR-SEATED: Brodart • Buckstaff • Gaylord • Highsmith • Mohawk Midland • Preston • Worden
WOOD: Brodart • Buckstaff • Demco • Fordham • Gaylord • Heller • Highsmith • Library Prods • Mohawk Midland • Porta-Struc-tures • Putnam • Texwood • Tuohy • Vecta • Worden
WORKROOM: Brodart • Buckstaff • Demco • Equipto • Fordham • Gaylord • Highsmith • Worden
WORKSTATIONS: Brodart • Buckstaff • Demco • Equipto • Fordham • Garrett • Gaylord • Heller • Highsmith • Kewaunee • Vecta • Worden

FURNITURE, FOLDING
CHAIRS: Demco • Fordham • Gaylord • Heller • Highsmith • Tuohy
LECTERNS (see Lecterns, Folding)
TABLES: Demco • Fordham • Gaylord • Heller • Highsmith • Tuohy • Wheelit
FURNITURE PLANNING
LAYOUT SERVICE: Buckstaff • Fordham • Gaylord • Kewaunee • Library Prods • Mohawk Midland • Worden
FURNITURE POLISH
Demco • Fordham • Gaylord • Library Store
GAMES
Demco • Garnet • Highsmith • Larlin
GLOBES (see Maps & Globes)
GLUE (see Adhesive, Glue)
GOVERNMENT PUBLICATIONS
Accents • Auto-Graphics • Blackwell NA • EBSCO Subscription Services • Pathway • Readex
GRAPHIC ART SUPPLIES
Demco • Kidstamps • Letterguide
GUIDES
CATALOG: Brodart • Demco • Fordham • Gaylord • Highsmith • Larlin • Library Store
CATALOG, CATHOLIC: Highsmith
CATALOG, INSTRUCTION: Demco • Fordham • Highsmith
CATALOG, PLASTIC: Brodart • Fordham • Gaylord • Highsmith
CHARGING TRAY: Brodart • Demco • Fordham • Gaylord • Heller • Highsmith • Larlin • Library Store
SHELFLIST: Brodart • Fordham • Gaylord • Highsmith
GUM REMOVER
Demco • Highsmith • Library Store
HAND CLEANER
Demco • Evans • Gaylord • Highsmith • Kole • Larlin • Library Store
HEADPHONES
Avedex • Brodart • Central AV • Gaylord • Highsmith
HINGE TAPE (see Tape, Mending)
HOLIDAY CUTOUTS
Gaylord • Highsmith
HUMIDIFIERS & DEHUMIDIFIERS
Highsmith
IDENTIFICATION CARDS (see Cards, Circulation, Identification)
INDEX TABLES (CBI) (see Furniture, Library)
INDEX TABS & DIVIDERS
Cel-U-Dex • Devoke • Esselte • Fordham • Larlin • Monaco • Permaseal
INDEXING SERVICES
Document Control • Magazine Article • Shelfmark • TV Guide • UMI
INFORMATION PROCESSING (see Data Processing—Equipment, Services, & Supplies)
INK
DUPLICATING MACHINE: Highsmith • Larlin • Multigraphics
MARKING: Highsmith • Pryor
STAMP PAD: Brodart • Demco • Fordham • Gaylord • Highsmith • Larlin • Library Store • Pryor
WHITE (book or spine marking): Highsmith
WRITING: Highsmith
INTERCOM SYSTEMS
Dukane • Talk-a-Phone
INTERIOR DESIGNERS
SPACE PLANNING: Fordham • Foster • Worden
INTERLIBRARY LOAN FORMS (see Forms, Interlibrary Loan)
INTERLIBRARY LOAN MATERIALS
Brodart • Demco • Gaylord • Larlin • Library Store • NSC
INVENTORY
Bar Code • Universal Library
JIFFY BOOK BAGS (see Book Mailing Bags)
JOBBERS, BOOKS (see Booksellers, Wholesale)
KEY FILING CABINETS (see Security Equipment)
KEY SORT (Tabulating Cards)
Block
LABEL GUMMING MACHINES
Demco • Larlin
LABEL HOLDERS (see Shelf-Label Holders)
LABEL PRINTING MACHINES
Demco • Gaylord • Larlin • Letterguide
LABELMAKERS & TAPE
Brodart • Demco • Esselte • Gaylord • Larlin
LABELS
BARCODE: Appleson • Bar Code • Catalog Card • CLSI • Computer Co • Data Recall • Data Trek • Demco • Follett Software • INLEX • NSC • Seton Name Plate • Sirsi • SOLINET • Universal Library
CALL NUMBER: Brodart • Computer Co • Data Trek • Demco • Fordham • Gaylord • Kapco • Larlin • Library Store • Sirsi • Specialized Service & Supply
CHARGE CARD: Fordham • Library Store
COLOR-CODED: Acme • Appleson • Brodart • Demco • Devoke • Gaylord • G M Assocs • Highsmith • Library Store
COMPUTER DISK: Appleson • Gaylord • Highsmith
DATE DUE: Demco • Fordham • Gaylord • G M Assocs • Highsmith • Library Store
FILMSTRIP CAN: Brodart • Demco • Fordham • Gaylord • Highsmith • Larlin
GUMMED: Brodart • Demco • Fordham • Gaylord • Highsmith • Larlin • Magafile
MACHINE-READABLE: Appleson • Computer Co • Data Trek • Sirsi
MAILING: Appleson • Demco • Follett Software • Highsmith • Kole • Learned Information • Message Movers • Seton Name Plate
OCLC: Data Trek • Demco • Follett Software • Gaylord • Highsmith • Library Store

OCR: Appleson • Gaylord • Highsmith • Sirsi
PHONOGRAPH RECORD: Brodart • Demco • Highsmith • Professional Media
PRESSURE-SENSITIVE: Appleson • Brodart • Demco • Gaylord • Highsmith • Kapco • Kole • Larlin • Library Store • Message Movers • Molex • Professional Media • Pryor • Seton Name Plate
PRINTED ("7 day book," etc): Acme • Appleson • Block • Brodart • Demco • Fordham • Gaylord • Highsmith • Message Movers • Professional Media • Seton Name Plate
SHELF (ENGRAVED PLASTIC): Brodart • Demco • Fordham • Gaylord • Highsmith • Library Store • Seton Name Plate
SHELF (MAGNETIC): Highsmith • Seton Name Plate

LACQUER, BOOK
Brodart • Gaylord • Larlin

LADDERS
Block • Equipto • Fordham • Highsmith • Kole • Larlin • Putnam

LAMINATING
MATERIALS & EQUIPMENT: Brodart • Demco • Follett Software • Fordham • Gaylord • Highsmith • Jackson-Hirsh • Kapco • Larlin • Library Store • Permaseal • Seal • Seton Name Plate
SERVICES (see Restoration & Preservation)
TACKING IRONS: Brodart • Demco • Gaylord • Highsmith • Larlin • Seal
VENDING MACHINE (see Coin-Operated Equipment)

LANGUAGE PROGRAMS (SELF-INSTRUCTIONAL)
Applause • Educational Servs • Fiesta • French & European • Norton • Professional Media

LAYOUT AIDS
Larlin

LEARNING SYSTEMS (LANGUAGE LABORATORIES) (see also Audiovisual Mobile Resource Center; Carrels, Audiovisual)
FIXED INSTALLATIONS: Avedex • Select AV
MOBILE-PORTABLE: Avedex • Select AV

LEASED BOOKS & EQUIPMENT (see Rental)

LEATHER BOOK BINDING (see Binding Materials & Equipment)

LEATHER PRESERVATIVE (see Binding Materials & Equipment)

LECTERNS
FOLDING: Buckstaff • Dahle • Demco • Fordham • Highsmith • Lawrence Metal • Select AV
MOBILE: Buckstaff • Demco • Fordham • Gaylord • Highsmith • Select AV • Texwood • Worden
SOUND: Buckstaff • Dahle • Demco • Gaylord • Highsmith • Lawrence Metal • Select AV • Texwood
STANDARD (see Furniture, Library)
TABLE: Buckstaff • Dahle • Demco • Fordham • Gaylord • Heller • Highsmith • Texwood • Worden

LETTERING PENS (see Pens)

LETTERS, DISPLAY
CERAMIC: Scott
CUTOUT: Arch Bronze • Designers Sign • Gaylord • Highsmith • Letterguide
MAGNETIC: Highsmith • Pryor
METAL: Arch Bronze • Designers Sign • Highsmith • Library Sign • Scott
PAPER & CARDBOARD: Gaylord • Highsmith • Scott
PLASTIC: Arch Bronze • Brodart • Demco • Designers Sign • Fordham • Gaylord • Highsmith • Library Sign • Pryor • Scott
PRESSURE-SENSITIVE: Demco • Designers Sign • Fordham • Gaylord • Highsmith • Library Sign • Pryor • Scott • Seton Name Plate
TRANSFER: Demco • Fordham • Gaylord • Highsmith • Larlin • Library Sign
VINYL: Demco • Designers Sign • Gaylord • Highsmith • Letterguide • Library Sign • Scott • Seton Name Plate

LIBRARY AIDE BUTTON (see also Award Pins)
Demco • Highsmith • Larlin

LIBRARY BUILDINGS, PORTABLE
Porta-Structures

LIBRARY LISTENING CENTERS (see also Learning Systems & Carrels, Audiovisual)
Brodart • Buckstaff • Gaylord • Highsmith

LIBRARY NETWORK SERVICE SYSTEMS (see Bibliographic Service Systems)

LIBRARY PUBLIC RELATIONS (see Publicity Services & Materials)

LIBRARY SKILLS
ACTIVITIES SOURCEBOOK: Highsmith • K-12 Micromedia • Larlin
FILMS: Applause • Cable • Coronet/MTI • Fordham • Highsmith • KECCō • Larlin
FILMSTRIPS, SILENT & SOUND: Applause • Brodart • Coronet/MTI • E M E • Guidance Assocs • Highsmith • KECCō • Larlin • Listening Library • Live Oak • Marshmedia • Merit AV • Nystrom • Pied Piper • Radmar • Right On • Troll • Vocational Media • Westport Media
FLASH CARDS: Applause • Highsmith • Larlin
GAMES: Afro-Am • Applause • Demco • Garnet • Highsmith • Larlin
K-8 PROGRAM: Follett Software • Larlin • Modern Book • Perma-Bound • Radmar
MANUALS & BOOKS: K-12 Micromedia • KECCō • Larlin
OVERHEAD TRANSPARENCIES: Demco • Devoke • E M E • Fay Inst • Fordham • Gaylord • Larlin • Letterguide
POSTERS & INSTRUCTION CHARTS: Brodart • Demco • Fordham • Gaylord • Highsmith • Larlin
PUZZLES: Afro-Am • Larlin • Preston
RECORDINGS: A A A Record • Afro-Am •

Applause • Jon-Tone • KECCō • Larlin • Live Oak • Norton • Phelps • Professional Media • Westport Media
TESTS: Highsmith • Larlin • Preston
LIBRARY SUPPLIERS (Firms listed offer extensive selections of library supplies & send catalogs free on request)
Brodart • Data Trek • Demco • Fordham • Gaylord • Highsmith
LIGHTING CONTROLS
Swivelier
LIGHTING FIXTURES
DESK: Fordham • Worden
DISPLAY: Gaylord • Scott • Swivelier • Video Space
EMERGENCY: Highsmith • Teledyne
FLUORESCENT: Swivelier
INCANDESCENT: Swivelier
STACK: Highsmith
TRACK: Highsmith • Swivelier • Worden
LISTENING CENTERS & TABLES (see Learning Systems)
LOCKERS
Demco • Equipto • Fordham • Library Bureau • Republic • Vogel
MAGAZINE
CHARGING DESKS (see Cards, Circulation, Magazine Charging)
DISPLAY RACKS (see Display, Racks)
INDEXING: Demco • Sirsi • TV Guide
MICROFICHE: Kraus • UMI • Univ Music
PREBINDERS (see Binding Services)
PROTECTIVE COVERS (see Binders, Magazine)
RECORD SYSTEM: Brodart • Gaylord • Message Movers • Phelps
REPRINTS (see On-Demand Publishing)
STORAGE: Brodart • Demco • Esselte • Gaylord • Gressco • Hannecke • Heller • Highsmith • Jones West • Kole • Larlin • Library Bureau • Library Prods • Library Store • Magafile • Vulcan • Worden
MAGAZINE DEALERS
BACK NUMBERS: Abrahams • Jaeger • Kraus • Turner
CHILDREN'S (see Children's Magazines, Indexed)
CONTINUATIONS: Accents • EBSCO Subscription Services • Jaeger • Kraus • Turner
DOMESTIC SUBSCRIPTIONS: Asia Society • Bowker • EBSCO Subscription Services • Fiesta • Ingram • Kraus • Turner
FOREIGN SUBSCRIPTIONS: Applause • EBSCO Subscription Services • Fiesta • French & European • Ingram • Kraus • Turner
MAGNETIC DEVICES
DISPLAY: Pryor
MAGNIFIERS (see also Physically Challenged, Reading Aids For)
Brodart • Gaylord • Highsmith • Larlin • Natl Inst for Rehabilitation
MAILING BAGS, BOOKS (see Book Mailing Bags)
MAILING LISTS
Pergamon • Tek Data
MAILROOM FURNITURE & EQUIPMENT
Demco • Fordham • Highsmith
MANAGEMENT
ENERGY: Motorola
MEDIA CENTER: Larlin
PROGRAM: Info Dimensions • K-12 Micromedia • Micro Data Base • OPL
TIME STUDIES: OPL
MAP TACKS
Fordham
MAPS & GLOBES
Applause • Brodart • E M E • Fordham • French & European • Gaylord • Hammond • Highsmith • Larlin • Nystrom • Rand McNally • Replogle • Riverside
MARC TAPE STORAGE & RETRIEVAL SYSTEMS
ATLIS • Auto-Graphics • Blackwell NA • CLSI • Computer Co • Data Trek • Dynix • Library Corp • NSC • Sirsi • SOLINET • Universal Library • VTLS
MARKING EQUIPMENT & SUPPLIES
CALL NUMBER LABELS: Brodart • Demco • Fordham • Gaylord • Highsmith • Larlin • Library Store • Sirsi
CALL NUMBER LABEL SHEARS: Gaylord
CALL NUMBER STAMPING EQUIPMENT: Highsmith
COLD TRANSFER CALL NUMBER: Brodart • Gaylord
ELECTRIC PENCILS (see Pencils, Electric)
ELECTRIC SEALING IRON: Brodart • Demco • Gaylord • Larlin
GENERAL: Gaylord • Kidstamps
LABEL PRINTING EQUIPMENT: Data Recall • Demco • G M Assocs • Larlin • Seton Name Plate
MARKING INK (see Ink, Marking)
MARKING KITS: Gaylord • Letterguide • Pryor • Select AV • Seton Name Plate
PENS (see Pens, Marking)
PENS, FELT-TIP (see Pens, Felt-Tip Marking)
SPINE MARKING EQUIPMENT: Brodart • Demco • Gaylord • Larlin
SUBJECT SYMBOLS: Demco • Gaylord
TRANSFER PAPER (see Paper, Transfer)
MEMORIAL BOOKS, PROMOTIONAL MATERIALS
Demco • OPL
MEMORIAL PLAQUES (see Signs, Metal)
MENDING
TAPE (see Tape, Mending)
TISSUE: Highsmith • Larlin
MICROCOMPUTER
DISK COPIER: ALF
FURNITURE: Brodart • Demco • Devoke • Fordham • Gaylord • Highsmith • Larlin • Library Bureau • Mohawk Midland • Sirsi • Wheelit • Worden
PERSONAL COMPUTERS: Auto-Graphics • CLSI • Data Trek • Document Control • Follett Software • K-12 Micromedia

• Magazine Article • Natl Inst for Rehabilitation • Ringgold • Sharp • Sirsi • UNISYS • VTLS • Worden

PRINTERS: CLSI • Data Recall • Data Trek • Demco • Follett Software • Natl Inst for Rehabilitation • Ringgold • Sharp • UNISYS

SOFTWARE: Applause • Auto-Graphics • Catalog Card • CLSI • Data Recall • Data Trek • Demco • Document Control • E M E • Follett Software • Gen Research • Highsmith • Ingram • Inst for Scientific Info • Islington • K-12 Micromedia • Larlin • Library Corp • Library Processes • Library Store • Marcive • Marshmedia • Meckler • Merit AV • Micro Data Base • Natl Inst for Rehabilitation • Nichols • Right On • Ringgold • Sirsi • Society for Visual Ed • Troll • UNISYS • VTLS

SUPPLIES: Demco • Elm • Follett Software • Gaylord • Highsmith • Library Store • Natl Inst for Rehabilitation • Pine Cone • Right On • Tech-Cessories

MICROFICHE (see also Ultrafiche)

CAMERA-PROCESSORS: Canon • Xidex

CAMERAS: Color Microimaging • Extek • Xidex

CATALOGING SERVICES: Advanced Library • Computer Co • Library Corp • Marcive • NewsBank • Shelfmark

CLEANING KITS: Highsmith • Realist • UMI • Xidex

COLOR CONVERSION: Color Microimaging

CUTTER: Extek

DEVELOPER: Micobra

DUPLICATORS: Extek • Micobra • Xidex

ENVELOPES: Brodart • Gen Microfilm • Highsmith • Larlin • Library Store • Molex • Univ Music

FORMS: Molex

GENERAL: Jaeger

GUIDES: Brodart • Faxon • Gaylord • Highsmith • Larlin

LAMPS: Sitler's

LIBRARY: Gaylord • Univ Music

PAPER: Molex • Xidex

PRINTER: Brodart • Xidex

PROJECTORS: Gaylord • Harris/3M • Highsmith • Univ Music

PROTECTORS: Gaylord • Highsmith • Molex • Library Bindery of PA • Univ Music

PUBLISHERS: Auto-Graphics • Bowker • Disclosure • Gen Microfilm • G K Hall • Kraus • Meckler • Readex • Research Pubns • UMI

READER-PRINTERS: Brodart • Canon • Highsmith • NewsBank • UMI • Xidex

READERS: Brodart • Color Microimaging • Dukane • Fordham • Gaylord • Gen Microfilm • Highsmith • Library Microfilms & Materials • Molex • Realist • UMI • Univ Music • Xidex

RETROSPECTIVE CONVERSION: Auto-Graphics • Computer Co • Library Corp • Readex

RETRIEVAL/DISPLAY UNITS: Xidex

SCREENS: Xidex

STORAGE BAGS: Jones West

STORAGE CABINETS (FILES): Brodart • Demco • Devoke • Fordham • Gaylord • Highsmith • Larlin • Liberty • Library Store • Micobra • Molex • Multigraphics • Realist • Russ Bassett • UMI • Univ Music • Worden • Xidex

TONER: Demco • Molex • Univ Music • Xidex

VIEWER: Auto-Graphics • Brodart • Radmar • Realist • Univ Music • Xidex

MICROFILM

BOXES: Demco • Gaylord • Highsmith • Larlin • Molex • Realist • Univ Music

CAMERA: Minolta

CAMERA-PROCESSORS: Canon • Color Microimaging • Xidex

CARTRIDGES: Xidex

CATALOGING SERVICES: Computer Co • Document Control • Marcive • Shelfmark

CLEANER: Extek • Xidex

COLOR CONVERSION: Color Microimaging

CONVERTERS (for reel & cartridge use): Color Microimaging

COPYING SERVICES: Garnet

GENERAL: Jaeger

INSPECTION EQUIPMENT: Extek • Neumade

JACKETS: Molex • Univ Music • Xidex

MICROFILMERS: Color Microimaging • Extek • Gen Microfilm • Xidex

PAPER: Xidex

PRESERVATIVE TREATMENT (see Films)

PROCESSORS: Extek

PROJECTORS: Harris/3M

PROTECTORS: Library Bindery of PA

PUBLISHERS: Auto-Graphics • Gen Microfilm • G K Hall • Readex • Research Pubns • Univ Music • TV Guide • UMI

READER LAMPS: Gaylord • Gen Microfilm • Harris/3M • Molex • Realist • Xidex

READER-PRINTERS: Brodart • Canon • Harris/3M • Minolta • UMI • Xidex

READERS: Brodart • Color Microimaging • Dukane • Gaylord • Gen Microfilm • Highsmith • Library Microfilms & Materials • Molex • Realist • UMI • Univ Music • Xidex

REELS: Molex • Univ Music

REWINDERS: Highsmith • Neumade

ROLLFICHE: Color Microimaging • Computer Co • Molex • Xidex

SCREENS: Highsmith

SHIPPING CASES: Highsmith • Kole • Molex • Neumade

STORAGE CABINETS (FILES): Acme • Adjustable Steel • Demco • Equipto • Fordham • Foster • Gaylord • Heller • Highsmith • Kole • Larlin • Liberty • Mico-

bra • Molex • Neumade • Putnam • Russ Bassett • Texwood • UMI • Univ Music • Worden
VIEWER: Highsmith • Realist
VIEWER-SORTER: Highsmith

MICRO-OPAQUE (MICROCARDS)
PUBLISHERS: Readex
READERS: Color Microimaging
STORAGE CABINETS (FILES): Equipto • Foster • Molex • Univ Music
VIEWER: Color Microimaging • Readex

MICROPHONES
Central AV • Dukane • Highsmith • Sharp

MICROPRINT (see Micro-Opaque, Publishers)

MICROTEXT (see Microfiche, Microfilm, or Micro-Opaque, Publishers)

MIRRORS
Brodart • Preston • Seton Name Plate

MODULAR DISPLAY SYSTEMS (see Display, Modular)

MOISTENER, BOOK POCKET
Demco • Gaylord • Larlin

MOTION PICTURES (see Films)

MOUNTING PAPER (see Paper)

MOVING (library relocation)
Action • Compass Van • S & G

MOVING EQUIPMENT
DESK: Demco • S & G
FILE: Demco • S & G

MULTIMEDIA KITS (see "Audiovisual Market Place: A Multimedia Guide," Bowker)

MUSEUM CASES (see Exhibit Cases)

MUSIC, SHEET
BINDERS (see Binders, Sheet Music)
BROWSERS: Worden
FILES (see Files, Pamphlet)

NAMEPLATES
Block • Brodart • Demco • Designers Sign • Fordham • Library Store • Seton Name Plate

NEWSPAPER
BINDERS (see Binders)
CLIPPING KNIFE: Gaylord • Highsmith • Larlin • Library Store
FILES (see Files, Newspaper)
INDEXES: NewsBank • Sirsi • UMI
MICROFORM (see Microfilm, Microfiche, & Micro-Opaque, Publishers)
RACKS (see Furniture, Library)
SUBSCRIPTIONS: French & European • Learned Information • UMI

NUMBERING MACHINES
Brodart • Demco • Fordham • Gaylord • Pryor

OFFICE LANDSCAPE PARTITIONS
Fordham • Vogel • Worden

OFFICE SUPPLY STORES
Garnet • Fordham • Highsmith

ON-DEMAND PUBLISHING (including periodicals)
Disclosure • Fay Inst • Gen Microfilm • UMI

ONLINE SYSTEMS
BACK ISSUES: Faxon • Jaeger • Turner • VU/TEXT
DOCUMENT ORDERING: Am Library Assn • Bowker • Faxon • Utlas • VTLS
ELECTRONIC MAIL: Am Library Assn • Data Trek • E B S • Faxon • Jaeger • UNISYS
FILE MAINTENANCE: Am Library Assn • Data Trek • Faxon • OCLC
NEWSLETTER: Am Library Assn • News-Net
NEWSPAPER: Am Library Assn • News-Net • VU/TEXT
PATRON ACCESS: Info Dimensions
RETRIEVAL: Am Library Assn • Auto-Graphics • Bowker • CLSI • Computer Co • Data Trek • Disclosure • Document Control • Dynix • Innovative Interfaces • NSC • OCLC • Sirsi • Utlas • VTLS • VU/TEXT
SOFTWARE: Am Library Assn • Auto-Graphics • Centel • CLSI • Computer Co • Data Research • Data Trek • Document Control • Dynix • Faxon • Info Dimensions • Inst for Scientific Info • NSC • OCLC • Right On • Ringgold • Sirsi • UNISYS • VTLS
SUBSCRIPTION SERVICE: Bowker • EBSCO Subscription Services • Faxon • Inst for Scientific Info • Learned Information • Turner • VU/TEXT

ORDER FORMS, BOOK OR RECORDING (see Forms, Book Order or Recording Order)

OUT-OF-PRINT BOOKS (see Booksellers, Out-of-Print Books)

OUT-OF-PRINT US GOVT DOCUMENTS (see Government Publications)

OVERDUE
NOTICES (see Forms, Circulation)
POSTCARDS (see Cards, Circulation, Overdue, Post)

OVERHEAD TRANSPARENCIES, PRODUCERS AND DISTRIBUTORS (see "Audiovisual Market Place: A Multimedia Guide," Bowker)

OVERHEAD TRANSPARENCIES—EQUIPMENT, SERVICES, & SUPPLIES
ENVELOPES: Highsmith
FILM: Brodart • Demco • Gaylord • Highsmith • Larlin • Multigraphics • Select AV • 3M Office Supply
GENERAL SUPPLIERS: Demco • Devoke • Esselte • Gaylord • Highsmith • 3M Office Supply
LETTERING SETS: Highsmith • Larlin • Letterguide • Select AV
MARKING EQUIPMENT: Demco • Highsmith • Larlin • Letterguide • Select AV • 3M Office Supply
MARKING PENS (see Pens, Overhead Transparency Marking)
MOUNTS: Demco • Gaylord • Highsmith • Larlin • Library Store • Select AV • 3M Office Supply
PROJECTORS: Brodart • Demco • Dukane • Gaylord • Highsmith • Select AV •

3M Office Supply
STORAGE CABINETS (FILES): Demco • Foster • Gaylord • Highsmith • Kalart • Liberty • Select AV
THERMAL DEVELOPER: Highsmith • Select AV

OVERNIGHT BOOKSLIPS (see Forms)
PACKAGE TYING MACHINES (see Carton Tying Machines)
PADS (see Office Supply Stores)
PAGE PROTECTORS (see Covers, Protective, Page)
PAMPHLET CASES (see Files, Pamphlet)
PAMPHLET DISPLAY CASES
LUCITE: Brodart • Fordham • Hannecke • Larlin
PAMPHLET JOBBERS
Bacon
PAPER
ACID-FREE (see Restoration & Preservation)
BOND: Follett Software • Highsmith
BOOKBINDING (see Binding Materials & Equipment)
COMPUTER: Devoke • Esselte • Follett Software • Highsmith
DISPLAY: R & D
MOUNTING: Demco
PHOTOCOPY: Highsmith • Kole
TISSUE & CREPE: Demco • Highsmith • Larlin
TRANSFER: Gaylord • Larlin
PAPER BOXES (see Files, Pamphlet or Periodical)
PAPER CLIPS
PLASTIC: Demco • Fordham • Gaylord • Highsmith • Kole • Larlin
STAINLESS STEEL (see Restoration & Preservation)
PAPER CUTTERS
Brodart • Dahle • Demco • Gaylord • Highsmith • Larlin • Library Store
PAPERBACKS (see Binding Materials & Equipment; Binding Services; Booksellers; Display, Racks; etc)
PARTITIONS
MOVABLE: Fordham • Vogel
OFFICE: Fordham • Vogel • Worden
PASTE (see Adhesive, Paste)
PATRON COUNTER
Laser Electronics
PAYROLL SYSTEMS (COMPUTER-BASED)
NSC
PEGBOARD (see Display, Panels)
PENCIL DATE HOLDERS
Brodart • Highsmith
PENCIL SHARPENER, ELECTRIC/MANUAL
Block • Brodart • Dahle • Demco • Fordham • Gaylord • Highsmith • Kole • Larlin • Library Store
PENCILS
ELECTRIC: Brodart • Demco • Fordham • Gaylord • Highsmith

PENS
BALLPOINT: Block • Brodart • Demco • Fordham • Gaylord • Highsmith • Kole • Library Store
BALLPOINT, CHAIN SECURED: Block • Brodart • Demco • Fordham • Gaylord • Highsmith • Larlin • Library Store
CHAIN SECURED: Brodart • Demco • Fordham • Gaylord • Highsmith • Larlin
DRAFTING: Fordham
FELT-TIP MARKING: Brodart • Demco • Fordham • Gaylord • Highsmith • Kole • Larlin
LETTERING: Demco • Fordham • Gaylord • Letterguide
LIBRARY: Demco • Fordham • Gaylord
MARKING: Demco • Fordham • Gaylord • Larlin • Library Store
OVERHEAD TRANSPARENCY MARKING: Brodart • Demco • Fordham • Gaylord • Highsmith • Larlin • Library Store
PASTE: Fordham • Gaylord
PERIODICALS (see Magazine Dealers)
PHONOTAPES & DISCS (see Recordings)
PHYSICALLY CHALLENGED
AUTOMATIC DOOR OPENER: Natl Inst for Rehabilitation
COMMUNICATION AIDS: Natl Inst for Rehabilitation • Preston • Telesensory
COMPUTER PROGRAMS: Data Research • Natl Inst for Rehabilitation • Telesensory • Universal Library
COMPUTERS: Natl Inst for Rehabilitation • Telesensory • Universal Library
DISPLAYERS/BROWSERS: Worden
LARGE PRINT JOBBERS (see "Large Type Books in Print," Bowker)
MAGNIFIERS FOR BLIND: Brodart • Gaylord • Natl Inst for Rehabilitation • Telesensory
MICROFILM READER: Gaylord
PAGE TURNERS: Natl Inst for Rehabilitation • Preston
PRINT-TO-BRAILLE SYSTEM: Telesensory
PRISMATIC GLASSES: Natl Inst for Rehabilitation • Preston
PROJECTORS: Gaylord
READING MACHINE: Preston
READING STANDS & BOOK HOLDERS: Elm • Gaylord • Preston
READ/WRITE SYSTEM: Natl Inst for Rehabilitation
TALKING BOOKS (RECORDINGS or CASCASSETTES): A A A Record • G K Hall • Professional Media
TAPE EQUIPMENT: Sharp
TYPE ENLARGERS & DUPLICATORS:
TYPING AID SYSTEM: Telesensory
VIEWERS: Telesensory
PICTURE
CARRYING CASES: Gaylord • Haddad's • Highsmith
COVERS, PROTECTIVE (see Covers)
FRAMES, ADJUSTABLE: Haddad's • Lawrence Metal

HANGERS & RODS: Demco • Walker
STORAGE: Jones West

PICTURE BINDINGS (see Binding Services)

PLAQUES, MEMORIAL (see Signs, Metal)

PLASTIC
ADHESIVE (see Adhesive, Plastic)
BOOK COATING (see Book Coating, Plastic)
BOOK COVERS (see Book Covers, Acetate or Polyester Film)
CATALOG GUIDES (see Guides, Catalog)
DISPLAY LETTERS (see Letters, Display)
SIGNS (see Signs, Plastic)

POCKET KNIVES
Warrentruss

POSTCARDS, LIBRARY
Demco • Gaylord • Haddad's • Highsmith • Riverside

POSTERS
CHILDREN'S: Asia Society • Demco • Gaylord • Haddad's • Highsmith
DECORATIVE: Haddad's • Highsmith • Larlin
FRAMES: Haddad's • Lawrence Metal
LIBRARY PROMOTION: Am Library Assn • Brodart • Demco • Gaylord • Highsmith • Video Space
LIBRARY SKILLS (see Library Skills)
SILK-SCREENED: Creative Library

PRACTICE CARDS (see Cards, Practice Index)

PREBINDERS (see Binding Services)

PRESENTATION BOARDS & ACCESSORIES (see Blackboards & Accessories)

PRESS, DRY MOUNTING/LAMINATING (see Laminating)

PRINCETON FILES (see Files)

PRINTED LABELS (see Labels)

PRINTING SERVICE
Gaylord • Science Pr

PRINTS & REPRODUCTIONS
ART REPRODUCTIONS: Afro-Am • Applause • Haddad's • Kraus • Publishers Book Bindery • Redpath
BROWSER UNITS: Gaylord • Redpath
CARRYING CASES: Gaylord
CATALOGED & PROCESSED:
FRAMED: Haddad's • Redpath
POSTCARDS, ART: Applause • Haddad's
REFERENCE WORKS: Haddad's • Publishers Book Bindery
SCULPTURE: Arch Bronze
STUDY PRINTS: Afro-Am • Haddad's • KECCō • Nystrom • Publishers Book Bindery • Redpath

PROCESSED BOOKS & A/V MATERIALS (see Cataloging Services)

PROCESSING KITS (see Books and/or Audiovisual Processing Kits)

PROGRAM CONTROL DEVICES (see Audiovisual Program Control Devices)

PROGRAMMED LEARNING MATERIALS (see also "Programmed Learning and Individually Paced Instruction: A Bibliography," Hendershot)
Afro-Am • Applause • Larlin • Norton • Nystrom • Teacher Support

PROJECTION SCREENS
CABINET & TABLE TOP: Brodart • Fordham • Highsmith • Larlin • Select AV
FRONT: Central AV • Demco • Gaylord • Highsmith • Larlin • Select AV
REAR: Central AV • Demco • Gaylord • Larlin • Select AV

PROJECTION TABLES & STANDS (see Stands, Audiovisual)

PROJECTORS
FILMSTRIP (see Filmstrip)
MAPPING: Demco
MICROFILM (see Microfilm)
MOTION PICTURE (see Films)
OPAQUE: Brodart • Central AV • Demco • Gaylord • Highsmith • Kalart • Select AV
OVERHEAD TRANSPARENCIES (see Overhead Transparencies)
PROJECTOR LAMPS: Brodart • Central AV • Demco • Gaylord • General AV • Radmar • Select AV • Sitler's
REAR SCREEN: Central AV • Demco • Select AV
TV (16MM): Brodart • Central AV • Demco • Select AV

PROTECTIVE COVERS (see Covers, Protective)

PROTECTORS, CALL NUMBER LABEL (see Call Number Label Protectors)

PUBLIC ADDRESS SYSTEMS
Avedex • Central AV • Dukane • Select AV • Sharp • Universal Library

PUBLICITY SERVICES AND MATERIALS (see also Bookmarks; Display; etc)
Larlin • Riverside • Video Space

PUNCHED CARDS (see Tabulating Cards Equipment & Supplies)

PUPPETS
Afro-Am • Applause • Brodart • Highsmith • Larlin • Playful Puppets • Renfro • Riverside

RADIO PROGRAMS (see Publicity Services & Materials)

RAILINGS
METAL: Larlin • Lawrence Metal • Sentronic • Tepromark
ROPE: Fordham • Larlin • Lawrence Metal • Sentronic • Tepromark

READERS (see type: Microfiche, Microfilm, Microform, Micro-Opaque)

REALIA
Applause

RECASING, LEATHER
Bridgeport • Gaylord

RECORD PLAYERS (see Recordings)

RECORDERS (see Audio)

RECORDINGS, BINDERS, PHONO DISCS (see Binder, Phono Discs)

RECORDINGS (DISCS & TAPES)
BINDERS, PHONO DISCS (see Binders)
BROWSERS & DISPLAY UNITS: Brodart

• Caedmon • Gaylord • Hannecke • Liberty • Texwood
CASSETTE BOOKS: A A A Record • Books on Tape • Cable • Clark • Fay Inst • G K Hall • Jon-Tone • Larlin • Listening Library • Norton • Professional Media • Story House
CASSETTE COPIERS & CLEANERS (see Audio Tape)
CASSETTE RECORDERS: Brodart • Demco • Select AV • Sharp • TEAC
CATALOGS, COMPREHENSIVE: A A A Record • Professional Media • Schwann
CLEANING PRODUCTS: A A A Record
FORMS (see Cards, Audiovisual)
GUIDES, BROWSERS': Professional Media • Worden
LABELS (see Labels, Phonograph Record)
LIBRARY: Gaylord • Professional Media • Schwann • Worden
PLAYERS (DISCS & TAPES): Brodart • Highsmith • Sharp • TEAC
PROTECTIVE COVERS (DISCS): A A A Record • Gaylord • Professional Media
SHIPPING CASES: Gaylord • Larlin
STORAGE CABINETS (FILES): A A A Record • Brodart • Equipto • Gaylord • Highsmith • Larlin • Neumade • Worden

RECORDINGS, VARIOUS SUBJECTS (DISCS & TAPES) (see "Audiovisual Market Place: A Multimedia Guide," Bowker)

RECORDS-BY-MAIL
A A A Record • Fay Inst • Jon-Tone • Professional Media

RECREATIONAL EQUIPMENT
Am Playground • Preston

REFERENCE TABLES (see Furniture, Library)

REGISTRATION CARDS (see Cards, Circulation)

REGISTRATION SUPPLIES
Larlin

REINFORCEMENTS, LOOSE-LEAF NOTEBOOK
Gaylord

REINFORCING TAPE (see Tape, Reinforcing)

RENTAL
BOOKS: Baker & Taylor • McNaughton
FILMS (see "Audiovisual Market Place: A Multimedia Guide," Bowker)
VIDEOCASSETTES (see "Audiovisual Market Place," Bowker)

REPRINTED BOOKS (see Booksellers, Reprints)

REPRODUCED BOOKS (see On-Demand Publishing)

REPRODUCTIONS (see Prints & Reproductions)

RESERVE BOOK CARD GUIDES (see Guides, Reserve Book Cards)

RESERVE BOOK CARDS (see Cards, Reserve Book)

RESTORATION & PRESERVATION—EQUIPMENT, SERVICES, & SUPPLIES
ADHESIVE, ACID-FREE: Demco • Gaylord • Highsmith • Kapco
DAMAGE SERVICE: Bridgeport
DEACIDIFICATION: Bridgeport • Library Bindery of PA
DEACIDIFIER SPRAY: Highsmith
DOCUMENT BOXES, ACID-FREE: Bridgeport • Demco • Foster • Gaylord • Highsmith • Wallaceburg
ENVELOPES, ACID-FREE: Demco • Foster • Gaylord • Highsmith • Molex
FILE FOLDERS, ACID-FREE: Demco • Foster • Gaylord • Gillotte • Highsmith
PAPER, ACID-FREE: Demco • Gaylord • Highsmith
PAPER CLIPS, STAINLESS STEEL: Highsmith
PREVENTIVE MAINTENANCE: Bridgeport • Plastic Window • VideoMedia
RESTORATION BINDING: Bridgeport • Library Bindery of PA • Wallaceburg
STAPLES, RUSTPROOF: Demco • Gaylord • Staplex
STORAGE: Jones West

RETRIEVAL SYSTEMS DESIGN
ATLIS • Auto-Graphics • Blackwell NA • Dynix • Minolta • NSC • OCLC • Sirsi • SOLINET • VTLS

REVIEWS (see also Book Review Cards or Film, Reviewing Services)
Am Library Assn • Bowker

RUBBER BANDS, FOUR-WAY
Demco • Gaylord • Highsmith • Larlin

RUBBER CEMENT (see Adhesive, Rubber Cement)

RULERS, CENTIMETER
Demco

SAFES & STRONG BOXES (see Security Equipment)

SCALES, POSTAL
Gaylord • Kole

SCHOOL LIBRARY FORMS (see Forms, School Library)

SCREENS, PROJECTION (see Projection Screens)

SEALS, HOLIDAY, GIFT, etc
Highsmith

SEARCH SERVICE
Internat Bookfinders • Jaeger

SECTION LABELS (see Labels)

SECURITY EQUIPMENT
BARCODING: Bar Code • Data Recall • Seton Name Plate
BURGLAR ALARMS: Detection Systems
CHAIN-SECURED PENS (see Pens, Chain-Secured)
CIRCULATION CONTROL: Data Recall • Sentronic
COMMUNICATIONS EQUIPMENT: Door Alarm • Motorola
COMPUTER CABINETS: Armor • Devoke • Omni Tech • Highsmith • Larlin • Omni Tech • Worden
CROWD CONTROL: Larlin • Lawrence

Metal • Sentronic
DOOR CONTROL DEVICES: Detection Systems • Detex • Door Alarm • Lock Corp • Phelps • Sentronic
EXIT ALARM LOCKS: Detex • Phelps
EXIT ALARMS: Door Alarm
IDENTIFICATION SYSTEMS: Buk Mark • Data Recall • Seton Name Plate
INTRUSION DETECTORS: Detection Systems • Door Alarm
KEY FILING CABINETS: Brodart • Equipto • Foster • Ke-Master • Kole • Larlin • Seton Name Plate • Telkee
LIGHTING: Buk Mark • Teledyne
LOCKS: Devoke • Door Alarm • Lock Corp • Phelps • Seton Name Plate • Tolmark • Worden
PARKING CONTROL EQUIPMENT: Detex • Seton Name Plate
PHOTO ID SYSTEMS: XCP
PHOTOELECTRONIC SENSORS: Checkpoint • Detection Systems
RECORDING LOCKS: Phelps
SAFES & STRONG BOXES: Block • Southsafe
SAFETY MIRRORS: Highsmith • Kole • Seton Name Plate
THEFT DETECTION SYSTEMS: Armor • Checkpoint • Sentronic • 3M Electronic Stanger • Surveillance
THEFT PREVENTION SYSTEMS: Checkpoint • Sentronic • Stanger • Telmark • 3M Electronic Surveillance • Tufnut
TRUCKS: Sentronic
TURNSTILES: Checkpoint • Lawrence Metal • Sentronic
WATCHLOCK SYSTEMS, PORTABLE: Detex

SERIALS
CONTINUATIONS: Brodart • EBSCO Subscription Services • Faxon • Jaeger • Turner
CONTROLS: CLSI • Data Research • EBSCO Subscription Services • Faxon • Info Dimensions • INLEX • Innovative Interfaces • NSC • Right On • Sirsi •• Utlas • Turner • UNISYS • Universal Library
GOVT DOCUMENTS: Brodart • EBSCO Subscription Services • Faxon • Readex • Sirsi • Turner
IRREGULAR: EBSCO Subscription Services • Faxon • Sirsi • Turner
MANAGEMENT: CLSI • Comstow • Data Trek • EBSCO Subscription Services • Faxon • NSC • Sirsi • Turner • UMI • Utlas

SHEARS, LEFT-HANDED
Dahle • Highsmith • Larlin • Preston

SHELF LABEL HOLDERS (card frames, index holders, range indicators)
Adjustable Steel • Brodart • Cel-U-Dex • Demco • Gaylord • Highsmith • Kole • Larlin • Seton Name Plate

SHELF LABELS (see Labels, Shelf)

SHELF PARTITIONS
Brodart • Gaylord • Larlin

SHELFLIST CARDS (see Cards, Shelf-List)

SHELFLIST GUIDES (see Guides, Shelf-List)

SHELLAC, BOOK
Gaylord • Larlin

SHELVING
BRACKET: Buckstaff • Demco • Equipto • Fordham • Gaylord • Heller • Highsmith • Library Bureau • Library Prods • Nieman Design • Worden
COMPACT (STORAGE): Acme • Adjustable Steel • Buckstaff • Demco • Equipto • Fordham • Foster • Gaylord • Highsmith • Larlin • Liberty • Library Bureau • Library Prods • Nieman Design • Porta-Structures • Putnam
DISPLAY: Adjustable Steel • Brodart • Buckstaff • Equipto • Fixturecraft • Fordham • Gaylord • Heller • Highsmith • InterMetro • Kole • Larlin • Library Bureau • Library Prods • Nieman Design • Porta-Structures • Putnam • Texwood • Worden
HIGH-DENSITY: Acme • Adjustable Steel • Buckstaff • Demco • Equipto • Fordham • Foster • Gaylord • Highsmith • InterMetro • Library Bureau • Library Prods • Lundia • Nieman Design • Porta-Structures
LOCKABLE: Acme • Adjustable Steel • Brodart • Buckstaff • Demco • Equipto • Fordham • Gaylord • Heller • Highsmith • Library Bureau • Library Prods • Nieman Design • Worden
MAGAZINE: Adjustable Steel • Brodart • Buckstaff • Demco • Fordham • Gaylord • Heller • Highsmith • Liberty • Library Bureau • Library Prods • Porta-Structures • R & D • Texwood • Tuohy • Worden
MOBILE: Acme • Adjustable Steel • Brodart • Buckstaff • Demco • Fordham • Gaylord • Highsmith • InterMetro • Library Bureau • Library Prods • Lundia • Porta-Structures • Spacesaver • Worden
MOVABLE: Acme • Adjustable Steel • Brodart • Buckstaff • Demco • Equipto • Fordham • Gaylord • Highsmith • Library Bureau • Library Prods • Lundia • Worden
MULTITIER (STACK): Adjustable Steel • Buckstaff • Equipto • Fordham • Gaylord • Highsmith • Library Bureau • Library Prods
NEWSPAPER: Adjustable Steel • Buckstaff • Demco • Fordham • Heller • Gaylord • Highsmith • Library Bureau • Library Prods • Nieman Design • Porta-Structures • Texwood • Tuohy • Worden
PAPERBACK: Adjustable Steel • Brodart •

Buckstaff • Demco • Fordham • Gaylord • Heller • Highsmith • Larlin • Liberty • Library Bureau • Library Prods • Nieman Design • Porta-Structures • Worden

RECORD ALBUM & PICTURE BOOK: Adjustable Steel • Brodart • Buckstaff • Fordham • Gaylord • Heller • Highsmith • Liberty • Library Bureau • Library Prods • Porta-Structures • Texwood • Tuohy • Worden

STEEL: Acme • Adjustable Steel • Brodart • Buckstaff • Demco • Equipto • Fixturecraft • Fordham • Gaylord • Highsmith • InterMetro • Kole • Library Bureau • Library Prods • Lundia • Neumade • Nieman Design • Republic • Russ Bassett

WALL-HUNG: Adjustable Steel • Buckstaff • Fixturecraft • Fordham • Foster • Gaylord • Highsmith • InterMetro • Library Bureau • Library Prods

WIRE: Buckstaff • Demco • Equipto • Fixturecraft • Fordham • Gaylord • Highsmith • InterMetro • Larlin

WOOD: Adjustable Steel • Brodart • Buckstaff • Demco • Fordham • Gaylord • Heller • Highsmith • Larlin • Library Bureau • Library Prods • Lundia • Porta-Structures • Putnam • Texwood • Tuohy • Worden

WORKROOM: Adjustable Steel • Buckstaff • Demco • Equipto • Gaylord • Highsmith • Kole • Library Prods • Lundia • Worden

SHIPPING CASES

FIBERBOARD: Brodart • Demco • Highsmith • Larlin • Neumade

PLASTIC: Highsmith

WOOD: Highsmith • Liberty

SHREDDING MACHINES

Block • Dahle • Demco • Devoke • Fordham • Gaylord • Heyer • Pryor

SIGNAL TABS

Cel-U-Dex • Demco • Fordham • Highsmith • Larlin

SIGNATURE STAMPS

Demco • Fordham • Gaylord • Highsmith • Kidstamps

SIGN MAKING

ENGRAVERS (PLASTIC): Demco • Fordham • Gaylord • Highsmith • Library Store

KITS: Brodart • Demco • Gaylord • Highsmith • Jackson-Hirsh • Letterguide • Library Sign • Seton Name Plate

MACHINES: Brodart • Demco • Gaylord • Highsmith • Jackson-Hirsh • Letterguide

SIGNS

DIRECTION & EXIT: Demco • Designers Sign • Highsmith • Lawrence Metal • Library Sign • Modulex • Scott

ELECTRONIC: Demco • Gamma • Scott • Seton Name Plate • Video Space

EXTERIOR: Designers Sign • Gamma • Highsmith • Library Sign • Modulex • Seton Name Plate

INTERIOR: Block • Designers Sign • Gamma • Highsmith • Lawrence Metal • Library Sign • Library Store • Modulex • Scott • Seton Name Plate

LOGOS (CUSTOM LETTERS): Brodart • Demco • Designers Sign • Gaylord • Library Sign • Modulex • Scott • Seton Name Plate

MATERIALS FOR (see Display, Materials)

METAL: Designers Sign • Library Sign • Seton Name Plate

MOVABLE LETTERS (BUILDING DIRECTORIES: Brodart • Demco • Designers Sign • Gaylord • Highsmith • Larlin • Lawrence Metal • Library Sign • Modulex • Pryor • Scott • Seton Name Plate

MOVING MESSAGE (PROGRAMMABLE): Demco • Designers Sign • Gamma • Scott • Seton Name Plate

PAINT: Seton Name Plate

PLASTIC: Designers Sign • Fordham • Larlin • Library Sign

SLIDES

CLEANING: Highsmith • World in Color

DUPLICATION SERVICE: Radmar • World in Color

ORGANIZERS: Highsmith • Right On

PROJECTORS: Brodart • Central AV • Demco • General AV • Highsmith • Radmar

REMOUNTING SERVICE: World in Color

SLIDE/SYNC RECORDERS & DISSOLVES: Highsmith

SLIDE/TALK THEATER:

SORTERS: Highsmith

STORAGE CABINETS (FILES): Demco • Elden • Foster • Franklin • Highsmith • Larlin • Neumade • Nieman Design • Worden

TRAYS: Demco • Franklin • Highsmith • World in Color

VIEWERS: Brodart • Demco • General AV • Highsmith • Larlin

SLIDES, PRODUCERS AND DISTRIBUTORS (see "Audiovisual Market Place: a Multimedia Guide," Bowker)

SLIPCASES

Demco • Highsmith • Library Store

SORTING EQUIPMENT

MANUAL: Demco

TRAYS (see Trays, Sorting)

SOUND DISTRIBUTION SYSTEMS (see Public Address Systems)

SPINE MARKING EQUIPMENT (see Marking Equipment & Supplies)

STAIN REMOVER

Demco

STAMPING MACHINES (see Marking Equipment & Supplies)

STAMPS

CLEANER: Highsmith

ELECTRIC TIME, DATE, NUMBER (see Numbering Machines)

LIBRARY EMBOSSING: Brodart • Demco • Fordham • Gaylord • Highsmith

PADS & INKS: Brodart • Demco • Fordham • Gaylord • Highsmith • Kidstamps •

Larlin • Library Store
RUBBER: Brodart • Demco • Fordham • Gaylord • Highsmith • Kidstamps • Larlin

STANDS
AUDIOVISUAL: Brodart • Buckstaff • Demco • Fordham • Gaylord • Heller • Highsmith • Larlin • Library Store • Wheelit • Worden
DICTIONARY (see Furniture, Library)
TYPEWRITER & OFFICE MACHINE: Buckstaff • Demco • Fordham • Gaylord • Heller • Highsmith • Larlin • Wheelit • Worden

STAPLES, RUSTPROOF (see Restoration & Preservation)

STAPLING MACHINES
ELECTRIC: Brodart • Demco • Fordham • Gaylord • Highsmith • Library Store • Staplex
MANUAL: Brodart • Dahle • Demco • Fordham • Gaylord • Highsmith • Library Store
SADDLE (ELECTRIC): Brodart • Demco • Fordham • Highsmith • Staplex
SADDLE (MANUAL): Demco • Fordham • Gaylord • Highsmith • Library Store

STATIONERS (see Office Supply Stores)

STATISTICAL REPORTS (see Forms)

STEP STOOLS
MOBILE: Block • Brodart • Demco • Fordham • Gaylord • Highsmith • Library Store • Preston
STANDARD (see Furniture, Library)

STORY HOUR LOUNGERS & FLOOR PADS
Brodart • Fordham • Gaylord • Highsmith

STUDY PRINTS (see Prints & Reproductions)

SUBSCRIPTION AGENCY
EBSCO Electronic Info • EBSCO Subscription Services • Faxon • Turner

TABLES, ALL TYPES (see Furniture)

TABLETS, BRONZE (see Signs, Metal)

TACKING GUNS
Fordham

TACKING IRONS (see Laminating)

TALKING BOOKS (see Physically Challenged)

TAPE
ATTACHING (BOOK JACKET COVER): Brodart • Demco • Fordham • Gaylord • Highsmith • Kapco • Larlin • Library Store
BOOK DISPLAY: Demco • Fordham • Gaylord • Hannecke • Highsmith • Liberty
DOUBLE-FACED: Brodart • Demco • Fordham • Gaylord • Highsmith • Kapco • Larlin • Library Sign • Library Store • Scott • 3M Office Supply
EDGING: Fordham • Highsmith • Larlin
IMPRINTED CLASSIFICATION: Brodart • Demco • Highsmith • Larlin
MAGNETIC: Central AV • Highsmith • Larlin • Pryor • Radmar • 3M Office Supply
MARKING: Fordham • Gaylord • Highsmith • Larlin
MENDING: Brodart • Demco • Fordham • Gaylord • Larlin • Library Store • 3M Office Supply
MOUNTING (PICTURES, POSTERS, etc): Brodart • Demco • Fordham • Gaylord • Highsmith • Kapco • Larlin • Library Store
NONSKID (FOR BOOK SUPPORTS): Demco • Highsmith • Kapco • Larlin
RED: Fordham • Gaylord • Highsmith • Larlin
REINFORCING: Brodart • Demco • Fordham • Gaylord • Highsmith • Larlin • Library Store
SHELF ARRANGING: Fordham • Highsmith • Larlin
SHELF, NONSKID: Demco • Highsmith • Larlin
TRANSPARENT PLASTIC: Brodart • Demco • Fordham • Gaylord • Highsmith • Larlin • Library Store

TAPE DISPENSERS (see Dispensers)

TAPE LEASING
Bowker

TAPE RECORDERS (see Audio Tape)

TAPEWRITERS (see Label Makers)

TEACHING AIDS
A A A Record • Afro-Am • Applause • Asia Society • Fordham • Haddad's • K-12 Micromedia • Larlin • Perma-Bound • Pied Piper • Preston • Radmar • Right On • Teacher Support

TELEPHONE ACCESSORIES
Malekos • Multiverse • R & D

TELEVISION MATERIALS (see Publicity Services & Materials)

TELEVISION SYSTEMS, CLOSED CIRCUIT (see Video Cameras, Receivers & Monitors)

THEFT DETECTION DEVICES (see Security Equipment)

TIME
STAMPS (see Numbering Machines)
SWITCHES (see Lighting Controls)

TISSUE, DRY MOUNTING (see Laminating)

TOOLS
HAND: Highsmith

TOTE TRUCKS
Block • Brodart • Equipto • Worden

TOYS
Garnet • Larlin • Preston

TRAFFIC CONTROL SYSTEMS (see Railings; also Security Equipment, Turnstiles)

TRANSFER PAPER (see Paper, Transfer)

TRANSPARENCIES (see Overhead Transparencies)

TRAVEL GUIDES
French & European

TRAYS
CHARGING: Brodart • Demco • Fordham • Gaylord • Heller • Highsmith • Larlin • Library Bureau • Library Store • Texwood
MEMO: Gaylord • Highsmith • Larlin
MICROFICHE: Brodart • Fordham • Gaylord • Highsmith • Larlin • Molex • Russ

Bassett • UMI
SORTING: Brodart • Fordham • Gaylord • Highsmith • Larlin

TROPHY CASES
Arch Bronze • Brodart • Fordham • Gaylord • Heller • Highsmith • Library Bureau • Texwood • Worden

TURNTABLES
Demco

TURNSTILES (see Security Equipment)

TYPE CLEANER
Demco • Garnet

TYPE, HOT STAMPING (see Marking Equipment)

TYPEWRITER CLEANER
Demco

TYPEWRITER RIBBON
Block • Demco

TYPEWRITERS
AUTOMATIC: Demco
CATALOGER'S: Demco
COIN-OPERATED: Demco • XCP
CONTROLS: Demco
ELECTRIC (STANDARD): Demco • Highsmith • Sharp
STANDARD & PORTABLE: Demco

TYPEWRITER STANDS (see Stands, Typewriter)

ULTRAFICHE
READER-PRINTERS: Minolta

UMBRELLA STANDS
Fordham • Vogel

US GOVT PUBLICATIONS (see Government Publications)

VACATION READING CLUB MATERIALS (see Publicity Services & Materials; Travel Guides)

VENDING MACHINES (see Coin-Operated Equipment)

VIDEO
CAMERAS: Brodart • Central AV • Demco • Gaylord • Micro Image • Select AV • Sharp
DISC-BASED INFORMATION SYSTEM: TEAC
DISCS: A A A Record • Gaylord • KECCō • Warner
DISPLAYERS: Alps • Brodart • Fordham • Gaylord • Gressco • Hannecke • Highsmith • Monaco • Video Trend • Worden
DUPLICATING SERVICE: Cable • Kartes • Radmar • Select AV
EDITORS: Select AV
FURNITURE: Central AV • Demco • Gaylord • Highsmith • Nieman Design • Porta-Structures • Russ Bassett • Select AV • Wheelit • Worden
PORTABLE EQUIPMENT: Eastin Phelan • Gaylord • Highsmith • Select AV • TEAC
RECEIVERS & MONITORS: Brodart • Central AV • Demco • Highsmith • Micro Image • Select AV • Sharp • Video Trend
RECORDING SYSTEM: Brodart • Select AV • TEAC
REELS: Central AV • Gaylord • Select AV
RENTAL: Cable • Professional Media • Select AV
SHIPPING CASES: Brodart • Gaylord • Highsmith • Jon-Tone • Select AV • Video Trend
STORAGE CABINETS (FILES): Alps • Brodart • Central AV • Demco • Fordham • Gaylord • Gressco • Highsmith • Liberty • Library Store • Nieman Design • Russ Bassett • Select AV • Video Space • Video Trend • Worden
TAPE, BLANK: A A A Record • Brodart • Central AV • Demco • Highsmith • Ingram • Jon-Tone • Kartes • Perma-Bound • Radmar • Select AV • Video Trend
TAPE CLEANER: A A A Record • Brodart • Central AV • Demco • Gaylord • Highsmith • Jon-Tone • Select AV • Video Trend • VideoMedia
THEATER: Cable • Select AV
TRIPODS: Central AV • Demco • Gaylord • Highsmith • Select AV
VIDEOCASSETTES (BETA or VHS): Afro-Am • Am Library Assn • Applause • Asia Society • Baker & Taylor • Brodart • Cable • Clark • Coronet/MTI • Demco • Discount Video • Eastin Phelan • E M E • Fay Inst • Gaylord • Guidance Assocs • Highsmith • Ingram • Jon-Tone • Kartes • KECCō • Listening Library • Live Oak • Marshmedia • Metacom • Norton • Perma-Bound • Pied Piper • Professional Media • Radmar • Rainbow • Select AV • Society for Visual Ed • TEAC • Troll • Video Trend • Vocational Media • Warner • Westport Media
VIDEOCASSETTE RECORDER (BETA or VHS): Brodart • Demco • Gaylord • Highsmith • Select AV • Sharp • TEAC

VIEWERS (see type: Microfilm; Filmstrip)

VOICE DATA ENTRY SYSTEM
Multiverse • Natl Inst for Rehabilitation

WARDROBE RACKS
Demco • Fordham • Heller • Highsmith • Vogel

WATER DETECTORS & ALARMS
Brodart • Dorlen • Motorola

WHOLESALERS, BOOKS (see Booksellers, Wholesale)

WORD PROCESSING EQUIPMENT (see Typewriters, Automatic)

Directory of Suppliers

A A A Record Hunter Dist Co
(507 Export Corp)
Contact: Ira Hirsch, Gen Mgr or Jay Sonin, Pres
507 5th Ave, New York, NY 10017; 212-986-6077, 697-8970
Maximum discounts, excellent service, complete catalog all labels, imports, domestic, compact discs, cassettes, records, accessories, experienced knowledgeable staff, established 1945.

Abrahams Magazine Service, Inc
Customer Service Dept, 56 E 13th St, New York, NY 10003; 212-777-4700; FAX 212-995-5413
Periodicals and serials—back volumes, runs, and sets—bought and sold. Write for our Buying List.

Accents Publications Service, Inc
Contact: N Katz, Dir
911 Silver Spring Ave, Suite 202, Silver Spring, MD 20910; 301-588-5496; telex 6503468108
Distributor of US government publications (GPO, NTIS, LC, etc); association, international/intergovernmental organization publications; and document retrieval and delivery service.

Acme Visible Records
Customer Services, 1000 Alview Dr, Crozet, VA 22932; 800-368-3275
Stationary and mobile shelving, lateral movable files, color-coded filing systems, visible record systems, computer room accessories.

Action Moving Co
Contact: Arlene Hopkins, Specialty Accts Rep
4109 Glencoe Ave, Marina Del Rey, CA 90292; 213-827-0442
Library consulting and moving specialists, nationwide. Services include: relocation planning, specialty handling of library collections, packing, shelving disassembly and assembly, storage, reshelving.

Adjustable Steel Products Co, Inc
276 Fifth Ave, New York, NY 10001; 212-686-1030
Shelving of exceptional quality. Shelves are strong, versatile, and "adjustable." Custom dimensions and attractive wood end panels and trim are our specialty.

Advanced Library Systems, Inc
Contact: John A Sammataro
93 Main St, PO Box 246, Andover, MA 01810
Library of Congress catalogs and technical publications and the National Union Catalog, pre–1956 imprints on microfiche.

Afro-Am Inc
Contact: Eugene Winslow
819 S Wabash Ave, Suite 610, Chicago, IL 60605; 312-922-1147
Distributors of black-oriented educational materials for grades K-12. Write for discounts extended to dealers, public libraries, and RIF subcontractors.

ALF Products Inc
Contact: Skip Greenleaf
3940 Youngfield St, Wheat Ridge, CO 80033; 303-423-0371
The Quick Copy family of portable, standalone disk copiers handle most any format quickly, easily, and reliably.

★**Alps, Inc** *(p 146)*
Contact: Joy G Renfrow
1517 E Sunrise Ave, Raleigh, NC 27608; 800-334-8363 or 919-834-4104
Alps, Inc. designs and manufactures storage cabinets and the Leaf-Thru Display for videocassettes, audiocassettes, and CDs. Inventory control system.

American Library Association
Contact: Ruth Ann Jones, Mktg Mgr/Pubns or Marcia Kuszmaul, Mktg Mgr/Lib Promotion
50 E Huron St, Chicago, IL 60611; 312-944-6780
Professional library science materials including monographs, reference books, training videotapes, electronic mail service, professional journals; also posters and library promotion items.

American Playground Corp
Contact: Mr Randall Coates, Pres
1801 Jackson St, PO Box 2599, Anderson, IN 46018; 317-642-0288
Bike racks, benches, picnic tables, playground equipment, park and sports equipment, spiral slides.

Applause Productions, Inc/Novacom Video
Contact: David Cole
85 Longview Rd, Port Washington, NY 11050; 516-883-7460, 516-979-6670
Distributes a wide variety of classroom materials to supplement foreign-language curricula, and videocassettes of opera, ballet, concerts, and theater.

Appleson Press Inc
Contact: Ken Sands
1120 Old Country Rd, Plainview, NY 11803; 516-937-6280; 800-888-APPLE; NY Showroom: 305 Madison Ave, Suite 2140, New York, NY 10017; 212-972-5255
Labels: barcode, color-coded, computer disk, machine-readable, mailing, OCR, pres-

sure-sensitive, printed.

Architectural Bronze & Aluminum Corp
3638 W Oakton St, Skokie, IL 60076; 312-539-0500, 312-674-3638
Plaques, medallions, signs, nameplates, bulletin boards, metal lettering, desk plates, service emblem pins, display cases, statues, cast bas relief portraits.

Armor Lock Corp
16 Fairlawn St, Ho-Ho-Kus, NJ 07423
We manufacture antitheft products for computers and related business machines.

Artisans' Guild Inc
Contact: Diane Hartzog, VP
311 Amhurst Ave, PO Box 345, High Point, NC 27261
Novelty seating for libraries and schools; specializing in lightweight urethane foam floor seating and cushions and NAPSAX® beanbag chairs.

Asia Society, The
(Education & Communications Dept)
725 Park Ave, New York, NY 10021
Educational video and print materials for teaching about Asia. "Focus on Asian Studies," resource journal; posters; teacher's guides; videocassettes. Free materials list.

Atlantic Book Binders, Inc
Contact: David A Bruso or Ronna Archbold
Box 599 Flagg St, South Lancaster, MA 01561; 617-365-4524
Binding services: Class A binding, leather binding, picture bindings; prebinders: hardbacks, magazines, paperbacks; restoration binding.

ATLIS Federal Services, Inc
Contact: Beryl L Feinberg, Prog Mgr
6011 Executive Blvd, Rockville, MD 20852
A comprehensive information management and database development firm for retrospective conversion, tape processing, acquisitions, cataloging, and database design and clearinghouse management.

Audio Language Studies, Inc
(Listen for Pleasure)
Contact: Brian Tierney
1 Colomba Dr, Niagara Falls, NY 14305; 716-298-5150 or 800-843-8056
A series of five read-alongs accompanied by word-for-word transcripts. Classics and best sellers with readability levels grade 3 to 12.

★**Auto-Graphics, Inc** ***(p 105)***
3201 Temple Ave, Pomona, CA 91768; 714-595-7204; 800-325-7961 or in CA 800-828-9585
Automation and systems design; bibliographic service systems; book catalog services; catalog card sets; classification guides; databases; MARC tape storage and retrieval.

Avedex, Inc
Contact: Robert D Hall, Pres
340 Anthony Trail, Northbrook, IL 60062; 312-480-7931 or 800-323-4239
Audiotape; cassettes; headphones; learning systems (language labs); sound distribution systems; tape recorders.

Bacon Pamphlet Service, Inc
Contact: Valva P Lawson
228 B—Hand Hollow Rd, East Chatham, NY 12060; 518-794-7722
For the past 51 years, service to libraries (school, college, public, special) in the United States and Canada—all pamphlet and paperbound materials.

★**Baker & Taylor** ***(2d cover, p 18)***
Contact: James Brooke
652 E Main St, Bridgewater, NJ 08807; 201-218-3822
Baker & Taylor is an international distributor of books, videocassettes, audio products, and related services including electronic ordering, standing order, and approval plans.

★**Bar Code Applications** ***(p 149)***
Contact: Mel Endelman
810 Peace Portal Way, #113, Blaine, WA 98230; 604-682-5497
Library barcode labels, scanners, PC circulation software—TLS, portable barcode scanners—inventory—since 1982.

★**Blackwell North America, Inc** ***(p 111)***
1001 Fries Mill Rd, Blackwood, NJ 08012; 800-257-7341 or in NJ 609-629-0700; FAX 609-629-0438; in Canada 800-631-3161; 6024 SW Jean Rd, Bldg G, Lake Oswego, OR 97035; 800-547-6426 or in OR 503-684-1140; FAX 503-639-2481; in Canada 800-626-1807
Bibliographic service systems; book catalog services; booklists; book processing kits; booksellers; catalog card sets; cataloging services; government publications; MARC tape storage and retrieval.

Block & Co, Inc
Contact: Barbara Cole, VP Merchandising
1111 S Wheeling Rd, Wheeling, IL 60090; 312-537-7200 or 800-323-7556; in IL 800-942-6088; in CA 800-55-BLOCK; in TX 800-94-BLOCK
Coin handling supplies, cash handling supplies, signs, bulletin boards, key control products, data processing supplies, business forms, writing instruments.

★**Books on Tape, Inc** ***(p 91)***
Contact: Jo Bradley, Admin Dir
PO Box 7900, Newport Beach, CA 92658; 714-548-5525 or Library Services 800-541-5525
Books on Tape produces full-length novels on cassette tape.

★**Bound To Stay Bound Books, Inc** ***(p 104)***
W Morton Rd, Jacksonville, IL 62650; 800-637-6586 or in IL 217-245-5191.
Books processed; catalog cards; jobbers, books; prebinders, processed books and materials; processing kits

★Bowker, R R *(p 2, 11, 25, 28, 29, 31)*
(Div of Reed Publishing USA)
245 W 17th St, New York, NY 10011; 212-337-6900
Information reference materials including: books, book series, annuals, and updates; CD-ROM; magazines; microfiche book and serial information; online databases; reviewing service; tape leasing.

Bretford Mfg Inc
Contact: Bob Redding, Natl Sales Mgr
9715 Soreng Ave, Schiller Park, IL 60176; 312-678-2545; telex 9102274925 Bretford SRPK; FAX 312-678-0852
Office equipment and library book trucks, audiovisual carts. Communication support system from Bretford.

Bridgeport National Bindery, Inc
Contact: James M Larsen, Pres
104 Ramah Circle S, PO Box 289, Agawam, MA 01001; 413-789-1981
Full-service library bindery; short-run edition binding; book conservation lab; custom binding and custom boxmaking; dependable service, competitive price.

Brodart Co
The Library Co
Contact: Bebe Bungo or Jeff Myers
500 Arch St, Williamsport, PA 17705; 1609 Memorial Ave, Williamsport, PA 17705; 800-233-8467 or 717-326-2461
Books, video: McNaughton Book Services. Acquisition systems, collection development services, continuation services, automated technical services, circulation systems, library furniture and supplies.

★Buckstaff® *(p 148)*
Contact: Thomas Madden, Natl Sales Mgr
1127 S Main St, Oshkosh, WI 54901; 414-235-5890
Atlas cases, bookcases, bookshelving, booktrucks, cabinets, carrels, chairs, charging desks, dictionary stands, exhibit cases, furniture, furniture planning, index tables (CBI).

Buk Mark Products, Inc
Contact: Richard Allison
15 Spinning Wheel Rd, Suite 108, Hinsdale, IL 60521; 312-850-9240
Line of decorative devices used for holding paperback books open while reading; also serves as bookmark, 50% discount.

Cable Films & Video
Contact: Todd Randall Miller, Gen Mgr
Country Club Sta, Kansas City, MO 64113; 913-362-2804
300 classics, 1920–1960. All formats. Public performance rights included. Ask for "Video Books" based on literature. Library/school discounts.

★Caedmon *(p 149)*
(Audio Div of Harper & Row Pubs, Inc)
Contact: Claire Curtin
1995 Broadway, New York, NY 10023; 800-C-HARPER
Pioneer producer of outstanding poetry, drama, mystery, science fiction on record and cassette; discounted library subscription plan; children's stories; original musicals.

Campbell-Logan Bindery, Inc
Contact: Gregor Campbell
212 Second St N, Minneapolis, MN 55401; 612-332-1313 or 800-942-6224
Binding services: Class A binding, leather binding, restoration binding.

Campus Copies Corp
(Kinko's Copies)
Contact: John Rinaldi
4810 Riverbend Rd, Boulder, CO 80301-2608; 800-448-5355
Management of copy vending facilities at larger institutions (15 or more copiers). We provide *on-site* technicians, couriers, and customer service staff.

★Canon USA, Inc *(p 97)*
(Micrographics Div)
1 Canon Plaza, Lake Success, NY 11042; 800-453-9000
Processor camera for microfilm; plain-paper copiers; plain-paper reader-printers.

★Carlyle Systems, Inc *(p 15)*
5750 Hollis St, Emeryville, CA 94608; 415-654-2600 or 800-274-4274; FAX 415-654-0464
Carlyle installs integrated systems: online catalog, circulation, catalog maintenance, authority control, and interfaces to cataloging utilities and other vendors' systems.

★Catalog Card Corp of America *(p 117)*
PO Box 1276, Burnsville, MN 55337; 800-328-2923 or in MN & Canada 612-894-5770
Dewey/Sears MARC records; retrospective conversion; circulation records.

★Cel-U-Dex Corp *(p 116)*
PO Box 4084, New Windsor, NY 12550; 914-562-4510
Desk-drawer dividers; filing signals; index dividers; index tabs; shelf label holders.

Centel Federal Services Corp
Contact: Janet R Bailin, DATALIB Prod Mgr
12730 Twinbrook Pkwy, Rockville, MD 20852; 800-843-4850 or 301-984-3636
DATALIB is a fully integrated library management system that includes cataloging, retrieval, serials management, circulation, and a MARC interface.

★Central Audio Visual Equipment *(p 147)*
340 Anthony Trail, Northbrook, IL 60062; 312-480-7560 or 800-323-4239
Studio and projector lamps; batteries; Polaroid film; screens, VCRs, monitors, VCR head cleaners; tripods; microphones; lecterns; headphones; CD cleaners; wireless PA systems.

Checkpoint Systems, Inc
Contact: Steven M Frazier, Natl Sales Mgr
550 Grove Rd, Thorofare, NJ 08086; 800-257-5540 x232

Checkpoint Systems, Inc. manufactures and markets library security systems to prevent the unauthorized removal of library materials.

Cheshire Corp
Contact: Mary Kay Opicka
PO Box 4544, Englewood, CO 80155; 303-333-3003
Award-winning filmstrips adapting some of the most popular contemporary books like *How To Eat Fried Worms*, *Anastasia Krupnik*, and more.

★Clark, Charles, Co, Inc ***(p 146)***
Customer Service Dept, 170 Keyland Ct, Bohemia, NY 11716; 800-247-7009 or 516-589-6643
Distributor of educational videocassettes, read-alongs, and filmstrips. Company offers a large product selection. Catalogs available upon request.

★CLSI, Inc ***(p 21, 23, 25)***
Contact: Richard Porter, Mgr Corp Communications
320 Nevada St, Newtonville, MA 02160; 617-965-6310 or 800-225-3076; FAX 617-969-1928
Develops turnkey library automation systems automating acquisitions, cataloging, online public access catalog, circulation, and serials management. New product: CD-ROM catalog.

Colonial "Out of Print" Book Service
PO Box 451, Pleasantville, NY 10570
We supply out of print books—specializing in literature, art, and history.

Color Microimaging Corp
Contact: Wayne Martin
5078 List Dr, Colorado Springs, CO 80919
The largest and most advanced color micrographic service company, providing specialized color micrographic services on 105mm color microfiche, rollfilm, or aperture cards.

Compass Van & Storage Corp
Contact: James Dowse
237 Main St, Hempstead, NY 11550; 516-486-6000
Library relocations specialist. Collections move on library bins, collections never boxed. Integration, segregations, rare collections, bid specifications, vacuuming.

★Computer Co, The ***(p 131)***
Contact: Kate Duval
1905 Westmoreland St, Richmond, VA 23230; 804-359-0193 or 800-327-5160
Experienced providers of: name/subject authority conrol; retrospective conversion; archive tape processing; database cleanup; MARC upgrades; barcode number processing.

Comstow Information Services
Contact: Jane Kalfus-Maine
302 Boxboro Rd, Stow, MA 01775-1161; 617-897-7163
BiblioTech is a family of integrated software modules, supporting cataloging, OPAC, circulation, acquisitions, serials/periodical management, and extensive report generation.

Continental Extrusion Corp
Contact: Hannah Kaltman
2 Endo Blvd, Garden City, NY 11530; 516-832-8111 or 800-645-6531
SUPERBAG—extra-strong, all-plastic carrier, can be custom printed.

★Copicard ***(p 147)***
Contact: Jeri Heidemann
12900 Valley Branch Lane #400, Dallas, TX 75234; in TX 214-243-4057 or 800-527-7639
Copicard Access Control System for copiers, IBM PC/compatibles, microfilm reader/printers. Uses magnetic stripe plastic cards encoded with value.

★Coronet/MTI Film & Video ***(p 147, 148, 149)***
(A Simon & Schuster Co—Secondary Education Group)
108 Wilmot Rd, Deerfield, IL 60015; 800-621-2131 or 312-940-1260
Distributors of Disney Educational Productions and Learning Corportation of America, award-winning film and video titles for schools, libraries, and the community!

Crawford Library Bindery, Inc
Contact: James H Poulson
2249 14th St, Akron, OH 44314; 216-745-9048
Providing complete binding services for monographs & periodicals! Hand binding lab specializes in phase boxes and micrographic copying for archival material.

Crystal Productions
Contact: Amy W Johns, Gen Mgr
PO Box Box 2159, Glenview, IL 60025; 800-255-8629
Producers and distributors of filmstrips, slides, videotapes, and films on art skills, art appreciation, careers for elementary through college levels.

Dahle USA
Contact: Janine Moore
6 Benson Rd, Oxford, CT 06483; 203-264-0505 or 800-243-8145; FAX 203-264-3714
Dahle has a full line of cutting and presentation products. Manufacture high-quality products for over 50 years. All products guaranteed.

★Data Recall, Inc ***(p 118)***
Contact: Brian K McBride
1711 Dell Ave, Campbell, CA 95008; 408-354-7555; FAX 408-379-9074
Your single source barcode supplier: barcode labels (all formats), laser scanners, decoders, and hand-held portables. Interfaces to all systems.

★Data Research Associates, Inc ***(p 103)***
Contact: James J Michael, VP
1276 N Warson Rd, St Louis, MO 63132; 800-325-0888 or 314-432-1100
ATLAS—A Total Library Automation Sys-

tem—is a fully integrated software package to perform the complete range of library functions.

★Data Trek, Inc ***(p 109)***
Contact: Tom Beaudin
167 Saxony Rd, Encinitas, CA 92024; 619-436-5055 or 800-875-5484
Data Trek specializes in library automation software and hardware for IBM, Apple "Macintosh," and DEC "Vax" minicomputer systems.

Demco, Inc
Contact: Colleen Goltz, Mktg Coord
Box 7488, Madison, WI 53707; 608-241-1201 or 800-356-1200; FAX 608-241-1799
Demco offers a full line of supplies and equipment to help your library operate efficiently. Call today for our catalogs!

Designers Sign Co
Contact: Judith Barbieri, VP Sales
352 Washington Ave, Carlstadt, NJ 07072
Manufacturer of sign systems and complete identification programs. In-house planning and design. Products with vandal resistance and maximum changeability.

Detection Systems, Inc
Contact: Mr Jan Landre
130 Perinton Pkwy, Fairport, NY 14450; 716-223-4060 or 800-521-0096
Detection Systems, Inc. designs, manufactures, and markets electronic instrumentation and control equipment for the security and facility management industries.

Detex Corp
Contact: Lee Graham
302 Detex Dr, New Braunfels, TX 78130; 512-629-2900 or 800-468-0112
Security hardware; exit control locks; exit alarms; access control equipment.

Devoke Co
Contact: John Ozmun, Mktg Dir
1500 Martin Ave, Box 58051, Santa Clara, CA 95052-8051; 408-980-1366
Our catalog offers a full range of computer-related furniture, supplies, accessories, and technical products. Quantity discounts available.

Digital Pr, Book Publishing
(Div of Digital Equipment Corp)
Contact: Willard M. Buddenhagen
12 Crosby Dr, Bedford, MA 01730; 617-276-1536
Publisher of computer books for professionals.

Disclosure Inc
(VNU [United Dutch Pub Co])
Contact: Michael Rittmann, VP Mktg & Sales
5161 River Rd, Bethesda, MD 20816; 301-951-1332
Publishes SEC financial information on more than 12,000 public companies in various products and services: microfiche/paper subscriptions, online database, CD-ROM, on-demand.

Discount Video Tapes, Inc
Contact: Woody Wise, Pres
PO Box 7122, Burbank, CA 91510; 818-843-3366
Specializing in the rare and unusual: classics, foreign films, serials, Westerns, and documentaries. Free catalog upon request.

Document Control Systems, Inc
Contact: Adam M Stack, VP
99 NW 183rd St, Suite 126, North Miami, FL 33169
Data processing equipment: general, mini & personal computers, software, storage & retrieval systems, terminals; automated electronic files; indexing services; microcomputer.

Door Alarm Devices Corp
Contact: Bert Harman
20 Lucan Dr, Deer Park, NY 11729; 516-586-2400
Manufacturer of the DADCO line of monitor panels and printers, exit alarms, power packs, and distributor of wireless paging systems.

Dorlen Products
(Div of Electro-Consultants, Inc)
Contact: Len Woloszyk
7424 W Layton Ave, Milwaukee, WI 53220; 414-282-4840
Manufacturer of surface water sensing alarm systems. Self-contained and remote wired-. . . for computer room subfloor and unattended areas.

★Dukane Corp ***(p 146, 147)***
Contact: Steve Kendall, Mktg Mgr
2900 Dukane Dr, St Charles, IL 60174-3395; 800-356-6540 or 800-634-2800; in IL 312-584-2300
New line of silent and sound filmstrip projectors/viewers, reliable microfilm readers, series of LCD panels for projecting computer data.

★Dynix, Inc ***(p 133)***
Contact: Jim Wilson
151 E 1700 S, Provo, UT 84601; 801-374-1888
Library automation systems. Software modules: circulation, public access, cataloging, acquisitions, etc. Fully integrated. User friendly. PICK™ operating system. Supports MARC/non-MARC formats.

Eastin Phelan Corp
1235 W 5th St, Davenport, IA 52801; 319-323-9735
We vend 16mm films from the Blackhawk Films collection and all types of prerecorded videocassettes. Leases also available.

E B S Inc Book Service
290 Broadway, Lynbrook, NY 11563; 516-593-1195
Wholesaler to libraries.

EBSCO Electronic Information
(Div of EBSCO Industries, Inc)
PO Box 13787, Torrance, CA 90503; 213-375-3588 or 800-888-3272
Develops, markets, and provides subscrip-

tion services for a wide range of CD-ROM databases including NLM's Medline® file and EBSCO Publishing's *The Serials Directory: An International Reference Book.*

EBSCO Publishing
(Div of EBSCO Industries, Inc)
PO Box 1943, Birmingham, AL 35201; 800-826-3024
The Serials Directory: An International Reference Book: 114,000+ serials, irregular series, annuals, ceased titles worldwide. 3d edition: November 1988. Also on CD-ROM.

★EBSCO Subscription Services *(p 120)*
(Div of EBSCO Industries, Inc)
Contact: Joe K. Weed, VP/Dir of Mktg
PO Box 1943, Birmingham, AL 35201; 205-991-6600
International subscription/serials management agency: order processing and customer service for magazines, regular/irregular series, continuations, annuals, microfiche/microform serials, CD-ROM database products.

Educational Services Corp
Contact: Barbara Bloch, Mktg Mgr
1725 K St NW, #408, Washington, DC 20006; 202-298-8424
Audiocassettes: LANGUAGE/30 self-teaching courses with book, 31 languages, $14.95. PSYCHOLOGY TODAY self-help series, $9.95. 20% library discount. Free racks.

Elden Enterprises
Contact: Ted Elden, Pres
PO Box 3201, Charleston, WV 25332; 304-344-2335; telex 9102403552 Elden USA CHAUQ
The Abodia Slide Storage System stores from 100 to 100,000 35mm slides. The cabinets have illuminated rear viewing.

Elm Products Corp
Contact: Erick Mott
PO Box 14988, N Palm Beach, FL 33408; 407-478-2690
The COPYGRIP reading stand firmly holds books, encyclopedias, manuals, and more at a comfortable and convenient reading angle. ONLY $6.95.

E M E Corp
PO Box 2805, Danbury, CT 06813-2805; 203-798-2050
Publishers of science and mathematics computer software, video, filmstrips, overhead projecturals, and maps. Write or call for FREE catalog.

Emery-Pratt Co
Contact: Maurice B Shattuck, Pres
1966 W Main St, Owosso, MI 48867-1372; 517-723-5291; orders 800-762-5683; customer serv 800-248-3887
A jobber/supplier to libraries representing over 40,000 publishing sources of "in-print" material, AV material. Cataloging also available.

Equipto
225 S Highland Ave, Aurora, IL 60507; 312-859-1000 or 800-323-0801; FAX 312-859-3255
EQUIPTO is a leading manufacturer of shelving, rack, mezzanines, modular drawers, benches, storage cabinets, and storage systems.

Esselte Pendaflex Corp
71 Clinton Rd, Garden City, NY 11530; 516-741-3200
Esselte Pendaflex Corp is a major North American manufacturer of brand name office supplies including: Pendaflex®, Oxford®, Dymo®, Boorum™, Ideal™, and Amberg®.

★Evans Specialty Co, Inc *(147)*
Contact: H L Daniels Sr, Pres
PO Box 24189-0189, Richmond, VA 23224; 804-232-8946 or 800-368-3061; FAX 804-233-7482
Antistatic sprays, antistatic computer cloths, cleaners for computer screens, hand cleaners, collators, fingertip moisteners, and message bars. Free catalog and name of local supplier.

Extek Microsystems, Inc
Contact: Elisa Abelleira
6955 Hayvenhurst Ave, Van Nuys, CA 91406; 818-989-2630
Extek Microsystems, Inc is a manufacturer of microfilming products. Included in this category is all you need to microfilm a document.

Eyring Library Systems
(Eyring Research Inst, Inc)
Contact: Mktg Dir
6918 S 185 W, Midvale, UT 84047; 801-561-1111; FAX 801-561-0910
Tandem-based library automation systems for large consortia, single libraries, and library systems. Virtually limitless growth by addition, not replacement.

Fairchild Books & Visuals
(Fairchild Publications)
Contact: Elaine Ross Bremer
7 E 12th St, New York, NY 10003; 212-741-4280
Publisher/producers of textbooks and visual programs in the fashion design, merchandising, textiles, and careers areas.

Faxon Co, The
Contact: Ron Akie
15 Southwest Pk, Westwood, MA 02090; 617-329-3350
Faxon offers online and microcomputer-based subscription check-in and routing services; acquisitions and collection development services and management.

★Fay Inst of Human Relations, Inc, The *(p 146)*
Contact: Catherine Blake
PO Box 5, CDN, Montreal, Quebec, Canada H3S 2S4; 514-737-1394
Multimedia publishing (audiocassettes, books, overhead transparencies, software, video) for sex education. Available from Bak-

er & Taylor, Bookpeople, Fitzhenry & Whiteside ....

Fiesta Book Co
Contact: Allan Sandler or Mercy Lopez
6360 NE 4th Ct, Miami, FL 33138; 305-751-1181
Spanish-language books, ESL materials, and magazine subscriptions. 3500 imported titles listed in free catalog. All categories.

Fixturecraft Corp
Contact: William P Mooney, Pres
443 E Westfield Ave, PO Box 292, Roselle Park, NJ 07204; 201-245-8440; FAX 201-245-2841
Display racks: literature, metal, paperbacks, wire; shelving: display, steel, wall-hung, wire.

Follett Software Co
(Follett Corp)
Contact: Lisa J. McManaman
4506 Northwest Hwy, Crystal Lake, IL 60014; 815-455-4660 or 800-323-3397
Follett specializes in complete automation and services for your library. Product line ranges from our single-concept programs to our Plus products, including Circulation Plus™.

Fordham Equipment Co
3308 Edson Ave, Bronx, NY 10469; 212-379-7300
Manufacturers, distributors full-line library supplies, furniture, and equipment. We can furnish and install custom quality hardwood and metal shelving.

Foster Mfg Co
Contact: C Stuart Goodwin
414 N 13th St, Philadelphia, PA 19108; 215-625-0500 or 800-523-4855; FAX 215-238-5457
Ask for free catalog with prices and descriptions of light tables, flat and vertical storage systems. New McSort Paper Management System—wall-mounted storage trays and bins.

Franklin Dist Corp
Contact: Alan Gill, VP Mktg
PO Box 320, Denville, NJ 07834; 201-267-2710
Archival materials for storage of photographic slides, prints, negatives, and documents, including, SAF-T-STOR™, PERMA-SAF™, polyester sheet protectors—archival, acid-free inserts.

French & European Publications, Inc
(The French & Spanish Bk Corp; The Dictionary & Learn-a-Language Co)
Contact: Emanuel Molho, Pres
115 5th Ave, New York, NY 10003; 212-673-7400
French and Spanish books and educational recordings. Dictionaries, language-learning books, recordings in more than 100 languages. General and technical.

Gamma Technologies, Inc
Contact: Harriet Dinari
12255 SW 132nd Ct, Miami, FL 33186; 800-522-SIGN; FAX 305-251-6713
Gamma Model features include wireless remote control keyboards, networking systems, three-color LEDs, and graphic and animation capability plus time/date.

Garnet Projects Inc
Contact: Ivan Gontko
PO Box 30241, Station B, Calgary, Alberta, Canada T2M 4P1; 403-250-5429; FAX 403-291-9401
General maintenance equipment for sensitive objects, educational games, development of new products to be announced when ready for marketing.

Garrett Industries
(Div of JSJ)
Contact: Duane Tuttle
PO Box 128, Hudson, IN 46747; 219-587-3231
Manufacturers of library carts, AV carts and cabinets, modular storage cabinets, computer tables, and adjustable seating.

★**Gaylord Bros** *(p 147, 149)*
Box 4901, Syracuse, NY 13221-4901; 800-448-6160
Library and office supplies, furniture, automation products. Compact disc, videocassette displayers and storage; microcomputer, audiovisual supplies; custom imprintables; contract furniture.

General Audio-Visual Inc (GAVI)
Contact: Michael Dituri
333 W Merrick Rd, Valley Stream, NY 11580; 516-825-8500; FAX 516-568-2057
Manufacturer of specialized AV equipment, including the only Automatic Lamp Changer for Kodak EIII. Also a rear screen 35mm filmstrip viewer.

General Microfilm Co
Contact: Mrs Cheryl A Copeland
70 Coolidge Hill Rd, Watertown, MA 02172; 617-926-5557
General Microfilm Company publishes 63+ micropublications. Its services and products include catalog card duplication and Easy-Access microfiche envelopes.

★**General Research Corp (GRC)** *(p 135)*
(Library Systems)
5383 Hollister Ave, Santa Barbara, CA 93111; 800-235-6788 or call collect 805-964-7724
CD-ROM patron access catalog, retrospective and current cataloging.

Ghent Mfg, Inc
Contact: Beverly K Worley
PO Box 410, South St at Cherry, Lebanon, OH 45036; 513-932-3445 or 800-543-0550; FAX 513-932-9252
Visual communication aids: markerboards, chalkboards, bulletin boards, easels, flannel boards, and letter/directory boards.

★**Gillotte, R P, Co** *(p 114, 149)*
(Div of National Service Industries, Inc)
Contact: Carol Heitlinger, Adv Mgr; Henry Berry, Customer Serv

PO Box 5735, Columbia, SC 29250; 803-799-5158 or 800-845-7068; telex 988501
Suspended filing systems for America's libraries.

G M Associates
14 Gustav Crescent, Willowdale, Ontario, Canada M2M 2C5
Date due systems (labels, label gun); porta-panel hinges, sign holders; Canadian Food Ingredient Information System helps people with allergies.

Gossage Regan Associates, Inc
Contact: Muriel Regan
15 W 44th St, New York, NY 10036; 212-869-3348
Consultation; personnel services: executive search/screening, permanent professional placement nationwide; permanent and temporary placement of professionals, paraprofessionals, clericals NYC area.

Graphic Learning Internat
Contact: Henry M Poirot, Dir of Sales & Mktg
1123 Spruce St, Boulder, CO 80302; 303-440-7620 or 800-423-0395
Earthbook: Explore earth sciences in the encyclopedia of the earth and the world in maps, featuring satellite-assisted, environmental cartography.

★**Gressco Ltd** *(p 148)*
Contact: George Histed, Pres
2702 International Lane, PO Box 7444, Madison, WI 53707; 608-244-4999; FAX 608-244-7212
Displayers and storage systems for paperbacks, audiocassettes, CDs, videocassettes, and periodicals. Most systems available with and without security.

Guidance Associates
Sales, Communications Park, Box 3000, Mt Kisco, NY 10549; 914-666-4100 or 800-431-1242
Guidance Associates produces videos on health, drug prevention, career development, study skills, and more. Most programs available for 30-day preview.

Haddad's Fine Arts, Inc
Contact: James J Haddad
3855 E Mira Loma, Anaheim, CA 92806; 714-996-2100
Publisher and manufacturer of fine art reproductions, art posters, photo art, and framed pictures. Master color catalog 432 pages, 2100 illustrations.

Hall, G K & Co
(Div of Macmillan)
70 Lincoln St, Boston, MA 02111; 800-343-2806 or in AK, HI, MA 617-423-3990; telex 94-0037
Unabridged books on cassette for adults and children; audio book albums; large print books for adults and children. Library catalogs and supplements on 35mm microfilm.

★**Hamilton Scale Corp** *(p 113)*
3350 Secor Rd, Toledo, OH 43606; 419-535-7667
Changemakers.

Hammond Inc
Contact: Lisa Cushine, Adv Mgr
515 Valley St, Maplewood, NJ 07040; 201-763-6000 or 800-526-4953; FAX 201-763-7658
Publisher of maps, atlases, and general reference books. Librarians get a 15% discount off of retail.

Hannecke Display Systems, Inc
(Hannecke Display Systems, Northeim, W Germany)
Contact: Bruce Dreher, Pres
370 Franklin Tpk, Mahwah, NJ 07430; in NJ 201-529-5995 or 800-345-8631; FAX 201-529-9343
Manufacturer of award-winning point-of-purchase display systems for audio, video, book publishing, and packaged products business; in-store custom-designed displays.

Harris/3M Document Products, Inc
Contact: Galen Bangsund
2300 Parklake Dr NE, Atlanta, GA 30345; 404-873-1711
A $650 million company; global marketing, sale, service of full line of copiers, facsimile, AV presentation equipment, distributing through direct sales and dealers.

Heller, W C & Co
Contact: Robert L Heller II
201 Wabash Ave, Montpelier, OH 43543; 419-485-3176
We manufacture and sell a complete line of wood library furniture including shelving, tables, carrels, card files, and counters.

Hendershot Programmed Learning Bibliographies
Contact: Dr Carl H Hendershot
4114 Ridgewood, Bay City, MI 48706-2499; 517-684-3148
Annotated bibliographies of self-study materials. Facts for ordering directly from each publisher. Instruction for business, industry, college, schools.

Hertzberg-New Method
E Vandalia Rd, Jacksonville, IL 62650; 800-637-6581
Binding services; book repairing; prebinders.

Heyer Inc
Contact: Thomas A Leach
1850 S Kostner Ave, Chicago, IL 60623; 312-277-0130
Manufacturer of spirit/stencil duplicators and supplies, stencil cutters, thermal processors, folding machines, labelers, and paper shredders.

★**Highsmith Co, Inc, The** *(p 102)*
W5527 Hwy 106, PO Box 800, Fort Atkinson, WI 53538; 414-563-9571
Direct mail catalog supplier of library equipment, supplies, and furniture. Featuring extensive lines of office, audiovisual/microcomputer equipment, supplies/furniture.

Information Dimensions, Inc
(A BATTELLE Subs)
Contact: Dick Lombard

655 Metro Place S, Dublin, OH 43017; 800-DATA-MGT or 614-761-7300
TECHLIB/STACS: Online, interactive text information management system (TIMS) for automating library functions: cataloging, acquisitions, circulation, serials control, patron access for special, corporate, technical libraries.

★Ingram Library Services, Inc *(3d cover)*
(Div of Ingram Distribution Group Inc) Library Services, 347 Reedwood Dr, Nashville, TN 37217; 800-251-5902 or 810-371-1092; FAX 615-793-3825
Ingram is the country's largest distributor of books, video- and audiocassettes, compact discs, microcomputer software, and special interest periodicals.

★INLEX, Inc *(p 136)*
Contact: Joseph Matthews
PO Box 1349, Monterey, CA 93942; in CA 408-646-9666 or 800-553-1202
INLEX/3000 provides a superior, user friendly automated library system with an online catalog, circulation, acquisitions, serials, and authority control modules.

Innovative Interfaces, Inc
Contact: Stephen Silberstein, Exec VP
2344 6th St, Berkeley, CA 94710; 415-644-3600
Re INNOPAC: An integrated turnkey automation system, comprising modules for online public catalog (including authority control), circulation, acquisitions, and serials control.

★Institute for Scientific Information (ISI) *(p 64, 98)*
Customer Services, 3501 Market St, Philadelphia, PA 19104; 800-523-1850 or 215-386-0100 x1405; telex 84-5305; European Branch: 132 High St, Uxbridge, Middlesex, UK UB8 1DP; +44-895-70016; telex 933693 UKISI
ISI, information supplier to libraries worldwide, has introduced the *Science Citation Index* compact disc edition and *Current Contents* on diskette.

InterMetro Industries Corp
Contact: William Chappell
651 N Washington St, Wilkes-Barre, PA 18705; 717-825-2741 or 800-321-1414 x100; telex 831-833
Shelving: display, high-density, mobile, steel, wall-hung, wire.

International Bookfinders, Inc
Contact: Richard Mohr
Box 1, Pacific Palisades, CA 90272
Free search service for OUT OF PRINT books. By mail, only (since 1950).

International Film Bureau Inc
Contact: Anne Hebert
332 S Michigan Ave, Chicago, IL 60604
Educational films and videos, color sound filmstrips, color sound slide sets, film guides (1-32 pages), language texts. Computer Latin program.

Islington Arbour Systems
Contact: Mr Arne J Almquist
PO Box 1324, Denton, TX 76202-1324; 817-387-1703
IAS develops and markets library-specific microcomputer applications programs. Excellent support and our *Technical Bulletin* are provided to registered users.

Jackson-Hirsh, Inc
Contact: Jim Brunenkant
700 Anthony Trail, Northbrook, IL 60062; 312-272-4193
We sell pouch laminators and plastic pouches for plasticizing patron cards, signs, labels, and protecting any document or paper.

Jaeger, Alfred, Inc
Contact: Don Jaeger, VP
66 Austin Blvd, Commack, NY 11725; 516-543-1500 or 800-453-0011; FAX 516-543-1537
Providing a comprehensive back-volume service including out of print and foreign publications. Appraisals and consulting for tax and insurance purposes.

Johnson Bookbinding Supply Co
Suite 175 Memorial Bldg, 610 N Main St, Blacksburg, VA 24060; 703-552-0876
Bookbinding supplies and equipment; conservation-quality imported cloth. Catalog and sample books available.

Jones West Co
PO Box 1084, Dept LJ, Rohnert Park, CA 94927; 707-795-8552 or 800-635-5673
Zip close plastic bags, see-thru, ideal for protection of periodicals, projects, documents, supplies, all sizes and quantities. Send for price list.

Jon-Tone Co, Inc
Contact: John Davis
109 E Main St, Clinton, CT 06413; 203-245-2968
Audio-video jobber for adult and children's recordings. Complete cataloging available. We serve only libraries and offer competitive discounts.

K-12 Micromedia Publishing
6 Arrow Rd, Ramsey, NJ 07446; 800-922-0401
Circulation control systems; educational software and books for microcomputer-based learning, including administrative and library management programs; software for catalog card/label generation.

Kalart Victor Corp
Contact: Bruce H Quartin, Sales Mgr
20 Hultenius St, Plainville, CT 06062; 203-747-1663
Manufacturers of audiovisual equipment: 16mm motion picture projectors, overhead and opaque projectors, film editing, accessories.

★Kapco *(p 123)*
Contact: Ed Small
930 Overholt Rd, Kent, OH 44240; 800-843-5368 or in OH 216-678-1626

Easy Cover™—self-adhesive book cover; Easy Bind™—self-aligning repair tape; Easy Lam™—easy-to-use laminating film.

Kartes Video Communications
7225 Woodland Dr, PO Box 68881, Indianapolis, IN 46268-0881; 317-297-1888; 800-331-1387 or in IN 800-523-5851; FAX 317-297-5892
Prerecorded videocassettes are offered to libraries and schools at a 30% discount off retail price.

KECCō
Contact: Ken Clouse
6020C Hwy 9, PO Box 2, Felton, CA 95018
KECCō is a producer/distributor of print and nonprint materials including videocassettes and discs, slides, filmstrips, audiodiscs, and cassettes.

Ke-Master
Contact: Peter M Lindley
300 S Pennell Rd, Media, PA 19063; 215-459-1129; FAX 215-459-1063
Manufacturer of single-tag and double-tag key control systems, key racks, and key tags for storing and securing ten to 800 keys.

Keystone Mfg Co
25481 Fortran Dr, Punta Gorda, FL 33950; 813-637-3933
Canvas library, film, and school supplies. Bags for transporting films, books, or supplies between rooms, departments, schools, and libraries. Free catalog.

Kidde, Walter
Contact: John Trinajstich
5036 Walter Kidde Dr, PO Box 1147, Wake Forest, NC 27587; 919-556-6811
Halon and carbon dioxide systems for quick extinquishment of fires—will not harm electrical equipment, books, papers, etc. Detection and control panels.

Kewaunee Scientific Corp
Contact: Brenda Rothrock
901 FM 20, PO Box 930, Lockhart, TX 78644; 512-398-5292
Manufacture a complete line of technical workstations and workbenches, storage cabinets, and market a complete line of technical seating.

Kidstamps
Contact: Larry Rakow, Pres
PO Box 18699, Cleveland Heights, OH 44118; 800-727-5437
Request our free catalog of over 600 rubber stamps designed by more than 70 leading children's illustrators—a $2 value!

Kole Industries
Contact: Mary Ponchio
3553 NW 50th St, Miami, FL 800-327-6085 or 305-633-2556
Factory direct storage, shipping, mailing, organizing, office and maintenance supplies.

Kraus Reprint & Periodicals
Contact: Kathryn Vail Maffucci, VP
Rte 100, Millwood, NY 10546; 914-762-2200 or 800-223-8323; FAX 914-762-1195; telex 6818112
One of the world's largest reprinters, with 20,000 titles in the form of books, monographs, journals, and microform. Original editions and special collections.

Larlin Corp
PO Box 1730, Marietta, GA 30061; 404-424-6210 or 800-548-8778
Call for free catalogs of library supplies; library/media skills and professional tools; AV/computer furniture, equipment, and storage.

Laser Electronics
Contact: Jay Ziolko
1420 W Walnut, Blytheville, AR 72370; 800-441-2665
The Laser Counter is an inexpensive but accurate electronic device that counts the people that enter your library.

Lawrence Metal Products, Inc
Contact: Louis Rabeno
PO Box 400-M, 260 Spur Dr S, Bay Shore, NY 11706; 800-441-0019 or in NY 516-666-0300; FAX 516-666-0336
Manufacturers of crowd control: ropes, posts, sign stands, gates, turnstiles, railing in brass, chrome, and stainless steel. Free 64-page catalog.

Learned Information, Inc
143 Old Marlton Pike, Medford, NJ 08055-8707
Learned Information, Inc. is a publisher of books, newspapers, and periodicals dealing with the computer industry and related fields.

Lectro-Stik Corp
Contact: Harold Press
3721 Broadway, Chicago, IL 60613; 312-528-8860
LECTRO-STIK: Wax adhesive and electronic applicator ($45). Pressure-sensitive coat cuts "paste-up" time over rubber cement.

Letterguide Inc
Contact: Howard R Waddle, Gen Mgr
PO Box 30203, 4247 O St, Lincoln, NE 68510; 402-488-0925
Manufacturers of mechanical lettering equipment. Letter direct in ink from ⅛" up to 2" in over 90 type styles.

Liberty Mfg Inc
Contact: Michele Bell
PO Box 8431, Stockton, CA 95208; 209-948-1176 or 800-553-3717; in CA 800-321-1175
We are a manufacturing company of quality wood audio, video, etc, display fixtures. We have a full color catalog available. Custom orders available upon request.

Library Bindery Co of PA
(Div of Information Conservation, Inc)
Contact: Val Scheckenbach
935 Horsham Rd, Horsham, PA 19044; 215-674-0486
Library Bindery Co offers a variety of services: Preservation microfilming/microfiche, conservation/preservation service, protec-

tive laminated covers, and commercial bookbinding.

★Library Bureau, Inc *(p 108)*
Contact: Len Black, VP Mktg
801 Park Ave, Herkimer, NY 13350; 315-866-1330; FAX 315-866-4430; telex 937440
A manufacturer of wood library furniture and shelving, steel bookstack, multitier shelving, and cantilever and four-post document storage shelving.

Library Corp, The
Contact: Brower Murphy or Mary Ann Zimmerman
PO Box 40035, Washington, DC 20016; 800-624-0559
BiblioFile automation tools provide superior automated library services exploiting the capacity of CD-ROM, making full use of PC speed, power, low cost.

Library Microfilms & Materials Co
Contact: Mrs Ina Spreitzer
38220 Dorn Rd, Cathedral City, CA 92234; 619-321-4842
Microfiche readers and microfilm readers: factory service and replacement parts of LMM readers.

Library Processes System
Contact: Fran Grant
919 W Canadian St, Vinita, OK 74301
CATALOG CARD/LABELS PROGRAM allows complete manipulation: stores entire inventory for printing card sets, booklists, and subject searches by any entry.

Library Products Inc
Contact: Steve Schneid, VP
4900 Hwy 33, Neptune, NJ 07753; 201-938-4492
Suppliers of library shelving and furniture, compact storage shelving, planning & design from concept to completion.

Library Reproduction Service
(Div of Microfilm Co of California, Inc)
1977 S Los Angeles St, Los Angeles, CA 90011; 800-255-5002
Duplicate catalog card service. Brochure and mailing kit available on request.

Library Sign Co, The
Contact: Dan Morganstern
1600 St Margarets Rd, Annapolis, MD 21401; 301-757-1661
Interior & exterior signage, badges, banners, sign kits, plastic & foam letters, directories, custom logo decals, changeable message boards, displays.

★Library Store, Inc, The *(p 148)*
Contact: Linda Scranton
Box 964, Tremont, IL 61568; 309-925-5571
Complete catalog of library supplies, lowest prices for premium products. Free shipping (most products). Free imprinting of pockets—special offer.

Listening Library, Inc
Contact: Diane Perlo
1 Park Ave, Old Greenwich, CT 06870-9990; 203-637-3616 or 800-243-4504
FREE 1989 catalog featuring on audiocassettes unabridged literature by the most popular and gifted writers for children through adult.

Live Oak Media
PO Box 34, Ancramdale, NY 12503; 518-329-6300
Publishers of audiovisual adaptations of children's books (audiocassettes, videocassettes, sound filmstrips, and book/cassette programs).

Lock Corp of America
Contact: Ronald L. Levin
6301 W Mill Rd, Milwaukee, WI 53218; 414-353-3600
Locker, sliding door, push-style, cabinet, drawer, showcase, plunger, cam and panel LOCKS; card-operated LOCKS; GSA/USPS approved LOCKS.

Ludlow Composites Corp
Contact: Richard W Zilles, Customer Serv Mgr
2100 Commerce Dr, Fremont, OH 43420; 419-332-5531; 800-628-5463 or in OH 800-223-2599; FAX 419-332-5531, 800-628-5463
Carpet top and antifatigue floor mats and matting.

Lundia
Contact: Janice Briggs, Adv & Sales Promotion
600 Capitol Way, Jacksonville, IL 62650; 217-243-8585 or 800-258-6342; FAX 800-262-8770
Manufacturer of space-saving mobile and stationary shelving systems. Double filing and storage space capacity. Nationwide sales and installation with full two-year warranty.

★McNaughton Book Services *(p 3)*
(Div of Brodart, Co)
500 Arch St, Williamsport, PA 17705; 717-326-2461 or 800-233-8467
Book leasing, rental services for adult and young adult books, large print books, books-by-mail service, and paperback service.

★Magafile Co, The *(p 149)*
Contact: Donna Detienne
606 S Maple, PO Box 66, Vandalia, MO 63382; 314-594-3713
A neat, *econ* attractive, and sturdy magazine filing system with a size for every need. Free Measure-Graph chart available.

Magazine Article Summaries
(Div of EBSCO Subscription Services)
Contact: Tim Collins
PO Box 325, Topsfield, MA 01983; 617-887-6667 or 800-221-1826
Timely and affordable abstracting and indexing service to over 200 general magazines, available in print, online, or CD-ROM.

Malekos Mfg Co, Inc
PO Box 956, Paradise, CA 95967; 916-872-0940
"Tele-Holder" supports the receiver so both hands are free for other tasks—typing, note

taking, etc. Special price for librarians—$5 each. Write for free brochure.

Marcive, Inc
Contact: Rose Marie McElfresh
PO Box 47508, San Antonio, TX 78265; 800-531-7678 or 512-646-6161
Marcive/PAC (library catalog on CD-ROM), GPO CAT/PAC (GPO database on CD-ROM), GPO depository cataloging, catalog cards, authorities processing, retrospective conversions.

Marshall Cavendish Corp
Contact: Richard Farley
147 W Merrick Rd, Freeport, NY 11520; 516-546-4200
Illustrated reference books, literary reference books, illustrated children's books.

Marshmedia
Contact: Joan K Marsh, Pres
PO Box 8082, Shawnee Mission, KS 66208; 806-523-1059 or 800-821-3303
Since 1969, producers and distributors of award-winning filmstrips, videos, and computer disks for K-12. Call or write for free catalogs.

Mat Makers Corp
Contact: Robert M Freedman
44 Norfolk Ave, Easton, MA 02375; 508-238-6999
Static dissipative clear chair mats and table top pads provide permanent protection against static for the life of the mat.

Meckler Corp
11 Ferry Lane W, Westport, CT 06880; 203-226-6967
Leading publisher of books, journals, software, and videos on library applications. Trade titles feature baseball topics and Swedish culture.

★**Meridian Data, Inc** *(p 110)*
Contact: Mike Rynas
4450 Capitola Rd, Suite 101, Capitola, CA 95010; 408-476-5858; FAX 408-476-8908; telex 988330
CD Net: Network CD ROM drives allow single or multiple, simultaneous access to CD-ROMs on a local area network.

Merit Audio Visual
Contact: Doris Hirsch
PO Box 392, New York, NY 10024; 212-787-4766
Producer of computer software, videocassettes, filmstrips for the educational market. Subject areas include language arts, mathematics, social studies, music.

Message Movers
Contact: P C Dobill
PO Box 5251, Oakbrook, IL 60522; 312-323-8736
Periodical labels, printed to each library's unique periodical collection. Professional, cost effective, each label shows title and issue date.

★**Metacom, Inc** *(p 139, 148)*
1401-B W River Rd N, Minneapolis, MN 55411; 800-328-0108
Audio- and videocassettes that are educational and entertaining for all ages. Free catalog.

Micobra Corp, The
176 King St, PO Box 1187, Hanover, MA 02339; 617-871-2610; FAX 617-982-1024
Leading suppliers of microfiche duplicating equipment for low- to medium-volume needs as well as the BERKSHIRE SERIES of oak microfilm cabinets.

Micro Data Base Systems (mdbs), Inc
Contact: Dyane Roesel, Mktg Coord
PO Box 248, 2 Executive Dr, Lafayette, IN 47902; 800-344-5832 or 317-463-2581; FAX 317-448-6428; telex 5106017487 (MDBS LAF UQ)
mdbs publishes database management, integrated business and expert system development software for business, government, and educational organizations. Discounts available.

MicroImage Video Systems
(Div of World Video Sales Co, Inc)
Contact: Jack Toylor
PO Box 331, Boyertown, PA 19512; 215-754-6800
Manufacturer of color and b&w video microscopy systems, color video monitors, audio program monitors, monitor amplifiers, and video test equipment.

★**Minolta Corp** *(p 8, 9)*
Micrographics Div
101 Williams Dr, Ramsey, NJ 07446; 800-821-7700, x327
Coin-operated equipment; computer-assisted retrieval; microfilm reader-printers; planetary microfilm camera; ultrafiche reader-printers.

Modern Book Co, The
(Div of Capital Resources, Inc)
Contact: Myra B Drew
5155 Kieley Place, Cincinnati, OH 45217; 513-641-4300
FREE library kits. Discount prices. Mail order hardcover books for grades K-8. Over 800 titles representing selections from 20+ publishers.

★**Modulex Inc** *(p 147)*
Contact: Jeffrey J Shortess
2920 Wolff St, Racine, WI 53402; 414-632-5330 or 800-632-4321; FAX 414-632-1851
MODULEX offers library signage for identification and direction. Signs with interchangeable text for directories, nameplates, and bookstacks.

★**Mohawk Midland Mfg** *(p 110, 146)*
Contact: Bill Drucker
7733 Gross Point Rd, PO Box 226, Skokie, IL 60067-0226; 800-533-5211; in IL 312-677-0333
Carrels: double-level & single-level, acoustical, computer, & wheelchair; furniture; furniture planning & computer 3D layout; lounge seating; study tables.

Molex Microfilm Products, Inc
Contact: C Pavlakis
PO Box 175 Inwood Sta, New York, NY 10040; 212-569-5340,5393; FAX 212-601-7226; telex 3792350-MOLEX///
Supplier of proprietary and other products used in micrographics: microfiche envelopes, title strips, fiche mastering system, film gloves, storage items.

Monaco
Contact: Audrey Harper
Box 765, Wilton, CT 06897
HangUp Storage Systems for the economical and efficient circulation and storage of audiovisual materials and software.

Mook & Blanchard
Contact: Jerry J Mook
PO Box 1295, La Puente, CA 91749; in CA 818-968-6424 or 800-532-3493
K-8 library book wholesaler with unique selective prebinding service. Cataloging/processing available optional micro entry for automated libraries.

★**Moroney Bookmobiles** ***(p 106, 141)***
(Div of Moroney Body Works, Inc)
Contact: Thomas Moroney
164 Southwest Cutoff, Worcester, MA 01604; 508-792-2878
Manufacturers of Monolite Bookmobiles, gasoline or diesel powered, for every type of library service.

Motorola, Inc
(Communications Sector)
Contact: Nadine M. Sudnick
1301 E Algonquin Rd, Schaumburg, IL 60196; 312-397-1000
Door closers, fire alarms, energy management, communications equipment, water detectors and alarms.

Multigraphics
(AM International Inc)
1800 W Central Rd, Mt Prospect, IL 60056-2983; 312-398-1900
Multigraphics offers quality reprographic and binding equipment plus supplies with nationwide service support for ours and competitive-make products.

Multiverse Communications
Contact: Arnold Bob, Sales Mgr
148 W 77th St, New York, NY 10024; 212-580-0541; demo 212-769-4792
Offers THE ANSWERS MACHINE that answers common patron questions via touch-tone telephones, also does voice mail, automated receptionist, Audiotext.

Nadex Industries, Inc
Contact: Rose Emerson
145 Ontario St, Buffalo, NY 14207; 716-873-6600
NADEX coin counter and packager. Quick wrap—reusable plastic coin packs.

National Institute for Rehabilitation Engineering, The
Contact: Donald Selwyn
PO Box T, Hewitt, NJ 07421; 201-853-6585
The NIRE is a nonprofit organization that, in addition to dispensing products, provides a variety of customized products and services.

Neumade Products Corp
Contact: Ron Jones
200 Connecticut Ave, Norwalk, CT 06856; 203-866-7600
Manufacturer of AV accessories particularly all types of media storage: film editing equipment, microfilm inspection stations, splicers, and film cleaners.

NewsBank Inc
Contact: Peter C Garrett, VP Mktg
58 Pine St, New Canaan, CT 06840; 203-966-1100 or 800-243-7694
A comprehensive current affairs resource. Index printed and CD-ROM updated monthly. Full-text articles from newspapers in over 450 cities on microfiche.

★**NewsNet, Inc** ***(p 32)***
945 Haverford Rd, Bryn Mawr, PA 19010; 215-527-8030
Online newsletters, wire service news.

Nichols Advanced Technologies Inc
Contact: Bruce Butler, Pres or Jim Van Thournout, VP Develop
1100, 10130 103rd St, Edmonton, Alberta, Canada T5J 3N9; 403-424-0091; FAX 403-420-1230
MOLLI—the keyword-searchable online catalog and circulation system for school and other libraries. Single and multiuser versions available.

Nieman Design Systems, Inc
PO Box 888, Mt Prospect, IL 60056; 312-259-7979; FAX 312-780-6028
Audio display shelving, book display shelving, custom displays, video display shelving, video storage cabinets.

Norton, Jeffrey, Pubs/Audio-Forum
Contact: Charlotte Currier
On-the-Green, Guilford, CT 06437; 203-453-9794
130 self-instructional language courses in 47 languages for adults and children; designed to teach conversational skills by leading language authorities.

★**NSC Inc** ***(p 148)***
Contact: Larry Nies
207 S Main St, Brillion, WI 54110; 414-756-5305
BOOKMARC™ is a software product for library automation. Including circulation, MARC record processing, online catalog, serials, and acquisitions.

Nystrom
(Div of Herff Jones)
Contact: Leo A Halbmaier, Mktg Servs
3333 Elston Ave, Chicago, IL 60618; 800-621-8086 or 312-463-1144
K-12 educational materials in social studies, science and health, language arts: maps, globes, models, Eye Gate Media filmstrips.

★**OCLC** ***(p 5)***
6565 Frantz Rd, Dublin, OH 43017-0702; 800-848-5878 x6243; in OH 800-848-

8286 x6243; in Canada 800-533-8201
Online systems, retrieval, bibliographic service.

Ohio Bus Sales, Inc
1324 Tuscarawas St W, PO Box 6210, Canton, OH 44706; 800-822-2083 or in OH 800-362-9592; FAX 216-453-0611
Highly innovative manufacturer of quality bookmobiles. All types and sizes from 1000-6000 volumes. Custom cabinetry, special equipment.

Omni Tech Corp
Contact: Terry Anderson
21850 Watertown Rd, Waukesha, WI 53186; 414-784-4112
We manufacture computer security cabinets for Apple IIGS, Apple IIe, Macintosh, IBM AT/XT and compatibles—of steel with multiple key options.

★**Omnifax-Telautograph Corp** *(p 148)*
Contact: Mktg Servs
8700 Bellanca Ave, Los Angeles, CA 90045; 800-221-8330 x115 or 213-641-3690; FAX 213-670-8578
Full line of facsimile from portable to store/forward units. Nationwide sales/service. Lease, lease/purchase, and purchase plans. Range of features and prices.

OPL Resources, Ltd
Contact: Guy St Clair
PO Box 948, Murray Hill Sta, New York, NY 10156; 212-515-5299
Consulting firm dedicated to one-person/one-professional libraries. Publishes newsletter, organizes seminars, and advises management about library problems.

★**Pathway Book Service** *(p 147)*
Contact: Wendell Johnson
Lower Village, Gilsum, NH 03448; 800-345-6665 or in NH 603-357-0236
General book jobber maintaining a 98% fulfillment rate that includes the lesser known publishers and other book sources. Catalog-ing available.

Pendragon House Ltd
Contact: John Badger, Pres
Suite 425, 107 Delaware Ave, Buffalo, NY 14202-2872; 416-822-9125
We import all British books. Discount 20%. No returns on imports. Specialize in HMSO books.

★**Perma-Bound Books** *(p 115)*
(Hertzberg-New Method)
Contact: Mike Puma
E Vandalia Rd, Jacksonville, IL 62650; 800-637-6581; FAX 217-243-7505
12,000+ titles; prebound paperbacks and trade; ages 4-adult; unconditional guarantee; online ordering; customized cataloging/barcoding; quantity discounts; special orders available.

Permaseal Corp
Contact: Easen Chapman, Pres
2124 Jody Rd, Florence, SC 29501; 800-845-4369
We specialize in bindery work (laminating, tabbing, etc) and sell laminating equipment and supplies.

Phelps Time Recording Lock Corp
Contact: Mike McGreen, Gen Mgr
53 Park Pl, New York, NY 10007-2497; 212-732-3791
Recording lock that records what time door is open—how long it is open—what time it is closed and any reentrys.

Pied Piper Productions
1645 Monrovia Ave, Costa Mesa, CA 92627; 714-646-4486 or 800-247-8308
Filmstrip and videos (language arts)—motivates INVOLVEMENT in reading and writing. Lessons are modules that fit into learning programs. Catalog.

Pine Cone, The
Contact: Joseph J Blake
PO Box 1378, Gilroy, CA 95021-1378; 408-842-7597
MINI-VAC—portable vacuum cleaner, absorbs minute debris, battery operated (not included), 5″ long, 6 oz., $19.95 plus $2.50 shipping.

Plastic Window Products Co
(Educational Materials Div)
Contact: Jay Smith
3104 Skokie Valley Rd, Highland Park, IL 60035; 312-432-6575
Manufacture and sell BOOK GUARD®—the permanent redi-cut cold lamination that repairs, restores, and extends the life of paperbound books and periodicals from 4″ x 7″ to 8½″ x 11½″.

Playful Puppets Inc
Contact: Patsy M Fann
9002 Stoneleigh Ct, Fairfax, VA 22031; 703-280-5070
PUPPETS THAT SWALLOW actually swallow objects such as "hairy bugs" and are excellent for storytelling, lending, and children's room.

Portage Newspaper & Supply Co
Contact: Robert Belter, Pres
1868 Akron Peninsula Rd, PO Box 5500, Akron, OH 44313; 216-929-4454 or 800-321-2183
Manufacturer and distributor of specialty newspaper products and manufacturer of prepress graphic arts equipment.

Porta-Structures Industries, Inc
Contact: Fred E Goodman, Pres
PO Box 30193, Bethesda, MD 20815; 301-951-0500
Ready-to-operate preengineered branches, kiosks, shopping mall boutiques, wood library furniture sold at discount. Quick delivery.

Potentials Unlimited, Inc
Contact: Stephanie L Konicov, VP
4606 44th St SE, PO Box 891, Grand Rapids, MI 49518; 616-949-7894 or 800-221-6121
Leading manufacturer of self-hypnosis/subliminal persuasion cassette tapes; tools to

help you mange your life; wholesale $5.50, retail $9.98.

Preston, J A, Corp
(Div of Bissell Healthcare)
60 Page Rd, Clifton, NJ 07012; 201-777-2700 or 800-631-7277; FAX 201-777-4071; telex 475-4139
Equipment for rehabilitation and special education. A free catalog is available upon request. We carry over 3000 products.

Professional Media Service Corp
13620 S Crenshaw Blvd, Gardena, CA 90249
Library jobbers of sound recordings and videocassettes, providing optional *AACR2* cataloging service: kits, tagged edit sheets, MARC-formatted machine-readable records on tape.

Pryor Marking Products
D J Wiiken, Pres
1006 S Michigan Ave, Chicago, IL 60605; 312-786-1143
Blackboards & accessories; bulletin boards: cork, electronic, magnetic, plastic; daters: automatic, band, numbering stamps, self-inking; exhibit cases; marking kits; numbering machines.

Publishers Book Bindery, Inc
Contact: B L Teel
21 East St, Winchester, MA 01890; 617-729-8000
Leather bindings; fine art reproductions for student use.

★**Putnam Rolling Ladder Co, Inc** ***(p 146)***
Contact: Gregg Peters Monsees
32 Howard St, New York, NY 10013; 212-226-5147
Custom-made oak rolling ladders, stools, and library carts. Other woods available. Brass-plated, chrome-plated, or black accessories.

★**R & D Products, Inc** ***(p 100)***
Contact: Dorothy Hansen
PO Box 2238, Rohnert Park, CA 94927-2238; 707-584-3484 or 800-523-6687
The curve of the PERKY display pocket prevents paper flop-over. Modular wall pockets, 12-pocket table or 28-pocket floor stands.

Radmar, Inc
Contact: Richard M Davidson, Pres
1263-B Rand Rd, Des Plaines, IL 60016; 312-298-7980
Manufacturers of audiovisual products: video/film/audio media duplication services; Carlos Campesino and Hanna-Barbera educational filmstrips.

★**Rainbow Educational Video** ***(p 149)***
Customer Service Dept, 170 Keyland Ct, Bohemia, NY 11716; 800-331-4047 or 516-589-6643
Producer of building-level, full-motion, educational videocassettes. Catalog available upon request.

Rand McNally & Co
Educational Publishing Div
PO Box 7600, Chicago, IL 60680; 800-323-1887 or in IL 312-673-9100; telex 210041 RMCN UR
The standard of excellence for over 132 years, bringing you the most extensive selection of educational maps, globes, and atlases.

Readex Microprint Corp
(Div of NewsBank)
58 Pine St, New Canaan, CT 06840; 203-966-5906
Readex is a microform publisher offering to libraries government document and historical collections (Evans, Shaw, drama) on microforms.

Realist
Contact: Julie Blanke
16288 Megal Dr, Menomonee Falls, WI 53051; 414-251-8100 or 800-732-5478
Realist manufactures a complete line of desktop and portable micrographic readers and accessories.

Redpath Art Service
Contact: James R Brown
304 Old Mountain Rd, Port Jervis, NY 12771; 914-856-5453
Framed/unframed art reproductions. Get on our special list for framed pictures at greatly discounted prices. Refurbishing help. Art browsers.

Renfro, Nancy, Studios
Contact: Lynn Irving
1117 W 9th St, Austin, TX 78703; 512-472-2140
Incredible variety of mitt-show-host puppets. Stages. Books: puppetry, storytelling, creative drama. Shadow puppet kits. Write for free catalog.

Replogle Globes, Inc
Contact: Robert W Jones, VP Mktg
2801 S 25th Ave, Broadview, IL 60153-4589; 312-343-0900; FAX 312-343-0923
World's largest manufacturer of geographic globes.

Republic Storage Systems Co, Inc
Contact: J M Keller, Mgr, Mktg Admin
1038 Belden Ave NE, Canton, OH 44705; 216-438-5800 or 800-321-0216
Industry leader in storage products—lockers, shelving, storage rack, etc. 100-year history. Employee owned. Made in America.

Research Publications
Contact: Helen Greenway, VP Mktg
12 Lunar Dr, Drawer AB, Woodbridge, CT 06525; 203-397-2600 or 800 REACH-RP
Micropublisher of rare books and manuscripts, journals, newspapers, patents, and reference books and indexes. International supplier with offices in Reading, England.

Right On Programs
Contact: Don Feinstein
755 New York Ave, Suite 210, Huntington, NY 11743; 516-424-7777
Easy to use, easy to learn. No manual required computer software for library man-

agement tasks . . . librarian friendly computer software!

Ringgold Management Systems, Inc
Contact: Ralph M Shoffner, Pres
PO Box 368, Beaverton, OR 97075-0368; 503-645-3502
Consulting and development to libraries since 1974. Product line: the Nonesuch Acquisitions System and the Nonesuch Circulation Control System.

Riverside Library Store
PO Box 3916, Rock Island, IL 61204; 309-787-7717
Summer reading awards, book sale promotions, buttons, puppets, imprinted pencils, magnets, masks, children's globes, Friends promotions, fundraising materials. Color brochure.

Roberts Book Mark Co
Contact: Norman Roberts
3038 N Federal Hwy, Ft Lauderdale, FL 33306; 305-563-6155
Holds any size book or magazine at convenient reading angle. Folds flat. Library discount 50% with order of 12 units.

Russ Bassett
Contact: Nate Babcock, VP Sales
8189 Byron Rd, Whittier, CA 90606; 800-624-4728 or in CA 213-945-2445; FAX 213-698-8972
Cabinets for high-density filing of microfilm, microfiche, and aperture cards. Visu-Flex tray-panel systems for microfiche and aperture cards.

S & G Enterprises, Inc
5626 N 91st St, Milwaukee, WI 53225; 800-233-3721
Manufacturers of the Lift-a-File® unique file cabinet dolly truck. Also, the Descolator® desk dolly. Terms are net 30 days.

San Val, Inc
Contact: Laura Davison
4127 Forest Park, St Louis, MO 63108; 314-652-8495 or 800-325-4465
Library Binding Institute member offering prebinding of paperbacks, oversewn bindings for books & periodicals, rebinding of textbooks. Service nationwide!

Science Pr
Contact: Alfred W Baker
PO Box 378
Sterling, VA 22170; 703-450-4477
Subject heading, catalog guide cards, printing service.

Scott Plastics Co
Contact: Scott Spear, Designer
PO Box 1047, Tallevast, FL 34270
Full line of signage, letters, and systems. We offer letters in vinyl, plastic, foam, and gypsum. Available in many different finishes.

Seal Products Inc
Contact: Laurene Guerrera
550 Spring St, Naugatuck, CT 06770; 203-729-5201
Manufacturer of mounting and laminating equipment and supplies including heat-activated and pressure-sensitive systems. Sold through library dealers.

Select Audio Visual, Inc
Contact: Robert A Menell
902 Broadway, 2d fl, New York, NY 10010; 212-598-9800
Select Audio Visual sells, rents, and repairs all of the major brands of audiovisual and video equipment.

Sentronic International
Contact: E M Trikilis
Box 815, Brunswick, OH 44212; 216-225-3029; FAX 216-225-3009
A broad line of access and theft (article surveillance) detection systems including accessory rail, etc., equipment for turnstiles, etc.

Seton Name Plate Co
PO Box 1331, New Haven, CT 06505; 800-243-6624
Signs, tags, labels for both interior facility and exterior use. Also, barcode and other property identification plates.

Sexton, Mark, Associates
Contact: Mark Sexton, Pres
152 Corlies Ave, Pelham, NY 10803; 914-738-5424
Management and marketing consultants to publishers, with a special interest in the library market.

Sharp Electronics Corp
(Professional Products Div)
Contact: Ron Colgan, Natl Sales Mgr
Sharp Plaza, Mahwah, NJ 07430; 201-529-8731
SHARP markets a full line of "audio/video" products for library use, including audio recorders, VCRs, TV/monitors, cameras, and LCD computer projection panels.

Shelfmark Original Cataloging
Contact: Irwin Feldman
277 Valley View Rd, Ukiah, CA 95482-6845; 707-468-8163
Shelfmark's CATALOGING ON DEMAND service provides quality *AACR2* cataloging for English-language materials in virtually all subject areas.

Sirsi Corp
2904 Westcorp Blvd, Suite 209, Huntsville, AL 35805; 205-536-5881
Sirsi Corporation develops and markets UNIX- and XENIX-based library automation products, turnkey or software-only.

Sitler's Supplies Inc
Contact: Wm C Sitler or John Prochaska
Box 10, 702 E Washington, Washington, IA 52353; 800-426-3938 or in IA 800-272-6459
General Electric–Sylvania–Wiko projector lamps 50% to 60% off.

Society for Visual Education, Inc
Customer Service, 1345 W Diversey Pkwy, Chicago, IL 60614; 312-525-1500
Producer and distributor of educational filmstrips, software, videocassettes, book cas-

settes, and study prints covering all curricula for grades K-12.

★SOLINET *(p 148)*
Contact: Laura Lazar, Prog Coord
Southeastern Library Network, Inc, Plaza Level, 400 Colony Sq, 1201 Peachtree St NE, Atlanta, GA 30361; 404-892-0943
Retrospective conversion and tape processing services. Full-service tape processing. Regional network providing access and support for OCLC products. Nationally recognized preservation program.

★Soper Sound Music Library *(p 148)*
Contact: Dennis Reed, Pres
PO Box 498, Palo Alto, CA 94301; 800-227-9980 or 415-321-4022
Production music for use in background with AV; multi-image slide and film productions. Available on compact disc.

Southsafe Corp
(Fichet-Bauche)
Contact: Randall Carter
1255-A Oakbrook Dr, Norcross, GA 30093; in GA 404-449-3076 or 800-323-4505
One- and two-hour high-security safes designed for computer data protection. Various sizes available to store all types of media.

★Spacesaver Corp *(p 125)*
Contact: James Franck
1450 Janesville Ave, Fort Atkinson, WI 53538; 414-563-6362
Spacesaver mobile storage systems can double your existing book storage capacity or reduce floor space requirements for storage by 50%.

Specialized Service & Supply Co
(Div of Capital Resources, Inc)
Contact: Myra B Drew
5155 Kieley Place, Cincinnati, OH 45217
Complete audiovisual cataloging. Book kits and/or processing, bulk only. Minimum 25 per title. Sears subject headings. Dewey Decimal Classification.

★Standard Change-Makers, Inc *(p 112)*
422 E New York St, Indianapolis, IN 46202; 317-639-3423; FAX 317-684-2134
$1/$5/$10/$20 bill changers and bill-activated card dispensers provide correct change or magnetic card to operate copy machines.

★Stanger Litho Graphics, Inc *(p 149)*
(Library Services Div)
921 Industrial Dr, W Chicago, IL 60185; 312-231-8000
Manufacture and distribute date due cards and pockets for use with CheckPoint® security systems.

Staplex Co, The
777 5th Ave, Brooklyn, NY 11232; 718-768-3333
Manufacturer of a complete line of automatic electric staplers, electric saddle staplers, and high-speed staples.

Stikki-Wax Corp
Contact: Harold Press
3721 Broadway, Chicago, IL 60613; 312-528-8860
E-Z-UP CLIP: Wax-adhesive backed "fingers" make any spot a bulletin board. Won't harm the papers put up. Always removable and remountable.

Story House Corp
Bindery Lane, Charlotteville, NY 12036; 800-847-2105
FREE PREBOUND BOOKS CATALOG. Get the best in prebound books grades K-12. Lower replacement costs. Satisfaction guaranteed.

Swivelier Co Inc
Contact: J Pitaro, Sales Mgr
33 Rte 304, Nanuet, NY 10954-2988; 914-623-3471; FAX 914-623-1861
Adjustable lighting products for stores, showrooms, displays, homes, museums, offices. Low voltage; track lighting; recessed lights; screw-in recesses light extenders.

Talk-a-Phone Co
5013 N Kedzie Ave, Chicago, IL 60625; 312-539-1100; FAX 312-539-1241
A complete line of intercom systems for office, industry, home, apartment house, self-service gas stations, fast food drive thrus, bank drive-ins.

★TEAC *(p 127)*
Contact: Lynn Yeazel
7733 Telegraph Rd, Montebello, CA 90640; 213-726-0303
Manufacturer of recordable laser videodisc products; videocassettes decks; computer data storage peripherals; and audiocassette/open reel decks, and CD players.

Teacher Support Software
PO Box 7130, Gainesville, FL 32605; 800-228-2871 or in FL 904-371-3802
Teacher Support Software is your reading-writing connection featuring basal correlation, semantic mapping, and the language experience approach.

Tech-Cessories Inc
Contact: Jeffrey Gesten
990 E Rogers Circle, Unit 2, Boca Raton, FL 33487; 407-994-9060
Full line of computer accessories including dust covers, printer stands, templates, monitor stands, diskette storage, tool kits, and keyboard shields.

Teledyne Big Beam
Contact: Nick Shah, Dir of Mktg & Engrg
290 E Prairie St, PO Box 518, Crystal Lake, IL 60014; 815-459-6100; FAX 815-459-6126; telex 72-2450
Manufacturer of battery-operated emergency and portable lighting equipment.

Telesensory Systems, Inc (TSI)
Contact: Anne Leahy, Mktg Communications Mgr
455 N Bernardo Ave, Mountain View, CA 94039-7455; 415-960-0920 or 800-227-8418; telex 278838 TSI UR
TSI is a company devoted exclusively to de-

signing, manufacturing, and marketing high-tech equipment for blind and low-vision people in over 70 countries.

Telkee Inc
(Subs of Sunroc Corp)
Rt 452, Glen Riddle, PA 19037; 215-459-1100; FAX 215-459-1063
World's oldest and largest manufacturer of key cabinets, key tag and key control systems that secure and organize from 22 to 2240 individual keys.

Telmark Technologies Corp
12203 SW 132nd Ct, Miami, FL 33186; 305-235-0770
SMART LOCK, library computer and equipment locking system. In five minutes you can make your instruments and equipment THEFT PROOF.

Tepromark International, Inc
Contact: Fred Sheinbaum, Pres
206 Mosher Ave, Woodmere, NY 11598; 516-569-4533 or 800-645-2622; telex 96-7799
Producers of wall guards, corner guards, handrails, and floor mats.

Terra Transit Div
(Turtle Top, Inc)
67819 S R 15, New Paris, IN 46553
Terra Transit manufactures bookmobiles to meet individual specifications. Welded-steel cage construction provides sturdy bodies with a bus-style stepwell.

Texwood Furniture Corp
Contact: Robert A Shoop
PO Box 6280, Austin, TX 78762; 512-385-3323
A complete line of wood library furniture.

★**Thomas Built Buses, Inc** *(p 107)*
Contact: Ken McDowell, Special Prods Sales Mgr
1408 Courtesy Rd, High Point, NC 27261
Every Thomas Built Bookmobile benefits from over 70 years of bus-building experience, with more than 30 years manufacturing bookmobiles to your demanding specifications.

3M Commercial Office Supply Div
Contact: Lynn Wilson
Bldg 223-3S-03, 3M Center, St Paul, MN 55144-1000; 612-736-0852; FAX 612-736-8261
General, special-purpose pressure-sensitive Scotch™ brand tapes, visual presentation products; Post-it™ brand note products; 3M brand magnetic media supplies, accessories.

3M Electronic Article Surveillance Systems
Contact: Joan Olseen
Bldg 223-3N-01, 3M Center, St Paul, MN 55144-1000; 612-736-1163
Library security systems to prevent the unauthorized removal of print and nonprint materials from the library.

Troll Associates
Contact: Jane Ireland, Customer Serv Mgr
100 Corporate Dr, Mahwah, NJ 07430; 800-526-5289
Troll Associates publishes children's books, read-along cassette tapes, book videos, library skills materials for ages 7-12, and microcomputer software.

Tufnut Works, The
Contact: Roland C Zinn
1414 4th St, Santa Fe, NM 87501; 800-227-0949 or in NM 505-983-2522
Supplies inexpensive theft protection systems for computers, audiovisual machines, and office equipment—$10 to $17 per secured machine.

Tuohy
Customer Service, 42 St Albans Pl, Chatfield, MN 55923; 507-867-4280
Tuohy offers a full line of library and general office furniture including desks, tables, and seating.

Turner Subscriptions/A Faxon Co
Contact: Stephen Kochoff
116 E 16th St, New York, NY 10003; 212-254-4454 or 800-847-4201
Efficient, economical periodical subscription service working to streamline college, school, public, corporate, government, and specialized libraries. Catalogs available upon request.

TV Guide Microfilm Library
Contact: Cathy Johnson
Radnor, PA 19088; 215-293-8947
TV Guide Microfilm, 1953–1986
TV Guide Indexes, 1953–1987

UMI (University Microfilms Inc)
(A Bell & Howell Information Co)
Contact: Carol Bamford
300 N Zeeb Rd, Ann Arbor, MI 48106; 313-761-4700
Periodicals, newspapers, dissertations, collections in microform; CD-ROM and online abstract and index databases; newspaper indexes; microform and CD-ROM equipment.

UNISYS Corp
Contact: Donna Gurdak
PO Box 500, B120, Blue Bell, PA 19428; 215-542-4061
Provides single source library automation software and accompanying hardware for all types/size libraries. Includes OPAC, circulation, serials, and acquisitions.

Universal Library Systems
Contact: AnaBela Taborda
2209-B Elm St, Bellingham, WA 98225; 206-733-1732 or 604-926-7421
ULISYS—Provides a total solution to medium and large libraries using digital VAX computers. Services include software support,

training, conversion.

University Music Editions
(Div of High Density Systems, Inc)
Contact: C Pavlakis
PO Box 192, Ft George Sta, New York, NY 10040; 212-569-5393,5340
Collections of music and music literature on microfiche and rollfilm: complete works of master composers, anthologies, journals, indexes, etc.

★Utlas ***(p 145)***
80 Bloor St W, 2d fl, Toronto, Ontario, Canada M5S 2V1; 416-923-0890
Online cataloging; authority and acquisition control; fund accounting; serials control; interlibrary loan; online catalogs; COM, book, and card catalogs.

Vecta
(Div of Steelcase Inc)
Contact: George Kordaris, VP Mktg & Sales
1800 S Great Southwest Pkwy, Grand Prairie, TX 75051; 214-641-2860; telex 214-660-1746
Vecta offers a full line of executive office furniture, including chairs, tables, area seating, and wood casegoods.

★VideoMedia Systems Inc ***(p 144)***
Contact: Peter Bourget or J-F Germain
840 Yonge St, Toronto, Ontario, Canada M4W 2H1; 416-920-5753 or for orders 800-387-0620; FAX 416-922-7806
Videotape wet wash cleaning system. CVTR1000—dual station unit cleans two 90-minute videos in seven minutes. "STOP SHOWING DIRTY MOVIES."

Video Space Products
9100 Jeffrey Dr, Cambridge, OH 43725; 614-432-2985 or 800-544-1585
Video movie box displays and storage of space-saving modular design. Movie Poster Marquee includes electric chase lights and all-gold color finish.

Video Trend, Inc
(A Chas Levy Circ Co)
Contact: Mary Zack
1011 E Touhy Ave, Suite 500, Des Plaines, IL 60618-2806; 313-591-0200 or 800-877-5414
Full-service video supplier, wholesale pricing to libraries with written purchase order, weekly title updates, 13,000 titles, VHS and Beta.

Vocational Media Associates
Sales, Communications Park, Box 1050, Mt Kisco, NY 10549; 914-666-4100 or 800-431-1242
Vocational Media Associates produces videos on automotive, business, computers, construction, food service, safety, and more. Most programs available for preview.

Vogel Peterson Co
Contact: Pat Gorman, Customer Serv Sup
Rt 83 & Madison St, Elmhurst, IL 60126; 312-279-7123 or 800-942-4332; FAX 312-279-9344
Manufacturer of coat racks, wardrobe equipment, movable partitions, and office screens. Purchases must be made through a dealer.

★VTLS ***(p 119, 121, 123)***
1800 Kraft Dr, Blacksburg, VA 24060; 703-953-3605
Automation and systems design; bibliographic service systems; cataloging services; circulation control systems; computers; data processing; library network service systems; retrieval systems design.

Vulcan Binder & Cover
(Div of EBSCO Inds)
PO Box 29, Vincent, AL 35178; 800-633-4526 or 205-672-2241; FAX 205-672-7159
Manufacturer of loose-leaf binders, index tabs, single-copy magazine binders, racks.

VU/TEXT Information Services, Inc
Contact: M Courtenay Willcox, Sales & Mktg Sup
325 Chestnut St, Suite 1300, Philadelphia, PA 19106; 215-574-4400 or 800-323-2940
An online database providing access to 39 full-text, regional newspapers, news and current event information, business and financial data.

★Walker Systems, Inc ***(p 148)***
Contact: W Jamar Jr
250 S Lake Ave, Duluth, MN 55802; 218-722-5945
Display and exhibit panel standards, bases, junctions; picture hanging rods, rails, hooks, holders, clips for paintings, posters, prints.

Wallaceburg Bookbinding & Mfg Ltd
95 Arnold St, PO Box 104, Wallaceburg, Ontario, Canada N8A 4L5; 519-627-3552
LBI certified library binder providing Class "A" and storage binding for books and periodicals. Computer "Binding—Preparation" software for libraries provided.

Warner Home Video Inc
(Subs of Warner Bros, Inc, a Warner Communications Co)
Contact: Dave Mount, VP/Sales
4000 Warner Blvd, Burbank, CA 91522; 818-954-6000; FAX 818-954-6540; telex 4720680WHV
Bringing to the prerecorded home video marketplace motion picture, TV products of Warner Bros; children's, educational, music, special interest products of other producers.

Warrentruss Co
Contact: Ed Matukonis
Box 74, Luzerne, PA 18709; 717-287-4375
Greeting card/round pocket knife: an excellent fundraising item.

Westport Media, Inc
Contact: Fred Hertz
155 Post Rd E, Westport, CT 06880; 203-226-3525
Exclusive distributor of The American Heritage Media Collection (videocassettes,

sound filmstrips, audio programs, sound/slides, etc.) for grades intermediate andup.

Wheelit, Inc
Contact: John Skilliter
PO Box 7350, 440 Arco Dr, Toledo, OH 43615; 419-531-4900 or 800-523-7508
Manufacturer of folding and nonfolding audiovisual and video carts, computer stands, and general duty transporting carts. Sells through dealers nationwide.

Woods Library Publishing Co
Contact: Margaret Woods
9159 Clifton Park, Evergreen Park, IL 60642; 312-423-5986
Cross-reference cards: 1,160 "See" and "See also" cards for typical school/children's library, plus Manual/List with Dewey numbers.

Worden Co, The
Contact: Laura Bringman
199 E 17th St, PO Box 1227, Holland, MI 49422; 616-392-1848 or 800-678-0199; FAX 616-392-2542; telex 5106013629
The Worden Company specializes in designing, manufacturing, and marketing library and contract furniture: technical furniture, shelving, storage units, reading chairs, upholstered lounge seating.

World in Color
Contact: Patrick & Ann Himmler
39½ Caledonia Ave, PO Box 170, Scottsville, NY 14546; 716-889-1910 or 800-288-1910
Slide and cassette duplication.

★XCP Inc *(p 126)*
Contact: Darrell G. Rademacher
40 Elm St, Dryden, NY 13053-0819; 607-844-9143; FAX 607-844-8031
Access Controls for vending/accountability for use on copiers, CD-ROM Public Access Cataloging, microfilm reader-printers, FAX, laser printers.

Xidex Microimage Display Div
(Xidex Corp)
Contact: Sue Stern
857 W State St, Hartford, WI 53027-1093; 414-673-3920 or 800-558-1703
Manufactures quality micrographic readers, reader/printers, cameras, and duplicators.

Part 6
Directory of Organizations

Directory of Library and Related Organizations

Networks, Consortia, and Other Cooperative Library Organizations

Alabama

Alabama Hospital Association Medical Library Program, c/o Alabama Hospital Association, Box 17059, East Station, Montgomery, 36193. SAN 322-4554. Tel. 205-272-8781. *Dir.* Ann Rhodes.

Gulf Coast Biomedical Library Consortium, c/o US Sports Academy Library, One Academy Dr., Daphne, 36526. SAN 322-2063. Tel. 205-626-3303. *Chmn.* Betty Dance.

Library Management Network, Inc., 915 Monroe St., Box 443, Huntsville, 35804. SAN 322-3906. Tel. 205-532-5963. *Pres.* Betty Warren; *System Coord.* Ann Talley.

Marine Environmental Sciences Consortium, Dauphin Island Sea Lab, Box 369-370, Dauphin Island, 36528. SAN 322-0001. Tel. 205-861-2141. *Libn.* Judy Stout.

Network of Alabama Academic Libraries, c/o Alabama Commission on Higher Education, 1 Court Sq., Ste. 221, Montgomery, 36197-0001. SAN 322-4570. *Dir.* Sue O. Medina.

Alaska

Alaska State Library, Film Services, Anchorage Center, 650 West International Airport Rd., Anchorage, 99518-1393. SAN 300-2411. Tel. 907-561-1132. *Supv.* Mary Jennings.

Arizona

Arizona Resources Consortium, c/o Northland Pioneer College, 1200 E. Hermosa Dr., Box 610, Holbrook, 86025-0610. SAN 329-5176. Tel. 602-524-6111, Ext. 265. FAX: 602-524-2772. *Head Libn.* Allen P. Rothlisberg; *Co-Dir.* Glen Tiller.

Maricopa County Community College District, Library Technical Services, 2325 E. McDowell Rd., Phoenix, 85006. SAN 322-0060. Tel. 602-275-3301, 275-0474, 275-3588. *Dir.* Shirley A. Lowman; *Bibliog. Coord.* Kathy A. Lynch; *Acq. Coord.* Jim A. Nader.

Arkansas

Arkansas-Central Area Health Education Center Consortium (AHEC), University of Arkansas for Medical Sciences, Mail Slot 599, 4301 W. Markham, Little Rock, 72205. SAN 329-3734. Tel. 502-661-5260. *Dir.* Grace Anderson.

Independent College Fund of Arkansas, Suite 610, Twin City Bank Bldg., 1 Riverfront Pl., North Little Rock, 72114. SAN 322-0079. Tel. 501-378-0843. *Pres.* Ben M. Elrod.

Northeast Arkansas Hospital Library Consortium, 223 E. Jackson, Jonesboro, 72401. SAN 329-529X. Tel. 501-972-1290. *Dir.* Peggy Smith.

South Arkansas Film Coop, Ash & E. Third, Malvern, 72104. SAN 321-5938. Tel. 501-332-5442. *Coord.* Mary Ann Griggs; *Project Dir.* Mary Cheatham.

California

Academic Business Librarians Exchange (ABLE), c/o University Library, San Diego

State University, San Diego, 92182-0511. SAN 322-4767. Tel. 619-265-6743. *Coord.* Michael J. Perkins.

Area Wide Library Network (AWLNET), 2420 Mariposa St., Fresno, 93721. SAN 322-0087. Tel. 209-488-3229. *Dir. Info. Serv.* Sharon Vandercook.

Bay Area Reference Center (BARC), San Francisco Public Library, Civic Ctr., San Francisco, 94102. SAN 322-0095. Tel. 415-558-2941. *Dir.* Fauneil McInnis.

Central Association of Libraries (CAL), 605 N. El Dorado, Stockton, 95202. SAN 322-0125. Tel. 209-944-8649. *Pres.* Larry Steuben; *Dir.* Janet Kase.

Coastal Health Library Information Consortium (CHLIC), c/o Betty Kroeze Student Health Services, California Polytechnic State University, San Luis Obispo, 93407. SAN 329-5427. Tel. 805-756-1211. *Chmn. of the Bd.* Marsha O'Neil.

Cooperating Libraries in Claremont (CLIC), c/o Honnold Library, 800 Dartmouth Ave., Claremont Colleges, Claremont, 91711. SAN 322-3949. Tel. 714-621-8045. *Dir.* Patrick Barkey.

Cooperative Library Agency for Systems & Services (CLASS), Suite 101, 1415 Koll Circle, San Jose, 95112-4698. SAN 322-0117. Tel. 408-289-1756. *Dir.* Ronald Miller; *Chmn.* Thomas E. Alford.

DIALOG Information Services, Inc., 3460 Hillview Ave., Palo Alto, 94304. SAN 322-0176. Tel. 415-858-3785. WATS: 800-3-DIALOG (800-334-2564). *Pres.* Roger K. Summit.

Forest Service Information (WESTFORNET), 1960 Addison St. (Mail add: WESTFORNET-BERKELEY, Box 245, Berkeley, 94701). SAN 322-032X. Tel. 415-486-3685. FTS 449-3173. *Mgr.* Dennis Galvin.

Health Information to Community Hospitals (HITCH), c/o Norris Medical Library, Univ. of S. Calif., 2003 Zonal Ave., Los Angeles, 90033. SAN 322-4066. Tel. 213-224-7414. TWX 910-321-2434. *Dir.* Nelson J. Gilman.

Information on Demand, Inc., 2020 Milvia, Box 1370, Berkeley, 94701. SAN 322-3809. Tel. 415-644-4500. WATS 800-227-0750. *Pres.* Christine Maxwell.

Inland Empire Academic Libraries Cooperative, c/o California Baptist College, 8432 Magnolia Ave., Riverside, 92504. SAN 322-015X. Tel. 714-689-5771, Ext. 228. *Chmn.* June Reeder.

Los Angeles County Health Sciences Library Consortium, c/o Rancho Los Amigos Medical Center, Health Sciences Library, 7601 E. Imperial Hwy., Downey, 90242. SAN 322-4317. Tel. 213-940-7696. *Coord.* Evelyn Marks.

Medical Library Consortium of Santa Clara Valley, Milton J. Chatton Medical Library, 751 S. Bascom Ave., San Jose, 95128. SAN 322-0184. Tel. 408-299-5650.

Mendocino-Lake Regional Library Consortium, c/o Ukiah Adventist Hospital, 275 Hospital Dr., Box 859, Ukiah, 95482. SAN 322-4090. Tel. 707-462-6631. *Libn.* Anna Chia.

Merced County Health Information Consortium, 301 E. 13 St., Merced, 95240. SAN 329-4072. Tel. 209-385-7058. *Dir.* Betty Madelena.

North Valley Health Science Library Consortium. Butte College Library, 3536 Butte Campus Dr., Oroville, 95965. SAN 329-5273. Tel. 916-895-2447. *Pres.* Donald Johanns.

Northern California & Nevada Medical Library Group, 2140 Shattuck Ave., Berkeley, 94704. SAN 329-4617. Tel. 916-752-6383. *Pres.* Jo Anne Boorkman.

Northern California Telecommunications Consortium, c/o Consumnes River College, 8401 Center Pkwy., Sacramento, 95823. SAN 329-4412. Tel. 916-938-4462. *Exec. Dir.* Robert Wynian.

Pacific Southwest Regional Medical Library Service, c/o Louise Darling Biomedical Library, 10833 Le Conte Ave., Los Angeles, 90024-1798. SAN 322-0192. Tel. 213-825-1200. *Dir.* Alison Bunting; *Assoc. Dir.* Elaine Graham.

Psychology Library Consortium, c/o Virginia Allan Detloff Library, C.G. Jung Institute of San Francisco, 2040 Gough St., San Francisco, 94109. SAN 329-4544. Tel. 415-771-8055. *Dir.* Joan Alpert.

Research Libraries Group, Inc. (RLG), Jordan Quadrangle, Stanford, 94305. SAN 322-0206. Tel. 415-328-0920. *Actg. Pres.* James Michalko.

Sacramento Area Health Sciences Libraries, Paul Guttman Library, 5380 Elvas Ave., Sacramento, 95819. SAN 322-4007. Tel.

916-486-2128. *Head Libn.* Kathleen D. Proffit.

San Bernardino, INYO, Riverside Counties United Library Services, 312 W. 20th St., Suite 2, San Bernardino, 92405. SAN 322-0222. Tel. 714-882-7577. *Dir.* Vaughn L. Simon.

San Francisco Consortium, S-224, 513 Parnassus Ave., San Francisco, 94143. SAN 322-0249. Tel. 415-476-2342. *Exec. Dir.* Malcolm S. M. Watts.

The Smerc Library, San Mateo County Office of Education, 333 Main St., Redwood City, 94063. SAN 322-0265. Tel. 415-363-5470. *Dir.* Karol Thomas; *Ref. Coord.* Mary Moray.

Southern California Answering Network (SCAN), c/o Los Angeles Public Library, 630 W. Fifth St., Los Angeles, 90071-2097. SAN 322-029X. Tel. 213-206-8875. *Dir.* Evelyn Greenwald.

SOUTHNET, c/o South Bay Cooperative Library System, 180 W. San Carlos St., San Jose, 95113. SAN 322-4260. Tel. 408-294-2345. *Systems Dir.* Craig Conover; *Ref. Coord.* Mary Clare Sprott.

Total Interlibrary Exchange (TIE), Black Gold Cooperative Library System, Box 771, Ventura, 93002. SAN 322-0311. Tel. 805-646-4377, Ext. 25. *Pres.* Carol L. Keator.

Colorado

Bibliographical Center for Research, Rocky Mountain Region, Inc., 1777 S. Bellaire, Suite 425, Denver, 80222-4310. SAN 322-0338. Tel. 303-691-0550. *Exec. Dir.* David H. Brunell.

Colorado Alliance of Research Libraries (CARL), 777 Grant, Suite 304, Denver, 80203. SAN 322-3760. Tel. 303-861-5319. *Exec. Dir.* Ward Shaw; *Assoc. Dir.* Patricia Culkin; *Sr. Libns.* Ted Koppel and John Garralda.

Colorado Association of Law Libraries, Box 13363, Denver, 80201. SAN 322-4325. Tel. 303-291-3000. *Pres.* Pamela K. Lewis.

Colorado Library Network (COLONET), c/o Colorado State Library, 201 E. Colfax, Rte. 309, Denver, 80203-1799. SAN 322-3868. Tel. 303-866-6736. *Coord.* Susan Fayad.

Colorado Technical Reference Center, c/o Norlin Library, Campus Box 184, University of Colorado, Boulder, 80309-0184. SAN 322-0362. Tel. 303-492-8774. *Dir.* Jo Chanaud.

Denver Area Health Science Library Consortium, National Jewish Center for Immunology & Respiratory Medicine, Gerald Tucker Memorial Library, 1400 Jackson St., Denver, 80206. SAN 329-5567. Tel. 303-398-1483. *Coord.* Kate Smith.

Irving Library Network, c/o Boulder Public Library Foundation, 1000 Cayon Blvd., Boulder, 80306. SAN 325-321X. Tel. 303-441-3105. *Dir.* Richard Luce.

Peaks and Valleys Library Consortium, c/o Arkansas Valley Regional Library Service System, 205 W. Abriendo Ave., Pueblo, 81004. SAN 328-8684. Tel. 719-542-2156. *Pres.* Jeanne Gardne.

Pueblo Library System Software Users' Group, 100 E. Abriendo Ave., Pueblo, 81004. SAN 322-4635. Tel. 719-543-9607. *Dir.* Charles E. Bates.

Connecticut

Capitol Area Health Consortium, 183 E. Cedar St., Newington, 06111. SAN 322-0370. Tel. 203-666-3304, Ext. 302. *Dir.* Steven Skorz.

Capitol Region Library Council, 599 Matianuck Ave., Windsor, 06095-3567. SAN 322-0389. Tel. 203-549-0404. *Exec. Dir.* Dency Sargent; *Assoc. Dir. for Automated Servs.* William Uricchio.

Connecticut Association of Health Sciences Libraries (CAHSL), Bridgeport Hospital, Reno Memorial Library, 267 Grant St., Bridgeport, 06610. SAN 322-0397. Tel. 203-344-6286. *Pres.* Kathleen Stemmer.

Council of State Library Agencies in the Northeast (COSLINE), Connecticut State Library, 231 Capitol Ave., Hartford, 06106. SAN 322-0451. Tel. 203-566-4301. *Pres.* Richard G. Akeroyd, Jr.

CTW Library Consortium (CTW), Olin Memorial Library, Wesleyan University, Middletown, 06457-6065. SAN 329-4587. Tel. 203-347-9411, Ext. 3143. *Dir.* Alan E. Hagyard; *Applications Programmer.* Elaine Blais; *Systems Programmer.* Bu Yang.

Eastern Connecticut Library Association, 15 Wilson St., Willimantic, 06226-1920. SAN 322-0427. Tel. 203-456-4343. *Pres.* Vivian Shortreed; *Coord.* Marietta Johnson.

Film Cooperative of Connecticut, Inc., 200 N. Main St., Wallingford, 06492. SAN 322-0435. Tel. 203-265-6754. *In-Charge.* Mary Capers.

Hartford Consortium for Higher Education, 260 Girard Ave., Hartford, 06105. SAN 322-0443. Tel. 203-236-1203. *Dir.* Ruth Billyou.

LEAP (Library Exchange Aids Patrons), c/o Adwater Library, Box 258, North Branford, 06471. SAN 322-4082. Tel. 203-488-7205. *Pres.* Robert Hull.

Libraries Online Inc. (LION), 123 Broad St., Middletown, 06457. SAN 322-3922. Tel. 203-347-1704. *Pres.* Joan Schneider; *Exec. Dir.* William F. Edge, Jr.; *Asst. Dir.* Open; *Admin. Asst.* Open.

Northwestern Connecticut Health Science Libraries, c/o Danbury Hospital, 24 Hospital Ave., Danbury, 06810. SAN 329-5257. Tel. 203-797-7279. *Libn.* Michael Schott.

Region One Cooperating Library Service Unit, Inc., 267 Grand St., Waterbury, 06702-1981. SAN 322-046X. Tel. 203-756-6149. *Coord.* Lee Flanagan; *Admin. Asst.* Vanessa Vowe.

Southeastern Connecticut Library Association (SECLA), Avery Point, Groton, 06340-9998. SAN 322-0478. Tel. 203-445-5577. *Dir.* James R. Benn; *Asst. Dir.* Patricia Holloway.

Southern Connecticut Library Council, 60 N. Main St.,Wallingford, 06492-3712. SAN 322-0486. Tel. 203-284-3641. *Dir.* Sharon W. Hupp.

Southwestern Connecticut Library Council, Inc., 925 Broad St., Bridgeport, 06604. SAN 322-0494. Tel. 203-367-6439. *Admin.* Ann Neary.

Delaware

Central Delaware Library Consortium, Dover Public Library, 45 S. State St., Dover, 19901. SAN 329-3696. Tel. 302-736-7030. *In Charge.* Paula Miller.

Delaware Library Consortium, Delaware Law School, Box 7475, Wilmington, 19803. SAN 329-3718. Tel. 302-478-5280, Ext. 354. *Dir.* Jacqui Paul.

Libraries in the New Castle County System (LINCS), Delaware Academy of Medicine, 1925 Loverling, Wilmington, 19806. SAN 329-4889. Tel. 302-656-1629. *Pres.* Joseph Tierney; *Treas.* Gail Gill.

Sussex Help Organization for Resources Exchange (SHORE), Laurel & Railroad Ave., Georgetown, 19947-1442. SAN 322-4333. Tel. 302-422-8896; 302-855-7890, Ext. 13. *Libn.* Carolyn Jarman.

Wilmington Area Biomedical Library Consortium (WABLC), 1925 Lovering Ave., Wilmington, 19806. SAN 322-0508. Tel. 302-656-1629. *Pres.* Gail P. Gill.

District of Columbia

CAPCON Library Network, 1717 Massachusetts Ave., Suite 101, Washington, 20036. SAN 321-5954. Tel. 202-745-7722. *Exec. Dir.* Dennis Reynolds.

Christian College Coalition, Suite 603, 1776 Massachusetts Ave. N.W., Washington, 20036-1996. SAN 322-0524. Tel. 202-293-6177. *Pres.* John R. Dellenback.

Cluster of Independent Theological Schools, 391 Michigan Ave. N.E., Washington, 20017. SAN 322-0532. Tel. 202-529-5244. *Dir.* M. Gongall.

Consortium of Universities of the Washington Metropolitan Area, 1717 Massachusetts Ave. N.W., Suite 101, Washington, 20036-2086. SAN 322-0540. Tel. 202-332-1894. *Coord. of Lib. Progs.* Darrell H. Lemke.

Division of Information & Library Services, Dept. of the Interior, 18 & C St. N.W., Mail Stop 2249, Washington, 20240. SAN 322-080X. Tel. 202-343-5821. *Dir.* Gail Kohlhorst.

ERIC—Educational Resources Information Center (Central ERIC), U.S. Dept. of Education, 555 New Jersey Ave. N.W., Washington, 20208. SAN 322-0567. Tel. 202-357-6919. *Head.* Bob Stonehill.

ERIC Clearinghouses

–ERIC Clearinghouse on Adult, Career, & Vocational Education, Natl. Ctr. for Res. in Vocation Educ., Ohio State Univ., 1960 Kenny Rd., Columbus, OH 43210-1090. SAN 322-0575. Tel. 614-486-3655. WATS 800-848-4815.

–ERIC Clearinghouse on Counseling & Personnel Services, School of Education, Rm.

2108, 610 E. University St., University of Michigan, Ann Arbor, MI 48109-1259. SAN 322-0583. Tel. 313-764-9492.

–ERIC Clearinghouse on Educational Management, University of Oregon, 1787 Agate St., Eugene, OR 97403-5207. SAN 322-0605. Tel. 503-686-5043.

–ERIC Clearinghouse on Elementary and Early Childhood Education (PS), College of Education, 805 W. Pennsylvania Ave., University of Illinois, Urbana, IL 61801-4897. SAN 322-0591. Tel. 217-333-1386.

–ERIC Clearinghouse on Handicapped & Gifted Children (EC), Council for Exceptional Children, 1920 Association Dr., Reston, VA 22091-1589. SAN 322-0613. Tel. 703-620-3660.

–ERIC Clearinghouse on Higher Education (HE), George Washington University, Suite 630, 1 Dupont Circle, Washington, DC 20036-1183. SAN 322-0621. Tel. 202-296-2597.

–ERIC Clearinghouse on Information Resources (IR), Syracuse University, School of Education, Huntington Hall, Rm. 030, Syracuse, NY 13244-2340. SAN 322-063X. Tel. 315-423-3640.

–ERIC Clearinghouse for Junior Colleges (JC), Mathematical Sciences Bldg., Rm. 8118, UCLA, 405 Hilgard Ave., Los Angeles, CA 90024-1564. SAN 322-0648. Tel. 213-825-3931.

–ERIC Clearinghouse on Languages & Linguistics (FL), Center for Applied Linguistics, 1118 22nd St. N.W., Washington, DC 20037-0037. SAN 322-0656. Tel. 202-429-9551.

–ERIC Clearinghouse on Reading & Communication Skills (CS), Indiana University, Smith Research Center, Bloomington, IN 47402. SAN 322-0664. Tel. 812-336-0583.

–ERIC Clearinghouse on Rural Education & Small Schools (RC), Appalachia Educational Laboratory, 1031 Quannier St., Box 1348, Charleston, WV 25325. SAN 322-0672. Tel. 304-347-0400.

–ERIC Clearinghouse for Science, Mathematics & Environmental Education (SE), Ohio State University, Rm. 310, 1200 Chambers Rd., Columbus, OH 43212-1792. SAN 322-0680. Tel. 614-422-6717.

–ERIC Clearinghouse for Social Studies Social Science Education (SO), Indiana University, Social Studies Development Center, 2805 E. 10 St., Bloomington, IN 47405-2373. SAN 322-0699. Tel. 812-335-3838.

–ERIC Clearinghouse on Teacher Education, American Association of Colleges for Teacher Education, Suite 610, 1 Dupont Circle N.W., Washington, DC 20036-2412. SAN 322-0702. Tel. 202-293-2450.

–ERIC Clearinghouse on Tests, Measurement & Evaluation (TM), American Institutes for Research (AIR), Washington Research Center, 1055 Thomas Jefferson St. N.W., Washington, DC 20007. SAN 322-0710. Tel. 202-986-1531.

–ERIC Clearinghouse on Urban Education (UO), Box 40, Teachers College, Columbia Univ., 525 W. 120 St., New York, NY 10027-9998. SAN 322-0729. Tel. 212-678-3433.

FEDLINK (Federal Library & Information Network), c/o Federal Library & Information Center Committee, Library of Congress, Washington, 20540. SAN 322-0761. Tel. 202-287-6454. *Network Dir.* James P. Riley; *Network Coord.* Milton Megee.

Interlibrary Users Association, Urban Institute Library, 2100 M St. N.W., Washington, 20037. SAN 322-1628. Tel. 202-833-7200. *Pres.* Camille Motta.

NASA Library Network ARIN (Aerospace Research Information Network), NASA Headquarters, Code NTT-1, Washington, 20546. SAN 322-0788. Tel. 202-453-2927. *Admin. Libn.* Adelaide DelFrate.

USBE, Inc. (Universal Serials & Book Exchange, Inc.), 3335 V St. N.E., Washington, 20018. SAN 322-0826. Tel. 202-636-8723. *Exec. Dir.* Claude Hooker.

Veterans Administration Library Network (VALNET), VA Library Div. (142D), 810 Vermont Ave. N.W., Washington, 20420. SAN 322-0834. Tel. 202-233-2711. *Chief.* Karen Renninger.

Washington Theological Consortium, 487 Michigan Ave. N.E., Washington, 20017-1585. SAN 322-0842. Tel. 202-832-2675. *Interim Dir.* Mark Heath.

Florida

Florida Computer Catalog of Monographic Holdings (Florida COMCAT), c/o State Library of Florida, R. A. Gray Bldg., Tallahassee, 32399-0250. SAN 322-0850. Tel. 904-487-2651. *State Libn.* Barratt Wilkins.

Florida Library Information Network, c/o Bureau of Interlibrary Cooperation, State Library of Florida, R. A. Gray Bldg., Tallahassee, 32399-0250. SAN 322-0869. Tel. 904-487-2651. *State Libn.* Barratt Wilkins; *Chief ILL Coop.* Freddie Mellichamp.

Library Affairs Committee of the Associated Mid-Florida Colleges, c/o Merl Kelce Library, University of Tampa, Tampa, 33606. SAN 322-0877. Tel. 813-253-6231. *Dir.* Lydia Acosta.

Saint Petersburg Junior College, Michael M. Bennett Library Processing Center, 8580 66th St. N., Pinellas Park, 34665. SAN 337-3185. Tel. 813-341-3693. *Libn. in Charge.* Mary Jane Marden.

Tampa Bay Library Consortium, Inc., University of Tampa, Merl Kelce Library, 401 W. Kennedy Blvd., Tampa, 33606. SAN 322-371X. Tel. 813-253-3333. *Pres.* David Reich; *Project Dir.* Robert A. Martin.

Tampa Bay Medical Library Network (TABAMLN), VA Medical Center Library, Box 527, Bay Pines, 33612. SAN 322-0885. Tel. 813-974-2775. *Chpn.* Mabel A. Costine.

Georgia

Atlanta Health Science Libraries Consortium, Kennestone Hospital, Health Sciences Library, 677 Church St., Marietta, 30060. SAN 322-0893. Tel. 404-426-2809. *Pres.* Alice DeVierno.

Central Georgia Associated Libraries, c/o Wesleyan College, Willet Memorial Library, 4760 Forsyth Rd., Macon, 31297. SAN 322-0907. Tel. 912-477-1110, Ext. 200. *Pres.* Tena Roberts.

Cooperative College Library Center, Inc. (CCLC), Suite 602, 159 Ralph McGill Blvd., Atlanta, 30365. SAN 322-0915. Tel. 404-659-6886. *Dir.* Hillis D. Davis.

East Georgia Library Triangle, c/o Georgia Southern College, Statesboro, 30460. SAN 322-0923. Tel. 912-681-5115. *Chpn.* Julius Ariail.

Emory Medical Television Network, 1440 Cliffton Rd. N.E., Atlanta, 30322. SAN 322-0931. Tel. 404-688-8736. *Dir.* Dan Joiner; *Bus. Mgr.* Julie Slavik.

Georgia Library Information Network (GLIN), c/o Division of Public Library Services, 156 Trinity Ave. S.W., Atlanta, 30303-3692. SAN 322-094X. Tel. 404-656-2461. *Dir.* Open.

Glynn Brunswick Regional Library (Formerly South Georgia Associated Libraries), 208 Gloocester St., Brunswick, 31523-0901. SAN 322-0966. *Secy./Treas.* Jim Darby.

Southeastern Library Network (SOLINET), Plaza Level, 400 Colony Sq., 1201 Peachtree St. N.E., Atlanta, 30361. SAN 322-0974. Tel. 404-892-0943. *Exec. Dir.* Frank P. Grisham.

University Center in Georgia, Inc., 50 Hurt Plaza, Suite 465, Atlanta, 30303-9983. SAN 322-0990. Tel. 404-658-2668. *Exec. Dir.* Charles B. Bedford.

Idaho

Health Information Retrieval Center, Saint Luke's Regional Medical Ctr., 190 E. Bannock St., Boise, 83712. SAN 322-1008. Tel. 208-386-2277. *Dir.* Pamela Spickelmier.

Southeast Idaho Health Information Consortium, Box 2077, Idaho Falls, 83403-2077. SAN 322-4341. Tel. 208-529-6077. *Pres.* Coleen C. Winward.

Illinois

Areawide Hospital Library Consortium of Southwestern Illinois (AHLC), c/o Memorial Hospital, 4509 N. Park Dr., Belleville, 62223. SAN 322-1016. Tel. 618-233-7750. *Contact.* Barbara Grout.

Capital Area Consortium, St. John's Hospital, Health Science Library, 800 E. Carpenter, Springfield, 62769. SAN 322-1024. Tel. 217-544-6464, Ext. 4567. *Coord.* Kitty Wrigley.

Center for Research Libraries, 5721 Cottage Grove Ave. & 6050 S. Kenwood, Chicago, 60637. SAN 322-1032. Tel. 312-955-4545. TWX 910-221-1136. *Pres.* Donald B. Simpson.

Champaign-Urbana Consortium, c/o Mercy Hospital Library, 1400 W. Park, Urbana, 61801. SAN 322-1040. Tel. 217-337-2283. *Coord.* Harriet Williamson.

Chicago Academic Library Council (CALC), c/o Roosevelt University, 430 S. Michigan Ave., Chicago, 60605. SAN 322-1059. Tel. 312-341-3640. *Chpn.* Adrian Jones.

Chicago & South Consortium, c/o Palos Community Hospital, 80 Ave. at McCarthy Rd., Palos Heights, 60463. SAN 322-1067. Tel. 312-361-4500, Ext. 5096. *Coord.* Gail Waldoch.

Conference of Directors of State University Librarians of Illinois (CODSULI), Northeastern Illinois University, Ronald Williams Library, 5500 N. St. Louis Ave., Chicago, 60625. SAN 322-1083. Tel. 312-794-2615. *Chmn.* John D. Gaboury.

Council of West Suburban Colleges, North Central College, Oesterle Library, 320 E. School, Naperville, 60566. SAN 322-1105. Tel. 312-420-3425. *Dir.* Edwin Meachen.

Fox Valley Health Science Library Consortium, 111 N. County Farm Rd., Wheaton, 60187. SAN 329-3831. Tel. 312-682-7372. *Coord.* Jan Aliccia.

Greater Midwest Regional Medical Library Network—Region 3, c/o Library of the Health Sciences, Univ. of Illinois at Chicago, 1750 W. Polk St., Box 7509, Chicago, 60680. SAN 322-1202. Tel. 312-996-2464. *Regional Med. Lib. Dir.* Irwin H. Pizer; *Assoc. Regional Med. Lib. Dir.* Ruby S. May.

Heart of Illinois Library Consortium, c/o The Health Sciences Library, Bromenn Health Care, 807 N. Main St., Bloomington, 61702. SAN 322-1113. Tel. 309-827-4321. *Coord.* Sue Stroyan; *Dir.* Mary Beth Klofas.

Illinois Department of Mental Health & Developmental Disabilities Library Services Network (LISN), Elgin Mental Health Ctr., 750 S. State St., Elgin, 60123. SAN 322-1121. Tel. 312-742-1040, Ext. 2660. *Chpn.* Jennifer Ford.

Illinois Health Libraries Consortium, Meat Indust. Info. Ctr., National Livestock & Meat Board, 444 N. Michigan Ave., Chicago, 60611. SAN 322-113X. Tel. 312-467-5520, Ext. 272. *Dir.* William D. Siarny, Jr.

Illinois Library & Information Network (ILLINET), c/o Illinois State Library, Springfield, 62756. SAN 322-1148. Tel. 217-758-0318. TWX 910-242-0575. *Dir.* Bridget L. Lamont; *Sr. Consult.* Preston Levi.

Illinois Library Computer Systems Organization (ILCSO) (Formerly Statewide LCS), Univ. of Illinois, 126 Administration Bldg., 506 S. Wright St., Urbana, 61801. SAN 322-3736. Tel. 312-996-7853 or 217-333-4895. *Dir.* Bernard G. Sloan; *Assoc. Dir.* Kristine Hammerstrand.

Libras Inc., c/o Elmhurst College, AC Buehler Library, 190 Prospeer Ave., Elmhurst, 60126. SAN 322-1172. Tel. 312-866-1322. *Pres.* Sally Chipman.

Metropolitan Consortium of Chicago, USA, Weiss Hospital, 4646 N. Marine Dr., Chicago, 60640. SAN 322-1180. Tel. 312-681-3000, Ext. 3215. *Coord.* Iris Sachs.

Metropolitan Periodical Service, 60 W. Walton St., Chicago, 60610. SAN 322-1199. Tel. 312-664-9366. *Dir.* Irma M. Lucht.

Northeastern Illinois Library Consortium, DuPont Critical Care, Information Center, 1600 Waukegan Rd., Libertyville, 60085. SAN 329-5052. Tel. 312-473-3000, Ext. 231. *Coord.* Cathy Syverson.

Northern Illinois Learning Resources Cooperative, 91 Sugar Lane, Suite 4, Box 509, Sugar Grove, 60554. SAN 329-5583. Tel. 312-466-4848. *Exec. Dir.* Alice Calabrese.

Sangamon Valley Academic Library Consortium, Schewe Library, Illinois College, Jacksonville, 62650-2299. SAN 322-4406. Tel. 217-245-7126, Ext. 227. *Dir.* Martin H. Gallas.

Shabbona Consortium, c/o Illinois Valley Community Hospital, 925 West St., Peru, 61354. SAN 329-5133. Tel. 815-223-3300, Ext. 529. *Dir.* Linda Ferrari.

Upstate Consortium of Illinois, Rockford Memorial Hospital, School of Nursing Library, 2400 N. Rockton Ave., Rockford, 61103. SAN 329-3793. Tel. 815-968-6861. *Coord.* Diane Fagen.

Indiana

Area Library Services Authority Region 2, 209 Lincolnway E., Mishawaka, 46544-2084. SAN 322-1210. Tel. 219-255-5262. TWX 810-297-2667. *Coord.* Martha Gardin.

Area 3 Library Services Authority (TRI-ALSA), 900 Webster St., Box 2270, Fort Wayne, 46801-2270. SAN 322-1229. Tel. 219-424-6664. *Coord.* Jane Raifsnider; *Ref. Ctr. Dir.* Karen Liston.

Central Indiana Area Library Services Authority, 1100 W. 42 St., Suite 305, Indianapolis, 46208. SAN 322-1237. Tel. 317-926-6561. *Exec. Dir.* Judith Wegener.

Central Indiana Health Science Libraries Consortium, 1701 N. Senate Blvd., Methodist Hospital Library, Box 1367, Indianapolis, 46206. SAN 322-1245. Tel. 317-929-8021. *Pres.* Marie Sparks; *Coord.* Dorothy Jobe.

Collegiate Consortium Western Indiana, c/o Cunningham Memorial Library, Indiana State University, Terre Haute, 47809. SAN 329-4439. Tel. 812-237-3700. *Dean.* Ronald G. Leech.

Eastern Indiana Area Library Services Authority, R.R. 1, Box 76-A, Daleville, 47334-9752. SAN 322-1253. Tel. 317-378-0216. *Admin.* Mary H. Frautschi.

Evansville Area Health Science Library Consortium, 3700 Washington Ave., Evansville, 47750. SAN 322-1261. Tel. 812-479-4151. *Coord.* E. Jane Saltzman.

Four Rivers Area Library Services Authority, Rm. 5, Old Vanderburgh County Court House, Evansville, 47708-1355. SAN 322-127X. Tel. 812-425-1946. *Exec. Dir.* Ida L. McDowell.

Indiana Cooperative Library Services Authority (INCOLSA), 1100 W. 42 St., Indianapolis, 46208-3379. SAN 322-1296. Tel. 317-926-3361. *Exec. Dir.* Barbara Evans Markuson.

Indiana State Data Center, Indiana State Library, 140 N. Senate Ave., Indianapolis, 46204-2296. SAN 322-1318. Tel. 317-232-3733. *Coord.* Jeff Barnett.

La Porte, Porter, Starke Health Science Library Consortium, Moellering Library, Valparaiso University, Valparaiso, 46383-9978. SAN 322-1334. Tel. 219-464-5366, Ext. 7177. *Coord.* Judith Miller.

Northern Indiana Automated Systems, c/o Brownsburg Public Library, 450 S. Jefferson, Brownsburg, 46112. SAN 322-4651. Tel. 317-852-3167. *Admin.* Wanda L. Pearson.

Northwest Indiana Area Library Services Authority (NIALSA), 1919 81st Ave. W., Merrillville, 46410. SAN 322-1342. Tel. 219-736-0631. WATS 800-552-8950. *Admin.* Deanna Snowden; *Admin. Asst.* Esther G. Maravilla.

Northwest Indiana Health Science Library Consortium, c/o N.W. Ctr. for Med. Educ., Indiana University School of Medicine, 3400 Broadway, Gary, 46408-1197. SAN 322-1350. Tel. 219-980-6852. *Coord.* Rachel Feldman.

Society of Indiana Archivists, Box 44074, Indianapolis, 46204. SAN 329-5508. Tel. 317-742-8411. *Pres.* Sally Cook.

Southeastern Indiana Area Library Services Authority (SIALSA), 428 Pearl St., Suite 5, New Albany, 47150-3420. SAN 322-1369. Tel. 812-948-8639. *Exec. Dir.* Brenda Blackburn.

Stone Hills Area Library Services Authority, 112 N. Walnut, Suite 500, Bloomington, 47401. SAN 322-1377. Tel. 812-334-8347. *Coord.* Sara G. Laughlin; *Prog. Mgr.* Karen Nissen.

Wabash Valley Area Library Services Authority, 224 S. Green St., Off. 201, Crawfordsville, 47933-2508. SAN 322-1385. Tel. 317-362-5839. *Admin.* Dennis Lawson; *Ref. Libn.* Becky Marthey.

Iowa

Bi-State Academic Libraries (BI-SAL), c/o Marycrest College, Davenport, 52804. SAN 322-1393. Tel. 319-326-9254. *Chmn.* Sister Joan Sheil.

Chiropractic Library Consortium (CLIBCON), c/o Palmer College Library, 1000 Brady, Davenport, 52803. SAN 328-8218. Tel. 319-326-9600. *Dir.* John Budrew.

Dubuque (Iowa) Area Library Consortium, c/o Mercy Health Center, AC Pfohl Health Science Library, Dubuque, 52001-7398. SAN 322-1407. Tel. 319-589-9620. *Lib. Mgr.* James H. Lander.

Iowa Computer Assisted Network (ICAN), Historical Bldg., E. 12 & Grand, Des Moines, 50319. SAN 322-1415. Tel. 515-281-4118. *State Libn.* Shirley George.

Iowa Online Users Group, Iowa Dept. of Education, Grimes State Office Bldg., Des Moines, 50319-0146. SAN 322-3728. Tel. 515-281-5286. *Chpn.* Mary Jo Bruett.

Iowa Private Academic Library Consortium (IPAL), c/o William Penn College, Oskaloohsa, 52577. SAN 329-5311. Tel. 515-673-1098. *Dir.* Edward Goedeken.

Linn County Library Consortium, Mercy Hospital, 701 10th St. S.E., Cedar Rapids,

52403. SAN 322-4597. Tel. 319-398-6166. *Pres.* Joy Stoker-Hadow; *Dir.* Linda Ravamitage.

Northeast Iowa Academic Libraries Association (NEIAL), Henderson-Wilder Library, Upper Iowa University, Box 1858, Fayette, 52142. SAN 322-1423. Tel. 319-425-5270. *Exec. Dir.* Becky Wadean.

Polk County Biomedical Consortium, c/o Iowa Methodist School of Nursing Library, 1117 Pleasant St., Des Moines, 50309. SAN 322-1431. Tel. 515-283-6453. *Coord.* Nancy O'Brien.

Quad City Area Biomedical Consortium, Illini Hospital, 801 Hospital Rd., Silvis, 61282. SAN 322-435X. Tel. 309-792-9363. *Coord.* Priscilla Swatos.

Sioux City Library Cooperative (SCLC), c/o Sioux City Public Library, 705 Sixth St., Sioux City, 51105-1998. SAN 329-4722. Tel. 712-279-6183. *Dir.* George Scheetz.

Southeast Iowa Academic Library Consortia, c/o Iowa Wesleyan University, Chadwick Library, Mount Pleasant, 52641. SAN 329-5095. Tel. 319-385-6315. *Dir.* Patricia Newcomer.

Tri-College Cooperative Effort, c/o Wahlert Memorial Library, Loras College, Dubuque, 52004-0178. SAN 322-1466. Tel. 319-588-7125. *Dirs.* Paul Roberts & Duncan Brockway; *Libn.* Robert Klein.

Kansas

Associated Colleges of Central Kansas, 105 E. Kansas, McPherson, 67460. SAN 322-1474. Tel. 316-241-5150. *Dir.* Robert Hinshaw.

Dodge City Library Consortium, 1001 Second Ave., Dodge City, 67801. SAN 322-4368. Tel. 316-225-0248. *Chmn.* Jane Hatch.

Kansas City Library Network, Inc., Shawnee Mission Medical Center Library, 9100 W. 74, Shawnee Mission, 66201. SAN 322-2098. Tel. 913-676-2101. *Pres.* Ann Marie Corry.

Kansas City Regional Council for Higher Education, 8016 State Line Rd., Suite 205, Leawood, 66208-3710. SAN 322-211X. Tel. 913-341-4141. *Dir.* D. Stanley Love.

Kansas Library Network Board, State Capital, 3rd fl., Topeka, 66612. SAN 329-5621. Tel. 913-296-3296. *Exec. Asst.* Michael Piper.

Kansas State Audiovisual Center, 223 S. Main, Wichita, 67202. SAN 322-1482. Tel. 316-262-0611. *Dir.* Sondra B. Koontz.

UTLAS, Inc., 8300 College Blvd., Overland Park, 66210. SAN 322-3701. Tel. 913-451-3111, 800-33-Utlas. Telex 065-24479. *Pres. & Chief Exec. Officer.* Sheldon I. Kramer; *V.P. & Gen. Mgr.* Richard W. Newman.

Kentucky

Association of Southeastern Research Libraries, M. I. King Library, University of Kentucky, Lexington, 40506-0391. SAN 322-1555. Tel. 606-257-3801. *Pres.* Paul A. Willis.

Coal Information Network of Kentucky (CINK), c/o University of Louisville, Laura Kersey Library, Louisville, 40292. SAN 322-4376. Tel. 502-588-5555. *Pres.* Janardan Kulkarni.

Council of Independent Kentucky Colleges & Universities, Box 668, Danville, 40422. SAN 322-1490. Tel. 606-236-3533. *Exec. Dir.* John W. Frazer.

Kentuckiana Metroversity, Inc., 3113 Lexington Rd., Louisville, 40206. SAN 322-1504. Tel. 502-897-3374. *Exec. Dir.* Thomas Diener.

Kentucky Cooperative Library Information Project, c/o Western Kentucky Univ., Helm Library, Off. 101, Bowling Green, 42101-3576. SAN 322-1512. Tel. 502-745-2904. *Dir.* Michael Binder.

Northern Kentucky Regional Library Consortia, c/o Northern Kentucky Regional Library, Covington, 41011. SAN 329-5079. Tel. 606-431-1043.

Theological Education Association of Mid America (TEAM-A), c/o Southern Baptist Theological Seminary, 2825 Lexington Rd., Louisville, 40280-0294. SAN 322-1547. Tel. 502-897-4807. *Dir.* Ronald F. Deering.

Louisiana

Baton Rouge Area Hospital Library Consortium, Our Lady of the Lake Regional Medical Center, 500 Hennessy Blvd., Baton Rouge, 70809. SAN 329-4714. Tel. 504-765-6565, Ext. 8140. *Dir.* Diane Whited.

Louisiana Government Information Network (LAGIN), c/o State Library of Louisiana, Box 131, Baton Rouge, 70821. SAN 329-5036. Tel. 504-342-4918. *Coord.* Dorothy White.

Louisiana Mississippi Microform Network, Louisiana State Univ. Library, Baton Rouge, 70803. SAN 322-1563. Tel. 504-388-2217. *Coll. Mgr.* Charles Hamaker.

Louisiana State University System Interlibrary Network (SINET), Louisiana State Univ., Baton Rouge, 70803-3322. SAN 322-1571. Tel. 504-388-2138. *Coord.* Jane P. Kleiner.

New Orleans Consortium, Loyola University, 6636 St. Charles Ave., Box 72, New Orleans, 70118. SAN 329-5214. Tel. 504-865-3092. *Chmn.* Gordon Mueller; *Dir.* Open.

Maine

Health Science Library Information Consortium, Gerris-True Health Science Library, Central Maine Medical Ctr., 300 Main St., Box 4500, Lewiston, 04240. SAN 322-1601. Tel. 207-795-2560. *Chpn.* Mary Ann Grevin.

Maine Health Science Libraries & Information Cooperative, Box 3395, Togus, 04330. SAN 329-4781. Tel. 207-872-1224. *Chmn.* Cora Damon.

Maryland

Cooperating Libraries of Central Maryland (CLCM), 115 W. Franklin St., Baltimore, 21201-4484. SAN 322-3914. Tel. 301-396-3921. *Coord.* Cecy Keller.

Criminal Justice Information Exchange Group, c/o National Institute of Justice/NCJRS, 1600 Research Blvd., Rockville, 20850. SAN 322-1717. Tel. 301-251-5101. *Coord.* Nancy Pearse.

ERIC Processing & Reference Facility, 4350 E. West Hwy., Suite 1100, Bethesda, 20814-3073. SAN 322-161X. Tel. 301-656-9723. *Dir.* Ted Brandhorst.

Maryland Interlibrary Organization (MILO), c/o Enoch Pratt Free Library, 400 Cathedral St., Baltimore, 21201-4484. SAN 343-8600. Tel. 301-396-5328. *Spec. Admin.* Open.

National Library of Medicine, MEDLARS, Medical Literature Analysis & Retrieval System, 8600 Rockville Pike, Bethesda, 20894. SAN 322-1652. Tel. 301-496-6193. *Head MEDLARS Mgt. Section.* Carolyn Tilley.

Southeastern-Atlantic Regional Medical Library Services (RML 2), Univ. of Maryland Health Sciences Library, 111 S. Greene St., Baltimore, 21201-1583. SAN 322-1644. Tel. 301-328-2855. WATS 800-638-6093. *Exec. Dir.* Suzanne Grefsheim; *Coords.* Nancy J. Nuell & Lisa Boyd.

Massachusetts

Boston Area Music Libraries (BAML), Boston University, Mugar Library, Waltham, 92254. SAN 322-4392. Tel. 617-253-5636. *Coord.* Frank Gramenz; *Dir.* Nina Davis Millis.

Boston Biomedical Library Consortium (BBLC), St. Elizabeth's Hospital, Stohlman Library, 736 Cambridge St., Brighton, 02135-2997. SAN 322-1725. *Pres.* Robin Braun.

Boston Library Consortium, c/o Boston Public Lib., Rm. 339, 666 Boylston St., Boston, 02117. SAN 322-1733. Tel. 617-262-0380. *Pres.* Arthur Curley; *Coord.* Marianne Burke.

Boston Theological Institute Library Program, c/o Andover-Harvard Library, 45 Francis Ave., Cambridge, 02138. SAN 322-1741. Tel. 617-495-5780. *Coord.* Donald S. Share; *Coord.* Open.

Consortium for Information Resources, Emerson Hospital, 133 Old Rd. to Nine Ave. Ctr., Framingham, 01742. SAN 322-4503. Tel. 617-879-7111, Ext. 2045. *Dir.* Nancy Callender.

Cooperating Libraries of Greater Springfield: A CCGS Agency, c/o Springfield City Library, 220 State St., Springfield, 01103. SAN 322-1768. Tel. 413-739-3871. *Chmn.* James H. Fish.

C W Mars (Central Western Massachusetts Automated Resource Sharing), One Sunset Lane, Paxton, 01612-1197. SAN 322-3973. Tel. 617-755-3323. *Mgr.* David T. Sheehan; *Supv., User Servs.* Gale E. Eckerson.

Essex County Cooperating Libraries, c/o Beverly Hospital Library, Herrick St., Beverly, 01915. SAN 322-1776. Tel. 617-922-

3000, Ext. 2920. *Chpn.* Victor Dyer; *Treas.* Rebecca Duschatko.

Fenway Library Consortium, c/o Wheelock College Library, 132 The Riverway, Boston, 02215. SAN 327-9766. Tel. 617-734-5200, Ext. 220. *Coord.* Andrea Hoffman.

HILC, Inc. (Hampshire Interlibrary Ctr.), 97 Spring St., Amherst, 01002. SAN 322-1806. *Admin. Asst.* Dora Tudryn.

Merrimac Interlibrary Cooperative, c/o Lawrence Public Library, 51 Lawrence St., Lawrence, 01841. SAN 329-4234. Tel. 508-682-1727. *Pres.* Joseph Dionne.

Merrimack Valley Library Consortium, c/o Memorial Hall Library, Elm Sq., Andover, 01810. SAN 322-4384. Tel. 617-475-6960. *Chmn.* Anne M. O'Brien; *Dir.* Evelyn Kuo.

Minuteman Library Network, 49 Lexington St., Framingham, 01701. SAN 322-4252. Tel. 617-879-8575. *Admin.* Joan Kuklinski.

NELINET, Inc., 385 Elliot St., Newton, 02164-1193. SAN 322-1822. Tel. 617-969-0400. *Exec. Dir.* Laima Mockus.

New England Deposit Library, 135 Western Ave., Allston, 02134. SAN 322-1830. Tel. 617-782-8441. *Dir.* Richard McCarty.

New England Law Library Consortium, Inc., Harvard Law School Library, Langdell Hall, Cambridge, 02138. SAN 322-4244. Tel. 617-495-9918. *Coord.* Elizabeth A. Snyder.

Noble (North of Boston Library Exchange), 82 Main St., Peabody, 01960-5592. SAN 322-4023. Tel. 617-532-8107.

Northeastern Consortium for Health Information (NECHI), Beverly Hospital, 75 Merrick St., Beverly, 01915. SAN 322-1857. Tel. 617-922-3000, Ext. 2920. *Chpn.* Ann Kowalski; *V. Chpn.* Margaret Duggan.

Southeastern Massachusetts Consortium of Health Science Libraries (SEMCO), c/o Medical Library, Cardinal Cushing General Hospital, 235 N. Pearl St., Brockton, 02401. SAN 322-1873. Tel. 617-588-4000, Ext. 1140. *Chpn.* Nancy Sezak.

Southeastern Massachusetts Cooperating Libraries (SMCL), c/o Bridgewater State College Library, Bridgewater, 02324. SAN 322-1865. Tel. 617-697-1256. *Chpn.* Owen T. P. McGowan; *Coord.* William E. Boyle.

Western Massachusetts Health Information Consortium, c/o Holyoke Community College Library, 303 Holmestead Ave., Northampton, 01040. SAN 329-4579. Tel. 413-584-4090. *Chmn.* Elizabeth Sheean; *Dir.* Susan LaForte.

Western Massachusetts Health Information Consortium, Franklin Medical Center, Health Science Library, 164 High St., Greenfield, 01301. SAN 329-5443. Tel. 413-772-2211. *Dir.* Marion Graney.

Worcester Area Cooperating Libraries, c/o Worcester State College Learning Resources Ctr., Rm. 301, 486 Chandler St., Worcester, 01602-2597. SAN 322-1881. Tel. 617-754-3964, 793-8000, Ext. 8544. *Res. Asst.* Gladys Wood.

Michigan

Berrien Library Consortium, Andrews Campus, Berrien Springs, 49104. SAN 322-4678. Tel. 617-471-3379, 983-7168. *Pres.* Anne Stobbe.

Cloverland Processing Center, c/o Bay de Noc Community College LRC, 2001 N. Lincoln Rd., Escanaba, 49829-2511. SAN 322-189X. Tel. 906-786-5802, Ext. 122. *Dean.* Christian Holmes.

Detroit Area Consortium of Catholic Colleges, c/o Marygrove College, 8425 W. McNichols Rd., Detroit, 48221-9987. SAN 329-482X. Tel. 313-862-8000. *Coord.* John Shay.

Flint Area Health Science Libraries Network, c/o Flint Osteopathic Hospital-Medical Library, 3921 Beecher Rd., Flint, 48502-3699. SAN 329-4757. Tel. 313-762-4587. *Chair.* Doris Blauet; *Lib. Tech. Asst.* Joanne Ellis.

Kalamazoo Consortium for Higher Education (KCHE), 6767 W. O Ave., Kalamazoo, 49009. SAN 329-4994. Tel. 616-372-5278. *Chmn.* Marilyn Schlack.

Library Cooperative of Macomb, 16480 Hall Rd., Mount Clemens, 48044. SAN 329-496X. Tel. 313-286-6660. *Dir.* Carol Goodwin.

Michigan Library Consortium (MLC), Suite 8, 6810 S. Cedar St., Lansing, 48911. SAN 322-192X. Tel. 517-694-4242. WATS 800-292-1359 (Mich. only). *Exec. Dir.* Kevin C. Flaherty.

Northern Interlibrary System, 316 E. Chisholm St., Alpena, 49707. SAN 329-4773. Tel. 517-356-1622. *Dir.* Susan S. Williams; *Info. Specialist.* Marsha Boyd.

Sault Area International Library Association, c/o Lake Superior State University Library, Sault Sainte Marie, 49783. SAN 322-1946. Tel. 906-635-2402. *Co-Chpns.* Charles E. Nairn & Brian Ingram.

Southeast Michigan Regional Film Library, 3700 S. Custer Rd., Monroe, 48161-9732. SAN 308-2814. Tel. 313-241-5277. WATS 800-462-2050. *Dir.* Bernard A. Margolis.

Southeastern Michigan League of Libraries (SEMLOL), c/o Mary Frances Ray, Henry Ford Community College, 5101 Evergreen, Dearborn, 48128-1495. SAN 322-4481. Tel. 313-845-9606, Ext. 373. *Chmn.* Shirley Smith.

State Council of Michigan Health Science Libraries, 401 W. Greenlawn Ave., Lansing, 48910-2819. SAN 329-4633. Tel. 517-334-2270. *Pres.* David Keddle.

Upper Peninsula of Michigan Health Science Library Consortium, c/o Marquette General Hospital, 420 W. Magnetic, Marquette, 49855. SAN 329-4803. Tel. 906-225-3429. *Chmn.* Mildred Kingsbury.

Upper Peninsula Region Library Cooperation, c/o Superior Land Library, 1615 Presque Isle Ave., Marquette, 49855. SAN 329-5540. Tel. 906-786-5802. *Dir.* Chris Holmes.

Minnesota

Arrowhead Professional Libraries Association, St. Mary's Medical Ctr., 407 E. Third St., Duluth, 55805-1984. SAN 322-1954. Tel. 218-726-4396. *Coord.* Elizabeth Sobczak.

Central Minnesota Libraries Exchange (CMLE), c/o Learning Resources, Rm. 122, Saint Cloud State University, Saint Cloud, 56301. SAN 322-3779. Tel. 612-255-2950. *Coord.* Patricia F. Peterson.

Cooperating Libraries in Consortium (CLIC), 1457 Grand Ave., Fourth & Market Sts., Saint Paul, 55105. SAN 322-1970. Tel. 612-227-9531. *Mgr.* Terrance J. Metz.

METRONET, 226 Metro Square Bldg., Seventh & Robert Sts., Saint Paul, 55101. SAN 322-1989. Tel. 612-224-4801. *Dir.* Mary Treacy Birmingham.

MINITEX (Minnesota Interlibrary Telecommunications Exchange), c/o S-33 Wilson Lib., Univ. of Minnesota, 309 19th Ave. S., Minneapolis, 55455-0414. SAN 322-1997. Tel. 612-624-4002. WATS 800-462-5348 (Minn.), 800-328-5534 (ND, SD). *Dir.* William DeJohn; *Asst. Dir., Doc. Delivery & MULS.* Anita Anker; *Asst. Dir., OCLC & Ref. Servs.* M. J. Dustin; *Sr. OCLC Servs. Coord.* Philip Youngholm; *OCLC Servs. Coord.* Neil Block; *Assoc. Admin.* Anne Stagg.

Minnesota Consortium of Theological Schools Libraries, c/o Luther Northwestern Theological Seminary, 2375 Como Ave., Saint Paul, 55108. SAN 322-1962. Tel. 612-641-3224. *Dir.* Norman Wente.

North Country Library Cooperative, c/o Arrowhead Library System, 701 11th St. N., Virginia, 55792-2298. SAN 322-3795. Tel. 218-741-3840. *Coord.* Sandra Isaacson.

Northern Lights Library Network, Box 845, Alexandria, 56308-0845. SAN 322-2004. Tel. 612-762-1032. *Coord.* Joan B. Larson.

SMILE (Southcentral Minnesota Inter-Library Exchange), Box 3031, Mankato, 56001. SAN 321-3358. Tel. 507-389-5108. *Coord.* Lucy Lowry; *Smiline I & R Dir.* Kate Tohal.

Southeast Library System (SELS), Education Service Center, 334 16th St. S.E., Rm. 6, Rochester, 55904. SAN 322-3981. Tel. 507-288-5513. *Multitype Libn.* Judith A. Rogers.

Southwest Area Multi-County Multi-Type Interlibrary Exchange (SAMMIE), Southwest State University, BAC 505, Marshall, 56258. SAN 322-2039. Tel. 507-532-9013. *Coord.* Open.

Tri-College University Library Consortium, Moorhead State University, Moorhead, 56560. SAN 329-4595. Tel. 218-236-2922. *Dir.* Darryl Meinke.

Twin Cities Biomedical Consortium, Abbott Northwestern Hospital, Health Sciences Library, 800 E. 28th St., Minneapolis, 55415. SAN 322-2055. Tel. 612-347-2713. *Chmn.* Elaine Trzebiatowski.

WESTLAW, c/o West Publishing Co., 50 W. Kellogg Blvd., Box 64779, Saint Paul, 55164-9990. SAN 322-4031. Tel. 612-228-2500. WATS 800-328-0109. *Mgr.* Thomas McLeod.

Mississippi

Mississippi Biomedical Library Consortium, VA Medical Center, Library Services

(142D), Biloxi, 39531. SAN 322-4422. Tel. 601-388-5541, Ext. 221. *Pres.* Chris Jones; *Dir.* James Caldwell.

Mississippi Delta Library Council, Roberts Memorial Library, Delta State University, Cleveland, 38733. SAN 322-2071. Tel. 601-846-4440. *Dir.* Myra Macon.

Missouri

Higher Education Center of Saint Louis, 928a N. McKnight Rd., Saint Louis, 63132-9898. SAN 322-208X. Tel. 314-991-2700. *Pres.* Samuel E. Wood.

Kansas City Metropolitan Library Network, Suite 215, 3675 S. Noland Rd., Independence, 64055. SAN 322-2101. Tel. 816-461-7001. *Coord.* Open.

Mid-Missouri Library Network, c/o Daniel Boone Regional Library, Box 1267, Columbia, 65205-1267. SAN 322-2136. Tel. 314-443-3161, Ext. 216, 217. *Actg. Dir.* Nina Sappington.

Missouri Library Network Corporation, 12166 Old Big Bend, Suite 215, Saint Louis, 63122. SAN 322-466X. Tel. 314-965-7030. *Dir.* Mary Ann Mercante.

Municipal Library Cooperative, 140 E. Jefferson, Kirkwood, 63122. SAN 322-2152. Tel. 314-966-5568. *ILL.* Vera H. Moeller.

Northeast Missouri Library Network, c/o Rm. 105, Pickler Memorial Library, Northeast Missouri State University, Kirksville, 63501. SAN 322-2160. Tel. 816-785-4542.

Northwest Missouri Library Network, 1904B N. Belt Hwy., Saint Joseph, 64506-3434. SAN 322-2179. Tel. 816-364-3386. *Dir.* Judith A. Muck; *Coord. Info. Servs.* April L. Fager.

PHILSOM Network (Periodical Holdings in Libraries of Schools of Medicine), c/o Washington University, 660 S. Euclid Ave., Saint Louis, 63110. SAN 322-2187. Tel. 314-362-2788. *Dir.* Loretta Stucki.

Saint Louis Regional Library Network, 9425 Manchester Rd., Big Bend, Saint Louis, 63119. SAN 322-2209. Tel. 314-965-1305. *Admin.* Bernyce Christiansen; *Dir.* Marty Knorr.

Sisters of Saint Mary Consortia, Saint Mary's Health Center, Health Sciences Library, 6420 Clayton Rd., Saint Louis, 63117. SAN 329-501X. Tel. 314-768-8112. *Dir.* Candy Thayer.

Southeast Missouri Library Network, 412 Kent Library, 900 Normal, Cape Girardeau, 63701. SAN 322-4457. Tel. 314-651-2152. *Dir.* Patricia Andermann.

Southwest Missouri Library Network, Box 760, Springfield, 65801. SAN 322-2217. Tel. 417-869-4621. TWX 910-775-4729. *Admin.* Jewell Smith.

Montana

Montana Information Network & Exchange (MINE), c/o Montana State Library, 1515 E. Sixth Ave., Helena, 59620. SAN 322-2241. Tel. 406-444-3004. *State Libn.* Sara Parker.

Nebraska

Lincoln Health Sciences Library Group, c/o Brian School of Nursing, 5000 Summer St., Lincoln, 68506. SAN 329-5001. Tel. 402-483-3801. *Pres.* Susan Echols.

Meridian Library System, Kearney Reference Interloan Center, c/o Kearney State College Library, Kearney, 68849-0376. SAN 325-3554. Tel. 402-234-8541. *Pres.* John Mayeski; *Admin. Secy.* Laurie Jarosz.

Midcontinental Regional Medical Library Program (RML4), c/o McGoogan Lib. of Medicine, Univ. of Nebraska Medical Ctr., 42 & Dewey Ave., Omaha, 68105-1065. SAN 322-225X. Tel. 402-559-4326, 800-MED-RML4. *Assoc. Dir.* Dorothy B. Willis.

NEBASE, c/o Nebraska Library Commission, 1420 P St., Lincoln, 68508-1683. SAN 322-2268. Tel. 402-471-2045. *Dir.* Rod Wagner; *Coords.* Pat Gildersleeve & Jacqueline Mundell; *Bus. Mgr.* Doreen Kuhlmann.

Northeast Library System, 2504 14th St., Columbus, 68601. SAN 329-5524. Tel. 402-564-7116. *Admin.* Carol Speicher.

Southeast Nebraska Library System, Union College Library, 3800 S. 48 St., Lincoln, 64506. SAN 322-4732. Tel. 402-486-2555. *Admin.* Georgia Robertson; *Staff Asst.* Rebecca Foster.

Nevada

Information Nevada, Interlibrary Loan Department, Nevada State Library, Capitol

Complex, Carson City, 89710-0001. SAN 322-2276. Tel. 702-887-2169. *In-Charge.* Millie L. Syring.

Nevada Cooperative Medical Library, 2040 W. Charleston Blvd., Suite 500, Las Vegas, 89102. SAN 321-5962. Tel. 702-383-2368. *Dir. Lib. Servs.* Aldona Jonynas.

New Hampshire

Merry-Hill Rock Coop, c/o Nesmith Library, Windham, 03087. SAN 329-5338. Tel. 603-432-7154. *Chmn.* Carl Heidenblad.

New Hampshire College & University Council, Library Policy Committee, 2321 Elm St., Manchester, 03104. SAN 322-2322. Tel. 603-669-3432. *Pres.* Henry Munroe; *V.P.* Douglas Lyon.

Nubanusit Library Cooperative, c/o Peterborough Town Library, Main St., Peterborough, 03458. SAN 322-4600. Tel. 603-924-6401. *Dir.* Ann Geisel.

Scrooge & Marley Cooperative, Park St., Tilton, 03276. SAN 329-515X. Tel. 603-286-8971. *Chmn.* Doris Ullrich.

Seacoast Libraries, Hampton Falls Free Public Library, 45 Exeter Rd., Box 69, Newmarket, 03844. SAN 322-4619. Tel. 603-926-3682. *Chmn.* Pamela Schwotzer.

New Jersey

AT&T Bell Laboratory Library Network, 600 Mountain Ave., Rm. 6A-412, Murray Hill, 07974. SAN 329-5400. Tel. 201-949-3456. *Mgr.* Tom Marsden.

Bergen County Cooperative Library System, 368A Paramus Rd., Paramus, 07652. SAN 322-4546. Tel. 201-652-8806. *Systems Admin.* Lila Cohen.

County of Essex Cooperating Libraries System (CECLS), 57 Kendal Ave., Maplewood, 07040. SAN 322-4562. Tel. 201-763-9006. *Admin.* Karen Lee.

Dow Jones News Retrieval, Box 300, Princeton, 08543-0300. SAN 322-404X. Tel. 609-452-1511. Telex 84-4450. WATS 800-257-5114. *Sr. Marketing Coord.* Carla Gaffney.

Essex-Hudson Regional Library Cooperative-Region Three, Federal Trust Bldg., 24 Commerce St., Suite 428, Newark 07102-4005. SAN 329-5117. Tel. 201-642-2923. *Dir.* Ray Murray.

LMX Automation Consortium, 155 Mill Rd., Box 3050, Edison, 08818-3050. SAN 329-448X. Tel. 201-906-2561. *Pres.* Sara Eggers; *Systems Dir.* Pamela Thornton.

Medical Resources Consortium of Central New Jersey (MEDCORE), c/o Medical Center Library, Medical Center at Princeton, 253 Witherspoon St., Princeton, 08540. SAN 322-2349. Tel. 609-921-7700, Ext. 4394. *Libn.* Louise M. Yorke.

Monmouth-Ocean Biomedical Consortium, Community Memorial Hospital, 99 Hwy. No. 37 W., Toms River, 08753. SAN 329-5389. Tel. 201-240-8117. *Dir.* Reina Reisler.

Morris Automated Information Network, 30 E. Hanover Ave., Whippany, 07981. SAN 322-4058. Tel. 201-285-6955. *Head of MAIN.* Margaret A. Trowbridge; *Automated Syst. Lib.* Jerrold P. Kuntz.

New Jersey Academic Library Network, c/o Montclair State College, Harry A. Sprague Library, Upper Montclair, 07043. SAN 329-4927. Tel. 201-527-2017. *Chmn.* Barbara Simpson.

Northwest Regional Library Cooperative, 31 Fairmount Ave., Box 486, Chester, 07930. SAN 329-4609. Tel. 201-879-2442. *Exec. Dir.* Keith Michael Fiels.

South Jersey Regional Library Cooperative, c/o Midway Professional Center, 8 N. Whitehorse Pike, Suite 102, Hammonton, 08037. SAN 329-4625. Tel. 209-561-4646. *Exec. Dir.* Karen Hyman.

New Mexico

New Mexico Consortium of Biomedical & Hospital Libraries, c/o Lovelace Medical Library, 5400 Gibson Blvd. S.E., Albuquerque, 87108. SAN 322-449X. Tel. 505-262-7158. *Contact.* Jeane Strub.

New Mexico Information System (NEMISYS), c/o New Mexico State Library, 325 Don Gaspar, Santa Fe, 87503. SAN 322-2403. Tel. 505-827-3820. WATS 800-432-4401. *Head.* Harold L. Bogart.

New York

Academic Libraries of Brooklyn, St. Francis College, 180 Remsen St., Brooklyn, 11201. SAN 322-2411. Tel. 718-522-2300. *Pres.* Joan Torrone.

Associated Colleges of the Saint Lawrence

Valley, Satterlee Hall, State University of New York at Potsdam, Potsdam, 13676-2299. SAN 322-242X. Tel. 315-265-2790. *Exec. Dir.* Judy C. Chittenden.

BRS Information Technologies, 1200 Rte. 7, Latham, 12110. SAN 322-2438. Tel. 518-783-1161. WATS 800-345-4277. *Pres.* Martin Kahn.

Capital District Library Council for Reference & Research Resources, 2255 Story Ave., Schenectady, 12309. SAN 322-2446. Tel. 518-382-2001. *Exec. Dir.* Charles D. Custer; *Admin. Secy.* Mary L. Schatke.

Central New York Library Resources Council, 763 Butternut, Syracuse, 13208. SAN 322-2454. Tel. 315-478-6080. In New York, 800-848-8448. *Exec. Dir.* Keith E. Washburn; *Asst. Dir.* Jeannette Smithee; *Bibliog. Servs. Coord.* Kathleen Davis.

Consortium of Foundation Libraries, c/o Carnegie Corporation of New York, 437 Madison Ave., New York, 10022. SAN 322-2462. Tel. 212-371-3200. *Dir.* Patricia Haynes.

Cornell Health Science Computerized Library Network (CORNET), 1300 York Ave., New York, 10021. SAN 329-5044. Tel. 212-472-6019. *Dir.* Jean Raibman.

Greater Northeastern Regional Medical Library Program, New York Academy of Medicine, 2 E. 103 St., New York, 10029-5293. SAN 322-2497. Tel. 212-876-8763. *Dir.* Brett Kirkpatrick; *Assoc. Dir.* Mary Mylenki.

Health Resource Council of Central New York, c/o St. Joseph's Hospital Libraries, 206-301 Prospect Ave., Syracuse, 13203. SAN 322-4511. Tel. 315-424-5054. *Pres.* Vincent Juchimek.

Library Consortium of Health Institutions in Buffalo, Office of the Consortium, c/o Info. Dissemination Service, SUNY, Buffalo, 14214. SAN 329-367X. Tel. 716-831-3351. *In Charge.* Cindy Bertuca.

Long Island Library Resources Council, Melville Library Bldg., Suite E5310, Stony Brook, 11794-3399. SAN 322-2489. Tel. 516-632-6650. *Dir.* Herbert Biblo.

Manhattan-Bronx Health Sciences Libraries Group, c/o Lincoln Medical Center Health Sciences Library, 234 E. 149th St., Bronx, 10451. SAN 322-4465. Tel. 212-579-5745. *Chmn.* Milagros M. Parades.

Medical & Scientific Libraries of Long Island (MEDLI), 1200 Stewart Ave., Garden City, 11530. SAN 322-4309. Tel. 516-832-2320. *Chpn.* Magdalene D. Aquilino.

Medical Library Center of New York, 5 E. 102 St., New York, 10029. SAN 322-3957. Tel. 212-427-1630. *Dir.* William D. Walker.

New York Metropolitan Reference & Research Library Agency (METRO), 57 Willoughby St., Brooklyn, 11201. SAN 322-2500. Tel. 718-852-8700. *Dir.* Joan Neumann; *Assoc. Dir. & Coord. of Progs. & Servs.* Alar Kruus.

New York State Interlibrary Loan Network (NYSILL), c/o New York State Library, Albany, 12230. SAN 322-2519. Tel. 518-474-5383. *State Libn.* Joseph F. Shubert; *Dir.* Jerome Yavarkovsky; *Principal Libn.* J. Van der veer Judd.

North Country Reference & Research Resources Council, Box 568, Canton, 13617-0568. SAN 322-2527. Tel. 315-386-4569. *Dir.* Richard H. Kimball.

Rochester Regional Library Council (RRLC), Rm. 300, 339 East Ave., Rochester, 14604. SAN 322-2535. Tel. 716-232-7930. *Dir.* Janet M. Welch.

South Central Research Library Council, 215 N. Cayuga St., Ithaca, 14850. SAN 322-2543. Tel. 607-273-9106. *Exec. Dir.* Janet E. Steiner; *Spec. Projects Dir.* Margaret De Bruine.

Southeastern New York Library Resources Council, Rte. 299, Box 879, Highland, 12528. SAN 322-2551. Tel. 914-691-2734. TWX 914-255-7340. WATS 800-251-1131. *Exec. Dir.* Ellen A. Parravano; *Asst. Dir.* Thomas A. Lawrence; *ILL Coord.* Christine Crawford-Oppenheimer; *Health Info. Libn.* Ronald Crovisier.

State University of New York OCLC Library Network (SUNY OCLC), Central Administration, State University of NY, State University Plaza, Albany, 12246. SAN 322-256X. Tel. 518-434-8141. WATS 800-342-3353 (New York only). *Dir.* Glyn T. Evans.

Western New York Library Resources Council, 180 Oak St., Buffalo, 14203. SAN 322-2578. Tel. 716-852-3844. *Exec. Dir.* Joyce D. Everingham.

North Carolina

Cape Fear Health Sciences Information Consortium, Fayetteville State University, Charles W. Chestnutt Library, 1100 Murchison Rd., Newbold Sta., Fayetteville,

28301. SAN 322-3930. Tel. 919-486-1111. *Dir.* Richard G. Griffin.

Microcomputer Users Group for Libraries in North Carolina, c/o Susan Speer, Health Sciences Library, ECU School of Medicine, Greenville, 27858-4354. SAN 322-4449. Tel. 919-551-2212. *Pres.* Robert Burgin.

North Carolina Department of Community Colleges, Media Processing Center, 200 W. Jones St., Raleigh, 27603-1337. SAN 322-2594. Tel. 919-733-7051. *Dir.* Pamela B. Doyle.

North Carolina Science & Technology Research Center, Box 12235, Research Triangle Park, 27709-2235. SAN 322-2608. Tel. 919-549-0671. *Actg. Dir.* Thil Wilson.

Northwest AEC Library at Salisbury, c/o Rowan Memorial Hospital, 612 Mocksville Ave., Salisbury, 28144. SAN 322-4589. Tel. 704-638-1081. *Dir.* Mary J. Peck.

NW AEC Library Information Network, Northwest Area Health Education Center, Bowman Gray School of Medicine, 300 S. Hawthorne Rd., Winston-Salem, 27103. SAN 322-4716. Tel. 919-777-3020. FTS 704-322-0662. *Coord.* Phyllis Gillikin.

Resources for Health Information Consortium (ReHI), 3000 New Bern Ave., Raleigh, 27610. SAN 329-3777. Tel. 919-755-8529. *Dir.* Karen Grandage.

State Library of North Carolina, 109 E. Jones St., Raleigh, 27611. SAN 329-3092. Tel. 919-733-2570. FAX 919-733-5679, Easy Link 62944775. *Dir.* Howard F. McGinn.

Triangle Research Libraries Network, University of North Carolina at Chapel Hill, Wilson Library, Chapel Hill, 27599-3940. SAN 329-5362. Tel. 919-962-8022. *Dir.* Jeanne Sawyer.

Unifour Consortium of Health Care & Educational Institutions, c/o NW AHEC Library at Hickory, Catawba Memorial Library, Hickory, 28602-9463. SAN 322-4708. Tel. 704-322-0662. *Dir.* Phyllis Gillikin; *Assoc. Dirs.* Carol M. Harris & Patricia A. Hammond.

North Dakota

North Dakota Network for Knowledge, c/o North Dakota State Library, Liberty Memorial Bldg., Capitol Grounds, Bismarck, 58505. SAN 322-2616. Tel. 701-224-2492. *State Libn.* Patricia Harris.

Tri-College University Libraries Consortium, c/o North Dakota State University, 306 Ceres Hall, Fargo, 58105. SAN 322-2047. Tel. 701-237-8170. *Coord.* Darrel M. Meinke; *Provost, Tri College Univ.* Marcia Kierscht.

Valley Medical Network, c/o Saint Luke's Hospital, Medical Library, 720 N. Fourth St., Fargo, 58122. SAN 329-4730. Tel. 701-234-6063. *Pres.* Janet Syrup.

Ohio

Cleveland Area Metropolitan Library System (CAMLS), 3645 Warrensville Center Rd., Suite 116, Cleveland, 44122-5210. SAN 322-2632. Tel. 216-921-3900. *Exec. Dir.* Nancy Wareham; *Project Libn.* Mildred Fry.

Cleveland Consortium, Health Medical Center, 1810 Lorain Ave., Cleveland, 44111. SAN 329-420X. Tel. 216-476-7118. *In Charge.* Susan Favorite.

Consortium for Higher Education in Religious Studies, Box 474, Wilberforce, 45384. SAN 329-4749. Tel. 513-376-2956. *Head Libn.* J. Dale Blasbaugh.

Consortium of University Film Centers, AV Services, Kent State University, 330 KSU Library, Kent, 44242. SAN 322-1091. Tel. 216-672-3456. *Exec. Dir.* John P. Kerstetter.

East Central Colleges, c/o Heidelberg College, Tiffin, 44883-2432. SAN 322-2667. Tel. 419-448-2047. *Exec. Dir.* Nancy Siferd.

Greater Cincinnati Library Consortium, Suite 605, 3333 Vine St., Cincinnati, 45220-2214. SAN 322-2675. Tel. 513-751-4422. *Exec. Dir.* Martha J. McDonald.

Miami Valley Libraries (MVL), c/o Washington Township Public Library, 6060 Far Hills Ave., Centerville, 45459. SAN 322-2691. Tel. 513-339-0502. *Pres.* Cynthia Klinck.

Mideastern Ohio Library Organization (MOLO), 403 N. Mill St., Louisville, 44641-1428. SAN 322-2705. Tel. 216-875-4269. *Dir.* Jane Biehl.

NOLA Regional Library System (Northeastern Ohio Library Association), Ohio One Bldg., 25 E. Boardman St., Youngstown, 44503-1802. SAN 322-2713. Tel. 216-746-7042. *Dir.* Ann J. Yancura.

North Central Library Cooperative, 27 N. Main St., Mansfield, 44902-1703. SAN 322-2683. Tel. 419-526-1337. *Dir.* David

Karre; *Media Spec.* Stephen Fought; *Staff Develop. Libn.* Jennifer Davis.

Northeastern Ohio Major Academic & Research Libraries (NEOMARL), University of Akron Library & Learning Resources, Akron, 44325. SAN 322-4236. Tel. 216-375-7496. *Dir.* George V. Hodowanec.

Northern Ohio Film Circuit, c/o Rodman Public Library, 215 E. Broadway St., Alliance, 44601-2694. SAN 322-2721. Tel. 216-821-2665. *Admin.* George W. S. Hays.

Northwest Library District (NORWELD), 251 N. Main St., Bowling Green, 43402. SAN 322-273X. Tel. 419-352-2903. *Dir.* Allan Gray.

Northwest Ohio Consortium, Bluffton College, Muscelman Library, Bluffton, 45817. SAN 329-4013. Tel. 419-358-8015, Ext. 271. *Dir.* Delbert Gratz.

Northwest Ohio Consortium, Defiance College, Anthony Wayne Library, Defiance, 43512. SAN 329-4692. Tel. 419-784-4010, Ext. 482. *Liaison Officer.* Maxie J. Lambright.

OCLC (Online Computer Library Center), 6565 Frantz Rd., Dublin, 43017-0702. SAN 322-2748. Tel. 614-764-6000. WATS 800-848-5878. *Pres.* Rowland C. W. Brown.

Ohio-Ky Coop Libraries, c/o Serials Department, University Library, Wright State University, Dayton, 45435. SAN 325-3570. Tel. 513-873-3034. *Man. Ed.* Kathryn E. O'Gorman.

Ohio Valley Area Libraries (OVAL), 252 W. 13 St., Wellston, 45692-2299. SAN 322-2756. Tel. 614-384-2103. *Dir.* Shirley Mills Fischer. *Consults.* Eric S. Anderson & Gwenyth Arnold.

OHIONET, 1500 W. Lane Ave., Columbus, 43221-3975. SAN 322-2764. Tel. 614-486-2966. WATS 800-282-8975 (Ohio). *Exec. Dir.* Ronald E. Diener; *Computer Operation Asst. Dir.* Robert Busick; *Dep. Exec. Dir.* Joel S. Kent; *TLM Project Mgr.* Sondra Sinder.

SOCHE, Library Division, 2900 Acosta St., Suite 141, Dayton, 45420. SAN 329-5346. Tel. 513-297-3150. *Pres.* Pressley C. McCoy.

Southwestern Ohio Council for Higher Education, 2900 Acosta St., Suite 141, Dayton, 45420-3467. SAN 322-2659. Tel. 513-297-3150. *Pres.* Pressley C. McCoy; *Chmn. Lib. Div.* Edward Garten.

Southwestern Ohio Rural Libraries (SWORL), 22½ W. Locust St., Wilmington, 45177-2274. SAN 322-2780. Tel. 513-382-2503. *Dir.* Corinne Johnson.

Western Ohio Regional Library Development System (WORLDS), 640 W. Market St., Lima, 45801-4604. SAN 322-2802. Tel. 419-227-9370. *Dir.* J. Kaye Schneider.

Western Ohio Video Circuit, c/o Lima Public Library, 650 W. Market St., Lima, 45801. SAN 322-2799. Tel. 419-228-5113. *Admin.* James Bouchard; *Coord.* Barbara Baker.

Oklahoma

Greater Oklahoma City Area Health Sciences Library Consortium, Box 60918, Oklahoma City, 73106. SAN 329-3858. Tel. 405-271-5699. *Pres.* Jeanie Cavett.

Midwest Curriculum Coordination Center, 1500 W. Seventh Ave., Stillwater, 74074-4364. SAN 329-3874. Tel. 405-377-2000, Ext. 260. *Reg. Dir.* Joyce Sawatzky.

Oklahoma Telecommunications Interlibrary System (OTIS), 200 N.E. 18 St., Oklahoma City, 73105-3298. SAN 322-2810. Tel. 405-521-2502. FAX 405-525-7804. *Head.* Mary Hardin.

Tulsa Area Library Cooperative, 400 Civic Ctr., Tulsa, 74103. SAN 321-6489. Tel. 918-592-7893. *Coord.* Judith Dennis-Burns.

Oregon

Chemeketa Cooperative Regional Library Service, c/o Chemeketa Community College, Box 14007, Salem, 97309-7070. SAN 322-2837. Tel. 503-399-5119. *Coord.* Linda Cochrane.

Cooperative Library Network of Clackamas County, 999 Library Ct., Oregon City, 97045. SAN 322-2845. Tel. 503-655-8545. *Coord.* Beverly Simpson.

Coos Cooperative Library Service, c/o Southwestern Oregon Community College, Coos Bay, 97420. SAN 322-4279. Tel. 503-888-7260. *Ext. Servs. Coord.* Dianne Hall.

Marine Valley Health Information Network, Linn Benton Community College Library, 6500 S.W. Pacific Blvd., Albany, 97321. SAN 329-3890. Tel. 503-928-2361. *Coord.* Charlene Fella.

Oregon Health Information Network, Oregon Health Sciences University Library, Box 573, Portland, 97207-0573. SAN 322-4287. Tel. 503-279-8026. *Coord.* Steve Teich.

Oregon State Library Network, State Library Bldg., Salem, 97310-0640. SAN 329-5230. Tel. 503-378-4367. *State Libn.* Wesley Doak.

Southern Oregon Library Federation, 3201 Campus Dr., Klamath Falls, 97601-8801. SAN 322-2861. Tel. 503-776-7294. *Pres.* Leonard H. Freiser.

Washington County Cooperative Library Services, 17880 S.W. Blanton St., Box 5129, Aloha, 97006. SAN 322-287X. Tel. 503-642-1544. *Coord.* Donna M. Selle.

Pennsylvania

Associated College Libraries of Central Pennsylvania, c/o Murray Learning Resources Center, Messiah College, Grantham, 17027. SAN 322-2888. Tel. 717-691-6006. *Coord.* Roger C. Miller.

Association for Library Information (AFLI), c/o Duquesne University, Pittsburgh, 15282. SAN 322-3965. Tel. 412-434-6138. *Exec. Dir.* Paul J. Pugliese.

Central Pennsylvania Consortium, c/o Dickinson College, Carlisle, 17013. SAN 322-2896. Tel. 717-245-1490. *Dir.* Stephen C. MacDonald.

Consortium for Health Information & Library Services, 15 St. & Upland Ave., Chester, 19013-3995. SAN 322-290X. Tel. 215-447-6163. *Exec. Dir.* Kathleen Vick.

Delaware Valley Information Consortium, Abington Memorial Hospital, 1200 York Rd., Abington, 19001. SAN 329-3912. Tel. 215-576-2096. *Coord.* Cathy Aharens.

Film Library Intercollege Cooperative of Pennsylvania (FLIC), c/o Bucks County Community College, Swamp Rd., Newtown, 18940. SAN 322-2926. Tel. 215-968-8004. *Dir.* John Bradley.

Health Information Library Network of Northeastern Pennsylvania, VA Medical Center, Medical Library, Wilkes-Barre, 18711. SAN 322-2934. Tel. 717-824-3521. *Chmn.* Bruce Reid.

Interlibrary Delivery Service of Pennsylvania, Pittsburgh Regional Library Ctr., Chatham College, Woodland Rd., Pittsburgh, 15232-2898. SAN 322-2942. Tel. 412-441-6409. WATS 800-242-3790 (PA only). *Admin.* H. E. Broadbent III.

Laurel Highlands Health Sciences Library Consortium, University Library, Rm. 209, University of Pittsburgh at Johnstown, Johnstown, 15904. SAN 322-2950. Tel. 814-266-9661, Ext. 305. *Dir.* Heather W. Brice.

Lehigh Valley Association of Independent Colleges, Inc., Moravian College, Bethlehem, 18018. SAN 322-2969. Tel. 215-691-6131. *Coord.* Galen C. Godbey.

Northeastern Pennsylvania Bibliographic Center, c/o D. Leonard Corgan Library, King's College, Wilkes-Barre, 18711-0850. SAN 322-2993. Tel. 717-826-5900, Ext. 643. *Dir.* Terrence Mech.

Online Database Information Network (ODIN), c/o Dauphin County Lib. System, 101 Walnut St., Harrisburg, 17101. SAN 322-4473. Tel. 717-234-4961. *Dir.* Rich Bowra.

PALINET & Union Library Catalogue of Pennsylvania, 3401 Market St., Suite 262, Philadelphia, 19104. SAN 322-3000. Tel. 215-382-7031. WATS 800-233-3401 (PA); 800-233-3402 (DE, MD & NJ). *Exec. Dir.* James G. Schoenung.

Pennsylvania Community College Library Consortium, Lehigh Community College, 2370 Main St., Schnecksville, 18078. SAN 329-3939. Tel. 215-799-1164. *Pres.* Sara Jubinski.

Pittsburgh Council on Higher Education (PCHE), 3814 Forbes Ave., Pittsburgh, 15213-3506. SAN 322-3019. Tel. 412-683-7905. *Exec. Dir.* Betty K. Hunter.

Pittsburgh-East Hospital Library Cooperative, c/o Forbes Center for Gerontology, Frankstown Ave. at Washington Blvd., Pittsburgh, 15206. SAN 322-3027. Tel. 412-665-3050. *Libn.* Susan Reeber.

Pittsburgh Regional Library Center (PRLC), Beatty Hall, Chatham College, 100 Woodland Rd., Pittsburgh, 15232-2898. SAN 322-3035. Tel. 412-441-6409. WATS 800-242-3790 (PA only). *Exec. Dir.* H. E. Broadbent III.

Somerset Bedford County Medical Library Consortium, Box 631, Somerset, 15501-0631. SAN 322-3043. Tel. 814-445-6501, Ext. 216. *Dir.* Eve Kline; *Libn.* Kathy Plaso.

State System of Higher Education Libraries Council (SSHELCO), Mansfield University, c/o Library, Mansfield, 16933-1198. SAN 322-2918. Tel. 717-662-4672. *Chmn.* Larry L. Nesbit.

Susquehanna Library Cooperative, Lycoming College Library, Williamsport, 17701-5192. SAN 322-3051. Tel. 717-321-4082. *Chmn.* Bruce Hurlbert; *Treas.* Kate Hickey.

Tri-County Library Consortium, 207 E. North St., New Castle, 16101-3691. SAN 322-306X. Tel. 412-658-6659. *Dir.* John Walter.

Tri-State College Library Cooperative (TCLC), c/o Kistler Memorial Library, Rosemont College, Rosemont, 19010. SAN 322-3078. Tel. 215-525-0796. *Pres.* Carolyn Dearnaley.

Rhode Island

Cooperating Libraries Automated Network (CLAN), c/o Providence Public Library, 150 Empire St., Providence, 02903. SAN 329-4560. Tel. 401-521-7722, Ext. 750, 751, 753. *Chpn.* Anne Toll; *V. Chpn.* Susan Reed; *Oper.* Peter Bennett & Doris Hornby.

Newport, Portsmouth Interlibrary Microform & Periodical Loan Cooperative, c/o Newport Public Library, Aquidneck Park, Newport, 02840. SAN 322-3108. Tel. 401-847-8720. *Circ. Supv.* Edna M. Welles.

Rhode Island College (Formerly Consortium of Rhode Island Academic & Research Libraries), 600 Mount Pleasant Ave., Box A, Rockefeller Library, Providence, 02908. SAN 322-3086. Tel. 401-863-2162. *Pres.* Merrily E. Taylor; *Dir.* Richard Olsen.

Rhode Island Library Film Cooperative, 600 Sandy Lane, Warwick, 02886. SAN 322-3116. Tel. 401-739-2278. *Interim Dir.* Janice B. DiFranco.

South Carolina

Catawba-Wateree Health Education Consortium, Springs Memorial Hospital, 800 W. Neeting St., Box 1045, Lancaster, 29720. SAN 329-3971. Tel. 803-286-4121. *Dir.* Martha Groblewski.

Charleston Consortium of Higher Education, 171 Ashley Ave., Charleston, 29425. SAN 329-4900. Tel. 803-792-3627. *Dir.* Ann Baker.

SC Consortium, 171 Ashley Ave., Charleston, 29425. SAN 329-3998. Tel. 803-792-4431. *Dir.* Dean Cleghorn; *Data Mgr.* Beth Kennedy.

South Carolina State Library, South Carolina Library Network, 1500 Senate St., Box 11469, Columbia, 29211-1469. SAN 322-4198. Tel. 803-734-8666. *State Libn.* Betty E. Callaham.

Upper Savannah Area Health Education Center (AHEC), Self Memorial Hospital, Spring St., Greenwood, 29646. SAN 329-4110. Tel. 803-227-4851, 227-4251. *Dir.* Jane Powers; *Head of Bd. of Dir.* Kenneth Flinchom.

South Dakota

American Indian Higher Education Consortium (AIHEC), Box 490, Rosebud, 57570. SAN 329-4056. Tel. 605-747-2263. *Pres.* Lionel Bordeaux.

Colleges of Mid-America, Inc. (CMA), 1501 S. Prairie, Sioux Falls, 57101. SAN 322-3132. Tel. 605-331-6670. *Pres.* John C. Koch.

Tennessee

Jackson Area Colleges, c/o Jackson State Community College Library, Jackson, 38301-3797. SAN 322-3175. Tel. 901-424-3520. *Dir.* Van Veatch.

Mid Tennessee Health Science Libraries Consortium, c/o Vanderbilt University Medical Center Library, 3400 Lebanon Rd., Nashville, 37232. SAN 329-5028. Tel. 615-893-1360. *Pres.* Joy Hunter.

Tri-Cities Health Science Libraries Consortium, East Tennessee State Univ., Quillen-Dishner College of Medicine, Medical Library, Box 23290A, Johnson City, 37614-0002. SAN 329-4099. Tel. 615-929-6252. *Dir.* Janet F. Fisher.

Texas

Abilene Library Consortium, c/o Abilene Public Library, 202 Cedar, Abilene, 79601-5793. SAN 322-4694. Tel. 915-677-2474.

Amigos Bibliographic Council, Inc., 11300 N. Central Expressway, Suite 321, Dallas, 75243. SAN 322-3191. Tel. 214-750-6130. WATS 800-843-8482 (national); FAX: 214-750-7921. *Exec. Dir.* Louella V. Wetherbee.

Association for Higher Education of North Texas (AHE), The Citicrest, Suite 125, 17811 Waterview Pkwy., Dallas, 75252-8016. SAN 322-3337. Tel. 214-231-7211. *Dir. Lib. Prog. & Servs.* Katherine P. Jagoe.

Coastal Bend Health Sciences Library Consortium, 2606 Hospital Blvd., Box 5280, Corpus Christi, 78405. SAN 322-3205. Tel. 512-881-4197. *Coord.* Angie Hinojosa.

Council of Research & Academic Libraries (CORAL), Box 290236, San Antonio, 78280-1636. SAN 322-3213. Tel. 512-695-8008. *Pres.* Antoinette Garza; *Exec. Dir.* Irene F. Scharf.

–*Circulation & Interlibrary Loan Group (CIRCILL)*, Univ. of Texas at San Antonio, San Antonio, 78285. SAN 322-323X. Tel. 512-691-4573. *Chpn.* Margaret Joseph.

–*Coral Periodicals-Serials Librarians Group (CORPSE)*, Af Human Resources Laboratory Library, Brooks AFB, 78235. SAN 322-3284. Tel. 512-536-2651. *Pres.* Orrine Woinowski.

–*Documents Users Groups (DOCS)*, San Antonio College Library, 1001 Howard St., San Antonio, 78284. SAN 322-3256. Tel. 512-733-2598. *Pres.* Christina Petimezas.

–*Instructional Media Services Group (IMS)*, Univ. of Texas Health Science Center, 7703 Floyd Curl Dr., San Antonio, 78284. SAN 322-3221. Tel. 512-567-2485. *Pres.* Martha Knott.

–*Reference and Instructional Services Interest Group (RISIG)*, Univ. of Texas Health Center Library, 7703 Floyd Curl Dr., San Antonio, 78284. SAN 328-753X. Tel. 512-567-2460. *Chpn.* Nancy Bierschenk.

–*San Antonio Area Online Users Group (SOLUG)*, Univ. of Texas at San Antonio, San Antonio, 78285, SAN 322-3264. Tel. 512-691-4573. *Chpn.* Rick McDonnell.

–*Special Collections Interest Group (SCIG)*, Univ. of Texas at San Antonio, San Antonio, 78285. SAN 324-2986. Tel. 512-691-4570. *Pres.* Dora Guerra.

–*Technical Services Interest Group (TSIG)*, Our Lady of the Lake University Library, 411 S.W. 24 St., San Antonio, 78284. SAN 322-3272. Tel. 512-434-6711, Ext. 328. *Chpn.* Linda Bloom.

Dallas-Tarrant County Consortium of Health Science Libraries, Methodist Medical Center, Medical Library, Dallas, 75265. SAN 322-3299. Tel. 214-944-8321. *Coord.* Mary Jarvis.

Del Norte Biosciences Library Consortium, c/o Reference Department Library, University of Texas at El Paso, El Paso, 79968-0582. SAN 322-3302. Tel. 915-747-5643. *Pres.* Esperanza A. Moreno.

Harrington Library Consortium, Box 447, Amarillo, 79178. SAN 329-546X. Tel. 806-371-5135. *Mgr.* Judabeth Floyd.

Houston Area Research Library Consortium (HARLiC), University of Houston Library, 4800 Calhoun, Houston, 77004. SAN 322-3329. Tel. 713-749-4241. *Pres.* Robin Downes.

Piasano Consortium, Victoria College, Univ. of Houston at Victoria, 2602 N. Ben Jordan, Victoria, 77901-5699. SAN 329-4943. Tel. 512-573-3291, 576-3151. *Dir.* S. Joe McCord.

Regional Information & Communication Exchange, Fondren Library, Rice University, Box 1892, Houston, 77251-1892. SAN 322-3345. Tel. 713-528-3553. FAX 713-523-4117. *Dir.* Una Gourlay.

South Central Regional Medical Library Program (TALON), 5323 Harry Hines Blvd., Dallas, 75235-9049. SAN 322-3353. Tel. 214-688-2085. TWX 910-861-4946. *Coords.* Nancy Comacho & Elaine Jones.

Texas Council of State University Librarians, 6300 Ocean Dr., Corpus Christi State Univ., Corpus Christi, 75962. SAN 322-337X. Tel. 512-991-6810. *Chmn.* Richard L. O'Keeffe.

Texas State Library Communications Network, Box 12927, Austin, 78711. SAN 322-3396. Tel. 512-463-5465. *Mgr.* Rebecca Linton.

USDA Southwest Regional Document Delivery System, c/o ILS, Texas A&M University Library, College Station, 77843-5000. SAN 322-340X. Tel. 409-845-5641. *ILL Head.* Jacque Halverson.

Utah

Utah College Library Council, c/o Utah State Library, 2150 S. 300 W., Salt Lake City, 84115. SAN 322-3418. Tel. 801-533-5875. *Chmn.* David A. Thomas; *Exec. Secy.* John Elsweiler.

Western Council of State Libraries, Inc., Utah State Library, 2150 S. 300 W., Suite

16, Salt Lake City, 84115. SAN 322-2314. Tel. 801-466-5888. *Chmn.* Wayne Johnson, Pat Murphey & Virginia Hendley.

Vermont

Vermont Resource Sharing Network, c/o Vermont Dept. of Libraries, State Office Bldg., Montpelier, 05602-2702. SAN 322-3426. Tel. 802-828-3261. *Head Ref. Servs.* Linda McSweeney.

Virginia

Consortium for Continuing Higher Education in Northern Virginia, 4400 University Dr., 214 E. Bldg., George Mason University, Fairfax, 22030. SAN 322-3434. Tel. 703-323-2399. *Admin.* Donna R. Bafundo; *Dir.* Sally Reithlingshoefer.

Defense Technical Information Center, Cameron Station, Bldg. 5, Alexandria, 22304-6145. SAN 322-3442. Tel. 703-274-6800. *Admin.* Kurt N. Molholm.

Lynchburg Area Library Cooperative, Mary Helen Cochran Library, Sweet Briar College, Sweet Briar, 24595. SAN 322-3450. Tel. 804-381-6139. *Pres.* John Jaffe.

Pergamon Orbit Infoline Inc. (Formerly Orbit Information Technologies Corporation), 8000 W. Park Dr., Suite 400, McLean, 22102. SAN 322-0273. Tel. 703-442-0900. *Pres.* James Terragno.

Richmond Area Film Library Cooperative, c/o Virginia Commonwealth Univ., James Branch Cabell Learning Resource Center, Richmond, 23284-2033. SAN 322-3469. Tel. 804-367-1088. *Assoc. Dir.* Richard Winant.

United States Army Training & Doctrine Command (TRADOC), Library & Information Network (TRALINET) Center, ATLS, Bldg. 117, Fort Monroe, 23651-5117. SAN 322-418X. Tel. 804-727-4491. *Dir.* James H. Byrn.

Virginia Tidewater Consortium, Old Science Bldg., Rm. 129, 5215 Hampton Blvd., Norfolk, 23529-0293. SAN 329-5486. Tel. 804-440-3012. *Dir.* Lawrence G. Dotolo.

Washington

Central Washington Hospital Consortium, Box 1887, Wenatchee, 98807. SAN 329-3750. Tel. 509-662-1511. *Libn.* Jane Belt.

Consortium for Automated Library Services, The Evergreen State College Library L2300, Olympia, 98505. SAN 329-4528. Tel. 206-866-6000, Ext. 6260. *Syst. Mgr.* Steven A. Metcalf.

Pacific Northwest Regional Health Sciences Library Service (PNRHSLS), c/o Health Sciences Library and Information Center, University of Washington, SB-55, Seattle, 98195. SAN 322-3485. Tel. 206-543-8262. *Dir.* Sherrilynne S. Fuller.

Seattle Area Hospital Library Consortium, c/o Virginia Mason Hospital Library, Box 1930, Seattle, 98111. SAN 329-3815. Tel. 206-223-6733. *Pres.* Ann Robertson.

Spokane Cooperative Library Information System (SCOLIS), c/o Spokane County Library District, N2901 Argonne Rd., Spokane, 99212-2101. SAN 322-3892. Tel. 509-924-4122. *Admin.* Michael J. Wirt; *Mgr.* Linda Predmore.

Western Library Network (WLN), Washington State Library, AJ-11W, Olympia, 98504-0111. SAN 322-3507. Tel. 206-459-6518. *Acting Dir.* Bruce Ziegman.

West Virginia

Huntington Health Science Library Consortium, Marshall University Health Science Libraries, Huntington, 25701. SAN 322-4295. Tel. 304-696-3170. *Chpn.* Sister Sylvia Rose.

Mountain States Consortium, c/o West Virginia Wesleyan College, Buckhannon, 26201. SAN 329-4765. Tel. 304-473-8000. *V.P.* David Thomas.

Southern West Virginia Library Automation Corporation, Box 1876 (221 N. Kanawha St.), Beckley, 25802. SAN 322-421X. Tel. 304-255-0511, Ext. 19. *Systems Mgr.* Bekki N. Ayers; *Systems Oper.* Michael Canada.

Wisconsin

Council of Wisconsin Libraries, Inc. (COWL), 728 State St., Rm. 464, Madison, 53706-1494. SAN 322-3523. Tel. 608-263-4962. *Dir.* Kathryn Schneider Michaelis.

Fox River Valley Area Library Consortium, c/o Riverside Community Hospital Library, 800 Riverside Dr., Waupaca, 54981. SAN 322-3531. Tel. 715-258-1063. *Coord.* Andrea Crane.

Library Council of Metropolitan Milwaukee, Inc., 814 W. Wisconsin Ave., Milwaukee, 53233. SAN 322-354X. Tel. 414-271-8470. *Exec. Dir.* Janis Trebby.

North East Wisconsin Intertype Libraries, Inc. (NEWIL), c/o Nicloet Federated Library System, 515 Pine St., Green Bay, 54301. SAN 322-3574. Tel. 414-497-3443. *Coord.* Mary Schmidt.

Northwestern Wisconsin Hospital Library Consortium, c/o Health Sciences Library, St. Michael's Hospital, 900 Illinois Ave., Stevens Point, 54481. SAN 322-3604. Tel. 715-346-5091. *Dir.* Barbara DeWeerd.

South Central Wisconsin Health Science Library Cooperative, c/o Methodist Hospital Library, 309 W. Washington Ave., Madison, 53703. SAN 322-4686. Tel. 608-251-2371, Ext. 3691. *Coord.* Robert Koehler.

Southeastern Wisconsin Health Science Library Consortium, c/o W. Allis Memorial Hospital Medical Library, 8901 W. Lincoln Ave., Milwaukee, 53227. SAN 322-3582. Tel. 414-546-6162. *Presiding Officer.* Joan Clausz.

Wisconsin Interlibrary Services (WILS), 728 State St., Rm. 464, Madison, 53706-1494. SAN 322-3612. Tel. 608-263-4962, 263-5051. FAX 608-263-3684. *Dir.* Kathryn Schneider Michaelis; *ILL & Ref. Coord.* Mary Williamson; *OCLC & New Technologies Coord.* Ed Van Gemert.

Wyoming

Southeast Wyoming Health Sciences Library Consortium, c/o Family Practice Library, 821 E. 18 St., Cheyenne, 82001-4393. SAN 322-3752. Tel. 307-777-7911. *Chmn.* Carol Seebaum.

Wind River Health Sciences Library Consortium, Lander Valley Regional Medical Center, 1320 Bishop Randall Dr., Lander, 82520. SAN 322-4228. Tel. 307-332-4420, Ext. 315. *Libn.* Jane Heuer.

Virgin Islands

VILINET (Virgin Islands Library & Information Network), c/o Div. of Libraries, Museums & Archives, 23 Dronnigens Gade, Saint Thomas, 00802. SAN 322-3639. Tel. 809-774-3407 (DLMAS) & 774-3725. *Chpn.* Fiolina B. Mills; *Dir.* Jeannette Allis.

Alberta

QL Systems Ltd., 150 Sixth Ave. S.W., Suite 2180, Calgary, T2P 3H7. SAN 329-403X. Tel. 403-262-6506. *Pres.* Hugh Lawford.

British Columbia

British Columbia Post-Secondary Interlibrary Loan Network, Net, University of BC Interlibrary Loan Library, 1956 Main Mall, Vancouver, V6T 1Y3. SAN 322-4724. Tel. 604-228-4430. *Head ILL.* Margaret Friesen.

Ontario

Bibliocentre, 80 Cowdray Court, Scarborough, M1S 4N1. SAN 322-3663. Tel. 416-299-1515. WATS 800-268-5560. *Dir.* Doug Wentzel.

Ontario Public Library Information Network, Ontario Ministry of Culture and Communications, Libraries and Community Info. Branch, 77 Bloor St. W., 3rd fl., Toronto, M7A 2R9. SAN 329-5605. Tel. 416-965-2696. *Mgr.* Maureen Killeen.

QL Systems Ltd., One Gore St., Kingston, K7L 2L1. SAN 322-368X. Tel. 613-549-4611. *Pres.* Hugh Lawford.

SIRLS, Faculty of Human Kinetics & Leisure Studies, University of Waterloo, Waterloo, N2L 3G1. SAN 322-4538. Tel. 519-885-1211, Ext. 2560. *Database Mgr. & Consult.* Betty Millman.

Toronto School of Theology, 75 Queen's Park Crescent E., Toronto, M5S 1K7. SAN 322-452X. Tel. 416-585-4551. *Coord.* R. Grant Bracewell.

Waterloo-Wellington Museum Computer Network, The Seagram Museum, 57 Erb St. W., Waterloo, N2L 6C2. SAN 329-4862. Tel. 519-885-1857. *Mgr.* Don Spencer; *Asst. Dir.* Wendy Hallman.

National Library and Information-Industry Associations, United States and Canada

American Association of Law Libraries

53 W. Jackson Blvd., Chicago, IL 60604
312-939-4764

Object

"To promote librarianship, to develop and increase the usefulness of law libraries, to cultivate the science of law librarianship, and to foster a spirit of cooperation among members of the profession." Established 1906. Memb. 4,100. Dues (Active) $65; (Inst.) $65; (Assoc.) $65 & $125; (Student) $10. Year. June 1 to May 31.

Membership

Persons officially connected with a law library or with a law section of a state or general library, separately maintained. Associate membership available for others.

Officers (June 1988–June 1989)

Pres. Margaret A. Leary, Univ. of Michigan Law Lib., 801 Monroe St., Ann Arbor, MI 48109-1210; *V.P./Pres.-Elect.* Richard A. Danner, Duke Univ. Law Lib., Durham, NC 27706; *Secy.* Gitelle Seer, Dewey, Ballantine, Bushby, Palmer & Wood, 140 Broadway, New York, NY 10005; *Treas.* Alan Holoch, Ohio State Univ. Law Lib., 1659 N. High St., Columbus, OH 43210; *Immediate Past Pres.* Albert O. Brecht, Univ. of Southern California Law Lib., University Park, Los Angeles, CA 90089-0072.

Executive Board (1988–1989)

Judy B. Dimes-Smith; Barbara L. Golden; Kathleen Larson; Melody Busse Lembke; Kay Todd; Donna Tuke Heroy.

Committee Chairpersons

Awards. Carol Yirka.

Call for Papers. Leah F. Chanin.

Citation Standards. Robert J. Nissenbaum, Cleveland State Univ. Law Lib., 1801 Euclid Ave., Cleveland, OH 44115-2403.

CONELL. Co-Chpns. Nancy P. Johnson, Georgia State Univ. Law Lib., University Plaza, Atlanta, GA 30303-3092; Janet Kasabian.

Constitution and Bylaws. Scott B. Pagel.

Copyright. Bruce M. Kennedy.

Council of Chapter Presidents Coord. Judith Meadows, State Law Lib. of Montana, Justice Dept., 215 N. Sanders, Helena, MT 59620.

Directory of Law Libraries. Eds. Anne H. Butler, Alston & Bird, 35 Broad St., Suite 1200, Atlanta, GA 30335; Randall T. Peterson, John Marshall Law School Lib., 315 S. Plymouth Ct., Chicago, IL 60604; Bardie C. Wolfe, Jr., St. Thomas Univ. Law Lib., 16400 N.W. 32 Ave., Miami, FL 33167.

Education. Joan S. Howland, Univ. of California, Law Lib., Boalt Hall, Berkeley, CA 94720.

Educational Policy–Special. Judith Wright.

Elections. Louis J. Covotsos.

Financial Advisory. Robert F. Jacobs.

Grants. Carol A. Suhre.

Index of Periodical Literature Advisory. Victoria Trotta, Lewis and Roca, 100 W. Washington, Phoenix, AZ 85003.

Index to Foreign Legal Periodicals. Ed. Thomas H. Reynolds, Univ. of California, School of Law Lib. (Boalt Hall), Berkeley, CA 94720.

Index to Foreign Legal Periodicals Advisory. Lance E. Dickson, Louisiana State Univ. Law Lib., Baton Rouge, LA 70803-1010.

Law Library Journal Advisory. Donald J. Dunn.

Law Library Journal Ed. Richard A. Danner, Duke Univ. Law Lib., Durham, NC 27706.

Legislation and Legal Developments. Mary B. Jensen.

Minorities. Cecilia Kwan.

National Information Policy–Special. Bob Oakley.

National Legal Resources. Kathie Pierce.

Newsletter. Mary Sworsky.

Nominations. Meg Chicco.

Organizational Structure of AALL. Kay M. Todd, Paul, Hastings, Janofsky & Walker, 133 Peachtree St. N.E., Atlanta, GA 30303.

Placement. Kathleen Carrick.

Preservation Needs of Law Libraries. Diana Vincent-Daviss, New York Univ. Law Lib., 40 Washington Sq. S., New York, NY 10012.

Publications. Merle J. Slyhoff, Univ. of Pennsylvania Law Lib., 3400 Chestnut St., Philadelphia, PA 19104-6279.

Relations with Information Vendors. Adrienne Adam.

Scholarships and Grants. Judith Anspach.

Sponsored Publications Advisory. Kaye V. Stoppel, Drake Univ. Law Lib., Des Moines, IA 50311.

Statistics. Dennis Stone.

Special-Interest Section Chairpersons

Academic Law Libraries. Lynn Foster, Univ. of Arkansas, Little Rock Law Lib., 400 W. Markham, Little Rock, AR 72201.

Automation and Scientific Development. S. Blair Kauffman, Univ. of Wisconsin Law Lib., 975 Bascom Mall, Madison, WI 53706.

Contemporary Social Problems. Arturo Torres, Univ. of Arizona Law Lib., Tucson, AZ 85721.

Foreign, Comparative and International Law. Daniel L. Wade, Yale Univ. Law Lib., 127 Wall St., New Haven, CT 06520.

Government Documents. Christine A. Corcos, Case Western Reserve Univ. Law Lib., 11075 East Blvd., Cleveland, OH 44106.

Legal Information Service to the Public. Elizabeth Schneider, Maricopa County Law Lib., 101 W. Jefferson, Phoenix, AZ 85003.

Micrographics and Audio/Visual. Kay Andrus, Northwestern Univ. Law Lib., 357 E. Chicago Ave., Chicago, IL 60611.

On-Line Bibliographic Services. Janice Anderson, Georgetown Univ. Law Lib., 600 New Jersey Ave. N.W., Washington, DC 20001.

Private Law Libraries. Susanne Gehringer, Piper and Marbury, 888 16th St. N.W., Washington, DC 20006.

Readers' Services. Pat Court, Univ. of Missouri, Kansas City, Law Lib., 5100 Rockhill Rd., Kansas City, MO 64110.

Special-Interest Sections Council. Carol Billings, Law Lib. of Louisiana, 100 Supreme Court Bldg., 301 Loyola Ave., New Orleans, LA 70112.

State, Court and County Law Libraries. Fred Baum, Assn. of the Bar of the City of New York, Law Lib., 42 W. 44 St., New York, NY 10036.

Technical Services. Renee Chapman, SUNY, Buffalo—Charles Sear Law Lib., Amherst Campus, John Lord O'Brian Hall, Buffalo, NY 14260.

Representatives 1988–1989

American Bar Association. Margaret Leary.

American Correctional Association. Jane (Charlie) Colokathis.

American Library Association. Sandra S. Coleman.

American Library Association Committee on Cataloging: Description & Access. Lee Leighton.

American Library Association Committee on Interlibrary Loan. Marjorie E. Crawford.

American Library Association Government Documents Roundtable (GODRT). Veronica MacLay.

American Library Association Machine Readable for Bibliographic Information (MARBI). Evelyn L. Smith.

American Library Association Publisher/Vendor Library Relations Committee. Margaret Maes Axtmann.

American Society for Information Science (ASIS). Mickie A. Voges.

Association for Information and Image Managements-Standards Board. Larry Wenger.

Association for Library and Information Science Education. Penny A. Hazelton.

Association of American Law Schools. Albert O. Brecht.

Association of Legal Administrators. Donald G. Ziegenfuss; Kenneth C. Halicki.

British-Irish Association of Law Libraries. David A. Thomas.

Canadian Association of Law Libraries. Frances H. Hall.

Coalition on Government Information. Charlotte White.

Council of National Library and Information Associations. James L. Hoover.
International Association of Law Libraries. Claire Germain.
International Federation of Library Associations. Laura N. Gasaway.
Library of Congress. Kathleen Price.
Library of Congress Network Advisory Committee. Robert L. Oakley.
Library of Congress Special Committee on Foreign Class K Schedule. Thomas H. Reynolds.
National Association of Secretaries of State. Judith Meadows.
National Information Standards Organization. Robert J. Nissenbaum.
Special Library Association. Virginia Wise.
State Justice Institute. Kai-Yun Chiu.
U.S. Congress Ad Hoc Committee on Depository Library Access to Databases. Stephen G. Margeton.
U.S. Copyright Office. Marlene C. McGuirl.

American Film and Video Association

(Formerly Educational Film Library Association)
Executive Director, Ron MacIntyre
920 Barnsdale Rd., Suite 152, La Grange Park, IL 60525
312-482-4000

Object

"To promote the production, distribution and utilization of educational films and videos, and other audiovisual materials." Incorporated 1943. Memb. 1,500. Dues (Inst.) $175; (Commercial organizations) $265; (Indiv.) $45; (Students and Retirees) $25. Floating membership year.

Officers

Pres. Sharon K. Chaplock, Milwaukee Public Museum, 800 W. Wells St., Milwaukee, WI 53233; *Pres.-Elect.* Mark Richie, Burlington County AVA Commission, 122 High St., Mt. Holly, NJ 08060; *Past Pres.* Judith Gaston, Univ. Film & Video, Univ. of Minnesota, 1313 Fifth St. S.E., Minneapolis, MN 55414; *Secy:* Linda Artel, Pacific Film Archive, Univ. Art Museum, Univ. of California at Berkeley, Berkeley, CA 94703; *Treas.* June McWatt, Macomb Intermediate School Dist., Beal Lib., 44001 Garfield, Mt. Clemens, MI 48044.

Board of Directors

Olga Knight, Univ. of California EMC, 2176 Shattuck Ave., Berkeley, CA 94704; Nora McMartin, Senior Libn., Chula Vista Public Lib., 365 F St., Chula Vista, CA 92010; Christine L. McDonald, Dir., Crandall Lib., City Park, Glens Falls, NY 12801; Beverly Teach, Indiana Univ., Audio-Visual Center, Bloomington, IN 47405-5901; Anthony Marshalek, Dir., North East Ohio Instructional Media Center, 2251 Atlantic St. N.E., Warren, OH 44483; Paul Neeb, Coronet/MTI Films & Video, 108 Wilmot Rd., Deerfield, IL 60015.

Publications

American Film and Video Association Bulletin (q.).
American Film and Video Evaluations (2 per year).
American Film and Video Festival Program Guide (ann.).
Sightlines (q.). *Ed.* Ray Rolf.

American Library Association

Executive Director, Thomas J. Galvin
50 E. Huron St., Chicago, IL 60611
312-944-6780

Object

The mission of the American Library Association is to provide leadership for the development, promotion, and improvement of library and information services and the profession of librarianship in order to enhance learning and ensure access to information for all. Memb. (Indiv.) 44,308; (Inst.) 2,941. Dues (Indiv.) 1st year, $38; renewing memb., $75; (Nonsalaried Libn.) $26; (Trustee & Assoc. Membs.) $34; (Student) $19; (Foreign Indiv.) $45; (Inst.) $70 & up, depending on operating expenses of institution.

Membership

Any person, library, or other organization interested in library service and librarians.

Officers

Pres. F. William Summers, Dean, School of Lib. and Info. Studies, Florida State Univ., Tallahassee, FL 32306; *Pres.-Elect.* Patricia W. Berger, National Institute of Standards and Technology, Info. Research and Service Div., Admin. Bldg. E 106, Rte. 270 & Quince Orchard Rd., Gaitersburg, MD 20899; *Treas.* Carla J. Stoffle, Assoc. Dir., Univ. of Michigan Libs., Ann Arbor, MI 48109. *Exec. Dir.* (*Ex officio*) Thomas J. Galvin, ALA Headquarters, 50 E. Huron St., Chicago, IL 60611.

Executive Board

Past Pres. Margaret E. Chisholm, Dir., School of Lib. and Info. Science, Univ. of Washington, 133 Suzzallo Lib., FM30, Seattle, WA 98195; Margaret L. Crist (1989); J. Dennis Day (1992); Sharon Hogan (1992); Duane F. Johnson (1990); Regina U. Minudri (Midwinter 1990); Patricia G. Schuman (Midwinter 1989); Robert D. Stueart (1991); Lucille C. Thomas (1991).

Endowment Trustees

Albert W. Daub (1991); Richard M. Dougherty (1989); Richard A. Olsen (1990). *Staff liaison.* Susan C. Odmark.

Divisions

See the separate entries that follow: American Assn. of School Libns.; American Lib. Trustee Assn.; Assn. for Lib. Service to Children; Assn. of College and Research Libs.; Assn. of Specialized and Cooperative Lib. Agencies; Lib. Admin. and Management Assn.; Lib. and Info. Technology Assn.; Public Lib. Assn.; Reference and Adult Services Div.; Resources and Technical Services Div.; Young Adult Services Div.

Publications

ALA Handbook of Organization and Membership Directory 1988–1989 (ann.).

ALA Yearbook (ann.; $80).

American Libraries (11 per year; free to membs.; available by subscription to organizations at $50 a year; foreign, $60; single copy, $5; foreign, $6).

Booklist (22 issues; U.S. & possessions, $56 a year; foreign, $70; single copy, $4.50).

Choice (11 issues; subscriptions, U.S., $125; foreign, $140).

Round Table Chairpersons

(ALA staff liaison is given in parentheses.)

Continuing Library Education Network and Exchange. Mary Y. Moore, Washington State Lib., Mail Stop AJ11, Olympia, WA 98504 (Elaine K. Wingate).

Ethnic Materials and Information Exchange. Marie F. Zielinska, National Lib. of Canada, 395 Wellington St., Ottawa, ON K1A 0N4, Canada (Sibyl E. Moses).

Exhibits. Roger J. Long, McGregor Subscription Service, 2 S. Seminary, Mt. Morris, IL 61054 (Walter M. Brueggen).

Federal Librarians. Doris Beachell Grimes, 5005 King Richard Dr., Annandale, VA 22003 (Anne A. Heanue).

Government Documents. Sandra S. McAninch, Government Publications Dept., Univ. of Kentucky Libs., Margaret I. King Lib., Lexington, KY 40506-0039 (Elaine K. Wingate).

Independent Librarians Exchange. Mary C. Chobot, Mary C. Chobot Assocs., 4950 Andrea Ave., Annandale, VA 22003-4166 (Margaret Myers).

Intellectual Freedom. Laurence A. Miller, Univ. Lib., Florida International Univ., Miami, FL 33199 (Anne Levinson).

International Relations. Miles M. Jackson, Grad. School of Lib. Studies, Univ. of Hawaii, 2550 The Mall, Honolulu, HI 96822 (Elaine K. Wingate).

Junior Members. Karin E. Ford, Idaho State Lib., 325 W. State St., Boise, ID 83702 (Marcia J. Kuszmaul).

Library History. Gordon B. Neavill, Grad. School of Lib. Service, Univ. of Alabama, Box 6242, Tuscaloosa, AL 35487-6242 (To be appointed).

Library Instruction. Tobeylynn Birch, California School of Professional Psychology, Los Angeles Campus Lib., 2235 Beverly Blvd., Los Angeles, CA 90057 (Jeniece Guy).

Library Research. Joe A. Hewitt, Walter Royal Davis Lib., Univ. of North Carolina, Chapel Hill, NC 27514 (Mary Jo Lynch).

Map and Geography Round Table. Mary Anne L. Waltz, E. S. Bird Memorial Lib., 222 Waverly Ave., Syracuse, NY 13244-2010 (Elaine K. Wingate).

Social Responsibilities. John B. S. Hostage, Harvard Law School Lib., Langdell Hall, Cambridge, MA 02138 (Sibyl E. Moses).

Staff Organizations. Gwendolyn J. Potier, Houston Community College Lib., 901 Yorkchester, Houston, TX 77079 (Elaine K. Wingate).

Committee Chairpersons

Accreditation (Standing). Herman L. Totten, 2100 Pembrooke Place, Denton, TX 76205 (June Lester).

"American Libraries" (Advisory). Allan J. Dyson, McHenry Lib., Univ. of California, Santa Cruz, CA 95064 (Arthur Plotnik).

Appointments (Advisory). Patricia Wilson Berger, National Institute of Standards and Technology, Info. Research and Service Div., Admin. Bldg. E 106, Rte. 270 & Quince Orchard Rd., Gaitersburg, MD 20899 (Miriam L. Hornback).

Awards. Ronald S. Kozlowski, Cuyahoga County Public Lib., 4510 Memphis Ave., Cleveland, OH 44144 (Elaine K. Wingate).

Chapter Relations (Standing). Patricia H. Mautino, Oswego County BOCES, County Rte. 64, Mexico, NY 13114 (Patricia A. Scarry).

Committee on Committees (Elected Council Committee). Patricia Wilson Berger, National Institute of Standards and Technology, Info. Res. and Services Div., Admin. Bldg. E 106, Rte. 270 & Quince Orchard Rd., Gaitersburg, MD 20899 (Miriam L. Hornback).

Conference Program (Standing) Dallas, 1989. F. William Summers, School of Lib. and Info. Studies, Florida State Univ., Tallahassee, FL 32306 (Roger H. Parent, Peggy Barber).

Constitution and Bylaws (Standing). Joel C. Rosenfeld, Rockford Public Lib., 215 W. Wyman St., Rockford, IL 61101 (Miriam L. Hornback).

Council Orientation (Special, Council). Julie A. Cummins, Monroe County Lib. System, 115 South Ave., Rochester, NY 14604 (Miriam L. Hornback).

Endowment Campaign (Special, Presidential). Patricia Schuman, Neal Schuman Publishers, 23 Leonard St., New York, NY 10013 (Peggy Barber).

Information Literacy (Special). Patricia Senn Breivik, Dir., Auraria Lib. and Media Center, Lawrence at 11 St., Denver, CO 80204 (JoAn S. Segal).

Instruction in the Use of Libraries (Standing). May Brottman, Glenbrook North H.S., Northbrook, IL 60062 (Andrew M. Hansen).

Intellectual Freedom (Standing, Council). C. James Schmidt, Research Libs. Group, Jordan Quadrangle, Stanford, CA 94305 (Judith F. Krug).

International Relations (Standing, Council). E. J. Josey, Assoc. Professor, School of Lib. and Info. Science, Univ. of Pittsburgh, Pittsburgh, PA 15260 (Robert P. Doyle).

Legislation (Standing, Council). Ella Gaines

Yates, State Lib. and Archives, 11 St. at Capitol Sq., Richmond, VA 23219 (Eileen D. Cooke).

Library Education (Standing, Council). Jane Robbins, School of Lib. and Info. Studies, Univ. of Wisconsin, Madison, WI 53706 (Margaret Myers).

Library Outreach Services, Office for (Standing, Advisory). Kenneth A. Yamashita, Branch/Book Mobile Supv., Stockton–San Joaquin County Public Lib., Stockton, CA 95202 (Sibyl E. Moses).

Library Personnel Resources, Office for (Standing, Advisory). Margaret M. Kimmel, School of Lib. and Info. Science, Univ. of Pittsburgh, Pittsburgh, PA 15260 (Margaret Myers).

Mediation, Arbitration, and Inquiry Review (Special). Robert D. Stueart, Dean, Grad. School of Lib. and Info. Science, Simmons College, 300 The Fenway, Boston, MA 02115 (Ernest Martin).

Mediation, Arbitration and Inquiry, Staff Committee on (Standing). Roger H. Parent, ALA Headquarters, 50 E. Huron St., Chicago, IL 60611.

Membership (Standing). Carol K. DiPrete, 26 Slater Ave., Providence, RI 02906 (Katherine G. Wilkins).

Minority Concerns (Standing, Council). Barbara Williams-Jenkins, 1594 Magnolia Ave., Orangeburg, SC 29115 (Sibyl E. Moses).

National Library Week (Standing). Dean Burgess, Portsmouth Public Lib., Portsmouth, VA 23704 (Linda K. Wallace).

Nominating—1989 Election (Special). Alphonse F. Trezza, School of Lib. & Info. Studies, Florida State Univ., Tallahassee, FL 32306 (Miriam L. Hornback).

Organization (Standing, Council). Norman Horrocks, Scarecrow Press, Box 4167, Metuchen, NJ 08840 (Roger H. Parent).

Pay Equity (Standing, Council). Janice Feye-Stukas, Minnesota State Lib. Agency, Lib. Development & Service, 440 Capitol Sq., 550 Cedar St., St. Paul, MN 55101 (Margaret Myers).

Planning (Standing, Council). William T. DeJohn, 2923 Northview St., Roseville, MN 55113 (Roger H. Parent).

Policy Monitoring (Council). Judith R. Farley, 1301 Delaware Ave. S.W., N-404, Washington, DC 20024 (Miriam L. Hornback).

Professional Ethics (Standing, Council). Gerald R. Shields, 546 College Ave., Niagara Falls, NY 14305 (Judith F. Krug).

Program Evaluation and Support (Standing, Council). Daniel J. Bradbury, Kansas City Lib., 311 E. 12 St., Kansas City, MO 64106 (Susan C. Odmark).

Publishing (Standing, Council). Bernard S. Schlessinger, School of Lib. and Info. Studies, Texas Woman's Univ., Denton, TX 76204 (Edgar S. McLarin).

Research (Standing). Janis C. Keene, Tulsa City-County Lib., 400 Civic Center, Tulsa, OK 74103 (Mary Jo Lynch).

Resolutions (Standing, Council). Bernard A. Margolis, Monroe County Lib. System, 3700 S. Custer Rd., Monroe, MI 48161 (Miriam L. Hornback).

Standards (Standing). Helen Lloyd Snoke, School of Lib. and Info. Studies, Univ. of Michigan, 580 Union Dr., Ann Arbor, MI 48109-1346 (Mary Jo Lynch).

Visionary Leaders for 2020 (Special). Brooke E. Sheldon, School of Lib. Science, Texas Woman's Univ., Denton, TX 76204 (Peggy Barber, Thomas J. Galvin, Margaret Myers).

Women in Librarianship, Status of (Standing, Council). Gail P. Warner, Whitman County Lib., N. 101 West St., Colfax, WA 99111 (Margaret Myers).

Joint Committee Chairpersons

American Correctional Association—ASCLA Committee on Institution Libraries (joint). Stephen Mallinger, Workplace Project Director, State Lib. of Pennsylvania, Harrisburg, PA 17105 (ACA); Mark E. Pumphrey (ALA/ASCLA).

American Federation of Labor/Congress of Industrial Organizations—ALA, Library Service to Labor Groups, RASD. Michele Leber, 1805 Crystal Dr., Apt. 911, Arlington, VA 22202 (ALA); Jim Auerbach, AFL/CIO, Dept. of Education, 815 16th St. N.W., Rm. 407, Washington, DC 20006 (AFL/CIO).

Anglo-American Cataloguing Rules Com-

mon Revision Fund. Edgar S. McLarin, Assoc. Exec. Dir. for Publishing (ALA); Laurie Bowes, Canadian Lib. Assn., 200 Elgin St., Suite 602, Ottawa, ON K2P 1L5, Canada (CLA); Joyce Butcher, British Lib., 2 Sheraton St., London W1V 4BH, England (British Lib. Assn.).

Anglo-American Cataloguing Rules, Joint Steering Committee for Revision of. Helen F. Schmierer, 5550 S. Dorchester, Apt. 408, Chicago, IL 60637 (ALA).

Association for Educational Communications and Technology–AASL. Frances M. McDonald, Mankato State Univ., Memorial Lib., Box 19, Mankato, MN 56001.

Association for Educational Communications and Technology–ACRL. James O. Wallace, Box 13041, San Antonio, TX 78213 (ACRL); Daniel D. Koenig, Piedmont Technical College, Box 1467, Greenwood, SC 29464 (AECT).

Association of American Publishers–ALA. F. William Summers, School of Lib. and Info. Studies, Florida State Univ., Tallahassee, FL 32306 (ALA); To be appointed (AAP).

Association of American Publishers–RTSD. Thomas L. Hart, School of Lib. and Info. Studies, Florida State Univ., Tallahassee, FL 32306; Peter Simon, R. R. Bowker Co., 245 W. 17 St., New York, NY 10011 (AAP).

Children's Book Council–ALA. Ellen E. Fader, Westport Public Lib., Arnold Bernhard Plaza, Westport, CT 06880 (ALA); James Giblin, Clarion Book/Ticknor & Fields, 52 Vanderbilt Ave., New York, NY 10017 (CBC).

Society of American Archivists–ALA (Joint Committee on Library-Archives Relationships). Robert S. Martin, Special Collections, Hill Memorial Lib., Louisiana State Univ., Baton Rouge, LA 70803-3300 (ALA); Nicholas Burckel, c/o Society of American Archivists, 600 S. Federal St., Suite 504, Chicago, IL 60606 (SAA).

American Library Association
American Association of School Librarians

Executive Director, Ann Carlson Weeks
50 E. Huron St., Chicago, IL 60611
312-944-6780

Object

The American Association of School Librarians is interested in the general improvement and extension of library media services for children and young people. AASL has specific responsibility for: planning of program of study and service for the improvement and extension of library media services in elementary and secondary schools as a means of strengthening the educational program; evaluation, selection, interpretation, and utilization of media as it is used in the context of the school program; stimulation of continuous study and research in the library field and to establish criteria of evaluation; synthesis of the activities of all units of the American Library Association in areas of mutual concern; representation and interpretation of the need for the function of school libraries to other educational and lay groups; stimulation of professional growth, improvement of the status of school librarians, and encouragement of participation by members in appropriate type-of-activity divisions; conduct activities and projects for improvement and extension of service in the school library when such projects are beyond the scope of type-of-activity divisions, after specific approval by the ALA Council. Established in 1951 as a separate division of ALA. Memb. 6,048.

Membership

Open to all libraries, school library media specialists, interested individuals, and business firms with requisite membership in ALA.

Officers

Pres. Jacqueline G. Morris, 5225 Leone Place, Indianapolis, IN 46226; *V.P./Pres.-Elect.* Retta B. Patrick, Box 22235, Little Rock, AR 72221; *Rec. Secy.* (1990). Delores Z. Pretlow, 1404 Antrim Ave., Richmond, VA 23230; *Past Pres.* Karen A. Whitney, 5320 W. Kings Ave., Glendale, AZ 85306.

Board of Directors

Officers; *Exec. Dir.* Ann Carlson Weeks; *Deputy Exec. Dir.* Barbara Herrin; *Regional Dirs.* Bernice (Bunny) L. Yesner, 16 Sunbrook Rd., Woodbridge, CT 06525; Sue Albertson Walker, 6065 Parkridge Dr., East Petersburg, PA 17520; Beverley C. Rentschler, 6095 Pontiac Trail, West Bloomfield, MI 48033; Phyllis (Rea) A. Monyakula, 5807 W. 99 St., Overland Park, KS 66207; Pamela Parman, 2312 Island Blvd., Sevierville, TN 37862; Marvene Dearman, 1471 Chevelle Dr., Baton Rouge, LA 70806; Mildred Lee, 5401 Santa Teresa, Santa Rosa, CA 95405; *Affiliate Assembly.* James F. Bennett, Shoreham-Wading River H.S., Rte. 2, Shoreham, NY 11786; *AA Delegates.* (1989) Gloria L. Davidson, Lib. Media Center, T. C. Williams H.S., 3330 King St., Alexandria, VA 22303; (1990) Anne Masters, 131 South Flood, Norman, OK 73069; *AASL Representative to Council* (1990) Helen Lloyd Snoke, 3352 Yellowstone Dr., Ann Arbor, MI 48105; *Non-Public Schools Sec. Chair* (1991) William M. Fabian, Principia Upper School, 13201 Clayton Rd., St. Louis, MO 63131; *School Library Media Educators Sec. Chair* (1990) Rosalind Miller, Apt. #15, 222 Forkner Dr., Decatur, GA 30030; *Supervisors Sec. Chair* (1989) Mary D. Lankford, Lib. & Media Services, Irving I.S.D.-Instructional Center, 820 North O'Connor Rd., Irving, TX 75061.

Publications

AASL Presidential Hotline (s. ann.; membs.).

School Library Media Quarterly (q.; memb.; nonmemb. $35). *Ed.* Judy Pitts, Barbara Stripling Fayetteville H.S. Lib., 1000 W. Stone St., Fayetteville, AR 72701.

Committee Chairpersons

Unit Group I – Organizational Maintenance

Unit Head. Jerry R. Wicks, 1359 W. Thorndale, Chicago, IL 60660.

Annual Conference Local Arrangements – Dallas, 1989. Cynthia A. Gray.

Annual Conference Program Planning – Dallas, 1989. Beverly Bashia and Sharon Harvey.

Budget. Judith M. King.

Bylaws and Organization. Barbara Nemer.

Membership. Nancy Zimmerman.

Nominating – 1989 Election. Blanche Woolls.

Unit Group II – Organizational Relationships

Unit Head. Donna J. Helmer, Loussac Lib., 3600 Denali, Anchorage, AK 99503.

AECT Liaison. Charles R. White.

ASCD Liaison. M. Ellen Jay.

IRA Liaison. Laura M. Benson.

Professional Organization Liaison. Hilda Jay.

Unit Group III – Media Personnel Development

Unit Head. Aileen Helmick, 318 Johnson, Warrensburg, MO 64093.

Continuing Education/Professional Development. Robert D. Little.

Joint Committee AECT/AASL. Frances McDonald.

Leadership Enhancement. Drucilla (Drucie) Reeves.

Unit Group IV – Media Program Development

Unit Head. Elizabeth (Bettie) B. Day, Office of County Supt. of Schools, 4400 Cathedral Oaks Rd., Box 6307, Santa Barbara, CA 93106-6307.

Intellectual Freedom. Pauletta Bracy.

International Relations. Marvene Dearman.

Legislation. Carol Diehl.

Research. Philip M. Turner.

Services to the School Community. Virginia Kalb; *Accessing Instructional Materials and Information.* Jane Terwillegar; *Evalu-*

ation of School Lib. Media Programs. Doris Epler; *Information Utilization Skills Instruction (Developing Critical Thinking Skills).* May Brottman; *Materials Selection.* Rosa Pressberry; *Standardization of Access to Lib. Media Resources.* To be appointed.

Technology. Robert Skapura. *Microcomputers and Telecommunications in Schools.* Lynn Livingston; *Networking.* Robert G. Hale; *Video Communications.* Daniel Callison.

Unit Group V—Public Information

Unit Head. Constance J. Champlin, Coord., Media Services, MSD Washington Township, 3801 E. 79 St., Indianapolis, IN 46240.

American University Press Services Publication Selection. Evelyn Schneider.

Awards. Joanne Troutner. *ABC/CLIO.* Doris Masek; *Distinguished Lib. Service Award for School Administrators.* Shirley D. Ross; *Distinguished Service Award (AASL/Baker & Taylor).* Clara J. Hoover; *Frances Henne.* Ann T. White; *Intellectual Freedom (AASL/SIRS).* Gayle Keresey; *Microcomputer in the Media Center (AASL/Follett).* Nancy Ellen Graf; *National School Lib. Media Program of the Year (NSLMPY/EB).* Eliza T. Dresang.

National School Lib. Media Month. Mary Lou Gregory.

Publications. Janie Schomberg.

School Lib. Media Quarterly Editorial Board of Directors. Judy M. Pitts and Barbara K. Stripling.

Special Committees

General Conference—Salt Lake City, Utah, 1989. Don Adcock.

NEA Mastery. Carol Stanke.

Task Forces

Guidelines for School Library Media Programs Implementation. Dan Barron.

Long-Range Planning. Karen A. Whitney.

WHCLIST Planning, 1989. Dianne Hopkins.

Interest Groups

Early Childhood Education. To be appointed.

School Library Media Programs in Vocational/Technical Schools. To be appointed.

Student Involvement in the Media Center. To be appointed.

Section Chairpersons

Non-Public Schools Section (NPSS). Ellen Mintz.

School Library Media Educators Section (SLMES). Margaret Denman-West.

Supervisors Section (SPVS). William Murray.

Representatives

ALA Appointments Committee. Retta B. Patrick.

ALA Dallas Conference (1989) Program Committee. Jacqueline G. Morris.

ALA Legislation Assembly. Carol L. Diehl.

ALA Chicago Conference (1990) Program Committee. Retta B. Patrick.

ALA Planning and Budget Assembly. Judith M. King.

Freedom to Read Foundation. Pauletta B. Bracy.

Library Education Assembly. Frank Birmingham.

RTSD-CCS Cataloging of Children's Materials Committee. To be appointed.

American Library Association
American Library Trustee Association

Executive Director, Sharon L. Jordan
50 E. Huron St., Chicago, IL 60611
312-944-6780

Object

The development of effective library service for all people in all types of communities and in all types of libraries; it follows that its members are concerned as policymakers with organizational patterns of service, with the development of competent personnel, the provision of adequate financing, the passage of suitable legislation, and the encouragement of citizen support for libraries. Open to all interested persons and organizations. Organized 1890. Became an ALA division 1961. Memb. 1,658. (For dues and membership year, see ALA entry.)

Officers (1988–1989)

Pres. Norma Buzan, 3057 Betsy Ross Dr., Bloomfield Hills, MI 48013; *1st V.P./Pres.-Elect.* Norman Kelinson, 1228 Coffelt Ave., Bettendorf, IA 52722; *2nd V.P.* Wayne Moss, 5329 Boulevard Place, Indianapolis, IN 46208; *Immediate Past Pres.* Gloria T. Glaser, 60 Sutton Place S., Apt. 8 C-S, New York, NY 10022; *Secy.* Ira Harkavy, 1784 E. 29 St., Brooklyn, NY 11229.

Board of Directors

Councillor. Deborah Miller; *PLA Rep.* Claudia Sumler; *Newsletter Ed.* Nancy Stiegemeyer; *Parliamentarian.* Ira Harkavy; *Historian.* James Hess; *Exec. Dir.* Sharon L. Jordan; *Council Administrators.* Gloria Dinerman; Jess Gardner; John Parsons; Aileen R. Schrader; Patricia F. Turner; *Regional V.P.s.* Mary Lou Dewey (1990); Cynthia Everett (1990); Leonard H. Freiser (1990); Robert G. Gaylor (1990); Esther Lopato (1989); Thomas M. McLaren (1990); Norma Lee Mihalevich (1989); Suzan Rickert (1989); Ramonda Wertz (1990); Holley Wilkinson (1990).

Publication

The ALTA Newsletter (6 per year; free to membs.). *Ed.* Nancy Stiegemeyer, 215 Camellia Dr., Cape Girardeau, MO 63701.

Committee Chairpersons

Action Development. Paulette Holahan, 6417 Fleur de Lis Dr., New Orleans, LA 70124; Patricia Pizzo, 2665 Sare Rd., Bloomington, IN 47401.

Awards. Minnie-Lou Lynch, 404 E. Sixth Ave., Oakdale, LA 71463.

Budget. Norman Kelinson, 1228 Coffelt Ave., Bettendorf, IA 52722.

Centennial (task force). Jess Gardner, 175 Idle Hour Dr., Lexington, KY 40502; Nancy Stiegemeyer, 215 Camellia Dr., Cape Girardeau, MO 63701.

Common Concerns ALTA/PLA. Mary Arney, 3646 Charlotte, Kansas City, MO 64109; William Ptacek, Louisville Free Public Lib., Fourth & York Sts., Louisville, KY 40203.

Conference Program and Evaluation. Patricia F. Turner, 3419 Redman Rd., Baltimore, MD 21207; Joyce E. Lottner, 5359 S. Geneva St., Englewood, CO 80111.

Education of Trustees. Ann Donoghue, 15411 Betty Ann Lane, Oak Forest, IL 60452.

Financial Development. Ronald C. Harley, 14840 Massasoit, Oak Forest, IL 60452; Virginia Young, 10 E. Parkway Dr., Columbia, MO 65203.

Intellectual Freedom. Madeleine Grant, 3300 Rance Terr., Lincolnwood, IL 60645; William Murray, 18011 E. 14 Dr., Aurora, CO 80011.

Legislation. Roslyn S. Kurland, 4400 N. Hills Dr., Hollywood, FL 33201; Terri C. Jacobs, 580 Longwood Ave., Glencoe, IL 60022.

Membership. Norman Kelinson, 1228 Coffelt Ave., Bettendorf, IA 52722.

Nominating. Gloria T. Glaser, 60 Sutton Place S., Apt. 8 C-S, New York, NY 10022.

Public Library Trusteeship. Donald J. Sager, 2943 N. Cramer, Milwaukee, WI 53211-3241.

Publications. Sharon Saulmon, 12228 High Meadow Ct., Oklahoma City, OK 73170.

Publicity. Cheryl Cooper, 206 N. 12 St., Oakdale, LA 71463; Joseph English, 220 25th St., Brooklyn, NY 11232.

Resolutions. Arthur Kirschenbaum, 750 S. 26 Place, Arlington, VA 22202.

Specialized Outreach Services. Catherine S. Wallace, 444 W. 44 St., Indianapolis, IN 46208.

Trustee Citations, Jury on. Aileen Schrader, 275 Promontory Dr., Newport Beach, CA 92660.

White House Conference (subcommittee). Barbara D. Cooper, 936 Intracoastal Dr., Apt. 6-D, Ft. Lauderdale, FL 33304; Lila Milford, 1225 Northwood Ct., Marion, IN 46952.

Representatives

ALA Committee on Professional Ethics. Aileen Schrader.

ALA Legislative Assembly. Roslyn S. Kurland.

ALA Membership Committee. Minnie-Lou Lynch.

ALA Membership Promotion Task Force. Norman Kelinson.

ALA Planning and Budget Assembly. Norman Kelinson.

ALA Standing Committee on Library Education. Ann L. Donoghue.

ASCLA Decade of Disabled Persons Committee. Arthur Kirschenbaum.

FOLUSA. Virginia Young.

Freedom to Read Foundation. Madeleine Grant.

PLA Board of Directors. Gloria T. Glaser.

American Library Association
Association for Library Service to Children

Executive Director, Susan Roman
50 E. Huron St., Chicago, IL 60611
312-944-6780

Object

Interested in the improvement and extension of library services to children in all types of libraries. Responsible for the evaluation and selection of book and nonbook material for, and the improvement of techniques of, library services to children from preschool through the eighth grade or junior high school age, when such materials or techniques are intended for use in more than one type of library. Founded 1901. Memb. 3,400. (For information on dues, see ALA entry.)

Membership

Open to anyone interested in library services to children.

Officers (July 1988–July 1989)

Pres. Marilyn Berg Iarusso, Office of Children's Services, New York Public Lib., 455 Fifth Ave., New York, NY 10016; *V.P.* Barbara Immroth, Grad. School of Lib. and Info. Science, Univ. of Texas at Austin, EDB564, Austin, TX 78712-1276; *Past Pres.* Mary Sommerville, 1611 N.W. 81 Way, Plantation, FL 33322.

(Address correspondence to the executive director.)

Directors

Barbara Barstow; Kathy A. East; Elizabeth Greggs; Karen Nelson Hoyle; Trevelyn Jones; Mary Ann Paulin; Linda Perkins; Frances Sedney; Kay E. Vandergrift.

Committee Chairpersons

Priority Group I: Child Advocacy

Consultant. Roslyn Beitler, 3601 Connecticut Ave. N.W., Apt. 719, Washington, DC 20008.

Boy Scouts of America (advisory). Carole De Jardin, Appleton Public Lib., 225 Oneida St., Appleton, WI 54912.

Legislation. Gretchen Wronka, Hennepin County Lib., 12601 Ridgedale Dr., Minnetonka, MN 55343.

Liaison with Mass Media. Virginia Walter, 48 Sunset Ave., Venice, CA 90291.

Liaison with National Organizations Serving the Child. Neel Parikh, 3027 Richmond Blvd., Oakland, CA 94611.

Priority Group II: Evaluation of Media

Consultant. Theresa B. Chekon, 84 Sunlit Circle, Sacramento, CA 95831.

Computer Software Evaluation. Susan J. Pine, Office of Children's Services, 455 Fifth Ave., New York, NY 10016.

Film and Video Evaluation. Rita Hoffman, 6647 N. Talman, Chicago, IL 60645.

Filmstrip Evaluation. Jane Kunstler, 41 W. 75 St., Apt. 2A, New York, NY 10023.

Notable Children's Books. Grace Ruth, 859 42nd Ave., San Francisco, CA 94121.

Recording Evaluation. Sarah McCarville, Oshkosh Public Lib., 106 Washington Ave., Oshkosh, WI 54901.

Selection of Children's Books from Various Cultures. Julie Carsaro, Univ. of Chicago, The Laboratory Schools, 1362 E. 59 St., Chicago, IL 60637.

Priority Group III: Professional Development

Consultant. Clara Bohrer, 4886 School Bell Lane, Birmingham, MI 48010.

Arbuthnot Honor Lecture. Ginny Moore Kruse, 1708 Regent St., Madison, WI 53705.

Education. Margaret Bush, Grad. School of Lib. & Info. Science, Simmons College, 300 The Fenway, Boston, MA 02115.

Managing Children's Services (Discussion Group). Sunny Strong, Sno-Isle Regional Lib. System, Box 148, Marysville, WA 98270; Eva-Maria Lusk, Children's Services Coord., Spokane Public Lib., W. 906 Main Ave., Spokane, WA 99201.

Putnam & Grosset Group Awards. Anne S. Boegen, 6451 S.W. 73 St., South Miami, FL 33143.

Scholarships. Melcher and Bound to Stay Bound. Ann Flowers, 8 Nob Hill Rd., Wayland, MA 01778.

State and Regional Leadership (Discussion Group). Anitra Steele, Mid-Continent Public Lib., 15616 E. Highway 24, Independence, MO 64050.

Teachers of Children's Literature (Discussion Group). Elizabeth F. Howard, 919 College Ave., Pittsburgh, PA 15232; Elizabeth M. Rosen, SLIS, Western Michigan Univ., Kalamazoo, MI 49008.

Priority Group IV: Social Responsibilities

Consultant. Ruth Toor, 61 Greenbriar Dr., Berkley Heights, NJ 07922.

Intellectual Freedom. Christine Jenkins, 321 Eighth St., Ann Arbor, MI 48103.

International Relations. Barbara Peterson, 2019 Coventry Rd., Columbus, OH 43212.

Library Service to Children with Special Needs. Faye Lander, 500 Harvey Ave., Kent, OH 44240.

Preschool Services and Parent Education. Floyd Dickman, 1786 Larkwood Place, Columbus, OH 43229.

Social Issues in Relation to Materials and Services for Children (Discussion Group). Joanne R. Long, 334 Woodland Rd., Madison, NJ 07940; Anitra T. Steele, Mid-Continent Public Lib., 15616 E. Highway 24, Independence, MO 64050.

Priority Group V: Planning and Research

Consultant. Deborah Weilerstein, 5513 S. Fourth St., Arlington, VA 22204.

Caldecott Medal Calendar. Bette Peltola, 4109 N. Ardmore Ave., Milwaukee, WI 53211.

Collections of Children's Books for Adult Research (Discussion Group). Gloria Smith, 8051 E. Rosewood St., Tucson, AZ 85710.

Grants. Carol Tarsitano, Portage-Cragin Branch, The Chicago Public Lib., 5108 W. Belmont, Chicago, IL 60641.

Local Arrangements—Dallas, 1989. Jo Ann Bell, 801 Carney Dr., Garland, TX 75041.

Membership. Mollie Bynum, 347-A 4 Dailey Ave., Anchorage, AK 99515.

National Planning of Special Collections. Linda Ward Callahan, 4841 W. Roscoe, Chicago, IL 60641.

Nominating. Adele Fasick, 4351 Bloor St. W., Unit 40, Etabicoke, ON M9C 2A4, Canada.

Organization and Bylaws. Anne V. Osborn, 2750 Orange, Riverside, CA 92501.

Program Evaluation and Support. Gail Sage, Sonoma County Lib., Santa Rosa, CA 95404.

Publications. Gayle Libberton, 900 Millbrook, Neenah, WI 54956.

Research and Development. M. Jean Greenlaw, 2600 Sheraton Rd., Denton, TX 76201.

"Top of the News" Editorial, Joint ALSC/YASD. Josette Lyders, 4322 Waycross Dr., Houston, TX 77035.

Priority Group VI: Award Committees

Consultant. Amy Kellman, 5441 Fair Oaks St., Pittsburgh, PA 15217.

Mildred L. Batchelder Award Selection—1989. Eliza T. Dresang, 440 Virginia Terr., Madison, WI 53705.

Mildred L. Batchelder Award Selection—1990. Elizabeth Hoke, 5700 Ridgefield Rd., Bethesda, MD 20816.

Caldecott Award—1989. Elizabeth Huntoon, Children's Services, The Chicago Public Lib., 425 N. Michigan Ave., Chicago, IL 60611.

Caldecott Award—1990. Amy Spaulding, 51 W. 74 St., New York, NY 10023.

Newbery Award—1989. Phyllis Van Orden, 2281 Trescott Dr., Tallahassee, FL 32312.

Newbery Award—1990. Caroline Ward, 971 Orienta Ave., Mamaroneck, NY 10543.

Representatives

ALA Dallas (1989) Conference Program. Marilyn Iarusso.

ALA Legislation Assembly. Cheryl Gage.

ALA Library Education Assembly. Margaret Bush.

ALA Planning and Budget Assembly. Gail Sage.

RTSD/CCS Cataloging of Children's Materials. Mary Beth Dunhouse; Adeline W. Wilkes.

Liaison with Other National Organizations

American Association for Gifted Children. To be appointed.

Association for Childhood Education International. Doris Robinson.

Association for Children and Adults with Learning Disabilities. Clara Bohrer.

Big Brothers and Big Sisters of America. Helen Mullen.

Boys Clubs of America. Carole De Jardin.

Camp Fire Inc. Anitra T. Steele.

Child Welfare League of America. Ethel Ambrose.

Children's Defense Fund. Effie Lee Morris.

Children's Theatre Association. Margaret Tassia.

Day Care and Child Development Council of America. James W. Hoogstra.

Four-H Programs, Extension Service. Elizabeth Simmons.

Freedom to Read Foundation. Christine Jenkins.

Girl Scouts of America. Margo M. Daniels.

Girls Club of America. To be appointed.

International Reading Association. Clara Bohrer.

National Association for the Education of Young Children. Jeanette A. Studley.

National Association for the Perpetuation and Preservation of Storytelling. Elizabeth Simmons.

National Multiple Sclerosis Society. Melanie Myers.

National Story League. To be appointed.

Parents without Partners. Lucy Marx.

Puppeteers of America. Frances J. McCurdy.

Reading Is Fundamental. To be appointed.

Salvation Army. Doris Robinson.

Young Men's Christian Association. To be appointed.

Young Women's Christian Association. To be appointed.

American Library Association
Association of College and Research Libraries

Executive Director, JoAn S. Segal
50 E. Huron St., Chicago, IL 60611
312-944-6780

Object

The mission of the Association of College and Research Libraries (ACRL) is to foster the profession of academic and research librarianship and to enhance the ability of academic and research libraries to serve effectively the library and information needs of current and potential library users. This includes all types of academic libraries—community and junior college, college, and university—as well as comprehensive and specialized research libraries and their professional staffs. Founded 1938. Memb. 10,170. (For information on dues, see ALA entry.)

Officers (July 1988–June 1989)

Pres. Joseph A. Boisse, Univ. of California, Santa Barbara, CA 93106; *V.P./Pres.-Elect.* William A. Moffet, Oberlin College, Oberlin, OH 44074; *Past Pres.* Joanne R. Euster, Rutgers Univ., New Brunswick, NJ 08903; *ACRL Councillor.* Thomas Kirk, Berea College, Berea, KY 40404; *Chpn., Budget & Finance.* Linda J. Piele, Univ. of Wisconsin-Parkside, Kenosha, WI 53141.

Directors-at-Large

Anne K. Beaubien; B. Ann Commerton; Mary Sue Ferrell; Melvin George; Larry Hardesty; Peter Malanchuk; Rochelle Sager; Elizabeth M. Salzer.

Publications

ACRL Publications in Librarianship (formerly *ACRL Monograph Series*) (irreg.). *Ed.* Jonathan A. Lindsey, Baylor Univ., Waco, TX 76998.

Choice (11 per year; $125); *Choice Reviews on Cards* ($195). *Ed.* Patricia E. Sabosik, 100 Riverview Center, Middletown, CT 06457.

College and Research Libraries (6 per year; memb.; nonmemb. $35). *Ed.* Charles R. Martell, Jr., California State Univ. at Sacramento, Sacramento, CA 95819.

College and Research Libraries News (11 per year; memb.; nonmemb. $15). *Ed.* George M. Eberhart, ACRL Headquarters.

Fast Job Listing Service (12 per year; 6 mo. $10 memb.; nonmemb. $15). ACRL Headquarters.

Rare Books and Manuscripts Librarianship (2 per year; $25). *Ed.* Alice D. Schreyer, Univ. of Delaware, Newark, DE 19717-5267.

Committee Chairpersons

Academic Library Statistics. Kent H. Hendrickson, Univ. of Nebraska-Lincoln, Libs., Lincoln, NE 68588-0410.

Academic or Research Librarian of the Year Award. Barry B. Baker, Univ. of Georgia Libs., Athens, GA 30602.

Academic Status. Charlene Mason, Univ. of Minnesota, 180 Wilson Lib., 309 19th Ave. S., Minneapolis, MN 55455.

Appointments (1988) and Nominations (1989). John C. Tyson, Univ. of Richmond, Richmond, VA 23173.

Appointments (1989) and Nominations (1990). Melvin R. George, Oregon State Univ., Corvallis, OR 97331.

Association of College and Research Libraries (ACRL) and Association for Educational Communications and Technology (AECT) (Joint Committee). Co-Chpns. James O. Wallace, Box 13041, San Antonio, TX 78213 (ACRL); Daniel D. Koenig, Piedmont Technical College, Box 1467, Greenwood, SC 29464 (AECT).

(Hugh C.) Atkinson Memorial Award. Ronald G. Leach, Indiana State Univ., Cunningham Memorial Lib., Terre Haute, IN 47809.

Audiovisual. Sandra K. Ready, Mankato State Univ. Lib., Mankato, MN 56001.

Awards (task force). Joan L. Chambers, Colorado State Univ., Ft. Collins, CO 80525.

Budget & Finance. Linda J. Piele, Univ. of Wisconsin-Parkside, Kenosha, WI 53141.

Conference Program Planning—Chicago, 1990. William A. Moffett, Oberlin College, Oberlin, OH 44074.

Conference Program Planning—Dallas, 1989. Joseph A. Boisse, Univ. of California, Santa Barbara, CA 93106.

Constitution & Bylaws. Barbara D. Bryan, Fairfield Univ., Nyselius Lib., Fairfield, CT 06430.

Continuing Education Courses (advisory). To be appointed.

Copyright. Barbara A. MacAdam, Univ. of Michigan, Ann Arbor, MI 48109-1185.

Distinguished Career Award (subcommittee of the ACRL National Conference Executive Committee). Carla Stoffle, Univ. of Michigan Libs., Ann Arbor, MI 48109-1608.

Doctoral Dissertation Fellowship. Stanton F. Biddle, Office of Vice Chancellor for Academic Affairs, CUNY, New York, NY 10021.

Extended Campus Library Services Guidelines (task force). Mary Joyce Pickett, Illinois Institute of Technology, Paul V. Galvin Lib., Chicago, IL 60616.

Faculty Workshops (ad hoc). Sharon J. Rogers, George Washington Univ., Washington, DC 20052.

Financial Development (task force). To be appointed.

Historically Black College and University Library Project (ad hoc). Beverly P. Lynch, Univ. of Illinois at Chicago, Univ. Lib., Chicago, IL 60680.

International Relations (task force). Maureen Pastine, Washington State Univ., Pullman, WA 99164-5610.

(Samuel) Lazerow Fellowship for Research in Acquisitions or Technical Services. Donald L. Lanier, Northern Illinois Univ., Founder Lib., DeKalb, IL 60115.

Legislation. Katherine F. Mawdsley, Univ. of California, General Lib., Davis, CA 95616.

Librarians as Instructors (task force). Marian C. Winner, Miami Univ., Science Lib., Oxford, OH 45056.

Library Access (task force). Kathleen Gunning, Univ. of Houston Libs., Houston, TX 77035.

Library School Curriculum (task force). William J. Studer, Ohio State Univ. Libs., Columbus, OH 43210-1286.

Membership. Susan B. Varca, Arizona State Univ. Libs., Mesa, AZ 85203.

National Conference Executive Committee. Martha A. Bowman, Univ. of Louisville, Louisville, KY 40292; Evan Ira Farber, Earlham College, Lilly Lib., Richmond, IN 47374.

Paraprofessionals in Academic Libraries (task force). Sheila D. Creth, Univ. of Iowa Libs., Iowa City, IA 52242-1093.

Performance Measures for Academic Libraries (ad hoc). Virginia M. Tiefel, Ohio State Univ. Libs., Columbus, OH 42310.

Planning. Carolyn Dusenbury, Arizona State Univ., 110 Hayden Lib., Tempe, AZ 85287.

President's Program Planning, Dallas, 1989. Joseph A. Boisse, Univ. of California, Santa Barbara, CA 93106.

Professional Association Liaison. Louise S. Sherby, Univ. of Missouri-Kansas City Libs., 5100 Rockhill Rd., Kansas City, MO 64110-2499.

Professional Education. George V. Hodowanec, Univ. of Akron, Bierce Lib., Akron, OH 44325.

Professional Ethics (task force). Doug Stewart, Univ. of California-San Diego, La Jolla, CA 92093-0175.

Publications. Ruth J. Person, Univ. of Missouri-St. Louis, St. Louis, MO 63121.

Recruitment of Underrepresented Minorities (task force). Edith M. Fisher, Univ. of California-San Diego, Univ. Libs., La Jolla, CA 92093.

Research. To be appointed.

Retired Librarians Service Corps Planning (task force). Evan Ira Farber, Earlham College, Lilly Lib., Richmond, IN 47374.

(K. G.) Saur Award for Best "College and Research Libraries" Article. Mary Reichel, Univ. of Arizona, Main Lib., Tucson, AZ 85721.

Small College Assessment Program (task force). Arthur H. Miller, Lake Forest College, Donnelley Lib., Lake Forest, IL 60045.

Social Responsibilities (and ACRL) (task force). Karyle S. Butcher, Oregon State Univ., Kerr Lib., Corvallis, OR 97330.

Sources of Revenue in Academic Libraries (task force). Anne K. Beaubien, Univ. of Michigan, Graduate Lib., Ann Arbor, MI 48105.

Special Grant Fund. Bob D. Carmack, Univ. of Wisconsin-Superior, Jim Dan Hill Lib., Superior, WI 54880-2898.

Standards and Accreditation. Barbara A. Lockett, Rensselaer Polytechnic Institute, Folsom Lib., Troy, NY 12180-3590.

Discussion Groups

Australian Studies. William Z. Schenck.

Black Studies Librarianship. Clarence E. Chisholm; Gloria Smith.

Canadian Studies. John A. Shuler.

Electronic Library Development in Academic Libraries. Nancy H. Evans.

English and American Literature. Lorraine A. Jean.

Extended Campus Library Services. Barbara Emmer.

Fee-Based Information Service Centers in Academic Libraries. Donna Rubens.

Heads of Public/Readers Services. Dorothy Christiansen.

Home Economics/Human Ecology Librarians. Suzanne D. Gyeszly.

Journal Costs in Academic and Research Libraries. James C. Thompson.

Librarians of Library Science Collections. Elizabeth J. Laney.

Microcomputer Services in Academic Libraries. Lee Jaffe.

Personnel Administrators and Staff Development Officer of Large Research Libraries. William K. Black; Lucy R. Cohen.

Popular Culture and Libraries. Allen Ellis.

Public Relations in Academic Libraries. Denise A. Forro.

Research. Timothy F. Richards.

Undergraduate Librarians. James R. Self.

Representatives

ACRL Academic Status Committee. Charlene Mason.

ACRL Librarians of Library Science Collections Discussion Group. Elizabeth J. Laney.

ACRL Professional Education Committee Chair (formerly *Continuing Education).* George V. Hodowanec.

ALA Committee on Appointments. William A. Moffett.

ALA Committee on Professional Ethics. Lucretia McCulley.

ALA Conference Program Planning Committee–Chicago, 1990. William A. Moffett.

ALA Conference Program Planning Committee–Dallas, 1989. Joseph A. Boisse.

ALA Legislation Assembly (Chair of ACRL Legislation Committee, Ex officio). Katherine F. Mawdsley.

ALA Membership Promotion Task Force (Chair of ACRL Membership Committee, Ex officio). Susan B. Varca.

ALA Planning and Budget Assembly. Joseph A. Boisse.

ALA Standing Committee on Library Education (SCOLE). To be appointed.

American Association for the Advancement of Science. Arleen N. Somerville.

American Association for the Advancement of Science, Consortium of Affiliates for International Programs. Arleen N. Somerville.

American Council on Education. Sharon J. Rogers.

ASCLA Decade of Disabled Persons, Committee on the. Cay Thomas.

Association for Asian Studies, Committee on East Asian Libraries. Tze-Chung Li.

BIS Education for Bibliographic Instruction Committee to SCOLE. Betsy Wilson.

Freedom to Read Foundation. Noreen S. Alldredge.

LC Cataloging in Publication Advisory Group. Heidi L. Hoerman.

Resources and Technical Services Division, Committee on Cataloging: Description and Access. Frank A. D'Andraia.

Sections

Activity Sections Council. Barbara Galik, Univ. of Michigan, Grad. Lib., Ann Arbor, MI 48109-1204.

Anthropology and Sociology Section. Stephen M. MacLeod, Univ. of California, Irvine, CA 92713.

Arts Section. Charles R. Smith, Texas A&M Univ., Sterling C. Evans Lib., College Station, TX 77843.

Asian and African Section. Basima Bezirgan, Univ. of Chicago, Joseph Regenstein Lib., Chicago, IL 60637.

Bibliographic Instruction Section. David N. King, Univ. of Kentucky, Lexington, KY 40506-0391.

College Libraries Section. Eleanor H. Pinkham, Kalamazoo College, Kalamazoo, MI 49007.

Community and Junior College Libraries Section. Shirley A. Lowman, Maricopa County Community Colleges, Phoenix, AZ 85006.

Education and Behavioral Sciences Section. Nancy P. O'Brien, Univ. of Illinois Lib., Urbana, IL 61801.

Law and Political Science Section. Natalie M. Schatz, Fletcher School of Law and Diplomacy, Tufts Univ., Edwin Ginn Lib., Medford, MA 02155.

Rare Books and Manuscripts Section. William L. Joyce, Princeton Univ. Lib., Princeton, NJ 08540.

Science and Technology Section. Laura M. Osegueda, North Carolina State Univ., D. H. Hill Lib., Raleigh, NC 27695-7111.

Slavic and East European Section. Barbara A. Galik, Univ. of Michigan, Ann Arbor, MI 48109-1204.

University Libraries Section. Karen S. Seibert, Univ. of North Carolina-Chapel Hill, Chapel Hill, NC 27514.

Western European Specialists Section. John B. Dillon, Univ. of Wisconsin, Madison, WI 53706.

Women's Studies Section. Beth Stafford, Univ. of Illinois-Urbana-Champaign, Urbana, IL 61801.

American Library Association
Association of Specialized and Cooperative Library Agencies

Acting Executive Director, Evelyn Shaevel
50 E. Huron St., Chicago, IL 60611
312-944-6780

Object

To represent state library agencies, specialized library agencies, and multitype library cooperatives. Within the interest of these types of library organizations, the Association of Specialized and Cooperative Library Agencies has specific responsibility for:

1. Development and evaluation of goals and plans for state library agencies, specialized library agencies, and multitype library cooperatives to facilitate the implementation, improvement, and extension of library activities designed to foster improved user services, coordinating such activities with other appropriate ALA units.

2. Representation and interpretation of the role, functions, and services of state library agencies, specialized library agencies, and multitype library cooperatives within and outside the profession, including contact with national organizations and government agencies.

3. Development of policies, studies, and activities in matters affecting state library agencies, specialized library agencies, and multitype library cooperatives relating to (a) state and local library legislation, (b) state grants-in-aid and appropriations, and (c) relationships among state, federal, regional, and local governments, coordinating such activities with other appropriate ALA units.

4. Establishment, evaluation, and promotion of standards and service guidelines relating to the concerns of this association.

5. Identifying the interests and needs of all persons, encouraging the creation of services to meet these needs within the areas of concern of the association, and promoting the use of these services provided by state library agencies, specialized library agencies, and multitype library cooperatives.

6. Stimulating the professional growth and promoting the specialized training and continuing education of library personnel at all levels of concern of this association and encouraging membership participation in appropriate type-of-activity divisions within ALA.

7. Assisting in the coordination of activities of other units within ALA that have a bearing on the concerns of this association.

8. Granting recognition for outstanding library service within the areas of concern of this association.

9. Acting as a clearinghouse for the exchange of information and encouraging the development of materials, publications, and research within the areas of concern of this association.

Memb. 1,420.

Board of Directors

Pres. Joseph F. Schubert, State Lib., Cultural Education Center, Empire State Plaza, Albany, NY 12230; *V.P./Pres.-Elect.* William G. Asp, Dir., Minnesota State Lib. Agency, Office of Lib. Development and Service, 440 Capitol Sq. Bldg., 550 Cedar St., St. Paul, MN 55101; *Past Pres.* Lorraine Schaeffer Summers, 505 Live Oak Plantation Rd., Tallahassee, FL 32312; *Div. Councillor.* Donna O. Dziedzic (1989); *Dirs.-at-Large.* William T. DeJohn (1989); Barratt Wilkins (1989); *Sec. Reps.* Stephen Prine, LSSPS chpn.; Jean A. Major, SLAS chpn.; Janet M. Welch, Multi-LINCS chpn; *Ex officio (nonvoting).* Mary Redmond, *Interface* ed.; *Organization and Bylaws Committee Chpn.* Sandra M. Ellison; *Acting Exec. Dir.* Evelyn Shaevel.

Publications

Bibliotherapy Forum Newsletter (q.; $5 memb.; $7 nonmemb.). *Newsletter Coord.* Lethene Parks, 8250 State Rd., State Highway 302 N.W., Gig Harbor, WA 98335.

Interface (q.; memb.; nonmemb. $10). *Ed.* Mary Redmond, State Lib., Legislative and Government Service, Cultural Education Center, Albany, NY 12230.

Committees

Awards. Lethene Parks, State Lib., AJ-11, Olympia, WA 98504.

Budget and Finance. William G. Asp, Dir., Minnesota State Lib. Agency, Office of Lib. Development & Service, 440 Capitol Sq. Bldg., 550 Cedar St., St. Paul, MN 55101.

Conference Program Coordination. Bruce E. Daniels, Dept. of State Lib. Services, 95 Davis St., Providence, RI 02908.

Decade of Disabled Persons (ad hoc). Laura J. Hodges, Lib. Consultant, State Lib. of Florida, RA Gray Bldg., Tallahassee, FL 32399-0250.

"Interface" Advisory. William Crowley, State Lib., 65 S. Front St., Columbus, OH 43266-0334.

Legislation. James A. Nelson, Dept. for Libs. and Archives, 300 Coffee Tree Rd., Frankfort, KY 40502.

Library Personnel and Education. Suzanne J. LeBarron, State Lib., 231 Capital Ave., Hartford, CT 06106.

Membership Promotion. Mary Flournoy, Free Lib., Logan Sq., Philadelphia, PA 19103.

Nominating. Barbara H. Will, California State Lib., 1001 Sixth St., Suite 300, Sacramento, CA 95814.

Organization and Bylaws. Nominating (1989). Sandra M. Ellison, Dept. of Libs., 200 N.E. 18 St., Oklahoma City, OK 73105.

Planning. Lorraine S. Summers, 505 Live Oak Plantation Rd., Tallahassee, FL 23212.

Publications. Bridget Later Lamont, Dir., State Lib., Rm. 275, Centennial Bldg., Springfield, IL 62756.

Research. Sally J. Drew, Dir., Reference and Loan Lib., 2109 S. Stoughton Rd., Madison, WI 53716.

Standards for Adult Correctional Institutions. Brenda Vogel, State Dept. of Educ., 200 W. Baltimore St., Baltimore, MD 21201.

Standards for Juvenile Correctional Institutions. Bonnie Crell, Principal Libn., CYA, 4241 Williamsbourgh Dr., Suite 227, Sacramento, CA 95823.

Standards for Multiple Library Cooperatives

and Networks (ad hoc subcommittee). Janice Beck Ison, Exec. Dir., Lincoln Trail Lib. System, 1704 W. Interstate Dr., Champaign, IL 61821.

Standards Review. Ann Joslin, Assoc. Dir., Lib. Development, State Lib., 325 W. State St., Boise, ID 83703.

Representatives

ALA Conference Program—Dallas, 1989. Joseph F. Shubert; *Chicago, 1990.* William G. Asp.

ALA Government Documents Round Table (GODORT). To be appointed.

ALA Legislation Assembly. James A. Nelson.

ALA Library Education Assembly. Suzanne J. Le Barron.

ALA Membership Promotion Task Force. Mary Flournoy.

ALA Planning and Budget Assembly. William G. Asp.

American Correctional Association. To be appointed.

Association for Radio Reading Services, Inc. To be appointed.

Freedom to Read Foundation. Ella Gaines Yates.

Interagency Council on Library Resources for Nursing. Frederic C. Pachman.

PLA Development Program. To be appointed.

RTSD/CCS Cataloging: Description and Access Committee. To be appointed.

Section Chairpersons

Libraries Serving Special Populations (LSSPS). Stephen Prine, Jr., NLSBPH, Lib. of Congress, Washington, DC 20542.

Multitype Library Networks and Cooperatives Section (Multi-LINCS). Janet M. Welch, Exec. Dir., Rochester Regional Lib. Council, 339 East Ave., Rm. 300, Rochester, NY 14604.

State Library Agency Section (SLAS). Jean A. Major, Colorado Dept. of Educ., 201 E. Colfax Ave., 3rd fl., Denver, CO 80203.

American Library Association
Library Administration and Management Association

Executive Director, John W. Berry
50 E. Huron St., Chicago, IL 60611
312-944-6780

Object

"The Library Administration and Management Association provides an organizational framework for encouraging the study of administrative theory, for improving the practice of administration in libraries, and for identifying and fostering administrative skill. Toward these ends, the division is responsible for all elements of general administration which are common to more than one type of library. These may include organizational structure, financial administration, personnel management and training, buildings and equipment, and public relations. LAMA meets this responsibility in the following ways:

1. Study and review of activities assigned to the division with due regard for changing developments in these activities.

2. Initiating and overseeing activities and projects appropriate to the division, including activities involving bibliography compilation, publication, study, and review of professional literature within the scope of the division.

3. Synthesis of those activities of other ALA units which have a bearing upon the responsibilities or work of the division.

4. Representation and interpretation of library administrative activities in contacts outside the library profession.

5. Aiding the professional development of librarians engaged in administration and en-

couragement of their participation in appropriate type-of-library divisions.

6. Planning and development of those programs of study and research in library administrative problems which are most needed by the profession."

Established 1957. Memb. 4,840.

Officers

Pres. Maureen Sullivan; *V.P./Pres.-Elect.* Dallas Y. Shaffer; *Past Pres.* Ann Heidbreder Eastman.

(Address correspondence to the executive director.)

Board of Directors

Dirs. Carol L. Anderson; Jonathan D. Eldredge; James G. Neal; Rebecca R. Martin; Norman L. Nelson; Larry T. Nix; Anne H. Rimmer; Patricia Wilson; Janis C. Keene; Donald E. Riggs; John J. Vasi; Peter R. Young; *Dirs.-at-Large.* Carol Lee Anderson; James G. Neal; *Councillor.* Carolyn A. Snyder; *Ex officio.* Joseph F. Boykin; Janice Feye-Stukas; Dottie R. Hiebing; Patricia H. Latshaw; Dana E. Smith; Lamar Veatch; John S. Wallach.

Publication

LAMA Magazine Library Administration & Management (q.; memb. and subscription $25 U.S., $35 foreign). *Ed.* Donald E. Riggs, 2120 E. Knoll Circle, Mesa, AZ 85203.

Committee Chairpersons

Budget and Finance. John J. Vasi, Asst. Univ. Libn., Univ. of California at Santa Barbara Lib., 3589 Library, Santa Barbara, CA 93106.

Editorial Advisory Board. Jennifer Cargill, Assoc. Dir. of Libs., Texas Tech Univ., Lubbock, TX 79409.

Governmental Affairs. Nancy M. Bolt, State Lib., 201 E. Colfax, Rm. 309, Denver, CO 80203.

Leadership Forum Steering. Donald E. Riggs, Dir. of Libs., Arizona State Univ., Tempe, AZ 85287.

Membership. Judith A. Adams.

Nominating—1989. Ronald P. Naylor.

Nominating—1990. Ronald Leach.

Organization. Janis C. Keene, Asst. Dir., City-County Lib., 400 Civic Center, Tulsa, OK 74103.

Orientation. Lynn Scott Cochrane.

Program. Robert F. Moran, Jr., Indiana Univ. Northwest Lib., 3400 Broadway, Gary, IN 46408.

Publications. John H. Martin, Jr., Head, Arts and Literature, Public Lib., 101 E. Central Blvd., Orlando, FL 32801.

Recognition of Achievement. Susan E. Stroyan, 1901 E. Oakland Ave., Bloomington, IL 61701.

Small Libraries Publications. Anders C. Dahlgren, 5814 Dorsett Dr., Madison, WI 53711.

Special Conferences and Programs Committee. William A. Gosling, 2005 Ridge Ave., Ann Arbor, MI 48104.

Discussion Group Chairpersons

Asst.-to-the-Dir. Robert E. Boyer, Assoc. Dir., Public Lib., 101 E. Abram St., Arlington, TX 76010.

Middle Management. Barbara M. Duke.

Women Administrators. Nancy L. Baker.

Section Chairpersons

Buildings and Equipment Section. Larry T. Nix, Bur. Dir., Wisconsin Bur. for Lib. Development, 125 S. Webster St., Box 7841, Madison, WI 53705.

Fund Raising and Financial Development Section. Norman L. Nelson, Oklahoma State Univ. Lib., Stillwater, OK 74078.

Library Organization and Management Section. Patricia Wilson, Schurwies 3, 8703 Erlenbach.

Personnel Administration Section. Anne H. Rimmer, Personnel Officer, Univ. of California—Irvine Lib., Box 19557, Irvine, CA 92713.

Public Relations Section. Jonathan D. Eldredge, Chief, Collection and Info. Resources Development, Univ. of New Mexico, Medical Center Lib., Albuquerque, NM 87131.

Statistics Section. Peter R. Young, 338 Gambrills Rd., Gambrills, MD 21054.

Systems and Services Section. Rebecca R. Martin, Assoc. Lib. Dir., San Jose State Univ., Div. of Lib. and Info. Science, Washington Sq., San Jose, CA 95192.

American Library Association
Library and Information Technology Association

Executive Director, Linda J. Knutson
50 E. Huron St., Chicago, IL 60611
312-944-6780

Object

"The Library and Information Technology Association provides its members and, to a lesser extent, the information dissemination field as a whole, with a forum for discussion, an environment for learning, and a program for action on all phases of the development and application of automated and technological systems in the library and information sciences. Since its activities and interests are derived as responses to the needs and demands of its members, its program is flexible, varied, and encompasses many aspects of the field. Its primary concern is the design, development, and implementation of technological systems in the library and information science fields. Within that general precept, the interests of the division include such varied activities as systems development, electronic data processing, mechanized information retrieval, operations research, standards development, telecommunications, networks and collaborative efforts, management techniques, information technology and other aspects of audiovisual and video cable communications activities, and hardware applications related to all of these areas. Although it has no facilities to carry out research, it attempts to encourage its members in that activity.

Information about all of these activities is disseminated through the division's publishing program, seminars and institutes, exhibits, conference programs, and committee work. The division provides an advisory and consultative function when called upon to do so.

It regards continuing education as one of its major responsibilities and through the above channels it attempts to inform its members of current activities and trends, and it also provides retrospective information for those new to the field."

Memb. 5,012.

Officers

Pres. Sherrie Schmidt, Sterling C. Evans Lib., Texas A&M Univ., College Station, TX 77843; *V.P./Pres.-Elect.* Carol A. Parkhurst, Univ. Lib., Univ. of Nevada, Reno, NV 89557; *Past Pres.* William Gray Potter, Hayden Lib., Arizona State Univ., Tempe, AZ 85287.

Directors

Officers. Walt Crawford (1991); Patricia H. Earnest (1990); Carolyn M. Gray (1991); Berna L. Heyman (1990); Charles Ray Hildreth (1990); Tamara J. Miller (1991); Bonnie K. Juergens (1989); Marianne D. Burke (1989); *Exec. Dir.* Linda J. Knutson.

Publications

Information Technology and Libraries (ITAL, formerly *JOLA)* (q.; memb.; nonmemb. $35; single copies $12.50). *Ed.* William G. Potter, Hayden Lib., Arizona State Univ., Tempe, AZ 85287. For information or to send manuscripts, contact the editor.

LITA Newsletter (q.; memb.; nonmemb. $15; single copies $5). *Ed.* Walt Crawford, The Research Libs. Group, Inc., Mountain View, CA 94041-1100.

Committee Chairpersons

Hugh C. Atkinson Memorial Award Committee, ACRL/LAMA/LITA/RTSD Award (HAMA). Ronald G. Leach, Cunningham Memorial Lib., Indiana State Univ., Terre Haute, IN 47809.

Budget Review. William Gray Potter, Hayden Lib., Arizona State Univ., Tempe, AZ 85287.

Bylaws and Organization. Marianne D. Burke, Boston Lib. Consortium, Boston Public Lib., Boston, MA 02117.

Education. Michael J. Gorman, Dean of Libs., Henry Madden Lib., California State Univ., Fresno, Fresno, CA 93740-0034.

Executive Committee. Sherrie Schmidt, Sterling C. Evans Lib., Texas A&M Univ., College Station, TX 77843.

ITAL Editorial Board. William G. Potter, Hayden Lib., Arizona State Univ., Tempe, AZ 85287.

Legislation and Regulation. Elaine M. Albright, Fogler Lib., Univ. of Maine, Orono, ME 04469.

LITA/CLSI Scholarship Subcommittee. Betsy Kruger, Univ. of Illinois Lib., Urbana, IL 61801.

LITA/Gaylord Award. Kathleen S. Jackson, 120 Perkins Lib., Duke Univ., Durham, NC 27706.

LITA Newsletter Subcommittee. Walt Crawford, Research Libs. Group, Inc., Mountain View, CA 94041-1100.

Membership. William Louden, Mail Location 33, Univ. of Cincinnati Libs., Cincinnati, OH 45221-0033.

Nominating. Karen A. Schmidt, 246 Lib., Univ. of Illinois-Urbana, Urbana, IL 61801.

Planning. Carol A. Parkhurst, Univ. Lib., Univ. of Nevada, Reno, NV 89557.

Program Planning. Betty Bengtson, Univ. of Washington, Seattle, WA 98195.

Publications. Don L. Tolliver, Univ. Libs., Kent State Univ., Kent, OH 44242.

Representation in Machine Readable Form of Bibliographic Information (MARBI). Kathleen Bales, The Research Libs. Group, Inc., Mountain View, CA 94041-1100.

Technical Standards for Library Automation (TESLA). Marilyn Nasatir, 1540 Summit Rd., Berkeley, CA 94708.

Technology and Access Committee. Brian G. Campbell, Vancouver Public Lib., Vancouver, BC V6Z 1X5, Canada.

Video Tutorial Project Subcommittee. Barry B. Baker, Univ. of Georgia Libs., Athens, GA 30602.

Interest Group Chairpersons

Artificial Intelligence/Expert Systems. Judy E. Meyers, Univ. of Houston Lib., Houston, TX 77004-2001.

Authority Control in the Online Environment LITA/RTSD. Kathleen R. Brown, D. H. Hill Lib., North Carolina State Univ., Raleigh, NC 27695-7111.

Desktop Publishing. Virginia Haynie, Pan American Univ. Lib., Edinburg, TX 78539-2999.

Distributed Systems. Phyllis Johnson, Univ. Lib., Virginia Polytechnic Institute and State, Blacksburg, VA 24061.

Electronic Mail/Electronic Publishing. Greg Zuck, Memorial Lib., Southwestern College, Winfield, KS 67156-2498.

Emerging Technologies. Brian G. Campbell, Vancouver Public Lib., Vancouver, BC V6Z 1X5, Canada.

Human/Machine Interface. Gail Persky, Elmer Holmes Bobst Lib., New York Univ., New York, NY 10012.

Imagineering Interest Group. Paul Evan Peters, New York Public Lib., New York, NY 10018-2788.

Innovative Micro-Cataloging. Robbin D. Ernest, 120 Perkins Lib., Duke Univ., Durham, NC 27706.

Library Consortia Integrated Systems. Gladys S. Shapera, The Carnegie Lib. of Pittsburgh, Pittsburgh, PA 15213.

Library Microcomputer Templates. Edward J. Valauskas, Merriam Center Lib., 1313 E. 60 St., Chicago, IL 60637.

Microcomputer Users. Elizabeth S. Lane, Lib. of Congress, Washington, DC 20540.

Online Catalogs. Christina Perkins Meyer, 160D Wilson Lib., Univ. of Minnesota, Minneapolis, MN 55455.

Optical Information Systems. Geraldine Hurley, SilverPlatter Information, 37 Walnut St., Wellesley Hills, MA 02181.
Programmer/Analysts. Michele I. Dalehite, Florida Center for Lib. Automation, 2002 N.W. 13 St., #202, Gainesville, FL 32609.
Retrospective Conversion, LITA/RTSD. Carolyn Dickinson, Salt Lake City Public Lib., Salt Lake City, UT 84111.
Serials Automation LITA/RTSD. Linda Sapp Visk, General Libs., Emory Univ., Atlanta, GA 30322.
Telecommunications. J. J. Hayden, III, SOLINET, 400 Colony Sq. Plaza Level, 1201 Peachtree St. N.E., Atlanta, GA 30361.
Vendor/User. Norene F. Allen, UTLAS, 8300 College Blvd., Overland Park, KS 66210.
Video and Cable Utilization. Mary Ellen Ritz, Libn., Lib. Dist., Buena Park, CA 90620.

American Library Association
Public Library Association

Executive Director, Eleanor J. Rodger
50 E. Huron St., Chicago, IL 60611
312-944-6780

Object

The Public Library Association will advance the development and effectiveness of public library service and public librarians. The following objectives represent priority actions for PLA:

1. To raise the awareness of public librarians about the issues related to free and equal access to information.
2. To develop a coordinated program for continuing education which includes conference programming, preconferences, regional workshops, and publications.
3. To provide a Public Library Information Service for inquiries on public library issues.
4. To initiate, support, and disseminate information on new research projects on public library service or management.
5. To develop and implement a public relations program at the national level to increase awareness of the diverse nature and value of public library services.
6. To provide public libraries with planning and evaluation tools and to advocate and encourage the utilization of these tools.
7. To ensure that ALA and other units within ALA keep literacy as a high priority.
8. To develop a strategic plan to address public library funding issues.
9. To develop a plan to assist PLA in addressing member interests regarding distinct constituencies by the public library.

Organized 1944. Memb. 6,298.

Membership

Open to all ALA members interested in the improvement and expansion of public library services to all ages in various types of communities.

Officers (1988–1989)

Pres. Melissa Buckingham, 8428 Shawnee St., Philadelphia, PA 19118; *V.P./Pres.-Elect.* Sarah A. Long, Multnomah County Lib., 205 N.E. Russell St., Portland, OR 97212; *Past Pres.* Susan S. Goldberg, Arizona Theatre Co., Box 1631, Tucson, AZ 85702.

Board of Directors (1988–1989)

Dirs.-at-Large. Carolyn Anthony; Ronald S. Kozlowski; John Allyn Moorman; Claudya B. Muller; Catherine A. O'Connell; Elliot Shelkrot. *Sec. Reps. AEPS Pres.* June E. Eiselstein; *AFLS Pres.* Elizabeth R. Snoke; *CIS Pres.* Honore L. Francois; *MLS Pres.* Mary Beth Babikow; *PLSS Pres.* Carolynn K. Johnson; *SMLS Pres.* Marianne K. Cassell;

Ex officio. Past Pres. ALTA. Gloria Glaser; *Public Libs. Ed.* Kathleen H. Heim; *ALA/PLA Councillor.* Rosemary S. Martin; *PLA/ALA Memb. Rep.* Linda P. Elliott; *PLA Exec. Dir.* Eleanor Jo Rodger.

Publication

Public Libraries (bi-mo. [beginning Jan. 1989]; sent to PLA membs.; subscriptions, U.S., $40 per year; Canada and foreign, $50; single copy, $10). *Ed.* Kathleen H. Heim, Louisiana State Univ., School of Lib. and Info. Science, Coates Hall, Rm. 267, Baton Rouge, LA 70803.

Section Heads

Alternative Education Programs (AEPS). June E. Eiselstein.

Armed Forces Library (AFLS). Elizabeth R. Snoke.

Community Information (CIS). Honore L. Francois.

Metropolitan Libraries. Mary Beth Babikow.

Public Library Systems. Carolynn K. Johnson.

Small and Medium-sized Libraries. Marianne K. Cassell.

Committee Chairpersons

Adult Readers Advisory Discussion Group. William T. Balcom, Villa Park Public Lib., 305 S. Ardmore Ave., Villa Park, IL 60181.

Affiliates Network Assembly. Nicola K. Stanke, Carnegie-Stout Public Lib., 11 and Bluff Sts., Dubuque, IA 52001.

Audiovisual. Phyllis Y. Massar, Arts and Media Dept., Ferguson Lib., One Public Lib. Plaza, Stamford, CT 06904.

Awards. Ronald A. Dubberly, Atlanta-Fulton Public Lib., One Margaret Mitchell Sq. N.W., Atlanta, GA 30303.

Budget and Finance. Sarah A. Long, Multnomah County Lib., 205 N.E. Russell St., Portland, OR 97212.

Business Council. To be appointed.

Bylaws and Organization. LaDonna T. Kienitz, Newport Beach Public Lib., 856 San Clemente Dr., Newport Beach, CA 92660.

Cataloging Needs of Public Libraries. Donna M. Cranmer, Sioux Falls Public Lib., 201 N. Main Ave., Sioux Falls, SD 57102.

Children, Service to. Mary K. Chelton, 1226 Cresthaven, Silver Spring, MD 20903.

Common Concerns (ALTA/PLA Joint Committee). Mary Arney, 3646 Charlotte, Kansas City, MO 64109 (ALTA); William H. Ptacek, Louisville Free Lib., Fourth and York Sts., Louisville, KY 40203 (PLA).

Conference Program Coordinating. Gordon S. Wells, Grande Prairie Public Lib. Dist., 3479 W. 183 St., Hazel Crest, IL 60429.

Cost Finding Discussion Group. To be appointed.

Division Program (1989). Bernard F. Pasqualini, Free Lib. of Philadelphia, Logan Sq., Philadelphia, PA 19103.

Division Program (1990). To be appointed.

Education Information Center (AEPS/CIS Joint Committee). Steven P. Lane, 10160 N.E. 112 Place, Kirkland, WA 98033.

Education of Public Librarians. Ryna H. Rothberg, 12271 Oakwood St., Garden Grove, CA 92640.

Goals, Guidelines and Standards for Public Libraries. June M. Garcia, Phoenix Public Lib., 12 E. McDowell, Phoenix, AZ 85044.

Intellectual Freedom. Susan M. Beck, 44 Fourth St., Box 56, South Range, MI 49963.

Internal Revenue Service on Tax Form Distribution, Advisory Committee. Toni A. Garvey, Loudoun County Public Lib., 208-B S. King St., Leesburg, VA 22075.

International Relations. Constance E. Cooke, 209-20 18th Ave., Bayside, NY 11360.

Leadership Development. John Allyn Moorman, Box 134, Oak Lawn, IL 60454.

Legislation. Don W. Barlow, Westerville Public Lib., 126 S. State St., Westerville, OH 43081.

Marketing of Public Library Services. Pamela J. Brown, 18 Fox Briar Lane, Baltimore, MD 21236.

Allie Beth Martin (1989) Award. Thomas C. Phelps, 4141 N. Henderson Rd., Arlington, VA 22203.

Membership. Linda P. Elliott, Palos Verdes Lib. Dist., 650 Deep Valley Dr., Palos Verdes, CA 90274.

Multilingual Material and Library Service. Tamiye M. Mehan-Trejo, 4714 N. Dover, Chicago, IL 60640.

1991 National Conference. Charles W. Robinson, Baltimore County Public Lib., 320 York Rd., Towson, MD 21204.

1991 National Conference: Exhibitor's Advisory. Fred A. Phillipp, Ingram Lib. Services, 347 Reedwood Dr., Nashville, TN 37217.

1991 National Conference: Local Arrangements. William W. Sannwald, San Diego Public Lib., 820 E St., San Diego, CA 92101-6478.

1991 National Cknference: Program. Kathleen M. Balcom, Downers Grove Public Lib., 1050 Curtiss St., Downers Grove, IL 60515.

1989 Nominating. Carol Ann Desch, Worthman Lane, Rensselaer, NY 12114.

1990 Nominating. Kathleen M. Balcom, Downers Grove Public Lib., 1050 Curtiss St., Downers Grove, IL 60515.

Output Measures for Children's Services (ALSC/PLA Joint Committee). Clara Nalli Bohrer, 4886 School Bell Lane, Birmingham, MI 48010 (ALSC); Sally D. Barnett, Huntsville-Madison County Public Lib., Box 443, Huntsville, AL 35804 (PLA).

Planning Process Discussion Group. Terry L. Weech, 1306 S. Orchard, Urbana, IL 61801.

Policy Manual Advisory. Susan D. Eason, 10408 Montrose Ave., Apt. 302, Bethesda, MD 20814.

Popular Materials Library Discussion Group. To be appointed.

Preschoolers' Door to Learning Discussion Group. To be appointed.

Public Libraries Advisory Board. Carolyn Anthony, Skokie Public Lib., 5215 Oakton, Skokie, IL 60076-3680.

Public Library Data Service Advisory. Charles W. Robinson, Baltimore County Public Lib., 320 York Rd, Towson, MD 21204.

Public Library Trusteeship (ALTA/PLA Joint Committee). James C. Baughman, Simmons College, GSLIS, 300 The Fenway, Boston, MA 02115 (ALTA); Donald J. Sager, 2943 N. Cramer St., Milwaukee, WI 53211 (PLA).

Publications. Karen J. Krueger, Janesville Public Lib., 316 S. Main St., Janesville, WI 53545-3971.

Publications Assembly. Susan S. Goldberg, Arizona Theatre Co., Box 1631, Tucson, AZ 85702.

Recruitment of Public Librarians. Sandra F. Reuben, Los Angeles County Public Lib., 7400 E. Imperial Hwy., Downey, CA 90242.

Research. Carolyn Moore, Clearwater Public Lib., 100 N. Osceola Ave., Clearwater, FL 33515.

Section Revitalization. Melissa Buckingham, 8428 Shawnee St., Philadelphia, PA 19118.

Technology in Public Libraries. Carol F. Liu, 162-20 Ninth Ave., Apt. 9C, Whitestone, NY 11357.

Technology in Public Libraries: Conference Program. Jean Armour Polly, Liverpool Public Lib., Tulip and Second Sts., Liverpool, NY 13088.

Technology in Public Libraries: Technology Awareness. Laura J. Seff, Baltimore County Public Lib., 320 York Rd., Towson, MD 21204.

Leonard Wertheimer Multilingual Award. Matthew C. Kubiak, 43 White Place, Bloomington, IL 61701.

White House Conference Planning. Nolan T. Yelich, Virginia State Lib., 11 St. at Capitol Sq., Richmond, VA 23219.

American Library Association Reference and Adult Services Division

Executive Director, Andrew M. Hansen
50 E. Huron St., Chicago, IL 60611
312-944-6780

Object

The Reference and Adult Services Division is responsible for stimulating and supporting in every type of library the delivery of reference/information services to all groups, regardless of age, and of general library services and materials to adults. This involves facilitating the development and conduct of direct service to library users, the development of programs and guidelines for service to meet the needs of these users, and assisting libraries in reaching potential users.

The specific responsibilities of RASD are:

1. Conduct of activities and projects within the division's areas of responsibility.

2. Encouragement of the development of librarians engaged in these activities, and stimulation of participation by members of appropriate type-of-library divisions.

3. Synthesis of the activities of all units within the American Library Association that have a bearing on the type of activities represented by the division.

4. Representation and interpretation of the division's activities in contacts outside the profession.

5. Planning and development of programs of study and research in these areas for the total profession.

6. Continuous study and review of the division's activities.

Formed by merger of Adult Services Division and Reference Services Division, 1972. Memb. 5,469. (For information on dues, see ALA entry.)

Officers (1988–1989)

Pres. Gail A. Schlachter, 6 Honeysuckle Lane, San Carlos, CA 94070; *Pres.-Elect.* Arthur S. Meyers, Hammond Public Lib., 564 State St., Hammond, IN 46320; *Secy.* Celia Hales-Mabry, 180 Wilson Lib., Univ. of Minnesota, Minneapolis, MN 55455.

Directors

Charles L. Gilreath; Joyce E. Jelks; Marcia J. Myers; Barbara Scheele; Suzanne D. Sutton; Rebecca Whitaker; *Councillor.* Rebecca A. Boone; *Past Pres.* Charles A. Bunge; *Ex officio. BRASS Sec.* Mark Leggett; *CODES Sec.* David F. Kohl; *History Sec.* Priscilla Ciccariello; *MARS Sec.* Julia M. Rholes; *Eds. RASD Update.* Constance R. Miller; *RQ.* Elizabeth Futas; *Council of State and Regional Groups Chpn.* Nancy Sherwin; *Exec. Dir.* Andrew M. Hansen.

(Address correspondence to the executive director.)

Publications

RASD Update (irreg.; memb.; nonmemb. $10). *Ed.* Constance R. Miller, Lib. W121, Indiana Univ., Bloomington, IN 47405.

RQ (q.; memb.; nonmemb. $35). *Ed.* Elizabeth Futas, GSLIS, Rodman Hall, Univ. of Rhode Island, Kingston, RI 02881-0815.

Section Chairpersons

Business Reference and Services Section (BRASS). Mark Leggett, 802 Lincolnwood Lane, Indianapolis, IN 46260.

Collection Development Section (CODES). David F. Kohl, 2575 Forest Ave., Boulder, CO 80302.

History Section. Priscilla Ciccariello, Port Washington Public Lib., 245 Main St., Port Washington, NY 11050.

Machine-Assisted Reference (MARS). Julia M. Rholes, Evans Lib., Microtext Dept., Texas A&M Univ., College Station, TX 77843.

Committee Chairpersons

Access to Information. Margaret Ann Reinert, 815½ N. Delaware, Independence, MO 60459.

Adult Library Materials. Janet W. Majilton, Raleigh Branch Lib., 3157 Powers, Memphis, TN 38128.

Adults, Library Service to. Gary O. Rolstad, Queens Public Lib., 89-11 Merrick Blvd., Jamaica, NY 11432.

Aging Population, Library Service to an. Allan M. Kleiman, Service to the Aging, Brooklyn Public Lib., 2115 Ocean Ave., 2nd fl., Brooklyn, NY 11229.

Bibliography. R. David Myers, 10614 Cavalier Dr., Silver Spring, MD 20901.

Catalog Use. Betsy Wilson, Undergrad. Lib., Univ. of Illinois, 1408 W. Gregory Dr., Urbana, IL 61801.

Conference Program. Danuta A. Nitecki, 11022 Cherry Hill Rd., Adelphia, MD 20783-1013.

Cooperative Reference Service. Dorothy E. Christiansen, 17 Hutchins Rd., Ballston Spa, NY 12020.

Council of State and Regional Groups. Nancy Sherwin, 3011 Corydon Rd., Cleveland Heights, OH 44118.

Dartmouth Medal. Donald J. Kenney, Virginia Tech, Blacksburg, VA 24061-0434.

Evaluation of Reference and Adult Services. Frances Benham, Univ. of Alabama Libs., Drawer 5, Tuscaloosa, AL 35487-9784.

Executive. Gail A. Schlachter, 6 Honeysuckle Lane, San Carlos, CA 94070.

Facts on File Grant. Virginia C. Hill, 3918 S. 16 St., Arlington, VA 22204.

Fee-Based Reference Services. Muriel J. Rossman, 1170 Cushing Circle, Apt. 212, St. Paul, MN 55108.

Interlibrary Loan. Ellen A. Parravano, Southeastern New York Lib. Resources Council, Box 879, Rte. 299, Highland, NY 12528.

Labor Groups, Library Service to, AFL/CIO-ALA (RASD) Joint Committee on. Michele Leber, 1805 Crystal Dr., Apt. 911, Arlington, VA 22202.

Legislation. Virginia Boucher, 845 Lincoln Place, Boulder, CO 80302.

Management of Reference. Ree DeDonato, Bobst Lib., New York Univ., 70 Washington Sq. S., New York, NY 10012.

Membership. Julia Gelfand, 22 Schubert Ct., Irvine, CA 92715.

Margaret E. Monroe Library Adult Services Award. Anne Kincaid, San Francisco Public Lib., Civic Center, San Francisco, CA 94102.

Isadore Gilbert Mudge Citation. Margaret L. Morrison, Torreyson Lib., Univ. of Central Arkansas, Conway, AR 72032.

Multilingual Subcommittee. Lee A. Krieger, North Carolina Foreign Language Center, 300 Maiden Lane, Fayetteville, NC 28301.

Nominating. Kay Ann Cassell, New School for Social Research, 65 Fifth Ave., New York, NY 10003.

Notable Books Council. William Gargan, Brooklyn College Lib., Bedford Ave. and Ave. H, Brooklyn, NY 11210.

Organization. Rebecca J. Whitaker, INCOLSA, 5929 Lakeside Blvd., Indianapolis, IN 46278.

Planning. Charles A. Bunge, Univ. of Wisconsin-Madison, SLIS, 600 N. Park St., Madison, WI 53706.

Professional Development. Joy M. Greiner, Univ. of Southern Mississippi, Southern Sta., Box 5146, Hattiesburg, MS 39406-5146.

Publications. Chris Ferguson, Undergrad. Lib. C-075-D, Univ. of California-San Diego, La Jolla, CA 92093.

Reference Service Press Award. Eric W. Greenfeldt, Princeton Public Lib., 65 Witherspoon St., Princeton, NJ 08542.

Reference Services for Children and Young Adults. Neel Parikh, 3027 Richmond Blvd., Oakland, CA 94611.

Reference Sources. Linda J. Sammataro, 3649 Taliluna Ave., Unit G-3, Knoxville, TN 37910.

Reference Sources for Small and Medium-Sized Libraries (5th ed.) ad hoc. Kevin M. Rosswurm, Mount Vernon Public Lib., 28 S. First Ave., Mount Vernon, NY 10550.

Reference Tools Advisory. La Verne Z. Coan, 2439 Cabot Rd., Canton, MI 48188.

RQ Editorial Advisory Board. Elizabeth Futas, GSLIS, Rodman Hall, Univ. of Rhode Island, Kingston, RI 02881-0815.

John Sessions Memorial Award. Paula O'Connor, American Federation of Teachers, 555 New Jersey Ave. N.W., Washington, DC 20001.

Spanish-Speaking, Library Service to the. Salvador Guerena, Collecion Tloque Nahuaque, Univ. Lib., Univ. of California, Santa Barbara, CA 93106.

Speakers and Consultants Directory. Mary A. Ryan, Reference Dept., Univ. of Missouri Lib., Columbia, MO 65201-5149.

Standards and Guidelines. Marta Lange, 4247-3 Avent Ferry Rd., Raleigh, NC 27606.

Wilson Indexes. Peter W. McCallion, 232 E. Fifth St., New York, NY 10003.

Discussion Group Chairpersons

Adult Materials and Services. Charlotte C. Clarke, Ramsey County Public Lib., Admin. Office, 1910 W. County Rd. B, Roseville, MN 55113.

Interlibrary Loan. Eva D. Godwin, Coord. of Access Services, Oregon State Lib., State Lib. Bldg., Salem, OR 97310.

Performance Standards for Reference/Information Librarians. Anna Donnelly, Reference Dept., St. John's Univ. Lib., Grand Central and Utopia Pkwys., Jamaica, NY 11439.

Reference Services in Large Research Libraries. Agnes Widder, 126 Centerlawn, East Lansing, MI 48823.

Reference Services in Medium-Sized Research Libraries. J. Douglas Archer, Reference

Dept., Hesburgh Lib., Univ. of Notre Dame, Notre Dame, IN 46556.

Women's Materials and Women Library Users. Sherry A. O'Brien, Wallace Lib., Wheaton College, Norton, MA 02776.

Representatives

Coalition of Adult Education Organizations. Hardy R. Franklin, 4417 46th St. N.W., Washington, DC 20016; Andrew M. Hansen, ALA, 50 E. Huron St., Chicago, IL 60611.

Freedom to Read Foundation. Carl Stone, Anderson County Lib., 202 E. Greenville St., Anderson, SC 29622-4047.

American Library Association Resources and Technical Services Division

Executive Director, Karen Muller
50 E. Huron St., Chicago, IL 60611
312-944-6780

Object

The division is responsible for the following activities: "acquisition, identification, cataloging, classification, reproduction, and preservation of library materials; the development and coordination of the country's library resources; and those areas of selection and evaluation involved in the acquisition of library materials and pertinent to the development of library resources. Any member of the American Library Association may elect membership in this division according to the provisions of the bylaws." Established 1957. Memb. 5,818. (For information on dues, see ALA entry.)

Officers (June 1988–June 1989)

Pres. Carolyn L. Harris, Asst. Dir. for Preservation, Columbia Univ. Libs., New York, NY 10027; *V.P.* Nancy R. John, Asst. Univ. Libn., Univ. of Illinois at Chicago Libs., Univ. Lib., Chicago, IL 60680.

(Address correspondence to the executive director.)

Directors

Officers; *Council of Regional Groups Chpn.* Dorothy J. McKowen, 7625 Summit Lane, LaFayette, IN 47905; *RTSD Councillor.* Frederick C. Lynden (1990); *Exec. Dir.* Karen Muller; *Past Pres.* Marion T. Reid; *Dirs.-at-Large.* Nancy J. Williamson (1989); Lizabeth Bishoff (1991); *Council of Regional Groups V. Chpn./Chpn.-Elect.* Joan W. Hayes; *LRTS Ed.* Sheila Intner; *RTSD Newsletter Ed.* Thomas W. Leonhardt; *RTSD Planning and Research Committee Chpn.* Pamela Bluh (1989); *RTSD Sec. Chpns.* Sheila Intner (CCS); Sherry Byrne (PLMS); Ann G. Swartzell (RLMS); Nora K. Rawlinson (RS); Alexander B. Bloss (SS); *LC Liaison.* Henriette D. Avram; *Parliamentarian.* Edward Swanson.

Publications

Library Resources and Technical Services (q.; RTSD memb. or $30). *Ed.* Sheila S. Intner, Winter Way, Box 53, Monterey, MA 01245.

RTSD Newsletter (6 per year; memb. or $20). *Ed.* Thomas W. Leonhardt, Dir. of Libs., Univ. of the Pacific, Stockton, CA 95211.

Section Chairpersons

Cataloging and Classification Section (CCS). Sheila Intner, Simmons College, Box 151, Monterey, MA 01245.

Preservation of Library Materials Section (PLMS). Sherry Byrne, Univ. of Chicago, Dept. B-3, Joseph Regenstein Lib., 1100 E. 57th St., Chicago, IL 60637.

Reproduction of Library Materials Section (RLMS). Ann G. Swartzell, SCM/NS (Preservation), New York State Lib., Albany, NY 12230.

Resources Section (RS). Nora K. Rawlinson, Library Journal, 249 W. 17th St., New York, NY 10011.

Serials Section (SS). Alexander B. Bloss, OCLC, 6565 Frantz Rd., Dublin, OH 43017.

Committee Chairpersons

Audiovisual. Michael D. Esman, 4849 Connecticut Ave. N.W., Apt. 832, Washington, DC 20008.

Budget and Finance. Arnold Hirshon, 916 Hedgelawn Dr., Richmond, VA 23235.

Catalog Form and Function. Wanda V. Dole, Pennsylvania State Univ., Ogontz Campus Lib., 1600 Woodland Rd., Abington, PA 19001.

Commercial Technical Services. Suzanne Sweeney, 405 Calderon, Apt. 3, Mountain View, CA 94041.

Conference Program – Chicago, 1990. Nancy R. John, Asst. Univ. Libn., Univ. of Illinois at Chicago Libs., Univ. Lib., Chicago, IL 60680.

Conference Program – Dallas, 1989. Carolyn L. Harris, Head, Preservation Dept., Columbia Univ. Libs., New York, NY 10027.

Duplicates Exchange Union. Kathryn Chilson O'Gorman, Head of Serials, 428 Lib., Wright State Univ., Dayton, OH 45435.

Education. Patricia G. Oyler, Simmons College, Grad. School of Lib. and Info. Science, 300 The Fenway, Boston, MA 02115.

International Relations. Merrily A. Smith, National Preservation Program, Office LM-G07, Lib. of Congress, Washington, DC 20540.

Legislative. Charlene Renner, Waldo Lib., Western Michigan Univ., Kalamazoo, MI 49008-3899.

LRTS Editorial Board. Sheila S. Intner, College Winter Way, Box 53, Monterey, MA 01245-1991.

Membership. Laverna M. Saunders, Head, Technical Services, Univ. of Las Vegas, 4505 Maryland Pkwy., Las Vegas, NV 89154.

Nominating. Judith N. Kharbas, Asst. Dir. for Technical Service, Univ. of Rochester, Rush Rhees Lib., Rochester, NY 14627.

Organization and Bylaws. Marion T. Reid, Louisiana State Univ. Libs., Baton Rouge, LA 70803-3300.

Esther J. Piercy Award Jury. Doris A. Bradley, Atkins Lib., Univ. of North Carolina, Charlotte, NC 28223.

Planning and Research Committee. Pamela Bluh, Marshall Law Lib., Univ. of Maryland School of Law, 20 N. Paca St., Baltimore, MD 21201.

Preservation Microfilming. Nancy E. Gwinn, Smithsonian Institution Libs., NHB 24 E., Washington, DC 20560.

Publications. Joseph J. Branin, Univ. of Minnesota, 180 Wilson Lib., 309 19th Ave. S., Minneapolis, MN 55455-0414.

Publisher/Vendor-Library Relations. Helen I. Reed, Acquisitions Dept., Perkins Lib., Duke Univ., Durham, NC 27706.

Representation in Machine-Readable Form of Bibliographic Information. Kathleen Bales, Research Libs. Group, Jordan Quadrangle, Stanford, CA 94305.

Strategic Long-Range Planning. Marion T. Reid, Louisiana State Univ. Libs., Baton Rouge, LA 70803-3300.

Technical Services Costs. Christian M. Boissonas, Acquisitions Dept., Cornell Univ. Lib., 110A Olin Lib., Ithaca, NY 14853-5301.

Representatives

ALA Legislation Assembly. Charlene Renner (1989).

ALA Library Education Assembly. Patricia G. Oyler (1989).

ALA Membership Promotion Task Force. Laverna M. Saunders (1989).

CONSER Advisory Group. Suzanne Striedieck (1989).

Freedom to Read Foundation Board. Karen Daziel Tallman (1989).

Joint Advisory Committee on Nonbook Materials. Katha D. Massey (1990); Verna Urbanski (1990).

Joint Steering Committee for Revision of AACR2. Helen F. Schmierer (1989).

National Information Standards Organization (NISO): Standards Committee Z39 on Library Work, Documentation, and Related Public Practices. Jean T. Hamrick (1989); *Alternate.* Sally H. McCallum.

National Institute for Conservation. Merrily A. Smith (1989).

American Library Association Young Adult Services Division

Executive Director, Evelyn Shaevel
50 E. Huron St., Chicago, IL 60611
312-944-6780

Object

The goal . . . is to advocate, promote, and strengthen service to young adults as part of the continuum of total library service. The following concerns and activities are interdependent in fulfilling the goal of YASD. The Young Adult Services Division:

1. Advocates the young adult's right to free and equal access to materials and services, and assists librarians in handling problems of such access.
2. Evaluates and promotes materials of interest to adolescents through special services, programs, and publications, except for those materials designed specifically for curriculum use.
3. Identifies research needs related to young adult service and communicates those needs to the library academic community in order to activate research projects.
4. Stimulates and promotes the development of librarians and other staff working with young adults through formal and continuing education.
5. Stimulates and promotes the expansion of young adult service among professional associates and agencies at all levels.
6. Represents the interests of librarians and staff working with young adults to all relevant agencies, government or private, and to industries that serve young adults as clients or consumers.
7. Creates and maintains communication links with other units of ALA whose developments affect service to young adults.

Established 1957. Memb. 2,488. (For information on dues, see ALA entry.)

Membership

Open to anyone interested in library services and materials to young adults.

Officers (July 1988–July 1989)

Pres. Susan B. Madden, King County Lib., 300 Eighth Ave. N., Seattle, WA 98109; *V.P./Pres.-Elect.* Gerald G. Hodges, 930 Sunset St., Iowa City, IA 52240; *Past Pres.* Vivian Wynn, Cuyahoga County Public Lib., Maple Heights Regional Branch, 5225 Library Lane, Maple Heights, OH 44137.

Directors

Jennifer Jung Gallant; Barbara Newmarx-Kruger; Elizabeth O'Donnell; Susan Rosenzweig; Roger Sutton; JoAnn Weinberg; Evie Wilson-Longbloom.

Publication

Journal of Youth Services in Libraries (formerly *Top of the News*) (q.; free to membs.; $30 nonmembs.). *Ed.* Josette Lyders, 4322 Waycross Dr., Houston, TX 77035.

Committee Chairpersons

Adolescent Health. Patty Campbell, 1437 Lucile Ave., Los Angeles, CA 90026.

Audiovisual Producers and Distributors Liaison. To be appointed.

Author Award. Roger Sutton, 807 W. Cornelia, Apt. 2E, Chicago, IL 60657.

Best Books for Young Adults. Eugene Lafaille, 769 Edgewood Ave., New Haven, CT 06515.

Budget and Finance. Margaret J. Harris, Maple Heights Regional Branch, Cuyahoga County Public Lib., 5225 Library Lane, Maple Heights, OH 44137.

Computer Applications to Young Adults Services. Holly Carroll, Geauga County

Public Lib., Bainbridge Lib., 17222 Snyder Rd., Chagren Falls, OH 44022.

Division Promotion. Ranae Pierce, Agency Head, Chapman Lib., 577 S. Ninth W., Salt Lake City, UT 84104.

Education. Timothea McDonald, Young Adults Libn., Brighton Branch, Boston Public Lib., 40 Academy Hill Rd., Brighton, MA 02135-3316.

Intellectual Freedom. Robert C. Small, Jr., Professor of English Education, Div. of Curriculum and Instruction, College of Education, Virginia Technical, Blacksburg, VA 24061.

Journal of Youth Services in Libraries. Josette Lyders, 4322 Waycross Dr., Houston, TX 77035.

Leadership Training. Gerald Hodges, Asst. Professor, School of Lib. and Info. Science, 3067 Lib., Univ. of Iowa, Iowa City, IA 52242.

Legislation. Cathy Monnin, Apt. 213, 3350 Tribune, Dallas, TX 75224.

Library of Congress, Advisory Committee to the National Library Service for the Blind and Physically Handicapped. Elizabeth Shorb, New Carrollton Lib., 7414 Riverdale Rd., New Carrollton, MD 20784.

Local Arrangements—Dallas, 1989. Teri Baker, Asst. Mgr., Children's Center, Dallas Public Lib., 1515 Young St., Dallas, TX 75201.

Long-Range Planning. JoAnn G. Mondowney, 2014 McElderry St., Baltimore, MD 21205.

Media Selection and Usage. To be appointed.

Membership Recruitment. Jennifer Jung Gallant, 482 Dover Center Rd., Bay Village, OH 44140.

National Organizations Serving the Young Adult Liaison. Marcia Miller Trent, Hammond Public Lib., 564 State St., Hammond, IN 46320.

Nominating. To be appointed.

Organization and Bylaws. Rosemary Kneale, 7020 Hunting Lane, Chagrin Falls, OH 44022.

Program Planning Clearinghouse and Evaluation. Gayle Keresey, 2148 Harrison St., Wilmington, NC 24801.

Public Relations. Betty Carter, 2310 Lexford Lane, Houston, TX 77080.

Publications. Anne Boegen, Youth Services Coord., Miami-Dade Public Lib., 101 W. Flagler St., Miami, FL 33130.

Publishers' Liaison. Barbara Newmark-Kruger, 24 Lancaster Lane, Monsey, NY 10952.

Recommended Books for the Reluctant Young Adult Reader. To be appointed.

Research. To be appointed.

Selected Films for Young Adults. To be appointed.

YASD/Baker and Tayor Conference Grant. Teri Baker, Asst. Mgr., Children's Center, Dallas Public Lib., 1515 Young St., Dallas, TX 75201.

Young Adults with Special Needs. Mary Flournoy, 3240 Midvale Ave., Philadelphia, PA 19129.

Youth Participation. Beth Wheeler Dean, Public Lib., Box 443, Huntsville, AL 35804.

Discussion Group Chairpersons

Booktalking. Joni Bodart-Talbot, School of Lib. and Info. Management, Emporia State Univ., 1200 Commercial St., Emporia, KS 66801.

Library Educators for Young Adult Services and Materials. To be appointed.

Storytelling. Rita Auerbach, 2 Shore Rd., East Patchogue, NY 11772.

Representatives

ALA Appointments Committee. Gerald G. Hodges.

ALA Budget Assembly. Susan B. Madden.

ALA Chicago Conference (1989) Program Committee. Gerald G. Hodges.

ALA Dallas Conference Program Committee. Susan B. Madden.

ALA Legislation Assembly. Cathy Monnin.

ALA Library Education Assembly. Timothea McDonald.

ALA Membership Promotion Task Force. Jennifer Jung Gallant.

Freedom to Read Foundation. Robert Small.

American Merchant Marine Library Association

(Affiliated with United Seamen's Service)
Executive Director, Vando Dell'Amico
One World Trade Center, Suite 1365, New York, NY 10048
212-775-1033

Object

Provides ship and shore library service for American-flag merchant vessels, the Military Sealift Command, the Coast Guard, and other waterborne operations of the U.S. government.

Officers

Honorary Chairman. John A. Gaughan; *Pres.* Hoyt S. Haddock; *Treas.* William G. Croly; *Secy.* Ellen Craft Dammond.

Board of Directors

F. Lee Betz; John Bowers; Robert A. Carl; Nick Cretan; William G. Croly; Ellen Craft Dammond; Richard Daschbach; John I. Dugan; Robert E. Fall; Florence R. Fleming; Arthur W. Friedberg; Charles Dana Gibson; Hoyt S. Haddock; John D. Hardy; Robert E. Hart; James J. Hayes; Edward Honor; Thomas A. King; James Kirk; Paul L. Krinsky; Edward R. Morgan; Thomas Murphy; Samuel B. Nemirow; Milton G. Nottingham, Jr.; Louis Parise; James F. Paterson; Lillian Rabins; Franklin K. Riley; Wallace T. Sansone; Robert H. Scarborough; R. J. Schamann; William Schuman; Allen Scott; Gerald Seifert; Talmage Simpkins; Thomas J. Smith; Adrian P. Spidle; John H. Stanford; A. Faulkner Watts; James R. Whittemore.

Committee Chairperson

AMMLA. Milton G. Nottingham.

American Society for Information Science

Executive Director, Linda Resnik
1424 16th St. N.W., #404, Washington, DC 20036
202-462-1000

Object

The American Society for Information Science provides a forum for the discussion, publication, and critical analysis of work dealing with the design, management, and use of information systems and technology. Memb. (Indiv.) 3,700; (Student) 480; (Inst.) 120. Dues (Indiv.) $85; (Student) $34; (Inst.) $350 and $550.

Officers

Pres. W. David Penniman, AT&T Bell Labs, 600 Mountain Ave., Murray Hill, NJ 07974; *V.P./Pres.-Elect.* Toni Carbo Bearman, Dean, SLIS, Univ. of Pittsburgh, Pittsburgh, PA 15260; *Treas.* N. Bernard Basch, EBSCO Subscription Services, 826 S. Northwest Hwy., Barrington, IL 60010; *Past Pres.* Martha Williams, Univ. of Illinois, CSL, 1101 W. Springfield, Urbana, IL 61801.

(Address correspondence to the executive director.)

Board of Directors

Chapter Assembly Dir. Sandra Killian; *SIG Cabinet Dir.* Carol Wasserman Diener; *Dirs.-at-Large.* Robert Baker; Marjorie Hlava; Randolph Hock; Helen Manning; Jessica Milstead; Gerard Salton.

Publications

Annual Review of Information Science and Technology. Available from Elsevier Science Publishers.

Bulletin of the American Society for Information Science. Available directly from ASIS.

Collective Index to the Journal of the American Society for Information Science (vol. 1, 1950–vol. 25, 1974). Available from John Wiley & Sons, 605 Third Ave., New York, NY 10016.

DataBase Directory Service 1985–1986. Available from Knowledge Industry Publications.

Journal of the American Society for Information Science; formerly *American Documentation.* Available from John Wiley & Sons, 605 Third Ave., New York, NY 10016.

Key Papers in the Design and Evaluation of Information Systems. Ed. Donald W. King. Available from Greenwood Press.

Library and Reference Facilities in the Area of the District of Columbia. Available from Knowledge Industry Publications.

Proceedings of the ASIS Annual Meetings. Available from Learned Information.

Committee Chairpersons

Awards and Honors. Roberta Maxwell, AT&T Bell Labs, 600 Mountain Ave., MH 6A-309, Murray Hill, NJ 07974.

Budget and Finance. N. Bernard Basch, EBSCO Subscription Services, 826 S. Northwest Hwy., Barrington, IL 60010.

Conferences and Meetings. To be appointed.

Constitution and Bylaws. Charles Sargent, Lib., Texas Tech Univ. Health Sciences Center, Lubbock, TX 79430.

Education. Julie Hurd, Univ. of Chicago, GLS, 1000 E. 57 St., Chicago, IL 60637.

Executive. W. David Penniman, AT&T Bell Labs, 600 Mountain Ave., Murray Hill, NJ 07974.

International Relations. Pamela Richards, Rutgers Univ., 4 Huntington St., New Brunswick, NJ 08903.

Inter-Society Cooperation. Ellen Sleeter, Getty Center, 401 Wilshire Blvd., Santa Monica, CA 90401.

Marketing. Michael O'Hara, 2032 Belmont Rd. N.W., #307, Washington, DC 20009.

Membership. Joan Mitchell, Carnegie-Mellon Univ., Hunt Lib., Schenley Pk., Pittsburgh, PA 15213.

Nominations. Martha Williams, Univ. of Illinois, CSL, 1101 W. Springfield, Urbana, IL 61801.

Professionalism. Jose Marie Griffith, King Research, 6000 Executive Blvd., Sta. 200, Rockville, MD 20852.

Public Affairs. Madeline Henderson, 5021 Alta Vista Rd., Bethesda, MD 20814.

Publications. Ethel Auster, Univ. of Toronto, CLIS, 140 St. George St., Toronto, ON M5S 1A1, Canada.

Research. Jeffrey Katzer, Professor, Syracuse Univ. School of Info. Studies, Syracuse, NY 13244.

Standards. Louise Levy, AT&T Bell Labs, 600 Mountain Ave., Murray Hill, NJ 07974.

American Theological Library Association

Executive Secretary, Simeon Daly, O.S.B.
St. Meinrad School of Theology, Archabbey Library
St. Meinrad, IN 47577

Object

"To bring its members into close working relationships with each other, to support theological and religious librarianship, to improve theological libraries, and to interpret the role of such libraries in theological education, developing and implementing standards of library service, promoting research and experimental projects, encouraging cooperative programs that make resources more available, publishing and disseminating literature and research tools and aids, cooperating with organizations having similar aims, and otherwise supporting and aiding theological education." Founded 1947. Memb. (Inst.) 170; (Indiv.) 480. Dues (Inst.) $75 to $400, based on total library expenditure; (Indiv.) $15 to $80, based on salary scale. Year. July 1–June 30.

ATLA is a member of the Council of National Library and Information Associations.

Membership

Persons engaged in professional library or bibliographical work in theological or religious fields and others who are interested in the work of theological librarianship.

Officers (July 1988–June 1989)

Pres. Channing Jeschke, Pitts Theology Lib., Emory Univ., Atlanta, GA 30322; *V.P./Pres.-Elect.* H. Eugene McLeod, Southeastern Baptist Theological Seminary, Box 752, Wake Forest, NC 27587; *Past Pres.* Rosalyn Lewis, United Methodist Publishing, 201 Eighth Ave. S., Lib. Rm. 122, Nashville, TN 37202; *Treas.* Robert A. Olsen, Jr., Libn., Brite Divinity School, Texas Christian Univ., Fort Worth, TX 76129.

Board of Directors

Mary Bischoff; Michael P. Boddy; Diane Choquette; Leslie R. Galbraith; Roger L. Loyd; Sharon A. Taylor.

Publications

Newsletter (q.; memb. or $10).
Proceedings (ann.; memb. or $20).
Religion Index One (formerly *Index to Religious Periodical Literature, 1949–date*).
Religion Index Two: Multi-Author Works.
Research in Ministry: An Index to Doctor of Ministry Project Reports.

Committee Chairpersons

Archivist. Gerald W. Gillette, Presbyterian Historical Society, 425 Lombard St., Philadelphia, PA 19147.

ATLA Newsletter. Donn Michael Farris, Ed., Divinity School Lib., Duke Univ., Durham, NC 27706.

ATLA Representative to the Council of National Library and Information Associations. Paul A. Byrnes, 69 Tiemann Place, Apt. 44, New York, NY 10027.

Bibliographic Systems. Ferne Weimer, Billy Graham Center Lib., Wheaton College, Wheaton, IL 60187.

Collection Evaluation and Development. Milton Joseph Coalter, Louisville Presbyterian Theological Seminary, 1044 Alta Vista Rd., Louisville, KY 40205.

Nominating. John Baker-Batsel, Grad. Theological Union, 2400 Ridge Rd., Berkeley, CA 94709.

Oral History. David Wartluft, Lutheran Theological Seminary, 7301 German Ave., Philadelphia, PA 19119.

Periodical Indexing Board. Norman Kansfield, Libn., Colgate Rochester/Bexley Hall/Crozer Divinity School, 1100 S. Goodman St., Rochester, NY 14620.

Preservation Board. Co. Chpns. John A. Bollier, Sterling Memorial Lib., Rm. 118, 120 High St., New Haven, CT 06511; Charles Willard, Dir., Speer Lib., Princeton Theological Seminary, Princeton, NJ 08540.

Program. Sara M. Myers, Ira J. Taylor Lib., Iliff School of Theology, 2201 S. University Blvd., Denver, CO 80210.

Public Service. Norman Anderson, Goddard Lib., Gordon-Conwell Theological Seminary, South Hamilton, MA 01982.

Publication. David. K. Himrod, United Lib.-GETS/SWTS, 2121 Sheridan Rd., Evanston, IL 60201.

Relationship with Learned Societies. Simeon Daly, ATLA.

Statistician and Liaison with ALA Statistics Coordinating Committee. Simeon Daly, ATLA.

ARMA International

Executive Director, James P. Souders
4200 Somerset Dr., Suite 215, Prairie Village, KS 66208
913-341-3808

Object

"To promote a scientific interest in records and information management; to provide a forum for research and the exchange of ideas and knowledge; to foster professionalism; to develop and promulgate workable standards and practices; and to furnish a source of records and information management guidance through education and publications."

Membership

Membership application is available through ARMA Headquarters. Annual dues are $65 for international affiliation. Chapter dues vary from city to city. Membership categories are chapter member ($65 plus chapter dues), student member ($10), and member-at-large.

Officers

Pres. and CEO. Martin Richelsoph, CRM, State Records Center, 1919 W. Jefferson, Phoenix, AZ 85009; *Exec. V.P.* David O. Stephens, CRM, Dataplex, Box 14975, Lefluer Sta., Jackson, MS 39236; *Secy.-Treas.* Manker R. Harris, CRM, 330 E. Klein Creek Ct., Carol Stream, IL 60188; *Past Pres. and Chairman of the Bd.* John Moss Smith, COAP, Corporate Records Management Admin., Atomic Energy of Canada, Ltd., 275 Slater St., Ottawa, ON K1A 0S4, Canada.

Board of Directors (1988–1989)

Regional V.P.s. Region I. Philip K. Albert, Sr., Johns Hopkins Univ./APL, Johns Hopkins Rd., Laurel, MD 20707; *Region II.* Beth A. Sherwood, League Insurance Co., Life Services, Box 33430, Detroit, MI 48232; *Region III.* Wendy Shade, Bell & Hawell Records Management, 4300 Highlands Pkwy. S.E., Smyrna, GA 30080; *Region IV.* Michael P. Flanagan, Union Pacific Railroad Co., 1416 Dodge St., Omaha, NE 68179; *Region V.* Patricia Britain Dixon, Southland Corp., 2828 N. Haskell Ave., Dallas, TX 75204; *Region VI.* Gabriel Forsberg, CRM, Lewis L. Roca, 100 W. Washington, Phoenix, AZ 85003; *Region VII.* Robert F. Calhoun, Aetna Life & Casualty, 151 Farmington Ave., Hartford, CT 06156; *Region VIII.* James Allin Spokes, Records Management, Manitoba Hydro, Box 815, Winnipeg, MB R3C 2P4, Canada; *Region IX.* Stephen E. Haller, Montgomery County Records Mgr., 451 W. Third St., Dayton, OH 45422; *Region X.* Dorris M. Schneider, Records Mgr., SAIF Corp., 400 High St. S.E., Salem, OR 97312; *Region XI.* Kristi Kay Woods, Heritage Security Centre, 4001 S.W. 47 Ave., Fort Lauderdale, FL 33314.

Publication

Records Management Quarterly. Ed. Ira Penn, Box 4580, Silver Spring, MD 20904.

Committee Managers

Audit/Budget/Compensation. Manker R. Harris, CRM, 330 E. Klein Creek Ct., Carol Stream, IL 60188.

Awards/Nominating. John Moss Smith, COAP, Corporate Records Management Admin., Atomic Energy of Canada Ltd., 275 Slater St., Ottawa, ON K1A 0S4, Canada.

Conferences. Mariyana L. Stamey, City of Sarasota, Box 1058, Sarasota, FL 34230.

Education and Scholarship. Gloria Bordenuk, Exec. Asst., Kent County Bd. of Educ., Box 1000, Chatham, ON N7M 5L7, Canada.

Industry Action. Jean K. Brown, Univ. of Delaware Archives, 78 E. Delaware Ave., Newark, DE 19716.

International Affairs. Judi Harvey, Pacific Press, Ltd., 2250 Granville St., Vancouver, BC V6H 3G2, Canada.

Legislative and Regulatory Affairs—Canada. Brenda Hobbs, City of Mississauga, Clerks Dept., 300 City Center Dr., Mississauga, ON L5B 3C1, Canada.
Legislative and Regulatory Affairs—U.S. Patrick Clarke, 2017 Northampton Way, Lansing, MI 48912.
Long Range Planning. Gail B. Pennix, CRM, 2364 South Ct., Palo Alto, CA 94301.
1989 Program Manager. Tyrone Butler, CRM, Asst. Mgr., NYC Dept. of Records and Info., 31 Chambers St., Rm. 107, New York, NY 10017.
Publications. Eldon Jones, CRM, 260 Riverside Dr., Apt. 6A, New York, NY 10025.
Standards Advisory and Development. Richard Weinholdt, Public Archives of Canada, 201 Weston St., Winnipeg, MB R3E 3H4, Canada.
Technical Research. Pat Vice, CRM, 9695 Desert Ave., Boise, ID 83709.
Technology Applications. Walter Moy, CRM, 120 Leslie Dr., San Carlos, CA 94070.
Teller. Roger Cooper, 5900 W. 85 St., Overland Park, KS 66207.

Art Libraries Society of North America (ARLIS/NA)

Executive Director, Pamela J. Parry
3900 E. Timrod St., Tucson, AZ 85711
602-881-8479

Object

"To promote art librarianship and visual resources curatorship, particularly by acting as a forum for the interchange of information and materials on the visual arts." Established 1972. Memb. 1,300. Dues (Inst.) $75; (Indiv.) $45; (Business Affiliate) $75; (Student) $20; (Retired) $25; (Unemployed) $30; (Sustaining) $175; (Sponsor) $500. Year. Jan.-Dec. 31.

Membership

Open and encouraged for all those interested in visual librarianship, whether they be professional librarians, students, library assistants, art book publishers, art book dealers, art historians, archivists, architects, slide and photograph curators, or retired associates in these fields.

Officers (March 1989–Feb. 1990)

Pres. Clive Phillpot, Museum of Modern Art Lib., 11 W. 53 St., New York, NY 10019; *V.P./Pres.-Elect.* Lynette Korenic, Arts Lib., Univ. of California, Santa Barbara, CA 93106; *Secy.* Anita Gilden, Baltimore Museum of Art Lib., Art Museum Dr., Baltimore, MD 21218; *Treas.* Jack Robertson, Univ. of Virginia, Fiske Kimball Fine Arts Lib., Bayly Dr., Charlottesville, VA 22903; *Exec. Dir.* Pamela J. Parry, 3900 E. Timrod St., Tucson, AZ 85711; *Past Pres.* Ann Abid, Cleveland Museum of Art Lib., 1150 East Blvd., Cleveland, OH 44106.

(Address correspondence to the executive director.)

Committees

(Direct correspondence to headquarters.)
AAT Advisory.
Cataloging Advisory.
Conference.
Development.
International Relations.
Membership.
Gerd Muehsam Award.
Nominating.
Professional Development.
Publications.
Standards.
Travel Awards.
George Wittenborn Award.

Executive Board

The president, past president, president-elect, secretary, treasurer, and four regional representatives (East, Midwest, West, and Canada).

Publications

ARLIS/NA Update (q.; memb.).
Art Documentation (q.; memb.).
Handbook and List of Members (ann.; memb.).
Occasional Papers (price varies).
Miscellaneous others (request current list from headquarters).

Chapters

Arizona; Central Plains; DC-Maryland-Virginia; Delaware Valley; Kentucky-Tennessee; Michigan; Midstates; Montreal-Ottawa-Quebec; New England; New Jersey; New York; Northern California; Northwest; Ohio; Southeast; Southern California; Texas; Twin Cities; Western New York.

Asian/Pacific American Librarians Association

President, Conchita J. Pineda,
Manager, Citicorp/Citibank, N.A.,
Citi Information Services, 153 E. 53 St., New York, NY 10043

Object

"To provide a forum for discussing problems and concerns of Asian/Pacific American librarians; to provide a forum for the exchange of ideas by Asian/Pacific American librarians and other librarians; to support and encourage library services to the Asian/Pacific American communities; to recruit and support Asian/Pacific American librarians in the library/information science professions; to seek funding for scholarships in library/information science schools for Asian/Pacific Americans; and to provide a vehicle whereby Asian/Pacific American librarians can cooperate with other associations and organizations having similar or allied interests." Founded 1980; incorporated 1981; affiliated with ALA 1982. Dues (Inst.) $25; (Indiv.) $10; (Students/Unemployed Librarians) $5.

Membership

Open to all librarians/information specialists of Asian/Pacific descent working in U.S. libraries/information centers and other such related organizations and to others who support the goals and purposes of APALA. Asian/Pacific Americans are defined as those who consider themselves Asian/Pacific Americans. They may be Americans of Asian/Pacific descent, Asian/Pacific people with the status of permanent residency, or Asian/Pacific people living in the United States.

Officers (June 1988–June 1989)

Pres. Conchita J. Pineda, Mgr., Citicorp/Citibank, 153 E. 53 St., New York, NY 10043; *V.P./Pres.-Elect.* Ichiko Morita, Ohio State Univ. Libs., 1858 Neil Ave. Mall, Columbus, OH 43210; *Treas.* Abdul J. Miah, Dir., J. Sargeant Reynolds Community College Lib., 700 E. Jackson St., Richmond, VA 23240; *Secy.* Dallas R. Shawkey, Brooklyn Public Lib., 109 Montgomery St., Brooklyn, NY 11225.

Advisory Committee

The president, immediate past president, vice president/president-elect, secretary, treasurer, chairpersons of the regional chapters, and an elected representative of the standing committees.

Publications

APALA Newsletter (q.; memb.). *Ed.* Sharad Karkhanis, Kingsborough Community College Lib., Oriental Blvd., Brooklyn, NY 11235.
Membership Directory.

Committee Chairpersons

Constitution and Bylaws. Connie Rebadavia, Head, Science and Technology Team, Alexander Lib., Rutgers Univ., New Brunswick, NJ 08903.

Membership. Chiou-Sen Chen, Serials Acquisitions Libn., Alexander Lib., Rutgers Univ., New Brunswick, NJ 08903.

Publicity and Program. Augurio Collantes, Hostos Community College/CUNY, 500 Grand Concourse, Bronx, NY 10451.

Recruitment and Scholarship. Ik-Sam Kim, Univ. of California, 405 Hilgard Ave., Los Angeles, CA 90024.

Associated Information Managers

Executive Director, Paul Oyer
3821-F S. George Mason Dr., Falls Church, VA 22041
703-845-9150

Object

To advance information management as a profession and to promote information management as an executive function by improving recognition of its applicability as a strategic and tactical tool in achieving organizational and executive effectiveness. AIM provides the meeting ground for the professionals responsible for meeting the present and future information needs of their organizations within the information management context. Established Jan. 1981. Memb. (Indiv.) 600; (Corporate) 23.

Membership

Corporate planners, vice presidents of communication and marketing, administration managers, on-line users, data processing, telecommunications, librarianship, records management, office automation, and management information systems (MIS) personnel. Its primary focus is on the management of these information activities and on making the total information base supportive of management and the decision-making process. Board of Directors made up of leading information professionals in industry, academia, and government. Dues (Corporate) sustaining $3,000, supporting $1,000, contributing $500; (Indiv.) private $100, public/Academician $60; (Foreign) $135; (Student) $35.

Board of Directors

Chpn. Ramona C. T. Crosby, Mgr. Technical Info. Services, AKZO Chemicals Inc.; *V. Chpn.* Robert O. Stanton, Mgr., Operations Libs. and Info. Systems Center, AT&T Bell Laboratories; *Treas.* Suzanne Geigle, Dir. Editorial Support Services, The Bur. of National Affairs; *Past Chpn.* Reed Phillips, Dir., Info. Resources Management, U.S. Dept. of Commerce; Floy Bakes, Account Development Mgr., Dow Jones News/Retrieval, Dow Jones & Co., Inc.; Herbert R. Brinberg, Pres. and CEO, Wolters Samson U.S. Corp.; Ina A. Brown, Dept. Mgr., Technical Publication Dept., AT&T Bell Laboratories; Cornelius F. Burk, Jr., DMR Group, Inc.; Christopher Burns, Pres., Christopher Burns, Inc.; M. Robert Kelly, Pres., St. James Group; Alan S. Linden, Mgr., Dist. Marketing Operations, Wang Laboratories, Inc.; Donald A. Marchand, Dean, School of Info. Studies, Syracuse Univ.; Melinda J. Scott, Management Consultant; E. Norman Sims, Dir., Dept. of State Services, Council of State Governments; Molly A. Wolfe, Pres., Knowledgeware Systems, Inc.; *Exec. Dir.* Paul Oyer, Pres., The Info. Exchange.

Publications

AIM Network (mo.; free to membs.). Newsletter.

AIM 1988 Membership Profile Survey (memb. $15; nonmemb. $25).
Marketing Yourself in Your Organization, by Morton Meltzer (memb. $9.95; nonmemb. $14.95).
Partners in Fact: Information Managers/ Information Company Executives Talk (memb. $14.95; nonmemb. $19.95).
Who's Who in Information Management (ann.; nonmemb. $50).

Association for Federal Information Resources Management (AFFIRM)

Chairperson, Margaret Skovira
U.S. Department of the Treasury, Washington, DC 20239
202-376-4204

Object

"Founded in 1979, AFFIRM is an organization of professionals associated to promote and advance the concept and practice of information resources management (IRM) in the government of the United States. AFFIRM carries out its goal through providing a forum for professionals in IRM to exchange ideas, exploring new techniques to improve the quality and use of federal information systems and resources, advocating effective application of IRM to all levels of the federal government, enhancing the professionalism of IRM personnel, and interacting with state and local government on IRM issues."

Membership

Regular membership is extended to professionals currently or formerly employed by the federal government in some capacity related to IRM. Persons who do not qualify for regular membership may join as associate members. The following component disciplines of IRM are represented: automatic data processing; library and technical information; paperwork management; privacy, freedom of information, and information security; records and statistical data collection; telecommunications; data administration; and other related areas. Dues (Regular Memb.) $20; (Assoc. Memb.) $30.

Officers (July 1988–June 1989)

Chpn. Margaret Skovira, Dept. of the Treasury; *Exec. V. Chpn./Chpn.-Elect.* Leon Transeau, Dept. of Interior; *V. Chpn., Finance.* James Clancy, Software Solutions; *V. Chpn., Admin.* Phil Casto, U.S. Info. Agency; *V. Chpn., Program.* Art Chantker, Dept. of Justice.

Committee Chairpersons

Membership. Patricia Jarrell.
Newsletter. Sarah Kadec.
Organizational Liaison. Marvin Gordon.
Publicity. Sahon Palmer.

Meetings

AFFIRM holds monthly luncheon-speaker meetings at the George Washington University's Marvin Center on 21 St. N.W. AFFIRM also sponsors an annual one-day seminar in Information Resources Management, usually in the autumn.

Association for Information and Image Management

(Formerly National Micrographics Association)
Executive Director, Sue Wolk
1100 Wayne Ave., Silver Spring, MD 20910
301-587-8202

Object

To provide a forum which contributes to the effective development and application of information and image management systems through a Trade Association to benefit companies and a Professional Society to benefit individuals. These companies and individuals are active in the design, creation, sale, and use of products and services for information and image management.

Officers (Apr. 1988–June 1989)

Pres. John A. Lacy, Eastman Kodak Co., BIS, 901 Elmgrove Rd., Rochester, NY 14653-5525; *V.P.* David T. Bogue, Zytron Corp., 2200 Sand Hill Rd., Menlo Park, CA 94025-6996; *Treas.* Kent P. Friel, Access Corp., 1811 Losantiville Ave., Suite 350, Cincinnati, OH 45237.

Publications

fyi/im newsletter (10 per year; memb.). *Ed.* Debbie Chase.

INFORM (mo. journal; memb.). *Ed.* Gregory E. Kaebnick.

Association for Library and Information Science Education

(Formerly Association of American Library Schools)
Executive Secretary, Ilse Moon
5623 Palm Aire Dr., Sarasota, FL 34243
813-355-1795

Object

"To advance education for librarianship." Founded 1915. Memb. 680. Dues (Inst.) $250; (Assoc. Inst.) $150; (International Affiliate Inst.) $75; (Indiv.) $40; (Assoc. Indiv.) $20. Year. Sept.–Aug.

Membership

Any library school with a program accredited by the ALA Committee on Accreditation may become an institutional member. Any school that offers a graduate degree in librarianship or a cognate field but whose program is not accredited by the ALA Committee on Accreditation may become an associate institutional member. Any school outside the United States and Canada offering a program comparable to that of institutional or associate institutional membership may become an international affiliate institutional member.

Any faculty member, administrator, librarian, researcher, or other individual employed full time may become a personal member. Any retired or part-time faculty member, student, or other individual employed less than full time may become an associate personal member.

Officers (Feb. 1989–Jan. 1990)

Pres. Miles M. Jackson, School of Lib. and Info. Studies, Univ. of Hawaii, Honolulu, HI 96822; *Past Pres.* Leigh S. Estabrook, Grad. School of Lib. and Info. Science, Univ. of Illinois, Urbana, IL 61801; *V.P./Pres.-Elect.* Phyllis Van Orden, School of Lib. and Info. Studies, Florida State Univ., Tallahasee, FL 32306; *Secy.-Treas.* Linda C. Smith, Grad. School of Lib. and Info. Science, Univ. of Illinois, Urbana, IL 61801.

(Address correspondence to the executive secretary.)

Directors

Charles Curran, College of Lib. and Info. Science, Univ. of South Carolina, Columbia, SC 29208; Adele Fasick, Univ. of Toronto, Faculty of Lib. and Info. Science, Toronto, ON M5S 1A1, Canada; Ronald R. Powell, School of Lib. and Informational Science, Univ. of Missouri, Columbia, MO 65211.

Publications

ALISE Library and Information Science Education Statistical Report (ann.; $30 plus postage, $2 domestic, $4 foreign).

Journal of Education for Library and Information Science (5 per year; $30 domestic; $40 foreign).

Committee Chairpersons

Awards and Honors. Desretta McAllister-Harper, School of Lib. and Info. Sciences, North Carolina Central Univ., Durham, NC 27707.

Communications and Public Relations. Daniel Callison, School of Lib. and Info. Science, Indiana Univ., Bloomington, IN 47405.

Conference. Robert Grover, School of Lib. and Info. Science, Univ. of South Florida, Tampa, FL 33620.

Editorial Board. Rosemary R. DuMont, School of Lib. Science, Kent State Univ., Kent, OH 44242.

Faculty Development. Elfreda Chatman, School of Info. and Lib. Science, Univ. of North Carolina, Chapel Hill, NC 27599.

Governmental. Arthur Gunn, Lib. Science Program, Wayne State Univ., Detroit, MI 48202.

Nominating. Jean Tague, Dean, School of Lib. and Info. Science, Univ. of Western Ontario, London, ON N6G 1H1, Canada.

Research. Marion Paris, Grad. School of Lib. Service, Box 870252, Tuscaloosa, AL 35487.

Representatives

ALA SCOLE. Ronald Powell (Missouri).

IFLA. Miles Jackson (Hawaii); Mohammed M. Aman (Wisconsin-Milwaukee); Josephine Fang (Simmons).

Association of Academic Health Sciences Library Directors

Administrative Assistant, Ann Fenner
Houston Academy of Medicine–Texas Medical Center Library, Houston, TX 77030
713-797-1230

Object

"To promote, in cooperation with educational institutions, other educational associations, government agencies, and other non-profit organizations, the common interests of academic health sciences libraries located in the United States and elsewhere, through publications, research, and discussion of problems of mutual interest and concern, and to advance the efficient and effective operation of academic health sciences libraries for the benefit of faculty, students, administrators, and practitioners."

Membership

Regular membership is available to nonprofit educational institutions operating a school of health sciences that has full or provisional accreditation by the Association of American Medical Colleges. Regular members shall be represented by the chief administrative officer of the member institution's health sciences library.

Associate membership (and nonvoting representation) is available to organizations having an interest in the purposes and activities of the association.

Dues (Inst.) $300; (Assoc. Inst.) $150.

Officers (Nov. 1988–Nov. 1989)

Pres. Nina W. Matheson, Welch Medical Lib., Johns Hopkins Univ. School of Medicine, 1900 E. Monument St., Baltimore, MD 21205; *Pres.-Elect.* Joan S. Zenan, Savitt Medical Lib., Univ. of Nevada, Reno, NV 89557; *Secy.-Treas.* Karen L. Brewer, Frederick L. Ehrman Medical Lib., New York Univ. Medical Center, 550 First Ave., MSB 197, New York, NY 10016; *Past Pres.* Shelley Bader, Himmelfarb Health Sciences Lib., George Washington Univ. Medical Center, 2300 Eye St. N.W., Washington, DC 20037.

Board of Directors (Nov. 1988–Nov. 1989)

Officers; Richard Lyders, Data Mgr., Houston Academy of Medicine, Texas Medical Center Lib., Jesse H. Jones Lib. Bldg., Houston, TX 77030; David Curry, Health Sciences Lib., Univ. of Iowa, Iowa City, IA 52242; Alison Bunting, UCLA Biomedical Lib., Center for the Health Sciences, Los Angeles, CA 90024; T. Mark Hodges, Medical Center Lib., Vanderbilt Univ., Nashville, TN 37232.

Association of Christian Librarians

Executive Secretary, Mr. Lynn A. Brock
Box 4, Cedarville, OH 45314
513-766-2211

Object

" . . . to meet the needs of evangelical Christian librarians serving in institutions of higher learning. The Association shall promote high standards of professionalism in library work as well as projects that encourage membership participation in serving the academic library community." Founded 1956. Memb. (Indiv.) 301. Dues (Indiv.) $16–$37, based on salary scale. Year. Conference to Conference (2d week in June).

ACL is a member of the Council of National Library and Information Associations.

Membership

A full member shall be a Christian librarian subscribing to the purposes of the corporation who is affiliated with an institution of higher learning. Associate members include those who are in agreement with the purposes of the corporation but who are *not* affiliated with institutions of higher learning or who are nonlibrarians.

Officers (June 1988–June 1989)

Pres. William Abernathy, Ozark Christian College, Joplin, MO 64801; *V.P.* Nancy Olson, Lincoln Christian College, Lincoln, IL 62656; *Secy.* Sharon Bull, Point Loma Nazarene College, San Diego, CA 92106; *Treas.* Stephen Brown, Cedarville College Lib., Cedarville, OH 45314; *Past Pres.* David Wright, SOLINET, 400 Colony Sq., Plaza Level, Atlanta, GA 30361; *Public Relations Dir.* Woodvall Moore, Evangel College, Springfield, MO 65803.

Board of Directors

Wava Bueschlen; Miles S. Compton; Richard Schuster; Paul Snezek; Roger Van Oosten.

Publications

The Christian Librarian (q.; memb. or $16).
The Christian Periodical Index.

Committee Chairpersons

Archivist. Jan Bosma, Cedarville College, Cedarville, OH 45314.

Bible College Section. Nancy J. Olson, Great Lakes Bible College, Box 40060, Lansing, MI 48901.

Christian Librarian. Ronald Jordahl, Ed., Prairie Bible Institute, Three Hills, AB T0M 2A0, Canada.

Christian Periodical Index. Douglas J. Butler, Asbury College, Wilmore, KY 40390.

Liberal Arts Section. Woodvall Moore, Evangel College, Springfield, MO 65802.

Program. David Twiest, Trinity Western Univ., Langley, BC V3A 4R9, Canada.

Seminary Section. David C. McClain, Baptist Bible College & Seminary, Clarks Summit, PA 18411.

Association of Jewish Libraries

c/o National Foundation for Jewish Culture
330 Seventh Ave., 21st fl., New York, NY 10001

Object

"To promote the improvement of library services and professional standards in all Jewish libraries and collections of Judaica; to serve as a center of dissemination of Jewish library information and guidance; to encourage the establishment of Jewish libraries and collections of Judaica; to promote publication of literature which will be of assistance to Jewish librarianship; and to encourage people to enter the field of librarianship." Organized in 1965 from the merger of the Jewish Librarians Association and the Jewish Library Association. Memb. 890. Dues (Inst.) $25; (Student/Retired) $18. Year. July 1–June 30.

Officers (June 1988–June 1990)

Pres. Marcia Posner, Judaica Lib. Consultant, Federation of Jewish Philanthropies Lib., 130 E. 59 St., New York, NY 10022. Tel. 212-836-1506; *Past Pres.* Edith Lubetski, Hedi Steinberg Lib., Stern College, Yeshiva Univ., 245 Lexington Ave., New York, NY 10016-4699; *V.P./Pres.-Elect.* Linda P. Lerman, Yale Univ., Sterling Memorial Lib., Box 1603A, Yale Sta., New Haven, CT 06520; *V.P. Membership.* David J. Gilner, Hebrew Union College Lib., 3101 Clifton Ave., Cincinnati, OH 45220; *Treas.* Toby G. Rossner, Bur. of Jewish Education of Rhode Island, 130 Sessions St., Providence, RI 02906; *Rec. Secy.* Esther Nussbaum, Ramaz Upper School Lib., 60 E. 78 St., New York, NY 10021; *Corresponding Secy.* Tzivia Atik, National Foundation for Jewish Culture, 330 Seventh Ave., 21st fl., New York, NY 10001; *Publns. V.P.* Ralph R. Simon, Sindell Lib., Temple Emanu El, 2200 S. Green Rd., Cleveland, OH 44121.

(Address correspondence to the Association.)

Publications

AJL Newsletter (q.). *Ed.* Irene S. Levin, Henry Waldinger Lib., Valley Stream, NY 11580.

Judaica Librarianship (2 per year). *Co-eds.* Marcia Posner and Bella Hass Weinberg, 19 Brookfield Rd., New Hyde Park, NY 11040.

Miscellaneous others (request current list from Ralph R. Simon, AJL Publications Coord., 2200 S. Green Rd., University Heights, OH 44121).

Divisions

Research and Special Library Division (R&S). Pres. Robert Singerman, Price Lib. of Judaica, 18 Lib. E., Gainesville, FL 32611.

Synagogue, School and Center Division (SSC). Pres. Judith Greenblatt, Lichtenstein Memorial Lib., Temple B'nai Israel, 2727 Kernwood Blvd., Toledo, OH 43606.

Association of Librarians in the History of the Health Sciences

President, Dorothy Whitcomb
Health Sciences Library, University of Wisconsin, Madison, WI 53706
608-262-2402

Object

To serve the professional interests of librarians, archivists, and other specialists actively engaged in the librarianship of the history of the health sciences by promoting an exchange of information and by improving standards of service, by identifying and making contact with persons similarly engaged, by providing opportunities to meet on appropriate occasions, by issuing a newsletter and such other materials as may seem appropriate to the association's interests, and by cooperating with other similar organizations in projects of mutual concern.

Membership

Voting members shall be limited to persons who have professional responsibilities for library and archives collections and services in the history of the health sciences. Nonvoting membership shall be open to persons interested in the concerns of the association.

Officers (May 1988–May 1989)

Pres. Glen Jenkins, Historical Div., Cleveland Health Sciences Lib., 11000 Euclid Ave., Cleveland, OH 44106; *Secy.-Treas.* Elizabeth Borst White, Houston Academy of Medicine Lib., Texas Medical Center, Houston, TX 77030; *Ed.* Judith Overmier, Wangensteen Lib., Diehl Hall, Univ. of Minnesota, Minneapolis, MN 55455.

Steering Committee

Mary Claire Cowen, Reynolds History Lib., Univ. of Alabama–Birmingham, Birmingham, AL 35294; Mary Teloh, Lib., Vanderbilt Medical Center, Nashville, TN 37232; Lilli Sentz, 93 Lehn Springs Dr., Williamsville, NY 14221.

Committees

Ad Hoc Committee on Genre Terms. Nancy Zinn, Lib., Univ. of California-San Francisco, San Francisco, CA 94143.

Publications. Nancy Zinn, Lib., Univ. of California, San Francisco, CA 94143.

Publication

Watermark (q.; memb.; nonmemb. $15). *Ed.* Judith Overmier, Wangensteen Lib., Diehl Hall, Univ. of Minnesota, Minneapolis, MN 55455.

Association of Research Libraries

Interim Executive Director, Duane E. Webster
1527 New Hampshire Ave. N.W., Washington, DC 20036
202-232-2466

Object

To initiate and develop plans for strengthening research library resources and services in support of higher education and research. Established 1932 by the chief librarians of 43 research libraries. Memb. (Inst.) 119. Dues (ann.) $7,000. Year. Jan.–Dec.

Membership

Membership is institutional.

Officers (Oct. 1988–Oct. 1989)

Pres. Charles E. Miller, Florida State Univ. Lib., Tallahassee, FL 32603; *V.P./Pres.-Elect.* Martin D. Runkle, Univ. of Chicago Libs., 1100 E. 57 St., Chicago, IL 60637-1502; *Past Pres.* Elaine F. Sloan, Columbia Univ. Libs., New York, NY 10027.

Board of Directors

David Bishop, Univ. of Illinois Libs.; D. Kaye Gapen, Univ. of Wisconsin Libs.; Ellen Hoffman, York Univ. Libs.; Charles B. Osburn, Univ. of Alabama Libs.; Carlton C. Rochell, New York Univ. Libs.; Martin D. Runkle, Univ. of Chicago Lib.; Thomas W. Shaughnessy, Univ. of Missouri Libs.; Merrily Taylor, Brown Univ. Lib.; Marilyn Sharrow, Univ. of California, Davis Lib.

Publications

ARL Annual Salary Survey (ann.; $60).

The ARL Index and Quantitative Relationships in the ARL. Kendon Stubbs ($5).

ARL Minutes (s. ann.; $15 each).

ARL Newsletter (approx. 5 per year; $15).

ARL Statistics (ann.; $60).

Cataloging Titles in Microform Sets. Report based on a study conducted for ARL in 1980 by Information Systems Consultants, Inc., Richard W. Boss, Principal Investigator ($12).

The Changing System of Scholarly Communication. Report of the ARL Task Force on Scholarly Communication ($1).

Cumulated ARL University Library Statistics, 1962–1963 through 1978–1979. Compiled by Kendon Stubbs and David Buxton ($15).

The Gerould Statistics, 1907/08–1961/62. A compilation of data on ARL libraries, begun in 1908 by James Thayer Gerould, and later continued as the "Princeton University Library Statistics." Compiled by Robert Molyneux ($25).

Linked Systems. Papers from the May 1988 ARL Membership meeting ($10).

Meeting the Preservation Challenge. Papers from the October 1987 ARL Membership meeting. Edited by Jan Merrill-Oldham ($28).

Microform Sets in U.S. and Canadian Libraries. Report of a Survey on the Bibliographic Control of Microform Sets contributed by the Association of Research Libraries Microform Project ($12).

Objective Performance Measures for Academic and Research Libraries, by Paul B. Kantor ($25).

Our Cultural Heritage: Whence Salvation? Louis B. Wright; *The Uses of the Past,* Gordon N. Ray; remarks to the 89th membership meeting of the association ($3).

Plan for a North American Program for Coordinated Retrospective Conversion. Report of a study conducted by the Association of Research Libraries, prepared by Jutta Reed-Scott ($15).

76 United Statesiana. Seventy-six works of American scholarship relating to America as published during two centuries from the Revolutionary Era of the United States through the nation's bicentennial year. Edited by Edward C. Lathem, dist. by the Univ. of Virginia Press ($7.50; $5.75 paper).

Technology and U.S. Government Information Policies: Catalysts for New Partnerships. Report of the ARL Task Force on Government Information in Electronic Formats ($5).

13 Colonial Americana. Edited by Edward C. Lathem, dist. by the Univ. of Virginia Press ($7.50).

Committee Chairpersons

ARL Statistics. Thomas W. Shaughnessy, Univ. of Missouri Libs., Columbia, MO 65201.

Bibliographic Control. Dorothy Greger, Univ. of California, San Diego Libs., La Jolla, CA 92037.

Collection Development. Susan K. Nutter, North Carolina State Univ. Libs., Raleigh, NC 27695.

Government Policies. Merrily Taylor, Brown Univ. Lib., Providence, RI 02912.

Management of Research Library Resources. Sul H. Lee, Univ. of Oklahoma Libs., Norman, OK 73069.

Nominations. Martin Runkle, Univ. of Chicago Libs., Chicago, IL 60637.

Preservation of Research Library Materials. Carole Moore, Univ. of Toronto Libs., Toronto, ON M5S 1A5, Canada.

Task Force Chairpersons

Membership of Nonuniversity Libraries. Elaine F. Sloan, Columbia Univ. Libs., New York, NY 10027.

Review of the Five-Year Plan. D. Kaye Gapen, Univ. of Wisconsin Libs., Madison, WI 53706.

ARL Membership in 1988

Nonuniversity Libraries

Boston Public Lib.; Canada Institute for Scientific and Technical Info.; Center for Research Libs.; Linda Hall Lib.; Lib. of Congress; National Agricultural Lib.; National Lib. of Canada; National Lib. of Medicine; New York Public Lib.; New York State Lib.; Newberry Lib.; Smithsonian Institution Libs.

University Libraries

Alabama; Alberta; Arizona; Arizona State; Boston; Brigham Young; British Columbia; Brown; California (Berkeley); California (Davis); California (Irvine); California (Los Angeles); California (Riverside); California (San Diego); California (Santa Barbara); Case Western Reserve; Chicago; Cincinnati; Colorado; Colorado State; Columbia; Connecticut; Cornell; Dartmouth; Delaware; Duke; Emory; Florida; Florida State; Georgetown; Georgia; Georgia Institute of Technology; Guelph; Harvard; Hawaii; Houston; Howard; Illinois, Chicago; Illinois, Urbana; Indiana; Iowa; Iowa State; Johns Hopkins; Kansas; Kent State; Kentucky; Laval; Louisiana State; McGill; McMaster; Manitoba; Maryland; Massachusetts; Massachusetts Institute of Technology; Miami; Michigan; Michigan State; Minnesota; Missouri; Nebraska; New Mexico; New York; North Carolina; North Carolina State; Northwestern; Notre Dame; Ohio State; Oklahoma; Oklahoma State; Oregon; Pennsylvania; Pennsylvania State; Pittsburgh; Princeton; Purdue; Queen's (Kingston, Canada); Rice; Rochester; Rutgers; Saskatchewan; South Carolina; Southern California; Southern Illinois; Stanford; SUNY (Albany); SUNY (Buffalo); SUNY (Stony Brook); Syracuse; Temple; Tennessee; Texas; Texas A & M; Toronto; Tulane; Utah; Vanderbilt; Virginia; Virginia Polytechnic; Washington; Washington State; Waterloo; Wayne State; Western Ontario; Wisconsin; Yale; York.

Association of Visual Science Librarians

c/o Bette Anton, Librarian, Optometry Library
University of California, Berkeley, CA 94720

Object

"To foster collective and individual acquisition and dissemination of visual science information, to improve services for all persons seeking such information, and to develop standards for libraries to which members are attached." Founded 1968. Memb. (U.S.) 55; (foreign) 13.

Officer

Chpn. Bette Anton, Libn., Optometry Lib., Univ. of California, Berkeley, CA 94720.

Publications

Opening Day Book Collection—Visual Science.

PhD Theses in Physiological Optics (irreg.).
Standards for Visual Science Libraries.
Union List of Vision-Related Serials (irreg.).

Meetings

Annual meeting held in December in connection with the American Academy of Optometry; midyear mini meeting with the Medical Library Association.

Beta Phi Mu

(International Library Science Honor Society)
Executive Secretary, Blanche Woolls
School of Library and Information Science
University of Pittsburgh, Pittsburgh, PA 15260

Object

"To recognize high scholarship in the study of librarianship and to sponsor appropriate professional and scholarly projects." Founded at the University of Illinois in 1948. Memb. 21,000.

Membership

Open to graduates of library school programs accredited by the American Library Association who fulfill the following requirements: complete the course requirements leading to a fifth year or other advanced degree in librarianship with a scholastic average of 3.75 where A equals 4 points. This provision shall also apply to planned programs of advanced study beyond the fifth year that do not culminate in a degree but that require full-time study for one or more academic years; receive a letter of recommendation from their respective library schools attesting to their demonstrated fitness of successful professional careers. Former graduates of accredited library schools are also eligible on the same basis.

Officers (1988–1989)

Pres. Elaine F. Sloan, V.P. for Info. Services and Univ. Libn., 313 Butler Lib., Columbia Univ., 535 W. 114 St., New York, NY 10027; *V.P./Pres.-Elect.* Joseph J. Mika, Dir., Lib. Science Program, Wayne State Univ., 106 Kresge Lib., Detroit, MI 48202; *Past Pres.* Edward G. Holley, Dean Emeritus and Professor, School of Info. and Lib. Science, Univ. of North Carolina, Chapel Hill, NC 27599-3360; *Treas.* Dennis K. Lambert, Collection Development Center, The Milton S. Eisenhower Lib., The Johns Hopkins Univ., Baltimore, MD 21218; *Exec. Secy.* Blanche Woolls, Professor and Chair of Lib. Science Dept., School of Lib. and Info. Science, Univ. of Pittsburgh, Pittsburgh, PA 15260; *Admin. Secy.* Mary Y. Tomaino, School of Lib. and Info. Science, Univ. of Pittsburgh, Pittsburgh, PA 15260.

Directors

Gordon N. Baker, Lib./Media Specialist, Edwin S. Kemp Elementary School, 10990 Folsom Rd., Hampton, GA 30228 (1989); John V. Richardson, Jr., Assoc. Professor, Grad. School of Lib. and Info. Science, Univ. of California–Los Angeles, Los Angeles, CA 90024 (1989); Patricia Oyler, Professor, Grad. School of Lib. and Info. Science, Simmons College, 300 The Fenway, Boston, MA 02115 (1990); Peggy Royster, 212½ W. Oklahoma, #3, Guthrie, OK 73044 (1990); Diane Carothers, Communications Libn., Communications Lib., 122 Gregory Hall, Univ. of Illinois, Urbana, IL 61801 (1991); Josephine McSweeney, Professor and Reference Libn., Pratt Institute Lib., School of Computer, Info. and Lib. Sciences, Brooklyn, NY 11205 (1991); *Dirs.-at-Large.* Betty J. Turock, Asst. Professor, School of Communication, Info. and Lib. Studies, Rutgers Univ., New Brunswick, NJ 08903 (1988); Mary E. Jackson, Head, Interlib. Loan Dept., Univ. of Pennsylvania, Philadelphia, PA 19104 (1990).

Publication

Newsletter (bienn.). Beta Phi Mu sponsors a modern Chapbook series. These small volumes, issued in limited editions, are intended to create a beautiful combination of text and format in the interest of the graphic arts and are available to members only.

Chapters

Alpha. Univ. of Illinois, Grad. School of Lib. and Info. Science, Urbana, IL 61801; *Beta*. Univ. of Southern California, School of Lib. Science, University Park, Los Angeles, CA 90007; *Gamma*. Florida State Univ., School of Lib. Science, Tallahassee, FL 32306; *Delta* (Inactive). Loughborough College of Further Education, School of Libnshp., Loughborough, England; *Epsilon*. Univ. of North Carolina, School of Lib. Science, Chapel Hill, NC 27514; *Zeta*. Atlanta Univ., School of Lib. and Info. Studies, Atlanta, GA 30314; *Theta*. Pratt Institute, Grad. School of Lib. and Info. Science, Brooklyn, NY 11205; *Iota*. Catholic Univ. of America, School of Lib. and Info. Science, Washington, DC 20064; Univ. of Maryland, College of Lib. and Info. Services, College Park, MD 20742; *Kappa*. Western Michigan Univ., School of Libnshp., Kalamazoo, MI 49008; *Lambda*. Univ. of Oklahoma, School of Lib. Science, Norman, OK 73019; *Mu*. Univ. of Michigan, School of Lib. Science, Ann Arbor, MI 48109; *Nu*. Columbia Univ., School of Lib. Service, New York, NY 10027; *Xi*. Univ. of Hawaii, Grad. School of Lib. Studies, Honolulu, HI 96822; *Omicron*. Rutgers Univ., Grad. School of Lib. and Info. Studies, New Brunswick, NJ 08903; *Pi*. Univ. of Pittsburgh, School of Lib. and Info. Science, Pittsburgh, PA 15260; *Rho*. Kent State Univ., School of Lib. Science, Kent, OH 44242; *Sigma*. Drexel Univ., School of Lib. and Info. Science, Philadelphia, PA 19104; *Tau* (Inactive). State Univ. of New York at Geneseo, School of Lib. and Info. Science, College of Arts and Science, Geneseo, NY 14454; *Upsilon*. Univ. of Kentucky, College of Lib. Science, Lexington, KY 40506; *Phi* (Inactive). Univ. of Denver, Grad. School of Libnshp. and Info. Management, Denver, CO 80208; *Pi Lambda Sigma*. Syracuse Univ., School of Info. Studies, Syracuse, NY 13210; *Chi*. Indiana Univ., School of Lib. and Info. Science, Bloomington, IN 47401; *Psi*. Univ. of Missouri, Columbia, School of Lib. and Info. Sciences, Columbia, MO 65211; *Omega* (Inactive). San Jose State Univ., Div. of Lib. Science, San Jose, CA 95192; *Beta Alpha*. Queens College, City College of New York, Grad. School of Lib. and Info. Studies, Flushing, NY 11367; *Beta Beta*. Simmons College, Grad. School of Lib. and Info. Science, Boston, MA 02115; *Beta Delta*. State Univ. of New York–Buffalo, School of Info. and Lib. Studies, Buffalo, NY 14260; *Beta Epsilon*. Emporia State Univ., School of Lib. Science, Emporia, KS 66801; *Beta Zeta*. Louisiana State Univ., Grad. School of Lib. Science, Baton Rouge, LA 70803; *Beta Eta*. Univ. of Texas at Austin, Grad. School of Lib. and Info. Science, Austin, TX 78712; *Beta Theta*. Brigham Young Univ., School of Lib. and Info. Science, Provo, UT 84602; *Beta Iota*. Univ. of Rhode Island, Grad. Lib. School, Kingston, RI 02881; *Beta Kappa*. Univ. of Alabama, Grad. School of Lib. Service, University, AL 35486; *Beta Lambda*. North Texas State Univ., School of Lib. and Info. Science, Denton, TX 76203; Texas Woman's Univ., School of Lib. Science, Denton, TX 76204; *Beta Mu*. Long Island Univ., Palmer Grad. Lib. School, C. W. Post Center, Greenvale, NY 11548; *Beta Nu*. St. John's Univ., Div. of Lib. and Info. Science, Jamaica, NY 11439; *Beta Xi*. North Carolina Central Univ., School of Lib. Science, Durham, NC 27707; *Beta Omicron*. Univ. of Tennessee, Knoxville, Grad. School of Lib. and Info. Science, Knoxville, TN 37916; *Beta Pi*. Univ. of Arizona, Grad. Lib. School, Tucson, AZ 85721; *Beta Rho*. Univ. of Wisconsin–Milwaukee, School of Lib. Science, Milwaukee, WI 53201; *Beta Sigma*. Clarion State College, School of Lib. Science, Clarion, PA 16214; *Beta Tau*. Wayne State Univ., Div. of Lib. Science, Detroit, MI 48202; *Beta Upsilon* (Inactive). Alabama A & M Univ., School of Lib. Media, Normal, AL 35762; *Beta Phi*. Univ. of South Florida, Grad. Dept. of Lib., Media and Info. Studies, Tampa, FL 33620; *Beta Psi*. Univ. of Southern Mississippi,

School of Lib. Service, Hattiesburg, MS 39406; *Beta Omega.* Univ. of South Carolina, College of Libnshp., Columbia, SC 29208; *Beta Beta Alpha.* Univ. of California, Los Angeles, Grad. School of Lib. and Info. Science, Los Angeles, CA 90024; *Beta Beta Gamma.* Rosary College, Grad. School of Lib. and Info. Science, River Forest, IL 60305; *Beta Beta Delta.* Europe, Univ. of Cologne; *Beta Beta Epsilon.* Univ. of Wisconsin, Madison, Lib. School, Madison, WI 53706; *Beta Beta Theta.* Univ. of Iowa, School of Lib. and Info. Science, Iowa City, IA 52242; *Beta Beta Zeta.* Univ. of North Carolina, Greensboro, Dept. of Lib. Science/Educational Technology, Greensboro, NC 27412.

Bibliographical Society of America

Executive Director, Irene Tichenor
Box 397, Grand Central Sta., New York, NY 10163
718-638-7957

Object

"To promote bibliographical research and to issue bibliographical publications." Organized 1904. Memb. 1,400. Dues. $30. Year. Calendar.

Officers (Jan. 1988–Jan. 1990)

Pres. Ruth Mortimer, Smith College, Box 775, Williamsburg, MA 01096; *V.P.* J. William Matheson; *Treas.* R. Dyke Benjamin, Lazard Freres and Co., One Rockefeller Plaza, New York, NY 10020; *Secy.* John Bidwell, Univ. of California at Los Angeles, 2520 Cimarron St., Los Angeles, CA 90018.

Council

(1989) William P. Barlow, Jr.; Ralph W. Franklin; Richard G. Landon; Bernard M. Rosenthal; (1990) Roland Folter; Paul Needham; Katharine F. Pantzer; William S. Peterson; (1991) Jonathan A. Hill; Robert Nikirk; Roderick D. Stinehour; G. Thomas Tanselle.

Publication

Papers (q.; memb.). *Ed.* William S. Peterson, Dept. of English, Univ. of Maryland, College Park, MD 20742.

Committee Chairpersons

Fellowship Program. Richard G. Landon, Thomas Fisher Lib., Univ. of Toronto, Toronto, ON M5S 1A5, Canada.

Publications. Paul Needham, J. Pierpont Morgan Lib., 29 E. 36 St., New York, NY 10016.

Canadian Association for Information Science (L'Association Canadienne des Sciences de L'Information)

140 St. George St., Toronto, ON M5S 1A1, Canada
416-978-8876

Object

Brings together individuals and organizations concerned with the production, manipulation, storage, retrieval, and dissemination of information with emphasis on the application of modern technologies in these areas. CAIS is dedicated to enhancing the activity of the information transfer process, utilizing the vehicles of research, development, application, and education, and serving as a forum for dialogue and exchange of ideas concerned with the theory and practice of all factors involved in the communication of information. Dues (Inst.) $150; (Regular) $65; (Student) $30.

Membership

Institutions and all individuals interested in information science and who are involved in the gathering, the organization, and the dissemination of information (computer scientists, documentalists, information scientists, librarians, journalists, sociologists, psychologists, linguists, administrators, etc.) can become members of the Canadian Association for Information Science.

Officers (Nov. 1, 1987–Aug. 31, 1989)

Pres. Michael Shepherd, Dept. of Mathematics, Statistics, and Computer Science, Dalhousie Univ., Halifax, N.S. B3H 3J5. Tel. 902-424-2572; *V.P./Pres.-Elect.* David Holmes, Univ. of Ottawa, Vanier Lib., 11 Somerset St. E., Ottawa, ON K1N 9A4. Tel. 613-564-2324; *Secy.-Treas.* Ron MacKinnon, Science Div., Univ. of Guelph Lib., Guelph, ON N1G 2W1. Tel. 519-824-4120 ext. 8535; *Publications Dir.* Charles Meadow, FLIS, Univ. of Toronto, 140 St. George St., Toronto, ON M5S 1A1. Tel. 416-978-4665; *Past Pres.* Michael Ridley, MacMaster Univ., Hamilton, ON L8S 4L6. Tel. 416-525-9140 ext. 2326.

Board of Directors

Ottawa Chapter. Remy Gaudet; *Quebec Chapter.* Jean Morel; *Atlantic Chapter.* Michael Shepherd; *Toronto Chapter.* Felicity Pickup; *CAIS West Chapter.* Helen Mayoh.

Publications

The Canadian Conference of Information Science: Proceedings (ann.).

The Canadian Journal of Information Science (q.; $95 Can., $110 outside Can.).

Canadian Library Association

Executive Director, Jane Cooney
200 Elgin St., Ottawa, ON K2P 1L5, Canada
613-232-9625

Object

To develop high standards of librarianship and of library and information service. CLA develops standards for public, university, school, and college libraries and library technician programs; offers library school scholarship and book awards; carries on international liaison with other library associations; makes representation to government and official commissions; offers professional development programs; and supports intellectual freedom. Founded in Hamilton in 1946, CLA is a nonprofit voluntary organization governed by an elected council and board of directors. Memb. (Indiv.) 4,000; (Inst.) 1,000. Dues (Indiv.) $100 to $160, depending on salary; (Inst.) from $150 up, graduated on budget basis. Year. Anniversary date renewal.

Membership

Open to individuals, institutions, and groups interested in librarianship and in library and information services.

Officers (1988–1989)

Pres. Vivienne Monty, Head, Government and Business Lib., York Univ., 4700 Keele St., Downsview, ON M3J 1P3; *1st V.P./Pres.-Elect.* Beth Barlow, Head, Info. Services, Saskatoon Public Lib., 311 23rd St. E., Saskatoon, SK S7K 0J6; *2nd V.P.* Jean Dirksen, Head, Adult Services, Regina Public Lib., Box 2311, Regina, SK S4P 3Z5; *Treas.* Patricia Cavill, Asst. Dir. of Admin., Calgary Public Lib., 616 MacLeod Trail S.E., Calgary, AB T2G 2M2; *Past Pres.* William Converse, Chief Libn., Univ. of Winnipeg, 515 Portage Ave., Winnipeg, MB R3B 2E9.

Board of Directors

Officers plus divisional presidents.

Council

Board of Directors plus councillors and provincial/regional representatives.

Councillors-at-Large

To June 1989: Jane Beaumont, Derek Frances; to June 1990: Ernie Ingles, Marnie Swanson; to June 1991: Marie DeYoung, Carrol Lunau.

Publications

Canadian Library Journal (6 issues; memb. or nonmemb. subscribers, Canada $40, U.S. $45 [Can.], International $50 [Can.]).

CM: Canadian Materials for Schools and Libraries (6 per year; $35).

Division Representatives

Canadian Association of College and University Libraries. Richard Greene, Dir., Biblo des Lettres et des Sciences Humaines, Univ. de Montreal, C.P. 6128, Succursale A, Montreal, PQ H3C 3J7.

Canadian Association of Public Libraries. Bessie Egan, Coord., Children's Services, The City of Winnipeg, Lib. Dept., 251 Donald St., Winnipeg, MB R3C 3P5.

Canadian Association of Special Libraries and Information Services. Sue Patrick, Mgr., Lib. Services, C.R.T.C., Ottawa, ON K1A 0N2.

Canadian Library Trustee Association. George Bothwell, Box 581, Regina, SK S4P 3A3.

Canadian School Library Association. Angela M. Thacker, 2561 Western Ave., North Vancouver, BC V7N 3L2.

Association Representatives

ASTED (Association pour l'advancement des sciences et des techniques de la documentation). Yvon Richer, Chief Libn., Univ. of Ottawa, 65 Hastey St., Ottawa, ON K1N 9A5.

Atlantic Provinces Library Association. Gwen Creelman, Ralph Pickard Bell Lib., Mount Allison Univ., Sackville, NB E0A 3C0.

British Columbia Library Association. Brian Owen, Fraser Valley Regional Lib., 34589 Delair Rd., Abbotsford, BC V2S 5Y1.

Library Association of Alberta. Ann Curry, Edmonton Public Lib., 48 Southgate Mall, 108 St. and 45 Ave., Edmonton, AB T6H 4M6

Manitoba Library Association. Earle Ferguson, Dir. of Libs., Elizabeth Dafoe Lib., Univ. of Manitoba, Winnipeg, MB R3T 2N2.

Ontario Library Association. Gerry Meek, Chief Libn., Thunder Bay Public Lib., 285 Red River Rd., Thunder Bay, ON P7B 1A9.

Quebec Library Association. Molly Walsh, Bibliotheque des Jeunes de Montreal, 1200 rue Atwater, Montreal, PQ H3Z 1X4.

Saskatchewan Library Association. Susan Clark, Saskatoon Public Lib., 311 23rd St. E., Saskatoon, SK S7K 0J6.

Catholic Library Association

Executive Director, John T. Corrigan, CFX
461 W. Lancaster Ave., Haverford, PA 10941
215-649-5250

Object

The promotion and encouragement of Catholic literature and library work through cooperation, publications, education, and information. Founded 1921. Memb. 3,250. Dues $35–$500. Year. July 1988–June 1989.

Officers (Apr. 1987–Apr. 1989)

Pres. Irma C. Godfrey, Lib. Consultant, St. Louis, MO 63109; *V.P./Pres.-Elect.* Brother Emmett Corry, OSF, Div. of Lib. and Info. Science, St. John's Univ., Jamaica, NY 11439; *Past Pres.* Mary A. Grant, Health Science Resource Center, St. John's Univ., Jamaica, NY 11439.

(Address general correspondence to the executive director.)

Executive Board

Rev. Kenneth O'Malley, C.P. (1989), Catholic Theological Union, Chicago, IL 60615; Sister Barbara Anne Kilpatrick, R.S.M. (1989), St. Vincent de Paul School, Nashville, TN 37208; Sister Jean R. Bostley, S.S.J. (1991), St. Joseph Central H.S., Pittsfield, MA 01201; Arnold Rzepecki (1991), Sacred Heart Seminary College, Detroit, MI 48206; Joy Choppin (1993), Georgetown Preparatory School, Rockville, MD 20852; Bert Thompson (1993), Illinois Benedictine College, Lisle, IL 60532.

Publications

Catholic Library World (6 issues; memb. or $35).

The Catholic Periodical and Literature Index (subscription).

Representatives

ALA Resources and Technical Services Division, Cataloging. Tina-Karen Weiner Forman, Los Angeles Lib., Univ. of California, 405 Hilgard Ave., Los Angeles, CA 90024.

American Theological Library Association. Rev. Kenneth O'Malley, Catholic Theological Union, Chicago, IL 60615.

Catholic Press Association. Michael W. Rechel, CLA Headquarters, 461 W. Lancaster Ave., Haverford, PA 19041.

Council of National Library and Information Associations (CNLIA). John T. Corrigan, CFX, CLA Headquarters, 461 W. Lancaster Ave., Haverford, PA 19041; Marie Melton, RSM, Dir. of Libs., St. John's Univ., Jamaica, NY 11439.

National Information Standards Organization (Z-39). John T. Corrigan, CFX, and Natalie A. Logan, CLA Headquarters, 461 W. Lancaster Ave., Haverford, PA 19041.

Society of American Archivists. H. Warren Willis, U.S. Catholic Conference, Washington, DC 20005-4105.

Special Libraries Association. Mary Jo DiMuccio, Sunnyvale Public Lib., Sunnyvale, CA 94087.

Section Chairpersons

Academic Librarians. Owen T. P. McGowan, Bridgewater State College, Bridgewater, MA 02324.

Archives. Brother Paul Ostendorf, FSC, St. Mary's College Lib., Winona, MN 55987.

Children's Libraries. Sister Mary Arthur Hoagland, IHM, Cardinal Dougherty H.S. Lib., Philadelphia, PA 19120.

High School Libraries. Sister M. Theodore Bollati, ASCJ, Cor Jesu Academy Lib., St. Louis, MO 63123.

Library Education. Mary June Roggenbuck, The Catholic Univ. of America, Washington, DC 20064.

Parish/Community Libraries. Lucy Wilde, Kansas State Univ. Lib., Manhattan, KS 66506.

Round Table Chairpersons

Bibliographic Instruction Round Table. Sister Margaret Ruddy, OSF, Cardinal Stritch College Lib., 6801 N. Yates Rd., Milwaukee, WI 53217.

Cataloging and Classification Round Table. Tina-Karen Weiner Forman, Los Angeles Lib., Univ. of California, 405 Hilgard Ave., Los Angeles, CA 90024.

Committee Chairpersons

Ad Hoc Committee on Grants and Development. Brother Emmett Corry, OSF, St. John's Univ., Jamaica, NY 11439.

Advisory Council. Brother Emmett Corry, OSF, Div. of Lib. and Info. Science, St. John's Univ., Jamaica, NY 11439.

Catholic Library World Editorial. Sister Jean R. Bostley, SSJ, St. Joseph Central H.S., Pittsfield, MA 01201.

The Catholic Periodical and Literature Index. Sister Ellen Gaffney, RDC, St. Joseph's Seminary, Yonkers, NY 10704.

Constitution and Bylaws. Thomas J. Neihengen, Gordon Technical H.S., Chicago, IL 60618.

Elections. Paul E. Pojman, St. Mary's School, Walton Hills, OH 44146.

Finance. Brother Emmett Corry, OSF, Div. of Lib. and Info. Science, St. John's Univ., Jamaica, NY 11439.

Membership. Nancy K. Schmidtmann, Our Lady of Mercy School Lib., Hicksville, NY 11801.

Nominations. Sister Mary Dennis Lynch, SHCJ, Rosemont College Lib., Rosemont, PA 19010.

Program Coordinator. Natalie A. Logan, CLA Headquarters, 461 W. Lancaster Ave., Haverford, PA 19041.

Public Relations. Sister Kathleen McCann, RDC, St. Joseph Seminary Lib., Yonkers, NY 10704.

Publications. Richard Fitzsimmons, The Pennsylvania State Univ., Dunmore, PA 18512.

Regina Medal. Betty Mahon, Cathedral of St. Thomas More School Lib., Arlington, VA 22203.

Scholarship. Mary June Roggenbuck, The Catholic Univ. of America, Washington, DC 20064.

Chief Officers of State Library Agencies

Thomas F. Jaques, State Librarian
State Library of Louisiana, Box 131, Baton Rouge, LA 70821
504-342-4923

Object

The object of COSLA is to provide "a means of cooperative action among its state and territorial members to strengthen the work of the respective state and territorial agencies. Its purpose is to provide a continuing mechanism for dealing with the problems faced by the heads of these agencies which are responsible for state and territorial library development."

Membership

The Chief Officers of State Library Agencies is an independent organization of the men and women who head the state and territorial agencies responsible for library development. Its membership consists solely of the top library officers of the 50 states and one territory, variously designated as state librarian, director, commissioner, or executive secretary.

Officers (1988–1990)

Chpn. Thomas Jaques, State Libn., State Lib. of Louisiana, Baton Rouge, LA 70821; *V. Chpn./Chpn.-Elect.* Richard Cheski, State Libn., State Lib. of Ohio, 65 S. Front St., Columbus, OH 43266-0334; *Secy.* Gary J. Nichols, Maine State Lib., State House, Sta. #64, Augusta, ME 04333; *Treas.* James Nelson, Kentucky Dept. of Libs. and Archives, 300 Coffee Tree Rd., Box 537, Frankfort, KY 40602.

Directors

Officers; immediate past chpn.; two elected members: Sara Parke, Pennsylvania State Lib., Box 1601, Harrisburg, PA 17105; Nancy Zussy, Washington State Lib., Olympia, WA 98502-0111.

Chinese-American Librarians Association

Executive Director, Amy Seetoo Wilson
c/o University Microfilms, Ann Arbor, MI 48106
800-521-0600

Object

"(1) To enhance communications among Chinese-American librarians as well as between Chinese-American librarians and other librarians; (2) to serve as a forum for discussion of mutual problems and professional concerns among Chinese-American librarians; (3) to promote Sino-American librarianship and library services; and (4) to provide a vehicle whereby Chinese-American librarians may cooperate with other associations and organizations having similar or allied interest."

Membership

Membership is open to everyone who is interested in the association's goals and activities. Memb. 400. Dues (Regular) $15; (Student/Nonsalaried) $7.50; (Inst.) $45; (Permanent) $200.

Officers (July 1988–June 1989)

Pres. Chang-chien Lee, Univ. of Central Florida, Orlando, FL 32816; *V.P./Pres.-Elect.* Peter R. Young, Faxon Co., Westwood, MA 02090; *Treas.* Sheila Lai, California State Univ., Sacramento, CA 95819; *Exec. Dir.* Amy Seetoo Wilson, Univ. Microfilms International, Ann Arbor, MI 48106.

Publications

Journal of Library and Information Science (2 per year; memb. or $15).
Membership Directory (memb.).
Newsletter (3 per year; memb.; nonmemb. $10/yr.).

Committee Chairpersons

Annual Program. Peter R. Young.
Awards. Hwa-wei Lee.
Books to China. Julia Tung.
Constitution and Bylaws. Roy Chang.
Finance. Clark Wong.
Foundation. Tze-chung Li.
Membership. Eveline L. Yang.
Nominating. Irene Yeh.
Public Relations. Robert Chang.
Publications. Marjorie Li.

Chapter Chairpersons

California. Gladys Chaw, College of San Mateo, San Mateo, CA 94402.
Mid-Atlantic. Julie Tsai, Lib. of Congress, Washington, DC 20540.
Mid-West. Margaret Todd, Brookfield Free Public Lib., Brookfield, IL 60513.
Northeast. Chiou-sen Chen, Rutgers Univ., New Brunswick, NJ 08903.
Southwest. Patrick Hsu, Texas Lutheran College, Sequin, TX 78155.

Journal Officers

Nelson Chou, Exec. Ed., Rutgers Univ., New Brunswick, NJ 08903. *Newsletter Co.-Eds.* Diana Shih, American Museum of Natural History, Central Park W. at 79 St., New York, NY 10024; Gladys Chaw, College of San Mateo Lib., San Mateo, CA 94402.

Church and Synagogue Library Association

Executive Director, Lorraine E. Burson
Box 19357, Portland, OR 97219
503-244-6919

Object

"To act as a unifying core for the many existing church and synagogue libraries; to provide the opportunity for a mutual sharing of practices and problems; to inspire and encourage a sense of purpose and mission among church and synagogue librarians; to study and guide the development of church and synagogue librarianship toward recognition as a formal branch of the library profession." Founded 1967. Dues (Contributing) $100; (Inst.) $75; (Affiliated) $50; (Church or Synagogue) $23; (Indiv.) $12. Year. July 1988–June 1989.

Officers (July 1988–June 1989)

Pres. Anne Greenwood, 4748 Eastern Ave. N.E., Washington, DC 20017; *1st V.P./Pres.-Elect.* Lin Wright, 27 Magna Dr., Gillette, NJ 07933; *2nd V.P. (Membership and Public Relations).* Eleanor S. Courtney, 115 Windy Ghoul Dr., Beaver, PA 15009; *Treas.* Vera G. Hunter, 5511 First St. N.E., Washington, DC 20011; *Past Pres.* Janelle E. Paris, 253 Normal Park Rd., Huntsville, TX 77340; *Publns. Ed.* Lorraine E. Burson, Exec. Dir. and Ed., Church and Synagogue Lib. Assn., Box 19357, Portland, OR 97219.

Executive Board

Officers; committee chairpersons.

Publications

A Basic Book List for Church Libraries, 3rd rev. ed. Bernard E. Deitrick ($3.75 memb.; $4.50 nonmemb.).

Church and Synagogue Libraries (bi-mo.; memb. or $15, Can. $18). *Ed.* Lorraine E. Burson. Book reviews, ads, $175 for full-page, camera-ready ad, one-time rate.

Church and Synagogue Library Resources, 4th rev. ed. Rachel Kohl and Dorothy Rodda ($3 memb.; $3.95 nonmemb.).

Church and Synagogue Library Resources: Annotated Bibliography ($3.95).

CSLA Guide No. 1. Setting Up a Library: How to Begin or Begin Again ($4.95).

CSLA Guide No. 2, rev. 2nd ed. *Promotion Planning All Year 'Round* ($4.95).

CSLA Guide No. 3, rev. ed. *Workshop Planning* ($6.50).

CSLA Guide No. 4, rev. ed. *Selecting Library Materials* ($3.95).

CSLA Guide No. 5. Cataloging Books Step by Step ($6.95).

CSLA Guide No. 6. Standards for Church and Synagogue Libraries ($4.95).

CSLA Guide No. 7. Classifying Church or Synagogue Library Materials ($3.95).

CSLA Guide No. 8. Subject Headings for Church or Synagogue Libraries ($4.95).

CSLA Guide No. 9. A Policy and Procedure Manual for Church and Synagogue Libraries ($3.95).

CSLA Guide No. 10. Archives in the Church or Synagogue Library ($4.95).

CSLA Guide No. 11. Planning Bulletin Boards for Church and Synagogue Libraries ($6.95).

CSLA Guide No. 12. Getting the Books Off the Shelves: Making the Most of Your Congregation's Library ($6.95).

CSLA Guide No. 13. The ABC's of Financing Church and Synagogue Libraries: Acquiring Funds, Budgeting, Cash Accounting ($5.95).

CSLA Guide No. 14. Recruiting and Training Volunteers for Church and Synagogue Libraries ($5.95).
CSLA Guide No. 15. Providing Reference Service in Church and Synagogue Libraries ($6.95).
The Family Uses the Library. Leaflet (10¢; $7/100).
Helping Children Through Books: Annotated Bibliography ($5.95).
Know Your Neighbor's Faith: An Annotated Interfaith Bibliography ($3.95).
Religious Books for Children: An Annotated Bibliography ($6.95).

Committee Chairpersons

Awards. Dorothy Lofton.
Chapters. Maryann Dotts.
Continuing Education. Claudia Hannaford.
Finance and Fund Raising. Marilyn Demeter.
Library Services. Barbara Mall.
Nominations and Elections. Margaret Korty.
Personnel. Janelle E. Paris.
Publications. Arthur W. Swarthout.

Council of National Library and Information Associations

461 W. Lancaster Ave., Haverford, PA 19041
215-649-5251

Object

To provide a central agency for cooperation among library/information associations and other professional organizations of the United States and Canada in promoting matters of common interest.

Membership

Open to national library/information associations and organizations with related interests of the United States and Canada. American Assn. of Law Libs.; American Lib. Assn.; American Society of Indexers; American Theological Lib. Assn.; Art Libs. Society of North America; Assn. of Christian Libns.; Assn. of Jewish Libs.; Catholic Lib. Assn.; Chinese-American Libns. Assn.; Church and Synagogue Lib. Assn.; Council of Planning Libns.; Lib. Binding Institute; Lib. Public Relations Council; Lutheran Church Lib. Assn.; Medical Lib. Assn.; Music Lib. Assn.; National Libns. Assn.; Society of American Archivists; Special Libs. Assn.; Theatre Lib. Assn.

Officers (July 1988–June 1989)

Chpn. Theodore Wiener, Hebraic Div., Lib. of Congress, Washington, DC 20546; *V. Chpn.* Tom Kemp, Box 4050, Stamford, CT 06907-0050; *Secy.-Treas.* John T. Corrigan, CFX, Exec. Dir., Catholic Lib. Assn., 461 W. Lancaster Ave., Haverford, PA 19041; *Past Chpn.* Christine Hoffman, New York Public Lib., 111 Amsterdam Ave., New York, NY 10023.

(Address correspondence to chairperson at 461 W. Lancaster Ave., Haverford, PA 19041.)

Directors

Margaret DePopolo, Rotch Lib., Massachusetts Institute of Technology, Cambridge, MA 02139; Sally Grauer (1987–1990), Lib. Binding Institute, 8013 Centre Park Dr., Austin, TX 78754; Mary A. Huebner (1986–1989), Dir. of Lib. Services, Concordia College, 171 White Plains Rd., Bronxville, NY 10708.

Council of Planning Librarians, Publications Office

1313 E. 60 St., Chicago, IL 60637-2897
312-947-2163

Object

To provide a special interest group in the field of city and regional planning for libraries and librarians, faculty, professional planners, university, government, and private planning organizations; to provide an opportunity for exchange among those interested in problems of library organization and research and in the dissemination of information about city and regional planning; to sponsor programs of service to the planning profession and librarianship; to advise on library organization for new planning programs; and to aid and support administrators, faculty, and librarians in their efforts to educate the public and their appointed or elected representatives to the necessity for strong library programs in support of planning. Founded 1960. Memb. 242. Dues (Inst.) $45; (Indiv.) $25; (Student) $5. Year. July 1–June 30.

Membership

Open to any individual or institution that supports the purpose of the council, upon written application and payment of dues to the treasurer.

Officers (1988–1989)

Pres. Catherine K. Harris, Texas Advisory Commission on Intergovernmental Relations, Info. Center, Box 13206, Austin, TX 78711; *V.P./Pres.-Elect.* June Crowe, Planning Lib., Tucson Planning Dept., Box 27210, Tucson, AZ 85726-7210; *Past Pres.* Katherine G. Eaton, 1631 E. 24 Ave., Eugene, OR 97403; *Secy.* Deborah Thompson-Wise, Univ. of Tennessee, Main Lib. Reference Dept., Knoxville, TN 37996-1000; *Treas.* Jane McMaster, Ohio State Univ., Engineering and Architecture Lib., 2024 Neil Ave., 112 Caldwell Lab, Columbus, OH 43210; *Memb.-at-Large.* Thelma Helyar, Institute for Public Policy and Business Research, 607 Blake Hall, Univ. of Kansas, Lawrence, KS 66045; *Ed., Bibliography Series.* Patricia Coatsworth, Merriam Center Lib., 1313 E. 60 St., Chicago, IL 60637.

Publications

CPL Bibliographies (approx. 24 published per year) may be purchased on standing order or by individual issue. Catalog sent upon request. The following is only a partial list of publications.

No. 192. *Municipal Codes of New Jersey.* Ted Kruse ($12).

No. 193. *American Dwellings in the 19th and 20th Centuries: A Bibliography.* Joan E. Draper ($12).

Nos. 194 & 195. *Port Planning.* Paul D. Marr ($16).

Nos. 196 & 197. *Innovators in Urban Planning: A Research Bibliography with Analytic Framework: Volume I—United States.* Cortus T. Koehler ($24).

Nos. 198 & 199. *Innovators in Urban Planning: A Research Bibliography with Analytic Framework: Volume II—British.* Cortus T. Koehler ($24).

Nos. 200 & 201. *Innovators in Urban Planning: A Research Bibliography with Analytic Framework: Volume III—Continental.* Cortus T. Koehler ($24).

No. 202. *Literature Review on Automobile Trip Characteristics.* Margaret E. Shepard ($16).

No. 214. *Environmental Consciousness—Native American Worldviews and Sustainable Natural Resource Management: An Annotated Bibliography.* Annie L. Booth and Harvey M. Jacobs ($16).

No. 215. *Groundwater Quality: Trends Toward Regional Management: A Review of the Literature.* Catherine H. Powell ($10).

No. 216. *Land Value Taxation and Urban Land Use Planning: An Annotated Bibliography.* Susan L. Roakes and Harvey M. Jacobs ($12).

No. 217. *The U.S. Agricultural Policy Debate: An Annotated Bibliography.* Jim Schwab ($12).

Council on Library Resources, Inc.

1785 Massachusetts Ave. N.W., Washington, DC 20036
202-483-7474

Object

A private operating foundation, the Council seeks to assist in finding solutions to the problems of libraries, particularly academic and research libraries. In pursuit of this aim, the Council conducts its own projects, makes grants to and contracts with other organizations and individuals, and calls upon many others for advice and assistance with its work. The Council was established in 1956 by the Ford Foundation, and it now receives support from a number of private foundations and other sources. Current program emphases include research and analysis; enhancing, preserving, and extending access to library resources; bibliographic services; the management of libraries; and professional education.

Membership

The Council's membership and board of directors is limited to 25.

Officers

Chpn. Maximilian Kempner; *V. Chpn.* Charles Churchwell; *Pres.* Warren J. Haas; *V.P.* Deanna B. Marcum; *Secy-Treas.* Mary Agnes Thompson.

(Address correspondence to headquarters.)

Publications

Annual Report.
CLR Reports (newsletter).

Federal Library and Information Center Committee (FLICC)

Executive Director, James P. Riley
Library of Congress, Washington, DC 20540
202-707-6055

Object

The Committee makes recommendations on federal library and information policies, programs, and procedures to federal agencies and to others concerned with libraries and information centers.

The Committee coordinates cooperative activities and services among federal libraries and information centers and serves as a forum to consider (1) issues and policies that affect federal libraries and information centers, (2) needs and priorities in providing information services to the government and to the nation at large, and (3) efficient and cost-effective use of federal library and information resources and services.

Furthermore, the Committee promotes (1) improved access to information, (2) continued development and use of the Federal Library and Information Network (FEDLINK), (3) research and development in the application of new technologies to federal libraries and information centers, (4) improvements in the management of federal libraries and information centers, and (5) relevant education opportunities. Founded 1965.

Membership

Libn. of Congress, Dir. of the National Agricultural Lib., Dir. of the National Lib. of Medicine, representatives from each of the other executive departments, and representatives from each of the following agencies: the National Aeronautics and Space Admin., the National Science Foundation, the Smithsonian Institution, the U.S. Supreme Court, U.S. Info. Agency, the Veterans Admin., the National Archives and Records Admin., the Admin. Offices of the U.S. Courts, the Defense Technical Info. Center, the Government Printing Office, the National Technical Info. Service, and the Office of Scientific and Technical Info. Ten additional voting member agencies shall be selected on a rotating basis by the permanent members of the Committee from the three branches of government, independent agencies, boards, committees, and commissions. These rotating members will serve two-year terms. In addition to the permanent representative of DOD, one nonvoting member shall be selected from each of the three services (U.S. Army, U.S. Navy, U.S. Air Force). These service members, who will serve for two years, will be selected by the permanent Dept. of Defense member from a slate provided by the Federal Lib. and Info. Center Committee. The membership in each service shall be rotated equitably among the special service, technical, and academic and school libraries in that service. DOD shall continue to have one voting member in the Committee. The DOD representative may poll the three service members for their opinions before reaching a decision concerning the vote. One representative from each of the following agencies is invited as an observer to committee meetings: General Accounting Office, General Services Admin., Joint Committee on Printing, National Commission on Libs. and Info. Science, and the Office of Management and Budget.

Officers

Chpn. James H. Billington, The Libn. of Congress; *Chpn. Designate.* Ruth Ann Stewart; *Exec. Dir.* James P. Riley, Federal Lib. and Info. Center Committee, Lib. of Congress, Washington, DC 20540.

(Address correspondence to the executive director.)

Publications

Annual FLICC Forum on Federal Information Policies.
Annual Report (Oct.).
FEDLINK Technical Notes (mo.).
FLICC Newsletter (q.).

The Federal Publishers Committee (FPC)

Chairperson, John E. Mounts
3700 East-West Hwy., Rm. 1-57, Hyattsville, MD 20782
301-436-8586

Object

To foster and promote effective management of data development and dissemination in the federal government through exchange of information and to act as a focal point for federal agency publishing.

Membership

Membership is available to persons involved in publishing and dissemination in federal government departments, agencies, and corporations, as well as independent organizations concerned with federal government publishing and dissemination. Some key federal government organizations represented are the Joint Committee on Printing, Government Printing Office, National Technical Information Service, National Commission on Libraries and Information Sciences, and the Library of Congress. There are 650 members at the present time. Meetings are held monthly during business hours.

Officers (1988–1989)

Chpn. John E. Mounts; *Secy.* Marilyn Marbrook.

Committee Chairpersons

Administration. Sandra Smith.
Task Force Activity. June Malina.

Information Industry Association

President, Paul G. Zurkowski
555 New Jersey Ave. N.W., Suite 800, Washington, DC 20001
202-639-8262

Membership

For details on membership and dues, write to the association headquarters. Memb. More than 460.

Staff

Pres. Paul G. Zurkowski; *Senior V.P.* Kenneth Allen; *V.P., Industry Relations.* Mary Crowson; *V.P., Meetings and Administration.* Linda Cunningham; *V.P., Marketing.* Peggy O'Hare. *Dir., Government Relations.* David Peyton; *Dir., Program Planning and Development.* Michael Atkin; *Dir., Membership Development.* Judith Angerman; *Controller.* Shad Ahmad; *Dir., Member Services.* Barbara Divver; *Dir. Communications.* Barbara Van Gorder; *Dir., Global Business Development.* Robert A. Vitro.

Board of Directors

Past Chair. Lois Granich, PsychINFO; *Chair.* Joseph J. Fitzsimmons, University Microfilms, Inc.; *Treas.* Vernon H. L. Tyerman, Pacific Telesis Group; *Secy.* Hugh H. Yarrington, Bureau of National Affairs, Inc. *Memb.* James P. McGinty, Dun & Bradstreet Corp.; Alan Brigish, Electronic Publishing Systems; Christopher Burns, Christopher Burns, Inc.; Matilda Butler, Knowledge Access, Intl.; Daniel H. Carter, Daniel Carter Consulting; Richard J. Cowles, Consultant; Robert Donati, DIALOG Information Services; T. Alec Edge, AT&T; Thomas E. Haley, New York Stock Exchange; Thomas Pace, Dow Jones, Inc.; L. John Rankine, IBM Corp.; Ian P. Sharp, I. P. Sharp Assocs., Ltd.; Jack W. Simpson, Mead Data Central; Stephen S. Smith, Consultant; Alan G. Spoon, Washington Post Co.; Rahul Srivastava, THEMIS Group, Inc.; Phyllis B. Steckler, Oryx Press; Kurt D. Steele, McGraw-Hill, Inc.; William T. Whitenack, Dun & Bradstreet.

Division Chairpersons

Database and Publishing. Richard F. Chappetto, Commodity Communications Corp.

Electronic Services. Paul M. Orne, Paul M. Orne & Assoc.

Financial Information Services. Thomas J. Jordan, Knight-Ridder Financial Information Group.

Voice Information Services. Bruce Fogel, Phone Programs, Inc.

Council Chairpersons

Global Business Development. Norman M. Wellen, Bear, Sterns, Intl.

Management and Technology. Lawrence L. Wills, IBM Corp.

Public Policy and Government Relations. Michael Brewer, Dun & Bradstreet.

Publications

Artificial Intelligence: Reality or Fantasy?

The Business of Information Report (1983).

Compensation Practices in the Information Industry: A Survey of Benefits and Salaries.

How to Succeed in the Electronic Information Marketplace.

The Information Executive's Guide to Intellectual Property Rights.

The Information Millenium: Alternative Futures (1986).

Information Sources (1987).

So You Want to Be a Profitable Database Publisher (1983).

Strategic Marketing: Techniques, Technologies and Realities in the Information Industry.

International Council of Library Association Executives

President, Sharilynn Aucoin
Louisiana Library Association, Box 3058, Baton Rouge, LA 70821
504-342-4928

Object

"To provide an opportunity for the exchange of information, experience, and opinion on a continuing basis through discussion, study and publication; to promote the arts and sciences of educational association management; and to develop and encourage high standards of professional conduct." Conducts workshops and institutes; offers specialized education.

Membership

Membership is available to chief paid executives engaged in the management of library associations. Founded 1975. Dues $25. Year. July 1–June 30.

Officers (July 1988–June 1989)

Pres. Sharilynn Aucoin, Exec. Dir., Louisiana Lib. Assn., Box 3058, Baton Rouge, LA 70821; *Pres.-Elect.* Margaret Bauer, Exec. Dir., Pennsylvania Lib. Assn., 3107 N. Front St., Harrisburg, PA 17110. Tel. 1-800-622-3308; *Secy.* Robert Greenfield, Exec. Secy., Maryland Lib. Assn., 115 W. Franklin St., Baltimore, MD 21201. Tel. 301-685-5760; *Treas.* Raymond Means, Exec. Secy., Nebraska Lib. Assn., Creighton Univ., California at 24th St., Omaha, NE 68178. Tel. 402-280-2705; *Past Pres.* Marianne Gessner, Michigan Lib. Assn., 415 W. Kalamazoo, Lansing, MI 48933.

Meetings

Two meetings are held annually in conjunction with those of the American Library Association in January and June. Elections are held during the June meeting.

Lutheran Church Library Association

122 Franklin Ave., Minneapolis, MN 55404
612-870-3623
Executive Director, Wilma Jensen
(Home address: 3620 Fairlawn Dr., Minnetonka, MN 55345
612-473-5965)

Object

"To promote the growth of church libraries by publishing a quarterly journal, *Lutheran Libraries*; furnishing booklists; assisting member libraries with technical problems; and providing meetings for mutual encouragement, assistance, and exchange of ideas among members." Founded 1958. Memb. 1,800. Dues $20, $30, $100, $500, $1,000. Year. Jan.–Jan.

Officers (Jan. 1989–Jan. 1990)

Pres. L. Edwin Wang, 6013 St. Johns Ave., Edina, MN 55424; *V.P.* Elaine Hanson, 1928 Limetree Lane, Mountain View, CA 94040; *Secy.* Gloria Landborg, 1109 W. 37 St., Sioux Falls, SD 57105; *Treas.* Robert Kruger, 15180 County Rd. 40, Carver, MN 55315.

(Address correspondence to the executive director.)

Board of Directors

Louise Anderson; Vernita Kennen; Ruth Martin; Sonja Nelson; George Qualley; Marcia Weltzin.

Publication

Lutheran Libraries (q.; memb.; nonmemb. $12). *Ed.* Ron Klug, 1115 S. Division St., Northfield, MN 55057.

Committee Chairpersons

Advisory. Anders Hanson, 4480 Parklawn Ave., Apt. 211, Edina, MN 55435.

Council of National Library and Information Associations. Wilma W. Jensen, Exec. Dir., and Mary A. Huebner, Libn., Concordia College, 171 White Plains Rd., Bronxville, NY 10708.

Finance. Rev. Carl Manfred, 5227 Oaklawn Ave., Minneapolis, MN 55436.

Library Services Board. Juanita Carpenter, Libn., Rte. 1, Prior Lake, MN 55372.

Membership. Betty LeDell, Libn., Grace Lutheran of Deephaven, 15800 Sunset Dr., Minnetonka, MN 55343.

Publications Board. Rod Olson, Augsburg Publishing House, 426 S. Fifth, Box 1209, Minneapolis, MN 55440.

Medical Library Association

Executive Director, Raymond A. Palmer
Six N. Michigan Ave., Suite 300, Chicago, IL 60602
312-419-9094

Object

The Medical Library Association (MLA) was founded in 1898 and incorporated in 1934. MLA's major purposes are: (1) to foster medical and allied scientific libraries, (2) to promote the educational and professional growth of health science librarians, and (3) to exchange medical literature among the members. Through its programs and publications, MLA encourages professional development of its membership, whose foremost concern is the dissemination of health sciences information for those in research, education, and patient care.

Membership

MLA has 1,295 institutional members and 3,758 individual members. Institutional members are medical and allied scientific libraries. Institutional member dues are based on the number of subscriptions (subscriptions up to 199 – $160; 200–299 – $215; 300–599 – $260; 600–999 – $315; 1,000 + – $375). Individual MLA members are people who are (or were at the time membership was established) engaged in professional library or bibliographic work in medical and allied scientific libraries or people who are interested in medical or allied scientific libraries. Dues (Indiv.) $95; (Emeritus) $32; (Student) $22; (Sustaining) $315.

Officers

Pres. Eloise C. Foster, AHA Resource Center, American Hospital Assn., 840 N. Lake Shore Dr., Chicago, IL 60611; *Pres.-Elect.* Frances Groen, McIntyre Medical Sciences Bldg., McGill Univ., 3655 Drummond St., Montreal, PQ H3G 1Y6, Canada; *Past Pres.* Holly Shipp Buchanan, NKC Hospitals, Corporate Info. Resources, Box 35070, Louisville, KY 40232.

Directors

Sherrilynne S. Fuller (1986–1989); J. Michael Homan (1986–1989); Rosanne Labree (1986–1989); Mickey Cook (1987–1990); Audrey Powderly Newcomer (1987–1990); Fred W. Roper (1987–1990); Gail A. Yokote

(1987–1990); Jo Anne Boorkman (1988–1991); Frieda A. Weise (1988–1991); Raymond A. Palmer (*Ex officio*).

Publications

Bulletin of the Medical Library Association (q.; $102).

Current Catalog Proof Sheets (w. plus mo. index; $115).

Handbook of Medical Library Practice, vols. 1–3 ($80 memb.; $100 nonmemb.).

Hospital Library Management ($67.50 memb.; $84 nonmemb.).

Introduction to Reference Sources in the Health Sciences ($27 memb.; $34 nonmemb.).

MEDLINE: A Basic Guide to Searching ($25 memb.; $32 nonmemb.).

MLA Directory (ann.; $35 memb.; $43.75 nonmemb.).

MLA News (10/year; $39.50).

Miscellaneous others (request current list from association headquarters).

Standing Committee Chairpersons

Awards Committee. Susan Starr, Biomedical Lib., Univ. of California-San Diego, Mail Code C-075-B, La Jolla, CA 92093.

Bulletin Consulting Editors Panel. Irwin H. Pizer, 6 N. Michigan Ave., Suite 300, Chicago, IL 60602.

Bylaws Committee. June H. Fulton, College of Physicians of Philadelphia, 19 S. 22 St., Philadelphia, PA 19103.

Committee on Committees. Frances Groen, Medical Lib., McGill Univ., 3655 Drummond St., Montreal, PQ H3G 1Y6, Canada.

Continuing Education Committee. Terry Ann Jankowski, Health Science Lib. and Info. Center, Univ. of Washington, SB-55, Seattle, WA 98195.

Credentialling Committee. Wenda Webster Fischer, Medical Lib., NKC Hospitals, Inc., Box 35070, Louisville, KY 40232-5070.

Editorial Committee for the Bulletin. Donna P. Johnson, Abbott-Northwestern Hospital, Lib./Media Services, 800 E. 28 St., Minneapolis, MN 55407.

Editorial Committee for the News. Rosemary Milner Kiefer, Box 1892, Pensacola, FL 32589.

Editorial Panel for Certification and Registration Examination. Rick B. Forsman, Ed., Denison Memorial Lib., Univ. of Colorado Health Science Center, 4200 E. Ninth Ave., Denver, CO 80262.

Elections Committee. Frances Groen, Medical Lib., McGill Univ., 3655 Drummond St., Montreal, PQ H3G 1Y6, Canada.

Exchange Committee. Maureen S. Battistella, Baptist Medical Center, 701 Princeton Ave. S.W., Birmingham, AL 35211.

Executive Committee. Eloise C. Foster, AHA Resource Center, American Hospital Assn., 840 N. Lake Shore Dr., Chicago, IL 60611.

Finance Committee. Sherrilynne S. Fuller, Health Science and Info. Center, Univ. of Washington, SB-55, Seattle, WA 98195.

Governmental Relations Committee. Valerie Florance, Welch Medical Lib., The Johns Hopkins Univ., 1900 E. Monument St., Baltimore, MD 21205.

Grants and Scholarship Committee. James Pat Craig, School of Medicine in Shreveport, Louisiana State Univ. Medical Center, 1501 Kings Hwy., Box 33932, Shreveport, LA 71130-3932.

Health Sciences Library Technicians Committee. Julia G. Pfau, Lister Hill Lib. of the Health Sciences, Univ. of Alabama at Birmingham, Univ. Sta., Birmingham, AL 35294.

International Cooperation Committee. Henry L. Lemkau, Jr., Louis Calder Memorial Lib., Univ. of Miami, School of Medicine, Box 016950, Miami, FL 33101.

Joseph Leiter NLM/MLA Lectureship Committee. Lois Ann Colaianni, National Lib. of Medicine, 8600 Rockville Pike, Bethesda, MD 20894.

Membership Committee. Nancy W. Clemmons, Lister Hill Lib. of the Health Sciences, Univ. of Alabama in Birmingham, Univ. Sta., Birmingham, AL 35294.

National Program Committee—1989. Irwin H. Pizer, 6 N. Michigan Ave., Suite 300, Chicago, IL 60602.

National Program Committee—1990. Robert M. Braude, Samuel J. Wood Lib., Cornell Univ. Medical College, 1300 York Ave., New York, NY 10021.

Nominating Committee. Frances Groen, Medical Lib., McGill Univ., 3655 Drummond St., Montreal, PQ H3G 1Y6, Canada.

Oral History Committee. David W. Boilard, Harley E. French Lib. of the Health Sciences, Univ. of North Dakota, Grand Forks, ND 58202.

Planning Committee. Holly Shipp Buchanan, NKC Hospitals, Inc., Corporate Info. Resources, Box 35070, Louisville, KY 40232-5070.

Professional Recognition Review Panel. Rick B. Forsman, Denison Memorial Lib., Univ. of Colorado, Health Science Center, 4200 E. Ninth Ave., Denver, CO 80262.

Program and Convention Committee. Marie C. Sparks, Sigma Theta Tau International, 1200 Waterway Blvd., Indianapolis, IN 46202.

Publication Panel. Dottie Eakin, Taubman Medical Lib., Univ. of Michigan, 1135 E. Catherine St., Ann Arbor, MI 48109.

Publishing and Information Industries Relations Committee. Barbara Halbrook, Medical Lib., Washington Univ., 4580 Scott Ave., St. Louis, MO 63110.

Status and Economic Interests of Health Sciences Library Personnel Committee. Lorraine M. Raymond, Health Sciences Lib. and Info. Center, Univ. of Washington, SB-55, Seattle, WA 98195.

Ad Hoc Committees

Ad Hoc Committee on Appointment of Fellows and Honorary Members. Holly Shipp Buchanan, NKC Hospitals, Inc., Corporate Info. Resources, Box 35070, Louisville, KY 40232-5070.

Ad Hoc Committee on the Position of Hospital Libraries. Mickey Cook, 8216 Rolla Ct., Orlando, FL 32819.

MLA Ad Hoc Committee to Establish Cunningham Endowment. Co-Chpns. Robert G. Cheshier, Lib., Cleveland Health Sciences, 2119 Abington Rd., Cleveland, OH 44106; Henry L. Lemkau, Jr., Louis Calder Memorial Lib., Univ. of Miami, School of Medicine, Box 016950, Miami, FL 33101.

The Miniature Book Society

President, Miriam O. Irwin
358 Oliver Rd., Cincinnati, OH 45215
513-761-5977

Object

Miniature books are those classified as under three inches tall. The Miniature Book Society is a nonprofit organization chartered in 1983 by the State of Ohio. Its purposes are to sustain an interest in all phases of miniature books; to provide a forum for the exchange of ideas; and to serve as a clearinghouse for information about miniature books. Memb. 450. Dues (U.S.) $10; (foreign) $15.

Officers

Pres. Miriam O. Irwin, 358 Oliver Rd., Cincinnati, OH 45215; *V.P.* Mae Hightower Vandamm, 2207 Highland Place, Wilmington, DE 19805; *Treas.* Rev. Joseph Curran, Box 127, Sudbury, MA 01776.

Directors

Evron Collins, 1008 Boone Ct., Bowling Green, OH 43402; Rev. Joseph Curran, Box 127, Sudbury, MA 01776; Frank Anderson, 229 Mohawk Dr., Spartanburg, SC 29301; John Lathourakis, 2245 Falcon Ridge Lane, Los Osos, CA 93402; James Yarnell, Wichita, KS 67213; Don E. Hildreth, 3841 Fourth Ave., Suite 113, San Diego, CA 92103.

Publication

The Newsletter of the Miniature Book Society (q.). *Ed.* John Lathourakis, 2245 Falcon Ridge Lane, Los Osos, CA 93402.

Music Library Association

Box 487, Canton, MA 02021
617-828-8450

Object

"To promote the establishment, growth, and use of music libraries; to encourage the collection of music and musical literature in libraries; to further studies in musical bibliography; to increase efficiency in music library service and administration." Founded in 1931. Memb. about 1,700. Dues (Inst.) $46; (Indiv.) $32; (Student) $16. Year. Sept. 1–Aug. 31.

Officers

Pres. Lenore Coral, Music Lib., Cornell Univ., Lincoln Hall, Ithaca, NY 14853-4101; *Past Pres.* Geraldine Ostrove, Music Div., Lib. of Congress, Washington, DC 20540; *V.P./Pres.-Elect.* Susan T. Sommer, N.Y. Public Lib., 111 Amsterdam Ave., New York, NY 10023; *Rec. Secy.* Jean Geil, 1403 S. Busey Ave., Urbana, IL 61801; *Treas.* Sherry L. Vellucci, 20 S. Main St., Pennington, NJ 08534; *"Notes" Ed.* Michael Ochs, Music Lib., Harvard Univ., Cambridge, MA 02138; *Exec. Secy.* A. Ralph Papakhian, Music Lib., Indiana Univ., Bloomington, IN 47405.

Members-at-Large

Marsha Berman, 2417 Fourth St., Santa Monica, CA 90405; James B. Coover, Music Lib., Baird Hall, SUNY, Amherst, NY 14260; Laura Dankner, 708 Hesper Ave., Metairie, LA 70005; John E. Druesedow, Jr., Music Lib., Duke Univ., Durham, NC 27707; Richard W. Griscom, Jr., Dwight Anderson Memorial Music Lib., Univ. of Louisville, 2301 S. Third St., Louisville, KY 40292; Diana Parr Walker, Music Lib., Old Cabell Hall, Univ. of Virginia, Charlottesville, VA 22903.

Special Officers

Business Mgr. James S. P. Henderson, Box 487, Canton, MA 02021.

Convention Mgr. Martin A. Silver, Music Lib., Univ. of California, Santa Barbara, CA 93106.

Placement. Paula D. Matthews, Ladd Lib., Bates College, Lewiston, ME 04240.

Publicity. Dawn R. Thistle, Music Lib., College of the Holy Cross, Worcester, MA 01610.

Publications

MLA Index Series (irreg.; price varies according to size).

MLA Newsletter (q., free to memb.).

MLA Technical Reports (irreg.; price varies according to size).

Music Cataloging Bulletin (mo.; $18).

Notes (q.; inst. subscription $42; nonmemb. subscription $28).

Committee Chairpersons

Administration. Nina Davis-Millis, Massachusetts Institute of Technology (Tel. 617-253-5636).

Awards. Publications. Karl Kroeger, Univ. of Colorado (Tel. 303-492-8093); *Walter Gerboth Award.* James W. Pruett, Lib. of Congress (Tel. 202-287-5503).

Bibliographic Control. J. Bradford Young, Univ. of Pennsylvania (Tel. 215-898-6715).

Development. Karen Nagy, Music Lib., Braun Arts Center, Stanford Univ., Stanford, CA 94305 (Tel. 415-725-1148).

Education. Ann McCollough, Sibley Music Lib., Eastman School of Music, Rochester, NY 14606 (Tel. 716-275-1078).

Finance. John E. Druesedow, Jr., Music Lib., Duke Univ., Durham, NC 27707 (Tel. 919-684-6449).

Legislation. Neil Ratliff, Univ. of Maryland, College Park (Tel. 301-454-6903).

Nominating. To be appointed.

Preservation. Deborah Hefling, Cleveland Public Lib. (Tel. 216-623-2813).

Program 1989. Shirlene Ward, Northwestern Univ. (Tel. 312-491-3434 or 2888).

Public Libraries. Anna M. Thompson, Indianapolis-Marion County Public Lib. (Tel. 317-269-1726).
Publications. Nancy Bren Nuzzo, State Univ. of New York, Buffalo (Tel. 716-636-2924).
Reference and Public Service. Bonnie Jo Dopp, Martin Luther King Memorial Lib., 901 G St. N.W., Washington, DC 20001 (Tel. 202-727-1253).
Resource Sharing and Collection Development. John H. Roberts, Univ. of California, Berkeley (Tel. 415-642-2428).

National Association of Government Archives and Records Administrators (NAGARA)

Executive Director, Bruce W. Dearstyne
New York State Archives
10A75 Cultural Education Center, Albany, NY 12230
518-473-8037

Object

Founded in 1984, the Association is successor to the National Association of State Archives and Records Administrators, which had been established in 1974. NAGARA is a growing nationwide association of local, state, and federal archivists and records administrators, and others, interested in improved care and management of government records. NAGARA promotes public awareness of government records and archives management programs, encourages interchange of information among government archives and records management agencies, develops and implements professional standards of government records and archival administration, and encourages study and research into records management problems and issues. NAGARA is an adjunct member of the Council of State Governments.

Membership

State archival and records management agencies are NAGARA's sustaining members, but individual membership is open to local governments, federal agencies, and to any individual or organization interested in improved government records programs.

Officers

Pres. John Burns, California State Archives; *V.P.* Roy Tryon, Delaware Bur. of Archives and Records Management; *Secy.* William Ptacek, Records Management Div., Nebraska State Historical Society; *Treas.* Deborah Skaggs, Alabama Dept. of Archives and History.

Publications

Clearinghouse (q.; free to memb.).
Government Records Issues.
Information Clearinghouse Needs of the Archival Profession (report).
Preservation Needs in State Archives (report).
Program Reporting Guidelines for Government Records Programs.

National Information Standards Organization (NISO)

Executive Director, Patricia Harris
Box 1056, Bethesda, MD 20817
301-975-2814, FAX 301-975-2128

Object

To develop technical standards used in libraries, publishing, and information services. Experts from the information field volunteer to lend their expertise in the development and writing of NISO standards. The standards are approved by the consensus of NISO's voting membership, which consists of 65 voting members representing libraries, government, associations, and private businesses and organizations. NISO is supported by its membership and corporate grants. Formerly a committee of the American National Standards Institute, NISO, formed in 1939, was incorporated in 1983 as a nonprofit educational organization. NISO is accredited by the American National Standards Institute (ANSI).

Membership

Open to any organization, association, government agency, or company willing to participate in, and having substantial concern for, the development of NISO standards. Dues $200 to $4,000 annually, based on voting member's budget.

Officers

Chpn. Mary Ellen Jacob, OCLC, Inc., Dublin, OH; *Past Chpn.* Ted Brandhorst, ERIC Processing and Reference Facility, Bethesda, MD; *V. Chpn./Chpn.-Elect.* Paul Evan Peters, New York Public Lib., New York, NY; *Treas.* Heike Kordish, New York Public Lib., New York, NY; Peter J. Paulson, OCLC-Forest Press, Albany, NY; Susan H. Vita, Lib. of Congress, Washington, DC; Toni Carbo Bearman, Univ. of Pittsburgh, Pittsburgh, PA; Richard Rowe, Faxon, Inc., Westwood, MA; Charles Bourne, DIALOG, Palo Alto, CA; Bill Bartenbach, The Foundation Center, New York, NY; Ernest Muro, Vendor Relations, Annandale, NJ; Carol A. Risher, Assn. of American Publishers, Washington, DC; Raymond J. Henderlong, Bantam Doubleday Dell Publishing Group, New York, NY.

Publications

Information Standards Quarterly (ISQ) (q.; U.S. $40, foreign $50). *Ed.* Walt Crawford.

NISO Published Standards. List available from headquarters; order from Transaction Publishers, Inc., Order Dept., Rutgers Univ., New Brunswick, NJ 08903.

National Librarians Association

Secretary-Treasurer, Peter Dollard
Box 586, Alma, MI 48801

Object

"To promote librarianship, to develop and increase the usefulness of libraries, to cultivate the science of librarianship, to protect the interest of professionally qualified librarians, and to perform other functions necessary for the betterment of the profession of librarians, rather than as an association of libraries." Established 1975. Memb. 200. Dues $20 per year; $35 for 2 years; (Students, Retired, and Unemployed Libns.) $10. Floating membership year.

Membership

Any person interested in librarianship and libraries who holds a graduate degree in library science may become a member upon election by the executive board and payment of the annual dues. The executive board may authorize exceptions to the degree requirements to applicants who present evidence of outstanding contributions to the profession. Student membership is available to those graduate students enrolled full time at any ALA accredited library school.

Officers (July 1989–June 1990)

Pres. Margaret Gibbs, Dir., Peoria Public Lib., Peoria, IL; *Secy.-Treas.* Peter Dollard.

Publication

The National Librarian (q.; 1 yr. $15, 2 yrs. $28, 3 yrs. $39). *Ed.* Peter Dollard.

Society for Scholarly Publishing

Secretary-Treasurer, Constance B. Kiley
2000 Florida Ave. N.W., Suite 305, Washington, DC 20009
202-328-3555

Object

To draw together individuals involved in the process of scholarly publishing. This process requires successful interaction of the many functions performed within the scholarly community. SSP provides the leadership for such interaction by creating the opportunities for the exchange of information and opinions among scholars, editors, publishers, librarians, printers, booksellers, and all others engaged in scholarly publishing.

Membership

Open to all with an interest in scholarly publishing and information dissemination. There are three categories of membership: individual, $50; contributing, $150; sustaining (organizational), $300. Dues are on a calendar year basis.

Officers (July 1, 1988–June 30, 1990)

Pres. Ann Reinke Strong, New England Journal of Medicine; *V.P.* Judy C. Holoviak, American Geophysical Union; *Secy.-Treas.* Constance B. Kiley, Waverly Press.

Board of Directors

Robert Baensch, Macmillan Publishing Co.; Barbara Drew, Canadian Medical Assn.; Shirley Echelman, Consultant; Edward J. Huth, American College of Physicians; Barbara J. Janson, Janson Publications, Inc.; Paula T. Kaufman, Univ. of Tennessee Lib.; William Kaufmann, William Kaufmann, Inc.; Herbert C. Morton, Bethesda, Maryland; Richard C. Rowson, Duke Univ. Press; Robert Shirrell, Univ. of Chicago Press; *Admin. Officer.* Alice O'Leary, SSP.

Committee Chairpersons

Annual Meeting Program. To be appointed.
Budget and Finance. Mark Mandelbaum.
Education. William Kasdorf; John Pugsley.
Executive. Ann R. Strong.
Membership. Christine Lamb.
Nominations and Awards. To be appointed.
Publications. Vicki Sullivan.

Meetings

An annual meeting is conducted each year in either May or June. The location changes each year. Additionally, SSP conducts three seminars throughout the year.

Society of American Archivists

Executive Director, Donn C. Neal
600 S. Federal St., Suite 504, Chicago, IL 60605
312-922-0140

Object

"To promote sound principles of archival economy and to facilitate cooperation among archivists and archival agencies." Founded 1936. Memb. 4,300. Dues (Indiv.) $45–$75, graduated according to salary; (Assoc.) $40, domestic; (Student) $30 with a two-year maximum on student membership; (Inst.) $65; (Sustaining) $150.

Officers (1988–1989)

Pres. Frank Evans, National Archives, Washington, DC 20408; *V.P.* John Fleckner, Smithsonian Institution, Washington, DC 20560; *Treas.* Linda Henry, National Archives, Washington, DC 20408.

Council

Nicholas Burckel; Richard J. Cox; Maygene Daniels; Linda Edgerly; Linda Matthews; Archie Motley; James O'Toole; Mary Jo Pugh; Joan N. Warnow.

Staff

Exec. Dir. Donn C. Neal; *Memb. Asst.* Bernice E. Brack; *System Admin.* Jim Sandler; *Managing Ed.* Teresa Brinati; *Publns. Assts.* Al Correa, Troy Sturdivant; *Education Officer.* Timothy L. Ericson; *Meeting Mgr.* Georgeann Palmer; *Program Asst.* Nancy VanWieren; *Program Officers.* Paul Conway, Marion Matters.

Publications

The American Archivist (q.; $30). *Ed.* David Klaassen; *Managing Ed.* Teresa Brinati. Books for review and related correspondence should be addressed to the managing editor. Rates for B/W ads: full-page, $250; half-page, $175; outside back cover, $350; half-page minimum insertion; 10% discount for four consecutive insertions; 15% agency commission.

SAA Newsletter (6 per year; memb.). *Ed.* Teresa Brinati. Rates for B/W ads: full-page, $300; half-page, $175; quarter-page, $90; eighth-page, $50; 10% discount for six consecutive insertions; 15% agency commission.

Special Libraries Association

Executive Director, David R. Bender
1700 18th St. N.W., Washington, DC 20009
202-234-4700

Object

"To provide an association of individuals and organizations having a professional, scientific, or technical interest in library and information science, especially as these are applied in the recording, retrieval, and dissemination of knowledge and information in areas such as the physical, biological, technical and social sciences, the humanities, and business; and to promote and improve the communication, dissemination, and use of such information and knowledge for the benefit of libraries or other educational organizations." Organized 1909. Memb. 12,500. Dues (Sustaining) $300; (Indiv.) $75; (Student) $15. Year. Jan.–Dec. and July–June.

Officers (June 1988–June 1989)

Pres. Joe Ann Clifton, Litton Industries, 5500 Canoga Ave., Woodland Hills, CA

91368; *Pres.-Elect.* Muriel B. Regan, Gossage Regan Assocs., 15 W. 44 St., New York, NY 10036; *Past Pres.* Emily Mobley, Purdue Univ. Libs., Stewart Center, West Lafayette, IN 47907; *Treas.* Catherine A. Jones, Lib. of Congress, Congressional Research Service, Washington, DC 20540; *Chapter Cabinet Chair.* M. Kay Mowrcy, California State Lib., Box 942837, Sacramento, CA 94237; *Chapter Cabinet Chair-Elect.* Marlene Tebo, Univ. of California, Davis, Davis, CA 95616; *Div. Cabinet Chair.* Carolyn Hardnett, Baltimore Sun, 501 N. Calvert St., Baltimore, MD 21278; *Div. Cabinet Chair-Elect.* Beth Paskoff, Louisiana State Univ., School of Lib. and Info. Science, Baton Rouge, LA 70803.

Directors

Judith J. Field, 20500 Clement, Northville, MI 48167; Catherine Scott, Smithsonian Institution, Washington, DC 20560; Mary Jane Miller, Plainsboro Free Public Lib., 506 Plainsboro Rd., Plainsboro, NJ 08536; James B. Tchobanoff, Pillsbury Co., 311 Second St. S.E., Minneapolis, MN 55414; Ann Talcott, 32 Lake Shore Dr., Short Hills, NJ 07078; Gloria Zamora, Sandia National Laboratories, Albuquerque, NM 87185.

Publications

Special Libraries (q.) and *SpeciaList* (mo.). Cannot be ordered separately ($48 for both; add $5 for postage outside the U.S. including Canada). *Ed.* Elaine Hill.

Committee Chairpersons

Association Office Operations. Joe Ann Clifton, Litton Industries, 5500 Canoga Ave., Woodland Hills, CA 91368.

Awards. Frank Spaulding, 910 River Rd., Piscataway, NJ 08854.

Bylaws. Lois Webster, American Nuclear Society, Info. Resources, 555 N. Kensington Ave., LaGrange Park, IL 60525.

Cataloging. Dorothy McGarry, UCLA, Physical Sciences & Technology, 8251 Boelter Hall, Los Angeles, CA 90024.

Committee on Committees. Barbara Semonche, Durham-Herald Sun Newspapers, Lib., 115 Market St., Durham, NC 27702.

Conference Program—1989 New York. William Woodruff, Hershey Foods, 1025 Reese Ave., Hershey, PA 17033.

Consultation Services. Ellen Steininger Kuner, Burson-Marstellar Lib., One E. Wacker Dr., Chicago, IL 60601.

Copyright Law Implementation. Laura N. Gasaway, Univ. of North Carolina, Law Lib., Chapel Hill, NC 27514.

Finance. Catherine A. Jones, Lib. of Congress, Congressional Research Service, Washington, DC 20540.

Government Relations. Donna Scheeder, Lib. of Congress, Congressional Reference Div., Washington, DC 20540.

Networking. Sharyn Ladner, 929 Majorca Ave., Coral Gables, FL 33134.

Nominating—1989 Elections. Sylvia Piggot, Bank of Montreal, Box 6002, 129 St. Jacques Pl d'Armes, Montreal, PQ H2Y 3S8, Canada.

Positive Action Program for Minority Groups. Stephanie D. Tolson, McDonnell Douglas Corp., ISG Lib. L034/300/2/220, Box 516, St. Louis, MO 63166.

Professional Development. Valerie Noble, Upjohn Co., Business Lib. 88-0, Kalamazoo, MI 49001; William H. Fisher, UCLA, Grad. School of Lib. and Info. Science, Los Angeles, CA 90024.

Public Relations. N. Bernard Basch, Ebsco Subscription Service, 826 S. Northwest Hwy., Barrington, IL 60010.

Publisher Relations. Barbara Best-Nichols, North Carolina State Univ., School of Textiles, Box 830L, Raleigh, NC 27695.

SLA Scholarship. Normand Varieur, U.S. Army, Sci-Tech Info. Div., Bldg. 59, Armament RD Center, Dover, NJ 07801.

Standards. Virgie Jo Sapp, Aluminum Co. of America, Info. Center, Alcoa Center, PA 15069.

Strategic Planning. Mary Jane Miller, Plainsboro Free Public Lib., 506 Plainsboro Rd., Plainsboro, NJ 08536.

Student Relations Officer. Marion Paris, Univ. of Alabama, GSLS, Box 6242, Tuscaloosa, AL 35482.

Tellers. Larry A. Himelfarb, Electronic Industries Assn., 2001 Eye St. N.W., Washington, DC 20006.

H. W. Wilson Company Award. Patricia Berger, U.S. National Bur. of Standards, Gaithersburg, MD 20899.

Theatre Library Association

Secretary-Treasurer, Richard M. Buck
111 Amsterdam Ave., New York, NY 10023

Object

"To further the interests of collecting, preserving, and using theatre, cinema, and performing arts materials in libraries, museums, and private collections." Founded 1937. Memb. 500. Dues (Indiv.) $20; (Inst.) $25. Year. Jan. 1–Dec. 31, 1989.

Officers (1988–1989)

Pres. Mary Ann Jensen, Curator, William Seymour Theatre Collection, Princeton Univ. Lib., Princeton, NJ 08544; *V.P.* James B. Poteat, Television Info. Office, 745 Fifth Ave., New York, NY 10022; *Secy.-Treas.* Richard M. Buck, Asst. to the Chief, Performing Arts Research Center, The New York Public Lib. at Lincoln Center, 111 Amsterdam Ave., New York, NY 10023; *Rec. Secy.* Lois Erickson McDonald, Assoc. Curator, The Eugene O'Neill Theatre Center, 305 Great Neck Rd., Waterford, CT 06385.

(Address correspondence, except *Broadside*, to the secretary-treasurer. Address *Broadside* correspondence to Alan J. Pally.)

Executive Board

Officers; Susan Brady; Elizabeth Burdick; Maryann Chach; Geraldine Duclow; John W. Frick; Brigitte Kueppers; Richard C. Lynch; Louis A. Rachow; Bob Taylor; Richard Wall; Wendy Warnken; Walter Zvonchenko; *Ex officio.* Barbara Naomi Cohen-Stratyner; Alan J. Pally; *Honorary.* Marguerite Loud McAneny; Paul Myers.

Publications

Broadside (q.; memb.). *Ed.* Alan J. Pally.
Performing Arts Resources (ann.; memb.). *Ed.* Barbara Naomi Cohen-Stratyner.

Committee Chairpersons

Awards. James Poteat.
Nominations. Richard Wall.
Program and Special Events. Richard M. Buck.
Publications. Martha Mahard, pro. tem.

Universal Serials and Book Exchange, Inc. (USBE)

Managing Director, Claude L. Hooker
3335 V St. N.E., Washington, DC 20018
202-636-8723

Object

"To promote the distribution and interchange of books, periodicals, and other scholarly materials among libraries and other educational and scientific institutions of the United States and between them and libraries and institutions of other countries." Organized 1948. Year. Jan. 1–Dec. 31.

Membership

Membership in USBE is open to any library that serves a constituency and is an institution or part of an institution or organization. The USBE corporation includes a representative from each member library.

Officers

Pres. Agnes M. Griffen, Dir., Dept. of Public Libs., Montgomery County Government, Rockville, MD 20850; *V.P./Pres.-Elect.* Nancy H. Marshall, Univ. Libn., College of William and Mary, Williamsburg, VA 23186; *Secy.* Helen Wiltse, Assoc. Dir. of Libs., Georgia Inst. of Technology, Atlanta, GA 30332; *Treas.* Sharon J. Rogers, Univ. Libn., George Washington Univ., Washington, DC 20052; *Past Pres.* Pat Molholt, Assoc. Dir. of Libs., Rennselaer Polytechnic Institute, Troy, NY 12180-3590.

Members of the Board

Susan J. Cote, Lib. Dir., Case Western Reserve Univ., Cleveland, OH 44106; Sara C. Heitshu, Asst. Univ. Libn. for Technical Services, Univ. Lib., Univ. of Arizona, Tucson, AZ 85721; Charlotta Hensley, Asst. Dir. for Technical Services, Univ. of Colorado Libs., Boulder, CO 80309; Sharon A. Hogan, Dir. of Libs., Louisiana State Univ., Baton Rouge, LA 70803-3300; Ellen Hoffman, Dir. of Libs., York Univ., 4700 Keele St., Downsview, Ont. M3J 2R2, Canada; Minna A. Saxe, Chief Serials Libn., Rees Lib., Grad. School and Univ. Center, City Univ. of New York, 33 W. 42 St., New York, NY 10036.

Publications

7,000 Most Available Titles. Microfiche listing of core serials collection.
USBE/NEWS. Monthly catalog and newsletter.
Subjects catalogs (irreg.).

State, Provincial, and Regional Library Associations

The associations in this section are organized under three headings: United States, Canada, and Regional associations. Both the United States and Canada are represented under Regional associations. Unless otherwise specified, correspondence is to be addressed to the secretary or executive secretary in the entry.

United States

Alabama

Memb. 1,450. Term of Office. Apr. 1988–Apr. 1989. Publication. *The Alabama Librarian* (9 per year). *Ed.* Kathy Vogel, 122 Plateau Rd., Montevallo 35115; *Business Mgr.* Sandra K. Sutton, Box 601, Helena 35080.

Pres. Mary Maud McCain, 2020 Melinda Dr., Birmingham 35214. Tel. 205-841-3642 (w), 205-798-7800 (h); *Pres.-Elect.* Regina Cooper, 4709 Calvert Rd., Huntsville 35816. Tel. 205-532-5954; *2nd V.P.* Linda Beving, 2055 Woodmeadow Dr., Birmingham 35216; *Secy.* Geneva Bush, Box 850935, Mobile 36685; *Treas.* Emily Eddy, Box 2418, Huntsville 35804; *Past Pres.* Pauline C. Williams, Sta. 6102, Univ. of Montevallo, Montevallo 35115; *ALA Chapter Councillor.* Joan Atkinson, GSLS, Univ. of Alabama, Box 6242, University 35486; *SELA Bd. Memb.* Billy Pennington, 397 Cambo Lane, Birmingham 35226.

Address correspondence to Sandra K. Sutton, Office of the Executive Secretary, Box 601, Helena 35080. Tel. 205-663-1130.

Alaska

Memb. 432. Term of Office. Mar. 1988–Mar. 1989. Publication. *Sourdough* (q.).

Pres. Mark Goniwiecha, Univ. of Alaska Lib., Box 2740, Fairbanks 99707. Tel. 907-474-7403; *Secy.* Dee McKenna, Box 963, Nome 99762. Tel. 907-443-5133; *Treas.* Audrey Kolb, 1215 Cowles St., Fairbanks 99701. Tel. 907-452-2999.

Address correspondence to the president.

Arizona

Memb. 1,164. Term of Office. Oct. 1988–Oct. 1989. Publication. *ASLA Newsletter* (mo.). *Ed.* David Buxton, Asst. Univ. Libn., Main Lib., Bldg. 55, Univ. of Arizona, Tucson 85721.

Pres. Dora Biblarz, Univ. Libs., Arizona State Univ., Tempe 85287-1006. Tel. 602-965-5250; *Pres.-Elect.* Jean Born, Mesa Community College, 1833 W. Southern Ave., Mesa 85202. Tel. 602-461-7661; *Secy.* Barbara Seperich, Mesa Public Lib., 64 E. First St., Mesa 85202; *Treas.* Caryl Major, Independence H.S., 6602 N. 75 Ave., Glendale 85303; *Exec. Secy.* Jim Johnson, Box 26187, Phoenix 85068.

Address correspondence to the president.

Arkansas

Memb. 800. Term of Office. Oct. 1988–Oct. 1989. Publications. *Arkansas Libraries* (q.); *ALA Newsletter* (bi-mo.).

Pres. Stephen Dew, Univ. of Arkansas, Mullins Lib., Fayetteville 72701; *Exec. Dir.* Sherry Walker, Arkansas Lib. Assn., 220 W. Third, Suite 300, Little Rock 72205. Tel. 501-372-1424.

Address correspondence to the executive director.

California

Memb. 2,747. Term of Office. Dec.–Nov. Publication. *The CLA Newsletter* (mo.).

Exec. Dir. Mary Sue Ferrell, California Lib. Assn., 717 K St., Sacramento 95814; *Pres.* Janice T. Koyama, Moffitt Undergrad. Lib., Univ. of California at Berkeley; *V.P./Pres.-Elect.* Catherine E. Lucas, San Diego County Lib.; *Past Pres.* Halbert Watson, Pomona Public Lib.; *Treas.* Linda D. Crowe, Peninsula Lib. System, Belmont; *ALA Chapter Councillor.* Betty J. Blackman, California State Univ., Dominguez Hills.

Colorado

Memb. 850. Term of Office. Oct. 1988–Oct. 1989. Publication. *Colorado Libraries* (q.). *Ed.* Brenda Bailey, Fort Lewis College Lib., Durango 81301.

Pres. Charles Hendrickson, Mesa State College Lib., Box 2647, Grand Junction 81502; *Pres.-Elect.* Donna R. Jones, Arkansas Valley Regional Lib. Service System, 205 W. Abriendo, Pueblo 81004; *Treas.* Maureen Crocker, Colorado State Lib., 201 E. Colfax Ave., Denver 80203; *Exec. Dir.* Judy Votisek, Colorado Lib. Assn. Box 4636, Englewood 80155. Tel. 303-779-1115: *Past Pres.* William A. Murray, Media Services, Aurora Public Schools, 875 Peoria St., Aurora 80011.

Address correspondence to the executive director.

Connecticut

Memb. 900. Term of Office. July 1, 1988–June 30, 1989. Publication. *Connecticut Libraries* (11 per year). *Ed.* David Kapp, 4 Llynwood Dr., Bolton 06040. Tel. 203-647-0697.

Pres. Ginny Vocelli, Avon Free Public Lib., 281 Country Club Rd., Avon 06001. Tel. 203-673-9712; *V.P./Pres.-Elect.* Laura Kahkonen, Windsor Public Lib., 323 Broad St., Windsor 06095. Tel. 203-688-6433; *Treas.* Mary Balmer, 54 Stone Pond Dr., Tolland 06084. Tel. 203-872-0267; *Managing Dir.* M. Suzanne C. Berry; *Assn. Administrator.* Sharon M. Sweeney, The Connecticut Lib. Assn., 638 Prospect Ave., Hartford 06105. Tel. 203-232-4825.

Delaware

Memb. 250. Term of Office. Apr. 1988–Apr. 1989. Publication. *DLA Bulletin* (3 per year).

Pres. Grace S. Husted, New Castle County Dept. of Libs., 187A Old Churchmans Rd., New Castle 19720. Tel. 302-323-6480; *Pres.-Elect.* Mary Tise, Concord Pike Lib., 3406 Concord Pike, Wilmington 19803. Tel. 302-478-7961; *Secy.* Sue Menson, Sanford School Lib., Box 888, Hockessin 19707; *Treas.* Jeff Ferris, New Castle County Processing Div., 2200 Wollaston, Wilmington 19808. Tel. 302-995-7686; *Past Pres.* Mart Titus, Concord Pike Lib., 3406 Concord Pike, Wilmington 19803.

Address correspondence to the Delaware Lib. Assn., Box 1843, Wilmington 19899.

District of Columbia

Memb. 1,000. Term of Office. Sept. 1988–Aug. 1989. Publication. *INTERCOM* (mo.).

Pres. William R. Gordon, Prince George's County Memorial Lib. System, 6532 Adelphi

Rd., Hyattsville, MD 20782. Tel. 301-699-3500; *V.P.* Shirley Loo, Lib. of Congress, CRS LM 221, Washington, DC 20540. Tel. 202-287-5804; *Secy.* Carol Henderson, ALA Washington Office, 110 Maryland Ave. N.E., Washington, DC 20002. Tel. 202-547-4440; *Treas.* Elizabeth Warren, Arlington County Public Lib., 1015 N. Quincy St., Arlington, VA 22201. Tel. 703-358-3352.

Address correspondence to the president.

Florida

Memb. (Indiv.) 1,000; (In-state Inst.) 80. Term of Office. July 1, 1988–June 30, 1989.

Pres. Althea H. Jenkins, USF Lib., 5700 N. Tamiami Trail, Sarasota 34243-2197; *V.P./Pres.-Elect.* Thomas L. Reitz, Seminole Community College Lib., 1333 Gunnison Ave., Orlando 33204; *Secy.* Linda Mielke, Clearwater Public Lib., 100 N. Osceola Ave., Clearwater 33515; *Treas.* Charles Parker, Gadsden County Public Lib., 919 W. King St., Quincy 32351.

Address correspondence to Dale Wagner, Executive Secretary, Florida Lib. Assn., 1133 W. Morse Blvd., Suite 201, Winter Park 32789.

Georgia

Memb. 975. Term of Office. 1988–1989. Publication. *Georgia Librarian. Ed.* Joanne Lincoln, Atlanta Public Schools, 2930 Forrest Hill Dr., Atlanta 30315. Tel. 404-827-8650.

Pres. James E. Dorsey, Chestatee Regional Lib. System, 127 N. Main St., Gainesville 30505. Tel. 404-532-3311; *1st V.P.* Bob Richardson, Young Harris College Lib., Box 38, Young Harris 30582; *2nd V.P.* Gail Lazenby, Cobb County Public Lib. System, 30 Atlanta St., Marietta 30060; *Treas.* Irma Harlan, Chatham-Effingham-Liberty Regional Lib., 2002 Bull St., Savannah 31499; *Secy.* Laura Lewis, Troup-Harris-Coweta Regional Lib., 200 Broome St., LaGrange 30240; *Exec. Secy.* Ann Morton, Box 833, Tucker 30084. Tel. 404-934-7118.

Address correspondence to the executive secretary.

Hawaii

Memb. 445. Term of Office. Mar. 1988–Mar. 1989. Publications. *Hawaii Library Association Journal* (irreg.); *Hawaii Library Association Newsletter* (4 per year); *HLA Membership Directory* (ann.); *Directory of Libraries and Information Sources in Hawaii and the Pacific Islands* (irreg.).

Pres. Donna Garcia, Lihue Public Lib., 4344 Hardy St., Lihue 96766. Tel. 808-245-3617; *V.P.* Sandy Akana, Kailuai Public Lib., 239 Kuulei Rd., Kailuai 96734; *Secy.* Cynthia Yen, c/o Research and Development Services, 465 S. King St., Honolulu 96813; *Treas.* Jeff Eldridge, Kaimuki Public Lib., 1041 Koko Head Ave., Honolulu 96816.

Address correspondence to the president.

Idaho

Memb. (Indiv.) 494; (Inst.) 34. Term of Office. Oct. 3, 1988–Oct. 6, 1989. Publication. *The Idaho Librarian* (q.). *Ed.* Gregg Sapp.

Pres. Margaret McNamara, 308 Roosevelt, American Falls 83211. Tel. 208-226-2335; *V.P./Pres.-Elect.* David Case, Lewis and Clark State College, Eighth Ave. and Sixth St., Lewiston 83501. Tel. 208-799-2395; *Treas.* Marjorie Shelby, Idaho State Lib., 325 W. State St., Boise 83702. Tel. 208-334-2153; *Secy.* Sandy Biermann, Bannock Regional Medical Center, Memorial Dr., Pocatello 83201. Tel. 208-232-6150.

Illinois

Memb. 4,000. Term of Office. Jan. 1, 1988–June 30, 1989. Publication. *ILA Reporter* (6 per year).

Pres. Marlene Deuel, Poplar Creek Public Lib. Dist., 1405 S. Park Blvd., Streamwood 60103. Tel. 312-837-6800; *V.P./Pres.-Elect.* Fred Peterson, Rte. 2, Box 160, Bloomington 61701-9626. Tel. 309-438-3446; *Treas.* Pat Llerandi, Schaumburg Township Public Lib., 32 W. Library Lane, Schaumburg 60194. Tel. 312-885-3373.

Address correspondence to Willine C. Mahoney, Executive Director, ILA, 33 W. Grand Ave., Chicago 60610. Tel. 312-644-1896.

Indiana

Memb. (Indiv.) 891; (Inst.) 152. Term of Office. May 1989–May 1990. Publications. *Focus on Indiana Libraries* (10 per year). *Ed.* Susan Humphrey, Box 44582, Indianapolis 46244. Tel. 317-266-0808; *Indiana Libraries* (q.). *Ed.* Danny Callison, School of Lib. and Info. Science, Indiana Univ., Bloomington 47401. Tel. 812-335-5113.

Pres. Bill Bolte, Jeffersonville Township Public Lib., Box 1548, Jeffersonville 47131. Tel. 812-282-7765; *V.P.* Betty Martin, Vigo County Public Lib., One Library Sq., Terre Haute 47807. Tel. 812-232-1113; *Secy.* Rosemary Saczawa, Anderson Univ. Lib., Anderson 46012; *Treas.* Charr Skirvin, Brown County Public Lib., Box 8, Nashville 47448.

Address correspondence to the association, 1500 N. Delaware St., Indianapolis 46202.

Iowa

Memb. 1,720. Term of Office. Jan. 1, 1989–Dec. 31, 1989. Publication. *The Catalyst* (bi-mo.). *Ed.* Naomi Stovall, Iowa Lib. Assn., 823 Insurance Exchange Bldg., Des Moines 50309. Tel. 515-243-2172.

Pres. Cynthia Dyer, Simpson College, Dunn Lib., Indianola 50125. Tel. 515-961-1519.

Address correspondence to Iowa Lib. Assn.

Kansas

Memb. 1,000. Term of Office. July 1, 1988–June 30, 1989. Publications. *KLA Newsletter* (q.); *KLA Membership Directory* (ann.).

Pres. Marlene Hendrick, Topeka Public Lib., Topeka 66604; *Pres.-Elect.* Karen Cole, Forsyth Lib., Fort Hays State Univ., Hays 67601; *Exec. Secy.* Leroy Gattin, SCKLS, 901 N. Main, Hutchinson 67501. Tel. 363-663-2501; *Secy.* Charlene Grass, Farrell Lib., Kansas State Univ., Manhattan 66506; *Treas.* Marcella Ratzlaff, Hutchinson Public Lib., Hutchinson 67501.

Address correspondence to the president or executive secretary.

Kentucky

Memb. 1,600. Term of Office. Oct. 1988–Oct. 1989. Publication. *Kentucky Libraries* (q.).

Pres. Jean Almand, Western Kentucky Univ., Bowling Green 42101. Tel. 502-745-3958; *V.P./Pres.-Elect.* John M. Bryant, Univ. of Kentucky, King Lib., Rm. 127, Lexington 40506-0039. Tel. 606-257-3801; *Secy.* Rose M. Gabbard, Box 313, Beattyville 41311; *Exec. Secy.* John T. Underwood, 1501 Twilight Trail, Frankfort 40601. Tel. 502-223-5322.

Address correspondence to the association, 1501 Twilight Trail, Frankfort 40601.

Louisiana

Memb. (Indiv.) 1,501; (Inst.) 82. Term of Office. July 1988–June 1989. Publication. *LLA Bulletin* (q.).

Pres. Marianne Puckett, 109 Southfield, #181, Shreveport 71105. Tel. 318-674-5450; *1st V.P.* Phyllis Heroy, 5768 Hyacinth Ave., Baton Rouge 70808. Tel. 504-295-8612; *2nd V.P.* Beth Vandersteen, Rte. 2, Box 361, Alexandria 71302. Tel. 318-445-6436; *Secy.* Jean Kreamer, Box 40077, USL Sta., Lafayette 70504. Tel. 318-231-6780; *Parliamentarian.* Dixie Jones, 421 Mayfair, Bossier City 71111. Tel. 318-424-6036; *Exec. Dir.* Sharilynn Aucoin, Box 3058, Baton Rouge 70821. Tel. 504-342-4928.

Address correspondence to the executive director.

Maine

Memb. 850. Term of Office. (*Pres., V.P.*) Spring 1988–Spring 1990. Publications. *Downeast Libraries* (4 per year); *Maine Memo* (mo.).

Pres. Reta Schreiber, Bangor Public Lib., 145 Harlow St., Bangor 04401; *V.P.* Nann Hilyard, Auburn Public Lib., Auburn 04210; *Secy.* Toni Katz, Miller Lib., Colby College, Waterville 04901; *Treas.* Steve Podgajny, Curtis Memorial Lib., Pleasant St., Brunswick 04011.

Address correspondence to Maine Lib. Assn., c/o Maine Municipal Assn., Local Government Center, Community Dr., Augusta 04330. Tel. 207-623-8429.

Maryland

Memb. 1,200. Term of Office. July 1, 1988–June 30, 1989. Publication. *The CRAB.*

Pres. Nadia Taran, South Maryland Regional Lib. Assn., La Plata 20646. Tel. 301-934-9442; *1st V.P.* Mary Landry, Dundalk Community College, 7200 Sollers Point Rd., Dundalk 21222. Tel. 301-285-5642; *Secy.* Lavern Pitman, Frostburg State College,

Frostburg 21532. Tel. 301-689-4313; *Treas.* Thomas Strader, A. S. Cook Lib., Towson State Univ., Towson 21204. Tel. 301-321-2450; *Exec. Secy.* Robert Greenfield, 115 W. Franklin St., Baltimore 21201. Tel. 301-727-7422 (h), 301-685-6705 (w).

Address correspondence to the Maryland Lib. Assn., 115 W. Franklin St., Baltimore 21201.

Massachusetts

Memb. (Indiv.) 950; (Inst.) 100. Term of Office. July 1988–June 1989. Publication. *Bay State Librarian* (12 per year).

Pres. Louise Brown, Wayland Public Lib., 5 Concord Rd., Wayland 01778. Tel. 508-358-2311; *V.P.* Anne O'Brien, Pollard Memorial Lib., 401 Merrimack St., Lowell 01852. Tel. 617-454-8821 ext. 247; *Secy.* Janet Husband, Rockland Memorial Lib., 366 Union St., Rockland 02370. Tel. 617-878-1236; *Treas.* Carl Sturgis, R.S. Storrs Lib., 693 Longmeadow St., Longmeadow 01106. Tel. 413-567-5500; *Past Pres.* Susan Flannery, Reading Public Lib., 64 Middlesex Ave., Reading 01867. Tel. 617-944-0840; *Exec. Secy.* Paula M. Bozoian, Massachusetts Lib. Assn., Box 556, Wakefield 01880. Tel. 617-438-0779.

Address correspondence to the executive secretary.

Michigan

Memb. (Indiv.) 2,200; (Inst.) 150. Term of Office. Oct. 1988–Oct. 1989. Publication. *Michigan Librarian Newsletter* (10 per year).

Pres. Colleen Hyslop, Head of Technical Services, Michigan State Univ., East Lansing 48823; *Treas.* Jule Fosbender, Adrian Public Lib., 14143 E. Maumee St., Adrian 49221; *Exec. Dir.* Marianne Gessner, Michigan Lib. Assn., 1000 Long Blvd., Suite 1, Lansing 48911. Tel. 517-694-6615.

Address correspondence to the executive director.

Minnesota

Memb. 850. Term of Office. *(Pres., V.P., & Secy.)* Jan. 1, 1989–Dec. 31, 1989; *(Treas.)* Jan. 1, 1988–Dec. 31, 1989. Publication. *MLA Newsletter* (10 per year).

Pres. Michael Haeuser, Dir., Learning Resources, Gustavus Adolphus College, St. Peter 56082; *V.P./Pres.-Elect.* M. J. Rossman, 1170 Cushing Circle, No. 212, St. Paul 55108; *ALA Chapter Councilor.* John D. Christenson, Dir., Traverse des Sioux Lib., Mankato 56001; *Secy.* Robbie LaFleur, 645 State Office Bldg., Legislative Reference Lib., St. Paul 55155; *Treas.* Carol LeDuc, 1633 Bohland Ave., St. Paul 55116.

Address correspondence to JoAnne Kelty, Administrative Secy., Minnesota Lib. Assn., North Regional Lib., 1315 Lowry Ave. N., Minneapolis 55411. Tel. 612-521-1735.

Mississippi

Memb. 1,200. Term of Office. Jan. 1989–Dec. 1989. Publication. *Mississippi Libraries.*

Pres. Sid Graves, Carnegie Public Lib., Box 280, Clarksdale 38614. Tel. 601-627-6268; *V.P./Pres.-Elect.* June Breland, 113 Apache Dr., Starkville 39759; *Treas.* Toni James, Pike-Amite-Wathall Lib., 114 State St., McComb 39648; *Secy.* Charmain Smith, Mississippi Lib. Commission, Box 10700, Jackson 39289-0700; *Exec. Secy.* Melissa Bailey, MLA Office, Box 20448, Jackson 39209-1448. Tel. 601-352-3917.

Address correspondence to the association, Box 20448, Jackson 39209-1448.

Missouri

Memb. 1,000. Term of Office. Oct. 1988–Oct. 1989. Publication. *MO INFO* (6 per year).

Pres. Dorothy Sanborn Elliott, Tenth and Felix Sts., St. Joseph 64501. Tel. 816-232-7729; *V.P./Pres.-Elect.* Ron Bohley, Curtis Laws Wilson Lib., Univ. of Missouri-Rolla, Rolla 65401. Tel. 314-341-4005; *Secy.* Barbara Moore, Missouri State Lib., Box 387, Jefferson City 65102. Tel. 314-751-3615; *Chpn., Budget & Finance.* Linda Medaris, Central Missouri State Univ., Warrensburg 64093. Tel. 816-429-4154.

Address correspondence to Jean Ann McCartney, Executive Coordinator, Missouri Library Association, 1015 E. Broadway, Suite 215, Columbia 65201. Tel. 314-449-4627.

Montana

Memb. 500. Term of Office. July 1, 1988–June 30, 1989. Publication. *Library Focus, the Newsletter of the Montana Library Association* (6 per year). *Ed.* Marilyn LeBlond, 807 S. Lincoln, #1, Sidney 59270.

Pres. Georgia Lomax, 94 Grandview Dr., Kalispell 59901; *V.P./Pres.-Elect.* Karen Hatcher, Mansfield Lib., Univ. of Montana, Missoula 59812; *Past Pres.* Bunny Morrison, 2135 Silver Sage Trail, Billings 59102; *Financial Secy.* Clara Sprague, Box 954, Bozeman 59771; *Rec. Secy.* Phelps Shepard, Butte-Silver Bow Lib., 106 W. Broadway, Butte 59701.

Address correspondence to MLA, Box 954, Bozeman 59771. Tel. 406-994-3126.

Nebraska

Memb. 1,000. Term of Office. Oct. 1988–Oct. 1989. Publication. *NLA Quarterly.*

Pres. Laureen Riedesel, 721 Grant St., Beatrice 68310; *V.P.* Dorothy Willis, 2602 N. 51 St., Omaha 68104; *Past Pres.* Dee Yost, 724 E. Seventh St., Hastings 68901; *Secy.* Clara Hoover, 13345 Madison, Omaha 68137; *Treas.* Rod Wagner, NLC, 1420 P St., Lincoln 68508; *Exec. Secy.* Ray Means, 678 Parkwood Lane, Omaha 68132. Tel. 402-556-0903 (h), 402-280-2217 (w).

Address correspondence to the executive secretary.

Nevada

Memb. 325. Term of Office. Jan. 1, 1989–Dec. 31, 1989. Publication. *Highroller* (4 per year).

Pres. Chuck Manley, Washoe County Lib., Box 2151, Reno 89505. Tel. 702-785-4545; *Pres.-Elect.* Lynn Ossolinski, Incline Village H.S., Box AA, Incline Village 89450. Tel. 702-831-1240; *Exec. Secy.* Allison Cowgill, Nevada State Lib., Capital Complex, Carson City 89710. Tel. 702-885-5160; *Treas.* Karen Albrethsen, Spring Creek School, Elko 89801; *Past Pres.* Danna Sturm, Douglas County Lib., Box 337, Minden 89423. Tel. 702-782-9841.

Address correspondence to the executive secretary.

New Hampshire

Memb. 555. Term of Office. June 1988–May 1989. Publication. *NHLA Newsletter* (bimo.).

Pres. Kathy E. Richardson, Nashua Public Lib., 2 Court St., Nashua 03060. Tel. 603-883-4141; *V.P./Pres.-Elect.* Patricia Topham, Plymouth Public Lib., Plymouth 03264; *Secy.* Barbara Young, 10 Leary Ct., Exeter 03833; *Treas.* Ellen Hardsog, Derry Public Lib., Derry 03038.

Address correspondence to the president.

New Jersey

Memb. 1,700. Term of Office. May–Apr. Publications. *New Jersey Libraries* (q.); *New Jersey Libraries Newsletter* (mo.).

Pres. Norma Yueh, Ramapo College Lib., 505 Ramapo Valley Rd., Mahwah 07430; *V.P./Pres.-Elect.* Irene Cackowski, Monroe Township Lib., Municipal Bldg., Perrineville Rd., Jamesburg 08831; *Past Pres.* Thomas J. Alrutz, 555 Parker St., Newark 07104; *Treas.* Sara Eggers, Old Bridge Public Lib., Old Bridge 08857; *Exec. Dir.* Danilo H. Figueredo, New Jersey Lib. Assn., 116 W. State St., Trenton 08608. Tel. 609-394-8032.

Address correspondence to the Executive Director, Box 1534, Trenton 08607.

New Mexico

Memb. 658. Term of Office. Apr. 1988–Apr. 1989. Publication. *New Mexico Library Association Newsletter. Ed.* Heidi Sims, Medical Center Lib., North Campus, Univ. of New Mexico, Albuquerque 87131.

Pres. Karen Watkins, New Mexico State Lib., 325 Don Gaspar, Santa Fe 87503. Tel. 505-827-3802; *V.P./Pres.-Elect.* Gloria Trujillo, General Delivery, Chimayo 87522. Tel. 505-753-2391; *Secy.* Louise Leon, 1922 Alabama St., Silver City 88061; *Treas.* Ellanie Sampson, Box 311, Truth or Consequences 87901.

Address correspondence to the Association, Box 25084, Albuquerque 87125.

New York

Memb. 3,200. Term of Office. Oct. 1988–Oct. 1989. Publication. *NYLA Bulletin* (10 per year). *Ed.* Richard Johnson.

Pres. Janet Steiner, SCRLC, 215 N. Cayuga St., Ithaca 14850; *1st V.P.* Frances R. Roscello, 19 Red Oak Lane, Rensselaer 12144; *2nd V.P.* Julia Van deWater, 219 Parsons Dr., Hempstead 11550; *Conference Mgr.* Angela Cappiello, New York Lib. Assn., 15 Park Row, Suite 434, New York 10038. Tel. 212-227-8033; *Exec. Dir.* Nancy W. Lian, CAE, New York Lib. Assn., 15 Park Row, Suite 434, New York 10038. Tel. 212-227-8032.

Address correspondence to the NYLA, 15 Park Row, Suite 434, New York 10038.

North Carolina

Memb. 2,011. Term of Office. Oct. 1987–Oct. 1989. Publication. *North Carolina Libraries* (q.). *Ed.* Frances Bradburn, Central Regional Education Center, 2431 Crabtree Blvd., Raleigh 27604.

Pres. Patsy Hansel, Asst. Dir., Cumberland County Public Lib., 300 Maiden Lane, Fayetteville 28301. Tel. 919-483-1580; *1st V.P./Pres.-Elect.* Barbara A. Baker, Durham Technical College, 1637 Lawson St., Durham 27703. Tel. 919-598-9218; *2nd V.P.* Ray A. Frankle, Atkins Lib., UNC-Charlotte, Charlotte 28223. Tel. 704-343-5440; *Secy.* Gloria Miller, Charlotte-Mecklenburg Schools, 800 Everett Place, Charlotte 28205. Tel. 704-331-9083; *Treas.* Nancy Clark Fogarty, Jackson Lib., Univ. of North Carolina, Greensboro 27412; *Dirs.* Janet Freeman, Campbell Lib., Meredith College, Raleigh 27607. Tel. 919-829-8531; Howard F. McGinn, Asst. State Libn., 109 E. Jones St., Raleigh 27611.

North Dakota

Memb. (Indiv.) 402; (Inst.) 36. Term of Office. Oct. 1988–Oct. 1989. Publication. *The Good Stuff* (q.). *Ed.* Gary Schultz, Fargo Public Lib., 102 N. Third St., Fargo 58102.

Pres. Diane Caley, Ward County Public Lib., 405 Third Ave. S.E., Minot 58701. Tel. 701-852-5388; *V.P./Pres.-Elect.* Delores Vyzralek, State Archives and Historical Research Lib., Heritage Center, Bismarck 58505; *Secy.* Jan Hendrickson, Hazen Public Lib., Box 471, Hazen 58545; *Treas.* Roann Masterson, 2877 A Warwick Loop, Bismarck 58504.

Ohio

Memb. 2,297. Term of Office. Nov. 1, 1988–Nov. 1, 1989. Publication. *Ohio Libraries* (6 per year).

Pres. Jo Riegel, Wagnalls Memorial Lib., 150 E. Columbus, Lithopolis 43136. Tel. 614-837-4765; *V.P./Pres.-Elect.* Judith Coleman, Euclid Public Lib., 631 E. 222 St., Euclid 44123. Tel. 216-261-5300; *Secy.* Margaret Cooper, Stow Public Lib., 3511 Darrow Rd., Stow 44224. Tel. 216-688-3295.

Address correspondence to the Ohio Lib. Assn., 40 S. Third St., Suite 230, Columbus 43215. Tel. 614-221-9057.

Oklahoma

Memb. (Indiv.) 1,000; (Inst.) 60. Term of Office. July 1988–June 1989. Publication. *Oklahoma Librarian* (bi-mo.).

Pres. Stephen Skidmore, Ponca City Lib., 515 E. Grand, Ponca City 74601. Tel. 405-762-6311; *V.P./Pres.-Elect.* Marilyn Hinshaw, Eastern Oklahoma Dist. Lib. System, 801 W. Okmulgee, Muskogee 74401. Tel. 918-683-2846; *Secy.* Joel Robinson, Chickasaw Lib. System, 801 Railway Express, Ardmore 73401. Tel. 405-223-3164; *Treas.* William Lowry, Pioneer Lib. System, 225 N. Webster, Norman 73069. Tel. 405-321-1481; *Exec. Secy.* Kay Boies, 300 Hardy Dr., Edmond 73013. Tel. 405-348-0506.

Address correspondence to the Association, 300 Hardy Dr., Edmond 73013. Tel. 405-348-0506.

Oregon

Memb. (Indiv.) 765; (Inst.) 51. Term of Office. Apr. 1988–Aug. 1989. Publication. *Oregon Library News* (mo.). *Eds.* Carole Dickerson and Dennis Moler, Newport Public Lib., 35 N.W. Nye St., Newport 97365. Tel. 503-265-3109.

Pres. Lynn K. Chmelir, 3540 16th Ct. S., Salem 97302. Tel. 503-472-4121 ext. 262; *V.P./Pres.-Elect.* Michael Gaston, Siuslaw Public Lib., Box A, Florence 97439. Tel. 503-

997-3132; *Secy.* Gary Sharp, North Bend Public Lib., 1925 McPherson, North Bend 97459. Tel. 503-756-0400; *Treas.* Wyma Rogers, 693 N.W. Jackson, Corvallis 97330. Tel. 503-757-6928 ext. 5851.

Pennsylvania

Memb. 1,750. Term of Office. Oct. 1988–Oct. 1989. Publication. *PLA Bulletin* (8 per year).

Pres. James L. Hollinger, Lancaster County Lib., 125 N. Duke St., Lancaster 17602. Tel. 717-394-2651; *Exec. Dir.* Margaret S. Bauer, Pennsylvania Lib. Assn., 3107 N. Front St., Harrisburg 17110. Tel. 717-233-3113.

Address correspondence to the Association, 3107 N. Front St., Harrisburg 17110.

Puerto Rico

Memb. 450. Term of Office. Apr. 1988–Apr. 1990. Publications. *Boletin* (s. ann.); *Cuadernos Bibliotecológicos* (irreg.); *Informa* (mo.); *Cuadernos Bibliográficos* (irreg.).

Pres. Digna Cruz de Escalera; *Pres.-Elect.* Aura Jiménez de Panepinto.

Address correspondence to the Sociedad de Bibliotecarios de Puerto Rico, Apdo. 22989, UPR Sta., Rio Piedras 00931.

Rhode Island

Memb. 543. Term of Office. Nov. 1988–Nov. 1989. Publication. *Rhode Island Library Association Bulletin. Ed.* Judith Paster.

Pres. Douglas A. Pearce, Warwick Public Lib., 600 Sandy Lane, Warwick 02886. Tel. 401-739-5440; *V.P./Pres.-Elect.* Carol Di-Prete, Roger Williams College Lib., Old Ferry Rd., Bristol 02809. Tel. 401-253-1040; *Secy.* Ruth E. Corkill, Barrington Public Lib., 281 County Rd., Barrington 02806. Tel. 401-247-1920; *Treas.* Judith H. Bell, Jamestown Philomenian Lib., 26 North Rd., Jamestown 02835. Tel. 401-423-1665; *Memb.-at-Large.* Eileen Socha, George Hail Lib., 179 Schoolhouse Rd., Warren 02885. Tel. 401-245-7686; *NELA Councillor.* Charlotte Schoonover, Kingston Free Lib., 1329 Kingstown Rd., Kingston 02881. Tel. 401-783-8254; *ALA Councillor.* Howard Boksenbaum, Rhode Island Dept. of State Lib. Services, 300 Richmond St., Providence 02903. Tel. 401-277-2726.

Address correspondence to the secretary.

St. Croix

Memb. 48. Publications. *SCLA Newsletter* (q.); *Studies in Virgin Islands Librarianship* (irreg.).

Pres. Wallace Williams, Florence A. Williams Public Lib., 49–50 King St., Christiansted, St. Croix 08820.

South Carolina

Memb. 712. Term of Office. Oct. 1988–Oct. 1989. Publications. *The South Carolina Librarian* (s. ann.). *Ed.* Katina P. Strauch, College of Charleston, Charleston 29424; *News and Views of South Carolina Library Association* (bi-mo.).

Pres. Betty Callaham, South Carolina State Lib. Tel. 803-734-8666; *V.P.* Joseph Boykin, Clemson Univ. Lib.; *Secy.* Yvette Pierce, Francis Marion College; *Treas.* Helen Callison, Irmo H.S. Lib.

South Dakota

Memb. (Indiv.) 448; (Inst.) 60. Term of Office. Sept. 1988–Sept. 1989. Publication. *Bookmarks* (bi-mo.). *Ed.* Donna Fisher, 3811 Brookside Dr., Rapid City 57706.

Pres. Nancy Sabbe, Madison Public Lib., 209 E. Center, Madison 57042. Tel. 605-256-4922; *V.P./Pres.-Elect.* Ethelle Bean, Mundt Lib., Dakota State College, Madison 57042; *Secy.* Gil Johnsson, Cozard Memorial Lib., 110 E. Lawler, Chamberlain 57325; *Treas.* Beth Marie Quanbeck, South Dakota State Lib., 800 Governor's Dr., Pierre 57501; *ALA Councillor.* Judy Johnson, Lib., Rapid City Central H.S., 433 N. Eighth, Rapid City 57701; *MPLA Rep.* Mary Caspers, Lib., South Dakota State Univ., Brookings 57007

Address correspondence to the Association, Box 673, Pierre 57501.

Tennessee

Memb. 1,161. Term of Office. Apr. 1988–Apr. 1989. Publication. *Tennessee Librarian* (q.).

Pres. David A. Kearley, Univ. Libn., Du-Pont Lib., Univ. of the South, Sewanee

37375. Tel. 615-598-1265; *V.P./Pres.-Elect.* Caroline Stark, Dir., Nashville Public Lib., Nashville 37203. Tel. 615-259-6045; *Treas.* Mary Lee Manier, Dir., Harpeth Hill School Lib., Nashville 37215. Tel. 615-297-9543; *Exec. Secy.* Betty Nance, Box 120085, Nashville 37212. Tel. 615-297-8316.

Address correspondence to the executive secretary.

Texas

Memb. 4,800. Term of Office. Apr. 1989–Apr. 1990. Publications. *Texas Library Journal* (q.); *TLAcast* (9 per year).

Pres. Patricia Doyle, McKinney Memorial Public Lib., Box 517, McKinney 75069. Tel. 214-542-2675 ext. 202; *Exec. Dir. (Continuing).* Patricia H. Smith, TLA Office, 3355 Bee Cave Rd., Suite 603, Austin 78746. Tel. 512-328-1518.

Address correspondence to the executive director.

Utah

Memb. 600. Term of Office. Feb. 1989–May 1990. Publication. *UTAH Libraries News* (q.).

Pres. Carolyn Dickinson, Dir., Technical Services, Salt Lake City Public Lib., Salt Lake City 84111. Tel. 801-363-5733 ext. 235; *1st V.P.* Eileen Longsworth, Dir., Salt Lake County Lib., 2197 E. 7000 S., Salt Lake City 84121. Tel. 801-943-4636; *2nd V.P.* Merna Smith, Assoc. Dir., Public Service, Salt Lake City Public Lib., 209 E. 500 S., Salt Lake City 84111. Tel. 801-363-5733 ext. 225; *Rec. Secy.* Mark A. Spivey, Reference Libn., Marriott Lib., Univ. of Utah, Salt Lake City 84112. Tel. 801-581-8103; *Exec. Secy.* Ruth Ann G. Hanson, Marriott Lib., Univ. of Utah, Salt Lake City 84112. Tel. 801-581-3852; *Assn. Office.* 2150 S. 300 W., Suite 16, Salt Lake City 84115.

Address correspondence to the executive secretary.

Vermont

Memb. 500. Term of Office. Jan. 1989–Dec. 1989. Publication. *VLA News* (10 per year).

Pres. Penelope Pillsbury, Brownell Lib., Essex Junction 05452. Tel. 802-878-6955; *V.P./Pres.-Elect.* Russell Moore, Springfield Town Lib., Springfield 05156; *Secy.* Linda Kramer, Johnson State College Lib., Johnson 05656; *Treas.* Rickie Emerson, Dorothy Ailing Memorial Lib., Williston 05495; *ALA Councilor.* Sally Reed, Ilsley Lib., Middlebury 05753; *NELA Rep.* Janet Nielson, Kellog-Hubbard Lib., Montpelier 05602.

Address correspondence to the president.

Virginia

Memb. 1,400. Term of Office. Jan. 1, 1989–Dec. 31, 1989. Publications. *Virginia Librarian* (q.). *Ed.* Jennilou Grotevant, Christopher Newport College, Smith Lib., 50 Shoe Lane, Newport News 23606; *VLA Newsletter* (10 per year). *Ed.* Sandy Heinemann, Hampden-Sydney College, Eggleston Lib., Hampden-Sydney 23943.

Pres. Wendell Barbour, Christopher Newport College, Smith Lib., 50 Shoe Lane, Newport News 23606; *Secy.* Stephen Matthews, Foxcroft School, Box 1233, Middleburg 22117; *ALA Councillor.* Sue Darden, Norfolk Public Lib., 301 E. City Hall Ave., Norfolk 23510; *Exec. Dir.* Deborah M. Trocchi, VLA, 80 S. Early St., Alexandria 22304. Tel. 703-370-6020.

Address correspondence to the executive director.

Washington

Memb. 1,000. Term of Office. Aug. 1, 1989–July 31, 1990. Publication. *Alki* (3 per year).

Pres. Mary Carr, Crosby Lib., Gonzaga Univ., E. 502 Boone Ave., Spokane 99258. Tel. 509-328-4220.

Address correspondence to the Washington Lib. Assn., 1232 143rd Ave. S.E., Bellevue 98007. Tel. 206-747-6917.

West Virginia

Memb. (Indiv.) 563; (Inst.) 95. Term of Office. Dec. 1988–Nov. 1989. Publication. *West Virginia Libraries. Ed.* Yvonne Farley, Raleigh County Public Lib., Box 1876, Beckley 25801. Tel. 304-255-0511.

Pres. Rebecca T. D'Annunzio, Adamston Elementary School, 403 Emerson Rd., Clarksburg 26301. Tel. 304-623-1281; *1st V.P.* Thomas Brown, J. Frank Marsh Lib., Concord College, Athens 24712-1001. Tel. 304-384-3115; *2nd V.P.* Peggy Bias, Putnam County Public Lib., 4219 State Rte. 34, Hurricane 25526. Tel. 304-757-7308; *Secy.* Charles A. Julian, Learning Resources Center, West Virginia Northern Community College, College Sq., Wheeling 26003. Tel. 304-233-5900 ext. 253; *Treas.* Dave Childers, West Virginia Lib. Commission, Cultural Center, Capitol Complex, Charleston 25305. Tel. 305-348-2041; *ALA Councillor.* Judy K. Rule, Cabell County Public Lib., 455 Ninth St. Plaza, Huntington 25701.

Address correspondence to the president.

Wisconsin

Memb. 1,650. Term of Office. Jan. 1989–Dec. 1989. Publication. *WLA Newsletter* (6 per year).

Pres. JoAnn Carr, Univ. of Wisconsin-Madison IMC, 225 N. Mills St., Madison 53706. Tel. 608-263-4962; *V.P./Pres.-Elect.* Patricia A. Geidel, 1302 E. Decorah Rd. No. 5, West Bend 53095.

Address correspondence to the association, 1922 University Ave., Madison 53705. Tel. 608-231-1513.

Wyoming

Memb. (Indiv.) 450; (Inst.) 21; (Subscribers) 24. Term of Office. Oct. 1988–Sept. 1989. Publication. *Wyoming Library Roundup* (tri-mo.). *Ed.* Linn Rounds, Wyoming State Lib., Cheyenne 82002.

Pres. Jerome W. Krois, Wyoming State Lib., Cheyenne 82002. Tel. 307-777-7281; *V.P./Pres.-Elect.* Susan M. Simpson, Albany County Public Lib., Laramie 82070. Tel. 307-745-4376; *Exec. Secy.* Kay Nord, Box 304, Laramie 82070. Tel. 307-745-8662.

Address correspondence to the executive secretary.

Canada

Alberta

Memb. 500. Term of Office. July 1–June 30. Publication. *Letter of the L.A.A.* (6 per year). *Ed.* Box 1357, Edmonton T5J 2N2.

Pres. Ann Curry, Southgate Branch Edmonton Public Lib., 48 Southgate Mall, Edmonton T6H 4M6; *V.P.* Alan MacDonald, MacKimmie Lib., Univ. of Calgary, Calgary T2N 1N4; *Treas.* Chandra Emann, 55 Rae Crescent S.E., Medicine Hat T1B 3C8; *Past Pres.* Peter Freeman, Cameron Lib., Univ. of Alberta, Edmonton T6G 2J8; *Exec. Secy.* Carol O'Hanlon, 356 Rehwinkel Close, Edmonton T6R 1M6.

Address correspondence to the president, Box 1357, Edmonton T5J 2N2.

British Columbia

Memb. 750. Term of Office. May 1988–Apr. 1989. Publication. *BCLA Reporter. Ed.* Tony Kelly.

Pres. G. W. Brian Owen. Tel. 604-430-6010; *V.P./Pres.-Elect.* Paula Pick.

Address correspondence to the president, BCLA, #300 3665 Kingsway, Vancouver V5R 5W2.

Manitoba

Memb. 300. Term of Office. Spring 1988–Spring 1989. Publications. *Manitoba Library Association Bulletin* (q.); *Newsline* (mo.).

Pres. Earle C. Ferguson, Box 176, Winnipeg R3C 2G9. Tel. 204-943-4567.

Address correspondence to the president.

Ontario

Memb. Over 3,300. Term of Office. Nov. 1988–Nov. 1989. Publications. *Focus* (q.); *Inside OLA* (mo.); *The Reviewing Librarian* (q.).

Pres. Peter Rogers, 145 Violet Dr., Stoney Creek L8E 3J2; *1st V.P.* Wil Vanderelst, 66 Fairview Ave., Toronto M6P 3A4; *2nd V.P.* Sandra Nash, Atikokan Public Lib. Bd., Civic Centre, Atikokan P0T 1C0; *Treas.* Larry Peterson, Metropolitan Toronto Reference Lib., 789 Yonge St., Toronto M4W 2G8; *Exec. Dir.* Larry Moore.

Address correspondence to Ontario Lib. Assn., 100 Richmond St. E., Suite 300, Toronto M5C 2P9. Tel. 416-363-3388.

Quebec

Memb. (Indiv.) 170; (Inst.) 42; (Commercial) 7. Term of Office. May 1988–May 1989. Publications. *ABQ/QLA Bulletin* (3 per year); *QASL Newsletter* (3 per year).

Pres. Molly Walsh, Montreal Children's Lib., 1200 Atwater, Montreal H3Z 1X4. Tel. 514-931-2304; *V.P./Pres.-Elect.* Barbara Hiron, Beaconsfield Public Lib., 303 Beaconsfield Blvd., Beaconsfield H9W 4A2. Tel. 514-697-9040; *Exec. Secy.* Marie Eberlin,

Quebec Lib. Assn., Box 2216, Dorval H9S 5J4. Tel. 514-630-4875.

Saskatchewan

Memb. 200. Term of Office. July 1988–June 1989. Publication. *Saskatchewan Library Association. Forum* (5 per year).

Pres. Susan Clark, Saskatoon Public Lib., 311 23rd St. E., Saskatoon S7K 0J6. Tel. 306-975-7566.

Address correspondence to the association, Box 3388, Regina S4P 3H1. Tel. 306-586-3089.

Regional

Atlantic Provinces: N.B., Nfld., N.S., P.E.I.

Memb. (Indiv.) 350; (Inst.) 40. Term of Office. May 1, 1988–Apr. 30, 1989. Publications. *APLA Bulletin* (bi-mo.); *APLA Proceedings; APLA Membership Directory.*

Pres. Gwen Creelman; *Past Pres.* Joy Tillotson; *V.P. Nova Scotia.* Gwyn Pace; *V.P. Prince Edward Island.* Bill Masselink; *V.P. New Brunswick.* Gerard Lavoie; *V.P. Newfoundland.* Allison Mews; *Secy.* Moira Davidson; *Treas.* Elaine Toms; *V.P. Membership.* Pat Belier; *APLA Bulletin Ed.* Andrea John.

Address correspondence to Atlantic Provinces Lib. Assn., c/o School of Lib. and Info. Studies, Dalhousie Univ., Halifax, N.S. B3H 4H8.

Middle Atlantic: Del., D.C., Md., N.J., W.Va.

Term of Office. June 1988–July 1989.

Pres. Kitty Hurrey, Southern Maryland Regional Lib., Box 459, Charlotte Hall, MD 20622. Tel. 301-934-9448; *V.P.* Ernest P. Kallay, Jr., Lib. Dir., Ohio County Lib., 52 116th St., Wheeling, WV 26003. Tel. 304-232-0244; *Secy.* Carolyn Royce, Ocean County Lib., 101 Washington St., Toms River, NJ 08753. Tel. 201-349-6200; *Treas.* Darrell Lemke, Consortium of Univs., Suite 101, 1717 Massachusetts Ave. N.W., Washington, DC 20036. Tel. 202-332-1894, 1895.

Address correspondence to the president.

Midwest: Ill., Ind., Minn., Ohio

Term of Office. Oct. 1988–Nov. 1991.

Pres. James L. Wells, Dir., Washington County Lib., 2150 Radio Dr., Woodbury, MN 555125. Tel. 612-731-8487; *V.P.* Patricia Llerandi, Schaumburg Township Lib., 32 W. Library Lane, Schaumburg, IL 60194. Tel. 312-885-3373 ext. 112; *Secy.* Barbara B. Fischler, IUPUI Univ. Libs., 815 W. Michigan St., Indianapolis, IN 46202. Tel. 317-274-0462; *Treas.* Bonnie Beth Mitchell, Ohio Lib. Assn., 40 S. Third St., Suite 230, Columbus, OH 43215. Tel. 614-221-9057; *Past Pres.* Walter D. Morrill, The Duggan Lib., Hanover College, Box 287, Hanover, IN 47243. Tel. 812-866-2151 ext. 333.

Address correspondence to the President, Midwest Federation of Lib. Assns.

Mountain Plains: Ariz., Colo., Kans., Mont., Nebr., Nev., N. Dak., S. Dak., Utah, Wyo.

Memb. 870. Term of Office. One year. Publications. *MPLA Newsletter* (bi-mo.). *Ed. and Adv. Mgr.* Jim Dertien, Sioux Falls Public Lib., 201 N. Main Ave., Sioux Falls, SD 57102. Tel. 605-339-7115; *Membership Directory* (ann.).

Pres. Jerry Kaup, Minot North Dakota Public Lib., 516 Second Ave. S.W., Minot, ND 58701. Tel. 701-852-1045; *Exec. Secy.* Joe Edelen, I.D. Weeks Lib., Univ. of South Dakota, Vermillion, SD 57069. Tel. 605-677-6082.

New England: Conn., Mass., Maine, N.H., R.I., Vt.

Memb. (Indiv.) 1,200; (Inst.) 100. Term of Office. One year (*Treas., Dirs.* two years). Publication. *NELA Newsletter* (6 per year). *Ed.* Frank Ferro, 35 Tuttle Place, East Haven, CT 06512.

Pres. Michael York, Univ. of New Hampshire/Manchester Lib., 220 Hackett Hill Rd., Manchester, NH 03102. Tel. 603-668-0700; *V.P./Pres.-Elect.* Richard Olsen, Adams Lib., Rhode Island College, 600 Mt. Pleasant Ave., Providence, RI 02908. Tel. 401-456-8052; *Secy.* Judith Allen, Springfield City Lib., 220 State St., Springfield, MA 01103. Tel. 413-739-3871 ext. 204; *Treas.* Libby Coombs, Fairfield Univ. Lib., Fairfield, CT 06430. Tel. 203-254-4404; *Past Pres.* Christine Kardokas, Worcester Public Lib., Salem Sq., Worcester, MA 01608. Tel. 617-799-1726; *Dirs.* Grace Greene, Vermont Dept. of Libs., State Office Bldg. PO, Montpelier, VT 05602. Tel. 802-828-3261; Janet A. Levesque, Cumberland Public Lib., 1464 Diamond Hill Rd., Cumberland, RI 02864. Tel. 401-333-2552; *Exec. Secy.* Paula M. Bozoian, New England Lib. Assn., Box 421, Wakefield, MA 01880. Tel. 617-438-7179.

Address correspondence to the executive secretary at association headquarters.

Pacific Northwest: Alaska, Idaho, Mont., Oreg., Wash., Alberta, B.C.

Memb. (Active) 982; (Subscribers) 220. Term of Office. (*Pres., 1st V.P.*) Oct. 1, 1988–Sept. 30, 1989. Publication. *PNLA Quarterly. Ed.* Kappy Eaton, 1631 E. 24 Ave., Eugene, OR 97403.

Pres. George Smith, Alaska State Lib., Box G, Juneau, AK 99801. Tel. 907-465-2910; *1st V.P.* Carol Hildebrand, Eugene Public Lib., 100 W. 13, Eugene, OR 97401; *2nd V.P.* Ann Joslin, Idaho State Lib., 325 W. State St., Boise, ID 83702; *Secy.* June Pinnell-Stephens, 3140 Roden Lane, Fairbanks, AK 99701; *Treas.* Adrien Taylor, Boise State Univ. Lib., 2120 Cataldo Dr., Boise, ID 83705.

Address correspondence to the president.

Southeastern: Ala., Fla., Ga., Ky., La., Miss., N.C., S.C., Tenn., Va., W. Va.

Memb. 2,000. Term of Office. Oct. 1988–Oct. 1990. Publication. *The Southeastern Librarian* (q.).

Pres. George R. Stewart, Birmingham Public Lib., 2100 Park Place, Birmingham, AL 35203. Tel. 205-226-3611; *V.P./Pres.-Elect.* James E. Ward, Southeastern Lib. Assn., Crisman Memorial Lib., Box 4146, David Lipscomb College, Nashville, TN 37204-3951; *Secy.* Myra Jo Wilson, 1604 Bellavista Rd., Cleveland, MS 38732; *Treas.* Wanda J. Calhoun, East Central Georgia Regional Lib., 902 Greene St., Augusta, GA 30901; *Exec. Secy.* Claudia Medori, SELA, Box 987, Tucker, GA 30085. Tel. 404-939-5080.

Address correspondence to SELA, Executive Secretary.

State Library Agencies

The state library administrative agencies in each of the states will have the latest information on their state plan for the use of federal funds under the Library Services and Construction Act. The directors and addresses of these state agencies are listed below.

Alabama

Blane Dessy, Dir., Alabama Public Lib. Service, 6030 Monticello Dr., Montgomery 36130. Tel. 205-277-7330.

Alaska

Karen Crane, Dir., Alaska State Lib., Dept. of Educ., Box G, Juneau 99811-0571. Tel. 907-465-2910.

Arizona

Sharon Womack, State Libn., Dept. of Lib., Archives, and Public Records, 1700 W. Washington, State Capitol, Phoenix 85007-2896. Tel. 602-542-4035.

Arkansas

John A. (Pat) Murphey, Jr., State Libn., Arkansas State Lib., One Capitol Mall, Little Rock 72201-1081. Tel. 501-682-1526 or 2848.

California

Gary E. Strong, State Libn., California State Lib., Box 942837, Sacramento 95814-3324. Tel. 916-445-2585 or 4027.

Colorado

Nancy M. Bolt, Asst. Commissioner, Colorado State Lib., 201 E. Colfax, Denver 80203. Tel. 303-866-6733.

Connecticut

Richard Akeroyd, State Libn., Connecticut State Lib., 231 Capitol Ave., Hartford 06106. Tel. 203-566-4192.

Delaware

Frances West, Secy., Dept. of Community Affairs, Box 1401, 156 S. State St., Dover 19903. Tel. 302-736-4456.

District of Columbia

Hardy R. Franklin, Dir., D.C. Public Lib., 901 G St. N.W., Washington 20001. Tel. 202-727-1101.

Florida

Barratt Wilkins, State Libn., State Lib. of Florida, R. A. Gray Bldg., Tallahassee 32399-0250. Tel. 904-487-2651.

Georgia

Joe Forsee, Dir., Div. of Public Lib. Services, 156 Trinity Ave. S.W., Atlanta 30303-3692. Tel. 404-656-2461.

Hawaii

Bartholomew A. Kane, Asst. Supt./State Libn., Office of Lib. Services, Research and Evaluation Services Section, 465 S. King St., Rm. B-1, Honolulu 96813. Tel. 808-548-5585 or 86, 87, 88.

Idaho

Charles A. Bolles, State Libn., Idaho State Lib., 325 W. State St., Boise 83702. Tel. 208-334-5124.

Illinois

Bridget L. Lamont, Dir., Illinois State Lib., Centennial Memorial Bldg., Springfield 62756-2296. Tel. 207-782-2994.

Indiana

C. Ray Ewick, Dir., Indiana State Lib., 140 N. Senate Ave., Indianapolis 46204-2296. Tel. 317-232-3692.

Iowa

Shirley George, Dir., State Lib. of Iowa, Dept. of Cultural Affairs, E. 12th and Grand, Des Moines 50319. Tel. 515-281-4105.

Kansas

Duane F. Johnson, State Libn., Kansas State Lib., 3rd fl., State Capitol, Topeka 66612-1593. Tel. 913-296-3296.

Kentucky

James A. Nelson, State Libn. and Commissioner, Kentucky Dept. for Libs. and Archives, Box 537, Frankfort 40602-0537. Tel. 502-875-7000.

Louisiana

Thomas F. Jaques, State Libn., Louisiana State Lib., Box 313, Baton Rouge 70821-0131. Tel. 504-342-4923.

Maine

J. Gary Nichols, State Libn., Maine State Lib., State House Sta. 64, Augusta 04333. Tel. 207-289-3561.

Maryland

Maurice Travillian, Asst. State Supt. for Libs., Div. of Lib. Development and Services, Maryland State Dept. of Educ., 200 W. Baltimore St., Baltimore 21201-2595. Tel. 301-333-2112.

Massachusetts

Roland R. Piggford, Dir., Massachusetts Bd. of Lib. Commissioners, 648 Beacon St., Boston 02215. Tel. 617-267-9400.

Michigan

James W. Fry, State Libn., Lib. of Michigan, Box 30007, Lansing 48909. Tel. 517-373-1580.

Minnesota

William G. Asp, Dir., Office of Lib. Development and Services, Minnesota Dept. of

Educ., 440 Capitol Sq. Bldg., 550 Cedar St., St. Paul 55101. Tel. 612-296-2821.

Mississippi

David M. Woodburn, Dir., Mississippi Lib. Commission, 1221 Ellis Ave., Box 10700, Jackson 39209-0700. Tel. 601-359-1036.

Missouri

Monteria Hightower, Assoc. Commissioner for Libs. & State Libn., Missouri State Lib., Box 387, Jefferson City 65102-0387. Tel. 314-751-2751.

Montana

Deborah Schlesinger, State Libn., Montana State Lib., 1515 E. Sixth Ave., Helena 59620. Tel. 406-444-3115.

Nebraska

Rod Wagner, Dir., Nebraska Lib. Commission, 1420 P St., Lincoln 68505. Tel. 402-471-2045.

Nevada

Joan Kerschner, State Libn., Nevada State Lib., Capitol Complex, Carson City 89710. Tel. 702-885-5130.

New Hampshire

Matthew Higgins, State Libn., New Hampshire State Lib., 20 Park St., Concord 03301-6303. Tel. 603-271-2393.

New Jersey

Barbara F. Weaver, Asst. Commissioner for Educ./State Libn., Div. of State Lib., Archives and History, 185 W. State St., Trenton 08625-0520. Tel. 609-292-6201.

New Mexico

Virginia Hendley, State Libn., New Mexico State Lib., 325 Don Gaspar St., Santa Fe 87503. Tel. 505-827-3804.

New York

Joseph F. Shubert, State Libn./Asst. Commissioner for Libs., New York State Lib., Rm. 10C34, C.E.C., Empire State Plaza, Albany 12230. Tel. 518-474-5930.

North Carolina

Jane Williams, Dir./State Libn., Dept. of Cultural Resources, Div. of State Lib., 109 E. Jones St., Raleigh 27611. Tel. 919-733-2570.

North Dakota

Patricia Harris, State Libn., North Dakota State Lib., Liberty Memorial Bldg., Capitol Grounds, Bismarck 58505. Tel. 701-224-2492.

Ohio

Richard M. Cheski, Dir., State Lib. of Ohio, 65 S. Front St., Columbus 43266-0334. Tel. 614-644-7061.

Oklahoma

Robert L. Clark, Jr., Dir., Oklahoma Dept. of Libs., 200 N.E. 18th St., Oklahoma City 73105-3298. Tel. 405-521-2502.

Oregon

Wesley A. Doak, State Libn., Oregon State Lib., Salem 97310. Tel. 503-378-4367.

Pennsylvania

Sara Parker, State Libn., State Lib. of Pennsylvania, Box 1601, Harrisburg 17105. Tel. 717-787-2646.

Puerto Rico

Awilda Aponte Roque, Secy., Dept. of Educ., Apdo. 759, Box 11496, Hato Rey 00919. Tel. 809-751-5572.

Rhode Island

Bruce Daniels, State Libn., Rhode Island Dept. of State Lib. Services, 300 Richmond St., Providence 02903-4222. Tel. 401-277-2726.

South Carolina

Betty E. Callaham, Dir., South Carolina State Lib., 1500 Senate St., Box 11496, Columbia 29211. Tel. 803-734-8666.

South Dakota

Jane Kolbe, State Libn., South Dakota State Lib. and Archives, 800 Governors Dr., Pierre 57501-2294. Tel. 605-773-3131.

Tennessee

Gentry Crowell, Secy. of State, G-13 John Sevier Bldg., Nashville 37219.

Edwin Gleaves, State Libn. and Archivist, Tennessee State Lib. and Archives, 403 Seventh Ave. N., Nashville 37219. Tel. 615-741-3158.

Texas

William Gooch, Dir. and Libn., Texas State Lib., Box 12927, Capitol Sta., Austin 78711. Tel. 512-463-5460.

Utah

Amy Owen, Dir., Utah State Lib., 2150 S. 300 West, Suite 16, Salt Lake City 84115. Tel. 801-466-5888.

Vermont

Patricia E. Klinck, State Libn., State of Vermont, Dept. of Libs., c/o State Office Bldg., Post Office, Montpelier 05602. Tel. 802-828-3256.

Virginia

Ella Gaines Yates, State Libn., Virginia State Lib., Richmond 23219. Tel. 804-786-2332.

Washington

Nancy Zussy, State Libn., Washington State Lib. AJ-11, Olympia 98504-0001. Tel. 206-753-2915.

West Virginia

Frederic J. Glazer, Dir., West Virginia Lib. Commission, Science and Cultural Ctr., Charleston 25305. Tel. 304-348-2041.

Wisconsin

Leslyn M. Shires, Asst. Supt., Div. for Lib. Services, Wisconsin Dept. of Public Instruction, 125 S. Webster St., Box 7841, Madison 53707-7841. Tel. 608-266-2205.

Wyoming

Wayne H. Johnson, State Libn., Wyoming State Lib., Supreme Court Bldg., Cheyenne 82002. Tel. 307-777-7283.

American Samoa

Sailautusi Avegalio, Federal Grants Mgr., Dept. of Educ., Box 1329, Pago Pago 96799. Tel. 633-5237.

Guam

Frank R. San Agustin, Territorial Libn., Nieves M. Flores Memorial Lib., 254 Martyr St., Agana 96910. Tel. 671-472-6417.

Republic of the Marshall Islands

Kinija Andrike, Secy., Dept. of Educ., Rep. of the Marshall Islands, Box 3, Majuro 96960.

Federated States of Micronesia

Duro Weitel, Dir., Office of Educ., Natl. Government, FSM, Kolomia, Pohnpei, East Caroline Islands 96941.

Northern Mariana Islands

Dir. of Lib. Services, Commonwealth of the Northern Mariana Islands, Saipan 96950.

Republic of Palau

William Tabelual, Dir., Dept. of Social Services, Bureau of Educ., Box 189, Koror 96940.

Virgin Islands

Jeanette Allis, Dir., Bureau of Libs., Archives and Museums, Dept. of Planning and Natural Resources, 179 Altona and Welgunst, Charlotte Amalie, St. Thomas 00802. Tel. 809-774-3407; St. Croix: 809-773-5715.

State School Library Media Associations

Unless otherwise specified, correspondence to an association listed in this section is to be addressed to the secretary or executive secretary in the entry.

Alabama

Alabama Lib. Assn., Children's and School Libns. Div. Memb. 450. Term of Office. Apr. 1988–Apr. 1989. Publication. *Alabama Librarian* (9 per year).

Chpn. Carol Johnson, 353 Lucerne Blvd., Birmingham 35209. Tel. 205-879-2361 or 205-321-4467; *Chpn.-Elect.* Edith Harwell, 2636 Buckboard Rd., Birmingham 35244. Tel. 205-991-7971 or 205-995-9931; *Secy.* Tywanna Burton, 607 Candle Lane, Birmingham 35214. Tel. 205-798-0979 or 205-979-3030.

Address correspondence to Sandra Sutton, Executive Secretary, Box 601, Helena 35080.

Arizona

School Lib. Media Div., Arizona State Lib. Assn. Memb. 440. Term of Office. Nov. 1988–Oct. 1989. Publication. *ASLA Newsletter*.

Pres. Sharon A. Herron, 3538 E. Ellington Place, Tucson 85713. Tel. 602-798-2552; *Pres.-Elect.* Betty Marcoux, Rincon H.S., 422 N. Arcadia Blvd., Tucson 85711. Tel. 602-745-4740; *Secy.* Jan Strell, Howell School, Tucson 85711. Tel. 602-798-2542.

Address correspondence to the president.

Arkansas

Arkansas Assn. of School Lib. Media Educators. Term of Office. Oct. 1988–Oct. 1989.

Chpn. Iris Tucker, Bayou Meto Elementary, Rte. 2, Box 200, Jacksonville 72076. Tel. 501-988-4131; *V. Chpn.* Kay Bland, Pulaski County Special School Dist., 1500 Dixon Rd., Little Rock 72216. Tel. 501-490-2000; *Secy.-Treas.* Carolyn Leonard, Greenland H.S., Box 57, Greenland 72737.

California

California Media and Lib. Educators Assn. (CMLEA), Suite 142, 1499 Old Bayshore Hwy., Burlingame 94010. Tel. 415-692-2350. Job Hotline. Tel. 415-697-8832. Memb. 1,400. Term of Office. June 1988–May 1989. Publication. *CMLEA Journal*.

Pres. Janis Kessler, Bakersfield City School Dist., 1300 Baker St., Bakersfield 93305; *Pres. Elect.* Jim Fryer, Alameda County Office of Education, 313 W. Winton Ave., Hayward 94544; *Secy.* Mary Morrison, Amador County Unified School Dist., 217 Bex Ave., Jackson 95642; *Treas.* Margery Findlay, Rio Linda U.S.D., 6450 20th St., Rio Linda 95673; *Business Office Secy.* Nancy D. Kohn, CMLEA, 1499 Old Bayshore Hwy., Suite 142, Burlingame 94010.

Colorado

Colorado Educational Media Assn. Memb. 680. Term of Office. Feb. 1988–Feb. 1989. Publication. *The Medium* (mo.).

Pres. Ted Benson, 7044 E. Maplewood Place, Englewood 80111; *Exec. Secy.* Terry Walljasper, Colorado Educational Media Assn., Box 22814, Wellshire Sta., Denver 80222.

Address correspondence to the executive secretary.

Connecticut

Connecticut Educational Media Assn. Term of Office. May 1988–May 1989. Publication. CEMA videotape "The School Library Media Specialist – A Continuing Story," available in ½″ ($35) or ¾″ Umatic ($40).

Pres. Harriet Selverstone, 31 Bonnie Brook Rd., Westport 06880. Tel. 203-226-6236; *V.P.* Eugene Lunch, Bill Hill Rd., Lyme 06371. Tel. 203-434-7062; *Secy.* Barbara Campbell, 88 Deepwood Dr., Avon 06001. Tel. 203-693-0594; *Treas.* William Secord, 87 Johnson Rd., Marlborough 06447. Tel. 203-295-9725.

Address correspondence to Anne Weimann, Administrative Secy., 25 Elmwood Ave., Trumbull 06611. Tel. 203-372-2260.

Delaware

Delaware School Lib. Media Assn., Div. of Delaware Lib. Assn. Memb. 92. Term of Office. Apr. 1988–Apr. 1989. Publications.

DSLMA Newsletter (irreg.); column in *DLA Bulletin* (3 per year).

Pres. Joseph Gates, Laurel Central Middle School, 801 Central Ave., Laurel 19956. Tel. 302-875-6110; *V.P./Pres.-Elect.* Marjorie Williams, Lake Forest North Elementary School, Main St., Felton 19943; *Secy.* Elizabeth Eldridge, McVey Elementary School, 908 Janice Dr., Newark 19713.

District of Columbia

D.C. Assn. of School Libns. Memb. 93. Term of Office. Aug. 1987–July 1989. Publication. *Newsletter* (4 per year).

Pres. Patricia Bonds, Elliot Jr. H.S., 18 and Constitution Ave N.E., Washington 20002. Tel. 202-724-4665; *Corres. Secy.* Sharon Sorrels, Stuart-Hobson Middle School, 410 E. St. N. E., Washington 20002. Tel. 202-724-4758.

Address correspondence to the corresponding secretary.

Florida

Florida Assn. for Media in Education, Inc. Memb. 1,450. Term of Office. Oct. 1988–Oct. 1989. Publication. *Florida Media Quarterly. Ed.* Mary Newman, Box 530425, Miami 33153-0425. Tel. 305-754-9345.

Pres. Shirley Pettit, 118 Lago Vista Blvd., Casselberry 32707. Tel. 305-423-9276; *V. Pres.* Jerry Barkholz, 12408 N. 52 St., Tampa 33617. Tel. 813-974-3460; *Pres.-Elect.* Maureen Skinner, 2015 Trescott Dr., Tallahassee 32312. Tel. 904-488-8184; *Secy.* Linda Edwards, 1641 Crescent Rd., Longwood 32750. Tel. 407-644-0229; *Treas.* Sherie Bargar, 143 Lago Vista Blvd., Casselberry 32707. Tel. 407-422-3200 ext. 636.

Address correspondence to the association executive, Mary Margaret Rogers, Box 13119, Tallahassee 32317. Tel. 904-893-5396.

Georgia

Georgia Lib./Media Assn. (GLMA). Memb. 1,050. Term of Office. May 1–Apr. 30. Publications. *The Media News Leader* (newsletter, q.); *The Media Educator* (journal).

Pres. Diane D. Myers, Fulton County Schools, Atlanta; *Exec. Dir.* Gordon N. Baker, Clayton County Schools, Jonesboro.

Address correspondence to the Georgia Lib./Media Assn., Box 793, Rex 30273. Tel. 404-961-9824.

School Lib. Media Div., Georgia Lib. Assn. Term of Office. Oct. 1987–Oct. 1989.

Chpn. Sharon Self, Hardaway H.S., 2901 College Dr., Columbus 31995. Tel. 404-327-6527.

Address correspondence to the Georgia Lib. Assn., Box 833, Tucker 30084. Tel. 404-934-7118.

Hawaii

Hawaii Assn. of School Libns. Memb. 240. Term of Office. June 1988–May 1989.

Pres. Patsy Suyat, McKinley H.S. 1039 S. King St., Honolulu 96814. Tel. 808-536-1061; *V.P./Pres.-Elect.* Karen Muronaga, Lincoln School, 615 Auwaiolimu St., Honolulu 96813.

Address correspondence to the association, Box 23019, Honolulu 96822.

Idaho

Educational Media Div. of the Idaho Lib. Assn. Memb. 125. Term of Office. Oct. 1988–Oct. 1990. Publication. Column in *The Idaho Librarian* (q.).

Chpn. Ned Stokes, Homedale Jr./Sr. High, Box 187, Homedale 83628. Tel. 208-337-4613; *Secy.* Marie Scharnhorst, Box 115, Genesee 83832.

Address correspondence to the chairperson.

Illinois

Illinois Assn. for Media in Education (IAME), Sec. of the Illinois Lib. Assn. Memb. 410. Term of Office. Jan. 1989–Dec. 1989. Publication. *IAME News for You* (q.). *Ed.* Charles Rusiewski, 207 E. Chester, Nashville 62263.

Pres. Nancy Bloomstrand, 2586 Point O'Woods, Rockford 61111. Tel. 815-229-2492.

Address correspondence to the president.

Illinois School Lib. Media Assn. Memb.

400. Term of Office. July 1988–June 1989. Publication. *Newsletter* (10 per year). *Ed.* Pamela Kramer, 1501 N. Milwaukee Ave., Apt. 8A, Libertyville 60048.

Pres. Kay Maynard, 609 W. Douglas, Fairfield 62837. Tel. 618-842-2649 ext. 139.

Address correspondence to the president.

Indiana

Assn. for Indiana Media Educators. Memb. 950. Term of Office. (*Pres.*) May 1, 1988–Apr. 30, 1989. Publication. *Indiana Media Journal*.

Pres. Ann Daniels, 11705 Eden Estates Dr., Carmel 46032; *Exec. Secy.* Lawrence Reck, School of Education, Indiana State Univ., Terre Haute 47809. Tel. 812-237-2926.

Address correspondence to the executive secretary.

Iowa

Iowa Educational Media Assn. Memb. 550. Term of Office. Apr. 1988–Apr. 1989. Publication. *Iowa Media Message* (q.). *Ed.* Pat Severson, Clear Lake Community School, Clear Lake 50428.

Pres. Karlene Garn, Ames H.S., 20th and Ridgewood, Ames 50010. Tel. 515-232-8440; *Pres. Elect.* Arletta Dawson, Western Hills AEA, 1520 Morningside, Sioux City 51106; *Secy.* Paula Murrell, 6400 Townsend, Urbandale 50322; *Treas.* Loretta Moon, Iowa Falls H.S., Iowa Falls 50126. Tel. 515-684-2500; *Dirs.* (1989) Jeanne Dugdale, Mark Henderson, Susan Schrader; (1990) Donna Granneman, Mary Jo Langhorne, Anita Jacob; (1991) Mary Lou Bayless, James Johnson, Kathy Kreykes.

Address correspondence to the president.

Kansas

Kansas Assn. of School Libns. Memb. 700. Term of Office. July 1988–June 1989. Publication. *KASL Newsletter* (s. ann.).

Pres. Joyce Funk, 916 S.E. Croco Rd., Topeka 66605. Tel. 913-233-1916; *V.P./Pres.-Elect.* Betsy Losey, Roosevelt Elementary School, 2000 MacArthur, Hays 67601. Tel. 913-625-2565; *Treas.* Dannette Schmidt, 2092 Norton, Salina 67401. Tel. 913-827-4018; *Secy.* Kathy Schneider, 1622 Center, Garden City 67846. Tel. 316-275-6859; *Busn. Mgr.* Kay Mounkes, Westridge Middle School, 9300 Nieman, Shawnee Mission 66214. Tel. 913-888-5214 ext. 14.

Address correspondence to the business manager.

Kentucky

Kentucky School Media Assn. Memb. 628. Term of Office. Oct. 1988–Oct. 1989. Publication. *KSMA Newsletter.*

Pres. Candace Wilson, Rte. 3, Box 375, Russell Springs 42642. Tel. 502-343-3644 or 502-866-2224; *Pres.-Elect.* Sandy Douglas, 442 U.S. 60, Ashland 41101; *Secy.* Judy Burchett, Rte. 1, Box 441, Springfield 40069; *Treas.* Hertha Smith, 8883 Valley Circle Dr., Florence 41042.

Address correspondence to the president.

Louisiana

Louisiana Assn. of School Libns., c/o Louisiana Lib. Assn., Box 3058, Baton Rouge 70821. Memb. 437. Term of Office. July 1, 1988–June 30, 1989.

Pres. Cathy Black, 13926 Katherine Ave., Baton Rouge 70815. Tel. (off.) 504-622-4004; (home) 504-275-2711.

Maine

Maine Educational Media Assn. Memb. 250. Term of Office. May 1988–May 1989. Publication. *Mediacy* (q.).

Pres. Abigail Garthwait, Asa Adams Elementary School, Orono 04473. Tel. 207-866-2151; *Pres.-Elect.* Jo Hipsher, Brunswick H.S., Brunswick 04011; *V.P.* Jeri Ann Holt, Erskine Academy, RFD 6, Augusta 04330; *Secy.* Lorraine Stickney, Gorham H.S., 41 Morrill Ave., Gorham 04038; *Treas.* Joyce Bell, Boothbay Region H.S., Boothbay Harbor 04538.

Address correspondence to the president.

Maryland

Maryland Educational Media Organization (MEMO). Term of Office. Nov. 1, 1988–Oct.

31, 1989. Publication. *MEMORANDOM* (q.).

Pres. Thea Jones, 4517 Alpine Rose Bend, Ellicott City 21043; *Secy.* Celeste Brecht, 4725 Salterforth Place, Ellicott City 21043; *Treas.* Richard Ashford, 420 Ridge Rd., #4, Greenbelt 20770.

Address correspondence to the president.

Massachusetts

Massachusetts Assn. for Educational Media. Memb. 500. Term of Office. June 1, 1988–May 31, 1989. Publication. *Media Forum* (q.).

Pres. Roxanne B. Mendrinos, EWT Jr. High, Westwood 02090. Tel. 617-326-7500 ext. 50 & 51; *V.P./Pres.-Elect.* Audrey Friend, 3 Wachusetts Circle, Lexington 02173. Tel. 617-862-4654. *Secy.* John LeBaron, Univ. of Lowell, One University Ave., Lowell 01854. Tel. 617-452-5000. *Treas.* John Earley, Redford H.S., 489 Winthrop St., Redford 02155. Tel. 617-396-5800.

Address correspondence to Nancy Johnson, Admin. Asst., 41 Waverly St., Brookline 02146. Tel. 617-566-5645.

Michigan

Michigan Assn. for Media in Education (MAME). Term of Office. One year.

Pres. Ricki Chowning, East Grand Rapids H.S., 2211 Lake Dr. S.E., Grand Rapids 49506. Tel. 616-459-9933; *Secy.* Normayne Jakubek, Lake Orion H.S., 455 E. Scripps Rd., Lake Orion 48035. Tel. 616-693-5420; *Treas.* Susan Schwartz, Charlotte H.S., 378 State, Charlotte 48813. Tel. 616-543-4340; *Past Pres.* Bernice Lamkin, REMC-7 Dir., OAISD, 13565 Port Sheldon Rd., Holland 49424. Tel. 616-399-6490; *Pres.-Elect.* Teddy Vandefifer, Carman-Ainsworth Community School, 1181 W. Scottwood, Flint 48507. Tel. 313-235-3565; *V.P. for Special Groups.* Jean Liming, Elementary Media Dept., Lapeer Community Schools, 1920 Oregon, Lapeer 48446. Tel. 313-664-9632; *V.P. for Regions.* Sally Kelly-Sewell, Vicksburg Middle School, E. Prairie St., Vicksburg 49097. Tel. 616-649-0552.

Address correspondence to M.A.M.E., c/o REMC-8, Ottawa Area Intermediate School Dist., 13565 Port Sheldon Rd., Holland 49424. Contact person: Bernice Lamkin. Tel. 616-399-6940.

Minnesota

Minnesota Educational Media Organization. Memb. 900. Term of Office. (*Pres.*) May 1988–May 1989 (other offices 2 years in alternating years). Publications. *Minnesota Media; ImMEDIAte.*

Pres. Shirley J. Christenson, 326 Rice St., Anoka 55303. Tel. 612-421-1016 or 612-422-5303; *Pres.-Elect.* Gail Jubala, 2831 Greysolon Rd., Duluth 55812; *Past Pres.* Tim Eklund, Rte. 1, Box 97, Rush City 55069; *Secy.* Susan Haggberg, 3116 Irving Ave. S., Minneapolis 55408.

Mississippi

Mississippi Lib. Assn., Educational Communications and Technology Roundtable. Memb. 86. Term of Office. Oct. 1988–Oct. 1989.

Chpn. Josie Roberts, Purvis Elementary School, Box 267, Purvis 39475. Tel. 601-794-2959. *V. Chpn.* Scott R. Johnson, Meridian Community College, 550 Hwy. 19 N., Meridian 39301. *Secy./Treas.* Kathey Abbey, 17 39th Ct., Meridian 39301; *Newsletter Ed.* Temple Lymbaris, MS. ETV, Drawer 1101, Jackson 39205.

Address correspondence to the association, Box 20448, Jackson 39289-1448.

Missouri

Missouri Assn. of School Libns. (MASL). Memb. 850. Term of Office. June 1988–May 1989.

Pres. Beth Lilleston, Clinton Middle School, 820 Fox Run Dr., Clinton 64735. Tel. 816-885-3353; *V.P./Pres.-Elect.* Floyd Pentlin, Lee's Summit H.S., 520 Grover, Warrensburg 64093. Tel. 816-747-2196.

Address correspondence to MASL, Box 22476, Kansas City 64113-2476. Tel. 816-361-9175.

Montana

Montana School Lib. Media, Div. of Montana Lib. Assn. Memb. 170. Term of Office. June 1988–June 1989.

Pres. Dale Alger, Central School, 600 First St. W., Roundup 59072. Tel. 406-323-1512; *V.P./Pres.-Elect.* John Meckler, Plains Public School, Plains 59859.

Address correspondence to the president.

Nebraska

Nebraska Educational Media. Assn. Memb. 350. Term of Office. July 1, 1988–June 30, 1989. Publication. *NEMA News* (4 per year). *Ed.* Dick Allen, 1420 P St., Lincoln 68508.

Pres. Alan Wibbels, Central City H.S., Central City 68826. Tel. 308-946-3086; *Pres.-Elect.* Bonnie Zetterman, Southeast Community College, 8800 "O" St., Lincoln 68520. Tel. 402-471-3333; *Past Pres.* LaJean Price, 1225 Idylwild Dr., Lincoln 68503. Tel. 402-464-6541; *Secy.* Eunice Parrish, Tecumseh H.S. Box 338, Tecumseh 68450. Tel. 402-335-3328; *Treas.* Mary Lou Bayless, IRC, Loess Hills AEA #3, Box 1109, Council Bluffs, IA 51502. Tel. 712-366-0507.

Address correspondence to the president.

Nevada

Nevada School and Children's Lib. Assn., Div. of Nevada Lib. Assn. Memb. 50. Term of Office. Jan. 1, 1989–Dec. 31, 1990. Publication. *NSCLA Newsletter* (q.). *Ed.* Lee Gordon, 3209 University Ct., Las Vegas 89121.

Pres. Christy Strange, Box 815, Virginia City 89440.

Address correspondence to the president.

New Hampshire

New Hampshire Educational Media Assn. Memb. 250. Term of Office. June 1988–June 1989. Publication. *Online* (5 per year).

Pres. Trudy Baldwin, Timberlane Jr. H.S., Plaistow 03865; *V.P.* Sandra Elder, Moultonborough Schools, Moultonborough 03254. Tel. 603-476-5517; *Treas.* Jeff Kent, Broken Ground School, Concord 03301; *Rec. Secy.* Joyce Kendall, Fall Mt. Regional H.S., R.R. 1, Alstead 03602; *Corres. Secy.* Marion Pierce, Merrimack Valley H.S., Penacook 03303.

Address correspondence to the president.

New Jersey

Educational Media Assn. of New Jersey (EMAnj). (Organized Apr. 1977 through merger of New Jersey School Media Assn. and New Jersey Assn. of Educational Communication and Technology.) Memb. 1,000. Term of Office. June 1988–June 1989. Publications. *Signal Tab* (newsletter, mo.); *Emanations* (journal, 2 per year).

Pres. Sheila Berkelhammer, 147 Laurel Rd., Princeton 08540; *Pres.-Elect.* Hilda Weisburg, 38 Indigo Lane, Aberdeen 07747; *Rec. Secy.* Patricia Priesing, 323 Burd St., Pennington 08534; *Corres. Secy.* Joan Robbins, Box 113, Dorothy 08317; *Treas.* Robert Bonardi, 41 Walnut Hill Lane, Freehold 07728.

Address correspondence to the president.

New Mexico

New Mexico Lib. Assn., School Libs. Children and Young Adult Services Div. Memb. 240. Term of Office. Apr. 1989–Apr. 1990.

Chpn. Claire Odenheim, 715 Sundown Ct., Las Cruces 88001. Tel. 505-522-8814.

Address correspondence to the chairperson.

New York

School Lib. Media Sec./New York Lib. Assn., 15 Park Row, Suite 434, New York 10038. Tel. 212-227-8032. Memb. 1,000. Term of Office. Oct. 1988–Oct. 1989. Publications. *SLMS-gram* (q.); participates in *NYLA Bulletin* (mo. except July and Aug.).

Pres. Julia C. Van de Water, Dir. of Media Resources, Freeport Public Schools, Box 50, Freeport 11520. Tel. 516-867-5334; *V.P./Pres.-Elect.* Sheryl Egger, Coord. of Libs., West Irondequoit School Dist., 260 Cooper Rd., West Irondequoit 14617. Tel. 716-266-7351; *V.P., Conferences.* Robert Berkowitz, Wayne Central School Dist., Ontario Center Rd., Ontario Center 14520. Tel. 315-524-2811 ext. 237; *V.P., Communications.* Judy Gray, Nottingham H.S., 3100 E. Genesee St., Syracuse 13224. Tel. 315-425-6533; *Secy.* Carolyn Giambra, Dodge Elementary School, 1900 Dodge Rd., East Amherst 14051. Tel. 716-689-7051; *Treas.* Robert Dobbs, Cayuga-Onondaga BOCES, 234 South St., Auburn 13021. Tel. 315-253-0361 ext. 126; *Past Pres.* James Bennett, Shoreham-Wading River H.S., Rte. 25A, Shoreham 11786. Tel. 516-929-8500 ext. 237; *Bur. of School Lib. Media Programs Liaison.* Robert Barron, Chief, Bur. of School Lib. Media Programs, State Educ. Dept., Rm. 676, Education Bldg. Annex, Albany 12234. Tel. 518-474-2468; *Div. of*

Lib. Development Liaison. Joseph Mattie, Associate, Div. of Lib. Development, 10B41 Cultural Education Center, Empire State Plaza, Albany 12230. Tel. 518-474-4970.

Address correspondence to the president or secretary.

North Carolina

North Carolina Assn. of School Libns. Memb. 900. Term of Office. Oct. 1987–Oct. 1989.

Chpn. Carol Southerland, Lib. Media Coord., South Lenoir H.S., Deep Run 28525; *Chpn.-Elect*. Laura Benson, Coord. of Media Services, High Point Public Schools, 900 English Rd., Box 789, High Point 27261; *Secy*. Augie Beasley, Dir. of Media Services, East Mecklenberg H.S., 6800 Monroe Rd., Charlotte 28212; *Treas*. Shirley Ledford, Lib. Media Coord., Pink Hill Elementary School, Pink Hill 28572.

Address correspondence to the chairperson.

North Dakota

North Dakota Lib. Assn., School Lib. Media Sec. Memb. 81. Term of Office. One year. Publication. *The Good Stuff* (q.).

Pres. Diana Schneider, Williston Jr. H.S., 612 First Ave. W., Williston 58801. Tel. 701-572-1651; *Pres.-Elect*. Mary Ellen Rue, 430 First Ave. N., New Rockford 58356. Tel. 701-947-5036; *Secy*. Kristi Engle, Cando Public School, Cando 58324. Tel. 701-968-3163.

Address correspondence to the president.

Ohio

Ohio Educational Lib. Media Assn. Memb. 1,300. Term of Office. Jan. 1989–Dec. 1989. Publication. *Ohio Media Spectrum* (q.).

Pres. Marjorie Pappas, Wright State Univ., Lib. Science Communications; *Exec. Dir*. Ann W. Hanning, 40 S. Third St., #230, Columbus 43215. Tel. 614-221-9057.

Oklahoma

Oklahoma Assn. of School Lib. Media Specialists. Memb. 277. Term of Office. July 1, 1988–June 30, 1989. Publications. "School Library News" column in *Oklahoma Librarian* (q.); "Library Resources" section in *Oklahoma Educator* (mo.).

Chpn. Carol Casey, Muskogee Public Schools, West Jr. High, 6200 W. Okmulgee Ave., Muskogee 74401. *V. Chpn./Chpn.-Elect*. Mona Hatfield, Cascia Hall Preparatory School, 2520 S. Yorktown, Tulsa 74114; *Secy*. Carol Stookey, Broken Arrow Public Schools, Broken Arrow 74012. *Treas*. Evelyn J. Healey-Freedman, Norman Public Schools, Norman 73069. *Past Chpn*. Pat Cunninghamn, Tuttle Public Schools, Box H, Tuttle 73089.

Address correspondence to the chairperson.

Oregon

Oregon Educational Media Assn. Memb. 650. Term of Office. Oct. 1, 1988–Sept. 30, 1990. Publication. *INTERCHANGE*.

Pres. Rebecca Macy; *Pres.-Elect*. Rod Hevland; *Past Pres*. Carol Abbott; *Exec. Secy*. Sherry Hevland, 16695 S.W. Rosa Rd., Beaverton 97007.

Pennsylvania

Pennsylvania School Libns. Assn. Memb. 1,450. Term of Office. July 1, 1988–June 30, 1990. Publications. *Learning and Media* (4 per year); *027.8* (2 per year).

Pres. Diana G. Murphy, 135 Wiltshire Circle, Monroeville 15146. Tel. 412-327-5976; *V.P./Pres.-Elect*. Janice Dysart, R.D. #1, Box 196, Orangeville 17859; *Secy*. Grace E. Shope, 318 Rodman Ave., Jenkintown 19046; *Treas*. Paulette Braucher-Watton, 108 Church Rd., Chalfont 18914; *Past Pres*. Margaret R. Tassia, Millersville Univ., Millersville 17551. Tel. 717-872-3630.

Address correspondence to the president.

Rhode Island

Rhode Island Educational Media Assn. Memb. 263. Term of Office. June 1988–June 1989. Publication. *RIEMA Newsletter* (9 per year).

Pres. Timothy Tierney, AV Center, Univ. of Rhode Island, Kingston 02881. Tel. 401-792-4273; *Pres.-Elect*. Harriet Lapointe, Resource Libn., Coelho Middle School, South Attleboro, MA 02703; *V.P.* Madeline Nixon, Libn. Rhode Island College, Henry Barnard School, Providence 02908. *Secy*. Carol Driver, Lib., Charleston Elementary School, Carolina 02812; *Treas.* Arlene Luber, Media Specialist, East Providence School Dept., East Providence 02915.

Address correspondence to the president.

South Carolina

South Carolina Assn. of School Libns. Memb. 925. Term of Office. One year. Publication. *Media Center Messenger* (5 per year).

Pres. Cecile H. Dorr, Rte. 2, Box 359, Frogmore 29920. Tel. 803-838-3781; *V.P./Pres.-Elect.* Debby Coleman, Rte. 2, Box 139F, Denmark 29042. Tel. 803-793-5836.

Address correspondence to the association, Box 2442, Columbia 29202.

South Dakota

South Dakota School Lib. Media Assn., Sec. of the South Dakota Lib. Assn. and South Dakota Education Assn. Term of Office. Oct. 1988–Oct. 1989.

Pres. Mary Homan, Patrick Henry Jr. H.S., 2200 S. Fifth Ave, Sioux Falls 57105. Tel. 605-331-7639; *Secy.-Treas.* Rosalie Aslesen, Spearfish H.S., Spearfish 57783. Tel. 605-642-2612.

Address correspondence to the president.

Tennessee

Tennessee Education Assn., School Lib. Media Sec. Term of Office. May 1988–May 1989.

Chpn. Wanda Mills, 203 Hidden Lake Rd., Hendersonville 37075. Tel. 615-822-3083 or 615-824-6162; *Chpn.-Elect.* Glenda Anderson, 472 Manor View Dr., Knoxville 37923. Tel. 615-691-1019; *Secy.-Treas.* Lana Wingo, 132 Wingo St., Bradford 38316. Tel. 901-742-3357.

Address correspondence to the chairperson.

Texas

Texas Assn. of School Libns. Memb. 2,300. Term of Office. Apr. 1988–Apr. 1989. Publication. *Media Matters* (4 per year).

Chpn. Ramona Kerby, 6916 Martha Lane, Ft. Worth 76112. Tel. 817-478-9829.

Address correspondence to an officer or to TASL, 3355 Bee Cave Rd., Suite 603, Austin 78746. Tel. 512-328-1518.

Utah

Utah Educational Lib. Media Assn. Memb. 280. Term of Office. Feb. 1989–Feb. 1990. Publication. *UELMA Newsletter* (5 per year).

Pres. Aleene B. Nielson, 659 S. 12 E., Salt Lake City 84102. Tel. 801-583-7108; *Pres.-Elect.* David Walton, Alpine School Dist., 50 N. Center, American Fork 84003. Tel. 801-756-9470; *Secy.* Janet Duane, Jordan Media Center, 9361 S. Third E., Sandy 84070. Tel. 801-565-7410; *Treas.* Shirleen Barrus, Westridge Elementary School, 1720 W. 1460 N., Provo 84604. Tel. 801-374-4870; *Past Pres.* George Weight, Juab H. S., 555 E. 750 N. Nephi 84648. Tel. 801-623-1764; *Exec. Secy.* Kathryn C. Gardner, 3690 N. Little Rock Dr., Provo 84604. Tel. 801-224-9920.

Address correspondence to the executive secretary.

Vermont

Vermont Educational Media Assn. Memb. 140. Term of Office. May 1988–May 1989. Publication. *VEMA News* (q.).

Pres. Tad Dana, Northfield H.S., Northfield 05663. Tel. 802-485-5751; *Pres.-Elect.* Juanita Platts, Morrisville Elementary School, Morrisville 05661. Tel. 802-888-3101; *Secy.* Karen Hennig, Craftsbury Academy, Craftsbury 05826. Tel. 802-586-2541; *Treas.* Christine Varney, Hinesburg Elementary School, Hinesburg 05461. Tel. 802-482-2106.

Address correspondence to the president.

Virginia

Virginia Educational Media Assn. (VEMA). Term of Office. Nov. 1988–Nov. 1989.

Pres. Richard Buck, Radford Univ., Box 5820, Radford 24142. Tel. 703-831-5736; *Pres.-Elect.* Helen DeWell, 8513 Claypool Rd., Richmond 23236. Tel. 804-796-5984; *Treas.* Ann Carter, 1695 Wilton Rd., Petersburg 23805. Tel. 804-733-4003; *Past Pres.* Nancy Vick, Longwood College, 103 Wynne Bldg., Farmville 23901. Tel. 804-392-9341. *Secy.* Judith Blankenburg, 551 Ott St., Harrisonburg 22801. Tel. 703-433-9277.

Address correspondence to the president.

Washington

Washington Lib. Media Assn. Memb. 800. Term of Office. Oct. 1988–Sept. 1989. Publications. *The Medium* (3 per year). *Ed.* Steve Goodwin; *The Newsletter* (irreg.).

Pres. Joan Newman, 12118 N.E. 64 St., Kirkland 98033. Tel. 206-882-0922; *Pres.-Elect.* Ginny Vogel, 3602 W. Ames Lake Dr. N.E., Redmond 98053. Tel. 206-823-6750; *Secy.* Irene Clise, 4015 60th S.W., Olympia 98502. Tel. 206-456-7740; *Treas.* Barbara J. Baker, Box 1413, Bothell 98041. Tel. 206-485-0258; *Past Pres.* Carol J. Hoyt, 14813 N.E. 13 St., Bellevue 98007. Tel. 206-485-0452.

Address correspondence to the president.

West Virginia

West Virginia Educational Media Assn. Memb. 350. Term of Office. Apr. 1988–Apr. 1989. Publication. *WVEMA Newsletter* (q.).

Pres. Debra Hickman, Media Specialist, Glenwood Jr. H.S., Rte. 1, Box 460, Princeton 24740. Tel. 304-425-5970; *Pres.-Elect.* Floyd K. Russell, 1416 Western Ave., Morgantown 26505. Tel. 304-598-0577; *Treas.* Kathleen Kawecki, Supr., School Services, WNPB-TV, 191 Scott Ave., Morgantown 26507. Tel. 304-293-6511; *Secy.* Barbara Aguirre, Libn., Logan Campus, Southern West Virginia Community College, Box 2900, Logan 25601. Tel. 304-752-5900 ext. 202; *Memb. Secy.* Mary Lou Brown, Media Specialist, Princeton H.S., 1321 Stafford Dr., Princeton 24740. Tel. 304-425-8101; *Past Pres.* Eleanor Terry, Dept. of Educational Media, Marshall Univ., Huntington 25701. Tel. 304-696-2330.

Address correspondence to the president.

Wyoming

Wyoming Lib. Assn., School Lib. Media Sec. Memb. 50. Term of Office. Sept. 1988–Sept. 1989.

Pres. Vickie Overcast, Worland H.S. 9–12, Worland 82401. Tel. 307-347-2414; *Secy.* Cindy Toth, Thermopolis H.S., Thermopolis 82443. Tel. 864-2144.

Address correspondence to the president.

State Supervisors of School Library Media Services

Alabama

Jane Bandy Smith, Educational Specialist, Lib. Media Services, 111 Coliseum Blvd., Montgomery 36193. Tel. 205-261-2746.

Alaska

B. Jo Morse, Alaska State Lib., School Lib./Media Coord., 3600 Denali, Anchorage 99503. Tel. 907-261-2977.

Arizona

Linda Edgington, Research Libn. II, State Dept. of Educ., 1535 W. Jefferson, Phoenix 85007. Tel. 602-255-5391.

Arkansas

Mary Lee Gillespie, Lib. Media Program Specialist, Arkansas Dept. of Educ., Arch Ford Bldg., Rm. 405B, Little Rock 72201. Tel. 501-682-4396.

California

John Church, Dir., Resource Services, State Dept. of Educ., Box 944272, 721 Capitol Mall, Sacramento 94244-2720. Tel. 916-322-0494.

Colorado

Nancy M. Bolt, Asst. Commissioner, Colorado State Lib., 201 E. Colfax Ave., Denver 80203. Tel. 303-866-6732.

Boyd E. Dressler, Supv., Curriculum and Instruction Project, Colorado Dept. of Educ., 201 E. Colfax Ave., Denver 80203. Tel. 303-866-6748.

John Hempstead, Supv. of School Media Services, Dept. of Educ., 201 E. Colfax Ave., Denver 80203. Tel. 303-866-6730.

Connecticut

Robert G. Hale, Senior Coord., Learning Resources and Technology Unit, and Instructional Television Consultant; Betty B. Goyette, Lib. Media Consultant, Learning Resources and Technology Unit; Linda Naimi, Assoc. Consultant, Computers in Instruction; and Dorothy M. Headspeth, Info. Specialist, Learning Resources and Technology Unit; State Dept. of Educ., Box 2219, Hartford 06145. Tel. 203-566-2250.

Delaware

Richard L. Krueger, Lib. Specialist, State Dept. of Public Instruction, John G. Townsend Bldg., Box 1402, Dover 19903. Tel. 302-736-4692.

District of Columbia

Bester Bonner, Dir., Lib. and Media Services, District of Columbia Public Schools, Lemmel Penn Center, 1709 Third St. N.E., Washington 20022. Tel. 202-576-6317.

Marie Harris, Supervising Dir., Lib. Services, District of Columbia Public Schools, Wilkinson Annex, Pomeroy Rd. and Erie St. S.E., Washington 20020. Tel. 202-767-8643.

James Murray, Supervising Dir., Media Services, District of Columbia Public Schools, Lemmel Penn Center, 1709 Third St. N.E., Washington 20002.

Florida

Sandra W. Ulm, Administrator, School Lib. Media Services, Florida Dept. of Educ., 303 Winchester Bldg. A, Tallahassee 32399. Tel. 904-488-8184.

Georgia

Nancy V. Paysinger, Dir., Media Planning Unit, Div. of Instructional Media, Georgia Dept. of Educ., Suite 2054, Twin Towers E., Atlanta 30334. Tel. 404-656-2418.

Hawaii

Patsy Izumo, Dir., Multimedia Services Branch, State Dept. of Educ., 641 18th Ave., Honolulu 96816. Tel. 808-732-5535.

Idaho

Mark A. Kuskie, Consultant, Educational Media Services, State Dept. of Educ., Len B. Jordan Bldg., 650 State St., Boise 83720. Tel. 208-334-2113.

Illinois

Marie Rose Sivak, Educational Consultant, Curriculum Improvement Sec., State Bd. of Educ., 100 N. First St., Springfield 62777. Tel. 217-782-2826.

Indiana

Phyllis Land Usher, Senior Officer, Center for School Improvement and Performance, Indiana Dept. of Educ., Indianapolis 46204. Tel. 317-232-9104.

Iowa

Betty Jo Buckingham, Consultant, Education Media, State Dept. of Educ., Grimes State Office Bldg., Des Moines 50319-0146. Tel. 515-281-3707.

Kansas

June Saine Level, Lib. Media Consultant, Educational Assistance Sec., Kansas State Dept. of Educ., 120 E. Tenth St., Topeka 66612. Tel. 913-296-3434.

Kentucky

Judy L. Cooper, Consultant for School Media Services, State Dept. of Educ., 1830 Capitol Plaza Tower, Frankfort 40601. Tel. 502-564-2672.

Maine

Walter J. Taranko, Coord., Media Services, Maine State Lib., LMA Bldg., State House Sta. 64, Augusta 04333. Tel. 207-289-5620.

Maryland

Rosa L. Presberry, Chief, School Media Services Branch, Div. of Lib. Development and Services, State Dept. of Educ., 200 W. Baltimore St., Baltimore 21201. Tel. 301-333-2125.

Massachusetts

Harold Raynolds, Jr., Commissioner of Education, Dept. of Educ., 1385 Hancock St., Quincy 02169. Tel. 617-770-7300.

Michigan

Stephanie Parentesis, Dir. of User Services, Lib. of Michigan, Box 30007, 717 W. Allegan St., Lansing 48909. Tel. 517-373-5506.

Minnesota

Joan C. Wallin, Supv., Media and Technology Unit, Minnesota Dept. of Educ., 683 Capitol Square Bldg., St. Paul 55101. Tel. 612-296-1570.

Mississippi

Lynn H. Conerly, State Dept. of Educ., Educational Media Services, Box 771, Jackson 39205. Tel. 601-359-3778.

Missouri

Carl Sitze, Dir. of Classification and Accreditation, Dept. of Elementary and Secondary Education, Box 480, Jefferson City 65102. Tel. 314-751-7754.

Beth Lilleston, Pres., Missouri Assn. of School Libns., 820 Fox Run Dr., Clinton 64735. Tel. (off.) 816-885-5586; (home) 816-885-4478.

Montana

Margaret Rolando, Lib. Media Specialist, Office of Public Instruction, Rm. 106, State Capitol, Helena 59620. Tel. 406-444-2979.

Nebraska

Jack Baillie, Dir., State Dept. of Educ., Box 94987, 301 Centennial Mall S., Lincoln 68509. Tel. 402-471-3567.

Nevada

Jody Gehrig, Lib. Media Consultant, State Dept. of Educ., Capitol Complex, 400 W. King, Carson City 89710. Tel. 702-885-3136.

New Hampshire

Susan C. Snider, Curriculum Supv., Lib. Media Services, State Dept. of Educ., Div. of Instructional Services, 101 Pleasant St., Concord 03301. Tel. 603-271-2632.

New Jersey

Jean E. Harris and Marcia Wolfe, Consultants, State Dept. of Educ., State Lib., 185 W. State St., CN 520, Trenton 08625-0520. Tel. 609-292-6245 (Harris), 609-984-6266 (Wolfe).

New Mexico

Mary Jane Vinella, Lib./Media Consultant, Dept. of Educ., Education Bldg., Santa Fe 87501-2786. Tel. 505-827-6561.

New York

Robert E. Barron, Chief, Bur. of School Lib. Media Programs, State Educ. Dept., Rm. 676 EBA, Albany 12234. Tel. 518-474-2468.

North Carolina

Elsie L. Brumback, Asst. State Superintendent, Dept. of Public Instruction, Raleigh 27603-1712. Tel. 919-733-3170.

North Dakota

Patricia Herbel, Dir., Elementary Education, Dept. of Public Instruction, State Capitol, Bismarck 58505. Tel. 701-224-2295.

Ohio

Jacqueline E. Wagner, Lib./Media Consultant, State Dept. of Educ., 65 S. Front St., Rm. 1005, Columbus 43266-0308. Tel. 614-466-2407.

Oklahoma

Barbara Spriestersbach, Dir.; John McGrath, Asst. Dir.; Betty Riley, Bettie Estes, and Linda Chapman, Coords.; Lib. and Learning Resources Div., State Dept. of Educ., 2500 N. Lincoln Blvd., Oklahoma City 73105. Tel. 405-521-2956.

Oregon

Don G. Erickson, Dir., Instructional Technology Unit, Oregon Dept. of Educ., 700 Pringle Pkwy. S.E., Salem 97310. Tel. 503-378-6405.

James W. Sanner, Specialist, Instructional Technology, Oregon Dept. of Educ., 700 Pringle Pkwy. S.E., Salem 97310. Tel. 503-378-6405.

Pennsylvania

Doris M. Epler, Div. of School Lib. Media, State Dept. of Educ., 333 Market St., Harrisburg 17126-0333. Tel. 717-787-6704.

Rhode Island

Richard Harrington, Coord. Grant Programs, State Dept. of Educ., 22 Hayes St., Providence 02908. Tel. 401-277-2617.

South Carolina

Pamela P. Pritchett, Lib./Media Consultant, State Dept. of Educ., Rutledge Bldg., Rm. 801, Columbia 29201. Tel. 803-734-8398.

South Dakota

Henry G. Kosters, State Superintendent, Div. of Education, Richard F. Kneip Bldg., 700 Governors Dr., Pierre 57501. Tel. 605-773-3243.

Tennessee

Betty Latture, State Dir. of Lib. Services, C1-103 Central Services Bldg., Tennessee Dept. of Educ., Nashville 37219. Tel. 615-741-0874.

Texas

Mary R. Boyvey, Dir., Lib. Media Program, Texas Education Agency, 1701 N. Congress, Austin 78701-1494. Tel. 512-463-9660.

Utah

Bruce Griffin, Assoc. Superintendent, Operations Div., State Office of Educ., 250 E. Fifth St., Salt Lake City 84111. Tel. 801-538-7762.

Vermont

Leda Schubert, School Lib./Media Consultant, Vermont Dept. of Educ., Montpelier 05602. Tel. 802-828-3124.

Virginia

Gloria K. Barber, Supv. of School Libs. and Info. Technology, Dept. of Educ., Box 6Q, 101 N. 14 St., Richmond 23219. Tel. 804-225-2958.

Washington

John Rutherford, Supv., Learning Resources Services, Office of State Superintendent of Public Instruction, Old Capitol Bldg., Olympia 98504. Tel. 206-753-6723.

West Virginia

Jeanne Moellendick, Coord., Lib./Media and Technology, c/o West Virginia Dept. of Educ., Capitol Complex, Bldg. 6, Rm. B-318, Charleston 25305. Tel. 304-348-2691.

Wisconsin

Carolyn Winters Folke, Dir., Bur. for Instructional Media and Technology, State Dept. of Public Instruction, Box 7841, Madison 53707. Tel. 608-266-1965.

Wyoming

Nancy Leinius, Education Programs Specialist, Wyoming Dept. of Educ., Hathaway Bldg., Cheyenne 82002. Tel. 307-777-6226.

American Samoa

Emma S. Fung Chen Pen, Program Dir., Office of Lib. Services, Dept. of Educ., Box 1329, Pago Pago 96799. Tel. 633-1181/1182.

Northern Mariana Islands (Commonwealth of the) (CNMI)

Malinda S. Matson, Dir. Lib. Services, Northern Marianas College, Box 1250, Saipan, CM 96950.

Pacific Islands (Trust Territory of)

Tamar A. Jordan, Public Libn., Government of the Republic of the Marshall Islands, Dept. of Interior and Outer Islands, Majuro, Marshall Islands 96960.

Puerto Rico

Elsadori de la Mata, Interim Dir., Public Lib. Div., Dept. of Educ., Box 759, Hato Rey 00919. Tel. 809-753-9191; 754-7227.

Virgin Islands

Fiolina B. Mills, State Dir., State Media Lib. Services, Virgin Islands Dept. of Educ., #44-46 Kongens Gade, St. Thomas 00802. Tel. 809-776-2573 or 809-774-5339.

International Library Associations

Inter-American Association of Agricultural Librarians and Documentalists

IICA-CIDIA, 7170 Turrialba, Costa Rica

Object

"To serve as liaison among the agricultural librarians and documentalists of the Americas and other parts of the world; to promote the exchange of information and experiences through technical publications and meetings; to promote the improvement of library services in the field of agriculture and related sciences; to encourage the improvement of the professional level of the librarians and documentalists in the field of agriculture in Latin America."

Officers

Pres. Nitzia Barrantes, UPEB, Panama; *V.P.* Guadalupe Bustamante, CENICANA, Cali, Colombia; *Exec. Secy.* Ana María Paz de Erickson, c/o CATIE, Turrialba, Costa Rica.

Publications

AIBDA Actualidades (irreg., 5 per year).
Boletín Especial (irreg.).
Boletín Informativo (q.).
Diccionario Histórico del Libro y de la Biblioteca (U.S. price: Memb. $15 including postage; nonmemb. $20 including postage).
Guía para Bibliotecas Agrícolas, by Olga Lendvay (U.S. price: Memb. $10 including postage; nonmemb. $15 including postage).
Páginas de Contenido: Ciencias de la Información (q.).
Proceedings. Cuarta Reunión Interamericana de Bibliotecarios y Documentalistas Agrícolas, Mexico, D.F., April 8–11, 1975 (U.S. price: Memb. $5 including postage; nonmemb. $10 including postage).
Proceedings. Quinta Reunión Interamericana de Bibliotecarios y Documentalistas Agrícolas, San José, Costa Rica, April 10–14, 1978 (U.S. price: Memb. $10 plus postage; nonmemb. $15 plus postage).
Proceedings. Tercera Reunión Interamericana de Bibliotecarios y Documentalistas Agrícolas, Buenos Aires, Argentina, April 10–14, 1972 (U.S. price: $10 including postage). Out of print. Available in Microfiche. (Price U.S. $10).
Revista AIBDA (2 per year; Memb. $12 including postage; nonmemb. $25 including postage).

International Association of Agricultural Librarians and Documentalists

c/o J. van der Burg, Acting Secretary–Treasurer,
PUDOC, Jan Kophuis, Box 4, 6700 AA Wageningen, The Netherlands

Object

"The Association shall, internationally and nationally, promote agricultural library science and documentation as well as the professional interest of agricultural librarians and documentalists." Founded 1955. Memb. 634. Dues (Inst.) $40; (Indiv.) $20.

Officers

Pres. E. J. Mann, England; *V.P.s.* P. J. Wortley, England; H. Haendler, Germany; *Secy.-Treas. (Acting)* Jan van der Burg, The Netherlands; *Ed.* Susan C. Harris, Colombia.

Executive Committee

L. Gregorio, Philippines; E. Herpay, Hungary; C. Joling, FAO; J. Kennedy Olsen, USA; Metcalfe, CABI; N.W. Posnett, U.K.; J. M. Schippers, The Netherlands; H. Schmid, Austria; A. T. Yaikova, USSR; representatives of national associations of agricultural librarians and documentalists.

Publication

Quarterly Bulletin of the IAALD (memb.).

International Association of Law Libraries

c/o The University of Chicago, Law School Library,
1121 E. 60 St., Chicago, IL 60637, USA

Object

"To promote on a cooperative, non-profit, and fraternal basis the work of individuals, libraries, and other institutions and agencies concerned with the acquisition and bibliographic processing of legal materials collected on a multinational basis, and to facilitate the research and other uses of such materials on a worldwide basis." Founded 1959. Memb. Over 600 in 60 countries.

Officers (1986–1989)

Pres. Adolf Sprudzs, The Univ. of Chicago, Law School Lib., 1121 E. 60 St., Chicago, IL 60637; *1st V.P.* John Rodwell, Kensington, Australia; *2nd V.P.* Yoshiro Tsuno, Tokyo, Japan; *Secy.* Timothy Kearley, Champaign, Illinois; *Treas.* Ivan Sipkov, Washington, D.C.

Board Members (1986–1989)

Katalin Balázs-Veredy, Hungary; Marga Coing, Fed. Rep. of Germany; David Combe, USA; Sng Yok Fong, Rep. of Singapore; Igor I. Kavass, USA; Arno Liivak, USA; Velma Newton, Barbados; Joachim Schwietzke, Fed. Rep. of Germany.

Services

1. The dissemination of professional information through the *International Journal of Legal Information*, through continuous contacts with formal and informal national groups of law librarians, and through work within other international organizations, such as IFLA.
2. Continuing education through the one-week IALL Seminars in International Law Librarianship periodically.
3. The preparation of special literature for law librarians, such as the *European Law Libraries Guide*, and of introductions to basic foreign legal literature.
4. Direct personal contacts and exchanges between IALL members.

Publications

The IALL Messenger (newsletter, irreg.).
International Journal of Legal Information (3 per year). *Ed.-in-Chief.* Ivan Sipkov, 4917 Butterworth Place N.W., Washington, DC 20016.

International Association of Metropolitan City Libraries

c/o W. M. Renes, City Librarian,
Dienst Openbare Bibliotheek, Bilderdijkstraat 1-3,
2513 CM Den Haag, The Netherlands

Object

"The Association was founded to assist the worldwide flow of information and knowledge by promoting practical collaboration in the exchange of books, exhibitions, staff, and information." Memb. 97.

Officers

Pres. Constance B. Cooke, Dir. of Libs., Queens Borough Public Lib., 89-11 Merrick Blvd., Jamaica, NY 11432; *Secy.-Treas.* W. M. Renes, City Libn., Dienst Openbare Bibliotheek, Bilderdijkstraat 1-3, 2513 CM Den Haag, The Netherlands; *Past Pres.* Sten Cedergren, Dir. and City Libn., Goteborg, Sweden. (Address correspondence to the secretary-treasurer.)

Publications

Annual International Statistics of City Libraries (INTAMEL).
Review of the Three Year Research and Exchange Programme 1968–1971.
Subject Departments in Public Libraries (Budapest 1983).

International Association of Music Libraries, Archives and Documentation Centres (IAML)

c/o Veslemöy Heintz, Secretary-General
Svenskt musikhistoriskt arkiv
Box 16326, S-103 26 Stockholm, Sweden

Object

To promote the activities of music libraries, archives, and documentation centers and to strengthen the cooperation among them; to promote the availability of all publications and documents relating to music and further their bibliographical control; to encourage the development of standards in all areas that concern the association; and to support the protection and preservation of musical documents of the past and the present. Memb. 1,800.

Board Members (1986–1989)

Pres. Maria Calderisi, National Lib. of Canada, 395 Wellington St., Ottawa, ON K1A 0N4, Canada; *Past Pres.* Anders Lönn, Musikaliska akademiens bibliotek, Box 16 326, S-103 26 Stockholm, Sweden; *V.P.s.* Bernard Huys, Bibliothèque Royale de Belgique, 4 blvd. de l'Empereur, B-1000 Brussels, Belgium; Catherine Massip, Bibliothèque Nationale, Département de la Musique, 2 rue Vivienne, F-75084 Paris Cedex 02, France; Svetlana Sigida, Moscow State Conservatoire, ul. Gerzena 13, Moscow K9, USSR; Malcolm Turner, British Lib., Music Lib., Great Russell St., London WC1B 3DG, England; *Secy.-Gen.* Veslemöy Heintz, Svenskt musikhistoriskt arkiv, Box 16326, S-103 26 Stockholm, Sweden; *Treas.* Don L. Roberts, Music Lib., Northwestern Univ., Evanston, IL 60208, USA.

Publication

Fontes Artis Musicae (4 per year; memb.). *Ed.* Brian Redfern, 27 Plantation Rd., Leighton Buzzard LU7 7HJ, U.K.

Professional Branches

Broadcasting and Orchestra Libraries. Finn Kaisner, Danmarks radio, Nodebiblioteket, Islands Brygge 81, DK-2300 København, Denmark.

Libraries in Music Teaching Institutions. Robert Jones, English Lib., Univ. of Illinois, Rm. 220, 1408 Gregory Dr., Urbana, IL 61801, USA.

Music Information Centers. Rogier Starreveld, Donemus, Box 7410, NL 1007 FK Amsterdam, The Netherlands.

Public Libraries. Ken Nein, Pariser Strasse 46, D-1000 Berlin 15, Fed. Rep. of Germany.

Research Libraries. Michael Ochs, Eda Kuhn Loeb Music Lib., Harvard Univ., Cambridge, MA 02138, USA.

Commission and Committee Chairpersons

Bibliography Commission. Joachim Jaenecke, Staatsbibliothek Preussischer Kulturbesitz, Musikabteilung, Potsdamer Strasse 33, D-1000 Berlin 30, Fed. Rep. of Germany.

Cataloguing Commission. Lenore Coral, Music Lib., Lincoln Hall, Cornell Univ., Ithaca, NY 14853, USA.

Constitution Committee. Heinz Werner, Berliner Stadtbibliothek, Breite Strasse 32-34, DDR-106 Berlin, German Dem. Rep.

Publications Committee. Catherine Massip, Bibliothèque Nationale, Département de la Musique, 2 rue Vivienne, F-75084 Paris Cedex 02, France.

Service and Training Commission. Marsha Berman, 2417 Fourth St., Santa Monica, CA 90405, USA.

US Branch

Pres. Susan T. Sommer, General Lib. for the Performing Arts, New York Public Lib., 111 Amsterdam Ave., New York, NY 10023, USA; *Secy.-Treas.* Charles Lindahl, Eastman School of Music, Sibley Music Lib., Rochester, NY 14604, USA.

Publication (US Branch)

Notes (4 per year; memb., subscr.). *Ed.* Michael Ochs, Eda Kuhn Loeb Music Lib., Harvard Univ., Cambridge, MA 02138, USA.

UK Branch

Pres. Malcolm Jones, Birmingham Central Lib., Birmingham B33 3HG, England; *Gen. Secy.* A. Helen Mason, Music and Drama Lib., Lincoln County Libs., Brayford House, Lucy Tower St., Lincoln LN1 1XN, England; *Treas.* Richard Priest, Allegro Music, 82 Suffolk St., Queensway, Birmingham B1 1TA, England.

Publication (UK Branch)

BRIO (2 per year; memb.). *Ed.* Ian Ledsham, Barber Institute of Fine Arts, Music Lib., Univ. of Birmingham, Box 363, Birmingham B15 2TS, England.

International Association of Orientalist Librarians (IAOL)

c/o Secretary-Treasurer, William S. Wong,
Assistant Director of General Services (for Asian Library) and
Professor of Library Administration,
University Library, University of Illinois at Urbana-Champaign,
1408 W. Gregory Dr., Urbana, IL 61801, USA

Object

"To promote better communication among Orientalist librarians and libraries, and others in related fields, throughout the world; to provide a forum for the discussion of problems of common interest; to improve international cooperation among institutions holding research resources for Oriental Studies." The term Orient here specifies the Middle East, East Asia, and the South and Southeast Asia regions.

Founded in 1967 at the 27th International Congress of Orientalists (ICO) in Ann Arbor, Michigan. Affiliated with the International Federation of Library Associations and Institutions (IFLA) and International Congress for Asian and North African Studies (formerly ICO).

Officers

Pres. Warren M. Tsuneishi; *Secy.-Treas.* William S. Wong; *Ed.* Om P. Sharma.

Publication

International Association of Orientalists Librarians Bulletin (s. ann.; memb.).

International Association of School Librarianship

c/o Executive Secretary, Jean Lowrie,
Box 1486, Kalamazoo, MI 49005, USA

Object

"To encourage the development of school libraries and library programs throughout all countries; to promote the professional preparation of school librarians; to bring about close collaboration among school libraries in all countries, including the loan and exchange of literature; to initiate and coordinate activities, conferences, and other projects in the field of school librarianship." Founded 1971. Memb. (Indiv.) 800; (Assn.) 41.

Publications

Books and Borrowers.
Getting Started: A Bibliography of Ideas and Procedures.
IASL Conference Proceedings (ann.).
IASL Monograph Series.
IASL Newsletter (q.).
Indicators of Quality for School Library Media Programs.
Persons to Contact for Visiting School Libraries/Media Centers, 6th ed.

Officers and Executive Board

Pres. Michael Cooke, Aberystwyth, Wales; *V.P.* Sigrunklara Hannisdöttir, Reykjavik, Iceland; *Treas.* Donald Adcock, Glen Ellyn, Illinois, USA; *Exec. Secy.* Jean Lowrie, Kalamazoo, Michigan, USA; *Dirs.* Carver Mparutsa, Harare, Zimbabwe; Lolita Brond, Melbourne, Australia; Shirley Coulter, Nova Scotia, Canada; Ylva Lindholm-Romantschuk, Helsinki, Finland; Takeshi Murofushi, Kanagawa, Japan; Joyce Wallen, Jamaica, West Indies; Wong Kim Song, Kuala Lumpur, Malaysia; Nelson Rodriguez-Trujillo, Caracas, Venezuela.

American Memberships

American Assn. of School Libs.; Assn. de Bibliotecarios Escolares de Puerto Rico; Educational Media Assn. of New Jersey; Hawaii School Lib. Assn.; Illinois Assn. for Media in Education; Louisiana Assn. of School Libns.; Maryland Educational Media Organization; Michigan Assn. for Media in Education; New York Lib. Assn., School Lib. Media Sec.; Oregon Educational Media Assn. Virginia Educational Media Assn.; Washington Lib. Media Assn.

International Association of Sound Archives

c/o Helen Harrison, Media Librarian, Open University
Library, Walton Hall, Milton Keynes MK7 6AA, England

Object

The International Association of Sound Archives (IASA) is a nongovernmental UNESCO-affiliated organization. It was established in 1969 in Amsterdam to allow international cooperation between archives which preserve recorded sound documents. IASA interests lie in a wide variety of recorded sound including music and cover problems common to the variety of collections with which the association deals: problems of acquisition, preservation, organization, documentation, copyright, accessibility, distribution, and the technical aspects of recording and playback. The association is actively involved in the preservation, organization, and use of sound recordings, techniques of recording and methods of reproducing sound in all fields in which the audio medium is used; the exchange of recordings between archives and of related literature and information; and in all subjects relating to the professional work of sound archives and archivists.

Membership

Open to all categories of archives and other institutions which preserve sound recordings, and to organizations and individuals having a serious interest in the purposes or welfare of IASA. The association includes members representing archives of music, history, literature, drama, and folklife recordings; collections of oral history, natural history, bioacoustic and medical sounds; recorded linguistic and dialect surveys; radio and television sound archives.

Officers (1987–1990)

Pres. Helen P. Harrison, Open Univ. Lib., Walton Hall, Milton Keynes MK7 6AA, England; *V.P.s.* Hans Bosma, Nederlandse Omroep Stichting, Divisie Radio Produktie, NL-1200 JB Hilversum, The Netherlands; Magdalena Cseve, Hungarian Radio, Documentation, Brody Sandor u.5-7, H-1800 Budapest, Hungary; Ulf Scharlau, Sueddeutscher Rundfunk, Archivwesen und Dokumentation, Box 837, Neckarstrasse 230, D-7000 Stuttgart 1, Fed. Rep. of Germany; *Ed.* Grace Koch, Australian Institute of Aboriginal Studies, Box 553, Canberra ACT 2601, Australia; *Treas.* Anna Maria Foyer, Sveriges Riksradio, Programarkivet, S-10510 Stockholm, Sweden; *Secy. Gen.* Jean Claude Hayoz, Radio DRS, Studio Bern, Phonothek, Schwartorstrasse 21, CH-3000 Bern 14, Switzerland.

Committees

Committees exist for Cataloguing, Copyright, Discography, the History of IASA, National Archives, Radio Sound Archives, and Technical and Training.

Publications

An Archive Approach to Oral History, by David Lance (1978).

Directory of Members, second edition, compiled by Grace Koch (1982. ISBN 0 946475 00 8).

Phonographic Bulletin (journal. ISSN 02533-004X). Index issues 1–40, 1971–1984.

Selection in Sound Archives, edited by Helen Harrison (1984. ISBN 0 946475 02 4).

Sound Archives: A Guide to Their Establishment and Development, edited by David Lance (1983. ISBN 0 946475 01 6).

International Association of Technological University Libraries (IATUL)

c/o President, Dennis Shaw,
CBE, Radcliffe Science Library, Oxford University,
Parks Rd., Oxford OX1 3QP, England

Object

To provide a forum where library directors can meet to exchange views on matters of current significance in the libraries of Universities of Science and Technology. Research projects identified as being of sufficient interest may be followed through by working parties or study groups.

Membership

Ordinary, official observer, sustaining, and nonvoting associate. Membership fee is $40 per year. Memb. 175 (in 39 countries).

Officers and Executives

Pres. Dennis Shaw, CBE, Keeper of Scientific Books, Radcliffe Science Lib., Oxford Univ.,

Parks Rd., Oxford OX1 3QP, England; *Secy.* Nancy Fjällbrant, Deputy Libn., Chalmers Univ. of Technology Lib., S-412 96 Gothenburg, Sweden; *Treas.* G. A. J. S. van Marle, Bibliotheek Technische, Hogeschool Twente, Box 217, 7500 AE Enschede, The Netherlands; *1st V.P.* D. Schmidmaier, Bibliothek "Georgius-Agricola," Agricolastrasse 10, DDR-9200 Freiberg, German Dem. Rep.; *2nd V.P.* Elin Törnudd, Dir., Helsinki Univ. of Technology Lib., Otaniementie 9, SF-02150 Espoo, Finland; *North American Regional Group. Chpn.* Jay K. Lucker, USA; *Study Group on Document Delivery. Chpn.* Nancy Fjällbrant, Sweden; *Study Group on Scientific Serials. Chpn.* Dennis F. Shaw, UK; *IATUL Quarterly Editorial Bd. Chpn.* Dennis Shaw, UK; *Ed.* To be announced; *Assoc. Ed.* Joan Shaw, UK; *Membs.* Tom Cochrane, Australia; Magda Czigany, UK; Anna Domotor, Hungary; Ulrich Fellmann, Fed. Rep. of Germany; Jay K. Lucker, USA; Christian Lupovici, France; Nurit Roitberg, Israel; Dieter Schmidmaier, German Dem. Rep.

Publication

IATUL Quarterly (q.).

International Council on Archives

Secretariat, 60 rue des Francs-Bourgeois,
F-75003 Paris, France

Object

"To establish, maintain, and strengthen relations among archivists of all lands, and among all professional and other agencies or institutions concerned with the custody, organization, or administration of archives, public or private, wherever located." Established 1948. Memb. 750 (representing 125 countries and territories). Dues (Indiv.) $30; (Inst.) $50; (Archives Assns.) $50 or $100; (Central Archives Directorates) $230 or $115 minimum, computed on the basis of GNP and GNO per capita.

Officers

Pres. Hans Booms; *V.P.s.* Angeline Kamba, Jean Favier; *Exec. Secy.* C. Kesckeméti; *Treas.* Klaus Oldenhage. (Address all correspondence to the executive secretary.)

Publications

Archivum (ann.; memb. or subscription to KG Saur Verlag, Possenbacker Str. 2, Postfach 71 1009, D-8 Munich 71, Fed. Rep. of Germany).

Guide to the Sources of the History of Nations (Latin American Series, 10 vols. pub.; African Series, 10 vols. pub.; Asian Series, 10 vols. pub.; Asian Series, 4 vols. pub.).

ICA Bulletin (s. ann.; memb., or U.S. $5).

List of other publications available upon request to ICA secretariat, Paris, France.

International Federation for Information and Documentation (FID)

Box 90402, 2509 LK The Hague, Netherlands

Object

To group internationally organizations and individuals interested in the problems of documentation and to coordinate their efforts; to promote the study, organization, and practice of documentation in all its forms; and to contribute to the creation of an international network of information systems.

Program

The activities of the federation are grouped under five major program areas: (1) Improvements in the availability and applicability of information resources; (2) developing the information marketplace; (3) developments of tools for information work; (4) increasing basic understanding of the fundamental properties of information; (5) professional development. The following committees have been established to execute FID's program of activities: Research on the Theoretical Basis of Information; Linguistics in Documentation; Information for Industry; Education and Training; Classification Research; Terminology of Information and Documentation; Patent Information and Documentation; Social Sciences Documentation; and Informetrics. It also includes a panel for the Broad System of Ordering (BSO), and a management board to manage the UDC (Universal Decimal Classification).

Officers

Pres. Michael W. Hill, Assoc. Dir., The British Lib. Science, Technology and Industry, 25 Southampton Bldgs., Chancery Lane, London WC1A 2AW, United Kingdom; *V.P.s.* S. Fujiwara, Kanagawa Univ., Research Institute on Info. and Knowledge, 3 chome 27, Rokkakubashi, Kanagawaku, Yokohama, Japan 221; A. I. Mikhailov, VINITI, Baltijskaja ul. 14, Moscow A219, USSR; M. H. Wali, Dir., National Lib. of Nigeria, PMB 12626, Lagos, Nigeria; *Treas.* P. P. Canisius, Dir., Bundesanstalt für Strassenwesen (BASt), Brüderstrasse 53, D-5060 Bergisch Gladback 1, Fed. Rep. of Germany; *Councillors.* J. R. P. Alvarez Ossorio, Madrid, Spain; T. Földi, Budapest, Hungary; E. Jirsa, Prague, Czechoslovakia; Ritva T. Launo, Helsinki, Finland; R. Ogwang-Ameny, Kampala, Uganda; J. Arias Ordoñez, Bogota, Colombia; T. S. Rajagopalan, New Delhi, India; W. L. Renaud, The Hague, Netherlands; M. Ristić, Belgrade, Yugoslavia; Vania M. Rodrigues Hermes de Araújo, Brasilia, Brazil; E. V. Smith, Ottawa, Canada; M. Thomas, Paris, France; *Belgian Memb.* J.-E. Humblet, Genval, Belgium; *Secy.-Gen.* Stella Keenan, The Hague, Netherlands; *Pres. FID/CLA.* R. A. Gietz, Buenos Aires, Argentina; *Pres. FID/CAO.* B. L. Burton, Hong Kong. (Address all correspondence to the secretary-general.)

Publications

FID Annual Report (ann.).
FID Directory (bienn.).
FID News Bulletin (mo.) with supplements on document reproduction (q.).
FID Publications (ann.).
International Forum on Information and Documentation (q.).
Newsletter on Education and Training Programmes for Information Personnel (q.).
R & D Projects in Documentation and Librarianship (bi-mo.).
Proceedings of congresses; Universal Decimal Classification editions; manuals; directories; bibliographies on information science, documentation, reproduction, mechanization, linguistics, training, and classification.

Membership

Approved by the FID Council; ratification by the FID General Assembly.

American Membership

U.S. Interim National Committee for FID.

International Federation of Film Archives

Secretariat, Coudenberg 70, B-1000 Brussels, Belgium

Object

"To facilitate communication and cooperation between its members, and to promote the exchange of films and information; to maintain a code of archive practice calculated to satisfy all national film industries, and to encourage industries to assist in the work of the Federation's members; to advise its members on all matters of interest to them, especially the preservation and study of films; to give every possible assistance and encouragement to new film archives and to those interested in creating them." Founded in Paris 1938. Memb. 76 (in 56 countries).

Executive Committee (June 1987–June 1989)

Pres. Anna Lena Wibom, Sweden; *V.P.s.* Hector Garcia Mesa, Cuba; Wolfgang Klaue, DDR; Eva Orbanz, RDR; *Secy.-Gen.* Guido Cincotti, Italy; *Treas.* Raymond Borde, France. (Address correspondence to B. Van der Elst, executive secretary, at headquarters address.)

Committee Members

Eileen Bowser, USA; Robert Daudelin, Canada; David Francis, UK; Maria-Rita Galvao, Brasil; PK Nair, India; Eva Orbanz, Fed. Rep. of Germany; Luis De Pina, Portugal; Robert Rosen, USA.

Publications

Annual Bibliography of FIAF Members' Publications.

Bibliography of National Filmographies.

Cinema 1900–1906, An Analytical Study.

Film Cataloging.

Glossary of Filmographic Terms in English, French, German, Spanish, and Russian.

Handbook for Film Archives (available in English or French).

International Directory to Film & TV Documentation Sources.

International Index to Film Periodicals (cumulative volumes).

International Index to Film Television Periodicals (microfiche service).

International Index to Television Periodicals (cumulative volumes).

The Preservation and Restoration of Colour and Sound in Films.

Proceedings of the FIAF Symposiums; 1977: L'Influence du Cinema Sovietique Muet Sur le Cinema Mondial/The Influence of Silent Soviet Cinema on World Cinema; 1978: Cinema 1900–1906; 1980: Problems of Selection in Film Archives; 1985: The Slapstick.

Study of the Usage of Computers for Filmcataloguing.

International Federation of Library Associations and Institutions (IFLA)

c/o The Royal Library, Box 95312,
2509 CH The Hague, Netherlands

Object

"To promote international understanding, cooperation, discussion, research, and development in all fields of library activity, including bibliography, information services, and the education of library personnel, and to provide a body through which librarianship can be represented in matters of international interest." Founded 1927. Memb. (Lib. Assns.) 178; (Inst.) 861; (Aff.) 174; 124 countries.

Officers and Executive Board

Pres. Hans-Peter Geh, Württembergische Landesbibliothek, Stuttgart, Fed. Rep. of Germany; *1st V.P.* Engelsina V. Pereslegina, All-Union State Lib. of Foreign Literature, Moscow, USSR; *2nd V.P.* P. B. Mangla, Delhi Univ. Campus, Delhi, India; *Treas.* Anthony J. Evans, Loughborough Univ. of Technology, Loughborough, UK; *Exec. Bd.* Marcelle Beaudiuez, Bibliothèque Nationale, Paris, France; P. J. Th. Schoots, City Lib., Rotterdam, Netherlands; M. Tørngren, Stockholms Stadsbibliothek, Stockholm, Sweden; R. Wedgeworth, School of Lib. Service, Columbia Univ., New York, New York, USA; *Ex officio Memb.* Joseph Price (Chpn., Professional Bd.), Lib. of Congress, USA; *Secy. Gen.* Paul Nauta, IFLA headquarters; *Programme Officer, IFLA International Programme for Universal Bibliographic Control. IFLA Office for Universal Bibliographic Control and International MARC.* Winston Roberts, c/o Reference Div., British Lib., London, UK; *Programme Officer, IFLA International Programme for UAP.* Marie-France Plassard, c/o British Lib., Document Supply Centre, Boston Spa, Wetherby, West Yorkshire, UK; *Dir., IFLA Office for Inter-*

national Lending. David Bradbury, c/o British Lib., Document Supply Centre, Boston Spa, Wetherby, West Yorkshire, UK; *IFLA Office for PAC.* Merrily Smith, c/o Lib. of Congress, Washington, D.C., USA; *IFLA Office for UDT.* Leigh Smith, c/o National Lib. of Canada, Ottawa, Canada; *Publications Officer.* W. R. H. Koops, Univ. Libn., Groningen, Netherlands; *Professional Coord.* A. L. van Wesemael, IFLA headquarters; *Programme Development Officer.* A. Wysocki, IFLA headquarters.

Publications

IFLA Annual.
IFLA Directory (bienn.).
IFLA Journal (q.).
IFLA Professional Reports.
IFLA Publications Series.
International Cataloguing and Bibliographic Control (q.).
PAC Newsletter.
UAP Newsletter (s. ann.).
UDT Newsletter.

American Membership

American Assn. of Law Libs.; American Lib. Assn.; Art Libs. Society of North America; Assn. for Lib. and Info. Science Education; Assn. for Population Planning/Family Planning Libs.; Assn. of Research Libs.; International Assn. of Law Libs.; International Assn. of Orientalist Libns.; International Assn. of School Libns.; Medical Lib. Assn.; Special Libs. Assn. *Institutional Membs.* There are 133 libraries and related institutions that are institutional members or affiliates of IFLA in the United States (out of a total of 861), and 89 Personal Affiliates (out of a total of 174).

International Organization for Standardization

ISO Central Secretariat
1 r. de Varembé, Case postale 56, CH-1211 Geneva 20, Switzerland

Object

To promote the development of standards in the world in order to facilitate the international exchange of goods and services and to develop mutual cooperation in the spheres of intellectual, scientific, technological, and economic activity.

Officers

Pres. R. Phillips, Canada; *V.P.* H. Reihlen, UK; *Secy.-Gen.* L. D. Eicher.

Technical Work

The technical work of ISO is carried out by over 160 technical committees. These include:

ISO/TC 46—Documentation (Secretariat, DIN Deutsches Institut for Normung, 4-10, Burggrafenstr., Postfach 1107, D-1000 Berlin 30). Scope: Standardization of practices relating to libraries, documentation and information centers, indexing and abstracting services, archives, information science, and publishing.

ISO/TC 37—Terminology (Principles & Coordination) (Secretariat, Osterreisches Normungsinstitut, Leopoldgasse 4, A-1020 Vienna, Austria). Scope: Standardization of methods for creating, compiling, and coordinating terminologies.

ISO/IEC JTC 1 (Joint International Organization for Standardization and International Electrotechnical Commission Technical Committee for Information Technology) (Secretariat, American National Standards Institute, ANSI, 1430 Broadway, New York, NY 10018, USA). Scope: Standardization in the field of information technology systems (including microprocessor systems) and equipments.

Publications

Bulletin (mo.).
Catalogue (ann.).
Liaisons.
Member Bodies.
Memento (ann.).

Foreign Library Associations

The following list of regional and national foreign library associations is a selective one. For a more complete list with detailed information, see *International Guide to Library, Archival, and Information Science Associations* by Josephine Riss Fang and Alice H. Songe (R. R. Bowker, 1980). The *Guide* also provides information on international associations, some of which are described in detail under "International Library Associations" (immediately preceding this section). A more complete list of foreign and international library associations also can be found in *International Literary Market Place* (R. R. Bowker).

Regional

Africa

International Assn. for the Development of Documentation, Libs., and Archives in Africa, *Secy.* Zacheus Sunday Ali, Box 375, Dakar, Senegal.

Standing Conference of African Lib. Schools, c/o School of Libns., Archivists & Documentalists, Univ. of Dakar, B. P. 3252, Dakar, Senegal.

Standing Conference of African Univ. Libs., Eastern Area (SCAULEA), c/o Univ. Lib., Univ. of Nairobi, Kenya.

Standing Conference of African Univ. Libs., Western Area (SCAULWA), c/o M. Jean Aboghe-Obyan, Bibliotheque Universitaire, Univ. Omar Bongo, Libreville, Gabon.

Standing Conference of Eastern, Central, and Southern African Libns., c/o Tanzania Lib. Assn., Box 2645, Dar-es-Salaam, Tanzania.

The Americas

Asociación de Bibliotecas Universitarias, de Investigación e Institucionales del Caribe—ACURIL (Assn. of Caribbean Univ., Research and Institutional Libs.), *Exec. Secy.* Oneida R. Ortiz, Apdo. Postal S. Estacion de la Universidad, San Juan, PR 00931.

Asociación Latinoamericana de Escuelas de Bibliotecologia y Ciencias de la Información (Latin American Assn. of Schools of Lib. and Info. Science), Colegio de Bibliotecologia, Universidad Nacional Autónoma de México, México 20, D. F., Mexico.

Seminar on the Acquisition of Latin American Lib. Materials, SALALM Secretariat, *Exec. Secy.* Suzanne Hodgman, Memorial Lib., Univ. of Wisconsin-Madison, Madison, WI 53706.

Asia

Congress of Southeast Asian Libns. (CONSAL), *Chpn.* Mastini Hardjo Prakoso, c/o National Lib. of Indonesia, Box 3624, Jalan Salemba Raya 28A, Jakarta 10002, Indonesia.

British Commonwealth of Nations

Commonwealth Lib. Assn. (COMLA), c/o *Hon. Exec. Secy.* Joan E. Swaby, Box 40, Mandeville, Manchester, Jamaica, West Indies.

International Assn. of Technological University Libs. (IATUL)/Association internationale des bibliothèques d'universités polytechniques, c/o Radcliffe Science Lib., Parks Rd., Oxford OX1 3QP, UK. *Pres.* Dennis Shaw.

Standing Conference on Lib. Materials on Africa (SCOLMA), c/o *Secy.* P. M. Larby, Institute of Commonwealth Studies, 27-28 Russell Sq., London WC1B 5DS, England.

Europe

LIBER (Ligue des Bibliothèques Européenes de Recherche), Assn. of European Research Lib., c/o H.-A. Koch, Staats-und Universitätsbibliothek, Postfach 330160, D-2800 Bremen 33, Federal Republic of Germany.

Nordisk Videnskabeligt Bibliotekarforbund – NVBF (Scandinavian Federation of Research Libns.), c/o Førstebibliotekar Ulla Højsgaard, I.D.E. Danish Institute of International Exchange, Amaliegade 38, DK 1256 Copenhagen K, Denmark.

National

Argentina

Asociación Argentina de Bibliotecas y Centros de Información Científicos y Técnicos (Argentine Assn. of Scientific and Technical Libs. & Info. Centers), Santa Fe 1145, Buenos Aires. *Exec. Secy.* Olga E. Veronelli.

Australia

LASIE Australia Company Ltd., *Pres.* Dorothy G. Peake, Box K446, Haymarket, N.S.W. 2000.

Lib. Assn. of Australia, *Exec. Dir.* Sue Kosse, 376 Jones St., Ultimo, N.S.W. 2007.

The School Lib. Assn. of New South Wales, c/o Secy., Box 80, Balmain, N.S.W. 2041.

State Libns.' Council of Australia, *Chpn.* D. W. Dunstan, State Libn., State Lib. of Tasmania, 91 Murray St., Hobart, Tasmania 7000.

Austria

Büchereiverband Österreichs (Assn. of Austrian Public Libs. & Libns.), *Chpn.* Franz Pascher; *Secy.* Heinz Buchmüller, Lange Gasse 37, A-1080 Vienna.

Österreichische Gesellschaft für Dokumentation und Information – ÖGDI (Austrian Society for Documentation and Info.), *Exec. Secy.* Bruno Hofer, c/o ON, Österreichisches Normungsinstitut, Heinestrasse 38, POB 130, A-1021 Vienna.

Vereinigung Österreichischer Bibliothekare – VÖB (Assn. of Austrian Libns.), *Pres.* Magda Strebl, c/o Österreichische Nationalbibliothek, Josefsplatz 1, A-1015 Vienna.

Belgium

Archives et Bibliothèques de Belgique/Archief-en Bibliotheekwezen in België (Archives and Libs. of Belgium), *Exec. Secy.* T. Verschaffel, Bibliothèque Royale Albert I, 4 bd. de l'Empereur, B-1000 Brussels.

Association Belge de Documentation-ABD/Belgische Vereniging voor Documentatie-BVD (Belgian Assn. for Documentation), Box 110, 1040 Brussels 26. *Pres.* Paul Hubot.

Institut d'Enseignement Superieur Social de l'Etat, Sec. Bibliothecaires-Documentalistes (State Institute of Higher Social Education, Libn., and Documentalist Sec.), Rue de l'Abbaye 26, B-1050 Brussels. *Dir.* R. Simon Saint Hubert.

Vereniging van Religieus-Wetenschappelijke Bibliothécarissen (Assn. of Theological Libns.), Minderbroederstr. 5, B-3800 St. Truiden. *Exec. Secy.* K. Van de Casteele, Spoorweglaan 237, B-2610 Wilrijk.

Vlaamse Vereniging voor Bibliotheek-, Archief-, en Documentatiewezen – VVBAD (Flemish Assn. of Libns., Archivists, and Documentalists), *Pres.* F. Heymans; *Secy.* L. Van den Bosch, Goudbloemstraat 10, 2008 Antwerp.

Bolivia

Asociación Boliviana de Bibliotecarios (Bolivian Lib. Assn.), *Pres.* Efraín Virreira Sánchez, Casilla 992, Cochabamba.

Brazil

Associação dos Arquivistas Brasileiros (Assn. of Brazilian Archivists), Praia de Botafogo 186, Sala B-217, CEP 22253 Rio de Janeiro, RJ. *Pres.* Jaime Antunes da Silva.

Fedração Brasileira de Associações de Bibliotecários (Brazilian Federation of Libns. Assns.), c/o *Pres.* Elizabet Maria Ramos de Carvalho, Rua Avanhandava, 40-cj. 110, Bela Vista, CEP 01306 São Paulo.

Bulgaria

Bulgarian Union of Public Libs., ul. Alabin, Sofia.

Sekciylna na Bibliotechnite Rabotnitsi pri Zentrainija Komitet na Profesionalniya Suyuz na Rabotnicite ot Poligrafičeskata Promišlenost i Kulturnite Instituti (Lib. Sec. at the Trade Union of the Workers in the Polygraphic Industry and Cultural Institutions), c/o Cyril and Methodius National Lib. Blvd., Tolbuhin. *Pres.* Stefan Kancev.

Canada

Association Canadienne des Écoles des Bibliothécaires (Canadian Assn. of Lib. Schools), *Pres.* L. J. Amey, School of Lib. Service, Dalhousie Univ., Halifax, NS B3H 4H8.

Canadian Assn. for Information Science (Association Canadienne de Science de L'Information), Univ. of Toronto, 140 St. George St., Toronto, ON M5S 1A1.

Canadian Council of Lib. Schools (Conseil Canadien des Ecoles de Bibliothéconomie) (CCLS/CCEB), *Chair.* Mary Dykstra, Dir., School of Lib. & Info. Studies, Dalhousie Univ., Halifax, NS B3H 4H8.

Canadian Lib. Assn., *Exec. Dir.* Jane Cooney, 200 Elgin St., 6th fl., Ottawa, ON K2P 1L5. (For detailed information on the Canadian Lib. Assn. and its divisions, see "National Library and Information-Industry Associations, United States and Canada"; for information on the library associations of the provinces of Canada, see "State, Provincial, and Regional Library Associations.")

La Société bibliographique du Canada (The Bibliographical Society of Canada), *Secy.-Treas.* W. P. Stoneman, Dept. of English, Univ. of Windsor, Windsor, ON N9B 3P4.

Chile

Colegio de Bibliotecarios de Chile A. G. (Chilean Lib. Assn.), *Pres.* Marcia Marinovic Simunovic; *Secy.-Gen.* Maria Antonieta Calabacero, Box 3741, Santiago.

China (People's Republic of)

Zhongguo Tushuguan Xuehui (China Society of Lib. Science—CSLS), *Secy.-Gen.* Liu Deyuan, 7 Wenjinjie, Beijing (Peking).

China (Republic of)

Library Assn. of China, c/o National Central Lib., 20 Chung-shan S. Rd., Taipei. *Exec. Dir.* Teresa Wang Chang.

Colombia

Asociación Colombiana de Bibliotecarios—ASCOLBI (Colombian Assn. of Libns.), Apdo. Aéreo 30883, Bogotá, D.E.

Asociación de Egresados de la Escuela Interamericana de Bibliotecologia—ASEIBI (International Lib. School Grad. Assn.), Apdo. Aéreo 49983, Medellín.

Costa Rica

Asociación Costarricense de Bibliotecarios (Assn. of Costa Rican Libns.), Apdo. Postal 3308, San José.

Cyprus

Kypriakos Synthesmos Vivliothicarion (Lib. Assn. of Cyprus), c/o Pedagogical Academy, Box 1039, Nikosia. *Secy.* Paris G. Rossos.

Czechoslovakia

Ústřední knihovnická rada CSR (Central Lib. Council of the Czechoslovak Socialist Republic), c/o Dept. of Libs., Ministry of Culture of CSR, Valdštejnská 10, 118 11 Praha 1-Malá Strana.

Zväz slovenských knihovníkov a informatikov (Assn. of Slovak Libns. and Documentalists), *Pres.* Vít Rak; *Exec. Secy.* Elena Sakálová, Michalská 1, 814 17 Bratislava.

Denmark

Arkivforeningen (The Archives Society), *Exec. Secy.* Steen Ousager, Rigsarkivet, Rigsdagsgarden 9, DK-1218 Copenhagen K.

Danmarks Biblioteksforening (Danish Lib. Assn.), *Pres.* Bent Sørensen, Trekronergade 15, DK-2500 Valby-Copenhagen.

Danmarks Forskningsbiblioteksforening (Danish Research Lib. Assn.), *Pres.* Niels-Henrik Gylstorff, Statsbiblioteket, Universitetsparken, DK-8000 Aarhus C.

Danmarks Skolebiblioteksforening (Assn. of Danish School Libs.), *Exec. Secy.* Ove Frank, Norrebrogade 159, DK-2200 Copenhagen N.

Dansk Musikbiblioteksforening, Dansk sektion of AIBM (Danish Assn. of Music Libs., Danish Sec. of AIBM/IAML), c/o *Secy.*, Duevej 14-6, DK-2000 Copenhagen F.

Dominican Republic

Asociación Dominicana de Bibliotecarios – ASODOBI (Dominican Lib. Assn.), c/o Biblioteca Nacional, Plaza de la Cultura, Santo Domingo. *Pres.* Prospero J. Mella Chavier; *Secy.-Gen.* Hipólito González C.

Ecuador

Asociación Ecuatoriana de Bibliotecarios – AEB (Ecuadorian Lib. Assn.), *Exec. Secy.* Elizabeth Carrion, Casa de la Cultura Ecuatoriana, Casilla 87, Quito.

Egypt

See United Arab Republic.

El Salvador

Asociación de Bibliotecarios de El Salvador (El Salvador Lib. Assn.), c/o *Secy.-Gen.* Edgar Antonio Pérez Borja, Urbanización Gerardo Barrios Polígono, "B" No. 5, San Salvador, C.A.

Ethiopia

Ye Ethiopia Betemetshaft Serategnoch Mahber (Ethiopian Lib. Assn. – ELA), *Exec. Secy.* Befekadu Debela, Box 30530, Addis Ababa.

Finland

Kirjastonhoitajaliitto-Bibliotekarieförbundet r.y. (Finnish Libns. Assn.), *Exec. Secy.* Jouko Lieko, Järnvägsmannagatan, Rautatieläisenkatu 6, SF-00520 Helsinki.

Kirjastonhoitajat ja informaatikot- Bibliotekarier och informatiker ry. (Assn. of Research & Univ. Libns.), *Exec. Secy.* Marketta Honkanen, Akavatalo, Rautatieläisenk 6, SF-00520 Helsinki.

Suomen Kirjastoseura-Finlands Biblioteksförening (Finnish Lib. Assn.), *Secy.-Gen.* Tuula Haavisto, Museokatu 18 A, SF-00100 Helsinki 10.

Tietopalveluseura-Samfundet för Informationstjänst i Finland (Finnish Society for Info. Services), Mannerheimintie 40A32, 00100 Helsinki.

France

Association des Archivistes Français (Assn. of French Archivists), *Pres.* Mlle. R. Cleyet-Michaud; *Exec. Secys.* Mme. M. P. Arnauld and Mme. E. Gautier-Desuaux, 60 r. des Francs-Bourgeois, F-75141 Paris, Cedex 03.

Association des Bibliothécaires Français (Assn. of French Libns.), *Exec. Secy.* Anne-Françoise Bonnardel, 65 rue de Richelieu, F-75002 Paris.

Association des Bibliothèques Ecclésiastiques de France (Assn. of French Theological Libs.), *Exec. Secy.* Jean-Marie Barbier, 6 rue du Regard, F-75006 Paris.

Association Française des Documentalistes et des Bibliotécaires Spécialisés – ADBS (Assn. of French Info. Scientists and Special Libns.), *Exec. Secy.* Serge Cacaly, 5, Av. Franco-Russe, 75007 Paris.

German Democratic Republic

Bibliotheksverband der Deutschen Demokratischen Republik (Lib. Assn. of the German Democratic Republic), c/o *Exec. Dir.* Klaus Plötz, Hermann-Matern-Str. 57, DDR-1040 Berlin.

Germany (Federal Republic of)

Arbeitsgemeinschaft der Kunstbibliotheken (Working Group of Art Libs.), c/o *Chpn.* Bernd Evers, Kunstbibliothek, Staatliche Museen, Preussicher Kulturbesitz, Berlin, Jebensstr. 2, 1000 Berlin 12.

Arbeitsgemeinschaft der Spezialbibliotheken (Assn. of Special Libs.), *Chpn.* Walter Manz, Zentralbibliothek der Kernforschungsanlage Jülich GmbH, Postfach 1913, D-5170 Jülich 1.

Deutsche Gesellschaft für Dokumentation e.V. – DGD (German Society for Documentation), *Scientific Secy.* Hilde Strohl-Goebel, Westendstr. 19, D-6000 Frankfurt am Main 1.

Deutscher Bibliotheksverband e.V. (German Lib. Assn.), *Secy.* Karin Pauleweit, Bundesallee 184/185, D-1000 Berlin 31.

Verband der Bibliotheken des Landes Nordrhein-Westfalen (Assn. of Libs. in the Federal State of North Rhine-Westphalia), *Chpn.* Ulrich Moeske, Ltd. Städtischer Bibliotheksdivektor, Stadtbücherei Dortmund, Vorsitzender, Markt 12, 4600 Dortmund 1.

Verein der Bibliothekare an Öffentlichen Bibliotheken e.V.—VBB (Assn. of Libns. at Public Libs.), *Chpn.* Birgit Dankert; *Secy.* Katharina Boulanger, Postfach 1324, D-7410 Reutlingen 1.

Verein der Diplom-Bibliothekare an wissenschaftlichen Bibliotheken (Assn. of Graduated Libns. at Academic Libs.), *Chpn.* Hans-J. Kuhlmeyer, c/o Nieders. Staats- u. Universitaetsbibliothek, Prinzenstr. 1, D-3400 Goettingen.

Verein deutscher Archivare—VdA (Assn. of German Archivists), *Chpn.* Hermann Rumschöttel, Generaldirektion der Staatlichen Archive Bayerns, Schönfeldstr. 5, Postfach 22 11 52, D-8000 Munich 22.

Verein Deutscher Bibliothekare e.V.—VDB (Assn. of German Libns.), *Pres.* Ltd. Bibliotheksdirektor Günther Wiegand; *Secy.* Else Maria Wischermann, Universitatsbibliothek, Olshausenstr. 29, D-2300 Kiel.

Ghana

Ghana Lib. Assn., *Exec. Secy.* D. B. Addo, Box 4105, Accra.

Great Britain

See United Kingdom.

Guatemala

Asociación Bibliotecológica de Guatemala (Lib. Assn. of Guatemala), *Pres.* Elizabeth Flores; *Secy.* Susana Prera de Meza, dir. O calle 15-70, ozna 15, Colonia El Maestro.

Guyana

Guyana Lib. Assn. (GLA), *Secy.* Alethea John, c/o National Lib., Box 10240, 76/77 Main St., Georgetown.

Hong Kong

Hong Kong Lib. Assn., *Pres.* David S. Yen, c/o Box 10095, G.P.O., Hong Kong.

Hungary

Magyar Könyvtárosok Egyesülete (Assn. of Hungarian Libns.), *Pres.* I. Billédi; *Secy.* G. Poprády, Úri U. 54–56, H–1014 Budapest.

Tájékoztatási Tudományos Tanács—MTESZ/TTT (Info. Science Council), c/o Pál Gágyor, Kossuth tér 6-8, Budapest 1055.

Iceland

Bókavarðafélag Islands (Icelandic Lib. Assn.), *Pres.* Thórdis Thorvaldsdóttir, Box 7050, 127 Reykjavík.

India

Indian Assn. of Special Libs. and Info. Centres (IASLIC), *Gen. Secy.* S. M. Ganguly, P-291, CIT Scheme 6M, Kankurgachi, Calcutta 700 054.

Indian Lib. Assn. (ILA), *Pres.* Krishan Kumay; *Gen. Secy.* C. P. Vashishth, A/40–41, No. 201, Ansal Bldgs., Dr. Mukerjee Nagar, Delhi 110 009.

Indonesia

Ikatan Pustakawan Indonesia—IPI (Indonesian Lib. Assn.), *Pres.* Prabowo Tjitroprawiro; *Secy.-Gen.* Nurhadi Sudarno, Jalan Salemba Raya 28A, Jakarta 10002.

Iran

Iranian Lib. Assn., *Exec. Secy.* M. Niknam Vazifeh, Box 11-1391, Tehran.

Iraq

Iraqi Lib. Assn., *Exec. Secy.* N. Kamal-al-Deen, Box 4081, Baghdad-Adhamya.

Ireland (Republic of)

Cumann Leabharlann Na h-Éireann (Lib. Assn. of Ireland), *Pres.* I. O'Deirg; *Hon.*

Secy. W. P. Smith, 53 Uppr. Mount St., Dublin 2.

Cumann Leabharlannaith Scoile—CLS (Irish Assn. of School Libns.), Headquarters: The Lib., Univ. College, Dublin 4. *Exec. Secy.* Sister Mary Columban, Loreto Convent, Foxrock Co., Dublin.

Italy

Associazione Italiana Biblioteche—AIB (Italian Libs. Assn.), *Secy.* G. Lazzari, Casella Postale 2461, 00100 Rome A-D.

Associazione Nazionale Archivistica Italiana—ANAI (National Assn. of Italian Archivists), *Secy.* Enrica Ormanni, Via Guido D'Arezzo, 18 00198 Rome.

Ivory Coast

Association pour le Développement de la Documentation des Bibliothèques et Archives de la Côte d'Ivoire (Assn. for the Development of Documentation, Libs., and Archives of the Ivory Coast), c/o Bibliothèque Nationale, B.P. 20915, Abidjan.

Jamaica

Jamaica Lib. Assn. (JLA), *Secy.* Gloria Y. Greene, Box 58, Kingston 5.

Japan

Information Science and Technology Assn., Japan (INFOSTA-NIPDOK), *Pres.* Yukio Nakamura; *Dir. and Secy.-Gen.* Tsunetaka Ueda, Sasaki Bldg., 5-7 Koisikawa 2-chome, Bunkyoku, Tokyo 112.

Nihon Toshokan Kyôkai (Japan Lib. Assn.—JLA), *Secy.-Gen.* Hitoshi Kurihara, 1-10, Taishido 1-chome, Setagayaku, Tokyo 154.

Senmon Toshokan Kyôgikai—SENTOKYO (Japan Special Libs. Assn.), *Exec. Dir.* Yoshitaro Tanabe, c/o National Diet Lib., 1-10-1 Nagata-cho, Chiyodaku, Tokyo 100.

Jordan

Jordan Lib. Assn. (JLA), *Pres.* Farouk Moaz; *V.P.* Nayef Khaleefa; *Secy.* Adeeb Agel; *Treas.* Reyad Barakat, Box 6289, Amman.

Korea (Democratic People's Republic of)

Lib. Assn. of the Democratic People's Republic of Korea, *Secy.* Li. Geug, Central Lib., Box 109, Pyongyang.

Korea (Republic of)

Hanguk Tosogwan Hyophoe (Korean Lib. Assn.), *Exec. Secy.* Dae Kwon Park, 100-177, 1-Ka, Hoehyun-Dong, Choong-Ku, CPO Box 2041, Seoul.

Laos

Association des Bibliothécaires Laotiens (Laos Lib. Assn.), Direction de la Bibliothèque Nationale, Ministry of Education, Box 704, Vientiane.

Lebanon

Lebanese Lib. Assn. (LLA), *Pres.* L. Hanhan; *Secy.* L. Sadaka, Univ. Lib., AUB, Beirut.

Malaysia

Persatuan Perpustakaan Malaysia—PPM (Lib. Assn. of Malaysia), *Secy.* Ahmad Ridzuan, Box 12545, 50782 Kuala Lumpur.

Mauritania

Association Mauritanienne des Bibliothécaires, des Archivistes et des Documentalistes—AMBAD (Mauritanian Assn. of Libns., Archivists, and Documentalists), c/o *Pres.* Oumar Diouwara, Dir., National Lib., Nouakchott.

Mexico

Asociación de Bibliotecarios de Instituciónes de Enseñanza Superior e Investigación—ABIESI (Assn. of Libns. of Higher Education and Research Institutions), *Pres.* Elsa Barberena, Apdo. Postal 5-611, México 5, D.F.

Asociación Mexicana de Bibliotecarios, A.C. (Mexican Assn. of Libns.), *Pres.* Rosa Maria Fernández de Zamora, Apdo. 27-651, 06760, Mexico, D.F.

Netherlands

Nederlandse Vereniging van Bibliothecarissen, Documentalisten en Literatuuronderzoekers—NVB (Dutch Lib. Assn.), p/a Mw. H. J. Krikke-Scholten, Nolweg 13 d, 4209 AW Schelluinen.

UKB—Samenwerkingsverband van de Universiteitsbibliotheken, de Koninklijke Bibliotheek en de Bibliotheek van de Koninklijke Nederlandse Akademie van Wetenschappen (Assn. of Univ. Libs., the Royal Lib., and the Lib. of the Netherlands Academy of Arts and Sciences), *Exec. Secy.* J. L. M. van Dijk, c/o Bibliotheek Rijksuniversiteit Limburg, Postbus 616, 6200 MD Maastricht.

Vereniging van Archivarissen in Nederland—VAN (Assn. of Archivists in the Netherlands), *Exec. Secy.* J. A. M. Y. Bos-Rops, Postbus 11645, 2502 AP Den Haag.

Vereniging voor het Theologisch Bibliothecariaat (Assn. of Theological Libns.), *Exec. Secy.* R. T. M. Van Dijk, Postbus 289, 6500 AG Nijmegen.

New Zealand

New Zealand Lib. Assn. (NZLA), *Pres.* J. Caudwell, 20 Brandon St., Box 12-212, Wellington 1.

Nicaragua

Biblioteca Universitaria, Universidad Centroamericana (UCA), Apdo. 69, Managua. *Dir.* Conny Mendez R.

Nigeria

Nigerian Lib. Assn. (NLA), *Pres.* J. A. Dosunmu; *Treas.* J. O. Fasanya; *Secy.* L. I. Ehigiator, c/o Bendel State Lib., James Watt Rd., P.M.B. 1127, Benin City.

Norway

Arkivarforeningen (Assn. of Archivists), *Secy.-Treas.* Kari Benedictow, Postboks 10, Kringsja, N-0807 Oslo 8.

Norsk Bibliotekforening—NBF (Norwegian Lib. Assn.), *Secy.-Treas.* G. Langeland, Malerhaugveien 20, N-0661 Oslo 6.

Norsk Fagbibliotekforening—NFF (Norwegian Assn. of Special Libs.), *Chpn.* Else-Margrethe Bredland, Malerhaugveien 20, N-0661 Oslo 6.

Pakistan

Pakistan Lib. Assn. (FBC), *Secy.* Bashir Chohan, c/o Lib., Quaid-i-Azam Univ., Box 2358, Islamabad.

Society for the Promotion & Improvement of Libs. (SPIL), *Pres.* Hakim Mohammed Said, Al-Majeed, Hamdard Centre, Nazimabad, Karachi-18.

Panama

Asociación Panameña de Bibliotecarios (Panamanian Assn. of Libns.), *Pres.* Amelia L. de Barakat, Estafeta Universitaria, Apdo. 10808, Republic of Panama.

Papua New Guinea

Papua New Guinea Lib. Assn. (PNGLA), *Pres.* Margaret Obi; *V.P.* Ursula Pawe; *Secy.* Haro Raka; *Treas.* Lewis Kusso-Aless; *Pubns. Mgr.* Maria Teka, Box 5368, Boroko.

Paraguay

Asociación de Bibliotecarios Universitarios del Paraguay—ABUP (Paraguayan Assn. of Univ. Libns.), c/o Zayda Caballero, Head, Escuela de Bibliotecología, Universidad Nacional de Asunción, Casilla de Correo, 1408 Asunción.

Peru

Agrupación de Bibliotecas para la Integración de la Información Socio-Económica—ABIISE (Lib. Group for the Integration of Socio-Economic Info.), *Dir.* Betty Chiriboga de Cussato, Apdo. 2874, Lima 100.

Asociación Peruana de Archiveros (Assn. of Peruvian Archivists), Archivo General de la Nación, C. Manuel Cuadros s/n., Palacio de Justicia, Apdo. 3124, Lima 100.

Asociación Peruana de Bibliotecarios (Assn. of Peruvian Libns.), *Exec. Secy.* Amparo Geraldino de Orban, Apdo. 3760, Lima.

Philippines

Assn. of Special Libs. of the Philippines (ASLP), *Pres.* Victoria S. Mercado, c/o The National Lib., Rm. 301, T. M. Kalaw, Manila.

Philippine Lib. Assn., Inc. (PLAI), *Pres.* Corazon M. Nera, The National Lib. Bldg., T. M. Kalaw St., Ermita, Box 2926, Manila.

Poland

Stowarzyszenie Bibliotekarzy Polskich – SBP (Polish Libns. Assn.), *Pres.* Stefan Kubów; *Gen. Secy.* Andrzej Jopkiewicz, ul. Konopczyńskiego 5/7, 00-953 Warsaw.

Portugal

Associação Portuguesa de Bibliotecários, Arquivistas e Documentalistas (Portuguese Assn. of Libns., Archivists, and Documentalists), *Exec. Secy.* Jorge Resende, Rua Ocidental ao Campo Grande, 83 1751 Lisbon.

Rhodesia

See Zimbabwe.

Romania (Socialist Republic of)

Asociatia Bibliotecarilor din Republica Socialista Romania (Association des Bibliothecaires de la République Socialiste de Roumanie), *Pres.* G. Botez, Biblioteca Centrala de Stat, Strada Ion Ghica 4, 7001 8 Bucharest.

Scotland

See United Kingdom.

Senegal

Commission des Bibliothèques de l'ASDBAM, Association Sénégalaise pour le Développement de la Documentation, des Bibliothèques, des Archives et des Musées (Senegal Assn. for the Development of Documentation, Libs., Archives, and Museums), *Gen. Secy.* Aïssatou Wade, B.P. 375, Dakar.

Sierra Leone

Sierra Leone Lib. Assn. (SLLA), c/o *Secy.* L. Hunter, Medical Lib., Connaught Hospital, Freetown.

Singapore

Congress of Southeast Asian Libns. (CONSAL), *Chpn.* Mastini Hardjo Prakaso, c/o National Lib. of Indonesia, Jalan Salemba Raya 28, Jakarta 10002, Indonesia.

Lib. Assn. of Singapore (LAS), *Hon. Secy.*, c/o National Lib., Stamford Rd., Singapore 0617.

South Africa

African Lib. Assn. of South Africa (ALASA), *Hon. Secy.-Treas.* G. K. Motshologane, c/o Lib., Univ. of the North, Private Bag X1112, Sovenga 0727.

Spain

Instituto de Información y Documentación en Ciencia y Tecnologia (ICYT), *Secy.* Milagros Villarreal de Benito, Joaquín Costa, 22, 28002 Madrid 6.

Sri Lanka

Sri Lanka Lib. Assn. (SLLA), *Pres.* C. L. M. Nethsingha; *Gen. Secy.* M. F. Hamid, OPA Centre, 275/75, Bauddhaloka Mawatha, Colombo 7.

Sudan

Sudan Lib. Assn. (SLA), *Exec. Secy.* Mohamed Omar, Box 1361, Khartoum.

Sweden

Svenska Arkivsamfundet (The Swedish Archival Assn.), c/o Riksarkivet, Box 12541, S-102 29 Stockholm.

Svenska Bibliotekariesamfundet – SBS (Swedish Assn. of Univ. and Research

Libs.), c/o *Secy.* Margareta Nordström, Universitetsbiblioteket, Box 1441, S-901 24 Umeå.

Sveriges Allmänna Biblioteksförening—SAB (Swedish Lib. Assn.), *Pres.* B. Zachrisson, Box 200, S-22100 Lund.

Sveriges Vetenskapliga Specialbiblioteks Förening—SVSF (Assn. of Special Research Libs.), *Pres.* Anders Ryberg; *Secy.* Birgitta Fridén, c/o Utrikesdepartementets bibliotek, Box 16121, S-10323 Stockholm.

Tekniska Litteratursällskapet—TLS (Swedish Society for Technical Documentation), *Secy.* Birgitta Levin, Box 5073, S-10242 Stockholm 5.

Vetenskapliga Bibliotekens Tjänstemannaförening—VBT (Assn. of Research Lib. Employees), *Pres.* Anders Schmidt, Lund Univ. Lib., Box 3, S-22100 Lund.

Switzerland

Schweizerische Vereinigung für Dokumentation/Association Suisse de Documentation—SVD/ASD (Swiss Assn. of Documentation), *Secy.-Treas.* W. Bruderer, BID GD PTT, CH-3030 Bern.

Vereinigung Schweizerischer Archivare—VSA (Assn. of Swiss Archivists), c/o Bernard Truffer, 7 rue des Vergers, CH-1950 Sion.

Vereinigung Schweizerischer Bibliothekare/Association des Bibliothécaires Suisses/Associazione dei Bibliotecari Svizzeri—VSB/ABS (Assn. of Swiss Libns.), *Exec. Secy.* W. Treichler, Hallwylstrasse 15, CH-3003 Bern.

Tanzania

Tanzania Lib. Assn., *Chpn.* T. E. Mlaki, Box 2645, Dar-es-Salaam.

Tunisia

Association Tunisienne des Documentalistes, Bibliothécaires et Archivistes (Tunisian Assn. of Documentalists, Libns., and Archivists), *Exec. Secy.* Mohamed Abdeljaoved, 43 rue de la Liberté, Le Bardo.

Turkey

Türk Kütüphaneciler Derneği—TKD (Turkish Libns. Assn.), *Exec. Secy.* Aydun Kuran, Headquarters, Elgün Sokağı 8/8, 06440 Kizilay, Ankara.

Uganda

Uganda Lib. Assn. (ULA), *Chpn.* P. W. Songa; *Secy.* L. M. Ssengero, Box 5894, Kampala.

Uganda Schools Lib. Assn. (USLA), *Exec. Secy.* J. W. Nabembezi, Box 7014, Kampala.

Union of Soviet Socialist Republics

USSR Lib. Council, *Pres.* N. S. Kartashov, Lenin State Lib., 3 Prospect Kalinina, 101 000 Moscow.

United Arab Republic

Egyptian School Lib. Assn. (ESLA), *Exec. Secy.* M. Salem, 35 Algalaa St., Cairo.

United Kingdom

ASLIB (The Assn. for Info. Management), *Dir.* Dennis A. Lewis, Information House, 26/27 Boswell St., London WC1N 3JZ.

Assn. of British Theological and Philosophical Libs. (ABTAPL), *Hon. Secy.* Alan Jesson, Bible Society's Lib., c/o University Lib., West Rd., Cambridge CB3 9DR.

Bibliographical Society, *Hon. Secy.* M. M. Foot, British Lib., Humanities and Social Sciences, Great Russell St., London WC1B 3DG.

British and Irish Assn. of Law Libns. (BIALL), *Hon. Secy.* H. C. Boucher, Libn., Pinsent & Co., Post and Mail House, 26 Colmore Circus, Birmingham B4 6BH.

The Lib. Assn., *Chief Exec.* George Cunningham, 7 Ridgmount St., London WC1E 7AE.

Private Libs. Assn. (PLA), *Hon. Secy.* Frank Broomhead, 16 Brampton Grove, Kenton, Harrow, Middlesex HA3 8LG.

School Lib. Assn. (SLA), *Exec. Secy.* Valerie Fea, Liden Lib., Barrington Close, Liden, Swindon, Wiltshire SN3 6HF.

Scottish Lib. Assn. (SLA), a branch of the Lib. Assn., Motherwell Business Centre, Coursington Rd., Motherwell ML1 1PW. *Exec. Secy.* Robert Craig.

Society of Archivists (SA), *Hon. Secy.* A. J. E. Arrowsmith, Suffolk Record Office, County Hall, Ipswich IP4 2JS.

The Standing Conference of National and Univ. Libs. (SCONUL), *Exec. Secy.* A. J. Loveday, Secretariat and Registered Office, 102 Euston St., London NW1 2HA.

Welsh Lib. Assn., a branch of the Lib. Assn., *Hon. Secy.* Dwynwen Roberts, Clwyd Lib. and Museum Service, County Civic Centre, Mold, Clwyd CH7 6NW.

Uruguay

Agrupación Bibliotecológica del Uruguay–ABU (Lib. Documentation, Numismatics and Archive Science Assn. of Uruguay), *Pres.* Luis Alberto Musso, Cerro Largo 1666, Montevideo.

Venezuela

Colegio de Bibliotecólogos y Archivólogos dc Venezuela–COL-BAV (Assn. of Venezuelan Libns. and Archivists), *Exec. Secy.* Zunilde Nuñez de Rojas, Apdo. 6283, Caracas 101.

Wales

See United Kingdom.

Yugoslavia

Društvo Bibliotečkih Radnika Srbije (Society of Lib. Workers of Serbia), *Chair.* Dragan Ćirović; *Exec. Secy.* Ljiljana Popović, Skerlićeva 1, YU-11000 Belgrade.

Društvo Bibliotekara Bosne i Hercegovine–DB BiH (Lib. Assn. of Bosnia and Herzegovina), *Exec. Secy.* Amra Rešidbegović, Obala 42, YU-71000 Sarajevo.

Hrvatsko bibliotekarsko društvo–HBD (Croatian Lib. Assn.), *Pres.* Anisja Čečuk; *Exec. Secy.* Daniela Živković, National and Univ. Lib., Marulićev trg 21, YU-41000 Zagreb.

Sojuz na Društvata na Bibliotékarite na SR Makedonija (Union of Libns. Assn. of Macedonia), Bul. "Goce Delčev" br. 6, Box 566, YU-91000 Skopje.

Zveza bibliotekarskih društev Slovenije–ZBDS (Society of the Lib. Assns. of Slovenia), *Exec. Secy.* Stanislav Bahor, Turjaška 1, YU-61000 Ljubljana.

Zaire

Association Zairoise des Archivistes, Bibliothecaires, et Documentalistes–AZABDO (Zairian Assn. of Archivists, Libns., and Documentalists), *Exec. Secy.* Mulamba Mukunya, Box 805, Kinshasa XI.

Zambia

Zambia Lib. Assn. (ZLA), Box 32839, Lusaka.

Zimbabwe

Zimbabwe Lib. Assn.–ZLA, *Hon. Secy.* D. M. Thorpe, Box 3133, Harare.

Directory of Book Trade and Related Organizations

Book Trade Associations, United States and Canada

For more extensive information on the associations listed in this section, see the annual issues of the *Literary Market Place* (Bowker).

Advertising Typographers Assn. of America, Inc., RD 3, Box 345, Stockton, NJ 08559. *Exec. Secy.* Walter A. Dew, Jr. Tel. 201-782-4055.

American Booksellers Assn., Inc., 137 W. 25 St., New York, NY 10001. Tel. 212-463-8450. *Pres.* Edward Morrow, Northshire Bookstore, Manchester Center, Vermont; *V.P.* Neal Coonerty, Bookshop Santa Cruz, Santa Cruz, California; *Secy.* Fern Jaffe, Paperbacks Plus, Inc., Bronx, New York; *Treas.* Michael Powell, Powell's Books, Portland, Oregon; *Publications Dir.* Ginger Curwen; *Conventions and Meetings Dir.* Eileen Dengler.

American Institute of Graphic Arts, 1059 Third Ave., New York, NY 10021. Tel. 212-752-0813. *Pres.* Nancye Green; *Dir.* Caroline W. Hightower.

American Medical Publishers Assn. *Pres.* Braxton D. Mitchell, Urban & Schwarzenberg, Inc., 7 E. Redwood St., Baltimore, MD 21202. Tel. 301-539-2550; *Pres.-Elect.* John Febigher Spahr, Jr., Lea & Febiger, 600 Washington Sq., Philadelphia, PA 19106. Tel. 215-922-1330; *Secy.-Treas.* Toni M. Tracy, Churchill Livingstone Inc., 1560 Broadway, New York, NY 10036. Tel. 212-819-5400.

American Printing History Assn., Box 4922, Grand Central Sta., New York, NY 10163. *Pres.* James Green; *V.P. for Programs.* John Lancaster; *V.P. for Publications.* Jeffrey Kaimowitz; *V.P. for Membership.* Edward Colter; *Secy.* Michael Hentges; *Treas.* Pat Taylor; *Ed., Printing History.* Renée I. Weber; *Ed., The APHA Newsletter.* Stephen O. Saxe.

American Society of Indexers, Inc., 1700 18th St. N.W., Washington, DC 20009. *Pres.* Bella Hass Weinberg, Div. of Lib. and Info. Science, St. John's Univ., Jamaica, NY 11439. Tel. 718-990-6200; *V.P.* Nancy Mulvany, Bayside Indexing Service, 265 Arlington Ave., Kensington, CA 94707. Tel. 415-524-4195; *Secy.* Trina E. King, 3530 Buford Hwy., #7, Atlanta, GA 30329. Tel. 404-636-2544; *Treas.* Clifton Anderson, 39 Lake Forest Dr., Box 4770, Charlottesville, VA 22905. Tel. 804-972-7600 ext. 238.

American Society of Journalists and Authors, 1501 Broadway, Suite 1907, New York, NY 10036. Tel. 212-997-0947. *Pres.* David W. Kennedy; *Exec. V.P.* Tom Bedell; *V.P.s.* Elaine Fein, Dodi Schultz; *Exec. Dir.* Alexandra Cantor; *Secy.* Gloria Hochman; *Treas.* Nona Aguilar.

American Society of Magazine Photographers (ASMP), 419 Park Ave. S., Suite 1407, New York, NY 10016. Tel. 212-889-9144. *Exec. Dir.* Richard Weisgrau; *Pres.* David MacTavish; *Admin. Dir.* Lucy Taylor.

American Society of Picture Professionals, Inc., Box 24201, Nashville, TN 37202. *National Pres.* Jane Kinne, Comstock, 30 Irving Place, New York, NY 10003. Tel. 212-353-8600; *Memb. Chpn.* Cathy Sachs, c/o Woodfin Camp Inc., 2025 Pennsylvania Ave. N.W., Suite 1011, Washington, DC 20006. Tel. 202-223-8442; *National*

Secy. Lynne Bachleda, Sterling Ct., A-3, 2101 Belmont Blvd., Nashville, TN 37212. Tel. 615-297-0640.

American Translators Assn., 109 Croton Ave., Ossining, NY 10562. Tel. 914-941-1500. *Pres.* Karl Kummer; *Pres.-Elect.* Deanna Hammond; *Secy.* Ann Sherwin; *Treas.* William I. Bertsche; *Staff Administrator.* Rosemary Malia.

Antiquarian Booksellers Assn. of America, Inc., 50 Rockefeller Plaza, New York, NY 10020. Tel. 212-757-9395. *Pres.* Michael Ginsberg; *V.P.* John R. Curtis, Jr.; *Secy.* Peter Stern; *Treas.* Raymond Wapner; *Admin. Asst.* Janice M. Farina.

Assn. of American Publishers, 220 E. 23 St., New York, NY 10010. Tel. 212-689-8920. *Pres.* Nicholas Veliotes; *Exec. V.P.* Thomas D. McKee; *V.P. School Div.* Donald A. Eklund; *Dirs.* Parker B. Ladd, Barbara J. Meredith; *Washington Office.* 2005 Massachusetts Ave. N.W., Washington, DC 20036. Tel. 202-232-3335; *Dirs.* Judith Platt, Diane G. Rennert, Carol A. Risher; *Chpn.* Lawrence Hughes, Hearst Trade Book Group; *V. Chpn.* Alberto Vitale, Bantam/Doubleday/Dell Publg. Group; *Treas.* Deborah E. Wiley, John Wiley & Sons.

Assn. of American University Presses, One Park Ave., New York, NY 10016. Tel. 212-889-6040. *Pres.* John G. Ryden, Dir., Yale Univ. Press; *Exec. Dir.* E. H. Phillips. Address correspondence to the executive director or to Hollis A. Holmes, Membership Services Manager.

Assn. of Book Travelers, c/o *Pres.* Donald Guerra, 175 Fifth Ave., Suite 2395, New York, NY 10010. Tel. 212-206-7715; *Treas.* Robert Evans; *Secy.* James King. Address correspondence to the president.

Assn. of Canadian Publishers, 260 King St. E., Toronto, ON M5A 1K3, Canada. Tel. 416-361-1408, FAX 416-361-0643. *Exec. Dir.* Hamish Cameron; *International Trade Officer.* P. Louise Smith; *Pres.* Clyde Rose; *V.P.* Patricia Dowdall; *Secy.* Margie Wolfe. Address correspondence to the executive director.

Assn. of Jewish Book Publishers, House of Living Judaism, 838 Fifth Ave., New York, NY 10021. *Pres.* Charles D. Lieber. Address correspondence to the president.

Assn. of the Graphic Arts, 5 Penn Plaza, New York, NY 10001. Tel. 212-279-2100. *Pres.* William Dirzulaitis; *Dir., Memb.* Maureen Christensen; *Dir., Govt. Affairs.* John J. Liantonio; *Dir., Ed.* Gail Zambrano; *Office Mgr.* Susan Shaw.

Book Industry Study Group, Inc., 160 Fifth Ave., New York, NY 10010. Tel. 212-929-1393. *Chpn.* Stephen Hill; *V. Chpn.* Neil Perlman; *Treas.* Seymour Turk; *Secy.* Robert W. Bell; *Managing Agent.* SKP Associates. Address correspondence to William G. Raggio.

Book Manufacturers Institute, 111 Prospect St., Stamford, CT 06901. Tel. 203-324-9670. *Pres.* John C. Wasson, Pres., Rand McNally Book Manufacturing Co.; *Exec. V.P.* Douglas E. Horner. Address correspondence to the executive vice president.

Book Publicists of Southern California, 6430 Sunset Blvd., Suite 503, Hollywood, CA 90028. Tel. 213-461-3921. *Pres.* Irwin Zucker; *V.P.* Sol Marshall; *Secy.* Suzy Mallery; *Treas.* Nina Mills.

Book Week Headquarters, Children's Book Council, Inc., 67 Irving Place, New York, NY 10003. Tel. 212-254-2666. *Pres.* John Donovan; *Chpn. 1989.* Brenda Bowen, Henry Holt and Co., 115 W. 18 St., New York, NY 10011. Tel. 212-886-9200.

The Bookbinders' Guild of New York, c/o *Secy.* Jeff Bernstein, Longacre, 85 Weyman Ave., New Rochelle, NY 10805. Tel. 212-824-8558; *Pres.* Sally McCravey, John Wiley & Sons, 605 Third Ave., New York, NY 10158. Tel. 212-850-6000.

Bookbuilders of Boston, Inc., c/o *Pres.* Paula Carroll, Simon & Schuster, Allyn & Bacon Div., 160 Gould St., Needham Heights, MA 02160. Tel. 617-455-1200; *1st V.P.* John Foley; *2nd V.P.* Nancy Seglin; *Treas.* Robert Delano.

Bookbuilders West, Box 883666, San Francisco, CA 94188. *Pres.* Larry Lazopoulos. Tel. 408-476-6990.

Canadian Book Publishers' Council, 45 Charles St. E., 7th fl., Toronto, ON M4Y 1S2, Canada. Tel. 416-964-7231. *Pres.* John Champ, Houghton Mifflin; *1st V.P.* George Bryson, Addison-Wesley; *2nd V.P.* Arnold Gosewich, Macmillan; *Secy.-Treas.* David Kirkwood, D.C. Heath; *Immediate Past Pres.* Brian E. Hickey, Harlequin Book Publg. Div.; *Exec. Dir.* Jacqueline Hushion; *Special Interest Groups.* The

School Group, The College Group, The Trade Group.

Canadian Booksellers Assn., 301 Donlands Ave., Toronto, ON M4J 3R8, Canada. Tel. 416-467-7883. *Convention Mgr.* Lynda Joyet; *Exec. Dir.* Serge Lavoie.

Chicago Book Clinic, 100 E. Ohio St., Suite 630, Chicago, IL 60611. Tel. 312-951-8254. *Pres.* Mercedes Bailey; *V.P.* Anita Constant; *Treas.* Richard McKee; *Secy.* Diane Tenzi; *Exec. Dir.* Anthony Cheung.

Chicago Publishers Assn., c/o *Pres.* Robert J. R. Follett, Follett Corp., 1000 W. Washington Blvd., Chicago, IL 60607. Tel. 312-666-4300.

The Children's Book Council Inc., 67 Irving Place, New York, NY 10003. Tel. 212-254-2666. *Pres.* John Donovan; *V.P.* Paula Quint; *Chpn.* Doris Bass, Bantam/Doubleday/Dell, 666 Fifth Ave., New York, NY 10103. Tel. 212-765-6500.

Christian Booksellers Assn., Box 200, Colorado Springs, CO 80901. Tel. 719-576-7880. *Pres.* William R. Anderson.

The Copyright Society of the U.S.A., New York Univ. School of Law, 40 Washington Sq. S., New York, NY 10012. Tel. 212-998-6194. *Pres.* Bernard Korman; *Secy.* E. Judith Hirschman Berger.

Council on Interracial Books for Children, Inc., 1841 Broadway, New York, NY 10023. Tel. 212-757-5339. *Pres.* Harriett Brown.

Evangelical Christian Publishers Assn., 950 W. Southern Ave., Suite 106, Tempe, AZ 85282. Tel. 602-966-3998. *Exec. Dir.* Doug Ross.

Graphic Artists Guild, 11 W. 20 St., 8th fl., New York, NY 10011. Tel. 212-463-7730. *Pres.* Kathie Abrams.

Guild of Book Workers, 521 Fifth Ave., 17th fl., New York, NY 10175. Tel. 212-757-6454. *Pres.* J. Franklin Mowery.

International Assn. of Printing House Craftsmen, Inc., 7599 Kenwood Rd., Cincinnati, OH 45236. Tel. 513-891-0611. *Pres.* Gordon D. Lindstrom; *Exec. V.P.* Patricia A. Milligan.

International Copyright Information Center (INCINC), c/o Assn. of American Publishers, 2005 Massachusetts Ave. N.W., Washington, DC 20036-1011. Tel. 202-232-3335. *Dir.* Carol A. Risher.

International Standard Book Numbering U.S. Agency, 245 W. 17 St., New York, NY 10011. Tel. 212-337-6971. *Dir.* Emery Koltay; *Coord.* Beatrice Jacobson; *Officers.* Erin M. Doyle, Lynn Ann Sahner, Albert Simmonds, Peter Simon.

JWB Jewish Book Council, 15 E. 26 St., New York, NY 10010. Tel. 212-532-4949. *Pres.* Abraham Kremer; *Dir.* Paula Gribetz Gottlieb.

Library Binding Institute, 8013 Centre Park Dr., Austin, TX 78754. Tel. 512-836-4141. *Exec. Dir.* Sally Grauer; *Counsel.* Dudley A. Weiss; *Technical Consultant.* Werner Rebsamen.

Magazine and Paperback Marketing Institute (MPMI), 1621 Cole St., Baltimore, MD 21223. Tel. 301-233-6764. *Exec. V.P.* Don DeVito.

Metropolitan Lithographers Assn., 950 Third Ave., Suite 1500, New York, NY 10022. Tel. 212-838-8480. *Exec. Dir.* Nichele Baum.

Mid-America Publishers Assn., c/o John Kremer, Ad-Lib Pubns., Box 1102, Fairfield, IA 52556. Tel. 515-472-6617.

Minnesota Book Publishers Roundtable. *Pres.* David Slater, Slater Studio, 211 Washington Ave. N., Minneapolis, MN 55401; *V.P.* Nordis Heyerdahl-Fowler, Minnesota Historical Society, 690 Cedar St., St. Paul, MN 55101; *Secy.-Treas.* Brad Vogt, The Liturgical Press, Collegeville, MN 56321. Tel. 612-363-2538. Address correspondence to the secretary-treasurer.

National Assn. of College Stores, 528 E. Lorain St., Box 58, Oberlin, OH 44074. Tel. 216-775-7777. *Pres.* Sarah Emerson, CSP, Hillsborough Community College Bookstore, Tampa, FL 33622; *Exec. Dir.* Garis F. Distelhorst.

National Council of the Churches of Christ in the U.S.A., Div. of Education and Ministry, Rm. 704, 475 Riverside Dr., New York, NY 10115-0050. Tel. 212-870-2271. *Assoc. Gen. Secy.* Rev. Dr. Arthur O. Van Eck.

New Mexico Book League, 8632 Horacio Place N.E., Albuquerque, NM 87111. Tel. 505-299-8940. *Exec. Dir.* Dwight A. Myers; *Pres.* Lawrence Clark Powell; *V.P.* Marc Simmons; *Treas.* C. Rittenhouse; *Ed.* Carol A. Myers.

New York Rights and Permissions Group, c/o

Chpn. Jeanne A. Gough, Gale Research Inc., 835 Penobscot Bldg., Detroit, MI 48226. Tel. 313-961-6813.

Northern California Booksellers Assn., c/o *Admin. Coord.* Elizabeth Bogner, 2141 Kittredge St., Box I, Berkeley, CA 94704. Tel. 415-644-3666; *Pres.* Melissa Mytinger, Cody's Books, 2454 Telegraph Ave., Berkeley, CA 94704. Tel. 415-845-9033.

Periodical and Book Assn. of America, Inc., 120 E. 34 St., New York, NY 10016. Tel. 212-689-4952. *Exec. Dir.* Michael Morse; *Pres.* Gerald Rothberg; *V.P.s.* Norman Jacobs, Marcia Orovitz; *Gen. Counsel.* Lee Feltman.

Periodical Marketers of Canada, c/o *Pres.* Cliff Connelly, Teck News Agency (1987), Ltd., 5 Kirkland St., Box 488, Kirkland Lake, ON P2N 3J6, Canada. Tel. 705-567-3318; *V.P.* Richard Bramall, Western Magazine Reshippers, 102-917 Cliveden Ave., New Westminster, BC V3M 6E8, Canada. Tel. 604-278-5642; *Secy.-Treas.* Steve Shepherd, Ottawa Valley News Co. Ltd., Box 157, Arnprior, ON K7S 3H4, Canada. Tel. 613-623-3197.

Philadelphia Book Clinic. *Secy.-Treas.* Thomas Colaiezzi, Lea & Febiger, 600 Washington Sq., Philadelphia, PA 19106. Tel. 215-925-8700.

Pi Beta Alpha, R.R. 2, Box 172, Bloomington, IL 61704. Tel. 309-378-4007. *Pres.* Ann Steinmetz, 2024 Kingsdale Dr., Stow, OH 44224; *Pres.-Elect.* David Gontz, 1138 S. Green St., Londonderry Farms, Palmyra, PA 17078; *V.P.* Mark Smith, 301 N. Meridian, Washington, IN 47501; *Dir., Memorial Loan Fund.* Glen Mallory, 10 Lake Park Rd., Champaign, IL 61821; *Exec. Secy.* Larry Efaw, R.R. 2, Box 172, Bloomington, IL 61704.

Proofreaders Club of New York, c/o *Pres.* Allan Treshan, 38-15 149th St., Flushing, NY 11354.

Publishers' Ad Club, c/o *Secy.* Catherine Grunewald, St. Martin's Press, 175 Fifth Ave., New York, NY 10010; *Pres.* Ken Atkatz, Franklin Spier, Inc., 650 First Ave., New York, NY 10016; *V.P.* Sarah Wright, Crown Publishers, 225 Park Ave. S., New York, NY 10003; *Treas.* Jerry Younger, New York Times Book Review, 229 W. 43 St., New York, NY 10036.

Publishers' Publicity Assn., c/o *Pres.* Arlynn Greenbaum, Little, Brown & Co., 205 Lexington Ave., New York, NY 10016. Tel. 212-683-0660; *V.P.* Susan Richman, Macmillan Publg. Co., 866 Third Ave., New York, NY 10022. Tel. 212-702-6757; *Secy.* Helen Atwan, Farrar, Straus, and Giroux, 19 Union Sq. W., New York, NY 10003. Tel. 212-741-6920; *Treas.* Karen Mender, Harper & Row, 10 E. 53 St., New York, NY 10022. Tel. 212-207-7250.

The Religion Publishing Group, c/o *Secy.* Mary Ruth Howes, Guideposts Books, 757 Third Ave., New York, NY 10017. Tel. 212-371-6060; *Pres.* Stephen Wilburn, Macmillan, 866 Third Ave., New York, NY 10022. Tel. 212-702-9865.

Research and Engineering Council of the Graphic Arts Industry, Inc., Box 639, Chadds Ford, PA 19317. Tel. 215-388-7394. *Pres.* Wendell M. Smith; *Exec. V.P./Secy.* James K. Henderson; *Exec. V.P./Treas.* Judith A. Booth; *Managing Dir.* Fred M. Rogers.

Society of Authors' Representatives, Inc., 10 Astor Place, 3rd fl., New York, NY 10003. Tel. 212-353-3709. *Pres.* Carl Brandt; *Exec. Secy.* Ginger Knowlton.

Society of Photographer and Artist Representatives, Inc. (SPAR), 1123 Broadway, Rm. 914, New York, NY 10010. Tel. 212-924-6023. *Pres.* Judith Shepherd; *1st V.P.* Rita Holt; *2nd V.P.* Robin Ritter; *Treas.* Alfred Forsyth; *Secy.* Edward Anthony.

Southern California Booksellers Assn., Box 92495, Pasadena, CA 91109. *Pres.* Adri Butler, Pacific Bookstore, 11755 Wilshire Blvd., Los Angeles, CA 90025. Tel. 213-312-1819; *V.P.* Gwen Feldman, Samuel French Theatre & Film Bookstore, 7623 Sunset Blvd., Hollywood, CA 90046; *Secy.* Sandra Patterson, Publisher's Rep., Addison-Wesley, 1322 Lantana, Camarillo, CA 93010. Tel. 805-987-2397; *Secy.* Barbara Schneyer, Bread & Roses, 13812 Ventura Blvd., Sherman Oaks, CA 91423. Tel. 818-986-5376; *Treas.* Tom Rusch, 166½ S. Sycamore Ave., Los Angeles, CA 90036. Tel. 213-931-9919.

Technical Assn. of the Pulp and Paper Industry (TAPPI), Technology Park/Atlanta, Box 105113, Atlanta, GA 30348-5113. Tel. 404-446-1400. *Pres.* Vincent A. Russo; *V.P.*

Clarence Hornsby; *Exec. Dir./Treas.* W. L. Cullison.

West Coast Bookmen's Assn., 27 McNear Dr., San Rafael, CA 94901. *Secy.* Frank G. Goodall. Tel. 415-459-1227.

Women's National Book Assn., 160 Fifth Ave., New York, NY 10010. Tel. 212-675-7805, c/o *National Pres.* Marie Cantlon, 8 Whittier Place, 21-A, Boston, MA 02114; *V.P./Pres.-Elect.* Patty Breitman, 20 Ross St., San Rafael, CA 94908. Tel. 415-456-3048. *Secy.* Lou Keay, 11684 Ventura Blvd., Studio City, CA 91604. Tel. 818-789-9175; *Treas.* Susan B. Trowbridge, Addison-Wesley Publishing Co., Reading, MA 01867; *Past Pres.* Cathy Rentschler, 60 W. 66 St., 16A, New York, NY 10023. Tel. 212-588-8400; *National Committee Chairs: Pannell Award Chpn.* Ann Heidbreder Eastman, Newman Lib., Virginia Polytechnic Institute and State Univ., Blacksburg, VA 24061; *Bookwoman Ed.* Nancy Musorafile-Lutz, 5222 St. Genevieve Place, Alexandria, VA 22310. Tel. 703-922-7174; *Book Review Eds.* Brenda Brienza and Adele Gorelick, Big River Publg., 9342 Big River Run, Columbia, MD 21045. Tel. 301-730-8744; *Corres. Membership Chpn.* Mary Glenn Hearne, Public Lib. of Nashville and Davidson County, Eighth Ave. N. and Union, Nashville, TN 37203. Tel. 615-244-4700; *Publicity.* Marilyn Abel, 325 E. 64 St., New York, NY 10021. Tel. 212-879-6850; *UN/NGO Rep.* Sally Wecksler, 170 West End Ave., New York, NY 10023. Tel. 212-787-2239; *Chapter Presidents: Binghamton.* Margiana T. Benza, School Libn., 2 Lowell Dr., Binghamton, NY 13901. Tel. 607-724-1306; *Boston.* Pamela M. Banks, Asst. Ed., Daedalus, 19 Garden St., #22, Cambridge, MA 02138. Tel. 617-576-5084; *Detroit.* Edith Phillips, Assoc. Professor, Lib. Science Program, Wayne State Univ., 25343 Maplebrook, Southfield, MI 48034. Tel. 313-577-1825; *Los Angeles.* Concetta diMatteo, 739 21st St., Santa Monica, CA 90402. Tel. 213-395-2494; *Nashville.* Carolyn Wilson, Acquisitions Libn., Crisman Memorial Lib., David Lipscomb College, 115 Grandview Dr., Nashville, TN 37204. Tel. 615-269-1000; *New York.* Diane Roback, Publisher's Weekly, 249 W. 17 St., New York, NY 10011. Tel. 212-463-6768; *San Francisco.* Patti Breitman, 4408 18th St., San Francisco, CA 94114. Tel. 415-552-1517; *Washington, DC/Baltimore, MD.* Kathleen Johnston, 1333 H St. N.W., Washington, DC 20005. Tel. 703-276-7748.

International and Foreign Book Trade Associations

For Canadian book trade associations, see the preceding section, "Book Trade Associations, United States and Canada." For a more extensive list of book trade organizations outside the United States and Canada, with more detailed information, consult *International Literary Market Place* (R. R. Bowker), which also provides extensive lists of major bookstores and publishers in each country.

International

Antiquarian Booksellers Assn., Suite 2, 26 Charing Cross Rd., London WC2H 0DG, England. *Secy.* Mrs. J. White.

International Booksellers Federation (IBF), Grünangergasse 4, A-1010 Vienna 1, Austria. *Pres.* Peter Meili; *Secy.-Gen.* Gerhard Prosser.

International League of Antiquarian Booksellers, c/o *Pres.* Anthony Rota, 9-11 Langley Ct., London WC2E 9RX, England.

International Publishers Assn., 3 av. de Miremont, CH-1206 Geneva, Switzerland. *Secy.-Gen.* J. Alexis Koutchoumow.

National

Argentina

Cámara Argentina de Editores de Libros (Council of Argentine Book Publishers), Talcahuano 374, p. 3, Of. 7, Buenos Aires 1013.

Cámara Argentina de Publicaciones (Argentine Publications Assn.), Reconquista 1011, p. 6, 1003 Buenos Aires. *Pres.* Augustin dos Santos.

Cámara Argentina del Libro (Argentine Book Assn.), Av. Belgrano 1580, p. 6, 1093 Buenos Aires. *Pres.* Jorge Naveiro.

Federación Argentina de Librerías, Papelerías y Actividades Afines (Federation of Bookstores, Stationers, and Related Activities), Balcarce 179/83, Rosario, Santa Fe. *Pres.* Isaac Kostzer.

Australia

Assn. of Australian Univ. Presses, c/o Univ. of Queensland Press, Staff House Rd., St. Lucia, Queensland 4067. *Pres.* L. C. Muller.

Australian Book Publishers Assn., 161 Clarence St., Sydney, N.S.W. 2000. *Dir.* Susan Blackwell.

Australian Booksellers Assn., Box 173, North Carlton, Victoria 3054. *Dir.* J. Stephens.

Austria

Hauptverband der graphischen Unternehmungen Österreichs (Austrian Master Printers Assn.), Grünangergasse 4, A-1010 Vienna 1. *Pres.* Komm.-Rat. Dr. Dkfm. Willi Maiwald; *Gen. Secy.* Dr. Hans Inmann.

Hauptverband des österreichischen Buchhandels (Austrian Publishers and Booksellers Assn.), Grünangergasse 4, A-1010 Vienna. *Gen. Secy.* Gerhard Prosser.

Oesterreichischer Verlegerverband (Assn. of Austrian Publishers), Grünangergasse 4, A-1010 Vienna. *Gen. Secy.* Gerhard Prosser.

Verband der Antiquare Österreichs (Austrian Antiquarian Booksellers Assn.), Grünangergasse 4, A-1010 Vienna. *Gen. Secy.* Gerhard Prosser.

Belgium

Association des Editeurs Belges (Belgian Publishers Assn. of French-language Books), Bd Lambermont, 140, Bte 1, B-1030 Brussels. *Pres.* Didier Plateau; *Dir.* Bernard Gerard.

Cercle Belge de la Librairie (Belgian Booksellers Assn.), rue de la Chasse Royale 35, 1160 Brussels.

Groupe des Editeurs de Livre de la CEE—GELC (Assn. of Book Publishers of the European Community), 111 av. du Parc, 1060 Brussels. *Pres.* G. J. van Roozendaal; *V.P. Exec.* J. J. Schellens; *Dir.* Bernard Gerard.

Syndicat Belge de la Librairie Ancienne et Moderne (Belgian Assn. of Antiquarian and Modern Booksellers), r. du Chêne 21, B-1000 Brussels.

Vereniging ter Bevordering van het Vlaamse Boekwezen (Assn. for the Promotion of Flemish Books), Frankrijklei 93, B-2000 Antwerp. *Pres.* M. Mertens. Member organizations: Algemene Vlaamse Boekverkopersbond; Uitgeversbond-Vereniging van Uitgevers van Nederlandstalige Boeken and Bond-Alleenverkopers van Nederlandstalige Boeken (Book Importers).

Bolivia

Cámara Boliviana del Libro (Bolivian Booksellers Assn.), Box 682, La Paz. *Pres. Lic.* Javier Gisbert.

Brazil

Associação Brasileira de Livreiros Antiquarios (Brazilian Assn. of Antiquarian Booksellers), Rua do Rosario 155, 2° p., Rio de Janeiro RJ. *Pres.* Walter Geyerhahn.

Associação Brasileira do Livro (Brazilian Booksellers Assn.), Av. 13 de Maio 23, andar 16, Rio de Janeiro. *Dir.* Alberjano Torres.

Cámara Brasileira do Livro (Brazilian Book Chamber), Av. Ipiranga, 1267-10 andar, 01039 São Paulo S.P. *Pres.* Alfredo Weiszflog.

Sindicato Nacional dos Editores de Livros (Brazilian Book Publishers Assn.), Av. Rio

Branco 37-15 andar, Salas 1503/6 e 1510/12, 20090 Rio de Janeiro. *Pres.* Alfredo C. Machado; *Exec. Secy.* Maria Christina Ramalho.

Bulgaria

Darzhavno Sdruzhenie "Bulgarska Kniga i Pechat" (Bulgarian State Book and Printing Assn.), 11, Slaveykov Sq., Sofia 1000.

Burma

Burmese Publishers Union, 146 Bogyoke Market, Rangoon.

Chile

Cámara Chilena del Libro, Av. Bulnes 188, Santiago. *Secy.* A. Newman.

Colombia

Cámara Colombiana de la Industria Editorial (Colombian Publishers Council), Carrera 17A, No. 37-27, Apdo. Aéreo 8998, Bogota. *Exec. Dir.* Miguel Eduardo Laverde Espejo; *Chpn.* Jorge Valencia Jaramillo.

Czechoslovakia

Ministerstvo Kultury CSR, Odbor Knižni Kultury (Ministry of Culture CSR, Dept. for Publishing and Book Trade), Staré Mésto, námesti Perštyně, 1, 117 65 Prague 1.

Denmark

Danske Antikvarboghandlerforening (Danish Antiquarian Booksellers Assn.), Box 2184, DK-1017 Copenhagen.

Danske Boghandlerforening (Danish Booksellers Assn.), Boghandlernes Hus, Siljangade 6, DK-2300 Copenhagen S. *Secy.* Elisabeth Brodersen.

Danske Forlaeggerforening (Danish Publishers Assn.), Kobmagergade 11, DK-1150 Copenhagen K. *Dir.* Erik V. Krustrup.

Finland

Kirja-ja Paperikauppojen Liitto ry (Finnish Booksellers and Stationers Assn.), Box 17 (Martinkyläntie 45), 01721 Vantaa, SF. *Secy.* Olli Eräkivi.

Suomen Antikvariaattiyhdistys Finska Antikvariatforeningen (Finnish Antiquarian Booksellers Assn.), P. Makasiininkatu 6, Helsinki 13.

Suomen Kustannusyhdistys (Publishers Assn. of Finland), Merimiehenkatu 12 A6, SF-00150 Helsinki. *Secy.-Gen.* Veikko Sonninen.

France

Editions du Cercle de la Librairie (Circle of Professionals of the Book Trade), 30, rue Dauphine, F-75263 Paris Cedex 06. *Dir.* Jean-Marie Doublet.

Fédération Française des Syndicats de Libraires (French Booksellers Assn.), 259 rue St.-Honoré, F-75001 Paris. *Pres.* Bernard Bollenot.

Office de Promotion de l'Edition Française (Promotion Office of French Publishing), 35, rue Grégoire-de-Tours, F-75279 Paris Cedex 06. *Managing Dir.* Pierre-Dominique Parent; *Secy.-Gen.* Marc Franconie.

Syndicat National de la Librairie Ancienne et Moderne (SLAM), 4 rue git-le-Coeur, F-75006 Paris. *Pres.* Jeanne Laffitte.

Syndicat National de l'Edition (French Publishers Assn.), 35, rue Grégoire-de-Tours, 75279 Paris Cedex 06. *Pres.* A. Gründ; *Dir.* Alain Roland Kirsch.

Syndicat National des Importateurs et Exportateurs de Livres (National French Assn. of Book Importers and Exporters), 35, rue Grégoire-de-Tours, 75279 Paris Cedex 06.

German Democratic Republic

Börsenverein der Deutschen Buchhändler zu Leipzig (Assn. of GDR Publishers and Booksellers in Leipzig), Gerichtsweg 26, DDR-7010 Leipzig.

Germany (Federal Republic of)

Börsenverein des Deutschen Buchhandels (German Publishers and Booksellers Assn.), Grosser Hirschgraben 17-21, Box 100442, D-6000 Frankfurt am Main 1. *Secy.* Hans-Karl von Kupsch.

Bundesverband der Deutschen Versandbuchhändler e.V. (National Federation of German Mail-Order Booksellers), An der Ringkirche 6, D-6200 Wiesbaden. *Dirs.* Stefan Rutkowsky; Kornelia Wahl.

Landesverband der Buchhändler und Verleger in Niedersachsen e.V. (Provincial Federation of Booksellers and Publishers in Lower Saxony), Arndtstr. 5, D-3000 Hannover 1. *Managing Dir.* Wolfgang Grimpe.

Presse-Grosso—Verband Deutscher Buch-, Zeitungs-und Zeitschriften-Grossisten e.V. (Federation of German Wholesalers of Books, Newspapers, and Periodicals), Classen-Kappelmann-Str. 24, D-5000 Cologne 41. *Mgr.* Hans Ziebolz.

Verband Bayerischer Verlage und Buchhandlungen e.V. (Bavarian Publishers and Booksellers Federation), Thierschstr. 17, D-8000 Munich 22. *Secy.* F. Nosske.

Verband Deutscher Antiquare e.V. (German Antiquarian Booksellers Assn.), Braubachstr. 34, D-6000 Frankfurt-am-Main 1.

Verband Deutscher Bühnenverleger e.V. (Federation of German Theatrical Publishers and Drama Agencies), Bismarckstr. 17, D-1000 Berlin 12.

Ghana

Ghana Booksellers Assn., Box 7869, Accra.

Great Britain

See United Kingdom.

Greece

Syllogos Ekdoton Vivliopolon (Publishers and Booksellers Assn. of Athens), 54 Themistocleus St., Gr-106 81, Athens. *Pres.* D. Pandeleskos; *Secy.* Th. Kastaniotis.

Hong Kong

Hong Kong Booksellers and Stationers Assn., Man Wah House, Kowloon.

Hungary

Magyar Könyvkiadók és Könyvterjesztök Egyesülése (Hungarian Publishers and Booksellers Assn.), Vörösmarty tér 1, H-1051 Budapest. *Pres.* András Petró; *Secy.-Gen.* Ferenc Zöld.

Iceland

Iceland Publishers Assn., Laufasvegi 12, 101 Reykjavik. *Pres.* Eyjólfur Sigurdsson, c/o Skjaldborg, Hólmgardur, 34 Reykjavík.

India

All-India Booksellers and Publishers Assn., 17L Connaught Circus, Box 328, New Delhi 11001. *Pres.* A. N. Varma.

Bombay Booksellers and Publishers Assn., c/o Bhadkamkar Marg, Navjivan Cooperative Housing Society, Bldg. 3, 6th fl., Office 25, Bombay 400 008. *Exec. Secy.* U. S. Manikeri.

Booksellers and Publishers Assn. of South India, c/o *Secy.* R. Seshadri, Routledge, Chapman and Hall, No. 32, II Main Rd., C.I.T. East, Madras 600 035.

Delhi State Booksellers and Publishers Assn., c/o The Students' Stores, Box 1511, 100 006 Delhi. *Pres.* Devendra Sharma.

Federation of Indian Publishers, 18/1-C Institutional Area, New Delhi 110 067. *Pres.* Ramdas Bhatkal; *Hon. Gen. Secy.* S. Balwant.

Indian Assn. of Univ. Presses, Calcutta Univ. Press, Calcutta. *Secy.* Salil Kumar Chakrabarti.

Indonesia

Ikatan Penerbit Indonesia (IKAPI) (Assn. of Indonesian Book Publishers), Jalan Kalipasir 32, Jakarta Pusat 10330. *Pres.* Azmi Syahbuddin.

Ireland (Republic of)

CLÉ: The Irish Book Publishers' Assn., Book House Ireland, 65 Middle Abbey St., Dublin 1. *Administrator.* Cecily Golden.

Israel

Book and Printing Center of the Israel Export Institute, Box 50084, 29 Hamered St., 68 125 Tel Aviv. *Dir.* Avital Katalan.

Book Publishers Assn. of Israel, Box 20123, 29 Carlebach St., Tel Aviv. *Chpn.* Racheli Eidelman; *International Promotion and Literary Rights Dept. Dir.* Lorna Soifer; *Managing Dir.* Arie Friedler.

Italy

Associazione Italiana Editori (Italian Publishers Assn.), Via delle Erbe 2, I-20121 Milan. *Secy.* Achille Ormezzano.

Associazione Librai Antiquari d'Italia (Antiquarian Booksellers Assn. of Italy), Via Jacopo Nardi 6, I-50132 Florence. *Pres.* Pietro Chellini.

Associazione Librai Italiani (Italian Booksellers Assn.), Piazza G. G. Belli 2, I-00153 Rome. *Pres.* Remo Croce.

Jamaica

Booksellers Assn. of Jamaica, c/o Sangster's Book Stores, Ltd., Box 366, 101 Water Lane, Kingston. *Managing Dir.* S. Kumaraswamy.

Japan

Antiquarian Booksellers Assn. of Japan, 29 San-ei-cho, Shinjuku-ku, Tokyo 160.

Books-on-Japan-in-English Club, Shinnichibo Bldg., 2-1 Sarugaku-cho 1-chome, Chiyoda-ku, Tokyo 101.

Japan Book Importers Assn., Chiyoda Kaikan, 21-4, Nihonbashi 1-chome, Chuo-ku, Tokyo 103. *Secy.* Mitsuo Shibata.

Japan Book Publishers Assn., 6 Fukuromachi, Shinjuku-ku, Tokyo 162. *Pres.* Toshiyuki Hattori; *Exec. Dir.* Sadaya Murayama; *Secy.* Masaaki Shigehisa.

Japan Booksellers Federation, 1-2 Surugadai, Kanda, Chiyoda-ku, Tokyo 101.

Textbook Publishers Assn. of Japan (Kyokasho Kyokai), 20-2 Honshiocho Shinjuku-ku, Tokyo 160. *Secy.* Masae Kusaka.

Kenya

Kenya Publishers Assn., Box 72532, Nairobi. *Secy.* J. M. B. Clarke.

Korea (Republic of)

Korean Publishers Assn., 105-2, Sagandong, Chongno-ku, Seoul 110–119. *Pres.* Byung-ill Kwoun; *V.P.s.* Nak-jun Kim; Chang-sung Huh; Byung-seok Chun.

Luxembourg

Confédération du Commerce Luxembourgeois-Groupement Papetiers-Libraires (Confederation of Retailers, Group for Stationers and Booksellers), 23, Centre Allée-Scheffer, Luxembourg. *Pres.* Raymond Daman; *Secy.* Léa Metz.

Malaysia

Malaysian Book Publishers Assn., 399A, Jalan Tuanku Abdul Rahman, 50100 Kuala Lumpur. *Hon. Secy.* Johnny Ong.

Morocco

Librairie-Papeterie, 344 Ave. Mohammed V, Rabat. *Contact* Kalila Wa Dimna.

Netherlands

Koninklijke Nederlandse Uitgeversbond (Royal Dutch Publishers Assn.), Keizersgracht 391, 1016 EJ Amsterdam. *Secy.* R. M. Vrij.

Nederlandsche Vereeniging van Antiquaren (Antiquarian Booksellers Assn. of the Netherlands), Nieuwe Spiegelstr. 33-35, 1017-DC Amsterdam. *Pres.* Mrs. C. F. M. van der Peet-Schelfhout.

Nederlandse Boekverkopersbond (Booksellers Assn. of the Netherlands), Waalsdorperweg 119, 2597-HS The Hague. *Pres.* J. van der Plas; *Exec. Secy.* A. C. Doeser.

Vereeniging ter bevordering van de belangen des Boekhandels (Dutch Book Trade Assn.), Frederiksplein 1, Box 15007, 1001 MA Amsterdam. *Secy.* M. van Vollenhoven-Nagel.

New Zealand

Book Publishers Assn. of New Zealand, Inc., Box 44146, Point Chevalier, Auckland 2. *Pres.* R. Ross; *Dir.* Gerard Reid.

Booksellers Assn. of New Zealand, Inc., Box 11-377, Wellington. *Dir.* John Schiff.

Nigeria

Nigerian Booksellers Assn., Box 3168, Ibadan. *Pres.* W. Adegbonmire.

Nigerian Publishers' Assn., G.P.O. Box 2541, Ibadan. *Pres.* F. S. Ogunniyi; *Contact Exec. Secy.* Tope Popoola.

Norway

Bok og Papiransattes Forening (Norwegian Book Trade Employees Assn.), Øvre Vollgate 15, 0158 Oslo 1. *Mgr.* Magda Sørevik.

Den norske Bokhandlerforening (Norwegian Booksellers Assn.), Øvre Vollgate 15, 0158 Oslo 1. *Dir.* Olav Gjerdene.

Norsk Antikvarbokhandlerforening (Norwegian Antiquarian Booksellers Assn.), Universitetsgt. 18, 0164 Oslo 1.

Norsk Musikkforleggerforening (Norwegian Music Publishers Assn.), Box 822, Sentrum, N-0104 Oslo 1. *Chpn.* Arne Damsgaard.

Norske Forleggerforening (Norwegian Publishers Assn.), Øvre Vollgate 15, Oslo 1. *Dir.* Paul M. Rothe.

Pakistan

Pakistan Publishers and Booksellers Assn., YMCA Bldg., Shahra-e-Quaide-Azam, Lahore.

Paraguay

Cámara Paraguaya del Libro (Paraguayan Publishers Assn.), Casilla de Correo 1705, Asunción.

Peru

Cámara Peruana del Libro (Peruvian Publishers Assn.), Jirón Washington 1206, of. 507-508, Lima 100. *Pres.* Andrés Carbone O.

Philippines

Philippine Book Dealers Assn., MCC Box 1103, Makati Commercial Centre, Makati, Metro Manila. *Pres.* Jose C. Benedicto.

Philippine Educational Publishers Assn., 927 Quezon Ave., Quezon City 3008, Metro Manila. *Pres.* Jesus Ernesto R. Sibal.

Poland

Polskie Towarzystwo Wydawców Książek (Polish Publishers Assn.), ul. Mazowiecka 2/4, 00-048 Warsaw.

Stowarzyszenie Ksiegarzy Polskich (Assn. of Polish Booksellers), ul. Mokotowska 4/6, 00-641 Warsaw. *Pres.* Tadeusz Hussak.

Portugal

Associação Portuguesa de Editores e Livreiros (Portuguese Assn. of Publishers and Booksellers), Av. dos Estados Unidos da Amêrica, 97-6 Esq. 1700 Lisbon. *Pres.* Francisco Espadinha; *Gen. Secy.* Jorge Sá Borges; *Service Mgr.* José Narciso Vieira.

Romania (Socialist Republic of)

Centrala editorială (Romanian Publishing Center), Piata Scînteii 1, R-79715 Bucharest. *Gen. Dir.* Gheorghe Trandafir.

Singapore

Singapore Book Publishers Assn., 865 Mountbatten Rd., No. 05-28, Katong Shopping Centre, Singapore 1543. *Hon. Secy.* N. T. S. Chopra.

South Africa (Republic of)

Associated Booksellers of Southern Africa, Box 326, Howard Place 7450. *Secy.* M. Landman.

Book Trade Assn. of South Africa, Box 326, Howard Place 7450. *Dir.* M. Landman.

South African Publishers Assn., Box 326, Howard Place 7450. *Secy.* M. Landman.

Spain

Centro del Libro y de la Lectura (Center for the Book and the Reader), Santiago Rusiñol 8, 28040 Madrid. *Dir.* Javier Abásolo Fernández.

Federacion de Gremios de Editores de España (Spanish Federation of Publishers Assn.), Juan Ramon Jiminez 45-9°izDA, 28036 Madrid. *Pres.* Pedro Vicens i Rahola; *Secy.-Gen.* Milagros del Corral.

Gremi d'Editors de Catalunya (Assn. of Catalonian Publishers), Valencia, 279, la Planta, Barcelona 08009. *Pres.* P. Vicens i Rahola.

Gremi de Llibreters de Barcelona i Catalunya (Assn. of Barcelona and Catalonia Booksellers), c. Mallorca, 272-274, 08037 Barcelona.

Sri Lanka

Booksellers Assn. of Sri Lanka, Box 244, Colombo 2. *Secy.* W. L. Mendis.

Sri Lanka Publishers Assn., 61 Sangaraja Mawatha, Colombo 10. *Secy.-Gen.* Eamon Kariyakarawana.

Sweden

Svenska Antikvariatföreningen, Box 22549, S-104 22 Stockholm.

Svenska Bokförläggareföreningen (Swedish Publishers Assn.), Sveavägen 52, S-111 34 Stockholm. *Managing Dir.* Urban Skeppstedt.

Svenska Bokhandlareföreningen (Swedish Booksellers Assn.), Skeppargatan 27, S-114 52 Stockholm. *Secy.* Thomas Rönström.

Svenska Tryckeriföreningen (Swedish Printing Industries Federation), Blasieholmsgatan 4A, Box 16383, S-10327 Stockholm. *Managing Dir.* Per Galmark; *Dir.* H. Hedberg.

Switzerland

Schweizerischer Buchhändler-und Verleger-Verband (Swiss German-Language Booksellers and Publishers Assn.), Baumackerstrasse 42, CH-8050 Zurich. *Managing Dir.* Peter Birchmeier.

Società Editori della Svizzera Italiana (Publishers Assn. for the Italian-Speaking Part of Switzerland), Box 2600, Viale Portone 4, CH-6501 Bellinzona.

Société des Libraires et Editeurs de la Suisse Romande (Assn. of Swiss French-Language Booksellers and Publishers), 2 av. Agassiz, CH-1001 Lausanne. *Secy.* Robert Junod.

Vereinigung der Buchantiquare und Kupferstichhändler der Schweiz (Assn. of Swiss Antiquarians and Print Dealers), c/o *Pres.* Walter Alicke, Schloss-Str. 6, FL 9490 Vaduz.

Thailand

Publishers and Booksellers Assn. of Thailand, 25 Sukhumvit Soi 56, Bangkok 10250. *Secy.* W. Tantinirandr.

Turkey

Türk Editòrler Derneği (Turkish Publishers Assn.), Ankara Caddesi 60, Istanbul.

United Kingdom

Assn. of Learned and Professional Society Publishers, 48 Kelsey-Lane, Beckenham, Kent 3RS 3NE. *Secy.* B. T. Donovan.

Book Trust, Book House, 45 E. Hill, London SW18 2QZ. *Chief Exec.* Keith McWilliams.

Booksellers Assn. of Great Britain and Ireland, 154 Buckingham Palace Rd., London SW1W 9TZ. *Dir.* Tim Godfray.

Educational Publishers Council, 19 Bedford Sq., London WC1B 3HJ. *Dir.* John R. M. Davies.

National Federation of Retail Newsagents, Yeoman House, Sekforde St., Clerkenwell Green, London EC1R OHD. *Admin. Secy.* E. D. McKinney.

Publishers Assn., 19 Bedford Sq., London WC1B 3HJ. *Chief Exec.* Clive Bradley; *Pres.* Robin Hyman. Home Trade & Services Council: *Dir.* Neil Morley; Book Development Council (International): *Dir.* Tony Read; Book Mktg. Council: *Dir.* Clare Middleton; Educational Publishers Council: *Dir.* John Davies; Univ., College and Professional Publishers Council: *Dir.* John Davies.

Uruguay

Cámara Uruguaya del Libro (Uruguayan Publishing Council), Carlos Roxlo 1446, piso 1, Apdo. 2, Montevideo. *Pres.* Arnaldo Medone; *Secy.* Walter Peluffo; *Mgr.* Ana Cristina Rodríguez.

Yugoslavia

Assn. of Yugoslav Publishers and Booksellers, Kneza Milosa str. 25, Box 883, Belgrade. *Pres.* Vidak Perić.

Zambia

Booksellers' and Publishers' Assn. of Zambia, Box 320199, Lusaka. *Chpn.* G. B. Mwangilwa.

Zimbabwe

Booksellers Assn. of Zimbabwe, Box 3916, 69 Stanley Ave., Harare. *Chpn.* C. K. Katsande.

Calendar, 1989–1990

The list below contains information (as of January 1989) regarding place and date of association meetings or promotional events that are, for the most part, national or international in scope. State and regional library association meetings also are included. For those who wish to contact the association directly, addresses of library and book trade associations are listed in Part 6 of this *Bowker Annual.* For information on additional book trade and promotional events, see the *Exhibits Directory,* published annually by the Association of American Publishers; *Chase's Calendar of Annual Events,* published by the Apple Tree Press, Box 1012, Flint, MI 48501; *Literary Market Place* and *International Literary Market Place,* published by R. R. Bowker; and the "Calendar" section in each issue of *Publishers Weekly* and *Library Journal.*

1989

May

1–3	New Hampshire Library Association	Manchester, N.H.
3–6	Oklahoma Library Association	Oklahoma City, Okla.
3–7	New Jersey Library Association	Atlantic City, N.J.
5–6	Manitoba Library Association	Winnipeg, Canada
8–9	Massachusetts Library Association	Sturbridge, Mass.
9–13	Florida Library Association	Jacksonville, Fla.
10–13	Indiana Library Association	Fort Wayne, Ind.
11–12	Maryland Library Association	Hunt Valley, Md.
19–20	American Society of Indexers	San Francisco, Calif.
21–23	Maine Library Association	Orono, Maine
19–25	Medical Library Association	Boston, Mass.
21–24	American Society for Information Science	San Diego, Calif.
22–26	International Association of Technological University Libraries	Ljubljana, Yugoslavia
24–25	Vermont Library Association	Poultney, Vt.
24–25	Women's National Book Association	Washington, D.C.
31	Bibliographical Society of Canada	Edmonton, Canada
5/31–6/2	Society for Scholarly Publishing	Washington, D.C.
*	American Merchant Marine Library Association	New York, N.Y.
*	Atlantic Provinces Library Association	Charlottetown, P.E.I.

*To be announced.

June

3–6	American Booksellers Association	Washington, D.C.
5–8	Association for Information and Image Management	San Francisco, Calif.
10–15	Special Libraries Association	New York City
11–14	Association of American University Presses	Cincinnati, Ohio
13–16	Association of Christian Librarians	Portland, Oreg.
16–22	American Association of Law Libraries	Reno, Nev.
18–21	Association of Jewish Libraries	Washington, D.C.
18–23	American Theological Library Association	Columbus, Ohio
22–25	Canadian Library Association	Edmonton, Canada
23–27	Canadian Booksellers Association	Vancouver, B.C., Canada
23	ALA Resources and Technical Services Division	Dallas, Tex.
24–29	American Library Association	Dallas, Tex.
25–26	Asian/Pacific American Librarians Association	Dallas, Tex.
26	Theatre Library Association	Dallas, Tex.
27	Chinese American Library Association	Dallas, Tex.
*	Book Industry Study Group Trends Seminar	New York, N.Y.

July

9–11	Church and Synagogue Library Association	Hartford, Conn.

August

6–9	International Association of Printing House Craftsmen	Reno, Nev.
16–18	Pacific Northwest Library Association	Coeur d'Alene, Idaho
20–25	International Federation of Library Associations and Institutions	Paris, France
*	International ISBN Advisory Panel	Paris, France

September

1–4	Miniature Book Society	Cincinnati, Ohio
8–9	Kentucky School Media Association	Louisville, Ky.
14	Book Industry Study Group	New York, N.Y.
18	National Information Standards Organization	Washington, D.C.

*To be announced.

September (*cont.*)

21–23	North Dakota Library Association	Grand Forks, N. Dak.
24–26	New England Library Association	Springfield, Mass.
25–29	New York Library Association	Saratoga Springs, N.Y.

October

1–3	Chief Officers of State Library Agencies	Helena, Mont.
2–5	ARMA International	New Orleans, La.
4–7	Wyoming Library Association	Laramie, Wyo.
6–8	Minnesota Educational Media Association	Brainerd, Minn.
11–13	Iowa Library Association	Cedar Rapids, Iowa
11–13	Kentucky Library Association	Louisville, Ky.
11–14	Pennsylvania Library Association	Pittsburgh, Pa.
11–14	South Dakota Library Association	Aberdeen, S. Dak.
11–16	Frankfurt Book Fair	Frankfurt, West Germany
12–14	Nevada Library Association	Boulder City, Nev.
12–14	Washington Library Media Association	Yakima, Wash.
17–20	Michigan Library Association	Lansing, Mich.
18–22	American Association of School Librarians	Salt Lake City, Utah
25–27	Mississippi Library Association	Natchez, Miss.
25–28	Georgia Library Association	Jekyll Island, Ga.
25–29	Society of American Archivists	St. Louis, Mo.
26–28	Nebraska Library Association/Nebraska Educational Media Association	Lincoln, Nebr.
26–28	Ohio Library Association/Ohio Educational Media Association	Toledo, Ohio
26–28	West Virginia Library Association	Canaan Valley, W. Va.
10/29–11/2	American Society for Information Science	Washington, D.C.
10/31–11/4	Arizona Library Association	Tucson, Ariz.
*	ISBN (U.S. Agency)	Paris, France

November

3–7	Colorado Library Association	Colorado Springs, Colo.
5–7	Arkansas Library Association	Little Rock, Ark.
5–7	Rhode Island Library Association	*
12	Hawaii Association of School Librarians	Honolulu, Hawaii
13–19	Book Week	U.S.A.
16–18	Virginia Library Association	Hot Springs, Va.
16–21	Montreal Book Fair	Montreal, Canada
15–17	South Carolina Library Association	Hilton Head, S.C.

*To be announced.

1990

January

2–5	Association for Library and Information Science Education	Chicago, Ill.
13–18	American Library Association	Chicago, Ill.
24–27	Special Libraries Association	St. Louis, Mo.
1/31–2/4	Association for Educational Communications and Technology	Anaheim, Calif.
*	Bibliographical Society of America	New York, N.Y.

February

9–15	Art Libraries Society of North America	New York, N.Y.

March

13–16	Louisiana Library Association	Monroe, La.
25–28	Association of American Publishers	Key Biscayne, Fla.
*	Alaska Library Association	Ketchikan, Alaska

April

9–12	Association of Information and Image Management	Quebec, Canada
16–19	Catholic Library Association	Toronto, Canada
18–21	New Mexico Library Association	Albuquerque, N. Mex.
18–22	Washington Library Association	Pasco, Wash.
20–23	Council of Planning Librarians	Denver, Colo.
22–28	National Library Week	U.S.A.
23–25	Arkansas Association of Instructional Media	Little Rock, Ark.
24–29	Quebec International Book Fair	Quebec, Canada
25–28	Pennsylvania School Librarians Association	Hershey, Pa.
*	Montana Library Association	Great Falls, Mont.
*	Tennessee Library Association	Memphis, Tenn.

May

2–5	Utah Library Association	Salt Lake City, Utah
2–5	Mountains Plains Library Association	Salt Lake City, Utah
3–6	Association of Jewish Libraries	Jerusalem
3–6	British Columbia Library Association	Victoria, B.C., Canada
6–11	Florida Library Association	Daytona Beach, Fla.
7–8	Massachusetts Library Association	Danvers, Mass.
18–21	Oklahoma Library Association	Tulsa, Okla.

*To be announced.

June

2–5	American Booksellers Association	Las Vegas, Nev.
9–14	Special Libraries Association	Pittsburgh, Pa.
11–15	Association of Christian Librarians	Cedarville, Ohio
23–28	American Library Association	Chicago, Ill.
23–26	Canadian Booksellers Association	Toronto, Canada
24–27	American Association of Law Libraries	Minneapolis, Minn.
24–27	Association of American University Presses	Philadelphia, Pa.
25	Theatre Library Association	Chicago, Ill.
25–30	American Theological Library Association	Evanston, Ill.
*	Canadian Library Association	Ottawa, Canada

August

3–5	Lutheran Church Library Association	Chicago, Ill
15–17	Pacific Northwest Library Association	Portland, Oreg.
8/30–9/3	Society of American Archivists	Seattle, Wash.
*	International Federation of Library Associations and Institutions	Stockholm, Sweden

September

23–25	New England Library Association	Sturbridge, Mass.
*	North Dakota Library Association	Minot, N. Dak.

October

3–6	South Dakota Library Association	Sioux Falls, S. Dak.
4–7	Minnesota Educational Media Association	St. Cloud, Minn.
10–12	Iowa Library Association	Des Moines, Iowa
10–14	New York Library Association	Rochester, N.Y.
10–14	Ohio Library Association	Dayton, Ohio
22–25	American Association of School Librarians	Baltimore, Md.
23–26	Michigan Library Association	Grand Rapids, Mich.
24–27	Ohio Educational Media Library Association	Cleveland, Ohio
10/28–11/1	Pennsylvania Library Association	Hershey, Pa.
*	Chief Officers of State Library Agencies	Lansing, Mich.
*	Frankfurt Book Fair	Frankfurt, West Germany
*	International ISBN Advisory Panel	Berlin, West Germany
*	Nebraska Library Association	Kearney, Neb.

*To be announced.

November

4–6	Rhode Island Library Association	*
4–8	American Society for Information Science	Toronto, Canada
5–8	ARMA International	San Francisco, Calif.
9–12	Ontario Library Association	Hamilton, Ont., Canada
12–18	Book Week	U.S.A.
15–20	Montreal Book Fair	Montreal, Canada
*	Theatre Library Association	Toronto, Canada

December

5–9	Southeastern Library Association	Nashville, Tenn.
5–9	Tennessee Library Association	Nashville, Tenn.

Index

B

C

D

E

F

G

H

I

O

P

T

U

V

W

Y

QUICK FIND INDEX